The United States

Experiment in Democracy

☆ ☆ ☆ ☆ ☆ ☆ ☆ ☆ ☆ ☆ ☆ ☆ ☆

By AVERY CRAVEN *and* WALTER JOHNSON

The University of Chicago

GINN AND COMPANY

BOSTON · NEW YORK · CHICAGO · ATLANTA · DALLAS · COLUMBUS
SAN FRANCISCO · TORONTO · LONDON

To

WILLIAM THOMAS HUTCHINSON

Gentleman and Scholar

CONTENTS

LIST OF MAPS

Black and White Maps

Colored Maps

The United States of America

THE HISTORY of the American people may be divided roughly into three periods. The first is the colonial period, in which different European groups, with differing cultural patterns, were adjusting themselves to one another and to the American environment and, thereby, evolving a new people and a new nation. The second is the national period, in which the young United States of America turned its back on Europe, marched steadily westward across the American continent, and transformed it, region by region, from a simple wilderness into a land of farms and towns and complex social-industrial institutions. Connections with the outside world were reduced to a minimum, and Americans, engaged in American tasks, sharpened and modified their own national characteristics, both personal and institutional, and emerged before the world as a powerful nation with positive interests and values uniquely its own. The third period is the one in which we find ourselves, at the present time, an integral part of the larger world. We are back where we started. The days of isolation are over. Just before the dawn of the twentieth century the United States found itself, half reluctantly, again facing outward. American goods and American capital had already invaded other lands; interests and values had forced a war with Spain and bequeathed us a colonial empire; and then the blunt fact of world interdependence pushed us into two great European wars. The cycle was thus completed, but the attitudes and assumptions inherited from the two earlier periods of American life, and their need of readjustment, have left much of mental confusion and much of uncertainty. We often appear to be a people whose bodies are in one age and whose minds are in an earlier one. The great task of adjustment still plagues the American people.

Many nationalities and much of good fortune have entered into the making of the United States. The first settlers on the North American continent came out of western Europe and brought with them the habits, the tastes, and the prejudices that they had acquired in that intensely active part of the world. It was a region where strong national governments, relying on taxes and gold and silver, not on personal services, had replaced feudalism; where commerce and trade, especially with the Orient, had greatly increased the importance of towns and townsmen; where great trading companies had been organized to exploit the riches of far-flung corners of the world; and where national churches, under the Protestant revolt, had defied the See of Rome and stressed anew the direct responsibility of the individual to his God.

The discovery of America came about as a result of the efforts of nations bordering on the Atlantic to escape the middlemen who controlled trade through the Mediterranean. In seeking the East they found the West. Some of the early American colonies were planted by the trading companies; others were founded by religious refugees who sought to escape the conformity required in most European nations; still others were made up of peoples set free by the great changes in rural Europe, and lured to the New World by hopes of better things than could be found amid the unsettled conditions at home. England furnished the greatest number of settlers, but Germany, Sweden, Holland, France, and Spain furnished enough to make the American colonies the children of Europe, not of Great Britain alone. Each of these groups made valuable contributions to American life.

From the English came the language which was to be the dominant one in use in the United States and with it the opportunity to share in the rich accumulations of English literature. Even the folk songs of Ireland and Wales and Scotland were a part of that heritage. The common law and most of the political forms and practices adopted in the colonies were of English origin. Much of the Protestant Reformation, but not all of it, came to America by way of England. The conception of classes in society, including the country-gentleman ideal, so important in the South, came from the same source. In fact, it would be difficult to find any part of life on the American continent that was not, to some degree, influenced by England.

The Dutch influenced only one colony, New York, but they left a decided impress on that colony. Their stanch Protestantism, their peculiar types of architecture, the great landed estates that they scattered along the Hudson, and the quaint, picturesque folklore that they created in both town and country added something rich to the American pattern.

Even greater was the contribution of the German people. They brought with them much of manual skill and a knowledge of farming, together with a taste for it, which the English sadly lacked. Their fields did not decline in fertility, and their great barns, soon known as "Pennsylvania Dutch barns," were symbolic of the interest and care that went into their efforts. They too were Protestants, and their Pietism, which came to them from Luther, flowered in various sects whose love of music, whose devotion to high social standards, and whose patient skill as craftsmen enriched the fiber being woven into American life.

The French Huguenots in New York and in South Carolina were comparatively few in number and were soon absorbed by the English stock. They did, however, reveal a peculiar aptitude for commerce and added something intellectual and artistic to the communities where they lived.

Farther away, and at first unconnected with these groups, were the French in Louisiana and the Spanish in the Southwest. Both were Catholic in religion, and both were strong enough in numbers to give the dominant color to life in the regions which they occupied. Each group had its type of houses and public buildings, which not only were different in appearance from those of the rest of the country, but exerted a strong and permanent influence on later American architecture. The Roman law, modified by French and Spanish influences, permanently shaped the legal code of Louisiana. The French love of music and the drama continued to characterize life in New Orleans and the neighboring region. In like manner, the Spanish missions and ranches colored life in California long after that state had become a part of the United States. Spanish influence in architecture was important; and, in later days, the cattle industry on the Plains carried the mark of its Spanish origin.

The contribution of the Negro to the Western world, to which he came first as a servant and then as a slave, is hard to measure. His labor helped to push the wilderness back and to open the way for the production of the great staples so necessary for trade. In places where his numbers were great, he altered and shaped both the economic and the social life. The plantation system and the caste system both rested in part on his shoulders. His strong sense of rhythm, his store of folk tales and superstitions, and the more subtle force of personality in the close contacts of rural living, all contributed something to the making of a new people in a new land.

All these early groups were augmented, both in colonial and in early national days, by new arrivals of the same stocks. Then, in the years after 1830, they were again increased, and new floods from wider areas also poured in. The Irish and the Germans headed the flow—the former settling in New England and along the canals and railroads which they helped to build into the West, and the latter finding places as tradesmen and farmers in Ohio, Texas, Missouri, and Wisconsin.

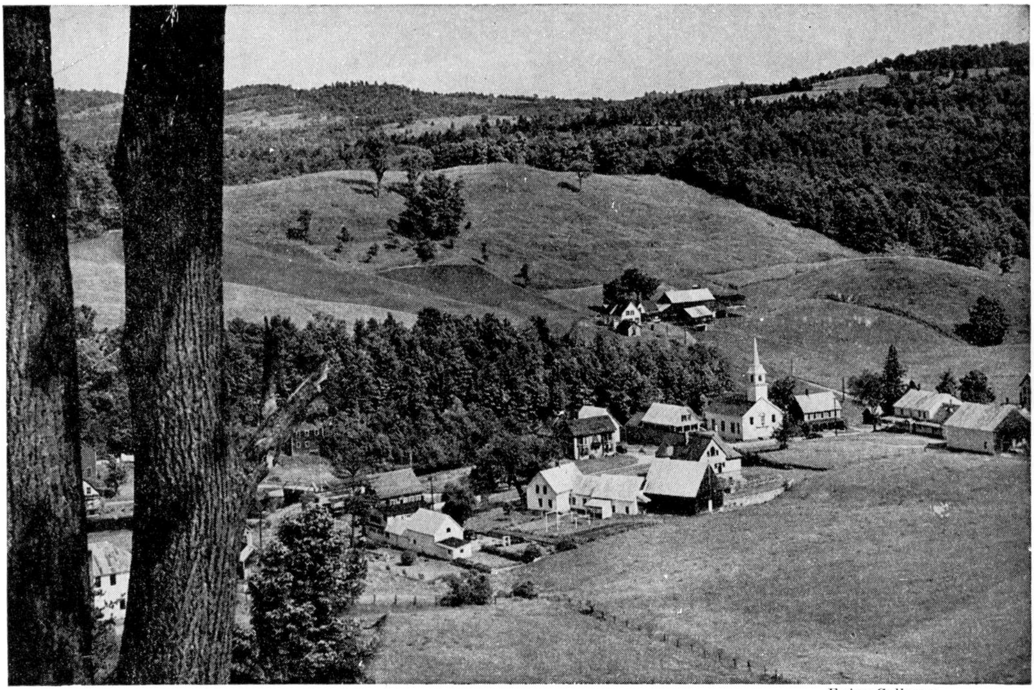

RURAL NEW ENGLAND

Ewing Galloway

Scenes from the Diverse

THE RURAL MIDWEST

Jerry Cooke, from Pix

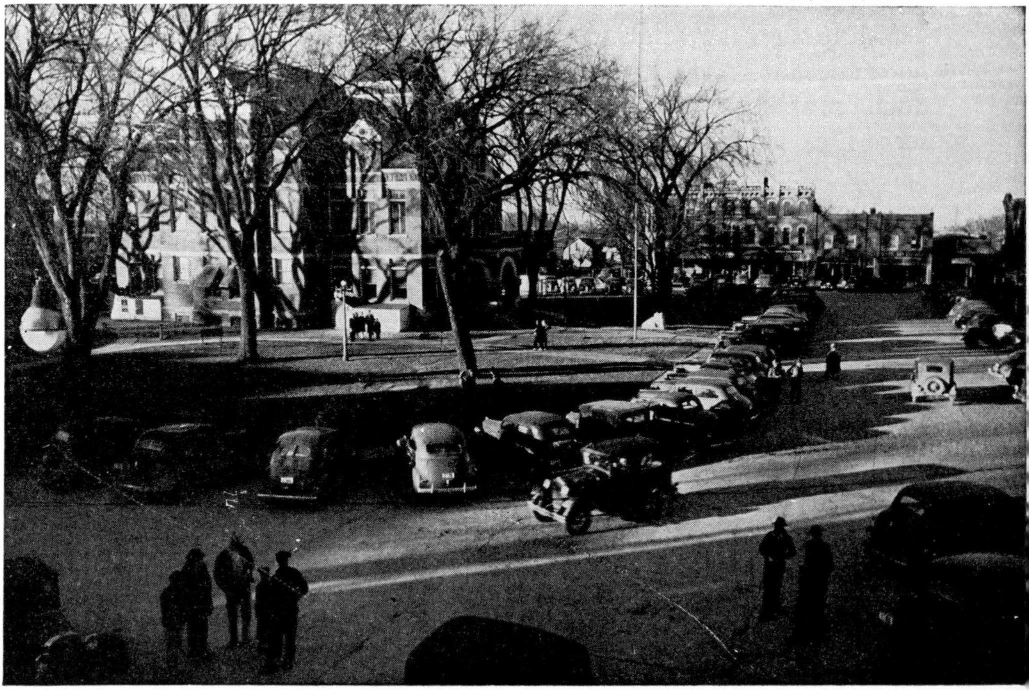

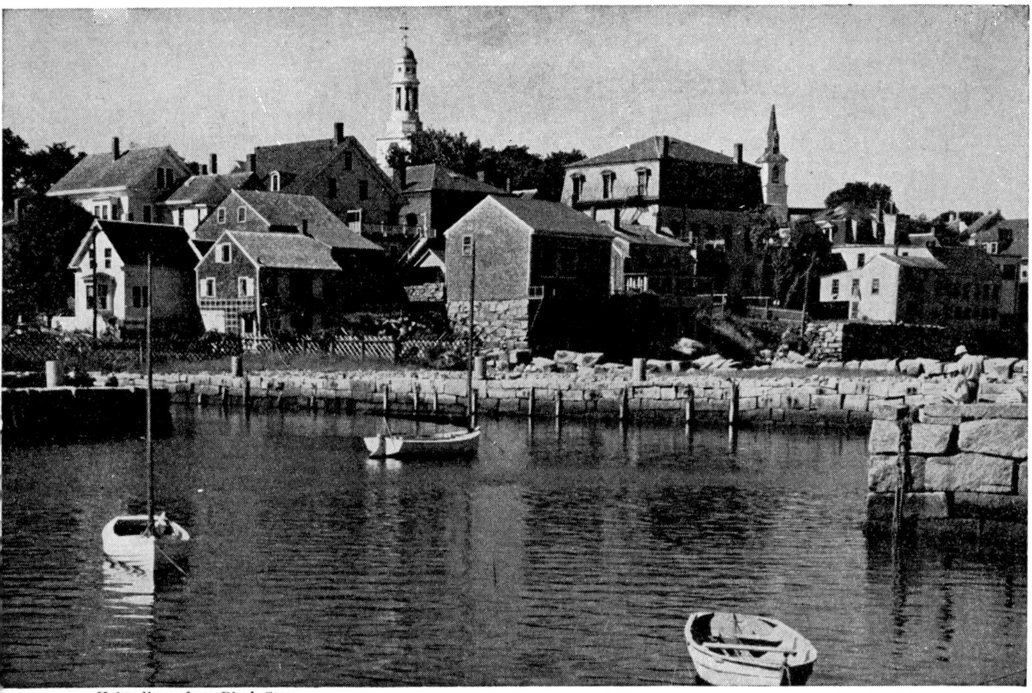

Helen Faye, from Black Star

EASTERN SEAPORT TOWN

American Landscape

Kaufmann-Fabry

URBAN CHICAGO

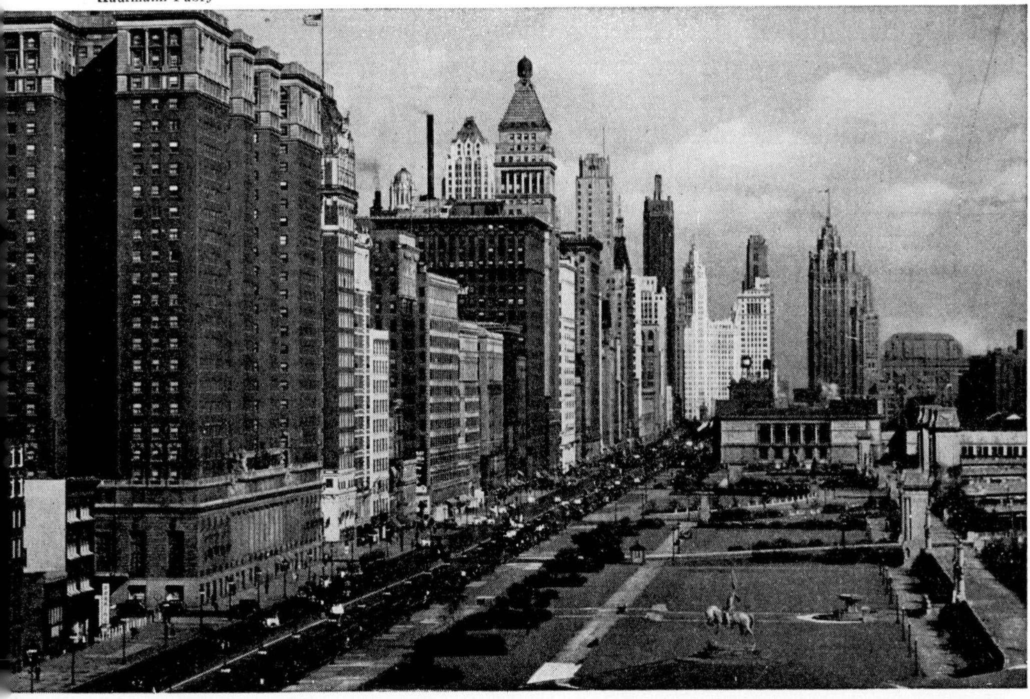

Both groups, long subject to harsh treatment at home, gloried in the freedom and the security that they enjoyed in the United States. The Civil War found them stanchly on the Union side. The Irish, already notable for their ready wit and romantic qualities, soon revealed a practical aptitude for politics, which matched their marked attachment to fellow countrymen and to their Catholic faith. The first Germans were joined, after 1848, by a group of intellectuals who, despairing of liberalism in the fatherland, hoped to realize their dreams in America. They showed less political acumen than the Irish, but not less of the desire to get ahead or to retain something of the joy of living.

After the Civil War great numbers of Scandinavians joined the few who had already come to make their homes largely in the newer states of the Old Northwest. Settlements now spread to Minnesota, northern Iowa, and out to the Dakota Territory. These were a hardy people, who settled in neighborhoods close together and revealed almost as much of thrift and eagerness for education as had the early Puritans themselves. The Jews, meanwhile, crowded into the cities to add something strangely different to the existing order—something older in tradition, but something intensely eager for success in the new urban-capitalistic society that was emerging. With them came from southern and southeastern Europe other new groups,—Italians, Poles, Greeks, and Czechs, —each with its own national traits and values, but nearly all alike in allegiance to the Catholic Church. The new flood was greater than the old; its birth rate was higher; its peoples tended to remain in the urban centers either as industrial laborers or as market gardeners on the outskirts of the cities. Members of these new groups, of the same nationality or race, often remained close together, retaining their national speech and, to some degree, their Old World customs. The problem of assimilation increased, but the public-school system and closer contact with the now established national ways of living worked wonders on second generations and brought unity of aspiration and feelings if not always of minor social practices. Thus, in spite of increased burdens, the "melting pot" continued its work of fusing divergent peoples into a new American race.

European peoples and ways, however, were only one factor in the making of the United States. Of equal importance was the influence of the continent itself, of the life it required of those who would make it their home. It was a continent great in size and rich in resources. Stretching nearly three thousand miles from the Atlantic to the Pacific, and more than fifteen hundred miles from the Great Lakes to the Gulf of Mexico, it lay between the parallels 26° and 55° north latitude in a climate where crops familiar to Europeans would yield bountiful harvests, where white men would be more healthy than in the tropics or in the extreme north, and where the change in seasons would be marked enough to stimulate a maximum of mental and physical activity. To the known European crops the continent added corn and potatoes and tobacco. It offered generous areas of fertile soils, well watered and easily accessible. Its rivers and lakes formed natural highways that interlocked in such manner as to provide, with only short portages, routes from ocean to ocean. In its mountains were convenient gaps through which trails might grow into wagon roads and these in turn give way to railroads and paved highways. Within its borders could be found rich deposits of all the important minerals save tin and potash. The iron and coal deposits were especially rich; copper and oil, so important in later days, were equally abundant. Great timber resources and almost limitless water power rounded out the picture of a land unmatched by any other of equal size on the face of the earth. For years the United States was to be known as a land of fabulous resources; in 1924 one writer estimated that it produced 38 per cent of the world's coal, 70 per cent of its petroleum, 38 per cent of its electric power, 54 per cent of its copper, 33 per cent of its iron ore, 53 per cent of its timber, and from 25 per cent to 75 per cent of its corn and cereals. With such great natural resources, and with some eight hundred million acres capable of being turned into improved farm lands, the potentialities for comfort and luxury were to be measured only by the abilities of those who undertook their realization.

But this great land, when the European first entered it, was only an untamed wilderness thinly occupied by tribes of Indians. It had to be possessed and transformed. Step by step, from east to west, the wilderness had to be pushed back, and farms and towns and all the complex agencies of civilization had to be set up in its place. First, the coast nearest Europe had to be won, then the regions farther inland. Trappers and traders and intrepid missionaries would lead the way and prepare the region for the first crude "cabineers," who would begin the cultivation of the soil. Sometimes lumbermen or miners or cattlemen took the lead when their special kind of natural wealth attracted. Sometimes the forward movement was too rapid; then the advance guard would be driven in by Indian massacres, by drought or pestilence. But always the frontier would again move forward, and behind it life would grow more complex and more like the pattern for living which men had brought with them from the Old World.

For nearly three centuries Americans and their institutions knew this great experience of forward movement into the wilderness, a return in some degree, at least, to more primitive ways than they had already known, and the uneven advance toward that complexity which, deservedly or not, was called "civilization." By this experience they were altered in person and in characteristics. They became Americans. Just what that meant is not easy to say, but there were definite marks left on men and on institutions that distinguished them from the original settlers and practices that had first come out of Europe. Men became natives. They fitted the continent and its needs. Outsiders recognized the differences.

In the colonial period intimate connections with the Old World and the fact that colonial life was modeled after European patterns held back change to a degree. Most of the colonists thought of themselves as Europeans and strove to look and act like their fellows in the homeland. Residents of the towns and those in the older areas of the colonies, and persons of wealth and officeholders,—in fact, most who could afford to do so,—read English books and magazines, decked themselves and their homes in English-made goods, and took a real interest, direct or indirect, in what was going on abroad. If permitted to prosper and enjoy a reasonable degree of freedom, they were content to remain as part of the growing British Empire. Those who moved farther out, however, and who were forced, of necessity, to supply their own needs, lost both the English contacts and the English patterns. For some time before the Revolution many felt the separateness of their world and were thoroughly conscious of the fact that, if they were to be content and were to realize the possibilities offered in the new land, they must live their own lives in their own way. Troubles with the mother country, therefore, divided the colonists into Tories and Patriots. The bitter struggle over the Declaration of Independence only stressed the conflict between the persistence of things old and the force of change to things new. The ultimate acceptance of independence confirmed the fact that long years and long miles apart had created two peoples. Sadly many Tories left the colonies; others reluctantly accepted the inevitable.

But the greater influence of frontier living and the steady advance into the wilderness came in the years after the second war with England, in 1812. Emigrants poured westward in ever greater numbers.

New Wests, one after the other in different geographic basins, sprang into being. Soon they had upset the old balance in American life and taken charge. Western men were elected to the Presidency; domestic issues occupied Congress; American traits and American assumptions deepened and became fixed. For eighty years and more the process went on until the end of the frontier was reached and new forces came to dominate. But even then the American was largely what he was because of these days under this great experience. His characteristics and outlook, for years to come, had been shaped.

Foreign writers and native observers generally agreed on the larger characteristics of this "new man," this American. They stressed the fact that he was an individualist—a man who had learned to stand on his own feet, care for himself, do all kinds of things fairly well; who kept the patent office busy with his inventions; who liked his freedom and resented even government's interference. Yet, with all his stanch individualism, he was a man who knew how to co-operate, to help to raise the neighbor's house or barn, husk his corn, or bring into being a vigilance committee or a more substantial government.

He was, moreover, a confirmed believer in progress. He was used to change, and his experiences in transforming the wilderness into farms, in seeing his towns grow into cities and his nation become powerful among the nations, gave him faith in the future. Anything could be done. Dreams were forever becoming realities. He saw things not as they were, but as he and his fellows could make them to be. Henry Adams tells how the early American was wont to boast of his wealth, his "solid mountains of salt and iron, of lead, copper, silver, and gold"; of his cities "broadcast to the Pacific," and his cornfields "rustling and moving in the summer breeze." But the visitor saw only "tremendous wastes," where "sickly men and women" were "dying of homesickness" or were being scalped by savages; mountains beyond reach or swamps "choked with their own rotten ruins." No wonder he called the American "a liar and swindler" and his story "a fraud." But what he did not realize was that the American was not talking about things as they were, but about things as they were to be. He was indulging in dreams that could and would come true. That became a national habit. The future, not the past, held America's Garden of Eden.

Yet with all his belief in progress and all his tolerance of change, the American was, at heart, a conservative and a conformist. Life on the frontier was rather simple, and the problems to be faced were rather restricted and definite. The men who successfully solved them were, therefore, much alike in ability and point of view. They were of the same general pattern, regardless of time and place. Their way of doing things also fell into a pattern and soon constituted the accepted way in which things should be done. Standards were thus set, and the notion was created that these were the means by which progress was achieved. Conformity to pattern of necessity became a virtue, and eccentricity a fault. Amid primitive conditions the price of survival was often the rigid adherence by all men to well-understood lines of conduct. Where men had to depend on one another and to know how each would react to a given situation, uniformity and conformity alone afforded security. The nonconformist was a weak link in the social chain.

And, in like manner, ways that had helped to give "progress" beyond anything known elsewhere were deemed superior to any "foreign" importations. A community that had struggled upward from simple crudeness to complex comforts and extravagance had, by that very fact, demonstrated its superiority. Most Americans lived in "the best town" in the world. Their form of government and business system were also "best." To hold fast to that which was "good" was as much an American trait as was the urge to change.

Out of the experience of crossing and transforming the continent came also a tendency to stress material things and accomplishments. The tasks that the American faced were largely those of clearing land, accumulating materials, extracting natural resources, and building things. His accomplishments represented victories over nature. He worked with his hands, bent his back, endured physical hardships. He measured his progress by the clearing he made in the forest, the acres he broke to the plow, the size of the buildings, the towns, and the factories that he erected. The measure of his success was the wealth he accumulated. He worked hard and glorified toil. He hated the lazy man. There were too many things that had to be done in a new country. The Massachusetts Bay Company instructed its governor to permit "noe idle drone . . . to live amongst us," and Virginia ordered slothful persons to be bound over to forced labor. Compulsory labor, in the form of Negro slavery, was long accepted as a "good."

Such a situation produced a quantitative valuation of almost everything. When an American talked about what a man was worth, he was speaking of his material accumulations. When he said that a girl had married well, he probably was referring to her husband's bank account. The words *big* and *great* became synonyms. Values were to be measured by statistics. The height of a building, the enrollment of a university, the acres of a farm—these were the things on which judgments were to be based. Men should be "practical." Theories and speculations served no purpose. "Doing something useful" did not include much that had to do only with beauty for its own sake.

Yet here, again, was contradiction. Behind the American's pride in national accomplishment lay the more profound fact of an incurable idealism. The men who transformed a wilderness had to be men of faith. The finished product was the substance of things hoped for. Big buildings, big universities, big farms, represented achievement— victory over difficulties. The skyscraper stood where, only a few years before, there was a one-story structure with a false front. The rich man probably began as a poor boy and was proof of the opportunity offered in this new land. Both seemed to justify American optimism. Both, in their way, seemed to prove, to the generations which saw their story repeated over and over again, that something better for mankind was always possible if the right effort was made.

A strong dislike of special privilege, sometimes interpreted as a belief in equality, also marked the American. He believed in every man's having a chance. After that, men could draw as far apart as their abilities permitted. Freedom to become unequal was an essential part of his democracy. Yet the game had to be played fairly; and when the rules sometimes permitted favors to the few, there was a "higher law." This was only saying that the purpose of law, after all, was to secure a just social order based on equality.

Then there was the American brand of humor, characterized by "exaggeration and extravagance"; there was a new place for women, and new attitudes toward their rights; there was ever a restless moving about—a nervous tension that kept the nation on wheels much of the time, put rockers on chairs, and kept people chewing at something from morning until night. These and other qualities marked the American, with his back to Europe and his face to the West. With boundless energy he created kingdoms of wheat and cotton, and cities where the Industrial Revolution reached new levels of efficiency; fought a Civil War in order to adjust conflicting interests and values to the needs of changing conditions; created a new age of big business, with larger problems of social justice and the question of what government could do about it. And then, as domestic problems grew more complex, he found himself again, unwilling and bewildered, an active participant in the affairs of the larger world.

The years following the Civil War were years of drastic change, in which industrial and financial capitalism definitely established their dominance in American life. Agriculture was slowly pushed into a secondary place, and the policies favorable to industry and capital were enacted into law. Natural resources were developed and exploited as never before, and the patterns of living were greatly altered by urban developments and mass production. It was a period of transition marked by conflict and strife. Agriculture and industry, capital and labor, East and West, North and South, were often in bitter conflict with each other. The relationships and assumptions which had come down from the great era of physical expansion did not always fit the facts of the new day. Nevertheless they continued to play a part in shaping the course of developments, and they made the problems of adjustment more difficult. Soon the very power of business interests threatened the whole democratic order and forced an effort to find a balance between *laissez faire* and government control and regulation. The clash of rival groups and interests also bore heavy at times on the public welfare and brought demands for reform that ranged all the way from the passage of new legislation to a complete reordering of the whole social-economic system. Urban growth brought greater emphasis on cultural achievements, such as music and the arts. The specialist began to take the place of the old Jack-of-all-trades, and a greater tolerance for the "expert" appeared. Group association for work and play and mutual development testified to a weakening of the old individualism of frontier days. More leisure was possible, and, though "the gospel of work" still persisted, men nevertheless began to talk of the good uses to which "spare time" could be put. The old American values were weakening.

Equally important was the gradual resumption of American participation in larger world affairs. External interests crowded in to turn the American face outward once again. The Monroe Doctrine was widened in its application; American capital and business interests looked outside for both raw materials and markets. We made Cuba's unhappy conditions our business, and, through a war with Spain, gained new territorial interests, which involved us in the affairs of areas as widely separated as the Caribbean and the Philippines in the far Pacific. That gave American isolationism a terrific jolt and brought sharp conflict over "imperialism" into American politics. But it was only a beginning. Soon American representatives were sitting at council tables where European problems were dealt with, and a world war, begun in 1914, soon drew us into the thick of it for the simple reason that our interests were as vitally affected as those of the other great nations of the earth. But our minds were not prepared to accept entirely the facts. The struggle over entrance into the war was a bitter one, and the conflict between the natural impulse to make the world safe for democracy and the equally good tradition of confining our interests to this hemisphere was never quite won or lost. Isolationism triumphed with peace, and the realization of how out of character we were as a participant in European strife was not the least of the reasons for our rejection of the League of Nations.

The conflict between necessary participation in world affairs and the bent to isolationism went on to the very outbreak of the Second World War. It was as confusing as was the struggle between "free enterprise" in our domestic economic life and government participation in business. It still finds many Americans torn between the necessity of accepting world responsibility for democracy and peace and the old urge to stay at home and "mind our own business." The American is still in the making.

The making of the American, however, is only one part of the story. The rest of it has to do with the great experiment in democratic government and the effort to create a more democratic social-economic order. Out of Europe, in early years, came much that favored the few and justified the exploitation of the many. There were "superiors" and "inferiors"; there were cliques that formed around the governors and enjoyed special privileges. There was an established church in some colonies; the franchise usually belonged to those with property; representation in the assemblies was seldom equitable.

But the harsh pressure of wilderness living brought aristocrats down and common men up, and the struggle for home rule in Revolutionary days forced concessions as the price of wider co-operation. Gradually the franchise was broadened and representation balanced. Church and State were separated, and freedom was granted to all sects. Freedom of speech, trial by an impartial jury, security of person and property, and the right to keep and bear arms were added, in the Bill of Rights, to the new national Constitution.

Nature, meanwhile, offered her riches impartially, and the pressure of sheer numbers gradually forced more liberal policies in their distribution. Free land became the symbol of democracy. And, though the speculator still held advantages, the demands of the actual settler forced the granting of pre-emption rights and the ultimate passage of homestead legislation. The right to begin over again on some new frontier was thereby guaranteed to all Americans.

The door of opportunity was thus kept open, and the chance to fight for more democratic advances was always possible. Inequalities and injustice still remained, but the frontier and the continent's riches were on the side of greater equality and greater justice. The American tradition favored the common man more and more. With increasing force, the nation's outstanding leaders spoke for democracy. In early national days Thomas Jefferson insisted on the sacredness of individual personality, and fought to free his countrymen from the burdens of too much governing and the tyranny of traditional practices. A generation later Andrew Jackson took up the fight against the threatening power of business and finance, and established the claim of the commonest of men to the nation's highest offices. Abraham Lincoln, for the next generation, struck down human slavery and forced the nation to understand the significance to all mankind of the great experiment in government of the people, by the people, for the people. Then, in turn, came the Populists, the Progressives, and the New Dealers to stress anew the claims of democracy on the American people. They kept alive the tradition of protest and the ideal that government exists only to promote the general welfare. They carried on the tradition that forced the nation to accept responsibility for making the world safe for democracy under Woodrow Wilson, and equally safe for the Four Freedoms under Franklin D. Roosevelt.

Never have the American people been allowed to forget that the United States is an experiment in democracy. Even, at times, they have been reminded, as August Belmont reminded them in 1850, that "the day is not far distant when self-preservation will dictate to the United States the necessity of throwing her moral and physical force into the scales of European republicanism."

THE UNITED STATES

EXPERIMENT
IN DEMOCRACY

I

The American Beginning

THE ROOTS of present-day America go deep down into the European past. During the expansion of Europe, following the opening of the New World by Christopher Columbus, the region which was to become the present-day United States felt the impact of European settlers, ideas, and institutions. English, French, Dutch, Spanish, and Portuguese were the chief rivals for control of the Western Hemisphere; but other peoples of European stock, particularly Germans, Swiss, and Swedes, also came to America in the period of colonization. North America, however, was not the only region of the world to be affected by the expansion of Europe. From the fifteenth century to the twentieth, Europeans explored, settled, and exploited areas of Central and South America, Asia, Africa, Australia, and the many islands of the oceans.

After the establishment of the United States as an independent republic, hordes of Europeans came to the country in search of opportunity to gain a better standard of living and to live in a freer environment than was possible in their homelands. The traits, customs, beliefs, and institutions that all these immigrants brought with them, from the period of colonization to the present day, have helped to mold the American way of life. These European traits, however, did not remain unchanged in America. The American environment, with its bountiful natural resources, its open land, and its climate, shaped and altered them. Much of the history of the United States, therefore, is the story of the impact of a rich and undeveloped American continent on a wide variety of European peoples with differing ideas, traits, and customs.

Since American life, in many of its aspects, is a projection of European culture and institutions, the forces that led to the expansion of Europe overseas are as much a part of United States history as they are of modern European history. Before Europe could expand in the fifteenth century and dominate the rest of the world during the next four centuries, new forces had to develop in Europe that would bring the Middle Ages to an end. After the conquest of the Roman Empire by the barbarians, Europe had lapsed into a state of lethargy and stagnation. Feudalism, developing in the place of the Roman Empire, brought the isolation of peoples into small communities, with each local area taking care of its own wants, and with trade and commerce in the modern sense virtually ceasing. European economic, intellectual, and cultural life would have to be reawakened before exploration and colonization could take place.

One force that helped to rejuvenate European life and break down the barriers of isolation came from the Norse people of Denmark, Sweden, and Norway. They explored and conquered as far east as Russia and as far south as Normandy, in France, and overran parts of England; in the west they colonized Iceland and Greenland. During the late tenth or the early eleventh century they probably visited America. Their activities, however, did not greatly affect the rest of Europe, and are more important as an evidence of a reawakening than as an ushering in of the new age of discovery.

The Crusades, undertaken, during the twelfth and thirteenth centuries, to free the Holy Land from the control of non-Christians, were another force that stirred European life. The crusaders, on landing in the Middle East, came into contact with a culture that was far richer than their own, one which contained many commodities that Europe lacked. This experience awakened in Europeans the desire to acquire the spices, fine cloth, and precious stones of the Orient and led them to establish new trading companies and to launch a revival of commerce and trade. The crusaders, sailing to Palestine, had also given an extraordinary impetus to shipbuilding. When the crusading had stopped, these ships were used to carry goods from the Holy Land back to Europe. Merchants of such Italian cities as Venice and Genoa soon waxed rich from the profits of transporting the luxury goods of the East to western Europe. Over the course of two centuries the Crusades awakened the desire of Europeans to reach the source of Oriental luxuries; they stimulated a zeal for adventure, travel, and exploration; and they also hastened the rise of national states, corporate enterprise, and merchant capitalism.

Of the goods of the East, spices especially, such as pepper, cinnamon, cloves, and ginger, were greatly desired by Europeans because spices made their food more palatable in an age before refrigeration. The feudal lords also desired the fine clothes and jewels of the East in order to set themselves apart in a conspicuous fashion from their serfs. The great demand for these goods led to a sharp revival of trade in Europe and to the rapid growth of a merchant class residing in the towns. Reports of the wealth of the Far East that were brought back by travelers like Marco Polo, who had lived in China from 1275-1292, only further stirred the European desire to explore and to seek new channels of trade.

The growing contacts of the new trade and the expanding horizons of European life were important factors in preparing the way for a great upsurge of European intellectual activity in the fifteenth century. This renaissance of European cultural life emphasized anew the importance of the individual, stimulated the desire for worldly fame through exceptional achievements, created a will to experiment and to criticize, and renewed the interest of Western men in the writings of the ancients. In the Greek classics Europeans read that the world was round and found suggestions that the East might be reached by sailing west from Europe. Such ideas, of course, were conducive to exploration. By the fifteenth century, too, the compass and the astrolabe, an instrument for determining latitude, were being widely used, and the improvement in maps and charts was so marked that the age of discovery was at hand.

All the forces thus far described—the revival of trade, the growth of a merchant class, travel, inventions, and the Renaissance—are not sufficient to explain the expansion of Europe. One other development—the rise of the national state—was necessary to channel all the other forces and turn the attention of Europeans to the opening of new worlds. In the period from 1200 to 1600 the modern European states of Portugal, Spain, France, England, and Holland gradually took form. These national states destroyed the feudal order of localism and replaced the isolated feudal world with the nation, organized as a compact region under one central government. As this took place, the spirit of patriotism developed to help unite people of the same traditions, language, and race into one country dominated by a central authority.

Along with the growth of the national state came the development of the power of kings. During the Middle Ages the king had really been just another feudal lord, and the various lords in a kingdom seldom paid him more than "lip service." As the national state emerged, the king gradually increased his power at the expense of the feudal lords. He found willing allies in the merchants of the towns, who were hostile to the attempts of the feudal lords to curb and tax their trade. As the merchant traveled through one feudal area after another, he was forced to pay a tax to each feudal lord; but a united kingdom would end these local payments and afford the merchant a great free-trade area within a country. The townsmen, therefore, paid the king a regular revenue and put the town militia at his disposal. In return the king granted the towns the right of local government and exemption from the taxes imposed by the various lords. With the money from the towns the king was able to hire troops and to break the military power of the nobles.

A factor of immense significance to future world history was that all the rising national states bordered on the Atlantic highway. Under their leadership the focus of world activities was soon to be shifted from the Mediterranean Sea to the Atlantic Ocean. From the standpoint of trade in the fifteenth century these national states found themselves in a disadvantageous position. The Italian merchants had a monopoly of the trade with the Middle East. They exacted a rich profit as middlemen, and the resulting prices paid for goods seemed unduly high. Between the Far East and the Middle East, also, innumerable rulers levied taxes on the heavily laden caravans as they creaked their way to the Mediterranean coast. As a result, the merchant groups in the new national states were naturally desirous of securing a better place in the Oriental trade; and since they could not control the established channels of commerce, they decided to find routes of their own. If any national state could find a new route to the Orient, its merchants and people would be freed of the charges paid to the Italians and to the Arabs. This state would also be in a position to supply all its neighbors with goods.

Portugal was the first of the national states to search for a new route. The Portuguese sought to reach the Orient by sailing around Africa. Under Prince Henry the Navigator (1394–1460) Portuguese seamen cautiously proceeded farther and farther down the African coast. In 1487 Bartholomeu Dias rounded the Cape of Good Hope, and eleven years later Vasco da Gama reached India. The new trade route was soon in wide use, and the Italian merchants suffered greatly from the competition. Gradually the commercial leadership of Europe shifted from the Mediterranean to the Atlantic world.

Portugal was not alone in the search for a new route to the Orient. While the Portuguese pushed southward along the coast of Africa, other men dreamed of finding the East by sailing directly westward across the Atlantic. Among these was a lowly Italian, Christopher Columbus, who for eight long years had wandered from court to court in search of aid for such an expedition. Portuguese successes now led the royal house of Spain to grant the necessary backing. Half reluctantly Ferdinand and Isabella yielded to Columbus's enthusiasm and thereby became the first heirs to the riches of a new world. On August 3, 1492, a little fleet of three vessels, the *Niña,* the *Pinta,* and the *Santa María,* left the coast of Spain. On September 9 the frail little vessels lost sight of the Canary Islands and ventured out into the great unknown waters of the Atlantic. Day after day they pushed on with growing fears. On October 10 a mutiny occurred, and the sailors demanded that the Admiral turn back. He persuaded them to sail on for three more days. His courage was rewarded, for on October 12 the island of San Salvador in the Bahamas was sighted. Columbus had found his "India." As Samuel Eliot Morison, distinguished biographer of Columbus, has written in *Admiral of the Ocean Sea:*

> Other discoveries there have been more spectacular than that of this small, flat sandy island that rides out ahead of the American continent, breasting the trade winds. But it was there that the Ocean for the first time "loosed the chains of things" as Seneca had prophesied, gave up the secret that had baffled Europeans since they began to inquire what lay beyond the western horizon's rim. Stranger people than the gentle Tainos, more exotic plants than the green verdure of Guanahaní have been discovered, even by the Portuguese before Columbus; but the discovery of Africa was but an unfolding of a continent already glimpsed, whilst San Salvador, rising from the sea at the end of a thirty-three-day westward sail, was a clean break with past experiences. Every tree, every plant that the Spaniards saw was strange to them, and the natives were not only strange but completely unexpected, speaking an unknown tongue and resembling no race of which even the most educated of the explorers had read in the tales of travelers from Herodotus to Marco Polo. Never again may mortal men hope to recapture the amazement, the wonder, the delight of those October days in 1492 when the New World gracefully yielded her virginity to the conquering Castilians.[1]

Following his epoch-making voyage in 1492, Columbus led three other expeditions to the New World, exploring the South American continent and founding the first Spanish colony in the Western Hemisphere.

While Columbus, in the course of his four voyages, was busy exploring the islands of the Caribbean and touching the mainland of

[1]Samuel Eliot Morison, *Admiral of the Ocean Sea* (one-volume edition), p. 236. Little, Brown and Company, Boston, 1942.

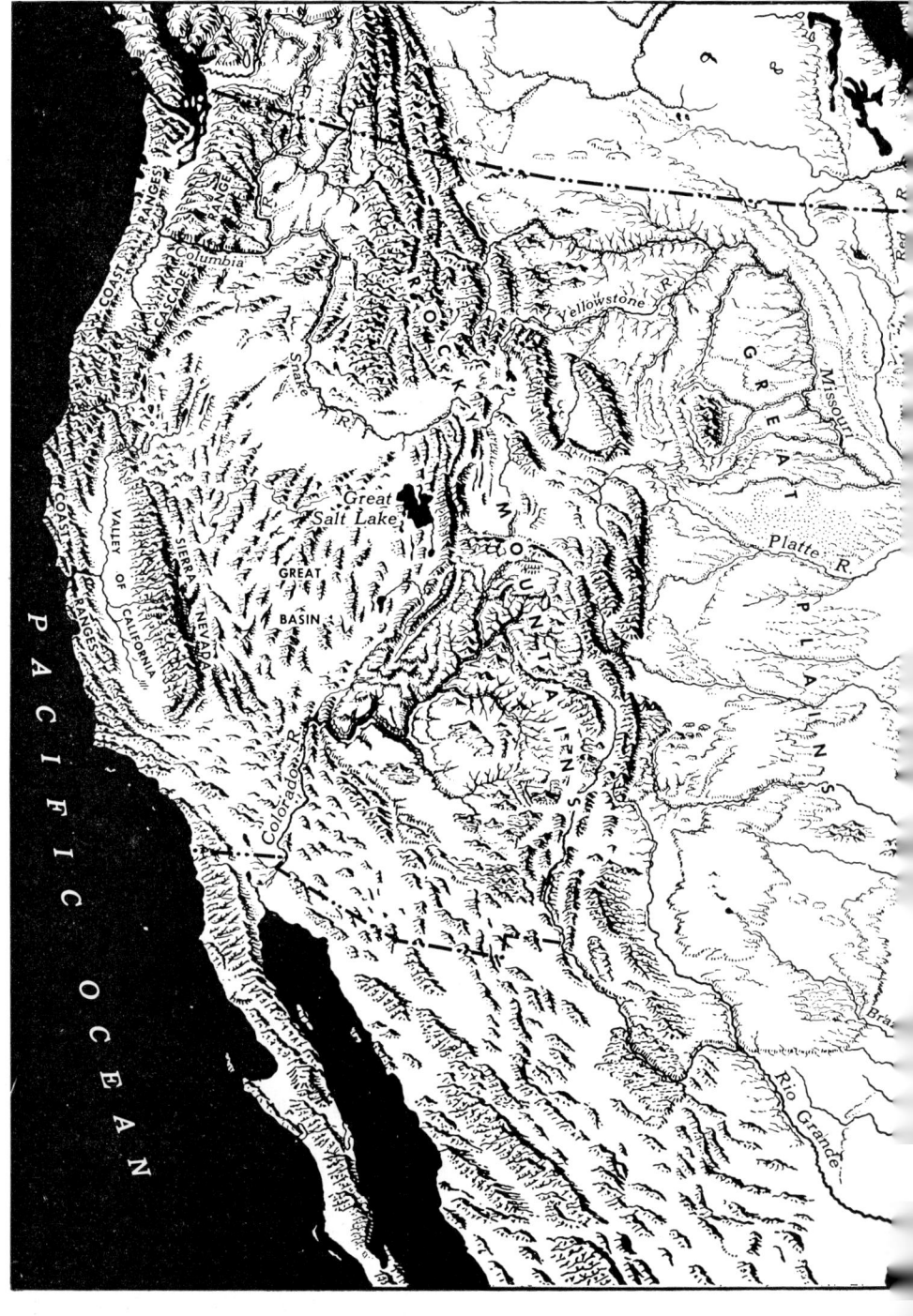

Relief Map

of the United States

European Exploration and Colonization of the New World

| | English | | French | | Spanish | | Portuguese | | Dutch |

South America, the English national state supported John Cabot in two voyages, in 1497 and 1498, to the North American continent. Although England did not follow up these discoveries for about three quarters of a century, they served to give her a "legal" title to North America against the claims of Spain and Holland. A Portuguese navigator, Pedro Álvares Cabral, on a voyage to India in 1500, landed on the shores of present-day Brazil and claimed it for Portugal. Other Spaniards made voyages to the South American continent, and with one of these trips, in 1499, was Amerigo Vespucci, a Florentine merchant. His account of the voyage made his name familiar to a German geographer, who suggested that the new continent be named *America*.

A warning from Portugal, to the effect that it felt that Columbus had trespassed on its territory, led Spain to seek confirmation of Spanish rights from Pope Alexander VI. In 1493 the Pope drew a demarcation line through a point a hundred leagues west and south of the Azores and the Cape Verde Islands. West of this line Spain was to have title to the lands that she discovered as well as a monopoly of the trade. Portugal objected, and a year later another line was drawn, three hundred and seventy leagues west of the Cape Verde Islands. This new line was to divide the whole world, outside of Europe, between Portugal and Spain. All the discoveries east of this line were to go to Portugal, and all west to Spain. The Line of Demarcation so fell in South America as to include Brazil in the Portuguese area; and when Cabral, in 1500, touched Brazil, Portugal had a "legal" right to establish a colony there.

THE ENGLISH BACKGROUND OF EXPANSION

England approached America cautiously. It was not until the seventeenth century, roughly a century after Spain had begun to have flourishing colonies in the Caribbean region, that England successfully established American colonies. English colonization was the result of profound economic and religious changes that had gradually altered English society. From 1350 to 1600 a basic revolution swept through English economic life. The raising of sheep for wool to supply the looms of Europe led many of the owners of feudal manors to drive their serfs off the land—the enclosure movement—and use their land for pastures instead of permitting it to be cultivated in small patches as in the past. The serfs thus became a foot-loose, unemployed group who could be used to develop industry and seafaring enterprises. Shortly after this change in agriculture, England began to develop her own woolen mills. Skilled artisans came from Europe to teach the new trade, and to make use of this bountiful supply of labor. With manufactured woolen goods to sell, England soon became interested in colonies and foreign trade. Joint-stock companies, with membership and control open to any purchaser of shares of stock, were organized to push trade and to forward colonization. The joint-stock company, through the device of selling stock, made it possible to raise the large sums of money necessary to finance colonizing expeditions. No one merchant could afford to run the risk attached to such an expedition; but when a group of merchants shared the risk, each with only part of his fortune, then it became feasible. From the English government the promoters of such companies received royal charters granting them monopolies of trade in the areas which they opened.

The growing industries of England were not able to absorb all the serfs turned off the land. This unemployed group led to the belief that the island was overpopulated and that colonies were needed where these Englishmen could live under their own flag. When the merchant capitalists organized companies to settle new areas, these unemployed furnished a supply of colonists. Another source of settlers was found among the younger sons of the landed aristocracy. English law provided that estates could pass only to the eldest son, and this rule of primogeniture cast the other sons adrift. They turned to colonization as a way to maintain their position as leaders of society. All these economic developments, preparing the way for expansion, were increased during the years from 1620 to 1635 by a severe depression that swept over England, and emphasized the need for new overseas markets.

At the same time that these economic changes were transforming England, the country was in the throes of religious unrest. The Protestant Reformation, which had been started by Martin Luther in 1519, now came to England. Under its influence Henry VIII (1509–1547) repudiated the authority of the Pope over the English Church, and Edward VI (1547–1553) made England a Protestant country. His successor, Queen Mary (1553–1558), reverted to Catholicism. Queen Elizabeth, who came to the throne in 1558, returned to Protestantism. She was the daughter of Henry VIII and Anne Boleyn, whose marriage had never been sanctioned by the Pope. When the Pope declared that Elizabeth could not become queen without his consent, Elizabeth refused to accept this statement, since it meant that her right to rule depended on an outside power. She began the development of the Church of England, or the Anglican Church, wherein the Pope was displaced by the sovereign as the head of the church. To obtain internal peace, Elizabeth imposed religious uniformity on the country, and laws against Catholics and more radical Protestants were passed, although they were not always rigorously enforced.

The Anglican Church was neither Roman Catholic nor radically Protestant, and the English Reformation really was a political compromise between the Catholic and Protestant groups. The Catholic hierarchy of archbishops and bishops was retained, while the Anglican creed was largely Protestant. Neither extreme Catholics nor extreme

Protestants were satisfied. This led to the development of various Protestant sects, among which were the followers of John Calvin.

Few men have had such a profound influence on American development as this French reformer. The religious beliefs of the Calvinists, more than those of any other religious group, helped to shape American institutions and life. An important part of the heritage of these Calvinist people was a belief in government by contract, intellectual freedom, and individualism. Calvin's *Institutes of the Christian Religion*, published in 1536, had a remarkable influence on world history. In four countries, during the period when the English were settling North America, that influence was far-reaching. Calvin's followers in France were the Huguenots, in Scotland the Presbyterians, in Holland the members of the Dutch Reformed Church, and in England the Puritans. From these four groups came the largest numbers of settlers for the English colonies. As a result, Calvinism was the most important religious force in the life of the colonies. In the twentieth century too, Calvinism, although modified in certain ways, is still a significant factor in American life, with such churches as the Presbyterian, Congregational, and Dutch and German Reformed, all displaying the mark of John Calvin.

The two major premises of Calvinism were the absolute sovereignty of God and the authority of the word of God. The word of God was to be found in the Scriptures as interpreted by the minister. The minister thus assumed a dominant position in any Calvinist group. Breaking with the Catholic position, Calvin held that man was justified in expecting salvation after death by faith alone, and that God had determined that some people were to be saved and others damned. The Calvinists naturally believed that they were the saved, or the elect of God. As a result of being an elect group, Calvin and his followers formulated the idea of a Holy Commonwealth on earth. This community consisted of the elect, whose duty it was to aid God in improving society.

Calvin developed the Presbyterian form of church organization. It was transplanted to Scotland, and a large segment of the English Puritans advocated its adoption. Under this type of organization the officers of the church—the minister, teacher, elder, and deacon—formed the Presbytery and were the dominant group in church affairs. Members of the various Presbyteries formed synods, which had the power to dictate to the individual congregations. The members of a congregation had some power in the selection of those who

formed the Presbytery, and thus approximated a form of representative government. The English Puritans who settled Massachusetts
followed Calvinism in its various beliefs and practices, except in church
organization. This wing of Calvinism emphasized the independence
of each congregation—hence they were termed Congregationalists—
but limited the power of synods to an advisory status only.

From the standpoint of political philosophy, the Calvinists believed
that the duty of government was to glorify God. Government, they
contended, had come about as a result of a contract between the ruler
and the people. This contract meant that there was a fundamental
written law, binding upon both the ruler and the subjects. This fundamental law guaranteed certain rights to the subjects; and if the ruler
violated these rights, then he had violated the fundamental contract and
thus forfeited his crown. When this occurred, the people, through
representatives of their own choosing, had the right to depose the ruler.
Here, in this political philosophy, were ideas that were to shape American development. The ideas of a fundamental written law (a constitution), representative government, and the right of resistance against
tyranny were basic concepts at the time of the American Revolution;
and when the belief in democracy is added to them, one has the basic
concepts of American political development.

In the field of economic endeavor also the Calvinists were to influence the history of America. Calvinism gave the rising capitalism of
western Europe a tremendous impetus. It offered theological justification to the trading middle class, since a Calvinist was supposed to
work hard in order to glorify God. In general, the Calvinists approved of business, trade, and profit-making, something which the
Catholic Church had long frowned upon. However, business activity
was subject to certain religious restraints. Private wealth was not
to be used in any way detrimental to the public welfare. Merchants
were entitled only to a fair profit, and were supposed to shun profiteering and monopoly. The community had the task of regulating prices,
wages, and the quality of commodities for the common good. The
holders of wealth and property had certain obligations to God to rule
justly, to enforce morality, and to advance education and religion.

This philosophy stimulated hard work, frugality, and thrift. The
sanction of hard work found fertile soil in the English colonies. The
wealth of the land and the sea was utilized by the Puritan groups to
the fullest extent. Under the influence of the bountiful resources and
the ever expanding frontier, however, the religious restraints on profit-

eering and the regulation of wages, prices, and the quality of goods gradually broke down. These Puritan characteristics of hard work, a belief in private property, the acquisitive spirit, profiteering, and social inequality (the idea of the elect as opposed to the damned) helped to form the American concept of rugged individualism.

While the Puritan group was developing in England, Queen Elizabeth was faced with opposition from Catholics at home and abroad. Philip II of Spain, with the wealth that came from the Spanish empire in the New World, determined to suppress Protestantism and place the Catholic Mary Stuart on the throne of England. This religious strife, together with the commercial rivalry between Spain and England, brought the two countries into open war in 1587. Before war actually occurred, such English seamen as Francis Drake, John Hawkins, and Thomas Cavendish raided Spanish treasure ships carrying gold and silver from Spanish America to Spain. When England destroyed the Spanish Armada in 1588, her mastery of the seas was established. She was now able to take advantage of colonization in the West.

An overseas empire in North America appealed greatly to Elizabethan England. It would be in a climate where the surplus population of England might live and provide a market for English manufactured goods. The colonies, it was hoped, could make England self-sufficient by supplying timber, gold and silver, spices, wines—in short, everything that England had to buy from foreign countries. In addition, the discovery of a route through America to the Far East would enhance national power. Richard Hakluyt, an English clergyman, stimulated interest in America by popularizing the exploits of the Elizabethan seamen through publishing accounts of their voyages. He also wrote a discourse advocating the planting of colonies in North America.

Sir Humphrey Gilbert made an unsuccessful attempt to found a colony in Newfoundland in 1583, and Sir Walter Raleigh sponsored three unsuccessful expeditions (1580's) to Roanoke Island, off the coast of present-day North Carolina. England was too busy warding off the Spanish invasion to pay much attention to these enterprises, but they did teach the English that founding a colony was too expensive for the purse of one man. The English sovereign, also, lacked the funds for colonization. English rulers could tax only with the consent of Parliament, and this check which Parliament had on the purse strings resulted in colonization being left to private persons. When English

America was being settled, the power of Parliament over the sovereign was growing, and by the Glorious Revolution, of 1688, Parliament's supremacy over the crown was definitely established. The fact that the king, during the early years of colonization, was not an absolute ruler, like the king of Spain, was a significant factor in the growth of self-government in America.

THE FOUNDING OF THE ENGLISH COLONIES

The land and climate of North America were exceedingly inviting to the English. A dense forest stretched from Maine to Georgia, and the temperate climate was extremely appealing. John Smith, in evaluating the climate of Virginia, wrote that "Heaven and earth never agreed better to frame a place for man's habitation." An early New England settler, Higginson, spoke in glowing terms of this region:

Experience doth manifest itself that there is hardly a more healthful place to be found in the world that agreeth better with our English bodies. Many that have been weak and sickly in Old England, by coming hither have been thoroughly healed and grown healthful strong. For here is a most extraordinary clear and dry air that is of a most healing nature to all such as are of a cold, melancholy, phlegmatic, or rheumatic temper of body.

The dense forest, with its bountiful pines, maples, beeches, oaks, and walnut trees, furnished the colonizers with lumber for homes, barns, furniture, and fuel. The settlers shipped pitch, tar, and resin to England, and constructed fine sailing ships to help in carrying the commerce of the empire. The Atlantic Ocean was teeming with all types of fish and other seafood. New England was to wax rich on the money made from cod-fishing in the cold waters off her coast and off the banks of Newfoundland. The land was teeming with turkeys, rabbits, partridges, quail, geese, deer, and elk, while the woods and bushes were a treasure house of many types of berries, grapes, crab apples, plums, and nuts. The soil and climate were admirably suited for such English crops as wheat, oats, barley, and rye. Swine, sheep, goats, chickens, and cattle, brought from the old country, flourished better than they had in England. To lend variety to the settlers' living, the Indian crops of peas, beans, maize, pumpkins, squash, melons, and cucumbers were cultivated.

From Maine to Georgia the land was so formed that, except in North Carolina and southern New Jersey, there were innumerable inlets and harbors. Inland from these harbors ran rivers, such as the Connecticut, the Delaware, the Potomac, and the James, which opened a way to the back-country regions. Settlers tended to establish their colonies along these rivers, which afforded them easy access to trade with England. Behind the coastal plain rose the Appalachian Mountains. These mountains, running in a chain from the White Mountains of New England to the Blue Ridge Mountains of the South, long checked western expansion and kept the colonies, for roughly a hundred and fifty years, in the narrow region between the mountains and the ocean. This geographical situation aided the English colonies in developing a more stable and unified society, whereas an open road to the West might have seriously scattered them.

The land and its resources shaped the economic activities of the colonies. Glaciated New England was so rock-strewn and rough that it was an inferior farming country. Its people turned to the rich forests and launched vigorous lumbering and shipbuilding industries. They took to the high seas as cargo-carriers and fishermen, and the Yankee trader became a well-known figure in other English colonies and in parts of Central and South America, Europe, and Africa. The soils of New York, New Jersey, and Pennsylvania were much better than that of New England, and this area became the great exporter of foodstuffs—the breadbasket of the English colonies. The soils of Maryland, Virginia, and North Carolina were admirably suited to tobacco-raising, while South Carolina and Georgia concentrated on rice, indigo, and sea-island cotton.

When the first settlers arrived, they found the land already inhabited by the Indians. The Indians of North America were far behind the Aztecs and Mayas of Mexico, the Chibchas of Colombia, and the Incas of Peru in their cultural, social, economic, and political development. The North American Indians were still mainly in the hunting stage of existence. Their agriculture was extremely primitive, and they had domesticated only the dog. The various tribes were thinly scattered over the area occupied by the English colonies, and their internal quarrels made the task of the English in subduing them relatively simple. The Indians sold the settlers food in times of crisis, taught them how to grow such valuable crops as tobacco and maize, opened up the wilderness trails to the white men, and revealed the secrets of forest life to the colonial citizens. The valuable fur trade was carried on with the aid of the Indians. Unlike the Spanish and Portuguese civilizations of the other Americas, the English society did not absorb the

Indians. The English exterminated them or pushed them westward, and they seldom intermarried.

The first successful English colony to be established on the shores of North America was sponsored by a group of merchant capitalists organized in a joint-stock company, the Virginia Company, which received a charter for the land from the crown. Three ships of settlers dropped down the Thames late in 1606 and reached the shores of Virginia early the following year. The Company expected to derive a profit from gold mines, to acquire goods that England lacked, to supply an outlet for the unemployed, to convert the Indian, and to discover the Northwest Passage. Across the bay from Jamestown, Virginia, twenty-seven years later, a proprietary colony was established by Lord Baltimore. Sir George Calvert, the first Lord Baltimore, desired a colony where he could create a great feudal domain for his family and where his fellow Catholics could settle. He did not live to carry out his project, but his son was granted a charter to the area of Maryland. Calvert, not a joint-stock company, held title to the land as the sole proprietor.

While the Southern colonies were being established, New England was settled largely as a result of the Puritan opposition to the Anglican Church. At the time when the great English merchants were settling Virginia, a small band of humble folk were worshiping at the village of Scrooby in Nottinghamshire in defiance of the state church. They were Puritans who believed in local, congregational control of the church, and they believed also in the separation of Church and State. From 1607 to 1609 groups of these Calvinists left England for Holland, where the religious climate was more favorable to them. They longed, however, to live in an English society, rear their children as Englishmen, and be in a land where there was more opportunity. Consequently a group of them decided to migrate to Virginia in 1620. The Virginia Company gave them permission to settle on its land, and King James I promised not to molest them if they lived peaceably. This decision of the king's opened English America to religious dissenters, and before long the English colonies became a great haven of refuge for the persecuted of Europe. The Pilgrims lacked capital to finance their expedition, and they made an arrangement with a group of London merchants whereby the profits of the colony were to go to the merchants for an agreed number of years in return for the financing of their colonization. Landing, by accident of weather, outside the Virginia Company's land and in territory that had been granted by the

Their manner of fishynge in Virginia

John White, a Member of Sir Walter Raleigh's Second Expedition (1585), Painted Water Colors of the Indians of North Carolina

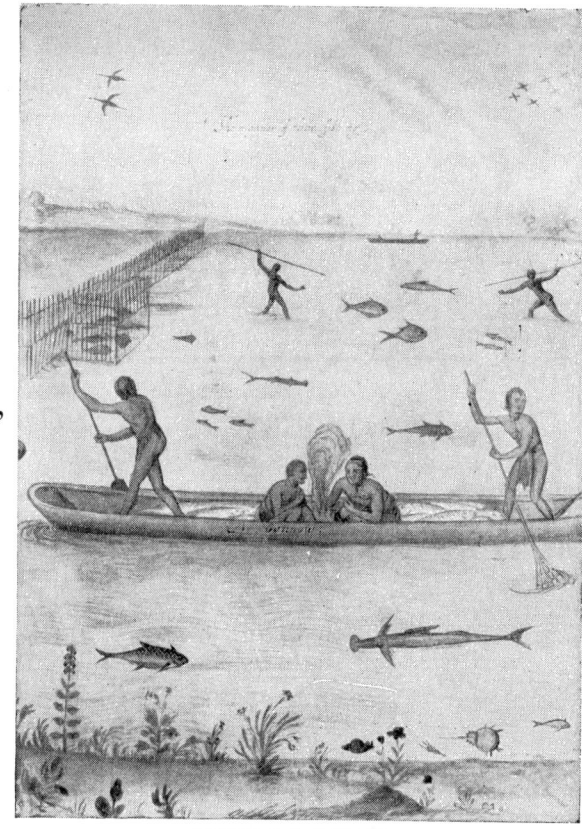

Their danses which they use att their hyghe feastes

Paintings in the British Museum
Photographs from the Library of Congress

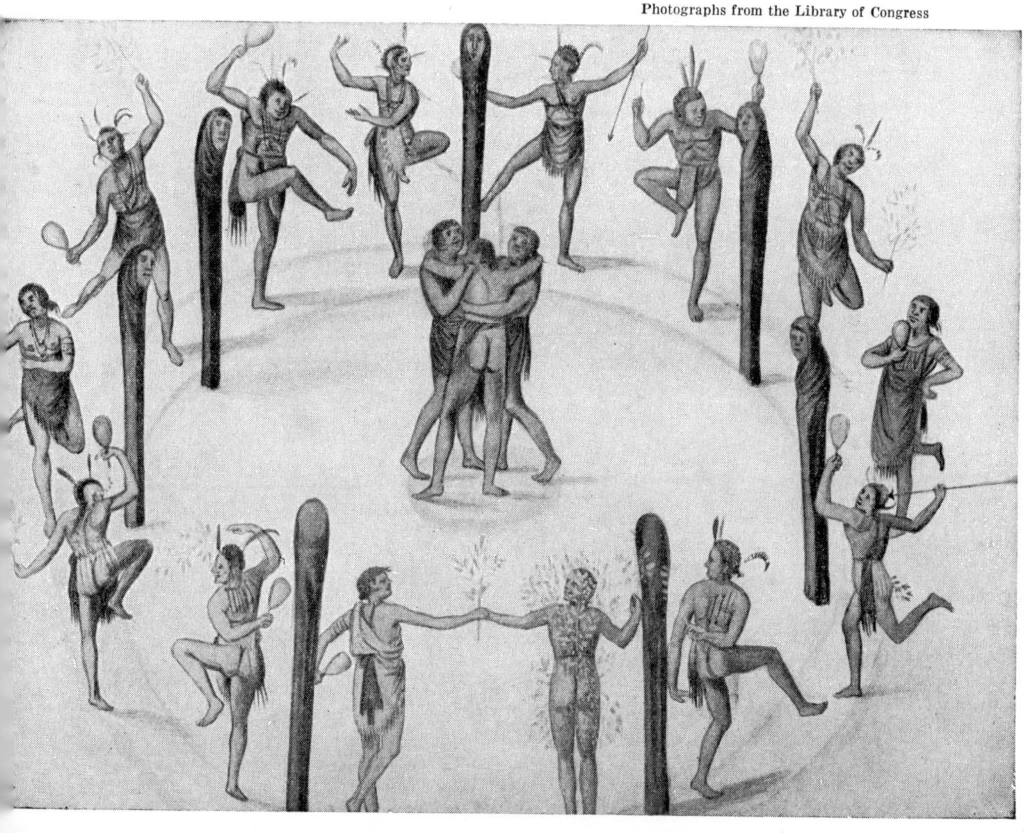

king to the Council for New England, headed by Ferdinando Gorges and John Mason, the Pilgrims quickly obtained permission to settle from the Council. The small colony never received a charter from the king, and in 1691 the king merged it with the larger Massachusetts Bay Colony. William Bradford, the first governor of Plymouth, left for posterity the story of the Pilgrims in a simple, moving book, *The History of Plymouth Plantation.*

Ten years after Plymouth was founded, a gigantic Puritan migration settled the Boston region. During the 1620's a group of businessmen in Dorchester, England, organized a company to engage in fishing activities off the coast of New England. A fishing settlement was established in 1623 at present-day Gloucester, Massachusetts, and moved to Salem three years later. The enterprise failed to pay, and the businessmen withdrew. The Reverend John White, pastor of these businessmen, persuaded a group of Puritans in England to take over the enterprise. A charter was obtained from the king, incorporating them as the Massachusetts Bay Company, a joint-stock company, and a large grant of land was secured from the Council for New England. In 1629 a group of the Puritan stockholders decided to migrate to the New World. They were suffering from the economic depression in England and from religious persecution. Led by John Winthrop, these Puritans looked forward to establishing the Holy Commonwealth of God in New England. Winthrop's group agreed to migrate, provided the charter and the government of the colony were transferred with them to the colony, not retained in England. They insisted upon this, since the Company was an open corporation and anyone could join it by purchasing stock. If the government of the Company were left in England, non-Puritans might secure control and destroy the Puritan commonwealth in New England. In 1630 Winthrop led the first large migration to Massachusetts and founded Boston. During the next ten years some twenty thousand people came to the colony.

The founders of the Massachusetts Bay Colony hoped to extend its borders to include all New England except Plymouth. In the 1630's settlers from Boston moved into New Hampshire and Maine. During much of the seventeenth century Massachusetts dominated New Hampshire, until the king established New Hampshire as a separate colony in 1679. Maine was incorporated as part of Massachusetts by the second charter, issued in 1691, and remained a part of Massachusetts until 1820. Connecticut was settled from two sources. The Reverend Thomas Hooker, dissatisfied with the conservative control of the Bay Colony and desirous of better land, led a band of people from the Bay Colony in 1635 to the richer lands of the Connecticut River area and established the towns of Hartford, Windsor, and Wethersfield. Two years later the three towns organized their own government, and in 1639 adopted a constitution known as the "Fundamental Orders of Connecticut." The colony of New Haven, founded in 1637 by an extreme Puritan preacher, John Davenport, and a London merchant, Theophilus Eaton, retained a separate existence from Connecticut until 1662.

These colonies were not basically different in point of view from Massachusetts. Rhode Island, however, which was founded as an emanation from Massachusetts in 1636, was decidedly contrary-minded. Massachusetts tried to force uniformity in religion, and Roger Williams, one of the outstanding liberals of the seventeenth century, objected. Williams believed in complete religious liberty wherein the individual could worship God as he chose, or not at all if he preferred. Williams challenged the right of Massachusetts to force people to worship in its Congregational Church, and he objected also to the control of the Massachusetts government by the few leading landowners and ministers. Banished from the colony, he founded Providence in 1636. Another thorn in the Massachusetts Puritan's flesh was Anne Hutchinson, who took upon herself the task of criticizing the preachers' sermons and expounding her own views on the Bible. Since the Puritan creed set forth that the minister was the sole interpreter of the word of God, Mrs. Hutchinson had to flee the colony. In 1638, with a group of friends, she founded Portsmouth, Rhode Island. Six years later the various Rhode Island settlements were federated into one government.

The Civil War in England and Cromwell's rule (1640–1658) temporarily stopped English colonization. When Charles II gained the throne in 1660, a new wave of colonization began. New Netherland was captured from the Dutch in 1664, the southern frontier was extended by the founding of the Carolinas, and the gap between New England and Maryland was filled by the colonies of New York, New Jersey, Pennsylvania, and Delaware. Charles II, in 1663, granted the area of Carolina to eight proprietors, who expected to create great landed estates on the feudal pattern and also to sell part of the land for revenue purposes. They made their first settlement in 1670 at old Charles Town, which was relocated at Charleston in 1680. The proprietors, furthermore, exerted control over settlements in the northern part that had been made by discontented Virginians. This area was later to become the separate colony of North Carolina.

In 1664 Charles II granted the Duke of York the region between the Connecticut and Delaware rivers. The Duke captured the weak Dutch colony of New Netherland that year and changed the name to New York. The land between the Delaware and Hudson rivers he gave to two proprietors, Sir George Carteret and John, Lord Berkeley, naming it New Jersey. These two men expected to realize money from New Jersey through a large-scale real-estate business. In 1674 Berkeley sold his share of New Jersey to two Quakers. Eight years later Carteret's widow sold her land to a group of proprietors, among whom were many Quakers.

The Society of Friends, or the Quakers, founded by George Fox, rejected the authority of the Church. Every man was his own priest and acted according to the "inner light" in the human soul. The Quakers believed in absolute equality and objected to all force and re- pression. They won to their faith William Penn, the son of an admiral of the royal navy. Through his father young Penn occupied a high place in English life. Penn inherited his father's estate and also a claim on the Duke of York because of a debt that the Duke owed the admiral. Visualizing a proprietary colony of his own, where the Quakers could build a commonwealth based on religious liberty, Penn obtained a grant of land from the king in 1681 in consideration of the debt owed by the royal family. Penn's estate was the largest, most valuable grant of land in America ever received by an individual from the crown. The king also gave Penn a charter making him the proprietor of the land with governmental powers. In the same year (1681) the first settlers were dispatched to Pennsylvania, which soon prospered as no other early colony did. Settlers poured in from the European continent, and the colony became a melting pot of different nationalities and religions. Looking to expand his dominion, Penn purchased the three "lower counties," as the future state of Delaware was then called, from the Duke of York. In 1702 Delaware was granted a separate legislature from Pennsylvania, although it had the same governor and constitution.

CONCLUSION

In looking back over the century of exploration and settlement, which had given England twelve colonies in North America, certain significant facts stand out. It had been not only a period of great physical expansion, but one also in which men's intellectual attitudes had been completely altered. They not only had found new physical

SELECTED BIBLIOGRAPHY

EDWARD P. CHEYNEY, *The Dawn of a New Era*, a book on the early European background that has insight and charm; CARLETON J. H. HAYES, *A Political and Cultural History of Modern Europe*, an excellent textbook survey of European development; HENRI PIRENNE, *Economic and Social History of Medieval Europe*, a significant book by one of the greatest scholars on the Middle Ages; PRESERVED SMITH, *The Age of the Reformation*, unexcelled on this subject; R. H. TAWNEY, *Religion and the Rise of Capitalism*, a profound study.

On the English background of American life: GEORGE M. TREVELYAN, *England under the Stuarts*, a brilliant survey of the religious turmoil of the day; GEORGE P. GOOCH, *The History of English Democratic Ideas in the Seventeenth Century*, an able study; EPHRAIM LIPSON, *The Economic History of England*, the best survey of this subject; CHARLES M. ANDREWS, *The Colonial Period of American History*, the best material on the work of the promoters of English colonies.

H. S. COMMAGER (Ed.), *Documents of American History*, pp. 1–25, contains source material.

II

Rivalries
in the Western Hemisphere

LONG BEFORE the English established colonies in the Western Hemisphere, the Spaniards had developed a powerful empire stretching from present-day Florida and New Mexico to Patagonia in the southernmost part of South America. In the half-century following Columbus's discovery of America, the world witnessed a series of exploits by the Spaniards that are unmatched in the history of exploration. In their search for slaves, gold, pearls, and a passage to the Orient, Spanish explorers, by 1525, had sailed along the entire Atlantic coast line from the Strait of Magellan to the northern boundary of the present-day United States. Thirty years after Balboa had discovered the Pacific Ocean in 1513, the entire Pacific coast line of the Americas, as far north as Oregon, had been traversed by Spanish pioneers.

While this was being accomplished, other Spanish explorers turned their attention to the inland regions, where the lust for gold, and the desire to establish huge landed estates and to subjugate the Indians and make them Christians, stimulated extraordinary achievements. The leaders of these expeditions, known as *adelantados*, obtained a license from the king to conquer a specified area. The leader was permitted, under this license, to recruit soldiers and settlers and to outfit ships. He was required to take a number of missionaries to convert the Indians, and to include royal agents to keep a record of the profits of the expedition, since one fifth of the profits automatically went to the king. After the conquest had been completed, the title to the land was vested in the king, although the leader was permitted to keep a vast estate for himself and distribute lands to his followers, and was also granted the right to put the Indians to forced labor on these estates, or encomienda grants as they were known. The most conspicuous and notorious of the *adelantados* were Hernando Cortes, Francisco Pizarro, and Gonzalo Jiménez de Quesada. Cortes with a small expedition landed in Mexico in 1519 and during the next two years succeeded in conquering the

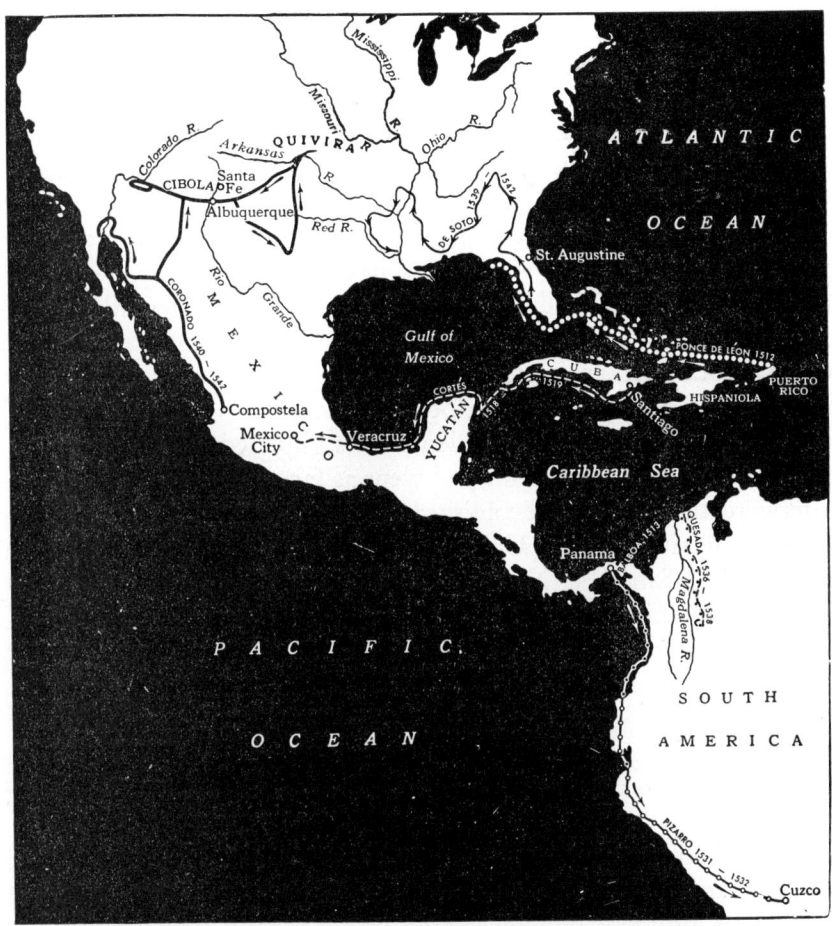

Spanish Explorations in the Sixteenth Century

highly developed Aztec Indians. He divided the land and the captive Indians among his men in encomienda grants. Some of his lieutenants led expeditions against the Mayas of Yucatán and succeeded in breaking their power by 1545. The second imposing and awe-inspiring conquest was that led by Pizarro. Pizarro had been a member of Balboa's expedition to Panama, and there he had heard tales of the rich Inca kingdom to the south. In 1531 he led a successful expedition to Peru and subdued the Incas, seizing their treasures of gold and silver and carving out large encomiendas for himself and his men. While Pizarro was busy in Peru, Quesada conquered the Chibchas of present-day Colombia. His expedition, consisting of only one hundred and sixty men, was unique in that it was cut off from the world for two years, and yet Quesada was able to defeat a far more numerous Indian group.

While the semicivilized Indians, their treasures of precious metals, and their lands were being added to the Spanish empire, other expeditions set out to conquer the less highly developed Indian groups. In 1528 Pánfilo de Narváez led an ill-fated expedition to Florida. Eleven years later Hernando de Soto landed in Florida and tramped overland as far north as the piedmont of North Carolina, then south toward Mobile Bay, from there to the Mississippi River, and then to the land of present-day Arkansas and Oklahoma. In 1540 Francisco Coronado set out from Mexico in search of the fabled land of Cibola, with its seven wealthy cities, whose golden towers glistened in the sun. Coronado crossed the Great Plains and went as far as central Kansas. Soon afterward the Spaniards established permanent settlements in what is now the territory of the United States, at St. Augustine, Florida, in 1565, and at Santa Fe, New Mexico, in 1610. In South and Central America, Spanish *conquistadores* explored vast regions of jungles, mountains, and plains, throwing a great deal of light on the geographical conditions and on the native inhabitants of the hemisphere.

THE SPANISH COLONIAL SYSTEM

Unity had been achieved in Spain under Ferdinand and Isabella, and a Spanish nationalism had come into being. In 1516 the united possessions of these two sovereigns passed into the hands of their grandson, Charles I. Spanish America was settled in a period when the absolute power of the crown was on the increase in Spain. The masses had acquired an unshakable faith in the divinity of kings, and the Cortes—the old legislative body—was ignored and rendered powerless. The nobility was either attracted to the royal court as satellites or suppressed, and royal officials—*visitadores*—were dispatched to the farthest bounds of the kingdom to infringe upon local independence. The ancient privilege of self-rule for the towns was openly violated, and the towns became mere administrative units of the central government. All this was in direct contrast with developments in England, where, during the seventeenth century, the power of the king was checked by Parliament and laws became supreme over the whims of the ruler.

The Spanish Church, under royal control, played a very important part in the creation of a strong centralized state. The enormous wealth and prestige of the Spanish Church placed it in the forefront of the battle against all opposition to the Catholic faith. Religious persecution was used to aid in the development of royal absolutism. The rulers of Spain, unlike the English kings, never permitted their colonies to become the refuge of religious dissenters. Heretics and recently converted Moors and Jews were not allowed to emigrate to Spanish America. Owing to the intolerant Catholicism of the rulers, the dissenting religious groups, which in English America contributed materially to the growth of the colonies, were never allowed to set foot in the Spanish dominions.

From the economic point of view, Spain lacked many of the qualities that were so influential in English colonization. Spain, interested in wars for the domination of the European continent, neglected her sea power. A strong commercial and industrial middle class was conspicuously lacking, too. Spain had to import her manufactured goods from England and Holland, and much of the treasure from her colonies went to pay for these goods.

The absolute monarchy of Spain, which regarded the colonies as personal possessions and not as belonging to the nation; the transplanting of the Spanish system of large landed estates; the intolerance of the Spaniards, which closed the colonies to non-Spaniards and heretics; and the central government's constant encroachment upon local autonomy, all these were factors that would mold the development of Spanish America. Furthermore, Spain's desire to dominate Europe resulted in the wasting of money and men on European wars, which in turn meant increased taxation of the colonies. All in all, the Spanish colonies were faced with a declining mother country after the turn of the seventeenth century. This, again, contrasts with the English colonies, whose mother country increased in wealth and power during the colonial period.

The Spaniards developed an elaborate colonial administration and policy. The king ruled the colonies without interference from the Cortes. Two agencies—the Council of the Indies and the *Casa de Contratación*—were set up by the crown to aid in administering the empire. The Council of the Indies selected colonial officials, superintended the administrative system, shaped policies, and served as a supreme court to review important cases arising in the colonies. The *Casa de Contratación* served as a board of trade, gathering information about commerce, regulating voyages to the colonies, and promoting imperial trade. In the colonization of the New World, Spain transplanted many of the institutions of the homeland. At all times colonial administration was closely supervised from Spain, and as a result the Spanish colonies did not suffer the degree of salutary neglect that the English colonies did.

In the sixteenth century the Spanish rulers divided the New World into two viceroyalties—New Spain (Mexico) and Peru. Over each ruled a viceroy as the personal agent of the king. The viceroy was the head of the civil government, the commander of the army, the vice-patron of the Church, and the head of the financial system. Two smaller administrative units—captaincies-general—were established in Guatemala and Chile. In this less important jurisdiction the captain-general had about the same functions as the viceroy. During the eighteenth century two more viceroyalties were added—New Granada (Colombia) and Rio de la Plata (Argentina). There were also by this time two additional captaincies-general—Cuba and Venezuela. The crown also set up *audiencias*, twelve of them by the eighteenth century. The *audiencias* were the supreme court of the colonies. They heard all cases appealed from lower courts, and they also had executive functions in that they were advisers to the viceroys and captains-general and, in times of the absence of any of these officials, could serve as the executive body. The *audiencia* frequently went over the head of the viceroy to the Council of the Indies. Conflicts between the *audiencia* and the viceroy were common. The entire Spanish colonial system of checking official against official—the use of the *audiencia*, for instance, to check the executive—frequently led to a paralysis of individual action and initiative.

Spaniards in the colonies did not enjoy the privilege of self-government, for representative assemblies were never granted by the king. Only the towns—two hundred and fifty of them by 1600—had any power of self-government. They had the right to elect a town council (*cabildo*), but these councils could act only with reference to such matters as sanitation, police regulation, and the use of the common land of the towns. In respect to fundamental policies of taxation and economic measures, the towns had no power. Even the right to choose the membership of their councils was gradually encroached upon by the central government. The central government appointed to the councils life members, who checked local influences. If self-government existed at all in the political life of Spanish America, it was in these town councils; but this modicum of self-government was constantly encroached upon by the absolute power of the central government. When the time came for independence from Spain, the Spanish colonists had had no training in political life outside of their participation in these town councils. But this participation was not an unmixed blessing when the freed colonies tried to establish governments, for the town councils never had had representatives in the central government of the empire, and as a result the towns were apt to lack a political-mindedness that could rise above purely local affairs.

The influence of the vast frontier was largely neutralized in Spanish America as a result of the close supervision exerted by the viceroy or directly by the king over the affairs of the people. The frontier, which in English America proved to be a leveling influence, stimulating freedom, individualism, and the growth of democratic ideals and practices, failed to serve this purpose in the Spanish colonies. In addition to the central government's checking the leveling influence of the frontier, a titled nobility was established, which served as a conservative bulwark against change, and the Inquisition was ever ready to support the nobility against heresies. New ideas had little chance to flourish in the face of such opposition. Education was left almost exclusively to the clergy, and their type of instruction did not emphasize progress and change.

Spanish America was prosperous only as long as Spain retained her prominence and prosperity. Soon after the reign of Philip II, Spain began to decline. This decline was manifested in America by the increasing corruption and venality of the officials of the central government and the imposition of arbitrary taxes and forced loans. Toward the end of the colonial period there were more than sixty distinct ways of exacting revenue from the colonists. Generally speaking, popular control over taxes and appropriations is the final measure of self-government. The Spanish colonists did not exercise such control, another contrast to the English colonists. Every Indian not under an encomendero (the holder of an encomienda) had to pay a yearly poll tax. A sales tax was levied on all goods sold within the colonies, and customs duties were collected on all imports and exports. For example, goods entering the colonies paid a 15 per cent duty, and goods leaving the colonies for Spain paid a $17\frac{1}{2}$ per cent duty. In addition to this, there was a convoy tax, which required every ship to pay 2 per cent of the value of its cargo. The king sold monopoly rights for the marketing of such common products as gunpowder, tobacco, salt, playing cards, ice, and quicksilver. The monopoly of quicksilver, so necessary in silver-mining, was one reason why the small mine-operator was never a figure in the Mexican ore mines. The king also sold the monopoly of the Negro slave trade, and the contractor who held the monopoly had to pay the crown a fee for every slave imported into the colonies. The sale of offices further added to the income of the king. Finally, he received a fifth of the gold and silver taken from the American mines. All this revenue made it unnecessary for him to ask his subjects for money, as the English king had to do; and since the Spanish colonists were not able to coerce him by withholding needed revenue, they could not compel him to concede political rights, such as self-government.

Spain applied the mercantile system to her colonies with a rigor unknown in the English system of colonization. Government control and monopoly extended to all branches of colonial commerce. Spanish exports to America consisted of wines, figs, olives, oil, quicksilver, iron, dry goods, and other manufactures, for which the colonists made payment with sugar, cacao, vanilla, cochineal, drugs, and gold and silver coin and bullion. Only Spanish vessels and merchants could engage in the trade. Spain was not very highly developed in manufacturing industries, and as a result had to buy many of her goods for the colonies from England and France; but she would not allow France or England to ship directly to the colonies. The goods had to be shipped to Spain and transshipped in Spanish vessels. To complete the control of colonial trade, the port of Seville was given a monopoly. From 1503 to 1718 this city alone was allowed to sell to the colonies or to import their products. Under control by the government, fleets were fitted out annually at Seville and provided with a naval convoy. Only a few colonial ports—Porto Bello, Havana, Cartagena, and Vera Cruz, for example—had the right to trade with the homeland.

This scheme of strict regulation imposed great hardships upon the colonists. The resulting scale of prices was atrocious; a barrel of wine worth 6 or 7 pesos in Spain cost 48 pesos in Mexico City. Under this system of permitting only a few ports to be open, a settler living on the banks of the Plata River in the Argentine was not allowed to ship his products to Buenos Aires to be sent directly to markets in Europe or to other parts of the Spanish American empire, nor was he able to import directly from Europe. If he bought goods made in England, they had to be shipped first to Seville, whence they went to the Plata by the way of Porto Bello on the Isthmus of Panama, to Peru, and then across the lofty Andes. The settler also had to send his exports over

Ewing Galloway

MISSION AT SANTA BARBARA, CALIFORNIA

Early Spanish Architecture in North America

GOVERNOR'S HOME BUILT IN 1598 IN ST. AUGUSTINE, FLORIDA

St. Augustine and St. John's County Chamber of Commerce

this roundabout route. As a result, he paid excessively high prices for European goods, while the lack of markets for his own products kept his prices at extremely low levels. Buenos Aires was not made a port of entry until late in the eighteenth century.

In the eighteenth century the Spanish government gradually relaxed some of its commercial controls, and by the time of the American Revolution any port in the colonies was allowed to trade with any port either in Spain or in the other Spanish dominions. But even at this late date the restriction against the colonists' owning ships and entering into the imperial trade was still continued. This was quite unlike the English system, where the colonists participated in the carrying trade of the empire. Even after restrictions were relaxed, the Spanish mercantile system was much more rigid than that which England applied to her colonies. The Spanish system encouraged a widespread smuggling trade, from which the English and the Dutch reaped most of the profit. In the early nineteenth century the stifling effects of such rigid regulation were a major cause of the Latin-American wars for independence.

Spain, in settling the New World, was confronted with a vast Indian population, variously estimated at from twenty-five to forty million. She amalgamated this population with her own settlers and produced the mestizo. The Indians were prepared for European civilization by various methods. Some were collected into missions, presided over by padres. After a period of ten years' tutelage these Indians were supposed to pass into the hands of the civil power. Another way of dealing with the Indians was to incorporate them into towns and place a royal official over them. The whites and mestizos were excluded by law from these Indian towns, but the law was not always obeyed. The third method of dealing with the Indians was through the encomienda. As has been indicated, the encomienda was a semifeudal institution imported from Spain. The Indians were assigned to some Spaniard who had rendered distinguished service to the crown. In Mexico the individual allotments were vast. That of Hernando Cortes, for instance, included twenty-two Indian towns with 23,000 vassals. In 1800 this entailed estate contained 15 villas, 157 pueblos, 89 haciendas, 119 ranchos, and 5 *estancias*, with a total of 150,000 people. Although this was the largest estate of its kind, there were many other encomiendas of considerable size. It was this type of land system that was to checkmate the development of small independent farmers. This farmer group, so important in English America, had little chance to flourish in Spanish America. The system of entailing estates from generation to generation, the character of the soil, and the system of forced Indian labor, all tended to concentrate vast holdings in the hands of a few. Independent Spanish America inherited this system of large landed estates, and the power of the landowners has been such as frequently to curb, to the present day, the development of democratic forces in these countries.

Mining ranked second to agriculture in importance among colonial economic pursuits. The silver mines of Mexico and Peru yielded the treasure which made it profitable for Spain to operate her vast imperial possessions. Colonial mining operations generally were not entrusted to ordinary prospectors, but to wealthy promoters, who set out with large numbers of workers and supplies to open new veins of ore. Of course not all Spanish settlers in America were large landowners or large-scale miners. A number of small farmers, attorneys, officials, traders, soldiers, and clergymen played important roles in colonial life. The manufacturing of goods for sale at a profit, although officially discouraged, appeared in some areas. Food-processing was universal; soap and gunpowder were made; pottery and glass were manufactured, and factories turned out velvet and textile goods; hats and wine also were made.

The prevention of non-Spanish Europeans from entering the colonies slowed up progress and developed a uniformity of European background unknown in the English colonies. The only outside element introduced by the Spanish was Negro slavery. Slavery spread rapidly, particularly in the Caribbean islands, where the hard work on the plantations had speedily killed off the Indians. Father Las Casas, struck by the plight of the Indians, persuaded the king, early in the sixteenth century, to adopt Negro slavery in place of Indian slavery. The importation of slaves followed a regular pattern. The king granted contracts, assientos, conferring monopoly rights upon private traders. Spain had to do this because she did not possess slave-trading stations of her own in Africa. The contractors paid the king a large bonus for the monopoly. Portuguese, Dutch, French, and English trading interests secured assientos at various times.

By 1700 Spain's administration was disordered, and her prestige and power in Europe were low. Her insistence on playing an imperial role on the European continent had reduced her power to a shadow. Then, in 1701, a French Bourbon prince ascended the throne. This ascension of a Bourbon, placing Spain under the influence of France, upset the

European balance of power and led to a great war. From the stand-point of Spain and the empire, the Bourbons brought new methods of government, a new stimulus, and reforms for Spanish America. The Bourbons helped to revive the nation; but their coming was not alto-gether a blessing, since they too attempted to play a dominating role in European politics, and they opposed the new ideas and movements of the eighteenth century—the belief in natural law, natural rights, self-government, and the rise of the middle class. For a time the Bour-bons did an amazing job. They extended the empire into upper Cali-fornia; graft and smuggling were largely stamped out; the Jesuits were disbanded because their power was a threat to the crown's; and the viceroys and captains-general who were sent to America were energetic rulers. The Bourbons also liberalized the commercial laws, as has already been described. They likewise sent over a new official—the intendant (used in France and French America)—to check on the financial system and the judicial system, and to encourage agriculture, mining, and economic life in general. The Bourbons continued to revive the empire until their dynasty decayed. However, many of their reforms trampled on vested interests in the colonies and helped to predispose this group in favor of independence.

In spite of the defects of the Spanish imperial system, the empire endured nearly a hundred and fifty years longer than England's rule of her colonies in North America. On the whole, given the defects of the society and the physical handicaps, the results in Spanish America were better than one might have expected. The Spanish faced the con-stant difficulty of expanding their frontiers beyond their man-power strength in order to head off encroachments by other countries. The long seacoasts made it difficult for Spain to stop smuggling or to enforce the acts of trade. The indolent kings of the seventeenth century made the Bourbons' task of reviving the empire a difficult one. The worst handicap, perhaps, was the immobile character of the colonial popula-tion. The titled nobility and the rigid caste system bred incompetency and killed initiative, and the immense concentration of land in the hands of a few completed the vicious circle.

The greatest damage done by Spain in the government of its colo-nies was the exclusion of the native white (creole) from political affairs. Only very infrequently did the creole obtain a position in the central administration. Usually participation in the local town government was all that was open to him. As a preparation for governing himself, when independence should be won, this local activity had the many defects already mentioned. It resulted in an intense local interest. The creole had little conception of a horizon of greater magnitude than his own community. Much of the chaos and many of the sectional quarrels of the national period of Latin America were a direct heritage of this situation. Spanish America was politically immature when it awoke and discovered that independence had been achieved.

The heavy hand of absolutism attempted to crush all democratic tendencies in the colonies. Although it succeeded to an amazing and appalling degree, it could not entirely wipe out love for local liberty. This local liberty was nurtured by the towns. The farther a town was from the seat of the central government, the greater was the degree of independence achieved. In terms of the central government, however, absolutism reigned supreme, and the words of Viceroy de Croix of New Spain aptly epitomized the situation: "The colonists were born to be silent and obey and not to discuss nor to proffer advice on the higher affairs of government."

Contrast this state of affairs with that of the English colonies in North America, where the development of self-rule was aided by the development of democratic, liberal ideas in England. No stifling policy of repression was instituted, as had been done by Spain in her empire. Even under the mercantile theory, the English colonies, particularly New England, were allowed a great deal of freedom. Permission to enter the carrying trade of the empire offered an opportunity for New England to grow rich and powerful. At all times the liberal ideas of the colonies had sympathetic listeners in the center of the empire, and during the troubled days before the War of Independence the rights of the colonies had many able defenders in England. The English colonies were fortunate in their political heritage from England. Having gained political experience through participation in government, they were to face the trials of a separate existence far better prepared than their Spanish-American neighbors.

THE FRENCH IN AMERICA

It has been written that the French dreamed of an empire while the Spanish established one. The explorations of Giovanni da Verrazano, Roberval, and Jacques Cartier, during the years from 1523 to 1543, gave France a legal claim to North America. European wars, the Protestant Reformation, civil disturbances, and lack of capital prevented other Frenchmen from continuing the work until the next century.

Cartier's work in exploring the St. Lawrence River valley, however, was to set the course for the French empire of the future. Obscure Breton fishermen, catching cod season after season on the Grand Bank of Newfoundland, were also foundation-builders of New France. With the coming of Henry of Navarre to the throne of France, in 1589, royal interest in American colonization was revived. French capitalists were attracted by the rich profits to be made in the fur trade. In 1608 Samuel de Champlain led an expedition which established Quebec, and under Champlain's guiding genius expeditions explored the Great Lakes, reached present-day Wisconsin, and heard rumors of a great river (the Mississippi) that might be the passage to the Orient. Momentous for the future was the inauguration in these early years of French-English rivalry for Acadia and the fishing regions, the French-Dutch rivalry for furs in the upper Hudson River valley, and the alliance of the French with the Algonquin tribes against the Iroquois.

Cardinal Richelieu, who had gained power in France by 1624, pushed colonization in New France. He organized the Company of New France, or the Hundred Associates, and gave the Company a monopoly of the fur trade and absolute title to the land. As part of its work, the Company had to transport four thousand agricultural settlers within fifteen years. It failed, however, to establish a flourishing agricultural colony. French Protestants were not allowed to settle there, and French Catholics were reluctant to leave the homeland. Fur trading still remained the main occupation of New France. By 1665 the French had about 3500 settlers in Canada, whereas the English, who had begun settlements at the same time, had about 25,000 people along the Atlantic seaboard.

Under Louis XIV, who came to the throne of France in 1661, the French empire received an important impetus. Colbert, Louis's finance minister, followed the English practice of developing colonies as areas to produce raw materials and to consume the manufactured goods of the homeland. Foreigners were excluded from the commerce between France and her colonies, and merchants at home, by monopoly grants and favors from the king, were encouraged to push imperial trade. The French colonies in the West Indies soon developed to a point where they made important purchases of French goods and supplied France with tobacco, sugar, indigo, cotton, ginger, and dyewoods. The settlements in Canada were expected to buy French goods and to supply the French West Indies with needed foodstuffs, work animals, and lumber. Canada, however, failed to supply these goods, and the French West

Indies had to buy them from the English in New England and New York. The French then began to think of acquiring New England and New York, and this created another source of controversy between the two rival empires. Other matters of conflict between the English and the French were the fur trade, which led the French to penetrate the Great Lakes region and the Illinois country, the control of the New-foundland fisheries, and other economic rivalries, and the religious differences between the Puritans in Maine and the French Catholics in adjoining Acadia.

Cardinal Richelieu, in order to stimulate agricultural settlement, developed a Canadian feudalism which continued during French control of Canada. Large grants of land were given to seigneurs. The seigneurs in turn made grants to their tenants, the habitants. Canadian feudalism had two ends in mind: one was to produce a semblance of French aristocracy; the other was to distribute land. It was a type of feudalism, however, that had lost its teeth, since the king completely controlled both the seigneur and the habitant. The great difference between the position of the Canadian seigneur and that of the lord of the Middle Ages lay in the extent to which the crown and its officials dominated the seigneur. A decree of the king, an edict of the superior council, or an ordinance of the intendant might at any time change old conditions, impose new ones, and interfere between the seigneur and the worker. The seigneur had to grant the habitant land on the condition of a small annual rent, and the habitant was required, in addition, to grind his grain at the seigneur's mill, work for him a stated number of days in the year, and give him one fish out of every twelve caught, for the privilege of fishing in the seigneur's streams. This land system, although similar in obvious ways to the encomienda of Spanish America, differed in certain important respects. The encomienda had a servile working class of different race from the landowner, whereas the seigneur and the habitant were both Frenchmen. In New France the seigneur, through necessity, worked in the fields with the habitant, and the habitant's son sometimes married the seigneur's daughter. These features made the French system somewhat more fluid than the Spanish.

The government of New France centered in the governor-general, the intendant, and the superior council, and all three were appointed by the king. The governor-general had real power. He was in command of the army and foreign affairs. The superior council was made up of the governor-general, the intendant, the Bishop of the Church, and five councilors appointed by the king. It issued decrees for governing the colony; it was the highest court of appeal; and it established lower courts. The intendant was virtually a spy. He wrote long reports back to the king about the actions of the governor-general, and had the power to call any law case before himself for judgment. He judged exclusively cases affecting the king and the relations of seigneur and tenant. The intendant, judged from his power, was the ruling force in New France. He had the power to issue ordinances that had the force of law, and he controlled all expenditures. The ordinances of the intendant covered a variety of subjects, from controlling chimney-sweeping to forbidding people to move from their farms without permits.

New France seems to have been cursed with too many restrictions. The minute regulation of life by the intendant's decrees; the monopoly of foreign trade held by the homeland; the restrictions on foreign trade; the regulation of the contacts of the white settlers with the Indians, were evidences of extreme paternalism. The more active and vigorous individuals in the colony took to the woods to be free of the restrictions. These *coureurs de bois*, as they were called, were the bane of the king. Francis Parkman, historian of New France, described the *coureurs de bois* in the following manner:

It was a curious scene when a party of *coureurs de bois* returned from their rovings. Montreal was their harboring place, and they conducted themselves much like the crew of a man-of-war paid off after a long voyage. As long as their beaver-skins lasted, they set no bounds to their riot. Every house in the place, we are told, was turned into a drinking shop. The new-comers were bedizened with a strange mixture of French and Indian finery; while some of them, with instincts more thoroughly savage, stalked about the street as naked as a Pottawatomie or a Sioux. The clamor of tongues was prodigious, and gambling and drinking filled the day and night. When at last they were sober again, they sought absolution for their sins; nor could the priests venture to bear too hard on their unruly penitents, lest they should break wholly with the church and dispense thenceforth with her sacraments.[1]

The work of the Jesuit missionaries was one of the most important phases of the history of New France. Their good work among the Indians was largely counteracted by the garrisons of French troops in the near-by forts. The soldiers, to eke out their pay, were allowed to

[1]Francis Parkman, *The Old Régime in Canada*, p. 312. Little, Brown and Company, Boston, 1915.

sell brandy to the Indians. According to many of the good fathers, this selling of brandy reduced the Indians to disorder, brutality, violence, injustice, impiety, impurity, insolence, scorn, and insult. One Jesuit declared, "All our Indian villages are so many taverns for drunkenness and Sodoms for iniquity, which we shall be forced to leave to the just wrath and vengeance of God." Although the missionaries opposed the selling of brandy to the Indians, it was not stopped, because the fur traders maintained that unless the French sold it, the Indians would take their furs to the English, and this would drive the Indians into the heretics' camp.

The clergy dominated the life of New France. The Jesuits were the most powerful but not the only clerical group in the colony. The Canadian priests held the manners of the people under rigid control. An example of this can be seen in the advice that the Bishop of New France gave to a new governor-general, his wife, and their daughter:

> Although balls and dances are not sinful in their nature, nevertheless they are so dangerous by reason of the circumstances that attend them, and the evil results that almost inevitably follow, that, in the opinion of Saint Francis of Sales, it should be said of them as physicians say of mushrooms, that at best they are good for nothing. . . . Nevertheless since the youth and vivacity of mademoiselle their daughter requires some diversion, it is permitted to relent somewhat, and indulge her in a little moderate and proper dancing, provided that it be solely with persons of her own sex, and in the presence of madame her mother; but by no means in the presence of men or youths, since it is this mingling of sexes which causes the disorders that spring from balls and dances.[1]

The Canadian curés saw to it that there was no heresy in Canada. They taught obedience, and there was little diversity of thought or of life. There were no newspapers, for instance, in the colony until after the English took it over.

In view of the sparse population of New France, the French scattered their settlements too widely from Acadia and Quebec to the Great Lakes and the region of the valley of the Mississippi and Ohio rivers. This made New France lack the unity and cohesiveness that characterized the thirteen English colonies. New France was closed to those who sought a haven because of religious persecution. Furthermore, the driving individual will of the English people was lacking. French

[1] Ibid. p. 344.

America, like Spanish America, was too dependent on the royal will. Self-government was entirely lacking. Despite the work of Colbert and Louis XIV, the French people were not a colonizing people. Canada was never a self-supporting area in agriculture, nor was it a great stock-raising region. French America was laggard in independent thought, and it lacked an alert public opinion struggling for freedom of action in political, religious, and economic fields. It produced little in art or letters, and contributed no political institutions to influence the world.

The French control of Canada was not of major importance to American history and culture except for the fact that the English colonies became involved in a number of wars with New France, which disturbed their peaceful development; and, since American independence, many French Canadians have migrated to the United States, particularly to New England, which necessitates an understanding of their colonial heritage from France before one can appreciate their difficulties in adjusting to American life and understand something of their contribution to America's growth.

THE DUTCH IN AMERICA

Four European powers—Spain, France, Holland, and Sweden—challenged England's growing dominance in North America. The Dutch created the most immediate threat by planting a colony along the Hudson River in 1624, which soon menaced the unity between England's northern and southern colonies. The Dutch in Europe had freed themselves from the control of Spain during the latter part of the sixteenth century, although Spain did not formally acknowledge their independence until 1648. They succeeded in developing an unexcelled textile industry, and they also built a flourishing merchant marine. A group of Dutch merchants dispatched Henry Hudson in 1609 to search for a passage to the East. His explorations in the Hudson River area gave Holland a claim to this region. In 1621 the Estates-General —the Parliament of Holland— incorporated the Dutch West India Company and gave the merchant capitalists power to establish colonies, build forts, maintain troops, and wage war against Spain.

The first settlers sent to North America, in 1624, were employees of the Company. Since the Company was mainly interested in the fur trade, the settlers were divided into groups: one group remained on Manhattan to construct Fort Amsterdam, another group proceeded up the Hudson and built Fort Orange at the site of present-day Albany, a third group went to the Delaware River and founded Fort Nassau, and the last group built a fort at the mouth of the Connecticut River.

While the Dutch were developing their area, the Swedish government chartered a company with authority to occupy the shores of Delaware Bay. Fort Christina was established in 1638 on the present site of Wilmington. A few other forts were constructed, and some farmers came to take up land; but New Sweden never numbered over four hundred people. The Dutch protested the Swedish encroachment; but since the two countries were allies in the Thirty Years' War (1618–1648) in Europe, the Dutch tolerated their competitors. Finally, in 1655, the Dutch conquered New Sweden and absorbed it into New Netherland.

During the forty-year period in which the Dutch controlled New Netherland, the colony grew only slightly. The Dutch people were not interested in migrating from the homeland in view of the fact that they enjoyed religious toleration and had favorable economic conditions at home. Nor did agricultural conditions in New Netherland attract settlers. The Company gave vast grants of land to landlords, or patroons, who were required to bring tenants from Europe to work their estates in order to fulfill the terms of the grants. The importance of this patroon system to American history was that it started a social cleavage in New York. The owners of the large landed estates were a powerful factor in New York history until the period of Jacksonian democracy, when a series of rent riots by the tenants led to the breaking up of many of the ancient grants. The permanent tenant status under the patroonship did not lure settlers to New Netherland. Settlers leaving Europe wanted to better their condition in life, and they could acquire ownership of land relatively quickly and easily in the English colonies.

Another weakness of the colony was the attitude of the Dutch West India Company, which was more interested in plundering the Spaniards in the Caribbean than in spending money on New Netherland. An even more fatal weakness lay in the government of the colony. The Company appointed all the officials of the colony and permitted no self-government; a director and a council were sent from the homeland, and they administered the laws passed by the Company in Amsterdam. The only thing that pointed in the direction of self-government was an unofficial advisory body of leading citizens, selected by the director. The advisory group frequently opposed the director and became the spokesman for the discontent of the colony. The three directors of the colony from 1633 to 1664, Wouter Van Twiller, William Kieft, and Peter Stuyvesant, were not equipped for the position. Van Twiller was so indecisive that he became known as "Wouter the Doubter," Kieft's blundering was so great that the settlers demanded his recall, and Stuyvesant ruled the colony with an iron hand and readily exploited the colonists. In 1649 the leaders among the settlers petitioned the Estates-General to take over the government of the colony in order to establish a suitable government which should encourage education, religion, and internal peace. The widespread discontent with the rule of the Company made the colony easy prey for the English in 1664.

Among the chief contributions of the Dutch occupation of New Netherland to American history were good racial stock; Dutch colonial architecture; the Dutch Reformed Church, with its tolerant attitude toward other sects; an unusual emphasis on such aspects of our folklore as Santa Claus and the Christmas tree; such sports as coasting and ice skating; and the significant work that the Dutch did in helping to break the power of the Spanish empire.

THE STRUGGLE FOR THE NORTH AMERICAN CONTINENT

England, in strengthening and expanding her foothold on the Atlantic seaboard, came into direct conflict with the Dutch in New Netherland, the French in Acadia and Canada, and the Spanish in Florida. The strife between England and these powers directly affected the course of colonial development. Border conflicts and rivalries over trade with the Indians naturally disturbed the peaceful development of the English colonies. New Netherland particularly was a thorn in the side of the English. It broke the continuity of the English settlements and furnished a base for smuggling goods into them. Holland was removed as a menace to England's imperial power by three commercial wars in the middle of the seventeenth century, and during the course of one war, in 1664, New Netherland was occupied.

The next struggle took place between France and England. The French and English fought in Europe, America, and India for the dominant position in world politics. The conflicts in America were only one part of this imperial struggle of Gargantuan nations for world domination. In America both powers chose to operate in much the same sphere; they came into conflict over the fur trade, the Newfoundland fisheries, and the encroachments of France on New England.

Events both in Europe and in America precipitated the outbreak of war, in the late seventeenth century. The territorial ambitions of Louis XIV on the European continent, the accession of William and Mary to the English throne, and the support of Louis XIV for the deposed James II led to war in 1689. King William's War (1689–1697) resulted in no change in American boundaries. Both England and France were too busy fighting in other regions to contribute much to the North American struggle. The English colonies captured Port Royal in Acadia, but failed to take Quebec. The French with their Indian allies ravaged English frontier settlements. The Treaty of Ryswick (1697) provided for a return to the *status quo ante bellum.*

Louis XIV precipitated war again in 1701, when he backed the ascension of his grandson to the throne of Spain. This tie-up of France and Spain was a serious threat to the continued independence of other nations in Europe. William of England organized the anti-French forces, and war broke out the following year. England and her allies recognized the claims of an Austrian Hapsburg to the Spanish throne and tried to place him on it. This War of the Spanish Succession (known as Queen Anne's War in America, since King William died just before hostilities broke out and Queen Anne succeeded him), with France and Spain allied, led to the extension of English attacks on Spanish territory in Florida and the Caribbean. The principal theater of action in the Western Hemisphere was the Caribbean, where English privateers and warships seized French and Spanish merchantmen. Fighting took place also along the New England, New York, and Carolina frontiers. Port Royal was captured again, in 1710, by a joint force of British marines and New England militia. This time England did not return Port Royal to France. She also kept Acadia. The Treaty of Utrecht (1713) was an important landmark in the expansion of England's empire. English sea power was strengthened by the acquisition of Gibraltar, and English merchants were given trading privileges in Spanish America, as well as a monopoly in the selling of slaves to that region. The Hudson Bay region was turned over to the English, as was Acadia except for Cape Breton Island. The English title to Newfoundland was recognized by France, and the English protectorate over the Iroquois was accepted.

In spite of these gains, the basic issue of the control of North America remained unsettled. Between 1713 and 1739 France, England, and Spain prepared for the reopening of the conflict. Spain and France remained allied, and England's antagonism to both countries continued active.

During this period of peace England founded the colony of Georgia partly to thwart Spanish designs in the region. West of the Alleghenies, English fur traders increasingly competed with the fur traders of the other two powers. The French tightened their hold on the Mississippi Valley and built the powerful fortress of Louisbourg on Cape Breton Island. Louisbourg stood as a threat to New England's fishing and commerce, since in time of war French privateers could use it as a base from which to prey on New England's seagoing activities.

Long-continuing trade bickerings between England and Spain in Spanish America led to open war in 1739. The fighting was desultory and indecisive in the Caribbean area and was overshadowed in 1740 by a general European conflict. Frederick the Great of Prussia and Louis XV of France tried to prevent Maria Theresa from ascending the throne of Austria. England backed Maria Theresa and secured the support of Holland, Russia, and Saxony for Austria. In 1744 England declared war on France.

The taking of Louisbourg by the English, in 1745, was the only event of the war in America of real significance to the colonies; and New England merchants and landowners were disgusted when, in the treaty of peace, in 1748, England restored the fortress to France in order to gain back from the French the British East India Company post at Madras, India.

In the short period of peace following this treaty, the English and French concentrated their activity in the Ohio River valley. The French built a line of forts to check the expansion of the English. By this time, merchants and landowners of Pennsylvania and Virginia were greatly interested in the trade and the land of this region. The Virginians formed the Ohio Company and received from the king a large grant of land between the Monongahela and Great Kanawha rivers. George Washington was sent by the governor of Virginia in 1753 to demand that the French withdraw from this area. They refused, and the following year armed conflict broke out when French soldiers and the Virginia militia, led by Washington, met at Great Meadows near the junction of the Allegheny and Monongahela rivers. Although England and France did not formally declare war until 1756, both sent soldiers to America before that year, and fighting raged along the frontier from Acadia to Virginia.

England, realizing the dangers of the situation, called a colonial congress to meet at Albany in 1754 for the purpose of discussing inter-colonial co-operation. The congress adopted a plan presented by Ben-

English Troops Storming Quebec in 1759

North America after the Treaty of Paris, 1763

jamin Franklin, calling for a president for all the colonies, to be appointed by the king, to act with a council of delegates chosen by the assemblies of each colony. This federal government was to have charge of Indian treaties, trade, defense, and settlement in the West. Neither England nor the individual colonies accepted the plan, but it was a step toward intercolonial union and the later Federal system.

From 1754 to 1757 the English suffered humiliating defeats in

America, such as Braddock's defeat on July 9, 1755, largely because of inefficient generals, hostile Indians, and the lack of colonial co-operation. By 1756 this colonial French and Indian war had grown into a general European conflict. France and Austria now joined hands against England and Prussia. Under the guidance of William Pitt, England, after 1757, won a series of remarkable victories. Pitt chose able commanders, inspired the nation with his zeal, and subsidized Prussia to keep France occupied in Europe. Generals Wolfe and Amherst had captured Ticonderoga, Crown Point, Quebec, and Montreal by 1760. English admirals were victorious on the sea, and Clive defeated the French in India. Spain entered the conflict on France's side in 1762, whereupon England captured Cuba and the Philippine Islands.

The Treaty of Paris, in 1763, marked the end of France as a great power in America. Canada, as well as the territory west to the Mississippi, was ceded to England. Spain gave Florida to England in return for the restoration of Cuba and the Philippines. France compensated Spain for the loss of Florida by giving her that part of Louisiana that lay west of the Mississippi and a small strip of land east of the mouth of the river. The English colonies now, for the first time in their history, were freed of the Spanish and French menace on their borders. This was to have profound significance for the relations of the colonies to England in the next few years. As long as France and Spain were threats to English America, England had to grant concessions to the colonies to gain their co-operation. As a result, England did not enforce certain parts of her colonial system. Once the menace was removed, England began to enforce her imperial plan, and revolt soon broke out.

SELECTED BIBLIOGRAPHY

F. A. KIRKPATRICK, *The Spanish Conquistadores*, a superb one-volume study; H. I. PRIESTLEY, *The Coming of the White Men*, the opening volume of the History of American Life Series; C. E. CHAPMAN, *Colonial Hispanic America*, a comprehensive study of the Spanish system; W. H. PRESCOTT, *The Conquest of Mexico* and *The Conquest of Peru*, brilliant pieces of writing.

FRANCIS PARKMAN's many works on the French and English in America are masterpieces. Especially recommended are *Pioneers of France in the New World*, *The Old Régime in Canada*, and *Montcalm and Wolfe*.

M. W. GOODWIN, *Dutch and English on the Hudson*, a readable account in the Chronicles of America Series.

J. F. JAMESON (Ed.), *Original Narratives of American History*, and A. B. HART (Ed.), *American History Told by Contemporaries*, contain source material.

III

Colonial Society

THE GROWTH OF REPRESENTATIVE INSTITUTIONS

MANY PRESENT-DAY offices and institutions of American government, such as the office of governor, the two-house legislature, written constitutions, and county and town governments, have their origins in the English and colonial past. When the kings of England granted charters to colonial proprietors or to joint-stock companies, these served to implant the idea of a written contract as the basis of government. The charters granted the settlers the rights of Englishmen—trial by jury, protection from arbitrary action by the State, and representative government. The charters specifically gave definite powers to governmental agencies, but retained all the rights of Englishmen for freemen.

In order to persuade settlers to come to the New World, the proprietors and commercial companies had to offer concessions. Settlers were not willing to face the dangers of a hazardous ocean voyage and the hardships of pioneer life without some reward. This compensation generally consisted of promises of free land to the settlers by the promoters of colonization. Once these people had free land, they, as Englishmen, had the right to vote and hold office, since ownership of property was accepted as the prerequisite for governmental rights. Many of the people who thus gained political rights in America had not had them in England, and before long political liberty was more widespread in the colonies than in the homeland. The proprietors and companies in charge of the various colonies were not necessarily in favor of representative government, but they had no other choice, since they wanted to attract settlers, and their charters, while confirming the sovereignty of the king over the colony, required that laws could be passed only with the advice and consent of the freemen.

During the early years of Virginia the colony was ruled by a governor and council appointed by the Company in England. Until 1618 all the settlers were employees of the Company, owning no property of their own, and thus having no right of self-government. In 1618, however, the Company granted land to these people, and they became entitled to a voice in the government. The following year the Company recognized this by allowing the election of a representative assembly, which from that time served as the House of Burgesses, or lower house, of the Virginia legislature. The nonelected council gradually became the upper house, and both the council and the governor had the power to veto laws drawn by the lower house. In spite of this restriction, however, representative government in the English colonies dates from 1619. Five years after this significant event, the king dissolved the Company and took over its powers. Henceforth, until the American Revolution, the king appointed the governor and council, while the House of Burgesses remained as before, elected by the freemen. During the early years of Virginia almost all freemen owned property. By about 1670, however, a group of freemen without property had developed, and a law was passed making it clear that only freemen who owned property could vote.

The Pilgrims, since they settled outside the territory of Virginia, had to create their own government. Before landing, the colonists drew up the *"Mayflower* Compact," by which they agreed to set up a government, enact laws, and at all times abide by the wishes of the majority of the freemen. The Pilgrims started a typically American process when they framed this compact. Later on, other groups, when they found themselves in frontier areas without government, simply got together as "squatters in the wilderness" and set up their own government, as the Pilgrims had done. The Pilgrims never received a royal charter or royal recognition, and in 1691 their settlements were placed under the government of Massachusetts.

The Puritan settlers of Boston, Salem, Dorchester, and many other towns in the Boston area brought the charter of their commercial company with them. This charter became the basis of the colony's government. It placed control of the company and the colony in the hands of the stockholders. Since only approximately thirteen stockholders came to the colony, technically a very few people were ruling the mass of settlers. This suited the ideas of Governor John Winthrop, Thomas Dudley, and others of the Puritan group in power who disliked democracy as a contemptible form of government. These men in control in Massachusetts in 1630 believed that only the rich and the well-born should rule. This idea, however, did not please the bulk of the settlers, who had come to the New World in search of more opportunities in the political, religious, and economic realms. Governor Winthrop soon found himself in an embarrassing position. Unless more people were given the right to vote for the officials and to make the laws, there was the danger that large numbers would leave for more friendly areas. If, on the other hand, all freemen received the right to vote, then the many would dominate the few. Winthrop and his small group worked out a compromise. Only members of the Puritan church were given the right to vote. This was in violation of the English principle that property was the basis of this privilege, but Massachusetts was able to ignore English law chiefly because England was torn with civil war. After the restoration of the Stuarts, however, England, in 1684, revoked the Massachusetts charter.

It was a difficult accomplishment to become a Puritan church member in Massachusetts. Everyone by law had to attend church, but only those approved by the minister and the other church members could have membership. A seeker after membership had to relate before the entire congregation the religious experience that he had had which he thought qualified him to join. Many people shrank from such an ordeal, and during the seventeenth century only a minority of people were church members. Massachusetts, until her charter was revoked, has been well described as a "speaking aristocracy in the face of a silent democracy."

As the colony spread out from the nucleus at Boston, it became necessary to establish a representative form of government for those privileged to vote, since it was physically impossible for all these people to assemble for the purposes of choosing new officials and passing laws. By 1644 a system had been worked out whereby the voters in each town selected men to represent them in a two-house legislature, and they also elected the governor. Church membership, as the basis of political rights, was to be replaced finally by the property requirement when the king gave the colony a new charter in 1691. The king also, at that time, made Massachusetts a royal colony by henceforth appointing the governor; the lower house remained elective, and this house nominated the upper house subject to the governor's approval.

The colonies that emanated from Massachusetts—Rhode Island, Connecticut, and New Hampshire—followed the same procedure of establishing a two-house legislature and electing a governor. In the case of Rhode Island the various towns that had been founded sent delegates to form a two-house legislature. Charles II issued a charter to them in 1664 which recognized the right of this colony not only to select its legislature, but also its governor. The towns of Connecticut convened in 1639 and adopted their frame of government, the "Fundamental Orders of Connecticut." Under this constitution the freemen elected the governor and the two-house legislature. Connecticut, unlike Rhode Island, did not stress religious freedom. Although not going so far as Massachusetts in allowing only church members to vote, Connecticut forced people to attend the Puritan church and allowed only a member of that church to be elected governor. In 1662 the king granted Connecticut a charter permitting that colony to elect its governor and two-house legislature. Rhode Island and Connecticut, to the outbreak of the Revolution, were the only two colonies permitted these privileges. The other colonies had their governors appointed by the king or a proprietor, and most of them had their upper house selected in the same manner. New Hampshire existed as part of Massachusetts until 1677 and sent representatives to the Massachusetts legislature. In 1679 the king made New Hampshire a royal colony whose governor and upper house he appointed, while the property-holders elected the lower house.

Government in the proprietary colonies did not vary greatly from the pattern established in Virginia, Massachusetts, Rhode Island, Connecticut, and New Hampshire. Ownership of all the land, as well as all political power, was placed in the hands of the proprietor or a group of proprietors. The proprietor appointed the governor and a council to advise the governor. All the proprietary charters required the advice and consent of the freemen for the passage of laws and the levying of taxes by the governor and council. In 1650 Lord Baltimore established the two-house-legislature system in Maryland, with the lower house elected by the freemen. Up to this point, his governor had obtained the advice of the freemen by calling them into general meetings at irregular intervals.

The early political history of the Carolinas is complex and tangled. The proprietors found it necessary to divide the area into North and South Carolina, and in 1712 each colony was given a separate governor. In addition to the governor, the proprietors appointed the upper house of each legislature. Proprietary rule was never satisfactory, and in 1719 and 1729 the king made South Carolina and North Carolina royal colonies. William Penn's colony tried a number of experiments before evolving its form of government in 1701. At that time Penn established the principle of a one-house legislature elected by the property-holders. The council, the upper house in the other colonies, in Pennsylvania served as adviser to the governor, and it had also certain judicial functions. Penn appointed the governor and the council, and the governor had the power of veto over the one-house assembly. Delaware was part of Penn's proprietorship and was included in Pennsylvania until 1702. At that time Penn made it a separate colony, retaining for himself the right to appoint the governor, as he did in Pennsylvania.

New York, under the proprietorship of the Duke of York from 1664 to 1688, was the most undemocratic of the English colonies, for the Duke was not required by his grant to make laws with the advice and consent of the freemen. He appointed a governor and council, and they ruled the colony with an iron hand. Discontent with this lack of self-government was so great among the property-holders that in 1683 the Duke permitted a representative assembly to be called. Two years later, however, the Duke became King James II, and he made New York a royal colony, at the same time abandoning the elected assembly. The Glorious Revolution, of 1688, ended James II's rule of England, and New York, as a royal colony under William and Mary, was permitted to elect a representative assembly in 1691, which became the lower house of the legislature. In New Jersey the political rights of the proprietors were confused. When the Duke of York gave them the land, it was not clear whether he had also given them governmental powers. For a portion of the time the proprietors exerted power, and for the remainder of the time the governor of New York ruled the colony. Finally, in 1702, the proprietors surrendered all governmental rights to the king. New Jersey then, as a royal colony, followed the characteristic pattern of an elected lower house and an upper house and governor appointed by the king.

By 1776 all the English colonies enjoyed representative government. Although the people who controlled the colonial ventures at the outset wanted to rule without interference from their settlers, certain circumstances altered their desires. In the first place, their charters (except New York's) required that all settlers were to have the rights of Englishmen—one such right, as stated above, was the privilege of voting and being represented in governmental affairs, provided one possessed property. Furthermore, in order to attract settlers, land and the right of self-government generally had to be offered. Gradually a two-house system developed except in Penn's proprietorship. The appointed council, originally designed to advise the governor, evolved into the upper house. Throughout colonial times the councils in the various colonies were controlled by the wealthy landlords or merchants. The lower houses, on the other hand, were generally in the control of the small property-holders. These middle-class people struggled with the wealthy councilors for control of the colonial governments, and this strife formed one of the major themes of colonial history. The lower house was not democratic in the modern sense, since only property-holders were permitted to vote for its members. This elected house, however, was a step toward a more democratic order, and by 1776 it had gained the right to initiate laws and taxes.

Although the colonies had diverse origins, all of them developed quite similar political institutions. By 1776 all colonies were royal except Maryland, Rhode Island, Connecticut, Pennsylvania, and Delaware. The people in the colonies did not achieve representative government without a struggle. To have even their limited form of democratic government had meant constant struggles with the appointed governors and councilmen, who were apt to despise the multitude and believe only in government by the few. The aspirations of the mass of colonists for control of their society were to be eloquently presented by Thomas Jefferson in the Declaration of Independence.

THE ECONOMIC BASIS OF LIFE

At the time of the American Revolution 90 to 95 per cent of the colonial citizenry were farmers. These farmers were Jacks-of-all-trades, able to build their own homes and barns, to make many of their own farm implements, and to fashion much of their household furniture. In the early years of the Virginia and Plymouth colonies, all the settlers worked as employees of the joint-stock companies, and any surplus that they produced belonged to the companies' stockholders. After a few years this system gave way to private ownership of the land and to individuals working for themselves. Private ownership of the land and profit-making, introduced by the Virginia and Plymouth colonies, was followed by the later colonies and proved to be the mainspring of American economic development.

The New England colonies and the middle colonies, stretching from Pennsylvania to New York, developed a diversified economy consisting of grains, livestock, household manufacturing, and some commercial manufacturing. The middle colonies, with their rich soil, produced a surplus of wheat, flour, beef, and pork for export. New England's soil, although most people tilled the land, was not rich enough to produce a surplus, and this region had to rely on such specialized industries as lumbering, shipbuilding, shipping, and fishing for its exports.

Virginia, Maryland, and, to a lesser extent, North Carolina produced tobacco for export. These colonies also engaged in home manufacturing and raised a good share of the foodstuffs for their own consumption. South Carolina's agriculture too was diversified, although its export crops consisted of rice and indigo. Tobacco, rice, and indigo culture required a large force of laborers. To obtain workers, the colonial citizens relied on a number of sources. England shipped some criminals to the colonies, who after a period of work were given their freedom. More important than this source was the indentured servant. European whites, who were unable to pay their passage to the colonies, were transported at the expense of colonial farmers and entrepreneurs, and they had to sign a contract to work for their employer for periods ranging generally from five to seven years. At the end of the period of indenture the employer usually gave the servant some clothes and tools, and the colonial government frequently gave him land. Thus the ex-servant was able to become a middle-class independent farmer himself. Another source of labor was Negro slavery, first introduced in 1619. The slaves were best suited to working in large gangs at simple tasks. The Northern farm, with its more diversified system, was not able to use the slave as profitably as the larger Southern plantation, and the Northern farmer turned to indentured servants and hired men.

Until the eighteenth century the small farm was the unit of production in the Southern agricultural system. In the eighteenth century the plantation tended to push the small farm out of the tidewater, or coastal, area into the upland, piedmont region. The growing of tobacco required a large amount of land, and new land had to be used constantly, since tobacco was a crop that wore out the soil. The small farmer bought more and more land until his holdings became large enough to be termed a plantation. As a plantation-owner, he tended to lead a different life from that of the ordinary Northern farmer. He supervised the work in the fields, but left the actual labor to an overseer and slaves. He also took charge of selling tobacco to merchants in London and buying imported goods in return. About 1670 the Negro slave began to replace the white indentured servant in Southern farming. The slave was cheaper to use, since he belonged to his owner as long as he lived, whereas the indentured servant received his freedom after a few years. Some slaves on the plantations were trained to raise food crops and do such tasks as carpentry and bricklaying. Many of the plantations were strategically located on rivers, so that ships could pick up tobacco at a planter's own wharf.

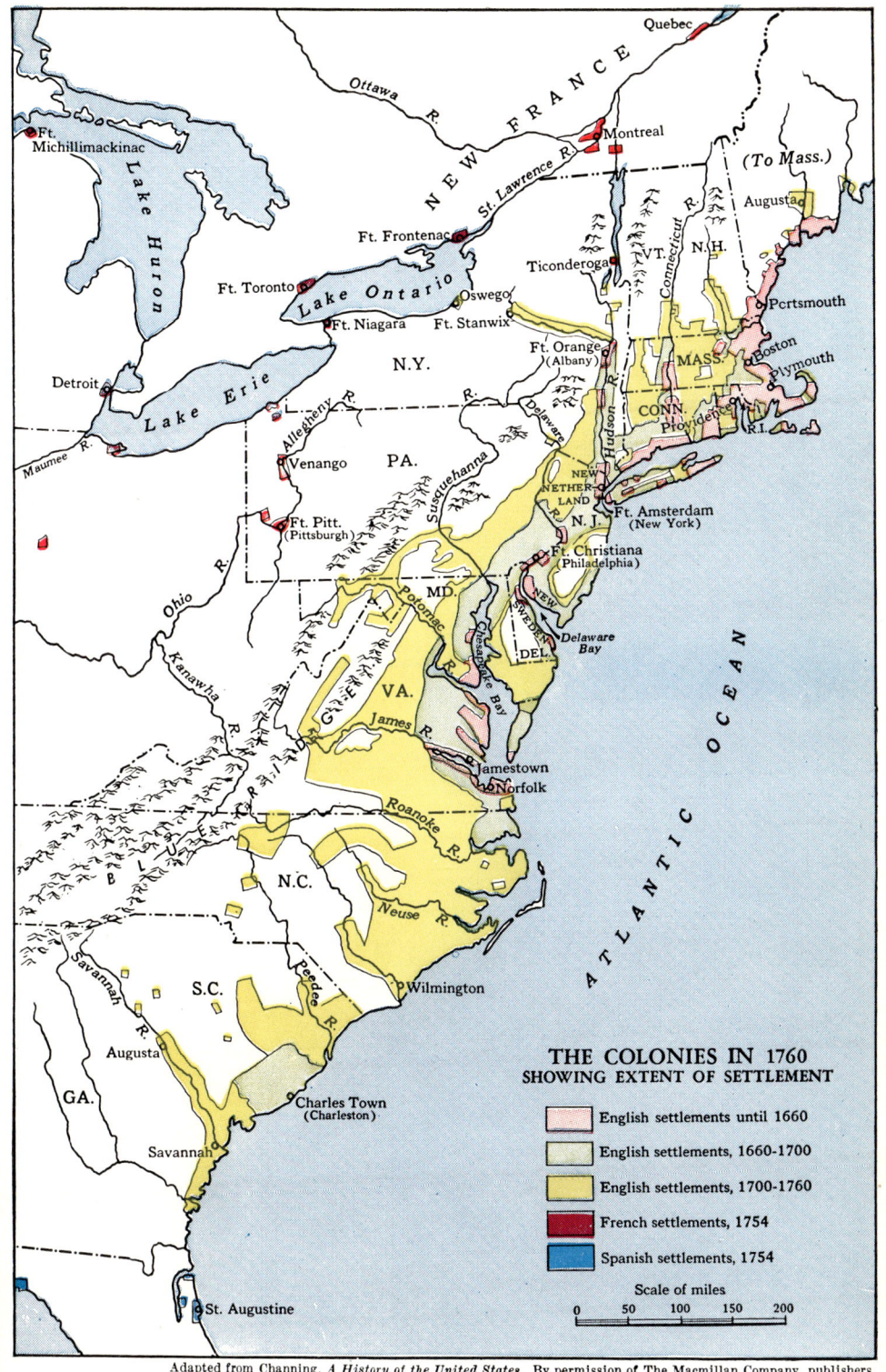

THE COLONIES IN 1760
SHOWING EXTENT OF SETTLEMENT

English settlements until 1660
English settlements, 1660-1700
English settlements, 1700-1760
French settlements, 1754
Spanish settlements, 1754

Scale of miles
0   50   100   150   200

Adapted from Channing, *A History of the United States.* By permission of The Macmillan Company, publishers

Slave labor flourished also in the production of rice and indigo in South Carolina and later in Georgia. Rice grew in the lowland swamp area, and conditions of work were such, particularly the danger of malaria, that the Negro slave was better suited for this than white indentured servants. During the malaria season the owners of the plantations left for the seacoast or the upland country. Since many planters resided part of the year in Charleston, this port soon became the center of Southern society. It was also the port from which the rice and indigo planters sent their crops to England.

Two types of manufacturing were carried on in the colonial economy, household and commercial. Most colonial Americans lacked the money to buy commercial goods, and they turned to making goods in their homes for their own consumption. Much of the clothing, bed and table linen, household and farm implements, leather goods, candles, and soap were made by the housewife, her husband, the children, and the servants. They made also their own bread, processed their meat, and brewed their own beer.

Commercial manufacturing differed from household manufacturing in that the goods were made for sale at a profit. The important commercial industries that developed during the seventeenth century were fishing, lumbering, shipbuilding, naval stores, flour-milling, and iron-manufacturing. The lumbering industry was carried on in all the colonies, although New England was the leading producing area. Massachusetts dominated the fishing industry with Gloucester, Marblehead, and Salem serving as the chief fishing ports. The better grades of fish were sent to the Catholic countries of Spain, Portugal, France, and Ireland, and the poorer grades were sold in the West Indies as food for the slaves. Shipbuilding, like fishing, flourished in New England because of the plentiful supply of the raw commodity. As early as 1614 John Smith had built some fishing boats on the Maine coast. Skilled shipbuilders came to the colonies from England to help to launch this industry, and England encouraged colonial shipbuilding as a source of supply for the ships needed by the empire. The cost of constructing ships was so high in England that it was found wiser to have the ships built in the colonies rather than import the timber for construction at home. By 1670 Massachusetts had built 730 ships, and in the single year 1721 all the New England shipbuilders constructed close to 160 vessels.

The best colonial iron was mined and worked in Pennsylvania, New Jersey, and Virginia. Lead mines were operated in Virginia and Pennsylvania, and brick kilns were busy in nearly all the colonies. Flour-milling was more widespread than iron-manufacturing. Gristmills sprang up as soon as a community was settled. Among the other colonial industries of lesser importance were rum-manufacturing, glass-works, paper mills, and shoe factories. England followed the policy of encouraging such industries as shipbuilding and lumbering, because her own raw materials had grown scarce. She did not allow the colonies, however, to manufacture goods in competition with English goods. For instance, the colonial manufacture of woolen goods was restricted by law in 1699 and of hats in 1732.

Trade within each colony, between the colonies, and with the rest of the British Empire, and certain lines of trade with foreign nations, formed an important part of colonial life. The colonists had to rely on England and Europe to supply them with many needed goods. Imports included canvas, cordage, hardware, nails, spades, shovels, knives, axes, hammers, guns, gunpowder, and miscellaneous household equipment. Wealthier families imported such luxury goods as wines, brandy, sugar, damask, linen, lace, and fine woolens. The great problem always facing the colonies was to find the means of paying for these goods.

Virginia, Maryland, and North Carolina paid for their goods by exporting tobacco and furs. Increasingly, during the eighteenth century, the price of tobacco fluctuated. The returns to the planters became so low that they failed to receive enough money to buy English goods. The English merchants, however, were willing to supply goods on credit, and more and more the planters' indebtedness increased. In this unfavorable situation it was not easy for the planters to shift to another type of production, because they had such a heavy fixed investment in land, labor, and equipment. Just before the American Revolution, Southern planters began to speculate in Western lands in the hope of acquiring enough money to free themselves of their debt to the English merchants. This speculation was cut off, however, when England passed the Proclamation of 1763, restricting settlers from going west of the Alleghenies. Gradually some planters decided that the only solution for them was to support a movement for independence from England, expecting that then debt repudiation would follow.

The middle and New England colonies had a far different trade relation with England. The home country, in 1660, in order to protect its own citizens, forbade the importation of colonial fish, flour, wheat, and meat into England. After this time, although the Northern colonies still purchased goods from England, what they were able to sell

England in return—chiefly ships, lumber, and furs—did not meet the cost of the English goods. This unfavorable balance of trade with England forced the Northern merchants to seek new outlets for their exports. Boston, Philadelphia, and New York were the three chief ports in this trade. Each town drew the products of the back country into the port and then shipped these goods out to world markets. In this way the Northern merchants and shipowners sold their goods to Newfoundland, to southern Europe, to the Canary Islands, and to the West Indies. From this trade they made more than enough money to pay for the goods imported from England. Many Northern ship-masters also engaged in the profitable African slave trade. Rum manu-factured at Newport, Rhode Island, served as the chief commodity with which to purchase Negroes. The Negroes were sold in the West Indies or the Southern colonies for money, molasses, sugar, and tobacco. The molasses and sugar were taken to Newport and turned into rum, while the tobacco and money were used to pay for English goods.

By the time of the War of Independence with England a distinct capitalistic group had developed in colonial society. Merchants, master artisans, and landowning farmers owned capital goods,—land, tools, shops, etc.,—and, dependent on them, was a group of laborers who did not share in the ownership of the capital goods. The rural capitalists of the South, as has been indicated, suffered from an unfavorable balance of trade with England and owed many debts to English merchants, which they attempted to pay off by speculation in Western lands. When this avenue was closed to them after 1763, this group of Ameri-can capitalists became increasingly in favor of breaking with England. The Northern merchant capitalists resented England's refusal to permit them to invest their money in industries that competed with England's own industries—leather goods, woolens, hats, and ironware. To pay for their imports of English goods, the Northern colonies followed the lines of trade mentioned above. Trade with the West Indies bulked larger than that with other regions. Up to 1700 the Northern merchants traded only with the British West Indies; but after that time the British West Indies did not offer large enough markets to consume Northern goods, and the French West Indies became an additional market. From the French West Indies the Northern shipmasters received molasses, sugar, and rum, which thus competed with the exports of the British West Indies. The British planters and their merchant representatives in London lobbied through Parliament the Molasses Act of 1733. This act placed extremely high duties on foreign molasses, sugar, and rum imported into the English colonies. Northern merchants immediately protested that these duties threatened to destroy their trade.

A serious crisis now developed within the British mercantile system. "The northern colonists, not permitted to manufacture in competition with English industry, were encouraged to produce a surplus of fish, lumber, provisions, and rum—products which had to be sold in outside markets to procure purchasing power for English goods," one historian has observed. "Yet the Molasses Act would have destroyed one of the necessary markets for that surplus."[1] The crisis was averted for the time being because England, engaged in struggles with the French, did not attempt to stamp out the evasions of the Molasses Act. When England, after 1763, favored English merchants and West Indian planters over colonial merchant capitalists and began to enforce her imperial system, then the colonial merchants became powerful factors in preparing the way for the Revolution.

SOCIAL CLASSES AND CONFLICTS

Colonial America had well-defined classes in its society. The upper class, numerically weak, consisted of those who owned so much wealth that they did not have to engage in manual labor. They generally wore finer clothes to set themselves off from the masses, and, in the seventeenth century, secured laws allowing only their group to wear silk and velvet clothing. The upper class in the South consisted of the large landowners, who had leisure time for politics, sports, and militia activities. This group had great power over the colonial governors and generally dominated the council. Similar to this group were the owners of the large estates in New York—the Van Rensselaers, the Livingstons, the Van Cortlandts, the Morrises, etc. In the Northern towns the wealthier merchants formed the upper class. These merchants owned warehouses, wharves, and ships. Generally, the governor's council in the Northern colonies was controlled by this group. Other elements in the upper class were the royal or proprietary governors, leading clergymen, and wealthy lawyers. Although there was a distinct upper class in the colonies, it never had titles, as the same class had in Europe. Furthermore, it was possible for poorer people, on acquiring wealth, to move into upper-class circles. Class mobility and fluidity tended to keep the upper class from being self-perpetuating.

[1]Curtis P. Nettels, *The Roots of American Civilization*, pp. 438–439. F. S. Crofts & Co., New York, 1939.

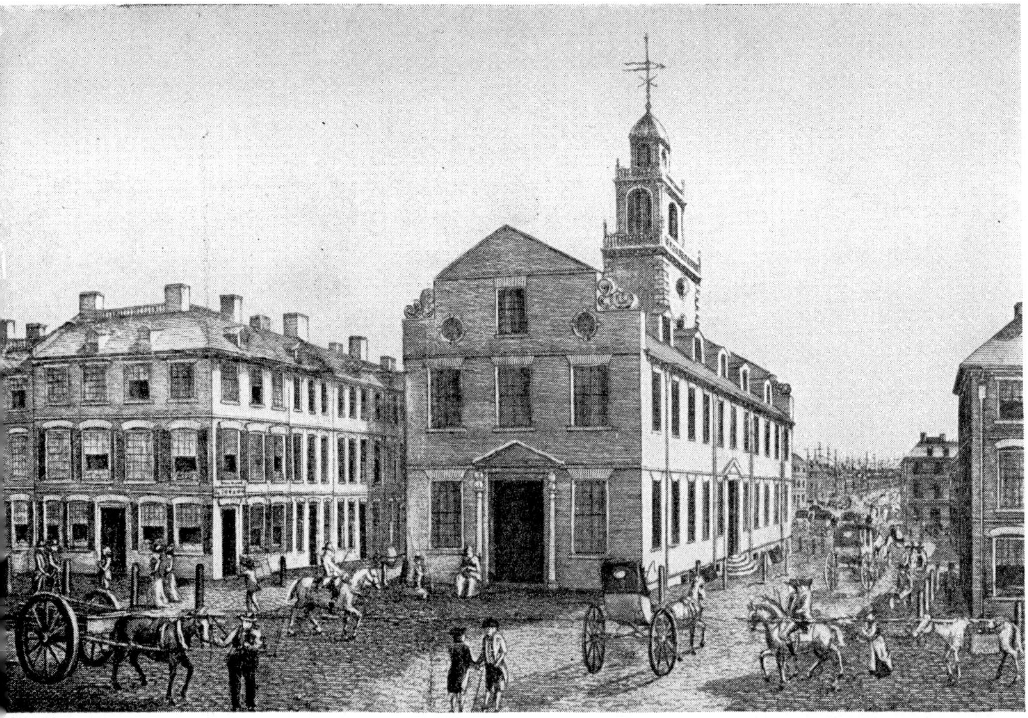

Boston about 1780

The Postrider Arrives

Mural painting by Edith C. Barry in the Post Office, Kennebunk, Maine

The great bulk of the population consisted of middle-class freemen who owned property—small farmers, skilled artisans, teachers, lesser clergy, shopkeepers, and minor government officials. Many of the middle class had sprung originally from the indentured-servant class. These middle-class folk possessed the acquisitive spirit and strove to acquire enough property to enter the upper class. The relative ease with which land could be acquired made this group much stronger than its counterpart in Europe. Their self-respect was highly developed, and they held the firm belief that they were as good as any other men. As they strove to enjoy more economic and political benefits, they came into open conflict with the upper class. Since they controlled the lower house of the colonial legislature, this conflict was conspicuous in the struggles of the lower house with the council and governor for power.

Immediately below the middle class was a group of freemen who owned no property—tenant farmers, farm hands, dock hands, fishermen, and sailors. Possessing no property, they had no right to vote. Below this group was the dependent class of nonfreemen, made up of indentured servants and Negro slaves. During the seventeenth century the indentured servants were more important than the slaves as a labor force. Each colony devised a legal code to govern indentured servants, and masters were supposed to feed and clothe them properly and not mistreat them. In many instances, however, the lot of these servants was so hard that they ran away from their masters. At the end of their indenture many were given land and were able to enter the ranks of the middle class. Another important group of the servant class consisted of boys and girls who were apprenticed to a master until they became of age. The lowest element in colonial society was, of course, the Negro slave. Most slaves were to be found in the Southern colonies, but some wealthy Northerners used them as household servants. The New England Puritans were not necessarily opposed to slavery, and their ships had brought many of the slaves to the colonies.

Social conflict between the classes was common in colonial days, particularly between the middle class and the aristocracy. These conflicts sometimes resulted in armed outbreaks. The smaller farmers were in competition with the larger landowners and frequently had to leave the coastal regions because they could not compete with the larger units of production. Also, small farmers had to borrow money from the merchants in order to buy supplies and equipment. This debt status, which sometimes led to foreclosures of mortgages, bred much of strife. The most critical contest in the seventeenth century between the small farmers and the upper class occurred in Virginia in 1675 and 1676. The small farmers were menaced by an economic revolution resulting from the introduction of more and more slaves, lower prices for their tobacco, inequitable taxes whereby they paid more taxes proportionally than the large landowners, and inadequate protection from the Indians. They could gain no relief from the government, which was dominated by Governor Sir William Berkeley in an alliance with the upper class. Led by Nathaniel Bacon, the small farmers revolted and seized control of the government. Berkeley organized the upper class to suppress the revolt; and while he was doing this, troops arrived from England to aid in putting down the uprising. Berkeley was removed from office by the king, but the grievances of the middle-class group were not wiped out.

The proprietary colonies had their troubles, too. Between 1660 and 1689 five revolts against the proprietor occurred in Maryland. Both North and South Carolina witnessed unsuccessful revolts on the part of the middle-class settlers. New York, in 1689, was torn by an uprising of small farmers and town workers led by Jacob Leisler, a merchant of democratic sympathies who seized control of the colony and ruled it for two years. William and Mary sent a new governor and soldiers to New York in 1691, and the revolt was suppressed. The sole gain for the democratic forces was the establishment by the new royal governor, in 1691, of the first legislative assembly in New York. The general attitude of England toward these class struggles was to support the colonial aristocrats in power. The middle class gradually realized, as trouble increased between them and the upper class in the eighteenth century, that they could not handle their own upper class until freedom from England should first be obtained. The upper class meanwhile developed a twofold strategy. When the middle class tried to improve its status, English backing was enlisted to check this movement. On the other hand, the upper class, disliking certain English commercial laws and acts, used the middle class to stir discontent and to try to frighten England into ameliorating oppressive features of her imperial system.

NEW BLOOD AND EXPANSION

European migration to America has been a continuing theme in American history from 1607 to the twentieth century. Before 1680 nine tenths of the colonists were of English stock. After that date England was replaced as the chief supplier of settlers by France, Germany, Ireland, Scotland, Switzerland, and Africa. The influx of immigrants made possible a vigorous expansion into new areas and into new lines of endeavor. By the time of the American Revolution there were over two and a half million people in the colonies, whereas in 1690 there had been only a quarter of a million. By 1776 the foreign-born accounted for one third of the population. Many of these foreign settlers, particularly the Scotch-Irish, felt a deep hostility to England, and this underlying antagonism toward Britain made it easier to snap the tie with the British Empire in 1776. Hector St. John de Crèvecœur, a French resident in New York at the time of the Revolution, in describing the mixture of various nationalities in America and the resulting American product, observed:

What then is the American, this new man? He is either a European or the descendant of a European; hence that strange mixture of blood which you will find in no other country. I could point out to you a family whose grandfather was an Englishman, whose wife was Dutch, whose son married a French woman, and whose present four sons have now four wives of different nations. He is an American, who, leaving behind him all his ancient prejudices and manners, receives new ones from the new mode of life he has embraced, the new government he obeys, and the new rank he holds. He becomes an American by being received in the broad lap of our great *alma mater.* Here individuals of all nations are melted into a new race of men whose labors and posterity will one day cause great changes in the world. Americans are the western pilgrims, who are carrying along with them the great mass of arts, sciences, vigor, and industry which began long since in the East. They will finish the great circle. The Americans were once scattered all over Europe. Here they are incorporated into one of the finest systems of population which has ever appeared and which will hereafter become distinct by the power of the different climates they inhabit.

The dominant force behind the immense non-English migration of the eighteenth century was lack of opportunity in Europe. The poverty of the great mass of workers and peasants was so great that many were attracted to the English colonies by the lure of cheap land and high wages. Thousands of German peasants fled from the Rhine country, repeatedly devastated by the Thirty Years' War, by the campaigns of Louis XIV, by the War of the League of Augsburg, and by the War of the Spanish Succession. Religious persecution of radical Protestants, such as the Mennonites, Moravians, Schwenkfelders, and Dunkers, was a further inducement to leave for the colonies. Louis XIV's persecution of the French Huguenots led many of them to flee that country and eventually reach the English colonies. The Scotch-Irish came in numbers comparable to those of the Germans. They were driven from northern Ireland as a result of England's prohibition of the export of woolen cloth from Ireland to any country. The Scotch-Irish had developed an industry that competed with England's for the world market, and, following the accepted mercantile theory, England suppressed the Scotch-Irish industry in favor of her own. The Scotch-Irish chose the American colonies in preference to poverty, and they came imbued with a violent hatred of England. From Scotland and Switzerland too came other poor people who were lured by the economic opportunity of America.

Colonial agents worked among the poor of Europe, persuading them that an El Dorado awaited them across the Atlantic Ocean. Since many of the immigrants were unable to pay the expense of the trip, they had to indenture themselves. The passage over was frequently attended with great hardships, for conditions on shipboard were indescribably bad. Immigrants were packed into small spaces and were given poor and little food, and the unsanitary conditions resulted in contagious diseases and high mortality.

New England did not attract the new settlers. The unfriendly attitude of the Puritans and the poor farming land discouraged the immigrant. And New York did not draw too many, because of the large landed estates worked by tenants and the presence of the Iroquois as barriers to western migration. Most of the settlers, therefore, landed in Pennsylvania, where access to land was relatively easy and where religious freedom prevailed. The Scotch-Irish usually pushed farther west, beyond the German settlers, and became a fighting frontier against the Indians. From Pennsylvania the Scotch-Irish migrated southward down the great valley of the Appalachians into the western part of Virginia and the Carolinas. These Scotch-Irish settlers were combative, politically aggressive, and opposed to paying quitrents, or yearly payments, to the proprietors or to the king. They demanded more adequate representation in colonial legislatures and became a definite threat to the political power of the tidewater upper class.

The new settlers exerted a profound influence on American life. They furnished a labor supply that made possible an expansion in farming, shipbuilding, lumbering, fur trading, and fishing. They created a frontier to which English thought and control, and the tidewater merchant and planter, seldom penetrated. Having come from persecution in Europe, they were opposed to all oppressive institutions in the colonies, such as taxes for the support of a state church, quitrents, and large landed estates. They weakened the large estates by squatting on the land and refusing to pay rent or money for its use. They strengthened the democratic movement in the colonies by joining with other middle-class people in fighting the domination of the upper class. And as they pushed westward, they came into conflict with French outposts and thus helped to precipitate the conflict between the two empires. The immigrants also brought an important diversity to the social and cultural life of the colonies, although they did little to change or modify the basic English political ideas and institutions.

During this period of expansion of the English colonies, Georgia was settled, in 1732, to serve as a buffer against the French and the Spanish. In addition, James Edward Oglethorpe persuaded the English government to make Georgia a haven of refuge for imprisoned debtors and other Englishmen who were victims of injustice and poverty. The charter given to the promoters of Georgia varied from all other charters given to English promoters. Control of the colony was placed in the hands of a board of trustees, who were empowered to grant land, raise money, pass laws, and levy taxes. The colony was financed by grants of money from philanthropic persons and by a yearly grant from Parliament. After twenty years the power of the trustees was to end and the colony was to become a royal province.

Georgia received not only settlers from England, but also many persecuted Protestants from Germany and Switzerland. The trustees tried to develop a small farming economy, to exclude Negro slavery, and to prevent the growth of land monopoly. These ends failed, and when the trustees relinquished their rights to the king, in 1752, Negro slavery and large-scale land ownership had developed. After 1752 Georgia followed the governmental pattern of other royal colonies, with the lower house of the legislature elected by the property-holders and the governor and council appointed by the king.

RELIGION AND COLONIAL CULTURE

Religious dissenters of all types found a haven in the English colonies. Only in Pennsylvania, Delaware, and Rhode Island was there religious liberty; that is, all religions were equal before the law, and there was no established church. By the eighteenth century, however, there was religious toleration in all the other colonies; that is, though there was a state church, other religions were permitted. Religious toleration in these colonies was won only after a hard struggle. The Puritans in Massachusetts, for instance, during the seventeenth century, persecuted anyone who did not accept their church. They assumed that they had the only correct religion and that everyone else must accept it or be persecuted. The need of enticing settlers, however, very early forced the controlling powers in a number of colonies to offer toleration to all types of religious sects. Developments in England too aided the growth of toleration in the colonies. The English Act of Toleration, of 1689, granted the right of public worship to all Protestants; and since all English liberties applied to the colonies, such toleration had to be established there too. The New England Puritans did their best to ignore the act and continued to persecute Baptists and Quakers, but England, in 1731 and 1734, forced the Puritans into line with English practice.

At the outset the Anglican faith was established in Virginia as the official religion. In the neighboring colony of Maryland, Lord Baltimore hoped to provide a haven for Catholics, but he could not establish a state church that varied from England's. Therefore he did not make Catholicism the official religion, nor did he persecute Anglicans or other Protestants, whom he needed to attract in order to build the colony. When the Puritans gained control of the English government during the Civil War, Lord Baltimore sent a Protestant governor to Maryland and officially proclaimed toleration for all Christians in 1649. From 1691 to 1716 the crown took control of the government of Maryland and officially established the Anglican Church. When the proprietor regained his governmental rights, he did not tamper with the established church. The Anglican Church in Maryland, however, was never as powerful as in Virginia. Other Protestant sects far outnumbered the Anglicans, and the Anglicans were only more numerous than the Catholics. The Carolina proprietors established the Anglican Church at the very beginning, but other "law-abiding" sects were permitted to worship. During the seventeenth century Quakerism was the dominant faith in North Carolina; and in South Carolina, Baptists, Quakers, and French Huguenots all had churches, and the Presbyterians and Congregationalists had a joint church.

New Jersey welcomed all groups of Protestants, and the Presbyterians became the dominant religious force in that colony. Even after New Jersey became a royal colony, in 1702, no church was established as the state church, and toleration continued to apply to all Protestants. New York had a different religious problem from that faced by other colonies. When the English took New Netherland, the Dutch Reformed Church was the state church, although toleration prevailed. The English disestablished the Dutch Reformed Church, and in 1693 the Anglican was established. The law establishing the church was vague, however, and the Dutch Reformed group claimed that it meant their church. As a result, outside of New York City, the Dutch Reformed Church received state aid, and the Anglicans in New York City accepted this situation in order to retain the support of the Dutch Reformed Church for an established Anglican Church in the city.

Theoretically, in those colonies where the Anglican Church was established, the Bishop of London ran the church. London, however, was so far away that actually the Anglicans in each colony ran their own church and generally selected their own ministers. In colonies like Virginia, where the distances were so great between the parishes, there was little central control. Also, the elaborate Anglican ritual proved so difficult to administer in frontier areas that it was frequently modified, and the American Anglican Church became more "popular" than the English Church.

The established church of New England, except for Rhode Island, was the Congregational. The Pilgrims at first did not establish a state church, but in 1659 Quakers were denied the right to vote, as were all opponents of "the true worship of God," Congregationalism. The rigid and intolerant nature of the established church in the Massachusetts Bay Colony led to the exile of Roger Williams and Anne Hutchinson, as well as to the persecution and the hanging of Quakers. Although the "Biblical Commonwealth" of Massachusetts tried to ignore the English Act of Toleration, as has been indicated, gradually it had to respect the rights of other Protestant groups. Connecticut, like Massachusetts, rejected the idea of toleration and established the Congregational religion. The power of Massachusetts over New Hampshire was such that even after New Hampshire became a royal colony the Congregational Church maintained its established position.

The colony of Rhode Island was the first to develop the complete separation of Church and State. Roger Williams had insisted, while he was still preaching in Massachusetts, that no one church enjoyed divine favor. This belief he carried out in his own colony. Civil power was not used to coerce people into worshiping in a particular church. The Baptists and the Quakers, particularly, flourished in this colony. William Penn and his fellow Quakers in Pennsylvania and Delaware, also, did not establish a state church. All who believed in God had the right to worship. During the eighteenth century all types of European Protestants poured into Pennsylvania to take advantage of this liberal environment. Although Rhode Island, Pennsylvania, and Delaware were the only colonies permitting religious freedom, their example later became the settled policy of the United States under the Constitution of 1787.

An incident occurred in the religious life of Massachusetts during the first and second decades of the eighteenth century which augured well for the growth of democratic ideals. A group of conservative ministers in Boston, led by Increase and Cotton Mather, attempted to take the control of the Puritan church away from each local congregation. To the defense of self-government rallied the Reverend John Wise, a village democrat whose father had been an indentured servant. He published two books, *The Churches Quarrel Espoused* and *Vindication of the Government of New England Churches*, which not only opposed the theory that the few should rule the many, but set forth the doctrine of the social compact. Wise argued that government had arisen as a result of an agreement between the people and the ruler, whereby certain rights were given to the ruler and the rest were retained by the people. According to Wise, rulers were always responsible directly to the people. Whenever a ruler overstepped his powers, then the people had the right to rise up and depose him. Wise's arguments supplied ammunition for the developing democratic cause, and his books were reprinted at the time of the American Revolution to provide the colonists with additional arguments.

The eighteenth century witnessed important developments in the religious history of the colonies. The English Society for the Propagation of the Gospel had done much to supply both clergymen and funds for work in America but it had not greatly altered the general decline in religion. Then, in the 1730's, came the Great Awakening, a series of religious revivals which swept through all the colonies. Jonathan Edwards, a Congregational preacher at Northampton, Massachusetts, complained in 1734 that a great part of the people were "very insensible of the things of religion, and engaged in other cares and pursuits. . . . Licentiousness for some years greatly prevailed among the youth of the town; they were, many of them, very much addicted to night walking, and frequenting the tavern, and lewd practices." The extraordinary revival in religious interest grew partly out of the low state of religion in the colonies, but was also greatly influenced by the Pietistic movement in Germany and the Methodist movement in England. The preachers of this rebirth in religion ignored formal creed and doctrines, and urged that everyone reform his own conduct and have a personal religious experience. The Great Awakening cut across denominational lines and appealed greatly to the small farmers and other middle-class folk. The Anglican clergy generally opposed the movement, the Baptists welcomed it and won many converts, and the Presbyterian, Congregational, and Dutch Reformed churches were split into factions over it.

In New England, Jonathan Edwards tried to win the people to Puritan beliefs by warning them that hell waited for any person who was not converted. He pictured God as holding the unsaved "over the pit of hell much as one holds a spider or some loathesome insect over the fire." The Great Awakening spread out of New England and became an intercolonial movement when men like George Whitefield came from England and toured the colonies, exhorting people to a rebirth. Whitefield's preaching was extremely effective, and according to Benjamin Franklin he so stirred the colonial people that, "from being thoughtless or indifferent about religion, it seemed as if all the world were growing religious." Pioneer evangelists among the Presbyterians of the middle colonies were William Tennent and his son Gilbert. The elder Tennent established a log college in 1736, where he trained zealous young preachers in the new evangelism.

The evangelists appealed to the emotions of the people rather than to their reason. The effects that powerful preachers had on their listeners were amazing. A contemporary, speaking of a Baptist revival in Virginia, said that he attended a meeting where two thousand people were present, and that he saw "multitudes, some roaring on the ground, some wringing their hands, some in extacies, some praying, some weeping; and others so outragious cursing and swearing that it was thought that they were really possessed of the devil. I saw strange things today." This type of religion appealed to the common people because wealth and rank were ignored by the revivalists.

The Great Awakening had many immediate effects on American life. The revival became the accepted American technique of winning the indifferent to religion. Revivals swept through the colonies from Maine to Georgia, flourished particularly in the frontier regions, and served as a colonial unifying force. The Great Awakening appealed to the common man, stirred emotions, and helped to prepare the way for the emotional aspects of the American Revolution. It increased the strength of the churches opposed to the state-church idea, and it tended to teach the right of self-determination in religion, which teaching could be transferred to the political sphere to mean the right to determine one's own form of government. In addition, four new colleges grew out of the religious rebirth: Princeton (Presbyterian), Brown (Baptist), Rutgers (Dutch Reformed), and Dartmouth (Congregationalist).

As a result of the religious stimulus of the Great Awakening, Virginia, for example, witnessed a series of revivals. The first wave was led by Samuel Davies and the Presbyterians who migrated into the great valley of Virginia in the 1730's and 1740's. Soon after, the Baptists poured in and, unlike the Presbyterians, openly attacked the established church. In the 1770's Methodist missionaries sent by John Wesley in England attempted to revive religious life among the Anglicans. At the end of the Revolutionary War the American Methodists withdrew from the Anglican Church and formed the American Methodist Episcopal Church. The Methodists and the Baptists, together with such leaders as Thomas Jefferson and James Madison, finally succeeded, in 1785, in disestablishing Church and State in Virginia.

While the colonies were being shaken by the Great Awakening, significant developments were taking place in other phases of colonial culture. The establishment of four colleges has just been mentioned. Long before this occurred, however, colonial education had made important strides. In 1647 the first school system was established when Massachusetts passed a law requiring all towns having fifty families to set up a primary school, and all towns having a hundred families to establish a grammar, or secondary, school as well. Compulsory education of the young had been required by law five years before this act of 1647. There were two main motives behind these laws. The Puritans feared that without the laws learning might disappear when the first generation of Puritans had passed away. Furthermore, it was necessary to supply students for Harvard College, founded in 1636, in order that the colony should be supplied with an educated clergy. New Hampshire and Connecticut soon copied these laws. The middle colonies had so many different religions that one system of education was impossible. As a result, each religious group educated its own citizens. In the Southern colonies the plantations and farms were so scattered that a public-school system similar to that of the New England town was impossible. Generally, education in this region was left to private schools and tutors. The College of William and Mary, however, was an exception.

The primary schools taught such subjects as reading, writing, arithmetic, and rules of good conduct. The grammar schools, or Latin schools, of New England trained the students in Latin, Greek, English composition, mathematics, modern languages, and philosophy. After grammar school or private academy the student could attend college. The cost of college meant that only the youth of the upper and middle classes could attend. Many of the richer Southern planters sent their sons to Oxford, Cambridge, or to the Inns of Court, a law school in London. By the end of colonial times there were nine colonial colleges: Harvard (1636), William and Mary (1693), Yale (1701), Princeton (1747), the Academy at Philadelphia, now the University of Pennsylvania (1749), Columbia, or King's College (1754) Brown (1764), Rutgers (1766), and Dartmouth (1769). All these, with the exception of the University of Pennsylvania, were founded by religious groups. In order to be admitted to college, the student had to be able to speak and write Latin, since textbooks and instruction were in that language. The college students studied such subjects as logic, rhetoric, Greek, Hebrew, ethics, and metaphysics. During the eighteeth century courses in science, literature, mathematics, and French were introduced. The possessor of a college education held a place of great prestige in his colonial community.

By the close of the colonial period colonial amusements and entertainment had reached a somewhat advanced state. In 1750, for instance, a company of English professional actors arrived in America to remain for twenty years, presenting classical English plays of Steele, Addison, and Shakespeare. New England was hostile to the theater, and as a result only in the middle and Southern colonies were theaters important. Musical recitals and concerts were so well developed by 1750 that they were a regular feature of life in the larger towns. Among the leading social clubs were the Philosophical Club of Newport, the Beefsteak Club of Philadelphia, and the French Club of New York City. These were composed of men of the same profession or ethnic group, or of men united by some other, less fundamental bond, such as an enjoyment of good beefsteaks. One club which had lodges in all the colonies was the Free Masons. Benjamin Franklin founded a debating society in 1727, which later became the American Philosophical Society.

Such sports as horse-racing, hunting, fishing, gambling, cockfighting, bowling, and skating were prominent in the everyday life of the citizen. When Virginia was founded, laws against such things as drunkenness, playing cards, and breaking the Sabbath were passed, just as in Massachusetts; but these laws were gradually abandoned as Virginia developed. The Puritan clergy of New England tried to discourage pleasure-seeking among their people. Card games, dancing, drinking, etc. were all denounced as devices of Satan. Actually, however, life in the Puritan colonies was not as somber as some might believe. The frequent reiteration in the laws of Massachusetts of pronouncements against drinking and dancing reveal that the laws were not very well obeyed. The college undergraduates were not so addicted to piety that they failed to enjoy the art of dissipation. A student at Yale, in 1738, recorded in his diary that "last night some of the freshmen got six quarts of rum and about two pails of cider and about eight pounds of sugar . . . and invited every scholar in college . . . and we made such prodigious rout that we raised the tutor. . . ." Clearly indicative that the clergy were not able to suppress courting and love affairs was a Massachusetts law of 1647 which complained that "it is a common practice in diverse places, for young men irregularly and disorderly to watch all advantages for their evil purposes, to insinuate into the affections of young maidens, by coming to them in places and seasons unknown to their parents for such ends, whereby much evil hath grown amongst us, to the dishonor of God and damage of parties." That this type of law was obeyed in the breach is shown by the following incident: a couple was hailed before the court in 1660 on the charge that "they sat down together, his arm being about her, and her arm upon his shoulder or about his neck; and he kissed her, and she kissed him or they kissed one another, continuing in this posture about half an hour."

Throughout all the colonies the taverns, or ordinaries, were centers of a great deal of social life. Residents of a town congregated at the tavern, or inn, to hear the latest news from travelers, and the tavern served also as the post office, where the postrider deposited or collected letters on his route from colony to colony. In 1710 Parliament placed the postal service of the colonies under the English post office. The outstanding Postmaster-General of the colonies was Benjamin Franklin, who served in that office from 1753 to 1774. Franklin lowered postal rates and speeded up the service by cutting the time of delivery on the Boston to Philadelphia route from three weeks to six days. The postal service was so essential to colonial unity that the patriots seized control of it immediately after the outbreak of the Revolution.

During the seventeenth century most of the colonists lived in relative isolation. In the next century means of transportation gradually tied

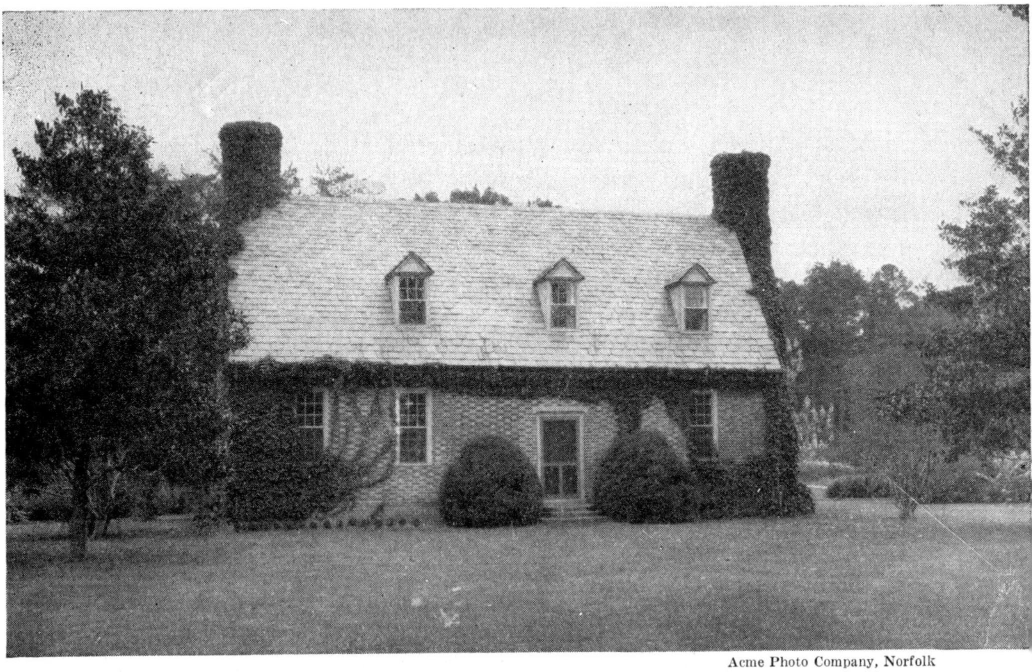

Acme Photo Company, Norfolk

The Thoroughgood House, Early Brick Home, Built in Virginia between 1636 and 1640

Colonial Home Built in Salem in 1684

Essex Institute, Salem

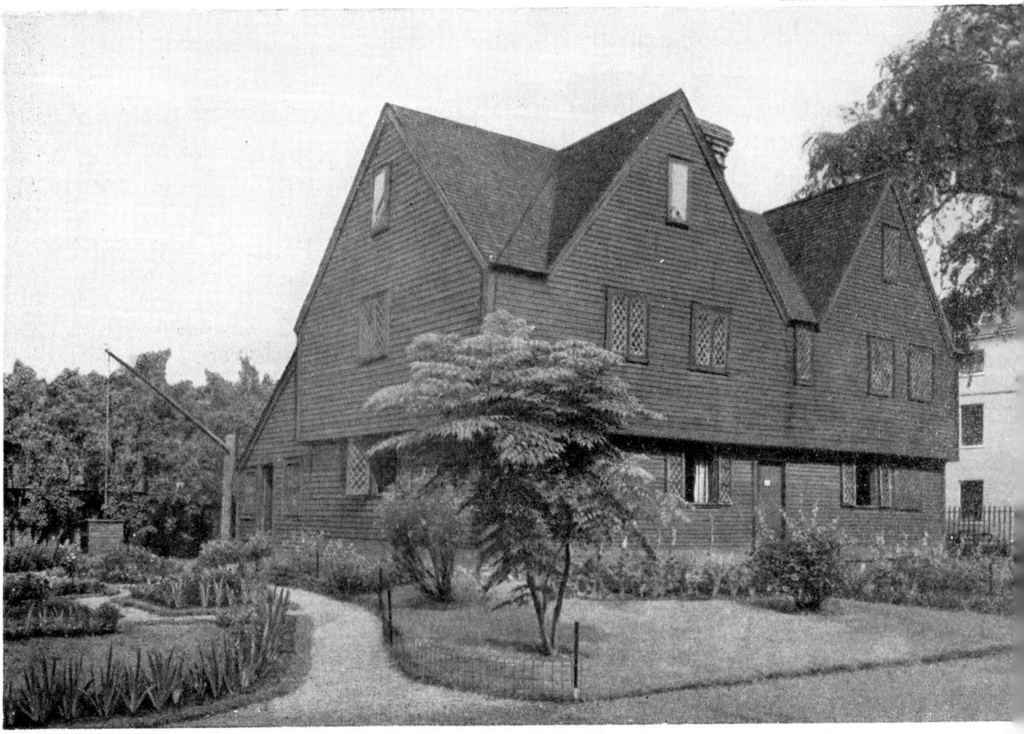

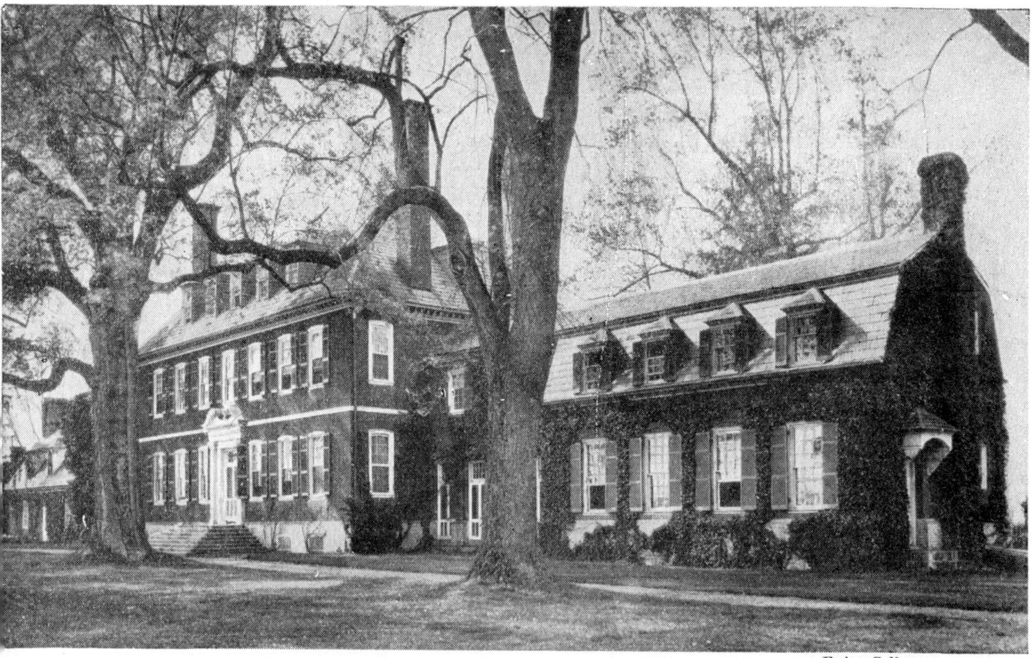

Ewing Galloway

Westover, the Georgian Ancestral Home of the Byrd Family, on the James River

Ronny Jaques, from Black Star

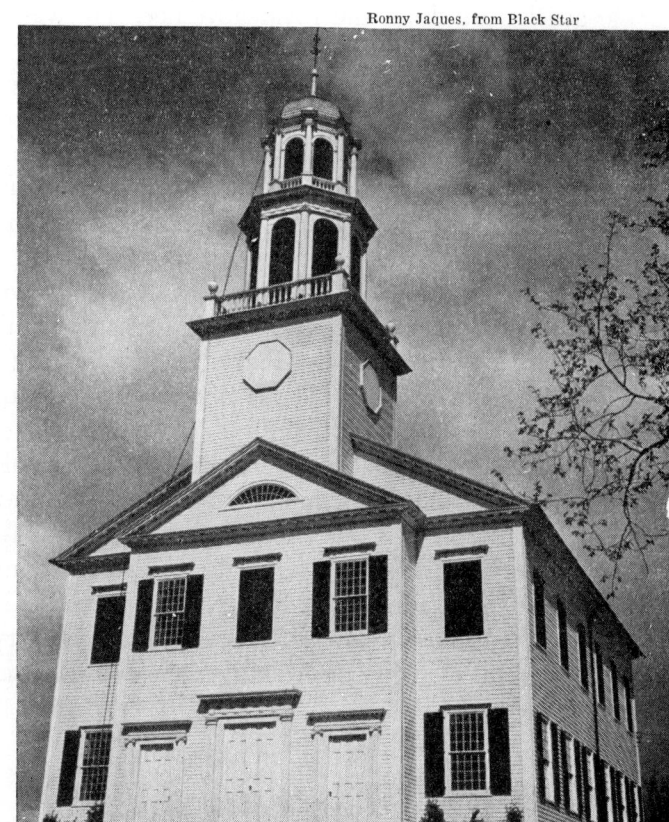

Colonial Church in Connecticut

them together. Towns like Boston, New York, and Philadelphia served as centers from which roads radiated out to the back country or to other towns. Travel overland between Boston and New York was so difficult, however, that it took six days to make the trip in 1704. But by 1776 a highway in fair condition made it possible to travel overland from Boston to Charleston. By 1776, too, regular stage service was in operation between Boston, New York, and Philadelphia. The sea, throughout the colonial period, served as a means of traveling from colony to colony.

Communication between the colonies was, of course, no speedier than transportation. Other than the postrider, the chief means by which one colony knew what was happening in another colony was the colonial press. The first colonial newspaper, the *Boston News-Letter*, was begun in 1704. By 1765 every colony, except Delaware and New Jersey, had at least one paper. Important articles from one paper were reprinted in other colonial papers. As the Revolutionary crisis approached, this reprinting increased and helped to bring unity to the colonial opposition to England. The freedom of the press to criticize acts of England and those of vested colonial groups was established in 1733, when Peter Zenger, a New York newspaper-publisher, printed articles attacking the royal governor. He was arrested for false and scandalous libel, but Zenger's lawyer, Andrew Hamilton, persuaded the jury to find him innocent. In addition to newspapers, the colonial press published magazines and almanacs, which circulated in all the colonies. The almanacs, the most famous of which was Benjamin Franklin's *Poor Richard's Almanack*, told about scientific agriculture and about the moon, stars, and seasons, listed important holidays, and printed essays, poems, jokes, and stories.

Colonial painting, architecture, and furniture-making leaned heavily on European examples and traditions. Benjamin West (1738–1820), Charles W. Peale (1741–1827), Gilbert Stuart (1755–1828), and John Singleton Copley (1738–1815) were the outstanding colonial artists. All of them studied painting in Europe and remained there many years, since the atmosphere and the financial support there were more favorable than in the colonies. West became court painter to George III, and Copley and Stuart won fame as outstanding portrait-painters. The upper class in the eighteenth century, with their added wealth, constructed fine homes, which presented a striking contrast to the small frame houses of the seventeenth century. English plans were generally used in constructing these colonial mansions. The wealthy people of New England and the middle colonies built rectangular houses, three stories high, with a pitched or slanting roof. In the South the buildings had roofs with less pitch than in the Northern colonies, since there was little snow to worry about. Another interesting difference between the architecture of the two regions was that of the construction of chimneys. The chimneys were built outside the house wall in the South, whereas in New England it was found that this caused the loss of too much heat and the chimneys were constructed within the house walls. The Southern homes were also different in that they generally had the kitchen in a separate building. Most of the colonial mansions copied the Georgian style of England. In the middle and Southern colonies these houses were built of brick; in New England they were built of brick, too, but clapboard was frequently used to cover the brick. Outstanding examples of colonial Georgian are Independence Hall in Philadelphia, built in 1735, and Mount Vernon, the home of George Washington.

The furniture of these houses followed prevailing styles in England and Europe. Oak furniture was a favorite, especially large and heavy cupboards and paneled chairs. The tendency was to put such furniture as chests of drawers, sideboards, and four-poster beds on high legs. During the seventeenth century prevailing styles of furniture in England called for heavy furniture in rectangular form. In the next century mahogany was widely used, and designers like Thomas Chippendale used curves instead of straight lines and right angles. Wealthy colonists imported Chippendale pieces, as well as furniture designed by the Adam brothers, Hepplewhite, and Sheraton. Sheraton had many followers in the colonies, particularly Duncan Phyfe of New York. The legs of Phyfe's tables and chairs were curved and carved in various delicate patterns. Many of Phyfe's designs have been copied by furniture-makers to the present day. Beautifully decorated glasses and pitchers were imported to grace fine homes, while the colonial glass industry, begun by Caspar Wistar in 1738, produced some treasured pieces. In fine silverwork the colonial craftsmen showed that they were as skilled as their European competitors. The rich merchants and planters had silver tumblers, tankards, bowls, candlesticks, and platters, which added to the elegance of their homes.

The upper class, in addition to having fine homes, furniture, and decorations to set themselves apart from the masses, wore elegant attire, far beyond the means of the majority of the people. English dressmakers and tailors were kept busy filling colonial orders. John Han-

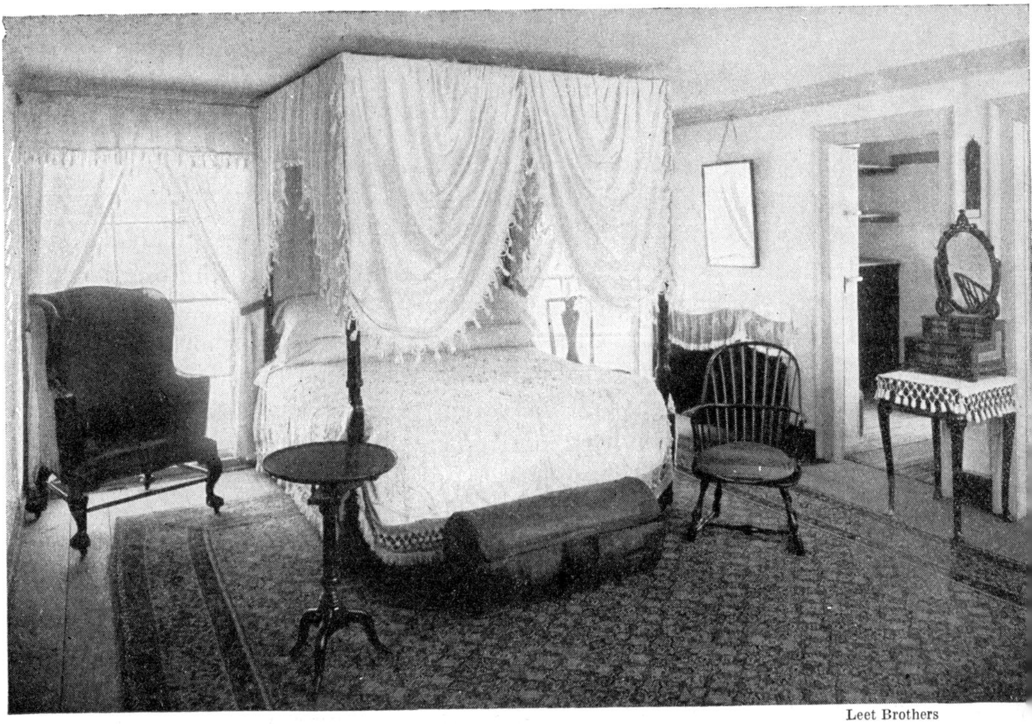

Leet Brothers

Bedroom at Mount Vernon

Dining-Room at Mount Vernon

© Leet Brothers, from Galloway

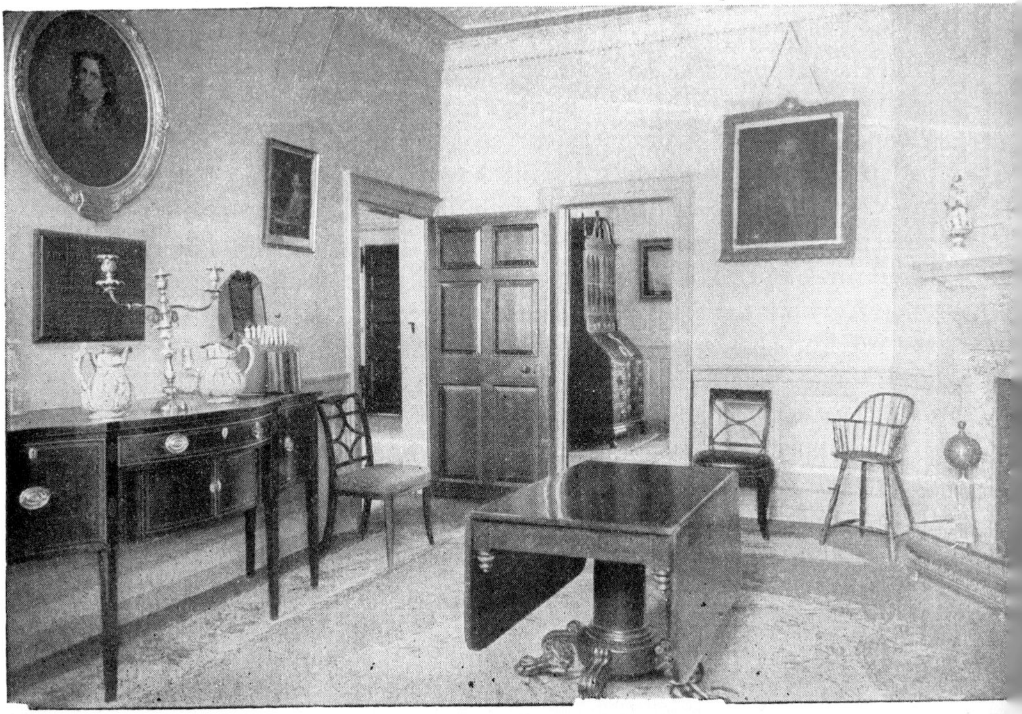

Dining-Room in the Dillingham House,
the Oldest House on Cape Cod

Great Room at Kenmore, the Home of Colonel Fielding Lewis
and His Wife, George Washington's Sister Betty

cock, a Massachusetts merchant, was likely to be seen at midday wearing a scarlet velvet cap, a blue damask gown lined with velvet, white satin embroidered waistcoat, black satin smallclothes, silk stockings, and red morocco slippers. For formal occasions powdered wigs and ornamented swords were added. The colonial lady wore richly embroidered gowns of silk or satin, innumerable petticoats, shoes covered with silk or satin, hoods of velvet, kid or silk gloves, and jeweled ornaments for the hands, neck, ears, and hair.

Such fancy clothes of colonial times were worn only by the rich. The middle class and lesser folk wore "homespun" clothes, made by the women of the family. Shoes were the one article of clothing that generally were made outside the less affluent home. Most of the table linen, pillowcases, towels, aprons, kitchen utensils, and furniture too were made by the housewife of the middle-class family. From the standpoint of dress, houses, furnishings, and amusements there was a clear-cut difference between the various classes in colonial society. It was possible, however, to move from one class to another; and although colonial society did not destroy class lines, class mobility existed as a reality for the hard-working citizen.

Here are no aristocratical families . . . [observed the French immigrant Hector St. John de Crèvecœur in 1782]. The rich and the poor are not so far removed from each other as they are in Europe. . . . We have no princes, for whom we toil, starve, and bleed; we are the most perfect society now existing in the world. . . . After a foreigner from any part of Europe is arrived, and become a citizen; let him devoutly listen to the voice of our great parent, which says to him: "Welcome to my shores, distressed European; . . . If thou wilt work, I have bread for thee; if thou wilt be honest, sober, and industrious, I have great rewards to confer on thee—ease and independence."

SELECTED BIBLIOGRAPHY

Curtis P. Nettels, *The Roots of American Civilization*, Chaps. VII, IX, X, XII, XIII, XV, XVI, XVII, XVIII, contains extremely valuable material, as do T. J. Wertenbaker, *The First Americans*, and J. T. Adams, *Provincial Society*, two volumes in the History of American Life Series.

V. L. Parrington, *The Colonial Mind*, a brilliant study of intellectual developments in colonial America; J. T. Adams, *The Founding of New England*, and S. E. Morison, *Builders of the Bay Colony*, very good reading; C. M. Andrews, *Colonial Folkways*, worth-while reading; W. W. Sweet, *Religion in Colonial America*, a good introduction to this subject.

H. S. Commager (Ed.), *Documents of American History*, pp. 15–31, 34–37, 39–42, contains source material.

IV

The American Revolution

THE AMERICAN Revolution and the French Revolution, which soon followed it, unleashed forces that were to shape world history in the nineteenth century. These two revolutions helped to destroy many of the things that had fettered mankind's progress for centuries. The ideal of liberty and equality for the common man, although not always achieved, was cast into the whirlpool of social, intellectual, and political life. Neither the United States nor France emerged from the revolutionary period completely democratic in the modern sense, but gradually, in the subsequent century, the common man in many parts of Western civilization acquired a greater control of government and a greater share of the benefits of society.

The American Revolution developed primarily from the problem of distributing governmental powers within the British Empire. After 1763 the English Parliament and the king strove to make the empire unitary with the power to regulate imperial affairs lodged in Parliament. The thirteen English colonies, on the other hand, struggled to achieve a federated empire, with some powers lodged in Parliament and others left to each colony. England, by attempting to create a unitary empire, overlooked the fact that in the years previous to 1763 a federated empire had developed and that any steps to make Parliament supreme threatened the existing situation.

BRITISH COLONIAL POLICY

The seeds of the American Revolution existed in the colonies from the outset. England, after 1763, ripened the seeds and added new grievances, which resulted in war. The different groups that had settled the colonies and the distance between England and the colonies scattered along the Atlantic seaboard made it impossible for England to establish a unified government during the age of colonization. Each colony was treated as a separate unit and permitted to exercise certain governmental powers, which gradually led to the development of a sense of independence.

English governmental acts during the century after 1650 were shaped largely by the principles of mercantilism. English statesmen believed that the colonies were chiefly desirable because they increased national wealth. To be powerful, a state had to have not only a strong military force, but also a sound economic life. It had to possess within its borders all the resources needed to free it from reliance on outside countries. Since England was not self-sufficient, colonization was pushed to those lands where the missing commodities could be found. Colonies would furnish essential raw materials and supply a market for English manufactured goods. Colonies existed, therefore, for the benefit of the mother country, and no mercantilist saw anything wrong in consigning colonies to a status of economic inferiority.

Laws of Trade, or Navigation Acts, were passed to achieve great national strength, and they aided England in her triumphs over Holland, Spain, and France in the struggle for world supremacy. The first Navigation Act, of 1651, declared that no goods from Asia, Africa, or America could be transported to England, Ireland, and the English colonies except in English, Irish, or colonial ships. The act was aimed mainly at the Dutch, who had been able to gain a heavy share of English colonial trade with England. This act still fell far short of the needs of a mercantile empire, since it allowed the colonists to ship their goods anywhere and buy manufactured goods wherever they pleased, provided the goods were carried in English or colonial ships. To tighten the mercantile system, a second Navigation Act was passed, in 1660, which required that certain "enumerated" commodities—sugar, tobacco, cotton, indigo, and dyewoods—be sent only to England. The colonists were not permitted to ship these articles directly to European markets, but had to send them to England for re-exporting to the Continent. During the eighteenth century England added whatever other products —rice, molasses, naval stores, and furs—strengthened her trading position with other nations. In 1663 the third Navigation Act, the Staple Act, was passed, prohibiting the colonies from importing goods directly from Europe. With some exceptions, European goods had to go to England, where, after the payment of customs duties, they could be shipped to the colonies. After the passage of these acts England concerned herself with the means of enforcing them and the tightening of her commercial monopoly of the trade with the colonies. By these measures the British Empire was changed from a free-trade area into a highly protected market, closed to foreign competition.

These acts worked hardships on the colonists, and, had they been strictly enforced, they might have precipitated revolution many years before 1775. At the same time, these measures conferred certain benefits on the colonists, such as English bounties to stimulate the production of certain goods, the promotion of colonial shipbuilding, protection by the British fleet, and monopoly markets. England dispatched naval officers and customs officials to the colonies, collected duties at the seaports, erected admiralty courts, and sought to suppress smuggling and piracy. In England the Lords of Trade, or Board of Trade, supervised the commerce of the empire and served as an advisory board to the king and Parliament.

The Northern colonies, particularly New England, did not easily fit into the mercantile empire. Raising no staple that England lacked, save some timber, the New England merchants competed with English merchants for the carrying trade of the empire, and they also violated the Navigation Acts by importing goods directly from Europe and by trading with the French, Dutch, and Spanish West Indies. The latter trade was virtually prohibited by the Molasses Act of 1733, but the Northern merchants evaded the act by smuggling. When England, after 1763, really tried to stamp out this smuggling, the merchants became vigorous opponents of the mother country. Long before all this occurred, however, England took unsuccessful steps to fit New England into the empire. In addition to the violations of the Navigation Acts, England, after the Stuart Restoration, in 1660, disliked the manner in which the Puritans had mistreated members of the Church of England, and had restricted the suffrage to members of the Congregational Church. The English also objected to the absorption of New Hampshire and Maine by Massachusetts. In 1684 the charter of Massachusetts was annulled. Two years later Edmund Andros was sent to Massachusetts as governor of all New England. New York and New Jersey were later added to his Dominion of New England. The colonial legislatures were disbanded, Rhode Island and Connecticut were reduced to the status of counties, efforts were made to collect quitrents and to interfere with long-established land titles, the church test for suffrage was abolished, and an Anglican Church was established in Boston.

New England had gone her own way too long to submit tamely, although from the standpoint of an effective mercantile empire much could be said in favor of the Andros consolidation. Two years after the establishment of the Dominion of New England the Glorious Revolution, of 1688, occurred in England. Parliament deposed James II in favor of William and Mary, and this overturn gave the New Englanders sufficient excuse to depose Andros and to bundle him off to England. Each of the colonies that had been placed under the Dominion now regained its separate identity. The new English rulers acquiesced in the *fait accompli*, for they could not afford to antagonize the colonies by retaining consolidated control in view of the war that was now raging with the French. In 1691 they granted Massachusetts a new charter, which placed Maine and Plymouth under the control of Massachusetts and permitted the election of a colonial legislature, although ownership of property rather than church membership henceforth became the basis of the suffrage. From this time on, England, through appointment of the governor, retained more control of Massachusetts than in the period from 1630 to 1684. The Glorious Revolution, however, had larger consequences for United States history than merely the overthrow of the Dominion of New England. Parliament became supreme over the king as a result of the Revolution, and this helped to inspire colonial legislatures in their quarrels with their governors. The Act of Religious Toleration too was extended to colonial America, and John Locke's treatise *Of Civil Government*, which justified the Glorious Revolution, was to furnish ammunition for the colonials at the time of their own revolution.

From the standpoint of Americans, the empire, during the eighteenth century, continued to be run for the benefit of British merchants and manufacturers at the expense of the colonists. Colonial debtors, for instance, tried to pay off their debts to English and colonial creditors by having the colonies print paper money; but in 1751 Parliament prohibited the issuing of paper money in New England, and thirteen years later the ban was extended to all the colonies. To protect British manufacturers the colonial manufacturing of woolen goods, hats, and iron for export from one colony to another was restricted. These acts tended to make the colonists realize that England was determined to prevent the colonies from growing too strong and powerful. During the troubled years from 1763 to 1775 the colonists hoped to gain a larger measure of economic freedom within the English mercantile system. The Northern merchants wanted to keep the trade that they had built up outside the empire; colonial capitalists wanted to invest in manufacturing; and Southern planters wanted the right to speculate in Western lands as a means of acquiring enough money to free them of their indebtedness to English merchants. The laws that England passed during these years, however, curbed these economic desires of the colonial peoples.

Another issue that precipitated trouble with England after 1763 was the invasion of American political rights. From the beginning England had permitted the tradition of local liberty to take root. All thirteen colonies possessed representative assemblies, which enabled the colonists to offer organized resistance to England. England made the mistake, for fifty years or more before 1764, of not directly taxing the colonies. The colonists, as a result, felt that only their own representative assemblies had the right to tax them; and when England began to tax them after 1764, they were strong enough to resist. Although the king had appointed most of the colonial governors after 1700, this in itself did not ensure strong imperial control. The assemblies regularly fought the governors on many issues and generally won. For instance, they gained control of appropriating money and supervising its expenditure. They appointed many administrative officers in spite of the governors' claim that they alone had the right of appointment. The most vital struggle between the assemblies and the king's representatives was over the question of salaries. The king regularly sent orders that the assemblies should grant permanent salaries to the governors and judges. To have complied would have meant that the assemblies would lose their control over the actions of these men. Virginia alone gave the governor a permanent salary. The rest of the colonial assemblies voted the salary each year. Whenever they objected to an action of a governor or a judge and he failed to pay attention to their objection, he received no salary. The royal governors thus found themselves in a dilemma. If they followed the orders of the king as to appointments and enforcing imperial laws, they were likely to go without any salary. If they gave in to the assemblies, they violated the royal orders. Most royal governors, rather than starve, gave in to the assemblies. Meanwhile, before 1763, the mother country did nothing significant to curb the growing power of the assemblies. The English applied the policy of "salutary neglect," or "let sleeping dogs lie," so that, by 1763, the assemblies had become virtually parliaments in their own right. It was not until this point had been reached that England began actively to curb colonial power.

During the Seven Years' War (1756–1763) the colonists still further increased their power at the expense of the empire. The assemblies gained exclusive control of the purse as the price of their voting supplies to aid in the war. The royal governors gave in rather than lose the war to the French. More infamous in English eyes than this failure to enter wholeheartedly into the war was the colonial practice of trading with the French and Spanish enemy in the West Indies. To prevent illegal trade, England issued writs of assistance, which permitted customs officials to search warehouses and private homes and seize illegal goods. The colonial merchants hired James Otis to plead against the writs as an invasion of the rights of Englishmen, but to no avail. The need of reorganizing the empire was clearly revealed during the Seven Years' War. The colonies had failed to co-operate sufficiently in the fight against the enemy, the English system of requisitioning money from each colony to help to meet the cost of the war had not been successful, and colonial taxation by Parliament now seemed necessary.

ON THE EVE OF REVOLUTION

The thirteen English colonies contained somewhat over two and a half million people in 1763, compared with the eight million people in Great Britain. They were a rural people, concentrated on the strip of land between the Appalachians and the Atlantic. They recognized that they were a part of the European-Atlantic world and had no desire to withdraw from it. "There was little sense of remoteness from the world's affairs and no desire to cut the ties that united them to the markets and culture of Europe," one writer has observed. "Far from wishing to live unto themselves, American merchants sought to range the world in search of markets, and the colonists in general, particularly the townspeople, attempted to identify themselves as closely as possible with the thought and life of Europe."[1]

Many of the common people had by this time caught the vision of a democratic America, where the ordinary citizen could shape his own destiny. These democrats had already fought many struggles against the colonial upper class for the control of government. In the years from 1763 to 1775 the colonial democracy waged a twofold war: against England and against their own upper class. They realized that England had to be disposed of before they could deal with their own aristocrats. Many of the upper class led in the agitation against England in order to gain freedom of action from imperial restrictions, but this group was hardly interested in granting more democracy to the underprivileged.

The removal of France from Canada by the Treaty of Paris of 1763 permitted England to attempt to consolidate her empire, long weakened by concessions to the colonists. Those who framed the reconstruction measures of the years from 1763 to 1775 were well-intentioned, but they refused to heed the warning of statesmen who understood the colonial situation. Leading authorities could be cited to prove that the English

[1]John C. Miller, *Origins of the American Revolution*, pp. 54–55. Little, Brown and Company, Boston, 1943.

legislation was or was not constitutional, but more important than this was the question of the expediency of the laws. To save the British Empire in these years, English statesmen needed to recognize that a federal system had developed over the past century; but they did not recognize this, and tried to create a unitary empire with Parliament as the supreme power. The series of laws passed by England from 1763 to 1775 to enforce her imperial idea only served to crystallize colonial opposition and lead to revolution.

At the close of the Seven Years' War, England was faced with the task of establishing a governmental system over the land stretching from the Appalachians to the Mississippi. In the Proclamation of 1763 she drew a line through the Appalachians, westward of which no British subject was allowed to settle or to purchase land. By this step England shut off colonial land speculation in the West. Colonial companies, even before the Seven Years' War, had been speculating in this region, and they naturally resented the Proclamation. When, in 1774, by the Quebec Act, this region was placed under the government of Quebec, colonials felt that their interests were being sacrificed in favor of English and Canadian speculators.

After 1763, too, England was faced with a heavy public debt, resulting from the Seven Years' War. In English eyes the colonists had not paid their fair share of the cost of the war, and there is no doubt that, compared with British taxes, the taxes of the colonists were light. To relieve British taxpayers, it was decided to place a duty on foreign molasses imported into the colonies. This had been attempted in the Molasses Act of 1733, but the colonial merchants had nullified it by smuggling. The Sugar Act of 1764 reduced the duty on foreign molasses from sixpence to threepence a gallon, but England now meant to collect the duty through a rejuvenated customs service. The colonial merchants insisted that the threepence duty could not be borne, since the margin of profit on the rum made from it was so low. They were now faced either with resistance or economic decay, since smuggling was no longer a way out. John Adams later said, "It is no secret that rum was an essential ingredient in the American Revolution." Samuel Adams of Massachusetts saw in the Sugar Act "taxation without representation." But colonial opposition was not well organized against this measure, which left the South largely unaffected, while the blow fell hardest on New England.

The second revenue bill of the Grenville ministry, however, stirred the colonials to well-organized resistance. The Stamp Act of 1765 required that a revenue stamp be affixed to all newspapers, broadsides, pamphlets, licenses, bills, notes, advertisements, and legal documents, and to a number of other similar papers. The revenue raised was to be spent solely for the purpose of "defending, protecting and securing the colonies." Grenville did his best to appease the colonials by appointing only Americans as stamp masters. In the eyes of the colonials, however, the Stamp Act was the culmination of a number of oppressive measures that were planned to destroy colonial prosperity.

The Stamp Act received such a violent reception in America that it left English leaders flabbergasted. It aroused the wrath of extremely powerful and articulate groups: colonial tavern-keepers, printers, lawyers, and merchants. It bore equally on all parts of the country. Colonial patriots held that the Stamp Act was the first step toward crushing out American liberties. If the principle of Parliamentary taxation were established, the colonial assemblies would lose control of the purse, and Parliament would then be able to make the governors and judges independent of colonial control. If the act were allowed to stand, all that the assemblies had struggled for would be wiped out.

In the Virginia assembly, Patrick Henry introduced a number of resolutions which denounced taxation without representation and asserted that Virginia alone had the right to tax Virginians. Soon rioting broke out in Boston and other seaports. Stamp masters were forced to resign, stamps were destroyed, and in Boston the home of Governor Thomas Hutchinson was gutted. Soon the colonies were covered with a network of clubs—Sons of Liberty—which served to organize resistance. Upper-class people often organized and guided the mobs. John Hancock of Boston, one of the wealthiest men in America, financed the Massachusetts mob which was directed by his friend Samuel Adams.

Shortly after Patrick Henry had introduced his resolutions in the Virginia assembly, James Otis persuaded the Massachusetts assembly to issue a call for an intercolonial congress to secure united action against the Stamp Act. At this Stamp Act Congress, held in New York, were some of the most distinguished men in the colonies. The Congress set forth the doctrine of no taxation without representation. It declared that "no taxes ever have been, or can be constitutionally imposed on them, except by their respective legislatures."

Colonial rioting and colonial manifestoes were not enough to induce England to repeal the Stamp Act, but a colonial boycott applied to English goods brought results. British merchants and manufacturers suffered so heavily from the boycott that they exerted pressure on Parlia-

John Locke

PAINTING BY
MICHAEL DAHL (?)

Thomas Paine

Benjamin Franklin

PAINTING BY
JOSEPH DUPLESSIS

Samuel Adams

PAINTING BY
JOHN SINGLETON COPLEY

Patrick Henry

PAINTING BY
THOMAS SULLY

James Otis

PAINTING BY
JONATHAN BLACKBURN

ment to repeal the act. Before Parliament complied, however, a Declaratory Act was passed, which asserted Parliament's right to "make laws and statutes of sufficient force and validity to bind the colonies in all cases whatsoever." The colonists were so occupied with celebrating the repeal of the Stamp Act, in March, 1766, that they paid no attention to this statement of Parliament's supremacy over them. The repeal of the Stamp Act removed the immediate menace to imperial peace, but there still remained deep-rooted sources of conflict. Had England refrained from further acts, a crisis might have been averted; but English leaders misunderstood the American mind.

From 1765 to 1775 Americans tried to impress American conceptions of law and liberty on the English government. The colonists tried to reform the empire, not break it up. They tried to win acceptance for their view of the British constitution and the rights of Englishmen. As George Mason of Virginia expressed it, "We claim nothing but the liberty and privileges of Englishmen." Most Americans supported the colonial cause as long as the dispute was on this basis; but after 1775, when the idea of independence was put forth, the colonists divided into pro-British and pro-American camps. The colonial assemblies, in their struggle for home rule, based their demand on natural law and the rights of Englishmen. The writings of John Locke furnished the colonials with ample ammunition. According to Locke, originally there had been a state of nature, in which all men enjoyed complete liberty; but because a few men transgressed on the rights of others, government was formed to protect man's natural liberties. This government was the result of a contract between the ruler and the people, and any time that the ruler transgressed on the natural rights of the people, they had the privilege of deposing him. There was no agreement on opposite sides of the Atlantic as to just what the laws of nature were. The colonials asserted that one such law was that taxes could not be levied without the people's consent. They quoted Locke: "If anyone shall claim a power to lay and levy taxes on the people by his own authority and without such consent of the people, he thereby invades the fundamental law of property, and subverts the end of government." Since Americans and Englishmen did not agree on the laws of nature, the colonists felt that their liberties would not be secure until the British constitution had been put into writing. Although they never accomplished this within the empire, as soon as they were free they put a constitution of their own into writing, in which were set forth the powers of government and the rights of the people.

Natural law served as the chief defense of colonial liberty. Some reliance was placed on the early colonial charters, but the argument based on them was gradually dropped, since the colonials realized that the king or Parliament, having frequently changed the charters in the past, might do so again. From 1763 to 1775 most of the colonists were willing to accept Parliament's right to regulate colonial trade and manufacturing, provided the right of direct taxation was placed solely in the assemblies. Sovereignty, according to the colonials, was divided between the crown, Parliament, and the assemblies. This argument actually meant that the empire was a federation of self-governing commonwealths. To the English of this time, however, sovereignty was indivisible. British political philosophy, like mercantile policy, emphasized that colonies should be dependent. Englishmen rejected the colonists' conception of natural law and the contention that there were bounds to Parliament's authority. Parliament could tax the colonies, argued the English, because "a country which we cannot tax is a country not subject to us." This position clearly excluded the colonial view of a federated empire.

Trouble broke out again between the colonies and England in 1767. The New York assembly refused to appropriate supplies, as was required by the Mutiny Act, for the British army stationed in New York. England felt that this was a threat to British sovereignty, but the New Yorkers held that they were fighting for the colonial liberty of determining their own taxes and expenditures. Parliament, led by Charles Townshend, Chancellor of the Exchequer, suspended the assembly of New York until it should comply with the Mutiny Act. Then Townshend persuaded Parliament to levy taxes on paint, lead, paper, and tea imported into the colonies. To collect the customs more efficiently, a Board of Commissioners of Customs was established in Boston. The money thus raised was to be used to defray "the charge of the administration of justice and the support of civil government."

The expressed intention of using the funds raised from the Townshend duties to pay the salaries of governors and judges, thus making these officials independent of the assemblies, naturally aroused colonial opposition. Patriots in Massachusetts drew up a circular letter which was sent to other colonies to unite British America against the Townshend Acts. This letter expressed the colonial desire of preserving colonial liberty within the empire. Parliament was acknowledged to be "the supreme legislative Power over the whole Empire," but, on the other hand, it was maintained that the power of both the crown and Parliament over the colonies was limited by the British constitution and natural law. The power of the purse belonged exclusively to the colonial assemblies, and no taxes, internal or external, could be levied by Parliament and imposed on the colonies. This letter had been drawn up by Samuel Adams. By this time Adams believed in independence from England, but he realized that public opinion had not yet accepted this belief. Therefore discretion led him to proclaim views that the public would accept.

At the same time that this circular letter was being debated, John Dickinson of Philadelphia wrote *Letters from a Farmer in Pennsylvania*, which, though moderate in tone, dealt with the same theme as the circular letter, namely that Parliament was sovereign but that the external taxation of the Townshend Acts was illegal. Real action against the Townshend duties developed when Boston merchants clamored for a boycott of English goods. These merchants suffered most, since the Board of Commissioners of Customs, stationed at Boston, stamped out smuggling at that port. The sailors and laborers thrown out of employment as a result of this step proved to be fertile ground for Samuel Adams's propaganda against England. By 1769 the boycott had spread to all the colonies. People dressed in homespun, substitutes were found for tea, and new colonial industries sprang up to make goods to take the place of those that were banned. Meanwhile British troops were sent to Boston to protect the customs officials from the Sons of Liberty. The patriots generally mobbed any American who tried to support England; and the press, under the patriots' control, regularly denounced English tyranny and served as an important device to consolidate public opinion. While the British troops were in Boston, Samuel Adams and the press stirred up strife between the citizenry and the soldiers, and altercations were numerous. On March 5, 1770, a mob of citizens jeered the sentry at the customhouse. Troops were called out, and someone gave the order to fire. Five Bostonians were killed, and the radical patriots, in their propaganda, inflated this "massacre" into proportions not warranted by the event.

On the same day as the Boston Massacre, Parliament repealed all the Townshend duties except the one on tea. To the utter disgust of Samuel Adams and the more radical leaders, the colonial merchants immediately dropped their nonimportation agreements. The radicals thus learned that in the future the Sons of Liberty must be entrusted with the enforcement of boycotts, and the merchants must be watched lest they "sell out" the colonial cause. From 1770 to 1773 imperial relations were peaceful. The radicals were forced to struggle against a widespread lethargy and indifference on the part of the people. Samuel Adams, always with an eye to ultimate independence, did his best to keep fires burning by attacks on Governor Hutchinson in the press and in the Massachusetts assembly. Late in 1772 he organized the Boston Committee of Correspondence and soon covered all New England with similar committees. These committees ultimately became a most formidable revolutionary machine. Through broadsides, pamphlets, and letters to the press the people were called to action. An example of patriot propaganda is a letter that appeared in a Rhode Island newspaper in 1773: "Rouse, my countrymen and townsmen, from your lethargic supineness! And convince your sister colonies, that the glorious spirit of patriotism and liberty, for which you have been celebrated in times past . . . is revived. . . . It is for Liberty! That Liberty for which our Fathers bled!" A popular liberty song of the day contained the following exhortations:

> Come Jolly Sons of Liberty . . .
> Come All with Hearts United,
> Our Motto is "We Dare Be Free,"
> Not easily affrighted!
> Oppressions band we must subdue,
> *Now* is the time or never.
> Let each Man Prove this Motto true,
> And Slavery from him sever.

In 1773 the East India Company and tea broke the calm in imperial relations. The English government gave the Company a monopoly of all tea sent to the colonies. The Company decided to sell the tea through its own agents, ignoring the colonial merchants, and to sell it at such a low price that smugglers could not compete. This action threw the colonial merchants, both smugglers and those who carried on only legal trade, into an alliance with the radicals. The merchants were afraid that a monopoly of tea might soon be increased to a monopoly of all colonial trade, which would drive the colonial merchant out of business. Also, the tax on tea threatened American political liberty. The money raised was to pay for the maintenance of an army and the civil list. Just as in the case of the other Townshend Acts, colonial assemblies were faced with a loss of their power over the governors and judges.

Sons of Liberty intimidated the tea agents in New York and Philadelphia, and the consignments were rejected and returned to England. In Charleston the tea was landed, but not sold. Boston used violence. On December 16, 1773, Sons of Liberty, dressed as Mohawk Indians, boarded three tea ships and dumped the tea into the ocean. The Boston Tea Party greatly stirred England. Demands for military reprisals and the destruction of Boston, "that nest of locusts," were heard. Lord North, however, decided to starve Boston into submission. The Boston Port Bill closed Boston to all shipping until the tea should be paid for, but the Boston radicals would not permit conservatively minded people to consider reimbursing the East India Company. They dispatched agents to other colonies for aid in the crisis. The radicals used the argument that Boston was the first line of defense of American liberties. If Boston went under, British tyranny would sweep all the colonies. Americans in other colonies quickly recognized that isolationism meant disaster. As George Washington expressed it, the question was whether Americans should "supinely sit and see one province after another fall a prey to despotism."

A Continental Congress was called for September, 1774, to secure colonial unity. This Congress became the battleground between colonial conservatives and radicals on the question of relations with England. Present were such extremists as John and Samuel Adams of Massachusetts, Stephen Hopkins of Rhode Island, Richard Henry Lee and Patrick Henry of Virginia, and Christopher Gadsden of South Carolina; moderates like George Washington of Virginia and John Dickinson of Pennsylvania; conservatives like John Jay of New York and Joseph Galloway of Pennsylvania. The conservatives expected that the Congress would advise Boston to pay for the tea and make peace with England. During the summer before the Congress met, Parliament adopted the "Coercive Acts," or "Intolerable Acts," which greatly strengthened the radicals. By these measures England transformed the government of Massachusetts. The holding of town meetings, without the governor's consent, was forbidden, the governor was given the power to appoint the upper house (previously chosen by the lower house), and juries were to be selected by the sheriffs (appointees of the governor) instead of by town meetings. An Administration of Justice Act provided that British officials or troops, charged with offenses committed in suppressing the Sons of Liberty, might be tried in another colony or in England. A Quartering Act provided that British troops might be quartered in the town of Boston.

The radicals charged that Parliament had treated the Massachusetts charter like a scrap of paper and might do the same to the charters of other colonies. At the Continental Congress, however, the radicals moved with care lest the conservatives charge them with desiring in-

*A Tense Meeting at the Old South Church
Leads to the Boston Tea Party*

MURAL PAINTING BY CHARLES HOFFBAUER

dependence. The two Adamses shrewdly stayed in the background and allowed the radical cause to be pushed by Virginians and Carolinians. The Congress drew up a list of grievances against England, which, though conceding that Parliament had the right to regulate colonial trade, stated that a settlement of the controversy might be had only on the basis of the repeal of all oppressive laws passed since 1763. By a majority of one the radicals secured the postponement of debate on conservative Joseph Galloway's Plan of Union. Galloway had proposed an American legislature elected by the assemblies. Each colony would continue to control its internal affairs, but the central legislature was to have control of general affairs, such as Indians, Western lands, and the raising of an army. Parliament might introduce acts relative to colonial affairs, but they would have to be approved by the American legislature. The assent of both Parliament and the American legislature was necessary to give validity to any law. Galloway's hopes of securing the adoption of his plan were completely dashed when, instead, Congress approved the Suffolk Resolves. These resolves, adopted by a convention of Suffolk County, Massachusetts, declared that no obedience should be paid to the "Coercive Acts" and that they should be resisted "as the attempts of a wicked administration to enslave America."

Throwing conciliation to the wind, the radicals now persuaded the Congress to draw up nonimportation, nonexportation, and nonconsumption agreements against England. The enforcement of the agreements was entrusted to local Continental Associations, which were usually run by the radicals. Samuel Adams and his group were not willing to let the merchants enforce them in view of the way that the boycott had broken down four years before. The Associations became a powerful extralegal machine to supervise the daily life of Americans. Every town or county in America set up a local Association to enforce the nonimportation, nonexportation, and nonconsumption agreements. Although the Adamses and Patrick Henry were ready for fighting in 1774, other colonials still hoped to work out a compromise within the British Empire. Thomas Jefferson and James Wilson of Pennsylvania, for instance, argued that each colony was a distinct state within the empire, held to the empire only by the crown. These two men thus envisioned an empire wherein the colonies had the dominion status which is now accorded to Canada, South Africa, New Zealand, and Australia. England, however, refused to accept any such constitutional theory.

THE OUTBREAK OF WAR

The continued presence of English troops in Boston stirred the Massachusetts patriots to collect materials of war and to train militiamen. Having a low opinion of the Yankees as fighting men, General Gage sent a contingent of troops to capture the patriots' supplies, accumulated at Concord, and to seize Samuel Adams and John Hancock, who were at Lexington. Learning of the plan, William Dawes and Paul Revere rode ahead and aroused the countryside. When the troops reached Lexington on the morning of April 19, 1775, they found themselves opposed by a band of militiamen. Shots were fired, and the patriots dispersed, leaving eight dead on the village green. The British pushed on to Concord, but on their return to Boston were subjected to a continuing fire from behind stone walls, houses, and trees. Within a week after the fighting at Lexington and Concord, patriot soldiers surrounded the British in Boston.

The bloodshed at Lexington was used by the radicals to rally support against England. Demands for vengeance rang throughout the colonies. The Second Continental Congress, which met on May 10, 1775, was in no conciliatory mood. It ordered that the colonies be immediately organized into a state of defense, and it created an army of twenty thousand men under the command of George Washington. In addition, it adopted a "Declaration of the Causes and Necessity of Taking Up Arms," which stated: "Our cause is just. Our union is perfect. Our internal resources are great, and, if necessary, foreign assistance is undoubtedly attainable." But the Congress also declared, "We have not raised armies with ambitious designs of separating from Great Britain, and establishing independent States." Until 1776 many Americans still hoped that something short of independence could be worked out. English statesmen, however, had not caught the vision of a world-wide empire of free colonies, which was necessary to forestall revolution.

In June, 1775, Washington started for Massachusetts to take command of the patriot army. Just before he reached his destination, he received news of the stirring battle of Bunker Hill. Late in 1775 the war was extended to Canada, when Congress authorized an expedition under Benedict Arnold to bring Canada into the union of colonies. England retaliated on August 23, 1775, by declaring that the colonies were in a state of rebellion, and, in December, closed all trade and intercourse with the colonies. The Continental Congress meanwhile authorized the construction of an American navy and appointed a committee to get in touch with foreign powers. When Thomas Paine published his remarkable pamphlet, *Common Sense*, in January, 1776, he gave the movement for independence a great stimulus. Paine had been in the colonies only two years, but he had had ample experience with English tyranny. As an excise officer in England, Paine had tried to organize the excise officers in order to win a raise in pay. For this activity he had been expelled from the service. Paine saw the issue in 1776 as one of slavery or independence. Liberties could not be defended by anything short of independence. After using both pen and musket in behalf of the American Revolution, Paine went to France and joined in the revolution there. Hating tyranny in all forms, he published *The Age of Reason* (1793-1795), an attack on organized religion as a fetter on mankind's progress. He published also an advanced scheme of social-security legislation, which in many ways was far beyond what was achieved under the New Deal, a century and a half later.

One hundred and twenty thousand copies of *Common Sense* were distributed in three months, and Paine's vigorous call for independence crystallized this latent thought in men's minds. With complete disregard for tradition, Paine ruthlessly attacked King George III, the British constitution, and the empire. One honest man, he stated, was worth "all the crowned ruffians that ever lived." George III, "the Royal Brute of Great Britain," was called the worst of possible kings. The British ruling class, Paine charged, lived by exploiting the common people of England and the colonies. After explaining that these factors were alone sufficient to warrant independence, he then went on to paint the glories of an independent, free America. In his statements Paine foreshadowed what America, as a shining light of freedom and liberty, was to mean to the world in the nineteenth century. "The Sun never shined on a cause of greater worth," he wrote. "'Tis not the affair of a City, a County, a Province, or a Kingdom; but of a Continent—of at least one eighth part of the habitable Globe. 'Tis not the concern of a day, a year, or an age; posterity are virtually involved in the contest, and will be more or less affected even to the end of time by the proceedings now." His peroration clearly demonstrated that it was of America as the hope of a free world that he was thinking:

O! ye that love mankind! Ye that dare oppose not only the tyranny but the tyrant, stand forth! Every spot of the old world is overrun with oppression. Freedom hath been hunted round the Globe. Asia and Africa have long expelled her. Europe regards her as a stranger, and England hath given her warning to depart. O! receive the fugitive, and prepare in time an asylum for mankind.

In the early months of 1776 events moved rapidly toward independence. North Carolina patriots defeated a force of loyalists on February 17 at Moores Creek. In April the North Carolina legislature instructed its delegates to the Congress to call for independence. The Congress, in May, 1776, moved toward independence by ordering the disarming of loyalists, the outfitting of privateers to prey on English shipping, and the opening of American ports to foreign vessels, and by advising all the colonies to wipe out England's authority and establish governments based on the will of the people. Then, on June 7, Richard Henry Lee rose in Congress and moved, "That these United Colonies are, and of right ought to be, Free and Independent States." On July 2 Lee's motion was carried, but not without some dissent. Certain members absented themselves on July 2, and New York did not approve the action until July 15. The formal Declaration of Independence, written by Thomas Jefferson, was adopted on July 4.

THE DECLARATION OF INDEPENDENCE

Democracy was not something inherent in American life. The main reason for its growth lay in the existence of interests and groups which, because of weakness or losses of opportunity, made democracy a cry, a weapon, with which to wage their fight for a better life. Democracy, to live, had to have spokesmen backed by practical interests. The quarrel with England required the use of the democratic doctrine. James Otis, Samuel Adams, Thomas Jefferson, and a host of others thoroughly established the relationship between American interests and the democratic dogma. They made democracy a weapon which future groups, disgruntled and oppressed, could use. Ever afterward America was on the side of the unfortunate and the oppressed. During the period of the American Revolution two struggles were taking place: the Revolution, a social and political struggle; and the War of Independence (1775-1783), a fight between the colonies and England. The latter had as its purpose the winning of independence from England; the former involved the aspirations of the democratic element, struggling against both English tyranny and the dominance of the colonial aristocrats. The most spectacular case of internal conflict took place in North and South Carolina. In May, 1771, in the battle at Alamance, men of the back-country region rose in open rebellion against the oppressive and irregular taxation of the government, under the control of the tidewater section. These so-called "Regulators," who had already been interfering with the holding of courts, opposed the Eastern militia sent against them. While this was perhaps the most extreme case of conflict, it nevertheless revealed the important fact that the oncoming struggle was not only to be one for home rule, but to decide who was to rule at home as well.

When Thomas Jefferson wrote the Declaration of Independence, he presented the principles of democracy and equality desired by the underprivileged groups. The preamble of the Declaration, far more important than the body of the document, expressed the spirit of the American Revolution and made democracy a weapon which neglected and oppressed groups in every generation have used. "When, in the course of human events," Jefferson wrote, "it becomes necessary for one people to dissolve the political bands which have connected them with another, and to assume, among the powers of the earth, the separate and equal station to which the laws of nature and of nature's God entitle them, a decent respect to the opinions of mankind requires that they should declare the causes which impel them to the separation."

The main body of the Declaration explained what the causes for the separation actually were. To the student of history, not all the causes set forth are the real ones. The reason for this, as Carl Becker has suggested, was that

... the framers of the Declaration were not writing history, but making it. They were seeking to convince the world that they were justified in doing what they had done. ... The Declaration was not primarily concerned with the causes of this rebellion; its primary purpose was to present those causes in such a way as to furnish a moral and legal justification for that rebellion. The Declaration was essentially an attempt to prove that rebellion was not the proper word for what they were doing.[1]

The colonists knew that rebellion was a serious matter. They had to prove, therefore, that they really were not engaged in rebellion against *just* authority, but against *unjust* usurptions. The theory that made rebellion respectable under these circumstances was explained in the preamble to the Declaration:

We hold these truths to be self-evident:—That all men are created equal; that they are endowed by their Creator with certain unalienable rights; that among these are life, liberty, and the pursuit of happiness. That, to secure these rights, governments are instituted among men, deriving their just powers from the consent of the governed; that, whenever any form of government

[1]Carl Becker, *The Declaration of Independence*, p. 6. Alfred A. Knopf, New York, 1922.

The Declaration of Independence Is Hailed in Boston

MURAL PAINTING BY CHARLES HOFFBAUER

becomes destructive of these ends, it is the right of the people to alter or to abolish it, and to institute a new government, laying its foundation on such principles, and organizing its powers in such form, as to them shall seem most likely to effect their safety and happiness.

In view of the charges against the king detailed in the body of the Declaration of Independence, revolution was necessary and meritorious. The colonists had to fight such usurpations and injustices, was the implication, or they would become slaves. Furthermore, they were fighting not only for their own rights, but also for the rights of all mankind. If this attack on liberty were to prevail without opposition, the rights of men everywhere would suffer.

The philosophy expressed by Jefferson in the Declaration was derived from the writings of Harrington, Sidney, and John Locke, and from the American colonial experience. Jefferson did not attempt to create a new philosophy; as he later observed, "I did not consider it as any part of my charge to invent new ideas altogether, and to offer no sentiment which had ever been expressed before." Jefferson gave his fellow patriots the goal of placing human rights above privilege and property rights. The new order that was to be achieved was to benefit the common man. Freedom of the individual and equality of opportunity for all men were the ideals for which to strive. During the Revolutionary days ahead, which were to "try men's souls," the Declaration's stirring phrases were needed to sustain Americans in their struggle for a better life for all, and the liberal reform movements of the nineteenth century in America and Europe based their philosophy on the Declaration of Independence.

THE WAR OF INDEPENDENCE, FROM 1776 TO 1778

Following the Declaration of Independence, America was far from united in the struggle against England. John Adams once said that he felt that one third of the people were for independence, one third were against, and one third were indifferent. Many of those who had participated in the argument against England up to 1776 were interested in solving the problem of imperial unity through evolution, and after the Declaration they became loyalists. In New York, New Jersey, and Georgia they probably made up a majority of the population. They were weakest in Virginia, Maryland, and Massachusetts. Seventy thousand loyalists left the colonies during the war, but the majority remained. Some took up arms to aid England, while others remained quiet, hoping for the defeat of the American cause. The majority of the loyalists were from the upper class. Royal officials, most of the Anglican clergy outside Virginia and Maryland, and some Northern merchants and lawyers, who feared that the war would unleash the masses, became Tories. The rest of the upper-class people joined in the American cause, but with the full intention of checking later the aspirations of the average citizen for a more democratic way of life.

The Americans started the war with the advantage of controlling almost every inch of the territory from Maine to Georgia, and England was faced with the enormous task of supplying and dispatching an army three thousand miles across the sea. Yet there was so much apathy in America that Congress had difficulty in keeping an army in the field and supplying it. Americans, therefore, instead of being able to win a quick victory, had to struggle for many years, and ultimate independence would have been lost had it not been for French aid. The English relied upon their regular army, augmented by German mercenaries, to subdue the Americans. They could also count upon some aid from American loyalists and from Indians, who were used to harass the frontier settlements. Many English officers, however, resigned their commissions rather than fight fellow Englishmen, and the English people were reluctant to enlist. The American patriots faced the grave disadvantage of having only a small number who were willing to fight. The American farmer enlisted only for a short time and then returned to care for his farm. This meant the frequent replacement of seasoned soldiers with raw recruits. Also, the American soldier was too individualistic to submit to the type of discipline necessary to build a powerful fighting force. The kind of warfare that the American desired was the kind which called him out to repel an invasion and then allowed him to return home. Regular service for a number of years was so distasteful that Washington had to endure disloyalty, disobedience, and neglect throughout the war. Not only did he have to be the commanding general of the army, but he had to beg Congress and state governments for men and supplies, and to placate his hungry men. Receiving no salary himself, he sometimes had to dig deep into his own pocket to buy equipment for his soldiers.

When the center of the warfare was in the South, it was difficult to persuade New Englanders to go there and fight; and when the war was in New England, Southerners were reluctant to leave their section to fight in the common cause. At peak strength, in 1776, Washington's army numbered eighteen thousand, but for the rest of the war it numbered about five thousand. Congress established quotas of men for the states to furnish to the army, but the quotas were not always filled. Volunteers were given cash and land bounties, but even these did not secure the necessary man power. No provisions were made for the families of men in service, and no pensions were paid to dependents of those killed. Thus those who enlisted were largely the young and the adventurous. A drafted army on a national scale was not used in this war, because Congress lacked the power and the people were not convinced that such a step was either necessary or justified.

Throughout the conflict Congress issued requisitions to the states for money, men, and supplies. The states honored these as they saw fit. Congress was able, however, to supply the army with arms and ammunition as a result of generous aid from France, of materials captured by privateers, and of supplies produced by local factories. On the other hand, Congress did not do too well in feeding and clothing the army; for it lacked the necessary power, and the people were not willing to endure taxation to pay for the cost of war. The war was financed by Continental currency, that is, paper money issued by Congress; state issues of paper money; and domestic and foreign loans. Congressional and state issues of paper money depreciated greatly in value. By 1780 Congress recognized that Continental currency was worth only one fortieth of its stated value. In all, Congress issued paper currency totaling about $241,000,000, and the states issued paper totaling $210,000,000. Domestic loans of $67,000,000 in paper were subscribed, which were worth about $10,000,000 in specie. France gave $1,800,000 and lent $6,352,000 after 1777. Spanish and Dutch bankers lent approximately $1,450,000.

The fighting war began in earnest with the patriots sealing up the British army in Boston following the battle of Bunker Hill, on June 17, 1775. Early in 1776 the British withdrew to Halifax, and in the summer sailed into New York Harbor with great reinforcements. By September, in spite of heroic efforts on the part of Washington, the English, under General Howe, occupied the town of New York and the surrounding territory. Washington divided his army, sending one force to New Jersey to protect Philadelphia, and dispatching the other under Charles Lee to White Plains to prevent the English from moving up the Hudson. When the British advanced on Washington's wing of the army, he was forced to call on Lee for reinforcements. Lee delayed and was captured by the English on December 13. The American cause now seemed to be lost. Washington, in order to repair the morale of his men, ordered a daring attack across the Delaware River on Christmas Eve and captured a thousand Hessians at Trenton. He followed this with a defeat of the British forces under Cornwallis at Princeton on January 3, 1777. Then Washing-

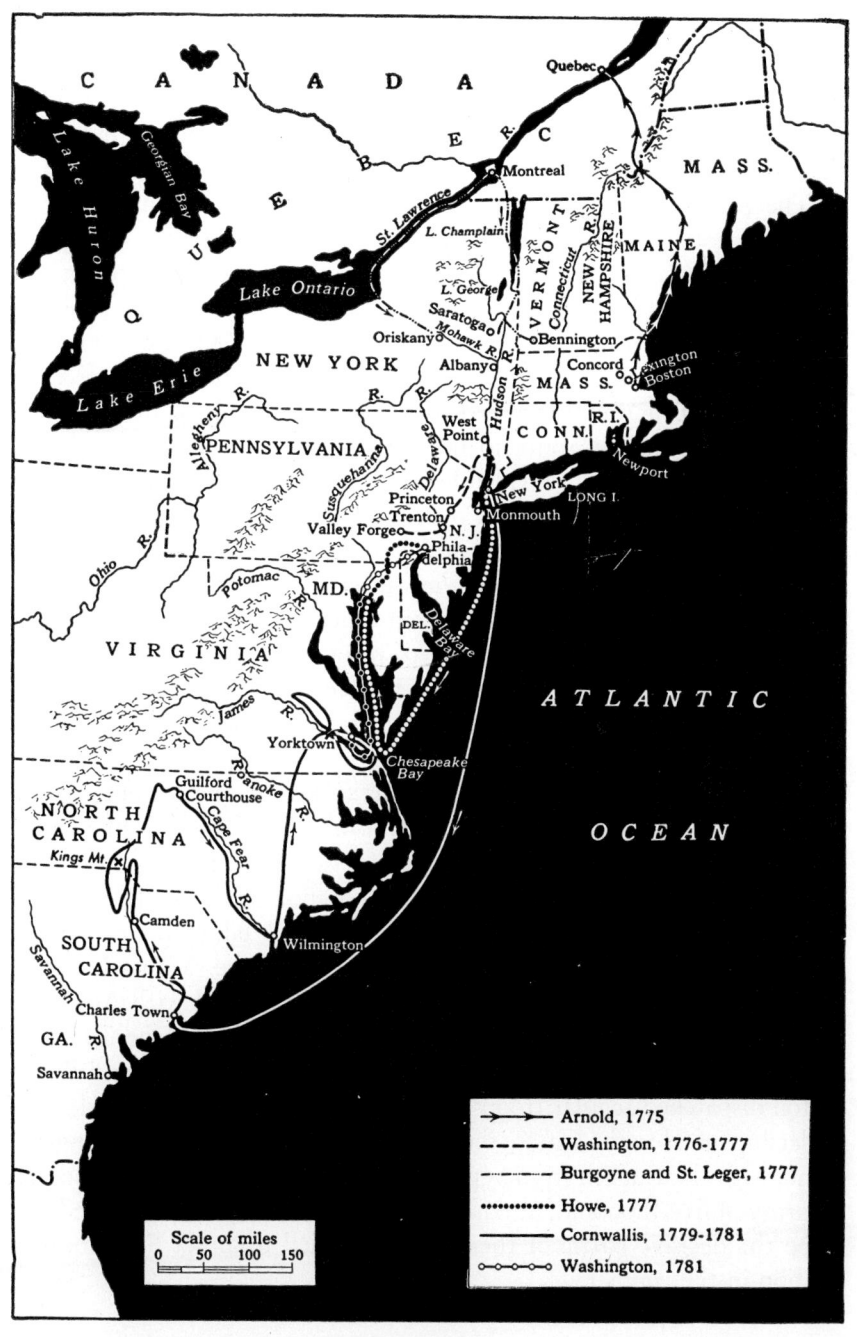

Important Campaigns in the War of Independence

ton went into winter quarters at Morristown, while the British returned to New York City. Congress tried to recruit for the army during the winter, but when spring came Washington had an army of only four thousand men.

The British strategy in 1777 was to split the New England colonies from the rest by an invasion of the Hudson valley. General Burgoyne was to lead an army from Canada to Albany via Lake Champlain; St. Leger was to lead an army to Albany via Lake Ontario and the Mohawk River; and an army from New York City was to sail up the Hudson to join the other two. General Howe, at New York, did not receive instructions that he was to proceed to Albany until most of his army was in Chesapeake Bay en route to take Philadelphia. During September, Howe's forces occupied Philadelphia after having defeated Washington's inferior army at Brandywine Creek on September 11. Washington's attack at Germantown on October 4 was repulsed, and Washington then retired to Valley Forge to spend the winter. Meanwhile Burgoyne was having his troubles in his invasion from Canada. The strategy that had been mapped out in England failed to recognize the physical problems that an army in the field would have to face. An enormous number of portable boats had to be carried for the transfers between Lake Champlain, Lake George, and the Hudson, and, at the same time, this amount of baggage slowed the march so much as to give ample warning to the patriots. On his way to the Hudson, Burgoyne detached an expedition of about seven hundred to forage for supplies in Vermont. John Stark and his "Green Mountain Boys" marched out from Bennington and overwhelmed the English force. While this was taking place, General Herkimer and the German-American settlers of the Mohawk valley checked St. Leger; and when Benedict Arnold arrived with American reinforcements, St. Leger returned to Canada. These American successes brought out the New England militia in great numbers, and Washington dispatched regular troops to help to check Burgoyne. Under the leadership of Horatio Gates, the Americans fought a series of engagements with the English from September 19 until Burgoyne surrendered his army of five thousand, at Saratoga, on October 17. This turned out to be the decisive battle of the war, since it led to direct French intervention in the conflict.

FROM THE FRENCH ALLIANCE TO THE TREATY OF PEACE

France had longed to revenge her defeat in 1763. French agents were present in the English colonies before 1776, adding to the fires of controversy between the mother country and the colonies. One Englishman likened France to a "vulture hovering over the British Empire, and hungrily watching the prey that she is only waiting for the right moment to pounce upon." Early in the war Congress sent a commissioner to France, who successfully purchased munitions and supplies, and France early showed enthusiasm for the American cause. Young Frenchmen like Lafayette joined Washington's army, and the French government, hoping to break up the British Empire and gain the trade of the colonies, permitted American privateers to use French seaports and sent Washington's army unneutral aid in the form of supplies. France, however, was reluctant to join the Americans in open war in view of the lack of military success of Washington's forces. Benjamin Franklin, who arrived in Paris in December, 1776, realized this, and he spent his time in gaining the confidence of the French leaders. Burgoyne's surrender at Saratoga altered the entire picture. Comte de Vergennes, who directed foreign affairs for Louis XVI, feared that England now would make concessions to the colonies and reunite the empire. Franklin encouraged this French belief; and the English government, in February, 1778, actually did approve of peace terms with the colonies, which would have given the colonies the kind of status now enjoyed by the Dominions.

Eleven days before Parliament acted, however, Franklin signed treaties of commerce and alliance with France. In the treaty of alliance France recognized the independence of the colonies and agreed to cooperate in a military fashion until independence was won. The Americans, in return, guaranteed to aid France in defending her possessions in the West Indies. Both parties agreed not to make peace without the approval of the other. Spain joined France in the war in 1779, although she refused to sign a treaty of alliance with the revolting colonies, for she detested the republicanism of the latter and feared that a successful revolt of the English colonies might inspire a similiar revolt in her own American dependencies. Spain entered the war to recover Gibraltar and Florida and also to acquire the land of the Mississippi Valley west of the Alleghenies. The Netherlands joined the war against the English in 1780, and Catherine II of Russia organized other European powers into a League of Armed Neutrality, which hampered England's maritime activities. Thus from 1778 to 1783, five of the eight years of the American Revolution, England's attention was divided among several enemies This, of course, was of great advantage to the colonies.

Washington early recognized that sea power would be decisive in the war. The work of American privateers and naval ships was not sufficient to win naval superiority, but the addition of the French, Spanish, and Dutch fleets gave the Americans the benefit of greatly needed naval strength. Great Britain had to divert a good share of her naval strength from the Atlantic seaboard to the West Indies, India, Africa, and the Mediterranean to fight her European enemies. Early in the summer of 1778 the British army, now under Sir Henry Clinton, evacuated Philadelphia and reached New York safely after fighting, on June 28, an indecisive battle with Washington at Monmouth. Thereafter to the close of the war there were few important military events in the middle colonies. In 1778 and 1779 George Rogers Clark, acting under a Virginia commission, cleared the English out of most of the Northwest and captured the English posts at Kaskaskia and Vincennes.

From 1779 to 1781 most of the warfare took place in the South. With the French fleet occupied elsewhere, the English moved troops from New York to the South. In December, 1778, the British captured Savannah, Georgia. Many colonists joined the English, and all went well until they reached the Carolina back country, where an army of patriots decisively defeated an English force at King's Mountain on October 7, 1780. General Cornwallis, in charge of an English army, met the Americans under General Nathanael Greene in an indecisive battle at Guilford Courthouse on March 15, 1781, and then retreated to Wilmington, North Carolina. Months later, after harrying Virginia and failing to capture an American army under Lafayette, Cornwallis withdrew to the Yorktown peninsula, where he expected to gain the support of the British fleet. Washington hurried overland with the American army and five thousand French soldiers under the Comte de Rochambeau to reinforce Lafayette and to lay siege to Cornwallis's army. Meanwhile the French fleet, under Admiral de Grasse, drove a British fleet from the Chesapeake capes, thus cutting off Cornwallis's escape by sea. On October 19, 1781, Cornwallis was obliged to surrender. This military-naval campaign at Yorktown was a well-conceived and brilliantly executed operation in its co-ordination of land and sea power. When Cornwallis's army stacked its arms before the conquering allied army, the British band expressed their army's sentiments by playing "The World Turned Upside Down."

By 1781 success in this six-and-a-half-year war, from the English standpoint, was as remote as ever. The financial burden of fighting many powers over the entire world was so heavy that peace negotiations were entered into in April, 1782. The American representatives were Benjamin Franklin, John Jay, Henry Laurens, and John Adams. These Americans, as a first consideration, demanded the territory west to the Mississippi and south from the Great Lakes to Florida. Spain, which was conducting separate negotiations with England, had, however, demanded Florida and all the land from the Alleghenies to the Mississippi. John Jay meanwhile became convinced that France was working with Spain to deprive the Americans of the West. France was indeed in a difficult position. She had not been able to win Gibraltar for the Spanish, and hoped instead to placate Spain by securing for her the land between the mountains and the Mississippi. A small and weak American republic, dependent on France, was preferred by both France and Spain. The English, seeing a division among their foes, chose to favor the Americans. In spite of instructions from Congress that they should proceed only with the knowledge and concurrence of France, Jay and Adams persuaded the hesitant Franklin to negotiate a separate preliminary treaty with England. This did not violate the Franco-American treaty of 1778, since the preliminary treaty was to be approved by France before it became effective. The preliminary treaty was signed on November 30, 1782, although it did not go into effect until France made peace with Great Britain. The final treaties among the various powers were concluded on September 3, 1783.

The new nation won a great victory in the peace treaty. Although the boundary line was vague and had to be adjusted later by such negotiations as the Webster-Ashburton Treaty, of 1842, America received the land south of the Great Lakes and west from the mountains to the Mississippi. America also received the privilege of fishing in the territorial waters of British North America. Congress was required to recommend to the various states that the confiscated property of loyalists be restored and that no more property be confiscated. Another article provided that no "lawful impediments" be placed in the way of prewar debts owed by Americans to British subjects. In the treaties between Spain, France, and England, Spain recovered Minorca and Florida. Spain now held all the land west of the Mississippi and Florida, and was not dislodged from this area until the nineteenth century. France received a few West Indian islands, a bankrupt treasury, the hope of an American market, and a future ally in the United States.

Thus, in 1783, the former British colonies joined the society of independent nations. The example of colonies throwing off the yoke of the mother country was later to inspire the Spanish American colonies to do likewise. The democratic ideology of the American Revolution influenced the French Revolution and the rise of democracy in nineteenth-century Europe. The United States meanwhile, in her sweep across the continent, was demonstrating the practical value of democracy and, by her example, offering new hope to the oppressed peoples of the world. Within a hundred years of winning independence, the United States emerged as one of the great powers, an event which shifted world thinking from complete absorption in European activities to the realization that the Western Hemisphere must be reckoned with in arriving at and maintaining the balance of power.

SELECTED BIBLIOGRAPHY

JOHN C. MILLER, *Origins of the American Revolution*, an excellent summary of the period from 1763 to 1776; C. M. ANDREWS, *Colonial Background of the American Revolution*, a discussion of the place of the colonies in the empire; CARL BECKER, *The Declaration of Independence*, an unexcelled study of this document; M. C. TYLER, *Literary History of the American Revolution*, and V. L. PARRINGTON, *The Colonial Mind*, valuable studies of the leading thinkers during the controversy from 1763 to 1776.

C. H. VAN TYNE, *The Causes of the War of Independence* and *The War of Independence*, worth-while studies; G. M. WRONG, *Washington and His Comrades in Arms*, good material on the military phase of the war; S. F. BEMIS, *The Diplomacy of the American Revolution*, the most accurate survey of this subject.

H. S. COMMAGER (Ed.), *Documents of American History*, pp. 45–103, contains valuable source information.

V

The Struggle for Stable Government

T HE WINNING of independence from England was a political, diplomatic, and military achievement. There were many on the patriot side, however, who hoped that the struggle would be also a social and economic revolution whereby the mass of the people would gain many democratic rights previously denied them. The democratic group, led by men like Thomas Jefferson, Thomas Paine, Samuel Adams, Benjamin Franklin, and Christopher Gadsden, assumed that man was a dignified, rational being capable of governing himself. Government in the past frequently had been tyrannical; therefore, these leaders believed, the powers given to government should be restricted. The people in their sovereign capacity, these leaders contended, should draw up a constitution clearly setting forth the powers allotted to government. Furthermore, the mass of people should have the right to vote and hold office, and should have proper representation in the legislature. These democrats also assumed that ownership of property was the basis of political rights, since only if a person owned property could he be independent in his actions. Ownership of property, however, did not imply the right to use such property in an antisocial and antidemocratic fashion. As Franklin said, "All the property that is necessary to a man, for the conservation of the individual and the propagation of the species, is his natural right, which none can justly deprive him of: but all property superfluous to such purposes is the property of the public, who by their laws have created it, and who may therefore by other laws dispose of it, whenever the welfare of the public shall demand such disposition."

Opposed to the colonial democrats was the conservative, upper-class group, led by men like Edmund Randolph, George Washington, Charles Cotesworth Pinckney, Gouverneur Morris, Alexander Hamilton, John Jay, and John Dickinson. These conservatively minded people were determined to prevent the war with England from resulting in a social upheaval in the colonies. Although they were radical in their attitude toward England, they were not interested in establishing democracy at home. One writer has said:

> They were not making war upon the principle of aristocracy and they had no more intention than had the Tories of destroying the tradition of upper-class leadership in the colonies. Although they hoped to turn the Tories out of office, they did not propose to open these lush pastures to the common herd. They did believe, however, that the common people, if properly bridled and reined, might be made allies in the work of freeing the colonies from British rule and that they—the gentry—might reap the benefits without interference. They expected, in other words, to achieve a "safe and sane" revolution of gentlemen, by gentlemen, and for gentlemen.[1]

These gentry denied that the common man was virtuous and rational. They held, instead, that he was ignorant, incompetent, and violent. As a result, the rich and the well-born should rule, all offices should be reserved for the upper class, and the constitutions of government should contain restrictions on majority rule. Those members of the upper class who sided with England were afraid that once war broke out, the upper class would not be able to restrain the passions of the plebeians. The Declaration of Independence, with its democratic ideology, seemed to the loyalists to be the first step toward "mob rule."

The patriots, desiring more democracy, naturally wanted to apply the doctrine of no taxation without representation to America, as well as to England. During the war their demands were not always met, but, on the other hand, certain important gains were made. These fighters for democracy realized that they had to push their demands during wartime if social progress was to be achieved. The gains that were made, however, generally were made at the expense of the loyalists and not at the expense of those members of the upper class who supported the American cause. The greatest change was the change in landownership. The various state governments seized the lands of the king and the proprietors. From the Penn family Pennsylvania took land valued at one million pounds, and Virginia confiscated five million acres from Lord Fairfax. The lands of the loyalists who fled to join the English cause were also confiscated. The acquisition of all this land put the state governments into the real-estate business. They gave the land as bounties to soldiers and sold a great deal of it at extremely low prices. These steps greatly increased the number of property-holders and hence increased the number of

[1]John C. Miller, *Origins of the American Revolution*, p. 498. Little, Brown and Company, Boston, 1943.

people who could vote. Feudal survivals like quitrents, entail, and primogeniture were swept away at the same time. Ever after in American development, individuals owned the land in fee simple and were not required to pay feudal dues to an overlord. The ending of the systems of entail and primogeniture meant that two of the props supporting concentrated land ownership were removed, and most of the states after the Revolution recognized, as legal, the division of estates equally among heirs.

During the war there was also a successful attack on the institution of the state church. Since the Anglican Church was the established church of England and many of the clergy were loyalists, the disestablishment of the church was carried out in Maryland and North Carolina in 1776, in New York and Georgia in 1777, and in South Carolina in 1778. Only in Virginia was there a long contest over this issue. Many of the leading Virginian patriots were Anglicans, and the clergy in this colony overwhelmingly supported the American cause. Thomas Jefferson, James Madison, and George Mason carried on a ten-year contest, with the aid of the Baptists and the Presbyterians, to disestablish the church. Many tidewater conservatives, on the other hand, looked upon the established church as a bulwark against social change and as a force which would "correct the morals of men, restrain their vices and preserve the peace of society." On December 17, 1785, Jefferson's famous Act for the Establishment of Religious Freedom was adopted. Jefferson's views on religious freedom were summarized in the following provision: "That no man shall be compelled to frequent or support any religious worship, place or ministry whatsoever, nor shall be enforced, restrained, molested or burthened in his body or goods, nor shall otherwise suffer on account of his religious opinions or belief; but that all men shall be free to profess, and, by argument, to maintain their opinions in matters of religion, and that the same shall in no wise diminish, enlarge or affect their civil capacities." Jefferson later was to list this act with the Declaration of Independence and the founding of the University of Virginia as the three great contributions that he had made to his country. Only in Massachusetts, Connecticut, and New Hampshire were the established churches retained during this period. Religious liberty was finally decreed in New Hampshire in 1817, in Connecticut in 1818, and in Massachusetts in 1833.

During the Revolutionary period a number of churches underwent reorganization. The Anglicans separated from the Church of England and formed the Protestant Episcopal Church of America, with Samuel

Seabury as their first bishop. The Methodists took the opportunity of withdrawing from the Anglican Church and organizing their own Methodist Episcopal Church, with Francis Asbury as their first bishop. The Presbyterians, at a series of meetings from 1785 to 1788, formed a national organization with a structure not unlike that worked out for the United States by the Philadelphia convention of 1787. Members of the Dutch Reformed and German Reformed churches, and the Lutherans, also worked out an American organization for their churches. The Congregationalists had no central organization to change, and the Quakers were so loosely organized that they too had no need of any change. The Catholics, numbering about thirty-two thousand in 1785, had, up to 1776, been under the jurisdiction of the London vicar-apostolic. In 1788 the Pope granted the American clergy the right to their own bishop, and John Carroll of Maryland was appointed the first Bishop of the Catholic Church in America, with his headquarters at Baltimore.

A movement against slavery gained strength during the Revolutionary years. This was in accordance with the views on liberty, equality, and natural rights that were adrift in the intellectual atmosphere of the day. On April 14, 1775, the first antislavery society was formed, at Philadelphia, and in 1774 the Continental Congress had decreed that the importing of slaves should cease. Rhode Island, in the same year, ordered that any more slaves brought into that colony should be free because "the inhabitants of America are generally engaged in the preservation of their own rights and liberties, among which that of personal freedom must be considered as the greatest, and . . . those who are desirous of enjoying all the advantages of liberty themselves should be willing to extend personal liberty to others." Six years later Pennsylvania passed an act of gradual abolition; Massachusetts, in 1781, ended slavery, as did Rhode Island and Connecticut, in 1784. New York, in 1799, and New Jersey, in 1804, took similar steps. Abolition in the South, where the greatest numbers of slaves were to be found, did not gain ready acceptance. Several states, like Virginia, encouraged masters to free their slaves, provided they did not become public charges. The antislavery forces also gained a victory in the Northwest Ordinance, which forbade slavery north of the Ohio.

As can be seen, important steps were made in social progress during the Revolutionary period. Feudal survivals like primogeniture, quitrents, and entails disappeared. Landownership, with resulting political power, was increased. The established-church idea suffered heavily. The humanitarianism of the day was applied to a certain extent to slavery.

All these gains, however, did not make the American Revolution primarily a social revolution. Democracy made strides, but had to wait for forces set in motion by such men as Jefferson and Jackson to move forward decisively. During the nineteenth century, however, American democratic forces would have been handicapped without the achievements of this Revolutionary period.

FROM COLONY TO STATEHOOD

Sometime before the Revolutionary movement sanctioned the Declaration of Independence, extralegal forms of government, such as provincial congresses, conventions, or committees, had appeared and had taken over the powers of government. The Continental Congress, naturally interested in strong governments in the thirteen rebellious colonies, recommended in May, 1776, that every type of authority under the crown be suppressed and that free governments based on the consent of the people be established. There was much speculation as to how the will of the sovereign people could best be ascertained. Colonial experience demonstrated that liberty under government required, for its protection, a written constitution. Therefore state constitutions were drawn up during the troubled days of the Revolution, which created a structure of government and defined that government's powers. These documents were drafted in a variety of ways by the different states. The constitutions of Virginia, South Carolina, and New Jersey were drawn up by temporary, Revolutionary congresses, which were not expressly authorized to undertake the task of constitution-making. Among the powers granted to congresses or conventions of the remaining states, with the exception of Massachusetts, was expressly the power of drawing up constitutions. These bodies, however, were not chosen for the sole purpose of framing constitutions, but had governmental powers as well. Although all the constitutions stated that they were based on the consent of the people, the constitution of Massachusetts was the first submitted to the people before being put into operation.

The procedure employed by Massachusetts was an outstanding, constructive achievement of this period. A special convention was called for the sole purpose of framing a constitution. After the convention had written the constitution, the document was submitted to the people for their approval or disapproval. This process clearly made the people the source of governmental authority. The device of a special constitutional convention also offered the people a peaceful way in which to express their discontent with the existing government and to change it without having to resort to revolution. This procedure adopted by Massachusetts was soon to gain wide acceptance, and some writers feel that the constitutional convention has been the most important contribution of the United States to the science of government.

The various state constitutions established institutions which were already familiar to the people from their colonial experience. A governor and a two-house legislature were set up, except in Georgia and Pennsylvania, where unicameral legislatures were established. Later these two states changed and followed the practice of the rest of the country. Suffrage was limited to property-holders, as in the past. Another direct product of colonial experience was the exalting of the power of the legislature and the curbing of the authority of the governor. In addition, bills of rights were provided to safeguard against encroachments on individual liberty. These bills of rights accepted the theory that government rested on the consent of the people and existed to protect their rights; also, the bills demonstrated that government was looked upon as something to be feared and, therefore, as something whose powers must be reduced to a minimum. As colonists, the Americans had seen how governmental powers might be used to curb the liberties of the people, and they attempted to prevent this in their new constitutions. In addition to bills of rights, another device to check government was the distribution of powers among the executive, legislative, and judicial branches of government. Colonial experience with appointed governors, elected assemblies, and appointed judges had taught the Americans that such separation of governmental functions provided each branch of the government with a check upon the other.

Although the new state constitutions followed the principle of the separation of powers, they tended to emphasize legislative power over that of the executive or the courts. This was natural in the light of the struggle from 1763 to 1775, when the colonial assemblies had fought for their rights against the governors and judges appointed by England. Under the new constitutions, usually the governor and judges were elected by the legislatures. In every state except Massachusetts and New York the executive was extremely weak. Only in Massachusetts was the governor given the veto power. On the whole, it was beneficial for the nation that there was no uniformity among these early constitutions, since the states became a laboratory from which the Constitutional Convention of 1787 was able to derive valuable lessons.

The formation of the new constitutions witnessed a severe struggle between the aristocratic and democratic elements. Although the constitutions stated that they were based on the consent of the people, the conservative forces had no desire to open the gates to popular rule. John Jay expressed the conservative viewpoint when he stated that "those who own the country ought to govern it." In the states of Pennsylvania, North Carolina, Delaware, Georgia, and Rhode Island the democratic element gained a large measure of its demands; in the rest of the states the conservative influence predominated.

The developments in Pennsylvania and South Carolina can be used as examples of the struggle between the two shades of opinion. The Pennsylvania constitution was adopted by a convention in which the democratic delegates outnumbered the conservatives two to one. A one-house legislature was established, to be elected annually by all the taxpayers. An elected council and a president replaced the old proprietary governor and council, and the council and president were deprived of the power of vetoing acts of the legislature. There were no qualifications for officeholding or voting other than the payment of a state tax. Representation was apportioned according to the number of taxable people, which gave the more numerous Scotch-Irish and German westerners a majority over the eastern, conservative Quakers.

The South Carolina constitution safely lodged control in the hands of the conservatives. Representation was so apportioned that the more populous back country received only 58 seats in the legislature, as compared with 144 seats for the tidewater region. Only men who owned fifty acres of land could vote, and to become the governor or a member of the upper house a man had to have an estate worth ten thousand pounds. To become a member of the lower house a man had to hold an estate worth two thousand pounds. The conservatives of the coastal region made the constitution, and they wrote it so as to retain control of the government, which they succeeded in doing until the Civil War.

THE ARTICLES OF CONFEDERATION

The Declaration of Independence did not markedly interrupt the course of American governmental development. The Revolution itself quickened progress toward certain constitutional objectives which had long been desired. The attainment of independence only transferred the task of attaining these objectives to the American people. Up to 1776 the patriots had been the party of opposition; after 1776 they were in power, and the responsibility of governing rested solely with them. As the result of a motion introduced in the Continental Congress by Richard Henry Lee on June 7, 1776, a committee, with John Dickinson as chairman, was elected to frame a constitution for a working central government. Congress, in 1777, adopted the Articles of Confederation, drawn up by that committee, and submitted this constitution to the states for ratification. Four years elapsed, however, before the thirteenth state approved the Articles.

Certain troublesome questions caused difficulties and delays in the formation of this new government. Should the states have equal voting power in the Congress of the Confederation, or should they have votes in proportion to their population or wealth? The outcome of the discussion was that each state was granted one vote in Congress. A second question was What should be the basis for determining how much each state should pay into the common treasury? It was finally decided that the expenses of the central government should be supplied by the states in proportion to the value of landholdings within each state. A third vital question was that of whether the states claiming vast stretches of land in the West should hold this land or whether it should be turned over to the central government. Rhode Island, New Jersey, Pennsylvania, Delaware, and Maryland had no claims to Western lands. They feared that if the other states could successfully lay claim to land to the Pacific on the basis of old colonial charters, then these landed states might become too powerful and overcome the landless states. Maryland suggested "that the United States, in Congress assembled, shall have the sole and exclusive right and power to ascertain and fix the western boundary of such states as claim to the Mississippi or South Sea, and lay out the land beyond the boundary, so ascertained, into separate and independent states, from time to time, as the numbers and circumstances of the people thereof may require." This proposal was not incorporated in the Articles. Maryland, however, refused to ratify the Articles until some states with Western-land claims ceded these to the central government. New York agreed to this in 1780, as did Connecticut and Massachusetts, and Virginia agreed in the following year. Maryland then ratified the Articles, and the Confederation was complete.

The preamble to the Articles described the Confederation as a "perpetual Union." According to Article II, "each state retains its sovereignty, freedom, and independence," and according to Article III the states will "enter into a firm league of friendship." The distribution of powers between the central and state governments was roughly the same as the distribution enjoyed by Parliament. the crown, and the colonies

PAINTING
BY CHARLES
WILLSON
PEALE

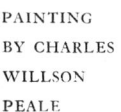

PAINTING
BY JOSEPH
WRIGHT

*John Dickinson,
Chairman of the Committee
to Draft the Articles
of Confederation*

*John Jay, in Charge
of Foreign Affairs under
the Articles of Confederation*

*The Most Reverend
John Carroll,
the First Catholic Archbishop
in the United States*

*Daniel Boone,
Kentucky Pioneer during
the American Revolution*

in the old colonial system of the British Empire before 1763. Congress was given the power of determining war and peace, carrying on foreign affairs, regulating the coinage system, fixing the standard of weights and measures, regulating Indian affairs, establishing post offices, borrowing money, maintaining an army and navy, making requisitions on the states for men and money, and deciding disputes between the states. These powers given the central government cast doubts on the reality of the sovereignty of the states under the Articles. In order to pass important laws, the vote of nine states in Congress was required. To amend the Articles, the unanimous vote of all thirteen states was necessary. Under the Articles each state gave full faith and credit to the records, acts, and judicial proceedings of other states, and citizens of one state were entitled to all the privileges and immunities of those of other states.

The states retained control over taxation and the regulation of commerce. Having just won these powers from Parliament, they were not willing to grant them to their central government, even though it was now located at Philadelphia and not at London. The central government's lack of power over taxation and commerce proved to be such a glaring omission that this was an important factor in bringing the Constitutional Convention of 1787 into existence. It has been customary to ridicule the weakness of the central government during the Confederation, but the Articles made the labors of those who drew up the Federal Constitution much easier, and the experiences of the Confederation period made it possible to develop an adequate central government in 1787.

WESTERN STATE-MAKING AND THE NEW COLONIAL SYSTEM

During the war and the period of reconstruction that followed, American pioneers developed new commonwealths in Vermont, Kentucky, and Tennessee. Vermont, an area claimed by both New York and New Hampshire, began to receive settlers as early as 1763, but was refused admission into the Confederation because New York still claimed it as part of its territory. In 1777 a Vermont Revolutionary convention adopted a state constitution modeled on that of Pennsylvania. Although the Vermonters, led by Ethan, Ira, and Levi Allen, aided in the war against England, they were primarily interested in autonomy for Vermont. Their land claims would be invalidated if New York could control the area. Before the war had broken out, New York had outlawed

Ethan Allen for destroying farms of New York grantees. When Congress refused to admit Vermont to the Confederation, Ethan Allen began making overtures to England for the recognition of Vermont as a separate province. During the 1780's Vermont maintained its independent status, and New York, in 1790, finally relinquished its claims. The following year Congress admitted Vermont as the fourteenth state of the Union.

Fur traders, land speculators, and pioneer settlers pushed west in the years after 1763 in violation of the English Proclamation of that year. By 1775 Pittsburgh was the most important settlement west of the mountains. The Vandalia Company instigated settlements along the headwaters of the Ohio River, an area in dispute between Virginia and Pennsylvania. The settlers unsuccessfully petitioned Congress during the 1780's for admission to the Union as the state of Westsylvania. The bulk of the settlers went west through the Cumberland Gap. Just east of the Gap, in present-day Tennessee, a settlement was started along the Watauga River in 1769. The settlers petitioned North Carolina to establish a government for the new community; but when North Carolina failed to act, they drew up their own government, the Watauga Association, in 1772. North Carolina finally made the new area into a county in 1777. From the Watauga settlement, pioneers like Daniel Boone pushed into the fertile plains of Kentucky and Tennessee. In 1775 Judge Richard Henderson organized the Transylvania Company and, accompanied by James Robertson and John Sevier, bought from the Cherokee Indians, at the Sycamore Shoals Conference, the region between the Kentucky and Cumberland rivers. Daniel Boone was sent by the Company to mark trails and establish settlements. In 1776 Virginia set up the County of Kentucky to regulate the area. Thirteen years later Virginia agreed to statehood for Kentucky, and three years after that Kentucky was admitted to the Union.

The third area of settlement in this western region was in central Tennessee. In 1779 James Robertson and eight others started a settlement at Nashborough, present-day Nashville. The number of settlers increased so rapidly that in 1780 they drew up their own constitution, the Cumberland Compact. Appeals from the settlers of the region south of the Ohio River were sent to Congress to form the new region into a state. Congress, however, was then busy persuading the states with Western-land claims to cede these to the central government and did not want to antagonize Virginia and North Carolina by any action in this region. The settlers in eastern Tennessee declared their independence in 1784 and formed the new state of Franklin. The state of Franklin collapsed from internal troubles, and North Carolina reasserted its control over the area. In 1789 North Carolina ceded its Western lands to the Federal government, and the following year Congress provided a territorial government for the region. Six years later Tennessee was admitted to the Union.

During the 1780's, when settlers in Kentucky and Tennessee were vainly trying to persuade Congress to admit them into the Confederation, Spanish agents were actively engaged in negotiations that might have led to a separation of these regions from the United States. As one writer has expressed it, "If the Federal Constitution had not been adopted when it was, or if a President unfamiliar with western problems had been placed at the head of the new government, it is likely that the United States would soon have been bounded by the Allegheny Mountains."[1] Congress, under the new government, admitted these areas into the Union as states, and President Washington took steps by which the West was held firmly to the Union.

The Congress of the Articles laid the foundation of the policy toward the West that was followed after 1789. Maryland's reluctance to ratify the Articles had led some states with Western claims to cede these claims to the Federal government. When New York ceded her claims in 1780, Congress adopted the following resolution: "The unappropriated lands that may be ceded or relinquished to the United States . . . shall be disposed of for the common benefit of the United States, and be settled and formed into distinct republican states, which shall become members of the Federal Union, and have the same rights of sovereignty, freedom and independence as the other states."

Congress appointed committees to investigate the problem of establishing governments in the West and disposing of the land. The Land Ordinance of 1785 contained the proposals of the committee on land. Townships six miles square were to be laid out; each township was to be divided into thirty-six sections, each containing 640 acres. Four sections in each township were to be set aside for the Federal government, and one section was to be reserved for the support of public schools. This land was to be sold; thus was established the principle of using the national domain for revenue purposes. After 1785 the unoccupied land west of the Alleghenies was laid out according to this plan as the frontier pushed farther westward every decade. Travelers in the Middle West

[1]T. P. Abernethy, *Western Lands and the American Revolution*, p. 359. D. Appleton-Century Company, Inc., New York, 1937.

The United States in 1783, Showing Land Cessions of the States

today, particularly travelers by air, can still see many of the old rectangular survey lines that were drawn over a century ago. The principle of selling the land to the settlers instead of giving it to them, was followed until the Homestead Act of 1862.

The problem of a government for the West was brought to a head by the activities of private land companies. In 1786 two Revolutionary War generals, Putnam and Tupper, organized the Ohio Company and petitioned Congress for a grant of land north of the Ohio River. Congress needed revenue so badly that it granted the Ohio Company 1,500,000 acres along the banks of the Ohio and Muskingum rivers for about eight cents an acre. The Scioto Company received an even larger grant, but it failed to make the down payment, and the sale was not completed. In 1788 John C. Symmes, a member of Congress from New Jersey, received a million acres of land west of the Little Miami. Symmes later defaulted on his payments, and his grant was reduced to 300,000 acres. The granting of land to the Ohio Company speeded up Congressional action on the governmental system for the West.

At the same time that a new constitution was being written in Philadelphia, the Congress of the Articles passed a remarkable measure, the Northwest Ordinance, on July 13, 1787. The principles of the Northwest Ordinance were accepted by the new government after 1789 and influenced the whole process of frontier advance to the Pacific. The Ordinance provided that the Old Northwest (the region north of the Ohio and east of the Mississippi) was to be divided, ultimately, into no less than three and no more than five states. Three stages of government were established. The Northwest Territory was to be ruled by a governor and three judges appointed by Congress. When the population reached five thousand free people, a territorial legislature could be elected and a nonvoting delegate could be sent to Congress. The third step was reached when the population in any one of the districts that were to become states numbered sixty thousand free people. Then a constitutional convention could be held and the prospective state could apply for admission to the Union "on an equal footing with the original States in all respects whatever." A bill of rights, similar to that later added to the Federal Constitution, and the prohibition of slavery were included in the Ordinance.

The provision that the new states were to be admitted "on an equal footing with the original States in all respects whatever" launched a new colonial policy in world history. Always before, colonies had been kept in a subordinate and inferior position in relation to the mother country.

The Northwest Ordinance repudiated this concept and established the principle that colonies, when they came of age, were to have equal rights with the older region. By drawing such a measure, Congress clearly demonstrated that it had learned an important lesson in the years from 1763 to 1783. Under the principle of the Northwest Ordinance the United States was able to expand to the Pacific without severe troubles between the new and the old areas of population.

THE TRIALS OF THE CONFEDERATION PERIOD

The troubles of the Confederation period revealed the need of a competent central government if the Union was to endure. The Revolution naturally had disturbed stability and social order. The Revolutionary philosophy that government was a necessary evil had prevented the Articles of Confederation from establishing a strong central government. Each state, too, was jealous of its rights and unwilling to sacrifice certain sovereign powers to a central government. "The contest for local rights under the old imperial system had strengthened the sense of state reality," one historian has noted; "men were conscious of their states; the states were in a sense their own creation. It was difficult, after the strain of war had gone, to feel acutely the reality of America and the dependence of its members one upon another. . . ."[1] Congress lacked the power to regulate commerce and to tax. Even more serious, however, than this was that Congress had no way to carry out the powers granted it. It made treaties with foreign powers and then witnessed the states violating these treaties, without being able to do anything about it. Congress sent requisitions to the states for money; but when a state failed to send the money, Congress had no power to force compliance. The basic problem of the Articles became how to compel the states to carry out their duties and obligations. For example, the states failed to carry out the terms of the Treaty of Paris of 1783. Few states complied with the treaty request that confiscated loyalist estates be returned, and the states failed to open their courts, as the treaty recommended, to English subjects trying to recover their prewar debts.

The governmental problem was made more difficult by the economic situation. The first years of independence were depression years. Unemployment in the seaports was rife, and foreclosures of farms were frequent. Now that the United States was outside the British Empire,

[1]Andrew C. McLaughlin, *Constitutional History of the United States*, p. 138. Copyright, 1936, D. Appleton-Century Company, Inc., New York.

she no longer was permitted to trade with Canada and the British West Indies. This severely handicapped American trading interests and shut off an important market for American farm produce. The United States had no power to force concessions from England. Congress had no control over commerce, and the efforts of the states to retaliate proved unsuccessful. One state might bar English goods from entering at its ports, but the merchants of a neighboring state would ship the goods overland to the state that was trying to boycott them and thus render the boycott useless.

The finances of the central and state governments were in a chaotic condition from 1783 to 1789. The people had been unwilling to pay taxes during the war, and as a result the various governments had issued paper money totaling about four hundred and fifty million dollars. Most of the states stopped issuing paper money at the close of the war and began to collect taxes in order to pay off the war debt. The loss of world trade, however, severely impeded this procedure. Merchants and bankers in the coastal towns, also, tried to collect debts owed them by rural people. This debtor class immediately tried to persuade the state legislatures to pass moratoriums on debt collections and to issue more paper money. In 1786 seven states did issue paper money, and the creditor group feared that their economic stake was in danger of being wiped out. The debtor movement, threatening propertied interests, contributed greatly to the calling of the Constitutional Convention, where a government was established which successfully checked the debtors.

Unrest in Massachusetts led to civil war. The farmers had no outlet in the British West Indies for their produce. Furthermore, the commercial interests had so drawn the state constitution as to shift the weight of taxation away from trade and on to the farmer. The courts were filled with suits against the farmers for failure to meet debt payments and taxes. Mobs of farmers in 1786, under the leadership of Daniel Shays, a Revolutionary soldier, prevented the courts from sitting and hearing any more debt cases. Militia was then sent from the seaboard, and the rebels were dispersed. The significance of Shays' Rebellion was that it frightened conservatives throughout the United States and led men of property to seek a stronger government. Washington, lamenting the disorder, wrote: "There are combustibles in every State which a spark might set fire to. I feel infinitely more than I can express for the disorders which have arisen. Good God! Who besides a Tory, could have foreseen, or a Briton predicted them?"

Proposals were offered during the 1780's to strengthen the central government. An amendment, which was not ratified by the states, would have permitted Congress to raise money by import duties. James Madison presented a proposal that Congress be permitted to use force to compel a "State or States to fulfil their federal engagements." This was never presented to the states for ratification. Noah Webster, in 1785, announced that "in all the affairs that respect the whole, Congress must have the same power to enact laws and compel obedience throughout the continent, as the legislatures of the several states have in their respective jurisdictions." Men who were concerned about achieving stability saw that the central government must be given the powers that it lacked, including especially the power to force states to carry out their obligations as members of the Union.

A step toward achieving this was taken when the state of Virginia called an interstate convention, which met at Annapolis, Maryland, in 1786, to work out a system of commercial regulation. Five states were present, but Alexander Hamilton persuaded the convention that commerce was too much involved with other questions to be solved by only five states. The convention then recommended that a convention meet in Philadelphia "to take into consideration the situation of the United States, to devise such further provisions as shall seem to them necessary to render the constitution of the federal government adequate to the exigencies of the Union." Congress approved the proposal, and in May, 1787, a convention met which finally brought forth the Constitution of the United States. A new government was instituted peaceably by this device, and the country was saved for the time being from the danger of disintegration.

SELECTED BIBLIOGRAPHY

J. F. JAMESON, *The American Revolution Considered as a Social Movement,* a valuable treatment of the revolution within American society; ALLAN NEVINS, *American States during and after the Revolution,* a good treatment of the transition from colonies to statehood; F. N. THORPE, *American Charters, Constitutions and Organic Law,* the state constitutions.

ANDREW C. McLAUGHLIN, *Confederation and Constitution* and *Constitutional History of the United States,* Chaps. XI, XII, XIII, excellent for the problems of the Articles government.

THOMAS P. ABERNETHY, *Western Lands and the American Revolution,* the best work on this subject; JOHN PELL, *Ethan Allen,* material on the Vermont situation.

H. S. COMMAGER (Ed.), *Documents of American History,* pp. 103–105, 107–116, 119–134, contains source material.

VI

The Federal Government

THE Constitutional Convention of 1787 was called to solve the difficulties that were facing the Articles of Confederation. The dynamic element in the movement for a new constitution was the propertied group, who feared that their stake in society was endangered by the weaknesses of the central government under the Articles. The central government's lack of control over commerce weakened the merchant and shipping interests in their competition with foreign powers, and the right of the state governments to issue paper money and pass stay laws threatened the basis of private property. Western land speculators and holders of government securities also found their investments jeopardized by the increasing ineptitude of the government of the Confederation. It was not only the propertied people, however, who would have suffered by the collapse of the government. The debtors and the nonvoting people as well stood to lose a great deal by disunity and chaos. A weak United States might invite foreign intervention, and the hard-won independence of the thirteen states might be lost. Although the propertied interests had an economic stake in the stronger government which was framed at Philadelphia in 1787, the Constitution was flexible enough to permit democratic forces in the years after 1787 to secure many of their demands within the framework of the Federal system. In the formation of the Constitution the landed group worked with the merchant-capitalist group to obtain a strong central government. After 1789 the agrarian interests struggled with the merchant capitalists and later the industrial capitalists for control of the government; but the two groups subordinated their antagonisms in the Constitutional Convention because of the danger of chaos, repudiation, and disunity.

THE FRAMING OF THE CONSTITUTION

Rhode Island alone was unrepresented at the Constitutional Convention, which met at Philadelphia during the spring and summer of 1787. The fifty-five delegates present comprised one of the ablest bodies of men in world history. All of them had had political experience in varying degrees. Forty-two of the delegates had served in Congress, eight had signed the Declaration of Independence, eight had helped to draw up state constitutions, seven had been chief executives of their states, and twenty-one had fought in the Revolution. They ranged in age and experience from the venerable Benjamin Franklin to the youthful Jonathan Dayton of New Jersey. The results of the Convention were reached only after long debate and deliberation. No one man dominated the proceedings, and no one person foresaw in its entirety the new system that was produced. The presence of George Washington at the Convention gave the meeting prestige

James Madison

and calmed some who feared that it was a plot against their liberties. The most effective man in the debates was James Madison, who brought to the Convention an intimate knowledge of all the federal leagues from antiquity to his own day. Madison believed in the need of framing a new constitution, and he told George Washington, "Conceiving that an individual independence of the States is utterly irreconcilable with their aggregate sovereignty, and that the consolidation of the whole into one simple republic would be as inexpedient as it is unattainable, I have sought for middle ground, which may at once support a due supremacy of the national authority, and not exclude the local authorities wherever they can be subordinately useful." Other extremely able men present were James Wilson and Gouverneur Morris of Pennsylvania, Roger Sherman and Oliver Ellsworth of Connecticut, William Paterson of New Jersey, John Dickinson of Delaware, Luther Martin of Maryland, and John Rutledge and Charles Pinckney of South Carolina. The only outstanding leaders not present at the Convention were John Jay, who was Secretary of Foreign Affairs under the Confederation, John Adams, who was our minister to England, and Thomas Jefferson, who held the same post in France.

The Convention met behind closed doors. No word of the agreements reached was permitted to go outside the meeting place. This secrecy permitted the members to speak freely without fear that the public would form opinions based on incomplete evidence. Each state was given one vote, and Washington was elected as the presiding officer. The delegates decided at the outset to frame a new constitution, not just to revise the Articles. They rejected a centralized government, as well as a league or confederation of the states. Instead they worked out a federal system, wherein a strong union was achieved without destroying the states as important entities. In working out this federal system, the delegates had their past to draw upon—their experiences with the British Empire, the Revolution, and the Articles of Confederation. They worked out a solution of the imperial problem, the same problem that had bedeviled Great Britain from 1763 to 1776, through the federal system that they adopted.

During the debates over this new governmental structure serious differences of opinion developed between the spokesmen for the big states and the spokesmen for the small states. Randolph of Virginia introduced a plan which called for a bicameral legislature, the members of the first branch to be elected by the people, and the members of the second to be chosen by the members of the first. The plan also called for a national executive and a national judiciary. Randolph attempted to solve the problem of getting the states to abide by the distribution of powers in the Constitution in three ways: the national legislature was to be empowered "to negative all laws passed by the several States, contravening the articles of Union"; the national legislature was "to call forth the force of the Union against any member of the Union failing to fulfill its duties under the articles thereof"; and the "Legislative, Executive, and Judiciary powers within the several States ought to be bound by oath to support the articles of Union." This third provision was the only one written into the finished Constitution.

The small states immediately objected to the proposal that the states should not be equally represented in the national legislature. They feared that the more populous states might oppress them. John Dickinson spoke for the small states when he said, "We would sooner submit to a foreign power, than submit to be deprived of an equality of suffrage, in both branches of the legislature, and thereby be thrown under the domination of the larger States." Paterson of New Jersey introduced a proposal acceptable to the small states. His plan called for amending the Articles to give Congress the power to regulate commerce and to tax; for the creation of a Federal executive and judiciary; and for a legislature in which each state was to have one vote. In order to ensure that the states carried out their duties, Paterson suggested that the acts of Congress should be "the supreme law of the respective States . . . and that the Judiciary of the several States shall be bound thereby in their decisions, anything in the respective laws of the Individual States to the contrary notwithstanding." The plan also suggested that force could be used by the central government to make the states carry out their obligations. Both the large-state and the small-state plan indicated a realization that the Union could not endure if the states obeyed laws only when they were so inclined.

The Convention deadlocked over these two plans. At times the members were ready to go home in despair. The critical issue was how to preserve the states as political bodies. When the Convention decided to elect the lower house of the legislature on the basis of population, Ellsworth of Connecticut suggested that the states should have equal representation in the upper house. Through this device Ellsworth hoped to assure the existence of the states and thus solve an agelong problem of imperial organization. The collapse of the Convention was averted by the adoption of Ellsworth's compromise proposal by a majority of one vote. The advocates of the Virginia plan were discouraged by equal representation in the upper house. They feared that this step would weaken the new government. Actually, however, in the history of the United States after 1789, the Senate did not develop into the guardian of the smaller states in the Union. This issue of small states versus large states, which nearly wrecked the Convention, was an unreal issue. After 1789, divisions within the country were those of East against West, North against South, farmer against merchant, creditor against debtor, never large state against small state.

Other compromises were adopted by the Convention, but of less significance than the one proposed by Ellsworth. Eastern conservatives, fearing the liberalism of the West, tried to prevent new states from being admitted into the Union. The Convention, however, refused to adopt a suggestion that the West be kept in a position inferior to that of the older region. To placate the conservatives, the decision of the Convention, as incorporated in the Constitution, read, "New States may be admitted by Congress into this Union." This meant that the admission of new states was not compulsory. The practice, however, has been to admit new states when qualified. Another problem was whether slaves should be counted in fixing the basis of representation in the lower house of Congress. Some men wanted all the slaves counted in fixing representation. Certain Northern members did not want to count any of them. A compromise was reached whereby three fifths of the slaves were counted both for representation and for the laying of direct taxes. Although the issue of free states versus slave states arose in the debates, it occupied very little attention. The Convention was decidedly not conducted on the basis of that issue. Two other questions raised some controversy. Some members wanted Congress to have the power to levy duties on exports. The Southern delegates objected, since these duties would fall largely on their goods. The second question was whether the foreign slave trade should be abolished. The compromises worked out on these two problems were that Congress was denied the right to tax exports, and that after twenty years Congress could prohibit the foreign slave trade.

There were no serious debates on such economic questions as the right of states to issue paper money and to pass any laws impairing the obligations of contracts. The states were expressly forbidden to do both these things. Shays' Rebellion, particularly, led to this action on the part of the delegates. Holders of government securities also were protected by the following statement, incorporated in the Constitution: "All debts contracted and engagements entered into before the adoption of this Constitution shall be as valid against the United States under this Constitution as under the Confederation."

THE NATURE OF THE NEW GOVERNMENT

The Constitution and the new government that it created were described as being Federal in order to allay current fears with regard to consolidated national governments. The central government was given clear-cut powers and in the exercise of these powers operated directly on the people. In working out the powers allotted to the central government, the delegates looked backward to the practices of the British Empire in its relations with the colonies and to the experiences of the Revolution and the Confederation. In answering the question How can the states be made to abide by their obligations and not destroy the Union? any thought of the coercion of sovereign states was abandoned. Instead the proposal that had first been made by the small-state plan was adopted:

Congress shall have power: . . . To make all laws which shall be necessary and proper for carrying into execution the . . . powers . . . vested by this Constitution in the government of the United States . . .

This Constitution, and the laws of the United States which shall be made in pursuance thereof; and all treaties made, or which shall be made, under the authority of the United States, shall be the supreme law of the land; and the judges in every State shall be bound thereby, anything in the Constitution or laws of any State to the contrary notwithstanding.

State legislators and state executive and judicial officers were "bound by oath or affirmation to support the Constitution." As Andrew C. McLaughlin has pointed out:

It is difficult to overemphasize the importance of this declaration in the Constitution. The significant word is not "supreme," but "law." If the Constitution is law, nothing contrary to it can also be law. There can be no such thing as illegal law. Furthermore, to make the declaration explicit beyond all chance of misunderstanding, the judges in their courtrooms are bound to recognize and apply the Constitution. . . . The very structure of the union, the very essentials of the federal system were thus intrusted to courts.[1]

The Congress of the Confederation had been powerless to enforce its law on the citizens of a recalcitrant state, but now the acts of the central government could be enforced through the Federal and state courts. Since the Constitution was the supreme law of the land, were the courts of the United States and the courts of the states given the power to declare an act of Congress unconstitutional? During the debates the right of the judiciary to declare legislative acts void was frequently mentioned. The Constitution failed to state that this should be the case, but most of the delegates seemingly took it for granted. While they had been English colonists, the framers had witnessed the Privy Council disallow acts of colonial assemblies, and state courts had already declared some laws passed by legislatures void for being contrary to state constitutions.

John Marshall, in 1803, in Marbury *v.* Madison, established the doctrine of judicial review. Since that time the Supreme Court has frequently declared acts of Congress or of the state legislatures to be void. Judicial review has meant that the nonelective and nonremovable branch of the government has rejected decisions reached by the two

[1]Andrew C. McLaughlin, *Constitutional History of the United States*, p. 184. Copyright, 1936, D. Appleton-Century Company, Inc., New York.

elective, removable branches. Judicial review has led directly to judicial legislation, since "whoever hath an *absolute authority* to *interpret* any written or spoken laws, it is *He* who is truly the *Law-Giver* to all intents and purposes, and not the person who first wrote or spoke them." Most of the cases involving judicial review have turned on such vague phrases in the Constitution as "to regulate commerce," "general welfare," and "due process of law." Every great leader of American democracy— Jefferson, Jackson, Lincoln, Theodore Roosevelt, Franklin D. Roosevelt —has charged that the courts have been biased against measures designed to aid the common man. As one writer has observed:

> The Court has effectively intervened, again and again, to defeat Congressional attempts to free the slave, to guarantee civil rights to Negroes, to protect working men, to outlaw child labor, to assist hard-pressed farmers, and to democratize the tax system . . . the Congress, and not the Courts, emerges as the instrument for the realization of the guarantees of the Bill of Rights. . . . The conclusion is almost inescapable that judicial review has been a drag upon democracy and—what we may conceive to be the same thing—upon good government.[1]

The powers that were granted to the central government by the Constitution included all those held by the Confederation government —the conduct of war and of Indian and foreign relations, the regulation of postal affairs, the coining of money, the fixing of standards of weights and measures, and the administering of Western territories. New powers, such as the power to regulate interstate and foreign commerce and the power to tax, were added. In working out this distribution of powers, the framers relied on past experience. They did not work in a vacuum, but used their knowledge of the structure of the British Empire in allotting these powers. In its distribution of powers the Constitution did not create a unitary government. The central government was supreme within its sphere, but that sphere was limited. To the states were left the administration and the development of civil and criminal law, the control of education, the supervision of religious organizations, the control of municipal and local government, the chartering of corporations, and the "police power" to pass laws to protect the health, safety, and welfare of the people. The Tenth Amendment, added to the Constitution in 1791, stressed that the power of the central government was limited to certain specified fields: "The powers not

[1]H. S. Commager, "Judicial Review and Democracy," *Virginia Quarterly Review* (summer, 1943), Vol. 19, p. 428.

delegated to the United States by the Constitution, nor prohibited by it to the States, are reserved to the States respectively, or to the people." The states were supreme in their sphere of power, as was the Federal government in its sphere.

In the allocation of powers between the Federal and state governments, the framers followed the same distribution that was present in the British Empire in 1763. The states had the powers once reserved to the colonies, and the Federal government had those once held by Parliament and the crown. The principle of the separation of powers in the central government was also followed by the delegates at the Convention. The distribution of powers among the executive, legislative, and judicial branches generally followed colonial practice and particularly was modeled after the Massachusetts constitution of 1780. The power to pass laws was given to a two-house legislature. The six-year term for the Senate was devised to serve as a curb on the popular will. Until 1913, when the Seventeenth Amendment provided for the popular election of the Senate, Senators were chosen by state legislatures. The United States Senate soon became an extremely powerful body by virtue of its sharing the legislative power equally with the House of Representatives and its sharing of power with the President. Presidential appointments of ambassadors, cabinet members, and judges could be made only with the advice and consent of the Senate. No treaty could be ratified without the approval of two thirds of the Senators present. James Madison opposed the two-thirds provision, but certain delegates insisted upon it for fear that the interests of one section of the country might be sacrificed for those of another section.

The Constitution gave the President clear-cut powers. In most of the state constitutions the executive had been weak, but Massachusetts had created a strong executive, and the Convention followed this example. The President was placed in charge of the executive and administrative branches of the government, he could veto acts of Congress, and he was made Commander in Chief of the army and navy. Although the President's powers were clear, the method of electing the President was cumbersome. Every four years each state legislature was permitted to select, or cause to be selected, Presidential electors equal to the state's representation in the House and Senate. The Presidential electors formed the electoral college and selected the President. When political parties developed, they selected the electors, who, in turn, simply carried out the will of the people as expressed by the vote in each state. This custom has become so generally accepted as to be almost part of

*Delegates
at the New York Convention
to Ratify
the Federal Constitution*

MURAL PAINTING
BY GERALD FOSTER
IN THE POST OFFICE,
POUGHKEEPSIE, NEW YORK

the written Constitution. The Constitution contains the provision that, if no candidate has a majority, the choice among the five highest candidates shall rest with the House of Representatives. The framers made this provision because they feared that the electors would select "favorite sons" from their own states and that therefore no candidate would have a majority. In spite of the expectation of the framers, the two-party system has avoided this exercise of the final choice by the House except in 1800 and 1824. If the framers had had complete faith in the people, this clumsy electoral mechanism probably would not have been set up.

Of the fifty-five delegates who had been at the Convention, only thirty-nine signed the completed document. A number refused to sign because of their disapproval of the Constitution, and the rest were absent. The completed Constitution was sent to Congress, with the recommendation that it be submitted to the states. As Andrew C. McLaughlin has pointed out:

The federal state which these men succeeded in formulating had the following salient features: (1) sovereign powers were distributed between the states and the national government; (2) the national government had only the powers granted it explicitly or by implication; the states individually retained the residue; (3) each government within its sphere of authority operated immediately over the individual citizen; (4) neither government was to be inferior to the other or in ordinary operation to come into contact with the other; (5) the constitutional system was established as law enforceable in courts and was superior to the authority of every state acting either through its government or by convention of its citizens; (6) the national government recognized and made applicable the principle of the separation of powers with certain modifications.[1]

Although it is true that the movement for the Constitutional Convention was inspired by the desire to check popular rule, the framers of the Constitution sincerely believed that a stronger government would bring peace and prosperity not just to themselves, but to all men. In this period it was the general conception that happiness was tied to property. Even as great a democrat as Benjamin Franklin felt that only property-owners should have political rights. Since there was no such thing as a popular will in 1787, it is difficult to say convincingly that the Constitution was made against the wishes of the people. The term

[1]*Constitutional History of the United States*, pp. 193–194. Copyright, 1936, D. Appleton-Century Company, Inc., New York.

popular will had little real significance until the time of Andrew Jackson.

From the standpoint of 1787 the Constitution was in some respects radical. The document prohibited a titled aristocracy. The short term of office for the President and for the members of the House of Representatives permitted an opportunity for frequent changes in personnel. More important has been the fact that although the Constitution was drawn up by a minority group, democracy has been able to develop under it. There was enough vagueness about certain terms in the document so that, when issues did arise, varying interpretations could be presented. Although Gouverneur Morris and Alexander Hamilton might be cynical about man and consider him depraved, delegates like James Madison, John Dickinson, and Benjamin Franklin feared the rise of a plutocratic aristocracy and felt that the Constitution protected the rights of the many. Dickinson said at the Convention that he "doubted the policy of interweaving into a Republican constitution a veneration for wealth. He had always understood that a veneration for poverty and virtue, were the objects of republican encouragement," and Franklin added that "some of the greatest rogues he was ever acquainted with, were the richest rogues."

By incorporating a method of amending the Constitution, unwieldy as it proved to be, the framers gave the future an opportunity to alter the document to fit a changing society. Thomas Jefferson once wrote:

Some men look at constitutions with sanctimonious reverence, and deem them like the ark of the covenant, too sacred to be touched. They ascribe to the men of the preceding age a wisdom more than human, and suppose what they did to be beyond amendment. . . . Laws and institutions must go hand and hand with the progress of the human mind. As that becomes more developed, more enlightened, as new discoveries are made, new truths disclosed, and manners and opinions change with the change of circumstances, institutions must advance also, and keep pace with the times. . . . The real friends of the constitution in its federal form, if they wish it to be immortal, should be attentive, by amendments, to make it keep pace with the advance of the age in science and experience.

The men of the Revolutionary period, from 1763 to 1789, made definite contributions to world thought and politics. The Declaration of Independence magnificently expressed the aspirations of the common man for freedom and equality of opportunity. The device of a constitutional convention afforded the world a peaceful method of changing governments. The Northwest Ordinance launched a new colonial policy based on the idea that colonies should not be retained perpetually in an inferior position. The Federal Constitution developed a solution for the problem of distributing powers between the central and local governments. The creation of this Federal system thus reconciled liberty with empire. The growth of democracy too helped to mark this period as one of the most constructive in world history.

RATIFYING THE CONSTITUTION

On September 28, 1787, Congress transmitted the Constitution to the state legislatures to be submitted by them to state conventions for approval or disapproval. Congress did this without any enthusiasm, since it was being invited "to light its own funeral pyre." As soon as nine states should ratify the Constitution, it was to go into effect. Ratification, however, had dangerous foes. The back country, except in the case of Virginia, was generally opposed to the Constitution. In New York the followers of Governor Clinton objected to the new government because they thought that it would be "productive of the destruction of . . . civil liberty." Richard Henry Lee of Virginia led an irreconcilable opposition to ratification, saying, "It cannot be denied, with truth, that this new Constitution is, in its first principles, highly and dangerously oligarchic." Robert Yates and John Lansing, two New York delegates who had failed to sign the completed document, warned Governor Clinton "of the impracticability of establishing a general government, pervading every part of the United States . . . however wise and energetic the principles of the general government might be, the extremities of the United States could not be kept in due submission and obedience to its laws, at the distance of many hundred miles from the seat of government." Other charges hurled at the Constitution were that it created a consolidated government, that it destroyed the rights of sovereign states, and that the President had the power of a king.

The Revolutionary generation had been nourished on the belief that all government, and particularly central government, should be viewed with suspicion and hostility. Localism and a narrow particularism were rampant. The question was Would the people be able to overcome their petty jealousies and local point of view in the interest of the common good of all the people of the United States? One person pointed out, "Some will oppose it from pride, some from self-interest, some from ignorance, but the greater number will be of that class who will oppose it from a dread of its swallowing up the individuality of the States."

The friends of the Constitution shrewdly chose the name *Federalists* and obliged their opponents to take the name *Antifederalists*. The Federalists were able to count on the support of most of the lawyers, merchants, landowners, officers of the Revolutionary army, the pulpit, and the press. The fact that George Washington approved the Constitution won the support of many of the common people for the document. The remarks of one "plain man" in the Massachusetts ratifying convention demonstrated that not all the common people were hostile to the Constitution:

Mr. President, I am a plain man, and get my living by the plough. I am not used to speak in public, but I beg your leave to say a few words to my brother ploughjoggers in this house. . . . I had been a member of the Convention to form our own state constitution, and had learnt something of the checks and balances of power, and I found them all here. I did not go to any lawyer, to ask his opinion; we have no lawyer in our town, and we do well enough without. I formed my own opinion, and was pleased with this Constitution. . . . I don't think the worse of the Constitution because lawyers, and men of learning, and moneyed men, are fond of it. I don't suspect that they want to get into Congress and abuse their power. . . . I don't know why our constituents have not a good right to be as jealous of us as we seem to be of the Congress; and I think those gentlemen, who are so very suspicious that as soon as a man gets into power he turns rogue, had better look at home.

The Federalists used wise strategy, as well as sound arguments, to secure ratification. In those states where the Antifederalists were slow in organizing, they rushed through the election of the conventions. In those states where the Antifederalists were well organized, they delayed the conventions until they had marshaled their supporters. Before the beginning of 1788 Delaware, New Jersey, and Pennsylvania had ratified the Constitution. Georgia and Connecticut ratified in January, 1788. In the following month Massachusetts ratified after a hard fight. The Federalists here won over many of the undecided delegates by proposing that amendments comprising a Bill of Rights be recommended to the other states as soon as the Constitution should go into operation. A letter from George Washington was published in a Boston paper while the state convention was meeting. "I am fully persuaded . . . that it [the Constitution] or disunion, is before us," wrote Washington, and his warning probably influenced many of the delegates to favor the new Constitution. Maryland and South Carolina

Ratifications of the Constitution. The Numbers Show the Order in Which the States Ratified

soon ratified, and by June, 1788, eight states had ratified. New Hampshire ratified June 21, thereby making the nine states necessary for adoption. The key states of Virginia and New York, however, had not yet ratified the Constitution, and no government could really operate without their co-operation.

Patrick Henry and George Mason led the fight against the Constitution in the Virginia convention. They were aided by *Letters from the Federal Farmer to the Republican,* written by Richard Henry Lee, which tried to arouse the people's localism by such statements as "It is to be observed that when the people shall adopt the proposed constitution it will be their last and supreme act; it will be adopted not by the people of New Hampshire, Massachusetts, &c., but by the people of the United States." The opposition to ratification was met by arguments from James Madison, John Marshall, and Governor Randolph. Randolph had at first been hostile to the Constitution, but Washington and Madison had won him over before the ratifying convention met. Patrick Henry attacked provision after provision of the Constitution, but he particularly emphasized that a consolidated government had been created. Madison's reply was a skillful explanation of the nature of the new government:

If Virginia was separated from all the states, her power and authority would extend to all cases; in like manner, were all powers vested in the general government, it would be a consolidated government; but the powers of the federal government are enumerated; it can only operate in certain cases; it has legislative powers on defined and limited objects, beyond which it cannot extend its jurisdiction.

The sectional division in Virginia varied from that of the other states. The Shenandoah valley, unlike the west of the rest of the states, was for ratification. This region was so eager for free interstate trade and a government strong enough to protect it from the Indians and to make treaties with Spain to gain it free navigation of the Mississippi that it cast a unanimous vote for the Constitution. The tidewater region too supported the Constitution. The opposition centered in the piedmont region. On June 25, 1788, Virginia ratified the Constitution by the narrow margin of eleven votes.

In New York the Antifederalists were so strong as to make ratification seem impossible. Madison, Hamilton, and John Jay published a series of essays in the New York press, explaining and defending the Constitution. These papers, called *The Federalist,* are among the greatest treatises on government ever published by political philosophers. They undoubtedly won considerable support for the Constitution. They ably explained the worth of the Constitution and wisely discussed the Federal principle of government. Essay No. 15 pointed out the humiliating condition into which the United States had fallen, with no treasury, no troops, and foreign nations controlling posts in American territory, and added:

> This is the melancholy situation, to which we have been brought by those very maxims and councils, which would now deter us from adopting the proposed Constitution; and which, not content with having conducted us to the brink of a precipice, seem resolved to plunge us into the abyss, that awaits us below. Here, my Countrymen, impelled by every motive that ought to influence an enlightened people, let us make a firm stand for our safety, our tranquillity, our dignity, our reputation. Let us at last break the fatal charm which has too long seduced us from the paths of felicity and prosperity.

Other essays warned that foreign powers were opposed to a firm United States, fearing that this would soon make the United States a world power, and that if the states remained completely independent units, they might fall under the influence of various foreign nations. Essay No. 2 closed with the warning

> They who promote the idea of substituting a number of distinct confederacies in the room of the plan of the convention, seem clearly to forsee that the rejection of it would put the continuance of the Union in the utmost jeopardy. That certainly would be the case, and I sincerely wish that it may be as clearly forseen by every good citizen, that whenever the dissolution of the Union arrives, America will have reason to exclaim, in the words of the poet: "Farewell! A Long Farewell To All My Greatness."

On July 26, 1788, New York ratified the Constitution by a vote of thirty to twenty-seven. North Carolina and Rhode Island alone now had not ratified, but the new government went into operation without waiting for these two states. (North Carolina ratified in November, 1789, and Rhode Island in May, 1790.) The Congress of the Confederation, on September 13, 1788, proclaimed that the new frame of government had been adopted. Dates were set for the choice of Presidential electors and for the inauguration of the new regime. Washington unwillingly accepted the office of President and on April 30, 1789, took the oath of office. Since a great deal of the opposition to the Constitution had developed because it lacked a Bill of Rights, ten amendments incorporating such a bill were added in 1791. Thomas Jefferson, following the adoption of the Constitution, prophesied, "The example of changing a constitution by assembling the wise men of the State, instead of assembling armies, will be worth as much to the world as the former examples we had given them."

SELECTED BIBLIOGRAPHY

ANDREW C. MCLAUGHLIN, *Confederation and Constitution* and *Constitutional History of the United States,* and MAX FARRAND, *Framing of the Constitution* and *Fathers of the Constitution,* excellent surveys.

CHARLES A. BEARD, *Economic Interpretation of the Constitution,* and *The Federalist Papers* (published in many different editions), should be read by the student.

O. G. LIBBY, *The Geographical Distribution of the Vote of the Thirteen States on the Federal Constitution, 1787–8,* contains useful material.

H. S. COMMAGER (Ed.), *Documents of American History,* pp. 134–150, contains source material.

VII

Establishing the Government at Home

IT IS NOT EASY for persons living in the twentieth century to understand the difficulties which had to be overcome in setting up the new government under the Constitution. It meant the establishment of an efficient government over a people which had only recently rebelled against Great Britain because of her attempts to build a more efficient empire. The colonists had objected to paying taxes not laid by their own local assemblies, to the laws passed by their assemblies being subject to judicial review, and to the efforts of the English Parliament to weld them into a smooth-working part of a larger political structure. In resisting, they had laid much stress on the rights of man as man, and had insisted that practices long existing, even though they represented only neglect, constituted rights which must not be violated. They had gone about as far as they thought desirable with central government when they set up the Articles of Confederation. Not all of them were convinced that these Articles were a failure.

And if habit and strongly held opinions were not enough, then there were all the difficulties of distance and poor communication. Compared with the areas familiar to Old World nations, the extent of territory in the United States then occupied or open for occupation was enormous. Citizens in Maine and Georgia were separated by nearly a thousand difficult and dangerous miles, made longer by the absence of even the poor roads and waterways of Europe. "The valley of the Ohio," says Henry Adams, "had no more to do with that of the Hudson, the Susquehanna, the Potomac, the Roanoke, and the Santee, than the valley of the Danube with that of the Rhone, the Po, or the Elbe." It took ninety-six hours of the hardest effort for express riders to go from Boston to New York, and eight or ten days for a passenger to make the trip by stage. As one went south or west, difficulties multiplied and speed slackened. Days stretched out into weeks, and at some seasons all communication ceased.

Sectional ignorance and indifference added their part to the problem of setting up a stronger government. Open hostility did not always exist, but the atmosphere was provincial, and natives, as well as foreign travelers, noted differences, real and imagined, between New England, the middle states, the South, and the West. The more careful observer understood that there were sharp divisions within these larger sections, marking each state off from its neighbors and distinguishing the habits and assumptions of one part of a state from those of another. Northern and southern New England varied from each other in greater or less degree, and the men of western Massachusetts had only a short time before been at odds with the men of the east in Shays' Rebellion. Like conditions were to be found elsewhere. Upper and lower New York, eastern and western Pennsylvania, tidewater and upcountry South, to say nothing of "Wests" that everywhere took their flavor from the widely scattered sources of settlement, all presented local interests and attitudes which made a greater unity desirable, but also made it difficult.

There were, however, forces favoring the new government. For one thing, the economic tide had turned, and a new prosperity not only aided political changes, but gave the impression that such changes had contributed to it. Washington himself remarked, "I expect that blessings will be attributed to our new government, which are now taking their rise from that industry and frugality, into the produce of which the people have been forced from necessity."

Then there was the fact that the men who had been behind the movement to form a new government were, in the main, the most prominent men in the different localities. They controlled the press; they were prominent in economic affairs, and many of them were known and trusted beyond the borders of their own localities because of services rendered in the Revolution and afterward. The natural fear that government would drift toward monarchy and turn back toward the undemocratic ways of England was tempered by confidence in such leaders—Alexander Hamilton's reference to the people as "a great beast" and to the Constitution as "a frail and worthless fabric" notwithstanding. And just as important was the fact that the new government was to be administered in its first days by the men who had promoted its formation. Eleven of the twenty-four Senators in the first Congress had helped to draft the Constitution. In the House were many others who had been framers or ratifiers. Washington's executive and judicial appointments strengthened this group and gave assurance that the new government would be in friendly hands in its formative years.

So the old order came to an end, and the young nation, reluctantly accepting the failure of its first attempt at government, prepared to launch its second trial.

FIRST THINGS

With the formation of the new Constitution, interest in government under the Articles of Confederation rapidly declined. Its Congress had a quorum for the last time on October 10, 1788. After that few attended; and in the days just before the new Congress was to meet, the young nation was without a central government of any kind.

The president of the old Congress, however, had designated the first Wednesday of the following January as the time for choosing Presidential electors in the different states and the first Wednesday in February as the day for casting their ballots. Then, perhaps in order to be ready to catch the spring shipping with taxes, March 4 was fixed as the day on which the new government should be launched.

When the electoral votes were counted, the name of George Washington appeared on every ballot. It was a way of winning confidence for the new government, as well as an expression of gratitude to a great leader. Eleven other persons received votes under the method prescribed by the Constitution. No one had a majority, but John Adams led the list. He would be the first Vice-President. The first steps toward the inauguration of the new government were thus completed, and messengers set out to notify the newly elected officials and to invite them to come to New York, where they would take their oaths and assume their offices. Then a nation settled back to await the arrival of its first public servants. And wait it did. March 4 came; only twenty-one members of Congress were present. Days and weeks passed while storms and indifference delayed a quorum. Not until the first day of April could the House be organized, and not until the sixth could the Senate choose a temporary presiding officer, whose duty it was to open and count the electoral votes. Two weeks passed before Washington could be notified and brought to New York. Adams arrived only two days before his chief. The spring trade remained untaxed while the task of organizing dragged on. "The people will forget the new government before it is born," wrote one observer. "The resurrection of the infant will come before its birth," wrote another.

At last, on April 30, all was ready. Troops and "distinguished gentlemen" escorted Washington to Federal Hall, newly made splendid by the French architect L'Enfant, at a cost of some twenty thousand pounds.

There committees of Congress greeted him and led him to the Senate chamber, where he was received with more than ordinary dignity by Vice-President Adams. He then proceeded to a gallery opening on the street, where the crowd had assembled, and took the oath of office, administered by Chancellor Livingston of New York. When the ceremony was ended, Livingston turned and "proclaimed in a loud voice": "Long live George Washington, the President of the United States!" The people shouted; ships in the harbor fired a salute. The new government was under way.

What happened in the next few months and years was of great importance not only for that time, but for all the future. Precedents had to be set and a practical, going government evolved out of the words and phrases which were the Constitution. The description of the government was only the skeleton on which flesh had to be put and into which life had to be breathed. What should Congress call its officers? Was John Adams Vice-President in the Senate as well as outside, or was he president of the Senate? How should Washington be addressed? Some wanted to call him "His Excellency" or "His Highness." Others, more democratically inclined, thought that "Mr. President" was enough. And should Congress stand or sit when the President appeared? And where was he to secure advice on important measures? These and other questions, some of them seemingly trivial, indicated the great areas where the personalities of leaders would shape not only the practice but sometimes the form of government. Alexander Hamilton put it this way: "'Tis with governments as with individuals, first impressions and early habits give a lasting bias to the temper and character. Our governments, hitherto, have no habits. How important to the happiness, not of America alone, but of mankind, that they should acquire good ones."

No man among those who came to New York understood the significance of first things better than George Washington. No man in all the United States was so well fitted in personal qualities and in patriotic devotion to the nation, to set precedents that were sound and constructive. No man accepted responsibility with more of humility and yet with more of understanding. He was a fortunate nation's first good fortune.

George Washington belonged to one of the leading families of tidewater Virginia. In the Old World kings had given the family lands, knighted its members, and even called its sons to serve as pages in the royal household. In the New World the first to bear the name, though driven to Virginia by poverty, quickly acquired property, became a "county officer, a burgess, and a colonel of militia," and left his sons to sign their wills as "gentlemen." Soon they had married into the best families and had established themselves firmly as belonging to the vigorous young aristocracy of achievement developing in the colony.

With such a background George Washington early took his place in tidewater society and was soon, like his neighbors, imitating the ways of an English country gentleman. An outdoor life of planting and hunting toughened his physical fiber, and long days in the wilderness to the west, surveying lands, deepened his understanding both of himself and of his fellow men. Early he caught the importance of military things, not only because English gentlemen had always borne arms for the king, but also as something vital to the interests of those who dwelt on the edge of the forest, where hostile Indians lurked and wily Frenchmen plotted for the control of a continent. "My inclinations are strongly bent to arms," he wrote, affirming a fact that his actions had already indicated. In 1753 he had gone to the West to warn the French from the forks of the Ohio, and in the French and Indian War, which followed, he had demonstrated skill great enough to make him the outstanding soldier in the colonies— one more capable in the rough-and-tumble fighting of the frontier than the British regulars. He emerged from the struggles against the French and Indians a veteran who understood the necessity for discipline among raw troops and who grasped the essential problems of warfare on the American continent. He alone appeared in uniform at the meeting of the Second Continental Congress. His choice as commander in chief of colonial troops in the Revolution was the reward of merit already clearly demonstrated.

During the next seven years he sustained the slender hopes of a people in their struggle for independence and, as much by his spirit as by his skill, made good their claims to a place among the nations of the earth. He proved himself an even greater soldier by his eagerness for peace, and won the admiration of men on both sides of the Atlantic by his quick retirement from the army to the sober work of farming at Mount Vernon. Arthur Young, the great English agriculturist, expressed this admiration when he wrote, "The spectacle of a great commander retiring . . . from ye head of a victorious army to the amusements of agriculture, calls all the feelings of my bosom into play."

He had been busy at the tasks of rebuilding his depleted soils, restoring his flocks and herds, and trying to find profitable crops for available markets when the call to serve as President of the nation interrupted. With sincere reluctance he left his lands, borrowed money to meet immediate expenses, and started northward again, this time for civil leadership, now as much required as had once been his military skill.

He was now fifty-seven years of age and thought of himself as an old man ready for retirement to private life. Years in power had not developed arrogance or spoiled the taste for simple, wholesome ways. He had that dignity which engenders spontaneous respect, and a sense of responsibility which often caused him to repress his natural inclinations to friendliness and good cheer. His dinners, said one guest, were cold and stiff, and he described one as "the most solemn dinner I ever sat at." He knew that respect for the office which he held depended on the respect which its incumbent could command, and that familiarity often breeds contempt. The same sense of responsibility made him eager for advice and sometimes brought a reliance on others which irritated those not consulted. Enemies even charged that he was sometimes used by designing friends; but even they soon discovered that although Washington was eager for advice, he carefully weighed opinions and then took a firm and independent stand. He was unselfish enough to consider his salary as President to be only expense money and set a standard of living in the interests of the office itself which later Presidents sometimes found embarrassing. He somehow seemed to know that his shadow was already stretching down the years and across a nation's life.

One illustration of Washington's influence on institutional development will suffice. The Constitution had authorized the President to require the opinion "in writing, of the principal officer in each of the executive departments," and to appoint inferior officers, but it had not created a cabinet. Acting under the Administrative Act, soon to be passed by Congress, Washington made Thomas Jefferson Secretary of State, Alexander Hamilton Secretary of the Treasury, Henry Knox Secretary of the War Department, and Edmund Randolph Attorney-General; and when the Senate proved cold to his advances for advice in certain Indian matters, he turned to his department heads and slowly welded them into a cabinet for consultation and advice. The practice, almost accidentally begun, stuck, and a precedent was set which in time made the cabinet an integral part of our governmental system. It was not like the British cabinet, but something American that belonged to the executive department and functioned along lines required by Washington's own personality.

Congress too, in these early days, felt the obligation to build wisely and with care. When it finally settled some of its problems of procedure, it turned, with what now seems to be unwarranted deliberation, to the problems of revenue and the setting up of administrative and judicial machinery. In spite of the fact that the government and everyone in it were desperately short of funds, a revenue bill became tangled with protective-tariff debate. Economic diversification and the protection of interests were matters of enough importance to outweigh financial necessity. States like Pennsylvania were determined that Congress should assume responsibility for encouraging industries. Some states wanted duties on iron, some on rum, some on textiles, and some on nails. Other states were as determined to prevent taxes which might raise the prices of favorite imports. The act, as finally passed on July 4, was a compromise. Duties of about 8 per cent were laid, and revenue was its larger purpose. It was apparent, however, that the act was only an emergency measure. The more involved financial matters remained for Alexander Hamilton to face.

Congress then turned its attention to the work of governmental organization. The Administrative Act set up the departments and significantly gave the President the power to appoint their heads and to hold them responsible to himself. Soon Congress recognized the President's right also to remove officials, thereby placing both the administrative and the diplomatic forces of government in his hands.

The Judiciary Act was one of great and enduring importance. It provided for a Supreme Court, composed of a Chief Justice and five associates, and thirteen district courts, each with its attorney, marshal, and deputies. State courts and even state legislatures were made subject to the central government through the provision that in any case in which a state court having final jurisdiction decided against the validity of a treaty or statute of the United States, or in which it upheld the statute of a state as against Federal authority, an appeal could be taken to the Supreme Court. Here was judicial review not greatly different from that once exercised by England over her colonies. But here also was protection for the individual in his personal and property rights against the acts of another state. The new government was to be an effective force in the affairs of men throughout the length and breadth of the land.

So far the acts of Congress all contributed to the establishing and building up of a strong central government. The questions of individual rights and states' rights which had been raised in the ratifying conventions and about which much of the opposition to the Constitution had centered had been largely ignored. Well might those who had feared a too powerful government begin to wonder whether pledges given to win their support would be kept. Why was not the suggestion for constitutional amendments, made by Washington in his inaugural address, acted upon? With Rhode Island and North Carolina still outside the Union and with strong minority opposition still to be found in many states, was it not of greatest importance to take up at once the amendments which had been suggested in the various ratifying conventions? Washington thought so. James Madison was equally insistent. Yet when amendments were drawn and presented, the committee to which they were referred showed little interest or inclination to hurry, and it was not until September 25, 1789, that twelve amendments were offered to the states for their consideration. Ten of these were approved. Eight had to do with the rights of the individual and the restraint of government from encroachment upon rights and privileges long held by Englishmen and their colonial offspring. The other two attempted to define the sphere of action granted to the new government and that retained by the people and the states. Those who feared the new order might gain something of comfort and assurance from these few added sentences, but the more important matter of how words and phrases were to be interpreted was left to the future.

THE WORK OF HAMILTON

These early acts of Congress were important, but the real work of laying foundations on which a permanently strong and efficient central government could rest fell to Alexander Hamilton, the brilliant young Secretary of the Treasury, who had served Washington so well in war and who now thought of himself as something of a prime minister in the first administration. His was the task of solving the problems on which the Confederation had gone to pieces. Most of them were financial, but around them clustered the larger issues of government efficiency and the ability of the central government both to survive and to prosper. Credit had to be established and debts paid, and the various government agencies had to be strengthened and made equal to their responsibilities. There was need not only for sound policies and smooth-working machinery, but also for an interpretation of the Constitution that would permit efficiency and expansion.

Alexander Hamilton was born on January 11, 1757, in the British colony of Nevis, one of the Leeward Islands in the West Indies. His mother was the daughter of a French Huguenot physician, and his father was a Scottish merchant of St. Kitts, another of the Leeward Islands. Their marriage was not quite regular, since the mother had not, at the time, obtained legal separation from a former husband, and was never satisfactory because of the business incompetence of the second husband. Family fortunes were always at a low level, and the mother was soon living with relatives, while the father wandered about in search of better things, which never appeared. Their son received only the most meager education and at twelve years of age was sent to work in a general store at St. Croix. The publication of a vivid description of a West Indian hurricane and the generosity of relatives enabled him to come to the United States in 1772 for further education. He entered a grammar school at Elizabethtown, New Jersey, and then King's College in New York City. Two years later the Revolution interrupted his studies and gave him the opportunity to take part in public affairs. He wrote pamphlets defending the colonial positions, which were good enough to be ascribed to John Jay, and was soon organizing military companies for service in the field.

Early in the war he met Washington, who recognized his unusual abilities and attached him to headquarters as secretary with the rank of lieutenant colonel. Here Hamilton proved invaluable as an aide, but always longed for active duty where the chance to become a popular hero could be found. Not until near the end of the war, however, did he see service. A slight quarrel with Washington detached him from the general's staff and permitted him to lead an infantry regiment at Yorktown. His conduct was of the highest order, but it was too late for a great reputation to be won.

With peace, Hamilton studied law and began practice in New York. He served for a time in Congress under the Articles of Confederation and was at Annapolis when plans for the Constitutional Convention were in the making. He represented his state at Philadelphia but was much absent, and was too extreme in his demands for a strong central government to have great influence. His masterly papers in *The Federalist* did much to promote the adoption of the Constitution, but he was not to reach real greatness until he again took his place alongside George Washington, in the cabinet.

Hamilton was a believer in administrative efficiency. A good government was one that could do the things required of it and one that gained and held the respect and support of those who had responsibility for securing a balance between agriculture, industry, and commerce. It should link the interests of the people with those of the government itself. It should enrich those whose support, in turn, would strengthen its hand. It should, in other words, rely on "the rich and the well-born."

It should force a respect for authority. "It should see to it that the masses secured the things which they did not have the wisdom to get for themselves."

Hamilton launched his program with his great report on public credit, presented at the request of Congress in January, 1790. Starting with the simple assertion that the way to maintain public credit is "by good faith, by a punctual performance of contracts," he proposed the funding of the foreign and domestic debt at par and the assumption by the central government of the state debts. He estimated the foreign and domestic national debt, including interest in arrears, at $54,124,464.56; the state debts at $25,000,000. The burden would be heavy, but the rewards, in terms of increased national self-respect, economic stability, and a closer union of the states, would more than compensate.

To the proposal to pay the foreign debts in full, there could be little objection. The necessity for foreign loans was well understood, and the idea of repudiation was not to be thought of. The domestic debt, however, was another matter. Much of the paper represented loans made by early patriots and a good deal of this had passed out of their possession and into the hands of speculators. Until very recently it had sold at only a fraction of its face value. If funded at par, great profits would be realized, and a group of men, already somewhat disliked by the common people, would be much benefited. Why put unearned money into the pockets of "speculators and money-changers"? Why favor those already rich at the expense of genuine patriots? A few advocated scaling down the old debts by paying the obligations at market, not face, value. James Madison, alarmed at recent trends toward class favoritism, proposed that the government pay the present holders of the certificates the highest price yet reached on the market and return the remainder to the original holders. Hamilton objected. A government that asked questions about its securities and went behind the fact of legal possession would not long retain the confidence so necessary for sound credit. The government could not risk its future stability by discriminating between different kinds of certificate-holders. The vote in the House was thirteen to forty-nine against Madison's proposal.

An even more bitter struggle took place over the question of assuming the state debts. Some states, including Virginia, New York, and Pennsylvania, had already reduced their debts, whereas others, notably Massachusetts and South Carolina, still labored under heavy burdens. The line of cleavage was sharp; the debate, at times, heated and personal. Defeat seemed certain. Then Hamilton turned to Thomas Jefferson, only recently arrived from Europe, and sought his influence to win Southern votes for the measure. A bargain was struck by which votes for assumption would be traded for votes to locate the seat of government for ten years in Philadelphia and then permanently at a place selected on the Potomac River. Men of that day, conscious that London and Paris were not only political capitals but great centers of industry, finance, and trade, believed that the capital city of the United States would one day become such an asset to the section in which it was located. Jefferson later regretted his part in the bargain and insisted that he had been more or less duped into it. Years later he wrote, "And so the assumption was passed and twenty millions of stock divided among the favored states and thrown in as pabulum to the stock-jobbing herd." Hamilton, however, was more than satisfied. He had succeeded in turning the interests of an important class from the states to the nation. Men who looked to a government for their profits would be inclined to support that government in its quest for funds.

To round out his financial program, Hamilton added two measures of major importance and of far-reaching consequence. In order to sustain this "magnificent paper edifice erected on the taxing power of the Federal government," as Charles A. Beard calls it, Hamilton proposed an excise tax on distilled liquors and an increase of customs duties laid in such a way as to encourage commerce and industry. Then to cap the whole structure and to facilitate and stabilize financial matters, he advocated the establishment of a great national bank. Three fourths of its capital stock was to consist of certificates of the funded public debt and the remainder of specie. One fifth of the capital stock was to be subscribed for by the government with funds borrowed from the bank itself. The whole procedure smacked of lifting oneself by one's bootstraps, but it followed Bank of England precedents closely enough to suggest to the investing class a further opportunity for sound profits.

Hamilton argued that the bank would be of great service to the government in the handling of revenue, in the obtaining of financial aid in times of stress, and in furnishing productive capital and a sounder currency. He was also conscious of the fact that bank stocks elsewhere were good investments and that "the rich" might be still further attached to the government through this agency. And what was more important, the establishing of a bank without expressed constitutional right to do so meant the beginning of a broad construction of the Constitution by which the scope of government might be greatly enlarged. That would be worth more in the long run than the most efficient of fiscal agencies.

George Washington

PAINTING BY GILBERT STUART

Alexander Hamilton

PAINTING BY JOHN TRUMBULL

Thomas Jefferson

PAINTING BY GILBERT STUART

John Taylor of Caroline

PAINTING BY HUBARD

As Hamilton phrased it, "every power vested in a government is in its nature *sovereign*, and includes, by *force* of the *term*, a right to employ all of the *means* requisite and fairly applicable to the attainment of the *ends* of such power, and which are not precluded by restrictions and exceptions specified in the Constitution, or not immoral, or not contrary to the *essential ends* of political society." He would, moreover, interpret the word *necessary* to mean "no more than *needful, requisite, incidental, useful* or *conducive to*." By such means the "frail and worthless fabric" would become a cloth of gold.

OPPOSITION TO HAMILTON

Opposition to Hamilton's measures was not long in developing and was not all to be found in Congress. John Taylor of Caroline, close friend of Jefferson, led the attack. Bluntly he charged that stockjobbing interests in Congress were backing Hamilton's schemes in order to fill their own pockets with ill-gotten gains. He thinly disguised the names of Congressmen who, rumor said, held certificates, and charged that the power of government to "distribute property by legislative favors" meant the end of popular rights. "A legislature, in a nation where the system of paper and patronage prevails, will be governed by that interest, and legislate in its favor." He was certain that the only productive group were those who tilled the soil. Those who relied on government favors to gain their profits lived at the expense of the farmers and turned government into an agent of exploitation. "Land," he said, "cannot be incorporated ... into a political junto—paper credit may. Land is permanent, paper, fluctuating." This "property transferring policy" of Hamilton's would impoverish the laboring masses, and it had been introduced "to enrich a few individuals, and also to revolutionize the revolution." He suggested that Congress be called "The royal American speculatum."

Jefferson himself was nearly as harsh in his criticisms. He had aided assumption, but, by the time the bank bill was under discussion, he had seen the folly of his ways and the dangers to agriculture which John Taylor pointed out. When Washington asked his opinion before signing the bank bill, he declared it unconstitutional and took occasion to expound the doctrine of strict construction of the Constitution. He could find no delegated power which authorized a bank. He did not believe that the bank was "necessary" under the meaning of that term in the Constitution. It might be convenient, but it was certainly not indispensable to the payment of taxes. He agreed with Taylor's statement that all capital employed in paper speculation is barren and useless, producing like that on a gaming table no accession to itself and is withdrawn from commerce and agriculture where it would have produced addition to the common mass; that it nourishes our citizens in habits of vice and idleness instead of industry and morality; that it has furnished effectual means of corrupting such a portion of the Legislature as turns the balance between honest voters whichever way it is directed.

Taylor and Jefferson took their opposition out in words. The plain farmers of western Pennsylvania, who were asked to pay an excise on whisky, resorted to action. Far from good markets, these men were accustomed to reduce their corn and rye into the less bulky and more profitable form of whisky. In this form it kept well, was transported more easily, and found a more ready market. Nearly every farmer in the back country from Pennsylvania to North Carolina manufactured liquor. Now these farmers were threatened not only with ruinous taxes, but with the searching of their homes. It began to look as though the benefits of independence were not to be so great.

In the summer and fall of 1794 open resistance developed in Pennsylvania in what is usually known as the Whisky Rebellion. Mass meetings were held at which "the most inflammatory language" was used; Federal officials were mobbed and driven back across the mountains. Washington and Hamilton were alarmed, and the militia of the several states was called out to put down rebellion and enforce the law. The governor of Pennsylvania insisted that Federal intervention was not necessary, but Hamilton, ignoring the governor's statement and the Secretary of War's authority, appointed Governor Henry Lee of Virginia to command the troops and prepared himself to join the expedition. He could not overlook the opportunity thus offered, said critics, for the government to prove its strength and to establish its taxing power over a group of people whose support did not count for much.

The "rebellion" vanished before the troops reached Uniontown. Representatives of the people presented the commander with resolutions saying that "offices of inspection may be immediately opened in the respective counties . . . without any danger of violence being offered to any of the officers, and that the distillers are willing and ready to enter their stills." But Lee and Hamilton went on to Pittsburgh, where a few of the more prominent leaders of the late resistance were hauled before the judiciary and all but two promptly discharged. The militia returned home, and the incident was closed. The new government had demonstrated its authority. The Pennsylvania farmers paid their taxes, but soon set about organizing "democratic societies," as suggested by Thomas Jefferson, who, meanwhile, had left the cabinet and was busy farming and writing letters to his many friends about the dangers of too much government.

It would be difficult to overestimate the importance of Hamilton's program to the young nation starting out under its new Constitution. He gave it more than sound national credit. He made it possible for it to be a real nation. He had favored certain classes and interests, but that was incidental to the larger purpose of building on sound and enduring principles. He had made enemies both for himself and for the administration, but he had risen to high levels of statesmanship at a time when statesmanship was both rare and indispensable.

He had been successful, in part, because the economic tide had turned. European disorders encouraged American trade in American ships. Exports rose sharply after 1790; the re-export of goods from the West Indies followed a like curve; American exports, lagging slightly behind, grew rapidly enough to indicate a condition of general prosperity such as had not been known for decades. Soon the position of the United States as a neutral carrier was the most significant fact in the determination of national policies.

Yet the fact of favoring economic conditions does not detract from the work which Hamilton and his associates had done. "For that work," says an eminent historian, "they will always deserve approbation from those who continue to believe that stable government and a well-organized Union are requisite even for developing democracy."

SELECTED BIBLIOGRAPHY

J. S. BASSETT, *The Federalist System, 1789–1801*; H. J. FORD, *Washington and His Colleagues*; EDWARD CHANNING, *A History of the United States*, Vol. IV, general surveys of the period.

Among the worth-while biographies are NATHAN SCHACHNER, *Alexander Hamilton*; A. McL. HAMILTON, *Intimate Life of Alexander Hamilton*; SHELBY LITTLE, *George Washington*; N. W. STEPHENSON and WALDO H. DUNNE, *George Washington*; CLAUDE G. BOWERS, *Jefferson and Hamilton*.

EUGENE T. MUDGE, *The Social Philosophy of John Taylor of Caroline*, and HENRY H. SIMMS, *Life of John Taylor*, throw light on a neglected figure.

LYNTON K. CALDWELL, *The Administrative Theories of Jefferson and Hamilton*; GEORGE FORT MILTON, *The Use of Presidential Power*; CHARLES WARREN, *The Supreme Court in United States History*, Vol. 1; *The Journal of William Maclay*, valuable for specific aspects of the Washington administration.

H. S. COMMAGER (Ed.), *Documents of American History*, pp. 151–162, 163–164, contains source material.

VIII

Establishing the Nation among the Nations

THE SECOND PROBLEM faced by those who administered the affairs of government was that of establishing the nation among the other nations of the earth. Its territory and its rights as an independent state were not always respected by those who had known and thought of "these United States" only as a group of disjointed colonies. England and France and Spain had not entirely abandoned plans for the expansion of their territories in the Western Hemisphere, nor did they think it necessary to conduct affairs with the United States in the same manner in which they conducted affairs with old and powerful nations. In many ways the years between the Revolution and the War of 1812 constituted "a lingering colonial period" for the American people—a period in which Old World ties still held.

This was not surprising in the light of the fact that the American people had been a part of western Europe and all its conflicts for a hundred and seventy years—a span nearly equal to that from independence to the present. Their life had been erected on Old World patterns, and these had been modified not from choice, but from the necessities of frontier living. Their best markets were in Europe; their credit was there; they dressed their bodies, and their minds as well, according to European fashions. Many leading citizens had been educated at Oxford and Cambridge; those best trained in law and medicine had graduated from schools in London and Edinburgh. Even the ideas with which the Revolution had been fought were borrowed from the liberals of England and France. For the rights of Englishmen, for the doctrines of the Enlightenment, the colonists had reluctantly accepted independence.

Nor did the break with England alter the situation. It only brought the colonists into closer alliance with France. Most Americans hoped that French markets and French goods would be substituted for those of the mother country. Many Frenchmen thought that the alliance formed in the Revolution would be a permanent one. This, however, was not to be. Habits and tastes were too strong. Peace found the states back where the colonies had been, buying from, selling to, and grumbling at England. We were not yet economically and socially independent from the life of which we had been so long a part.

If American interests in the Old World were still strong, the interests of European nations on the American continent were equally so. England owned Canada, and her traders still reached far down into what was then the northwest corner of United States territory for furs and profits. Through this trade the Indians secured arms and ammunition with which to hold back American settlers and to keep the frontiers in a state of constant turmoil. Conditions had become so bad in that area by the time that Washington took office that it was necessary to send out a series of expeditions aimed at the Indians, but expected also to warn their British sympathizers. The first (1790), under General Harmar, was ambushed and beaten; the second (1791), under St. Clair, governor of the Territory, was almost destroyed. Not until "Mad Anthony" Wayne, with a well-drilled body of troops, struck the Indians a decisive blow at Fallen Timbers and forced the signing of a treaty at Greenville (1795) did they cease to bother or the British cease to encourage them.

Spanish territory and interests on the west threatened the United States even more than did those of the British on the north. In possession of the Mississippi River and the great Louisiana territory beyond, Spain controlled the destiny of all those who dwelt west of the Alleghenies. The pioneers of the great interior of the continent had left behind them the comforts of an older society and had staked their hopes of regaining those comforts on their ability to produce a surplus in the new West and find a market for it. Only in this way could they buy the things which their young frontier could not produce. And the way to markets where their surplus could be exchanged lay down the rivers which poured into the Mississippi and ultimately into the Gulf of Mexico. Without the free navigation of the Mississippi and a port of deposit at its mouth, they were destined to remain for long in primitive simplicity and want.

Furthermore, Spain owned both East and West Florida, which extended along the Gulf from the Atlantic to the Mississippi. Her influence with the southern Indian tribes added to her power and to the threat that she carried to the interests of American citizens. Her claims to California and to the Pacific coast northward, though not dangerous at the moment, did emphasize her paramount interest in the Western Hemisphere and the possibilities of future conflicts. The fact that Spanish strength was declining and that other land-hungry European nations looked with eager eyes at her rich territories, so feebly held, made Spain a more dangerous neighbor than those with stronger arms and more promising futures.

France too had her American interests. She had lost in the long struggle with England for the control of the great interior of the North American continent, and she had ceded Louisiana to Spain; but she still kept her hold in the West Indies and planned to make them a steppingstone back to the mainland. At the peace conference following the American Revolution, Vergennes even hoped to regain for France all the lands between the Alleghenies and the Mississippi as the reward for assistance given the colonies, and French ministers continually supported Spain's contention that American rights did not extend beyond the mountains. When these efforts failed, France favored the setting aside of the whole region as an independent Indian country. During the next few years her ministers "employed every means of persuasion 'to induce Spain, already so rich in possessions beyond the sea, to give France her ancient colony.' "

IMPACT OF THE FRENCH REVOLUTION

What American interests in Europe and European interests in America meant to the youthful United States was soon demonstrated by a series of events, some of which occurred on this side of the Atlantic and some on the other. First of all was that violent political upheaval the French Revolution, and the wars which it brought in its wake. In the spring of 1789 the contradictions in French life, symbolized by the fact that France had been the home of liberal thought since the days of the Enlightenment and at the same time the home of a weak and extravagant monarchy, flared up in a demand for reform. Under the pressure of bankruptcy, the king consented to the calling of the old Estates-General and thereby opened the floodgates which had held back the impounded bitterness of years of oppression. Aroused by the impassioned eloquence of Mirabeau, the Third Estate swept the king and nobles aside and began the remaking of French society according to the liberal pattern already set by the people of the United States. Old feudal privileges were swept away; a constitution was framed; a national assembly created. In the ringing phrases of a Declaration of the Rights of Man a new political ideal for France was proclaimed.

Soon, however, violence and excesses took the place of constructive building, and factions struggled against rival factions for control and power. The king and queen were put to death. Day after day the guillotine took its toll. Quickly the Revolution passed from one phase to another, each more bloody and extravagant in its drive toward equality than its predecessor, until, at last, the inevitable conservative reaction set in. That brought Napoleon, with his "whiff of grapeshot," into control.

Meanwhile the broad international character of revolutionary thinking caused its force to spread far beyond French borders and to become a potential threat to social-political stability in other countries and soon, under Napoleon's control, an actual military threat to their national existence. Europe became an armed camp in which war and peace alternated until 1815. French principles, as well as French armies, fought and were opposed from Spain and Italy to the very gates of Moscow. Reverberations of the struggles reached across the Atlantic.

Reaction in the United States to the French Revolution was, in the beginning, generally favorable. Men recognized the part which the American Revolution had played in stirring liberal action in France, and they remembered the aid given the colonies, in their darkest hour, by the French nation. The fact that Lafayette and Thomas Paine were repeating their American exploits in France emphasized the kinship of the two struggles. Jefferson and Madison and others who stressed the virtues and abilities of common men were particularly pleased and saw in the French upheaval the spread of their doctrines to wider fields.

As the French Revolution entered its later phases and violence increased, conservatives began to draw back. English reaction, under the leadership of Edmund Burke, who took it upon himself to check the spread of revolutionary principles, had its effects; but the natural inclination of Alexander Hamilton and his fellow Federalists needed no Old World stimulation to turn them sharply away from lawlessness and lack of respect for authority. The attacks on religion, the threats to family life, the wanton shedding of blood, these were things in the French Revolution which Americans who stressed practice, not theory, could not accept. Nor could they resist the temptation to use the French excesses to discredit their opponents at home and to hurl the term *Jacobin* at those who followed Thomas Jefferson in both his admiration of liberal France and his dislike of the programs which Alexander

Hamilton had launched. As England and France drifted toward war, a sharp line of cleavage began to appear between those in the United States who favored England and those whose sympathies were with France.

A crisis in the situation was reached when word came that the Girondist party, then in control of the revolutionary government of France, had dispatched a minister, "Citizen" Edmond Charles Genêt, to the United States for the definite purpose of securing aid against England. Here was a situation that required action. Should he be received and the old alliance with France continued? Were we under obligation to the revolutionary government to carry out all the pledges made to the French monarchy? And what was more important, should we risk the fortunes of the new American government by becoming embroiled directly in the conflicts of western Europe? Washington was troubled. He turned to his cabinet for advice. Hamilton, bluntly but unsoundly, declared that our treaty had been made with the king and that his overthrow had erased all our obligations. Jefferson, more correctly, held that treaties are made between nations and are unaltered by shifts in domestic control. Both agreed that for the present, at least, the United States should not become involved in the European struggle. Thus encouraged, Washington issued a proclamation of neutrality with which to greet the enthusiastic Genêt.

April storms drove Genêt's ship out of its course and forced him to land in Charleston, South Carolina. The welcome received from good Carolinians encouraged him to action. Quickly he fitted out a privateer, in part manned by Americans, to prey on British commerce, and proceeded with plans for aggressions against the Spanish in Florida and Louisiana. He sent two representatives, Tate and Hammond, to stir up the frontiers of Carolina and Georgia and commissioned George Rogers Clark "Major General in the Armies of France and Commander in Chief of the French Revolutionary Legion on the Mississippi River." He suggested that the United States should pay the debt owed France ahead of time and hinted at Canada as a reward for aid given. He even presided at the formation of a Charleston Jacobin Club. Then he turned northward toward Philadelphia to face Washington and the United States government. Receptions and banquets marked his course and probably encouraged him in the belief that the people were far less neutral than their rulers. The rulers, however, proved to be as harsh as expected. Washington's stern dignity and the cold reception given his proposals by other officials quickly convinced him that co-operation was not to be expected. Rebuff after rebuff met his efforts. Only Jefferson seemed friendly. Even he advised moderation. In despair, Genêt determined to appeal to the people over the heads of their officials. Boldly he asked Jefferson to transmit directly to both houses of Congress certain documents which he expected to assist his cause. That was going too far. Washington ordered the letter and documents returned to Genêt, with a sharp reminder of the undiplomatic character of his conduct. He then asked the French government for Genêt's recall. France complied but, on their part, requested the recall of Gouverneur Morris, who represented the United States at Paris and who had been open in his sympathy for the Bourbons.

It has been customary to view Genêt as something of a foolish young man who misrepresented France and misunderstood the United States. A more just estimate, however, would take into consideration the fact that he seems only to have carried out his instructions and that French leaders, down to the time when Napoleon sold Louisiana, persisted in their scheme for a restored colonial empire in the Western Hemisphere. Furthermore, it should be noted that Genêt's repudiation was made easy by the fact that his party at home had fallen. So significant was this event that Genêt dared not return home, but remained in America to marry Governor Clinton's daughter and to become a successful gentleman farmer who dabbled, at times, even with such matters as the navigation of the air.

TROUBLES WITH ENGLAND

England, meanwhile, was showing no more respect for American rights and neutrality than was France. Back in 1790, when the Spaniards had seized her ships at Nootka Sound on the Pacific coast, England had temporarily been more friendly and had even expressed a willingness to make commercial agreements and to live up to past promises. But when Spain yielded, she quickly returned to her earlier attitudes. Soon American spokesmen were complaining of press gangs that "entered American vessels with as little ceremony as those belonging to Britain" and seized American seamen for service in the British navy. Matters grew worse in the next few years when war broke out between England and France. British officials naturally expected the United States to side with the nation that had aided her in the Revolution, and therefore ordered the seizure of all vessels engaged in the provision trade with the West Indies. Hundreds of American vessels were seized and condemned. Impressment of seamen rose to new proportions. When American ships sought to take advantage of the interruption of trade between the French colonies and the mother country, England applied the "rule of 1756," which held that trade not open to a nation in time of peace could not be open to it in time of war. That was in direct conflict with the doctrine that "free ships make free goods," which the United States had subscribed to in her treaties with France, Holland, and Prussia. It gave further excuses for what sometimes amounted to open plundering. Jefferson's protests went unheeded. Congress, in anger and despair, placed an embargo of a month's duration on foreign trade. Americans who followed Jefferson began to talk of war against England.

There was, however, another side to the matter. In spite of growing losses, the general level of profits to be made from a world at war was very high. Furthermore, most of them came from British sources. Trade with England was more than three times as great as that with France and more than double that with the rest of Europe. Would it not be better to go on protesting than to resort to force? Might there not be some chance of England's seeing the advantages of American friendship and the usefulness of neutral trade in such a period of turmoil and strife? Washington thought so. In the face of rising indignation at England's actions, he dispatched Chief Justice John Jay to London for the purpose of negotiating a treaty which might settle the difficulties existing between the two nations. At the same time, James Monroe was sent to Paris to replace Morris, and Thomas Pinckney, then in England, was moved down to Spain in the hope that better relations might also be established with that country.

Jay found the British ministers in a receptive mood. Rumors were afloat to the effect that certain Baltic countries had approached the United States regarding the formation of a league for the enforcement of neutral rights. This might add new difficulties to those which British statesmen had begun to realize were about as heavy as the nation could bear. Jay's advances were accepted and negotiations begun. A treaty was ready for signing in November, 1794.

The provisions of the Jay Treaty, however, were anything but generous to the United States. England had struck a hard bargain. She knew that the strength of her opponent was not great, and, besides, Alexander Hamilton had already assured a British official in private that the United States would neither go to war nor join an armed-neutrality group. Jay thus started under a handicap. He gained about all that could have been expected. England agreed to abandon the Northwest posts by June 1, 1796. Mixed commissions were to settle the questions of boundaries, debts, and payments for unlawful captures. Some concessions were made in regard to trade with the East Indies, but trade with the West Indies, the thing in which the United States was most interested, was restricted to vessels under seventy tons, with the understanding that, while this privilege remained, molasses, sugar, coffee, and cotton, the principal products of the islands, should not be re-exported from the United States. A few matters in regard to neutral trade were also cleared up, but nothing was said about the seizure of ships and the impressment of sailors.

When the treaty reached the United States, Washington was bitterly disappointed. He had hoped for more. His one great purpose was "to be upon friendly terms with, but independent of, all the nations of the earth," but he did not wish peace at the price of humiliation. Only after much hesitation did he pass the treaty on to the Senate, where the section dealing with the West Indies trade was quickly rejected and the remainder grudgingly ratified by a two-thirds vote.

Even while the treaty was before the Senate in secret executive session, its terms leaked out to the public. A storm of indignation greeted them. Federalists and Republicans alike considered them disgraceful and humiliating. The rejection of the section dealing with the West Indies trade allayed some of the excitement, but did not prevent the mobs from burning Jay in effigy and stoning Hamilton in the streets of New York. In some quarters flags hung at half-mast, and it was reported that "on the walls inclosing the home of Robert Treat Paine were chalked these words: 'Damn John Jay. Damn everyone who won't damn John Jay; damn everyone who won't put lights in his windows and sit up all night damning John Jay!'"

When passions cooled, men began to see that acceptance of the Jay Treaty had not been a blunder. It had ended threats of war, and it had smoothed trade relations when trade was particularly profitable. In conjunction with Wayne's victories over the Indians and the treaty of Greenville, it had opened the great Northwest to further and more secure settlement. It had, moreover, greatly assisted in getting a much needed treaty with Spain.

This latter benefit was the result of Spanish fear that the United States was about to join with England at the very moment when Spain herself was entering the war on the side of France. In the light of demands which American frontiersmen had long been making, this might mean the quick loss not only of Florida but of most of Spain's American possessions. With a speed quite foreign to Spanish diplomatic practice, Don Manuel de Godoy, prime minister to King Carlos, proposed the settlement of all difficulties between his nation and the United States. The Treaty of San Lorenzo (1795), negotiated between Godoy and Thomas Pinckney, was the result. In it a satisfactory boundary between Natchez and New Orleans was drawn; the principle of "free ships, free goods" was recognized; a commission was appointed to settle the claims of American citizens against Spain; and the right of deposit without duty at New Orleans was granted for three years, with the understanding that if it did not prove injurious, it would be continued or some other satisfactory place substituted.

This was the young nation's second treaty with a major power, and it was a highly favorable one. It was, moreover, an important step toward gaining the loyalty of Western men, who, as Washington had said, stood "as it were on a pivot. A touch of a feather would turn them either way."

Treaties with England and Spain did not improve relations with France, nor solve increasingly irritating problems. When Morris was recalled and James Monroe took his place, the latter was warmly welcomed as a friend of the Revolution. The president of the Convention embraced him and kissed him so warmly that he was moved to speak enthusiastically, if not wisely, in praise of France and the victories of her armies. Relying on instructions which said, "You will be amply justified in repelling with firmness any imputation of the most distant intention to sacrifice our connection with France to any connection with England," he gave assurance that the negotiations then being carried on by Jay in England had to do only with Negroes and furs and forts. The publication of the treaty itself revealed the folly of his assurances and led him in embarrassment to even more foolish words. He went so far as to publish a harsh condemnation of the Federalists at home, which brought a quick recall from Washington.

C. C. Pinckney was offered in his stead, but France, angry at all that had happened, rejected him, refused him the usual hospitality, and forced him, even in the interests of personal safety, to retire to Amsterdam. Friends of Monroe and of France in the United States made little effort to conceal their approval of such actions. They were rapidly and openly becoming an opposition party.

This was the situation when George Washington let it be known that he would not accept a third term as President and issued his Fare-

well Address to the American people. In it he pled for the continuation
of union under the Constitution, which had benefited all sections alike.
He denounced the growing tendency toward rival political factions and
declared that they would destroy the nation. They encouraged selfish
leaders, introduced foreign influences, and destroyed that unity so
necessary for national preservation. He would encourage friendship
with all nations alike. He would have no favorites. He would maintain peace at all costs. In this way the United States could develop a
detached attitude toward Europe, whose affairs were remote, and it
could soon become a respected neutral in European struggles. This
nation, he insisted, had nothing to gain by entangling its "peace and
prosperity in the toils of European ambition, rivalship, interest, humor,
or caprice." It would do well to steer clear of permanent alliances with
any portion of the foreign world in so far as this was possible.

With these words of sound advice still in their ears, the partisan
factions, against which Washington had warned, set about naming his
successor. Parties and party machinery in the modern sense had not
yet developed, but the split between Jefferson and Hamilton and the
divisions over foreign and domestic policies had drawn a wavering line
between those who favored the general program of the Washington-
Hamilton administration and those who opposed its measures. The one
settled upon John Adams and Thomas Pinckney for President and
Vice-President, while the other favored Thomas Jefferson and Aaron
Burr. The contest was close. In its midst Alexander Hamilton, who
thought his influence with Adams was none too great, began an intrigue to reverse the Federalist ticket and to make Pinckney President.
At the same time, Adet, the French minister, openly worked for Jefferson and talked of war between France and the United States if the
Federalists were not defeated. These acts probably determined the
outcome. Some New Englanders withheld their votes from Pinckney,
and some patriots, resentful of foreign interference, turned against
Jefferson. Adams won the Presidency with 71 votes; Jefferson, his rival,
ran second, with 68 votes, and became Vice-President. George Washington, his advice unheeded, went back to Mount Vernon and the life
of a Virginia planter.

JOHN ADAMS IN OFFICE

John Adams, then sixty-four years of age, has been described as
"robust, rotund, learned, consequential and fully conscious of his merits,
which were great." John T. Morse insists that "his supreme quality was

John Adams
PAINTING BY GILBERT STUART

John Marshall
PAINTING BY THOMAS SULLY

James Monroe
PAINTING BY REMBRANDT PEALE

General Anthony Wayne
FROM A SKETCH BY JOHN TRUMBULL

stubbornness." J. T. Adams calls him "bull-headed" and "utterly lacking . . . in a sense of humor." Edward Channing says that he was "honest and high-minded" but possessed of "infirmities of temper and habits of expression which made him an unpleasant team-mate." All, however, agree on his industry and on his high devotion to the causes of liberty and good government. Some rank him among the great political thinkers of his day.

The son of sturdy, New England rural stock, Adams had graduated at Harvard fourteenth in a class of twenty-four. He had then studied law in the office of one Mr. Putnam and, soon after admission to the bar, had married Abigail Smith, "the most distinguished woman who had yet appeared in the annals of the family." He had also begun the Adams habit of writing, writing, writing. From then on his career had been linked with the colonial struggle for independence and had become so much a part of it that the name *Adams* and the word *revolution* had much the same effect on those in authority. After valiant service at home, he had gone abroad to help to win foreign support for the colonies and had served on the commission which wrote the final peace. He was the young nation's first minister to England and its first Vice-President. In ability and experience he was well qualified to take over the office which Washington had both dignified and made efficient.

The first task which Adams faced as President was that of attempting a settlement of the difficulties which had developed with France. Not only had that nation rejected our representative and informed him that aliens could not remain in France more than two months without permission, but it had, in addition, adopted a policy of "retaliation" which permitted the seizure of American ships on the ground that England was profiting by like seizures! These acts had deepened Federalist hatred of France, and some members were ready for the declaration of war. They approved when Adams bluntly informed Congress that to treat us so was "to treat us neither as allies, nor as friends, nor as a sovereign state" and that the effort to separate the people from the government of the United States "ought to be repelled with a decision which shall convince France and the world that we are not a degraded people, humiliated under a colonial spirit of fear and sense of inferiority, fitted to be the miserable instruments of foreign influence, and regardless of national honor, character and interest."

Adams, however, was not yet ready for war. He knew that some Americans still sympathized with France and that the nation was totally unprepared for fighting. He therefore determined to send John Marshall and Elbridge Gerry to join Pinckney in an effort to secure both peace and a satisfactory adjustment of difficulties. On October 5, 1797, these men announced their arrival in Paris to the Directory and patiently awaited word from the government as to the date of their reception and the opening of negotiations. Weeks passed, but no word came. Instead certain unofficial and mysterious persons approached them with suggestions that the United States lend money to France and pay certain sums of money to the Directory and to the Minister of Foreign Affairs. The invitation to bribery was clear. One of the agents, however, reinforced it with the blunt statement "It is money; it is expected that you will offer money." This the Americans refused, more because a loan to France violated our neutrality than because they were against buying peace. Attempts to negotiate ended. Marshall left for home, Pinckney went to southern France because of his daughter's illness, and only Gerry remained in Paris under the threat that war would be declared if the mission was entirely abandoned. The correspondence between the Americans and the irregular agents was sent home to John Adams.

When this correspondence was laid before Congress, with the letters X, Y, and Z substituted for the names of the French emissaries, a storm of indignation swept the country. In words that fitted the temper of the times, Adams let it be known that he would "never send another minister to France without assurance that he [would] be received, respected, and honored as the representative of a great, free, powerful and independent nation." Pinckney's reported answer to the agents in Paris—"Millions for defense, but not one cent for tribute"—became the cry of a united people. Congress set to work to put the country in a state of defense and to protect our shipping on the high seas. Harbors were fortified, a Navy Department was created, ships were built, and the army was strengthened by the creation of a new regiment of artillery and the authorization of ten thousand new volunteers. For a period of time a state of actual but unrecognized warfare existed, in which both French and American vessels were seized with reckless abandon. Frigates and armed merchantmen slugged it out on the high seas while comfortable citizens enjoyed the profits of privateering. A more romantic citizen provided the young nation with a stirring song, "Hail Columbia."

The move to enlarge the army revealed an interesting political situation, which in turn brought a settlement of the immediate troubles with France. When Adams took office, he retained Pickering, Mc-Henry, and Wolcott from Washington's cabinet in his own. Long used to taking advice from Hamilton, these men continued to look to him and, in time, considered him, not Adams, as their leader. On one occasion Wolcott wrote Hamilton: "Either nothing will be done or your opinion will prevail."

Hamilton rather foolishly accepted this attitude, and a rift in Federalist ranks began to develop. When war threatened, Hamilton took the initiative in calling upon Washington to head the army and made sure that he himself would be placed in a position of importance.

Adams had early resented Hamilton's interference with affairs, but had seldom resisted. He now saw that unless he asserted himself, he would hardly occupy the place granted him by the electorate. He therefore officially asked Washington to take command of the army and suggest a group of subordinates. In his reply Washington agreed to serve if he were permitted to name his own associates. He then submitted a list of names, including that of Hamilton as Inspector-General, a position which would place him "second in command and actual chief while the army was being recruited." The President accepted Washington's suggestions, but when Major General Henry Knox, also on the list, protested that he (Knox) had outranked Hamilton in the Revolution and would not accept the present appointment, Adams took his side and ordered the commissions dated so as to give Knox first rank. Hamilton, who seems to have been entertaining dreams of a great military career, perhaps even of driving Spain from the Western Hemisphere, was furious. His friends turned to Washington and persuaded him to refuse to serve unless Hamilton were given the first place. Adams yielded, but not gracefully. Evidently he concluded that it would be easier to deal with France than to contend with Hamilton and his military intrigues, for he suddenly sent to Congress the nomination of William Vans Murray as envoy to France.

This move, coming just after the British had administered a crushing naval defeat to the French, exactly suited the purposes of Talleyrand, the French foreign minister. He let it be known that an American envoy would be received and treated well. American citizens in France, such as Dr. George Logan and Joel Barlow, gave assurance of French sincerity and urged an effort at negotiations. Adams might have peace for the asking.

Hamilton and his friends were bitterly angry at the turn of events. A committee of the Senate even attempted to persuade Adams to withdraw his nomination of William Vans Murray. He countered with the nomination of Oliver Ellsworth and Patrick Henry, as well as Murray. Reluctantly the Senate confirmed the nominations. Henry refused to serve, but William R. Davie accepted in his place, and the commission set sail for France. There they found the Directory overthrown and Napoleon Bonaparte in control as First Consul. Fear that this might upset plans was quickly dispelled. Napoleon too wanted peace. Without delay he appointed a commission to deal with the Americans. A treaty was signed on September 30, 1800. It provided that the citizens and the commerce of each country should henceforward be treated fairly, and all vessels that had been seized by either nation should be restored. Earlier treaties were abrogated, and the much desired principle that free ships make free goods was recognized. Adams had won his point, secured peace for his nation, and asserted his independence against the intrigues of Hamilton. Warlike contemporaries were inclined to continue their criticisms, but time has justified John Adams in his quest both for peace and for Presidential independence. His acts proved to be important steps in the establishment of the young nation among the nations of the earth.

SELECTED BIBLIOGRAPHY

T. A. Bailey, *Diplomatic History of the American People*, and S. F. Bemis, *A Diplomatic History of the United States*, general surveys.

S. F. Bemis, *Jay's Treaty* and *Pinckney's Treaty*, are valuable studies of the diplomacy of the period, as are A. B. Darling, *Our Rising Empire, 1763–1803*; Frank Monaghan, *John Jay, Defender of Liberty*; Gilbert Chinard, *Honest John Adams*; A. P. Whitaker, *The Spanish-American Frontier*; G. W. Allen, *Our Naval War with France*; W. P. Cresson, *James Monroe*. The West and Indian affairs are covered in C. W. Alvord, *The Illinois Country*, and in T. Boyd, *Mad Anthony Wayne*.

H. S. Commager (Ed.), *Documents of American History*, pp. 162–163, 165–175, contains source material.

IX

Political Parties
and Domestic Problems

THE BASIS OF PARTIES

IN ESTABLISHING the nation at home and among the nations of the world, differences of opinion as to policies and purposes had gradually developed. Just when such differences may be said to have created political parties in any modern sense it is hard to say. When the Constitution itself was being formed, there were sharp conflicts between those who favored a strong central government and those who wanted the rights of local governments preserved in large degree. The same line of cleavage had been apparent in the struggles over ratification in the various states. Washington's popularity and the unanimous desire that he be the first President had, for a time, silenced the disagreements, but the launching of Hamilton's several programs had stirred old fears and resentments and added new ones of greater intensity. Hamilton's expressed opinion that "the rich and the well-born" should rule and his reference to the Constitution as "a frail and worthless fabric" alarmed opponents almost as much as his measures themselves. His insistence on "implied powers" to justify the National Bank and his eagerness to use force against the Whisky Rebellion led some to believe that he even hoped to establish a monarchy.

Gradually Thomas Jefferson took the lead in opposition. First, he attempted to win Washington to his way of thinking, and when this failed, he withdrew from the cabinet. In the next few years he corresponded widely with others who feared a strong central government and encouraged them in the formation of "democratic societies" for the purpose of greater unity and more efficient opposition. Differences of opinion on foreign policies completed the break, and by 1796, at least, a rather distinct division into two political parties had developed and the names *Federalist* and *Republican* were being applied to them.

Something of sectionalism and class consciousness, as well as political convictions and personalities, entered into the formation of parties.

There were Federalist groups in all the states, but the party was strongest in New England and along the Atlantic seaboard to the South. It attracted the commercial and financial elements in the urban centers. In certain areas it maintained a firm hold on the rural groups, which had early adopted the faith and which seldom made quick changes. It was the party of Hamilton and his friends. Its emphasis was on efficient government and stable conditions, as against individual freedom.

The Republicans, on the other hand, were strongest in most back-country regions and found their greatest spokesmen in the South. There were, of course, Republicans among the lesser men in all the towns, and there were men who could justly call themselves gentlemen who espoused the democratic doctrines. Yet, on the whole, "the opposition" in the years when Washington and Adams were in office was to be found in the rural-agricultural groups and their allies among the mechanics and other laborers. These people insisted that governments were not ends in themselves, but existed only to promote the happiness and well-being of men. They found in Thomas Jefferson the virtues and attitudes which best accorded with their views.

Nor was the consolidation of rural-agricultural groups into a political faction the result of mere agreement on abstract doctrines. Farming in the nation had profited little from funding, banking, and tariffs. Markets for agricultural produce, closed by the Revolution, were slow to open; new ones had not developed. From New England to Georgia those who tilled the soil found little in the new order to make them happy and much to alarm them. The old tobacco regions, particularly, were in the depths of depression. Their great staple of colonial days had long languished under British regulations, the heavy burdens of indirect marketing, and the wasteful practices of frontier farming methods. Soils had been depleted as crop after crop had been taken from the land and as destructive rainfall, under clean cultivation, had swept away the surface soil. A traveler through the region found the farmers "in low circumstances, the inferior rank of them wretched in the extreme." He declared that agriculture in Virginia "had arrived at its lowest state of degradation."

It is clear that this first political uprising of rural-agricultural groups, like the uprisings which were to follow in after years, had behind it economic pressure of a very real kind.

ALIEN AND SEDITION ACTS; VIRGINIA AND KENTUCKY RESOLUTIONS

Emotions stirred by the troubles with France magnified both differences and economic conditions and brought the parties into open strife. In defying France and in asserting the dignity of the United States, John Adams intensified the Federalist belief that Federalists alone represented the true national interests. The foolish actions and words of French refugees and other foreigners in the United States who had failed to get on with their governments at home added to this feeling. Most of them were Republicans, and many of them had openly criticized the President. Federalists began to say, as did Robert G. Harper of South Carolina, "It is high time to recover from the mistake which we set out under the Constitution of admitting foreigners to citizenship, for nothing but birth should entitle a man to this privilege." The result was the Alien and Sedition Acts of June and July, 1798.

These acts were four in number. The first increased the period required for complete admission to the rights of citizenship from five to fourteen years. (It did not apply to persons actually in the country in January, 1795.) The next two acts gave the government control of alien enemies and authorized the President to order any alien out of the country or to force him to live in some designated place. The fourth act was aimed at any person who conspired against the government or brought any of its officers into disrepute through writing or printing. Jurisdiction in all cases was given to Federal courts, and punishment was limited to five years' imprisonment and five thousand dollars' fine.

Although "designed to afford the President of the United States an effective weapon against what was deemed an especially pernicious and dangerous form of domestic opposition in time of war," these acts became, in fact, a Federal weapon to be used against outspoken Republicans. Adams himself was not aggressive in their use, but Timothy Pickering, Secretary of State, Justice Chase, and certain Federal district attorneys and marshals were. A few aliens were driven out of the country; the columns of Republican newspapers were constantly scanned to detect possible material for sedition charges; a few individuals were seized, convicted, and subjected to fines and imprisonment. In all, about twenty-four or twenty-five persons were arrested, and at least fifteen were indicted. Only ten or eleven cases came to trial; but some lesser men, such as David Brown, served long terms in prison, and a few prominent men, such as Matthew Lyon, a Vermont Congressman, Jedediah Peck, a member of the New York legislature, and Thomas Cooper, the great scholar, were made Republican martyrs by harsh treatment.

Such partisan action brought an answer from Republican leaders in the form of the Kentucky and Virginia Resolutions. The first were drawn up by Jefferson and sponsored in the Kentucky legislature by John Breckinridge; the second were drafted by James Madison and introduced into the Virginia assembly by John Taylor of Caroline. Together they constituted a statement of Republican-party principles—a call to party action. The Federalists must be turned out and the government brought back to its original principles.

Briefly, the Resolutions declared that the states were not united on the principle of unlimited submission to the central government, but that they had formed a general government for special purposes and had delegated to it certain definite powers. They charged that the Federalists had gone far beyond the limits of the compact thus made in passing the Alien and Sedition Acts and that it was the duty of the states "to interpose for arresting the progress of the evil." The states, not the Federal government, were to be the judges as to which powers had been delegated and which had been retained. They should, therefore, declare these acts "void and of no force" and should request their repeal by the next Congress.

The purpose behind the Resolutions was political. They "viewed with alarm" the way in which the Federalists had departed from the plans and purposes of the Fathers. They gave the "correct" interpretations and all but said that the only way to save the great American experiment from degenerating into a monarchy was to elect Thomas Jefferson President. They stated clearly the then popular doctrine that the union of the states was a compact between equals who retained their right to judge of infractions. They were the Republican-party platform.

"REVOLUTION OF 1800"

The appeal was successful. When the electoral vote of 1800 was counted, Jefferson and Burr had a majority of eight. In spite of all that Adams and Hamilton had been able to do, the Federalists had lost control. The enemies of strong government had come to power.

As a matter of statistics, the shift in votes in 1800 was not great. All of it was in the state of New York, where Burr had built something of a machine. Adams actually had more votes outside that state in 1800 than he had in 1796. and Jefferson had fewer. And what was more embarrasing, Jefferson and Burr had received the same number of votes and were tied for the Presidency. Some Federalists saw in this a chance, even yet, to keep the hated Jefferson out of office. They talked of electing Burr or of declaring a deadlock and giving control of the administration to the leaders of the House or the Senate. Wiser heads, however, including that of Hamilton, saw the danger involved and, after six days of delay and thirty-six ballots, chose Jefferson for the office originally intended.

It was a close squeeze from every angle. Yet Jefferson always spoke of what had happened as "the Revolution of 1800." He seemed to think it was almost as significant as that of 1776! Federalists seemed to agree. They saw the coming of the Republicans to power in terms of the French Revolution. Timothy Dwight, an intelligent and educated New Englander, declared:

The great object of Jacobinism, both in its political and moral revolution, is to destroy every trace of civilization in the world and force mankind back into a savage state. We have now reached the consummation of democratic blessedness. We have a country governed by blockheads and knaves; the ties of marriage with all its felicities are severed and destroyed; our wives and daughters are thrown into the stews; our children are cast into the world from the breast and forgotten; filial piety is extinguished, and surnames, the only mark of distinction among families, are abolished. Can the imagination paint anything more dreadful on this side of hell?

He expected the Bible to "be cast into a bonfire" and "our holy worship changed into a dance of Jacobin phrensy." He even believed that American "wives and daughters" would be "dishonored" and their "sons converted into the disciples of Voltaire and the dragoons of Marat." The Federalist Congress, in alarm, passed a new Judiciary Act in the hope of keeping control in one department of the government, and John Adams himself co-operated by the questionable procedure of making last-minute appointments to the courts. Opponents always spoke of these as "midnight appointments."

With changes so slight and reactions so extreme and diverse, the question immediately arises, What was the real meaning of the election of 1800? Was it revolutionary in its import? Were social as well as political consequences involved? Had the young nation begun a new era in its development? The answer to these questions lies in the man Thomas Jefferson and his political-social philosophy. Thomas Jefferson is one of the great controversial figures of United States history. In his own lifetime men adored him or hated him with equal blindness. The century and more that has elapsed since his death has not greatly changed the situation. True democrats from Jackson to Lincoln to Wilson have viewed him as the great spokesman of their faith. Men who have called themselves liberals throughout the years have turned to him for support. On the other hand, those who have not quite trusted the masses have always feared and resented his power. Even in 1907 Theodore Roosevelt saw him as an ever dangerous force in American life and wrote his friend Lodge, "The more I study Jefferson the more profoundly I distrust him and his influence." He wanted Hamiltonians, not Jeffersonians, in office. A recent writer sums up the matter in this way: "The controversial discussion which Thomas Jefferson excited in his own time has grown, until today, two hundred years after his birth, it has become a habit of the American political imagination." Another has said that Jefferson "still stalks our streets."

It is, therefore, not surprising that some have called Jefferson's ideas "mere glittering generalities," "self-evident lies," doctrines "both false and foolish," to be applied, if at all, only to superior races and times. Nor is it surprising that Abraham Lincoln called the same ideas "truths, applicable to all men and all times"—truths which "in all coming days . . . shall be a rebuke and a stumbling block to the every harbinger of reappearing tyranny and oppression."

But contradiction does not end here. The man himself was a bundle of contradictions. The great apostle of freedom was a slaveholder. The champion of the common man was a blue-blooded aristocrat who built for himself the finest house in all America. He was a citizen of the world, as much at home in London and Paris as in Virginia; yet he was the spokesman of localism.

Champion of crude, rude, back-country farmers, he was at one and the same time a philosopher, a scientist, an architect, and something of a musician. He was a master of speculation and theory, yet practical enough to invent the swivel chair, a machine to make copies of letters, a bed lamp, a weather vane that registered inside the house, and a dozen other helpful gadgets. He was shy and bashful, almost afraid of his own voice, yet pushed himself to the head of a political party and organized "the first American rabble."

Born in the upcountry of Virginia in what is now Albemarle County and living part of the time at "Tuckahoe," down near Richmond, with his mother's people, Jefferson came to know the new and the old, the cultured and the raw in American life. Over the red hills of Albemarle, on their way south, drifted the Germans, the Scotch-Irish, the Welsh, and the lesser English peoples who were swarming out of Pennsylvania, America's first "great mixing bowl." Lutherans, Mennonites, Quakers, Methodists, Baptists, and Presbyterians they were—poor folks looking for a spot where they could build a house and better their social-economic condition. And at "Tuckahoe" was a bit of Old England, reproduced a little on the homespun side, but merry and cultured and gentle.

Educated at home and then at William and Mary, where, strangely enough, he seems to have learned how to think, Jefferson turned to the study and then to the practice of law. That led quickly to politics and public life. In the Virginia House of Burgesses and in the Continental Congress he took advanced ground in defense of colonial rights and from his pen came, first, *A Summary View of the Rights of British America* and then the immortal Declaration of Independence. This much accomplished in the general cause, he returned to his native state and the task of local reform. During the next two years he set in motion a program to end primogeniture and entail, to establish religious freedom, and to provide a complete system of free public education in Virginia. He succeeded only in part, but opened the way for others to continue the effort while he served as governor of the state, and later as representative of the United States in France. Late in 1789 he came home to sit in Washington's cabinet and to build a political party.

Jefferson was in his fifty-eighth year when he assumed the office of President. A secretary of the British legation, none too friendly, described him as "a tall man with a very red, freckled face and gray, neglected hair; it had once been red. . . . He wore a blue coat, a thick, gray colored hairy waistcoat, with a red underwaistcoat lapped over it, green velveteen breeches with pearl buttons, yarn stockings, and slippers down at the heels—his appearance being very much like that of a tall, large-boned farmer." An American Senator said that his clothes seemed too small for him, that he sat in a lounging manner on one hip, that he talked incessantly, and that his looks and talk were loose and rambling. Both observers noted his friendly, "sunny" expression.

Historians since that day have generally commented on the fact that Jefferson was the first President to be inaugurated in the new capital city of Washington. The removal of government had taken place during John Adams's administration, but the city and the government buildings were still unfinished when Jefferson took over. These facts seemed to symbolize a new day just beginning. The heavy investments which capitalists like Robert Morris, James Greenleaf, and John Nicholson had made in city lots and buildings, in the belief that Washington would become another Paris or London, seemed to be in accord with the promise of a greater democracy which Jefferson was inaugurating. A new setting for a new order was indeed fitting.

Jefferson's political-social philosophy began with the simple doctrine that "the end of life is individual happiness" and "the purpose of the state is to secure and increase that happiness." He was certain that "liberty, security in the possession of material goods and freedom from arbitrary coercion by others were essentials to a happy life." He believed that the great majority of men were, by nature, potentially intelligent enough to seek happiness in these terms and inherently just enough to be trusted with the freedom necessary to achieve it. Their intelligence would enable them to make the most of freedom, and their sense of justice would prevent them from using their freedom to encroach upon the rights of their fellow men. The good society, therefore, would be one in which "liberty and equality" dwelt together.

The functions of government, according to Jefferson, were of two kinds. Its first business was to keep order at home and defend the nation against outside aggressions; its second business was to promote those institutions and activities which made citizens more fit to live in the good society. Since a few men would not respect the rights of others, they had to be restrained and punished. Since the work of promoting education and the arts, and of regulating and encouraging sound economic effort, was of such wide social importance, it too belonged to government. And since the end of all such activities was the general welfare, the best government was one in which the people ruled and the laws represented the free will of the majority.

It was Jefferson's conclusion that all governments tend to become ends in themselves; that they were inclined to fall into the hands of small groups and interests and to become heavy burdens on the backs of the masses, who had to pay the bills and fight the battles. He would, therefore, limit governments by written constitutions in which powers were specifically delegated and the rights of individuals jealously guarded. He would leave as much governing as possible to local authorities and construe strictly all grants made to the central government. He would avoid complexity in its forms and limit its activities to essentials. Economy would be his watchword; strict construction, his policy.

In this way men would be freed from the greatest burden they had borne in the past. Taxes would be light; wars would be few; privileged classes would be avoided. Officials would become servants of the people, not their masters. Then, to make certain that even limited government would not become tyrannical, there should be periodic inspection of constitutions and a definite time set when all laws would come to an end if not again approved. Provision for the payment of government debts should be made when they were contracted, and they should never run beyond the lifetime of the generation which benefited from the expenditure. The same idea, carried farther, would discredit all customs, creeds, and doctrines which enabled one age to bind another. The tyranny of the dead should be broken on all sides and men made free indeed.

Granted so much of freedom, men should be equipped to make the most of it. The State should educate the people at public expense to the limit of each man's capacity to benefit. The press should be free from all restraints. Agriculture should be encouraged and promoted because those who own and till the soil are hard to corrupt and form the most solid of foundations on which to erect an enduring society. Men thus equipped could be trusted with self-government. Majorities would not oppress minorities; an aristocracy of ability would rule, and democratic government would have a chance to prove its worth.

JEFFERSON TAKES OVER

These were high ideals—some of them, perhaps, a bit impractical. Jefferson was conscious of that fact and hardheaded enough to compromise with reality when necessary. He could at least change the direction in which things were going, and the ends sought. There were, moreover, plenty of practical things which could be done, and the time was ripe for doing them. With a cabinet which contained James Madison, as Secretary of State, and Albert Gallatin, as Secretary of the Treasury, he set to work. In order that there might be "a due participation in office," and, since "vacancies caused by death" were "few and by resignation, none," some Federalists were removed and Republicans, now sometimes called Democrats, put in their places. The hated Naturalization Act and the excise tax were repealed; persons convicted under the Alien and Sedition Acts were pardoned, and the acts themselves allowed to expire; the court system, which the Federalists had altered to their advantage, was restored to its original form, and commissions not already delivered to "midnight appointees" were withheld. Then began the more solid effort at instituting "a wise and frugal government," which was to occupy Jefferson throughout his years in office.

With economy an avowed objective, Gallatin insisted that the payment of the national debt should take precedence over all other expenditures. And since "debt, taxes, wars, armies, and navies were all pillars of corruption," obviously saving should begin with army and navy expenditures. "Natural estimates" for these branches were, therefore, cut in half, and an act to reduce the number of ships and officers in the navy, which Adams had already signed, was put quickly into force. What was left of the navy was then sent off to the North African coast, where Jefferson had long insisted it was cheaper to fight the Barbary corsairs than to pay them tribute.

The background to the North African situation was this: For years the rulers of Algiers, Tunis, Tripoli, and Morocco had made a practice of plundering the Mediterranean trade of Christian nations and granting immunity only to those who paid tribute. England had escaped by this method during the colonial period, and Washington had reluctantly used the same method in his administration. Jefferson's move was, therefore, something new both in American policy and in international practice. But it worked. Tripoli took the lead in resistance, and Commodore Preble, with the aid of a group of brilliant young lieutenants and the assistance of local rebels, quickly forced the Pasha to sign a treaty on terms, as Preble wrote, "more honorable . . . than any other nation had ever been able to command."

The Tripolitan War served two purposes. It gave valuable experience to American naval officers, such as Decatur, Porter, Bainbridge, Burrows, and Macdonough—names that would one day make their way permanently into history. It convinced those in control of affairs that American-built gunboats were the cheapest and best means of defense and led to the building of some two hundred of them as the backbone of American naval strength.

But there was another side to it. War and ships cost money. In the long run they might be cheaper than tribute, but they did bring immediate expenses to an administration dedicated to economy. So hard put was Gallatin to maintain his financial program that on one occasion he refused the money for a ship authorized by Congress until a special duty was laid for the purpose. Increasing revenue from expanding trade came to his assistance, but a second unexpected occurrence piled expenditures to unheard of heights. Thomas Jefferson, who preached economy, paid fifteen million dollars for Louisiana! Thomas Jefferson, who insisted on a strict construction of the Constitution, made the purchase, by his own admission, without constitutional sanction!

PURCHASE OF LOUISIANA

The importance of the free navigation of the Mississippi River to Western men and the desire of France to restore her empire on the American continent have been discussed in an earlier chapter. Both matters took a new turn with Napoleon's rise to power. In 1800 he brought pressure on Spain to cede all her North American possessions to France and began preparations for the reconquest of Santo Domingo as a base for French activities. The Spanish king, Don Carlos IV, was a weakling who gave most of his attention to hunting and dabbling in mechanics and left affairs of state to his minister, Manuel de Godoy. For the promise of a kingdom in Italy for his daughter, Don Carlos readily agreed to Napoleon's demands, but Godoy had vigor enough to reduce the grant to the territory of Louisiana alone. On October 15, 1802, the order of transfer was signed.

Meanwhile an expedition under Napoleon's brother-in-law Leclerc had been sent to Santo Domingo, where the brilliant Negro general Toussaint L'Ouverture had taken control following a wave of revolts and massacres produced by news of revolution in France. The island was to be conquered and slavery restored. Toussaint's defense, however, and the outbreak of yellow fever were too much even for troops seasoned in European campaigns. Toussaint himself was at length tricked into yielding, but neither resistance nor disease ended, and the whole effort ultimately failed. With the renewal of war in Europe, Napoleon was glad to abandon the venture.

Americans had watched these developments with genuine alarm. Spain in Louisiana was one thing; France in Louisiana was quite another. Jefferson expressed the meaning of the latter by saying, "The day that France takes possession of New Orleans . . . we must marry ourselves to the British fleet and nation." On another occasion he declared that "the inevitable consequences of their taking possession of Louisiana" would be a war that would annihilate France on the ocean and place England in control of the seas, a development which might be dangerous for the United States. His worst fears seemed justified when on October 29, 1802, Governor Claiborne (of the Mississippi Territory) informed him that Americans had been forbidden longer to deposit their merchandise at New Orleans. The Mississippi had been closed. Western men were back where they were in 1794.

Under bitter protest the right was restored after a five months' interval, but the reactions in Ohio, Kentucky, and Tennessee had been violent

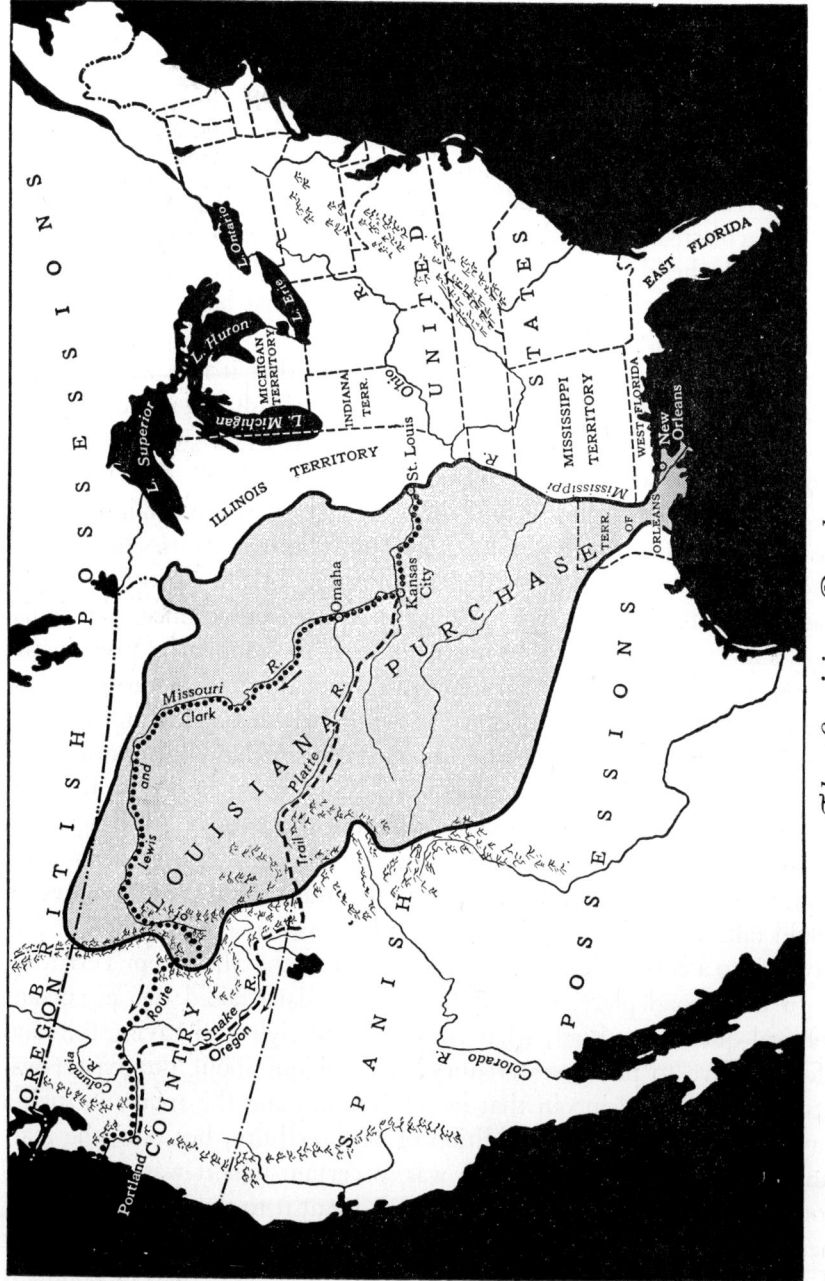

The Louisiana Purchase

enough to cause Jefferson to send James Monroe to France as minister extraordinary with instructions to join with Robert Livingston in an effort to purchase the Isle of Orleans and West Florida. Fortunately this move coincided with the collapse of French hopes in Santo Domingo and with the certainty that war was about to be renewed in Europe. Napoleon's interests, therefore, had begun to shift. Even before Monroe's arrival, his minister, Talleyrand, had surprised Livingston by breaking into a discussion regarding the purchase of a place to deposit American goods, with the blunt question as to what we would give for the whole of Louisiana. Negotiations now went forward on that basis, with the final agreement that the United States should have Louisiana with the boundaries "that it now has in the hands of Spain and that it had when France possessed it," for the sum of 60,000,000 francs in cash and the assumption of 20,000,000 francs in American claims against France. The total was about $15,000,000 in United States money.

In the light of future development, few steps of greater importance have ever been taken in the history of the United States. In the first place, we had purchased a boundary dispute. In the various wars and transfers of territory between England, Spain, and France in colonial days, surveys had never been made and definite boundaries fixed in the various treaties signed. Differing claims were advanced at times, but no one knew exactly where the lines between British Canada and Spanish Louisiana ran on the north, whether Texas was included on the west, or whether West Florida or what part of it, if any, was included on the east. As an expansionist, Jefferson chose to make the most of his bargain, as Napoleon probably intended. But in that decision lay significant consequences for the future. Congress revealed the general trend that events would take when, in 1804, it erected West Florida, as far as the Perdido River, into a customs district and annexed it to the Mississippi Territory.

In the second place, the purchase of Louisiana raised two important political questions. First, what constitutional right did Livingston and Monroe have to purchase territory? So dubious about the matter was Attorney-General Lincoln that he advised framing the treaty in such a way as to make it not the addition of new territory, but only the rearranging of boundaries. Jefferson was so certain that it was unconstitutional that he drew up an amendment and sent it to the cabinet for comment. Later he told Congress that he would "rather ask an enlargement of power from the nation, where it is found necessary, than to assume it by a construction which would make our powers boundless." But few seemed to think the question important after the purchase was an accomplished fact, and interest in constitutional sanction dwindled to the point where Jefferson confessed that, while he thought an amendment desirable, he was willing to acquiesce, "confiding in the good sense of our country . . . to correct the evil of construction when it shall produce ill effects." That was a long step from the Virginia and Kentucky Resolutions!

The second political question had to do with government in Louisiana. The treaty had stated that the inhabitants of the ceded territory should, as soon as possible, "be incorporated in the Union of the United States" and should enjoy "all the rights, advantages and immunities of citizens of the United States." There was, however, considerable objection to the immediate incorporation of a foreign people into our system. A committee of Congress even proposed the continuation of the existing Spanish government, putting the President in the place of the Spanish king and permitting him to name all officers. Those who objected to this did so more because it increased Jefferson's powers than because they were interested in the rights of the people of Louisiana or the terms of the treaty. In the end, after much debate, the territory was divided into two parts at the thirty-third parallel. The northern part, containing few inhabitants, was subjected to the government of Indiana Territory, while the southern part, containing some fifty thousand persons, was organized as the Territory of Orleans. Here the people were to have no share in government. The President was to appoint a governor, secretary, legislative council, and judicial officers. Proposals for such a government brought sharp debate and talk of "despotism," "royal powers," and "conquered country," but these objections produced only a reduction in the length of time that the act was to apply. The new Americans were to be subjects, not citizens, "lower in the political scale," as Henry Adams says, "than the meanest tribes of Indians."

Such was the first decision on the vital question of the powers of government over national territory. One day, in the Dred Scott decision, men who believed in states' rights would alter the implications.

The purchase of Louisiana was "an event so portentous as to defy measurement." By it the threat of European aggressions and restrictions, which had so greatly affected the United States up to this time, was in large part removed. Spain would be, from now on, in a position to offer little more than temptation, and England would not matter greatly again until English and American settlers met in far-off Oregon. The Mississippi River would run undisturbed from its source to its mouth through United States territory. The young nation was free to expand into what in the Old World would have been a half-dozen king-doms. Its area ranged from one to two million square miles, depend-ing on which boundaries were accepted. Within its confines lay all the opportunities and problems suggested by the words *Texas, Kansas-Nebraska, trans-Missisippi*, and *The Great Plains*. Along its rivers lay the routes to California and the Pacific Northwest. New wealth in soil and minerals and grass awaited settlers. Another powerful force was thus added to those already at work to turn the American people around to face their continent. Nor were the gains all material. The Constitution, even in the hands of strict constructionists, was, by the act of purchase, being slowly adjusted to the necessities of widening horizons. Something also of breadth and color was added to a people's life as tales of great riches and stirring adventure drifted back from these vast open spaces. When, in the winter of 1803–1804, Meriwether Lewis and William Clark, under instructions from President Jefferson, made their way up the Mis-souri and over the continental divide to the waters of the Columbia, they were doing more than securing information on geography, Indian tribes, and plant and animal life; they were, in fact, blazing the trail for the expansion of a nation from the Atlantic to the Pacific.

JEFFERSON AND THE COURTS

One of the important tasks which Jefferson had set for his administra-tion was that of reducing the power of the courts. It will be remembered that the Federalists had, in desperation, passed a new Judiciary Act in 1801 after the election of Jefferson had become a certainty. This act had reduced the size of the Supreme Court by providing that the next va-cancy should remain unfilled. It had then discontinued the practice of sending Supreme Court members on circuit duty, and had created a distinct set of new judges for the circuit courts, with a corresponding group of attorneys and marshals. John Adams's "midnight appoint-ments" had filled these courts with Federalists, and Adams had capped the whole structure by the appointment of John Marshall, one of Thomas Jefferson's real enemies, as Chief Justice.

What all this meant was quickly revealed when one William Mar-bury, who had been commissioned a justice of the peace in the District of Columbia in the closing days of Federalist rule, brought suit against Madison, as Secretary of State, for the delivery of his commission. He asked the Supreme Court for a mandamus compelling Madison to act, and Chief Justice Marshall seized the opportunity to reprimand Madison for failure to perform his legal duty, and to render a startling decision on the powers of the Court. In this opinion, in the case of Marbury *v.* Madison, Marshall denied Marbury's request for a writ on the ground of lack of authority. True, Congress had given the Court such power, but in doing so it had, he said, exceeded the powers granted it by the Constitution. It was, therefore, the duty of the Court to exercise the right of judicial review and to void acts of Congress which, in its opinion, violated the Constitution. In Marshall's own words: "It is emphatically the province and duty of the judicial department to say what the law is. . . . If two laws conflict with each other, the courts must decide on the operation of each. So if a law be in opposition to the Constitution . . . the court must determine which of these conflicting rules governs the case." And since in declaring "what shall be the *supreme* law of the land, the Constitution itself is first mentioned and not the laws of the United States generally," it may be assumed that they rank in that order. Thus the very "phraseology" confirms the principle "that a law repugnant to the Constitution is void."

This claim of power for the Court by a Federalist justice was not only a threat to Republican legislation; it was a move to bestow on one of the three departments of government a power which lifted that department well above the others and which gave it authority such as no other similar body in the world enjoyed. There were, indeed, precedents for judicial review in the decisions of colonial and state judges, but the Constitution had not expressly given such authority to the Supreme Court, nor had justices always claimed it. Coming now from a Virginia Federalist linked with the political faction in Richmond and the Northern Neck of Virginia which had long fought Jefferson and his political allies, the Court's claim, however much it might be in line with future developments, seemed to smack of a Federalist effort to thwart the will of the people.

The attitude of certain judges in the lower courts seemed to confirm this charge. This was particularly true of Justice Samuel Chase of Maryland, who not only ruled his court in a despotic manner, but on occasion left the bench without a quorum in order to make Federalist political speeches. Chase had, moreover, been particularly offensive in applying the Alien and Sedition Acts and later in his condemnation of the repeal of the Judiciary Act. He talked about the people's being no longer free and about the triumph of a mobocracy.

Was it not time to place some check on these dangerous trends among judges who felt secure behind life or good-behavior appointments?

Ironworks in Pennsylvania in 1800 · MURAL PAINT

The Lewis and Clark Expedition on Its Way to the Pacific, 18

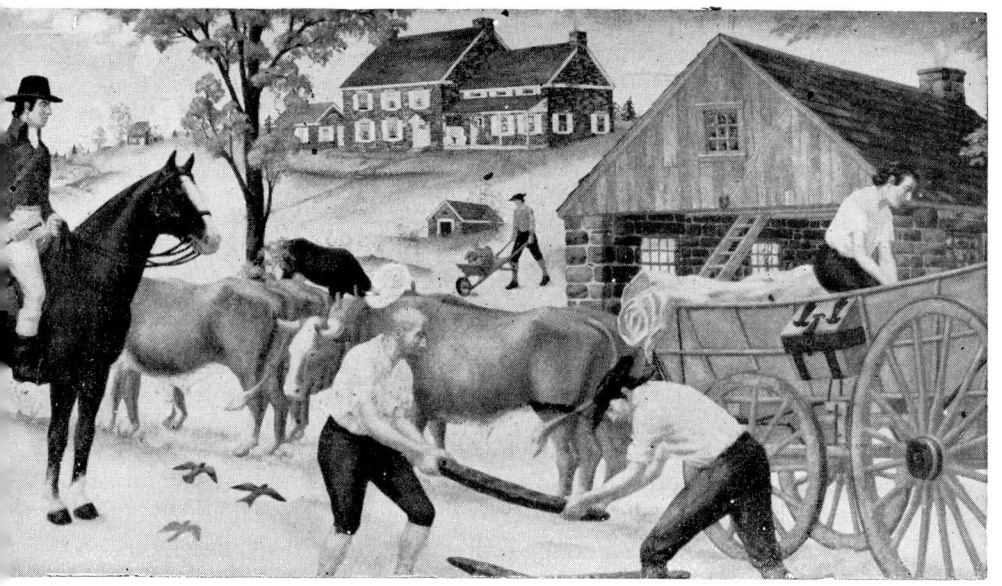

ROBERT LARTER IN SOUTHWARK STATION, PHILADELPHIA

AL PAINTING BY FRANK SCHWARZ IN THE STATE CAPITOL, SALEM, OREGON

Hagelstein Brothers

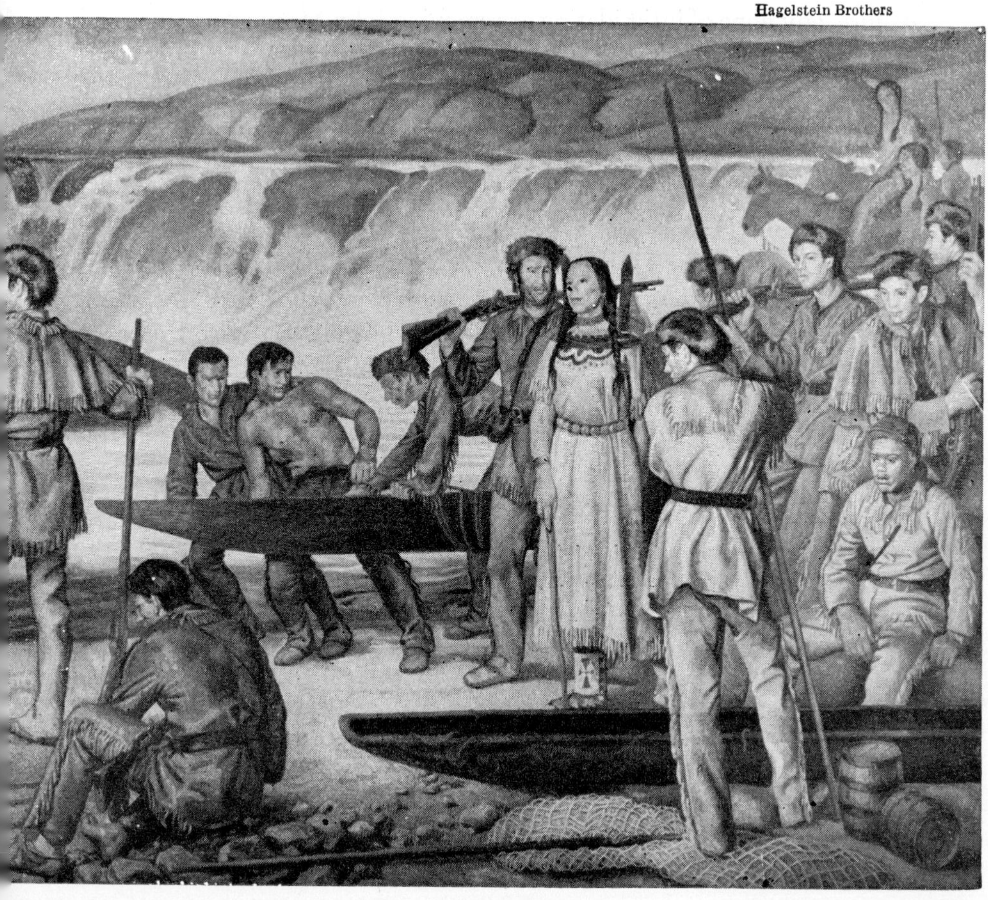

Ought such "sedicious and official" attacks "on the principles of our Constitution and on the proceedings of a State," as Jefferson called Chase's outbursts, to "go unpunished"? Republicans thought not. Spurred on by Jefferson's belief that the Judiciary Act of 1801 and the "midnight appointments" under it were "an outrage on decency," Congress had already repealed the obnoxious act. It had then added one new justice to the Supreme Court and returned its members to circuit duty. Now, after more than a year's delay (1803), Republicans began an effort at impeachment as a remedy.

The first case selected was that of John Pickering, district judge of New Hampshire, whose habits of intoxication and periods of mental derangement had long been a scandal to the bench. The House accepted Jefferson's opinion that Pickering's conduct constituted a "misdemeanor" within the meaning of the Constitution and promptly impeached him. Then, after some delay, the same charges were brought against Justice Chase. This time, however, the case was badly handled by the House managers, and the idea that Chase was being tried for mere errors of judgment was allowed to creep in. No lawyer could permit this to happen, and after much bitter discussion Chase was acquitted. With this failure, any hope of intimidating or removing John Marshall or other high officials was lost. Impeachment was only a scarecrow, an "impractical thing" for partisan purposes. John Marshall added the final touch to the whole episode soon afterward in a trial that grew out of the strange behavior of Aaron Burr.

Checked in his willingness to profit by the tie vote of 1800, Burr had soon gone over to the side of certain disgruntled Federalists, who talked of seceding from the Union and making New York and New England into a new confederation. He had, moreover, continued his clever political manipulations in New York and had, while still Vice-President, announced himself as a candidate for the governorship of the state. With these plans Alexander Hamilton interfered. A duel followed, and Hamilton was slain. The nation was horrified; opinion ran sharply against dueling and the man who had won. Politically ruined by these events, Burr turned toward the recently acquired Louisiana territory, where William C. C. Claiborne was governor and General James Wilkinson was in charge of the army. It was a region where intrigue and disorder flourished. Here political fortunes might be restored. Here a badly soiled reputation might be improved. Just how Burr planned to do this we do not know. Perhaps he planned the independence of Louisiana and subsequent union with Great Britain; perhaps he planned a buffer state between Louisiana and Mexico or even a great new confederation of states carved out of Spanish territory. At any rate, he was able to enlist the support of a number of Western men, including one Harman Blennerhassett, whose home on an island in the upper Ohio became headquarters for an expedition against New Orleans, and to create the impression that something very important was about to take place. Unfortunately for Burr, General Wilkinson, who seems to have been in on the whole affair, suddenly changed sides and secretly informed President Jefferson of what was going on. Burr was seized soon after he reached Natchez and charged with treason. It looked like a good chance for Jefferson to square accounts with Burr.

At this point John Marshall entered the picture. Burr was ordered to trial before the circuit court at Richmond—the court over which Marshall himself, on circuit, would preside and in the city where Federal opposition to Jefferson was most bitter. The next step was Marshall's blunt ruling that treason under the Constitution could be established only by an overt act in which the accused actually participated. And since the only act which met this requirement was the assembling of the group on Blennerhassett's Island, at which Burr had not been present, acquittal was a certainty before the trial had fairly begun. Even the effort to shift the charges from treason to misdemeanor failed and only resulted in allowing Marshall to order the President himself to appear and produce all the documents which the government possessed relating to the affair. That was carrying the effort at humiliation too far, and Jefferson refused. Yet even he saw clearly that any further attempt to check the courts or to advance partisan interests through them was hopeless. John Marshall had proved more than a match at the game.

It would thus appear that Jefferson had largely failed in his two great efforts, at economy and at the reduction of the courts' place and power. A war and the purchase of Louisiana had wrecked the first; John Marshall had taken care of the second. Nor had things always gone smoothly within the party itself. One group, under the leadership of John Randolph, had become openly hostile over the settlement of a Georgia land scandal, sometimes known as "the Yazoo frauds." It was a case of corruption in the sale of the state's Western lands by one legislature, the repudiation of the sale by a later one, and the proposal of the national government to compensate those who had lost money in the transaction when Georgia ceded her Western lands. The "Quids," as Randolph's followers were called, opposed such payments and, with this as a start, had become "insurgents" against the administration in general.

Also, Jefferson had been unable to win over the New England Federalists to the degree that he had hoped when, in his first inaugural, he declared, "We are all Republicans; we are all Federalists." Efforts at simplicity in relationships with the foreign representatives in Washington had met with little more success. The British and Spanish representatives especially had resented the failure to follow old, established customs and had heaped ridicule on Republican simplicity. Yet in 1804, even before the Burr trial, Jefferson had been re-elected, with George Clinton of New York as Vice-President. His electoral vote was 112, as against 14 for C. C. Pinckney, the Federalist candidate. Even New England, with the exception of Connecticut, had voted for him. Perhaps, after all, he had been successful in spite of failures.

SELECTED BIBLIOGRAPHY

HENRY ADAMS, *History of the United States, 1801–1817* (9 vols.), the classic work on this period; CHARLES A. BEARD, *Economic Origins of Jeffersonian Democracy*, and S. E. MORISON, *Maritime History of Massachusetts*, valuable studies of economic developments. Among the worth-while biographies are H. J. ECKENRODE, *The Randolphs*; DUMAS MALONE, *Thomas Cooper*; NATHAN SCHACHNER, *Aaron Burr*; W. B. HATCHER, *Edward Livingston*; A. J. BEVERIDGE, *John Marshall* (4 vols.).

GILBERT CHINARD, *Thomas Jefferson*; CLAUDE BOWERS, *Jefferson in Power*; ADRIENNE KOCH, *The Philosophy of Thomas Jefferson*; ALLEN JOHNSON, *Jefferson and His Colleagues*; CHARLES M. WILTSE, *The Jeffersonian Tradition in American Politics*, throw light on Thomas Jefferson's contribution to American life.

E. D. WARFIELD, *The Kentucky Resolutions of 1798*; W. F. MCCALEB, *Burr Conspiracy*; J. A. ROBERTSON, *Louisiana under Spain, France, and the United States*; E. WILSON LYON, *Lousiana in French Diplomacy*; I. J. COX, *The West Florida Controversy*; L. M. SEARS, *Jefferson and the Embargo*; LOUIS B. WRIGHT and JULIA H. MACLEOD, *The First Americans in North Africa*, important studies of various phases of this period.

H. S. COMMAGER (Ed.), *Documents of American History*, pp. 175–197, contains source material.

X

National Growth

and Neutral Trade

SOCIAL AND CULTURAL DEVELOPMENTS

IN ORDER to understand foreign affairs as they developed under Jefferson and ultimately culminated in the War of 1812, it is necessary to notice certain great social-economic changes which were taking place in the nation. Since the establishment of government under the Constitution, growth of population and expansion of settlement had been rapid. In 1790 the estimated population was about 3,950,000, fairly equally distributed between North and South. By 1800 it had reached 5,300,000 and by 1810, 7,250,000—an increase for the two decades of 84.2 per cent. It contained, along with its other elements, a new generation of Americans, who had grown to maturity in a nation independent of European control. They were natives in a new sense.

The spread of population had been equally rapid. In 1790 the great majority of Americans lived within a hundred miles of the Atlantic seaboard. Timid lines of settlement reached up the rivers into the interior, and the advance guard had pushed out into central New York, into southwestern Pennsylvania, and through the mountain gaps in the Carolinas to form islands of settlement in Kentucky and Tennessee. Since the Revolution the tide had been running strong. It now seemed to gain momentum every year. By 1810 population in New England had pushed northward into Maine and to the farthest borders of New Hampshire and Vermont. It had crowded south and west against the Indians in Georgia and had moved westward across New York along the lakes into Ohio, and from Pennsylvania, Virginia, and the Carolinas in a great wedge down the Ohio River to its mouth. In 1810 Kentucky had a population of over 400,000, and Tennessee and Ohio each had more than half that number. All three had been admitted to the Union as states. The purchase of Louisiana had started another stream northward along the Mississippi River and had added groups of population in the Illinois and Mississippi territories. A great, new, internal section, facing westward and down the rivers that ran to the Gulf, was in the making. It was one step farther removed from Europe, and its people, like most frontiersmen, were a bit more self-reliant and aggressive than those in older sections.

These developments had been accompanied by a less spectacular but important increase in urban population. In 1790 the United States was, like most young countries, a land of rural peoples. In that year only 3.3 per cent of the total population lived in towns of 8000 or more, and only Philadelphia, New York, Boston, Charleston, and Baltimore were in that bracket. Philadelphia, the largest of these, had only 42,444, and Baltimore, the smallest, had 13,503. During the next two decades urban growth more than kept pace with the national increase and in 1810 constituted 4.9 per cent of the total. New York outstripped all rivals and stood at the head of the list, with a population of over 96,000. Other Northern cities grew steadily if not quite so rapidly, and Western towns like Pittsburgh, Cincinnati, and St. Louis began to dispute the strictly rural character of that region. In the South, only Baltimore showed unusual gains, but Norfolk, Charleston, and Savannah grew rapidly enough to keep alive their confidence in the future.

What was equally important was that these cities were rapidly becoming the center of a more or less self-reliant, native culture. Comforts, and sometimes enough of luxury to surprise the European traveler, had come with expanding trade. Gardens and servants and fine carriages, on the material side, indicated enough of wealth and leisure to permit some interest in things intellectual and artistic. Along these lines Philadelphia took the lead. It "had long prided itself on its culture and it was on chatty terms with the fine arts, with books and music and painting, with actors and plays and playhouses." Especially while it was the seat of the national government, 1790–1800, it attracted intellectuals and stimulated creative effort. In the early nineties Philip Freneau, who had come on Jefferson's invitation to edit the *National Gazette*, paused now and then in his work as official spokesman for the Republican party to give the young nation a start in poetry. A little later Mathew Carey set up a publishing house and sent agents, like the good Parson Weems, up and down the countryside to peddle his books, and, in Weems's case, to gather materials for the writing of popular biographies of Washington and other national dignitaries. Carey published a magazine, the *American Museum*, which gave much of its space to disputes with William Cobbett and Joseph Dennie, rival Fed-

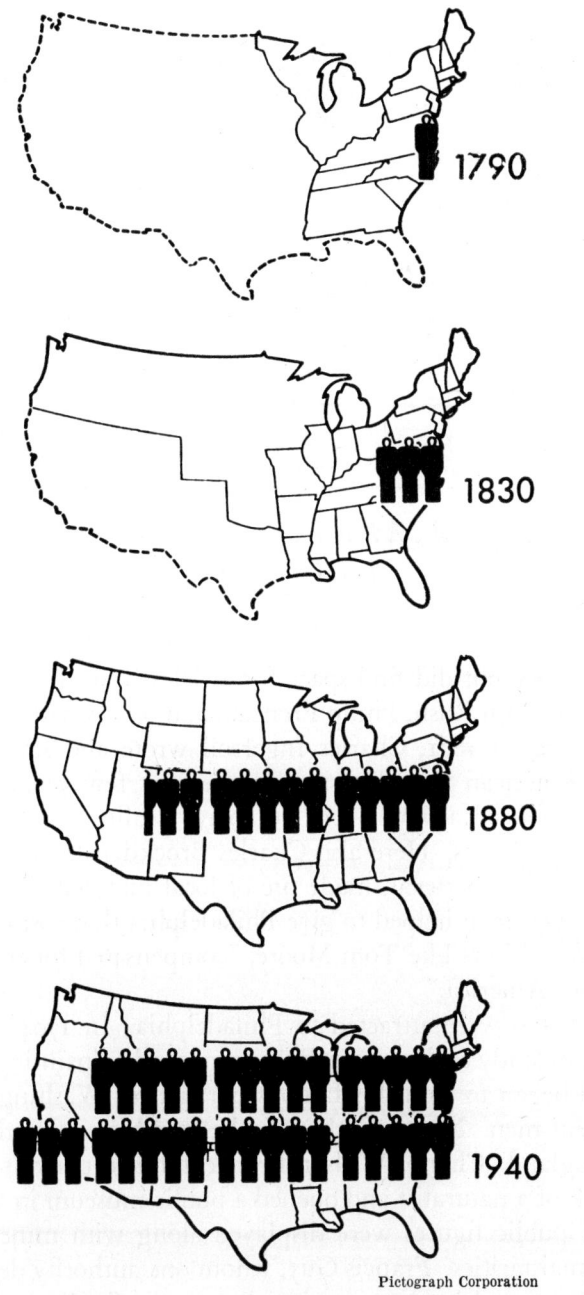

1790

1830

1880

1940

Growth of the Continental United States. Each Man
Represents 4 Million People

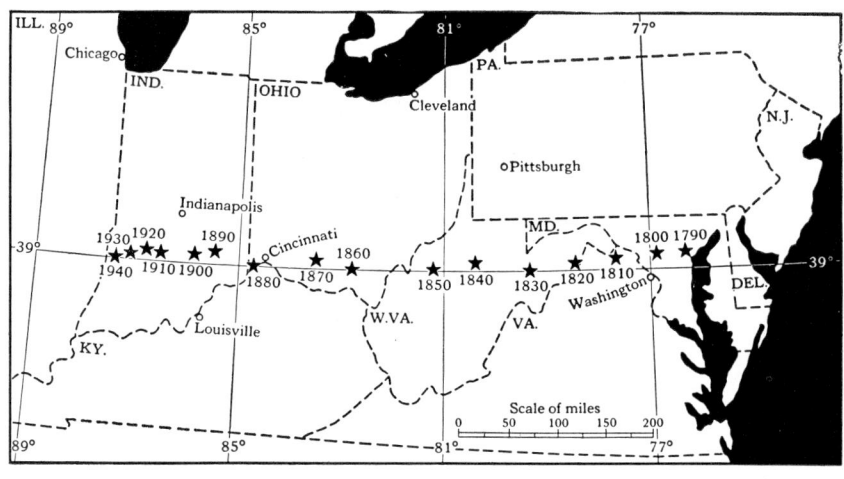

The Westward Movement of the Center of Population from 1790 to 1940

eralist editors, but did find space for articles from the pens of Thomas Paine, Benjamin Rush, Philip Freneau, and others with literary inclinations. Here, in 1801, Charles Ingersoll wrote and staged one of the earliest American tragedies, and in the next few years James Nelson Barker produced a whole series of plays dealing with local and contemporary subjects. Here also Charles Brockden Brown, although following English patterns, made use of local materials in the writing of novels. Such men helped to give Philadelphia that cosmopolitan flavor which, for visitors like Tom Moore, "compensated for the meanness of the rest of America."

Artists too were attracted to Philadelphia. In 1794 Gilbert Stuart, fresh from study and work in Europe, opened a "painting room" in the city and began to paint his famous portraits of Washington and other prominent men. Not until 1805 did he find his way back to his native New England. Charles Willson Peale combined portrait-painting with the work of a naturalist and opened a public museum in which the portraits of public figures were displayed along with mineral, vegetable, and animal rarities. Francis Guy, whom one authority describes as "the first [American] landscape painter" to make "a direct and independent" approach to nature, came to Philadelphia for a time in the late nineties, and Benjamin Latrobe settled there about the same time to reveal equal independence as an architect in the designing of both public and private buildings. His Bank of Pennsylvania has been described as "unlike any bank built before the Revolution, . . . unlike any British prototype, . . . unlike any known classic structure." His Baltimore cathedral was equally revolutionary and was "the first attempt to break completely with the Wren-Gibbs tradition in church design." One of his houses, built in Philadelphia, contained a bathroom, bathtub, washbasin, and water closet complete!

Nor was the scientific interest which Franklin had awakened in Philadelphia lost in this period. William Bartram continued the botanical garden which his father had developed, and with the publication of his *Travels* established himself both as an authority on American plants and flowers and as a man of literary ability. Alexander Wilson arrived from Scotland in 1794 and, between 1808 and 1813, published seven volumes of his magnificent *American Ornithology*. "He has treated of American birds better than those of Europe have yet been treated," said Baron Cuvier. Joseph Priestley came from England in the same year to continue his work in chemistry, and Benjamin Rush, who had already established himself as the leading American medical scholar, went on with his varied, if somewhat shallow, observations and writings.

New York and Boston had fewer distinguished individuals. Business occupied more attention. In New York the Dutch influence, which still showed itself in brick houses with their stepped-gable ends to the streets and in Dutch shop signs and Dutch Reformed churches, had somewhat retarded interest in things aesthetic and intellectual. Yet William Dunlop's theater was the best in the nation and Chancellor Kent, with his legal writings, was already well on his way to becoming "the American Blackstone." The young Washington Irving was just beginning to publish, in the years after 1800, his first efforts at satire on theatrical and social affairs in the city. These things, however, counted for less in the growth of local pride and self-assurance than the forward rush of commerce and the beginnings of industry, which had already pushed New York to the head of American cities.

Talent in Boston also turned to trading, and Long Wharf, which jutted a third of a mile out into the water, was the symbol of her strength. Later writers spoke of the period as the "ice age" in Massachusetts history and declared that not a book, a speech, or a thought had been produced. Conservative Federalists dominated society. Many of them still dressed in colored coats, figured waistcoats, and short breeches buttoned at the knee, although most other Americans had abandoned them. Confidently they awaited the breakdown of popular government and openly talked of secession from the Union. Yet there was something highly suggestive of growing local pride in the fact that Jeremy Belknap was writing first-class local history and biography, and with some friends had already founded the Massachusetts Historical Society. There was something American also in some of the buildings which Charles Bulfinch was designing in Boston, and some breaking away from the English Adam style in the exquisite wood-carvings with which Samuel McIntire glorified Salem houses. In like spirit, Jedidiah Morse, over in Charlestown, was producing *The American Geography*, and Nathaniel Bowditch of Salem was making a sound contribution to commercial expansion by the publication of his book *The New American Practical Navigator*. Noah Webster of Hartford was at the same time publishing his American spelling books, one of which contained in its introduction a literary declaration of independence from England. He insisted that he had "too much pride to stand indebted to Great Britain for books to learn our children the letters of the alphabet." "Europe is grown old in folly, corruption, and tyranny," he wrote, . . . "manners are licentious, literature is declining, and human nature is debased. For America in her infancy to adopt the present maxims of the old world would be to stamp the wrinkle of decrepit age upon the bloom of youth, and to plant the seed of decay in a vigorous institution."

No one of these writers was as effusive in his Americanism as Joel Barlow, the Connecticut poet, whose ponderous *Columbiad* appeared in 1807; but each revealed a solid, practical quality that belonged to future national trends as certainly as the reactionary religious writings of President Timothy Dwight of Yale belonged to a slipping past. They all had something strikingly American about them which had not been present in earlier writers.

Nor were all the developments in the North. The South had fewer towns, but the cultural tradition was strong, and the plantation system offered opportunity for the achievement of wealth and the enjoyment of leisure. In houses and gardens and writing, Southerners also revealed the slow breaking away from colonial patterns and the birth of a new national spirit. In Virginia, Thomas Jefferson was already designing houses that drew their inspiration from Roman sources, but which early took on something of both Jefferson and America. Monticello, Farmington, Bremo, and the Virginia state capitol all revealed a "quiet and gracious sobriety" of taste that did not come from any Old World

Carolina Art Association

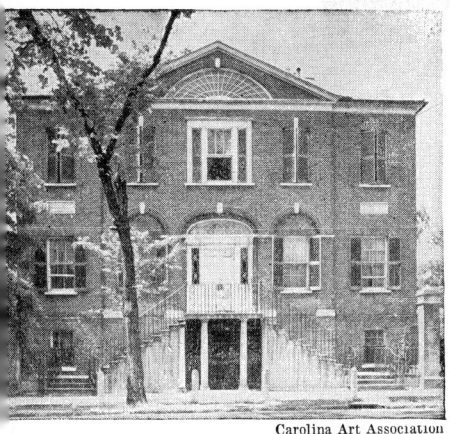

The Blacklock House, Built in Charleston in 1800

Maryland Historical Society

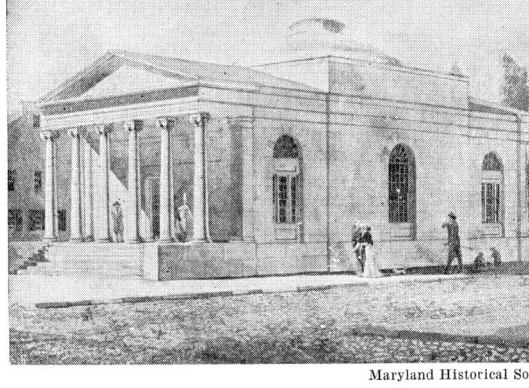

The Bank of Pennsylvania, Designed by Benjamin Latrobe

Fourth of July in Centre Square, Philadelphia. This Picture Shows the Pumping Station of the Water Works, Designed by Latrobe

PAINTING BY JOHN LEWIS KRIMMEL

The Pennsylvania Academy of the Fine Arts

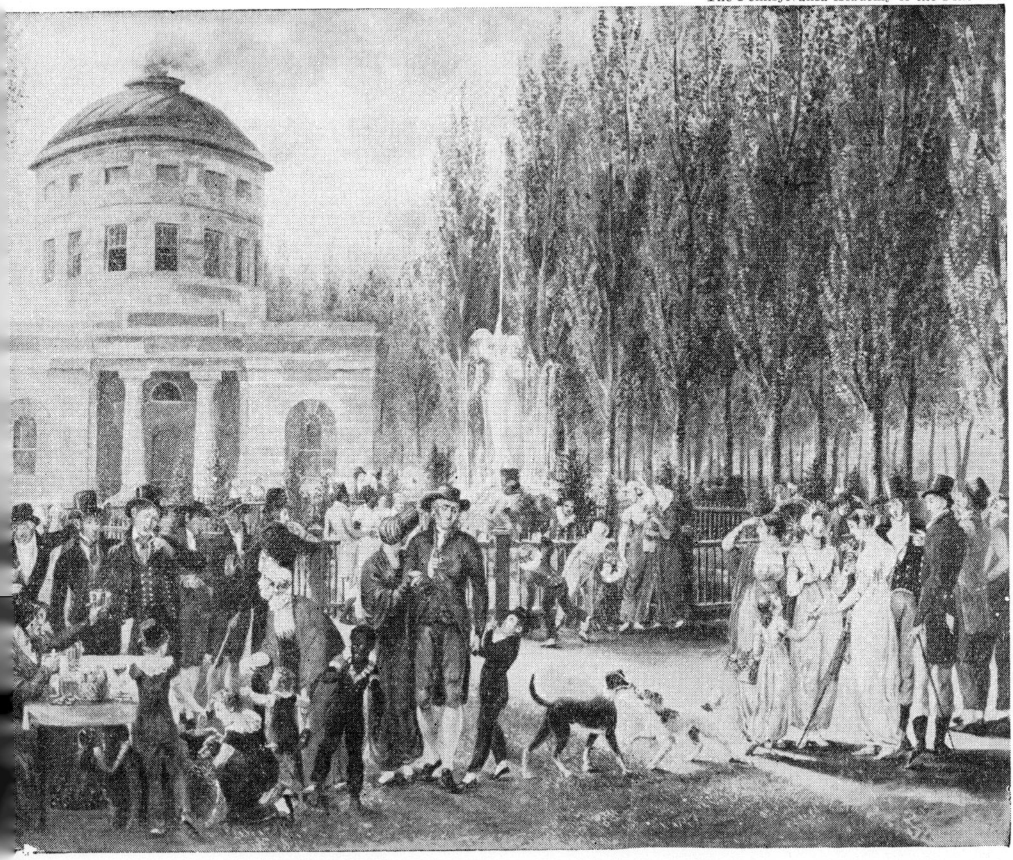

source. In forwarding plans for the new national capitol both Washington and Jefferson instinctively "realized the futility of trying here in the United States to reconstruct another England."

Literary effort in the region was far less satisfactory. Yet William Wirt of Richmond did publish his *Letters of the British Spy* in 1803, and followed it in 1804 with *The Rainbow*. Neither had great merit, but the very fact that a Virginia lawyer was trying to write about life in his native state was not without significance. John Taylor of Caroline, on the other hand, was both profound and original in his writings on political and economic subjects and justly found a place alongside Thomas Jefferson as one of the great spokesmen of the agricultural way of life.

The city of Charleston in South Carolina had long been distinguished for its quiet dignity and the fact that it seemed to have grown out of the very earth on which it stood. Its houses were adapted to the peculiarities of the local climate; its citizens were noted for a self-reliance born of many successful battles against storms and Indians and Spaniards. Its commerce rested on the rice and cotton fields behind and reached out through a magnificent harbor to the West Indies and the Mediterranean. It had a library society, orchestra concerts, a race course, a city college, a public museum, and a botanical garden. Its historian, David Ramsay, wrote a two-volume *History of the Revolution of South Carolina* and also a history of South Carolina. Its architects were breaking away from English patterns, experimenting with octagonal and oval rooms and with stairways that "floated from floor to floor," and were building some of the most satisfactory homes in a city of fine homes.

Another fact of significance was that all this growth and development of the new nation had been achieved without great aid from foreign immigration. European wars had kept peoples at home, and arrivals for the period 1790–1810 averaged not more than five or six thousand per year. Some of these were common folk who sought a home in upper New York, in western Pennsylvania, or out on the banks of the Ohio. Some were political refugees whose liberal attitudes had made flight to America imperative and whose residence in the United States added something of color and maturity to the cultural patterns evolving. An example of these was Joseph Priestley, the scientist, who was a discoverer of oxygen, who introduced the study of modern history and science into the schools, and who was a pioneer in the Unitarian movement in the United States. Another was Thomas Cooper, "the publicist from Oxford," who came to teach at the University of Virginia and went on to the College of South Carolina, where he influenced the thinking of a generation in political economy. They and others like them left England largely because of persecution incident to their enthusiasm for the French Revolution, and they understood the growing difference between life in the New World and the Old as native sons could not.

There were others, like Talleyrand, Louis Philippe, Du Pont de Nemours, the Duc de La Rochefoucauld-Liancourt, and the Vicomte de Noailles, who, as refugees from the French Revolution, lived in seaboard cities for longer or shorter periods of time. They were the more prominent individuals among the ten or twenty thousand Frenchmen who sought to escape the terrors of social conflict either in France itself or in Santo Domingo. Both intentionally and unintentionally they emphasized the fact that freedom in the United States was something more than a theory, and they paid a part of their debt to its existence by contributing something of urbanity and intellectual sophistication to society in New York and Philadelphia.

In sharp contrast to these were some seventy thousand Negro slaves who came to the United States in this period, not from choice but from compulsion. Most of them were destined to serve on Southern plantations. The spread of cotton cultivation called for new laborers, and necessity stilled the more liberal attitudes about human rights which the Revolution had awakened. Jefferson, however, was determined to check the slave trade, which still went on under the compromise reached in the Constitutional Convention, and, after a somewhat bitter struggle, forced the passage of an act which forbade further importations after January 1, 1808. That satisfied liberal demands for the moment, but left slavery itself to trouble future generations.

RISE OF NATIONAL CONSCIOUSNESS

As a result of all these developments, the colonial character of American life was slowly being altered, and a national feeling and outlook was taking its place. Foreign travelers spoke of the "sanguine and self-confident" attitude of the people. One of them described a Pennsylvania miller, to whom he had talked, as "a sound American patriot, persuading himself that nothing good is done, and no one has any brains, except in America: that the wit, the imagination, the genius of Europe are already in decrepitude." "This error is to be found in almost all Americans," added the traveler. A later visitor said: "The national vanity of the United States surpasses that of any other country. ... It blazes out everywhere, and on all occasions." "We already rival Europe in portraits and engravings," boasted Benjamin Latrobe, who had given Philadelphia her first public water system in 1801 and who had not set foot on the continent until 1796! This nation is "the freest and most enlightened in the world" was a Congressman's opinion.

Nor was confidence expressed in words alone. Speculation in lands and in various developments revealed unbounded confidence in the nation's future. Mention has already been made of the speculation produced by Hamilton's financial measures. Stories of fast ships that were sent to the South to purchase securities before news of national assumption reached that region were common. A traveler from Philadelphia to Alexandria in 1791 declared that the whole way was "one continued scene of stock gambling; agriculture commerce & even the fair sex relinquished, to make way for unremitted exertion in this favorite pursuit." Bank stock, state certificates, and real estate attracted excited purchasers. Patrick Henry and a group of friends invested in Yazoo land and Georgia paper money, and became financially independent. Another group, including Henry Knox and Hamilton himself, purchased ten townships on the southeastern shore of the St. Lawrence, and Oliver Phelps and Nathaniel Gorham bought six million acres in upper New York. More daring than any of these was William Duer, who joined with Knox and others to secure pre-emption rights to some three million acres in Maine and then organized what he called the Scioto Company for huge speculations in Ohio lands. He sent Joel Barlow, the poet, to France to sell shares and to forward emigrants who would raise some of the enormous crops which the promotion literature said were possible. His dealings in United States securities were so extensive that his failure produced a panic of major importance in New York.

More significant for future developments were the speculations of Robert Morris and his associates in building-lots in the city of Washington, D. C. When the location had been chosen for the permanent Federal capital and Major L'Enfant had drawn plans for its streets and parks, these men, who had already been associated in what they called the North American Land Company, turned eagerly toward the profits which seemed assured in the future replica of London or Paris or Rome. They even talked of "the seven hills" and named a little stream, which now finds its way down a Washington sewer, the Tiber! They built warehouses for expected trade on the Potomac; they erected a brewery to cater to anticipated thirst; they staged a great barbecue, with tables set up in the streets in front of houses that they were building to accommodate prospective citizens, and invited the public to come and feast and buy. But they were ahead of their time. The city grew all too slowly. Government officials went to live in the older and more comfortable Georgetown. Even in Jefferson's day Washington consisted largely of one cluster of buildings about the half-finished Capitol and another about the President's mansion a mile away. The road in between was only a stretch of almost impassable "ruts and puddles" in wet weather and a yellow streak of "blinding dust" in dry weather. Morris and his friends struggled valiantly against fate, then yielded to bankruptcy and a debtors' prison. "God help us," wrote Morris, "for men will not."

GROWTH OF TRADE

Closely related to all the growth and prosperity and failure that have been described was the fact that Europe had been at war most of the time since the new United States government had been functioning, and this nation had become the most important neutral carrier in the world. The growth of foreign trade and shipping had, in turn, both increased and altered the demands made on American agriculture and manufactures. Between 1790 and 1807 the total exports of the country rose from $20,000,000 to $108,000,000. Part of this reflected a rising price level; some $60,000,000 of it represented the re-export of goods imported largely from the West Indies. The residue, however, was large; and the increase of imports from $23,000,000 to $138,000,000 and of total tonnage in foreign trade from 127,000 to 1,089,000 tons indicated an astonishing expansion of the nation's commercial life. "The maritime industry of Massachusetts, New York, Pennsylvania and Maryland in 1807," says one writer, "had no precedent in the history of any nation." American goods, says another, "filled the warehouses of Cádiz and Antwerp to overflowing. They [American exporters] glutted the markets of Emden and Lisbon, Hamburg and Copenhagen, with the produce of the West Indies and the fabrics of the East, and, bringing back the products of the looms and forges of Germany to the New World, drove out the manufactures of Yorkshire, Manchester and Birmingham."

Commerce in the days just after the Revolution had been greatly injured by British regulations which barred American vessels from trading with Britain's West Indies colonies and which, when war first broke out, enforced the "rule of 1756" against trade with the French colonies. Necessity, however, soon altered the situation. Unable to secure sufficient shipping and supplies as the war dragged on, local governors in the West Indies openly invited American vessels into their ports, and England herself soon accepted the principle of the "broken voyage," by which goods from forbidden areas might be first landed in a neutral country and then reshipped to a nation at war. This meant that cities like New York, Philadelphia, and Baltimore, with great food-producing areas behind them, might supply both the West Indies planters and the contending armies of Europe. Even Alexandria, Norfolk, and Charleston might have a share in such trade. It meant also that New England states, such as Massachusetts, with little to export, but with many ships and great skill in building and sailing them, might regain their colonial supremacy, which, in spite of new Chinese and South American trade, had weakened.

Most of the exports from the United States were, of course, agricultural produce. Wheat was especially in demand. As one merchant wrote in 1789, "It appears to us that all the world is after wheat." "Take up any good double-decked vessel that can be chartered and load with wheat," he advised; "it will be a very safe speculation." "If I were there [the West Indies] at this present moment," wrote Stephen Gerard, the great Philadelphia merchant, "I should sell all I have in the world to speculate in this article even at 7 gourdes a barrel."

Fields in New York, Pennsylvania, and Virginia that had once been planted in corn or tobacco now were turned to wheat. Mills sprang up on every stream, and the harbors of coastal cities were filled with vessels loading with grain and flour. An agricultural depression that had begun well before the Revolution and had become worse with its ending now lifted. Prosperity took the place of "benumbing poverty." The price of flour rose from $5.41 per barrel to $9.12. Farmers were paid prices for their wheat that one merchant called "beyond the bounds of prudence." In some places merchants waited along the highways in order to have the first chance at grain on its way to market. The value of exports from small towns like Alexandria rose from $381,242 in 1791 to over $1,100,000 in 1796, and from larger ports like Baltimore from $1,576,588 to over $8,500,000. In 1800 the British consul at Philadelphia reported that 22,678 barrels of flour left that port during the month of July for England, and the next year he declared that "almost every large ship upon her arrival in the Delaware is taken up for the purpose of conveying flour to England." New York's exports of "flour, rye-flour and Indian-meal," meanwhile, had risen to over 296,475 barrels per year. Rice from the Charleston area supplemented wheat and became a part of the cargoes not only out of the ports of that area, but out of New York, Philadelphia, and other ports where the aggressive New England carriers first unloaded it. Agriculture in the United States was being remade by Old World events.

It must be remembered, however, that this activity in shipping and farming was largely in response to demands caused by war and the loosening, incident to war, of trade regulations. It expanded with battle; it shrank with peace or rumors of peace. When, in November, 1801, rumors were noised about that England and France were discussing terms of peace, "it instantly operated almost like the hand of death upon all business." "Wheat, corn, and flour have been constantly on the fall," wrote one observer. "No earthquake I suppose ever produced a greater crush than peace has amongst the merchants," wrote another. "Everything you know depends upon the will of Napoleon," was a merchant's comment.

DIFFICULTIES OF NEUTRAL TRADE

The next few years were not happy ones for either the farmers or the merchants. Prices fell, business houses failed, and farmers shifted crops again, as of old. Then, in 1805, war was resumed, and a new wave of even greater prosperity followed. Wheat again poured from American ports, and timid merchants complained that "our flour dealers are mad or something worse." The boom, however, was short-lived. British merchants had watched with jealous eyes the growth of American trade, and navy officials had become somewhat alarmed when British seamen, attracted by the higher wages on United States ships, had deserted to become American citizens. One James Stephens had written a pamphlet, *War in Disguise; or the Frauds of Neutral Flags*, in which he bitterly declared that aid was being given to the enemy under the guise of neutral trade. It was, therefore, not surprising that the British Admiralty Court, which had, in the *Polly* case, accepted the principle of the "broken voyage" now reversed itself in the *Essex* case (1805) and held that entrance to a neutral port and the payment of duties before proceeding to a once forbidden area did not constitute bona fide importation.

If this decision were rigidly enforced, it would mean the destruction not only of the rich West Indies trade, but also of a heavy trade that rugged New England sailors had built up in the Baltic. Americans protested loud and long. The British, however, now strengthened by Nelson's great naval victory at Trafalgar, which destroyed Napoleon's plans for invading English soil, became more active in seizing ships and condemning them before British admiralty courts. More seamen were removed from American crews as deserters from the British navy. Jefferson's answer was a return to the old policy of commercial restrictions. On April 18, 1806, he approved a Nonimportation Act, which declared that after the fifteenth day of November next, it should be unlawful to import such British goods as Americans could make for themselves or secure from nations other than Great Britain. The direct object of the act was, of course, to apply economic pressure, but it had also another purpose. The commercial clauses of the Jay Treaty were soon to expire, and William Pinkney of Maryland was being sent to England to join James Monroe, the regular minister, in an effort to secure better terms in a new treaty. Nonimportation would serve as a threat in their hands.

Britain, however, was now too secure in her position, and the necessity for holding seamen to their ships and returning any who might have escaped was too great for compromise. The only treaty that could be secured refused to yield the right of impressment or to pay indemnity for captures under the *Essex* decision. Jefferson refused to submit such a treaty to the Senate, even though his representatives had signed it, and Madison informed Monroe and Pinkney that no treaty would be ratified that did not contain satisfactory guarantees on impressment.

Difficulties for the United States, however, had scarcely begun. England, and France under Napoleon, were locked in a life-and-death struggle in which the rights of neutrals counted for little. Foiled, by England's sea power, in his attempt to strike the island directly, Napoleon had turned to the conquest of the continent of Europe. He was now in a position where he could use the domination won there to strike England in a vital spot. To a nation of shopkeepers dependent on outside trade, the loss of Continental markets would be fatal. England could be brought to her knees by economic pressure through the closing of all Continental ports to her ships. By threats against other nations this might be widened and extended.

Consequently, on November 21, 1806, Napoleon began to issue from different conquered capitals a series of decrees for the carrying out of his policy. The first, from Berlin, declared the British Isles to be in a state of blockade. All trade with them was prohibited, and merchandise coming from them was good prize, as was any ship which attempted in any way to evade the regulations. England answered this, on January 7, 1807, with an Order in Council forbidding the coastal trade of France and her allies to neutral ships; and, when French seizures became frequent, she added a new provision, prohibiting all trade with ports closed to England unless ships first called at a British port, paid duties, and obtained proper clearance. Napoleon countered with his Milan Decree (December 17, 1807), threatening confiscation to any ship which complied with British regulations, or was on its way to or from a British port. Ships which had submitted to British search or had on board any British goods were also subject to seizure and confiscation.

Such regulations placed American shipping between the devil and the deep sea. Ships could not enter a French port without having paid duties at a British customhouse, ranging from three cents per pound on tobacco to two dollars a barrel on flour; and if they did this, they immediately became liable to capture and condemnation by any French vessel or French official that they met. This actually reduced American shipping to a happy hunting ground for the privateers of both nations. British and French men-of-war and other ships boldly put into American harbors or patrolled the coasts where vessels must pass. For weeks at a time British ships lay off Sandy Hook, or anchored in New York Harbor or inside the capes of the Chesapeake, stopping all vessels bound in or out and actually firing on them if they refused immediate obedience. The French were less aggressive only because their naval strength was weaker. Both searched vessels for deserters and impressed them when there was the slightest excuse for doing so. Both showed an utter disregard for the three-mile limit, the zone of national control.

These outrages reached a climax on June 22, 1807, when the British fifty-gun ship *Leopard* followed the United States frigate *Chesapeake* out from Norfolk and, just beyond the three-mile limit, stopped her and demanded the surrender of seamen who were said to have deserted from the British service. When the request was refused, the *Leopard* opened fire. The *Chesapeake*, whose gun deck was littered with stores of various kinds and some of whose guns were not properly placed, could offer no resistance. When twenty-one of her men had been killed or wounded, she pulled down her flag and submitted to search. Four alleged deserters were seized.

News of the outrage committed on the *Chesapeake* stirred American resentment as no other event in the short national life of the country had done. Mobs in Norfolk ran riot at the sight of their dead and wounded comrades. Threats were hurled against the British fleet still anchored in the bay, and supplies were refused. "The whole American people," says Henry Adams, "roared with pain and stood frantic on the shore, hurling abuse at their enemy, who taunted them from his safe ships." "The feeling of a true national emotion" had been awakened by a national insult and injury.

JEFFERSON'S PROGRAM FOR PEACE

When Jefferson's cabinet met, on July 2, a proclamation was issued, ordering all British men-of-war out of United States waters, forbidding others to enter, and prohibiting all intercourse, including the furnishing of supplies, with such ships. James Monroe, in England, was instructed to demand satisfaction for the attack on the *Chesapeake* and to insist that this include the avowal of a change of policy on the whole subject of impressment. Soon afterward he was recalled from his post for failure to secure satisfactory agreements. Meanwhile Congress was called to meet on the fourth Monday of October. Even Gallatin thought that war would be a "necessary result."

War did, indeed, seem certain when, after an early note expressing regret, Britain suddenly ordered her naval officers to carry out impressment to the fullest extent and then sent a special envoy to the United States, with instructions to secure a withdrawal of Jefferson's proclamation before the opening of any discussions of the *Chesapeake* affair! A London paper, officially inspired, declared, "A war of a few months ... would be sufficient to convince her [America] of her folly by a necessary chastisement of her insolence and audacity."

Thomas Jefferson, however, did not want war. He still believed in peaceable coercion. On December 18, 1807, he sent a message to Congress, pointing out the advantages to be gained "from an inhibition of the departure of our vessels from the ports of the United States," and a bill, which he had evidently drawn, for the immediate establishment of an embargo for an indefinite period of time. Four days later the bill was passed and signed. Under the provisions of this bill, and those of two supplementary acts passed to facilitate its enforcement, all ships, except foreign ships in ballast, were forbidden to leave the United States for any foreign country, and a heavy bond was required of all ships engaged in the coastal trade to ensure that their cargoes would be landed in the United States.

It was Jefferson's hope that the withdrawal of the great neutral carrier would soon bring the warring nations to their senses. He had not, however, foreseen all the difficulties in his method. Strict enforcement proved impossible. Many ships loaded quickly before the act went into force and hurried off to markets. Ships already at sea remained away, and convenient storms blew a surprising number of coastal traders to outside ports. Others deliberately left without clearance papers, and British officials winked at irregularities. New England shippers were particularly active in evading the law, and the flour trade of the North suffered far less than the tobacco and cotton trade of the South.

The embargo, however, thoroughly upset the normal run of business. Although some large owners, whose ships were out when the embargo became effective, increased their profits as risks increased, the majority of small owners and some of the smaller ports, such as New Haven, were utterly ruined. Where a traveler, in early 1807, had found the wharves of New York crowded with produce of all kinds and the people "scampering in all directions to trade with each other," he found them, in April of the next year, so empty and dismantled that he might have "thought that a malignant fever was raging in the place." In Boston also the harbor was filled with dismantled ships and not "a box, bale, cask, barrel or package" was to be seen on the wharf.

Agriculture also suffered as shipping dwindled, but the Southern planters were less inclined to grumble than were those who lived in regions where both shipping and Federalism centered. Here was a chance for the disgruntled New England element to strike back at Jefferson, with economic suffering adding strength to their opposition.

Senator Pickering of Massachusetts, who had talked of secession even in 1804, issued a public letter boldly asserting that the embargo had been dictated by Napoleon himself and was being used by Jefferson to destroy the shipping interests and to impoverish New England. Abusive letters from lesser men called the President fool and knave, and some even threatened him with assassination. One Boston correspondent called him "the greatest tirant in the whole world" and announced that he had agreed to pay his friends the sum of four hundred dollars "to shoot you." Another wrote, "Thomas Jefferson, you are the damdest fool that God put life into." Jefferson did not answer, but wrote on the outside of such letters the word *nonsense*. He probably found some comfort in the correspondence of John Taylor, who expressed complete confidence in the President and told of his own ability to sleep soundly because Jefferson was in control.

Fourteen months were enough to convince even Jefferson that the embargo was not a success. By connivance with American vessels that had escaped and by increasing her own carrying power, England avoided any great amount of injury; Napoleon used the embargo as an excuse for seizing any American ships that he could find, on the ground that they had no business being where they were. The rising storm of protest at home, which Federalists used to rebuild their political strength and which seemed about to split the Republicans, added the final pressure. Jefferson's second term was drawing to a close. He had refused to run again, but he was anxious that his Secretary of State, James Madison, should be his successor. Federalists were supporting C. C. Pinckney, and the ills of the embargo were their chief weapon of attack. How effective that weapon had become was revealed when the votes were cast. All New England, with the exception of Vermont, returned to the Federalist fold. The Republicans retained control of Congress, but their majority was much reduced. Madison was elected, but fifty-two electoral votes were cast against him, as compared with fourteen against Jefferson in 1804.

The election determined the fate of the embargo. In spite of a "Force Act," passed in January, 1809, increasing the bonds required, and permitting officials without warrant to seize any goods which they suspected were bound for exportation, evasion went on and protests became louder. The legislatures of the New England states, in phrases reminiscent of the Virginia and Kentucky Resolutions, talked of interposing state power for the protection of their interests. John Randolph and his friends kept up their opposition. Jefferson could not stem the tide. A few days before he left office, he signed a bill for the repeal of the embargo. James Madison took over with a clean slate on which to write his own program.

The new administration began with what seemed to be a diplomatic triumph. David Erskine, the British resident minister in Washington, suddenly informed the new President that the British officials would withdraw the Orders in Council if the United States would, at the same time, lift all her commercial interdicts from England and allow England to enforce nonintercourse with France. To this Madison readily agreed and on June 10, 1809, issued a proclamation renewing trade with Great Britain. This proved, however, to be only a temporary pause before the storm. In a few months Madison was forced to order commercial nonintercourse again with both England and France. This was repealed early in 1810 and an offer of exclusive trade made to whichever country would repeal its restrictions. Even that was to prove futile.

SELECTED BIBLIOGRAPHY

MERLE CURTI, *The Growth of American Thought*; RALPH GABRIEL, *The Course of American Democratic Thought*; V. L. PARRINGTON, *Main Currents in American Thought*, Vol. 2, extremely valuable studies of the intellectual currents; TALBOT HAMLIN, *Greek Revival Architecture in America*, which contains fine illustrations; BEATRICE S. RAVENEL, *Architects of Charleston*; J. T. FLEXNER, *America's Old Masters*; FISK KIMBALL, *Thomas Jefferson: Architect*; VAN WYCK BROOKS, *The Flowering of New England*, important works on the cultural, artistic, and literary developments.

JAMES TRUSLOW ADAMS, *New England in the Republic, 1776–1850*; EDWARD CHANNING, *History of the United States*, Vol. IV; ROBERT G. ALBION, *The Rise of the New York Port*; AVERY CRAVEN, *Soil Exhaustion—in Virginia and Maryland*, throw light on significant economic and political changes.

ANN C. CLAUDER, *American Commerce as Affected by the Wars of the French Revolution and Napoleon, 1793–1812*; W. F. GALPIN, *The Grain Supply of England during the Napoleonic Period*; W. W. JENNINGS, *The American Embargo*, deal with the diplomatic events.

H. S. COMMAGER (Ed.), *Documents of American History*, pp. 198–205, contains source material.

XI

The War of 1812

BACKGROUND OF THE WAR

EHIND THE declaration of war, which came in 1812, was more than the immediate irritations caused by England's refusal to alter her rules or to stop impressment. These things had only hastened the development of attitudes and feelings which growth and expansion and accomplishment had already promoted. The United States was becoming a nation in outlook and temper, as well as in material ways. Patriotism now reinforced resentment of injuries and snubs. Respect for American rights meant more than just allowing a chance for profits. On the score of material damage, there was as much reason for war with France as with England. Napoleon's withdrawal of decrees had never gone beyond words, and Madison's efforts to believe that they did were naïve to say the least. Yet the drift to war with England had been sure and steady, even though logic and interest both were against it. Nationalism required it; tradition justified it; the location of Canada and the presence of British ships made it practical.

The larger factor in this drift was the rise of the West to greater political influence and to a larger part in determining national policies. Men from that section took the lead in declaring war. Always a bit aggressive and a bit resentful of those in more sheltered places, they had, in the last few years, become increasingly disturbed. For a time after Wayne's victory over the Indians in the Northwest (1794), the cession of land to settlers had gone steadily forward. Indiana, Michigan, and Illinois had all become territories by 1809. Under the leadership of William Henry Harrison, governor of Indiana Territory and superintendent of Indian affairs in that area, the Indians had seemingly ceased to be a barrier to the white man's advance. Then something happened. An Indian chieftain by the name of Tecumseh began a move to organize all the tribes east of the Mississippi River into a strong confederacy to resist further land cessions and to restore and preserve Indian strength. With the aid of his brother, the Prophet, he induced his people to give up intoxicating liquor and to reduce relations with white men to those of trade alone.

216

He even began a new settlement at the point where Tippecanoe Creek empties into the Wabash.

Governor Harrison answered these moves by the old trick of rounding up a few renegade Indians and signing a treaty with them for the cession of most of Tecumseh's hunting grounds and for a new boundary line within fifty miles of his Tippecanoe village. Tecumseh rightly declared the treaty illegal and increased his efforts at organizing the tribes. Harrison, in November, 1811, collected a force of some eleven hundred men and marched up the Wabash, where the Indians, in spite of the Prophet's efforts to keep peace, attacked and were repulsed after killing or wounding sixty-eight of Harrison's men.

Western men called it an Indian massacre and convinced themselves that the British in Canada were behind the whole affair. The Indians were only "hired assassins." The British were the real murderers. The Kentucky *Reporter* declared:

The war on the Wabash is purely British. The British scalping knife has filled many habitations both in this state as well as in the Indiana Territory with widows and orphans. This is what comes of dignified "moderation." On both land and sea Britain with impunity violates sacred personal rights. The crisis in the West does not affect ships and cargoes, or *"British agents or importing merchants"* or *"British callicoes or bags of coffee"* but something "ten thousand times more valuable. . . . *The lives* of the women and *children on the frontiers* are at stake, and the settlement of the western territories is deeply involved."

"The cause of the impressed seamen and the LIVES and wounds of hundreds of American FARMERS" were one and the same. Both blows proceeded "from one common source—the English cabinet." War was the only remedy! Canada must be conquered!

Another factor, almost as important as Indians and land in producing hatred of England, was the matter of markets. When men went to the West, they were usually forced to return to a more or less primitive way of living, from which they escaped only when they produced a surplus of some kind and found a profitable market for it. Thus markets determined the speed with which progress could be made and the comforts and luxuries of older regions secured. Next to land itself a profitable market was the object of greatest desire. Also, the need of markets was a source of special bitterness against outsiders because it represented a great degree of dependence upon them.

Markets in the Northwest had never been entirely satisfactory. Until the purchase of Louisiana there had been constant trouble because of uncertainty regarding the navigation of the Mississippi. After that time markets had not expanded as rapidly as population, and, in spite of the effort to reach out through New Orleans and the Gulf for a share in the neutral trade of the period, hopes were never quite realized. A commercial situation which, in 1802, one Kentucky paper said could not "be worse than it is at present" did become worse in the next few years. With only two short periods of improvement, one in 1805 and one in 1809, conditions remained bad to the opening of the War of 1812. Prices of Western produce in New Orleans dropped steadily, while the prices of imported goods to be purchased there remained unaltered or increased. A state of constant depression settled down upon the whole region served by the Mississippi River and its tributaries. Provisions, hemp, tobacco, and cotton, all became a drug on the market.

For this depression blame was quickly lodged against England. "The Farmer who is complaining of the low price of Cotton, of Tobacco, of any other produce cannot now be deceived of the real cause," wrote a Western editor. ". . . [he] will see clearly that the orders in council prohibiting and interrupting all commerce to the continent is the only cause for his embarrassments." "The dispute between us and the belligerents is not about the carrying trade," said Senator Pope of Kentucky, "but whether we shall be permitted to carry our surplus produce to foreign markets. . . . The necessity . . . of restricting the British orders and forcing our way to those markets where there is a demand for the article, must be evident to everyone who will consider the subject."

A war for markets was demanded—a war "to procure a market for our tobacco, flour and cotton," said the Kentucky *Reporter*. "Today we are asserting our right to export our cotton, tobacco and other domestic produce to market," said Henry Clay. Whereupon Eastern men accused Western people of being "willing to plunge our country into war for . . . base and precarious motives." John C. Calhoun was quick to refute the charge with the assertion that Western men saw "in the low price of produce the hand of foreign injustice"—and that they were "not prepared for the colonial state to which again that Power [Great Britain] is endeavoring to reduce them."

The Southwest was somewhat less excited than the Northwest. Yet its people too shared the desire for markets, especially markets for cotton, and they wanted to drive the Spaniards out of Florida. They were pleased when Madison, in 1810, ordered the governor of Louisiana to extend his control over that portion of Spanish territory adjacent to the Mississippi known as West Florida, but they wanted East Florida as well. American control there would check the harboring of runaway slaves and the attacks of hostile Indian tribes. The people of the Southwest too, as "expansionists," were ready for war.

THE YOUNG "WAR HAWKS"

This was the situation when the Congressional elections of 1810–1811 brought a new group to the fore. Nearly half the members of the preceding Congress failed of re-election. Younger men were sent in their places. Among them were John C. Calhoun, Langdon Cheves, and William Lowndes from South Carolina; Richard Johnson and Henry Clay from Kentucky; Felix Grundy from Tennessee; and John Harper from New Hampshire. The youngest of these was twenty-nine; the oldest, thirty-four. Josiah Quincy called them "young politicians, half hatched, the shell still on their heads, and their pin feathers not yet shed." Yet they knew what they wanted, and they lost no time in getting at it. When Congress assembled on November 4, 1811, these "young politicians" quickly elected Henry Clay as Speaker—Clay, who had written in August, "I look upon war with Great Britain as inevitable," and who was a member of the House that day for the first time. Then they began to make speeches.

During the next weeks they flaunted their patriotism, denounced England, and talked of conquest. Madison's message of November 5 spoke of the "tramping on rights which no independent nation can relinquish," and expressed the hope that Congress would feel the duty of putting the country "into an armour and an attitude demanded by the crisis." The Committee on Foreign Relations, under the chairmanship of young Peter Porter of upper New York, answered with a report which recommended the strengthening of the army by the addition of ten thousand regulars and fifty thousand volunteers, arming merchantmen, and putting warships into fighting condition. It concluded with these words:

> To wrongs so daring in their character, and so disgraceful in their execution it is impossible that the people of the United States should remain indifferent. We must now tamely and quietly submit, or we must resist by those means which God has placed within our reach. . . . We have bourne with injury until forbearance has ceased to be a virtue.

In the debates on these proposals Grundy, Johnson, Calhoun, and Clay urged the United States to defend her rights, protect her seamen, secure her territory, and force markets for her produce. "Which shall we do," asked Calhoun, "abandon or defend our own commercial and maritime rights, and the personal liberties of our citizens employed in exercising them?" "These rights are vitally attacked," he added, "and war is the only means of redress." Clay was equally emphatic. England's actions were born of jealousy. Her tyranny could "never be arrested by submission." We must carry the war to her borders. Canada was within our reach. "I am not for stopping at Quebec," he said, "but I would take the whole continent."

John Randolph of Roanoke, "brilliant to the limits of sanity" and bitter foe of both war and the administration, led the opposition. He talked about "agrarian cupidity" and the "scuffle and scramble for plunder." He dubbed the young leaders "War Hawks" and charged that "the cry 'Canada! Canada! Canada!' ran through their speeches like the monotonous call of the whip-poor-will." He warned them that the acquisition of Canada would so increase the power of the North as to force the slave states to secede. He accused them of being "bound to France as Sinbad the sailor was bound to the putrifying corpse of his deceased wife." He pointed out the folly of rushing into a war for which the nation was totally unprepared.

New England Federalists disliked the idea of war with England as much as did John Randolph. They saw in the rash acts of the young Republicans, however, a chance to discredit the party and sometimes gave assistance to war measures with that in mind. They were confident always that Madison would not permit affairs to drift into actual fighting. But they kept the threat of secession handy in case their interests were too seriously menaced. When Madison took over West Florida, Josiah Quincy of Boston openly declared that if Louisiana were admitted to the Union as part of Clay's "new United States," New Englanders would withdraw "amicably if they can, violently if they must." Quincy was now as willing to act if commercial interests were sacrificed. Boston papers, in like vein, were again talking of "*an eternal separation* between the northern states and the nabobs of the South."

Quincy and Pickering meanwhile were manifesting considerably more friendship for British officials than for administration leaders. Americans abroad reported that agitation for the repeal of the Orders in Council was constantly checked by reports of division and internal weakness coming from Federalist sources. What this might mean was revealed on March 9 when President Madison laid before Congress the instructions and dispatches of one Captain Henry, who had been sent to Boston as a secret agent by the governor of Canada "for the purpose of bringing about resistance to the laws, and eventually, in concert with British force, of destroying the Union and forming the eastern portion thereof into a political connexion with Great Britain."

THE DRIFT TO WAR

Under such conditions action on war measures in Congress was discouragingly slow. Not until January, 1812, was a bill to increase the army to twenty-five thousand men passed. Another month went by before the President was authorized to secure fifty thousand volunteers. The effort to vote an appropriation of seven and a half million dollars for a navy of twenty frigates and twelve ships of the line was hopelessly beaten. Men from the interior were not interested in defending the seacoast. They distrusted, as one of them said, all water animals. And what was more alarming was the reluctance of Congress to pass the internal-revenue measures which Gallatin recommended and the refusal to recharter the National Bank, which was now allowed to wind up its business and close its doors.

Yet the drift was unmistakably toward an early declaration of war. Madison was reluctant to commit himself and his country, but the pressure was becoming too strong to be resisted. As one editor put it, the President either had to secure an "honorable peace" or begin hostilities. His almost unanimous renomination by a Congressional caucus on May 18 seemed to indicate that he had at last yielded to the advocates of war. His message of June 1 removed all doubt. It opened with a clearcut recital of wrongs suffered because of impressment and the violation of neutral rights and closed by leaving to Congress the question whether we should "continue passive under these progressive usurpations and these accumulating wrongs" or should oppose "force to force" in defense of national rights, allowing the issue to rest "in the hands of the Almighty Disposer of Events." On June 18 Congress took the latter course in a declaration of war. It mattered little that twenty-four hours earlier Britain had abandoned her Orders in Council.

For the war thus declared the United States was pitifully unprepared. The regular army was neither well organized nor well equipped. Its original ten regiments, with half-filled ranks, were scattered over a vast territory on garrison duty. Its officers were old and inefficient. Congress had authorized new enlistments, but the number of men that responded was small. In June the number was less than that of regular recruits. The situation in regard to the state militia was as bad. The President had been given permission to call out one hundred thousand men, but some states hesitated, and no one knew whether such troops would serve beyond the frontier. Even in states like Kentucky and Tennessee, where the war was popular, the militia showed a decided tendency to fight when and as they pleased. With far-flung borders to defend, both on the Canadian side and along the seacoast, and with few roads, none of which were located advantageously for present purposes, the military tasks were, indeed, stupendous.

Added to material difficulties was the solemn fact that many Americans doubted the wisdom and justice of the war. Was not England, by fighting Napoleon, serving the interests of all mankind? Had the drive for war come from New England, whose ships and sailors were supposed to be the real sufferers from England's policies? Had France really withdrawn her measures, and was she any less than England the enemy of neutral rights? Men like John Marshall thought not. "The declaration of war," he said, "has appeared to me to be one of those portentous acts which ought to concentrate on itself the effort of all those who can take an active part in rescuing their country from the ruin it threatens." Robert Smith, Madison's first Secretary of State, actually issued a public address against the war. There was enough opposition in Baltimore to incite a mob against those advocating war, one of whom was the father of Robert E. Lee. Flags hung at half-mast in New England. Congressmen who voted for war were hissed in Boston, and one from Plymouth was seized by a crowd and "kicked through the town." The Massachusetts House of Representatives urged the formation of a peace party throughout the country and suggested that "there be no volunteers except for defensive war." "Let the sound of your disapprobation of this war be loud and deep," it advised. This was "Mr. Madison's war," and responsibility for its conduct rested with him.

BEGINNING OF MILITARY ACTION

It was against such a background that the War of 1812 began. Canada was the obvious point of attack, and its conquest seemed to the young "War Hawks" an easy matter. The plan was for William Hull, governor of Michigan Territory, to move on Detroit; for Major General Henry Dearborn to drive along Lake Champlain toward Montreal; and for Stephen Van Rensselaer, with a force largely composed of New York militiamen, to strike from Fort Niagara, near the eastern end of Lake Erie. The Canadians, with only four or five thousand regulars and with

The War of 1812

not more than one tenth as many militiamen as the United States had enrolled, were not expected to offer serious resistance. Help from England was out of the question; she was too deeply engaged with Napoleon on the Spanish peninsula. Indian support might be counted on, but how much of an advantage that might be was something of a question.

A week before the declaration of war Hull was ordered forward with some fifteen hundred men for the purpose of strengthening Detroit and controlling the upper lakes. He was still ignorant of the fact that war had been declared when he reached Detroit. General Isaac Brock, the British commander who opposed him, not only was a man of energy and ability, but had the advantage of knowing that a state of war existed. He had learned this from the agents of John Jacob Astor, who had been given advance information in order that they might secure fur-trading property from capture. Upon hearing that the British commander at Sault Ste. Marie had forced the American garrison at Michilimackinac to surrender and that this event had brought Tecumseh's confederacy to the British side, Brock moved quickly to Detroit, captured Hull's baggage, containing his plans of campaign, and demanded the surrender of all the American forces. He hinted in his note that he might have difficulty in controlling the Indians under his command if open fighting developed. The threat of massacre had the desired effect. Hull surrendered without striking a blow. The first effort at the invasion that was to put Canada completely in our hands was over. With the surrender of Fort Dearborn on Lake Michigan, on August 15, 1812, the military frontier in the Northwest was pushed back to the line of the Wabash and Maumee valleys. Hull, who was largely responsible for this disaster, was court-martialed and ordered to be shot; but President Madison, remembering his services in the Revolution, granted him a pardon.

Meanwhile Major General Dearborn, in charge of the operations against Montreal, was frittering away his time on the coast defenses of Massachusetts and doing nothing about his main job. That was why Brock had been able to concentrate all his forces against Hull at Detroit. In early August, Dearborn did request Major General Stephen Van Rensselaer of the New York militia to take command at Fort Niagara, but quickly nullified the benefits of this action by agreeing to an armistice proposed by an agent sent from the Canadian government in an abortive effort to end hostilities because the Orders in Council had been withdrawn. Even before the peace efforts were shown to be hopeless, Brock was back at Fort George with Hull's army as captives and with plans for aggression in that area.

It was, therefore, not until the middle of October that the Americans under Van Rensselaer, in the Fort Niagara sector, were ready for action. On the morning of the thirteenth a body of troops was ferried across the Niagara River for an attack on Queenston. In the first action Van Rensselaer was wounded, but a small body of regulars under Captain John Wool seized the heights above the river, repulsed a strong counterattack, in which General Brock was killed, and might have won a brilliant victory had they received reinforcements. The New York militia, however, on the opposite bank, stood by their constitutional rights, which exempted them from serving outside the United States, and watched their gallant comrades, slowly enveloped by fresh reserves, driven back to the water's edge to die or surrender.

Van Rensselaer immediately resigned his command, and Brigadier General Alexander Smyth of the regular army, who had done little but quarrel with him up to this point, was placed in command. Smyth's contribution consisted of a few bombastic proclamations about what he intended to do to "the ruffian power of the British king" and then a decision to go into winter quarters. His troops were delighted and celebrated by firing their guns in all directions, particularly toward the general's tent. Congressman Peter Porter publicly accused Smyth of cowardice. The general immediately challenged him to a duel, which was dramatically staged after the seconds had removed the balls from the pistols. That ended Smyth.

To complete the fiasco, General Dearborn, who had collected a force larger than the forces of both Hull and Smyth combined, at Plattsburg on Lake Champlain, marched out on November 19 to the Canadian border, twenty miles away. There his militia refused to cross, and he marched back again. That should have been his end, but Madison had no one to put in his place. Dearborn therefore continued his incompetent course for a few months longer.

THE WAR ON THE SEA

In sharp contrast to the dismal story of failure on the Canadian front was that of American exploits on the sea. In 1812 the navy consisted of sixteen seagoing vessels, ranging from heavy frigates carrying forty-four guns to small brigs carrying only twelve or fourteen. Three fourths of them were as good as any ships in the world—heavily timbered and planked, "yet with such fine, clean lines under water that they could outsail almost anything that floated." Their commanders, moreover, were seasoned veterans of the wars with Tripoli and France. They accepted with tough pride the slur of a British paper which referred to our navy as a "few fir-built frigates, manned by a handful of bastards and outlaws." In spite of the fact that only a few ships were actually ready for sea and that the British navy consisted of two thousand or more ships, at least a hundred of them assigned to transatlantic duty, the men were eager for a chance to test their mettle against an old foe.

Events of the next few months justified their confidence. Only three days after his uncle had surrendered at Detroit, young Isaac Hull, captain of the frigate *Constitution*, met the long-hated British brig *Guerrière* in the North Atlantic and in a stirring battle, lasting less than half an hour, left her, as Hull himself reported, "without a spar standing, and the

Ewing Galloway

"Old Ironsides" Today
in the Boston Navy Yard

New England Mutual Life Insurance Company, Boston

The Frigate Constitution
Is Launched at Boston, 1797

MURAL PAINTING BY CHARLES HOFFBAUER

hull cut to pieces in such a manner as to make it difficult to keep her above water." Then, in October, the eighteen-gun sloop *Wasp* captured the equal-sized *Frolic*, and the *United States*, under Captain Stephen Decatur, outfought the *Macedonian* off the Azores and brought her a prize into an American port. In December the *Constitution*, this time commanded by Captain Bainbridge, so completely wrecked the *Java* off the coast of South America that she could not be got to port and had to be blown up. American privateers, meanwhile, had taken more than five hundred British merchantmen in the first seven months and were rapidly turning British surprise into consternation.

Such unbroken success could not be expected to continue. In February, 1813, the American ship *Hornet*, under Captain James Lawrence, did sink the *Peacock* in short order, but in June the British frigate *Shannon* more than equaled the score by decisively defeating the *Chesapeake*, to which Lawrence had been transferred. Not only was his ship destroyed, but the brave captain lost his life. His dying words, "Don't give up the ship," became at once an American battle cry. Then slowly the numerically superior British fleet began to effect a stringent blockade of the American coast south of New London, the region above that point being exempted because of its well-known hostility to the war. The frigates *United States*, *Macedonian*, *Constellation*, and *Adams*, together with the *Hornet* and other lesser ships, were driven into American ports and penned there for the duration. The *Essex* and the *President*, which remained at sea, were both destroyed in the course of the next year. Only the *Constitution* and a few other hardy vessels were able to continue the fight, and American exports from New York fell from $12,000,000 in 1811 to $200,000 in 1814, and those from Virginia dropped from $4,800,000 to $17,500. Britain was again complete mistress of the sea.

American naval exploits, however, had contributed something vital to the warp and woof of the national fabric. The victory of the *Constitution* over the *Guerrière*, says Henry Adams, "raised the United States in one half hour to the rank of a first-class Power in the world." In spite of all that had happened along the Canadian border, the nation's seamen were showing the world that Americans could fight. As victory followed victory, the startled reaction of the British press and the even greater chagrin of British naval officials added to the satisfaction. It was indeed pleasant to hear George Canning tell the British Parliament that "it cannot be too deeply felt that the sacred spell of the invincibility of the British navy was broken by those unfortunate captures," or to have the London *Times* tell its readers that "anyone who had predicted such a result of an American war this time last year would have been treated as a madman or a traitor." Even New Englanders were elated. They did not like the war, but the sea was so much their own province that they could not be indifferent to skill and courage in men who handled ships. Pride in native accomplishment was a rather good substitute for enthusiasm whipped up about a war that many substantial citizens thought unnecessary.

Neither defeat nor victory, however, seemed to alter the general political situation. In the Presidential election of 1812 Madison, as the avowed advocate of war and with the support of the "War Hawks," defeated his opponent, De Witt Clinton, with 128 electoral votes to 89. Vermont alone of the New England states supported Madison, and the middle states, including Maryland and Delaware, showed a decided preference for Clinton. The South and West thus were the strongholds of both Madison and the war spirit. The Federalists, however, doubled their number of representatives in Congress, where the problem of financing the war had to be met. With widespread hostility to internal taxation and with revenue from tariff declining rapidly under the British blockade, this was no easy matter. At first, tariff rates were doubled; then duties were revised on sugar, salt, wines, liquors, carriages, and auction sales. At last, a direct tax of three million dollars was apportioned among the states, and even a stamp tax was imposed on notes and bills of exchange. Returns, however, were never more than a third enough to meet expenses, and resort to loans was necessary. All of which gave the opponents of war a chance to resist and to indulge in that most satisfying of all human refrains, "I told you so." New England, with more than half the specie of the nation in her banks, subscribed for less than one million of the eleven-million-dollar loan of 1812, and during the entire struggle paid into the Treasury less than three millions of its total receipts of forty-one millions.

THE WAR ON THE GREAT LAKES

The year 1813 saw the effort to invade Canada renewed. Events of the preceding year had shown the necessity of controlling the Great Lakes if success was to be expected. Consequently, during the winter and spring of 1812–1813, a small fleet of sturdy vessels was constructed and Captain Oliver Hazard Perry sent to equip them and to take command. While this was being done, William Henry Harrison, governor of Indiana Territory, was commissioned brigadier general and put in charge of a greatly enlarged northwestern army. Bad weather and supply difficulties hindered his plans for a winter campaign, and in January a detachment of troops from his army, foolishly pushing ahead to Frenchtown on the Raisin River, was thoroughly defeated, five hundred of its men captured, and its wounded massacred in cold blood by the Indian allies of the British general, Henry Proctor. It was a miserable start, and Harrison did not improve on it in the months which followed. He retreated to Fort Meigs on the Maumee, but did little to better the efficiency of his army. Only through the excellent work of one of his subordinates was the fort put in condition to withstand the attack which Proctor made in April. Harrison was just as inefficient after he moved his headquarters to the upper Sandusky and to Cleveland, and was saved from ruin when Proctor moved against that area only by the gallant defense of Fort Stephenson by the young Kentuckian, Major Croghan.

This was the situation when Captain Perry moved his battle fleet out across the bar which guarded the harbor where it had been building and sailed up Lake Erie to a point off the mouth of the Sandusky River. Short of seamen, he borrowed a hundred Kentuckians from Harrison's army and awaited the arrival of the British fleet under Captain Barclay, who had served with Nelson at Trafalgar and who until now had dominated the lake and made military success possible to the British. The battle began a few minutes before noon on September 10 and lasted three hours. The American advantage in heavier guns was in part counteracted by the close-in character of the fighting, and Perry's flagship, the *Lawrence*, was at length so riddled that it had to be abandoned. Undaunted, the young captain went over her side into a small boat and was rowed, under the heavy fire of British guns, to the *Niagara*, which now closed in to complete the destruction of the English ships. Few deeds of greater daring grace the pages of naval history. A commander with such spirit could not be denied victory. One by one the British ships struck their colors, and the battle ended. With real justification Perry penned his famous message to General Harrison: "We have met the enemy and they are ours: two ships, two brigs, one schooner, and one sloop."

Perry's victory left the British positions at Detroit and Malden so exposed that General Proctor was forced to abandon them and fall back toward the eastern end of the lake. His Indian allies were disgusted. Tecumseh likened him to a fat dog that had carried its tail erect, but now dropped its tail between its legs and ran in fright. Many of Proctor's Indians deserted, and Harrison, reinforced by Kentucky volunteers, fell upon the retreating army at Moravian Town on the Thames and gave it a thorough beating. Proctor's baggage, artillery, small arms, and stores were captured, and the general himself barely escaped. Tecumseh was among the killed. His confederation was broken up, and most of the tribes submitted. All that Hull had lost was thus regained.

While these events had been taking place around Detroit, affairs on the Niagara front had remained nearly at a standstill. In April, Dearborn led a raiding party against York (later Toronto), and his troops, incensed by the explosion of a powder magazine which killed General Pike and some three hundred men, burned two brick parliament buildings and the governor's residence. Another raiding expedition, at the end of the year, burned Newark and much of Queenston. The chief results of these moves were to give the British, the next year, an excuse for burning United States government buildings in Washington, and for permitting Indian allies to pillage the American countryside when the British captured Fort Niagara in late December. Meanwhile James Wilkinson and Wade Hampton, who had replaced Van Rensselaer and Smyth, had spent the summer quarreling with each other and now, after each had made a futile advance and a successful retreat, went into winter quarters and soon, with Dearborn, into well-deserved retirement.

The spring of 1814 saw Napoleon defeated in his efforts to conquer Europe and forced to abdicate the French throne. England was now free to provide Canada with an army that could assume the offensive. Her ships were in control of the sea, and her generals planned invasion from Niagara, Lake Champlain, and New Orleans. The Americans, however, were not inclined to sit idly by and wait for British reinforcements to reach America. They had got rid of their most inefficient generals, and young Winfield Scott and General Jacob Brown, the Quaker, had begun to make a real army out of the troops around Niagara. On July 4, with Brown in command and Scott as his subordinate, they pushed across the river and forced the capitulation of Fort Erie. The next day Scott, attempting to stage a belated Independence Day military parade, ran squarely into the British forces advancing against Brown's position and won an unexpected but brilliant victory on the Chippewa River. Brown followed this with an even more spectacular fight when he advanced to Lundy's Lane on July 25. He was forced to retreat in the face of heavy British reinforcements, but the battle had been inconclusive, and Brown had shown greater skill in command than any other American had shown so far in this war. A British invasion from Niagara was thus rendered quite improbable.

When the British blow came in September, it was aimed down Lake Champlain, probably with the idea of cutting New England off from the rest of the country. Sir George Prevost, in command, had more than five times the number of troops with which General Alexander Macomb could oppose him at Plattsburg. He did, however, have to face formidable forts, which the Americans had constructed, and he did believe that it was necessary to gain complete control of the lake before he advanced too far. He therefore delayed while his vastly superior fleet cornered the small American flotilla under Commodore Thomas Macdonough at Plattsburg Bay. On the morning of September 11 the British closed in. At the end of two hours it seemed probable that the American fleet would be destroyed or captured. Then, by a superior handling of his ships, Macdonough turned defeat into victory. The British gunboats at length drew off, and three smaller ships surrendered. Control of the lake belonged to the Americans, and Prevost, with his magnificent army, retreated to Canada without striking a blow. A second line of invasion was thus closed.

WASHINGTON AND NEW ORLEANS

Throughout the summers of 1813 and 1814 the British navy had ranged along the Atlantic coast at will and had, on a few occasions, actually occupied a port or shelled some object on land. As part of their 1814 invasion plans the British now sent General Robert Ross with a body of troops to co-operate with the navy in a series of attacks on the Chesapeake Bay region. The object was in part to aid the invasions from Canada and in part to retaliate for the destruction of property committed by the Americans in some of their forays against Canada. To meet this attack a fleet of American gunboats was stationed in the bay and a feverish call sent out for militia. Only about seven thousand responded, and these were stationed at the town of Bladensburg, on the East Branch of the Potomac River, for the purpose of protecting the city of Washington. Neither boats nor troops proved effective. The gunboats fled up the Patuxent River ahead of the British fleet, and the militia at Bladensburg, "innocent of war and unmindful of its method," scattered before the British regulars, who, for five days, had marched leisurely along country roads where a handful of men with axes and guns might have held them up indefinitely. On the evening of August 24 the British entered Washington, and burned the Capitol and other public buildings, while the Americans themselves destroyed the Navy Yard and the vessels there.

A second day of destruction was well under way when a violent storm and drenching rain weakened the desire for plunder and caused the British to fall back for better contact with their fleet.

Encouraged by easy success, the invaders now turned toward Baltimore. But here the defense on land was better, and the fleet was unable to reduce Fort Henry, which guarded the water approach to the city. A night of bombardment left the Star-Spangled Banner still flying and gave a people their national anthem. The effort to take Baltimore was abandoned; and though the British remained in the bay until October 20, no further raiding took place.

The last British effort at invasion was planned to begin at New Orleans and to result in the conquest of the whole Southwest. During the summer of 1813 the Creek Indians in that general region had been on the warpath. Inspired in part by Tecumseh's efforts and British friendship, they had, in August, stirred the whole Southern frontier by the massacre of some two hundred and fifty persons at Fort Mims in Mississippi Territory, just above Mobile. For revenge and protection a committee of public safety had turned for leadership to Andrew Jackson of Tennessee.

This superbly American man had been born somewhere on the border between North and South Carolina and had come to Tennessee with one of the early immigrant trains. There he had made his way to the top as a lawyer and fighter in the rough-and-tumble frontier town of Nashville. When the request to lead the militia against the Creeks came, he was in bed from a bullet wound in the arm, received in a recent hot-tempered quarrel with Thomas Hart Benton and his brother. Doctors had advised the amputation of the arm. Jackson barely understood. "I'll keep my arm," he said. Then, propped against a pillow, he wrote: "The health of your general is restored. He will command in person."

A few days later he was on his way, his arm in a sling and his face pale and haggard. In the next months, by sheer force of personality, he held his troops together and waged a successful campaign against the Creeks, which culminated in a great victory at Tohopeka in the "horseshoe" bend of the Tallapoosa River. Once, when his militia threatened to return home before new troops had arrived, he planted himself with two small cannon across their path and forced them back into service. On another occasion, when ordered by the governor of Tennessee to return home before his task was done, he bluntly refused to obey. He asked the governor:

And are you my Dear Friend, sitting with yr. arms folded, . . . recommending me to retrograde to please the whims of the populace . . .? Let me tell you it imperiously lies upon both you and me to do our duty regardless of consequences or the opinion of these fireside patriots, those fawning sycophants or cowardly poltroons who . . . would . . . let thousands fall victims to my retrograde.

And for his courage and skill the War Department now made him commander of the Seventh Military District, which embraced Tennessee, Louisiana, and Mississippi Territory.

It was thus clear that when the British began their next invasion of the United States, planned to start at New Orleans late in 1814, they would find the Americans well equipped in leadership. And so it proved. When the British fleet appeared at Pensacola in Spanish East Florida, and began to distribute arms and scarlet jackets to the natives, Jackson did not hesitate. With complete disregard for the supposed neutrality of Spain, he marched against the town and forced its surrender. Whereupon the British fled to their ships and put to sea. He was back at New Orleans some three weeks later, ready to face Sir Edward Pakenham and ten thousand British regulars who had fought under Wellington against Napoleon.

There, in a series of clashes culminating in a great battle on January 8, 1815, this raw frontier leader, with as strange an army as ever assembled on a battlefield, won one of the most astonishing victories in history. Behind the "mud ramparts of Rodrigues Canal," American riflemen intently awaited the charge of compact British columns with orders to pick their targets and "to aim above the cross plates." With the kind of marksmanship which made life for a Kentucky squirrel unsafe at two hundred yards, they reduced columns to skirmish lines and left the cane stubbles red with British coats. "Never before," related an English lieutenant, "had British veterans quailed. But it would be silly to deny that they did so now. . . . That leaden torrent no man on earth could face. I had seen battle-fields in Spain and in the East . . . but nowhere . . . such a scene" as this. The British lost nearly two thousand men, the Americans only thirteen!

THE HARTFORD CONVENTION AND PEACE

New Orleans ended the fighting. Both sides had had quite enough of it. Opposition in New England had already reached the point of open resistance. From the very beginning of the war, enlistment had been discouraged there, and when asked to place their militia at the service of the national government, Massachusetts, Connecticut, and Rhode Island had refused on constitutional grounds. Individuals had gone even farther. In August, 1814, Sir George Prevost wrote his superiors in England, "Two-thirds of the army in Canada are at this moment eating beef provided by the American contractors, drawn principally from the states of Vermont and New York; . . . large droves are daily crossing the lines, coming into Lower Canada." Boston papers meanwhile talked of the nation as already "separated" when "one section . . . perseveres in measures fatal to the interests and repugnant to the opinion of another section"—an attitude all the more remarkable in the face of the fact that New England escaped the blockade until the spring of 1814 and as a result received practically all the imports of the nation and most of its specie. In addition, manufacturing in New England had secured a good start, and war conditions had afforded it the very best of protection. Yet communications in the newspapers contained such statements as "The federal constitution is nothing more than a treaty between independent sovereignties"; "It was by the assent of nine states, considered as such, that it became a compact"; "If they violate the terms of that compact, its validity is annihilated, and the parties to it are released from their obligations."

The real trouble evidently seemed to be that Virginia was furnishing the nation with its Presidents and that the South, with the co-operation of an expanding West, had purchased Louisiana, destroyed the National Bank, and declared the War of 1812. What was even worse, these sections seemed destined to continue their control indefinitely because of greater growth and expansion. The Federalists were doomed. Action was demanded now or never.

The legislature of Massachusetts took the lead. On October 17, 1814, it summoned a New England Convention to meet at Hartford for the purpose of discussing "public grievances and concerns" and "defense against the enemy," and to take steps, if deemed necessary, "to revise the Constitution" of the United States. The Convention assembled on December 15, 1814, with delegates principally from Massachusetts, Connecticut, and Rhode Island. A division of opinion quickly developed, with one group, under Harrison Gray Otis, wishing only to improve conditions and win concessions, and another, under Timothy Pickering, who wanted a new Federal Constitution, with clauses protecting New England interests, and a separate peace with England if this was rejected. The result was a compromise report and resolutions. In these there was talk of "the right and duty of a state to interpose its authority" in case of "deliberate, dangerous, and palpable infractions of the Constitution," and a series of constitutional amendments was demanded, which would put an end to the three-fifths rule in apportioning Representatives; require a two-thirds vote in both houses of Congress to admit a new state, declare war, or interdict trade with any foreign country; limit all embargoes to sixty days; and prohibit a President from serving a second term or being elected from the same state two terms in succession. Virginia, the South, and the West could, by these restrictions, be held in check. This much done, Massachusetts and Connecticut sent commissioners off to Washington to make arrangements with the national government for the separate defense of New England interests. On the way they learned of Jackson's victory.

A better reason why the battle of New Orleans marked the end of hostilities was the fact that, even before it was fought, American and British representatives, on the other side of the Atlantic, had come to peace terms. This was not surprising. Almost from the day that war was declared there had been talk of peace and some efforts to make peace on both sides. Once, in October, 1813, the Czar of Russia attempted the role of mediator, and Madison went so far as to appoint commissioners to negotiate under his proposals. England refused on this occasion, but offered to negotiate directly with the United States. Thus peace was always a possibility. To be sure, England's official interest usually varied in warmth according to the success or failure of her war efforts on the Continent, but some group was always eager for peace. The summer of 1814 provided enough uncertainty in European affairs to warrant Lord Castlereagh in sending commissioners to meet with the American representatives, three of whom, Gallatin, Bayard, and John Quincy Adams, had been sent at the time of the Czar's proposal, and two of whom, Henry Clay and Jonathan Russell, had been recently appointed. The meeting place was Ghent in Belgium. Anticipating military success in 1814, England probably had no notion of bringing anything to a conclusion before the advantage was all on her side. The instructions to her commissioners were in line with that idea. They were to limit or reject all discussion of impressment; to demand the prohibition of American forts on the Great Lakes; to ask for the cession of lands in Maine and upper New York which would connect Halifax and Quebec and give control of the St. Lawrence basin; to insist on the formation of an Indian state in the Northwest under British protection, the right of British navigation of the Mississippi, and the exclusion of Americans from the Newfoundland and Labrador fisheries. American instructions, of course, asked for the end of impressment, indemnity for prizes illegally taken, the cession of Upper Canada, and the exclusion of Britain from the Great Lakes.

With demands so conflicting, satisfactory negotiations seemed hopeless. John Quincy Adams was justly agitated over the British demands in regard to fisheries; when the proposal for an Indian state was made, he was ready to break off negotiations and go home. Bayard was of the same mind. American successes on the Canadian border, however, and the failure of British troops to win any major success in the Chesapeake region softened the British attitude, and even the Duke of Wellington, who had been asked to take command in America, assured British officials that he could accomplish little without control of the Lakes—a thing which he believed could not now be regained. Heavy taxes at home and troubles at the Congress of Vienna, where European problems were being threshed out, made the British ministry more eager for peace than it had been at first. New instructions to their commissioners and "the extraordinary patience and judgment of Gallatin," who somehow kept a balance between the convivial Henry Clay and the stern, unbending John Quincy Adams, finally made agreement possible. That is, both parties agreed to stop fighting. The Treaty of Ghent, signed on December 24, 1814, conceded nothing. Impressment and blockades were not mentioned. The fisheries and the boundaries were left to future settlement by joint commissions. For the time being things were to stand as they had stood before war began. Both nations were left free to claim victory and to get as much satisfaction out of empty claims as possible. The world was entering a new era, and the peoples in both England and the United States were impatient to be about the more important things ahead.

SELECTED BIBLIOGRAPHY

J. W. Pratt, *The Expansionists of 1812*, a pioneer work in re-evaluating the causes of the war; A. T. Mahan, *Sea Power in Its Relation to the War of 1812* (2 vols.), the best study of naval history; Freemon Cleaves, *Old Tippecanoe*, discusses military events in the West; Henry Adams, *History of the United States*, Vols. VII–IX; C. P. Lucas, *The Canadian War of 1812*, worth-while general studies; F. A. Updike, *Diplomacy of the War of 1812*, the most important monograph.

Among the valuable biographies are Bernard Mayo, *Henry Clay*; C. G. Van Deusen, *The Life of Henry Clay*; Marquis James, *Andrew Jackson: The Border Captain*; S. E. Morison, *The Life and Letters of H. G. Otis*.

H. S. Commager (Ed.), *Documents of American History*, pp. 207–211, and William Wood, *Select British Documents of the Canadian War of 1812*, contain source material.

XII

The Beginning of a New Era

THE WAR of 1812 marks the end of the lingering colonial period in United States history. We had, indeed, fought a second war for American independence. The forces that had led us into that struggle grew out of the constant clash between a lingering European dependence and a growing national consciousness, combined with a new spirit of national self-reliance. In one sense we simply had to fight someone in order to convince both ourselves and the rest of the world that we were a nation with ends of our own to be sought and protected. The war might have been avoided had everyone wanted to avoid it. It might have been fought against France instead of England, or against both of them with equal justice. The important thing, when it was over, was that we had fought in defense of our own rights and interests and had done a fairly creditable job. At least we could remember with pride Lundy's Lane, New Orleans, and many gallant fights on the lakes and the seas. The rest could easily be forgotten, for we had satisfied all our inner demands and proved beyond a doubt that we were free from the apron strings of England and Europe. Now we could go our own way in confidence.

In the period after 1815 the people of the United States turned completely around. Where before they had faced the Atlantic, they now faced westward, toward their own continent. Until now their commerce had been foreign commerce; their major problems had been those of a neutral in European conflicts; their leaders had been those experienced in diplomacy; even their political divisions had been influenced by a preference either for England or for France.

Now the word *commerce* meant, more and more, trade with the interior; the national problems had to do with land, internal improvements, and home markets; the leaders were men who had fought Indians or who had helped the people to get lands and to prosper; political issues were concerned increasingly with domestic problems, and political parties were made up of sectional blocs. As John Randolph said, we became a great land animal dragging its bulky form across a continent toward the setting sun. The "isolationist" period in American history had begun.

The first few years immediately after the signing of the Treaty of Ghent were years in which conflicting forces, old and new, were so evenly balanced that open political conflict ceased. Old interests were weakening; new ones had not yet become articulate. Peace silenced those who had opposed the war; it left those who had fought it without an issue. Furthermore, the national weaknesses revealed by war were apparent to all, and enough of national pride had been awakened by the conflict to give Congress and the President rather wide support in passing legislation to remedy them. A certain kind of harmony and a certain kind of nationalism appeared to characterize the political scene, which enabled later historians to talk about the "era of good feeling" and the "rise of American nationality." Yet a closer view shows that neither phrase accurately describes the situation. It was, in fact, a period of transition rather than one of definite quality. The United States was entering a new era. What actually had happened was that embargoes and war had stimulated manufacturing in New England and had begun to shift the center of her economic life from her harbors to her fall line. What this would ultimately mean to this section and to the other sections of the nation and what shifts it would require in politics, local and national, no one could quite foresee. The rapid spread of cotton to the upland South and the corresponding spread of wheat to the greater Northwest were bringing changes equal in degree to these sections, with as little immediate indication of political consequences. Certain it was, however, that conflict of interests and sections, and rivalry of leaders, were inherent in such developments, regardless of present "good feelings" and "national attitudes." The period was simply one of readjustment, a time of quiet before a storm.

The war itself had done much to end the old order and to hurry on the new. It enabled Clay and Calhoun, Webster and John Quincy Adams, Felix Grundy, William Lowndes, and other young leaders to establish themselves firmly in the places once occupied by the elder statesmen. It made a national reputation for William Henry Harrison and for Andrew Jackson, both of whom would one day reach the highest office in the land, with the support of men whose lands and thoughts they had cleared of Indians. For a generation, political leadership belonged to those who had come to the fore in the War of 1812.

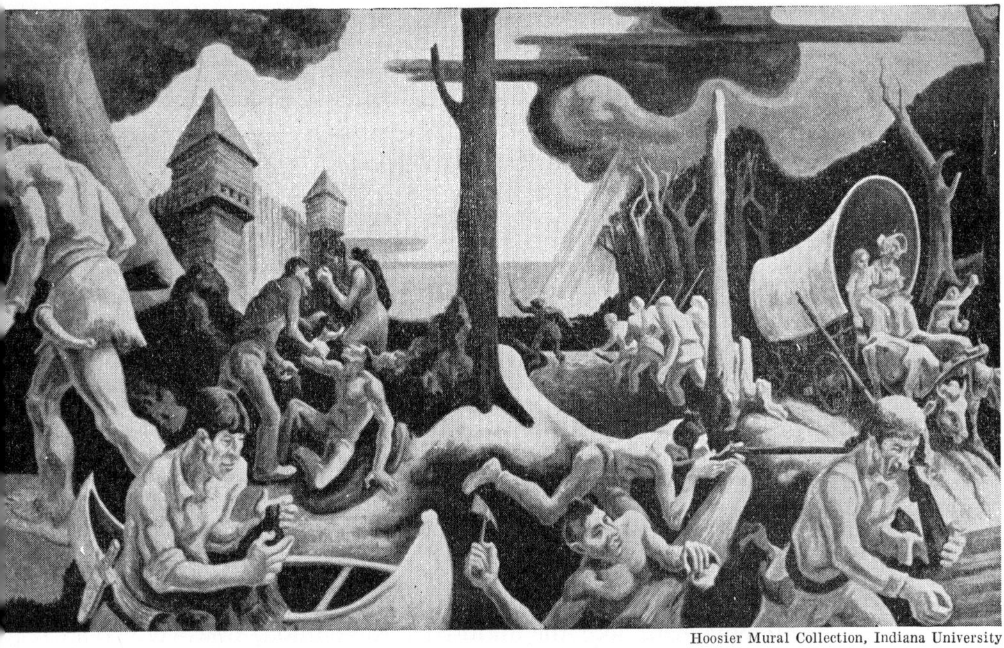

Hoosier Mural Collection, Indiana University

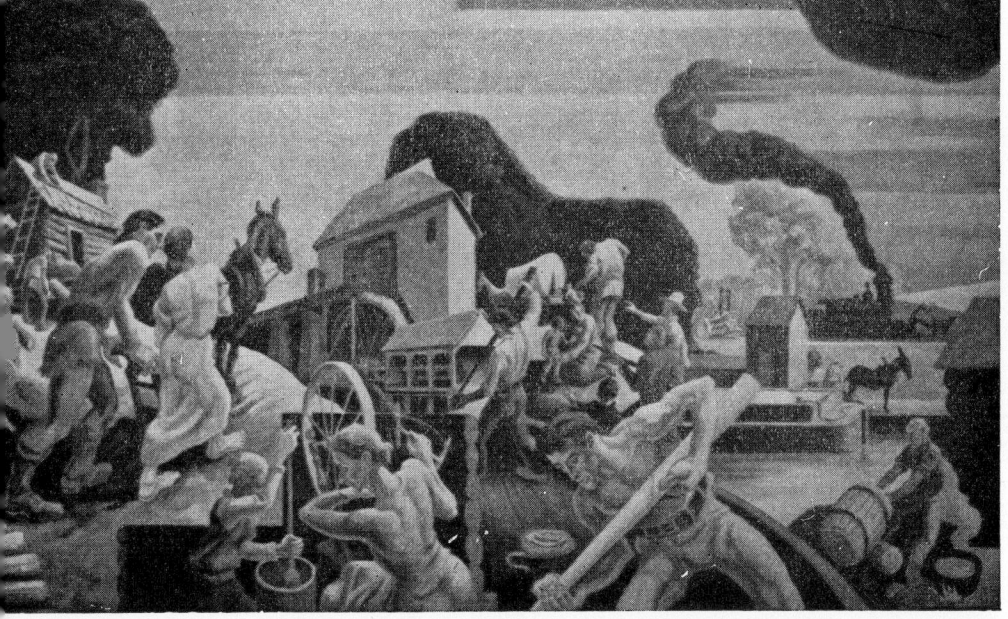

The Struggle for Control of the Old Northwest

Indians, Fur Traders, George Rogers Clark, and Pioneer Settlers Symbolize Waves of the Frontier

PAINTINGS BY THOMAS HART BENTON

The Conquest of the Old Northwest from Log-Cabin, Pioneer-Agriculture, and Home-Manufacturing Days to the Advent of the Railroad Age

Hoosier Mural Collection, Indiana University

THE RISE OF INDUSTRY

The war, with much aid from the embargoes, carried manufacturing in the United States into the factory stage. In the colonial period almost every household had manufactured some of the clothing and furnishings which it required, but restrictive legislation and a natural preference for British goods held back larger developments. During the Revolution such industries as the making of powder and firearms flourished, and household manufactures, especially textiles, greatly increased. Peace, however, brought back English goods and made rapid development impossible. Acts of Parliament prohibiting the exportation of machines or models also interfered and helped to keep the great majority of Americans at the agricultural tasks which Jefferson and his kind thought were "the most beneficial and productive object of human industry."

A great movement like the Industrial Revolution, however, could not be monopolized by England or any other country, and gradually machines began to appear in the United States. In 1789 Samuel Slater, who had worked in an English textile factory, came to New York and soon found his way into the employment of Moses Brown, a Quaker merchant in Pawtucket, Rhode Island. With the aid of a local carpenter and a blacksmith, Slater reproduced from memory some of the machines on which he had worked in England. In a short time, with Brown's financial backing, he had the first successful cotton factory in the United States in operation. With a Negro workman to break the ice about the water wheel on cold winter mornings, his machinery spun the yarn, which was later woven into cloth in the homes of the neighborhood. Here and there in the next five years other spinning machines were devised, and thus the first great "bottleneck" in the textile industry was broken. No longer need the womenfolk of the countryside go about with distaff and spindle, using every spare hour of the day to accumulate the yarn which their hungry looms could consume in so short a time.

But the great opportunities for agriculture and commerce during the Napoleonic wars in Europe kept manufactures at a minimum until restrictive measures cut down outside supplies and weakened other economic efforts. Then, on the foundations already laid, progress was rapid. By 1809 some sixty-two cotton mills were turning 31,000 spindles, a number which one year later had increased to two hundred and sixty-nine mills with 87,000 spindles. Most of these were in southern New England, where some capital, formerly employed in commerce, was being transferred to manufacturing.

Household manufactures, however, more than kept pace with factory developments. In a report to the House of Representatives made by Secretary of the Treasury Albert Gallatin, in 1810, it was stated that probably "two-thirds of the clothing, including hosiery, and of the house and table linen, worn and used by the inhabitants of the United States, who do not reside in cities, is the product of family manufactures." Gallatin estimated the domestic manufactures of iron and steel at from twelve million to fifteen million dollars, and thought that we were producing an excess above domestic needs of wood, leather, soap, candles, flaxseed oil, refined sugar, and coarse earthenware. He might have added that the New England peddler had already begun scattering the domestic surplus of shoes and clocks, tinware and linen, up and down the countryside from New York to Georgia.

The war, of course, brought industrial development to its climax. In 1816 the amount of capital invested in manufacturing in the United States was estimated at one hundred million dollars, of which some forty million dollars was in cotton textiles alone. This industry employed one hundred thousand persons and consumed twenty-seven million pounds of cotton. In one place, at least, a power loom was in operation, and the entire process of converting cotton into cloth was being performed under a single roof. The industry had definitely entered the factory stage and, in so doing, heralded the coming of the Industrial Revolution to the United States, as it had, much earlier, heralded the coming of this great change to Europe.

Peace again threatened to destroy the developments which war had permitted. After 1815 British merchants and manufacturers emptied their overstocked warehouses onto American markets, and Henry Brougham told Parliament that it was "worth while to incur a loss upon the first exportation in order, by a glut, to stifle in the cradle those rising manufactures in the United States which the war had forced into existence contrary to the natural course of things." Importations jumped in value from thirteen millions in 1813 to one hundred and forty-seven millions three years later. Newspapers were crowded with advertisements of British goods for sale, and credit was widely extended to tempt further the purchaser. One by one the weaker mills closed their doors. In the mill district of Rhode Island nearly one hundred and fifty small concerns ceased operations, and only the old Slater mill was able to weather the storm.

The young leaders who were at the head of national affairs, however, were quite unwilling to stand idly by and see American industry wrecked.

Acting on President Madison's recommendation that a tariff should be laid to protect manufactures "whose interests are now at stake," Secretary of the Treasury Dallas drafted a bill which Lowndes of South Carolina introduced into the House. After some alterations, under the sharp prodding of John Randolph, who would "not agree to lay a duty on the cultivator of the soil to encourage exotic manufactures," it was passed in 1816. Under its provisions the duty on woolen and cotton goods was fixed at 25 per cent for a period of three years, after which it should be reduced to 20 per cent. The principle of minimum valuation was applied to cotton goods, whereby all fabrics costing less than twenty-five cents a square yard should be deemed to have cost that amount. The idea was unquestionably that of protection for infant industries.

Support for the bill came from all sections of the nation, and opposition was likewise distributed. Industrialists in both New England and the middle states threw their strength behind it; Southerners, like Lowndes and Calhoun, urged its passage. Calhoun, with a broad national sweep, declared, "Neither agriculture, manufactures, nor commerce, taken separately, is the cause of wealth; it flows from the three combined, and cannot exist without each." He would protect industry for the purpose of securing a balanced national economy independent of foreign sources of supply. He thought that "the industrial system would increase mutual dependence of the parts of the Union and thus promote internal improvements as a consequence of expanding intercourse."

Randolph expressed the attitude of certain planting interests when he declared that the duties bore "on poor men and slave holders," and young Daniel Webster voiced the opinion of commercial groups, both in New England and the middle states, when he insisted that he was unwilling to rear manufactures "in hot beds" or "to push the capital into extensive manufactures faster than the general progress of our wealth and population propels it." He would rue the day when the great mass of American laborers would "immerse themselves in close and unwholesome workshops"; when they would "open their ears in dust, and smoke, and steam, to the perpetual whirl of spools and spindles, and the grating of rasps and saws."

THE BANK AND INTERNAL IMPROVEMENTS

Another thing which the War of 1812 did was to reveal the weaknesses in the national financial structure. It will be remembered that Congress, in 1811, had refused to recharter the old Bank of the United

States. This had resulted in the increase of state banks from eighty-eight in that year to two hundred and forty-six in 1816, and in the export of some seven million dollars of foreign stockholders' funds. The waging of war, of course, greatly increased the demand for credit,—a demand already heavy as a result of the large purchase of public lands under the act of 1800,—and tempted the state banks, now free from the restraints of a national bank, greatly to overexpand their note circulation. Inflation resulted, and by August, 1814, all banks, except those in New England, were forced to suspend specie payment. The situation was desperate. Henry Clay, who had led in the fight against the first Bank of the United States, now confessed his error, and James Madison surmounted "the prejudices of a life time." Both gave their support to a bill which John C. Calhoun, as chairman of the Committee on Currency, introduced for the establishment of a new national bank. As to the question of constitutionality, which Clay had stressed in 1811, Calhoun dismissed it as "a useless consumption of time." Randolph and Webster again opposed. The Bank "would be an engine of irresistible power in the hands of any administration," said Randolph. "It would be in politics and finance what the celebrated proposition of Archimedes was in physics,—a place, the fulcrum, from which at the will of the executive the whole nation could be hurled to destruction." He was anticipating Andrew Jackson by more than a decade.

But opposition was in vain. The bill was passed, and in January, 1817, the Bank began operations. Its capital was thirty-five million dollars, one fifth subscribed by the government, the remainder by individuals, companies, or corporations. Seven millions of this latter amount was to be in gold and silver, the remainder in the funded debt of the United States. The charter was to run for twenty years, and five of the twenty-five directors were to be appointed by the President of the United States. The Bank was to be the depository for government money, and it was permitted to establish branches in different parts of the nation. For these privileges it was to pay a bonus of one million five hundred thousand dollars to the government in three equal installments.

The same forces which favored the re-establishment of a national bank worked for the improvement of transportation. Roads in colonial America had been bad—"worse than any I ever met with elsewhere," said an English traveler. Some improvement had been made in early national days when the various states had chartered companies for the building of turnpikes and authorized the collection of tolls for their use. A further step was taken when the enabling act which admitted Ohio as a state to the Union provided that 5 per cent of the proceeds of the sale of public lands within her borders should be used for the construction of roads to and within the state. This led to the building of the famous Cumberland, or National, Road, which was to run from Maryland westward across Ohio and ultimately to St. Louis. Contracts for its construction were let in 1811, and in 1817 it was opened to traffic as far as Wheeling in western Virginia.

This was an important step not only in rendering the West more accessible and encouraging internal trade, but in developing the stagecoaches and the great freight wagons with which America would continue her way across the whole continent. It cut rates. It furnished a model for other roads in other parts of the country. It helped to bind the Union together.

It was the War of 1812, however, which dramatized the nation's lack of adequate communication facilities. The lack of roads had hindered troop movements and the securing of adequate supplies. Sectional indifference to national dangers and sectional opposition to national effort in the war had revealed the need for easier and cheaper communication between the different parts of the country. Where before the war Gallatin's plan for a great national system of roads and canals (1808) had stirred little interest in Congress and had raised serious questions as to the constitutionality of internal improvements at national expense, now all saw the need for such improvements, and even some Republicans were willing to accept the doctrine of implied powers for that purpose. President Madison, in his message of December 3, 1816, urged the use of existing powers and the enlargement of them for the construction of "a comprehensive system of roads and canals" for the purpose of "drawing more closely together every part of our country by promoting intercourse and improvements and by increasing the share of every part in the common stock of national prosperity." Calhoun would not pause to argue over the question of whether the power to make improvements was already granted or whether "the enlargement of them" would be necessary. "I am no advocate of refined arguments on the constitution," he said. "The instrument was not intended as a thesis for the logician to exercise his ingenuity on. It ought to be construed with plain good sense." Nor were these idle words. Already he had introduced a bill appropriating the bonus of one million five hundred thousand dollars which the Bank of the United States was to pay, together with all future dividends on bank stock held by the government, for the building of roads and canals. Clay gave ardent support to this measure, but Madison, still a bit worried over constitutional powers, vetoed the bill and thus set a precedent which Monroe followed in 1822 by rejecting a measure for the erection of toll gates on the National Road. Randolph said that it was all a question of "whether or not we [are] willing to become one great consolidated nation, or whether we still [have] respect enough for those old, respectable institutions [the states] to regard their integrity and preservation as a part of our policy."

But the need for internal improvements was too great to be thwarted by constitutional objections. When the central government hesitated, the states and the private corporations chartered by them went on with their building. New York took the most important step with the Erie Canal, begun in 1817 and completed eight years later at a cost of seven million dollars; but other states were not idle, and the rapid development of the steamboat, both on Eastern and Western waters, played an important part in forwarding a new era of internal transportation and communication.

JOHN MARSHALL AND THE SUPREME COURT

More indicative of a stronger national attitude than anything done by Presidents or Congressmen in this period was the work of John Marshall as Chief Justice of the United States. Appointed to office in the closing hours of John Adams's administration, he served continuously until his death, in 1835. Born in Virginia and reared in "the simple, crude environment of the near frontier," he took part in the Revolution, studied law under Chancellor Wythe at the College of William and Mary, and, when elected to the state assembly from his native Fauquier County, settled down to practice law and fulfill his official duties in the city of Richmond. His carelessness in dress and his "lax, lounging manners," hampered his progress for a time, but great native ability soon pushed him forward both in legal practice and in political prominence.

Early he threw his influence on the side of strong central government and played a prominent part in Virginia's ratification of the Constitution. He championed Washington's administration and Hamilton's financial measures from the first, and soon was recognized as the leader of Federalist interests in Virginia. His ingenious defense of the Jay Treaty and his services on the famous X Y Z mission won the gratitude of John Adams and led to his appointment, first, as Secretary of State and then as Chief Justice.

William Wirt pictures Marshall at this time as a "tall, meagre, emaciated" individual, loose-jointed, careless in "dress, attitudes, gesture." He liked people, and his countenance was marked by "great good humor and hilarity." He was now a successful man. The clear, close reasoning of his legal opinions had brought wide patronage and many friends. His accounts recorded "considerable losses at whist and backgammon, generous contributions to churches, horse-races, festivals, card games, and balls, liberal purchases of wines and other drinkables, sundry fees to the Masons, 'The Jockie Club,' and 'Farmicola's.'" His regular income was large for the period, and he had recently joined a syndicate for the purchase of the remnant of the old Fairfax estate. As commissioner for this group he had received nearly twenty thousand dollars "over and above his expenses." He had, moreover, become the recognized political and personal enemy of his distant cousin, on his mother's side, Thomas Jefferson.

The office which he now occupied was one which John Jay surrendered with the remark that "he left the bench perfectly convinced that under a system so defective, it would not obtain the energy, weight, and dignity, which were essential to its affording due support to the National Government, nor acquire the public confidence and respect which, as a last resort of the justice of the nation, it should possess." How badly Jay had underestimated the possibilities of the Court in the hands of a man like Marshall, we have already seen in the case of Marbury *v.* Madison. And that was but the beginning. In 1809 Marshall again found the opportunity to assert the supremacy of the Federal government in the case of the United States *v.* Judge Peters. The dispute in this case had begun during the Revolution when a committee of the old Congress had reviewed the decision of a Pennsylvania court and had decided that prize money from the sale of a captured British sloop belonged to one Gideon Olmstead and others. The decision was very unpopular in Pennsylvania, and her legislature immediately took steps to prevent the payment ordered by the Federal judge. Olmstead, a Connecticut Yankee, persisted in his claims and secured a mandamus from the Federal Supreme Court, directing Judge Peters to issue process for carrying out the order. Marshall accompanied it with a sharp statement that "if the legislatures of the several states may, at will, annul the judgements of the Courts of the United States, and destroy the rights acquired under those judgements, the constitution itself becomes a solemn mockery, and the nation is deprived of the means of enforcing its laws by the instrumentality of its own tribunals." When the state called its militia to prevent action,

Federal officers accepted the challenge and a clash seemed inevitable. This was prevented by a clever ruse in serving the writ, but the commander of the state troops and his aides were haled before the Federal courts, convicted, and sentenced to fines and imprisonment. Madison wisely pardoned the offenders, but not until Federal supremacy had been adequately asserted.

Then, decision by decision, Marshall continued to strengthen Federal authority under the Constitution and the right of the Court to interpret that instrument. In Fletcher *v.* Peck (1810) he denied the right of the legislature of Georgia to rescind a grant of public lands, even though that grant had been secured by open bribery and corruption. The "obligation of contract" clause in the Constitution applied to states, as well as to individuals, regardless of moral issues involved! Then came the opportunity to settle matters with Virginia rivals—Virginia, where Jefferson still dominated and where Spencer Roane, whom Jefferson would have named Chief Justice of the United States had John Adams not so rudely pushed Marshall forward, presided as chief justice of the state court. During the Revolution, Virginia had seized lands in her Northern Neck which had been granted by English kings to Lord Fairfax and which, in spite of the seizure, he attempted to pass on to his nephew Denny Martin. Both the state and the Fairfax heir had, meantime, continued to dispose of the lands. Disputes over titles, of course, developed, and cases were brought before state courts. In one of these, Martin *v.* Hunter's Lessee, Judge Roane upheld the state's seizure of the Fairfax lands and, when appeal on error was taken to the Federal Supreme Court and the decision reversed, denied the appellate jurisdiction of the Federal court. Claimants to lands under the Fairfax title, including Marshall and his brother, immediately took the case back to the Supreme Court under another writ of error, and Judge Story, speaking for Marshall, wrote his famous decision (1816) asserting the constitutional right of the Supreme Court to review the decisions of "the highest court of a sovereign state."

Shortly afterward, in another case, Cohens *v.* Virginia (1821), Marshall went even farther and not only reasserted the right of appeal from state courts, but accepted appeal in a suit against the state of Virginia itself. In so doing he asserted the oneness of the people and of the states of the United States. "America has chosen to be, in many respects, and to many purposes, a nation," he said, "and for all these purposes, her government is complete; to all these objects, it is competent. . . . It can, then, in effecting these objects, legitimately control all individuals or governments within the American territory."

Virginia Republicans were furious. Under the pen name of "Algernon Sidney," Roane declared that this judgment would "not be less disastrous in its consequences" than any of those of the courts of Charles I. "It completely negatives the idea that the American states have a real existence, or are to be considered, in any sense, as sovereign and independent states." Bitterly he chided his fellow Republicans: "I greatly fear that the day of retribution is at hand. The scepter of power is about to depart from you. . . . The hair of the federal Samson has again begun to grow and with it power and strength." John Taylor of Caroline was less emotional, but more logical. In his book *Construction Construed and Constitutions Vindicated*, he insisted that the Supreme Court could receive appeals only from lower Federal courts and that the whole question of a Federal negative on state action had been discussed and rejected in the Constitutional Convention. Marshall's decisions were clearly a usurpation of power.

Opposition, however, did not check Marshall. Even while Virginians protested, he declared, in the Dartmouth College case (1819), that a charter granted by a legislature to a corporation was a contract which could not be impaired by later action. In a day when the important work of improving internal communication was being turned over to private corporations, such a decision might place great business concerns well out of the control of the states in which they functioned. In the same year, in the case of McCulloch *v.* Maryland (1819), he checked the efforts of Maryland to tax the Baltimore branch of the Bank of the United States and in so doing found occasion to give approval to the Hamiltonian doctrine of implied powers. Rejecting completely the Maryland contention that the powers of the Federal government were delegated by the sovereign states and must be exercised in subordination to the states, Marshall declared that "the government of the Union is emphatically, and truly, a government of the people. In form and in substance it emanates from them. Its powers are granted by them, and are to be exercised directly on them, and for their benefit." And as to the power to establish a bank, though not specifically granted, it was "necessary and proper" to the exercise of powers conferred. "Let the end be legitimate, let it be within the scope of the constitution, and all means which are appropriate, which are plainly adapted to that end, which are not prohibited, but consist with the letter and spirit of the constitution, are constitutional." Sovereignty belonged both to the states and to the "government of the Union," "with respect to the objects committed to" each. If a state could tax a legitimate creation of the Federal government, it could destroy it and with it the Federal government's rightful power.

Here was all that Alexander Hamilton had ever desired. Here it was declared to be a part of that very Constitution which Hamilton had distrusted and called "a frail and worthless fabric." And as though this were not enough, in Gibbons *v.* Ogden (1824) Marshall held that a monopoly granted by the state of New York to a steamship company for the use of the waters between New York and New Jersey was unconstitutional. He declared that the power granted to Congress over commerce included the right to regulate all trade across state lines and also the right to regulate all instruments involved in such trade. The Federalist party was dead, but through John Marshall and the Supreme Court its doctrines were very much alive. Marshall had accepted the responsibility for the triumph of Federalist principles. The old fight with Jefferson was not over. In Virginia's opposition to his decisions he saw "a deep design to convert our government into a mere league of states." "The whole attack, if not originating with Mr. Jefferson," he wrote, "is obviously approved and guided by him. . . . An effort will certainly be made to repeal the 25th section of the judicial act." Those who would avoid "dismemberment" of the Union must rally to the support of the judiciary.

JAMES MONROE AS PRESIDENT

But Marshall's fears were unfounded. The Republicans themselves had come a long way since Hamilton's day, and political lines were in the process of re-forming. There was little to suggest "dismemberment." As a matter of fact, the decline of the Federalist party after the Hartford Convention and the blunt acceptance of Federalist doctrines by leading Republicans robbed the election of 1816 of all color and left the impression of general political harmony. Madison made no secret of the fact that he favored James Monroe, his Secretary of State, as his successor, and a Congressional caucus nominated him over William H. Crawford of Georgia by a vote of 65 to 54. The Federalists did not bother to name a candidate, and Monroe received the votes of all but three states, whose electors supported Rufus King of New York.

The "Virginia dynasty," against which the New England Federalists had complained so bitterly, was thus still in power. But James Monroe was not a Thomas Jefferson or even a James Madison. He had had wide experience in public service,—state, national, and foreign,—

but his record had not been brilliant. It was, for the most part, that of a middle-of-the-road man. He had, however, been highly useful, and even when he blundered or failed, as he did in France and in England, he somehow managed to keep the loyalty of his friends and to avoid intense hatred on the part of his enemies. His personality and his way of doing things seemed eminently fitted to a day of uncertainty and transition. With a cabinet containing such men as John Quincy Adams (Secretary of State), John C. Calhoun (Secretary of War), William H. Crawford (Secretary of the Treasury), and William Wirt (Attorney-General), even a weak President might accomplish much for the nation.

FLORIDA AND THE FISHERIES

One of the first problems which had to be faced by the Monroe administration was that of Florida. There Spanish occupation had dwindled to a handful of garrison at the three military posts of Pensacola, St. Marks, and St. Augustine. The wide stretches of semitropical forest and swamp in between provided a home for a few Seminole Indians and a refuge for small bands of runaway slaves from neighboring plantations in the United States. One "village" of the latter kind, established on the Apalachicola by a renegade British lieutenant colonel after the battle of New Orleans, had become particularly obnoxious as a center of disorder and resistance to advancing settlement. A Scottish trader, named Arbuthnot, and a young English adventurer, named Ambrister, had sought trade and adventure among these peoples and had encouraged them to resist the American advance and to assert their rights against the treaty which Andrew Jackson had forced upon the Indians in 1814. Open resistance followed, and a few American settlers lost their scalps. By 1817 conditions had become so bad that President Monroe ordered Jackson and his Tennessee militia to move against the offenders and to follow them into Spanish territory if necessary. With characteristic zeal Jackson hurried into Florida, destroyed the Indian villages, and then marched directly to St. Marks. Ignoring the governor's protest, he hauled down the Spanish flag, hanged the Indian leaders who had taken refuge there, and seized Ambrister and Arbuthnot. A hurried court martial was set up, and the two British subjects were put on trial for their part in the Indian troubles. Conviction followed, and in a few hours Ambrister was before a firing squad and Arbuthnot was hanging from the yardarm of his trading vessel.

This much accomplished, Jackson turned toward Pensacola. There the Spanish governor was ejected, and an American garrison was stationed in the fortress. Trouble in Florida was at an end. But it was only beginning elsewhere. Such methods in dealing with international affairs were effective, but not regular. War both with Spain and with England was a possibility. Monroe and Calhoun were alarmed. The cabinet was hastily called into session. All but the Secretary of State were certain that an act of war had been committed and that Jackson's conduct must be promptly disavowed. Adams, however, insisted that everything Jackson had done was necessary and was implied in his orders. In the end Adams had his way. The return of the captured forts was pledged, but Jackson's acts were not repudiated.

Regardless of the fact that Jackson's methods had not been exactly in accord with accepted international procedures, they had the desired effect on Spain. They enabled John Quincy Adams to insist that she either adequately police Florida or relinquish her claims to it. With troubles enough on her hands in her other colonies, Spain was now ready to be rid of both Florida and Jackson. In 1819, therefore, she agreed to cede the province on condition that the United States should settle all claims held by Americans against the Spanish government. These amounted to some five million dollars, and the settlement of them by the United States constituted the purchase price. In 1821 Jackson himself, as governor, accepted the surrender of Florida to the United States, and his government accepted a boundary line between Spanish and American territory west of the Mississippi which followed the Sabine River and left what was later to be Texas in Spanish hands. One day that would be considered a serious blunder.

Shortly afterward, in the face of intense excitement stirred by a hostile press, the British Foreign Secretary examined the reports received from Washington and refused to take action in behalf of Englishmen who had been engaged in "unauthorized practices of such a description as to have deprived them of any claim on their own government for interference." Jackson was vindicated. His hold on the people of the back country was more secure. He did not yet know of the harsh criticisms which Calhoun and others in Washington had lodged against his impetuous deeds.

Meanwhile the boundary and fishery problems left unsettled by the Treaty of Ghent were being faced by joint commissions. A beginning was made toward establishing the boundary line between Canada and the United States along the Lakes to near Sault Ste. Marie, but negotiations broke down over the northern boundary of Maine, which had to be left to Webster and Ashburton in 1842. Some rights were granted American fishermen along the Newfoundland and Labrador coasts, but not enough to prevent nearly a hundred years more of constant bickering. The one great accomplishment, made not by a commission but by agreement between Rush, for the United States, and Bagot, for England, was the limitation of naval force on the Great Lakes to the minimum required for police protection. That was the beginning of a policy which created one of the few unfortified international boundaries in the world and constituted an important step toward an enduring peace between the two countries. In fact, the friendly attitude of Lord Castlereagh and the firm, dignified methods of John Quincy Adams in this period may be said to have done much toward weakening old prejudices and toward establishing better Anglo-American relations.

THE MONROE DOCTRINE

One of the first fruits of this new friendliness and one of the clearest statements of America's new self-reliance was the Monroe Doctrine. It grew out of Spain's troubles with her colonies in the Western Hemisphere and the inclination of other European nations to take a hand in Spanish affairs. To understand the situation it must be remembered that when Napoleon extended his control over Spain and Portugal in 1807–1808, the Spanish colonies in the New World began, one after the other, to revolt and to set up little republics modeled after the government of the United States. They established a profitable trade with England and looked to that country and to the United States for recognition. Public opinion in both countries approved, but England hesitated because of her connections with those who had helped to defeat Napoleon; the United States hesitated because the transfer of Florida had not been completed.

Both countries, however, realized that failure to recognize the independence of these colonies might produce serious consequences. Moved by the fears of democracy and revolution which France and Napoleon had stirred, the Continental monarchs had allied themselves together and had been holding a series of conferences in which a program for checking all such movements was being developed. They bluntly asserted the right of intervention in the affairs of nations where revolution threatened and, on another occasion, frankly discussed intervention to suppress the revolts in Spain's American colonies. That would, of course, check England's trade and destroy American prestige in these aspiring republics. It would, most certainly, re-establish and strengthen Old World influence in the Western Hemisphere.

The situation was a delicate one. It became more so for the United States when some of the Latin-American colonies began to waver in their enthusiasm for the republican form of government and when Alexander I of Russia invited the United States to join the European Holy Alliance. Action could no longer be delayed. Secretary Adams, therefore, told the Czar that "to stand in firm and cautious independence of all entanglements in the European system has been a cardinal point of their [American] policy under every administration of their government," and, in March, 1822, President Monroe and Congress extended recognition to the five South American republics and opened diplomatic relations with them.

England hesitated until the following year, when France, now completely in reactionary hands, invaded Spain for the avowed purpose of destroying the constitution which a rebellious people had forced upon their king and when rumors of a Franco-Spanish expedition to South America began to spread around Europe. Then George Canning, who had succeeded Lord Castlereagh at the British Foreign Office, suggested to Richard Rush, the American minister at London, a mutual agreement as to the Spanish American colonies and a joint declaration to the world of our "opinions and feelings." Rush was without instructions, but, after further pressure, agreed to a joint statement, provided England granted immediate recognition to the former Spanish colonies. This Canning would not do; but when Rush's report of the conversations reached America, the effect was profound. England had treated the United States as an equal. The young republic was in a position to take new and firmer ground in diplomatic affairs.

Monroe sought the advice of Jefferson and Madison. The Sage of Monticello advised co-operation, yet confessed himself out of touch with current affairs. He was generally convinced that we should have a system "distinct from Europe." Madison agreed and even favored Anglo-American support of Greek independence. John Quincy Adams, however, needed no advice. He had early sought British co-operation and had found it lacking. He now saw the opportunity to face the whole problem of European aggression in the Western Hemisphere. Not only were the Spanish republics in danger, but the Russians were pushing their trading posts as far south as San Francisco Bay on the western coast of North America. "It would be more candid, as well as more dignified," he said, "to avow our principles explicitly to Great Britain and France, than to come in as a cockboat in the wake of the British man-of-war." It would be "a very suitable and convenient opportunity for us to take our stand against the Holy Alliance."

Such an attitude well fitted the temper of the day. Already Henry Clay had declared that "we look too much abroad. Let us no longer watch the nod of any European politician; let us become real and true Americans and place ourselves at the head of the American system." The public was ready to support such a move. So when Adams insisted that the ground he wished to take was "that of earnest remonstrance against the interference on our part with Europe; to make an American cause and adhere inflexibly to that," President Monroe fell into line and, in December, 1823, sent to Congress his now famous message known as the Monroe Doctrine.

The first section of this message was aimed at Russia. It expressed our willingness "to arrange by amicable negotiation the respective rights and interests of the two nations on the northwest coast of this continent," but laid down as a fundamental principle "that the American continents, by the free and independent condition which they have assumed and maintained, are henceforth not to be considered as subjects for future colonization by any European powers." The second section dealt with European affairs and noted the fact that "in the wars of the European powers in matters relating to themselves we have never taken any part." It pointed out, however, our peculiar interests in movements in the Western Hemisphere and the differences between political systems here and in Europe, and made it perfectly clear "that we should consider any attempt on their [the Europeans'] part to extend their system to any portion of this hemisphere as dangerous to our peace and safety." It went on to say that with existing colonies or dependencies of European powers we had not interfered and would not interfere. But in the case of governments which had declared their independence and maintained it, we would not view any interposition for the purpose of oppressing them or controlling their destiny, by any European power, "in any other light than as the manifestation of an unfriendly disposition toward the United States."

In these clear-cut statements the United States "came forward," independent of Europe, "as the champion of the autonomy and freedom of America, and declared that the era of European colonization in the New World had passed away." John Quincy Adams and James Monroe had given the United States something of a new foreign policy. Its immediate effects were not great, but the years ahead would see its simple statements expanded to meet the needs of a nation widening its international interests. For the present it stood as the climax of the new self-consciousness and independence which had come in the years immediately following the War of 1812.

SELECTED BIBLIOGRAPHY

W. P. Cresson, *James Monroe*; Marquis James, *Andrew Jackson: The Border Captain*; Charles M. Wiltse, *John C. Calhoun, Nationalist*; Henry H. Simms, *Life of John Taylor*, valuable biographies of some of the leading figures. Constitutional changes under John Marshall are covered in E. S. Corwin, *John Marshall and the Constitution*; A. J. Beveridge, *John Marshall* (4 vols.); A. C. McLaughlin, *A Constitutional History of the United States*.

Important economic developments are described in R. M. Tryon, *Household Manufactures in the United States*; J. S. Clark, *History of Manufactures in the United States, 1607–1928* (3 vols.); M. T. Copeland, *The Cotton Manufacturing Industry in the United States*; F. W. Taussig, *The Tariff History of the United States*; R. C. H. Catterall, *The Second Bank of the United States*; A. B. Hulbert, *The Paths of Inland Commerce*.

Dexter Perkins, *Hands off: A History of the Monroe Doctrine*, and his three-volume history of the Monroe Doctrine are valuable studies; J. F. Rippy, *Rivalry of the United States and Great Britain for Latin America*; E. H. Tatum, *The United States and Europe, 1815–1823*; F. A. Golder, *Russian Expansion on the Pacific, 1641–1850*; A. P. Whitaker, *The U.S. and the Independence of the Latin-American States*, worth while on the diplomacy of the period.

H. S. Commager (Ed.), *Documents of American History*, pp. 211–224, 228–237, contains source material.

XIII

Westward Expansion to 1840

U P TO OUR own day American history has been in a large degree the history of the colonization of the Great West." Steadily population has moved forward, pushing the wilderness back and supplanting it with farms and cities and a more complex social order. During the colonial period, settlement spread back from the coast up the rivers and out over the piedmont and upland valleys. Here and there it broke through the mountain barriers that marked the eastern borders of the great interior basin of the continent and formed islands of settlement in what was to become Kentucky, Tennessee, and Ohio. Already men drew a distinction between the peoples and society of the seaboard and those which were designated as "frontier," "upcountry," or "backwoods." Conflict over the franchise and representation, and even over governmental policies, had developed between coast and interior in different colonies, and some men were beginning to understand that moving west and living on the frontier were altering the characteristics of both persons and society.

In the years immediately following the Revolution the tide of emigration rose sharply. By the first Federal census, of 1790, Kentucky's population was 73,677, and Tennessee's 35,691; by that of 1810 the first was 406,511, and the second 261,727. Ohio, meanwhile, had grown from a mere handful of people to 230,760, and a deepening line of population had pushed on down the Ohio River into the territories to the west. With the purchase of Louisiana a new line of expansion was opened up the Mississippi River, which, by 1810, gave Louisiana and what was to become Missouri and Arkansas a population of more than 96,000.

An English traveler through Pennsylvania, in 1796, said that he had seen "ten and twenty waggons at a time . . . on their way to Pittsburg and other parts of Ohio, from thence to descend down the river to Kentucky. These waggons were loaded with the clothes and necessaries of a number of poor emigrants, who follow on foot with their wives and families, who are sometimes indulged with a ride when they are tired, or in bad weather."

From Tennessee, in 1795, a visitor wrote:

To a person who observes the migration to this country, it appears as if North and South Carolina, and Georgia, were emptying themselves into it. It is not infrequent to see from 2 to 300 people in a body coming from those southern climates, oppressed with diseases to revive and enjoy health in this salubrious air.

Into the lake region of western New York and on out into the Connecticut Reserve in northern Ohio another stream of population moved. Some of it came from New England, where southern Maine, northern Vermont, and New Hampshire were rapidly filling up, and the surplus was pouring over into the neighboring states. Even in Georgia, where the Indians blocked the way, population crowded westward against the Indian barrier, and land-hungry settlers, who had already begun the cultivation of cotton, talked of Indian removals and the clear open road that would then lie south and west around the mountains and along the Gulf of Mexico.

THE GREAT MIGRATION

All this expansion played its part in bringing on the War of 1812. The war itself played its part in a new westward movement which began after 1815 and which, by comparison with all that had gone before, was soon known as "the Great Migration."

This movement was not confined to any one section. From Maine to Georgia eager emigrants crowded the roads leading toward the West. Up the Connecticut and the Housatonic into northern New England and on into upper New York; up the Hudson and out along the Mohawk into Ohio and Michigan; across Pennsylvania and down the Ohio as far as Missouri; up through the mountain gaps from the Carolinas into Kentucky and Tennessee and on across the Ohio; south and west in Georgia to the very edges of the Indian lands; south from Tennessee into Alabama and Mississippi along the path that Andrew Jackson had recently cleared—a steady human stream poured its flood into the great interior basins.

To one of the emigrants it seemed that "Old America" was "breaking up, and moving westward." On the "grand trek, towards the Ohio," he said, "we are seldom out of sight . . . of small family groups, behind and before us." In Ohio the roads were "literally covered with waggons moving out families." "On the road," wrote another, "every emigrant tells you he is going to Ohio; when you arrive in Ohio its inhabitants are moving to Missouri and Alabama." "Missouri and Illinois exhibit an interesting spectacle at this time," said Hezekiah Niles's *Weekly Register* in 1816. "A stranger to witness the scene would imagine that Virginia, Kentucky, Tennessee and the Carolinas had made an agreement to introduce them soon as possible to the bosom of the American family. Every ferry on the river is daily occupied in passing families, carriages, wagons, negroes, carts, &c. &c." In southern Indiana the traveler was "continually coming in view of new cabins, or wagons, the inmates of which had not yet sheltered themselves in cabins." In Ohio "fifty wagons . . . passed the Muskingum at Zanesville in a day." "Emigration powerfully sets westward," was Niles's comment.

Meanwhile, back East, a writer, humorously inclined, spoke of "that alarming disease, denominated the Ohio fever which continues to rage in various parts of New England, by which vast numbers are taken off." In North Carolina it was "the Alabama fever" which struck men "with great violence." "You, Sir, can't conceive of the anxiety and confusion that pervades all ranks of people in this section of the country to remove to Alabama," wrote one of North Carolina's citizens, who saw the lands around him "diminishing in point of value, and the country loseing many of its most respectable inhabitants." "Thousands of our wealthy and respectable citizens are annually moving to the West," wailed Archibald Murphy. He estimated (1816) that in the past twenty-five years North Carolina had given more than two hundred thousand people to the West.

The whole nation seemed to be in constant motion. A writer from upper New York, in 1815, said that "during the past winter our roads have been thronged with families moving westerly. It has been remarked by our oldest settlers that they never before witnessed so great a number of teams passing, laden with women, children, furniture, &c., to people the fertile forests of New York, Pennsylvania, and Ohio." In nine days (1817) some two hundred and sixty wagons, "besides many persons on horseback and on foot," passed a given point on the road through New York and down the Allegheny. One caravan consisted of one hundred and sixteen persons, all from the same town in Maine, on their way to Indiana. In the same year a traveler, returning to Georgia from "the Alabama country," told of meeting some 3800 persons on the road. "Mississippi," boasted one of her newly acquired citizens, "will settle faster than any new country ever did." "By the

Main Routes to the West

time the land can be sold," wrote one of his fellows from Alabama, "these countries will contain a dense population." "The emigration is wonderful—and seems daily to acquire new power." So great was the pressure that Andrew Jackson, as the commanding officer in the region, found it necessary to warn "all white men settling on Cherokee lands," without a permit, that they must "drive off their stock" and "remove themselves and families" under penalty of prosecution and forfeiture of stock.

Frequently "a cart and a single horse" afforded the means of transfer for the emigrant; sometimes "the back of the poor pilgrim" bore "all his effects," while "his wife, naked-footed," followed behind, "bending under the hopes of the family." Others were more fortunate. Timothy Flint, in Missouri, saw a train of "nine wagons harnessed with from four to six horses." Each wagon was accompanied by "a hundred cattle, besides hogs, horses and sheep . . . and from three or four to twenty slaves." These emigrants were evidently planters from the older South. They did not, however, represent the usual Southern emigrant, who, as a rule, belonged to the lesser people, with little to move and more reason for doing so. "Few people of extensive wealth," says Abernethy, "moved into the Alabama region during the period of early settlement. . . . Those who had slaves rarely owned but a small number, and many who later became planters had no slaves at all to begin with. In other words, the small farmer of the piedmont region became the pioneer planter of the Southwest."

By these shifts of population six new Western states were added to the Union between 1812 and 1821: Louisiana (1812), Indiana (1816), Mississippi (1817), Illinois (1818), Alabama (1819), and Missouri (1821). With heavy percentages of increase of population in Kentucky, Tennessee, Ohio, and the western parts of New York, Pennsylvania, and Georgia, the political power of a new section in American life was becoming great enough to upset old balances. This section now had about four million population and was growing much faster than any other. What it wanted in the way of land legislation, internal improvements, and markets would, henceforward, have to be considered.

During the 1820's and 1830's the tide of emigration, thus begun, ran even heavier. Wagons on the roads and flatboats and soon steamboats on the rivers and lakes became more numerous. In the first decade travel was heaviest in the southern portions of the Old Northwest and in upper Mississippi and Alabama, but after 1830 the movement along the Great Lakes into Michigan, northern Ohio, Indiana, Illinois, and southern Wisconsin more than matched it. In 1825 the great Erie Canal, connecting Lake Erie and New York City, was completed with what one writer called "pompous show and parade, not unlike those triumphal games and processions that were given to some of the Roman Emperors." In that year the tolls collected amounted to nearly five hundred thousand dollars, and some thirteen thousand one hundred and ten boats and over forty thousand persons passed Albany and Utica. New England and New York now had easier access to the great interior. Individuals, families, and even whole church congregations, which drew up community compacts not unlike that signed in the cabin of the *Mayflower*, sought new homes in more favored places where old customs and values might be preserved and made to flourish. A greater New England, with its elms, its Congregational churches, its Puritan conscience, and its Yankee thrift, was beginning to stretch from New York to Illinois and Wisconsin.

In the period 1830–1840 the removal of the southern Indian tribes, begun a few years earlier, was completed, and a great crescent-shaped world, reaching from the piedmont region of the Carolinas to Texas and Arkansas, was opened for the spread of cotton plantations and slave labor. Led first by small farmers and joined later by large planters, settlement swept south and west around the mountains and across the "deep South." Lands and slaves rose to almost unbelievable prices as the call for cotton increased. A new South, built according to old Southern patterns but altered by pioneering experiences and conditions, was also in the making.

Between 1820 and 1830 Alabama, Arkansas, Mississippi, and Indiana each more than doubled its population. In 1840 Illinois had three times as many people as in 1830, and Michigan seven times as many. A Buffalo newspaper told of "steamboats, and other vessels . . . literally crammed with passengers, and a great part of them emigrants from the East, intending to settle in the fertile parts of Michigan and Ohio," and an Arkansas paper reported that "not only is every steamboat crowded with cabin and deck passengers, but the roads are also lined with wagons, conveying families to the Eden of Arkansas—as it is considered abroad—the counties of Washington and Crawford."

In this same period there was considerable activity in the trans-Mississippi West. It was a huge, raw world, which began with the grassy prairies of the recently organized territory of Iowa, faded into the semiarid plains beyond the hundredth meridian, and then swept across the great ridges of the Rocky Mountains and inland empires to the Pacific coast. Most of it was as yet unoccupied, and its boundaries were not firmly drawn. To the south, first Spain and then Mexico held Texas, New Mexico, and California, and laid claim to a portion of what was to be Colorado, Arizona, Utah, and Nevada. England and Russia both disputed American claims in the Pacific Northwest, where Robert Gray had discovered the mouth of the Columbia River and Lewis and Clark, under Jefferson's inspiration, had explored the great interior. Open conflict had occurred during the War of 1812, when British traders seized the trading post (Astoria) which John Jacob Astor had established in the region. In the agreements reached after the war, however, the post was returned, and a policy of joint occupation of Oregon was accepted by England and the United States. In 1824 Russia agreed to confine her interest to the region north of the line of latitude fifty-four degrees and forty minutes; the permanent settlement of claims, however, was left to the future.

Conditions on the southern border were equally disturbed and unsettled. Throughout the 1820's and early 1830's individual Americans crossed the border into Texas to secure lands and establish colonies. In 1835 these Americans rebelled against Mexico and set themselves up as an independent republic. Their request for annexation to the United States was denied, but they had launched "manifest destiny" on its course and could well afford to bide their time. Meanwhile trappers and traders from the Rocky Mountain and the American fur-trading companies were wandering about over the whole great interior of the continent in quest of peltries. James Bridger had already visited the Great Salt Lake and Jedediah Smith had made his way overland to California. A lively trade between St. Louis and Santa Fe had developed. Missionaries were at work among the Indians. Trading posts were being set up at strategic points. A system of forts was already projected. In fact, the first stages in the occupation of another American frontier were well under way.

FORCES BEHIND EMIGRATION

Ahead of these great waves of emigration were, of course, the lure of cheap lands and the fact that the Indian menace had been removed. The long debate as to whether the public lands should be sold primarily for revenue purposes or be disposed of to actual settlers was gradually being decided in the interest of the latter. The first general national-land law had been passed in 1796. Under it certain lands in

Ohio were to be surveyed and sold—half in quarter-townships at Philadelphia, and half in tracts of 640 acres at Pittsburgh and Cincinnati Sales were to be made at auction, with a minimum price of two dollars an acre—one twentieth to be paid at the time of application; the remainder, one half in thirty days and the final half within a year. This was a compromise between speculators, who would provide revenue by large purchases, and actual settlers, who desired the smaller tracts for homes. However, it proved unsatisfactory to both groups and was superseded in 1800 by an act which reduced the minimum tract which could be purchased to a half-section and extended credit to a four-year period. In 1804 the minimum tract was still further reduced to a quarter-section of 160 acres. Both the reduction in size of tract and the extension of credit were supposed to be concessions to the actual settler and checks on the speculator. But the results were not satisfactory when emigration grew heavy. The credit system brought only ruin to the overanxious settler and failed to impede speculation. The hard times of 1819, therefore, brought demands for new legislation. In 1820 the minimum price was cut to $1.25 an acre, to be paid in one cash payment, and the smallest unit of purchase was reduced to 80 acres. Thus the settler, for $100, could secure immediate ownership of his farm, and the speculator would, theoretically at least, be forced to use greater ingenuity in order to secure profits.

These changes in the land laws were, of course, in large part the result of pressure brought by "the Great Migration." In turn, they augmented the urge to emigrate. Cheap land has ever been the lure that has drawn men westward. Without new favors to "the actual settler" the great expansion of these years would not have been possible. Yet the pull ahead was not stronger than the economic pressure behind. The men who had peopled the new West had been crowded, as well as lured. In New England the period immediately following peace in Europe and America was one of extreme uncertainty. Manufacturing, as we have seen, was seriously checked by renewed Old World competition and was able to establish itself as the dominant interest of the section only after years of struggle. Commerce suffered even more and never quite resumed its former place. The soundness of New England's maritime life was indeed on trial in these years. At first, shipping seemed to be on its way back. The demand for goods was strong, and the need for carriers was great. Then Europe began slowly to recover her own carrying trade and only gradually to open her colonial ports to Yankee ships. Meanwhile the heavy western shift of population in the United States tended to favor ports like New Orleans, Baltimore, and, especially, New York with her Erie Canal. Pessimists began to predict "the decline of Boston to a fourth-rate seaport, and the total extinction of Salem." Farsighted men began to place their capital and their abilities in manufacturing, and political influence slowly shifted in this direction. Daniel Webster signaled the change by dropping the cause of free trade and taking up the fight for protective tariffs. The fall line was slowly establishing its superiority over the harbor.

The pressure was particularly heavy on the smaller centers, such as Salem, Beverly, Marblehead, and Newburyport. Some of them began a permanent decline. Others saved themselves by turning industrial. Boston, however, was able to absorb the foreign commerce and shipping of these lesser places to a degree and, in twenty years' time, to recover the losses of embargo and war years. New York outstripped her and even drew some of her trade and traders away. Yet her store of Yankee grit was sufficient to weather the storm and, with new markets in California, Australia, and South Africa, to merit the title "Hub of the Universe," which proud citizens bestowed.

In the rural areas of New England, where large families and stingy soils had always demanded much of toil and more of courage, there was suffering to match that of the old trading centers. Markets for agricultural produce had never been large, and families had long supplemented their farming with home manufacturing. Self-sufficiency in all ways was the general rule. A few supplies for the ships that went out from New England's harbors, now and then a boatload of horses for the West Indies, a little produce for the neighboring town—this was about the extent of New England's agricultural surplus. It never was great enough to alter the general pattern of rural life and labor. It never dispensed with the necessity of making and selling a few straw hats, a few yards of cloth, a few chairs, or other articles for which skill had been developed.

The rise of manufacturing, under embargoes and war, stimulated agriculture to a degree and offered to a few people, in a few places, the chance to expand their efforts. The call for wool encouraged the raising of more sheep, and the demands of the army for food supplies led to an increase of stall-fed cattle. Factory workers, here and there, provided a market for produce and milk, and the employment of girls and boys at the looms lightened the burden on those who remained behind on the land. It was only a beginning; yet it was enough to stir the Berkshire plan of agricultural society, advocated by Elkanah Watson, into being and to make fairs and cattle shows the order of the day. In these, practical dirt farmers exchanged ideas, exhibited their stock and vegetables, and sought ways to improve the life and profits of those who farmed. Observers sensed a new spirit in agriculture.

Peace, however, checked the expansion of markets and threw agriculture back to its old levels. Agriculture dwindled, and improvements ceased. The depression that had already fallen on commerce and manufacturing spread to the farms, where the pinch had always been greatest. The slight upward swing of the past few years now only served to emphasize normal difficulties and to add a bit to normal restlessness. The pressure to emigrate was thus increased, and the New England states, where the number employed in agriculture (1820) was two and a half times greater than the number employed in commerce and manufacturing combined, had a surplus of people, if not of goods.

The rapid development of manufacturing in the next two decades did not ease the pressure in rural areas. In the first days factory towns encouraged enterprising farmers who lived near by to increase the supply of vegetables, fruits, and dairy produce. Travelers noted improvements in methods and in the general appearance of farms. Better breeds of stock were introduced, and farm machinery was more widely used. Farther back in the hills, beef cattle were raised and sold in the Brighton (Massachusetts) market. Sheep increased so rapidly that whole areas were given over to them. By 1835 Vermont had more than a million sheep, and half her people had become shepherds. Western Massachusetts was not far behind and had specialized to the point where wheat and pork had to be imported.

Then disaster fell. Many families on the less favorable lands had already been crowded aside to make way for cattle and sheep. Now the rapid building of canals and railroads accompanied by the steady westward spread of wheat opened Eastern markets to a widening group of Western farmers. As wheat moved into Ohio, Michigan, Indiana, and Illinois, New York farmers turned to cattle and sheep, and even to vegetables and the dairy. They poured their surplus into New England and other Eastern markets at prices such as farmers on stingy soil could not match. Step by step, the Northeastern farmer yielded ground. New crops were tried; lands were mortgaged; lesser men gave in and moved West or to the rising urban centers; sheep and cattlemen followed. In the 1830's the *New England Farmer* was saying that thousands had gone down, and gone down in poverty. Migration was the only thing left.

Conditions in the South were even worse. The old Virginia tobacco region, which had turned to wheat during the Napoleonic wars, now found its markets, both in Europe and the West Indies, closed and its new staple badly damaged by the ravages of the Hessian fly. In 1821 the town of Norfolk, the great port for tobacco and wheat, was described as a place of "grass-grown streets and deserted wharfs," and the rural areas outside as worked "down to utter sterility, . . . gullied fields interspersed with broom-straw and stunted pines."

Under such circumstances, the efforts at better farming which had come with the recent prosperity were rapidly abandoned. While the region was feeding the armies of Europe, a spirit of optimism had dominated. Crop rotation, horizontal and deep plowing, and the use of fertilizers had been tried. Even the publication of agricultural papers and the organization of agricultural societies had made considerable progress. John Taylor of Caroline had taken the lead and his little volume *The Arator*, which both criticized old methods and advocated new ones, was hailed as marking a new day in Southern agriculture.

All this was now forgotten. Wheat was no longer in demand; markets for tobacco were not what they had been years ago. As one farmer wrote, "It is not worth while to make crops—we can get nothing for them . . . neither is it any object to improve our lands." Public men, such as Jefferson, Madison, and Monroe, found themselves facing bankruptcy, and lesser men by the thousands were willing to leave the land of their fathers and seek a better chance in the new West.

Political conflicts added their part to an already bad situation. Bitter struggles developed between the old coastal areas and the back country over the franchise and representation, the right and duty of the government to build internal improvements, and taxation, especially as it affected slavery. Western men demanded a new constitution and raised fundamental questions regarding the rights of minorities, the evils of slavery, and the part which government ought to play in re-establishing economic conditions on a more sound basis. Nowhere in the nation were men more disturbed; nowhere was the social-economic order more uncertain. For more than two decades after the peace of 1815, depression and conflict continued unbroken, and complaints against the central government for its tariffs and its broadening activities went on unchecked. It was, therefore, not surprising that many sighed for "another Napoleon to restore to us by his wars, the feeding of all Europe."

Conditions farther south were equally bad. North Carolinians had never known great prosperity, and they had not shared to any extent in the trade which war had brought. As self-sufficient farmers, they had always moved about easily under economic pressure. Now dissatisfaction with slavery and the failure of the state to provide adequate transportation facilities for their small surpluses added to the usual restlessness and turned men's faces westward. Only Connecticut, in New England, contributed proportionately to emigration.

South Carolinians from the upcountry joined the trek, for the same reasons and for the added one that they were already trying cotton and had heard of better lands to the west. Nor were planters near the coast entirely indifferent. Indigo had ceased to yield profits when independence had put an end to British bounties, and Charleston's shipping had suffered even more than that of New England under embargoes and war. The markets for rice, the best of which were always in southern Europe, had been largely cut off, and the West Indies trade had, of course, been badly disrupted. In a region where agriculture and commerce were so closely united, the result was doubly disastrous. Already the rumblings of protest against the new protective tariffs and other evidences of consolidation in government were beginning to be heard. Soon men were ready to nullify the acts of Congress and to fall back on states' rights for protection.

LIFE IN THE WEST

These were some of the pressures behind the great flood of migration which, in the period from 1815 to 1840, was building the new West. Only the middle states seemed to lack them; yet even here the rapid development of upper New York and of western Pennsylvania, when accompanied by the development of superior transportation, meant sharp competition for the farmers in the older regions. Many found it easier to move than to alter their crops and methods, and joined the steady flow of immigrants from Europe who landed at New York and Philadelphia and then moved on into the West. Thus from Maine to Georgia the pressure was being applied, while from the Lakes to the Gulf rich lands at low rates, now cleared of the Indian menace, invited settlers.

Life in the West, as a rule, meant, for the majority, a return to a more or less primitive existence. In both North and South, first settlers were often part farmer and part trapper and trader. Many were squatters on the public domain who readily sold the improvements they had made to a more substantial newcomer and moved on farther into the wilderness. Houses were of logs, and lands were "cleared" by girdling the trees, which caused the branches to wither and die. First crops were often planted while the dying trees still stood, but in time the trees were cut and burned or split into rails for fencing. Later the stumps were removed, and the task of making a homestead was completed.

It was backbreaking toil, but it raised the value of lands, and it made possible the food necessary for survival. It might later provide the opportunity for sale to a newcomer with more capital, and the chance to begin again in the same way farther out with funds to secure more land or to make better improvements. Some, of course, were shiftless and lazy. Indifferent to progress, they merely squatted on the public domain, with no intention of acquiring title to land. Content to hunt and to own a few cattle and hogs, which ranged the woods, they lived in squalor and poverty. They moved easily and drifted with the frontier ever westward. They did, however, with their more thrifty neighbors, help to break the dominance of the forest and to drive in the wedge of civilization.

Such backwoodsmen formed the outer edge of advance. Behind them came the more substantial farmers, who made possible the school and church, the mill and the local store, the doctor, the lawyer, and, after a time, simple manufactures. The American frontiersman was thus engaged in a process of social-economic evolution not unlike that which has marked the course of human development from primitive to modern times. In a relatively short time it revealed something of the different periods through which man has passed in his long journey to modern times.

The process of settlement and growth, although alike in general characteristics, differed somewhat in the Northwest and the Southwest. Settlers in both regions early depended on corn and hogs for sustenance. In developing a surplus, however, the Northwest turned to wheat, while the lower South turned to cotton. In the Northwest the farm was ever the unit of production, and the family the source of the labor supply. In the South, while the farm predominated, the plantation early made its appearance, and Negro slaves on plantations and on many farms supplemented the family or completely replaced it as the labor employed.

As time went on, differences in the social patterns of the sections increased. Men who went into the Old Northwest found their political forms and even their economic system already shaped, in part, for them by the Land Ordinance of 1785 and the Northwest Ordinance of 1787. Their lands were surveyed according to a regular formula; townships were established, provisions were made for public schools and a territorial government, a system of inheritance was set up, and slavery was prohibited. In regions where New Englanders settled, elm-lined streets, well-proportioned houses with green shutters, and Congregational churches with tall spires soon gave outer expression to the inner fact of Yankee-Puritan forces at work. The early establishment of schools and colleges gave further evidence of these forces, and a lively interest in community affairs, backed by a genuine demand for the maintenance of high moral standards, revealed a firm determination to retain New England values in the new Western home. Where Pennsylvania settlers or those directly from the Old World dominated, their houses and barns and fences soon betrayed that fact, as did their institutions and their ways of living—even to the covers on their beds and the utensils in their kitchens. Great barns and Conestoga wagons, as much as sauerkraut and well-kept fields, characterized the "Pennsylvania Dutch" wherever they went, and an attempt to reproduce Old World ways, whether English, German, or Scandinavian, marked the regions where the immigrant fresh from Europe settled. Even the upland Southerners who early pushed across the Ohio River into Ohio, Indiana, and Illinois kept something in speech and easygoing ways of the region of their origin. The Quaker groups, especially, carried a definite hatred of slavery and an unusual interest in education. The Methodists brought the circuit rider and, together with Baptists and Presbyterians, a fondness for revival meetings of a somewhat boisterous character.

Also, settlers from Virginia and the Carolinas who went into Alabama and Mississippi carried the ways of parent states into the wilderness with them and, as soon as the sale of a surplus permitted, began to put up houses somewhat like the one that Jefferson had built in Virginia or Miles Brewton had fashioned in Charleston. As they widened their acres and acquired slaves, they paid more attention to good manners, and held their honor as something to be defended, at times in personal combat. There were more Methodist, Baptist, and Presbyterian churches, and fewer using Episcopalian forms, than there were in the Old South; but these settlers respected the ways of "gentlefolk" even in religion and were wont to boast of ancestors who deserved that title. Education remained more a private than a public matter, and they found more time for, and gave a wider expression to, amusements and social affairs. Where there were French and Spanish backgrounds, as around Mobile and New Orleans, the Catholic Church flourished, and music and drama occupied a solid place in the order of things. Creole and American met there to resent each other and to quarrel, but, in the end, to blend and adjust, as did the New Englander and the German in Wisconsin.

EFFECTS OF THE FRONTIER

Yet with all these differences, the more basic fact was that of common experience on an American frontier. In the West of both North and South, men were beginning over again and living under conditions where the wilderness predominated and where they faced the task of pushing it back and replacing it with their own forms of complexity. It was this experience that made all Wests more or less alike and, in turn, shaped, in unusual degree, the whole of American character.

Professor Frederick Jackson Turner, the great historian of the frontier, insists that the West served as a great "mixing-bowl" in which differing nationalities were fused into "a composite nationality for the American people." By it the powers of the national government were expanded to meet new requirements, and soon the problems of land, internal improvements, and markets which it raised occupied the major part of the government's time and effort. A new national attitude came to men who looked to the central government for the satisfaction of their needs. And what is of most importance, the wide existence of opportunity in an area of free land and the greater interdependence of men in a primitive society fostered a practical democracy that stressed individualism, a larger freedom for those who had to rely on their own initiative, and a greater equality among those who had to accept their share of responsibility for the survival of the whole.

Living and working together in a region where men were scarce and nature abundant soon produced certain intellectual traits. "That coarseness and strength combined with acuteness and inquisitiveness; that practical, inventive turn of mind, quick to find expedients; that masterful grasp of material things, lacking in the artistic but powerful to effect great ends; that restless nervous energy; that dominant individualism, working for good and for evil, and withal that buoyancy and exuberance which comes with freedom"—these traits, says Professor Turner, are the frontier's contribution to the American mind. He and others have stressed the idealism characteristic of men who stake their all on the future and build anew in the wilderness. They have noted the provincialism of those wrapped up in domestic affairs; the wastefulness of those with abundant natural resources, but little labor and capital; the boastfulness of those who have done a great deal in a short time; even the coarseness and vulgarity of people who are young enough to be rude without embarrassment and rash enough to believe their ways superior to those of all other lands.

THE WEST AND NATIONAL PROBLEMS

In a more immediate way the rise of the new West affected the national life. The heavy buying of land on credit, and the unsound practices of Western banks in making loans in the years following the War of 1812, led to overspeculation and played a part in producing the panic of 1819. The efforts of the Bank of the United States to force specie payments wrecked most of the local banks in the South and West, drove land values down, and led to the foreclosure of mortgages throughout the region. In towns like Cincinnati much of the property fell into the hands of the Bank of the United States, which caused Thomas Hart Benton to exclaim: "All the flourishing cities of the West are mortgaged to this money power. They may be devoured by it at any moment. They are in the jaws of the monster. A lump of butter in the mouth of a dog! one gulp, one swallow, and all is gone!"

One day, not many years ahead, Andrew Jackson would reveal a like attitude and, with Benton's aid and the West's consent, would strike down the Bank as an enemy of common men and state banking. He too would call it a "monster." Western states, meanwhile, passed laws for the relief of debtors and forced the national government to revise its land laws to the advantage of the actual settler.

The rise of the new West also hastened developments in transportation. Where in earlier days Western needs had been served by the flatboat, which was little more than a large raft for down-river trade, and the keelboat, which could be moved upstream only by poles or sails or the cordelle, better means of transportation were now required for both passengers and freight. The first step in this direction came in 1811, when Nicholas J. Roosevelt launched his steamboat *New Orleans* at Pittsburgh. On October 28 of that year it reached the city for which it was named after a voyage of only sixty-four days! Experiments showed that it could move upstream at the rate of some thirteen miles in two and a half hours, but it was put to use only as a Natchez packet during the next few years. The first steamboat to reach Louisville from New Orleans was the *Enterprise*, in 1815.

By 1817 the number of steamboats on the Ohio and Mississippi was twenty—a number that increased to one hundred and twenty-five by 1825. Round trips from New Orleans to Louisville were being made at the later date in twenty-five days, and fares, under stiff competition, were being reduced at a rapid rate. Many boats were fitted out in luxurious fashion with two decks, cabins, bars, and richly carpeted social rooms. A river life that had long had something of a unique flavor in its vigorous boatmen and its notorious bad men now added its gamblers and its swaggering planter passengers, on whom the gamblers preyed. Fires and snags always offered dangers and excitement, and an urge to speed well beyond the limits of safety kept losses at a maximum.

Transportation on the Great Lakes and in the region south of them grew rapidly in this period. The first steamboat on the Lakes was the *Walk-in-the-Water*, launched in 1817; but sailing vessels had already pioneered the way, and the completion of the Erie Canal (1825) definitely opened a new era of ever increasing traffic. Not to be outdone by New York, Pennsylvania began, in 1826, to build a great system consisting of canals, tramways, and a series of inclined planes over the mountains. Horsecars ran out from Philadelphia to the Susquehanna, where a canal took over and carried passengers and freight to the foot of the mountains; there stationary engines and cables lifted them some fourteen hundred feet and lowered them on the other side to a canal that reached Pittsburgh. It was an interesting but unprofitable undertaking, which soon gave way to the Pennsylvania Railroad.

Virginia and Ohio both built canal systems, and by 1833 the Cumberland Road had been pushed westward as far as Columbus, Ohio. The railroad, however, was making a beginning, and the future belonged to it. John Stevens and Oliver Evans pioneered the way and popularized the idea of steam transportation. In 1827 a short line was constructed in Massachusetts from Quincy to the Neponset River, and another was built in Pennsylvania for hauling coal from the mines to a river for shipment. Then, also in 1827, charters were granted for both the Charleston-Hamburg line in South Carolina and the Baltimore and Ohio in Maryland. The Charleston road was begun in 1830 and the Baltimore line in 1828. Both were to use steam engines. Together they opened a new era in transportation in the United States.

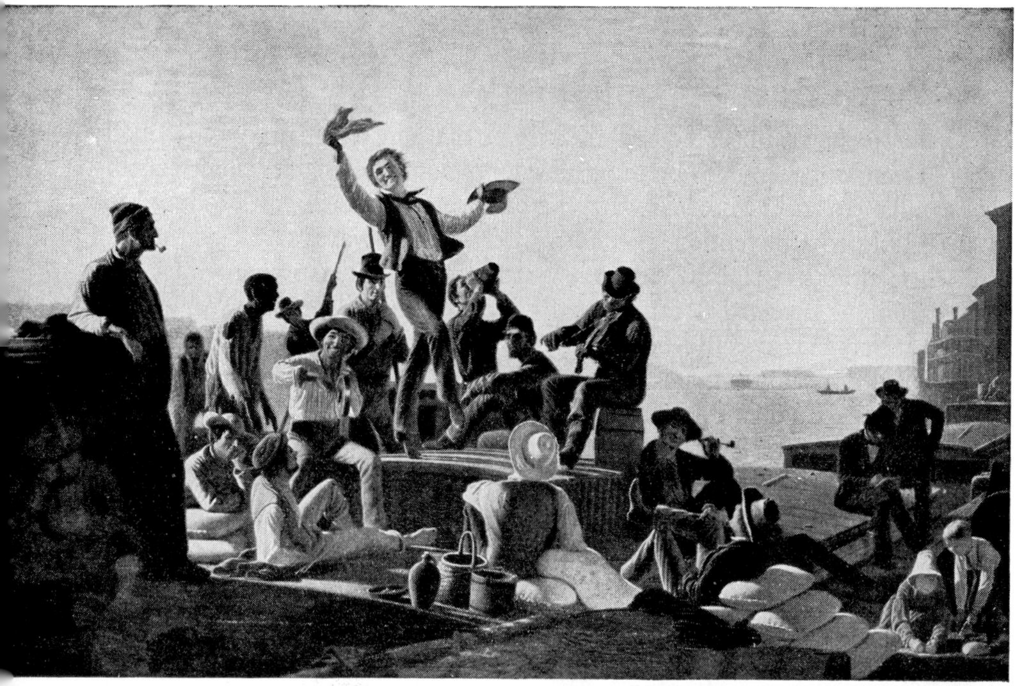

From the Collection of the City Art Museum, St. Louis

Flatboatmen on the Mississippi River

CONTEMPORARY PAINTING BY GEORGE C. BINGHAM

Detroit, Michigan, in 1837, from the Canadian Shore

Stokes Collection. The New York Public Library

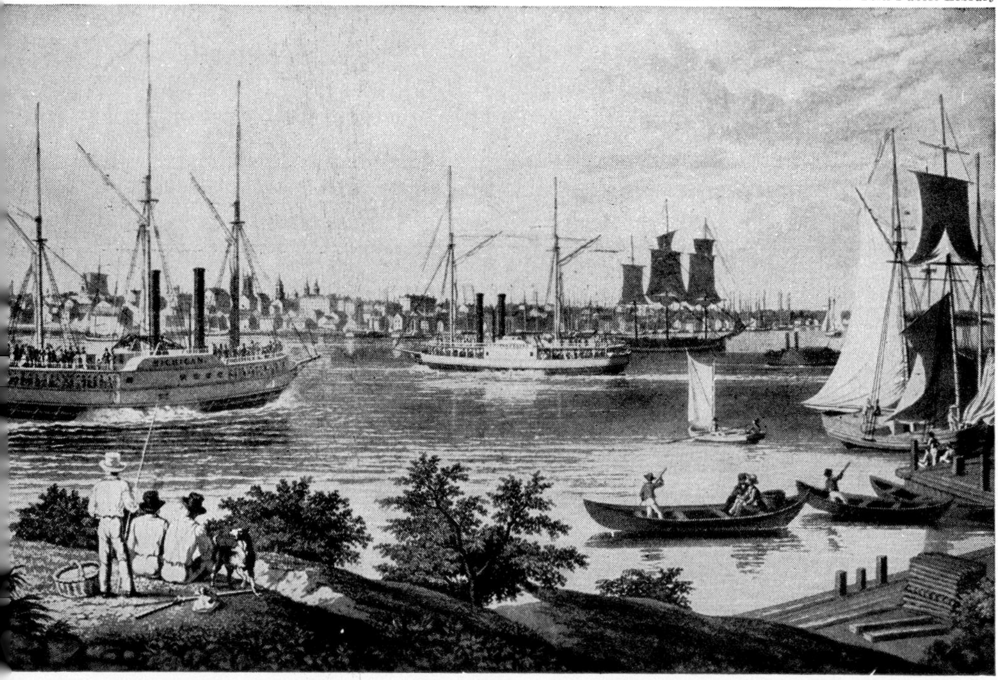

In the realm of politics the rise of the new West produced equally important results. The rapid development of new states upset existing balances and pressed forward the old problem which had produced the Hartford Convention. Western interests and ways were not those of the older states. Furthermore, Western states had shown a tendency to combine with the South in their voting. All the ills of the War of 1812 and afterward could be laid to such a combination. Now, if a whole group of Western states were suddenly introduced into the American family,—Indiana had been admitted in 1816, Illinois in 1818, and Alabama in 1819,—did this not threaten both the interests of the older members and the sound, safe practices which they had established? Was it not time to place some checks on these developments?

THE MISSOURI COMPROMISE

Woven into this problem was another of growing importance. Slavery was now localized. Where, in early days, Northern as well as Southern states had accepted the institution, it was now largely confined to the South and was being carried westward by Southern emigrants. The Ordinance of 1787 had excluded it from territory north of the Ohio River, and both Indiana and Illinois, after some effort to establish it under a system of indenture, had finally forbidden its existence. It was, however, spreading to the lower South with cotton, and many slaves had been carried from Kentucky and Tennessee into the Missouri territory.

Ironically enough, this expansion of slavery came at a time when criticism of the system was widespread and open. Antislavery societies had been springing up, especially in the back sections of the South, where the Quakers took the lead. The American Colonization Society for the transportation of freed Negroes to Africa had been organized in 1816, and Charles Osborne and Benjamin Lundy were already publishing antislavery periodicals. Economic depression in the older slaveholding regions added something to the move, and soon a series of Negro insurrections played a part. Some Southerners also noted the fact that their section—the slaveholding part of the nation—was falling behind the North in population and, consequently, in political power. By 1820 the North had 5,152,000 people; the South, only 4,485,000. Even with three fifths of the slaves counting as population, the slave states could muster only 81 votes in the House of Representatives, as against the free states' 105. Only in the Senate were these sec-

tions equal. The stage was thus set, when Missouri asked for admission
to the Union as a slave state, for one grand tangling of interests, morals,
and sectional rivalry.

The struggle began in the House of Representatives when Tallmadge
of New York proposed an amendment to Missouri's application, prohibiting the further introduction of slavery and providing for the freeing of all children of slaves, born within the state after admission, at
the age of twenty-five years. Behind this amendment lay not only the
rising moral objections to slavery, but also the resentment which men
of the Northeast felt for the three-fifths rule, the prevalence of Southerners in high office, and the political combinations of South and West,
which often opposed the Federalists and the various programs for the
advancement of their interests. The opposition which the amendment
immediately met had behind it, in like fashion, the Southern fear of
loss of power and the Western resentment of Eastern interference.
Debate became intense and bitter. It centered about two larger issues:
the evils of slavery itself and the constitutional right of Congress to lay
restrictions on a new state at admission. James Tallmadge and John W.
Taylor in the House and Rufus King in the Senate took the lead in
pushing the amendment. Their attacks on slavery were so harsh that
slaveholders "gnawed their lips and clenched their fists" and talked of
a fire that had been kindled which only "seas of blood" could extin-
guish. The proponents of the amendment held that the power to prohibit slavery in the territories had already been granted in the Northwest Ordinance and in certain restrictions placed on Louisiana; that the
three-fifths rule applied only to the original slave states and not to those
created from the territories; and that the Louisiana treaty did not
guarantee property rights in slaves to the people of Missouri. Taylor
followed the passage of the amendment in the House with an unsuccessful amendment that prohibited slavery also in the territory of
Arkansas.

The constitutional issue was best stated by Pinkney of Maryland. He
argued that the United States was a union of equals and that if Congress could place special restrictions on a prospective new state as a
condition of admission, that state would be a pygmy among giants. If
Congress could pluck power after power from an applicant for admission, the new state would enter the Union "shorn of its beams," a servant of the majority.

The Senate rejected the amendment as passed by the House, but
in the next session of Congress combined a bill for the unrestricted

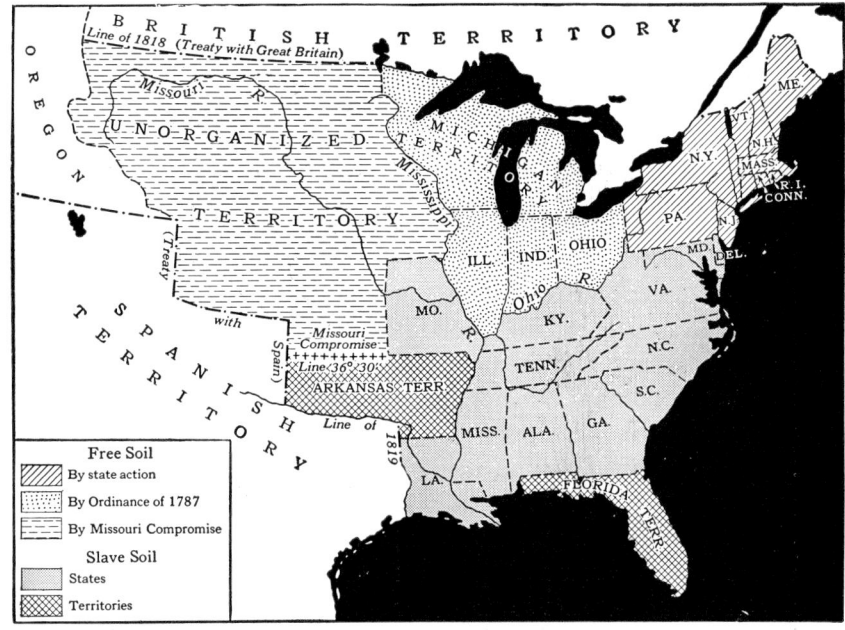

Free States and Slave States after the Missouri Compromise

admission of Missouri with one for the admission of Maine, which had just received permission for separation from Massachusetts. To this bill Senator Thomas of Illinois moved an amendment providing for the prohibition of slavery north of the line 36° 30′ in the rest of the Louisiana Purchase.

This proposal was ultimately accepted by the House and became known as the Missouri Compromise. It was not a popular measure with either party, and much of the bitterness engendered by the debates flared up again when Missouri, in her constitution, incorporated not only guarantees of slavery, but also a provision against the admission of free Negroes into the state. Henry Clay, however, engineered a second compromise, by which Missouri promised never to construe the provision in such a way as to exclude citizens of other states or of the Union from the enjoyment of such privileges and immunities as these citizens were entitled to under the Constitution of the United States.

The importance of the Missouri struggle lay not in its immediate effects, but rather in what it revealed of future possibilities. Passions soon subsided. The Federalists were already on their way out. Opposition to the West did not die with them in Eastern breasts, but new combinations were soon possible that softened fears. The more important facts were that the slavery issue had been raised and that politicians had learned the value of its moral force in support of other interests. John Taylor saw it as an excuse to use slavery as an instrument for effecting a balance of power between sections and prophesied that it would one day bring about the dissolution of the Union. Jefferson spoke of it as "a fire-bell in the night" and declared that "a geographical line, coinciding with a marked principle, moral and political, once conceived and held up to the angry passions of men, will never be obliterated; and every new irritation will mark it deeper and deeper."

Equally important was the entangling of slavery with expansion and with the struggles of certain sections for dominance in new Western territories. Even if a sharp difference of opinion on the good and evil in slavery could be accepted within the constitutional framework, was it possible to avoid open conflict in the territories when freedom and slavery both wished to enter? That might change the issue from the merits of slavery per se to the desirability of extending it and bringing it into open competition with freemen and their interests.

So the great era of expansion went on upsetting the balance in American life and pressing forward new forces and new problems. It slackened a bit in the late 1830's, when another depression—produced, again, in part, by Western optimism and overexpansion—settled down upon the nation. It was, however, only gathering strength for another great wave, which, in the next decades, would reach the western edge of the continent in California and Oregon.

SELECTED BIBLIOGRAPHY

FREDERICK JACKSON TURNER, *The Rise of the New West*, is the best single volume on this period, and his *Frontier in American History* and *Sections in American History* contain pertinent material; L. K. MATHEWS, *The Expansion of New England*; D. E. CLARK, *The West in American History*; R. E. RIEGEL, *America Moves West*, general accounts.

S. D. SMEDES, *A Southern Planter*; T. P. ABERNETHY, *From Frontier to Plantation in Tennessee*; C. H. AMBLER, *Sectionalism in Virginia*; L. C. GRAY, *History of Agriculture in the Southern States to 1860*; W. P. WEBB, *The Great Plains*, valuable studies of developments in the Old South and the Southwest; H. C. HUBBART,

The Older Middle West; EVERETT DICK, *The Sod House Frontier*; JOSEPH SCHAFER, *Four Wisconsin Counties*; C. H. AMBLER, *A History of Transportation in the Ohio Valley*; F. C. SHOEMAKER, *Missouri's Struggle for Statehood*; CARL WITTKE (Ed.), *The History of the State of Ohio*, deal with changes in the Midwest; S. E. MORISON, *Maritime History of Massachusetts*, and P. W. BIDWELL and others, *History of Agriculture in the Northern United States, 1620–1860*, reveal something of the impact of the new West on the old Northeast.

B. H. HIBBARD, *A History of the Public Land Policies*, and PAYSON J. TREAT, *The National Land System, 1785–1820*, special studies of importance.

H. S. COMMAGER (Ed.), *Documents of American History*, pp. 224–227, 233–234, 237–238, 242–244, contains source material.

XIV

Politics and the Age of Jackson

T HE POLITICAL situation indicated by the expression "era of good feeling" altered sharply in the last years of Monroe's administration. The Federalist party continued to decline. It maintained an organization in a few states, but offered only local candidates for office. It was no longer a national force. New issues, however, had produced sharp differences of opinion among Democrats (Republicans), and the leaders of factions within the party were making a strong bid for popular support. As early as April, 1822, Niles's *Weekly Register* remarked that there were already sixteen or seventeen aspirants in the field for the office which Monroe was about to relinquish. An interesting comment on changing conditions was the fact that not one of them was from the state of Virginia. The dynasty of the Old Dominion, like the harmony within the Democratic party, was evidently coming to an end.

By election year (1824) the list of active candidates had been reduced to five. They represented both different sections of the country and differences of opinion in regard to all the new issues of the new day.

At the head of the list was John Quincy Adams, Secretary of State and son of John Adams, second President of the United States. He was every inch a New Englander and every inch an Adams. He was cold and reserved, intelligent, independent, and patriotic. A short, thickset body and a bald head added nothing to his personal charm. Trained in public life from the day when, as a lad of seventeen, he had accompanied his father to Paris, he now stood before the American people as the most cosmopolitan and the best-equipped man in public life. His understanding of national problems was clear and comprehensive. He was a nationalist in the best sense of the term.

Yet Adams was not popular. In spite of acute sensitiveness to public opinion, he lacked the ability to win popular favor. Harsh and critical of weakness in others, he met his own standards, but somehow gained no forgiveness by doing so. Few men have ever merited more of affection and received less of it. What he achieved came by sheer merit, hard work, clear insight, and a stern sense of duty. He was, therefore, always a bit thwarted and a bit cynical. Denied personal satisfaction, he found compensation by pouring out his bitterness on the pages of one of America's great diaries.

In sharp contrast to Adams was the somewhat youthful Henry Clay. Born in Virginia and matured in Kentucky, he spoke for the older West in favor of protective tariffs and internal improvements at Federal expense. He called it the American System. He was as "distinctly and warmly human" as Adams was reserved. He was equally honest, and not a single dollar of public money ever stuck to his fingers. Yet he was no Puritan. He had gambled heavily in his younger days; "his relations with several pretty women were unquestionably something more than fraternal"; "his attentions to the wine bottle were frequently more ardent than discreet." Yet men loved him even when they disapproved, and with good reason. His approach was that of the conciliator. He thought peace was better than conflict. As Gerald Johnson has said of him, "He escaped the greatest arrogance of all, the arrogance of believing that God had endowed him with a peculiar and infallible capacity to distinguish between good and evil." He knew that sometimes he might be mistaken.

Then there was the even younger John C. Calhoun of South Carolina, who, as Secretary of War, sat in the cabinet with Adams. He too was a nationalist with a record for supporting the tariff, the Bank, and internal improvements. Although born and reared in a frontier region, Calhoun had acquired the culture and grace of a Carolina gentleman. He made friends and held them, but more through admiration than warmth. The word *correct* seems best to describe both his ways and his personality. He was tall and spare and handsome; he sowed no wild oats; he took the business of living seriously; he was a devoted husband both to the aristocratic Floride Bonneau Calhoun and to the state of South Carolina. As Puritanical as Adams himself, he was as unhumorously certain of his own righteousness and of the soundness of his principles. For the good of the South and of the nation he wanted to be President of the United States.

William H. Crawford of Georgia was the other Southern candidate. He was a man of gigantic stature and handsome face who had made his mark in the Senate, since 1807, by "a studious disposition, a clear judgment, a native sagacity, an engaging affability, and a fund of entertaining anecdotes." He was now Secretary of the Treasury. Less a personal aristocrat than Calhoun, he nevertheless represented the older, the more well-to-do, and the more conservative states'-rights part of the

South. He was, moreover, the choice of the Congressional caucus, against which the tide of public opinion was rapidly rising. He was thus viewed, with some justice, as the politicians' candidate—one who favored the spoils system and whose record in connection with the Bank and the public lands was not everywhere satisfactory.

The last and most colorful candidate was Andrew Jackson of Tennessee. He represented not only the new West, but all the great democratic forces which were stirring in the South and East as well. Although allied with the conservative, aristocratic element in his own state and somewhat vague in his attitudes toward Clay's American System and other issues of the day, he enjoyed immense popularity as a military hero and as a self-made man. That was enough to open wide the door to politics and to give the impression that he was the people's friend. Even before his triumphs on the battlefield, he had served his state in Washington in both the House and the Senate. Now, with added prestige, he was being thrust forward by devoted friends for the highest office in the land.

Jackson was always a man to be reckoned with. What he did he did with vigor and precision. Private enemies had discovered that on the dueling ground; the Indians had learned it at Horse Shoe Bend; the British, at Pensacola and New Orleans. He was direct to the point of rashness. He was as brave as he was blunt. Enemies charged him with being "intemperate, arbitrary and ambitious for power." Yet there was a certain coldness in his impetuosity that produced fear in timid souls and gave unbounded confidence to friends. Jefferson is supposed to have referred to him as "a dangerous man," and, according to Van Buren, "Thomas Ritchie of the *Richmond Enquirer* 'scarcely ever went to bed . . . without apprehension that he would wake up to hear of some *coup d'état* by the General.' " Friends, on the other hand, spoke of his unswerving loyalty, his unflinching courage, and his crystal-clear frankness. Women generally liked him—a fact that emphasizes the personal charm, the aristocratic bearing, and the inborn gentility which lay behind his sometimes blustering exterior. He was thus something of a contradiction but, all in all, sound enough in judgment and strong enough in personality and character to create an age and to give to it his name.

THE ELECTION OF 1824

Events such as the panic of 1819, the Missouri Compromise struggle, and the sharp clash over the tariff in 1824 kept the political waters troubled and brought embarrassments to most of the candidates. The panic permitted enemies to criticize Crawford's handling of finances, and the struggle over slavery in Missouri injured him, as it did the other slaveholders among the candidates, Clay and Calhoun. Clay's ardent support of the tariff lost Southern friends as the older portions of that section began their fight against protection. The tariff placed Calhoun in an even worse position. His constituents were now sharply divided on the issue, and any decision on his part meant trouble. Adams, meanwhile, as the only Northern candidate, may have gained something from the Missouri conflict and might have gained more from the acquisition of Florida if Clay and his Western friends had not delayed ratification. Only Jackson seemed to remain untouched by events and to be growing in public favor. He was far enough removed from the center of sectional and interest conflict to escape injury. He governed Florida with a strong hand, while his rivals quarreled and did their best to discredit one another in the eyes of the people.

As election day drew near, the situation was somewhat simplified when Crawford suffered a stroke of paralysis and when Calhoun, pushed to second place in Pennsylvania, was content to accept the Vice-Presidential nomination behind either Adams or Jackson. Crawford continued in the race, but lost ground as his condition became generally known and finished third in the electoral vote, behind Jackson and Adams, who ranked in that order. The vote, however, was close, and no candidate had the required majority. The election, therefore, went to the House of Representatives, where Clay, now out of the race, threw his support to Adams, who had received both fewer popular and fewer electoral votes than Jackson. The combination made Adams President, with his great rival Calhoun as Vice-President, and his other rivals as bitter critics. Crawford went home, a cripple in body and none too clear in mind, to nurse a futile hope for later success; Jackson went back to Tennessee "to rest, recruit and then sally forth to smash Henry Clay," whom he dubbed "the Judas of the West."

This unhappy situation bore fruit at once when Adams made Henry Clay his Secretary of State. Jackson's friends, through the person of one George Kremer, charged a "corrupt bargain," in which Adams had entered into a deal to appoint Clay Secretary of State in return for support for the Presidency. The charge was false. Some contacts had been made by friends, but there was no "corrupt bargain." Clay found in Adams the best expression of his own political principles, domestic and foreign, and Adams, coldly and without much enthusiasm, independently reached the conclusion that Clay was the best man for the office. That was the true basis of Clay's appointment and acceptance. The charge, however, was kept alive to stress "the fact" that Jackson, who was supported by the majority of the people, had been cheated out of the Presidency. The Adams administration thus became one long campaign for Jackson in 1828. It opened, even before Adams had met his Congress, when the legislature of Tennessee, in October, 1825, nominated Jackson, and he accepted in a speech before both houses.

ADMINISTRATION OF JOHN QUINCY ADAMS

Few men of ability equal to that of John Quincy Adams have ever served as President of the United States. As few have ever had a more unsuccessful administration. Both his virtues and his weaknesses contributed to that end. He absolutely refused to appoint men to office for political reasons and insisted on leaving where they were those who had served efficiently in past years. Only twelve removals were made in his term. Adopting the principle of broad constitutional construction, he urged the building of a great national system of roads and canals, the establishment of a national university, and the passage of laws for the advancement of agriculture, manufactures, commerce, literature, science, and even "the elegant arts."

With equally broad international feeling he nominated delegates to represent the United States at the Panama Congress, a movement initiated by President Bolívar of Colombia for the purpose of consolidating the new South American republics against attacks by Spain and other aggressor nations. Participation in an organization where a general assembly could, in time of war, determine the contribution of each nation in funds and troops by majority vote ran counter to American ideas of predominance, as well as of national independence. But the prospect of an American system without the participation of the United States was not pleasing, and the threatened move by Colombia and Mexico to seize Cuba and presumably to free the slaves there was something that should be opposed from the inside. Adams believed, with Henry Clay, that we must take part.

Then there was the case of the Creek Indians in Georgia, against whose lands the eager cotton planters of the state were pressing and who held that the agreement of 1802 for their removal had been secured against the wishes of the majority of the tribe. They now appealed to the Adams administration for protection and justice.

With a characteristic sense of fair play, Adams secured a new treaty, which gave the Indians until January 1, 1827, to remove themselves and their possessions. He was willing to use "all the means under his control to maintain the faith of the nation by carrying the treaty into effect."

But unfortunately both for Adams and for the nation, none of his plans and purposes were allowed to succeed. The friends of Jackson saw to that. With Jackson himself declaring, among other things, that "By me no plans were concerted to impair the pure principles of our republican institutions, nor to prostrate that fundamental maxim, which maintains the supremacy of the people's will," his supporters took the hint and bluntly set about frustrating every move of the man who, Jackson implied, *had* done such things. As one of them exclaimed when the administration forces had carried a minor point, "Too bad,— if they had taken the other side we could have whipped them."

Under such circumstances, Adams's plans for a national system of internal improvements came to little. In December, 1825, Senator Van Buren of New York went so far as to introduce resolutions which would have denied to Congress any right to build roads or canals within a state. The resolutions failed of passage, but they showed the temper of the day. Even the Cumberland Road, now authorized as far as Zanesville, Ohio, was neglected, and relinquishment to the states through which it passed was being considered. Constitutional objections reduced Federal action to the mere appropriation of funds; and even when this was done, local interests, by political pressures, monopolized them. Thus gradually the states and private corporations took over the work of building roads and canals to suit their own needs. The Federal government played little part in this vital development except as a subscriber to local stocks.

The Panama Congress project fared no better. Southern Congressmen professed to fear that the slavery question would come up for discussion, and Northern men objected to the control of affairs by a congress. Delay after delay occurred; and when, at last, two delegates were selected and started on their mission, one died on the way and the second reached Panama after the Congress had adjourned.

In the Creek Indian affair Governor Troup of Georgia denied the right of the Federal government to reopen the question and boldly declared that his state was sovereign on her own soil. He announced his intention to use military force against the government if necessary and proposed to free his surveyors should they be arrested by Federal authorities. A House committee recommended the purchase of all the Indian lands in Georgia and the upholding of the Washington treaty, but the Senate committee, under the leadership of Thomas Hart Benton, upheld Georgia under the earlier treaty and refused military aid for the coercion of the state. Fortunately the issue was avoided by the Indian acceptance of a treaty extinguishing all their claims, but Adams was, nevertheless, thoroughly discredited and the nation defied by a state.

The political intrigue behind these developments was even more clearly revealed in conflicts over the tariff. The demands for protection had increased after the crash of 1819, and a bill, backed primarily by the middle and Western states, had passed the House that winter, but had failed in the Senate. Pressure continued, however, and in 1824 an act was passed increasing duties on iron, lead, wool, hemp, cotton-bagging, and other less important articles. It was carried mainly by the votes of Western and middle states, with New England divided between the manufacturers, who favored the act, and the commercial leaders, who opposed it, and the South in sharp opposition. As John Randolph said, "The merchants and manufacturers of Massachusetts and New Hampshire repell this bill, while men in hunting shirts, with deerskin leggings and moccasins on their feet, want protection for home manufactures."

For a period of time agitation weakened, but the woolen manufacturers soon revived their demands for the application of the minimum principle to their product, and in 1827 an act to meet their demands passed the House, but failed in the Senate by the deciding vote of Vice-President Calhoun.

The manufacturers answered this with a "national convention of protectionists," held in the midsummer of 1827 at Harrisburg, Pennsylvania. The convention considered all industries and recommended aid to agriculture, to the manufacturers of cotton, hemp, flax, iron, and glass, and, of course, to the woolen industry.

With the election of 1828 so near, and with the sections and interests so divided, the politicians saw their opportunity. Jackson's friends were now in control of the House. They charged that the Harrisburg meeting had been got up by Adams men. They understood, however, the popularity of protection in New York, Pennsylvania, and Ohio. They also knew that they must somehow widen Jackson's support in these states without weakening his hold on the South. With this in mind, the new Speaker, Stephenson of Virginia, placed five Jackson men and two Adams men on the Committee on Manufactures, from which any tariff bill must come. The result was the notorious "Tariff of Abominations," the purpose of which, said John Randolph, was related "to manufactures of no sort or kind but the manufacture of a President of the United States."

The plan, as Calhoun frankly explained it nine years later, was to offer a bill containing not only a high general range of duties, but especially high rates on raw materials used in the New England mills. This would satisfy the middle and Western states, but meet opposition in both the South and New England. The combined vote of these sections, with the regular Jackson vote, would defeat the bill purely on grounds of equity and not because it was protective in character. Thus the country would escape the tariff, Adams men could be charged with aiding in its defeat, and Jackson men could parade themselves as true friends of protection.

It was a clever scheme, but it failed. In the end, New England men saw the advantage in higher rates, even when raw materials were included, and cast their votes in favor of the bill. The South was bitter. The politicians were chagrined. Jackson, however, suffered little. Even the South did not hold him responsible for what many citizens there viewed as a sectional disaster.

THE ELECTION OF ANDREW JACKSON, 1828

Long before his term of office was ended, Adams knew that he could not be re-elected. He had built no political machine. He had retained opponents in office, even though he knew it would end his own control. The aggressive efforts of Jackson's friends and the charges of a "corrupt bargain" not only had kept their hero before the public eye, but had ruined Adams's plans and robbed him of credit due. The personal factor alone was enough to drive the one out, and to bring the other into the Presidency. Yet that was the least of the factors at work which were to sweep Jackson triumphantly into office in 1828.

Behind that triumph, and behind most that was to happen in the next administration, lay the fact that all the great changes which had been going on in American life had now reached the point of permanent effectiveness. The period of transition was ended. New forces —some national, some sectional, some individual, and some social— were at work, and new groups representing conflicting interests and values were already struggling for control. The back of the nation was

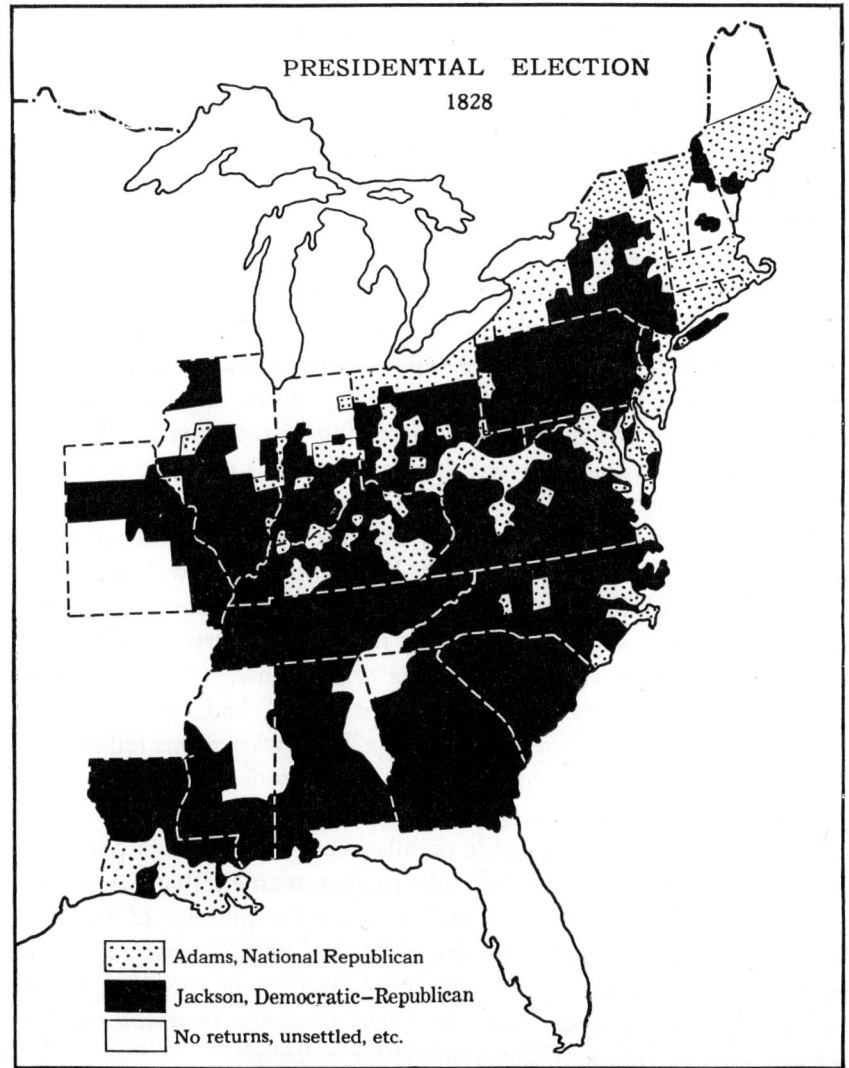

PRESIDENTIAL ELECTION
1828

.... Adams, National Republican

▓ Jackson, Democratic–Republican

☐ No returns, unsettled, etc.

Presidential Election of 1828

now squarely turned on Europe. American problems and local forces monopolized the stage. Sectional and national interests and feelings were both on the increase. Industry was mature enough to give something of a class feeling to capitalists and workers. Cotton had established its kingdom and had given slavery a new hold. The West was a power in politics and a positive force in shaping attitudes and reactions. The basic problem of a consolidated central government versus local control was sharpening and was becoming menacing. In an age of widening opportunity and increasing power in the hands of the few, the questions of individual rights, majority control, and property influence were beginning to be faced. Under American conditions all these things had to do with politics. They had to be phrased in terms of the democratic intent and character of our government. A political revolution as an expression of these forces was inevitable.

Andrew Jackson was the first President who came out of the heart of the continent and from the ranks of common men, and whose reputation was based on his dealing with strictly domestic affairs. As a popular hero he profited by the widening of the franchise and the interest in voting which had been increasing in recent years. Between 1816 and 1830 ten states revised their constitutions or made new ones. All the new Western states, except Mississippi, granted manhood suffrage, and Mississippi required only that the voter be a taxpayer or a member of the militia. Connecticut, Massachusetts, New York, Maryland, and New Hampshire liberalized their old requirements and either granted manhood suffrage or set very nominal property qualifications. In states like New York the struggle was intense. Chancellor Kent insisted that the "extreme democratic principle" had "been regarded with terror by the wise men of every age," and warned his fellows that "the men of no property, together with the crowds of dependents connected with the great manufacturing and commercial establishments, and the motley and undefinable population of the crowded ports may predominate in the assembly." He further warned that "there is a tendency in the poor to covet and to share the plunder of the rich; in the debtor to relax or avoid the obligation of contracts; . . . in the indolent and profligate to cast the whole burden of society upon the industrious and virtuous, and *there is a tendency in ambitious and wicked men to inflame these combustible materials*."

The *Albany Register*, however, was willing to "let the whole government go into the hands of the people; there is no danger that they will commit political suicide. . . . Do not let us deceive ourselves with the idea that our ancestors knew almost everything . . . it is no fiction to say that they lived in ages comparatively dark . . . had too much of the prejudice derived from the musty schools of feudalism, monarchy and despotism." Thomas Jefferson, evidently, was coming back into style in some corners in the 1820's!

Such were the changes and temper which brought out some eight hundred thousand more votes in 1828 than had been cast in 1824. Much less than half of this increase was due to changes from legislative selection to direct voting, so that the additional vote of 1828 was larger than the total vote of 1824. Indeed, Jackson could consider himself, in a peculiar way, the spokesman of the people. Perhaps that was one reason why he viewed the Presidency as having a new importance which required it to assert independence of both Congress and the Supreme Court.

The distribution of votes also reflected the changing conditions. Sectionalism, economic interests, and class consciousness all played a part in the voting. Adams's support came largely from New England and the parts of New York and Ohio to which New Englanders had migrated. It embraced the industrial areas and those in the older West, especially Kentucky and the "sugar bowl" in Louisiana, where home markets were breaking and a place in the national economy had to be found. He secured votes because of his support of internal improvements in Maryland and Virginia and in regions, like North Carolina, where such improvements were badly needed. Jackson, on the other hand, had the backing of most of the West and South, of Pennsylvania and the interior of New York. Back-country men in Maine and New Hampshire and the new laboring classes in Eastern cities voted for him. Some Southern planters may have given their support in the belief that Calhoun would be his successor, but most others viewed him as the friend of common men and accepted his vagueness on issues as a possible support of their interests. At any rate, most of them now thought of government under Jackson as a means to certain definite ends.

In a larger way Jackson's election meant that the West had grown to the point where it could elect one of its own to the Presidency. It meant also that a great new middle class, through the opportunities in land and the places offered in a steadily expanding social-economic order everywhere, had come to dominance in the United States and was asserting and applying new notions of what was meant by the term *democracy*. So far, it had usually suggested the equality of all men in voting and holding office. Now, however, in its attitudes and assumptions with regard to the public lands, public schools, and, recently, the government's relations to social-economic activities, it threatened, vaguely, to give a wider meaning to both liberty and equality.

Some men had sensed these deeper meanings, and the campaign of 1828 had reflected this awareness in unusual bitterness and in unrestrained indulgence in personalities. Adams was maligned equally for what he had done and for what he had not done. The cry of "corrupt bargain" never ceased. His cold dignity was made to appear as indifference to the general welfare, and his loyalty to principle was distorted into disloyalty to friends and supporters. It was Jackson, however, who suffered most. He was pictured as a fiery murderer whose bloody deeds included the killing of opponents in duels, the putting of soldiers to death without sufficient reasons, and the bold execution of British subjects in Florida. To the charge of murder one of his defenders replied: "Yes! He murdered in the coldest kind of blood fifteen hundred British soldiers for merely trying to get into New Orleans in search of booty and beauty." An unintentional irregularity in Jackson's marriage to Mrs. Rachel Robards was distorted into a brazen case of wife-stealing, and the name of one whom Jackson loved with all the passion of his ardent nature was subjected to scandal and abuse. Her death in December, just after the election, may or may not have been hastened by knowledge of all that had been said. At any rate, a "sinewy hatred" was born in Jackson himself, which found expression in these words: "May God Almighty forgive her murderers as I know she forgave them. I never can." The lonely grave in the garden at the Hermitage thus became a driving force in Jackson's political relationships.

The inauguration also revealed the fact that men thought something significant had happened in Jackson's election. "I have never seen such a crowd before," wrote an observer. "Persons have come five hundred miles to see General Jackson and they really seem to think that the country is [to be] rescued from some dreadful danger." Lean, unkempt, unlovely back-country folks filled the town. Homespun clothes became a familiar sight on the crowded streets. "It was like the inundation of northern barbarians into Rome," wrote one observer. ". . . Strange faces filled every public place, and every face seemed to bear defiance on its brow." Jackson arrived earlier than expected and went quietly to Gadsby's Hotel; but when his presence became known, bedlam broke loose. Cannons roared in salute; drums kept time for marching crowds; men and women shouted themselves hoarse in welcome to their hero. Washington had never experienced anything like it in all its days.

With harsh memories of the fact that Adams had made no effort to silence the attacks on Rachel, Jackson ignored the retiring President and coldly asked for the White House for the inaugural reception. He walked bareheaded to the Capitol to take the oath and then rode back to the White House, where the crowd followed. Through the unpaved streets they plodded, stood with their muddy boots on the damask-covered furniture, stormed into the rooms where waiters were serving orange punch out of barrels, broke the glasses, and almost crushed Jackson until some friends formed a solid phalanx around him, and others, more thoughtful, carried the punch out to the lawn. The people had truly taken charge of their government.

JACKSON'S FIRST ADMINISTRATION BEGINS

Jackson's first administration took its character largely from the personal friendships and antagonisms that had been formed in recent years. Soon it added its own share of attachments and hatreds. The cabinet, as Jackson formed it, contained elements of serious discord. Against the advice of friends, Major John H. Eaton of Tennessee was made Secretary of War. He had only recently married the widow Margaret Timberlake, whom, some said, public opinion would not permit in Washington society. Eaton, in turn, had approved Berrien of Georgia as Attorney-General, and Branch of North Carolina as Secretary of the Navy. McLean of Ohio, the Postmaster-General, and Ingham of Pennsylvania, the Secretary of the Treasury, were supposedly friends of Vice-President Calhoun, and Martin Van Buren of New York, the Secretary of State, was a clever and ambitious politician whose hold on the democratic element in the powerful Empire State machine made his appointment necessary.

Two factions, one looking to Van Buren, the other to Calhoun, quickly developed. Both were conscious of the fact that Jackson was old and feeble and was expected to serve only one term. Around the matter of Mrs. Eaton's acceptance in society, they and their good wives soon raised a feud which rendered the official cabinet useless to Jackson as an advisory body. Because she, as Peggy O'Neale, had sometimes helped out in her father's tavern, and, as Mrs. Timberlake, had indulged in flirtations while her husband was at sea, the Calhoun group considered her quite unfit for their society. The widower Van Buren thought otherwise, and Jackson, who had only recently buried his much abused Rachel at the Hermitage, found in these divergent attitudes the test of loyalty and democratic common sense.

Soon he turned to a little group of outside friends, appropriately dubbed the "kitchen cabinet," and relied on them for both advice and companionship. The ablest of these were Amos Kendall and Francis Preston Blair, who were soon to edit the *Globe* and make it the official voice of the administration. Then there were Isaac Hill, the crippled New Hampshire editor, soon to be in the Senate, and William B. Lewis, an old Tennessee friend, who came to live in the White House. They, with such ardent Democrats as Thomas Hart Benton in the Senate and James K. Polk in the House, provided Jackson with whatever counsel his own vigorous, independent mind required. They never dictated or controlled. Jackson was the President, and both he and they were thoroughly conscious of that fact.

While these developments were in their early stages, the problem of appointments to office crowded upon the administration and revealed certain new factors at work. The wider participation of common men in voting had stressed the democratic belief not only in the capacity of all men to hold public office, but in their right to take turns in doing so. Earlier Presidents had been somewhat reluctant to remove incumbents, and, except in the case of Jefferson, there had been no sharp party overturnings. Now the situation was different. Jackson represented a complete break with the Adams regime, and behind him was now forming a well-organized political machine. Practical politicians like Van Buren and Hill believed that, if things were to run smoothly, all offices should be in the hands of friends. If the party expected to remain in power, it should use offices to reward its supporters. "Cleanse the Augean Stables," cried the *United States Telegraph*. And Isaac Hill echoed: "Shall we . . . appoint to office and continue in office men who have . . . libel[ed] the purest patriots in the country? . . . Forbid it, Heaven!" To the victors belonged the spoils. Even a hearse-driver in an obscure village, who had voted for Adams, had no right to his job. Every "traitor" should go.

Jackson was far more moderate in his attitude. He did not remove all those who had voted against him, nor were "the barnacles . . . scraped clean" from the "Ship of State," as Hill demanded. He did, however, fall in with the trend enough to give a new turn to party developments. From that day forward those who served the party expected rewards in offices or in favors. As Jackson himself observed in regard to his own support, "It appeared that instead of love of principle it was love of office that had induced [many of] them to support the good cause as they pleased to term it, . . . that self-exertion was about to be abandoned and dependence for a livelihood placed upon the government."

The danger in such attitudes, of course, was not immediate. A new and wider interest in government was certainly all for the best. A

Andrew Jackson

PAINTING BY
THOMAS SULLY

John Quincy Adams

The Corcoran Gallery of Art

Henry Clay

John C. Calhoun

PAINTING BY
EUGENIUS DE BLOCK

Carolina Art Association

Dartmouth College

Daniel Webster

PAINTING BY
JOHN POPE

Stephen A. Douglas

notion that government existed only for personal gain through party service, however, might lead to both inefficiency and corruption. A too great emphasis on the party as the sole agent of political interest might reduce all social-economic progress to a matter of political-party support. Then all reform movements would, of necessity, be forced into politics. That would bring moral issues and political interests together in a way that one day would divide the political parties along sectional lines and, because of moral tangling, place problems beyond solution by the democratic process of rational discussion, compromise, and mutual adjustment.

DISCORD IN THE ADMINISTRATION

But the immediate effect of Jackson's removals was only to add to the growing discord that had begun to develop among his associates. When the Senate was asked to approve the appointment of one hundred and twenty-one persons named to take the places of those removed, there was much bitter opposition. Some, including Isaac Hill himself, were bluntly rejected; Amos Kendall was passed only by Calhoun's deciding vote. When literally thousands of minor civilian officers, especially postmasters, were removed in the first eighteen months, men began to talk of the feasibility of impeaching the President. They even consulted Justice Kent regarding the constitutionality of such a procedure.

All this added to the fury which had developed about Peggy O'Neale and which now assumed real political importance. Eaton, with Jackson's urging, pushed his wife forward for social recognition. The alignment for and against her was now perfectly clear. Van Buren and his friends were on her side; Calhoun and his friends were against her. Cabinet meetings became strained and irritating. Rumors of agreements among cabinet ladies to boycott Mrs. Eaton came to Jackson's ears, and even clergymen visited him with ugly tales of her early misconduct. Jackson only became more resolute. *"Eaton is the last man on earth I ought or would abandon,"* he said. "I would sooner *abandon life."* Furthermore, he threatened that if Ingham, Berrien, and Branch did not alter both their own conduct and that of their wives, dismissals would be in order. So cabinet meetings and official dinners were abandoned. Some men passed without speaking. And all the while everyone observed that Van Buren's influence over Jackson increased, while a coldness grew between the old General and Calhoun.

Disagreement over public issues also contributed to the unhappy situation. Jackson had entered office with only a few positive convictions on public issues, and friends had represented him to each part of the nation as favoring policies beneficial to that part. In his first message to Congress he recommended a modification of the existing tariff, with "utmost caution," so as to diminish "any burthen" on any section. He favored such internal improvements as were constitutional, but suggested that most "internal affairs" should be left to the state governments. He advocated the setting aside of "an ample district west of the Mississippi" to which Eastern Indian tribes should be removed, and in closing, as almost an afterthought, he declared that the Bank of the United States, whose creation was questionable on grounds both of constitutionality and expediency, had failed to establish a uniform and sound currency. Perhaps it would be well, he said, to think about some other kind of institution, founded upon the credit of the government and its revenues.

There was little here to suggest either reform or an aggressive program. Some of the ideas were perhaps a bit sharper than had been expected of Jackson, but the temper was, on the whole, one of conciliation and compromise. In May, 1830, however, a new note appeared, in which Van Buren's influence was apparent. A bill to construct a turnpike from Maysville to Lexington, Kentucky, had passed both the House and the Senate and had come to the President for final action. Because the road lay entirely within one state,—Henry Clay's state,— it offered an excellent test of constitutionality. It offered also splendid opportunity to strike a blow at Clay and his American System. It was just the kind of case that Martin Van Buren, long an aggressive opponent of such measures, was waiting for. Under his guiding hand Jackson penned a stinging veto. It combined a deep emotional appeal to preserve the fundamental principles of our constitutional government with the more practical suggestion that all government funds were needed to eliminate the national debt and reduce taxes. It called men back to the principles of Jefferson.

Such an attitude toward internal improvements, however, was not popular in older corners of the West, where home markets were breaking, or in newer ones, where ways to markets had not been developed. Coming, as it did, at a time when Benton was unsuccessfully urging the passage of new public-land legislation embodying the ideas of pre-emption for the actual settler and the gradation of prices where lands had long remained unsold, Jackson's veto caused many Westerners to believe that their interests were being neglected and suggested to them a closer alliance with the South, where dissatisfaction over the tariff was reaching new levels of bitterness.

Indications of such a move had already appeared when on December 29, 1829, Senator Foot of Connecticut introduced a resolution to inquire into the expediency of limiting the sale of public lands to those already surveyed and abolishing the office of Surveyor-General. Benton of Missouri led the opposition, and Robert Y. Hayne of South Carolina came quickly to his support. A combination of West and South which might affect both lands and tariff seemed in the making. New England leaders were alarmed. Unless that combination could be broken, their section was doomed. With shrewd insight Daniel Webster moved. The charge that New England had always been hostile to the West and Hayne's support of the doctrine of state sovereignty in one of his speeches enabled the great Massachusetts orator to turn the debate from one on the merits of particular land policies to one of sectional recriminations. Skillfully he drove a wedge between his rivals. Relying on the strong national sentiments of the West, he cleverly phrased the conflict in terms of states' rights versus national unity. With unmatched eloquence he voiced the aspirations of all the great new forces working toward political consolidation and nationalism and by so doing both checked the threatened coalition of West and South and forwarded the strictly sectional interests of his own Northeast. His closing words, "Liberty *and* Union, now and forever, one and inseparable!" became a national slogan, even though both he and his industrial friends clearly understood the sectional purpose behind his oratorical efforts.

CALHOUN AND JACKSON

Calhoun was keenly disappointed. His position was now anything but comfortable. In Washington, Jackson had definitely turned toward Van Buren, and the Peggy O'Neale situation had grown steadily worse. Back in South Carolina economic conditions had become desperate, and Calhoun's constituents were badly divided on causes and remedies. While men in the western part of the state still supported Jackson, opposition to the tariff in the eastern section was reaching the point of open resistance. More and more of Calhoun's old supporters joined the protest and looked suspiciously at his past record of ardent support of nationalistic measures. In an attempt to appease without inviting violence, he had, in 1828, penned on their behalf a document known as the "South Carolina Exposition," but had not yet openly admitted his authorship. It provided what he thought was a legal method by which a state might escape what it believed to be an unconstitutional act. As he explained it, the sovereign people of a state in convention assembled could declare an act of Congress null and void and appeal to the people of the other states for like action. If three fourths of the states—the number required to pass an amendment—agreed, then the act was everywhere annulled. It sounded peaceful enough, but Calhoun said nothing about what might happen if the President of the United States did not agree to the method suggested and viewed nullification as an ordinary refusal to obey Federal law. Then Calhoun and those who followed his advice might be in serious trouble.

As a nationalist forced to justify states' rights, Calhoun had reason enough to be uneasy, but Van Buren and his friends now made his situation worse. A dinner to honor the memory of Thomas Jefferson was so arranged as to bring the toasts of Jackson and Calhoun together. Obviously directing his words at South Carolina and her spokesman, the President toasted, "Our Federal Union—it *must* and *shall* be preserved!" To which Calhoun, with the air of one reluctantly pushed into a corner, responded, "The Union—next to our liberty most dear!" and after a pause, "May we all remember that it can only be preserved by respecting the rights of the states and by distributing equally the benefits and burdens of the Union."

The ground was now prepared for the final break. Some of Jackson's friends had long known that, at the time of Jackson's invasion of Florida, Calhoun had, in cabinet meetings, favored his arrest and trial. Jackson, on the other hand, had always thought of Calhoun as one of his defenders. The truth was now revealed to Jackson, and letters from William H. Crawford were produced to prove the fact. The effect was all that Calhoun's most bitter enemies desired. In a blunt note Jackson demanded to know whether the information contained in Crawford's letters was correct; and when Calhoun's answer failed to satisfy, he closed the correspondence with the curt sentence "Understanding you now, no further communication with you on the subject is necessary."

Reconciliation was now impossible. Soon Jackson let it be known that he would accept a second term, and Van Buren suggested, as a means of getting rid of Calhoun's friends in the cabinet, that he and Eaton resign and then force the others to do likewise. Jackson at first objected. but in the end agreed. Calhoun's friends hesitated and then reluctantly stepped out. Van Buren was named ambassador to the Court of St. James's. Eaton celebrated his return to private life by challenging first Ingham and then Berrien to a duel. Neither accepted, but the husband of Peggy O'Neale roamed the streets of Washington for days with a pistol, seeking to interview his late colleagues. Calhoun found consolation in making sure that the Senate would not approve Van Buren's appointment, even though that gentleman had already reached London. Jackson, undaunted by the whole affair, named a new cabinet, made up of men favorable to the Van Buren group. He was now ready and willing to face the problems which foreign relations, sectional interests, and ambitious leaders were pushing forward.

FOREIGN AND DOMESTIC PROBLEMS

In the handling of foreign affairs Jackson was surprisingly successful. Where earlier efforts had failed, he now induced England to remove restrictions from American produce and ships in the West Indies. Where John Quincy Adams had clashed with Canning over Mexico and South America, Jackson simply forgot the Monroe Doctrine and let things quiet down. His dealings with France were more stormy, but, in the end, no less satisfactory. Here trouble arose over American claims for spoliations under the Berlin and Milan decrees, which the French government had agreed to pay, but for which no funds were provided. When a draft for the first installment was protested, Jackson, in good frontier fashion, ordered the navy to prepare for action. France was deeply offended. American businessmen were greatly alarmed. War seemed possible. Finally, however, the French legislature voted the money on condition that it should be paid only when the President's words had been satisfactorily explained. A year went by. Then Jackson let it be known that he would not apologize, but that he had not intended to insult the French people. With British aid the matter was closed and the money paid. Americans were well pleased with their President's conduct; foreigners gave him added respect.

In the domestic field, first of all was the problem of Georgia and the Indians, which had flared up again when the Cherokees, in July, 1827, adopted a national constitution and declared themselves a sovereign and independent nation with complete jurisdiction over their territory. Georgia countered, as she had done in the case of the Creeks, with an assertion of her authority and an extension of her laws over

worlds, but had gained an entirely new outlook on life, as important as the physical discoveries. Until the intellectual and economic revolutions of the sixteenth and seventeenth centuries, men's faces were turned toward the past. They looked backward to lost perfections, gardens of Eden where humanity had been free and happy. Pessimism ruled men's minds. Man himself was depraved, and helpless to improve his status. An angry God had cursed the world, and salvation was to be found only in the Heavenly City of life after death.

With the great revolutions men discovered their world anew. Science revealed a world of laws, not of arbitrary curses. The universe was found to be a rational place, and man could understand and control its forces. Its God was not angry; man was not condemned to a hopeless fate. A more rational study of the past banished the golden ages of the past to the realm of myth and assured mankind that Utopia was not behind, but might be achieved through man's own efforts in man's own future. Thus the modern doctrine of *progress* was born. Out of it stemmed the democratic dogma. The political side of this notion of a universe run by law was the idea of a divinely planned human economy which men could comprehend as easily as they could comprehend the rational order. This reduced the whole matter of government to the discovery of natural law and natural rights and to making human conduct and institutions conform to that law and those rights. Men might catch the fundamental law on which the universe rested and incorporate it into their written constitutions. Such a conception lifted the individual to new heights of dignity and power. Through reason he could find truth, and the divinity which once rested in kings now belonged to common men. The voice of men became the voice of God. Self-government was a natural right.

The second result of this notion of progress in a universe of law had to do with the relation of the State to the individual's social-economic activity. Business too had its natural laws, which if applied could give the greatest prosperity and well-being. Through reason again, man himself might put an end to want and poverty. All that was necessary was to let natural law operate. Then the individual would find the tasks that he was best fitted for, and competition with others would produce the maximum of goods; the law of supply and demand would establish just prices; and the State would need only to restrain and punish those who cheated at the game. Economic utopias also lay just around the corner.

Such ideas fitted the conditions of the new age that was dawning and of which the settlement of the Americas was a part. Everywhere new groups were rising in response to the new forces astir, and new groups needed new philosophies and ideologies with which to make their way. The old order of despair and pessimism had been one in which governments under absolute rulers and the all-powerful Church dominated the lives of common men and monopolized the good things of life for the few. Everywhere there was oppression and restraint. Caste and tradition held men in place and regulated their actions; custom and law forced the masses to old ways and robbed them of the chance to assert themselves.

With the development of these new ideas, and with the rise of the towns and the stirring of the lesser clergy, the basis of revolt was laid. Freedom from the tyranny of kings, freedom from the dominance of the Pope, freedom from the restraints on trade, commerce, and manufacturing—these were the great demands of the age. The *bourgeoisie* of the towns, backed by the rural masses, upset the old order and made freedom the battle cry of the Reformation and the Industrial Revolution. The philosophy of the Enlightenment, with its emphasis on the rational individual and on the universe of law, understandable and subject to control by intelligence, became the weapons by which an old order was overturned and a new one established.

As a product of the Commercial Revolution, which was a part of all this stirring and which set the European nations to planting colonies, and as a victim of mercantilism, which condemned all colonies to a status of dependence on the mother country, the destiny of the English colonies in America would be strangely wrapped up with all that had broken the old Europe to pieces and had produced a new Europe. They would be the heirs of its philosophies and its procedures. Life in the American wilderness would sharpen the emphasis of the colonists on the individual and reinforce their bent to freedom. In their colonial governments they would put into practice as much as possible the new theories of self-government. In their economic pursuits they would practice the doctrine of let alone, or *laissez faire*. When restraints upon their pursuit of self-interest became unbearable, they would resort to revolution in perfectly good Enlightenment fashion and justify their course by an appeal to all the doctrines of the new day—the natural rights of man, the constitution of the empire, the fundamental law of the universe. Then they would draw up their own Constitution, incorporate in it all the philosophy and practice of the new liberalism, and begin the great American experiment in government.

all Indians after June 1, 1830. The discovery of gold in the region and the inrush of miners brought the situation to a climax. Jackson, with true Western sympathy for settlers who coveted Indian lands, withdrew the Federal troops already there, but the Supreme Court accepted jurisdiction in the matter. Georgia, however, refused to appear and announced her determination to uphold her sovereignty. When Chief Justice John Marshall, in the case of Worcester *v.* Georgia, declared the Indians a domestic dependent nation under the sole control of the national government, neither Jackson nor the House of Representatives was willing to use Federal agents for the enforcement of the decision. Jackson is said to have remarked, "John Marshall has made his decision; now let him enforce it." He did, however, in the end, secure the cession of the disputed lands and the creation of an Indian territory west of the Mississippi. To this the four Southern tribes, which had caused so much trouble, were soon removed.

Jackson's sympathy for a state's upholding its "sovereignty" against Federal authority did not, however, extend to South Carolina and its talk of nullifying tariff legislation. Here the situation was complicated by the fact that the high tariff and the sale of public lands were creating a heavy Treasury surplus. Jackson's attitude toward internal improvements prevented relief from that direction. His insistence on the immediate payment of all debts cut off hope of other lavish expenditures. The only other remedy was a reduction of the tariff or of the price of government lands. Here the matter of sectional interest entered, and politicians had to face it. The Northeast wanted protection and favored high-priced land to check emigration. It was divided on internal improvements. The South wanted the tariff lowered, but its eastern and western parts disagreed over cheap lands and internal improvements. The West wanted cheap lands and internal improvements, but was divided on the tariff. The opportunity for political bargaining was thus excellent, but the chances that had to be taken were great. South Carolina's pressure against the tariff made that issue the first point of attack, but left it linked securely with that of the public lands.

Seeing the danger in the situation to his American System, Henry Clay now proposed some slight reductions of the tariff on noncompetitive items and a distribution of the proceeds from the sale of public lands to all the states of the Union according to the Federal ratio of representation. Calhoun, who had resigned as Vice-President and had returned to the Senate, began to talk of ceding the public lands to the states in which they lay, and, of course, advocated a sharp reduction of the tariff. Each aimed to serve his own sectional ends as to the tariff and to win Western support. John Quincy Adams, who now represented his district in Congress, brought forward a tariff measure which was, on the whole, a compromise, but which left enough of protection to retain the hostility of the southern Atlantic states. The Adams measure, slightly amended, was the only one able to secure a majority. The others, such as Benton's pre-emption and gradation bill, again under consideration, were defeated by strictly sectional voting.

JACKSON AND THE BANK OF THE UNITED STATES

Jackson's hostility to the Bank of the United States was now injected into the picture, and the whole tangled situation became part of the campaign of 1832. In both his first and second annual messages Jackson had expressed doubts concerning the Bank, but had, in the meantime, given Nicholas Biddle, its president, reason to believe that nothing drastic was to be done. Opinion, even among Jackson's supporters, was enough divided to give the impression that the administration wished to avoid the issue in the coming election. Jackson's new Secretary of the Treasury, McLane, went so far as to declare publicly for the rechartering of the Bank.

Thus, seemingly, Jackson had failed to arouse interest and to make the rechartering a political issue. But where he failed, Henry Clay and George McDuffie, close friend of John C. Calhoun in South Carolina, now succeeded. Under their influence a new political party, calling itself the National Republicans, met in convention at Baltimore, December 12, 1831, and declared for the rechartering of the Bank. They named Clay as their candidate for the Presidency. Support of Clay also implied support of the American System. Biddle then asked for the rechartering of the Bank, even though its present charter did not expire until 1836. In response, the Senate passed a bill for a modified recharter, and the House gave its approval. It then went to Jackson, to provide him with what Clay thought was the chance to commit political suicide.

No man was ever more mistaken than Clay. Jackson vetoed the bill, as was expected, but his veto message was one of the shrewdest political documents ever penned in these United States. Not an American prejudice or conviction was overlooked. The Bank, he insisted, was a great monopoly with exclusive privileges. A recharter would increase the value of the stock and put millions into the pockets of the

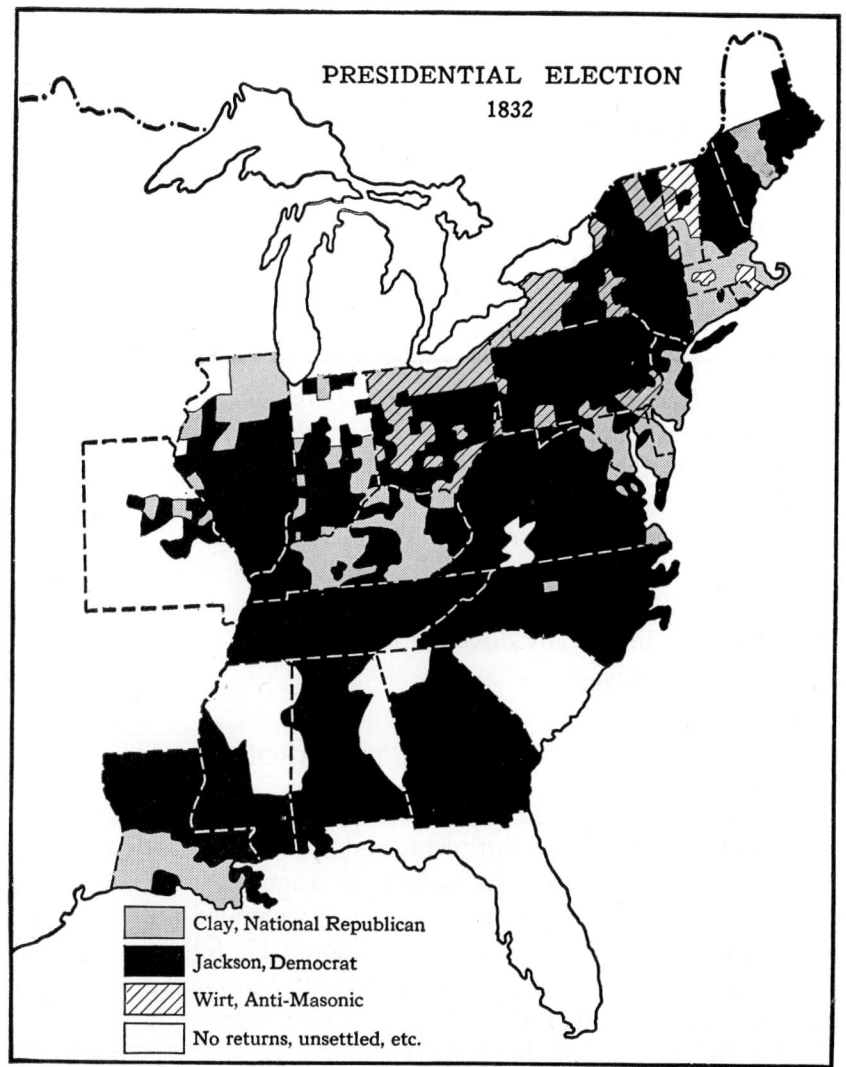

PRESIDENTIAL ELECTION
1832

Clay, National Republican

Jackson, Democrat

Wirt, Anti-Masonic

No returns, unsettled, etc.

Presidential Election of 1832

few. Many "of these few" were Englishmen, and the rest our citizens "of the richest class." Poor men were being plundered by the already rich. The Court had said that the law incorporating the Bank was constitutional, but the people's President had an equal right to an opinion on the subject. And his opinion was that the Bank was both unnecessary and dangerous.

Much of this was mere opinion; some of it was guess; all of it over-looked the benefits rendered by the Bank both to debtors and to the nation. Of the 4145 stockholders only 466, owning 79,159 shares, were foreigners. As against this, stockholders in the middle Atlantic states held 88,206 shares, and those in the southern Atlantic states 96,415 shares. New Englanders relied largely on their own banks; the middle Atlantic states used less than a fourth of the Bank's currency; the southern Atlantic states, one fourth; the Southwest, one fourth; Ohio, Kentucky, and Tennessee, about as much as New England and the middle Atlantic region combined.

Jackson's statements and inferences were, in fact, so extreme that Biddle and Clay reprinted them and scattered them widely at their own expense as campaign material. How wrongly they had judged was revealed in the November vote. Clay carried only six states, and the electoral vote stood 219 to 49. Jackson's personal popularity and the growing belief that he represented the people against the business interests outweighed his failures in connection with internal improve-ments, the tariff, and the public lands. He was now in a position to act with confidence in any direction that he might choose. His rivals were out of the way.

JACKSON AND SOUTH CAROLINA

Clay had been thoroughly beaten. Calhoun had been thrown back upon his South Carolina constituents and forced reluctantly to accept the stand that the extremists had taken. In August, 1832, he had issued his "Fort Hill Letter," in which he openly expounded nullification in even sharper fashion than in the "Exposition." He followed this with a report and address to the legislature of South Carolina in November, and that body responded with a call for a state convention.

With the meeting of this body, Calhoun's control weakened. Im-petuous men were turning his theories into action. He was not quite prepared for that. On November 24 the convention passed an ordi-nance of nullification, declaring the tariff acts of 1828 and 1832 not binding on the people of South Carolina, forbidding appeals to the Federal courts for the enforcement of tariff laws, and requiring state officials to take oath to uphold the ordinance. When the legislature reassembled, it passed a replevin act, by which owners of goods seized might recover twice their value from the official who had seized them. Then the state settled back to see what Jackson would do.

Encouraged by a strong Union party in South Carolina, under the leadership of Joel Poinsett, the President merely kept his eye on the situation and dropped a hint here and there to the effect that the laws of the nation must be obeyed. Soon seven revenue cutters and a United States battleship appeared in Charleston harbor, and on December 10 Jackson's answer to nullification appeared in the form of a proclamation. Bluntly he rejected the theory which Calhoun had provided, and closed by saying:

The laws of the United States must be executed. I have no discretionary power on the subject; my duty is emphatically pronounced in the Constitution. Those who told you that you might peaceably prevent their execution, deceived you; they could not have been deceived themselves. They know that a forcible opposition could alone prevent the execution of the laws, and they know that such opposition must be repelled. Their object is disunion. But be not deceived by names. Disunion by armed force is *treason*.

Such a statement left no room for misunderstanding. The national sentiment that had stirred at Webster's words now manifested itself. Union sentiment was strong in the North, and only small groups in other Southern states supported nullification. To Clay and Calhoun and their friends it was perfectly clear that Jackson was about to achieve another triumph. A compromise tariff, the Verplanck Bill, was rushed before Congress. Even Van Buren, now certain that he would be Jackson's successor, favored its passage, and Jackson himself at least did nothing to check the move. He nevertheless sent a special message to Congress, dealing with the situation, and his friends introduced a bill authorizing the President to call out the army and navy to enforce the laws of Congress. Jackson's supporters called it "the Force Bill"; Calhoun's friends spoke of it as "the bloody bill."

South Carolina, however, stood her ground. She had not faced the Spaniards and the Indians and the West Indian hurricanes all these years without developing iron in her blood. She prepared to defend herself. An outbreak of hostilities seemed imminent. Only the sullen resistance of the Union group in South Carolina and the firm determination of Henry Clay to stay Jackson's triumphal course seemed to stand in the way.

Clay accepted the responsibility. He alone could get enough Northern votes to pass a bill lowering the tariff. To check Jackson, he was willing to try. On February 12 he introduced a bill to reduce the tariff gradually during the next ten years to the point where a general minimum of 20 per cent would be reached. But Jackson insisted on his Force Bill, and Calhoun, who had always assumed that nullification was a legal and peaceful method of protecting the minority, agreed not to oppose him if the compromise tariff was assured.

This ended the controversy. Both Jackson and South Carolina could claim a victory. Clay had won back some prestige. Only John C. Calhoun had lost national standing. Jackson later expressed regret that he had not seized the opportunity to hang the Carolina leader. At the time, however, he was content to have driven him out of the Democratic party and to have made certain that Van Buren was next in line for the Presidency. He could, moreover, now give attention to Nicholas Biddle and his National Bank.

SELECTED BIBLIOGRAPHY

A. M. Schlesinger, Jr., *The Age of Jackson*; Gerald Johnson, *America's Silver Age*; Claude G. Bowers, *The Party Battles of the Jackson Period*, all entertainingly written books that capture the flavor of the period.

Marquis James, *Andrew Jackson: Portrait of a President*; B. C. Clark, *John Quincy Adams*; Bernard Mayo, *Henry Clay*; C. M. Fuess, *Daniel Webster* (2 vols.); Charles M. Wiltse, *John C. Calhoun, Nationalist*; J. S. Bassett, *Life of Andrew Jackson* (2 vols.); Quenna Pollock, *Peggy Eaton*, some of the better biographies of the individuals who dominated these years.

Alexis de Tocqueville, *Democracy in America*, a classic contemporary picture of the Age of Jackson. Among the more specialized works of importance are C. S. Boucher, *The Nullification Controversy in South Carolina*; D. F. Houston, *Critical Study of Nullification in South Carolina*; U. B. Phillips, *Georgia and State Rights*.

H. S. Commager (Ed.), *Documents of American History*, pp. 249–251, 253–270, contains source material.

XV

The Bank, the Sections, and Slavery

STRICTLY SPEAKING, the Bank of the United States was not a national institution. It was a private concern, located in Philadelphia. The government was connected with it through the fact that it had subscribed one fifth of the capital, used it as a repository of public funds, and appointed one fifth of its directors. For the privilege of using government deposits for its own banking purposes and of issuing bank notes, the Bank paid and transferred government funds without charge and paid a bonus of one and a half million dollars. In other respects the Bank operated like other private banks.

Government connections, however, gave the Bank enormous prestige, which, in turn, gave it great power. Lesser banks were at its mercy, and the national financial stability was in its hands. Through loans to public officials and newspaper editors it had become a political influence, and its officers were not always either businesslike or entirely ethical in the use of funds or power.

Jackson's distrust of the Bank, which represented both a personal and a sectional point of view, was not shared by all those in his official and unofficial family. Some, of course, agreed; Amos Kendall spoke of a "nobility system" whose head was the Bank and which, like such systems everywhere, enabled the few "to live upon the labor of the many." Benton and Blair were equally violent in their attitudes, and the *Globe*, under Blair's editorship, kept up a steady stream of charges and denunciations. On one occasion it even asserted "that members of the defeated party were prompting 'the minions' of the bank" to assassinate the President. Van Buren, on the other hand, hesitated. He had to think of his own political future, which seemed to include a Presidential term. McLane, Cass, and Duane, who now held cabinet posts, were equally hesitant, and all of them were opposed to any extreme measures against the Bank. It would, therefore, have been easy for the President to avoid the issue.

Jackson, however, did not waver. He longed for "retirement and repose" at the Hermitage; but, as he said, "until I can strangle this hydra of corruption, the Bank, I will not shrink from my duty, or my part." To Blair he confided, "Providence may change me but it is not in the power of man to do it."

Ill and often prostrated by hemorrhage of the lungs, Jackson went ahead with his plans for removing the government deposits from the Bank of the United States and scattering them among local banks selected for that purpose. Even the favorable report of Treasury agents on the safety of Western loans, and a vote of 109 to 46 in the House, upholding the opinion that the government deposits were perfectly safe in the keeping of the Bank, did not alter his plans. Knowing that McLane, Secretary of the Treasury, was opposed to removal, he sent Livingston, Secretary of State, to France as minister and made McLane Secretary of State. He then appointed William J. Duane as Secretary of the Treasury for the avowed purpose of making the removals. Duane, however, hesitated and almost immediately received a curt note from the President, saying that his "further services" were no longer required. Immediately Roger Taney was named in his place, and the required orders for removal were issued. Clay took the lead in Congress in opposing Taney's orders and secured the passage of resolutions censuring Jackson for acting illegally in regard to the deposits. Biddle struck, too, by presenting the notes of state banks for redemption and by reducing the Bank's discounts and call-in loans. A new financial panic resulted. Credit tightened, businesses failed, and men were thrown out of work. Money rates rose to 12 and 18 per cent. Protests poured in to Congress. Jackson only pointed to these results as proof of the power unwisely bestowed on the Bank. But Biddle wrote a friend: "This worthy President thinks that because he has scalped Indians and imprisoned Judges, he can have his way with the Bank. He is mistaken—and he may as well send at once and engage lodgings in Arabia."

As depression deepened, delegations from business centers called on the President for relief. Jackson only told them to see Nicholas Biddle. "We have no money here, gentlemen," he told one group. "Biddle has all the money. He has millions of specie in his vaults, at this moment, lying idle, and yet you come to me to save you from breaking." "Go to the monster," he told another group. "The government will not bow to the monster." To all of which Justice Story sadly said, "Though we live under the form of a republic we are in fact under the absolute rule of a single man." Time, however, was with Jackson, and soon even businessmen began to see that he was right. The Bank was too powerful. Biddle was producing the hard times. Slowly public opinion turned against the Bank, and delegations began visiting Biddle to inform him that the people "ought not and would not sustain him in further pressure, which he very well knew was not necessary for the safety of the bank, and in which his whole object was to coerce a charter through the distress of the mercantile community."

Soon Biddle saw the light, eased his restrictions, and slowly began to make plans to continue his business under a charter from the state of Pennsylvania. The war on the Bank was over. Biddle had taken his place alongside Clay and Calhoun in the rear of Jackson's chariot. He summed up his feelings about the whole matter by saying: "For the last few years the Executive power of the Govt. has been weilded by a mere gang of banditte. I know these people perfectly . . . and in my deliberate judgement, there is not on the face of the earth a more profligate crew."

With the Bank question out of the way, Jackson now turned to the problem of reducing the paper money in circulation and putting the country on a "hard money" basis. This was to be done by forbidding the new deposit banks to issue small notes and by refusing to accept such notes in payment of taxes. In this way notes under twenty dollars would be eliminated. The great exponent of this program was a Philadelphia editor named William M. Gouge, but the real force behind it in Congress was Thomas Hart Benton. So ardent were Benton's efforts that he acquired and ever afterward carried the nickname "Old Bullion."

Hard-money advocates believed, as Thomas Jefferson had contended in his fight against Alexander Hamilton's policies, that paper issues encouraged speculation, produced periodic depressions, and created a moneyed aristocracy that exploited the poor and lived without service to society. It was again the question of whether the people or property should control. That was the way in which Jackson viewed the whole Bank struggle. To complete it, the paper banking system also had to go.

Benton took the lead. A measure revising the valuation of gold from the ratio 15 to 1, to 16 to 1, was pushed through Congress, and gold coins, not minted since 1805, soon made their appearance. Where in October, 1833, there was only thirty million dollars of specie in the country, by December, 1836, there was seventy-three millions. Then a Treasury circular banned all notes under five dollars and, later, notes of ten and twenty dollars' value. Many states passed acts to control local banks. The effect, due to a great economic boom now well under way, was not all that Jackson had hoped, but he at least had followed Jefferson another step along the democratic way.

Jackson's final domestic move was one designed to solve the problem of a growing surplus. The debt was now paid, the tariff had been fixed until 1842, and no remedy for the growing surplus had been suggested other than the distribution of funds to the states. In view of the great speculative boom that was sweeping the country, this seemed unwise. Besides, Henry Clay was now advocating such a move. In 1832 he had carried a bill for this purpose through both houses of Congress, only to meet Jackson's "pocket veto." In 1835 he put through a similar modified bill, providing that all the surplus in the Treasury on January 1, 1837, above five million dollars, should be deposited with the states in four equal quarterly installments as a loan to be repaid at the discretion of Congress. It was, of course, understood that a demand for repayment would never be made. Jackson accepted this plan temporarily, but was determined to find some other way to handle the problem. Since much of the revenue came from the sale of public lands, and since these sales, now very heavy under the speculative boom, were being paid for with the notes of insecure Western banks, Jackson ordered the public-land offices in the future to accept only specie in payment for lands. This famous "Specie Circular" immediately reduced the revenue, and the surplus on January 1, 1837, was only $36,000,000. When, therefore, two and a half installments were paid to the states, the Treasury was empty, and local banks were everywhere suspending payment on their notes. Jackson had accomplished his purpose, but distribution and the Specie Circular had played havoc with an already unsound economic situation.

VAN BUREN AND THE PANIC OF 1837

The first crash, however, did not come at once. It held off until after the election of 1836. The political pot had boiled fiercely throughout Jackson's second administration. His friends had become more aggressive; his enemies, more sullen and determined. Van Buren had held his place in Jackson's affections, and his nomination as the Democratic candidate was everywhere taken for granted. Opponents, on the other hand, regardless of the fact that they differed widely among themselves on every subject except Andrew Jackson, had slowly drawn

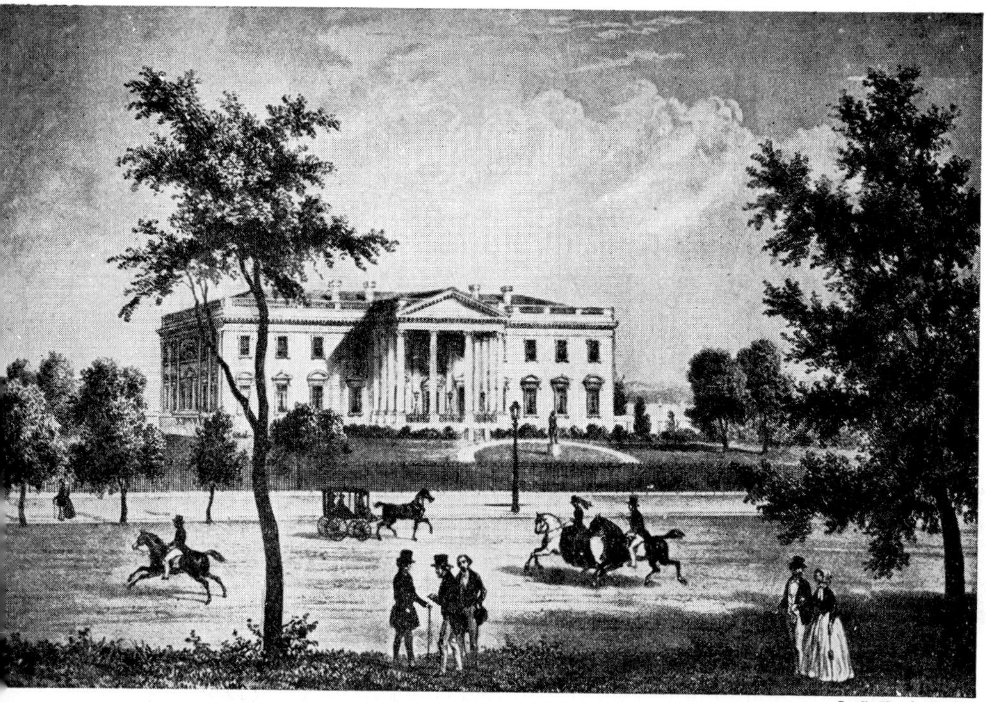

L. C. Handy Studios

The White House about 1835.
The Statue Is That of Thomas Jefferson

Broadway, New York, about 1834

Eno Collection. The New York Public Library

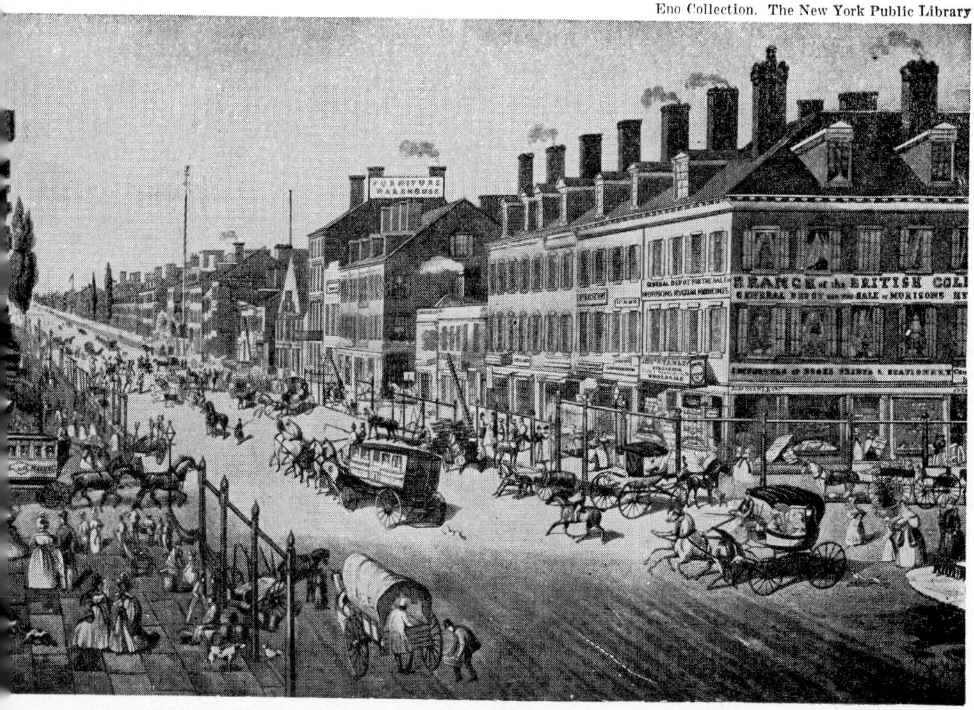

together into a new party, now widely called the Whig party, with the implication that it, like the English party of that name, was opposing tyranny. Some of them had been Federalists; some were the followers of Henry Clay and his American System; some were states'-rights men, who did not like the way in which Jackson had dealt with South Carolina; some were bitter about the Bank; some just disliked "King Andrew," as they called him.

Clay was the logical man to head this party, but his position on issues was too well known, and his enemies were too numerous to make success a certainty. It seemed better to split the votes, if possible, by putting forward several candidates. First, there was Hugh Lawson White, from Jackson's own state, who, for some reason not quite clear, had broken with the President and had been voting against his measures; then there was Webster, favorite son of Massachusetts; and William Henry Harrison, from Ohio, with a good Virginia background and a fair record as a soldier against both the Indians and the British. Mangum of North Carolina could draw votes from the South. Perhaps the election could be thrown into the House, where the chances were better.

Such scheming, however, came to nothing. Van Buren carried the country, with a popular majority of less than twenty-eight thousand votes, but with a comfortable lead in the Electoral College. Jackson went home to Tennessee for a well-deserved rest and left the man he had placed in the Presidency to reap the whirlwind of depression.

The causes of the panic which now swept the country were many. Behind it lay the speculative fever which had rushed forward the building of canals and railroads and had created banks in quantity far beyond the capacity of the country to supply capital. Between 1829 and 1837 the number of banks rose from 329 to 788, and their circulation tripled. The states vied with one another in chartering banks and building internal improvements, and their debts grew from $12,790,728 in 1820 to over $170,000,000 in 1839. Europe invested heavily in these enterprises, and her merchants extended easy credit to American purchasers of her goods. Between 1830 and 1836 the total value of American imports rose from $71,000,000 to about $190,000,000. Export increases lagged far behind, and the balance of trade became increasingly "unfavorable." The sale of public lands, meanwhile, kept pace with other developments. Between 1830 and 1836 more than 57,000,000 acres were disposed of, and in the single year 1836–1837 over 20,000,000 more were sold.

A financial crisis in England now combined with Jackson's financial measures to precipitate a crash. In October, 1837, the Bank of the United States in Pennsylvania closed its doors and thus forced most of the other Pennsylvania banks, as well as banks throughout the South, to do likewise. Values of all kinds depreciated, state after state declared its inability to meet its obligations, and a few, like Mississippi, repudiated their bonds or disavowed their responsibility to meet obligations. Bankruptcies increased, and nearly a half-billion dollars of debt was wiped out by a Federal Bankruptcy Act in 1841. Labor, of course, suffered heavily. By September, 1837, authorities asserted that nine tenths of the Eastern factories were closed and that the almshouses were crowded to the doors. The West and South suffered even more in the next few years, as a lingering depression settled down upon them to check expansion and to stress their status as debtors.

Van Buren struggled to check the disaster. While Horace Greeley talked of a public-works program to relieve unemployment and urged many to move West, friends of the Bank clamored for the repeal of the Specie Circular and the re-establishment of their pet institution. Van Buren called Congress in special session and proposed the Independent Treasury system. Under this system government subtreasuries would collect all revenue in specie and make all payments. The government would thus be divorced from all banking, and the circulation of specie would be promoted. Opposition to the measure came not only from Whigs, but from some Democrats as well, and final passage of the act was delayed until 1840.

The political effects of the depression and of the relief measures taken by Van Buren and his supporters were apparent at once. Whig strength increased rapidly. Criticism of the President became open and widespread. With the great personality of Andrew Jackson, plus his popularity, removed from the stage, all the forces which were shaping a new America now began to manifest themselves and to produce new alignments of men and interests and sections. Van Buren was forced to bear the brunt of these reactions.

THE NORTHWEST

To understand the new political situation, it is necessary to turn back and notice certain developments that were taking place in the different corners of the nation. Life and relationships were being strangely altered in the Northwest, the Northeast, and the South, and these changes, in turn, were altering the attitudes which men took toward national issues.

The Northwest, under the lures and pressures already described, grew rapidly in the days of Jackson and Van Buren. By 1840 its population was three and one third millions—deepest in Ohio, but spreading rapidly across the Mississippi River. Upland Southerners, augmented by emigrants from Pennsylvania, predominated in the older, hilly, wooded counties of the southern half of the region, while men from New England and New York, now heavily reinforced by European immigrants, occupied the counties to the north around and below the Great Lakes. First pioneer days had passed in all but the outermost western areas, and definite progress had been made toward the reproduction of the social-economic patterns which men had carried with them from the older regions. This threw a sharp line of cleavage across the section, reflected in politics and in the lesser things that made up life and values. Something of the Old South on the one side and of the Northeast on the other still persisted in spite of the great forces of common living in pioneer commonwealths. There was an Ohio valley with Southern backgrounds; there was a Lakes region that looked back in memory and habits to New England and Europe. The one had more of Quakers, Disciples of Christ, Methodists, and Baptists; the other, more of Congregationalists and Catholics. The one had more of illiteracy than the other, held to the Democratic party a bit more regularly, and, when state debts grew heavy, was more inclined toward repudiation than was its northern neighbor. In the later decades the line between those who resented the abolitionist and those who gave him support followed the line of cleavage fixed by the origin of population.

This general division in the Northwest, however, did not mean complete unity in either part. The Germans, who settled around Chicago, Milwaukee, St. Louis, and Cincinnati, differed greatly from the Irish, who helped to build the roads and canals and then settled along their courses. Both differed from the New Englanders, who lived near them and frowned upon their religious practices and their greater tolerance of what the Puritans called the pleasures of this world. Sharp conflict developed over the morality of dancing, beer-drinking, the theater, and even a too great fondness for music. Settlers from Kentucky did not always agree with those who came from North Carolina, and the Quakers and the Methodists sometimes stood as far apart in their social values as in their religious expression. Yet all these

Sections of the United States in 1840

peoples viewed their section as a land of opportunity and gradually found a surprising amount of agreement in their outlook on national affairs.

Most of the people in the Northwest were farmers. Small crossroad and river towns, however, had sprung up widely, and Cincinnati, Cleveland, Detroit, Chicago, and Milwaukee now counted their population by the thousands. Wheat was the great agricultural surplus crop, but general farming gave great numbers of cattle and hogs to the markets, and Cincinnati had become a meat-packing center of importance. Manufactures to satisfy local needs had early developed; and as improved transportation brought more goods from the East, Western factories had turned to the production of things for which natural resources and conditions gave them advantage enough to meet outside competition. Sawmills had already begun to cut deep into the rich timber resources of Michigan and Wisconsin, and lead-mining, in the region where Iowa, Illinois, and Wisconsin meet, added to the growing quantity of materials to be exported.

In the early period, when most of the population lived along the streams that joined the Ohio and Mississippi rivers, the greater part of the surplus of the Northwest went to New Orleans. As the northern counties filled up, more and more produce went east by way of the Lakes. The value of the surplus products of the West reaching New Orleans in 1860 was estimated at $26,000,000. In 1850 it was over $108,000,000. Tonnage on the Great Lakes, meanwhile, rose from less than 6000 in 1829 to over 184,000 in 1850. In 1841 the value of the Lakes trade by way of the Erie Canal had reached $65,000,000, and in 1846 Buffalo received more grain and flour from the interior than did New Orleans. The old balance in the section was being upset.

The rapid spread of population and the increasing surplus of goods for export called for better ways to market. Following the example set by New York, Ohio launched, in 1825, a canal-building program which ultimately connected Portsmouth and Cincinnati on the Ohio River with Cleveland and Toledo on Lake Erie and linked up with Indiana's great Wabash-and-Erie project. Illinois fell in line with a canal joining Lake Michigan and the Illinois River, and only the panic of 1837 held back other canal schemes until the railroad, which had already made a start, could definitely demonstrate its superiority.

Under these wild efforts to secure internal improvements, the states borrowed heavily at home and abroad. By 1842 Ohio had an indebtedness of $10,924,000; Indiana, one of $11,751,000; Illinois, one of $10,371,000; and Michigan, one of $5,420,000. Banking facilities were overstretched to meet demands, and the crash which followed in 1837 led to serious efforts at repudiation and a general hostility to banks for their part in the disaster. The demand for national aid to local efforts increased, and Whig strength in internal-improvement areas reflected this demand.

The temper of the Northwest was decidedly democratic. Its democracy stressed the individual and his rights more, perhaps, than it did social reform, but it was not without its social purposes. It stressed equal opportunity and the capacity of individuals to achieve their purposes and to make a good society if given a free and equal chance. The Northwest wanted the public lands placed in the hands of actual settlers. The law of 1832, which reduced the minimum tract to be purchased to 40 acres, and that of 1841, which granted general and permanent pre-emption, received the support of the majority of its representatives in Congress. "Claim Associations," in the meantime, were active in some localities for the protection of squatters. Bluntly one of them would ask "that if any member of this club finds his or any of his friends Clames has been Jumpt that they inform this Club of the fact and that this Club forthwith put them off said Clame without trobling the sivel law." Now men in the Northwest were talking of a homestead act which would give every deserving man a farm of his own.

In the constitutional conventions held in Northwestern states in this general period (1835–1851) there were shown a decided distrust of legislatures and a tendency to refer important matters directly to the people. Judiciaries were made elective, the property rights of married women were recognized, and the questions of naturalization and land limitation were thoroughly discussed.

On practical issues attitudes reflected concrete needs. Men favored the Bank of the United States or opposed it because of loyalty to Andrew Jackson or Henry Clay, or, in many cases, because of recent experiences with state banks and with National Bank branches in their neighborhoods. Kendall, Blair, and Benton, all good Westerners, furnished Jackson with stanch political support in his struggle with Biddle, and lesser men all over the section echoed their dislike of banks and credit systems.

Interest in river and harbor improvement made Western men less sympathetic to strict-construction ideas than Jackson might have wished, and the emigration of New England and New York men, with long-held Whig attitudes, to the region dependent on the Great Lakes, strengthened this attitude toward strict construction. Abstractions weighed less than needs, and those who would win and hold Western votes had to recognize the force of internal-improvement demands, which were soon expressing themselves in great conventions held to discuss the subject.

THE NORTHEAST

Great changes were taking place also in the Northeast. There manufactures multiplied rapidly, and capital, once invested almost exclusively in shipping, now went in part into the building of factories. In the earlier period most of these were small concerns, largely located in communities where there was water power and owned and manned by those who lived in the communities. In 1813, however, young Francis Lowell and his brother-in-law, Patrick Jackson, organized the Boston Manufacturing Company with a capital of four hundred thousand dollars, purchased the property of an unsuccessful paper-cum-spinning mill at Waltham on the Charles River, and began a new era in industry. Improved machinery, largely the work of Paul Moody of Amesbury, was installed, and all the processes required to turn raw cotton into cloth were performed under a single roof. Soon they built the mill towns of Lowell and Lawrence. Where the older mills, which Slater and others had established in Rhode Island, had used children and whole families as laborers, the Boston Manufacturing Company employed girls between the ages of eighteen and twenty-two. They lived in boardinghouses under the strict supervision of carefully selected matrons, who saw that they went to bed at reasonable hours, attended religious services, and lived according to the strictest Puritan code. This company made a single type of cloth, which it sold through one agent on commission. Its profits were always large; and when slack times closed the weaker and less efficient mills, the Boston Manufacturing Company continued to prosper.

Other companies followed the pattern set by this successful concern, and soon the factory town, with its rows of company houses and its clumsy factory buildings, was a definite part of the New England landscape. The larger companies tended to monopolize the favorable power sites, and absentee ownership became the rule rather than the exception. Because the business was new, its early years were marked by alternate periods of overproduction and slack times, which permitted the factory to be carried to all favored spots, but which forced the speeding up of production and much of pinching and uncertainty for labor. By 1845 uncertain pioneer days began to pass, and industry assumed the more mature characteristics which had marked its course in the Old World. Then capital and labor began their endless struggle.

When the factory first came to New England, its laborers were countryfolk, who, on the farm, expected women and children to carry their share of the work burden, and to toil from sunrise to sunset. Children of ten years and under tended the first machines, and a workday of from twelve to thirteen hours was considered normal. In one Rhode Island factory a boy of thirteen years, with seven years of experience already behind him, was employed to repair the machinery and set it in operation. In another a boy of nineteen, with eleven years of experience, was made superintendent of production. Wages varied from place to place, but were generally low. Women earned about two dollars a week in the 1820's, and children from thirty-three cents a week to a dollar or more. Men might make from a dollar and a half to three dollars, and a family of seven, with all its members employed, might receive from ten to fifteen dollars a week.

To farm people, who seldom had ready money, all this seemed good. The fact that they had become dependent on others for the chance to work and that unemployment was a constant threat did not at first make much difference. Life in a factory town for the country girl was far more exciting than it was at home, and the chance to save something with which to aid the family back on the farm, to send a brother to college, or to provide herself with a trousseau was not to be missed. The idealistic picture of life in these early factory towns given by travelers and by the girls themselves shows that conditions were better here than abroad and quite satisfactory to the workers.

But this was before the sharp competition of later days developed and before the workers became industrially conscious. When the memories of pinched farm days had faded and the pressure of immediate industrial ills was felt on every hand, all was changed. The paternalism that marked relations between employers and employees gradually weakened as millowners refused to employ workers discharged from other mills or workers who quit against the owners' wishes. The speeding up of work and the bad living conditions which soon existed in some mill towns added to the workers' discontent. Strikes began to occur. Employers sometimes refused to re-employ those who had struck, and Irish and Canadian girls began to take their places. Communities caught between employer and workers usually took the side of capital, but certain discontented elements in the section defended labor. Farmers in the back country whose fortunes were being ruined by Western competition and commercial groups in the old coastal towns who saw their capital and talents steadily drawn away to Boston and New York began now to talk of "the cotton lords" and their "wage slaves," of capitalists who grew rich on "the unremunerated toil of their workers," and of "the disparity between Capital and Labor," which left "the latter almost entirely within the control of the former."

Soon writers were telling of a single house in Lowell occupied "by one store and twenty-five families, embracing 120 persons, more than half of whom were adults," and of another in Holyoke in which a "man and woman . . . six children . . . six boarders . . . a sow and ten pigs" made their home. The factory girls at Garland declared in 1844 that "our *corporation slaves* receive *less* compensation, and are required to work a *greater* number of hours, than in some parts of that detested dynasty, . . . old despotic England," and the *Voice of Industry* insisted "that the factory system contains in itself the elements of slavery . . . [and] every day continues to add power to its incorporate sovereignty, while the sovereignty of the working people decreases in the same ratio."

These great changes in industry coincided with the equally great changes which were taking place in agriculture and commerce, and which were adding to the discontent of the day. The factory towns, as has already been noted, had provided the farmers near by with new and better markets. More capital had been put into farming, and some specialization had been attempted. Sons and daughters left the farms to work at the looms and spindles or to pioneer in the West. Household manufactures were gradually given up as the factories and their machines turned out cheaper cloth and shoes and hats. The old rural self-sufficiency was thus destroyed—a fact that in the end spelled disaster, first for the farmers of New England and then for those of New York, as wheat moved steadily westward and the regions behind altered their crops to meet the competition. The heaviest blows from such developments always fell on those in the older regions. Soon rural peoples of New England and then of New York seemed to be about as disturbed and unhappy as the factory workers.

The shifts in commerce, which lifted Boston and New York to new heights, but which weakened or destroyed some of the other old coastal centers, produced much the same results. As the glory passed from Salem, Beverly, and Newburyport, and as their old important families moved away, envy and bitterness filled the hearts of those who remained. Once, at least, they had to turn to Robert Y. Hayne of South Carolina to present their petitions against the mounting tariffs advocated by the newer representatives of New England. The lesser men who labored on the wharves of Boston and New York, and the working element that grew so rapidly as these great commercial centers expanded, also felt the loss of independence and the growing power of the few who more and more had the keeping of the many in their hands. The great expansion of banking, now largely controlled by those who owned the mills and the great mercantile establishments, added both to their dependence and their apprehensions. When the Suffolk Bank in Boston forced all country banks to keep deposits with it sufficient to cover their paper, and regularly returned their notes for immediate discount, lesser men needed no further proof of their bondage. A moneyed aristocracy was about to end men's freedom and their equality. Democracy was not functioning well in America. Perhaps Christianity was not serving the practical ends that it should.

Social-intellectual developments in this section reflected these conditions. Reaction to the great changes that were so drastically altering the lives of all groups, high and low, varied greatly from place to place and from group to group, but all expressed alarm at growing social ills and a genuine desire for change. Democracy was endangered by the growth of wealth and power in the hands of the few. The well-being of common men—workers and farmers—was becoming less secure. Perhaps even the Christian virtues and the better society promised by their practice were being neglected and unrealized.

From the Old World came men and ideas to criticize the materialism of the day and to urge social reform. Out of the American West came the hint of greater opportunities for the individual and the chance to build new and, perhaps, better social conditions. A strange restlessness appeared as men began to realize that their old ways of thinking and the old assumptions on which they had built their relations somehow failed to comprehend and meet the requirements of the new day of greater interdependence.

Lowell humorously described the situation as one in which

every possible form of intellectual and physical dyspepsia brought forth its gospel. Bran had its prophets. . . . Plainness of speech was carried to a pitch that would have taken away the breath of George Fox. . . . Not a few impecunious zealots abjured the use of money . . . professing to live on the internal revenues of the spirit. Some had an assurance of instant millennium so soon as hooks and eyes should be substituted for buttons. Communities were established where everything was to be common but common sense.

The ferment which now developed took different forms in different places and often produced bitter conflicts between conservatives and those who demanded change. Some men struck sharply at the inequalities that were developing between rich and poor and at the power which corporations exercised over the lives of lesser people. In Massachusetts the farmers organized a Workingmen's Movement as "a protest against the 'accumulations' in Boston society" and the "exclusive privileges of the wealthy." Samuel C. Allen, their candidate for governor, spoke of "the poor as a class" and insisted that government had become "but the combination of the rich and powerful to increase their riches, and extend their power." "All wealth," he wrote, "is the product of labor and belongs of right to him who produces it, and yet how small a part of the product of its labor falls to the laboring class!" He felt that Christianity was failing in its mission because the preachers had "attached themselves to the privileged classes, and had . . . lent themselves to uphold an order of things wholly irreconcilable with its principles."

George Bancroft, teacher and historian, soon joined hands with the Workingmen's Movement to unite the support of disgruntled men in the old, Eastern commercial centers and the unhappy farmers of the West behind Andrew Jackson and his war on the Bank. These Democrats talked much of a ten-hour day, the ending of imprisonment for debt, and better opportunities for public education; but underneath was the constant thought of the rich arrayed against the poor as a denial of the true intent of the democratic dogma.

In New York City, Frances Wright and Robert Dale Owen, two young idealists recently come from England, joined with George H. Evans to publish the *Free Enquirer* for the purpose of uniting the workingmen in their struggle for greater rights. Miss Wright spoke of this struggle as "a war of class" in which "the ridden people of the earth" were "struggling to throw from their backs the 'booted and spurred' riders whose legitimate title to starve as well as to work them to death will no longer pass current." They wanted the public lands placed at the disposal of the poor, who would actually use them, the establishment of public schools, the end of credit and banking evils, shorter hours for labor, and the end of militia service and imprisonment for debt. Thomas Skidmore went so far as to suggest the redistribution of all property in the state.

These early efforts at change reached their climax in the so-called "Locofoco" movement. The Bank struggle and the inflation, which came with it after 1834, caused the working groups to enter politics in an effort to influence Democratic nominees. The name came from the use of "locofoco" matches to furnish light at one of their meetings where conservatives had cut off the gas, but the ideas for which they stood came from the older Workingmen's Movement and the new drive of the Jacksonian Democrats. The Locofoco movement spread to the more remote agricultural areas and widened its program into the nearest approach to Christian-democratic expression to be found in the period.

Philip Hone, a rich merchant, once said that the Locofocos waged their fight entirely "upon . . . grounds of the poor against the rich." They did indeed condemn the banking system as a "plan by which the idle few live by the labor of the many" and they accepted the Declaration of Independence as an integral part of the national creed. To this they added a Christian slant, and a contemporary called them "these Methodists of Democracy," who had "revived these heaven-born principles which had been so long trodden under the foot of monopoly." Another referred to "the light of Locofocoism as an outward sign of the inward light of Christianity."

In Pennsylvania unrest was equally intense, but less widely spread. In the textile industry, which had developed rapidly in the Delaware valley, and in the iron industry, which had made rapid strides in both the eastern and the western part of the state, conditions were about the same as in New England factories. The Pennsylvania farmers, however, had suffered less than those of New England. Their soils were better, and thrifty methods had retained the fertility. Markets were better developed, and self-sufficiency on the farm had seldom been surrendered. Social protest, therefore, came largely from Philadelphia, where the rich merchants and bankers exercised unusual control and where wealth and poverty were more sharply contrasted.

In 1828 the Mechanics Union of Trade Associations of Philadelphia declared:

We, the Journeymen Mechanics of the City and County of Philadelphia, conscious that our condition in society is lower than justice demands it should be, and feeling our inability individually to ward off from ourselves and families those numerous evils which result from an unequal and very excessive accumulation of wealth and power into the hands of a few, are desirous of forming an Association which will avert as much as possible those evils which poverty and incessant toil have already inflicted and which threaten ultimately to overwhelm and destroy us.

The labor movement, thus started, grew rapidly in the early thirties under the leadership of John Ferral, a hand-loom weaver, and William

English, a journeyman shoemaker. They saw the coming of a war between capital and labor and boldly declared that "even in this . . . boasted land of liberty, has the omnipotence of wealth . . . rendered the condition of labor little better than that of the slave." William Gouge, meanwhile, denounced the banking system, and Henry Carey sought to give new freedom to every American youth in the choice of occupations by a wider diversification of economic occupations under a paternal tariff program.

While these groups struggled to make democracy and Christianity function practically in the removal of inequality, others set about destroying evils and restoring justice and morality in the world. William Lord, David Dodge, Noah Worcester, and their kind drew up plans for international organization and the bringing of peace to all mankind; Lyman Beecher, Abner Clopten, John B. Gough, and dozens of others fought the evils of intemperance; Dorothea Dix labored for prison reform and a more intelligent care of the insane; Lucretia Mott, Lucy Stone, Susan B. Anthony, Margaret Fuller, and many more did all they could for woman's rights both before the law and in the political world; Horace Mann and Henry Barnard sought to awaken interest in public education and to improve the teaching profession. While these labored in the more spectacular movements, others attempted to found ideal societies where high thinking and just social relationships should predominate. At Brook Farm, at Fruitlands, at New Harmony, and elsewhere, they tried their fortunes at common living and common toil. They usually ended in failure, but they did reveal their thorough dissatisfaction with society as it was and their willingness to sacrifice for its improvement.

Part and parcel of these movements, flourishing in the same regions and under the same leadership in most cases, was the antislavery movement. Slavery was an evil which more bluntly violated the democratic ideals of liberty and equality and the Christian doctrine of justice than any other in the United States. It had once existed in both North and South. It was now localized in the South. Opposition to slavery had also existed at an earlier time, the movement, strangely enough, centering in the Southern states. The unsuccessful American Colonization Society for the removal to Africa of Negroes who had been set free had also received its greatest support from Southerners. The new antislavery movement in the Northeast, however, was of a different kind. Its most prominent leader was William Lloyd Garrison, who founded and edited in Boston an abolition paper called the *Liberator*. Its temper was indicated in the first issue, in which Garrison wrote: *"I do not wish to think or speak or write with moderation.* I will not retreat a single inch, and I will be heard." To Garrison slavery was a sin, and immediate emancipation was the remedy.

Abolition fell in with the larger ferment of the day, and soon antislavery societies, local and national, were at work advancing the cause and generating moral fervor toward its ends. Out in upper New York and Ohio, closely connected with a series of great religious revivals, another center developed, and from Lane Theological Seminary came a group of young students, under the leadership of Theodore Weld, to carry the antislavery crusade into the evangelical churches and to pour petitions into Congress. When Southerners objected to the clogging of public business by the reception of so many petitions and laid down the rule that all petitions dealing with slavery, whether within or without the legislative competence of Congress, should be laid on the table, the crusaders dubbed the measure the "gag resolution" and turned the battle against slavery into a defense of civil rights. Ex-President John Quincy Adams, then a member of the House, won the title of "Old Man Eloquent" by his gallant fight to save the fundamental right of petition. The slavery struggle was now well into the open, and its appeal was definitely broadened. Soon the movement overshadowed all other reform efforts and to a surprising degree swallowed up their zeal. In this way one of the great and effective moral crusades of all time was launched and carried forward.

THE SOUTH

The third section which was developing in form and consciousness in this period was the one that lay below Mason and Dixon's line. This was not a single unity, but was primarily a rural-agricultural section with few important cities, though it differed greatly from region to region. There was the old tobacco world in Maryland and Virginia, a rice world about Charleston in South Carolina, a "sugar bowl" around New Orleans, a land of hemp and tobacco and livestock in Kentucky and Tennessee, and now a new cotton kingdom that stretched south and west across the upcountry of the Carolinas through Alabama, Mississippi, and upper Louisiana into Arkansas and the edges of Missouri across the Mississippi River. Then, too, there were great mountain areas, and swamp and bayou regions, and sandy, pine-covered lands, and other places where self-sufficing farmers, like those of the West and the Northeast, lived their simple lives.

The pattern of life and labor in the section had been evolved in the older states in earlier days. Most men were yeoman farmers and remained that throughout their lives. They lived in simple homes on moderate-sized farms and raised such crops as supplied their needs and for which there were marketing facilities at hand. But because tobacco, rice, sugar, and cotton were staples for which there was a world demand, the opportunity for capitalistic farming also presented itself to those of wealth, ability, and imagination. These enlarged their acres, secured more of tools and labor, established marketing connections, and developed plantations. Because their undertakings were large-scale, they tended to monopolize the areas best fitted for each staple, and became the "big business" men of their communities. Like such men in other lines, they dominated also the social order and often the political life of their states.

A typical plantation, whether for tobacco, rice, sugar, or cotton, would include a big house, built perhaps in the Greek Revival type of architecture, with white pillars across the front at least, and a wide hall running through the center; barns for the horses and mules; a tool shed and a generous smokehouse; an overseer's house of modest proportions; a cluster of Negro cabins scattered among shade trees or neatly arranged along a single street; a hospital; a nursery; and last, and sometimes least, a church, where those who toiled might find rest and peace in worship. Not all plantations had all these things, but a few did. If rice were the major crop, a rice mill might also be found, where the owner and probably several of his neighbors might care for their crop. If the plantation were engaged in making sugar, then there would be a great sugarhouse, with its elaborate machinery and its towering smokestacks—an establishment that might represent an investment of a hundred thousand dollars or more.

Plantation labor consisted of Negroes, who worked under the system of slavery; that is, the workers were owned, not hired. The status of the worker and of his children was permanent unless the owner chose to terminate it. The slave could be sold, hired out, given away, or left as an inheritance. He seldom had anything to say about whose possession he should be.

Such a labor system provided a permanent supply of workers, but it tied up much capital that might have been better employed. It provided a more complete control of the workers, but denied them incen-

THE UNITED STATES MINT, PHILADELPHIA. ENGRAVING MADE IN 1830

THE HERMITAGE,
ANDREW JACKSON'S HOME
NEAR NASHVILLE

Examples of Greek-Revival Architecture

"THE WHITE HOUSE
OF THE CONFEDERACY,"
IN RICHMOND,
USED BY PRESIDENT
JEFFERSON DAVIS.
BUILT IN 1818

tive to their best efforts. It removed from the worker the fear of unemployment and worry about care in old age, but it denied him the dignity that comes with responsibility for self-care and with the need of formal education for self-improvement. It subjected him to the humiliation of corporal punishment and exposed him to the brutality of those masters who were cruel and inconsiderate. In practice it was as mild or as vicious as good men and morons could make it. Few men made it pay. Few men were able to check its inherent wasteful-ness or its dangers to the character of both master and slave.

But it had, through more than a century, become a part of Southern life, and its elimination would mean the loss of millions of dollars in property and the creation of a serious race problem. It would upset a whole section's economy and social arrangements. No group of men could welcome such drastic changes.

Most Southerners, however, lived on farms, not plantations, and had little to do with slavery. Out of a white population of over eight million there were only 383,637 slaveholders, and of these only 48,566 held twenty slaves or more—a number sufficient to constitute a planta-tion force. Nearly half of the slaveholders held fewer than five slaves, and nearly a third of them held only one or two. Thus three fourths of all the Southern people, in 1860, had nothing directly to do with slavery, and there were regions in the South as large as New England where there were practically no slaves at all.

These farmers ranged all the way from those with nearly enough slaves to belong to the planter class to the so-called "poor whites," who lived on infertile lands in poverty or allowed their herds of cattle to roam the forests while they, in leisurely fashion, loafed and hunted and fished. Most of them owned their own farms and seemed to be growing in prosperity throughout the decades.

A few free Negroes in the cities and a goodly number of white folk who dwelt in the mountains rounded out the Southern population. Neither played an important part in the life of the section, which in this period was shifting its center steadily toward the region along the Gulf, where the cotton kingdom was in the making.

That shift was the most important fact of the day. It lifted the section as such to new economic importance in national life as cotton poured out, first from Charleston and Savannah, and later from Mobile and New Orleans, to feed the hungry machines of the great Industrial Revolution. The cotton kingdom *became* the South. The older regions, dwarfed in their efforts, became allies of the great new kingdom or drifted into the position of border states, whose interests looked north, as well as south. Virginia, under the lead of Edmund Ruffin, struggled to restore her wasted fields, to produce grain and livestock, and to find special crops, such as new types of tobacco, fruits, and vegetables, which were as often marketed in Philadelphia, New York, and Boston as they were in the lower South. Kentucky, Missouri, and Tennessee engaged in an increasing sale of livestock, cotton-bagging, liquor, and tobacco to the cotton-planters, and also in trade with states that lay north of the Ohio River.

The spread of cotton was the extension of old Southern ways and values into a new Southern frontier. It did not produce a sharp break in men's ways of life or thought patterns. Old institutions and assumptions were simply thrust into a new locality, and men there simply reproduced the old order under conditions similar to those in the regions from which they had come. The section, therefore, escaped most of the social ferment so marked in the West and the Northeast. The task of the emigrants became one of defending old ways and institutions, not of rushing about in search of new ones.

The values of men in this region were highly personal. They stressed a man's honor and the necessity for good manners. Men were quick to resent any breach of the chivalric code or any "raw intrusion on the sacred individual." Their hospitality was traditional, and their children were taught to say "sir" and "ma'am" to their elders. They were much given to conversation, and the Church—Episcopal among gentlemen, Methodist, Baptist, Christian, and Presbyterian among lesser folk—was the center of both their emotional and their social lives.

They generally opposed a consolidated central government and held to states' rights as the original intent of the Constitution. In like fashion they defended slavery, first as an inherited evil for which they could not be held responsible, then as a positive good. In the Virginia Convention of 1829–1830, and in the debates in the Virginia legislature of 1832, men denounced slavery as "a blighting, withering curse," "ruinous to the whites" and unjust to the Negro. But that was about the last Southern protest. That very year, at the request of the legislature, Professor Dew of the College of William and Mary wrote the first great defense of slavery, proclaiming it beneficial to the Negro and necessary for the South. It could not be removed without bankrupting the section and without producing an insoluble race problem. Southern society, with slavery, he concluded, was the perfect order in which white men, freed from the drudgery of toil, realized republican government at its best. With this as a start, Calhoun, on the floor of Congress, was soon proclaiming slavery a positive good. The proslavery argument was on its way to meet the abolition attack. Freedom of thought in this field came to an end.

Such were the sections as they now had evolved. Such were the conflicting interests and attitudes that now troubled the politicians. Western men, caught between their needs and their resentments, were badly divided on both the banking and the internal-improvement issue. Southerners were as badly divided between those who, like John C. Calhoun, now saw in Van Buren's Independent Treasury sound Democratic policy and those who, like John Tyler, still bitterly resented Jackson's stroke against nullification. Men in the Northeast, whose conservative business interests called for wider government activity, were now more sharply divided from the working groups and farmers than at any previous time. New political alignments were in order, and the Democrats, as the party in power, of course suffered most from these new developments.

When the Whigs nominated William Henry Harrison, Virginia-born resident of Ohio, for the Presidency and placed John Tyler of Virginia on the ticket with him as Vice-Presidential candidate, they recognized the possibilities in the situation. Then by proclaiming the true democratic qualities of their candidate and refusing to write a platform, they allowed all dissatisfied elements in all sections to assume that they would gain their ends. Van Buren, meanwhile, for his liberal support of Jacksonian policies, was dubbed a Locofoco and then, in complete contradiction, pictured as an aristocrat of the worst sort. A campaign developed that was all sound and fury, all slogans and bitter attacks. Young men rolled huge balls across the country; built log cabins to symbolize Harrison's modest beginnings and ways; sang and shouted, "Tippecanoe and Tyler Too" and "Little Van Is a Used-up Man."

Issues were forgotten. Harrison, sick and old, was elected President for no reason of policies, and Van Buren went back to New York to brood over the injustice done him, even by many Democrats. Thus an old era closed, and a new one opened for an unsuspecting nation.

SELECTED BIBLIOGRAPHY

Political developments are best to be seen in MARQUIS JAMES, *Andrew Jackson: Portrait of a President*; A. B. DARLING, *Political Changes in Massachusetts, 1824–1848*; S. R. GAMMON, *The Presidential Campaign of 1832*; R. B. NYE, *George Bancroft*; W. E. SMITH, *The Francis Preston Blair Family in Politics* (2 vols.). Jackson's war on the bank is described in R. C. H. CATTERALL, *The Second Bank of the United States*, and in R. C. McGRANE (Ed.), *Correspondence of Nicholas Biddle, 1807–1844*. R. C. McGRANE, *The Panic of 1837*, is an important monograph.

The ferment and change of the era are to be found in A. M. SCHLESINGER, JR., *Orestes Brownson* and *The Age of Jackson*; W. R. WATERMAN, *Frances Wright*; ALICE TYLER, *Freedom's Ferment*; R. W. LEOPOLD, *Robert Dale Owen*; and F. BYRDSALL, *History of the Loco Foco Party*; GILBERT H. BARNES, *The Anti-Slavery Impulse*, a pioneer work in stressing the revivalistic background of the abolition movement.

Significant changes within the sections are described in R. G. WELLINGTON, *Political Influence of the Public Lands, 1828–1842*; H. C. HUBBART, *The Older Middle West*; AVERY CRAVEN, *Sources of Culture in the Middle West* (D. R. Fox, ed.); U. B. PHILLIPS, *Life and Labor in the Old South*; J. T. CARPENTER, *The South as a Conscious Minority*; C. EATON, *Freedom of Thought in the Old South*.

H. S. COMMAGER (Ed.), *Documents of American History*, pp. 270–282, 283–287, 291–292, 300–304, contains source material.

XVI

Expansion and Conflict

GROWTH OF POPULATION

THE YEARS from 1840 to 1860 were heavy with meaning for the United States. The nation had achieved enough of size and strength to awaken a just national pride and to permit something of swagger. By the end of the period its population had passed that of the United Kingdom and was rapidly catching up with that of France and Germany. With its 31,443,321 people, it was now one of the great powers in the Western world.

Most of this growth represented an increase of native stocks, which, even in 1860, constituted a heavy majority of the total. A growing proportion, however, came from immigrants. Between 1820 and 1830 less than half a million foreigners came to the United States. In the next two decades nearly two and a half million arrived. The peak was reached in 1854, when over four hundred and twenty-seven thousand came. By 1860 the foreign-born constituted 12.9 per cent of the total population.

Most of these immigrants came from England, Wales, Scotland, Germany, and Ireland. In the later years, owing to unusual circumstances, Germany and Ireland furnished the greater number. In Germany hard times combined with political oppression to drive people out. Crop failures in the Rhine valley and the replacing of household manufactures by factory machine-made goods forced lesser people to migrate; the persecution of political liberals by despotic princes, who held back German national unification and opposed all democratic efforts, gave America such intellectuals as Carl Schurz and Franz Sigel. Forced military service affected all classes and added to the growing flood. In Ireland dissatisfaction with English rule and with much of absentee landlordism, and a series of famines, due to potato-crop failures, were the principal forces behind the heavy emigration of these years. In few lands was the pressure on the poor greater.

The majority of early immigrants to the United States had been attracted to rural areas by cheap lands, but these newcomers, in growing numbers, remained in the cities, where expanding commerce and industry offered opportunities. The Irish found the New England towns particularly attractive; the Germans turned to Cincinnati, St. Louis, Milwaukee, and Chicago. Many of both groups, of course, went to New York and Philadelphia. Many sought work on the canals and railroads or did what their predecessors had done, cleared a farm on some remote frontier. The majority, however, played a part in increasing the number of cities with a population of eight thousand and over from 13 in 1820 to 141 in 1860. With their aid New York (including Brooklyn) grew to 1,174,799; Philadelphia, to 565,529; and Boston, to 177,812. Where in 1790 only 3.3 per cent of the population lived in cities (incorporated places of eight thousand and over), in 1860 over 16 per cent were urban dwellers.

WESTWARD EXPANSION

The growth of cities and the increasing tendency of immigrants to remain there did not mean that Western expansion had halted. In fact, the completion of the Erie Canal had greatly stimulated the movement of population along the Great Lakes, and by 1834 had given Michigan Territory a population of more than eighty-seven thousand. Encouraged by such rapid growth, the people east of Lake Michigan quickly drafted and adopted a constitution, but, because of a boundary dispute with Ohio, did not secure admission as a state until 1837. Population, meanwhile, had crossed the Mississippi into the lands opened by the defeat, in 1832, of the Sauk and Fox Indians under the leadership of Chief Black Hawk, and soon Iowa Territory came into being, and then the state of Iowa (1846). Wisconsin became a state in 1848, and Minnesota a decade later. By 1860 these states, together with the older states of the Northwest, had a population of 7,773,820.

This growth and expansion in the Northwest was balanced in the South by the admission of Arkansas in 1836, and by Florida and Texas in 1845. The first two of these were a part of the great sweep of cotton to the south and west; the third represented a new expansive force at work in the nation, which soon, also, brought California (1850) and Oregon (1859) into the Union.

In the early period of national life, politicians had sometimes talked about the Pacific Ocean as the natural western boundary of the United States and even of the possible extension of United States territory beyond the existing southwestern border. The people, however, knew little of the region south and west of Missouri and had accepted Zebulon Pike's and Stephen Long's notions that it constituted the "Great American Desert," suited only to wandering tribes of Indians and herds of buffalo. They knew, of course, that the United States had once had a claim to Texas, but had yielded it in 1819 in order to gain Florida. They knew, even when they talked of the Pacific as a western boundary, that the Oregon country was held jointly by Great Britain and the United States and that California had been Spanish territory until the revolutions of the 1820's had made it, like Texas, a part of Mexico. Other than that, knowledge was not important, because needs did not exist.

The first break in this attitude of near indifference came when Missourians discovered the profits possible in trade with Santa Fe. Some efforts along this line had been made while the town was under Spanish control, but it was not until after Mexican independence that William Becknell made the first profitable trip (1822). Thereafter trade flourished, and in 1834 a Missouri newspaper reported that "the company of Traders to Santa Fe" had brought back one hundred and eighty thousand dollars in gold and silver and some twenty-five thousand dollars' worth of furs, wool, and mules. Not all expeditions were so successful, but one such kept interest high and the trade steady. Year by year their wagons cut deep the ruts of the first great Western trail, and hardy frontiersmen learned the methods of travel on the plains and prepared the way for the acceptance of American rule in these regions when it should come.

While these events were taking place, a new interest in the Oregon country was developing. During the 1820's, in spite of the efforts of John Floyd and Thomas Hart Benton, Congress refused to provide for American occupation of the Columbia River region, and the British Hudson's Bay Company, under its chief factor, Dr. John McLoughlin, extended its activities from Vancouver throughout the entire Oregon country. Only the work of Hall Kelley and Nathaniel Wyeth, two Massachusetts men who promoted an overland expedition, kept American interest alive. Then came a series of missionary efforts, the first, in 1834, under Jason and Daniel Lee for the Methodist Board of Missions, and the second, in 1836, under Marcus Whitman, Henry Spalding, and W. H. Gray for the American Board of the Presbyterian, Congregationalist, and Dutch Reformed churches. These groups set up missions in the Willamette and Walla Walla regions. Soon thereafter Father Pierre Jean de Smet began his work in the Bitterroot region for the American Catholics.

Exploration and Settlement in the Southwest
MURAL PAINTINGS BY TOM LEA IN THE COURTHOUSE, EL PASO, TEXAS

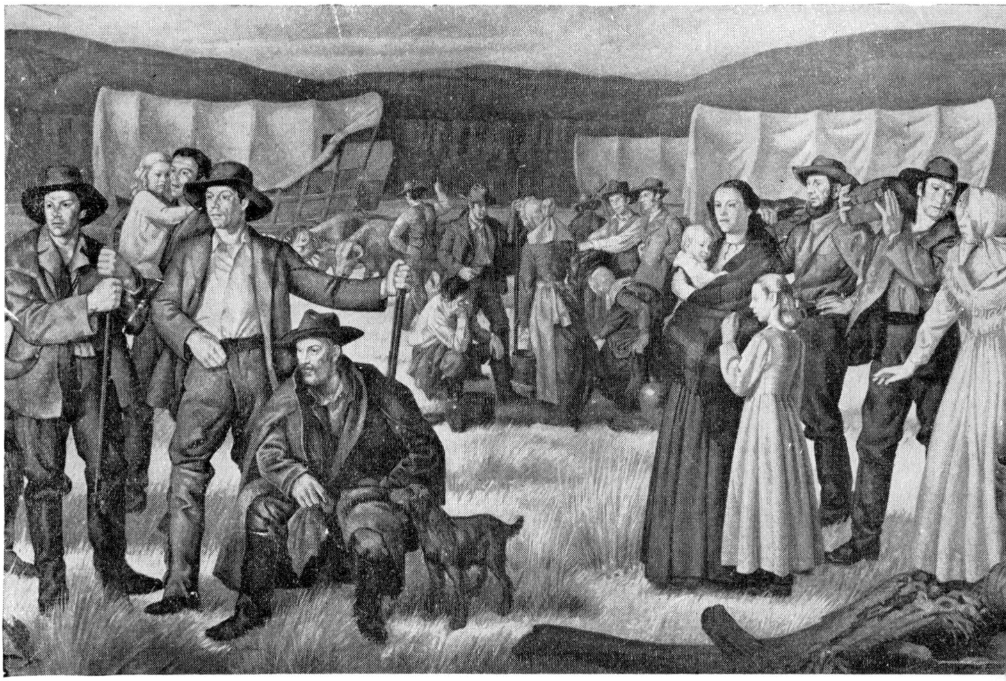

Hagelstein Brot[illegible]

An Overnight Camp on the Oregon Trail about 1847

MURAL PAINTING BY FRANK H. SCHWARZ IN THE STATE CAPITOL, SALEM, OREGON

A Pioneer Home at Old Fort Sales, Washington

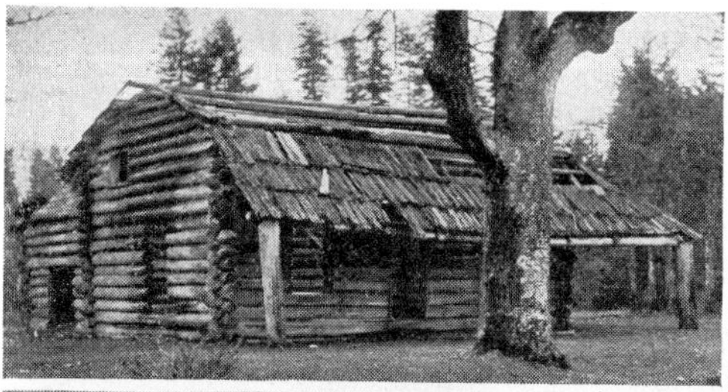

Crossing the Rockies

Currier and Ives, 1

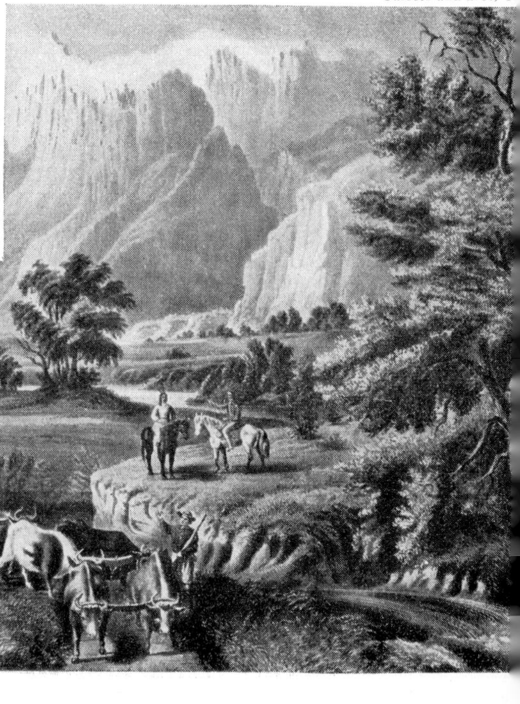

These missionaries not only carried the gospel to the Indians and trappers of a far-off country; they also began farming operations, which revealed the remarkable fertility of the soil. Their reports reached the Old Northwest just when home markets were faltering and the hard times following the panic of 1837 were at their height. An "Oregon fever" suddenly broke out, and in 1843 a thousand people crossed the plains and began cutting a new and more wonderful trail into the Far West. The next year fourteen hundred new settlers arrived in Oregon, a figure that reached nearly five thousand in 1847. The slumbering problem of boundary lines in a region jointly occupied by Britain and the United States was thus rudely awakened.

THE MORMONS; CALIFORNIA AND TEXAS

While the Oregon migrations were still running in full tide, a strangely different band of Americans were making their way into the region around Great Salt Lake, then in Mexican territory. They were the patient, much harassed Mormons, moving for the fourth time in search of a promised land where they could worship God and build a social-economic order in their own way. The sect had its beginnings in western New York during the restless twenties, when revivals flourished, millenniums seemed at hand, and men dared to dream of perfection in men and in society here on earth. Its founder was the young Joseph Smith, who suddenly announced the finding of golden plates, on which, he believed, were inscribed sacred scriptures, comparable to the books of the Bible, and which, when translated, became the Book of Mormon.

As Smith's converts grew in number, a church was organized and located first at Kirtland, Ohio, and then at Independence, Missouri. Troubles with native "gentiles," however, soon led to persecution and the arrest of leaders. The sect moved to Nauvoo, Illinois. For a time the Mormons prospered, and their city reached a population, in 1846, of some fifteen thousand. But trouble began again, with rumors of the practice of polygamy. Smith and his brother were thrown into prison and then murdered by a mob. The Mormons were soon on the move again, this time under the shrewd leadership of Brigham Young, and their destination lay across the plains to the southeastern shores of Great Salt Lake. There they plowed their lands, planted their fields and learned to irrigate them, laid out their city with its spacious streets and Temple lot, and founded a new type of Western community, held in social-economic unity by the cement of a new religious revelation.

With these great western sweeps attracting national attention, it was only natural that interest in California should also quicken. Even in 1841 one caravan had started for that region, and by 1846 it was estimated that at least one fourth of those who followed the Oregon Trail turned off to California. They usually headed for the fort which John A. Sutter had built on the American fork of the Sacramento River. There they found a bit of the United States lodged in this Spanish-Mexican outpost—fields of grain, herds of cattle and horses, a gristmill, and all the paraphernalia of a prosperous fur trade. Such an establishment, set up in a region once jealously guarded by a long line of picturesque Spanish missions under able Franciscan friars and scattered ranches in the hands of easygoing colonials, testified to weakening Mexican control and enlarging opportunities for Americans. Already Thomas O. Larkin of Massachusetts had opened a store in Monterey; already Commodore Thomas Jones, commander of the American fleet in the Pacific, acting under instructions to seize that port in case of war between Mexico and the United States, had, in 1842, landed a force, seized public property, and raised the American flag. He had, as Larkin showed him, acted too soon, and he was forced to apologize and retire. But his action showed the American temper and general purpose.

National horizons had definitely widened as Oregon and Utah and California came into the news and as some Americans sought homes in these distant places. The full measure of "manifest destiny," however, showed itself best in relation to Texas. That region was nearer and had been long a part of American territorial interest. When the Florida treaty of 1819 had fixed the southwestern boundary of the United States at the Sabine River, both Clay and Benton denounced it as a surrender of rightful American territory. Louisiana newspapers spoke of "territory belonging to the U. S. . . . ceded away to a despot" and of Texas being worth ten Floridas. Some Americans even marched across the border with the avowed intention of establishing the independence of that region. Had it been known that Napoleon, when he sold Louisiana, regarded the Rio Grande, not the Sabine, as the western boundary, they would probably have had enough support to accomplish their purpose.

Spanish control, however, had not prevented American migration to Texas. Moses Austin, a Connecticut man who had lived in Missouri when it was under Spanish control and who had fallen into financial difficulties during the panic of 1819, led the way. In 1820 he went to San Antonio and petitioned the local authorities for the right to establish a colony in that province. The right was granted, but Austin died before receiving word to that effect, and the grant fell to his son, Stephen F. Austin. Stephen's appeal for settlers, coinciding with hard times, brought ready response. Land grants were generous and prices low. Poor men of Missouri, Arkansas, and Tennessee moved easily to such lures. By 1830 from sixteen to twenty thousand Americans lived in Texas, along with some three or four thousand Mexicans.

The attempts of both John Quincy Adams and Andrew Jackson, when they were in the Presidential chair, to purchase Texas, and the predominance of Americans there, soon alarmed the Mexican government. Troops were stationed in various settlements; a series of restrictive laws, culminating in one forbidding further immigration from the United States, were passed. Self-rule, so essential to Americans, was denied. Even property rights were endangered. Efforts at improvement only brought more moves toward consolidation on the part of the Mexican government. The inevitable result of all these developments was revolt, and, after the massacre of one body of Texans, defending themselves in the Alamo, the people rallied under General Sam Houston and won victory and independence. In November, 1835, a provisional government was established, and a year later independence was declared and a permanent constitution adopted. The next step was a vote in favor of annexation by the United States.

With the election of 1836 approaching, President Jackson was unwilling to act. The existence of slavery in Texas, a normal result of the migration of peoples from the regions adjacent, endangered Northern support. The recognition of Texas as an independent republic was all that could be accomplished. "Manifest destiny" had not yet done its work.

Interest in Texas, however, did not die. The great expansion fervor of the next few years not only kept it alive, but turned it into a burning issue. The demand that the United States should round out its natural borders; the feeling that we were a chosen people with a preordained mission to extend our system of government to others; the notion that we had a right, based on divine sanction, to dominate the Western Hemisphere—all these attitudes, which made up "manifest destiny," somehow touched Texas and made annexation inevitable. But the actual step was a political one, and politics, as we shall see, were becoming highly complicated in the "roaring forties."

GROWTH OF INTERNAL TRADE AND TRANSPORTATION

The spectacular nature of territorial expansion tends to hide certain other highly important features of American growth in this period. Among them the development of trade and the facilities for trade were of greatest importance. Here the most significant facts were the comparatively slow growth of foreign trade and the unusually rapid development of internal commerce. Foreign trade rose rapidly in the early 1830's, fell off as rapidly after the panic of 1837, and picked up again after 1846, when the British corn laws were repealed and prosperity became general. The steamship and the clipper ship both came in this period to facilitate ocean shipping, and the American merchant marine, in 1860, almost equaled that of Great Britain. Yet foreign commerce did not hold the important place in the nation's life that it had held in early national days, and the single item cotton made up nearly two thirds of the value of all exports. Foodstuffs, almost entirely from the North, formed a larger part after the repeal of the British corn laws, but never constituted more than one sixth of the total. Imports, meanwhile, exceeded exports, and the annual value of the total foreign trade per capita was well below that of the earlier period.

In sharp contrast to developments in foreign trade were those in the domestic field. Here trade followed the line of sectional specialization. The South, with its heavy concentration on cotton, sugar, tobacco, rice, and naval stores, formed a splendid market for the horses, mules, tobacco, cotton-bagging, and surplus slaves of the border states, the manufactures of the Northeast, and the foodstuffs of the Northwest. It offered great opportunities to the ships and shippers of the North and to the bankers of Eastern cities, who often financed both the production and the marketing of the crops. The Northwest, as an expanding frontier region, needed manufactured goods beyond its capacity to produce, and in its wheat and hogs and cattle had the surplus with which to pay for them. It could secure cash, as well as sugar and other Southern produce, by way of the great Ohio-Mississippi riverway, which bore also so much of its produce to Southern plantations. The Northeast, more and more, needed raw materials for its factories and food for its workers and had the products of its machines to give in exchange. Imports and exports of the whole nation poured in and out of the harbors of the Northeast. The task of gathering capital at home and abroad for national development was in the keeping of its citizens.

Trade of such proportions hurried forward the agents of transportation. Steamboats in use increased from one hundred and twenty-five in 1825 to over six hundred in 1856, and one estimate placed the steamboat tonnage on Western rivers, in 1847, as above that of the whole British Empire. Speed also increased, as did accidents. Soon vessels were moving upstream as rapidly as once they had made their way downstream. By the fifties, boats were going from New Orleans to Louisville in five days, a trip that once required seven times that long.

Steamboats also increased on the Great Lakes as population deepened along their borders, but the sailing vessel more than held its own. As the surplus of wheat reached its crest in the fifties, the tonnage of vessels on the Lakes surpassed that of the Mississippi River system. The balance of trade in the Northwest was shifting.

More important than water transportation was the coming of the railroad. Back in 1804 Oliver Evans of Philadelphia had driven "a five-horsepower steamboat on wheels" through the streets of the city, and some years earlier he had petitioned the state legislature for the sole right to use "wagons propelled by steam" on the highways of Pennsylvania. Then, in 1820, John Stevens built and operated a narrow-gauge steam railroad on his estate in New Jersey. Both men were considered somewhat demented, and most people agreed with the statement of the Ohio school board that refused the use of the schoolhouse for the discussion of the practicability of railroads:

> You are welcome to use the schoolhouse to debate all proper questions in, but such things as railroads and telegraphs are impossibilities and rank infidelity. There is nothing in the word of God about them. If God had designed that His intelligent creatures should travel at the frightful speed of fifteen miles an hour, by steam, He would have clearly foretold it through His holy prophets. It is a device of Satan to lead immortal souls down to Hell.

But railroads could not be held back by such skepticism, and soon English and American experiments on local projects opened the way for larger undertakings. A Baltimore group pioneered the way with the first major undertaking and in 1827 incorporated the Baltimore and Ohio Railroad Company. On July 4 of the next year Charles Carroll of Carrollton, Maryland, the last surviving signer of the Declaration of Independence, turned the first shovelful of dirt in its construction. In that same year the Charleston and Hamburg road was incorporated, and by 1834 it had one hundred and thirty-seven miles in operation. Then followed short lines radiating out from Boston, New York, and Philadelphia, serving local needs, but destined, in the case of the Mohawk and Hudson, and the Philadelphia and Columbia, to become the first links in the New York Central System and the Pennsylvania Railroad of later days.

With these beginnings, the railroad came into its own. Engineering difficulties were overcome, disjointed links were united into systems, and local and foreign capital was secured. Public prejudice against railroads turned into a frantic demand for their construction. By 1840 the railroad mileage of the country totaled 2818 miles, and by 1860 more than 30,000 miles. Most of this mileage was in the North and connected the eastern seaboard with the growing cities of the Old Northwest. A few lines had even crossed the Mississippi River.

Southern building had been slower, and lines joining the North and the South were few. This fact, combined with the more rapid growth of population in the northern half of the Old Northwest, helps to explain the trade shifts of the period. Where in early days most of the surplus of the Northwest went south by river and canal, the balance was now definitely in favor of the East. Not that trade with New Orleans ceased to grow, but rather that trade with New York, Philadelphia, and Baltimore grew much more rapidly. And the shift in economic interest, unquestionably, played a part in the shifts in political alliances which were also taking place.

INTELLECTUAL PRIDE AND INDEPENDENCE

Such great strides in expansion and development could not help stirring in the American a new sense of national pride. We had become a nation among the great nations. Pride might center about a local section, but it also reflected a consciousness of national achievement and a sense of being a part of it. Even the close co-operation of Americans with Englishmen in peace and slavery crusades and the strident efforts of the "Young America" groups for official intervention in behalf of the European liberals after their defeats in 1848–1849 were evidence of the aggressive belief that the United States was the peculiar guardian of freedom and the hope of mankind. And from the same sources, combined with a marked provincialism, came the sharp reaction against the foreign immigrant, which expressed itself in various forms of nativism and reached a climax in the American, or Know-Nothing, party. Its basic drive came from a feeling that the foreigner might damage the great American dream; that his Catholic religion, centered in Rome, and its expression did not accord with the old, dominant Protestant values. Its moves to check immigration and to lengthen the period required for the attainment of citizenship expressed not only prejudice against that which was different, but also a firm belief in the superiority of that which already made up the United States.

National consciousness, of course, lay behind the slogan "manifest destiny" and the idea that God and nature "had designed a unique geographical arena for the American experiment." Whitman wrote of the

> . . . flag of man . . . run up above them all,
> Flag of stars! thick-sprinkled bunting!

The song "America," written in 1832, now achieved national popularity. A whole series of monuments, starting with one at Bunker Hill, began to rise to the memory of national heroes. Through the efforts of Sarah Hale, the last Thursday of November soon was recognized in different states as a national Thanksgiving Day.

Literary men also felt the new impulse. One writer asked:

> Why cannot our literati comprehend the matchless sublimity of our position among the nations of the world—our high destiny—and cease bending the knee to foreign idolatry, false tastes, false doctrines, false principles? When will they be inspired by the magnificent scenery of our own world, imbibe the fresh enthusiasm of a new heaven and a new earth, and soar upon the expanded wings of truth and liberty?

Some writers were already answering. In 1837 Ralph Waldo Emerson delivered his great address "The American Scholar," which has been called the "declaration of American intellectual independence." Boldly he declared: "Our day of dependence, our long apprenticeship to the learning of other lands, draws to a close. . . . The millions that around us are rushing into life cannot always be fed on the sere remains of foreign harvests." He continued: "We have listened too long to the courtly muses of Europe. We will walk on our own feet; we will work with our own hands; we will speak our own minds." A few years earlier Washington Irving had come home from a prolonged stay in Europe to discover the romantic charm in the vast changes that had come to the United States in his absence, and to portray one phase of those changes in his *Astoria* and in *The Adventures of Captain Bonneville*. Eagerly he embraced the new world that had proven so disconcerting to his own bewildered Rip van Winkle at an earlier date. In so far as it was possible for one whose chief "business in life was to loaf and invite the picturesque," he identified himself with the new democratic forces of the day.

Even more occupied with American themes were the novels of James Fenimore Cooper. The clash of Patriot and Tory in the Revolution, the life of the rugged pioneer and the "noble" Indian in the American forest, even the relative merits of Federal aristocracy and the new democratic order, furnished materials for work that brought quick response at home and, for the first time, made Europe "aware of a dynamic country beyond the Atlantic Ocean." Romancer and critic by turns, Cooper sharply revealed both the strong appeal to liberal minds of the democratic urge and the instinctive fears which aristocratic groups felt at the changes that it brought.

William Gilmore Simms of South Carolina used similar materials, finding in the Revolution on the Southern frontier themes for an astonishing number of novels. An ardent Southerner, steeped in the history and traditions of his Charleston world, he created a group of characters as native in their homespun vices and virtues as any to be found in American literature. His defense of planter life and slavery stressed his provincialism, but did not hide the fact of intense Americanism in language, subject matter, and values. Vernon L. Parrington calls him "an American Fielding with a dash of Smollett."

Somewhat less appreciated in their day, but destined to hold high place with later critics, was another group: Nathaniel Hawthorne, who occupied himself with the problem of evil as it presented itself in an age when older, Calvinistic views were being mellowed by Unitarianism; Emerson and Thoreau, who stressed the sacredness of the individual and the possibility, through the free individual, of greater perfection in society; and Edgar Allan Poe, whose mastery of the short story and whose ability to create and convey intense moods through prose and verse have seldom been equaled. And then there was Herman Melville, who had known life at naked, elemental levels of excitement and brutality on a Pacific whaling vessel and among the simple natives of tropical islands. He too had come home to tell, in *Typee, Mardi,* and *Moby Dick,* tall tales of the seas and to express grave doubts about the smug assumptions that Americans of his day were making about God and man and the merits of democratic institutions. He saw little difference between the conquests of "manifest destiny" and those of the savages on Pacific islands; he found only mystery where his fellows found certainty; he was not so sure that democracy was the final and perfect order that would one day bring Utopia to the whole world.

Ralph Waldo Emerson, Washington Irving, and
William Gilmore Simms

Henry David Thoreau, Edgar Allan Poe, and
Herman Melville

Henry Wadsworth Longfellow, Walt Whitman, and
George Bancroft

A group of poets also played a part in proving to the world that the United States had reached enough of maturity to produce a native literature. Longfellow and Whittier and Bryant and Lowell, all did work that satisfied the standards of their day, if not those of later ones. Walt Whitman, on the other hand, reached true greatness. More than any other he voiced both the temper and the ideals of democracy. About him were a largeness and a coarseness that were America itself. His words were native; what he said was original; the way he said it was new. Truly in *Leaves of Grass*, published in 1855, Whitman put into poetry all that Emerson had preached and all that Thoreau at Walden had tried to live.

The historian also played his part in expressing the new national temper. In 1834 George Bancroft began the publication of his ten-volume *History of the United States*, which fairly reeked with patriotism. Even the dullest reader could not escape the conclusion that the hand of Providence worked in American affairs and that a new and better force had appeared among the nations of the earth. Richard Hildreth also set out to tell the national story. His approach was more restrained and more scientific than that of his great contemporary. Yet he too, by his very interest in the working of the Federal system, showed the new consciousness of national entity. Francis Parkman, turning his attention toward Canada and the West, produced work of enduring historical and literary value. William Prescott and John Motley, writing in the same period, chose their subjects outside the national sphere. Prescott told of the conquest of Mexico and Peru; Motley wrote of the Dutch republic. Both did their work with enough of mature scholarship to impress European readers and, thereby, to add their part to the growing understanding that the United States was now something more than a raw wilderness occupied by an uncouth people.

Nor were all the evidences of intellectual maturity confined to literature. A group of scientists were also doing creditable work. Benjamin Silliman at Yale was assembling a chemical laboratory and making a first-class collection of minerals; Louis Agassiz at Harvard was carrying on research in zoology; Matthew Maury at the United States Naval Observatory was exploring the physical geography of the sea; and the botanist Asa Gray, teaching at the new University of Michigan and then at Harvard, had begun the study and classification of North American flora. Friend and correspondent of Charles Darwin, Gray not only made American data available to that scholar, but became a champion of his theories.

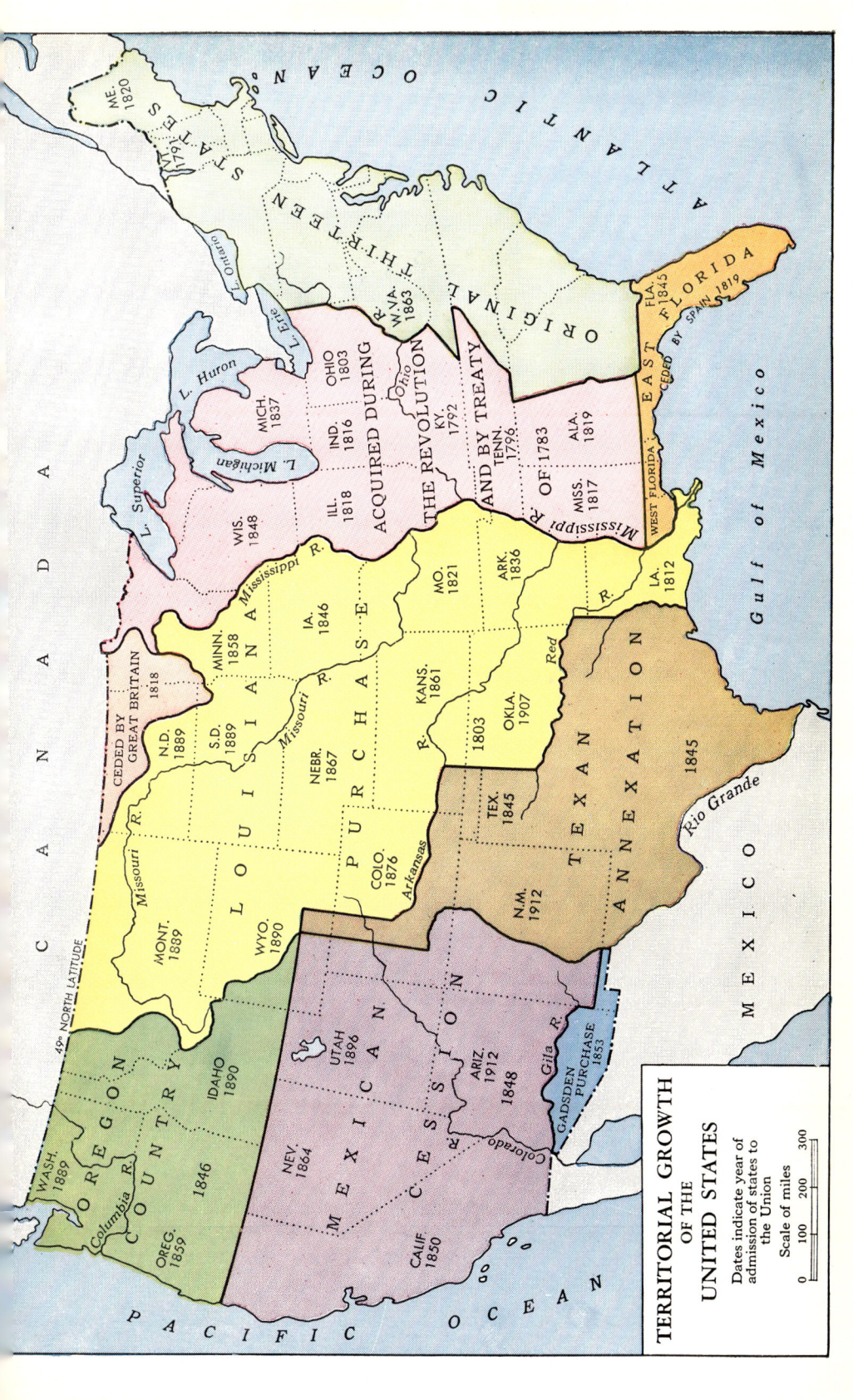

TERRITORIAL GROWTH
OF THE
UNITED STATES

Dates indicate year of
admission of states to
the Union

Scale of miles

0   100   200   300

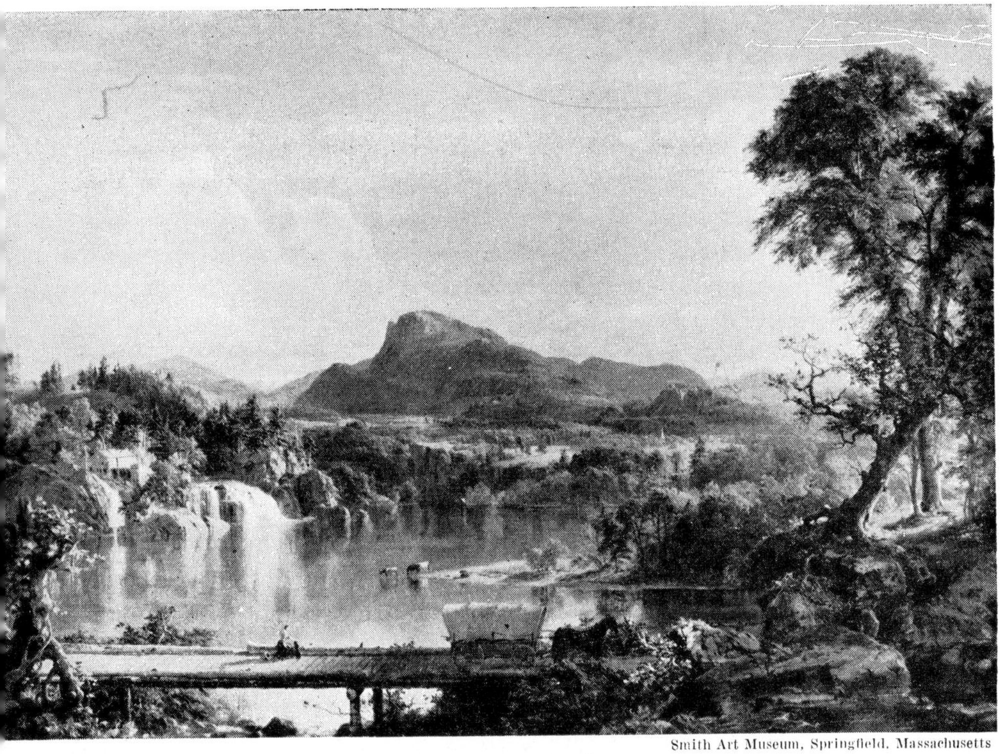

Smith Art Museum, Springfield, Massachusetts

In the Catskills

PAINTING BY F. E. CHURCH, 1851

Western Landscape

PAINTING BY THOMAS MORAN, 1864

Art Museum of the New Britain Institute

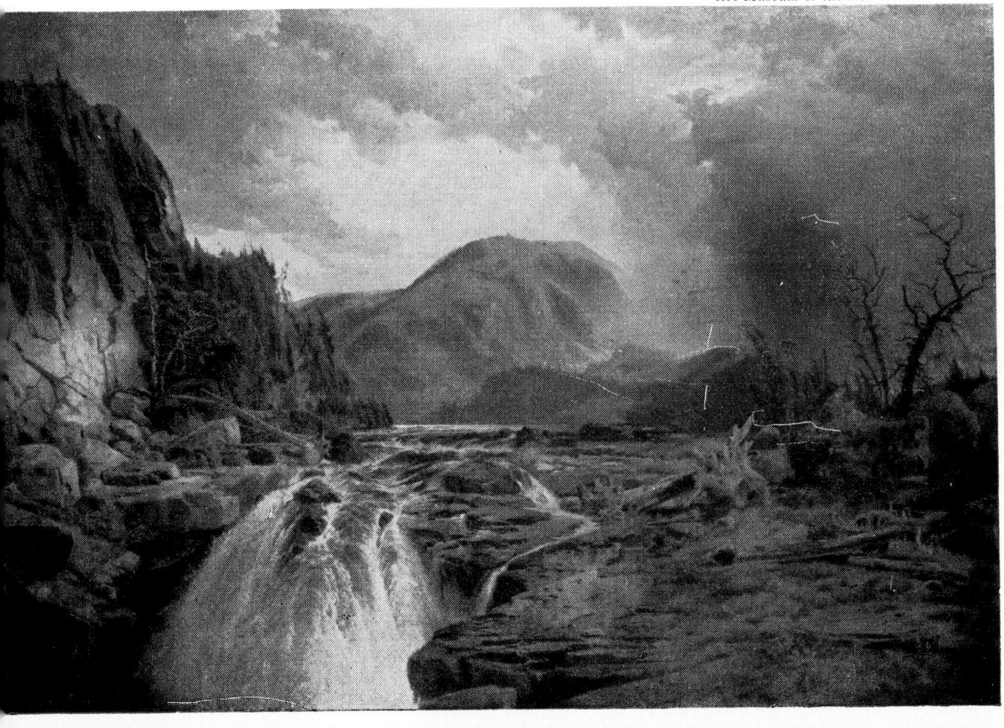

The Hudson River school of artists, including such painters as Thomas Cole, Washington Allston, Samuel Morse, Thomas Doughty, Asher Durand, John Kensett, Frederick Church, Thomas Moran, and Albert Bierstadt, not only produced a native art, but showed an interest in the American landscape that had earlier been lacking. Over and over again they pictured Niagara Falls, the coast of New England, the Palisades of the Hudson, the rugged beauty of the Catskills, and soon the wild, majestic splendors of the Far West. William Mount and George Bingham caught on canvas bits of everyday American life. In architecture Robert Mills and William Strickland gave an American touch, in both structure and integrity, to the buildings that they designed to fit the needs of a new people in a new land. The charge of romanticism which hangs over all these creative spirits only serves to stress their national pride, links them with poet and novelist, and establishes their firm relationship with Andrew Jackson and James K. Polk.

POLITICS AND EXPANSION

The strain and stress which expansion and a degree of national maturity brought to the political order proved serious. Issues involving fundamental rights and interests were thrust forward, and decisions that had to do with the very structure of American society had to be faced. Economic developments in different corners of the nation magnified normal sectional differences and intensified sectional strife. Uneven growth raised, in more bitter form, the question of majority and minority rights for groups and interests and sections. The growth of industry and finance to levels where the well-being of the many was placed at the mercy of the few pushed forward the question of government's obligation to regulate business, as well as to assist it. Expansion into new areas brought conflict over the rights of slavery in territories and raised constitutional questions regarding the powers of government to interfere with developments there. Here and there men began to question the ability of democracy itself to survive changed conditions. Others began to wonder how long the democratic process of the settlement of problems by discussion could go on where such divergent interests and values were involved. It had worked quite well when issues had to do only with policies. Could it cope with issues involving the very structure of society and those phrased in terms of honor, right, and wrong?

Already the political parties had felt the pressure. The Democrats had lost enough strength in 1840 to lose the election. The Whigs had won without a platform and with a President and a Vice-President who held diametrically opposing views on most issues. The result kept the country at a standstill during the next four years.

On April 4, 1841, just one month after delivering his long and labored inaugural address, President Harrison, whom the Clay faction expected to dominate, died, and John Tyler took his place. Strife began at once. Clay and his friends had hoped to re-establish the Bank, increase the protective tariff, and distribute to the states the funds from the sale of public lands. Tyler informed Congress that while the Independent Treasury had plainly been repudiated and Congress could decide on the advisability of chartering a bank to take its place, he reserved to himself the ultimate power of rejecting any measure which he thought conflicted with the Constitution or would otherwise jeopardize the prosperity of the country. Two attempts by Congress to find such a bank met his veto, and there that issue rested. As a Southern agriculturist, he refused to disturb the 20 per cent tariff level reached in 1842 under the compromise tariff or to distribute the funds from the sale of public lands, which would weaken the Treasury to a point where increased tariffs could be justified. The best that could be done along this line, therefore, was a bill by which distribution would cease if the tariff was raised above 20 per cent.

A stalemate resulted, and threats of impeachment were heard. Editors referred to Tyler as "His Accidency" or the "Lilliputian Dictator." Clay and his friends were furious. The cabinet, with the exception of Daniel Webster, resigned. Webster remained only to complete the negotiations that he was conducting with Lord Ashburton for the settlement of the long-standing dispute between England and the United States over our northeastern boundary. This dispute had existed since the Treaty of Paris after the Revolution, and had led to friction between the citizens of Maine and of Canada in the so-called "Aroostook War" of 1838, and to some American interference in the abortive Canadian rebellion against England in the same decade. The burning of an American ship, the *Caroline*, which had been used in aiding the insurgents, and British anger at the seizure, by New York State officials, of one Alexander McLeod, who boasted that he had taken part in the burning of the ship, showed the necessity for settlement; and Webster, placing country before party pique, remained at his post to complete, in 1842, the first of the only two real accomplishments of the administration.

The second accomplishment of the Tyler administration had to do with Texas, and that, in turn, had to do with politics. Strife inside the Whig party upset what little political equilibrium existed and started the Presidential campaign of 1844 prematurely. Clay resigned his seat in the Senate and went home to make sure of his party's nomination two years ahead. Tyler, deserted by the Clay faction, began trying to build a party of his own and to look for new issues that would help. The friends of Martin Van Buren, meanwhile, strengthened their hold on the Democratic machine, and John C. Calhoun trimmed his attitudes on the tariff in an effort to increase his own popularity. He had already sought Western favor by advocating the cession of public lands to the states in which they lay.

SLAVERY AND EXPANSION

Out of these circumstances came one of the most fateful developments in American history. The annexation of Texas was pushed forward as a political issue and linked with the question of slavery. Subsequently the matter of settling the Oregon boundary was joined with these issues, and all the forces of party and sectional feelings were tangled with the basic American urge to expansion and "manifest destiny."

How this came about is not entirely clear. We do know that the antislavery forces had been greatly strengthened by the debates in Congress over the receiving of petitions; that they had openly charged that the move to annex Texas was a deliberate effort to extend and perpetuate slavery; and that they had entered politics with the Liberty party in 1840. We know also that both Tyler and Calhoun, sometime in 1843, began to advocate annexation for the purpose of advancing their Presidential aspirations and that Calhoun, at least, gave as one of the important reasons for annexation the efforts of English antislavery groups to end slavery in Texas.

The Texas issue took hold quickly, but profited the Presidential prospects of neither Tyler nor Calhoun. Tyler's support never developed, and Calhoun soon found that Van Buren had a majority of Democrats already pledged to his nomination. Fate, however, now took a hand. When Webster had completed his negotiations with Lord Ashburton, he gave up his cabinet post and permitted first Legaré and then Upshur, stanch advocate of the annexation of Texas, to take his place. Negotiations toward that end were already under way when an explosion on the gunboat *Princeton*, where Upshur had gone to witness the demonstration of a new type of gun, caused his instant death. Friends now forced Tyler to make Calhoun Secretary of State, and the latter, without delay, completed the Texas treaty and sent it off to the Senate. At the same time, he seized the opportunity, in a letter addressed to the British minister, to let it be known that the protection of slavery was the basic reason for our action.

The Senate held up the treaty, but annexation with a slavery flavor was now thrust into the Presidential campaign, where Van Buren and Clay confidently awaited nomination by their parties. Both had expected the campaign to be waged on all the old issues, but now they were forced to speak on Texas. On the same day they issued letters saying, in effect, what everyone now knew was untrue, that the annexation of Texas was not an issue. The quick course of events revealed their fatal blunder. When the Democrats met in convention, a combination of Southern and Western expansionists put through a two-thirds rule to affect Van Buren's pledged majority and made James K. Polk, who had favored annexation, the party's candidate. Their platform, in true expansive mood, declared for the reoccupation of Oregon and the reannexation of Texas. Their candidate let it be known in Pennsylvania that he was not an enemy of protective tariffs.

The Whigs took Clay in spite of his mistake. He made repeated efforts to show that he was not against annexation, but the damage had been done. In November, Polk carried the country by a more than thirty-eight-thousand majority. The people had spoken for expansion; and in spite of the fact that the Liberty party had increased its vote nearly ninefold over that of 1840, Tyler and Calhoun accepted the verdict as final on Texas. Congress agreed and by joint resolution passed an act for annexation to complete the second positive contribution which the Whigs under Tyler would make to the country.

Polk's administration is one of the most remarkable in American history. After years of uncertainty and deadlock, the country was ready to move forward, and Polk, blunt, honest Presbyterian that he was, took his party's platform seriously. On the domestic front the Independent Treasury system was re-established, and all thoughts of a new National Bank were pushed aside until the Civil War. Then, in December, 1845, Secretary of the Treasury Robert J. Walker submitted his report, recommending a new, "free trade" tariff schedule in which rates on luxuries, including wines and liquors, would be high; an average duty of 25 per cent would be laid on most imports competing with American cotton, wool, and iron manufactures; and a long list of articles in common use would be duty-free. The industrial interests were bitterly dissatisfied, and only one member of Congress from Pennsylvania, a man named David Wilmot, voted for the schedule. Nevertheless it became law "and remained the cornerstone of the Democratic structure" until 1861.

The so-called "Walker tariff," of course, pleased the South, and the next step in the program was one especially designed to satisfy the Northwest, whose leaders had loyally supported the tariff measure. It was a bill for liberal internal improvements on the rivers and lakes of that section. Both houses gave it support strong enough to indicate previous agreement among leaders on the whole program. But members from the South, under the leadership of Robert Barnwell Rhett of South Carolina, fought the measure at every step, and Polk, accepting their view, vetoed the measure on constitutional grounds. Western men were furious and began to talk of a bargain that had not been kept. The full fury of their anger, however, would come later.

The more important phases of Polk's administration had to do with foreign affairs. Southern leaders, such as Robert J. Walker, had, in the recent campaign, demanded the whole of Oregon, as well as the "re-annexation of Texas." That had pleased the men of the Northwest and also the merchants of Boston and New York, who saw Oregon as a steppingstone to wider commercial expansion in the Pacific. The campaign cry of "Fifty-four forty or fight!" had indicated about as much pressure for all of Oregon as there was for annexing Texas. Polk's diplomatic problems, therefore, had to do both with getting Mexico to accept our annexation of Texas with satisfactory boundaries, and with adjusting the Oregon boundary to England's satisfaction, as well as our own. Accordingly, in August, 1845, he sent John Slidell to Mexico, with instructions to adjust the Texas boundary by offering as much as twenty-five million dollars for Upper California and New Mexico, and to settle all American claims against Mexico. He also ordered General Zachary Taylor to concentrate troops as rapidly as possible at Corpus Christi, at the mouth of the Nueces River, to protect Texas interests while negotiations proceeded. Unfortunately Mexico refused to receive Slidell or to negotiate for the alienation of territory. Even more unfortunately it viewed the movement of Taylor's troops as an invasion of Mexican territory.

While these developments were taking place, Congress, in April, 1846, at Polk's insistence, authorized the President to notify England that joint occupation in Oregon would cease at the expiration of a year. Polk was convinced, as he said, "that the only way to treat John Bull was to look him straight in the eye." He believed that "a bold and firm course on our part was the pacific one; that if Congress faltered or hesitated in their course, John Bull would immediately become arrogant and more grasping in his demands; and that such had been the history of the British nation in all their contests with other powers for the last two hundred years."

British public opinion was deeply stirred by Polk's action, and the possibility of war was accepted. Britain's officials, however, were more calm, and her business groups were more interested in whether the Walker tariff, with its trade advantages, would be passed. When this was assured, the British government offered to compromise the Oregon boundary at the forty-ninth parallel. Polk, with troubles enough on the Mexican front, accepted the offer, and on June 12, 1846, a treaty to that effect was ratified. Northwestern Democrats, who insisted that they had been promised all of Oregon, were sorely disappointed. One of their leaders declared in the Senate, "James K. Polk has spoken words of falsehood, and with the tongue of a serpent." Another "asserted distinctly that the Oregon and Texas annexation projects had their birth in the Baltimore convention . . . that they were 'cradled together' with a distinct understanding that if the West sustained the South in securing Texas, the South would sustain the West in her claims to Oregon." A game "treacherous to the West" had been played.

WAR WITH MEXICO

Polk's willingness to compromise with England was due in part to his growing conviction that war with Mexico was inevitable. As early as April 25, 1846, he had decided to send a message to Congress, recommending a declaration of war. On May 9 he told his cabinet that there was ample cause for war and that he could no longer remain silent. Mexico, however, saved him the trouble, for on that very day word was received from General Taylor that his troops had been attacked. All that Polk had to do was to notify Congress that "the two nations are now at war." Mexico had "invaded our territory and shed American blood upon the American soil."

The war which followed was brief and conclusive. General Taylor's army, though without adequate preparation or supplies, moved forward to defeat the Mexicans at Palo Alto, Resaca de la Palma, and

Matamoras and then, on September 24, 1846, to capture the key city of Monterrey. Meanwhile General John E. Wool advanced from San Antonio to Parras, where he established communication with Taylor's army, and Colonel A. W. Doniphan, marching from Santa Fe, captured the city of Chihuahua and then joined Taylor at Saltillo in May, 1847. More spectacular was the expedition under Colonel Stephen Kearny, which captured Santa Fe in August, 1846, and then pushed on to California, where it joined the marines operating there under Commodore R. F. Stockton. Kearny found California already under American control. Settlers there had revolted, in 1846, and with the aid of General John C. Frémont, who was there on one of his numerous exploring expeditions, had set up the "Bear Flag Republic." It was short-lived; but soon after war had broken out between the United States and Mexico, Commodore John D. Sloat raised the American flag at Monterey and took possession of all California. A few days later he turned control over to Commodore Stockton, whom Kearny found in command.

These brilliant victories gave the swaggering young nation the kind of heroes it needed, and soon men were talking of Zachary Taylor for the Presidency. Polk and his Democratic friends were alarmed. Whig leaders began to make inquiry regarding Taylor's political affiliations. They found that he had none, but that he had become somewhat dissatisfied with the treatment which the administration in Washington had given him after his victories. That was all the Whigs needed, and it was enough to cause the administration to pass Taylor by when a leader for the final drive against Mexico City, by way of Vera Cruz, was being chosen. Not only that, it was reason enough to cause the administration to withdraw most of Taylor's regular-army troops to add to the expedition.

That was a fatal blunder. For the Mexicans, under Santa Anna, whom Polk had recently allowed to return from exile in the hope of securing peace, suddenly turned on Taylor's weakened forces on the battlefield of Buena Vista. Although greatly outnumbered, Taylor stood his ground and won a smashing victory. Much of the credit for success belonged to General Wool, Colonel Jefferson Davis, and the artillery under Sherman and Bragg. Taylor had exhibited marked personal bravery and had inspired his troops by deeds and words, but his preparations for battle had been none too good. The country, however, only knew that a general, already badly treated by the administration and now deprived of his best troops, had gained a great victory. The

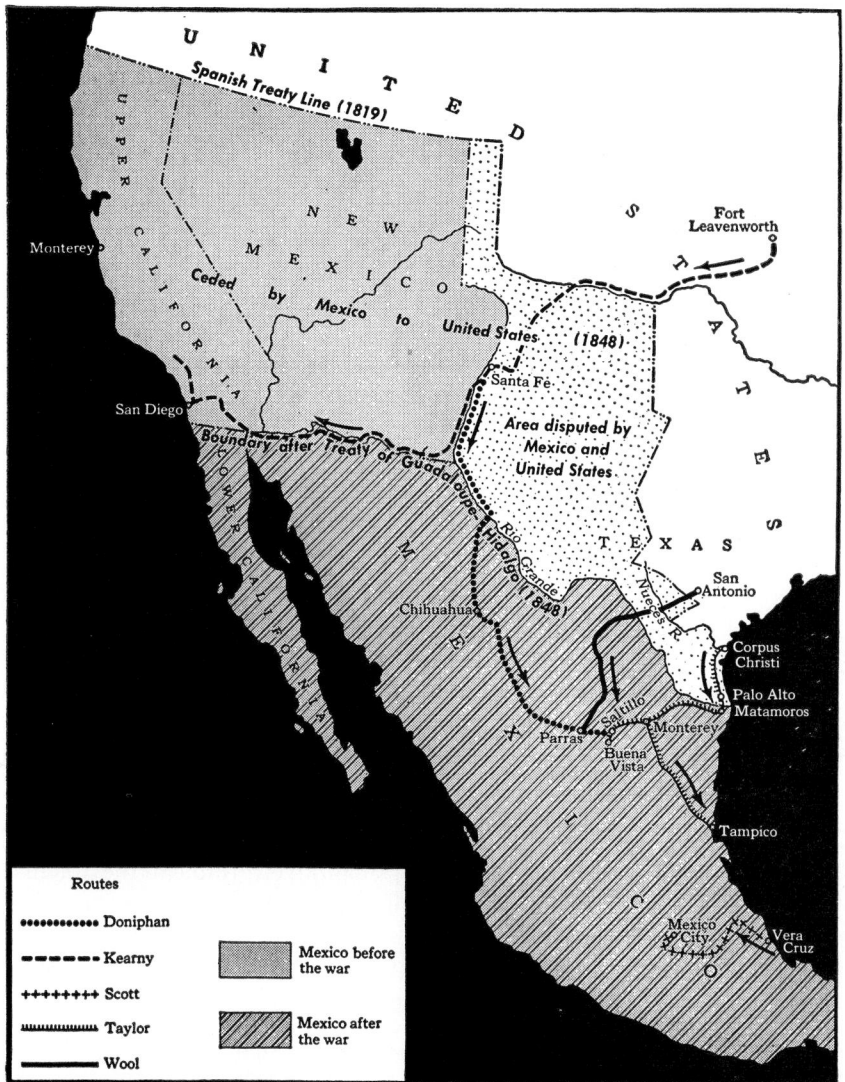

Important Campaigns of the Mexican War

Whigs could rest content while General Winfield Scott, in command of the new army, swept on from Vera Cruz to capture Mexico City and to make peace possible.

Peace came in a strange way. Knowing that General Scott was a Whig, Polk sent one Nicholas P. Trist, the chief clerk in the Department of State, along with the army to negotiate peace and to order

Scott to cease fighting when he thought it expedient. Of course the general and the clerk quarreled, but in the end began to work together in a way that alarmed Polk. Trist was recalled, but stayed on after the fall of the Mexican capital to negotiate a treaty of peace. Polk was badly upset, but his cabinet advised that the treaty be sent to the Senate for ratification.

This Treaty of Guadalupe Hidalgo, ratified May 30, 1848, fixed the boundary at the Rio Grande and ceded California and New Mexico to the United States. The United States, for its part, agreed to pay Mexico fifteen million dollars and to assume all the claims held by Americans against that government. The United States thus acquired new lands equal to more than one third of its former territory. What was equally important, conquest gave a new turn to the slavery question, a turn that was to prove tragic.

SLAVERY AND THE COMPROMISE OF 1850

New England antislavery men had been open and violent in their opposition to the annexation of Texas and especially to the Mexican War. In their eyes it was all a great scheme to expand slavery and provide new markets for excess human property. Emerson urged that annexation be resisted "with tooth and nail." Charles Sumner chided one of his friends who had voted for army supplies in Mexico, saying:

Rather than lend your vote for this wickedness you should have suffered the army of the United States to pass submissively through the Caudine Forks of Mexican power,—to perish, it might be irretrievably, like the legions of Varus. Their bleached bones in the distant valley where they were waging war, would not tell to posterity such a tale of ignominy as this lying act of Congress.

James Russell Lowell broke into verse to insist that

> They just want this Californy,
> So's to beg new slave states in.

Far more serious, in the closing days of the war, was the attitude of Northwestern political leaders. The whole section, with the exception of the Western Reserve area, had been expansionist in temper and had gone for Polk on both Texas and Oregon. When the Oregon boundary of fifty-four forty had been surrendered without a fight and the Texas boundary had been insisted on with a war, they bluntly charged betrayal. When the bill for the improvement of rivers and harbors in the Northwest was vetoed by Polk, they saw the whole situation as one in which their interests were being ignored and those of the slaveholding South were being forwarded at any cost. In November, 1846, the Chicago *Democrat* disclosed that "this harbor question is not a political one, but a sectional one. It is between North and South." The Chicago *Daily Journal* insisted that "the lives and property of the freemen of the North, her free laborers, sailors, and those passing to and fro upon her Great Lakes and Rivers," when "weighed against a Virginia abstraction, or that idol of the South, *negro slavery*," were nothing in the sight of James K. Polk. Southerners had shown themselves "to be slaveholders, but not Americans."

It was, therefore, not surprising that when, in August, 1846, Polk asked Congress to appropriate two million dollars to be used in purchasing territory from Mexico, a group of men from the Northwest and a few others friendly to their attitude should have introduced a resolution in the House to the effect that "as an express and fundamental condition" to such purchase "neither slavery nor involuntary servitude shall ever exist in any part of said territory." This was the famous Wilmot Proviso. It said, in effect, that if the North was to be slighted, then the South, as a slaveholding section, was not to gain at the expense of the North. For the next few years that Proviso was attached to every bill dealing with new territory. It became the symbol of Northern interests in conflict with those of the South.

The introduction of the Wilmot Proviso linked slavery and expansion more firmly than ever and stirred deeply sectional bitterness and fears. The slavery question, in the form of slavery extension, made a new kind of appeal. Northerners talked of "a slave power" and of the need that the "lovers of freedom" unite to check the common enemy by fixing bounds to its aggression. The legislatures of Ohio and Michigan passed resolutions against further extension, a thing which every legislature in the North would ultimately do. Opposition to slavery extension began to be the test of a desirable candidate for office. Parties began to divide on the issue.

In the South the reaction was even more violent. Calhoun led off with resolutions in the Senate, asserting the common ownership of territories and denying the right of Congress to pass any law which discriminated between free and slave states or which deprived any citizen of any state of the right to emigrate to any territory with his property—meaning, of course, his slaves. Virginia passed similar resolutions, and both Mississippi and Alabama endorsed them. Texas, Georgia, and South Carolina took like ground, and some began to talk of a dissolution of the Union if the hated Proviso were insisted upon.

That was the situation when the election of 1848 came round. Polk deserved the Democratic nomination, and Calhoun had long hoped for it. But the war and sectional reactions had ruined the chances of both. The convention, therefore, turned to Lewis Cass of Michigan, a Westerner who had recently suggested the leaving of slavery in the territories to the people thereof. The Whigs took up Zachary Taylor because he was popular, and did their best to keep him quiet on issues and to keep him from telling people that he was not a party candidate. They wrote letters for him to sign, which he immediately contradicted in private letters. Also, he accepted nomination by independent groups, often with a Democratic Vice-Presidential nominee attached to his nomination. Before election day he had, with his pen, almost destroyed the popularity won with his sword. But he was a Southern slaveholder, and though good abolitionists called him this cup "offered by slaveholders for us to drink," enough Southern Democrats deserted their party to more than offset Northern losses. And what was most important, a new Free-Soil party, based on the Wilmot Proviso and advocating free lands to settlers, river and harbor improvements, and a protective tariff, arose in upper New York, with Martin Van Buren as its candidate.

Election day found Taylor in the lead by virtue of the votes which Van Buren took from Cass and the heavy swing of Southern voters to the Whig side. A military man, without strong party leanings, but with honest, sincere purpose, became President of a disturbed and uncertain nation.

Trouble began in Congress at once when bills for the organization of New Mexico and California, with slavery excluded, were introduced and efforts were made to check the slave trade in the District of Columbia. The South stirred. A caucus of Southern Congressmen issued an "Address to the People of the Southern States," written for the most part by Calhoun. In October, 1849, a Mississippi state convention issued a call for a Southern convention to meet in Nashville in June. Many believed that this was the first step toward secession.

With excitement at white heat, news suddenly arrived of the discovery of gold in California. A rush of settlers quickly turned a scantily settled territory into a region populous enough to demand, and lawless enough to require, the organization of a state government. In

ST. LOUIS ABOUT 1849

American Scenes about 1850

SUPPERTIME
AT THE CALIFORNIA
"DIGGIN'S"

By William R. Ryan, 1848-1849

WINTER SCENE

N. Currier, 1854; from Bland Gallery, New York

September, 1849, its people met, framed a constitution, elected senators, prohibited slavery, and asked for admission to the Union. The fat was in the fire. The question of slavery in the new territories had to be faced at once.

When the new Congress met in December, Whigs and Democrats were so nearly equal in the House that the new Free-Soil members held the balance of power. Attempts to elect a Speaker produced a prolonged deadlock. Behind the scenes, pledges were demanded and bargains attempted. Debate became acrimonious. Weeks went by without an election. At length men's patience gave way, violence broke out, and the House became uncontrollable. When some semblance of order was restored, Toombs of Georgia took the floor. Bluntly facing the fact that the slavery issue was behind the difficulty, he warned his fellows that if the efforts to drive the South from the territories were continued, he was for disunion. He was willing to go to war in defense of his section's rights.

The effect of these words was sobering. Debate was suspended, and voting for a Speaker was resumed. At length, on December 23, 1849, Howell Cobb of Georgia was elected, and Congress was organized.

Understanding the danger to the nation which these issues threatened, Henry Clay now evolved a plan. His chances for high office were now gone; only love of the Union prompted him. Ill and weary, he had hoped to escape hard work in this session of Congress. But he could not see younger men destroy the government that he had done so much to build. Securing Webster's promise to help, he now introduced a series of resolutions which he believed would secure an amicable settlement of all difficulties. California should be admitted as a state, without Congressional action on slavery; a territorial government should be set up in the remaining territory secured from Mexico, also without provisions regarding slavery; boundaries should be drawn for Texas, and she should be compensated by Federal assumption of her debts, for any losses of territory; the slave trade in the District of Columbia should be abolished, but slavery should be continued until the people of Maryland and of the District should accept compensation for abolition; a new and more effective fugitive-slave law should be passed, and the principle that Congress had no power over the domestic slave trade should be recognized.

Here was compromise. Here was enough to protect Southern interests, enough to satisfy Northern reformers. Eloquently he defended his plan. North and South alike should "conjure . . . at the edge of the precipice before the fearful and disastrous leap" was taken.

A month later Calhoun tottered up the steps of the Capitol and sat while Mason of Virginia read his (Calhoun's) speech. He was too ill to attend the sessions or to speak. He too saw the Union in danger. The agitation against slavery was the reason. The South, by yielding to the North in the Northwest Ordinance, the Missouri Compromise, and on Oregon, was now in the minority. A consolidated government, which the South had tried so long to prevent, was now completed and in Northern hands. The Union could be saved only by justice granted the South as a minority. California was a test question.

Daniel Webster spoke three days later. He too pleaded for the Union. He defended the North against Calhoun's charges, but he begged the North not to abuse its power. Nature had already prohibited slavery in all the territories acquired from Mexico. It would never go there; so why push the Wilmot Proviso? He would support Clay's proposals. Abolitionists at home called him traitor, and Whittier wrote,

> All else is gone; from those great eyes
> The soul has fled:
> When faith is lost, when honor dies,
> The man is dead!

Southern writers, however, noticed a decided cooling of tempers in their region after Webster had spoken.

Lesser men followed these giants. William H. Seward and Salmon P. Chase would have nothing to do with compromise. The issues were moral issues. Slavery smacked of the Dark Ages. A democracy owed its territories freedom. Jefferson Davis was equally uncompromising on the other side. To him Clay's proposals were a complete surrender of the South's contentions. The South must have equal rights in the territories. The line 36° 30′ should be extended to the Pacific. David Wilmot, Albert G. Brown, and others added heat to the debate, but little light. For a time it looked as though the Union would go to pieces.

Then gradually the tide turned. The Whigs did not relish the thought of their second administration being a failure, like their first. Their old leaders, Clay and Webster, had advised compromise. That was good Whig practice. Even Southerners began to falter. "Our politicians have gone over to the compromisers," wrote a Virginian. Calhoun's death, on the last day of March, 1850, completed the breakdown. By June, when the Nashville Convention met, the violent tem pers had cooled, and nothing more than a set of rather mild resolutions and a call for a later meeting resulted. Then the opposing hand of President Taylor was removed. He had not liked Clay's proposals, because he felt that if the people in California and New Mexico were left alone, the nation would escape bitter controversy on the subject of slavery. He would face each problem as it arose. He dubbed Clay's proposals the "Omnibus Bill." But he too died, in July, and Millard Fillmore, who favored compromise, became President. The way was then cleared for settlement.

Through the summer, under the leadership of Stephen A. Douglas, measure after measure was debated and passed. September saw the task completed and the Compromise a reality. That the crisis had been safely passed was soon evident in the public acceptance of the Compromise. The second meeting of the Nashville Convention was a decided anticlimax. Its membership was small, and its resolutions, asserting the sovereignty of the states, attracted little attention. South Carolina's efforts to call another great Southern convention met with no response. A Georgia convention, called to deliberate on issues, was thoroughly Union in sentiment, but issued the so-called "Georgia Platform," which said in effect that it accepted the present Compromise, but expected the North to maintain faithfully all its provisions. In the state election which followed, a combination of Whigs and Democrats, who favored compromise, triumphed. Other Southern states fell into line. In Mississippi, Senator Foote, who had favored compromise, defeated Jefferson Davis, who had opposed, for the governorship. Alabama, under the leadership of William L. Yancey, was more divided, but was unwilling to probe the issues further. The other Southern states generally accepted Georgia's position and were glad to see the danger passed. The real question for the future was whether a compromise on issues that had become tangled with morals and sectional honor had settled anything permanently.

SELECTED BIBLIOGRAPHY

Ralph Gabriel, *The Course of American Democratic Thought*; Vernon L. Parrington, *Main Currents in American Thought*, Vol. II; Merle Curti, *The Growth of American Thought*; Van Wyck Brooks, *The World of Washington Irving*; Frederick Jackson Turner, *The United States, 1830–1850*; Avery Craven, *The Coming of the Civil War*, valuable accounts of the life and thought of this period.

Robert G. Cleland, *The Cattle on a Thousand Hills*; R. N. Richardson and Carl C. Rister, *The Great Southwest*; Justin H. Smith, *The Annexation of Texas*; E. C. Barker, *The Life of Stephen F. Austin, Founder of Texas, 1793–1836*; J. S. Reeves, *American Diplomacy under Tyler and Polk*, contain important material on American expansion in the Southwest. The influx of immigrants, which helped to make expansion possible, is described in Marcus L. Hansen, *The Atlantic Migration, 1607–1860*, and in G. M. Stephenson, *A History of American Immigration*.

Various phases of American expansion in the Far West are to be found in A. C. Laut, *Pathfinders of the West*; R. F. Duffus, *The Sante Fe Trail*; Josiah Gregg, *Commerce of the Prairies*; Katherine Coman, *Economic Beginnings of the Far West*; Joseph Schafer, *A History of the Pacific Northwest*; Archer Hulbert, *The Call of the Columbia* and *The Oregon Crusade*; W. A. Linn, *The Story of the Mormons*; Bernard De Voto, *The Year of Decision*; Robert G. Cleland, *A History of California*; Allan Nevins, *Frémont, the West's Great Adventurer* (2 vols.); Levi E. Young, *The Founding of Utah*. Important studies of expansion and slavery are O. P. Chitwood, *John Tyler, Champion of the Old South*; E. I. McCormac, *James K. Polk*; Brainerd Dyer, *Zachary Taylor*; Justin H. Smith, *The War with Mexico* (2 vols.); C. B. Going, *David Wilmot*.

The crisis over slavery and the Compromise of 1850 are described in Laura White, *Robert Barnwell Rhett*; Richard H. Shryock, *Georgia and the Union in 1850*; Cleo Hearon, *Mississippi and the Compromise of 1850*; M. J. White, *The Secession Movement in the United States, 1847–1852*; Henry T. Shanks, *The Secession Movement in Virginia*; G. G. Van Deusen, *The Life of Henry Clay*; Claude Fuess, *Daniel Webster* (2 vols.); W. E. Smith, *The Francis Preston Blair Family in Politics*.

H. S. Commager (Ed.), *Documents of American History*, pp. 306–314, 319–325, contains source material.

XVII

Trial and Failure

POLITICIANS now proclaimed the finality of the Compromise of 1850. The causes of sectional and party conflict were now removed, they said. The extremists, who had stirred the troubles and who had wanted a drastic settlement of issues, had been defeated. Party and sectional harmony were now possible.

Such wishful thinking overlooked two very significant facts. First, the recent controversy had pushed the slavery question to the fore, had enlarged its scope to include the extension of slavery, and had made it definitely a symbol of the basic differences between the sections. Northern men who earlier had been indifferent now saw slavery as a moral question, as one opposed to the basic democratic intent of the great American experiment, and as one which constituted a test of their religious sincerity. In 1844 Northern Methodists had refused to recognize the right of a clergyman to hold slaves, and the church had split along sectional lines. The next year the Baptists, after a bitter quarrel over support for slaveholding missionaries, had followed a like course. Right and wrong, as well as democracy itself, were involved in every phase of the slavery question. And did that not apply to the return of fugitive slaves, which the new law under the Compromise required?

The second fact had to do with Southern attitudes. The recent controversy had led Southern men to stress the benefits and justice of slavery, the tendency to discriminate against Southerners because they held slaves, and the necessity for strengthening the South as a section in all ways. They had accepted compromise on the assumption that their attitude toward slavery and their rights as slaveholders would be respected and protected in the North. They would, in the meantime, prepare to act if this were not done. And did this not mean that they were asking the North to change its moral values and that they were expecting the South to become even more determined in its ways?

The politicians, however, ignored these basic questions. In January, 1851, a group of fifty-four Congressmen, representing both parties and both sections, signed a pledge to oppose any candidate for public office who did not accept the Compromise as a finality. Regardless of political irregularity in the last few years, the drift was now back into the old parties. When the Presidential election of 1852 came round, the Democrats stood firmly by the Compromise and chose Franklin Pierce of New Hampshire as their candidate on a platform similar to that of 1844. The Whigs again tried a military man, in the person of Winfield Scott, on a platform "acquiescing in the Compromise measures, as a settlement in principle and substance of the dangerous and exciting questions which they embrace" and agreeing to abide by them until experience should prove further legislation necessary. The Free-Soil party, weakened by Van Buren's return to the Democrats, nominated John P. Hale as a symbol of their return to old Liberty-party days. Pierce carried the election by a majority of only two hundred and fifteen thousand. Democrats talked of another period of glorious national expansion under this "New England Polk."

While the politicians went on their wishful-thinking way, other events, more indicative of real attitudes, were occurring. Late in October, 1850, a group of prominent Boston citizens, calling themselves a Vigilance Committee, "rescued" two runaway slaves, Ellen and William Croft, from officials who would have returned them to their owners under the new Fugitive Slave Law. In the following February they broke open the jail to liberate the fugitive Shadrach and to send him off to Canada and freedom. Violently they assailed Judge Curtis, who had attempted to enforce the law and held him up, as they said, "to receive the hootings and rotten eggs of the advancing generation." Then, shortly after Pierce's inauguration, they organized a mob to rescue the Negro Anthony Burns, and when they failed, draped the streets of Boston in black and hung their flags at half-mast. Like rescues took place in upper New York, and out in Chicago the common council pronounced the Fugitive Slave Law "cruel, unjust and unconstitutional, a transgression of the laws of God." Even Emerson, calm philosopher that he was, wrote in his journal: "This filthy enactment was made in the nineteenth century, by people who could read and write. I will not obey it, by God!"

Then, late in 1852, Harriet Beecher Stowe published her melodramatic *Uncle Tom's Cabin*, which, besides having a sale of millions of copies, supplied something that the antislavery crusade had until now lacked. Where before, slavery, to most Northerners, had been a rather vague, general matter, it now was made real and personal in the character of Uncle Tom. They saw him as a near-perfect Christian, as a long-suffering father attempting to reunite his family. They understood his feelings. They suffered with him. Never again could they be indifferent to the institution under which he toiled. No matter what politicians said about the Compromise ending the conflict over slavery, they knew in their hearts that slavery must be put on the road to ultimate extinction.

When Franklin Pierce took office, the country was enjoying prosperity, and business was in an expansive mood. Immigration was at its height; railroad-building was progressing rapidly; settlers were pouring into the West; industry was again prospering. The country was ready for another forward advance. Gold in California had brought pressure for a transcontinental railway, and, to facilitate its building, one of the first acts of the new administration was the acquisition of territory from Mexico, thereafter known as the Gadsden Purchase (1853). Efforts were also made to secure Cuba, but the blustering methods of Pierre Soulé, our minister to Spain, in demanding redress for the illegal seizure of an American ship, the *Black Warrior*, in Havana, ruined any chances of success. This was made even worse when, in August, 1854, Soulé joined with our ministers to England and France, at Ostend, in Belgium, to issue an astonishing Manifesto to the effect that if Spain would not sell Cuba, it would be well to consider whether the domestic peace and security of the United States did not justify its acquisition by other means. The Manifesto was repudiated, but the damage had been done.

These moves for expansion had stirred some antislavery feeling, and Joshua Giddings, Congressman from Ohio, had denounced them as an effort "to meanly and piratically steal Cuba, in order that the chains of slavery [might] . . . be more securely riveted upon her bondsmen." He had bluntly asserted that the North would "set at defiance all low and unworthy machinations of this Executive, and of the minions of its power." There had been some response to these statements, but no reopening of the old, bitter slavery controversy. That came from a quite unexpected quarter.

THE KANSAS-NEBRASKA BILL

On January 23, 1854, Stephen A. Douglas, Senator from Illinois, introduced a bill for the organization of the territory west of Missouri and Iowa, in which "all questions pertaining to slavery in the Territories, and in the new States to be formed therefrom," were "left to the decision of the people residing therein, through their appropriate representatives." In the final bill the territory was divided into two units, Kansas and Nebraska. To the Kansas-Nebraska Bill was appended a section specifically declaring the Missouri Compromise, of 1820, inoperative and superseded "by the principles of legislation of 1850, commonly called the compromise measures."

This bill climaxed a long series of efforts on the part of Congressmen from Iowa and Missouri to have this territory organized. The section repealing the Missouri Compromise followed the threat, made earlier by Senator Dixon of Kentucky, to attach such a proviso to any territorial bill presented.

The reaction to Douglas's bill was immediate and violent. A group of antislavery leaders, including Chase of Ohio and Sumner of Massachusetts, quickly issued "The Appeal of the Independent Democrats in Congress to the People of the United States." It declared that the freedom of our institutions was endangered, that Douglas's bill opened all our unorganized territories to slavery, and that a sacred pledge, a precious right, had been violated. It urged all honest men to rise in protest.

The response to the Appeal was immediate. "Its inflammable sentences fell like sprays of oil upon fires." Protest meetings resolved and petitioned; excited editors took up their pens to enlarge on the sentiments of the Appeal. "This measure [Douglas's bill]—the scheme of a weak and imbecile administration; of a corrupt and ambitious demagogue; of grasping, dishonorable Slaveholders," cried one Ohio editor, "has filled the cup of bitterness which has been pressed to Northern lips so long." "His bill," asserted an Illinois editor, ". . . practically contemplates the introduction of human slavery into that territory, and proves beyond peradventure, that the Illinois Senator, although pretending to represent a free State, is wedded to slavery, and is using his influence for its extension." Soon Douglas was pictured as a slaveholder about ready to take up his residence in Mississippi. He had sold out to the South in order to secure votes for the Presidency. He had fallen in with slavery's "insatiate demands for more slave territory and more slave States."

Stephen A. Douglas, whose act had so stirred the North, was one of the most capable young men of this generation of capable men. Admirers called him "the Little Giant." He had been born in Vermont and at the age of twenty had gone West, first to Cleveland, Ohio, and then to Jacksonville, Illinois. He had made his way forward by sheer drive and ability, as a teacher, as a lawyer, and then as the recognized leader of the Democratic party in his state. Few men, in personal qualities, have ever better represented the region in which they have lived. Vigorous, forceful, rough, and audacious, Douglas came to understand the great Northwest as few men understood it, and to champion, first as a Representative and then as a Senator, those measures necessary for its development. He had been an ardent expansionist in regard to Oregon and Texas; he had not been satisfied with Polk's policies, but had thrown himself into the work of passing the various bills which made up the Compromise of 1850 and deserved much of the credit for what was then accomplished. He had always been interested in the organization of new territories, and his zeal in promoting railroads had been matched only by his zeal in speculating in Western real estate.

He was a good Democrat. He believed in the people and in their right to decide matters for themselves. As applied to slavery, this came to be spoken of as popular or squatter sovereignty. He would grant slavery its constitutional rights, and he had no use for abolitionists. But neither was he a slaveholder, nor did he wish to extend slavery. His first wife, Martha Martin of North Carolina, had inherited a plantation and slaves from her father, but Douglas himself had refused this same property as a wedding present. For both abstract and practical reasons he viewed slavery as "a curse beyond computation" to blacks and whites alike. He was certain that "the laws of climate, and production, and physical geography" had excluded slavery from Kansas and Nebraska.

Nor had Douglas's bill come in response to Southern demands. The moves for organization had originated with settlers anxious to enter the new lands and with the promoters of a Pacific railroad. A Missouri political conflict, in which Thomas H. Benton sought to regain the Senatorial seat occupied by David Atchison, also played a part. Benton made his bid by advocating the organization of the territories and the making of St. Louis the eastern terminus of a great central railroad. He expected organization to be under the provisions of the Missouri Compromise, which would make the territory free. Atchison countered by also advocating organization of the territories, but without the restriction of slavery in them. He most certainly appealed to Senator Douglas, as chairman of the Committee on Territories, for assistance in his schemes. And Douglas himself was not without interest in the matter. Chicago was now his home, and he was as determined to make Chicago the eastern terminus of the Pacific railroad as Benton was to

bring it to St. Louis. Both of them realized that Southern interests, working through Jefferson Davis, Secretary of War, were already busy with plans to run any Pacific line west from New Orleans.

Since all believed that only one line would be built, the part that organized territory would play in locating its course was very important. Here Southern interests had an advantage, and the Gadsden Purchase seemed to indicate a near victory. If Chicago were to have a chance, the organization of Northern territories was imperative. Atchison's interests in slavery and Dixon's threat to attach his proviso to any territorial bill were reasons enough for Douglas's adding the Missouri Compromise repeal to the Kansas-Nebraska Bill. It was his reason for doggedly pushing the bill, almost singlehanded, to final passage.

The matter of real motives, however, was of little importance in the excited state of public opinion in the North. The question as to whether Kansas and Nebraska were physically fitted to slavery mattered as little. The important thing was that Northern men had come to believe that an aggressive slave power had pushed aside a sacred agreement, made in 1820, that it ruled the nation through the Democratic party, and that it had blocked Northern interests in tariffs, internal improvements, and the Oregon boundary. It had failed to pass homestead legislation, and Polk, then Pierce, had vetoed a river-and-harbor bill. It had corrupted Northern leaders and turned them into "doughfaces." It was now seemingly determined to push the institution of slavery to every corner of the nation. The time to resist had come.

EFFECTS OF KANSAS-NEBRASKA BILL, NORTH AND SOUTH

The first important result of this attitude was the birth and development of a new political party, based on the principle of opposition to the further extension of slavery. Local moves in this direction occurred in different places, but those at Ripon, Wisconsin, and Jackson, Michigan, seem to have been the first to take on the name *Republican*. Both Whigs and Democrats had a hand in developments. Old Free-Soilers and even a few Liberty-party men joined the move. Some believed the effort to be only a temporary one to meet a specific issue, but some Democrats, dissatisfied since the election of 1844, and many Whigs, certain that the crushing defeat of 1852 had permanently ended their party's chances, saw in the new Republican party a permanent political roof over their heads.

Local elections quickly revealed the strength of the new appeal. Anti-Nebraska candidates swept the spring elections in three New England states and the fall elections in two more. A candidate with Free-Soil backing became governor of Iowa, and fusion candidates for Congress won victories throughout the section. As one writer said, political fusion "literally slaughtered" the administration Democrats in the Northern, middle, and Western states. The next year (1855) a like combination of discordant elements made Salmon P. Chase governor of Ohio and in February, 1856, elected Nathaniel Banks, an avowed anti-Nebraska man, Speaker of the House. Whether such disjointed groups could be fused into a permanent organization of national scope depended, of course, entirely on what happened in the South and in the Kansas-Nebraska territory.

As far as the South was concerned, it had been remarkably quiet since 1850. The section had been deeply stirred in the conflict which ended in the great compromise of that year, but the reaction from that excitement was equally sharp. As the Richmond *Enquirer* said, in 1854:

> Throughout the South there prevails a repugnance to agitation. We had enough, and too much, excitement during the Compromise Controversy of 1850, and now there exists an indisposition to popular meetings and legislative resolves.

Very little was said about the slavery question in Southern newspapers during the period when Douglas was introducing his bill and when it was being debated in Congress. Southern representatives in Washington, of course, took sides in the debates, but, of the more than fifty who spoke, only two expressed any confidence that slavery would ever go to either Kansas or Nebraska. More than half of them said positively that it would not. Some went so far as to agree that Douglas's bill was a bill to extend free soil. Some felt that its introduction was a serious mistake. It would only renew sectional strife. They voted for the measure largely because it granted an abstract right to their section rather than concrete advantages. Even at the end of April, 1854, Benton could say:

> It is now four months since this movement for the abrogation of the Missouri Compromise commenced in this Congress. It began without a memorial, without a petition, without a request from a human being. It has labored long and hard in those Halls, and to this hour there is not a petition for it from the class of States for whose benefit the movement professes to have been made!—not a word in its favor from the smallest public meeting or private

assemblage of any Slave State. This is the response of the South to this boon tendered to it by Northern members under a Northern President. It is the response of silence—more emphatic than words.

The thing which finally did arouse the South was the organization of the New England Emigrant Aid Society, which accepted Douglas's statement that the people of a territory should decide for or against slavery, and began to send out settlers. The Society also had an economic aim of land profits, but the triumph of free soil was the thing most talked about. The efforts of the Society and the arrival of settlers in Kansas greatly disturbed the proslavery men of Missouri. Citizens of that state, they thought, had a peculiar interest in Kansas. For years they had crossed it on their way to trade at Santa Fe. In later days they had carried on trade with the missions, the military posts, and the Indians across the border. And always, like the good citizens in any Western state, they had looked with longing eyes at the fertile lands in the territories beyond, which someday would be open to settlement.

THE STRUGGLE FOR KANSAS

It is, therefore, not surprising that, when Missourians and Kansas colonists of the Emigrant Aid Society came together in a frontier region where land surveys were not yet completed, trouble should have begun. Claim-jumping and disputes over prospective town sites brought assault and murder. Interest in the spread or the checking of slavery added bitterness and confusion. The moves to establish a government, of course, brought fraud and violence. When, on November 29, 1854, an election to choose delegates to Congress from the territory was held, and again, in March, 1855, when a territorial legislature was to be elected, Missourians in numbers crossed the border and voted for candidates satisfactory to themselves. Then the legislature adopted the laws of Missouri and enacted a slave code.

This was more than the free-soil settlers, centering about the town of Lawrence, could accept. They refused to recognize either the legislature or the laws. In September, 1855, they too held a convention, elected a delegate to Congress and a governor, framed a constitution, and asked to be admitted to the Union as a free state. The House, under Republican control, voted in their favor; the Senate checked the movement.

That was a signal for renewed violence in Kansas. It reached a climax when a posse, assembled by a proslavery marshal, marched on Lawrence, served writs on the free-state officials there, destroyed the local newspaper plant, and set fire to several buildings, including the town's only hotel. "The sacking of Lawrence," in turn, stirred the Emigrant Aid Society to new efforts and lifted the avenging hand of John Brown. Recently come to Kansas, this strange man not only had experienced the disorders due to contested land titles, but also had felt the heavy responsibility on antislavery men to win the territory for freedom. His code was one of violence to meet violence; his honest conviction, that the God of vengeance had commissioned him to service. Gathering a little band of equally fanatical followers, all but two his relatives, he proposed to destroy all the proslavery men along Pottawatomie Creek. Under the cover of night five helpless men were dragged from their cabins and "mortally hacked and slashed with cutlasses" or shot with pistols at short range. Thus was the territory turned into "Bleeding Kansas."

News of events in Kansas, some of it correct, most of it badly distorted, stirred both North and South. Funds poured into the Emigrant Aid treasury. New committees were organized. Speakers urged the sending of "none but armed emigrants" to Kansas. Republicans in Congress, conscious of the value of such disorder to their cause, hurried off an investigating committee to the territory. Southerners, not to be outdone, praised the "gallant" fight which Missourians were waging in Kansas, and began recruiting emigrants to go to their assistance. It was difficult to get genuine slaveholders to risk their property in the confusion and uncertainty of Kansas, but planters could and did contribute funds. Before long, small but determined bands of Southerners were on their way to add to the confusion in Kansas.

BROOKS AND SUMNER

Hatred and violence now broke out in Congress. The day before the so-called "border ruffians" marched on Lawrence, Charles Sumner of Massachusetts delivered one of the most stinging and abusive speeches ever uttered in the Senate of the United States. He called his speech "The Crime against Kansas." He assumed as absolutely true all the charges made against the "slave power" in Kansas. He spoke of the "murderous robbers from Missouri, hirelings picked from the drunken spew and vomit of an uneasy civilization," from whose crimes "the soul recoils, and which language refuses to describe." He became personal and poured abuse and disdain upon the unoffending head of the aged Senator Butler of South Carolina, who was absent at the time. When he had finished his speech, Senator Cass of Michigan called it "the most un-American and unpatriotic speech that ever grated on the ears" of Congress, and Senator Douglas of Illinois tersely remarked, "That damn fool will get himself killed by some other damn fool."

Two days later, as Sumner sat at his desk, Representative Preston S. Brooks, from South Carolina, a relative of Butler, approached him with a gutta-percha cane in hand. While friends stood by to prevent interference, he struck the Massachusetts Senator blow after blow upon the head. Sumner attempted to rise, then fell to the floor. For the next five years his seat in the Senate was vacant.

With excitement over Kansas at its height, this episode only served to intensify sectional attitudes. The *New York Times* asserted that "Bully Brooks" had "sneaked and lain in wait" for Sumner, with the intention of murdering him. It assumed that the whole South approved, and spoke of the "self-appointed oligarchy" whose scepter was "a guttapercha cane, backed by pistols and bowie knives" and whose patron saint was "Bully Brooks." South Carolina, on the other hand, generally approved of what had happened. When Brooks resigned his seat in the House, South Carolina re-elected him and, on his visit home, showered him with gifts. Other Southerners, however, were not so enthusiastic. Most thought that Sumner "got what he deserved," but that Brooks had chosen a poor place and a poor method of avenging a wrong. Some openly condemned his act as one highly injurious to his section. As G. B. Lamar wrote, "Viewed dispassionately in every light, the assault was unquestionably unjustifiable, unmanly, ill-timed, ill-advised, injudicious to the cause of the South, and totally indefensible as to time, place, and manner."

THE ELECTION OF 1856

With "Bleeding Kansas" and "bleeding Sumner" both playing into its hands, the young Republican party entered the campaign of 1856. It chose John C. Frémont as its candidate. Its platform declared that "it is both the right and the imperative duty of Congress to prohibit in the territories those twin relics of barbarism—polygamy and slavery." It denounced the administration's policy in the territories and asked for the immediate admission of Kansas as a free state. It favored the building of a central Pacific railroad and advocated appropriations for other internal improvements.

In addition to the new Republican party, there was another new party, to testify to the chaotic condition into which political affairs had fallen. As the Whig party weakened and slowly went to pieces under the impact of the slavery issue, the sharp reaction against the foreigners, who had been pouring into the country, proved strong enough to draw disgruntled voters into a new political organization. It insisted that "Americans must rule America." It opposed parochial schools as un-American; it pointed out the danger of papal influence in American affairs; it saw crime and pauperism on the increase because of the foreign invasion. Opponents called it the Know-Nothing party because of its semisecret character and the refusal of members to answer questions. Its appeal, however, had proved strong, especially in Eastern communities where foreigners were numerous, and now, in 1856, it had achieved national extent and organization. It offered Millard Fillmore as its candidate.

The Democrats again ignored the man who had headed their party during the past four years, and named James Buchanan of Pennsylvania as their candidate. He had been out of the country for several years, in foreign service, and therefore had the advantage of having escaped the damage done to political reputations by sectional conflict.

The election which followed was highly important for several reasons. Buchanan was elected. That proved that the Democrats still had enough unity, North and South, to win with a Northern candidate whose views on slavery were satisfactory to the South. Fillmore was a poor third, but his vote was widely scattered over the entire nation. He had evidently taken over much of the old Whig strength, especially in the South, but elsewhere to a lesser degree. Frémont, though a strictly sectional candidate, polled over a million votes. He carried ten free-soil states and had a strong minority vote in all the others. Only Illinois, Indiana, Pennsylvania, California, and New Jersey had been lost by the Republicans. If that much could be achieved in two years, what of the future? Farsighted Southerners saw the danger. As one formerly conservative editor wrote:

It is evident . . . that Col. John C. Frémont, the candidate for the Presidency of the free-soilers, abolitionists and haters of the South generally, has received the electoral votes of a large majority of the Northern people! Almost as a mass, the North has gone for him, and gone for him too on a platform the carrying out of the principles of which would inflict immeasurable degradation upon the Southern people—would reduce them to the level of serfs—would deprive them of every real vestige of manly equality, strip them of respect at home and abroad and render them the laughing stock of the governments of the old world.

THE DRED SCOTT DECISION

Buchanan's inaugural was a labored affair. He spoke with confidence regarding the slavery controversy. The simple rule that the will of the majority should prevail would settle everything. Let the people of the territories determine their own destiny. True, a difference of opinion as to the time at which the people of a territory might accept or reject slavery had arisen, but the Supreme Court of the United States was "speedily and finally" about to settle it.

And the Court did settle it quickly, for two days after the inauguration the famous Dred Scott decision was made public. The facts in the case were as follows: Dred Scott, a St. Louis Negro slave, was sold, in 1833, by one Elizabeth Blow to Dr. John Emerson, a surgeon in the United States army. Emerson carried him first to Fort Armstrong, in Illinois, and then to Fort Snelling, near the present site of St. Paul, Minnesota—regions made free soil by the Northwest Ordinance and the Missouri Compromise. Sometime later Scott was returned to Missouri and, on the death of Dr. Emerson and the removal of Mrs. Emerson to Massachusetts, fell back on the Blow family for support. With the aid of Henry Blow, who evidently wanted relief from his burden, Scott sued in the state court for his freedom on the ground that residence in free territory had ended his bondage. He lost his first case, but won on a second trial. Then followed reversals and appeals in the state courts, and finally the whole matter became involved in the slavery controversy.

This came about because Mrs. Emerson had married one Dr. Chaffee, an ardent antislavery man, who, in turn, transferred Scott to Mrs. Chaffee's brother, John F. A. Sandford, a citizen of New York and an equally ardent opponent of slavery. Under their direction, Scott now claimed citizenship in Missouri, and, because it was a case of action by a citizen of one state against a citizen of another state, brought suit in the United States Circuit Court of Missouri. Sandford, in answer, brought a plea in abatement, which denied the jurisdiction of the court on the grounds that Scott was born a slave and could not, therefore, bring suit. This plea was overruled, but Sandford's suit was upheld on other grounds. Scott then appealed his case to the Supreme Court of the United States on writ of error.

The decision which the Supreme Court now handed down was delivered by Chief Justice Roger B. Taney. He denied the right of the lower Federal court to assume jurisdiction, because Dred Scott was not, and could not have been, a citizen of the United States. Members of the African race and their descendants, said Taney, were not, at the time when the Constitution was adopted, citizens of any state. They were regarded as of an inferior order of beings who, emancipated or not, "had no rights or privileges but such as those who held the power and the government might choose to grant them." The justice or injustice of this was not a matter for the Court to decide. That meant, of course, that Dred Scott's suit should never have been entertained. Nor had his residence in free territory changed his status and given him the right to sue in the courts. Each state had the right to determine for itself the status of a slave, regardless of temporary residence elsewhere, and Missouri courts had held that Dred Scott was still a slave.

The Justice then went a step farther. He asserted that Congress, in passing the Missouri Compromise, forbidding slavery in that part of the Louisiana Purchase north of 36° 30', had exceeded its authority. Slave property, like any other property in the territories, was protected by the Constitution.

Justices Curtis and McLean offered dissenting opinions. They denied the assertion that Negroes had not been regarded as citizens at the time of the adoption of the Constitution, and they offered evidence to show that Congress had the right to prohibit slavery in the territories. They were quite unwilling to see the doctrines of John C. Calhoun become a judicial decision.

Historians have pointed out the fact that much that Taney said was mere *obiter dicta*. If Dred Scott was not a citizen, then that was all that needed demonstration. As the *New York Times* said, the opinions of the Chief Justice on the Missouri Compromise and slavery in the territories deserved "no more respect than any pro-slavery stump-speech made during the late presidential canvass." Historians have also shown that the majority of the Court agreed to dispose of the case without raising the question of jurisdiction and without discussing the territorial question, but had been forced to go farther because Justices McLean and Curtis were determined to cover all the issues in dissenting opinions. Historians have not, however, always noted that in discussing questions that did not have to be decided, Taney was only following a precedent established by John Marshall. As Carl Swisher has said: "Some of the landmark decisions of the Marshall period would be completely unknown today had Marshall limited his opinions to statements which were essential to the decision of the case." Nor have the historians always noted the fact that Taney's *obiter dicta* would never have been uttered if the two Republican justices on the Court had been willing in the first place to go along with the others.

The important point, however, is that both Buchanan and Taney expected the Court's decision, as Taney had delivered it, to settle the bitter question of slavery in the territories. The fact of *obiter dicta* and the sharp dissenting opinion of two members, in reality, worked in exactly the opposite direction. Republicans took it all as mere partisan action, and the only result was injury to the Court's prestige. Its dignity was gone. Its reputation for impartiality was destroyed. Men began to talk of adding new members or reconstructing the Court for their own ends. From now on to the outbreak of war, Republicans viewed the Court as an agent of the Democratic party. The slave power, through control of the courts, had opened all territories to its peculiar institution. The Wilmot Proviso doctrine, on which Republicans relied, had unjustly been declared illegal!

"BLEEDING KANSAS"

The Dred Scott decision would have been a serious blow to the Republican party if conditions in Kansas had not continued to work for the party. It was to prove a nearly fatal blow to the political fortunes of Stephen A. Douglas, whose squatter-sovereignty ideas would have no meaning if slavery could legally exist in all territories. To Buchanan and the Democrats, who hoped that it would settle the whole matter once and for all, it was to prove even more disastrous.

Buchanan's first step was to send Robert J. Walker, Polk's Secretary of the Treasury from Mississippi, to Kansas as governor. His task was to establish order and a permanent government. He promptly called an election to choose delegates to a constitutional convention. Free-soil men, distrusting the Buchanan administration, refused to participate. The proslavery interests, therefore, completely dominated the convention, held at Lecompton, and drew up a proslavery constitution. This was then submitted to the people, but not to be approved or rejected; instead their ballots were to be endorsed either "Constitution with slavery" or "Constitution with no slavery." Should the first proposition carry, slavery would be definitely fixed on the state; should the second prevail, slavery as it already existed in Kansas "would in no manner be interfered with."

Again the free-state men refused to vote, and the first proposition carried. In the fall elections for a territorial legislature, however, the free-soil men did vote and, when Governor Walker threw out many fraudulent votes, carried the election. The legislature, so chosen, now resubmitted the Lecompton Constitution, to be accepted or rejected. This time the proslavery element refused to vote, and of course the constitution was rejected. Lecompton men, however, held their ground and turned bitterly against Walker, whom they held responsible for what had happened.

In Washington, meanwhile, President Buchanan became convinced that a settlement of affairs in Kansas could never be reached by the groups there. He recalled Walker and urged upon Congress the admission of Kansas under the proslavery Lecompton Constitution. He saw the way in which politicians were using Kansas and declared that the antislavery group had rejected the constitution not on the basis of merit, but simply because they wished to resist the government authorized by Congress—meaning, of course, the government of his administration. He insisted that by the Dred Scott decision Kansas was "at this moment as much a slave state as Georgia or South Carolina."

DOUGLAS AND THE DEMOCRATIC ADMINISTRATION

That was too much for Stephen A. Douglas. He had defended himself against the attacks of Chase and Sumner on the ground of the democratic right of the people to decide for themselves. The rule of the majority—and in this case the majority were clearly for free soil—was the very heart of his doctrine. He had not intended to introduce slavery into Kansas. He could not stand idly by and see the administration do so. Squatter sovereignty must be given a chance. "By God, Sir," he is reported to have said, "I made James Buchanan, and by God, Sir, I will unmake him."

Such defiance brought an open break. The personnel of Douglas's Committee on Territories was altered so as to place him in a minority; newspapers in Illinois which supported him were deprived of official advertising and post-office printing; pressure was brought on local officeholders to denounce him and to foster meetings for the same purpose. He was read out of the Democratic party.

Douglas, however, more than held his own. His doctrine of self-rule was not easily pushed aside, and Democrats of the Northwest were not easily divorced from their great leader. His superb courage in defying the administration and in risking his Southern popularity brought allies to his side. With Republican aid, the administration's plans were checked, and Kansas, under the so-called "English Bill," was allowed to reject the Lecompton Constitution at the cost of delay in achieving statehood. Some Republicans began to see Douglas as a possible leader for their party. Some said that he should not be opposed for re-election to the Senate in 1858. A few even talked of Republican support for his candidacy for the Presidency in 1860.

Illinois Republicans, however, were not so enthusiastic. They had been fighting Douglas too long. As one of them said, it was "asking too much for human nature to bear, to now surrender to Judge Douglas . . . , to quietly let him step foremost in our ranks and make us all take back seats. . . . When Judge D. is made our Leader, with all his sins yet unrepented for, the party is scattered and disbanded in Illinois." It was hard enough on Republicans for them to realize that the slavery-extension issue in Kansas, from which their party had originated and on which it had grown, was now settled in their favor and was not likely to arise elsewhere. To surrender leadership to Douglas might be the end of the party.

A candidate for the Senate to oppose Douglas was, therefore, a necessity, and the choice fell on Abraham Lincoln. This Springfield lawyer had been a Whig in early days and had served one term in Congress for that party during Polk's administration. He had not been a great success in the national House, but something about him had won and held the people of Illinois. He was moderate in his views, intensely human in his attitudes, and deeply sincere in his belief in democracy as expressed in the Declaration of Independence. He had a strong sense of humor of the Western kind, a real love of justice, and more than an ordinary degree of plain common sense. More than that, he was a man with the capacity for steady growth. He had been slow to take up with the Republican move. He did not believe in the equality of the Negro and the white man, and he recognized the constitutional right of Southerners to hold slaves. Yet somehow he understood that in a democracy every man, white or black, has a right to eat the bread that his hands have produced; that the road of opportunity to go forward must be open to all; that the holding of men in bondage, even legally, does not square with the great purposes of democratic society.

He accepted the nomination with a frank, honest facing of the increasingly apparent fact that "a house divided against itself cannot stand"; that "this government cannot endure permanently half slave and half free. . . . It will become all one thing or all the other." Boldly he challenged Douglas to a series of debates on issues and in them proved his ability to hold his own against one of the nation's most tried and able speakers. The debates themselves, seven in number in different parts of the state, were not all "reason and light." There was much of bantering, much of maneuvering for party advantage, and considerable "shaping of appeals for local effect." Debate centered about the position of each party and each speaker on the "vexed question" of slavery in the territories. Douglas tried hard to associate Lincoln with the abolitionists and chided him with changing his attitude toward slavery to suit the part of the state in which he was speaking. The Republicans had "got up" this strife, he charged, and were disrupting the Union; the mission of the Democrats was to save it. Illinois Republicans had even allied themselves with the Democratic administration in Washington "to beat a man [Douglas] merely because he [had] done right," because he had advocated the only just solution of the whole slavery issue: for each state and each territory to make its own popular decision.

Lincoln was quick to sense the conflict between Douglas's position and that of the Dred Scott decision. How, under that decision, could slavery be excluded from a territory, even if the people wished to exclude it? he asked. By "local police regulations" was Douglas's answer. The passing of unfavorable regulations, or the failure to pass those necessary for slavery's protection, would make its existence impossible, regardless of what the Supreme Court had said. It was a good answer for the time and place, but Lincoln understood that such an answer would not suit the South nor the future. And what about the gradual advance of Douglas and his party along proslavery lines? Could a nation trust men who did not care whether slavery was voted up or down? The repeal of the Missouri Compromise and the Dred Scott decision were but forerunners of new steps to legalize slavery in all the states. "The real issue in this controversy," said Lincoln, ". . . is the sentiment . . . of one class that looks upon the institution of slavery as a wrong, and of another class that does not look upon it as a wrong." The Republicans, said Lincoln, were the class that viewed it "as being a moral, social, and political wrong."

The campaign ended, and Douglas was re-elected to the Senate. The

people of the North, however, had learned that there was a man in Illinois who could match Douglas in debate, one who had stumbled onto the Declaration of Independence and had paused to give it serious consideration.

Men in the South had not been indifferent to Douglas's recent conduct. In many ways he represented the only hope they had of Northern support. Many in the South had expected him to be the next Democratic nominee. His position on the Lecompton Constitution, his break with the administration, and now his position on territorial rights and slavery had given them a severe jolt. Many renounced him at once; others, understanding that the unity of their party was at stake, were inclined to hesitate. As a farsighted Mobile editor said,

> The inevitable consequence of the triumph of Mr. Douglas will be, either that the political character of the Democratic party as the great conservator of the constitutional rights of the South will be essentially demoralized, or that the party will be completely broken up and denationalized.

What this editor was saying was that if it was necessary for Douglas to take these positions on slavery in the territories in order to hold the Northwest, then it would be necessary for the Democratic party to accept both Douglas and his doctrines in order to keep itself a national party united for victory. And if the party did this, where was slavery, in spite of the Constitution and of what the Dred Scott decision had said about the Constitution's application to slavery in the territories?

Southern radicals who had opposed the Compromise of 1850 were, of course, encouraged by these developments. They had been busy trying to make their section economically and socially independent of the North by encouraging direct trade with Europe, the improvement of Southern agriculture, the increasing of manufactures, and the building up of Southern schools and summer resorts. They wanted their children to remain in the South for their education, to study Southern textbooks, and to read Southern novels and periodicals. Men like William L. Yancey, Robert Barnwell Rhett, and Edmund Ruffin had organized Leagues of United Southerners to "fire the Southern heart, instruct the Southern mind, give courage to each other, and ... by one organized concert action, ... precipitate the cotton states into a revolution." Slowly their efforts and the unfortunate developments in the territories were stirring the fears and the prejudices of the masses. If the North was alarmed over the slave power, the South was becoming equally alarmed over what they symbolized by the term "Black Republicans."

SECTIONAL CONFLICT AND JOHN BROWN

Economic conditions now contributed to sectional animosities. In 1857 a panic had broken upon the nation. Northern industrial and financial interests were particularly affected. The South was scarcely touched by the panic, but planters found the New York banks unable to meet the payments due for their cotton crops and soon noticed a sharp renewal of Northeastern demands for protective tariffs. Men from the Northwest matched these demands with new efforts to pass the Homestead Bill. They talked of a man's "inalienable right to a reasonable share and proportionate part" of the public lands. They scoffed at "the bogus Democracy" which denied this right; and when President Buchanan vetoed their bill, an Iowa newspaper referred to him as "the old reprobate, who sits in the Presidential Chair at Washington," and charged that he had acted as the "pliant tool" of the slaveholders. New efforts at river-and-harbor legislation also met with Presidential opposition. Again the charge of slave-power influence was made. "Millions to subjugate Kansas," said an Ohio paper, "but not one cent to relieve the internal necessities of the country."

Southerners answered these complaints by insisting that every Northern demand was unconstitutional and had been checked on that ground. Northern indignation only showed how little Northerners respected the Constitution and how frail that document had become for the protection of rights. It was all in keeping with the "higher law" doctrine which Republican politicians were expressing in regard to slavery, and with Republican lack of respect for the Supreme Court and its decisions.

Into this troubled situation of growing distrust and sectional recrimination, suddenly, on October 16, 1859, the strange figure of John Brown, of Kansas fame, appeared again. That night, with a little band of followers collected at a near-by Maryland farm, he swept down on the arsenal at Harpers Ferry in Virginia. His men were heavily armed with rifles and carried with them a wagonload of hand pikes. Their object was to seize the arsenal, arm the Negro slaves of the neighborhood, and turn them against their "hated" masters.

The effort was a pitiful failure. The slaves failed to respond. A small body of United States troops, under the command of Robert E. Lee, who was at his home in Arlington, Virginia, on leave from his post in Texas, quickly overcame the invaders. Brown was wounded, and a few weeks later tried and hanged for "treason, murder, and inciting slaves to rebellion."

The raid was a mere fiasco. Its importance, however, was national in extent. Here was an attempt to do all the things which Southerners, in their wildest imaginings, had ever conjured up. "The public mind," wrote an observer, "rolled and tossed like the storm-whipped billows of an enraged sea." Who was behind such a move? Where did Brown get his money and supplies? Was this not the logical conclusion of abolition agitation? Words were now being turned into action. The horrors of Santo Domingo were to be held as a threat over the South. If this could happen in the Union, was it not time to begin planning for an independent future?

Northern reactions to the John Brown raid did not help matters much. The first impulse was one of condemnation. Conservatives and politicians alike drew back. Respectable men could have nothing to do with such violence. Northern radicals and idealists, however, saw something else in John Brown. He had the courage of his convictions. If slavery was the great evil which violated every Christian and every democratic ideal, was it not time to do more than talk? Emerson wished that men had "health enough to know virtue" and would "not cry with fools, 'madman,' when a hero pass[ed]." He called Brown a "new saint awaiting his martyrdom, and who, if he shall suffer, will make the gallows glorious like the cross." Others called him "an angel of light," "Saint John the Just," "the Noble John Brown." Soon even conservatives were suggesting that Virginia deal gently with the old man.

Unfortunately it was the rabid spokesman who was quoted in the Southern newspapers. In the strained atmosphere of the day Brown's attitudes were ascribed to the whole North, and all the fear, all the unreason, that go with any race problem stirred in Southern breasts. As never before to this moment, men talked of "an independent Southern confederacy." For the first time white men who held no slaves and who might have to face the freed Negro as an economic and social rival were deeply stirred. That had not been the case in 1850.

THE ELECTION OF 1860

In this excited state of mind the parties prepared for the election of 1860. How deep sectional cleavage had gone was quickly revealed when the Democrats met in Charleston. Douglas, on a squatter-sovereignty platform, was their logical candidate; but the Buchanan administration threw its weight against him, and Southern radicals, under the lead of William L. Yancey, demanded a platform sanctioning Federal protection of slavery in the territories. Agreement was impossible. The Douglas faction, by seating the contested New York delegation and discarding the unit rule for voting where possible, were able to reject the Southern platform and to substitute their own, but they could not muster the two-thirds majority required to nominate Douglas. Defeated in their platform demands, Yancey and his followers walked out of the convention. The Douglas group adjourned to meet later in Baltimore. A great national political party, like the Methodist and Baptist churches, was split along sectional lines.

The Republicans met in Chicago a few weeks later, thoroughly conscious of the opportunity for victory offered by the Democratic split. They had come a long way since 1856. Their organization was more complete; their party principles were definitely wider. The platform that they adopted opposed slavery in the territories, but pledged non-interference in the states. The John Brown raid was flatly condemned; the Declaration of Independence was at first ignored, then reluctantly included. Settlers were pledged a quarter-section of public land, and the old Henry Clay American System of internal improvements and a protective tariff was enthusiastically endorsed. It was a practical, politically sound platform. Crusading days for the party were over. Sectional interests, as well as ideals, had to be recognized. Whigs, who had taken a turn with the now defunct Know-Nothings, had to be attracted; Pennsylvania tariff interests and Northwestern land and railway interests had to be looked after, even if early slavery attitudes had to be somewhat slighted.

Of candidates there were many. William H. Seward of New York headed the list, and behind him were Bates of Missouri, Cameron of Pennsylvania, Chase of Ohio, and Lincoln of Illinois. There was much of trading, and much of shrewd political manipulation to win the Northern states which, in 1856, had gone Democratic. Here Lincoln had an advantage, and, on the third ballot, he was nominated.

The Douglas Democrats, meeting in Baltimore, named their candidate without opposition, and the seceding Democrats, moving on to Richmond, named John C. Breckinridge of Kentucky. Each group took the platform that it had demanded at Charleston.

In the interval between the two Democratic conventions another group, made up of Whigs and Know-Nothings who had not joined one of the other parties, also assembled in Baltimore, took the name of Constitutional Union party, and named John Bell of Tennessee as its

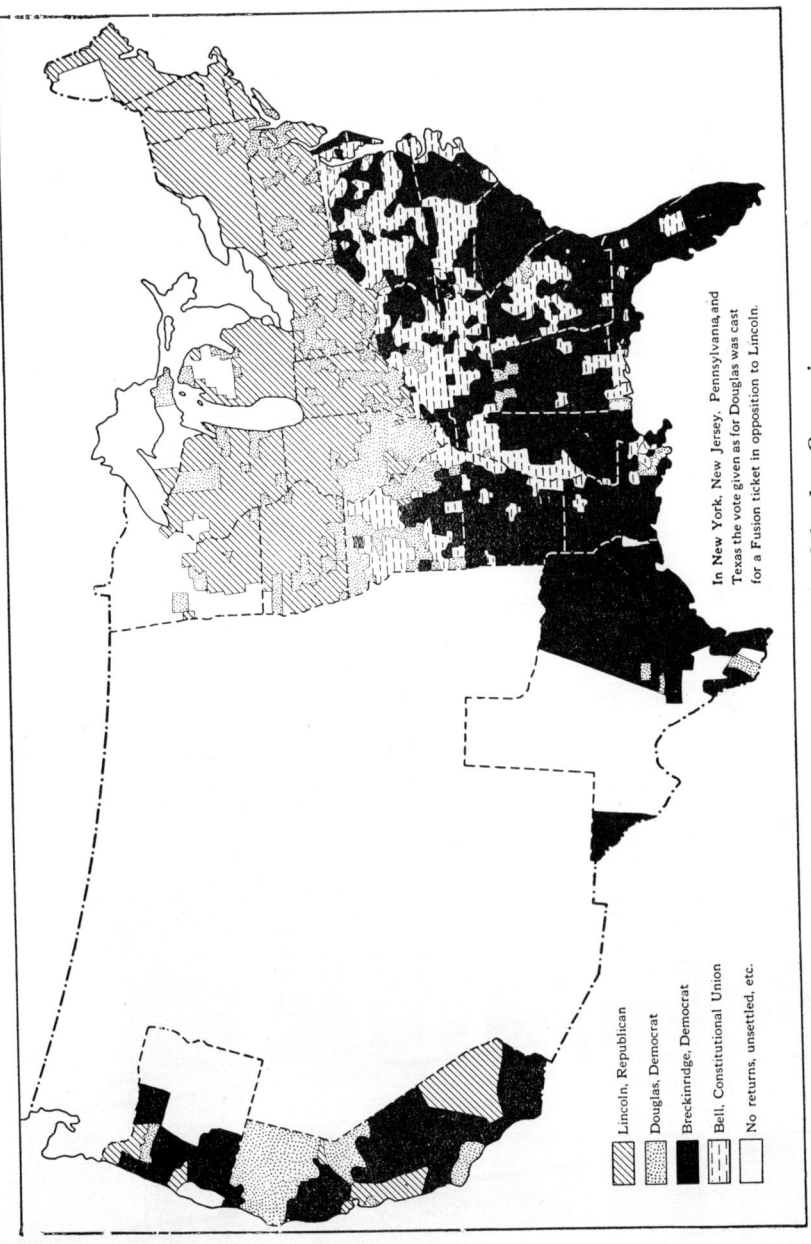

Lincoln, Republican

Douglas, Democrat

Breckinridge, Democrat

Bell, Constitutional Union

No returns, unsettled, etc.

In New York, New Jersey, Pennsylvania, and Texas the vote given as for Douglas was cast for a Fusion ticket in opposition to Lincoln.

Presidential Election of 1860 by Counties

Chicago Historical Society

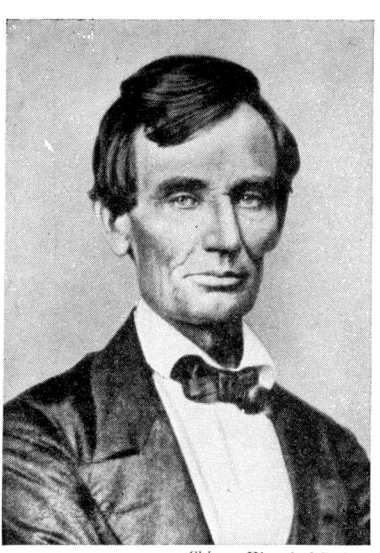

Abraham Lincoln in 1860

Brady photog

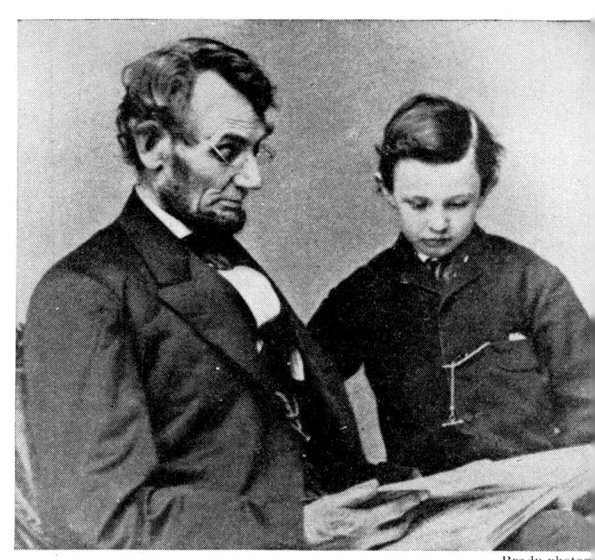

President Lincoln and His Son Tad in 1864

Lincoln in Front of His Springfield Home, Receiving a Procession of His Neighbors in the Autumn of 1860

The Abraham Lincoln Associa

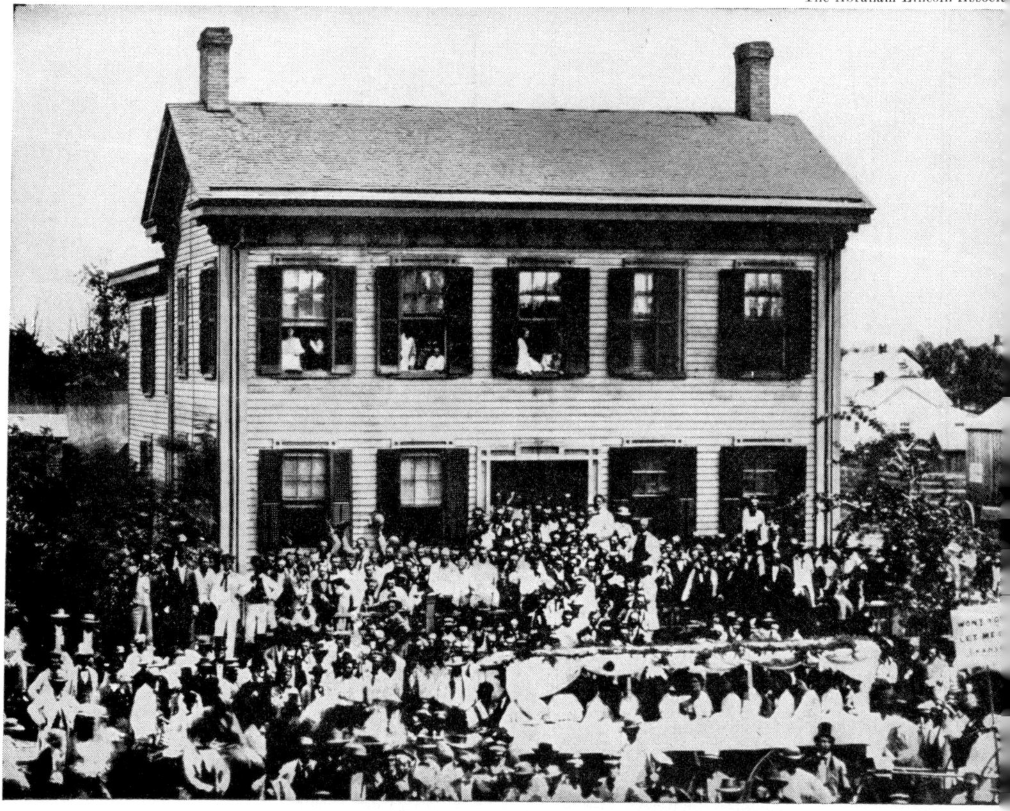

candidate. Its only platform, if such it could be called, was the duty of all patriots to recognize "no political principles other than the Constitution of the country, the Union of the states, and the enforcement of the law."

The campaign which followed was a strange one. In the North it was a contest between Lincoln and Douglas; in the South, one between Breckinridge and Bell. Douglas, Breckinridge, and Bell all received some support from the nation as a whole; Lincoln's support, with the exception of a few votes in his native Kentucky, was strictly sectional. The Republicans organized the "Wide-awakes," who marched with torches and fence rails and songs, much as the Whigs had done in 1840. They stressed the new conservative attitudes of the party in business circles, but permitted Seward and Sumner to woo the antislavery element as well. Douglas struck hard at the danger in Republican antislavery attitudes and urged again the right of the people to decide for themselves. In the South the issue quickly became one between the extremists, who insisted that the time for final resistance had come, that the North was intent on carrying the "irrepressible conflict" to a finish, and the conservatives, who still believed that Southern rights could best be preserved within the Union by democratic methods, not by rebellion.

The vote in November proved only one thing: the majority of the people, North and South, were still conservative. Lincoln polled 1,866,452 votes, against 2,815,617 for all opponents (Douglas, 1,376,957; Breckinridge, 849,781; Bell, 588,879). His vote was sectional, as was the bulk of that polled by Breckinridge. The major parties, like most other things in the nation, had become sectional. Yet behind this lay the fact that the majority of the people had not voted for either sectional candidate.

THE DIVIDING NATION

What happened in the next five months was only a logical concluding of events as they had shaped themselves since the middle of the 1840's. Fears and resentments had grown to the point where the rational discussion and adjustment of issues, as required under the democratic process, was difficult, if not impossible. Radical minorities had more influence under such circumstances than was normal. Fundamental issues involving right and wrong, honor and dishonor, had arisen, and many lesser issues, involving only material interests, had taken on the coloring of more fundamental ones. Some men wanted to break the Union to pieces. Many felt that they might be forced to accept that alternative. Most Southern men believed in a constitutional right to secede from the Union if necessary. When Virginia ratified the Federal Constitution, she did so with the proviso that her people should have the right to rescind ratification "whenever the powers granted unto it [the Union] should be perverted to their injury or oppression." South Carolina had more than once shown her sincere belief in such a right, and Calhoun had applied logic in abundance to its demonstration. The cotton kingdom had accepted the doctrine as a part of its heritage from the Old South.

What they all overlooked, however, were the facts of national growth, of the new technology in production and communication, of the new interdependence which business and finance were creating, of the new moral forces astir in the world. Men's minds had not everywhere kept pace with their bodies, which lived in a modern world. Men could be absolutely right in their theories and in their historical analyses in this changing world, and yet find themselves completely overrun by the blunt forces of necessity under change.

The election of a sectional President by a sectional party clearly proved to Southern radicals that the political machinery no longer gave protection to their interests. Republican attitudes, such as those of the "higher law" and contempt for the Supreme Court, seemed to end all chance of protection from the Constitution. The sweep of events in California and Kansas assigned the South to the role of a permanent minority in Congress. Why, when you had a legal right to withdraw, remain in a Union where your interests and your social security were to be ignored? Why await some overt act?

Such were the arguments of South Carolina radicals as they began their steps toward secession. Conservatives, such as Benjamin F. Perry, James Petigru, and even James H. Hammond, still held back, but "the unconciliatory and defiant course of the Republican leaders," as the Louisville *Journal* said, "[had] rendered the advocates of patience and steadiness in the South all but powerless." On December 17, 1860, a convention met in Columbia and three days later passed an ordinance of secession. Within six weeks similar action had been taken by Mississippi (January 9), Florida (January 10), Alabama (January 11), Georgia (January 19), Louisiana (January 26), and Texas (February 1).

Opposition to secession, in every state, was intense. In many cases a motion to secede was carried in spite of the fact that a majority of the people were clearly against hasty action. "Fools & wicked fools," wrote Benjamin Perry in his diary, "they know not what they do & may God forgive them." A Georgia editor wrote, "We have loved the Union with an affection pure and unselfish ... we would cheerfully . . . lay down our life to preserve the Union, as our fathers made it." Secession was "Bloody Revolution," said Judge William Sharkey in Mississippi. It was "no remedy at all." It would only make the affairs of the South worse than they had been. "The only thing that makes the thought [of separating "from the land of our birth and the graves of our ancestors"] supportable," wrote a member of the Alabama convention, "is the hope that we may be again reunited."

From *Frank Leslie's Illustrated Newspaper*, February 2, 1861

"A Job for the New Cabinetmaker"

The deed, however, had been done, and in February delegates from the seceded states met in Montgomery, Alabama, to form the Confederate States of America. They chose Jefferson Davis of Mississippi president, and Alexander H. Stephens of Georgia vice-president. They then adopted a constitution, which, with a few variations, made to avoid the "evils" of recent days, was that of the United States.

While Lincoln waited in Springfield for the fourth of March to arrive, James Buchanan informed Congress of what had happened and of his firm conviction that it was all unconstitutional. He added that, in spite of his conviction, he had no authority to coerce a state. He did urge Congress to act and to pass an amendment to protect slavery in the states where it already existed, and he did make every effort to prevent open violence. He permitted the Southern states to seize government property within their borders and to take over the national forts, with the exception of Pickens at Pensacola in Florida and Sumter in Charleston harbor. Here he asserted the nation's authority.

The border states, meanwhile, hesitated, and William H. Seward, who was to be Lincoln's Secretary of State, did everything in his power to keep them in line. Union leaders in Kentucky and Missouri quickly gained permanent control. Conservatives dominated in Virginia, North Carolina, Tennessee, and Arkansas. Efforts of radicals to rush them into hasty action failed. Some even talked of a border-state confederacy to avoid the extremes on either side. The final decision of the border states, however, would depend on the statesmanship of leaders in Washington.

EFFORTS AT COMPROMISE

Some men in and out of Congress were already trying to find a solution to the national difficulties. J. J. Crittenden of Kentucky introduced, in the Senate, a series of resolutions aiming at compromise. He would extend the line 36° 30′ to the Pacific, clearly define the power and the lack of power of Congress over slavery, and provide Federal compensation to owners of rescued fugitive slaves. A Senate committee of thirteen, representing all factions, struggled to frame satisfactory legislation along these lines, but Lincoln's refusal to accept any compromise on slavery extension forced the committee to report only failure to agree. A House committee tried to frame an amendment to satisfy all parties, but failed as completely. Then the Virginia legislature invited the states to a great peace convention in Washington, with ex-President John Tyler in the chair. It deliberated for three weeks and recommended a constitutional amendment dividing the territories along the 36° 30′ line and requiring concurrent majorities of free-state and slave-state Senators in the acquisition of any new territories. Its recommendations, however, came too late to be effective, and the Senate rejected them. That left the problem still in Lincoln's lap.

LINCOLN AND THE SOUTH

Sad and weary, the President-elect left Springfield late in February. He had selected his cabinet largely from the candidates whom he had defeated in the Republican convention and from politicians in doubtful states who had received promises from his campaign managers. He was not entirely satisfied with all his choices, but the task of selection had occupied most of his time and energy since election day. Now he had to take charge of a divided nation. On March 4 he took the oath of office and delivered his inaugural. It was a cautious statement, but left no doubt as to his purpose to "preserve, protect, and defend" the Union. He would not interfere with slavery where it already existed, but he would hold government property and enforce the laws in all the states. He would not recognize the right of a state to secede from the Union.

During the first few weeks in office Lincoln did little. Seward became alarmed, and foolishly attempted to supply a policy which included the declaration of war against Spain and France as a means of uniting the divided American people. Lincoln firmly put Seward in his place and then turned to the problem of the Southern forts.

Here the question was whether to continue holding Fort Pickens and Fort Sumter. Efforts under Buchanan to send supplies to the latter fort had been resisted, and the ship making the attempt, the *Star of the West*, had been fired upon. Now the fort must either be supplied or, as the Confederate government was demanding, abandoned. Lincoln's decision was to relieve both forts. Confusion in authority, which involved Secretary Seward, Secretary of the Navy Gideon Welles, and Lincoln himself, resulted in success at Fort Pickens, but in the sending of an inadequate force to Fort Sumter. Still greater confusion, which resulted in failure to give South Carolina prompt and correct information on the government's plans, created an impression of trickery. Hotheads in Charleston seized the occasion to justify an attack on Fort Sumter. On the morning of April 12, 1861, they opened fire. Major Anderson, in command of the fort, replied. The Civil War had begun.

News of the firing on Sumter and its final surrender stirred both sections. Lincoln called for seventy-five thousand men to begin the subjugation of rebellion. To fight against their fellow Southerners was more than most of the border states could bring themselves to do. Reluctantly Virginia, North Carolina, Tennessee, and Arkansas moved to join the Confederacy. Groups in both Missouri and Kentucky also threw their lot in with the South, but the official governments remained loyal to the Union. A rump government held on in Virginia and soon gave its consent to the division of the state and the formation of West Virginia.

Thus the long, bitter conflict was transferred to the field of battle. The democratic process for dealing with problems had failed. A war testing whether "a government of the people, by the people, for the people" would survive or would "perish from the earth" had taken its place.

SELECTED BIBLIOGRAPHY

Avery Craven, *The Coming of the Civil War*, and A. C. Cole, *The Irrepressible Conflict*, present sharply conflicting points of view as to the origins of the war; James C. Malin, *John Brown and the Legend of Fifty-six*, a pioneer work that questions many accepted ideas; Dwight L. Dumond, *Anti-Slavery Origins of the Civil War*; T. C. Smith, *Parties and Slavery, 1850–1859*; W. S. Jenkins, *Pro-Slavery Thought in the Old South*; R. W. Shugg, *Origins of Class Struggle in Louisiana*; William A. Barringer, *A House Dividing*; Henry H. Simms, *A Decade of Sectional Controversy*; A. W. Crandall, *Early History of the Republican Party*; L. W. Spring, *Kansas*; P. O. Ray, *The Repeal of the Missouri Compromise*, contributions to various aspects of the coming of the war.

Among the best biographies of Northern men are George Fort Milton, *The Eve of Conflict: S. A. Douglas and the Needless War*; Roy F. Nichols, *Franklin Pierce*; Allen Johnson, *Stephen A. Douglas*; Albert J. Beveridge, *Abraham Lincoln*; James G. Randall, *Lincoln, the President*; G. G. Van Deusen, *Thurlow Weed, Wizard of the Lobby*. Among the biographies of Southern leaders are Lillian A. Kibler, *Benjamin F. Perry, South Carolina Unionist*; J. B. Ranck, *Albert Gallatin Brown*; Harvey Wish, *George Fitzhugh*; Robert Meade, *Judah P. Benjamin*; W. E. Dodd, *Jefferson Davis*; Avery Craven, *Edmund Ruffin, Southerner*.

R. A. Billington, *The Protestant Crusade, 1800–1860*, and Madeleine H. Rice, *American Catholic Opinion in the Slavery Controversy*, throw light on religious developments; the Supreme Court in the slavery crisis is described in C. B. Swisher, *Roger B. Taney*, and Charles Warren, *The Supreme Court in United States History*.

R. H. Luthin, *The First Lincoln Campaign*, and Ollinger Crenshaw, *The Slave States in the Presidential Election of 1860*, deal with the critical election of 1860, and David M. Potter, *Lincoln and His Party in the Secession Crisis*, is a real contribution; C. P. Denman, *The Secession Movement in Alabama*; Percy Rainwater, *Mississippi, Storm Center of Secession*; Dwight L. Dumond, *The Secession Movement, 1860–1861*, important studies of secession.

Dwight L. Dumond, *Southern Editorials on Secession*; H. C. Perkins, *Northern Editorials on Secession*; H. S. Commager (Ed.), *Documents of American History*, pp. 329–384, contain source material.

XVIII

Civil War

FROM THE SPRING of 1861 until the spring of 1865, for four long and trying years, every aspect of American life was affected by the Civil War. By force of arms the majority sought to enforce its will upon a determined minority. "You aggress upon our rights and homes," Jefferson Davis had warned Republican members of the United States Senate on January 10, 1861, "and under the will of God we will defend them." While Southerners felt that they were fighting for their rights, antislavery men in the North were fighting to prevent Southern secession from destroying the Republic and from wrecking the United States as the hope of a free world. "No people of the world were ever sheltered under institutions as genial and benign as ours," declared a Northern preacher. "... Our cause, we love to think, is specially God's. ... We associate God and religion with all we are fighting for."

During the early weeks of the first Republican administration, President Lincoln, besieged with office-seekers, unaccustomed to the intricacies of Washington, and confronted with the problem of the secession of the lower South, seemed to many people to be completely indecisive and to lack mastery of the Presidential office. The Fort Sumter incident, however, brought an end to indecision. On April 15 Lincoln issued a call for "the militia of the several States of the Union," to the number of seventy-five thousand, and this appeal to arms precipitated the secession of Virginia on April 17, of Arkansas on May 6, of North Carolina on May 20, and of Tennessee on June 8. With Virginia leaving the Union, the action of the border state of Maryland became crucial, since her secession would isolate Washington. Federal troops were stationed in Maryland, secessionist leaders were arrested, and Maryland was won for the North. As for the remaining border states, Missouri, throughout much of the war, was torn by civil conflict and was under two governments; Kentucky refused Lincoln's call for volunteers and tried to remain neutral, but at the close of 1861 joined the North; Delaware was stanchly with the North from the outset.

In every state that seceded after Sumter there was a strong Union minority. On the other hand, the Confederate army included men

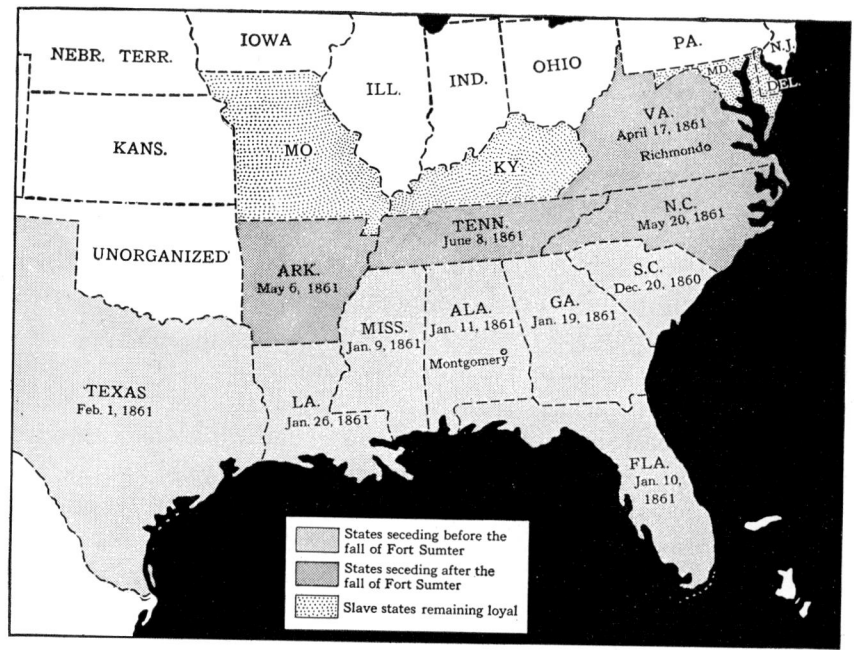

The Confederate States after the Fall of Fort Sumter

from every Northern state. Robert J. Walker, former Mississippi Senator, served Lincoln as an agent in Europe, while the ablest Confederate agent in Europe was from Massachusetts. Secession and war divided families. Three of Mrs. Lincoln's brothers died for the South, and Robert E. Lee's nephew commanded the Union naval forces on the James River while his uncle was opposing General Grant in the Wilderness campaign.

The Confederate States of America, a loose confederacy of eleven states, contained nine million people, of whom three and a half million were slaves. The North, with twenty-three states, numbered twenty-two million people. The North had an overwhelming superiority in wealth, manufacturing, shipping, railway equipment, and technical facilities. Yet, as the Confederate general Beauregard remarked, "No people ever warred for independence with more relative advantages than the Confederates." To win, the South had to fight a defensive war, protecting her territory until the North tired and sued for peace. The South had "the immense advantage," as General Beauregard pointed out, of "the interior lines of war." Furthermore, the South had the moral stimulus provided by the fact that it was fighting for independence and for self-government. The North, on the other hand, frequently found that the sentiment for Union was not sufficient to stir people from apathy. The men of the South had also the advantage of possessing a more martial spirit than the North. Southern youth were handier with horse and gun, and Southern generals were leading products of West Point. "When to these factors," J. G. Randall has written, "it is added that many Federal forts and arsenals fell into their hands, that they fought with high courage on interior lines in their own country, and that much was expected from the international situation, it will be seen that they were not unreasonable in their hope of winning the war, if it should not be too long drawn out."[1]

The first important battle of the war, fought near a stream called Bull Run, on July 21, 1861, ended any thought of the war's being of short duration. The Confederates, under Beauregard and Jackson, administered a real defeat to the Northern army, and only Confederate inexperience saved that army from complete destruction. As the Union army retreated toward Washington, it broke into a confused mob. "There was never anything like it," noted a Congressman who had journeyed to the battlefield to watch the destruction of the Confederates. "The further they ran the more frightened they grew. . . . To enable them better to run, they threw away their blankets, knapsacks, canteens, and finally muskets, cartridge-boxes, and everything else."

The Union defeat made the North realize that the war was a serious affair. "What we need," General Sherman told President Lincoln, "is cool, thoughtful, hard-fighting soldiers—no more hurrahing, no more humbug." With a long war in mind, Congress, the day after Bull Run, voted loans and authorized five hundred thousand three-year volunteers; and after Bull Run, too, the North launched the threefold strategy of trying to strangle the South economically by a blockade of her ports, of splitting the Confederacy in two, and of defeating the Southern armies of the East in the field.

As the war unfolded, the Northern blockade became increasingly effective, and the South was prevented from importing essential manufactured goods. The strategy of splitting the South was accomplished by the fall of Vicksburg in July, 1863; but the attempts to defeat the Southern armies in the East and to capture Richmond failed until the Union successes in the West greatly weakened the Confederacy.

Shortly after Bull Run thirty-four-year-old George B. McClellan, a

[1] *The Civil War and Reconstruction*, p. 263. D. C. Heath and Company, Boston, 1937.

West Point graduate who had performed distinguished service in the Mexican War, was appointed to command the army about Washington. An excellent organizer, McClellan formed an efficient army out of his volunteers; and since he was a man of real personal magnetism, he soon was worshiped by his men. He was, however, overcautious and seemingly lacked an understanding of the role of a general in a democracy. He was rude to Lincoln and, in addition, made public statements advising the politicians how to run the government. McClellan's frequent inaction prompted Lincoln once to remark, "If General McClellan does not want to use the army I would like to *borrow* it."

THE WAR IN THE WEST

After Bull Run the war in the East was inactive for many months, and the West became the main theater of operation. In this region General D. C. Buell commanded the army in Ohio and General H. W. Halleck commanded the army that was to capture the Mississippi from the enemy. Serving under Halleck was Ulysses S. Grant, who had had to resign from the army after the Mexican War in order to avoid a court-martial for drunkenness. The war rescued Grant from an unsuccessful career as a clerk in the family store at Galena, Illinois, and he received a brigadier's commission in August, 1861.

On January 11, 1862, Grant led an army against Fort Henry on the Tennessee River and Fort Donelson on the Cumberland River, two Confederate posts which controlled the route into Tennessee, Alabama, and Mississippi. On February 6 Grant captured Fort Henry, and ten days later Donelson fell. When the Confederate commander at Donelson asked for surrender terms, Grant replied, "No terms except an unconditional and immediate surrender can be accepted."

The news of these Union successes thrilled the victory-starved North. "The monster is already clutched and in his death struggle," commented the overenthusiastic *New York Times*. Grant's victory compelled the Confederates to withdraw their last forces from Kentucky and to abandon Nashville, and it advanced the Northern front two hundred miles. Soon after Donelson, Grant moved down the Tennessee River, where the Confederates, under the able leadership of Albert Sidney Johnston, launched a surprise attack at Pittsburg Landing. The resulting battle of Shiloh, on April 6, saw the Confederates dislodge the Union forces from their positions, but at the cost of the death of their commander, Johnston. On April 7 Grant was strengthened by

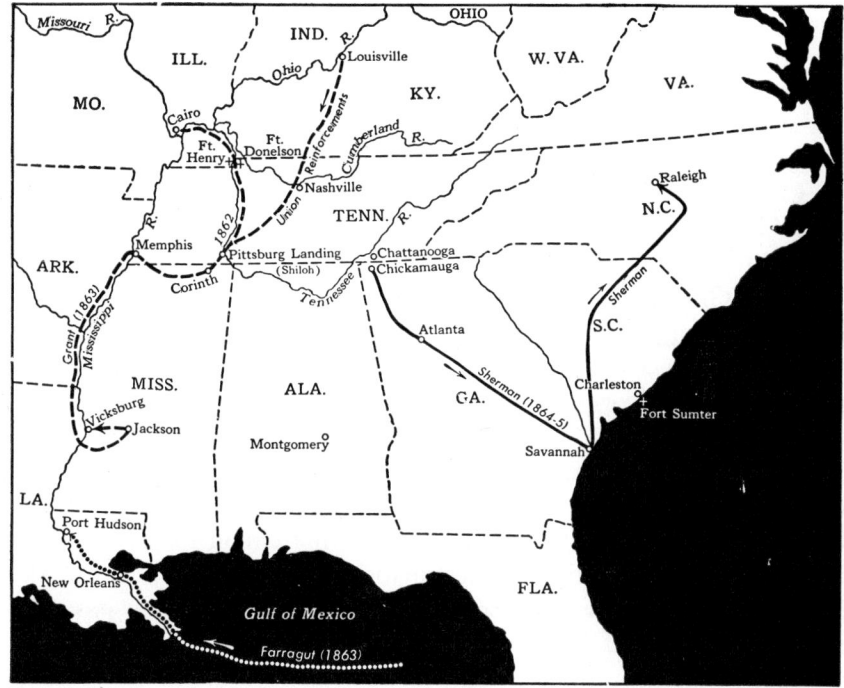

The War in the West

reinforcements under General Lew Wallace and from General Buell's Army of the Ohio, and the Confederates were driven back to Corinth, Mississippi. The Union victory cost the North thirteen thousand lives and the South eleven thousand lives. Little more was accomplished by the army in the Western theater in 1862, but the river gunboats advanced down the Mississippi and joined Admiral Farragut's fleet, which, after destroying the Confederate ships defending New Orleans and capturing the city, had advanced to a point above Vicksburg. At the close of 1862 the Union held all Kentucky, western and central Tennessee, and all the Mississippi except the area between Vicksburg and Port Hudson.

As long as the Confederacy held Vicksburg, troops and supplies from Arkansas, Louisiana, and Texas could pour into the heart of the South. Vicksburg, on a high bluff commanding a hairpin bend in the Mississippi, was difficult to assault because it was protected by swamps, lakes, creeks, and bayous. The remarkable campaign that Grant conducted against Vicksburg ranks as his outstanding achievement. In a twenty-day period in late April and early May, 1863, Grant marched his army two hundred miles through difficult terrain, defeated the Confederates in five battles, and on May 22 laid siege to Vicksburg. For six weeks the Confederates were subjected to bombardment from the Union fleet in the river and from Grant's forces on land. On July 4 the Confederate Gibraltar surrendered, and five days later Port Hudson capitulated; thus was the entire Mississippi placed in Union hands and the Confederacy split in two.

While Grant was laying siege to Vicksburg, General Rosecrans, in June, 1863, marched the Army of the Cumberland to the neighborhood of Chattanooga and began a campaign that eventuated in Sherman's march through Georgia and the splitting of the eastern portion of the Confederacy in two. On September 9, 1863, Rosecrans outmaneuvered the Confederates under General Bragg and occupied Chattanooga without fighting a battle. Nine days later the two armies met at Chickamauga, and the Confederates drove the Union forces back into Chattanooga. The battle of Chickamauga was extremely bloody. The North had 1600 soldiers killed, 5000 captured, and slightly less than 10,000 wounded. The South suffered 2300 killed, 1500 captured, and approximately 14,000 wounded. Only the brilliant generalship of George H. Thomas, a Virginian, saved the Union army from destruction. For six hours Thomas, "the Rock of Chickamauga," held the Union line against repeated Southern assaults. "The *élan* of the Southern soldier," wrote D. H. Hill, "was never seen after Chickamauga."

The Confederates then laid siege to Rosecrans in Chattanooga. At this point Grant was made supreme commander of Union operations in the West, and he replaced Rosecrans with Thomas. Grant opened up a line of supplies to Thomas, and Sherman brought his army eastward from Memphis to strengthen the Union position. On November 24 Grant ordered Generals Thomas, Sherman, and Hooker to take the offensive, and the Confederates, in spectacular battles, were driven from Missionary Ridge and Lookout Mountain.

In May, 1864, with Grant now in the East as commander of all the Union armies, Sherman launched the armies of the West on the march through Georgia. Slowly the smaller Confederate army, under the skillful generalship of Joseph E. Johnston, fell back, destroying bridges and railroad tracks and fighting defensive battles. Jefferson Davis, however, made the mistake of removing Johnston, and the new commander lost Atlanta to Sherman on September 2. The news of

Atlanta's fall gave new hope to the North, weary of the heavy casualty lists, and it immeasurably aided Lincoln's re-election. Although Lincoln was "anxious, if not fearful," in November of 1864, Sherman, with about sixty thousand men, cut loose from his base of supplies and started for the Atlantic Ocean. On December 20 he wired Lincoln: "I beg to present you as a Christmas gift the city of Savannah." Sherman's army destroyed everything that could be useful to the Confederacy on a path thirty miles on each side of the line from Atlanta to Savannah. The army burned bridges, ruined crops, removed livestock, and looted private houses. "The extent of line destroyed was enormous," reported one Northern general. "So great a destruction would have been a long and serious interruption even at the North; but the blockade of Southern ports and the small facilities for manufacture in the Confederate States made the damage practically irreparable."

While Sherman was marching on Savannah, the Confederates, under Hood, started for Tennessee, hoping that this threat of an invasion of the North would force the recall of Sherman. Hood was successful in his invasion until he met Thomas at Nashville, where, on December 27, 1864, Thomas inflicted a smashing defeat and ended effective Confederate military power in the West.

THE WAR IN THE EAST

For six months after Bull Run (July, 1861) the new commander of the Union army, George B. McClellan, trained and drilled his soldiers. While the public bitterly complained of the inaction, Lincoln supported McClellan, even though, as John Hay, Lincoln's secretary, remarked, McClellan displayed the "unparalleled insolence of epaulettes" to the President. McClellan's caution and policy of long preparation were correct in that every day that the war was prolonged increased Northern strength and made Southern success the more unlikely. It was the South, not the North, that needed quick victory; but Jefferson Davis interfered with Robert E. Lee's plans and advocated a policy of defense and delay. On February 22, 1862, Lincoln's patience ended, and he ordered McClellan to advance. Two weeks later the President took the supreme command of all the armies from McClellan and left him only the command of the Army of the Potomac. During the next few months Lincoln and Secretary of War Stanton interfered with McClellan's campaign against Richmond and contributed somewhat to its failure.

McClellan chose to attack Richmond by moving his troops by sea and marching up the York peninsula. Such a campaign would require speed and audacity, but McClellan followed the cautious policy of gradual victory by constriction. One hundred thousand well-armed and well-trained men landed on the peninsula, and forty thousand men, under General McDowell, were left at Washington, at Lincoln's insistence, to defend the city. At this point the Confederates followed the advice of General Robert E. Lee and delayed McClellan at Yorktown, while Stonewall Jackson made a feint at Washington and drew McDowell away so that he could not assist in the Richmond campaign.

On May 14, 1862, McClellan, now within three days' march of Richmond, wired Washington for more men, to be sent by sea. McDowell, however, was ordered to advance on Richmond by land, and, as a result, his army was never really co-ordinated with McClellan's. Meanwhile Lee and Jackson took full advantage of McClellan's caution and the failure of Union co-ordination. After harrying Union forces in the Shenandoah valley and preventing reinforcements from being sent to McClellan, Jackson joined Lee's army for the bloody Seven Days' Battle, from June 26 to July 2. Although McClellan had to withdraw and regroup his lines, he was by no means defeated, and the casualties inflicted on Lee's army were far greater than those that McClellan's suffered. McClellan wanted to continue the campaign, but Lincoln, having withheld the full use of the armies in the East from McClellan, now gave in to radical Republican clamor and removed the "Democratic General," McClellan. The army was withdrawn from the Peninsula, and General John Pope was brought in from the West to lead the attack on Richmond by land.

Pope's appointment was a mistake. He advanced his army without proper precautions, and Lee, following a brilliant plan, sent Jackson on a flanking move behind Pope. On August 29–30, 1862, at the second battle of Bull Run, Pope's army was thoroughly defeated and retreated in disorder toward Washington. Lincoln quickly turned to McClellan, and McClellan rode out to take charge of the weary troops. One Union soldier declared that when the men saw "Little Mac," they "threw their caps high into the air, and . . . frolicked like school-boys." With the army's morale restored, McClellan set out in pursuit of the audacious Lee, who, with his ragged army, was invading Maryland. On September 17 McClellan stopped Lee and Jackson at Antietam Creek, forcing them to retreat; but he failed to pursue Lee and thus lost a possible chance to destroy the Confederate army.

President Jefferson Davis   *General Robert E. Lee*

President Lincoln and Pinkerton, Head of the Secret Service,
Visiting the Union Camp at Antietam in 1862

Just before Antietam the Confederates reached their high point. Their army was in a position to attack Washington, Baltimore, or Philadelphia, and France and England seemingly were only waiting for the next Confederate victory to recognize the independence of the Confederacy. Antietam, therefore, was a decisive battle of the war. McClellan, by his victory, rendered valuable service, even though he did not follow up his advantage. The battle ended the danger of foreign recognition of the Confederacy, and it afforded Lincoln the opportunity of securing the support of liberal European opinion by issuing the Emancipation Proclamation.

McClellan's failure to follow Lee cost him his command, and General A. E. Burnside was appointed to take charge of the army. Burnside's incompetence was revealed when he rashly attacked the entrenched position of Lee at Fredericksburg on December 13. The Northern soldiers bravely charged six times, only to be hurled back each time. As Lee watched the bloody battle, he observed: "It is well this is so terrible! We should grow too fond of it." Burnside lost 12,600 men, of whom 9600 were wounded and 1284 were killed; Lee had only 600 killed and fewer than 5000 wounded.

On January 25, 1863, Lincoln replaced Burnside with "Fighting Joe" Hooker, who did much to restore morale, but who soon revealed that he had only mediocre ability as a commanding general. With an army of one hundred and thirty thousand Hooker moved on toward Richmond and was stopped by Lee at Chancellorsville on May 2. Lee, with an army of just sixty thousand, courageously divided his forces and sent Stonewall Jackson on a flanking movement to strike the Union army's right wing. It was a brilliant success, and the Federal forces were routed; but the battle cost the life of Jackson, whose skill and energy could not be replaced.

Shortly after Chancellorsville, Lee decided to launch a second invasion of the North, and by the end of June his army was in Pennsylvania. The North was now reeling, and a stunning blow might have secured a negotiated peace; but President Davis lacked the imagination necessary for a sweeping defeat of the North at this point. He refused to add other forces to Lee's army, and the invasion had to be made by an army of seventy-three thousand men. In the late days of June the Confederate army moved north across Maryland into Pennsylvania. To the men in gray the fertile fields and prosperous farms of Pennsylvania must have contrasted sharply with their own, battle-scarred northern Virginia. On July 1 advance guards of the two armies met at Gettysburg and for the next two days struggled for position on opposite ridges about the town. On the third day the fighting reached a violent climax when, after deafening cannon fire, Lee staked the fate of his army and unknowingly the fate of the Confederacy on a final charge against the Union line. Majestically the men under Pickett, with flags flying, moved out from Lee's position on Seminary Ridge. Almost as on dress parade they covered the first ground. Then the Union guns opened fire. Huge gaps appeared in the Confederate line. Gallantly they closed their ranks and moved on, only to break in one last futile effort at the foot of the Round Tops. For a moment a handful of Confederates reached their objective and then fell back exhausted and defeated. Never again would the Confederate army be the same after that fateful charge. Realizing that the battle was lost Lee turned his army southward. The Northern army too had suffered heavily, and General Meade failed to take advantage of his victory. Lee was allowed to withdraw his troops across the Potomac. President Lincoln was bitterly disappointed. "Our army held the war in the hollow of their hand," observed Lincoln, "and they would not close it."

After Gettysburg there was little hope left for either a Southern victory or even a stalemate war. "It is for us the living," remarked Lincoln in his Gettysburg Address four months after the battle, "to be dedicated here to the unfinished work which they who fought here have thus far so nobly advanced." The unfinished work, however, would still require a year and a half of fighting before the Confederacy was conquered. After Gettysburg the war in the East entered a quiet phase, and it was not until early in 1864 that significant developments occurred.

On March 9, 1864, U. S. Grant was called from the West, commissioned lieutenant general, and given general command of the Union armies. This Midwesterner from Galena, Illinois, an "ordinary, scrubby-looking man with a slightly seedy look," was in sharp contrast to the pomp associated with most of the Eastern generals. Grant's determination and earthiness won Lincoln's confidence, and Lincoln resisted powerful pressures to remove Grant when the casualties piled up in staggering numbers.

Soon after being placed in charge of the Union armies, Grant launched his strategy of ruthlessly using his superior numbers to wear out the Confederates. While Sherman in the West was moving toward Atlanta, Grant, on May 4, 1864, crossed the Rapidan and, after marching halfway through the Wilderness, came into battle with Lee's army.

For two days the armies struggled in dense thickets, and the casualties were heavy. Union losses were eighteen thousand, and the Confederate losses were ten thousand. In spite of the casualties, Grant ordered his army to move ahead, to the great disappointment of the South. As one Southern writer said:

We had been accustomed to a program which began with a Federal advance, culminated in one great battle, and ended in the retirement of the Union army. . . . But here was a new Federal general, fresh from the West, and so ill-informed as to the military customs in our part of the country that when the battle of the Wilderness was over, instead of retiring . . . he had the temerity to move . . . to a new position.

From May 8 to 12 there was continuous fighting at Spottsylvania Court House. Although Grant's losses were heavy, he wrote his famous dispatch: "I propose to fight it out on this line, if it takes all summer." At Cold Harbor, on June 3, Grant hurled his army at the strongly entrenched Confederates and lost between eight and nine thousand men in three hours. It was a serious mistake on Grant's part. After this battle the Union forces moved on to Petersburg. From the Wilderness to Cold Harbor, Grant had suffered losses of about fifty-five thousand. He had, however, ample man power and excellent food and equipment. Lee, by this time, not only lacked man power, but his army was hungry and there were acute shortages of many supplies.

After failing to take Petersburg by assault from June 15 to 18, Grant sat down to a nine months' siege of the city. Late in 1864 General Sheridan, under Grant's orders, drove the Confederates from the Shenandoah valley. This victory, in addition to Sherman's capture of Atlanta, cheered the North, which had been disheartened by Grant's stupendous losses. Grant's incessant hammering, however, had prevented Lee from detaching any of his troops to try to stop Sherman's march on Atlanta, and Grant's attacks had resulted in Confederate losses which could not be replaced.

The re-election of Lincoln, Sherman's march to Savannah, and the efficiency of the Union blockade proved disastrous to Southern morale as the operations of 1865 began. Desertions were heavy in Confederate ranks by February 1, when Sherman started north from Savannah. At Petersburg, Grant's army now numbered one hundred and fifteen thousand to Lee's fifty-four thousand. To keep from being outflanked, Lee had to abandon Petersburg, and Richmond with it, and attempt a juncture with General Johnston's forces; on April 2 and 3, therefore,

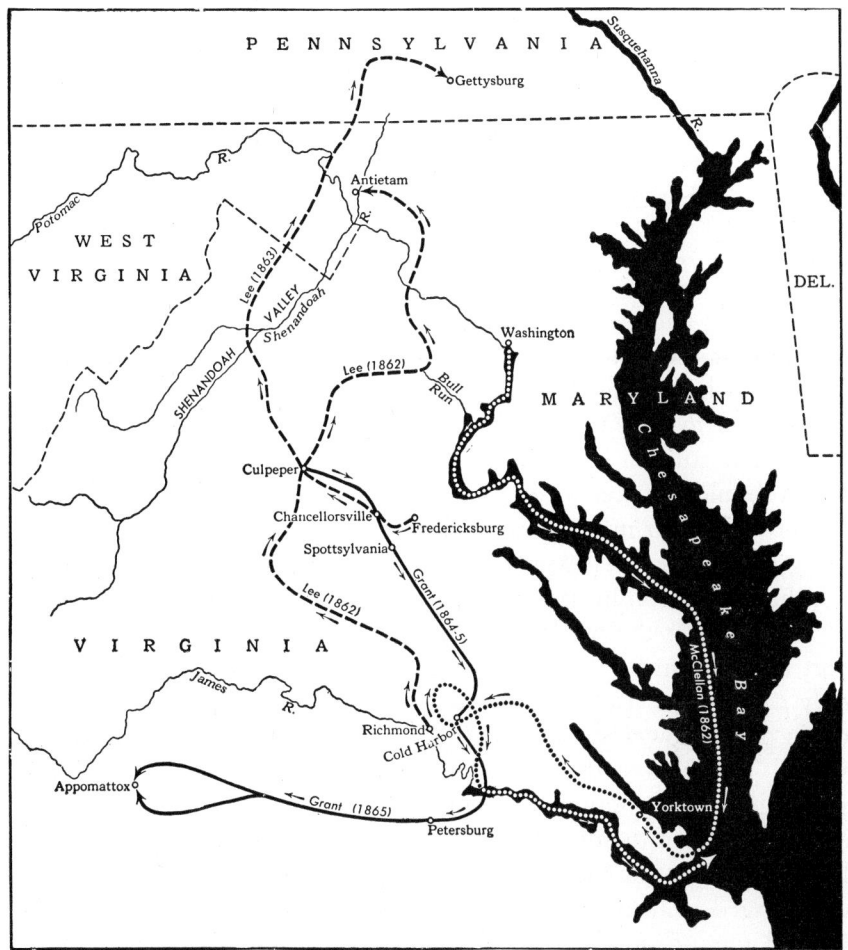

The War in the East

Lee slipped out of Petersburg, and the Union army occupied Richmond
the next day. A large Union force under Sheridan very quickly blocked
Lee's escape, and on April 9, 1865, Lee surrendered at Appomattox
Court House. At the conference between the begrimed Grant and the
faultlessly dressed Lee, Grant allowed the Confederate officers to retain
their side arms and both the officers and the men to keep their horses
and mules "to work their little farms." After bidding his army farewell, Lee set out for Richmond. In the meantime the Confederate
government had fled that city, and the war was virtually over. A few

weeks later President Jefferson Davis and Vice-President Alexander Stephens were captured and hurried off to Northern prisons. The Confederate States of America had come to the end of its troubled existence. The last real organized resistance stopped when Johnston surrendered his army to General Sherman on April 26, and when General Kirby Smith, on May 26, surrendered the Confederate forces west of the Mississippi.

POLITICAL PROBLEMS

Not only had Abraham Lincoln to face crucial military problems during four years of war, but he had groups within the civilian population which were hostile to the war effort and which did all within their power to force the North into a negotiated peace. Before the outbreak of hostilities, in April, 1861, the North was divided as to what action should be taken against the seceded states. Some urged that they be allowed to go in peace; others warned that, if force were used to bring them back, civil war would break out in the North; still others felt that the Union must be preserved, regardless of cost.

Shortly after the outbreak of war, Stephen A. Douglas rallied support for Lincoln by declaring, "There can be no neutrals in this war, *only patriots*—or traitors." The defeatist movement within the Democratic party, however, grew as the Union suffered severe military reverses. Throughout the war this movement had its greatest strength when the military situation was unfavorable to the North. The most extreme wing of the defeatist cause was the secret Copperhead societies like the Knights of the Golden Circle and the Sons of Liberty, which discouraged enlistments, opposed conscription, aided the escape of Confederate prisoners, and shipped arms to the Confederacy.

Another group which caused Lincoln great concern was the peace Democrats, who opposed the war effort and demanded a negotiated peace. Early in 1862, led by the Ohio Congressman C. L. Vallandigham, this group warned that it would not aid in a war to free the slaves:

Democrats recognize it as their duty as patriots to support the government in all constitutional, necessary, and proper efforts to maintain its safety, integrity, and constitutional authority; but at the same time they are inflexibly opposed to waging war against any of the States or people of this Union . . . for any purpose of conquest or subjugation, or of overthrowing or interfering with the rights of established institutions of any State.

The military situation at the time of the mid-term elections in 1862 was so disastrous that peace Democrats were elected to office in Ohio,

Indiana, and Illinois. Urging a negotiated peace on the floor of Congress, Vallandigham declared, on January 14, 1863: "Defeat, debt, taxation, sepulchres, these are your trophies. . . . The war for the Union is, in your hands, a most bloody and costly failure." The fall of Vicksburg and the stopping of Lee at Gettysburg, in July, 1863, gave the North renewed hope of victory; after that time the peace Democrats had less and less influence and success.

Confronted with opposition from the Copperheads and the peace Democrats, Lincoln could not count on unity within the remaining forces in the North. Although he had the support of war Democrats like Andrew Johnson and Stephen A. Douglas, and of moderate Republicans like W. H. Seward and Montgomery Blair, radical Republicans, such as Wade of Ohio, Chandler of Michigan, and Stevens of Pennsylvania, were continually criticizing him for not conducting the war as a crusade to free the slaves.

Lincoln made it clear from the outset that he was waging the war to preserve the Union. When, because of the diplomatic situation and the radical clamoring, he issued the Emancipation Proclamation, the radicals shifted their criticism to his conduct of the war. Through a Congressional committee to investigate the war, they forced Lincoln to replace Democratic generals with radical Republicans, and they tried to determine military policy. When Grant was being checked with heavy losses in August, 1864, Wade of Ohio demanded the removal of Grant and told Lincoln, "You are the father of every military blunder that has been made during this war." Then Wade cried, "This government is on the road to hell, sir, by reason of your obstinacy, and you are not a mile from there this minute." At this point Lincoln quietly observed that a mile was just the distance to the Capitol, where Congress met.

In 1864 the radicals opposed Lincoln's renomination, but they reluctantly supported him and Andrew Johnson when they realized that a third candidate would probably mean the election of the Democratic candidate, General McClellan. In spite of a peace plank in the Democratic platform, McClellan went to the country as a war leader, and Lincoln was sure that he himself could not be re-elected. Sherman's capture of Atlanta in September, however, and the now approaching end of the war made Lincoln's election possible.

While Lincoln was under constant attack for his conduct of the war, Jefferson Davis was having a difficult time in the Confederacy. Davis had been chosen provisional president by a convention that assembled at Montgomery, Alabama, on February 4, 1861. This convention also drafted a constitution, which closely resembled the Federal Constitution in most ways. The new constitution, however, called for the protection of slavery in any territory to be acquired, forbade the levying of protective tariffs, limited the term of the president to one term of six years, permitted the president to veto single items of an appropriation bill without vetoing the entire bill, and allowed cabinet members to hold seats in Congress.

In the fall of 1861 Davis and Alexander Stephens were elected president and vice-president, and their provisional term thus was replaced by a permanent one. In spite of the many brilliant victories won by Confederate armies, the new government was continually beset by troubles. The South lacked money and manufactured goods; the international support that had been expected proved to be disappointing; and an extreme emphasis on states' rights made efficient prosecution of the war difficult. When, for instance, the Confederate government found that it had to institute conscription in April, 1862, in order to secure man power for the army, certain state governments objected to the step. Davis's power to suspend the writ of habeas corpus also stirred opposition, particularly from the governors of North Carolina and Georgia. In certain areas of the South there was widespread evasion of the draft law. Also, desertions from the army were heavy, and the deserters and draft-dodgers in remote areas waged guerrilla war against troops sent to defeat them.

THE DIPLOMATIC FRONT

During four years of war the North and the South waged a dramatic diplomatic duel. When the war began, leaders in the Confederacy were confident that Southern cotton was so important to Europe's welfare that recognition of Confederate independence would be immediately forthcoming. "King Cotton," however, did not prove to be the overwhelming factor that Southerners had hoped it would be. Although by 1862 the lack of cotton had forced many English mills to close, the English worker favored the Northern cause, particularly after Lincoln's Emancipation Proclamation. Non-American sources of cotton eased the situation somewhat after 1862, and at all times the English government had to remember the importance of Northern wheat for the English masses. As a result, "King Wheat" was to offset the importance of "King Cotton" in the diplomatic struggle.

In March, 1861, President Davis dispatched W. L. Yancey, P. A. Rost, and A. D. Mann to Europe to secure recognition. Two months later England recognized the belligerent status of the South, but did not go so far as to recognize its independence. Lincoln sent Charles Francis Adams, son of John Quincy Adams, to England to counteract the work of Confederate agents. Charles Francis Adams, throughout the war, was an able representative struggling against an unfavorable press, Confederate propaganda, and the animosity of the British ruling class. The British Foreign Secretary, Lord John Russell, chose to ignore Adams. As Henry Adams, who accompanied his father to London, has written: "Personally the Minister was to be kindly treated; politically he was negligible; he was there to be put aside. London and Paris imitated Lord John. Everyone waited to see Lincoln and his hirelings disappear in one vast *débâcle*."[1]

The first real campaign carried on between Federal and Confederate agents was that waged for control of the munitions market of Europe. Although the Confederate agents generally placed their orders first, the Union representatives had superior financial resources. As a result, they were able to outbid Confederate agents, and snapped up Confederate orders when the South failed to make payments.

After England and other European nations had recognized the belligerency of the South, there was the grave danger that Europe might intervene in the conflict and demand an armistice. In November, 1861, intervention seemed near when a Union warship stopped the British steamer *Trent* and removed two Confederate agents, J. M. Mason and John Slidell, who were en route to Europe. Immediately sections of the English press clamored for war, while the North hailed the patriotism of the American captain's action. England demanded an apology, and, although Secretary of State Seward sent no real apology, the two agents were released and allowed to proceed to Europe.

When, in 1862, Confederate victories were plentiful and Confederate hopes seemed brightest, Napoleon III urged England and France to force an armistice. At this point the English cabinet seriously considered recognizing the independence of the South. "We may anticipate with certainty the success of the Southern States so far as regards their separation from the North," declared William E. Gladstone, the Chancellor of the Exchequer, on October 7, 1862. Two developments, however, checked recognition and possible intervention. Lee's armies

[1] *The Education of Henry Adams*, p. 123. Houghton Mifflin Company, Boston, 1918.

had been stopped at the battle of Antietam in September, 1862, and Lincoln's Emancipation Proclamation was having widespread effect among the English working people.

Lincoln approached the slavery question cautiously while abolitionists clamored for the war to become a crusade against slavery. Lincoln had to retain the support of the war Democrats and the support of the border states, both of which might be lost by emancipation. "My paramount object," Lincoln wrote Horace Greeley on August 22, 1862, "is to save the Union, and is not either to save or to destroy slavery. If I could save the Union without freeing any slave, I would do it; and if I could save it by freeing all the slaves I would do it. . . . What I do about slavery and the colored race, I do because I believe it helps to save the Union."

By this time, Lincoln was convinced that a proclamation of emancipation was essential to the preservation of the Union. The clamor of the abolitionists at home and the dangerous international situation convinced him that the moment had arrived when "slavery must die that the nation might live." After Lee's invasion of the North had been stopped at Antietam, Lincoln issued a preliminary Emancipation Proclamation on September 22, 1862. He declared that on January 1, 1863, slaves in the rebellious states would thenceforth be free. None of the Union slave states were affected by the decree; the Proclamation applied only to areas of the Confederacy not occupied by Union troops, where the North obviously had no power to execute the measure.

Lincoln's Proclamation had the effect of strengthening the support of the English working class, and of such English liberals as Cobden and Bright, for the Northern cause. Charles Francis Adams, by his warning that, if England recognized the Confederacy, diplomatic relations would be severed, also played an important part in averting English action in 1862. Another threat to the delicate relations between the two nations was the building of Confederate ships in English shipyards. The *Florida* and the *Alabama* sailed from England to prey upon Northern commerce, but the construction of other ships was stopped when Adams warned the British foreign minister, "It would be superfluous in me to point out to your lordship that this is war." Years later England was to compensate the United States for the damages inflicted by the *Florida* and the *Alabama*.

Relations with England improved in 1863, particularly after the victories at Vicksburg and Gettysburg had improved Northern chances of victory. During 1863 Napoleon III represented the greatest danger

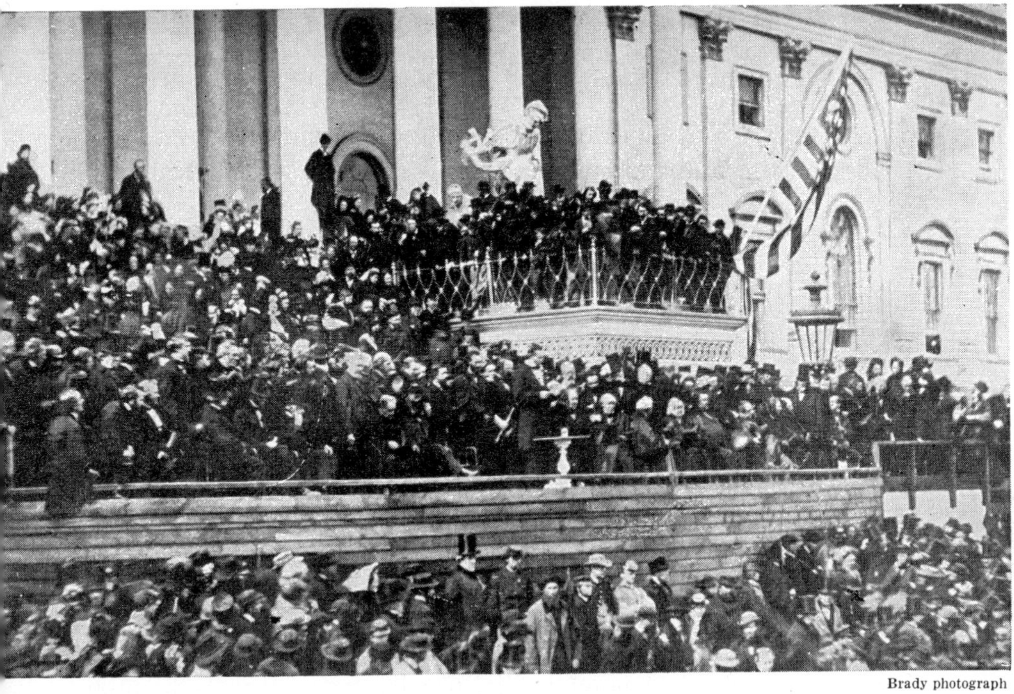

Brady photograph

President Lincoln Delivering the Second Inaugural Address, March 4, 1865

The Union Fleet, under Admiral Porter, Running the Confederate Blockade at Vicksburg, April 16, 1863

Lithograph by Currier and Ives, 1863; from The Library of Congress

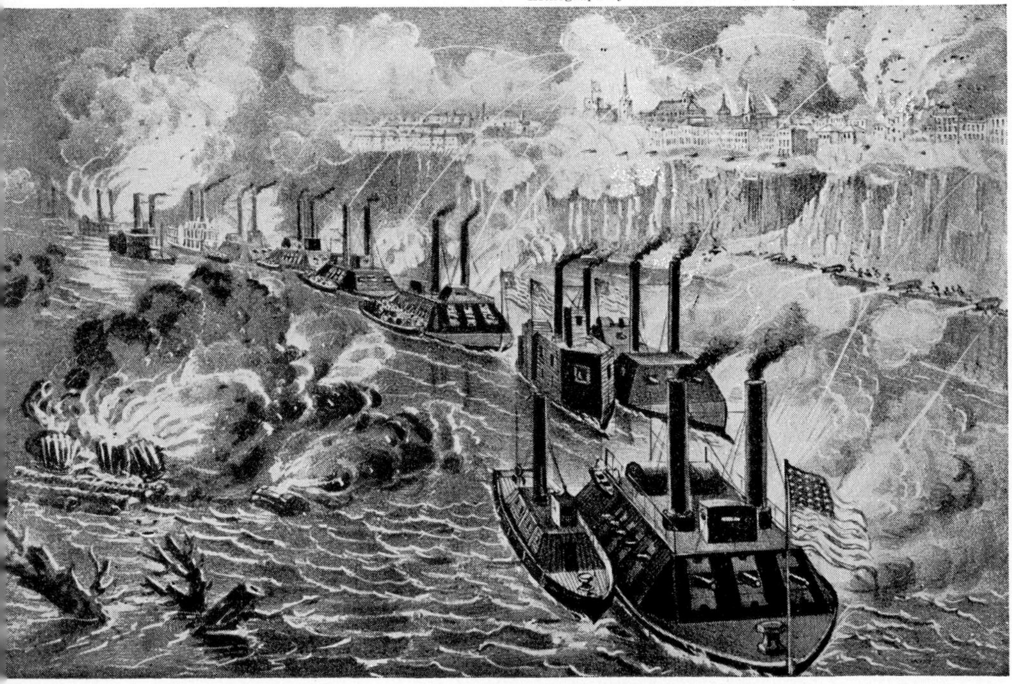

of recognition and intervention. Napoleon's actions, however, depended on England and on their possible effect on his intervention in Mexico. When England abandoned the idea of recognizing the Confederacy, Napoleon also failed to act, since he had no desire to take the step alone. Napoleon's Mexican adventure and his placing of Maximilian on the Mexican throne brought continued warnings from the United States; but as long as the Civil War continued, Napoleon ignored Secretary of State Seward's notes. By the end of 1863 the Confederate hope of European recognition and intervention had ended, and in December, 1863, President Davis remarked that the attitude of European nations was "positively unfriendly."

LIFE IN THE CONFEDERACY

When Lee's army invaded the North in the summer of 1862, thousands of his soldiers were "barefooted, blanketless, and hatless!" For four years the South, a nonindustrial people, struggled with the problem of supplying its army and its people with war equipment and with the necessities of life. Hope for supplies from Europe was shattered by the effective Union blockade of Southern ports. "The blockade was the real destroyer of the South," N. W. Stephenson has written. "Besides ruining the whole policy based on King Cotton, besides impeding to a vast extent the inflow of munitions from Europe, it also deprived Southern life of numerous articles which were hard to relinquish—not only such luxuries as tea and coffee, but also such utter necessities as medicines."[1]

Throughout four years of conflict the supply of manufactured goods was wholly inadequate to the task of waging a great war. For instance, there were only two plants in the South capable of casting the heavy ordnance required by the armies, and the supplies captured from Northern soldiers were constantly needed to equip the Confederate soldier. The railway system was another critical Southern weakness. The inadequacies of Confederate railroads made total mobilization of Southern resources impossible. Before the war the South had neglected its railroads, since its commerce went by rivers to the ocean ports. Many of the existing railroads were short lines, and the narrow point of view of their owners prevented the Confederate government from organizing the lines into a coherent system. At the strategic military city of

[1] *The Day of the Confederacy* (Vol. 30, The Chronicles of America), p. 105. Yale University Press, New Haven, 1920.

Petersburg, Virginia, for example, two railroads terminated, but did not connect. The town, wishing to retain its transfer business, resisted Confederate attempts to link the two lines. The crying need of the armies for ordnance made it impossible for the South to produce railroad rails throughout the war. It became necessary at times to tear up the rails of less important roads to repair the lines essential to the war effort. There was congestion at many points on the railroads, which prevented food and other supplies from reaching the cities and the battle fronts. Hunger in Confederate cities and in Lee's ranks, near the end of the war, was largely the result of the inability of the transportation system to meet the situation.

Cut off from the foodstuffs of the Midwest, Southern state governments encouraged the sowing of corn, wheat, and other foodstuffs in place of cotton. Shortages in many lines, including food, led to widespread speculation. As Confederate currency became less and less valuable, the story was circulated that one could take money to market in a basket and bring the supplies home in a pocketbook. "Extortion, pitiless extortion is making havoc in the land," declared a Southern minister in 1863. "We are devouring each other. Avarice with full barns puts the bounties of Providence under bolts and bars, waiting with eager longings for higher prices." The high cost of living bore hardest on the masses in the Southern cities. In spite of relief work by the Y.M.C.A. and local governments, there were real suffering and squalor in these localities. Soldiers' families particularly suffered unless they owned farms. The desperate condition of soldiers' families was the probable cause of the widespread desertions from the army that occurred near the close of the war.

War-financing in the South was a difficult problem for the Davis government. Although direct taxes were levied, they failed to yield large sums. The blockade precluded income from customs, and the Confederate government had to rely on paper money to defray war expenses. By 1864 there was $1,000,000,000 in Confederate notes in circulation to be paid the bearer "two years after the ratification of a treaty of peace between the Confederate States and the United States of America." The value of these notes in gold depreciated from 90 cents in 1861 to 1.7 cents in 1865.

During the first year of war the South relied upon volunteering for its armies. Compulsory service, however, became "absolutely indispensable," and the first conscription law was passed on April 16, 1862. By 1864 white men between seventeen and fifty were liable for military

service. Exemptions were numerous. Government officials, persons engaged in war industry, and overseers of twenty slaves did not have to
serve. In addition, people with money could escape service by hiring
substitutes. As conditions became increasingly difficult in the Confederacy, this method by which the wealthy escaped military service led
to considerable grumbling in the ranks that it was "a rich man's war
and a poor man's fight." The government generally had in service an
active military machine of about four hundred thousand men, and
something over a million men served under the Confederate banner in
the course of the four-year struggle. With white man power being
called to service, it became increasingly necessary to rely upon slave
labor for food and cotton production. Though there were some fears
that there would be a slave insurrection, with the white males away in
the service, slave revolts failed to occur.

LIFE IN THE NORTH

Although the first year of the war resulted in serious economic dis-
locations in the North, by 1863 the *New York Times* remarked that
"the prosperity of the country [was] the greatest disadvantage of the
war." The war resulted in a vigorous expansion of business and trade in
the North. At first, the end of trade with the South and the closing of
the Mississippi crippled the nation, but by 1862 a new prosperity was
sweeping the land. Railroads, for instance, greatly increased their earnings, and the stock of the Erie Railroad soared from 17 to $126\frac{1}{2}$ in three
years. Speculation on the stock market became so widespread that one
writer declared, in 1864: "The city exchanges and their approaches are
already crowded with a frenzied throng of eager speculators. . . . The
number of brokers has more than quadrupled in a few months, such
has been the enormous increase of stock-jobbing."

Manufacturing boomed with the war prosperity. The high protective tariff passed by the Lincoln government stimulated the building
of new industrial plants, as did the government contracts for war
supplies. The woolen industry, shoe-manufacturing, and the coal and
iron industries were those that felt the greatest impetus from the war
effort. War-transportation requirements brought new prosperity to the
railroads, and some of the shorter lines were consolidated into trunk
lines. The military need of a railroad to the west coast led Congress to
subsidize the construction of the Union Pacific–Central Pacific project
in 1862.

Agriculture too expanded during the war. Although young men left the farms to fight in the army, the introduction of farm machinery replaced hand labor and greatly increased the yield of the land. Poor crops in Europe and the need of feeding the soldiers and of feeding the workers in the expanding cities brought war prices for agricultural produce. As part of the expansion in agriculture, between 1862 and 1865, under the Homestead Act, about two and a half million acres of land were given to agricultural settlers.

The need of man power for the armies and for the new Northern industries resulted in an acute labor shortage. Negroes, women, and immigrants were recruited for the factories. In 1864 Congress passed a law allowing the importation of workers by contractors under regulations established by the Commissioner of Immigration. In 1864, partly as a result of this law, 191,000 immigrants entered the country, and 180,000 came in 1865.

Prices rose rapidly during the war, and the worker did not share equally with the industrialists in the widespread prosperity. Wages failed to keep abreast of prices, and the workers turned to unionization to aid them in their struggle for higher wages and better working conditions. There were over a hundred strikes in 1864, and by 1865 there were assemblies of trade-unions in all major cities.

As in the South, the need of supplying man power for the armies resulted in the passage of a conscription law. Volunteering continued as a policy, but in addition, after March 3, 1863, all able-bodied male citizens between the ages of twenty and forty-five were made liable for military service. A drafted man, however, as in the South, was permitted to hire a substitute and escape service. Before long this provision of the law became a national scandal. Of the drafted men, approximately 46,000 were bona fide draftees and 118,000 were substitutes, which brought the total of the conscripted roll to about 160,000. But volunteering remained the main source of man power. In all, about two and a half million men served under the Union flag.

There was bitter opposition to the draft in many areas. Draft officials were mobbed in Wisconsin; an "insurrection" was suppressed in Holmes County, Ohio; there was rioting in Troy and Albany, New York; and secret societies created real disturbances in Ohio, Indiana, and Illinois. Most serious of all was the riot that broke out in New York City. From July 13 until July 16, 1863, rioters stormed through the streets of the city, setting fire to buildings and overpowering police and militia. A number of Negroes were killed, and Horace Greeley's

Tribune office barely escaped destruction. Troops from the Gettysburg campaign had to be dispatched to quell the riot. J. G. Randall has observed,

> Party feeling, race prejudice, agitation for peace, disgust with the oft-mentioned "incompetence" of the Lincoln administration, belief in the hopelessness of subjugating the South, resentment born of blunders in the conscription act and the manner of its execution, outraged personal independence reacting against an effort to force a man into a service contrary to his sympathies and convictions, anger at the "rich man's war" with its fraud and profiteering,—these were among the motives which resulted in mass obstruction of the draft.[1]

An unfortunate phase of the Northern war effort was the profiteering and graft. Political allies and personal friends of government officials reaped a harvest from supplying the government. Enormous commissions were paid to men by producing companies to secure war contracts. The government was cheated a number of times by paying for sugar but receiving a great deal of sand, by being sold guns that had been condemned, and by paying for coffee and receiving some substitute such as rye. In 1864, the *New York Herald* denounced the "gross corruption prevailing in nearly every department of the government," and a Congressional committee charged that the mania of corruption permeated the army and that officers colluded with "contractors, bartering away and dividing contracts for horses and other supplies to enrich personal favorites; purchasing articles and compelling false invoices to be given."

The corruption of the war period and the loose ethics displayed in many war contracts were to continue after the war and besmirch the Grant administration. On the whole, of course, the country's business during the war was carried on with honesty and integrity. To pay for the vast amount of material needed to subdue the Confederacy, the government at first relied on loans and taxes. Income-tax laws were passed, excise taxes were levied, and customs rates were raised. By 1864 taxation was meeting one third of the cost of the war. In addition to loans and taxes, the government issued legal-tender notes, or greenbacks, to help to defray expenses. The value of the greenbacks varied with the success of the Northern armies, and they did not reach parity with gold until many years after the conflict.

[1] *The Civil War and Reconstruction*, p. 416. D. C. Heath and Company, Boston, 1937.

The Civil War ended Negro slavery, and, at the same time, it gave a remarkable impetus to the growth of American industrialism. The war speeded up the advent of the age of industrial capitalism and stimulated the organization of American business into larger and larger units. With the vision of a poet, Stephen Vincent Benét, in his *John Brown's Body*, explained the significance of the Civil War for the growth of American industrialism in the following words:

> Out of his body grows revolving steel,
> Out of his body grows the spinning wheel
> Made up of wheels, the new, mechanic birth,
> No longer bound by toil
> To the unsparing soil
> Or the old furrow-line,
> The great, metallic beast
> Expanding West and East,
> His heart a spinning coil,
> His juices burning oil,
> His body serpentine.
> Out of John Brown's strong sinews the tall skyscrapers grow,
> Out of his heart the chanting buildings rise,
> Rivet and girder, motor and dynamo,
> Pillar of smoke by day and fire by night,
> The steel-faced cities reaching at the skies,
> The whole enormous and rotating cage
> Hung with hard jewels of electric light,
> Smoky with sorrow, black with splendor, dyed
> Whiter than damask for a crystal bride
> With metal suns, the engine-handed Age,
> The genie we have raised to rule the earth,
> Obsequious to our will
> But servant-master still,
> The tireless serf already half a god—[1]

[1]Stephen Vincent Benét, *John Brown's Body*, p. 376. Copyright, 1927, 1928, by Stephen Vincent Benét.

SELECTED BIBLIOGRAPHY

J. G. RANDALL, *The Civil War and Reconstruction*, and GEORGE FORT MILTON, *Conflict: The American Civil War*, valuable single volume; PHILIP S. FONER, *Business and Slavery*, analyzes Northern business attitudes toward secession; D. L. DUMOND, *The Secession Movement*, provides necessary material.

The following biographies are valuable: L. A. WHITE, *Robert Barnwell Rhett*; AVERY CRAVEN, *Edmund Ruffin: Southerner*; U. B. PHILLIPS, *Robert Toombs*; CARL SANDBURG, *Lincoln: The War Years*; J. G. RANDALL, *Lincoln from Springfield to Gettysburg*; W. E. DODD, *Jefferson Davis*; B. J. HENDRICK, *Statesmen of the Lost Cause*; D. S. FREEMAN, *R. E. Lee* and *Lee's Lieutenants*; J. A. WOODBURN, *Thaddeus Stevens*; CLAUDE FUESS, *Carl Schurz*; L. PENDLETON, *Alexander H. Stephens*.

On the military situation the following are valuable: R. S. HENRY, *Story of the Confederacy*; M. F. STEELE, *American Campaigns*; J. F. RHODES, *History of the Civil War, 1861–1865*; A. T. MAHAN, *Farragut*; J. P. BAXTER, *Introduction of the Iron Clad Warships*; M. ROBINSON, *The Confederate Privateers*.

Domestic and diplomatic problems are covered in T. H. WILLIAMS, *Lincoln and the Radicals*; GEORGE FORT MILTON, *Lincoln and the Fifth Column*; WOOD GRAY, *The Hidden Civil War*; N. W. STEPHENSON, *Day of the Confederacy*; E. D. FITE, *Social and Industrial Conditions in the North during the Civil War*; A. C. COLE, *The Irrepressible Conflict, 1850–1865*; E. D. ADAMS, *Great Britain and the American Civil War*; F. L. OWSLEY, *King Cotton Diplomacy*; F. BANCROFT, *W. H. Seward*.

H. S. COMMAGER (Ed.), *Documents of American History*, pp. 362–448, contains source material.

XIX

Reconstruction, South and North

WITH THE ENDING of the Civil War the United States faced not only the problem of returning a nation, keyed to the tasks of war, back to the pursuits of peace, but also that of restoring unity and co-operation to a people part of whom were jubilant in victory and part of whom were bitter in defeat. These were not simple tasks. Great armies had to be disbanded and absorbed again into civilian life. The intensified production of goods needed for war had to be shifted to the production of peacetime goods. Huge war debts had to be paid. Some four million Negroes, just out of bondage, had to assume the responsibility of freedom in the very neighborhoods where they had recently been slaves. A broken, bankrupt South, which for four years had been the Confederate States of America, somehow had to find a place again in the national pattern.

And all of this had to take place in an atmosphere overcharged with energy, still poisoned by the propaganda necessary to stir men to warlike deeds, and sharply characterized by the notion that ends justify means.

The significance of this to national life as a whole becomes apparent only when we remember that the Northern victory was more than just the victory of one army over another. It was, to be more exact, the victory of one section over another; of one social-economic system over another; of one political group over another. It was, in fact, the climax of a revolution in American life that had been under way for many years. The North had triumphed under the banner of a great moral-patriotic drive for freedom and union, but this victory carried with it drastic changes for every phase of national life. Modern America could now swiftly emerge.

The Northern victory meant that certain forces and interests, long held in check by the combination of the agricultural South and West, could now have free and full play. The bitter controversies over lands, tariffs, internal improvements, finances, and immigration could now be settled in the way that the Northeast and the Northwest wanted them settled. Finance and industrial capitalism could move forward to completion without effective opposition from the old agricultural interests. Already much had been accomplished. Since the withdrawal of Southern representatives from Congress at the beginning of the war, a Homestead Act had been passed, the tariff had been substantially raised, lavish aid had been granted to railroad-builders, a national banking system had been established, and foreign immigration had been consistently encouraged. These were all positive gains for the victorious section and for its dominating classes.

EFFECTS OF THE WAR ON NATIONAL LIFE

The financing of the war had played a significant part in pushing forward a new economic order. The first decision was to borrow heavily and to hold taxes down. This was later modified, and taxes, even including an income tax, were widely extended. Yet, in all, loans amounted to $2,621,000,000 and taxes to only $667,000,000.

Interest on these loans was generous. In a few cases it ran to 7 per cent and over. At times depreciated greenbacks were received at face value in payment for bonds which were later to be redeemed in gold. Then, with the new National Banking Act of 1863, banks, organized under national authority, could purchase bonds and emit notes of their own up to 90 per cent of the par value of bonds held. They would thus receive interest on the bonds purchased and also interest on their own notes issued as loans to their customers. In this way certain large Eastern bankers made great profits in the original disposal of bonds for the government and also on the bonds that they held and the notes that they issued to meet the demands of a rapidly expanding business world. Local banks in widely separated communities were, by the same system, linked to these larger concerns, and thus a strong financial group was created which had a deep interest in any financial policy that the government might adopt in the settlement of its huge $2,846,000,000 debt. The work of Andrew Jackson in his fight against "the money powers" was thus largely undone.

The flat repudiation of all Confederate debts and obligations was also important. These amounted to something over $2,350,000,000. The wiping out of slave property, once worth millions, added to the Southern losses. Since the South's true wealth, in 1860, was less than $3,500,000,000, this meant that one section of the new united nation would be totally bankrupt. It would be quite outside the financial interests of the new day; the Civil War had put the South at the bottom of the financial ladder.

The tariff legislation which had been passed during the war had even greater social-economic significance. The issue had been thoroughly fought out before the war. All the arguments for and against protection had been stated. The drift was definitely toward free trade. Even Lincoln, in 1859, had said that, though he favored a moderate protective tariff, it was his opinion that the issue could not be raised. "We have been beaten on it," he stated.

Business conditions just before the war, however, had brought new demands, and the Republicans, largely under Pennsylvania pressure, had favored protection in their platform of 1860. The war, in turn, favored tariffs, both for increased revenue and as a means of compensating domestic interests for the higher taxes assessed. By 1862 tariff rates, which had been fixed at about 19 per cent by the act of 1857, were up to about 37 per cent; by 1864 they stood at 47 per cent. These increases had been hastily passed, with no scientific study of rates, after inadequate debate, and often with the idea that they were only temporary increases to meet an immediate emergency. Nevertheless they bestowed matchless favors on industry—a near monopoly and high prices in the world's most valuable market. Continued into the days of peace, such favors, combined with lower taxes and an immigration act that permitted, for a time, the importation of workers bound for a term of service, bestowed upon industry benefits that even surpassed those granted to finance. A great new power in American life had been created. From now on, the once dominant farmers of the nation, divided and out of favor, would constitute only a protesting minority.

Another effect of the war can best be described by the phrase "the emergence of nationalism." The South had long championed the idea of states' rights. From the days of the Virginia and Kentucky Resolutions, such Southerners as Thomas Jefferson, John Taylor, and John C. Calhoun had taken the lead in opposing a consolidated national government, and in 1860–1861 the Southern states had justified secession on the ground of confederation as against organic unity. Men of the North, in step with the facts of modern interdependence, refused to accept such a doctrine, and the necessities of the war days greatly strengthened their stand. Lincoln, without calling a special session of Congress in the spring of 1861, increased the army, issued "general orders" for its regulation in the field, and soon set up the draft in states which lacked conscription acts, ordered the Treasury to pay money to individuals without security, ordered arbitrary arrests, suppressed newspapers, and suspended the right of habeas corpus. As Professor W. A. Dunning says, "In the interval between April 12, and July 4, 1861, a new principle thus appeared in the constitutional system of the United States, namely that of temporary dictatorship." The widespread acceptance of this "avowed ignoring of the organic law" emphasized "the completeness of the revolution which was in progress. The idea of government limited by the written instructions of a past generation had already begun to grow dim in the smoke of battle."

The climax of these developments came with the adoption of the Fourteenth Amendment in 1868. Its apparent purpose was to bring pressure on the Southern states to grant political rights to the Negro; but it defined citizenship and made it a national, not a state, matter, and then declared that "No state shall make or enforce any law which shall abridge the privileges or immunities of citizens of the United States; nor shall any State deprive any person of life, liberty, or property, without due process of law, nor deny to any person within its jurisdiction the equal protection of the laws." By these provisions a heavy hand was laid on the state legislatures, and also by the fact that the Supreme Court granted to the central government the constitutional power to check local action in a broad and uncertain field. When the courts interpreted the term *citizens* to mean all persons and then accepted corporations as persons, the "nationalism" won on Civil War battlefields became both a social and an economic thing. Business in the United States need no longer fear "unsound" restrictions and regulations by state legislatures. The defeat of the South had indeed been a serious blow to the rights once granted to the states.

In the political realm the Civil War sharply altered the party situation. The Republican triumph in 1860 was the triumph of many divergent elements fused together and given a working unity by a single issue, the nonextension of slavery. Without that, the disjointed mass of Democrats, Whigs, Free-Soilers, and Know-Nothings that was the Republican party could not have been held together. Lincoln understood this when he insisted that the sole object of the war was to save the Union. No other appeal would have sufficed, and even that did not satisfy the extreme antislavery group. He had the same thing in mind when he placed in his cabinet individuals who represented each of the factions in the party. That had its disadvantages, as he soon learned, but the effort for unity required it.

It was, therefore, not surprising that war problems soon brought strife. Some Republicans early stressed the freeing of the slaves as an open objective; others held, with Lincoln, to the single purpose of saving the Union. Some believed that the control of the army should be entirely in the hands of antislavery men; others asked only military skill of the generals. Some soon wearied of war and asked for peace at any price, but Lincoln insisted on carrying the struggle to a victorious end, regardless of the cost. Since the Democrats were divided in the same way, party lines began to break, and, by the Congressional election of 1862, it was clear that the war Republicans and the war Democrats would have to combine if political success were to be achieved. The term *Union party* began to be heard in local elections as these groups co-operated. The move reached its climax in the national election of 1864.

In this election those who supported Lincoln, regardless of party, met in a great Union convention. It was called by the Republican National Executive Committee, but was thought of, and spoken of, as a Union-party convention. The temporary chairman said:

"I see before me not only primitive Republicans and primitive abolitionists but I see also primitive Democrats and primitive Whigs. As a Union party I will follow you to the ends of the earth and to the gates of death; but as an Abolition Party, as a Republican Party, as a Whig Party, as a Democratic Party, as an American Party, I will not follow you one foot."

The permanent chairman was equally explicit. "In no sense," he said, "do we meet as members or representatives of either of the old political parties. . . . The extraordinary condition of the country . . . has compelled the formation of substantially new political organizations." Mr. Tremain of New York was even more emphatic: "We meet here not as Republicans; if we meet as Republicans, I have no place in this convention. I have been a lifelong Democrat."

In keeping with this attitude, the convention renominated Lincoln and placed on the ticket with him Andrew Johnson, a Democrat from Tennessee. Its platform centered about the preservation of "the Federal Union" and the suppression of "the rebellion" by "force of arms." As Professor Dunning has said, "The Republican party did not exist in 1864."

The Democrats were as badly divided, but, being out of power, maintained their organization without a break. They did, however, draw to themselves many of those who did not like Lincoln's methods and many who wanted peace at any cost. They lost many *war* Democrats to the Union party, and thus laid themselves open to the charge of harboring the disloyal. This was all the more unfortunate because the most ardent secessionists had been Democrats and because the so-called "Copperhead" movement in the Northwest had often been strongest in Democratic areas. That put the party somewhat under a cloud and subjected it to what was often unfair criticism. In the days ahead Democrats would have to fight against insinuations of disloyalty and open charges of hostility to the war effort.

When the Republican party was "reborn" in the next few years, it quickly fell under the leadership of a group long opposed to Lincoln's policies. Soon it allied itself with the forces of corporate industry, which represented a greater investment of capital and, consequently, a greater concentration of power in politics and economic life than the slave-holders had ever dreamed of possessing. Soon men were talking of the danger "from another kind of slavery, namely the slavery that would result from aggregations of capital in the hands of a few." That left to the Democrats the task of opposition; and in spite of Civil War handicaps, the opposition party was soon able to talk of needed reforms and of a return to the democratic ideals of Jefferson and Lincoln.

THE PROBLEMS OF SOUTHERN RECONSTRUCTION

The so-called "period of reconstruction," after 1865, presents a bewildering tangle of forces and motives. There was much of the past in it, and much that had to do only with the future. The war had shaped men's thinking and feelings and kept them looking backward; yet the basic fact of the day was that modern urban-industrial America was emerging. What was done about the past somehow always had to do also with the future. Behind the political parties, shaped by the war, there now lay great, new social-economic groups, whose interests were only indirectly related to the war record of the parties. Interwoven with every political move or situation were economic considerations. Congress was angry because the Executive had exercised so much power in war days and because the courts had upheld him; its members were now sullen and determined. Yet the drive to set a new balance in government could not be divorced from the conflicting attitudes on Southern reconstruction and the favors being doled out to business. These two matters were, in turn, closely related, for the return of the South to a place in the national life had political and economic implications. The majority of Southerners had been Democrats; they had

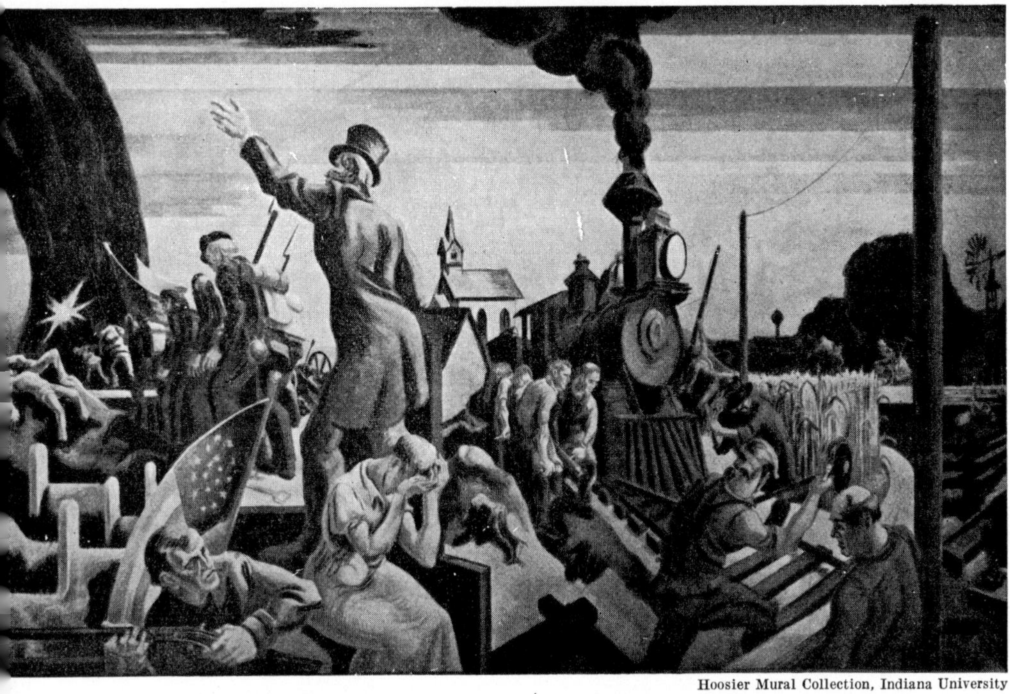

Hoosier Mural Collection, Indiana University

Civil-War Scenes and Post-Civil-War Expansion

PAINTING BY THOMAS HART BENTON

An Urban Scene in 1870

The Bettmann Archive

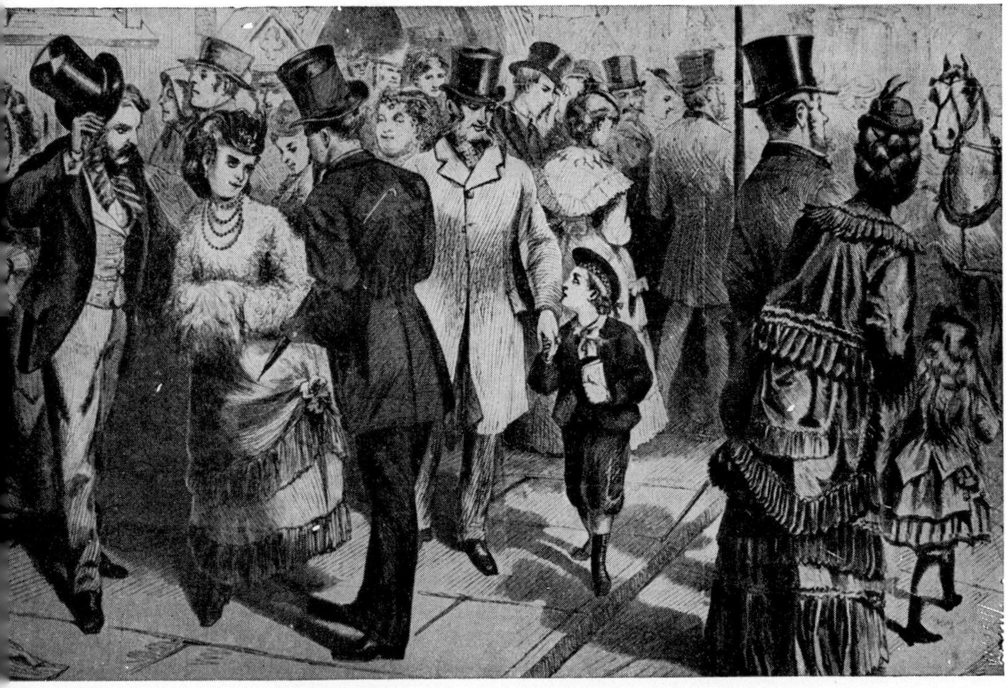

held agrarian attitudes toward finance and tariffs. If they were permitted to resume their old place, might not all the recent gains for
business be endangered? And what effect might Southern resurgence
have on the future of the Republican party, which, just now, was
assuming that it alone had saved the Union and now alone stood for
loyalty? And to make matters even more complicated, the appeal to
old war hatred and patriotism could still be made to serve selfish ends.

The point about which all these tangled forces and purposes now
revolved was the reconstruction of the South. Because victory in the
war had been a victory for certain new forces and values, and because
all issues were now closely interwoven, what was done to the South,
and how it was done, would shape and fix the future of the whole
nation. What was gained would be national gain. Where the South
suffered, the Constitution, democracy itself, and the agricultural interests everywhere would suffer. What men did not always understand
was that in reconstructing the South, they were unconsciously remaking
the nation for the modern age.

The Civil War left the South in physical, economic, and social ruin.
Her lands, always subject to heavy depletion from erosion and harmful
organisms, had "tumbled down" badly under neglect and abuse. The
armies of both North and South had tramped and fought over large
areas and had often wrought complete destruction. Sheridan and
Hunter had left their mark on the Valley of Virginia. A farmer from
that region described the country from Harpers Ferry to New Market
as "almost a desert." "We had no cattle, hogs, sheep, or horses or anything else," he wrote. "The fences were all gone. Some of the orchards
were very much injured, but the fruit trees had not been destroyed.
The barns were all burned; chimneys standing without houses, and
houses standing without roof, or door, or window." A traveler in
Tennessee told of "burnt-up [cotton] gin-houses, ruined bridges, mills,
and factories," lands stripped of fencing, roads in disorder and, in
places, impassable. Where Sherman's army had gone, there was even
greater ruin. A hardened newspaper correspondent for the *New York
Herald*, who witnessed the destruction, spoke of "scenes that would
have driven Alaric the Goth into frenzied ecstasies." He told of
"planter's houses . . . overrun in a jiffy; boxes, drawers, and escritoirs
. . . ransacked, . . . sorghum barrels . . . knocked open, bee-hives
rifled, . . . hogs . . . bayonetted, . . . chickens, geese, and turkeys . . .
knocked over, . . . mules and horses . . . fished out of the swamps,
. . . cows and calves . . . driven along, . . . furniture . . . smashed in

pieces, . . . music . . . pounded out of four-hundred-dollar pianos with the ends of muskets," mirrors, cushions, and carpets carried off, and, when all was "cleared out," the house burned down. "This is the way," he concludes, "Sherman's army lived on the country."

The cities especially had suffered. In Richmond, "as far as eye could reach, the business portion of the city lay in ruins. Beds of cinders, cellars half filled with bricks and rubbish, broken and blackened walls, impassable streets deluged with *debris*." Atlanta and Columbia had been burned. An eyewitness to the burning of Atlanta told how "the sun looked, through the hazy cloud [of black smoke], like a blood-red ball of fire; and the air, for miles around, felt oppressive and intolerable." "The Tyre of the South," the same eyewitness added, "the 'Gate City,' was a thing of the past." Charleston had been burned twice; the business section of Mobile had been torn out by an explosion; half the stores in New Orleans had been locked and their owners driven into exile.

The supply of livestock was badly depleted. It was estimated that from one third to one half of all the horses, mules, cattle, and hogs were gone. In places, if the plow was to be used, men and women would have to drag it through the ground. In other places oxen came back into general use.

Southern railroads had suffered heavily. Except those captured and repaired for the use of Federal troops, all were "in a state of physical dilapidation little removed from destruction." Stations were gone; the rolling stock had been captured and carried away or destroyed; the rails had been torn up, then heated and twisted into useless shapes. The companies were bankrupt.

Capital for recovery was, of course, entirely lacking. Confederate stocks, bonds, and currency were worthless paper souvenirs. Banks had failed early in the war. Insurance companies had collapsed before its end. To make matters worse, the efforts of the United States Treasury Department to seize all property on which the Confederate government once had a claim led to a wide confiscation of cotton stores, regardless of their ownership. Agents made huge fortunes by fraudulent seizures and rendered all legitimate trade, in the one asset that the South possessed, absolutely impossible. The breakdown of government, as the Confederacy ended, completed the picture. Outlaws, pretended Treasury agents, horse thieves, cattle thieves, and deserters took over in many localities to render property insecure and recovery more difficult.

The labor situation was equally bad. The war had cost the South about half its white military population; it had freed all the slaves, who had constituted the majority of workers in the homes and on the plantations. The problem was, therefore, largely one of working out a new system satisfactory to the Negro as a freedman. The absence of capital and the persistence of old racial attitudes made that extremely difficult.

Slavery had been a poor school in which to learn self-reliance and self-care. Many Negroes had early "deserted" to follow the Union army and were now in camps, in the towns, in colonies set up on seized lands, or in the Union army itself. With the coming of peace, others joined in migrations that had no particular destinations. Freedom often meant only the right to wander, to change one's name, or to secure a new wife. It certainly meant less work under supervision and more regular pay for whatever was done. Many, of course, remained where they were, too bewildered to do anything else. The old and the weak always stayed behind.

Health and manners and morals all suffered heavily in the first years. Thousands, especially children, died of disease and starvation. Theft became general. Ex-slaves stole from their former masters and called it "spilin de gypshuns" (despoiling the Egyptians). Many who received a little money spent it for "finery" or were swindled out of it by the ever present rascal. Politeness was rejected as a mark of servitude, and abandoned. Charmed by the promise of "forty acres and a mule," many refused to accept their former masters' offers of their old places on the plantations, and not a few left the older regions on promises of better opportunities in the Southwest.

Nor had slavery been a good training school for the master, who now had to deal with freedmen. Too often he showed his belief in the inferiority of the Negro, and too often he expected to go on with old ways, with the exception of payment for labor. He wanted to re-establish the gang system. He wanted the Negro to live in "the quarters." He expected to employ an overseer and to ride about on his horse to supervise procedures. He wanted to retain control over the Negro when out of the fields and to fix wages and hours as he thought necessary.

He might have had his way if there had been no Freedmen's Bureau and no army of occupation. They represented an outside element and one that held Northern opinions about slavery and Negroes and Southerners. The Freedmen's Bureau had been created by an act of March 3, 1865, for the purpose of caring for refugees, freedmen, and abandoned lands. It was to advise the Negro and protect him in the labor contracts that he signed. It set up Negro schools, organized a Negro bank, and, in general, worked with the army in the attempt to smooth the path from slavery to freedom. It unquestionably did much good; it unquestionably, at times, by its lack of understanding and its overzeal, did much harm. At any rate, it was there, and the economic fate of the section had to be worked out with the Bureau as the third factor in the situation.

POLITICAL RECONSTRUCTION UNDER LINCOLN AND JOHNSON

How economic affairs would develop, however, would depend on how the South was reconstructed politically. That would determine everything. Until order and security were established, little could be accomplished. Yet agreement on political matters was hard to secure. What was the relation of the Southern states to the Union now? Were they conquered territory, to be disposed of in any way the victors chose? Had they ever been legally out of the Union? Were the states, or just the citizens of the states, out of their proper relationship to the Union? And who was to decide these things, and who was to do the work of restoration to normal conditions? The people of the states? The President? Congress? The answers would come only through blood and sweat and tears.

Lincoln had early given his answer. He dismissed the question as to whether the seceded states were out of the Union as "a pernicious abstraction . . . good for nothing at all." "We all agree," he said, "that the . . . States . . . are out of their practical relation with the Union, and that the sole object of the government . . . is to again get them into that proper political relation." He proposed, therefore, that when in any state one tenth of the number of persons who had voted in 1860 should form a loyal government and ratify the Thirteenth Amendment, that state should be restored to its old place in the Union. He would leave internal affairs largely to such governments, suggesting, however, in one case, that the state itself grant the vote to educated Negroes.

Senators like Sumner, Chandler, and Wade had opposed this procedure when applied to Louisiana, and in the so-called Wade-Davis Bill (1864) had offered a different policy and implied that Congress, not the President, was to take the initiative. Lincoln's death by an assassin's bullet prevented an open clash and left the next steps to his successor, Andrew Johnson.

Those who opposed Lincoln welcomed the change. George W. Julian wrote, on the day of Lincoln's death:

> I spent most of the afternoon in a political caucus, held for the purpose of considering the necessity for a new cabinet and a line of policy less conciliatory than that of Mr. Lincoln: and while everybody was shocked at his murder, the feeling was nearly universal that the succession of Johnson to the Presidency would prove a godsend to the country. Aside from Mr. Lincoln's known policy of tenderness to the Rebels . . . his . . . views of the subject of reconstruction were as distasteful as possible to radical Republicans.

Andrew Johnson, on whom the hard task of leadership now fell, was a man of positive quality. Like eastern Tennessee, which molded him, he was rough and rugged, honest, blunt, and stubborn. He was a self-made man with intense love for, and confidence in, the institutions that had permitted him to rise from obscurity to national prominence. He was polished in manners, neat in dress (as a tailor should be), and possessed of that self-assurance and determination which is learned only in "the school of hard knocks."

As a child in North Carolina, he had been apprenticed to learn his trade, had run away from his employer, and had "struck out" for the Tennessee frontier. There, in the little town of Greenville, he had "set up shop," married the woman who taught him to read and write, and broadened his world by having the newspapers read to him as he sat, cross-legged, plying his needle. He entered politics early and began a career that led from alderman in Greenville to the state legislature, to Congress, to the governorship of Tennessee, and then to the Vice-Presidency of the United States. He was both a democrat and a Democrat. His ideal was Andrew Jackson, who had fought the fight for common men. He loved the Constitution as few men in the history of America have loved it.

Johnson's early talk had pleased the radicals. The responsibilities of office, however, sobered him, and in a short time he was moving along lines very similar to those that Lincoln had pursued. He added the demands that the Southern states should repeal secession and repudiate Confederate debts; he excluded from amnesty diplomats, army officers above the rank of colonel, governors, and holders of taxable property worth over twenty thousand dollars, but permitted the people to go on organizing their own governments.

Johnson's plans soon brought trouble. Old Confederate leaders were chosen to high offices, and the Southern legislatures, faced with the dual problem of labor and race, began passing Black Codes. These were not new. In ante bellum days slavery had solved this problem, in the main. But, because some masters had been too lenient in their controls and allowed their slaves to wander about, assemble as they pleased, buy and sell produce, etc., it had become necessary for society to act. Abolition activities had added further pressure. The result was that every Southern state, before the Civil War, had had its Black Codes, which restricted and controlled the Negro. Their repassage at this time, therefore, did not mean an effort to restore slavery. It did mean a return to old methods of solving old problems at a time when new methods were imperative, since slavery had been destroyed.

The Codes varied from state to state, but generally limited the Negro to agriculture or domestic work, restricted his possession of firearms, limited his testimony in courts to cases involving his own race, provided for discipline in cases where labor contracts were violated, and allowed corporal punishment for vagrancy. They contained also some guarantees for the Negro, but generally accepted the idea of his inferiority.

To Northern radicals all this seemed like open defiance—perhaps even an effort to restore slavery. They held meetings, protested, railed at the arrogance of the South. Said the *Chicago Tribune*, "Men of the North will convert Mississippi into a frog-pond before allowing these codes to disgrace one foot of soil in which the bones of our soldiers sleep." At Dartmouth College the Phi Beta Kappa speaker asked, "Shall the horrors of Salisbury and Andersonville prisons, the murdering of innocent prisoners be forgotten and forgiven to unrelenting or lip-serving, lying rebels, whose oath is as nought under compulsion?" Evidently men who had failed to understand each other to the point of civil war were still failing to understand.

It is, therefore, not surprising that the favorable reports now brought back from the South by agents officially sent there to investigate were largely ignored and that the more biased and critical reports were accepted. Men were willing to believe, with Carl Schurz, that Southerners lacked a "hearty attachment to the great republic," that they were not in "communion with the progressive ideas of the times," and that they were possessed of a "self-admiration" that resented criticism.

By the time Congress met, in December, 1865, distrust of the South and resentment against the Lincoln-Johnson reconstruction program had driven radical leaders into open revolt. The clerk of the House did not include the names of the newly chosen Southern Representatives in the roll call, and a Joint Committee of Congress on Reconstruction was quickly formed. Under the leadership of Thaddeus Stevens in the House and Charles Sumner in the Senate, an aggressive drive was launched to destroy confidence in the President and to place the whole reconstruction program in the hands of Congress. The motives behind this were, as we have seen, highly complex. It is quite clear that Congress was jealous of the executive power and eager to reassert itself. Wade had written Sumner that "if something isn't done the people will crown Johnson king before Congress meets. So much success will reconcile the people to anything." Fear that the Republican party would be upset was as clearly expressed. "To admit the [Southern] states on Mr. Johnson's plan," wrote Benjamin Wade, "is voluntarily ... to surrender our political rights into the hands and keeping of those traitors we have just conquered. . . . It is nothing less than political suicide." And to increase Democratic-party strength was a serious matter to men who believed, as Henry Wilson said, that the Republican party contained "more of moral and intellectual worth than was ever embodied in any political organization in any land . . . created by no man . . . but brought into being by Almighty God himself," and who also believed, with Oliver Morton, that "the Democratic party may be described as a common sewer and loathsome receptacle," containing "every unregenerate rebel, . . . every sneak who ran away from the draft, . . . every man who murdered Union prisoners," every man who "invented dangerous compounds to burn steamboats" and to introduce yellow fever into Northern cities, "every dishonest paymaster," and every "officer in the army who was dismissed for cowardice." To increase Democratic-party strength would also endanger both the tariff and the financial policies which were proving so beneficial to the business interests now forming solidly behind the Republican party.

Andrew Johnson understood all this. He was thoroughly convinced of the constitutional soundness of his program and as stubbornly determined to carry it forward as the radical Republicans were to check it. He was not the kind of man to yield ground or to surrender the right as he understood it. To him the issue was simply one of whether the Southern states should be restored under the Constitution and the Union remain what it had been, or whether both the Constitution and the past should give way to new and arbitrary procedures.

CONGRESS AND RECONSTRUCTION

The fight which the grim and determined Thaddeus Stevens and the dapper Charles Sumner now launched against the equally stubborn Andrew Johnson was, therefore, to be a fight to the bitter end. A sense of righteousness, on both sides, made compromise impossible. A vindictive spirit, on both sides, robbed the contest of sportsmanship. It opened, early in 1866, when Congress passed a bill extending the time of the Freedmen's Bureau and Johnson vetoed it. Then a Civil Rights Bill, intended to push forward Negro suffrage, met a like fate, but the effort to secure the two-thirds vote necessary to pass it over the President's veto was successful. Then came the Fourteenth Amendment, which, if adopted, would practically make the Congressional reconstruction program a part of the Constitution. In addition to its provisions on citizenship and on state limitations, already discussed, it reduced the representation in Congress of any state which denied the vote to any of its citizens, barred Confederates from office unless restored by a two-thirds vote of Congress, and repudiated all Confederate debts. To this Johnson was also opposed, and the whole issue was thereby thrown into the Congressional election of 1866.

This was indeed the "critical year," for victory or defeat in this election would determine the relative strength of the radical Congressional group and the President. Unfortunately there had been a strong drift back into old party lines; and though a Union convention of Johnson's supporters was held, it did not create a new party for the new issues. That gave the Republicans a decided advantage. Then three unfortunate events occurred. In April a race riot broke out in Memphis, Tennessee, in which some forty Negroes were killed and many Negro churches and schools were burned. Then, in July, an even more serious race riot occurred in New Orleans. Again the Negroes suffered heavily. Although the blame for trouble in each case must, by the careful scholar, be rather widely distributed and in large part ascribed to the unsettled state of local affairs, yet, coming at this particular time, these riots enabled radical Republicans to place the blame entirely on Johnson's reconstruction methods and the Southern arrogance which these methods were supposed to create. The third event was Johnson's trip to Chicago to speak at the dedication of the Stephen A. Douglas monument. A rather large party accompanied the President, and stops and speeches were made at the principal cities en route. Opponents seized the opportunity to hiss and heckle Johnson, and he, in turn, retorted in kind. The effect, especially as reported in Republican newspapers, was decidedly bad. It caused the real issues to be forgotten and centered attention largely on personalities. It permitted appeal to party prejudices and to the emotions left by the war. It unquestionably played a part in the election of enough radicals to Congress to give Johnson's opponents a clear two-thirds majority. They could now "reconstruct" as they pleased.

Accepting the election as a clear-cut referendum on the differences between Congress and the President, the radicals inaugurated an entirely new program. The voting public had probably never intended to go much beyond approval of the Fourteenth Amendment. Yet, in March, 1867, existing governments were repudiated, and the South was divided into five military districts, to be occupied and ruled by military authority. Under military supervision voters were to be registered, conventions held, and loyal governments eventually set up. Disabilities of Confederates were to be strictly enforced, and Negroes were to vote on the same basis as whites. The South was back where the war had left it. Peace *with victory* was to have a trial.

The radicals in Washington now set about plotting the ruin of Andrew Johnson. To ensure effective action, the Congressional vacation was abandoned, and the new Congress, instead of first meeting in December, was scheduled to open in March, immediately following the adjournment of its predecessor. Then a Tenure of Office Act followed, making it a misdemeanor, punishable by fine and imprisonment, for the President to remove civil officeholders without the consent of the Senate. This was followed by an act forbidding the President, who, by the Constitution, is commander in chief of the army, to issue military orders except through the General of the Army. The purpose of each act was perfectly clear. In the first case Congress intended to keep matters constantly in its own hands; in the second the removal of radicals from office was to be prevented; and in the third it was hoped that General Grant would yield to the wishes of Congress and go against the President. The radicals hoped that, somewhere along the line, Johnson, by opposing such questionable acts, would provide an excuse for impeachment.

The President, however, carefully avoided the trap set, and faithfully enforced the measures passed over his vetoes. Not until he attempted to remove Edwin M. Stanton, who, as Secretary of War, had constantly betrayed the administration and had worked hand in glove with his opponents, could the latter find any excuse for action. The

President had asked for Stanton's resignation and had named General Grant as his ad interim successor. When the Senate refused to confirm these actions, Grant, in direct violation of promises made to the President, turned the office back to Stanton. This evidence of duplicity turned the ever popular Grant into an open enemy, but did nothing to get rid of Stanton, who, behind the Tenure of Office Act, held tenaciously to the war office.

With Stevens leading, the House of Representatives now brought impeachment charges to the Senate. These ranged from Johnson's harsh words against Congress to his defiance of the Tenure of Office Act. The trial began in March (1868), with Chief Justice Chase presiding. Chase's firm insistence that proceedings should be strictly judicial in character prevented the trial from degenerating into frank political persecution. Johnson's lawyers accepted their task as a defense of our constitutional form of government and insisted on the actual facts in the case and not the irritations involved. Intelligent partisans soon began to understand the seriousness of what was taking place and to realize that Johnson's "political" offenses did not constitute "high crimes and misdemeanors." When the vote was taken, seven Republicans voted with twelve Democrats for acquittal. Thus by a single vote the President retained his office. The damage done to the executive department of government, however, was serious. Congress had browbeaten the President. He had suffered indignities. His standing and that of his office had definitely been weakened in the eyes of the people.

THE SOUTH UNDER CONGRESSIONAL RECONSTRUCTION

While these events were taking place in Washington, the South was experiencing military rule. Under it, conditions varied from state to state. Some army officers acted like dictators and removed officials at will; some respected public opinion and needs. All began the work of registering voters, with strict regard to securing the kind of conventions desired. In South Carolina 46,882 whites and 80,550 Negroes were registered; in Alabama 61,295 whites and 104,518 Negroes; in Florida, Mississippi, and Louisiana the Negroes outnumbered the whites and in Georgia equaled them. The army and the Freedmen's Bureau were, of course, active in securing these results. They were now assisted by a new organization, the Union League, a group formed to further Republican-party interests in the South. It took the form of lodges with a ritual. nocturnal meetings, emblems, etc., which caught the fancy of the Negro and rendered him a political tool in the hands of radical leaders.

The conventions chosen by the registered electorate contained large blocs of Negroes, a considerable number of Northern whites, whom the old ruling element called "carpetbaggers," and a smaller group of Southern whites (men from the little people), who were called "scalawags." In South Carolina, to take an extreme case, sixty-six of the one hundred and twenty-four delegates were Negroes, forty-seven were Southern whites (scalawags), and eleven were from the North. Yet of the Southern whites only twenty-three were from South Carolina, and the whole group together paid only $761.21 in taxes. Of this amount one man paid all but $252.76. The comment of the *New York Times* was that "there is scarcely a Southern white man in the body whose character would keep him out of the penitentiary." In North Carolina, to take an extreme in the other direction, there were only fifteen Negroes and eighteen "carpetbaggers" out of one hundred and seven Republicans and thirteen conservatives.

The other conventions ranged between these extremes, but all of them showed a strong Negro element, which often worked closely with the native whites for the establishment of a better deal than either had known in ante bellum days. Alignment was not just whites against blacks, but more often class against class for social-economic advantage.

The constitutions framed by these conventions were, on the whole and from an abstract point of view, fairly good. The franchise was broadened where necessary, public-school systems were extended, reforms in local government, finances, and judicial procedure were instituted, and, in some cases, the rights of women were enlarged and better defined. In all of them the equality of the races was established. Yet with all their advances, one thing was lacking: the approval of the group that had once ruled the South. The members of this group were the traditional leaders of the section, and until they could have at least a share in government, all would not be right. Ratification was, therefore, defeated in Mississippi and in Alabama by its failure to secure a majority of the registered votes. The Negroes and their white friends secured majorities elsewhere, but left great groups of important persons eager to overthrow the new governments at the first opportunity.

In this way, between June, 1868, and July, 1870, governments in the control of those whom the radicals favored were set up in each of the Southern states and their representatives admitted to Congress. The Fifteenth Amendment, forbidding the denial or abridgment of the rights

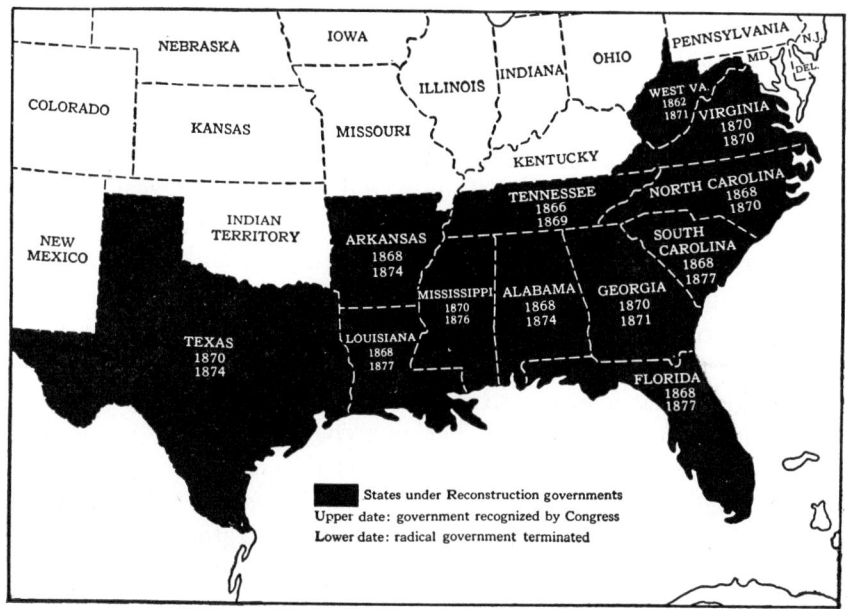

The Readmission of the Confederate States

of citizens on account of race, color, or previous condition of servitude, was, in the meantime, added to the reconstruction program as a further restriction under which the Southern states were to live until Rutherford B. Hayes removed the United States troops from the section in 1877. The period was characterized by strife between local groups, extravagance, and corruption. Of the fourteen United States Senators from the South in these years, ten were Northerners. Twenty of the thirty-five Representatives were from the North, as were seven of the governors. A few Negroes went to Congress, and many more served, often with ability, in the state legislatures. Debts mounted. In the eleven Southern states, already bankrupt, the increase was more than $131,717,000. Land steals, fraudulent railway grants, and extravagant purchases were the rule. In South Carolina the statehouse was refurnished. Four-dollar mirrors were replaced by French imports costing $650; chairs were purchased at $60 apiece; 40-cent spittoons were replaced by $60 cuspidors; $600 was paid for a clock. Legislative supplies included champagne, Westphalian hams, imported mushrooms, feather beds, suspenders, ladies' hoods, bonnets, chemises, corsets, gold watches, garters, perfumes, and one metal coffin.

Much, however, was spent on railroads, and Southern businessmen, as well as outsiders, were willing to mix politics and business where gains were possible. This was especially true in Georgia and Alabama. Here charters were flung about recklessly, and huge sums of money were granted for a limited mileage. Men like John B. Gordon, James W. Sloss, Henry Clews, Joseph Brown, and Albert Fink revealed themselves as worthy members of that band of unscrupulous railroad-promoters who were making history in the North and West.

In the agricultural realm changes were equally great. Planters who attempted to return to the old system soon discovered that they were attempting the impossible. As the *Southern Cultivator* said, in 1867: "It is evident that a new system of farming (not planting) must be inaugurated in the South. . . . The first change that must occur, and which will eventually prove beneficial, is the subdivision of landed estates." Gang labor, living in "quarters" and working under an overseer, was too much like the old days to suit the Negro. He wanted to rent land and live on it. Scarcity of labor permitted him to have his way. Here and there planters sold off their stock, cut their lands into farms, and contracted for rent in cash or kind. They usually furnished the seed, the mules, the plows, the hoes, etc., and secured credit from the village stores that began to spring up all around. Thus "crop-sharing" and soon the "lien system," by which the merchant secured himself against losses by a lien on the crops, appeared. Then a second step was taken when the Negro borrowed directly from the merchant and thus became a tenant in the purest sense. The owners often retired to the rising country towns to turn merchant, banker, gin-owner, or mule dealer. Soon industry, particularly the cotton factory, gave opportunity for investment or management. A few Negroes, in the meantime, bought their farms, and, either as owners or sharecroppers, they tended to live in small homes on individual farms and to direct their own efforts.

Some planters refused to accept these changes. A few left the country and went to South America. Others tried to import foreign laborers or to dispense with labor by the wider use of machinery. The majority, however, yielded to necessity, gave the Negro his way, and let the "agrarian revolution" take its course.

THE SUPREME COURT IN RECONSTRUCTION

All through the period an effort was made to escape the ills of re-construction by an appeal to the Supreme Court on the constitutionality of the whole program. There was much in it that might be questioned. In the case of the Fourteenth Amendment, for instance, the Southern states, while being held out of the Union, were forced to ratify the amendment as a condition for admission. They were forced also to incorporate Negro suffrage into their constitutions before being ad-mitted. In other words, the effects of the amendment were applied as a qualification for being made a state with the right to ratify! Further-more, the Court had, in the ex parte Milligan case (1866), held that "martial rule can never exist where the courts are open, and in the proper and unobstructed exercise of their jurisdiction." This seemed to offer hope that arbitrary measures might be avoided legally.

Yet when the trials of those supposedly involved in Lincoln's assas-sination, and the trial of Henry Wirz, Confederate head of Anderson-ville Prison, were held before strictly military commissions, the Court said nothing. The protests and threats that had met its Milligan deci-sion and the treatment that Andrew Johnson was receiving kept it quiet. The very suggestion that test cases might be brought before the Court caused men like Wendell Phillips and John A. Bingham to talk of abolishing the Court. Others suggested "packing" the Court, or reducing it to three members, or taking from it jurisdiction in any case involving the South. On July 23, 1866, in order to prevent Johnson from appointing Court members, a law was passed providing that vacancies among associate justices could not be filled until the number of such justices was reduced to six. In 1868 a bill which required the agreement of two thirds of the justices for any decision passed the House, but failed in the Senate. Then, on March 27, 1868, jurisdiction was taken from the Court in appeals from lower Federal courts in cases where the right of habeas corpus was involved. This was to check the case of one McCardle, a Mississippi editor, on trial for criticizing the radical program, who had been denied a writ of habeas corpus. The Federal court in Mississippi had upheld the military officer involved, and an appeal to the Supreme Court was already pending. The Supreme Court bowed to Congress, as it did in all other cases of a like kind that were brought forward.

Thus the third unit in the American system of government was cowed into impotency. Congress was supreme. In reconstructing the

South, it had done much to the national life as a whole. And that is the thing which stands out so clearly in a long-time view of reconstruction. What was happening in the South was only one phase of what was happening everywhere else. If, in reconstruction, there were evasion of law and something of wholesale corruption, that was only the Southern side of the worst corruption and disregard for law that the nation had ever known. The Tweed Ring, the Crédit Mobilier scandal, and the "salary grab" were just another part of the same story. If the Northern army ruled the South, the returned soldiers, through the Grand Army of the Republic, were soon dominating Northern politics and offices and drawing heavily on the Treasury for pensions. If the South lost self-government, so did many a Northern city and state through corrupt rings and powerful economic interests. The "solid South," always voting the Democratic ticket, was nearly matched by great blocs of Northern states that always went Republican. The destruction of the Southern planter weakened the Northern farmer as a political force and left him, as Granger and Populist, to grumble and complain and revolt throughout the remainder of the century.

Nor was this all, for the general level of American culture lost something when the values which Southern gentlemen had fostered were discredited and the newer ones of business were enthroned. The name *Gilded Age* has been used to suggest the cheap, surface quality of taste, and the worship of wealth that went with it. The beauty and dignity that distinguished the homes of early New England, the Dutch houses of the Hudson valley, the classical homes of the Southern plantations, were now superseded by styles that seemingly had only one purpose— to advertise the possession of wealth. Bay windows, useless gables, mansard roofs, and "gingerbread" woodwork were "stuck on" at every opportunity; diverse types of architecture were combined in a single building; size, not good proportions, was the thing desired.

Taste in literature was equally bad. A few writers from the romantic age of Emerson, Melville, and Whitman lingered on for a time as a sort of afterglow of a brighter age. Sidney Lanier and Bayard Taylor both kept something of the worship of beauty in their verses, but were so clearly out of step with the day that neither spoke with much assurance. A few writers caught the local color of unique corners in the nation and produced sketches of enduring value. Bret Harte did it for the mining world; George Cable, Irwin Russell, Mary Murfree, and Joel Chandler Harris did it for different parts and different groups of the South; Sarah Orne Jewett and Mary Wilkins Freeman did it for

New England. The more popular writers, however, were such as E. P. Roe, Lew Wallace, and Mrs. Southworth. Their romances dripped with sentiment and paid lip service to the high morality which was everywhere being so emphatically neglected. There was about their work much of historical glitter, and more of a superficial gesture toward religion. Nowhere was there any appreciation of the problems of the time, nor any effort to come to grips with the shallow character of the age. That had to await the stinging pens of Mark Twain and William Dean Howells, who were already breaking with their day and moving forward toward a new realism.

The reconstruction era thus belonged to the "doers" and not to the thinkers and those with gentle tastes. There was something magnificent about the ruthlessness, the waste, the daring, of the men who were on the stage. Their life was poor in culture, but rich in energy. The era had little notion of where it was going, but its head was up, and its self-confidence was somewhat terrifying. The men who dealt with the South were no different from those who were dealing with the Indians and the buffaloes on the plains, or from those who, like Jim Fisk and Jay Gould, were busy with railroads. It was fortunate for the South that Huntington, Stanford, Hopkins, and Crocker operated in California. It was not good to be numbered among the weak of any sort in such an age.

SELECTED BIBLIOGRAPHY

Howard K. Beale, *The Critical Year*, a valuable study of the national implications of reconstruction; George Fort Milton, *The Age of Hate*; Allan Nevins, *The Emergence of Modern America*; Claude G. Bowers, *The Tragic Era*; R. B. Brooks, *The Agrarian Revolution in Georgia*, present various impressions of the significant changes transforming American life.

J. G. Randall, *The Civil War and Reconstruction*; W. A. Dunning, *Essays on the Civil War and Reconstruction*; H. C. Warmoth, *War Politics and Reconstruction*, important books. Reconstruction in the various states is presented in J. H. Garner, *Reconstruction in Mississippi*; J. G. de R. Hamilton, *Reconstruction in North Carolina*; H. J. Eckenrode, *The Political History of Virginia during the Reconstruction*; W. L. Fleming, *Civil War and Reconstruction in Alabama*; F. B. Simpkins and R. H. Woody, *South Carolina during Reconstruction*; J. W. Patton, *Unionism and Reconstruction in Tennessee*; W. M. Caskey, *Secession and Restoration of Louisiana*; J. R. Ficklin, *History of Reconstruction in Louisiana*; Ella Lonn, *Reconstruction in Louisiana after 1868*; C. W. Ramsdell, *Reconstruction in Texas*; T. S. Staples, *Reconstruction in Arkansas, 1862–1874*; C. M. Thompson, *Reconstruction in Georgia*; E. M. Coulter, *The Civil War and Readjustment in Kentucky*; W. W. Davis, *Civil War and Reconstruction in Florida*.

The problem of the adjustment of the freedmen to competitive society is presented in W. E. B. Du Bois, *Black Reconstruction*; S. Pierce, *The Freedman's Bureau*; A. A. Taylor, *The Negro in South Carolina during Reconstruction*; A. A. Taylor, *The Negro in the Reconstruction of Virginia.* James Pike, *The Prostrate State: South Carolina under Negro Government*; J. T. Trowbridge, *The South*; Sidney Andrews, *The South since the War*, offer contemporary pictures of reconstruction.

Paul H. Buck, *The Road to Reunion*, a significant study of the reuniting of the sections; R. W. Winston, *Andrew Johnson, Plebeian and Patriot*, and D. M. DeWitt, *Impeachment and Trial of Andrew Johnson*, important for new light on President Johnson.

W. L. Fleming, *Documentary History of Reconstruction* (2 vols.), and H. S. Commager (Ed.), *Documents of American History*, pp. 1–54, 59–63, 84–91, contain source material.

XX

Urban-Industrial America

THE RAPID development of industrial America in the last four decades of the nineteenth century marked the replacement of the small-town, friendly world that had characterized the nation before the Civil War by a society in which life was conducted on an impersonal basis. The Machine Age meant the subordination of the craftsman to the unskilled job of the assembly line, and the substitution of the corporation as the employer for the old-time boss, who had known his workers in an intimate and friendly way. With the growth of industry came vast, sprawling, dirty cities like Chicago, whose population jumped from one hundred thousand in 1860 to three hundred thousand in 1870. Scattered around the industrial plants were the slum tenements of the workers, who poured in from Europe to build industrial America. The new industries meant a wide variety of goods for the material betterment of the American people, but in addition the industrial age meant that the United States one day would have serious labor conflicts and deplorable living conditions for many of its people, and, as a result of its industrial power, would be cast into the crosscurrents of world politics.

The Republican party's policy of subsidizing industry with a protective tariff, a favorable banking system, and a contract labor law was an important aspect of the growth of American industry, but undoubtedly industrial growth would have been inevitable without these political supports. The United States was richly endowed with coal, iron, and oil—the sinews of the new age. The first commercial oil well was drilled in Pennsylvania in 1859, and the rich deposits of oil that were found in all parts of the country gave the United States a great advantage over other nations in both war and peace. The country had also extremely rich deposits of coal, located in regions from which the coal could readily be transported to the industrial cities. Also, there was an abundance of iron ore, which was soon to make the United States the world's leading producer of iron and steel. By 1870, as a result of the Kelly-Bessemer process, the Age of Steel had arrived as the basis of both modern industry and modern transportation. Another

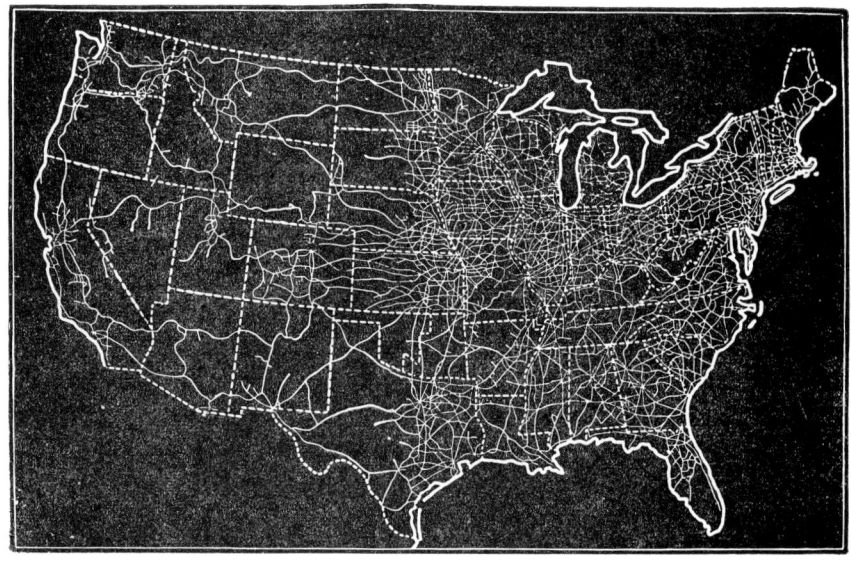

The Railroads in 1900

natural resource that served as a sinew of America's industrial age was the highly productive wheat, corn, and grazing lands of the trans-Mississippi and trans-Missouri West. From these areas flowed a torrent of produce to feed the industrial workers.

Technological improvements were another factor in the expanding industrial age. The development of the rotary drill, for instance, after 1900, made possible a faster rate of boring new oil wells; and constantly improved refining processes produced a gasoline of much higher power. The introduction of electricity into homes and factories and its application to transportation increased the comfort and efficiency of life and brought new inventions in its wake. The improvements in steel-manufacturing quickly led to widespread demands for steel for factories, bridges, skyscrapers, and automobiles. As invention after invention transformed American industry, the techniques of mass production and interchangeable parts were developed. This was to characterize many industries, but was to be most highly developed in the automotive field.

Rapidly expanding railroad mileage was still another factor in the growth of industrial America. Whereas total mileage in 1850 had been only nine thousand and twenty-one, it had jumped to approximately two hundred thousand by 1900. By this time great trunk lines, with heavy steel rails, standardized gauge, and Pullman sleepers and dining-cars, spanned the continent. The growth of railroads ended the isolation of various regions of the country and made it possible for goods manufactured in large cities to be distributed to a national market. Soon in small-town America the local craftsman was to find it extremely difficult to compete with cheaper industrial goods made under mass production.

Railroad expansion was accomplished by direct aid from local, state, and Federal governments. In 1850 the Federal government established the principle of subsidizing railroad construction when it gave the Illinois Central a right of way and alternate sections of land along the track. Federal land grants were instrumental in the construction of such transcontinental lines as the Union Pacific and Central Pacific, the Northern Pacific, the Southern Pacific, and the Atchison, Topeka, and Santa Fe. By 1870 the Federal government had given the railroads land equal to the combined areas of New England, New York, and Pennsylvania.

State and county governments, particularly west of the Mississippi, gave lands to the railroads and issued bonds to encourage construction through their areas. Towns vied with neighboring towns to secure the railroad, and this competition naturally increased the subsidies given to the railroads. The state of Texas, for instance, gave the railroads thirty-two million acres of land and for a time granted a subsidy of six hundred dollars in bonds for each mile of railroad construction.

It has been estimated that the combined land and financial grants from all public sources had accounted for three fifths of the cost of railroad construction by 1870. Many of the railroads were unsoundly financed and poorly constructed. In some cases the original owners of a railroad had voted themselves such lucrative contracts for building the road that they left the completed road insolvent. Those people who had mortgaged their property to buy railroad bonds were frequently left with a worthless investment; and when the various state and county railroad and bond issues came due in the depression of the 1870's, the states and counties involved found such great difficulty in meeting payments that some of them repudiated the bonds.

The milking of the railroads by the original owners, the worthless bonds, and high freight and passenger charges provoked the Midwestern farmer into action in the 1870's. Government subsidies were stopped, and some states enacted laws regulating railroad rates. Closely allied with the economic grievances of the farmers was their objection

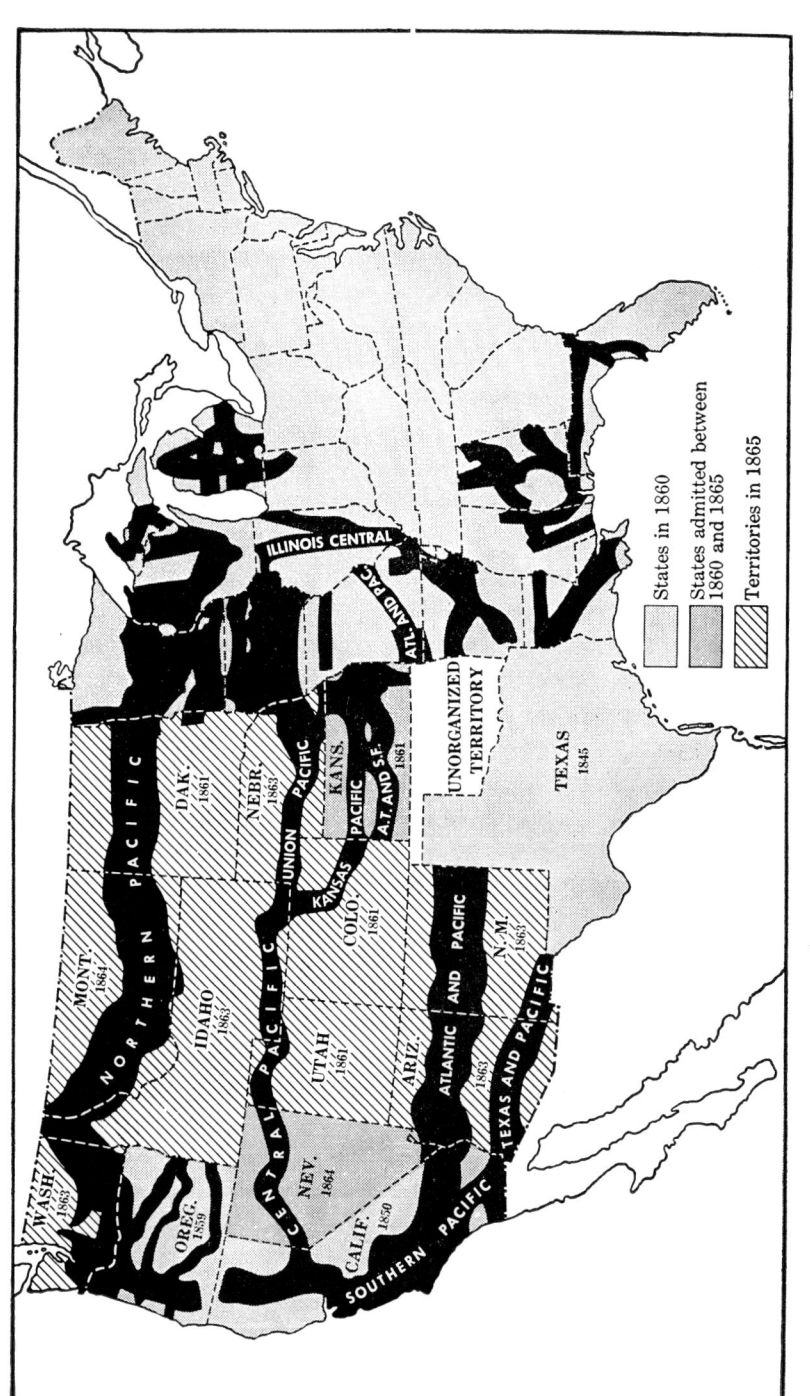

The Federal Railroad Land Grants

States in 1860

States admitted between 1860 and 1865

Territories in 1865

NORTHERN PACIFIC

ILLINOIS CENTRAL

UNION PACIFIC

CENTRAL PACIFIC

KANSAS PACIFIC

A.T. AND S.F.

ATLANTIC AND PACIFIC

SOUTHERN PACIFIC

TEXAS AND PACIFIC

A.T. AND PACIFIC

WASH.
1863

OREG.
1859

CALIF.
1850

NEV.
1864

IDAHO
1863

MONT.
1861

UTAH
1861

ARIZ.

DAK.
1861

NEBR.
1863

COLO.
1861

N.M.
1863

KANS.
1861

UNORGANIZED
TERRITORY

TEXAS
1845

to the power of railroads in politics. Charles Francis Adams, grandson of President John Quincy Adams, remarked, in 1871:

If individuals have, as a rule, quietly pursued their peaceful vocations, the same cannot be said of certain single men at the head of vast combinations of private wealth. This has been particularly the case as regards those controlling the rapidly developed railroad interests. These modern potentates have declared war, negotiated peace, reduced courts, legislatures, and sovereign states to an unqualified obedience to their will.

THE GROWTH OF MONOPOLY

In both railroading and industry, business units grew to mammoth proportions, and many competing companies were consolidated into monopolies. The joint-stock-company device made it possible to raise vast amounts of capital, and corporation lawyers developed techniques to make monopoly possible. The first device was the trust, created by the Standard Oil Company. A number of competing companies were merged by establishing a central board of trustees to which individual stockholders in the various companies surrendered their stock in return for certificates from the trust. The Standard Oil trust was declared illegal in 1892, and its place was quickly taken by the holding-company device. This was a plan which made it possible for corporations—the holding companies—to buy stock in competing corporations and thus control the policies of these corporations. The state of New Jersey, in 1888, made the holding company legal when it passed a law declaring that "any corporation may purchase, hold, sell, assign, transfer, mortgage, pledge, or otherwise dispose of the capital stock of . . . any other corporation . . . [and] may exercise all the rights, powers or privileges of ownership, including the right to vote thereon." The holding company has been the principal way by which monopolistic corporations have flourished, in spite of the Sherman Antitrust Act of 1890.

In addition to holding companies, there have been "gentlemen's agreements" whereby competing corporations have divided the business in a given field or pooled the profits on an agreed basis. During the 1920's trade associations were developed as the most significant technique of monopoly. Encouraged by the government, businessmen organized trade associations in the various fields of economic endeavor to standardize products, conduct research, handle labor relations, serve as a lobby to check governmental regulation, and in many cases to stifle competition. From 1928 to 1937 sixty-five industries were arraigned before the Federal Trade Commission for forming trade associations in unlawful restraint of trade. An example of these associations is the trade association that was formed by the combination of thirty-one corporations in the water-valve and hydrant industries; this association divided the United States into zones and established uniform prices for its products. It was estimated in 1938 that there were about seventy-eight hundred trade associations, two thousand of which were national in scope and nearly six thousand of which were local. The trade associations, as well as holding companies and various pooling agreements, represented a type of economic development far removed from the pre-Civil-War America of craftsmen, shopkeepers, and individual corporations operating under a system of competition and free enterprise. Walter Lippmann once analyzed the attitude of the monopolists correctly when he remarked that "competition is something of which producers have only as much as they cannot eliminate."

During the late nineteenth century the growth of monopolistic power was most impressive in the oil and steel industries. John D. Rockefeller dominated the American oil industry. In 1872, as head of the Standard Oil Company of Ohio, Rockefeller acquired the South Improvement Company and launched a ruthless policy to destroy his competitors. Standard's strength was so great that Rockefeller forced the railroads to pay him not only a rebate on all Standard oil carried by them, but also a rebate on all competitors' oil as well. The protests against the South Improvement Company were so bitter that this company was abandoned, but Rockefeller continued to utilize unfair methods to drive competitors out of business or at least to make them bow to Standard's will. In 1911, when the United States Supreme Court ordered the dissolution of the Standard Oil Company of New Jersey as a monopoly in restraint of trade, Rockefeller controlled roughly 80 per cent of American oil production.

The growth of monopolistic power in steel centered around Andrew Carnegie, who came to the United States as a Scottish immigrant boy. After building his steelworks near Pittsburgh, Carnegie won control of the coke industry through a tie with Henry Clay Frick; he secured long-time leases of valuable ore deposits in the Lake Superior region; and he purchased steamship and railroad lines to ensure a consolidated control from raw material to finished product and the consumer. When Carnegie decided to retire from business, J. P. Morgan and Company, in 1901, organized the United States Steel Corporation as a holding

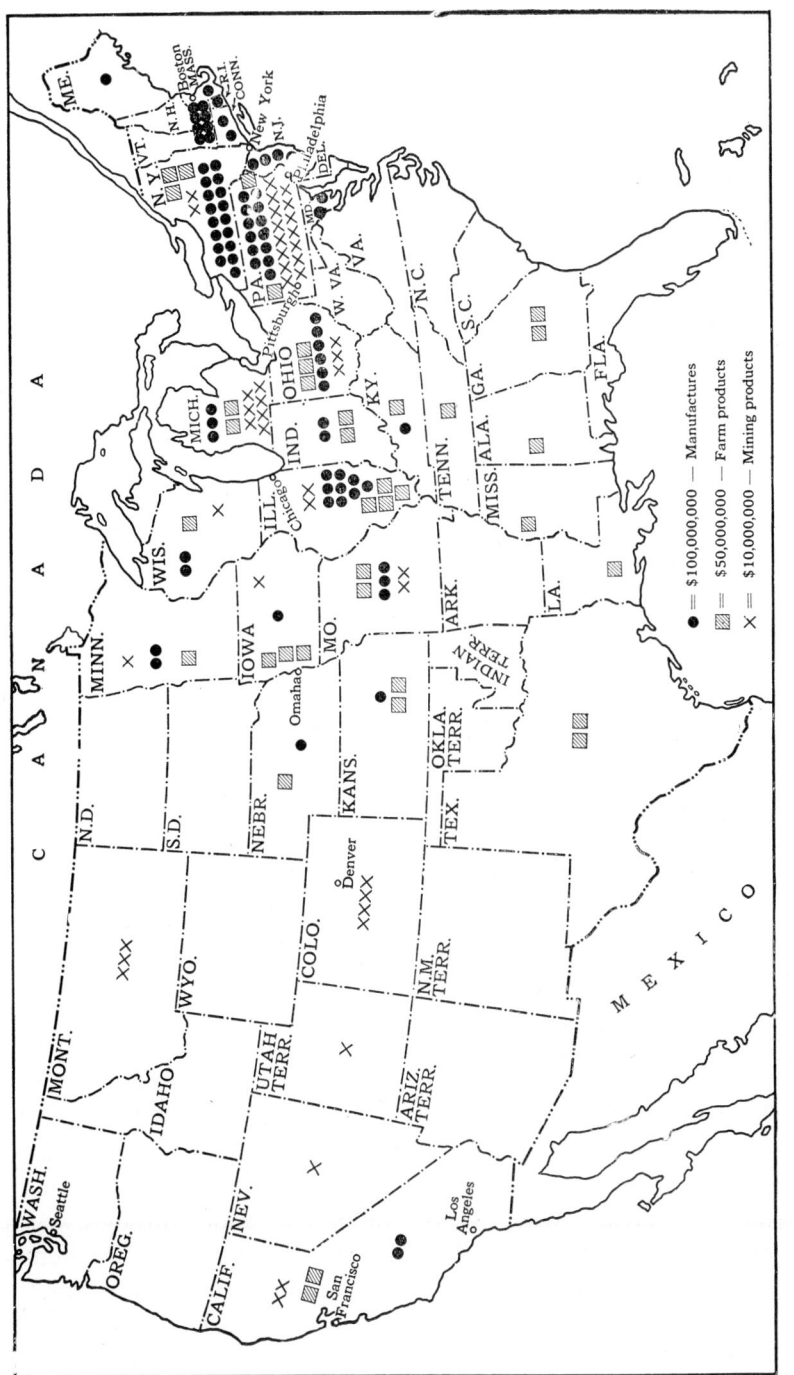

The Industrial United States in 1890

company and consolidated their steel interests with the Carnegie empire. In the years after the organization of the United States Steel Corporation, in order to ensure that such smaller companies as the Bethlehem Steel Company and the Youngstown Sheet and Tube Company should not establish lower prices through competition, the steel industry, led by the United States Steel Corporation, agreed on a price-stabilization scheme.

The periods of greatest industrial consolidation were the period just after the Spanish-American War and the period just after the First World War. In 1904, for instance, John Moody published his book *The Truth about the Trusts*, listing three hundred and eighteen monopolies representing mergers of fifty-three hundred formerly competing plants. In 1938 a government committee revealed that thirty corporations had assets of more than one billion dollars each. Among these were the Metropolitan Life Insurance Company, the American Telephone and Telegraph Company, the Prudential Insurance Company, the Pennsylvania Railroad Company, and the New York Central System.

A significant factor in the consolidation of American business was the activity of powerful banking houses, such as J. P. Morgan and Company. The bankers marketed corporation stock and engineered many mergers of competing enterprises. In return for their aid, they usually retained stock in a new enterprise. As a result, a few banking firms soon had a powerful hold on many segments of American industry. The Populist party of the 1890's and twentieth-century Progressives were to charge that Wall Street bankers were a great menace to democracy because of their concentrated economic power. "The great monopoly in this country is the money monopoly," Woodrow Wilson declared while he was governor of New Jersey; and Louis D. Brandeis, soon to be placed on the Supreme Court by Wilson, warned that "we must break the Money Trust or the Money Trust will break us." After the immense growth of monopoly following the First World War, the Temporary National Economic Committee, established to investigate the concentration of economic power, reported, in 1941, "If democracy is really to survive, then all organizations through which man operates—industrial, social, and political—must also be democratic. Political freedom cannot survive if economic freedom is lost."

THE SUPREME COURT AND BUSINESS AND LABOR

Henry Adams remarked, in his *Education*, that after the Civil War "the whole government, from top to bottom, was rotten with the senility of what was antiquated and the instability of what was improvised." A reconstruction of the Constitution was needed, he added, since the Constitution was as incapable of meeting the new problems of the day as the Articles of Confederation had been in their day. The Constitution, drafted for a rural society, was now faced with the problem of adapting itself to the dynamics of an urban-industrial America. A lengthy lag was to develop, however, before this process of adaptation was undertaken.

In such advanced commonwealths as Massachusetts, New York, Kansas, and Oregon, progress was made in the 1870's and 1880's in passing laws to protect workers from industrial accidents and from widespread exploitation. Many of these states, under the police power, —the reserved right of a state to protect the people's health, safety, and welfare,—passed laws limiting the operation of business. Business quickly carried these laws to the Supreme Court of the United States, contending that they violated the Fourteenth Amendment, which declared that no state shall "deprive any person of life, liberty, or property, without due process of law."

For twenty years the Supreme Court supported the police power and refused to interpret the Fourteenth Amendment as protecting business from state legislation. An excellent example of the Supreme Court's refusal to increase the power of the central government at the expense of state governments in the field of regulating business is the Slaughterhouse cases of 1873. The radical legislature of Louisiana had granted to one corporation a monopoly of the slaughtering of animals in the New Orleans district, thus depriving other butchers of the right to practice their trade. Former Associate Justice of the Supreme Court J. A. Campbell, who had resigned to go with the South in 1861, argued the case for the dispossessed butchers. Campbell asserted that the Fourteenth Amendment was not just a social revolution in the field of Negro rights, but that it was a political revolution as well. The amendment, he contended, had created a national citizenship with privileges and immunities for all citizens, beyond state control. Among these privileges was the right to work at one's profession for oneself. The Supreme Court, by a five-to-four decision, contended that the amendment applied only to the rights of Negroes and refused to interpret it as making the Supreme Court "a perpetual censor upon all legislation of the states."

During the 1870's the Fourteenth Amendment was used by railroads in a futile attempt to curb state laws controlling freight and passenger rates. In 1876 these laws, passed at the request of the National Grange, were brought before the Supreme Court on the ground that such laws violated the due-process clause of the Fourteenth Amendment. In the case of Munn *v.* Illinois the Supreme Court held that private property became clothed with a public interest when it was so used that it affected the community at large. Under such circumstances, the states had the right to regulate private property. On the same day the Supreme Court, in Peik *v.* Chicago and Northwestern Railroad and in Chicago, Burlington and Quincy Railroad *v.* Iowa, declared that, as long as Congress took no action to regulate interstate railroads, the states could regulate railroads to promote the general welfare.

The decisions in these "Granger cases" and in the Slaughterhouse cases reveal that the Supreme Court was reluctant to expand the power of the national government at the expense of the states. The concept of an expanding national government had not yet permeated the Court.

In spite of this attitude, a large number of cases were brought by business groups to the Court under the Fourteenth Amendment. In 1885 the Court protested that it was not a "harbor where refuge" could be had from state legislation. It was soon, however, to become just such a refuge. The Court began to change its attitude in the 1880's. There was a steady increase in state regulation, and there was much social unrest, led by groups like the Knights of Labor, which challenged the private-property system. Increasing pressure was exerted on the Court to induce it to become a conservative bulwark against any regulation of the free individual. New judges, too, were appointed to the Court, and these judges thoroughly accepted the attitude of the Gilded Age that property was a divine right and that business should not be regulated by the government.

In 1886 the Court, by declaring that a corporation was a person, opened the way for business to seek protection from state laws under the Fourteenth Amendment. Four years later, in Chicago, Milwaukee, and St. Paul Railroad *v.* Minnesota, the Supreme Court struck down state rate regulation on the ground that this violated the due-process clause. After this case business found the Court more sympathetic to its desire to escape controls. The right of the states to regulate under the police power, however, was not entirely destroyed. In 1898 the

Court, in Holden *v*. Hardy, upheld the right of Utah to limit the hours of work in mines to eight a day. Seven years later, on the other hand, the police power was dealt a stunning blow in Lochner *v*. New York. On the ground that excessive hours of work in bakeries hurt the health of its citizens, New York passed a law limiting the hours of work to ten a day. The Court maintained that this law interfered with the workers' freedom of contract and that "the limit of police power has been reached and passed in this case." Associate Justice Oliver Wendell Holmes delivered a ringing dissent, objecting to the freezing of *laissez faire* into law. "This case is decided upon an economic theory which a large part of the country does not entertain," declared Holmes.

It is important to note that it took the doctrine of *laissez faire* a long time to secure protection by the Court. It was twenty years after the Civil War before the Fourteenth Amendment was used to protect corporations, and it was not until 1905 that the police power received a staggering defeat. The Court began to adopt *laissez faire* about the turn of the century, when the doctrine had ceased to be common sense in the light of the growth of monopoly. Even after 1905, however, *laissez faire* and the due-process clause had to share sovereignty with the police power.

In Mueller *v*. Oregon, for instance, in 1908, the Court upheld an Oregon law limiting the working hours of women to ten. During the hearings in this case, Louis D. Brandeis, the lawyer for Oregon, introduced economic and sociological data to establish the just nature of the law. By permitting this material, the Court admitted that it must sometimes go beyond the law and the Constitution to reach a decision in the industrial age. As a result of this case, most states, by 1930, had laws limiting the hours of work of women and strictly regulating child labor. The setting of maximum hours for men, however, was not secured until the New Deal. Minimum-wage legislation had a difficult time before the Court. In 1916 Louis Brandeis, then a justice of the Supreme Court, persuaded the Court to uphold an Oregon minimum-wage law for women. Seven years later, in Adkins *v*. the Children's Hospital, minimum-wage legislation was declared unconstitutional. Not until 1937 did the Court return to its 1916 position.

The Court's upholding of the right of states to regulate railroads has been mentioned in the discussion of the decisions in the "Granger cases." In 1886, however, in the Wabash case, the Court reversed itself and held that states had no power over railroads engaged in interstate commerce. This decision made Federal regulation necessary, and in the following year Congress extended the power of the national government by passing the Interstate Commerce Act. This law ordered all rates to be "reasonable and just"; forbade pooling agreements, rebates, and any other form of discrimination; and established a Commission to administer the law. The Supreme Court, in subsequent years, threw many obstacles in the path of the Commission. Every rule and order was subjected to judicial investigation, and fifteen out of sixteen cases heard between 1887 and 1905 were decided against the Commission. The Court's crippling of the Commission's regulation of the railroads was climaxed in the Maximum Freight Rates case of 1897. The Commission had ordered certain rates stopped and had fixed a fair rate. The Court held that only Congress could fix rates and that, therefore, all the Commission could do was to inquire as to whether a given rate was reasonable. As a result of popular discontent with such Court decisions, Congress, in 1906, passed the Hepburn Act, specifically granting to the Interstate Commerce Commission the right to fix rates.

The passage of the Sherman Antitrust Act in 1890 marked another way in which the power of the national government was extended to meet the conditions of a new day. This law was the result of a concerted attack on the menace to democracy of monopolies, launched by the Farmers' Alliance, various labor groups, and such writers as Henry George, Henry Demarest Lloyd, Peter Cooper, and Edward Bellamy. Justice Harlan, in the Standard Oil case (1911), said:

All who recall the conditions of the country in 1890 will remember that there was everywhere among the people generally a deep feeling of unrest. The nation had been rid of human slavery . . . but the conviction was universal that the country was in real danger from another kind of slavery, namely the slavery that would result from the aggregation of capital in the hands of a few . . . controlling, for their own advantage exclusively, the entire business of the country.

The Sherman Antitrust Act declared: "Every contract, combination in the form of a trust or otherwise, or conspiracy, in restraint of trade or commerce among the several States, or with foreign nations, is hereby declared to be illegal. . . . Every person who shall monopolize, or attempt to monopolize . . . any part of the trade or commerce among the several States, or with foreign nations, shall be deemed guilty of a misdemeanor." Such terms as *trust, monopoly,* and *restraint of trade* were vague in meaning, and the act proved to be ineffective in curbing monopoly. Under President Harrison only seven suits were instituted, under President Cleveland only eight, and under President McKinley only three. In 1895 the Supreme Court weakened the law in a case against the sugar trust. The Attorney-General unwisely tried to prosecute the case on the basis that the sugar trust owned 98 per cent of the refineries and thus was a monopoly in restraint of trade. The Supreme Court declared that refineries were within the borders of states and that the act did not apply to manufacturing within states. It was not until Theodore Roosevelt's administration that the Sherman Antitrust Act was really enforced. Woodrow Wilson added the Clayton Antitrust Act, prohibiting tying or pooling agreements and the purchase of competitors' stock by a rival corporation; outlawing interlocking directorates and making officials of corporations responsible for antitrust violations; and exempting labor unions from the laws and limiting the use of injunctions in labor disputes.

During the First World War the antitrust laws were suspended, and in the 1920's the laws were seldom enforced, except that, in 1922, in a case involving the United Mine Workers, the antitrust laws were held to apply to labor unions. On the whole, the Sherman Antitrust Act and the Clayton Antitrust Act, either through adverse Supreme Court decisions or through ineffective prosecution, have failed to solve the problem of monopoly.

Since the 1880's the Supreme Court has sat as a continuous constitutional convention. Before the Civil War the Court had declared only two laws of Congress unconstitutional, but with the advent of industrial control of the country's economic life, many laws regulating business were struck down. With the growth of corporations, many lawyers became corporation lawyers and exerted strong influence on the Court's decisions. The Court, in its interpretation of such phrases as *due process of law, police power, liberty,* and *property clothed with a public interest,* has handed down decisions which Roscoe Pound, for long Dean of the Harvard Law School, has described as "purely personal and arbitrary." Only a few justices, such as Louis Brandeis, Benjamin Cardozo, and Oliver Wendell Holmes, had a deep enough understanding of economic and sociological problems to deal with the question of governmental extension of controls over industry in terms of the situation created by the development of technology. The Supreme Court, of course, was not alone in its slowness to adjust to the conditions required by the rise of urban-industrial America. President Herbert Hoover's Committee on Social Trends, commenting on the difficulty of keeping institutions adjusted to the Machine Age, declared, during the great depression:

Social institutions are not easily adjusted to inventions. The family has not yet adapted itself to the factory; the church is slow in adjusting itself to the city; the law was slow in adjusting to dangerous machinery; local governments are slow in adjusting to the transportation inventions; international relations are slow in adjusting to the communication inventions; school curricula are slow in adjusting to the new occupations which machines create. There is in our social organizations an institutional inertia, and in our social philosophies a tradition of rigidity. Unless there is a speeding up of social invention or a slowing down of mechanical invention, grave maladjustments are certain to result.

THE LABOR SCENE

"Democracy is an assertion of the right of the individual to live and to be treated justly as against any attempt on the part of any combination of individuals to make laws which will overburden him or which will destroy his equality among his fellows in the matter of right or privilege," declared Woodrow Wilson in 1919. With the growth of corporations and other large-scale units of business, workers found that they had to organize into trade-unions to protect their rights and privileges. The ranks of labor have been torn, however, with disunity and doubts over what policies to follow. Although the vast majority of workers have believed in the profit system, a small, radical wing has demanded the rejection of private capitalism. Also, labor has been torn by the question of whether to form a workingmen's party or to support specified candidates in the two regular parties. In addition, there has been no agreement as to whether unions should be organized on a narrow craft basis or should encompass entire industries.

As American industry expanded and railroads spanned the continent, labor was faced with a national market; goods from Boston competed with goods made in Minneapolis. The worker had to realize that labor conditions were no longer local problems. Poor wages in one area existed as a threat to the wage structure everywhere. National unions would have to be launched.

The development of mass production brought a tremendous increase in production, and at the same time it destroyed the old craftsmen Jobs on the assembly line usually required little training, and the work became routine and monotonous, as Charlie Chaplin depicted it in his satirical movie *Modern Times.* The growth of the powerful corporation too was a serious problem for the worker. No longer did he know his boss and call him by his first name. Huge, impersonal corporations hired or fired men with little consideration for the social problems of the workers. The directors of the corporations, even though they might be willing to treat labor fairly, had to satisfy stockholders' desires for dividends. With the advent of the corporation, the individual worker lost his freedom of contract, his ability to bargain as an individual with his employer. Andrew Carnegie noted in his *Autobiography:*

Labor is usually helpless against capital. The employer, perhaps, decides to shut up the shops; he ceases to make profits for a short time. There is no change in his habits, food, clothing, pleasures—no agonizing fear of want. Contrast this with his workman whose lessening means of subsistence torment him.

Laborers found it necessary to organize unions to represent them collectively in negotiations with corporations. Many corporations, however, viewed unions as interlopers and hired detectives to spy on the unions, engaged lawyers to force unions into court, imported strikebreakers to wreck strikes, and sometimes locked out the workers and starved them into submission. The National Association of Manufacturers was the spearhead of the employers' antiunion activities. "We are not opposed to good unionism," a president of the N.A.M. once remarked, "if such exists anywhere. The American brand of unionism, however, is un-American, illegal, and indecent."

The hordes of immigrants swarming into the country were another serious problem to labor. Most of these immigrants were unskilled workers, and they increased the supply of cheap labor available to the antiunion employer. Also, the employer was able to play national group against national group, and it became difficult to organize these conflicting workers for common action. As union leaders tried to build unions, they discovered that their task was made even more difficult by the lack of class consciousness on the part of the workers themselves. The worker, as well as other Americans, was imbued with the idea of "from farm boy to financier in one generation." Social mobility was a fact, and assembly-line workers looked on their present occupation as only temporary, since soon they would be starting out in business for themselves.

Above all, union leaders discovered that they received impressive emotional opposition. Businessmen who had built powerful monop-

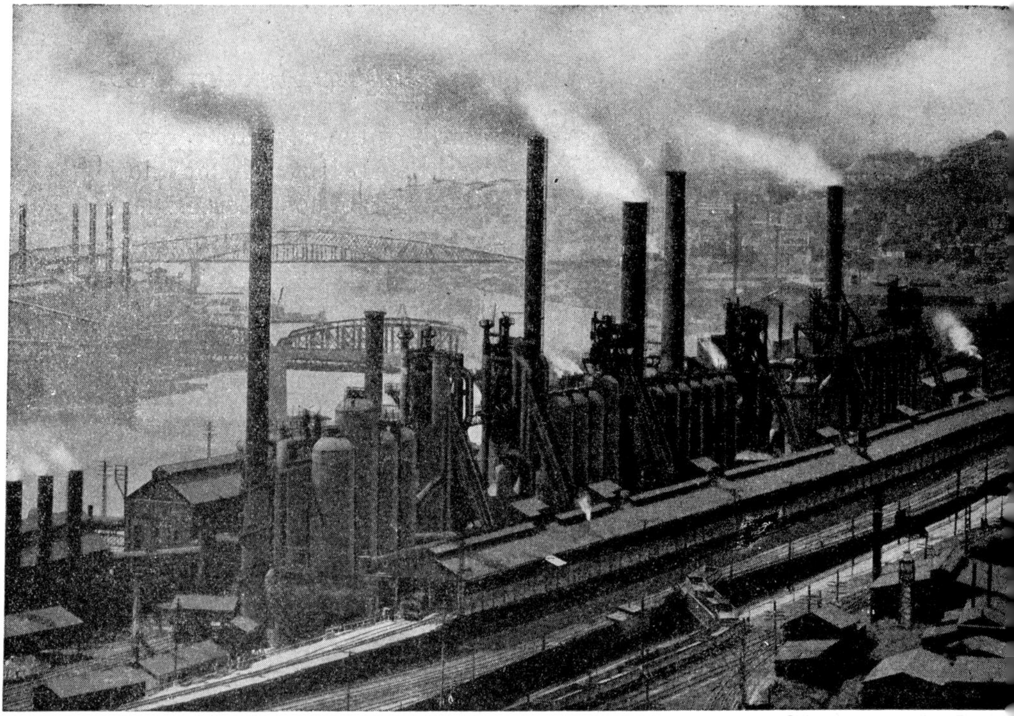

© Altwater and Brother, Pittsbu

BLAST FURNACES
IN PITTSBURGH'S
STEEL INDUSTRY

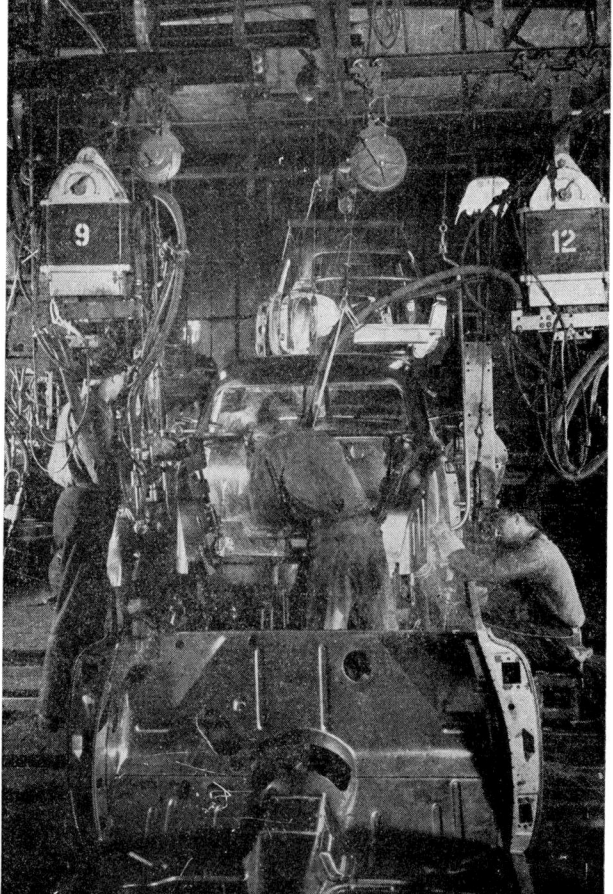

Studebaker Corporation

America

AN AUTOMOBILE
ASSEMBLY LINE

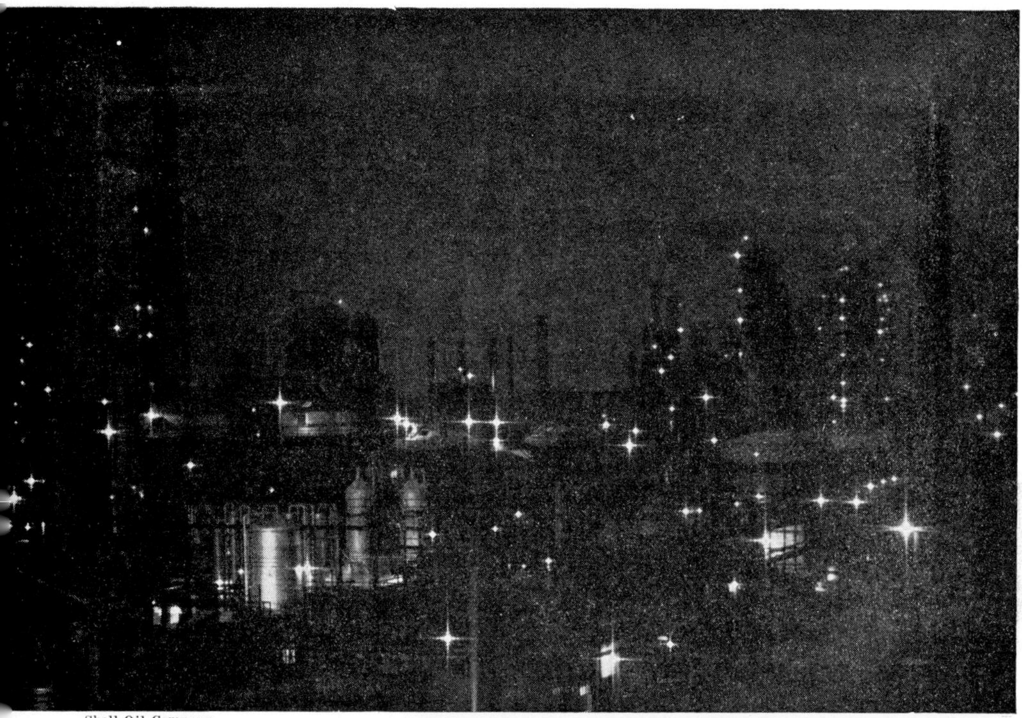

Shell Oil Company

AN OIL REFINERY
AT NIGHT

Robert Y. Richie, from American Locomotive Company

dustry

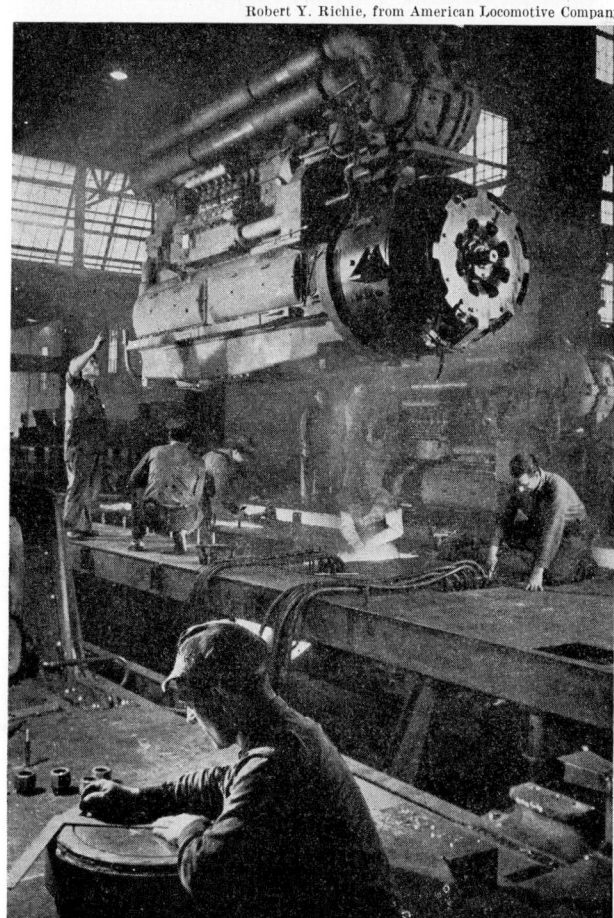

A DIESEL ENGINE
FOR A LOCOMOTIVE

olies asserted that for labor to organize was a threat to society. These same monopolists, who felt that it was shrewd on their part to crush out competition, became apoplectic when unions asked for the closed shop. Businessmen also advocated that government should aid industry with tariffs and other subsidies, but that it must not help labor, because to do so would be socialism. When business organized powerful lobbies and influenced legislation and elections, this was viewed as salutary, but when labor took the same step, that was denounced as "un-American." "The task of employers' associations," declared one businessman, at the turn of the century, "is to pull up root and branch the un-American institution of organized labor as at present conducted."

The year following the close of the Civil War witnessed the first attempt of city trade-unions to organize on a country-wide basis in the National Labor Union. In its six years of existence this national union organized over six hundred thousand workers and helped to build public opposition against the Contract Labor Law. The 1870's were years of chaos and extreme suffering for many workers. The country underwent a severe depression, and unemployment was widespread. Dissatisfied laborers in the Pennsylvania coal country organized the "Molly Maguires," a secret terroristic group, and violence swept the coal fields. Major cities like Baltimore, Pittsburgh, and Chicago witnessed, in 1877, battles between strikers and militia after railroads had arbitrarily slashed wages. Order was restored only when President Hayes dispatched Federal troops to break the strike. The average American was shocked by this industrial violence and placed the blame at the door of "foreign agitators." The *Nation* commented:

The optimism in which most Americans are carefully trained . . . has concealed from most of the well-to-do and intelligent classes of the population, the profound changes which have during the last thirty years been wrought in the composition and character of the population, especially in the great cities. Vast additions have been made to it within that period, to whom American political and social ideals appeal but faintly, if at all, and who carry in their very blood the traditions which give universal suffrage an air of menace to many of the things which civilized men hold most dear.

Actually, these severe railway strikes signified the fact that the country had reached the point where it had a serious labor problem. Now, after two hundred and fifty years of exploiting a frontier economy, the United States was acquiring a complex and complicated society with problems not too dissimilar from those of industrialized European nations.

The most powerful labor organization in the 1880's was the Noble Order of the Knights of Labor, which had existed as a secret organization from 1869 to 1881. The Knights were a radical union movement in their advocacy of public ownership of public utilities, and workers' co-operatives for the production and distribution of goods. The Knights attempted to organize all workers into one big union, and their main appeal was to the unskilled. Led by T. V. Powderly, the Knights increased their power in 1884 by winning a railway strike against Jay Gould. Something of the hold that Powderly had on his rank and file was revealed in the following prayer from the *Journal of United Labor*, in 1886: "Our father, who sits in Scranton, Pa., T. V. Powderly is thy name . . . Lead us not in the way of monopoly, but deliver us from the Republican and Democratic parties, and thine shall be the power and the glory and the honor. Amen."

In 1886 the Knights of Labor, in an alliance with independent unions, some of them socialist, struck for an eight-hour day. A riot occurred on May 3 outside the Chicago McCormick Harvester works, and the police killed or wounded six of the strikers. The next day, while a great mass protest was being held in Haymarket Square, the police arrived to disperse the meeting and a bomb was thrown, killing seven policemen and injuring over sixty. At the subsequent trial of eight anarchists, although the culprit could not be discovered, the presiding judge held that those who had incited violence, even by word, were guilty of murder. The press demanded revenge, and the *Chicago Tribune* charged that "there seems to be no doubt that the Anarchists planned wholesale murder, arson, and pillage." Seven anarchists were sentenced to death and one to life imprisonment. Four were executed, one killed himself, and the other two had their sentences commuted to life imprisonment. Six years after the trial Governor John Peter Altgeld pardoned these two, declaring that "the judge conducted the trial with malicious ferocity."

Although the Knights of Labor were not responsible for the Haymarket bombing, the public's reaction to all radical movements was so extreme that the Knights began to decline. In general, the Knights helped to improve the condition of labor, and they were instrumental in securing the Chinese Exclusion Act of 1882 and the repeal, in 1885, of the Contract Labor Law.

In 1886, as the Knights of Labor began to decline, the American Federation of Labor appeared on the scene. Led by Samuel Gompers, the A. F. of L. repudiated all radical theories and supported private capitalism and the profit system. It relied on strikes and bargaining to increase labor's position within the existing economic order. It avoided third-party politics and instead supported those candidates of the two major parties who were most favorable to labor. The Knights' idea of one big union was replaced by that of a number of craft unions.

The 1890's were bitter years for labor. From 1893 to 1897 there was a serious depression, with bloody strikes and widespread unemployment. In 1892 strikers and Pinkerton detectives fought it out at the Homestead plant of the Carnegie Steel Company, and the workers lost public support when an attempt was made on the life of President Henry C. Frick. The steel industry was a powerful antiunion force from that time until 1937. In 1919, for instance, four hundred thousand workers launched an unsuccessful strike for union recognition, higher wages, and an eight-hour day. The strike, bitterly fought by every means at the steel industry's disposal, failed because the public was undergoing a great Red scare and was hostile to union activity.

Two years after the Homestead strike of 1892 the workers at the Pullman plant near Chicago went on strike when George M. Pullman refused to arbitrate a wage dispute with his employees. The American Railway Union, led by Eugene Debs, then refused to handle any Pullman cars on the railroads. Quickly the General Managers' Association of Railroads upheld the Pullman Company, and a paralysis of transportation set in. At this point the Federal government interfered and issued an injunction against Debs's union, restraining it from obstructing the mails. Disorders broke out, and President Cleveland dispatched Federal troops to break the strike. Until the Federal injunction had been issued, Governor Altgeld had the situation under control with state militia. He would not, however, use the militia to break the strike. Over his protests, the Federal troops came into Illinois. It was clear from this action that the Federal government was supporting business against labor; and Debs, who defied the injunction, was sentenced to six months in jail for contempt of court. Governor Altgeld, by his opposition to Federal action, futilely tried to check the trend toward the centralization of power in the Federal government which had been developing since the Civil War.

In spite of the difficult times of the 1890's, the American Federation of Labor had a half-million members by 1900. At the outbreak of the First World War it numbered two million. During the 1920's, however, the death of Samuel Gompers, the rise of company unions, and the development of vigorous, independent unions, such as Sidney Hillman's Amalgamated Clothing Workers, led to a decline in strength for the A. F. of L. At no time in its history has the A. F. of L. represented a majority of American workmen. In the 1930's a new national union, the Committee for Industrial Organization (since 1938, the Congress of Industrial Organizations), was to emerge and organize great industries like steel, automobiles, and rubber hitherto unorganized.

While the A. F. of L. was expanding its membership between 1900 and 1914, a militant, radical union, the Industrial Workers of the World, was organized, in 1905. It denounced the capitalist system and tried to organize all workers into one great industrial union. The "Wobblies," as the members of the I.W.W. were called, led a bitter strike against the textile industry in 1912. When the I.W.W. opposed American participation in the First World War, its leaders were indicted under the Espionage Act and the union collapsed.

One other trade-union development in the years following the Civil War deserves attention. The Railroad Brotherhoods, consisting of the Locomotive Engineers, the Railway Conductors, the Locomotive Firemen and Enginemen, and the Railroad Trainmen, were all in existence by the 1870's. In this period railroad workers found it difficult to buy insurance, and the Brotherhoods were organized as benevolent associations to insure their members. The vast sums of money that these unions accumulated led them to adopt a cautious policy toward strikes for fear of damage suits that might be instituted against them.

THE FLOOD OF IMMIGRANTS

"The height of our civilization, it seems to me," wrote Wendell Willkie, in 1943, "has been reached not by our assembly lines, our inventions, or any of our great factitious development, but by the ability of peoples of varying beliefs and of different racial extractions to live side by side here in the United States with common understanding, respect, and helpfulness."[1] From 1607 to the 1920's the story of America was in large part the saga of the immigrant; a great folk migration poured into the United States to develop its resources, and in the process the foreign peoples modified their inherited traits to fit the new environment.

[1]Reprinted from *One World*, by permission of Simon and Schuster, Inc., copyright, 1943.

Until the 1880's the bulk of the immigrants came from northern and western Europe. After that date southern and eastern Europe furnished the majority of the new settlers.

Period	Total Admitted	Number and Percentage from North and West Europe		Number and Percentage from South and East Europe	
1861–1870	2,314,824	2,031,624	87.8	33,628	1.4
1871–1880	2,812,191	2,170,373	73.6	201,889	7.2
1881–1890	5,246,613	3,778,633	72	958,413	18.3
1891–1900	3,687,564	1,643,492	44.6	1,915,486	51.9
1901–1910	8,795,286	1,910,135	21.7	6,225,981	70.8
1911–1920	5,735,811	997,438	17.4	3,379,126	58.9
1921–1930	4,107,209	1,284,123	31.3	1,193,830	29

The immigrants from southern and eastern Europe added diversity to the basic Anglo-Saxon cultural traits of the United States. "The United States is a new civilization," Louis Adamic has pointed out, "owing a great deal to the Anglo-Saxon strain, owing much to the other elements in its heritage and growth. . . . The actual American norm is not only not exclusively Anglo-Saxon, but . . . it is not yet formed, . . . it is still in progress."

Millions of immigrants poured into the United States to meet the demand for workers in the rapidly expanding industrial plants, while a smaller number, like the Scandinavian settlers, bought farm land along the transcontinental railroads. By the 1880's the industries of northern and western Europe, particularly those of England and Germany, were prospering and offering adequate employment for their own people. Southern and eastern Europe, however, lacked industry and had a backward farm economy. To the people of this area, and to the Jewish citizens of Russia, who were undergoing persecution, America was the golden land of opportunity.

As the new immigrants from Russia, Italy, and the Balkan area poured into the United States, many old-stock Americans became frightened lest their traditional ways and habits be destroyed. The Catholicism of many of the immigrants stirred fears, and some Protestants organized the American Protective Association in 1887 to counteract the new forces. One of the A.P.A.'s tracts asked:

Can a good Romanist be at the same time a loyal American citizen? . . . The Vatican claims absolute and supreme authority in all things, civil as well as spiritual, and every member of that Church is bound to render to the

Pontiff absolute and unquestioning obedience. This being true, is it not quite certain that whatever his personal opinions and feelings may be as an American citizen, he must support the Church against the State? . . . Can any person who is loyal to Romanism be true to Republicanism? Can a Romanist be a good citizen of America?

The immigrants, of course, have been no less faithful to democracy than the earlier settlers, and they have supplied the labor force to build the country into a great world power. The United States Immigration Commission observed, in 1911, that the immigrants were not "beaten men of beaten races," but were "composed largely of the peasantry and unskilled laboring classes," and that they represented "the stronger and better element of the particular class from which . . . [they were] drawn." Organized labor believed that the horde of immigrants lowered wages and debased standards in general; and undoubtedly the ability of the employer to turn one religion against another and one ethnic group against another did make the task of organizing the immigrant worker extremely difficult. It is to be remembered, however, that sweatshops and poor working conditions had existed long before the Italian, Slav, and Jewish immigrants reached America.

The immigrant usually took the poorest job and lived in the worst slum area; but as he improved his economic position, he moved into a better area and into a better position in industry. Social mobility was a significant factor for the latter-day immigrant, just as it had been before the Civil War. The achievements of immigrants like Carl Schurz in politics, Joseph Pulitzer in journalism, Samuel Gompers in labor, Alexander Graham Bell in invention, Rabbi Stephen S. Wise in religion, and Walter Damrosch in music reveal something of the rich contribution that immigrants have made to American life. The problem of assimilation in the American melting pot was not so serious as some people feared. The contributions of these immigrant groups in two world wars revealed that Old World ties generally had been severed and that the immigrants were as able defenders of American liberties as were the older groups.

THE RESTRICTION OF IMMIGRATION

Toward Oriental peoples the United States rather quickly adopted a policy of exclusion. After Chinese workers had been imported to develop the California mines and build the railroads, great waves of anti-Chinese agitation swept the west coast. The Chinese were hard workers to compete with, and they accepted a lower standard of living than American workers. In 1882 Congress passed a law suspending the immigration of Chinese laborers for ten years. Twenty years later the exclusion was adopted for an indefinite period. Nonimmigrant classes, such as government officials, students, merchants, and visitors, were not affected by the law. The same policy was applied to the Japanese in 1907. To forestall a Congressional bill, President Theodore Roosevelt made an executive agreement with Japan, providing that Japan would not issue passports to workers. In 1924 Congress terminated this "Gentlemen's Agreement" and wrote into the Immigration Act of that year the exclusion of Japanese. The exclusion of both the Chinese and the Japanese was based on the assumption, for which there was no scientific data, that Oriental peoples were inferior. This exclusion policy was an unnecessary affront to the national honor of China and Japan and played no small part in Japanese propaganda aimed at stirring up hatred of the United States from 1924 to 1941.

Toward European peoples the United States adopted a policy of virtually free immigration up to 1882. At that time the policy became selective in that convicts, lunatics, idiots, and others likely to become public charges were excluded. This list was added to over the years until, in 1917, a literacy test was passed, permitting entry to no immigrant over sixteen unless he could read some language.

During the 1920's the United States adopted a definitely restrictive policy on immigration. In 1921 a law was passed reducing the percentage of immigrants allowed to enter the United States annually to 3 per cent of the total of each national group present in 1910. Three years later, in order to favor northern and western Europeans over southern and eastern Europeans, Congress fixed the rate at 2 per cent and took 1890 as the base year. Five years later, in 1929, Congress put into operation the National Origins Act, establishing the total number of immigrants to be admitted in any year as one hundred and fifty thousand and apportioning this number according to the national origins of the American people in 1920. With the adoption of this policy of restricting European immigration, the inscription on the base of the Statue of Liberty no longer applied:

> Give me your tired, your poor,
> Your huddled masses yearning to breathe free,
> The wretched refuse of your teeming shore,
> Send these, the homeless, tempest-tossed, to me:
> I lift my lamp beside the golden door.

SELECTED BIBLIOGRAPHY

ALLAN NEVINS, *The Emergence of Modern America;* A. M. SCHLESINGER, *The Rise of the City;* IDA M. TARBELL, *The Nationalizing of Business,* the three volumes in the History of American Life Series that cover the material in this chapter.

V. L. PARRINGTON, *Main Currents in American Thought* (Vol. 3), a thought-provoking interpretation of the Gilded Age; JOHN MOODY, *The Truth about the Trusts,* and IDA M. TARBELL, *The Standard Oil Company,* early attacks on monopoly; DAVID LYNCH, *The Concentration of Economic Power,* an analysis of the findings of the Temporary National Economic Committee with regard to the American economy.

H. V. FAULKNER and MARK STARR, *Labor in America,* a concise, lucid history of American labor; SAMUEL GOMPERS, *Seventy Years of Life and Labor—An Autobiography,* indispensable; ANDREW C. MCLAUGHLIN, *Constitutional History of the United States;* FELIX FRANKFURTER and W. V. GREEN, *The Labor Injunction;* C. O. GREGORY, *Labor and the Law,* contain information on labor's legal position.

GRACE ABBOTT, *The Immigrant and the Community,* and MAURICE DAVIE, *World Immigration with Special Reference to the United States,* valuable studies.

H. S. COMMAGER (Ed.), *Documents of American History,* pp. 51, 71–75, 78–80, 91–93, 96, 109–110, 122–123, 129–136, 155–156, 180, 215–221, 223, 235–238, 279–280, 287–289, contains source material.

XXI

The Revolution in Agriculture

IN THE ENTIRE history of the United States up to 1870, only 407,734,041 acres of land had been incorporated into farms. In the thirty years after 1870 more than 430,000,000 acres were added. One generation of men, from 1870 to 1900, turned more land into farms than all their predecessors combined. During the Civil War and immediately afterward, a new era of agricultural expansion began, bringing into the American economy the cattle, sheep, wheat, and corn kingdoms of the trans-Mississippi West. The war had brought about a wide adoption of such farm machines as the corn-planter, the two-horse cultivator, the mower, the reaper, and the steam thresher. Although invented earlier, these machines were not widely used until man power left the farms to fight the war.

After the Civil War thousands of Northern veterans poured into the flat, fertile prairies of Iowa, Minnesota, Kansas, Nebraska, and the Dakotas. The Homestead Act of 1862 made free land available, agricultural machinery made it possible to farm large areas, and the expanding railroads made markets seem close to the farm. The twenty-five years after 1865 witnessed the peopling, in one mad rush, of the last great American frontier and the end of a pioneer economy.

The Federal government's policy of rapid disposal of the land increased the tempo of farm expansion. Under the Homestead Act 147,146,830 acres were removed from the public domain between 1862 and 1914. As a result of the Homestead Act, of land grants to the railroads, of gifts of land to states for educational and for irrigation purposes, and of the setting aside of land for Indian and forest reserves, the Federal government, in the period from 1860 to 1914, disposed of over 700,000,000 acres of land.

The trans-Mississippi West was peopled not only by blue-coated war veterans, but also by a portion of the immigrants pouring in from Europe. Farm population between 1880 and 1910 showed an absolute increase of almost five million. This was a slower rate of growth, however, than cities were undergoing, and as a result, even though farm population increased in these years, by 1910 only about one third of the gainfully employed were in agriculture. But the wide application of farm machinery to the fertile prairies made it possible for this proportionally smaller farm group to supply food for the workers of American and European cities. By 1910 the farm machinery in use totaled a billion and a quarter dollars, whereas in 1860 it had represented only a quarter of a billion dollars. The increased application of farm machinery greatly increased the productivity of the American farm. The story of wheat is spectacular. Yields rose from 173,000,000 bushels in 1860 to 498,000,000 in 1880 and to over 522,000,000 in 1900. "Year after year," one writer has observed, ". . . came from widening acreage . . . torrents of wheat, of pork, of cattle, of corn, swelling the channels of trade and spreading over the whole civilized world. Year after year, more and more freight cars creaked wearily with heavier and heavier loads to cities whose prosperity waxed higher and higher and higher."

One result of this remarkable revolution in American agriculture was, in many cases, the ruination of the farmer. As increasing torrents of farm produce poured into the world market, and as such other nations as Australia and Canada began to produce foodstuffs, prices suffered a disastrous drop. The American wheat farmer received $1.05 per bushel from 1866 to 1875; $.92 from 1878 to 1885; $.67 from 1886 to 1895; and $.62 by 1900. The prices of cattle and sheep followed a similar pattern, corn prices fell 32 per cent from 1866 to 1878, and cotton fell 58 per cent. Only the price of farm machinery, the charges of railroads, and mortgage rates seemed to increase. By 1900, 31 per cent of the nation's farms were mortgaged, with middle border states like Wisconsin, Iowa, and Nebraska running from 45 to 50 per cent. Farm tenantry too showed a rapid increase, reaching 35 per cent by 1900 and close to 50 per cent by 1930.

As rural incomes declined and tenantry increased, the farm country witnessed a steady stream of enterprising boys and girls leaving the farms for the cities—the new zone of opportunity, adventure, and culture. Not only did the American farmer tend to wreck his own economic position, but his produce was disastrous to the European farmer. European farmers could not compete with this flood of foodstuffs from the richer lands of America, and many peasants had to migrate to industrial centers or emigrate to the United States. Much of the social unrest in Europe from 1870 to the outbreak of the First World War can be attributed to the impact of the American agricultural revolution on the European economy.

Until the time of the Civil War the farmers of the South and Mid-

A One-Man Hay-Baler Picking Up Cut Hay and Binding It into Compact Bundles

The Latest Development in Mechanizing the Farm

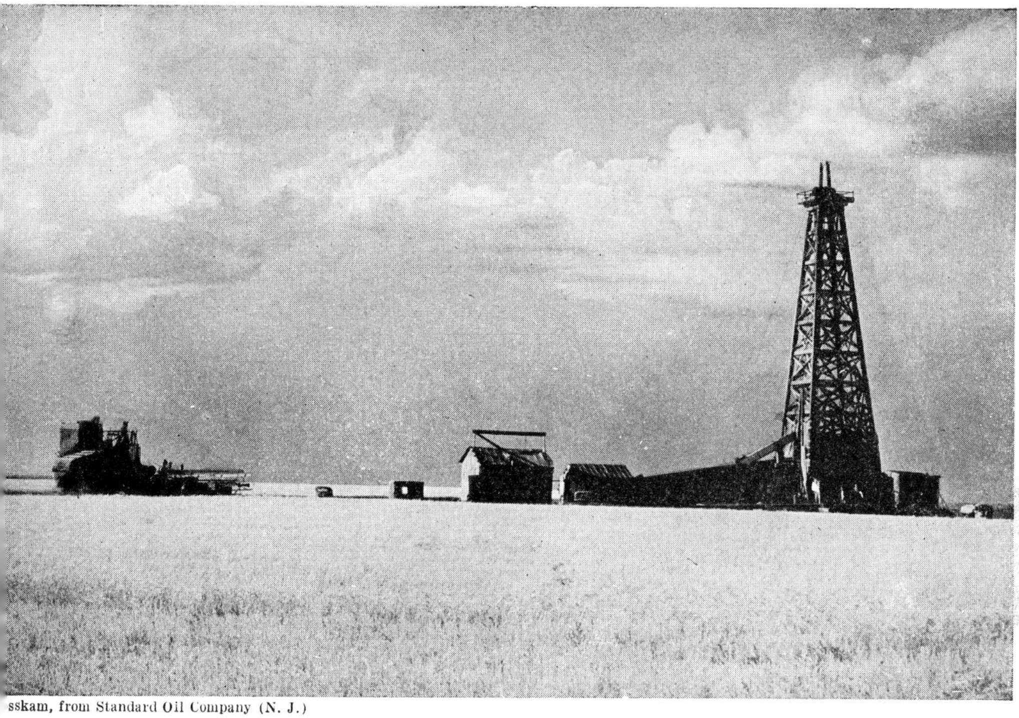

sskam, from Standard Oil Company (N. J.)

Harvesting Grain and Pumping Oil on the Same Field in Montana

Irrigation on a Truck Farm in Arizona

Ewing Galloway

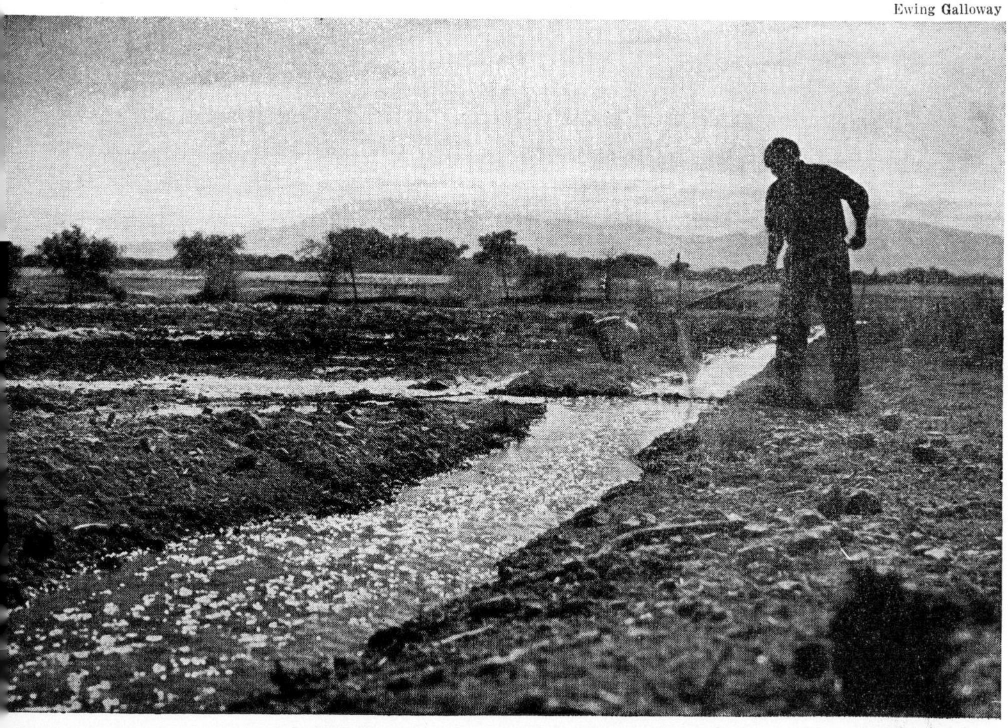

west, united in the Democratic party, had dictated the major policies of the nation. Abraham Lincoln's liberalism, however, drew many Midwestern farmers into the Republican party, and from that time on, the farmers of the country were to be so divided that they never again dominated the government. Four years of war further split the farmers, and the Grand Army of the Republic and Republican politicians told the Midwestern farmer, after 1865, that the only patriotic vote was a vote for the Republican party. "It was natural to be a Republican," Brand Whitlock once recalled about the Ohio of his childhood. ". . . It was merely a synonym for patriotism, another name for the nation. . . . It was inconceivable that any self-respecting person should be a Democrat."[1] Senator George W. Norris was also to remember that as a youngster in Ohio he was told that "hell is crowded with two types of people. Democrats and those who don't read the Bible."

The grain farmer of the Midwest continued to vote the "right" ticket long after Lincoln's liberalism had been replaced by industrial domination of the Republican party. He thus voted for policies that economically were often not to his best interests. He had to sell his produce in a market where competition decided the price, and he had to buy in a protected market where many tariff policies were speeding the growth of the monopolies. Yet, thoroughly convinced that the Republican party was the party of God and patriotism, the Northern farmer supported the high-tariff party.

The Midwestern farmer was more likely, however, to attribute his economic troubles to railroad abuses and high mortgage rates than to the tariff. One Nebraska editor commented,

> There are three great crops raised in Nebraska. One is a crop of corn, one is a crop of freight rates, and one a crop of interest. One is produced by farmers who by sweat and toil farm the land. The other two are produced by men who sit in their offices and behind bank counters, and farm the farmers.

The Midwestern farmer was particularly irritated by the "absentee" Eastern ownership of the railroads and mortgage firms.

A more complex factor in the economy that added to the farmer's woes was the rising value of the currency. During the Civil War large debts had been contracted, when the value of money was depreciated. These debts had to be paid back in a period when money had increased

---

[1] Reprinted from Brand Whitlock, *Forty Years of It.* Copyright, 1914, D. Appleton and Company, New York.

in value from 15 to 20 per cent. It therefore required many more bushels of wheat and corn to pay off a loan than it had taken at the time when the loan had been contracted. In 1867, for instance, wheat prices in gold had been one dollar and forty-five cents a bushel, but by 1894 they were forty-nine cents. The farmer and debtor group in general faced a contracting, inelastic currency, controlled by private banking interests under the National Bank Act of 1863. For years farm groups were to lead the demand for a flexible currency controlled by the government in the interest of all the people.

Equally serious for the Midwestern farmer were the physical problems that he faced. Drought, erosion, wind storms, and grasshopper plagues were all too frequent. "I have seen it dry," commented one Kansas editor, "so dry that you had to prime the mourners at a funeral so that they could shed tears for the departed." During the years 1880 to 1887 the western areas of Kansas, Nebraska, and the Dakotas had such abundant rain that a number of farmers moved into that region. A series of droughts in the next ten years drove them back east. William Allen White, youthful Kansas editor in 1895, described this exodus in the following editorial:

There came through Emporia yesterday two old-fashioned "mover wagons," headed east. The stock in the caravan would invoice four horses, very poor and very tired, one mule, more disheartened than the horses, and one sad-eyed dog, that had probably been compelled to rustle his own precarious living for many a long and weary day. A few farm implements of the simpler sort were loaded in the wagon, but nothing that had wheels was moving except the two wagons. All the rest of the impedimenta had been left upon the battlefield, and these poor stragglers, defeated, but not conquered, were fleeing to another field, to try the fight again. These movers were from western Kansas—from one of those counties near the Colorado line which holds a charter from the state to officiate as the very worst, most desolate, God-forsaken, man-deserted spot on the sad old earth. They had come from that wilderness only after a ten years' hard, vicious fight, a fight which had left its scars on their faces, had bent their bodies, had taken the elasticity from their steps, and left them crippled to enter the battle anew. For ten years they had been fighting the elements. They had seen it stop raining for months at a time. They had heard the fury of the winter wind as it came whining across the short burned grass and cut the flesh from their children huddling in the corner. These movers have strained their eyes watching through the long summer days for the rain that never came. They have seen that big cloud roll up from the southwest about one o'clock in the afternoon, hover over the land, and stumble away with a few thumps of thunder as the sun went down. They have tossed through hot nights wild with worry, and have arisen only to find their worst nightmares grazing in reality on the brown stubble in front of their sun-warped doors. They had such high hopes when they went out there; they are so desolate now.

The remoteness, the loneliness, the lack of educational opportunities and health facilities, added to the tribulations of the farmer. One cannot read such realistic novels of the farm country as Ed Howe's *Story of a Country Town*, Ole Rölvaag's *Giants in the Earth*, and Hamlin Garland's *Main-Traveled Roads* without being impressed with the drabness of life, the backbreaking labor, and the toll in human lives that the farm country faced.

According to Ed Howe, in *The Story of a Country Town*, the people in his Midwestern farm town "seemed to be miserable and discontented," and he wondered why they did not leave a place "which made all the men surly and rough, and the women pale and fretful." Howe answered his own question:

There were cheap lands farther on, where the people raised a crop one year, and were supported by charity the next; where towns sprang up on credit, and farms were opened with borrowed money; where no sooner was one stranger's money exhausted than another arrived to take his place; where men mortgaged their possessions at full value, and thought themselves rich, notwithstanding, so great was their faith in the country; where he who was deepest in debt was the leading citizen, and where bankruptcy caught them all at last. On these lands the dusty travelers settled, where there were churches, school-houses, and bridges—but little rain—and railroads to carry out the crops should any be raised.[1]

The older folks might gamble on another trial in a new rural area, but youth, in increasing numbers, made another choice. To them, the city must have seemed a veritable utopia, with its theaters, concerts, and fine educational facilities. Year after year farm boys and girls poured into the cities, and the great agrarian democracy of Thomas Jefferson was relegated to the position of one of the cogs in the industrial order.

THE SOUTHERN AGRARIAN SCENE

While the North came out of the Civil War with a new, expanding industrial economy, the Old South, which had played such a significant part in the life of the country up to the war, was cast aside and crushed.

[1]Copyrighted by E. W. Howe, 1882.

For years after the war and reconstruction, the area that had once been the spokesman for the agrarian interests played only a minor role in national affairs. Its interests were primarily focused on its own economic and social recovery.

A pressing race question robbed the South of the advantages of the two-party system and helped to form the "solid South," where differences of opinion on varied problems were not expressed politically. The great exploited groups in American life—the unorganized worker and the white and Negro farmer—were to predominate in the South. Southern agriculture witnessed the replacement of the old plantation system by tenantry and sharecropping and by what Jonathan Daniels, North Carolina newspaper editor, has termed "the economy of want."

Although some industry was introduced into the South in the decades following the war, chiefly in the field of cotton textiles, the region remained predominantly a staple-crop section. The well-organized cotton plantation, however, was broken up, and farm tenantry took its place. Attempts at maintaining the plantations intact, with the Negro now receiving wages for his work, generally failed. There was a natural reluctance among many former slaves to remain on the old plantations, and the plantation-owners lacked ready cash to pay wages. The great majority of plantations were broken up into units—one-mule farms—and rented on a money basis or more likely on a share basis. Generally, under the share system, the owner supplied the land, the house, the seeds, and the equipment and received in return a fixed per cent of the crop. Laws were passed permitting the landlord to take a mortgage—a lien—on the tenants' crops.

As the farm-tenantry system developed, the tenants, frequently to escape supervision by the old plantation-owner, went directly to the bankers and merchants in the crossroad town to secure food and farm equipment. The liens that the merchants and bankers took on the tenants' crops helped, over the years, to prostrate Southern agriculture. The merchants charged excessive prices for the foodstuffs sold the tenants, and as cotton prices dropped 58 per cent from 1866 to 1878, the tenants fell hopelessly into debt. Meanwhile independent small farmers borrowed money from the merchants and, as prices failed, saw their mortgages foreclosed.

The development of the sharecropping system made the South a greater one-crop region than it had been before 1860. In the years before the war many plantation-owners had been shifting away from tobacco and cotton to food production, but this effort at diversification was checked by the sharecropping system. The merchant, with his lien on the crop, wanted a product that he could quickly turn into cash, and furthermore he wanted to sell the sharecropper food at an exorbitant price.

The breakup of the plantation, of course, increased the number of Southern farms in the years from 1865 to 1880. Yet statistics in this case are misleading. The increase in farms generally represented an increase in tenant farms. As far as the South was concerned, tenant farming, instead of leading to farm ownership, signified a life of increasing debt and hopelessness. Furthermore, the tenant, as he ran more hopelessly into debt, neglected the upkeep of the land and failed to conserve the soil.

As a result of the breakup of the plantations and the development of the sharecropping system, the South soon had more tenant farmers than any other section. Over half of the Southern farmers were to be found in that category by 1930. Farm tenantry meant the perpetuation of economic slavery, and also it helped to link the South as a vassal area to the industrial, commercial North. The merchant class found their economic interests closely intertwined with those of the Northern manufacturers, and they exerted their full power to prevent the Southern farmer from uniting with the Midwestern farmer in the days of the Populist crusade.

The Southern agrarian revolution, the rise of the crossroad merchants to power, the growth of some industries, and the emergence of a Southern industrial class created the new South. This section's emphasis on a staple crop and its economic bondage to the financial North brought about the conditions that led Franklin D. Roosevelt to list the South in 1933 as economic problem number one of the nation.

THE PASSING OF THE FRONTIER

American schoolbooks, in the years from 1820 to 1850, described the area of what is now the central and western portions of Kansas, Nebraska, and the Dakotas as the Great American Desert. This was the area of the high plains, differentiated from the richer farm lands of the prairies to the east by insufficient rainfall. Settlers poured into all sections of the Midwestern prairies before the Civil War; but when they reached, roughly, the ninety-eighth meridian, they stopped. Instead of settling the vast area of the high plains stretching to the Rockies, the pioneer traveled across this area to reach California and the Northwest.

The Cattle Kingdom

The farming frontier jumped the high plains until new methods of tilling the soil, of fencing the range, and of securing water could be developed. During the period from 1840 to 1885 the cattle kingdom and the mining kingdom, therefore, flourished in this area.

The cattle kingdom, with the use of the horse distinguishing it from Eastern stock farming, developed a civilization which was the first really to utilize the high plains. The range-cattle industry grew to gigantic proportions and produced a great supply of meat, which made the nation a beef-eating people. The first boom came in 1866. Texas, which long had raised cattle, launched the idea of driving its cattle across the plains to meet the nearest railroad. In 1867 Abilene, Kansas, on the Kansas Pacific Railroad, became the focal point for Texas cattle.

Over the next few years, as railroads stretched farther and farther west, towns like Wichita and Dodge City replaced Abilene as the great cow towns. From 1867 to 1872 it has been estimated that nearly a million and a half head of Texas cattle reached Abilene over the Chisholm Trail, and the number of Texas cattle reaching all Kansas shipping points is said to have reached nearly four million.

With the great demand for beef in the industrial cities, the Texas cattle industry spread quickly into the rest of the high-plains area. In Nebraska and Wyoming cow towns quickly appeared to rival those of Kansas. The range-cattle industry, in so far as it was characterized by the long drive, came to an end when the transcontinental railroads were completed. The railroads brought farmers, who settled on the grazing grounds used by herds being driven north. Since the farmers were citizens of the states and the cattlemen only migrants, the farmers secured laws curbing the long drive. By 1885 the long drive and the open range were disappearing. Now the range was fenced, and the cattle were kept on the ranches, where they were reared and sold.

During the 1880's the cattle industry in the northern high plains underwent an immense boom. Capital from the East and Europe poured into the industry, and in Wyoming alone, in 1883, twenty companies, with a total capitalization of twelve million dollars, were incorporated. Wherever the cattle industry became important, cattlemen's associations were quickly organized. These associations had real political power in territories and states, and they adopted rules regulating the use of the public domain for grazing areas. They also organized to crush out cattle thieves, to drive Indian war parties back to their reservations, and to check the encroachment of sheepherders and agricultural settlers on the grazing land.

The old range-cattle industry at its height, in the 1870's and 1880's, has been preserved for future generations in literature, songs, and paintings. Andy Adams's *Log of a Cowboy*, E. D. Branch's *Cowboy and His Interpreter*, and E. E. Dale's *Range Cattle Industry* reveal much of the flavor of the Old West. John A. Lomax's collections *Cowboy Songs and Other Frontier Ballads* and *Songs of the Cattle Trail and Cow Camp* furnish splendid examples of the balladry of the open range. The novels of Zane Grey and James Oliver Curwood, as well as the numerous Western-story magazines and most Western motion pictures, present an overromantic and less authentic picture. The paintings of Frederic Remington and Charles M. Russell, Montana's famous cowboy artist, have added to the glamour associated with the Old West.

A Dash for Timber

PAINTING BY

FREDERIC REMINGTON

Sod Houses on the Nebraska Frontier, 1887

The Rush for Oklahoma Land in 1889

MURAL PAINTING BY

JOHN STEUART CURRY

The most picturesque character of the range-cattle industry was the cowboy who drove the cattle to market on the long drive. Later generations have found the cowboy's attire gay and colorful, but actually it was admirably adapted to life on the high plains. The large sombrero, for instance, served as protection against sun, rain, snow, and sleet. Folded, it became a pillow, and in times of severe drought it could be used to give the horse precious water from the canteen. The cowboy's amusements were few. On his infrequent trips to the cow towns he gambled his money in poker or faro, and drank straight whisky. Johnny Ritch, who worked on Montana ranges in the 1880's, in a poem entitled "Shorty's Saloon," drew the following picture of a cow-town saloon:

> And up from the vast, silent stretch of the range,
> From line camps and roundups, and all of the strange,
> Lone places in Cow-land, men came there to play
> In that drama whose artists all lived by the way;
> Their sky-line of life blazed crimson and gold,
> For hope gave them wealth and youth made them bold
> And strong in life's strife to dare any task,
> And "licker" was theirs when Shorty would ask
> > "What's yours, Pard?"
>
> They danced and they drank, and they sang that old song,
> "I'm just a poor cow-boy, and know I've done wrong,"
> While the click of the chips in the games that were played,
> And the sob in the music the violin made
> Rang out through the smoke that clouded the room,
> For joy held the top-hand and drink drowned all gloom
> The future might hold for him who made gay,
> And life filled with sunbeams, when Shorty would say
> > "What's yours, Pard?"

The cowboy gave American culture excellent folk ballads. "I'm a Poor Lonesome Cowboy," "The Dying Cowboy," and "Rosalie the Prairie Flower" are samples of the more popular ones. Perhaps the saddest of all cowboy ballads is

> "Oh, bury me not on the lone prairie,
> Where the wild coyotes will howl o'er me;
> Where the rattlesnakes hiss and the wind flows free,
> Oh, bury me not on the lone prairie."

They heeded not his dying prayer,
They buried him there on the lone prairie,
In a little box just six by three,
His bones now rot in the lone prairie.

When the range-cattle industry was at its height, the mining industry also flourished in certain areas of the high-plains country, as well as in the Rocky Mountain states. The California gold rush was only a harbinger of many others to follow. Gold brought settlers to Bannack City, Alder Gulch, Virginia City, and Last Chance Gulch (later Helena), in Montana. The discovery of gold in the Pikes Peak district of Colorado in 1858 drew a stream of one hundred thousand people across Nebraska to the mines. At the same time the fabulous Comstock lode was opened in Nevada. Mining, by this time, was an expensive proposition. Large sums were necessary to purchase mining machinery, and corporations replaced the old prospector as the key factor in the industry.

The last important gold rush in the United States came in the 1870's in the Black Hills of South Dakota. To Deadwood, in the heart of the Sioux country, came prospectors, as well as Wild Bill Hickok, Calamity Jane, and the rest of the floating population of the West. Stagecoach and ox team were the means of transportation for a decade, and Wells, Fargo & Co., an early express company, carried sixty million dollars' worth of bullion out of Deadwood by stagecoach.

The West of the cowboy, of the miners, and of the stagecoach was by no means a peaceful and law-abiding region. Professional bad men made life exciting and short. The most famous, or infamous, of all the bad men of the West was Billy the Kid, who, before he was killed at the age of twenty-one, boasted that he had murdered twenty-one men, not counting Mexicans and Indians.

While the range-cattle industry and mining were flourishing in the high-plains country in the 1870's and 1880's, the agricultural civilization was making the adjustments necessary to occupy the region. Once the farm frontier had solved the problems of transportation, fencing, water, and arid farming, it could proceed to the conquering of the high plains. As the transcontinental railroads pushed their ribbons of steel tracks across the short-grass country, the transportation problem was solved.

The fencing problem took a little longer. The farmer had to fence his crops to protect them from cattle and sheep grazing on the open range. Wood was too expensive to import from the East, and for a time an unsuccessful effort to substitute hedge fences was made. The

From *The Pacific Tourist,* 1879

Busted

invention of barbed wire, however, in 1873, solved the problem and soon brought the decline of the range-cattle kingdom as more and more of the open range was fenced. Barbed wire made stock farming, rather than the old type of ranching, the occupation of the high-plains area.

Barbed wire, then, made it possible for farmers to move from the prairies into the plains region, but the problem of sufficient water still remained. The available supply of water on the high plains fell far short of what was needed for successful agriculture. The region might have remained uninhabitable for farmers if the Industrial Revolution had not brought the mass production of windmills. The railroads and cattlemen were the first to introduce windmills into the plains. After the development of barbed wire farmers made wide-scale use of the factory-manufactured windmill, and without it large areas of the region would have remained uninhabited. Irrigation was another means of securing water in the region. At first, individuals organized irrigation associations, but gradually irrigation became accepted as a government task. The Federal government, by the Carey Act of 1894, gave to the states millions of acres of land for irrigation purposes, but eight years later the Federal government itself took charge of irrigation and, under the Reclamation Act of 1902, constructed gigantic dams and irrigation projects.

Irrigation, however, took care of only a small area of the short-grass country. By necessity, irrigation could be used, largely, only on the land close to the mountains. Wheat production in other areas could not have succeeded without the development of dry farming. By rapid plowing, which produced a blanket of dust, moisture was retained in the soil. This type of plowing would have been impossible without the advances in farm equipment that came with the Industrial Revolution.

THE FARMER ORGANIZES

Increasingly in the Machine Age, as the individual was more and more dwarfed, it became necessary for individuals to organize into groups to secure influence and to wield political power. As the farmers began to see mortgages mount and farm tenancy spread, and railroad rates and the prices of industrial goods remain constant or increase, they turned to farm organizations for protection. Over the years farm organizations helped to secure such beneficial legislation as the Interstate Commerce Act, the Sherman Antitrust Act, and the raising of the Department of Agriculture to cabinet rank.

Two years after the close of the Civil War, Oliver H. Kelley, a government clerk, founded the National Grange of the Patrons of Husbandry. The year before, while on a government survey of the South, Kelley had been impressed by the drabness of life and the need of education for rural people. From 1872 to 1874, years when farm prices were depressed, the Grange gained a large membership, and by 1875 it numbered eight hundred thousand people, located principally in the Midwest and the South.

The Grange labored to increase the comforts of the farm home, to teach scientific farming, and to establish co-operative buying and selling and co-operative manufacturing units. The Grange admitted women to membership and through its meetings and picnics afforded a social life seriously needed in isolated rural communities. It had little success in its economic ventures, however. Private manufacturers and bankers fought co-operative industries and banks, and this opposition, in addition to poor management, spelled the ruin of most of the economic undertakings.

Although the Grange announced that it was not an organization with political purposes, it proved to be a rallying point for discontented farmers. Farmers' parties, closely allied to the Grange, captured political offices in such states as Illinois, Iowa, Kansas, and California, and soon secured the enactment of laws regulating railroad and warehouse charges. The Grange was replaced as the organ of farm protest, however, in the 1880's, by the more militant Farmers' Alliance. During that decade a Northern Alliance and a Southern Alliance were organized, and these two groups demanded more effective government regulation of railroads, abolition of the national banking system, a currency controlled by the government, a more equitable system of taxation, and political reforms, such as the initiative, the referendum, and the direct election of United States Senators. The Alliances also promoted social functions for the farmers, as well as educational activities, and sponsored co-operative elevators and insurance companies.

But it was in the field of political action that the Alliances were to make their most significant contribution. In 1890 they became the basis of the Populist, or People's, party. The Populists were to launch the first real, significant revolt against the dominance of American economic and political life by the industrial forces. They were to try to rally the American people to an understanding of the new problems created by the growth of urban industrialism and the end of the frontier era in American development.

THE END OF AN ERA

By 1890 the farming civilization had so completely assumed control of the plains region that the census of that year announced that, for the first time in American development, there was no longer a frontier zone. There was still, of course, some free land to be had in the West, but there was no longer any large, definable area in which there were fewer than two to six people per square mile. The end of the frontier, as Frederick Jackson Turner has pointed out, "marked the closing of a great historical movement."

President Theodore Roosevelt, from 1901 to 1909, had to call frequent meetings of governors and conservation authorities to consider the sad state of our depleted resources. At the same time, it became clear that in the past the American farmer had made the largest percentage of his profits from the rising value of his lands and from the squandering of the natural fertility of the soil. Land prices would rise in the future, but not so steadily as in the past, and depleted soils would require more scientific and more expensive care. If young people were to be retained on the farms, life had to be drastically altered. The future of America, after 1890, belonged to the city, to industry, and to

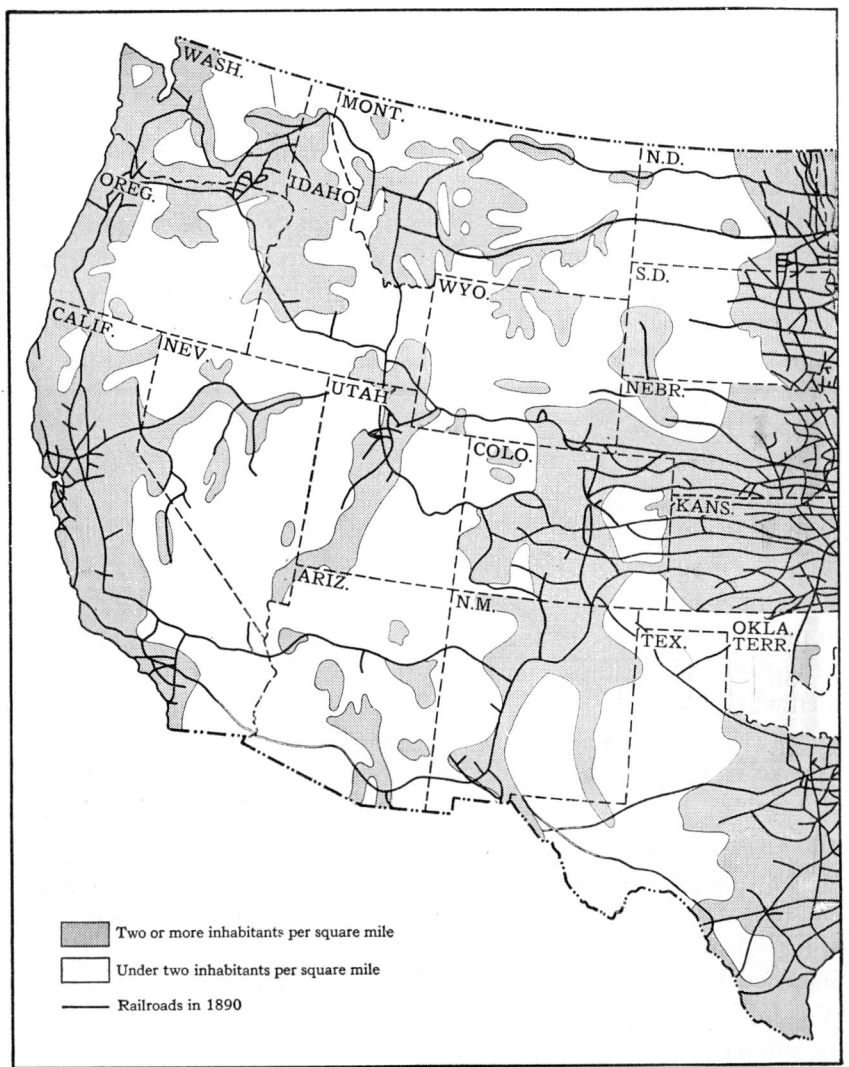

Railroads Pushing East and West Closed the American Frontier

a new kind of agriculture. Also, America was turning back to face Europe after sixty years of relative isolation.

Until the 1890's the great natural forces in American economic and social life had dictated a democratic way of life based mainly on a high average standard of living. All that was necessary to utilize the resources of America and to increase the standard of living was to turn the individual loose to exploit and to develop these resources. Opportunity for all was so great during this development that the question of equality of opportunity for all took care of itself. The frontier, free land, and isolation from world troubles made possible and encouraged the full development of the rugged individualist. Well might the government "keep its hands off." But freedom under urban industrialism had proved to be something quite different from the American experience of freedom up to the Civil War. Freedom for the individual under industrialism too often meant freedom to exploit and freedom to lift the few above the many. It created America's first real crop of millionaires, her first permanent paupers, her first slums, and her first serious class hatreds—hatreds that could not be solved, as in the past, by social mobility.

If democracy was to live, the emphasis in American life had to shift from freedom of the individual to another ingredient of the democratic faith, equality of opportunity. For men to have an equal chance under industrialism, it was necessary that government should become more active in American life. Government would have to establish controls to prevent the misuse of freedom by the selfish few. It would have to struggle to enforce these controls in the face of the opposition of strong men who had no interest in or desire for freedom or equality for anyone except themselves. The American people, to preserve democracy, would have to chart a path whereby government would prevent the misuse of freedom, but, at the same time, would not go too far and stifle initiative. The Populist crusade of the 1890's and Bryan's campaign of 1896 were the first real acknowledgments that the frontier economy had passed and that now the people would have to turn to government to help them to secure democracy under industrialism. Years later Ray Stannard Baker, one of the leading muckrakers and the biographer of Woodrow Wilson, looking back on the decade of the 1890's, wrote, in his autobiography, *Native American:*

Most of my ancestors on both sides had been pioneering for two hundred and fifty years before I was born, exploring, surveying, opening new land, building up small frontier communities. My own generation saw the end of that process. Professor Frederick J. Turner, authority upon the pioneer era, has said that the early 90's marked the end of the frontier in America. I had been brought up on the "last frontier," and I was, presently, to be turned back into crowds, and life in the city. I have had the rare experience of having in my own life passed through all the stages of American development from pioneering to the complicated and dangerous civilization of today; from the intense individualism and the simplicities of the frontier to the advancing, jostling, uneasy, more or less unacceptable socialism of the present hour. When I went to Chicago at the age of twenty-two (1892) I had not the slightest idea that the old free life of the frontier, in which I had grown up, had become a thing of the past, that the American people and I with them were entering into a new world with new problems and a new kind of civilization.[1]

SELECTED BIBLIOGRAPHY

L. B. SCHMIDT and E. D. Ross, *Readings in the Economic History of American Agriculture*; F. A. SHANNON, *The Farmer's Last Frontier*; W. T. HUTCHINSON, *Cyrus Hall McCormick*, valuable on various aspects of the farm story.

HOWARD ODUM, *Southern Regions of the United States*; RUPERT VANCE, *Human Geography of the South*; H. C. NIXON, *Forty Acres and Steel Mules*, throw light on Southern agriculture and its problems.

The literature of the farm country is voluminous, but among the best items are HAMLIN GARLAND, *Main-Traveled Roads*; ED HOWE, *The Story of a Country Town*; OLE RÖLVAAG, *Giants in the Earth*; WILLA CATHER, *O Pioneers*; MARI SANDOZ, *Old Jules*; FRANK NORRIS, *The Octopus*.

JOHN D. HICKS, *The Populist Revolt: A History of the Farmers' Alliance and the People's Party*, and S. J. BUCK, *The Agrarian Crusade: A Chronicle of the Farmer in Politics*, valuable for farm organizations.

R. E. RIEGEL, *America Moves West*; L. R. HAFEN and COKE RISTER, *Western America*; DAN CLARK, *The West in American Life*, general material on the settlement of the West; W. P. WEBB, *The Great Plains*, the classic treatment of this region.

H. S. COMMAGER (Ed.), *Documents of American History*, pp. 122, 125, 132–135, 138, 146, contains source material.

[1] Charles Scribner's Sons, New York, 1941.

XXII

Politics and Personalities,
1868-1896

N O PERIOD so thoroughly ordinary had been known in American politics since Christopher Columbus first disturbed the balance of American Society," Henry Adams once remarked of the years following the Civil War. The years from the Presidency of General Grant to the election of 1896 were characterized by a lack of brilliance and color in the White House. From Rutherford B. Hayes to Benjamin Harrison the Republican Presidents were respectable mediocrities who, in their social and economic thinking, were thoroughly convinced that the Republican party's support of the industrial forces was in accord with some divinely ordained plan. As to the Presidency of Grant, Henry Adams trenchantly observed:

> Grant was archaic, pre-intellectual. . . . He had no right to exist. He should have been extinct for ages. The idea that, as society grew older, it grew one-sided, upset evolution, and made education a fraud. That, two thousand years after Alexander the Great and Julius Caesar, a man like Grant should be called —and should actually and truly be—the highest product of the most advanced evolution, made evolution ludicrous. One must be as commonplace as Grant's own commonplaces to maintain such an absurdity. The progress of evolution from President Washington to President Grant, was alone evidence enough to upset Darwin.[1]

With the hero of Appomattox as their candidate in 1868, the Republicans, in the first postwar Presidential election, made widespread use of the patriotic slogans and issues arising from the war. Voters were urged to vote as they had shot during the conflict, and the Democrats were denounced as a disloyal party and as a force opposing political rights for the Negroes. Such issues of the new industrial age as tariffs, money policy, and governmental subsidies to business were carefully avoided in the Republican campaign.

[1] *The Education of Henry Adams*, p. 266. Houghton Mifflin Company, Boston, 1918.

The Democratic party found itself in a difficult situation in 1868. The activities of the peace Democrats during the war served to cripple the party at a time when the Republicans were thoroughly utilizing appeals to past emotions. Furthermore, disgruntled agrarian forces were demanding that the party frankly oppose the new industrial groups, which were using the government. An occasional gesture was made to these agrarians, led by William Allen and George Pendleton of Ohio, but actually, from 1868 to 1896, the party was in control of men who supported the new industrial group almost as ardently as did the Republicans. Conservative Horatio Seymour, Democratic war governor of New York, was nominated for the Presidency on a platform which criticized radical reconstruction as "unconstitutional," which praised President Johnson's administration, and which made a concession to the agrarian forces by endorsing the "Ohio idea," which was to pay the public debt in greenback, paper currency rather than in specie, as the Republican platform advocated.

In spite of Grant's military prestige, he received only 52 per cent of the popular vote and a popular majority of only three hundred thousand. Grant could not have been elected without the radical reconstruction policy, which still deprived three Southern states of the right to vote, the disfranchisement of two hundred thousand whites, and the enfranchisement of seven hundred thousand Negroes. In view of this situation, there is little doubt why Grant, who in 1866 had urged moderate reconstruction, pursued a radical policy during his administration. Through a continuation of radical reconstruction, the Republicans hoped to establish Republican supremacy so firmly that when Federal troops were withdrawn from the South, that area would still support the Republican party. The radical Republicans did not succeed in this attempt, however, and after 1876 the South reverted to an unswerving allegiance to the Democratic party.

While the Southern agrarians were still an impotent force in national life, the Grant administration continued the wartime policy of subsidizing and otherwise encouraging the growth of industry. When Grant left office, the industrialists were so firmly entrenched that the agrarians were not to be a serious threat until 1896. The repeal of war taxes, for instance, was not followed by a lowering of the tariff. Duties on wool and woolens had been raised in 1867, and during Grant's first term rates were raised on such products as copper and steel rails. Fear of the Liberal Republican movement in 1872 led to a 10 per cent reduction of the tariff, but the depression of 1873 was used as an excuse to return the tariff to its former high level. As the high tariff remained year after year, what had been justified as a war expedient became an entrenched economic policy. As a result, more and more people became convinced that the high tariff was the "American way" and that it was responsible for the American standard of living. By 1876 industrialists had succeeded in winning general acceptance of the idea that the support of an economic policy of benefit to themselves was a patriotic duty.

The Grant administration was also a handmaiden of the new age in the field of financial policy. The principal issues centered around the question of the national debt and the circulating medium. Eastern banking groups advocated the payment of the debt in gold, even though they had purchased the government bonds with depreciated paper currency during the war. The agrarian forces supported the "Ohio idea" of paying off the debt in greenbacks. The banking circles followed the prevailing English theory that coin or bullion was the only real money. They maintained that gold did not fluctuate in price, and therefore was the only true monetary standard.

The National Banking Act of 1863 was the first step of private bankers to control the currency, since under this measure they received the right to issue paper money based on the amount of government bonds that they owned. In order to remove the government from the field of emitting money, the bankers set out to retire the government's greenback currency. In 1866 Congress, under this pressure, authorized the retirement of greenbacks at the rate of four million dollars a month. A mild depression in 1867 provoked such vigorous opposition to this policy that the retirement of any more greenbacks was stopped. The panic of 1873 stirred a great demand for more currency, but President Grant vetoed a bill that would have restored the greenbacks to their original quantity before the passage of the act of 1866. Although banking forces were not able to secure the removal of greenback currency, in 1875 Congress did pass a law declaring that the greenbacks would be redeemed in gold. As a result, the bankers achieved their objective of basing the currency system on the bullion theory of money. There was bitter opposition to the hard-money policy, not only from the debtor class, but also from such men as Thaddeus Stevens, Peter Cooper, Horace Greeley, and Wendell Phillips. These men argued that gold was only a commodity and its value depended on the amount in circulation. It was the duty of the government, they contended, to regulate the circulation of money in accordance with the business needs of the nation. The only rational currency, they maintained, was a national

Harper's Weekly, 1871, from Library of Congress

The Tammany Tiger Loose.

"What are you going to do about it?"

Thomas Nast conducts a cartoon war against the corruption
of Tammany Hall in New York politics

currency based on the credit of the Federal government and issued by
the government in the interests of all the people. Although these men
were characterized as repudiationists and menaces to the sanctity of
property, their ideas were to be carried out in the administrations of
Woodrow Wilson and Franklin D. Roosevelt.

Although the public's attention during the Grant era seemed to be
focused on Southern reconstruction, and politicians garnered votes by
appeals "to vote as you shot," the basic issue of the day was the economic change to urban industrialism. The corruption of politics by
business, in the years from 1868 to 1876, to secure favorable legislation
was rampant. Expensive business lobbies bought the votes of city councilmen, state legislators, and Congressmen. Even cabinet officials were
involved in scandals, and one Senator charged that corruption "haunted
the footsteps of the trusted companions of the President."

Boss Tweed in New York, whose ring, from 1863 to 1871, looted the
city of something between twenty and two hundred million dollars,

was just a symbol of similar politicians elsewhere, who, with their machines, ran government in the interest of seekers of special privilege.

Harper's Weekly, 1875

Calling in Frauds. "Step up, gentlemen. Don't be bashful."

Thomas Nast assails corruption in the Grant administration

President Grant himself, in a general and indirect way, was responsible for some of the most unsavory scandals of the day. Two examples will suffice to demonstrate how even the President of the United States contributed to the low moral tone of the era. During the Grant administration a Whisky Ring was organized for the purpose of evading the Federal tax on distilled liquor. With the connivance of internal-revenue officials, this ring deprived the Federal government of vast sums of money. When Grant's Secretary of the Treasury, B. H. Bristow, investigated the affair and discovered that Grant's secretary, General O. E. Babcock, was closely connected with the ring, Grant shielded Babcock and eventually forced Bristow to resign from the Cabinet. In another case, where Grant's Secretary of War, General W. W. Belknap, was involved in scandals connected with the administration of Indian affairs, the President protected his friend by allowing him to resign his post. "The role he [Grant] played in crippling both the Whiskey Ring prosecutions and the impeachment of Belknap," Allan Nevins has written, "offers the darkest page in the history of the Presidency . . . other loose and scandalous times— in Buchanan's day, in Hanna's, in Harding's—have been repellent enough, but the Grant era stands unique in the comprehensiveness of its rascality."

In 1872 moderate Republicans, in various sections of the country, repelled by Grant's Southern policy and by the unsavory influences and events of his Presidency, called a Liberal Republican convention to oppose "Grantism" in all its forms. This Liberal Republican movement was a resurgence of the moral idealism that had controlled the party in its early days, and its advocates wanted to turn away from war issues and focus attention on such current issues as the tariff.

Unfortunately the Liberal Republican convention was packed by small-time politicians, who nominated Horace Greeley of the *New York Tribune* for the Presidency, an incredible choice in view of his past record. Greeley was a high-tariff man, he had once advocated utopian socialism, he had supported many fads, and he had signed Jefferson Davis's bail bond. Although Greeley was honest and sincere, his idiosyncrasies wrecked the Liberal Republican campaign.

Grant's followers, making the most of the bloody-shirt appeal, won the votes of Negroes and Northern veterans. Grant received also the support of business and industrial groups, which feared that the opposition would check government subsidies to business; and he received a heavy vote from urban workingmen, who were wallowing in a post-war boom. The Liberal Republicans, backed by Democrats who had abandoned their own ticket, fared poorly in the election. Grant received 56 per cent of the popular vote, and he was re-elected in the Electoral College by a vote of 286 to 63.

THE DISPUTED ELECTION OF 1876

The panic of 1873 and the resulting depression marked a rebirth of the Democratic party and a decline in the value of the bloody-shirt appeal and war issues in general. In the mid-term elections of 1874 the voters punished the incumbent party for their economic woes by placing the Democrats in control of the House of Representatives for the first time since the outbreak of the war. As resulting Congressional investigations unfolded the corruption of the Grant administration, the Democratic chances for 1876 reached a new high.

The Democrats nominated Governor Samuel J. Tilden of New York, who had attracted nationwide attention by helping to crush the Tweed Ring in New York City. His war record, however, subjected him to the charge of copperheadism by the worried Republicans. His attitude toward the new issues of the day was thoroughly in step with that of the industrial forces. He himself had acquired a large fortune by serving as an attorney for such promoters as Jay Gould and Jim Fisk.

The promise of the Democrats that they would remove "Grantism" from Washington was weakened in its effect by the Republican nomination of Rutherford B. Hayes, governor of Ohio, who had supported the merit system for the civil service in that state and who was in no way tainted by "Grantism." Hayes had risen to power in Ohio politics by his "sound-money" policy and his opposition to the agrarian forces in their demand for a more flexible greenback currency. The Hayes-Tilden nominations clearly signified that both parties had placed candidates on their tickets who were deeply in accord with the industrial and financial forces.

On election day Tilden obtained a popular majority, but the Republicans asserted that Hayes had received one hundred and eighty-five electoral votes and therefore was elected. Actually the electoral votes of South Carolina, Florida, and Louisiana were in dispute, and Hayes needed all these votes to be elected, whereas Tilden needed only one. With the aid of Federal troops, Republican returning boards in these three states, which still did not have home rule, sent returns to Washington for Hayes. The Democrats, however, filed their own returns, and Congress was faced with these two sets of conflicting votes. A Republican Senate and a Democratic House finally decided that a special Electoral Commission would have to judge which returns to accept. The Commission was composed of five Senators, three of whom were Republicans; five Representatives, three of whom were Democrats; and five Supreme Court justices, two from each party and a nonpartisan justice, David Davis of Illinois. At this juncture the Illinois legislature elected Davis to the Senate, causing him to withdraw from the Commission, and leaving only Republican justices from which to draw. Hayes was elected President as the result of the eight Republican votes in the Commission.

One student of this election has reached the conclusion that the Democrats stole the election in the first place and then the Republicans stole it back. It is the opinion of P. L. Haworth, in *The Hayes-Tilden Disputed Presidential Election of 1876*, that Hayes would have won in a free election. Many Southern Negroes, who would have voted Republican, were deprived of the right to vote in those states where the Southern whites were back in control. "All things considered, it appears, both legally and ethically, the decision was a proper one," declares Haworth.

While the Electoral Commission was reaching its decision, Southern Democrats, who desired home rule more than a Tilden victory, reached an agreement with friends of Hayes that military rule in the South would end if Hayes were elected. Although Hayes was not a party to this agreement, he did withdraw the Federal troops during his term in office.

When the Federal troops were withdrawn from the South, the states quickly threw off their reconstruction governments and returned to home rule. Since 1866 a secret organization known as the Ku Klux Klan had been at work attempting to intimidate the Negro and to weaken his participation in public affairs. Arrayed in ghostly white robes and other disguises, Ku Klux members rode about the country-side at night, threatening and frightening "objectionable" Negroes, breaking up meetings of the Union League, and, now and then, resorting to the use of violence to accomplish their purposes. So effective did their efforts become that Congress passed a series of laws laying heavy penalties on those found guilty of using force or bribery to prevent "citizens" from voting, or of forming conspiracies, wearing disguises, or intimidating witnesses. The President was even authorized to suspend the writ of habeas corpus, where necessary, to suppress Klan activities. Backed by the Union army, such measures were more or less effective, but they lost all force when the troops were gone.

One by one, the Southern states pushed the Negro and the carpet-bagger aside and took steps to repeal much of the legislation that the reconstruction legislatures had passed. Debts were repudiated, ingenious laws were passed to prevent the Negro from voting, and a "solid South," always voting the Democratic ticket, took its place in national politics. The fight was most bitter in South Carolina and Louisiana, and recovery was longer delayed there. Much of the internal strife between local groups in these states in the next decades grew out of conditions generated in these early years. In fact, much of the backwardness in industry and in education, as well as the bitter strife between "Bourbons" and the "wool-hat boys," which characterized a good deal of the South for a generation, was a result of reconstruction. Not until near the end of the nineteenth century did the new South begin to emerge. Even then, when factories, better schools, and a better use of Southern resources had come, the South, with its share tenantry, its racial tensions, and its one-party system, was still a colonial dependency of the North.

FROM HAYES TO HARRISON

President Hayes had a difficult four years in the White House. The Democrats constantly referred to him as "His Fraudulency," and, being in control of the House all four years and of the Senate from 1879 to 1881, they hamstrung executive action. Even with his own party Hayes had none too pleasant a relation. His appointment of reformer Carl

Schurz as Secretary of the Interior and David M. Key of Tennessee, a Democrat and an ex-Confederate, as Postmaster-General alienated such powerful Old-Guard Republican bosses as Roscoe Conkling, Thomas Platt, James G. Blaine, and Simon Cameron. He alienated the Old Guard, particularly, by his attempt to improve the quality of the civil service. Although Hayes was unable to secure Senate approval of a law forbidding the assessment of officeholders for political purposes, he did force the removal of Chester A. Arthur as collector of the port of New York, a post which had long been a lucrative political plum for Senator Conkling and his partisans.

As for the economic issues of the day, President Hayes revealed his firm opposition to organized labor and to the agrarian demands for a more flexible currency. In the midst of the great railroad strike of 1877, Hayes called out the Federal troops and broke the back of the strike. In connection with the question of currency he vetoed the Bland-Allison Act of 1878, authorizing the purchase and coinage of not less than two million and not more than four million dollars' worth of silver per month. By 1878 those forces desiring an increased supply of money found their ranks augmented by the adherence of the silver-miners. Before 1873 silver had been too valuable to make into coins, and the silver dollar had been dropped from the currency list. The increased mining of silver, however, soon brought a drop in price and a clamor for silver to be returned to the coinage system. The greenback and silver forces joined together in 1878 and passed the Bland-Allison Act over President Hayes's veto.

President Hayes removed himself from the 1880 election by announcing early that he was not a candidate. This election revealed how close the Republican and Democratic parties actually were from the standpoint of strength. The Old-Guard Republicans, thirsting for the days of Grant, launched a third-term boom for the general, but James G. Blaine rallied the opposition and deadlocked the convention. As a result, dark horse General James A. Garfield of Ohio was a compromise choice. In order to smooth the ruffled feathers of Senator Conkling of New York, who had been the main support behind the Grant boom, the convention nominated his henchman Chester A. Arthur, ex-collector of the port of New York, for the Vice-Presidency. The Democrats too nominated a Civil War veteran, General W. S. Hancock of Pennsylvania, and their platform avoided the major issues of the industrial age as thoroughly as did the Republican platform. Garfield won over Hancock by a margin of 7018 in a total vote of about nine million.

Scenes from Late Nineteenth-Century Rural America

MURAL PAINTING BY THOMAS HART BENTON

A Meeting of the Grangers in Illinois

From *Frank Leslie's Illustrated Newspaper*, 1873

In the election of 1880, as indeed in all the elections from 1868 to 1892, the major-party platforms were so filled with ringing platitudes that third parties arose to carry to the public the issues created by an industrial society. The chief strength of these third parties came from depressed Midwestern farmers, and the platforms of these parties reflected the farmer's bitterness over his role in the new age. Advocating such reforms as government regulation of the railroads and the ending of monopoly, a more flexible currency, and such political reforms as the direct election of United States Senators, these parties, variously named Anti-Monopoly, Independent, Reform, and Greenback, made little impression during the 1870's and 1880's. Peter Cooper, for instance, running on the Greenback-Labor ticket in 1876, polled only eighty-one thousand votes out of a total cast of eight million.

Although these third parties had little immediate success at the polls, they did have a long-range value for American life. They planted the seeds of harvests that others were to reap. After they had agitated for many years on the necessity of reforms to adjust government to the needs of the new day, one of the two major parties would finally adopt their reform planks. William Jennings Bryan was to spearhead the Democratic absorption of these third-party demands in 1896, and Theodore Roosevelt was to lead the Republican. party into a similar course after 1901. It was, then, as harbingers of what was to come in American politics that the third-party movements of the Gilded Age have significance.

President Garfield had held office only six months when he was assassinated by a disappointed office-seeker. To the joy of the Old Guard Grant-supporters, Chester A. Arthur succeeded to the Presidency. Arthur, a New York City lawyer who had been educated at Union College, had achieved an unsavory reputation because of his administration of the port of New York in complete acceptance of the spoils principle. The tragic circumstance under which he assumed the Presidency, in addition to his reputation as collector, handicapped his term in the White House. Though he disappointed the spoilsmen by not prostituting his office to their purposes, he failed in the eyes of the reform element to rise far enough above his previous political background. Through his support of the Pendleton Civil Service Act (1883), however, Arthur did aid in the securing of a Civil Service Commission and the launching of a real merit system for government employees.

By 1884 President Arthur had so completely lost the support of the major elements in the Republican party that he was dropped in favor of James G. Blaine, "the Plumed Knight from the State of Maine." Blaine, however, had serious handicaps as a candidate. As a member of Congress, for instance, he had helped a railroad to secure subsidies from the government and, in return, had received private financial rewards. Blaine was a magnetic personality, but he was the type of leader who, during this Gilded Age, aided business interests in making use of the government. He manipulated votes in Congress for the benefit of the new forces, and he helped to lower the moral tone of government. His nomination cost the party the support of such independent Republicans as Carl Schurz and George William Curtis; and Roscoe Conkling, Blaine's bitter foe in the Old Guard, refused to campaign for Blaine because, he declared, "I don't engage in criminal practice."

The Democrats, who had won the popular vote in 1876 and just missed in 1880, were now in a favorable position. They nominated Grover Cleveland, reform mayor of Buffalo and governor of New York, who had won fame for his honesty and integrity and his willingness to fight Tammany Hall. "We love him for the enemies he has made," one of his supporters said in the nominating speech before the convention.

The resulting campaign was the most colorful and personal since 1860, and also it split party ranks wide open. Blaine's willingness to be a servant of special interests was thoroughly aired. The Republicans retaliated by charging that Cleveland had an illegitimate child, a charge which Cleveland did not deny.

In the midst of all the personal abuse of the campaign, one of Cleveland's supporters from Buffalo concluded that "the obvious course of wisdom would be to retain Cleveland in the public office where he had been so conspicuously faithful and relegate Blaine to that private life for which he was so eminently fitted by his domestic virtue." The election turned on New York State, where Blaine, because of family connections, had strong support among the Catholic population. A visiting preacher, S. D. Burchard, however, described the Democrats as the party of "Rum, Romanism, and Rebellion," and Blaine's failure to rebuke his supporter cost him New York's vote by a plurality of 1149, and the New York electoral vote put Cleveland in the White House.

The new President was a huge hulk of man, rather austere and frigid, but with an amazing capacity for hard work. His biographer Allan Nevins has written:

In Grover Cleveland the greatness lies in typical rather than unusual qualities. He had no endowments that thousands of men do not have. He possessed honesty, courage, firmness, independence, and common sense. But he possessed them in a degree that others did not. His honesty was of the un-deviating type which never compromised an inch; his courage was immense, rugged, unconquerable; his independence was elemental and self-assertive.[1]

Cleveland was a rank individualist, who acted according to what he considered right, regardless of party or public opinion. Although he was conservative in his economic attitudes and lacked an understand-ing of the problems facing the Midwestern and Southern farmers, he did defy the special interests which had been using the government in the past. He vetoed innumerable pension grabs on the part of Civil War veterans, he challenged the protective-tariff principle, he supported civil-service reform, and he led a fight against those groups that were raiding the public domain for their own interests.

Cleveland thoroughly believed that "a public office is a public trust." Many Democrats were angry because he did not turn all the spoils of office over to the party. The Grand Army of the Republic was furious when, in 1887, he vetoed a general pension bill which would have granted pensions to all veterans suffering from disabilities, regardless of how contracted. The lumber companies, the cattle interests, and the railroads, which had been despoiling the public domain, were incensed when he forced them to disgorge their illegal holdings. In 1887 Cleve-land devoted his entire annual message to Congress to the tariff ques-tion. Convinced that the protective system had bred trusts and had increased the price of protected goods, Cleveland denounced protection as "the vicious, inequitable, and illogical source of unnecessary taxation" and demanded a reduction in the interests of society as a whole. Pro-tectionists in the Senate blocked a resulting bill to lower the tariff, and Cleveland's stand became the issue in the campaign of 1888.

Although Grover Cleveland waged a courageous struggle against the use of the government by special interests, he had only a dim under-standing of the problems created by the industrial age. He did mention in his annual message of 1886 that the country was faced with a labor problem, and earlier he had been concerned over the paradox of wealth and luxury sharing the American scene with poverty and toil. Yet toward such problems as labor and taxation he revealed a basically conservative temper, a temper which was to become acute in his second term.

The Democrats renominated Cleveland in 1888, with no apparent

[1] *Grover Cleveland: A Study in Courage.* Reprinted by permission of Dodd, Mead and Company, New York, 1933.

ardor. To the Republican candidate, Benjamin Harrison of Indiana, rallied G. A. R. veterans, bitter at Cleveland's veto of outrageous pension bills, and business forces antagonistic to Cleveland's tariff message. The "bloody shirt" was once more waved because Cleveland had returned captured Confederate flags to the Southern states and had gone fishing on Memorial Day. The Republicans also utilized a trick to help to defeat Cleveland. A naturalized Anglo-American was persuaded to write the British ambassador and ask him which candidate would be best for England. The ambassador foolishly fell into the trap and answered, "Cleveland." When the ambassador's letter was published, it alienated key Irish votes in New York City. Tammany Hall, the Democratic organization in that city, also deserted Cleveland, because he was not a spoils politician, and Cleveland lost New York State by thirteen thousand votes. He polled 48.66 per cent of the popular vote and defeated Harrison by one hundred thousand, but the loss of New York's electoral vote gave Harrison the Presidency.

Grandson of a former President, Benjamin Harrison was a dignified and aristocratic man who had little comprehension of the social and economic problems of the day. With the Republicans in control also of both the House and the Senate, the business forces once more had an administration which would not check their special privileges. President Cleveland's civil-service reforms were wrecked, and Harrison so reverted to the spoils policy that the *Nation* denounced him as a "subservient disciple of the spoils doctrine."

Unlike Cleveland, Harrison allowed the G. A. R. to raid the Treasury, and he signed a pension bill in 1890 granting any veteran pension aid who could not perform manual labor, regardless of how the disability had been incurred. In the same year the Republican party pushed through a new tariff bill. In the light of Cleveland's margin of votes over Harrison, there was no mandate for the Republicans to increase the tariff, but special interests like the wool-manufacturers, the steel industry, and the sugar-growers clamored for increased rates. William McKinley of Ohio led in the drafting of the bill in the House, and protective rates were raised from about 38 to close to 50 per cent.

The Republican party had a difficult time in securing enough Congressional votes to pass the McKinley tariff. The Speaker of the House, Thomas B. Reed, had to be ruthless to push the bill through the House. In order to secure passage the protectionist forces also had to make a bargain with the silver group, promising to support a new silver-purchase measure in return for votes for the tariff. The Sherman

Silver-Purchase Act, also passed in 1890, pledged the government to buy four and a half million ounces of silver each month.

The McKinley tariff boomeranged on the Republican party. In the Congressional election of 1890 McKinley went down to defeat, and only eighty-eight Republicans were sent back to the House, whereas two hundred and thirty-five Democrats and nine Populists were elected. This election was more than just a protest against the tariff measure and Harrison's spoils politics; it was a warning that forces were developing to check the use of government by special interests—forces that would rally behind the new Populist party in 1892 and behind William Jennings Bryan in 1896; forces that were discontented with the submergence of the farmer, concerned over the rise of urban slums and industrial exploitation, and fearful that democracy would be destroyed unless government ceased to back special interests.

THE REVOLT OF THE NINETIES

"We meet in the midst of a Nation brought to the verge of moral, political, and material ruin," the Populist platform of 1892 declared. "Corruption dominates the ballot box, the legislatures, the Congress, and touches even the ermine of the bench. The people are demoralized; . . . The newspapers are largely subsidized or muzzled, public opinion silenced, business prostrated, our homes covered with mortgages, labor impoverished, and the land concentrating in the hands of the capitalists. From the same prolific womb of governmental injustice we breed the two great classes—tramps and millionaires."

The Populist party, launched in 1890, had behind it a mixture of anger over difficult times and the special favors going to the business group, and a genuine belief in and desire for a purer American democracy. It expressed all the resentments of rural people against the growing power of the urban world; it represented the fears of the farmers of the South and West that their political power was failing and that the two major parties no longer represented their interests; and it revealed an aroused hatred of the concentration of wealth and power in the hands of the few to the detriment of American democracy.

Before the Populists launched their revolt, Henry George, Edward Bellamy, and Henry Demarest Lloyd had taken stock of the industrial age and had asked how the American dream was faring, how democracy had come out in all the mad rush to build an industrial civilization. Henry George, walking the streets of New York in 1869, saw the violent contrast between the showy extravagance of the rich and the appalling poverty of the poor. The Gilded Age of the business rich and the filth and despair of the tenement districts made no sense to Henry George's democratic mind. Back to the Declaration of Independence he went for the expression of the democratic dream. "Insidious forces" were producing "inequality" and destroying liberty, he charged. He explained:

It is not enough that men should vote; it is not enough that they should be theoretically equal before the law. They must have liberty to avail themselves of the opportunities and means of life; they must stand on equal terms with reference to the bounties of nature. Either this or liberty withdraws her light! Either this or darkness comes on, and the very forces that progress has evolved turn to powers that work destruction.

Poverty, George explained, in *Progress and Poverty* (1879), was a social evil that had no place in the good society. The great trouble, George found, was that man's God-given right to the use of the land had been denied by private ownership of the land, which led to inequalities. By the single tax on land, which would wipe out the gain from rent, George proposed to achieve equality. The State, through the single tax, would become the instrument by which freedom and equality would be realities.

Edward Bellamy, in *Looking Backward* (1888), also faced the problem of happiness in the Machine Age and reached the conclusion that the destruction of competition by monopolies was responsible for the terrible gap between what seemed possible and what really existed. "Equality is the vital principle of democracy," he wrote. Until we recognized the "worth and dignity of the individual" and made material conditions subservient to man's well-being, democracy could not exist. Bellamy urged planning so that the economic and social forces might give a new equality and a new security to every man, woman, and child.

During the 1880's, in a series of articles, Henry Demarest Lloyd too attacked the menace of monopoly to democracy, and in 1894 he published his great work, *Wealth against Commonwealth*. Lloyd warned that "liberty permits wealth and wealth destroys liberty." He charged, on the opening page of this detailed study of monopoly:

Nature is rich, but everywhere man, the heir of nature, is poor. . . . The World . . . has reached a fertility which can give every human being a plenty undreamed of even in the Utopias But between this plenty . . . and the people hungering for it step the "cornerers," the syndicates, trusts, combinations, with the cry of "overproduction." . . . Holding back the riches of earth, sea, and sky from their fellows who famish and freeze in the dark, they declare . . . that there is too much light and warmth and food. . . . The majority have never been able to buy enough of anything; . . . [the] minority have too much of everything to sell.[1]

Although not directly connected with the Populist crusade, George, Bellamy, and Lloyd, in their writings, emphasized the developing tendency to look to government as an agent of social betterment, and they revealed that Americans still accepted the idea that Christianity offers a sound basis for a genuine democracy. The Populist party itself represented a close fusion of democracy and Christianity. "The upheaval that took place," one writer has observed, "can hardly be diagnosed as a political campaign. It was a religious revival, a crusade, a pentecost of politics in which a tongue of flame sat upon every man, and each spake as the spirit gave him utterance." "It was a fanaticism like the crusades," wrote William Allen White, bitter enemy of the Populists; and he continued:

Indeed, the delusion that was working on the people took the form of religious frenzy. Sacred hymns were torn from their pious tunes to give place to words that deified the cause [of silver] and made gold—and all its symbols, capital, wealth, plutocracy—diabolical. At night, from ten thousand little white schoolhouse windows, lights twinkled back vain hope to the stars. . . . Far into the night the voices rose—women's voices, children's voices, the voices of old men, of youths and of maidens, rose on the ebbing prairie breezes, as the crusaders of the revolution rode home, praising the people's will as though it were God's will and cursing wealth for its iniquity.[2]

The Populists were particularly strong in Kansas, Nebraska, and the Dakotas. They elected a United States Senator, for instance, in Kansas in 1890 and captured the governorship twice before their merger with the Democrats in 1896. In Kansas they were led by "Sockless" Jerry Simpson and by Mary E. Lease, who gained fame for telling the farmers that the only way for them to get anywhere was to "raise less corn and more hell." In 1891 Tom Watson of Georgia launched the Southern wing of the party and tried to organize the farmers for a fight against the merchants and industrialists of the new South.

The Populist convention in 1892 nominated General James B. Weaver for the Presidency and adopted a platform calling for a grad-

[1] Harper & Brothers, New York, 1894.
[2] *Stratagems and Spoils.* The Macmillan Company, New York, 1901.

uated income tax, a postal savings bank, government ownership of the railroads, telegraph, and telephone, the free and unlimited coinage of silver at a ratio of sixteen to one, a legal-tender currency issued only by the government, the initiative and the referendum, the direct election of United States Senators, the eight-hour day, and the prohibition of the use of labor spies. Although their platform was widely denounced as dangerous radicalism, most of its demands had been incorporated into the law of the nation by 1917.

In 1892 the Republicans renominated the incumbent, President Harrison, and the Democrats renominated Grover Cleveland. Both parties dodged the question of free silver, and the Democrats campaigned mainly against the McKinley tariff, which they characterized as the "culminating atrocity of class legislation." The elections went overwhelmingly Democratic, with both the executive and legislative branches in that party's hands. The new Populist party had a surprising degree of success for a third party in its first Presidential election, capturing over a million popular votes and twenty-two electoral votes for Weaver and electing two Senators and eleven Representatives to Congress.

The election, however, revealed serious weaknesses in the new party. It had made no impression on urban labor. Although it had appealed to the worker in its platform, the laboring man remained suspicious of the "employing farmer." The Rocky Mountain states supplied Weaver with half his electoral votes, but this region was interested solely in the free-silver plank in the platform. Also, from Iowa east the new party secured little support from farm people. It was too radical for the corn-belt farmer. The Populists also failed to crack the "solid South." Although Tom Watson tried to rally white and Negro farmers against the forces controlling the Democratic party, he was faced with the charge that he and his party were threatening "white supremacy." Nevertheless the Populists did force many people to consider seriously the new industrial age and to question how democracy was faring in this new environment.

CLEVELAND'S SECOND TERM

Later generations of Americans were to view the decade of the 1890's in a nostalgic fashion, believing that the era was characterized by lovers riding on bicycles built for two and singing the popular song "Daisy, Daisy . . . I'm half crazy all for the love of you!" For many people, of course, the nineties were gay. Good, solid, middle-class folk, undisturbed by the labor and farm revolts, lived in big Victorian houses with broad verandas and spacious lawns and spent the summers at the seashore or in the mountains. Lawn tennis was just in its infancy as a sport, and professional baseball was beginning to capture the imagination of the public. During this decade DeWolf Hopper gained fame by reciting and acting E. L. Thayer's "Casey at the Bat" in theaters across the land.

. . . .
There was ease in Casey's manner as he stepped into his place,
There was pride in Casey's bearing, and a smile on Casey's face;
And when, responding to the cheers, he lightly doffed his hat,
No stranger in the crowd could doubt 'twas Casey at the bat.
. . . .
Oh! somewhere in this favored land the sun is shining bright,
The band is playing somewhere, and somewhere hearts are light;
And somewhere men are laughing, and somewhere children shout,
But there is no joy in Mudville—mighty Casey has struck out.

Yet by the nineties even the most optimistic American had to admit that something had gone awry. The Gilded Age, as it had forged ahead, had left many shattered lives in its wake. Mark Twain and Charles Dudley Warner, in their novel, *The Gilded Age* (1873), presented a harsh description of the political corruption of the day, and novelist William Dean Howells, in *The Rise of Silas Lapham* (1884), portrayed the selfish aspects of American life against the panorama of the good society. Utopian novelist Edward Bellamy charged that American society presented the following picture:

I cannot do better than to compare society as it then was to a prodigious coach which the masses of humanity were harnessed to and dragged toilsomely along a very hilly and sandy road. The driver was hunger, and permitted no lagging, though the pace was necessarily slow. Despite the difficulty of drawing the coach at all along so hard a road, the top was covered with passengers who never got down, even at the steepest ascents. These seats on top were very breezy and comfortable. Well up out of the dust, their occupants could enjoy the scenery at their leisure, or critically discuss the merits of the straining team. Naturally such places were in great demand and the competition for them was keen, everyone seeking as the first end in life to secure a seat on the coach for himself and to leave it to his child after him.[1]

[1]*Looking Backward.* Houghton Mifflin Company, Boston, 1888.

Ulysses S. Grant

Horace Greeley

Grover Cleveland

William Jennings Bryan

Marcus A. Hanna

William McKinley

Grover Cleveland's second term was launched amid troublesome times. Two months after his inauguration a grave depression broke on the nation. Already there had been serious industrial troubles, symbolized by the violent Homestead strike in 1892. President Cleveland was not too well equipped to handle the acute problems facing the nation after 1893. Although he was honest, courageous, and hardworking, he lacked a comprehension of the social forces that were unloosed during his second term in office.

In the years from 1889 to 1893, while Cleveland was out of the White House, he had practiced corporation law in New York City and had become closely associated with some of the financial leaders of the day. As a result, he failed to appreciate the aspirations behind the farm and labor protests of the nineties. For instance, he appointed as his Attorney-General Richard Olney, a corporation lawyer who had a record of fighting the Sherman Antitrust Act in the courts. It was Olney who allowed the sugar trust to escape conviction by the Supreme Court in 1895, since, as the Court observed, Olney "had failed to submit any evidence that the law was violated." It was Olney, too, who used the Sherman Antitrust Act against the railroad strikers in 1894 and persuaded Cleveland to send Federal troops to Chicago to break the strike.

Soon after Cleveland took office, he was faced with a steady depletion of the government's gold reserve. Harrison's extravagant pension grants and the loss of government revenue because of the high McKinley tariff left the government, in 1893, with only about a hundred million dollars in gold. After the beginning of the depression, holders of government paper money began a run on the Treasury to secure the redeeming of the paper with gold. At this point Cleveland called a special session of Congress and forced through the repeal of the Sherman Silver-Purchase Act of 1890, which he held responsible for the draining of the government's gold. The silver had been paid for in government paper, and frightened people, after the start of the panic, demanded that this paper be redeemed with gold.

Cleveland, with his belief that the government's outstanding paper currency should be backed, dollar for dollar, by gold, was disturbed that the repeal of the Sherman Act did not stop the run on the Treasury. By January, 1894, there was less than seventy million dollars in gold in the government's coffers, while four hundred and fifty million dollars in paper could conceivably be presented for redemption. Cleveland moved to borrow gold to meet this situation, but a public bond issue failed to help. In desperation he went to his friend J. P. Morgan and exchanged government bonds for gold, with the agreement that the banking firm would obtain at least half the gold from abroad. The bankers made a good profit, and Cleveland was attacked for being a tool of Wall Street.

To the disgruntled agrarian and labor forces the bond agreement seemed further evidence that the government was on the side of the capitalists. When, the next year, the sugar trust escaped prosecution, and the Supreme Court declared an income tax to be unconstitutional, the agrarians particularly were convinced that the government was supporting one special interest against the rest of the nation.

In order to increase the government's revenue, Cleveland tried to force his party to redeem its campaign pledge of a tariff for revenue only. Eastern Democrats, however, allied themselves with protectionist Republicans, and between them they emasculated the administration's tariff measure. Although Cleveland allowed the Wilson-Gorman tariff to become a law without his signature, he did charge that the bill signified "party perfidy and party dishonor."

The mid-term election of 1894 reflected the grim economic depression and the growing revolt within the Democratic party against Cleveland's leadership. The Republicans captured both houses of Congress, and the Populists also cut into the Democratic vote. The struggle for control of the Democratic party during the next two years was to be most bitter. "Silver Dick" Bland of Missouri and young William Jennings Bryan called upon the rank and file to rescue the party from its conservative Eastern leadership. Although Cleveland fought this move, Bryan was destined to capture the party and repudiate its past support of the industrial forces.

While the Democrats were torn with internal strife, the Republicans boasted of an easy victory in 1896. William McKinley, governor of Ohio, was nominated for the Presidency by a convention dominated by Marcus A. Hanna, Cleveland businessman. Hanna was a shrewd, aggressive, hard fighter who wanted results from politics. He believed that the government should grant favors to business, agriculture, and the railroads. Good government, to Hanna, was synonymous with Republican control.

Hanna was one of the first businessmen of his day to deal with organized workers through contract agreements, and in 1894 he had been extremely critical of George Pullman's refusal to arbitrate with his workers. "A man who won't meet his men halfway is a fool," asserted Hanna. William McKinley too had a record that attracted labor support to the Republican ticket. As a young lawyer in 1876, he had defended thirty-three strikers indicted for rioting, when no other lawyer in Canton, Ohio, would risk his career. In the following year McKinley had entered Congress, and he served in the House of Representatives for fourteen years, where, as a member of the powerful House Ways and Means Committee, he collected valuable information on industry and the tariff question.

In 1896 Governor McKinley was nominated on a platform that praised the achievements of thirty years of Republican rule and contrasted this record with the "unparalleled incapacity, dishonor, and disaster" of the Cleveland administration. The Republican platform endorsed the protective tariff, asserting that "it secures the American market for the American producer. It upholds the American standard of wages for the American workingman; it puts the factory by the side of the farm, and makes the American farmer less dependent on foreign demand and price." The platform also opposed the free coinage of silver and announced its support of the gold standard. When the gold plank was adopted, Senator Teller of Colorado and thirty-three other silver advocates withdrew from the convention.

The Democrats, meeting three weeks later in Chicago, witnessed a turbulent struggle between the agrarian forces and the Eastern group, led by Senator Hill of New York. The agrarians captured the convention and adopted a platform calling for the unlimited coinage of silver and gold and blaming the gold standard for the hard times. The national banking system was denounced, and government control of the currency was advocated. The Cleveland-Morgan bond agreement was repudiated, and the McKinley tariff of 1890 was characterized as "a prolific breeder of trusts and monopolies," which "enriched the few at the expense of the many." The Supreme Court was criticized for its decision against the income tax, and government intervention in the Pullman strike was censured as "a crime against free institutions."

William Jennings Bryan, a delegate from Nebraska, made the concluding speech on the platform and dramatized himself as the spokesman for the bitter discontent that had been developing over the past few years. Except for his golden voice, Bryan, who enjoyed being called "the Christian Statesman," was a typical Midwesterner. The men of the Mississippi Valley understood him and respected him, even if they did not always vote for him. His ancestors were typical pioneers of upland-Southern stock who had followed the trails into Illinois and who had repeated the experience of other pioneers in seeking new opportunity in the West. Referring to his ancestors Bryan once wrote,

There is not among them so far as I know, one of great wealth or a great political or social prominence, but so far as I have been able to learn they were honest, industrious, Christian, moral, religious people . . . not a black sheep in the flock, not a drunkard, not one for whose life I would have to apologize.

Bryan was born in Salem, Illinois, in 1860 and grew to manhood in an extremely religious environment. His father was a Baptist, his mother a Methodist, which made it possible for him to attend both Sunday schools every Sunday. In the end he was to become a Presbyterian, thus merging in his own experience these three leading Protestant churches. His favorite songs for a lifetime were hymns, and he was always to be bitterly intolerant of all unbelief. He was confident, for instance, in 1908 that the American people would never elect William Howard Taft to the Presidency, because Taft was a Unitarian.

Bryan graduated from Illinois College, a small denominational institution, studied law in Chicago under Lyman Trumbull, Lincoln's old friend, and then moved to Nebraska. In 1892 he ran for Congress and carried on such a whirlwind campaign that he was elected in a normally Republican district. During his two years in Congress he fought the tariff and was an outspoken champion of the common man's struggle against privilege. In his thinking Bryan was typically rural. He believed that the farmers were the real producers and that the cities and industry depended on the farmers for their prosperity. At a time when corporations and trusts were prosperous and the farmers were suffering from droughts, mortgages, and high freight rates, Bryan fused the economic discontent of the farmers and the old Jeffersonian ideals of freedom and equality of opportunity into a new Western revolt.

He was more than just the Democratic candidate in 1896. He was the head of the whole bitter revolt of lesser men against the new urban-industrial America and its values. The whole substance of Bryan's appeal lay in his perfect fusing of the democratic ideal, Christian principles, and the farmers' bitterness over both loss of prestige and failure to prosper. He expressed it all in his speech before the Chicago convention in 1896. "I come to speak to you," he announced, "in defense of a cause as holy as the cause of liberty—the cause of humanity." To Bryan it was not a question of personalities; it was a question of principle. He accused Eastern businessmen of disturbing the business interests of the West and of making the definition of *businessman* too limited. The worker, the country lawyer, the farmer, and the small-town merchant, as well as those who ran industry and finance in the huge cities, should be classed as businessmen. What America needed, charged Bryan, was "an Andrew Jackson to stand, as Jackson stood, against the encroachments of organized wealth." He stood with Thomas Jefferson on the money question and insisted that "the issue of money is a function of government, and that the banks ought to go out of the governing business."

"There are two ideas of government," he told the convention. "There are those who believe that if you will only legislate to make the well-to-do prosperous, their prosperity will leak through on those below. The Democratic idea, however, has been that if you make the masses prosperous, their prosperity will find its way up through every class which rests upon them."

Thunderous applause greeted every sentence. The highest emotional fervor of the convention was reached when Bryan uttered his peroration:

> You come to us and tell us that the great cities are in favor of the gold standard; we reply that the great cities rest upon our broad and fertile prairies. Burn down your cities and leave our farms, and your cities will spring up again as if by magic; but destroy our farms and the grass will grow in the streets of every city in the country. . . . Having behind us the producing masses of this nation and the world, supported by the commercial interests, the laboring interests and the toilers everywhere, we will answer their demand for a gold standard by saying to them: You shall not press down upon the brow of labor this crown of thorns, you shall not crucify mankind upon a cross of gold.

In William Jennings Bryan, "the Boy Orator of the Platte," the whole rural world became articulate. He had uttered the protest of the old America against the overshadowing dominance of a new urban-industrial order. He had talked as farmers wanted to talk; he had talked like hardhanded men who daily read their Bibles, said their family prayers, and listened on the Sabbath to their Protestant minister's sermons. He had expressed their distrust of privilege and of corruption in politics for the sake of private gain, their contempt for the new city aristocracy, and their feeling that honest toil should give prosperity. He had called America back to old principles—as old as Jefferson, Jackson, and Lincoln. He had launched another democratic revolt.

Eastern interests understood this even better than Bryan himself. The *New York Herald* declared that his speech was "a shot as dangerous and treasonable as that fired on Sumter in '61." This paper also accused him of being "a puppet in the blood-imbued hands of Altgeld, the anarchist, Debs, the revolutionist, and other desperadoes of that stripe." The fact that John P. Altgeld, progressive governor of Illinois, who had freed the anarchists indicted at the time of the Haymarket bombing and who had secured laws limiting child labor and requiring factory inspection and the arbitration of labor disputes, supported Bryan was used against Bryan to demonstrate that he favored the curbing of free enterprise.

The Democratic party selected Arthur Sewall of Maine to be Bryan's running mate. The Bryan nomination and the progressive platform adopted by the Democrats wrecked the Populist party. When the Populists met in convention, they decided to fuse with the Democrats. The Populists, however, refused to accept Sewall, a bank-director and shipbuilder, and instead they nominated Tom Watson of Georgia for the Vice-Presidency. The silver Republicans threw their support to Bryan, while the gold Democrats, although nominating their own ticket, actually supported McKinley.

Mark Hanna raised the largest campaign fund ever used in American politics up to that election. Hanna did not subscribe to the hysteria against Bryan. "There won't be any revolution," he told the frightened members of the Cleveland Union Club. The country was flooded with campaign literature, and Hanna skillfully shifted the emphasis of the campaign from Bryan's attack on special privilege to the proposition that the Republicans alone could guarantee the full dinner pail. Republicans warned workers that if Bryan were elected, business would have to close, orphans and widows would lose their investments, and the farmers' crops would wither in the fields.

Bryan launched a colorful campaign, traveling eighteen thousand miles and speaking to nearly five million people. Although many people became hysterically pro-Bryan, victory was not in the air for the Democrats.

According to Governor Altgeld the Democratic cause faced impossible odds:

> It was confronted by all the trusts, all the syndicates, all the corporations, all the great papers. It was confronted by everything that money could buy, that boodle could debauch, or that fear of starvation could coerce. It was confronted by the disgust which the majority of the American people felt toward the National Administration, for which they held us responsible. It was confronted by the unfounded charge of being partly responsible for the hard times. It was confronted by a combination of forces such as had never been united before and will probably never be united again, and worse still, the time was too short to educate the public.

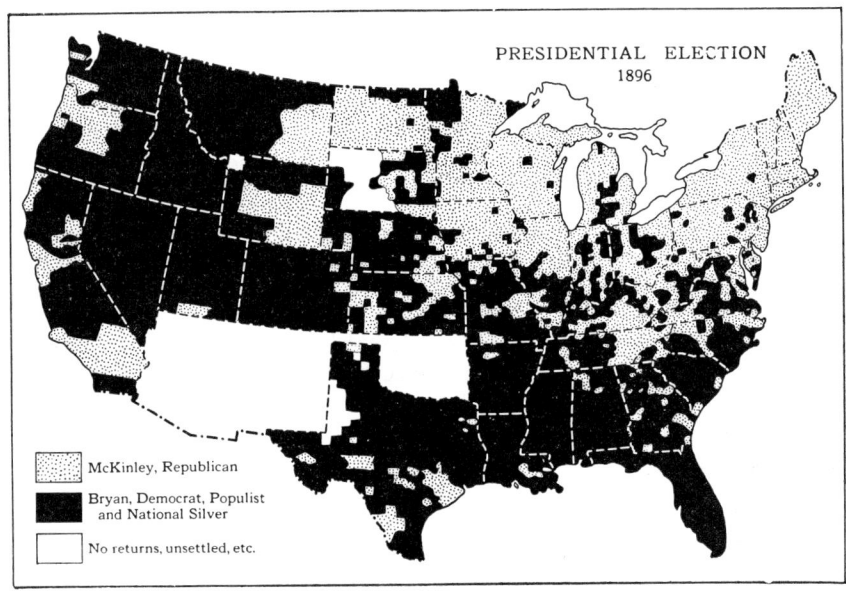

PRESIDENTIAL ELECTION
1896

McKinley, Republican

Bryan, Democrat, Populist
and National Silver

No returns, unsettled, etc.

The Presidential Election of 1896 by Counties

McKinley received a half-million more votes than Bryan, who carried only the South and the Mountain states. The electoral votes of the East, the Old Northwest, and such trans-Mississippi states as Iowa, Minnesota, North Dakota, Oregon, and California went to McKinley. Bryan's appeal to the rural population was impaired by a rise in farm prices and also by the entangling of the basic democratic revolt with the money question. Bryan made silver the symbol of democracy, and gold too became a symbol, with the result that the fight was reduced to one between the metals, losing its character as a struggle between democrats and aristocrats of the new industrial age. Mark Hanna's clever campaign, centering around the imaginary full dinner pail, confused the issue completely. The fate of the old agrarian, democratic America was linked with the soundness or unsoundness of "16 to 1." The question of equality and security for the masses in urban-industrial America was never faced.

After the defeat of Bryan one Eastern religious magazine commented:

Praise the Lord! The cause of National honor and righteousness has triumphed, and triumphed gloriously. The leaders of the forces of Free Silver and Repudiation, anarchy and class hatred have been overthrown, and their unrighteous cause is lost forever. The result shows that the people are leavened with the leaven of Christianity, and only things honest and of good report can command the support of the Christian conscience of this country.

The Bryan revolt was like that led by Jefferson, like that led by Jackson, and like that led by Lincoln in many of its essentials. By Bryan's time, however, basic changes had taken place in America, and the democratic problem was different. Two years after Bryan's defeat the United States was to fight a war with Spain and become a great imperial power. The old isolation of the past eighty years had ended. The passing of the frontier and the triumph of the industrial order required a shift in emphasis from freedom of the individual to equality of opportunity. Bryan's advocacy of the positive state was to prepare the way for the progressive reforms of Theodore Roosevelt, Woodrow Wilson, and Franklin D. Roosevelt.

SELECTED BIBLIOGRAPHY

W. E. BINKLEY, *American Political Parties*, and E. M. SAIT, *American Parties and Elections*, provide ample material on party platforms, elections, and candidates.

Among the better biographies are ALLAN NEVINS, *Grover Cleveland: A Study in Courage;* D. S. MUZZEY, *James G. Blaine;* H. J. ECKENRODE, *Rutherford B. Hayes;* ALLAN NEVINS, *Abram S. Hewitt* and *Hamilton Fish and the Grant Administration;* CLAUDE FUESS, *Carl Schurz;* W. A. WHITE, *Masks in a Pageant.*

There is a wealth of material in such autobiographies as J. G. BLAINE, *Twenty Years in Congress;* T. C. PLATT, *Autobiography;* HENRY ADAMS, *The Education of Henry Adams;* G. F. HOAR, *Autobiography of Seventy Years;* JOHN SHERMAN, *Recollections of Forty Years.*

Valuable books on special topics are T. S. BARCLAY, *The Liberal Republican Movement in Missouri;* HENRY and C. F. ADAMS, *Chapter of Erie;* MATTHEW JOSEPHSON, *The Robber Barons;* P. L. HAWORTH, *The Hayes-Tilden Disputed Presidential Election of 1876;* C. R. FISH, *The Civil Service and the Patronage.*

JOHN D. HICKS, *The Populist Revolt;* C. VANN WOODWARD, *Tom Watson, Agrarian Rebel;* WALTER JOHNSON, *William Allen White's America*, provide valuable material on various phases of the Populist movement; D. C. MCMURRAY, *Coxey's Army*, information on the troubles and unrest of the second Cleveland administration; W. H. HARVEY, *Coin's Financial School*, a contemporary bit of propaganda for the silver cause; HERBERT CROLY, *Marcus Alonzo Hanna;* THOMAS BEER, *Hanna;* C. S. OLCOTT, *William McKinley*, the Republican situation in 1896; W. J. BRYAN, *The First Battle*, Bryan's own view of the campaign; M. R. WERNER, *Bryan*, and PAXTON HIBBEN, *The Peerless Leader*, useful biographies of Bryan.

H. S. COMMAGER (Ed.), *Documents of American History*, pp. 54, 56–57, 64–66, 70, 81–82, 97–99, 104–107, 118–120, 126–128, 138–150, 155–170, 173–180, contains source material.

XXIII

Social Protest
and Industrial America

AMERICAN LIFE from 1901 to 1917 was greatly influenced by
the Progressive movement. Political activities, business attitudes, labor history, and social and intellectual trends were all
deeply affected by the ardor and intensity of the militant gladiators
who were fighting for the principles of a Progressive democracy. The
Progressive revolt was clearly in the American tradition. It was an
attempt to return to the older spirit of America, to the spirit of justice,
fairness, and honesty in dealing with one's fellow man. It tried to adjust the ideas of Jeffersonian democracy—the principles of freedom
of the individual and equality of opportunity—to the facts of the
twentieth-century industrial and urban economy, which were threatening to crush out equality of opportunity for the mass of Americans.
The Progressives, in order to achieve their ends, demanded that power
be concentrated in the hands of the Federal government and that
the government regulate industry, finance, transportation, agriculture,
labor, and morals. The Progressives thus rejected *laissez faire* and
justified public control of social and economic institutions on the principle that this was the only way to retain a liberal democracy in a society
where so much power had been concentrated in the hands of the few
who controlled industry and finance.

The Progressive movement also called for a new standard of honesty
in politics and business through the reform of political machines and
the restoration of ethics in business practice. The movement was liberal
in nature, not radical, since it did not want to abolish private ownership of the means of production, but, instead, to regulate and control
private ownership in an intelligent and orderly manner for the benefit
of society. In short, the goal was a liberal, democratic republic where
private ownership worked for society and not for its own selfish interest. The movement was optimistic, not pessimistic. Leaders like
Theodore Roosevelt, Woodrow Wilson, William Jennings Bryan, and

Robert M. La Follette were confident that they could achieve this goal within the existing framework.

THE LITERATURE OF PROGRESSIVISM

The most sensational aspect of the Progressive movement was the muckraking episode. A group of writers exposed, in concrete terms, the corruption and fraud to be found in business and political life. Theodore Roosevelt applied the name *muckrakers* to these writers as a term of derision, but the name was accepted by the writers themselves and soon lost its scornful implication. The phenomenal success that muckraking had after 1903 was due in part to the fact that popular magazines which had built up great circulations devoted themselves wholeheartedly to the business of exposure. Muckraking was really launched in October, 1902, when *McClure's Magazine* printed an article by Claude Wetmore and Lincoln Steffens entitled "Tweed Days in St. Louis" and, in November, one by Ida M. Tarbell, "History of the Standard Oil Company." In January, 1903, *McClure's* carried muckraking articles by Steffens, Tarbell, and Ray Stannard Baker. The public response to these articles was so great that other magazines entered this field, and by 1904 most of the major magazines were carrying a ringing attack on the abuses and evils in American life. Millionaires, United States Senators, clergymen, and politicians were all drawn and quartered by the muckrakers. The historian of the movement, C. C. Regier, has observed:

> Pure sensationalism some of this was, but much of it was the result of a real passion for social justice and an honest desire to set the truth before the people. The leading muckrakers were not cheap journalistic specialists in billingsgate; they were intelligent, educated, honest men and women. But they were nauseated by the spectacle of grab and graft presented in these United States. They were enraged at the corruption in municipal, state, and national governments. And they were shamed and sickened by the complacency of the majority of citizens, who remained utterly indifferent to the purulent condition of the political and industrial order. They were fighting for principles, and they did not hesitate to hit hard and often.[1]

Lincoln Steffens was the real inaugurator of the muckraking movement. After writing his article on St. Louis with Claude Wetmore, Steffens wrote a series on the American cities entitled *The Shame of*

[1] Reprinted from *The Era of the Muckrakers*, p. 10. University of North Carolina Press, Chapel Hill, copyright, 1932.

TWEED DAYS IN ST. LOUIS

*Joseph W. Folk's Single-handed Exposure of Corruption,
High and Low*

BY CLAUDE H. WETMORE AND LINCOLN STEFFENS

ST. LOUIS, the fourth city in size in the United States, is making two announcements to the world : one that it is the worst governed city in the land ; the other that it wishes all men to come and see it. It isn't our worst governed city ; Philadelphia is that. But St. Louis is worth examining while we have it inside out.

might have won. But a change occurred. Public spirit became private spirit, public enterprise became private greed.

Along about 1890, public franchises and privileges were sought not only for legitimate profit and common convenience, but for loot. Taking but slight and always selfish interest in the public councils, the big men misused

From McClure's Magazine, October, 1902

the Cities. Among the most important articles in the series were "The Shame of Minneapolis" and "Philadelphia: Corrupt and Contented." Other muckrakers followed in Steffens's footsteps and described corrupt conditions in other American cities. They soon learned that corruption was not confined to the cities, and they turned to the state governments. Steffens ranks first, too, among the muckrakers in state exposures. The conclusion that Steffens reached, after this lengthy study of city and state corruption, was extremely important from the standpoint of the future of American democracy. This conclusion he ably presented in his *Autobiography*, which ranks as one of the great books on American life produced in the last forty years. Steffens discovered that the source of bad government was not the politician, but the man who corrupted the politician in order to obtain favors. Captains of industry, for instance, who desired to gain a streetcar franchise from a city might buy up the politicians and thus corrupt politics. According to Steffens, the man most to blame for poor government was not the bribetaker, but the bribegiver. He said:

"Big Business" was, and it still is, the current name of the devil, the root of all evil, political and economic. It is a blind phrase, useless; it leads nowhere. . . . As early as St. Louis I had seen and written that the big businesses which were active in political corruption were the railroads, public service corporations, banks, etc., which are "big," but also saloons, gambling and bawdy houses, which are small. And I had seen and written that what these big and little businesses all had in common was not size but the need of privileges: franchises and special legislation, which required legislative corruption; protective tariffs, interpretations of laws in their special interest or leniency or "protection" in the enforcement of laws, calling for "pulls" with judges, prosecutors, and the police. . . . It was "privilege" that was the source of the evil; it was "privileged business" that was the devil.[1]

From city and state government the muckrakers turned to the Federal government. Here the most sensational articles, *The Treason of the Senate*, were written by David Graham Phillips for the *Cosmopolitan*. Senators Chauncey M. Depew and Nelson Aldrich were singled out as representatives not of the people, but of special interests. Phillips opened his series with expressive words:

> The Treason of the Senate! Treason is a strong word, but not too strong, rather too weak, to characterize the situation in which the Senate is the eager, resourceful, indefatigable agent of interests as hostile to the American people as any invading army could be, and vastly more dangerous: interests that manipulate the prosperity produced by all, so that it heaps up riches for the few; interests whose growth and power can only mean the degradation of the people.

While Steffens and other muckrakers were discovering that corruption in politics could be explained only if one realized the role of the seekers of special privilege, who corrupted politics, Ida M. Tarbell was corroborating this by her articles on the Standard Oil Company, which revealed the effect of this company on politicians in its machinations to obtain special privileges.

After the appearance of Miss Tarbell's series on the Standard Oil Company, other muckrakers battled valiantly against the evils in the business world. In 1904 *Everybody's Magazine* began the publication of articles by Thomas Lawson, called *Frenzied Finance*, which created a sensation. Lawson was not a reporter, but a great, colorful figure of the financial world. He was a stock-manipulator who had been forced out by his former allies, and his articles were a revelation of how ruthless financiers manipulated the stock market for their own benefit. The relations of labor and capital too received a great deal of attention at the hands of writers like Ray Stannard Baker, who described the techniques by which employers destroyed labor unions.

A campaign was carried on also against impure-food and patent-medicine frauds. S. H. Adams, writing in *Collier's* for October 28, 1905, gave an amazing description of the amounts of straight alcohol contained in some patent medicines. He discovered that many tem-

[1] *The Autobiography of Lincoln Steffens*, p. 492. Harcourt, Brace and Company, New York, 1931.

W. A. Rogers in *Harper's Weekly*, 1887

Nothing but Feed and Fight

FARMER JONATHAN (*who has just been rooting out foreign thistles*). "I guess this new breed of cattle has got to go next." (An early cartoon attack on the growing power of American monopolies.)

perance advocates drank some of these medicines to excess and were treated by doctors as simple alcoholics. According to Adams:

A distinguished public health official and medical official made this jocular suggestion to me: "let us buy in large quantities the cheapest Italian vermouth, poor gin, and bitters. We will mix them in the proportion of three of vermouth to two of gin with a dash of bitters, dilute and bottle them by the short quart, label them *Smith's Revivifier and Blood-Purifier;* dose one wineglassful before each meal: advertise them to cure erysipelas, bunions, dyspepsia, heat rash, fever and ague, and consumption; and to prevent loss of hair, smallpox, old age, sunstroke, and near-sightedness, and make our everlasting fortune selling them to the temperance trade."

The press of the nation also came in for attack. It was alleged that newspapers were in the pay of the special-interest groups. The Associated Press was frequently charged with being a monopoly, and Upton Sinclair, in one article, quoted an editor as referring to the AP as "the damndest, meanest monopoly on the face of the earth—the wet-nurse for all other monopolies."

Muckraking was militant and active from 1903 to 1912. The muckrakers contributed greatly to the Progressive belief that government regulation of business was necessary to protect the rights of the common man. The muckrakers undoubtedly exerted real influence on Federal and state laws that were passed to curb business excesses. Perhaps the happiest comment, and at the same time a penetrating remark, on the muckrakers was made by Finley Peter Dunne, American humorist and creator of the two Irishmen Mr. Dooley and Mr. Hennessy, whose views on all subjects were greatly cherished by the American public. Said Mr. Dooley to his friend Hennessy:

> Th' noise ye hear is not th' first gun iv a rivolution. It's on'y th' people iv th' United States batin' a carpet. . . . What were those shots? That's th' housekeeper killin' a couple iv cockroaches with a Hotchkiss gun. Who is that yellin'? That's our ol' frind High Finance bein' compelled to take his annual bath.[1]

Finley Peter Dunne expressed, in these words of Mr. Dooley's, the firm intention of the muckrakers not to destroy private capitalism, but rather to ensure the continued existence of this form of economic organization by necessary reforms before it was too late.

In addition to the muckraking literature, the Progressive era produced many novels of political and economic reform. Among the leading novelists were Jack London, Upton Sinclair, Winston Churchill (not the British statesman), Booth Tarkington, David Graham Phillips, and William Allen White. The Progressive novels of Churchill, White, Tarkington, and Phillips were written with the general assumption that private capitalism was satisfactory, provided businessmen had the proper ethical code. Phillips was the most strenuous of the novelists of the movement, writing twenty novels in ten years. White, in *A Certain Rich Man* (1909) and *In the Heart of a Fool* (1918), and Churchill, in *Coniston* (1906) and *Mr. Crewe's Career* (1908), from their own experience in practical politics, thoroughly presented the fight of the Progressives against unscrupulous businessmen.

The most effective pamphleteer of the Progressive movement was Upton Sinclair. Sinclair wrote against all oppression. *The Jungle*, published in 1906, was a book of great power. Into this book Sinclair

---

[1]Quoted by Elmer Ellis, *Mr. Dooley's America*, p. 215. Alfred A. Knopf, New York, 1941.

packed all the information that he had learned about the Chicago stock-yards from living in "Back of the Yards" with a workman's family. He described how diseased cattle were butchered and sold as clean meat; he related how the packers sold meat that had been condemned; and his descriptions of the conditions under which labor worked were revolting. After reading this book many people temporarily lost their appetite for meat. Sinclair once remarked that he had aimed at the public's heart in this book and by accident had hit them in the stomach. President Roosevelt was greatly influenced by *The Jungle,* and the book helped to prepare sentiment for the passage of the first Federal Pure Food and Drugs Act, shortly after the publication of the book. Mr. Dooley's description of the effect of the book on Roosevelt was one of his richest comments:

Tiddy was toyin' with a light breakfast an' idly turnin' over th' pages iv th' new book with both hands. Suddenly he rose fr'm th' table, an' cryin': "I'm pizened," begun throwin' sausages out iv th' window. Th' ninth wan sthruck Sinitor Biv'ridge on th' head an' made him a blond. It bounced off, exploded, an' blew a leg off a secret-service agent, an' th' scatthred fragmints desthroyed a handsome row iv ol' oak trees. Sinitor Biv'ridge rushed in thinkin' that th' Prisidint was bein' assassynated be his devoted followers in th' Sinit, an' discovered Tiddy engaged in a hand-to-hand conflict with a potted ham. Th' Sinitor fr'm Injyanny, with a few well-directed wurruds, put out th' fuse an' rendered th' missile harmless. Since thin th' Prisidint, like th' rest iv us, has become a viggytaryan, an' th' diet has so changed his disposition that he is writin' a book called *Suffer in Silence*, didycated to Sinitor Aldrich.[1]

Sinclair published innumerable other books demanding social justice. He varied from most other Progressive writers of this period in that he repudiated private capitalism and believed in socialism. With Sinclair, in the ranks of the socialist pamphleteers, belongs Jack London, who is still a staple in the literary diet of Scandinavia and Soviet Russia. In such books as *The War of the Classes* (1905), *Revolution* (1910), and *The Iron Heel* (1907), London prophesied a violent socialistic revolution, which would destroy private capitalism.

While the muckrakers were keeping the magazine world afire with exposures, and the novelists were publishing books on the need of reform, a group of more serious writers were publishing studies in which they showed their concern over the problem faced by an equalitarian democracy in an industrialized world. Among these writers

[1]Ibid. p. 217.

were Gustavus Myers, Thorstein Veblen, Frederick Jackson Turner, and Herbert Croly. Myers was primarily interested in the power politics of such families as the Vanderbilts, the Goulds, and the Morgans. His study *The Great American Fortunes* (1909–1910) charged that the history of huge accumulations of property was largely a narration of plunder. With the aid of the government, the plunderers gained concessions of land from the public domain, obtained public-utility franchises, and secured rich mineral deposits. Myers's book was a careful study based on the records of legislative investigations and court decisions. It aided the Progressive political leaders by offering them adequate facts to justify their work of regulating predatory wealth.

Frederick Jackson Turner's main interest during this era was in expressing the importance of the frontier to American development. In his great essay, *The Significance of the Frontier in American History* (1893), he insisted that freedom of the individual and equality of opportunity, made possible by free land, were the basic elements in the growth of democratic America. In other essays Turner explained that the Populists and the Progressives had turned to the government to secure for the common man the equality of opportunity that had disappeared when the expansion of industrial America had closed the frontier. Thus Turner's writings tended to give historical background for the activities of the Progressives.

Thorstein Veblen, through his *Theory of the Leisure Class* (1899) and *Theory of Business Enterprise* (1904), contributed greatly to Progressivism. His genius was that of a phrasemaker; we owe to him such phrases as *conspicuous leisure, conspicuous waste,* and *conspicuous consumption.* According to Veblen, the leisure class was composed of those who had secured ownership of land and resources, and thus did not have to do manual tasks. In order to display that status in society, they enjoyed their leisure in a conspicuous fashion, they wasted time and money conspicuously, and they consumed goods in a conspicuous manner. Perhaps the most vital distinction made by Veblen was that between the businessman and the industrialist. In *Theory of Business Enterprise* Veblen contended that the businessman was interested only in profit, whereas the industrialist was a technologist who was interested in making the machine produce the most goods for the satisfaction of mankind's wants. The businessman checked the work of the technocrat and actually sabotaged the machine by not permitting it to produce as much as it might, since the businessman was more interested in profit than in service to mankind. Veblen's writing helped

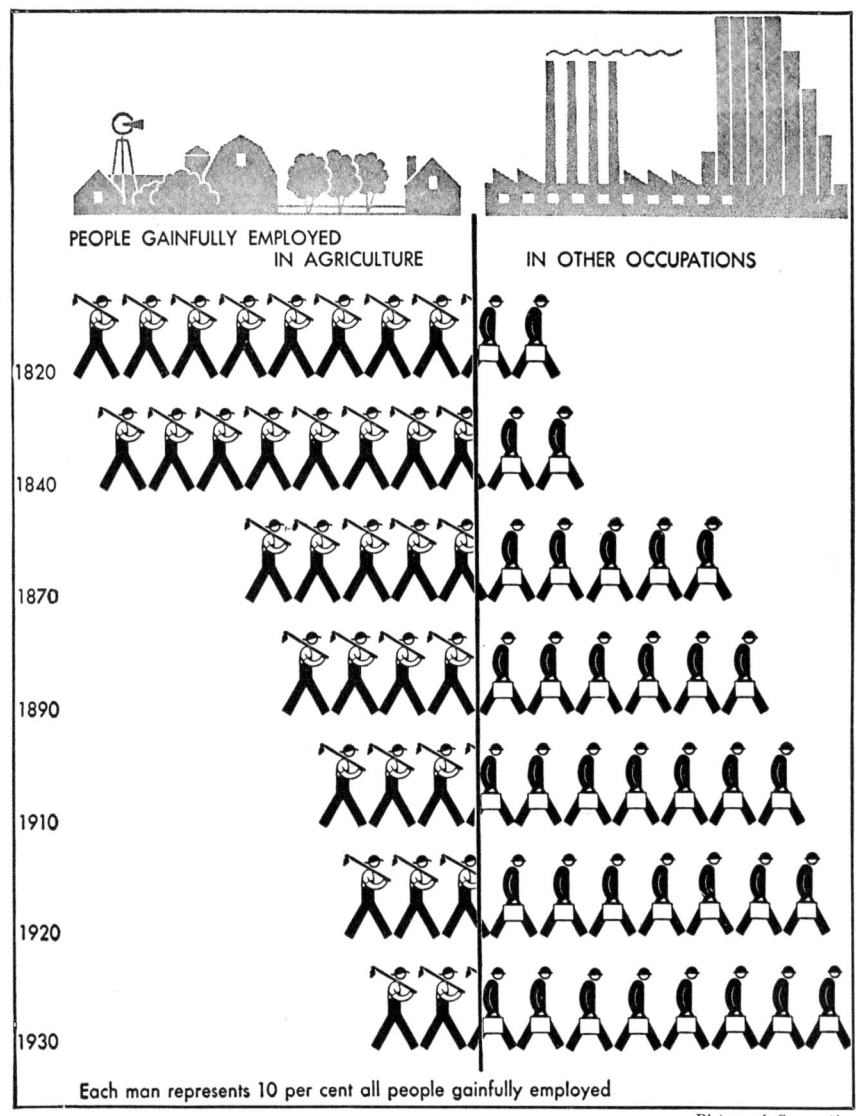

PEOPLE GAINFULLY EMPLOYED
IN AGRICULTURE   IN OTHER OCCUPATIONS

1820

1840

1870

1890

1910

1920

1930

Each man represents 10 per cent all people gainfully employed

Pictograph Corporation

Agriculture Surpassed by Industry

to awaken the public to the power of "vested interest" groups, and thus helped to furnish a more realistic approach to the problems facing American society.

The spirit that pervaded a good many Progressives was that of a desire to return to the simpler order of things in the American past—

to return the control of business to the small businessman, instead of permitting a few monopolists to control the industrial structure. During Theodore Roosevelt's Presidency the "good" man was the trust-buster. But by 1912 the inner circle of Roosevelt followers, who themselves had shaken the big stick at the trusts from 1903 to 1908, had decided that concentration in industry was here to stay and that, therefore, regulation of trusts, not trust-busting, was now in order. The campaign of 1912 clearly revealed this conflict among Progressives. The Wilson Progressives still talked of trust-busting and returning to the day of the small businessman. Theodore Roosevelt and the Bull Moosers, however, called for the regulation of industry instead of trust-busting. A book which influenced the Rooseveltians in their change of mind was *The Promise of American Life* (1909), written by Herbert Croly, founder of the *New Republic* magazine. Croly advocated a strong central government equipped to co-ordinate all activities in the United States. Croly was a Hamiltonian in emphasizing the importance of the central government, but he did this with a Jeffersonian bias in favor of opportunity for the common man. According to Croly,

In becoming responsible for the subordination of the individual to the demand of a dominant and constructive national purpose, the American state will in effect be making itself responsible for a morally and socially desirable distribution of wealth.

In 1914 Croly published *Progressive Democracy* in which he expressed his skepticism of Wilson's type of Progressivism. In describing the philosophy of the Bull Moosers, Croly observed, "Its advocates are committed to a drastic reorganization of the American political and economic system, to the substitution of a frank social policy for the individualism of the past, and to the realization of this policy, if necessary, by the use of efficient governmental instruments."

The above-mentioned serious writers of this era by no means exhaust the list of those who wrote influential serious books. For instance, if time and space permitted, one might discuss the following men and their books: Edward A. Ross, *Sin and Society* (1907), J. Allen Smith, *The Spirit of the American Government* (1907), Walter Weyl, *The New Democracy* (1912), Walter Lippmann, *A Preface to Politics* (1913), and Charles A. Beard, *Economic Interpretation of the Constitution* (1913). All these works made contributions by arousing the public to militant action in support of Progressive political measures. The part played by Louis Brandeis of Boston, though it was not, chiefly, that of a writer of books, deserves attention. As a lawyer arguing cases before the Supreme Court, Brandeis was the first man to introduce sociological data to prove that laws regulating hours of work and conditions of labor should be upheld. In 1914 Brandeis published a book based upon a Congressional investigation which revealed the dangers to democracy of a moneyed monopoly which, through interlocking directorates, could control the industrial structure and raise prices to the consumer. To illustrate how the financial oligarchy controlled American industry, Brandeis wrote the following description:

J. P. Morgan (or a partner), a director of the New York, New Haven & Hartford Railroad, causes that company to sell to J. P. Morgan & Co. an issue of bonds. J. P. Morgan & Co. borrow the money with which to pay for the bonds from the Guaranty Trust Company, of which Mr. Morgan (or a partner) is a director. J. P. Morgan & Co. sell the bonds to the Penn Mutual Life Insurance Company, of which Mr. Morgan (or a partner) is a director. The New Haven spends the proceeds of the bonds in purchasing steel rails from the United States Steel Corporation, of which Mr. Morgan' (or a partner) is a director. The United States Steel Corporation spends the proceeds of the rails in purchasing electrical supplies from the General Electric Company, of which Mr. Morgan (or a partner) is a director. The General Electric sells supplies to the Western Union Telegraph Company, a subsidiary of the American Telegraph and Telephone Company; and in both Mr. Morgan (or a partner) is a director. The Telegraph Company has an exclusive wire contract with the Reading, of which Mr. Morgan (or a partner) is a director. The Reading buys its passenger cars from the Pullman Company, of which Mr. Morgan (or a partner) is a director. The Pullman Company buys (for local use) locomotives from the Baldwin Locomotive Company, of which Mr. Morgan (or a partner) is a director. The Reading, the General Electric, the Steel Corporation and the New Haven, like the Pullman, buy locomotives from the Baldwin Company. The Steel Corporation, the Telephone Company, the New Haven, the Reading, the Pullman and the Baldwin companies, like the Western Union, buy electrical supplies from the General Electric. The Baldwin, the Pullman, the Reading, the Telephone, the Telegraph and the General Electric companies, like the New Haven, buy steel products from the Steel Corporation. Each and every one of the companies last named markets its securities through J. P. Morgan & Co.; each deposits its funds with J. P. Morgan & Co.; and with these funds of each, the firm enters upon further operations.[1]

[1]Louis D. Brandeis, *Other People's Money and How the Bankers Use It*, pp. 52–54. Frederick A. Stokes Company, New York, 1914. Quoted by permission of J. B. Lippincott Company, Philadelphia.

PROGRESSIVISM IN LOCAL POLITICS

The work of the muckrakers, novelists, and more serious writers of this period aided the political leaders of Progressivism in winning the public to a support of their measures. In many cities of the country alert political leaders carried out the ideals of the Progressive movement. Mayor Hazen Pingree of Detroit; Charles E. Merriam, Jane Addams, Raymond Robins, and Harold Ickes in Chicago; Fremont Older in San Francisco; Judge Ben Lindsey in Denver; Tom Johnson in Cleveland; and "Golden Rule" Sam Jones and Brand Whitlock in Toledo were the most conspicuous leaders of the Progressive movement in the American city.

These city Progressives did their best to change the conditions that had led James Bryce, in *The American Commonwealth* (1888), to state that the government of the American cities was the most conspicuous failure in the American system. The city reformers discovered the same thing that Lincoln Steffens was learning in his *Shame of the Cities*, that behind political corruption was economic corruption; that certain businessmen who wanted to control the street railways or who wanted their property undervalued so that they could pay lower taxes were the cause of a great deal of the political corruption of the day. These reformers generally came to the conclusion that in order to have good city government, the privileges that led to corruption must be eradicated. The best way to accomplish this was to have public ownership of the utilities; but many of the Progressives found that this could not be carried out, because the cities did not have home rule. The state legislatures usually had control of or supervision over a number of city activities, and thus the state legislatures too had to be controlled by the Progressives if Progressive measures were to be gained. The Progressives did not always succeed in winning control of state legislatures, and to this day state governments still control some of the vital activities of many American cities. As long as state governments were in the hands of conservatives, Progressives in the cities found their work checked. The city Progressive movements in Cleveland and Toledo, Ohio, deserve some detailed treatment as examples of the difficulties faced by Progressives in local government.

Tom Johnson of Cleveland was the most prominent Henry George mayor of the Progressive period. He came to office in Cleveland in 1901, and for ten years carried on a resourceful, hard fight against the Cleveland traction ring. Johnson had as his aides in this struggle Newton D.

Baker, later to be Woodrow Wilson's Secretary of War, and Frederic C. Howe, who in 1925 published a revealing autobiography, *The Confessions of a Reformer*. Johnson was a rich man, and the spectacle of a rich man battling to rid the land of some of the sources of easy wealth astounded many other rich men. One newspaper thought that Johnson had some sinister motive in his work for better government and called him "the fat casuist of Cleveland." Johnson knew all the methods of monopoly, since, in his earlier career, he had been a first-rate monopolist himself. At the age of twenty-two he had controlled the streetcar franchise of Indianapolis. When he entered the traction business of Cleveland, he learned the relationship between the granting of streetcar franchises and political corruption. Mark Hanna completed his education in how seekers of business privilege corrupted politics in order to gain means to exploit the people.

Johnson's conversion to devoting his life to serving the public, rather than exploiting it, came in a dramatic fashion. One day, while Johnson was riding on his own railroad, a "train butcher" refused to take no for an answer, and virtually forced him to buy one of Henry George's books on social problems. Johnson was so impressed with it that he then read *Progress and Poverty*. He did not want to believe all that George had to say about the exploitation that had taken place in America since the Civil War, but he could not find any loopholes in George's argument. Johnson took the books to his lawyer, and when the lawyer was unable to refute George's statements, Johnson went to New York City to see George. From that time on, Tom Johnson was an outstanding supporter of Henry George and the single-tax theory. While he was mayor of Cleveland, Lincoln Steffens called him "the best mayor of the best governed city in America." Johnson prevented the city from giving a valuable streetcar franchise to a private company, and he forced the fares to be reduced to a three-cent level. He was unable, however, to obtain public ownership of the street railways, because a law passed by the state legislature prevented this step. According to Frederic C. Howe, who helped Johnson in his fight for decent government:

Mr. Johnson called his ten years' fight against privilege a war for "A City on a Hill." To the young men in the movement, and to tens of thousands of the poor who gave it their support, it was a moral crusade rarely paralleled in American politics. The struggle involved the banks, the press, the Chamber of Commerce, the clubs and the social life of the city. It divided families and destroyed friendships. You were either for Tom Johnson or against him. If for him, you were a disturber of business, a Socialist, to some an anarchist.

Had the term "Red" been in vogue, you would have been called a Communist in the pay of Russia. Every other political issue and almost every topic of conversation was subordinated to the struggle.[1]

While Cleveland was witnessing the struggle between Johnson and the special-interest groups, Toledo was faced with much the same situation. A sucker-rod manufacturer, Sam Jones, had been elected mayor by the business groups and the Republican boss of the town. They had selected Jones because they were confident that he would grant the street-railway and electric-light companies valuable franchises. Jones, however, refused. He fought for the interests of the public, and when the next election occurred, he ran as an independent with the golden rule as his platform. Jones had been so successful in curbing the predatory desires of the streetcar company that when he died in office, the stock of the company went up twenty-four points on the following morning. Jones also contributed to city government the idea of nonpartisanship in municipal affairs. He was not interested in political parties and felt that efficiency in municipal affairs was more important than party affiliation. Brand Whitlock, who succeeded Jones as Progressive mayor of Toledo, wrote of his predecessor:

Jones used to herald himself as "a Man without a Party," but he was a great democrat, the most fundamental I ever knew or imagined; he summed up in himself, as no other figure of our time since Lincoln, all that the democratic spirit is and hopes to be. Perhaps in this characterization I seem to behold his figure larger than it was in relation to the whole mass, but while his work may appear at first glance local, it was really general and universal. No one can estimate the peculiar and lively force of such a personality; certainly no one can presume to limit his influence, for such a spirit is illimitable and irresistible.[2]

PROGRESSIVISM IN STATE POLITICS

While Progressives were active in a number of cities, many states had vital struggles between the Progressives and the standpat conservatives. In Kansas, W. R. Stubbs, William Allen White, and Victor Murdock fought within the Republican party to elect Progressive Republicans to office and then to enact Progressive laws. Stubbs was elected governor for several terms, and Murdock went to Congress for a number of years. White refused to run for office, but used his *Emporia Gazette* as a

[1] *The Confessions of a Reformer*, p. 113. Charles Scribner's Sons, New York, 1926.
[2] *Forty Years of It*, p. 138. D. Appleton & Co., New York, copyright, 1914.

powerful organ for the Progressive movement. From 1910 to 1912 Governor Woodrow Wilson brought New Jersey to the front rank of Progressive states, and California witnessed a strong movement to check untrammeled exploitation, led by Fremont Older, Francis J. Heney, and Hiram Johnson. Just before the California Progressives began their fight, the Southern Pacific Railroad group controlled the state legislature, courts, and city and county governments. Hiram Johnson was elected governor in 1910 on the platform "Kick the Railroad out of Politics." During his governorship the railroad was dethroned as the controlling force in state politics; a commission was set up to regulate the railroads; the initiative, the referendum, and the recall were adopted; and a workmen's-compensation law was passed. Meanwhile Progressive fires in Colorado were kept burning by Judge Ben Lindsey and Edward P. Costigan, and in Iowa by Albert Cummins and Jonathan P. Dolliver. Michigan, Missouri, Texas, and North Carolina likewise felt the imprint of Progressivism, but the states with outstanding movements were Wisconsin and Oregon.

The place at the head of the pre-First-World-War Progressive movement belongs rightfully to Robert Marion La Follette of Wisconsin. La Follette tried to bring his state, and later the nation, to new vistas of democracy. He said:

> The essence of the progressive movement, as I see it, lies in its struggle to uphold the fundamental principles of representative government. . . . The people have never failed in any great crisis in our history. The real danger to democracy lies not in the ignorance or want of patriotism in the people, but in the corrupting influence of powerful business organizations upon the representatives of the people. The real cure for the ills of democracy is more democracy.

Wisconsin, during the twenty years before La Follette's governorship, was firmly in the hands of railroad and lumber interests. The decade of the 1890's marked a turning point in La Follette's career. While practicing law at Madison, he came to question the validity of McKinley's talk about a full dinner pail and the gold standard and about a billion-dollar country being the chief concern of the United States. The chief concern, he felt, should be to have a democracy. The people, he thought, had permitted their government to fall into the hands of a few party bosses, and these bosses were running the government in the interest of corporate wealth. There were railroad governors, trust senators, canal representatives, but very few people's governors, senators, and representatives. The politicians in the pay of the special interests granted these interests franchises, rights of way, and the right to exploit the public domain. La Follette and his followers, faced with this situation, felt that the solution was to return the control of government to the people, preserve the natural resources for the use of the people, and make the public utilities the servant, rather than the master, of the State.

In 1900 La Follette won the governorship of Wisconsin in spite of the opposition of the old-time Republican party bosses. He fought his campaign chiefly on the issues of the need for a direct primary and adequate taxation of the railroads. To obtain real democracy in Wisconsin, La Follette looked forward to the direct election of United States Senators, the initiative, the referendum, and the recall, remedial and regulatory legislation for business, and an awakened public conscience. In order to obtain candidates for office who represented the people, not the special-interest groups, he led the state to adopt the direct-primary law. With this law in operation, the people could choose their own nominees for office, and not have the doubtful privilege of voting for candidates hand-picked by conventions controlled by seekers of special privileges. After the people had elected their own candidates for the legislature and governorship, then the rest of the Progressive platform could be carried out. This platform, known as the "Wisconsin idea," called for the following: (1) a railroad commission with power to fix rates based on the value of the railroad investment; (2) a law taxing railroads in proportion to their actual property value; (3) an income-tax law; (4) an antipass law forbidding railroads to give passes to politicians; (5) an antilobby law; (6) a corrupt-practices act limiting the amounts that could be spent on campaigns by candidates; (7) the initiative, the referendum, and the recall; (8) conservation, particularly of the forests; (9) the co-operation of the University of Wisconsin in improving the state. In addition to regular courses, an extension department was to give various courses throughout the state.

From 1900 to 1905 La Follette pushed through most of this program, despite the machinations of the special interests. In this fight party lines became meaningless. You were either a La Follette man or against La Follette. La Follette himself became a national figure, and the state a model for other states to follow. When Lincoln Steffens visited Wisconsin, he was told by an attorney of the vested-interest group that La Follette was a dangerous fanatic. According to the attorney, "the way that man goes around spreading discontent is a menace to law, property, business and all American institutions." After Steffens investigated the situation, he came to the conclusion that "Bob La Follette's measures seemed fair to me, his methods democratic, his purposes right but moderate, and his fighting strength and spirit hopeful and heroic. . . . Bob La Follette was restoring representative government in Wisconsin. . . . It was a great experiment." In 1906 La Follette was elected to the United States Senate, and the rest of his career was devoted to fighting nationally for the Progressive movement. During the period of conservatism from 1920 to 1932 his ideas suffered an eclipse, but after 1933 they were found to be filled with value and wisdom. The basic philosophy of the New Deal was similar to La Follette's, particularly the New Deal's interest in the common man and its desire to curb the power of special-interest groups over American life.

La Follette's influence on Progressivism in other states was great. He spoke many times for Progressives in order to help them in their state fights, and he was always ready to offer advice from his own experience. William Allen White spoke for the Progressives when he wrote, in 1929:

> Wisconsin has put a statue of the late Senator Robert M. La Follette in the National Hall of Fame in the capitol building at Washington. America, in the first quarter of this century, developed three statesmen of the first order, Roosevelt, La Follette and Wilson. Each had his elements of greatness. Wilson was great in the thing to which he aspired—his realizable ideals. Roosevelt was an agitator, who stirred the people to anger against the injustice of his day—comparable with Lincoln and the revolutionary group in that. La Follette was great as a practical law giver—a man who crystallized noble ideals into reality, a statesman who clinched like a wrestler at the neck of wrong, and downed it. He fought without surrender, without mercy, without compromise—a warrior for the justice of God.
>
> A great man was "Fighting Bob."

Oregon was another state that was influential wherever Progressives were battling conservative forces. In 1891 Oregon adopted the secret ballot; in 1899 a general registration law to combat wholesale election frauds was passed; in 1902 the initiative and referendum were enacted; in 1904 the direct primary was passed; in 1908 a corrupt-practices law was adopted; and in 1910 the recall was approved. These were the chief ingredients of the "Oregon system." In Oregon the initiative worked in the following manner: a voter, by obtaining the signatures of a given proportion of the people who had voted in the last election, could have any measure placed on the ballot for the voters' approval or disapproval. By the referendum a voter, following the same procedure, could place on the ballot, for final decision by the people, a measure which had passed the legislature. The fate of a measure, whether initiated or referred, was determined not by a majority of the voters of the state, but by a majority of those voting on that particular measure. As a result, many bills became laws in Oregon when less than 40 per cent of the voters supported them; and the governor of the state had no veto over laws passed by the people.

The weakness that developed under the initiative and referendum stemmed from the fact that all that was necessary to secure the passage of a bill was the support of a majority of those voting in a given election. This situation permitted an organized minority to push through measures favorable to its point of view. The Progressives in Oregon, as well as in the rest of the nation, soon realized that only an aroused and alert public opinion could check this evil. If a majority of the voters turned out on election day, then these Progressive devices could not be perverted by organized minorities. The Progressives discovered, however, that, unfortunately, vast numbers of voters never bothered to go to the polls on election day. Nonvoting played directly into the hands of vested-interest groups and political machines, since the machine always delivered its supporters' vote. Political machines, it was clear, hoped that the average person would not vote, since no machine could survive a large turnout of voters. The Progressives generally agreed that where machine rule existed in American life, it could be attributed directly to the lethargy of the people in that community, many of whom did not bother to vote or to take an active interest in political matters.

It was largely through the work of W. S. U'Ren that Oregon was so advanced in the adoption of Progressive political measures. Not only was he the father of direct legislation in Oregon, but he aided many other states in adopting similar laws. U'Ren started out in Oregon politics as secretary of the Populist state committee. From this position he flooded the state with pamphlets advocating the initiative and referendum. After the death of the Populist party U'Ren became secretary of a number of different organizations, all favoring varying types of Progressive legislation. He was wise in the ways of politics, and he knew how to guide bills shrewdly through the state legislature. Working closely with U'Ren was Jonathan Bourne, who was sent to the United States Senate, where he was a leading Progressive figure. U'Ren's power in Oregon was described in 1915 in the following fashion:

In Oregon the state government is divided into four departments—the executive, judicial, legislative and Mr. U'Ren—and it still is an open question which exerts the most power. One fact must be considered in making comparisons: That the legislature does not dare to repeal the acts of Mr. U'Ren, the executive has no power to veto them, and thus far the judiciary has upheld all his laws and constitutional amendments. On the contrary, Mr. U'Ren has boldly clipped the wings of the executive and legislative departments, and when he gets time will doubtless put some shackles on the supreme court. To date, the indications are that Mr. U'Ren outweighs any one, and perhaps all three, of the other departments.[1]

The Progressive era in city and state governments decidedly raised the tone of governmental practices. New horizons of democracy were opened to the people. While the cities and states were feeling the leaven of Progressivism, the government in Washington was undergoing the same experience. The Progressives discovered that in a highly industrialized, urban world it was futile to limit the curbing of predatory wealth to a state only, because industry and finance were so organized that they transcended state lines. Therefore, to regulate industry in the interest of the people, to make democracy really work in America, the Progressives had to fight for control of the Federal government, as well as of city and state governments. During the administrations of Theodore Roosevelt and Woodrow Wilson real progress was made in the nationwide adoption of Progressive ideas.

SELECTED BIBLIOGRAPHY

JOHN CHAMBERLAIN, *Farewell to Reform*, extremely provocative; C. C. REGIER, *The Era of the Muckrakers*, a good survey of the work of the muckrakers.

FREDERIC C. HOWE, *The Confessions of a Reformer*, one of the ablest autobiographies produced in the last few decades; BRAND WHITLOCK, *Forty Years of It*, good material on the struggles of the city Progressives; LINCOLN STEFFENS, *Autobiography*, a *must* book for any intelligent American, brilliantly written and by far the best autobiography produced in recent years; ROBERT M. LA FOLLETTE, *Autobiography*, suffers because it was written while La Follette was still busily engaged in politics, but throws a great deal of light on his background and philosophy; HAROLD U. FAULKNER, *The Quest for Social Justice*, the volume in the History of American Life Series that covers the Progressive era.

H. S. COMMAGER (Ed.), *Documents of American History*, pp. 215–225, 228–232, 233–239, contains source material.

[1] James Barnett, *The Operation of Initiative, Referendum and Recall in Oregon*, p. 17. The Macmillan Company, New York, 1915.

XXIV

Progressivism
in the National Government

FEW MEN have ever captured the public imagination as completely as did Theodore Roosevelt in the first decade of the twentieth century. Many people worshiped him as a hero, and he is still often referred to in glowing and nostalgic terms. His jutting teeth, his pince-nez eyeglasses, the Roosevelt scowl, and his constant talk about the strenuous life won him great popularity. Roosevelt always was a great showman; his showmanship not only won him the admiration of the middle class, but caused Lord Morley to say that the two outstanding things he had seen in America were Niagara Falls and Theodore Roosevelt.

Roosevelt was close to the English ideal of the gentleman in politics. He enjoyed inherited wealth—an aristocrat in a democracy. He was a colorful personality and an amusing talker. When Rudyard Kipling was in the United States in 1889, one of his diversions was to drop in at the Cosmos Club, where Theodore Roosevelt would be holding forth on politics, literature, and world affairs. "I curled up on the seat opposite, and listened and wondered until the universe seemed to be spinning around and Theodore was the spinner," commented Kipling. Henry Adams, in his *Education*, recalled that, at a White House dinner, President Roosevelt characteristically monopolized the conversation, and "we were overwhelmed in a torrent of oratory, and at last I heard only the repetition of I—I—I."

During his years in the White House, Theodore Roosevelt constantly exhorted Americans to lead a strenuous life. He frequently put his words into practice by going to the War Department and making the fat and aged generals get out of their armchairs and go horseback-riding with him across rugged terrain. It was reported that, after one of these excursions, the generals, unused to exercise, were scarcely able to appear for work the next day.

Roosevelt swept across the American scene like a meteor. He stirred public opinion and popularized and dramatized the Progressive cause. He was a typical Progressive in that he wanted to bring control of the government back to the people, and also because he desired to curb the greed and lust for power of the plutocracy. In 1912 he expressed his philosophy in these words:

We are engaged in one of the great battles of the age-long contest waged against privilege on behalf of the common welfare. We hold it a prime duty of the people to free our government from the control of money in politics. For this purpose we advocate, not as ends in themselves, but as weapons in the hands of the people, all governmental devices which will make the representatives of the people more easily and certainly responsible to the people's will.

This country, as Lincoln said, belongs to the people. So do the natural resources which make it rich. They supply the basis of our prosperity now and hereafter. In preserving them, which is a National duty, we must not forget that monopoly is based on the control of natural resources and natural advantages, and that it will help the people little to conserve our natural wealth unless the benefits which it can yield are secured to the people. Let us remember, also, that Conservation does not stop with the natural resources, but that the principle of making the best use of all we have requires with equal or greater insistence that we shall stop the waste of human life in industry and prevent the waste of human welfare which flows from the unfair use of concentrated power and wealth in the hands of men whose eagerness for profit blinds them to the cost of what they do.

In Roosevelt's opinion the United States was a middle-class country. Capital and labor and minority interests had to respect this situation. Gilson Gardner has summed up thus Theodore Roosevelt's attitude on this matter:

"More honesty. By George, they musn't do it. The rich must be fair and the poor must be contented—or, if not contented, at least they must be orderly. I will tell them both. No restraining of trade by the great corporations and no rioting by the toiler. Give me the power and I will make them behave."

Roosevelt had a long background of political training before assuming the Presidency. He had been a member of the New York legislature in the 1880's, Civil Service Commissioner under Presidents Harrison and Cleveland, New York police commissioner, Assistant Secretary of the Navy in McKinley's first administration, governor of New York from 1898 to 1900, and Vice-President of the United States in McKinley's second term. His work as police commissioner of New

York City in 1895 brought him face to face, for the first time, with the social problems created by the Machine Age. He saw slums and poor housing conditions at first hand. While in this work, he abandoned his opposition to governmental regulation of industry and became, as he observed in his *Autobiography*, "more set than ever in my distrust of those men, whether business men or lawyers, judges, legislators or executive officers, who seek to make of the Constitution a fetish for the prevention of the work of social reform."

While police commissioner, he did his best to stamp out corruption and laxity in the police force. At night, after dinner, he prowled through the streets of New York in the hope of finding a policeman asleep or off his beat. One time he found a policeman drinking beer at the side door of a saloon. The policeman ran when he recognized the stern visage of Roosevelt, but Roosevelt caught him after a fifty-yard run and made the policeman report for trial. Cartoonists caricatured Roosevelt's activities and made his face familiar to the nation. When the Spanish-American War broke out, he resigned as Assistant Secretary of the Navy and organized the Rough Riders. The fame gained from his Cuban exploits helped to elect him governor of New York in 1898 against the wishes of Republican boss Thomas Platt. In 1900, in order to get Roosevelt out of New York politics, Platt had him nominated for the Vice-Presidency in the belief that this position would end Roosevelt's political career. Fate, however, decided otherwise, and on the death of McKinley in September, 1901, Roosevelt became President.

When Roosevelt took the oath of office, he assured the country that he would continue and carry out McKinley's policies. From the record of the Roosevelt administration, it is safe to observe that he did—he carried them to their grave and buried them! Mark Hanna had some premonition of all this in 1900 when he objected to the nomination of Roosevelt as Vice-President. He opposed the nomination because, he said, only one life would stand "between this madman and the Presidency." Under Roosevelt's Presidency, Hanna lost the great influence that he had had while McKinley was in that office. On the other hand, Roosevelt never fought the Old Guard, conservative Republicans to the same extent that Senator Robert La Follette did. Roosevelt generally followed a middle-of-the-road position, attempting to retain control over both the Progressives and the conservatives.

THE ROOSEVELT ADMINISTRATION

One of Roosevelt's chief claims to fame in his own day rested on his activities as a trust-buster. Cartoons portrayed him wielding a big stick against the trusts. Actually, for all his work in dissolving them, the trusts were more firmly entrenched when he left office than when he entered it. In 1900 there were 185 trusts, with a capitalization of over three billion dollars, and in 1909 there were 10,020 trusts, with a capitalization of thirty-one billion dollars. These figures may suggest that the desire to smash the trusts and return the control of industry to the small businessman was opposed to economic trends, and that the policy of trust regulation, advocated by Roosevelt and the Bull Moosers in 1912, was more in line with the needs of the situation.

When Roosevelt took office, he believed that the future of American democracy was imperiled by the concentration of power in the hands of a few financial groups, like the houses of Morgan, Rockefeller, and Vanderbilt. The organization of the United States Steel Corporation, with half of its capitalization watered stock, and Morgan's wrecking of the New England railroads through financial manipulation demonstrated the need of governmental action. Roosevelt, however, approached the problem cautiously. After all, he was the head of the party of big business. He differentiated between good and bad trusts, and pointed out that he was not opposed to corporations per se, but just to the evil in them. Roosevelt's policy of arguing both sides of the trust question led Mr. Dooley to satirize the President:

"Th' thrusts are heejous monsthers built up be th' inlightened intherprise iv th' men that have done so much to advance progress in our beloved counthry," he says. "On wan hand I wud stamp thim undher fut; on th' other hand not so fast. What I want more thin th' bustin' iv th' thrusts is to see me fellow counthrymen happy an' continted. I wudden't have thim hate th' thrusts. Th' haggard face, th' droopin' eye, th' pallid complexion that marks th' inimy iv thrusts is not to me taste. Lave us be merry about it an' jovial an' affectionate. Lave us laugh an' sing th' octopus out iv existence. Betther blue but smilin' lips arny time thin a full coal scuttle an' a sour heart."[1]

In order to eradicate the evils in corporations, President Roosevelt persuaded Congress to establish a Department of Commerce and Labor, in 1903, whose secretary should be of cabinet rank, and a Bureau of Corporations with power to investigate the activities of interstate cor-

[1] Quoted by Elmer Ellis, *Mr. Dooley's America*, p. 170. Alfred A. Knopf, New York, 1941.

porations. Then Congress enacted a law expediting trust cases through the courts and appropriated money to prosecute the cases. To the horror of Wall Street, in 1902 Roosevelt instructed his Attorney-General Philander C. Knox to enter suit under the Sherman Antitrust Act against the Northern Securities Company. J. P. Morgan tried to dissuade the President, and, according to Roosevelt, J. P. Morgan's attitude in this case was that the President was a rival operator trying to take control away from Morgan.

The Northern Securities case is one of the most famous in American industrial history and was the result of an episode that furnishes an excellent example of the workings of railroad consolidation. E. H. Harriman controlled the Union Pacific, Central Pacific, and Southern Pacific railroads, and had a working agreement with the Santa Fe.

Broncobusting in the West Amuses Us and Don't Hurt the Hoss

Theodore Roosevelt launches his antitrust program[1]

Only the Northern Pacific and Great Northern were outside his overlordship. These two railroads were in the control of J. P. Morgan and J. J. Hill. Hill and Morgan bought control of the Chicago, Burlington and Quincy, which alarmed Harriman as being a threat to his control of Western transportation. Harriman began to buy stock in the Northern Pacific in order to wrest control from the Hill-Morgan group. Hill and Morgan now became alarmed and began buying more Northern Pacific stock. This competition resulted in an insane contest on Wall Street, where the price of a single share of the stock increased from $350 to $1000 in one hour. Finally, a compromise was worked out between the two groups. The Northern Securities Company, a holding company, was chartered, with directors from both sides. The

[1] W. A. Rogers in *Harper's Weekly*, 1903. From The Bettmann Archive.

purpose of the holding company was to bring harmony between the two factions and also to stop competition between them. The Supreme Court, in 1904, decided that this holding company was a trust in restraint of trade and ordered it dissolved. This decision demonstrated that the trusts were not above the law, and the case greatly enhanced Roosevelt's popularity.

Old-Guard Republicans, in 1904, would have liked to drop Roosevelt from their Presidential ticket, but by this time he was so popular that to have done so would have courted disaster for the party. The Democrats, expecting to win the support of reactionary Republicans, dropped Bryan as their candidate in favor of conservative Alton B. Parker, a New York judge. The election was a decisive victory for Roosevelt, and he now was President by election—President in his own right. Encouraged by his election, Roosevelt pushed the antitrust proceedings. During his second administration the beef trust, the fertilizer trust, and the American Tobacco Company were dissolved. The dissolution of these trusts, however, seemed to have little effect. The component parts were able to reintegrate in a different form and continue their monopoly control. Trust-busting seemed ineffective, and Roosevelt came to the conclusion that the government should prosecute only "bad" trusts, those which did not pass the benefits of their economies on to the consumer. The Supreme Court accepted this moral distinction of good and bad trusts in the Standard Oil case of 1911, when it ruled that only "unreasonable" restraint of trade was to be considered a violation of the antitrust law. The Standard Oil Company was ordered dissolved because its operations were in "unreasonable" restraint of trade. But in another case, in 1920, the United States Steel Corporation was left intact because its operations were only in "reasonable" restraint of trade.

Roosevelt extended the arm of governmental regulation of business through his antitrust work. In other ways also he extended governmental regulation of economic activities. He saw to it that Congress passed a Workmen's Compensation Act for all government employees, and factory-inspection and child-labor laws for the District of Columbia. By "executive action" Roosevelt settled the anthracite strike of 1902. The mine-operators had refused to confer with the union over a demand for a wage increase and union recognition. The miners went on strike, and, as the months dragged on, the United Mine Workers union won public sympathy. As winter approached, the country was faced with no coal. The President intervened and called a parley of the two sides. The operators, at the conference, were insolent to Roosevelt and openly hostile to John Mitchell, the union president. According to Roosevelt, "There was only one man in the room who behaved like a gentleman, and that man was not I [it was Mitchell]." The operators adopted the attitude that the President should break the strike, as past Presidents had broken strikes. Faced with such an intransigent attitude on the part of the owners, Roosevelt threatened to take over the mines and operate them with the army. To head this off, J. P. Morgan persuaded the operators to submit the case to an arbitrating commission. The operators agreed to this, but only if no labor representative was on the commission. Roosevelt circumvented this condition by appointing a union man as an "eminent sociologist." The outcome of the arbitration was a victory for the miners, an increase of popularity for the President, and a loss of prestige for the operators because of their defiance of public opinion. During the course of this controversy, humorist Finley Peter Dunne was led to comment on the blind and selfish attitude of the operators:

"It'll be a hard winther if we don't get coal," said Mr. Hennessy.

"What d'ye want with coal?" said Mr. Dooley. "Ye'er a most unraisonable man. D'ye think ye can have all th' comforts iv life an' that ye mus' make no sacryfice to uphold th' rights iv property? Ivrybody will have plinty iv fuel this winther. Th' rich can burn with indignation, thinkin' iv th' wrongs inflicted on capital, th' middle or middlin' class will be marchin' with th' milishy, an' th' poor can fight among thimsilves an' burn th' babies. I niver thought iv babies befure as combustible, but they are. At wan stroke ye can keep th' baby warrum an' th' rest iv th' fam'ly comfortable. Befure th' winther is over I expict to hear ye callin'; 'Packy, go out to th' woodshed an' bring in a scuttleful iv little Robert Immitt. Th' fire is burnin' low.' They'll be nawthin' else to burn."[1]

Governmental control was applied also to the railroads. The Interstate Commerce Act of 1887 had been weakened by the courts, and Presidents Harrison, Cleveland, and McKinley had disregarded it. Rebates, discrimination, and favoritism had continued after 1887. By 1904 six major railway systems controlled about three fourths of the mileage of the country. In 1903 the railroads supported the Elkins Act, which enforced the prohibition of rebates. Under this measure the government indicted certain railroads and shippers for granting and accepting rebates. The next step was to give the Interstate Commerce Commission specific power to regulate rates, which was accomplished

[1] Quoted by Elmer Ellis, *Mr. Dooley's America*, p. 174. Alfred A. Knopf, New York, 1941.

in 1906 by the Hepburn Act. This act, however, did not go to the roots of the problem, as Senator La Follette pointed out, since the Commission was not given power to evaluate railroad properties and the cost of services. Only if it knew this, of course, could the reasonableness of rates be determined. It was not until 1913 that the Commission gained this power.

In the field of foods and drugs too the government's power was extended. Experts had revealed that the use of adulterants and preservatives in food was a common practice of the packers and manufacturers. In 1905 Roosevelt urged Congress to pass a law to ensure pure foods. The meat trust fought this proposal as dangerous, "socialistic" interference with the rights of business, but the publication of Sinclair's *Jungle*, in 1906, stirred the public to demand action. In June, 1906, a Federal meat-inspection law was passed. During the same year Congress passed a Pure Food and Drugs Act to protect the public from the frauds that Samuel Hopkins Adams had described in his muckraking articles *The Great American Fraud*.

The most important and lasting achievement of the Roosevelt administrations was that in the conservation of the natural resources. Some check had to be placed on the greedy and wasteful destruction of the resources of the country. Of the original eight hundred million acres of virgin forest land only two hundred million acres remained in 1900. Four fifths of the timber was in private hands. Under a law of 1891, which permitted the President to set aside as a national forest reserve unsold government timberland, Roosevelt set aside over three times as much land as Cleveland, Harrison, and McKinley together had done. The forests were placed under the Department of Agriculture, where they were ably administered by Gifford Pinchot, head of the Forest Service. Another phase of conservation that interested Roosevelt was the interrelation of rivers, soil, forests, water-power development, and water transportation. In 1907 he appointed an Inland Waterways Commission to study this problem, and the recommendations of the Commission led to a great national conservation conference. This conference gave the conservation movement an impetus and prestige which were needed to overcome the many obstacles to carrying out conservation policies, and also it led many states to establish state conservation commissions. The conference recommended that the government retain all lands containing coal, oil, natural gas, and possible power sites; regulate timber-cutting on private land; improve navigable streams; and conserve the watersheds. The irrigation of land was

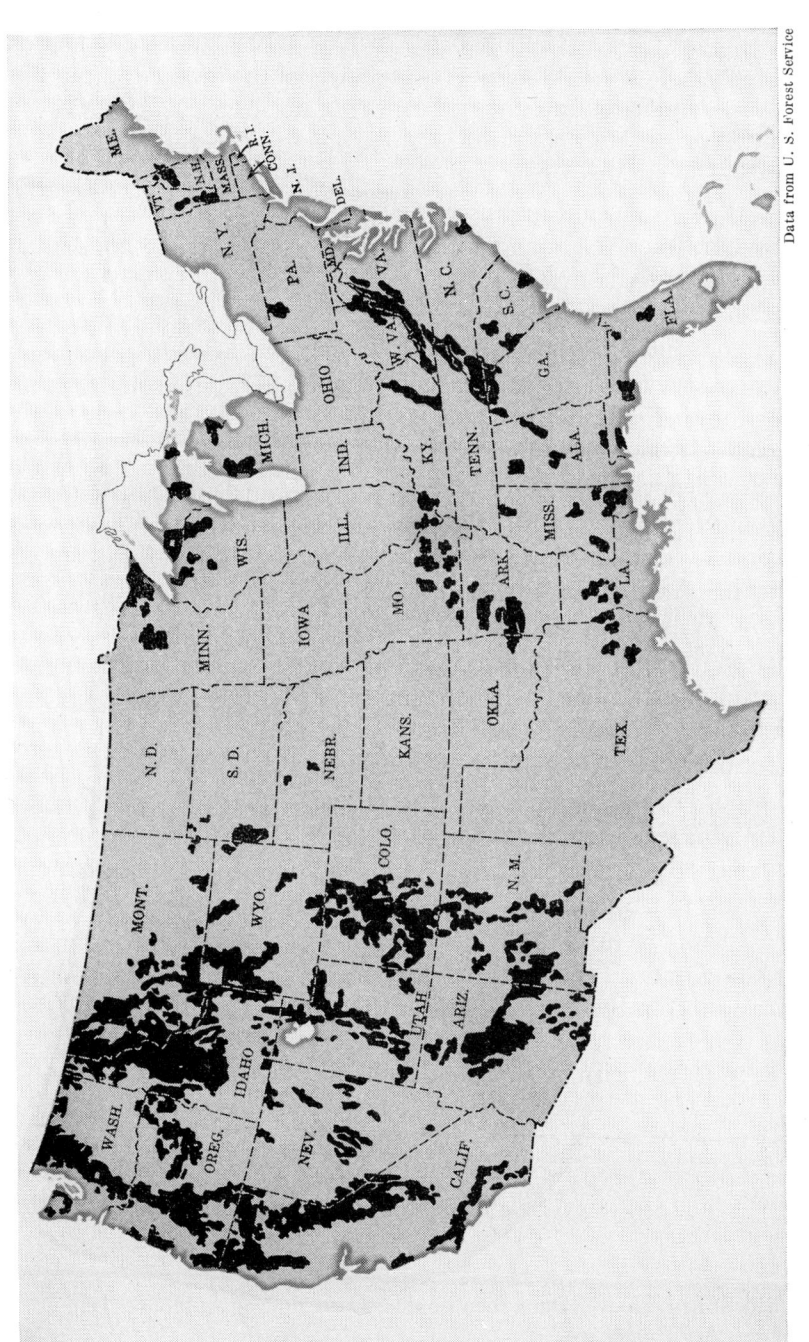

The National Forests of the United States

carried on under the Reclamation Act of 1902, which allowed irrigation
to be financed by the Federal government out of the proceeds of public-
land sales. Under that act the government later constructed Roosevelt
Dam in Arizona, Hoover[1] Dam on the Colorado River, Grand Coulee
Dam on the Columbia River, and many smaller projects, thus bringing
millions of acres of land into use.

Theodore Roosevelt inaugurated work in the field of conservation
that was sadly needed. After 1909 much remained to be done. Coal,
oil, and natural gas were wasted yearly through inefficient methods.
Lumber companies continued to devastate great areas. After Theodore
Roosevelt, however, no President had broad enough vision to carry on
the work until Franklin D. Roosevelt.

Theodore Roosevelt brought certain definite ideas to the fore while
in the Presidency. He felt that the executive branch should dominate
the legislature and the courts. To him the President had all the power
not expressly forbidden him by the Constitution. This was the same
concept that Andrew Jackson and Abraham Lincoln, before him, and
Woodrow Wilson and Franklin D. Roosevelt, after him, had of the
Presidency. The other concept of the Presidency, held by men like
William H. Taft, James Buchanan, and most of our weaker Presidents,
was that the President had only the powers expressly granted by the
Constitution. These two points of view help to explain the difference
between our "strong" and "weak" Presidents.

During his seven years in the White House, although Roosevelt took
vigorous action along many lines, he did nothing to change the basic
organization of American life. He was interested in eradicating bad
men and bad practices from industry, finance, and the government,
and nothing more. In this he represented the will of middle-class
America. Lincoln Steffens observed of Roosevelt in the Presidency:

> T. R. was a politician much more than he was a reformer; in the phrase-
> ology of the radicals, he was a careerist, an opportunist with no deep insight
> into issues, but he was interesting, picturesque . . . . T. R. was an honest
> mind . . . he was a careerist on the people's side, . . . working to wangle some
> concessions from the powers that be and make them do some things for the
> country at large.[2]

[1] Called, at first, Hoover Dam, then Boulder Dam, now again Hoover Dam (act
of Congress, April 30, 1947).

[2] *The Autobiography of Lincoln Steffens,* pp. 506, 514. Harcourt, Brace and
Company, New York, 1931.

THE TAFT ADMINISTRATION

Roosevelt could have been renominated by the Republicans in 1908. The Old Guard disliked him because of his growing "radicalism"; his willingness to compromise and take half a loaf instead of a whole loaf had lost him the support of liberals like La Follette; he had sacrificed the confidence of professional reformers by scornfully calling them muckrakers; but with the average American he was the most popular President since the days of Andrew Jackson and Abraham Lincoln. Instead of running, however, he selected his successor, William Howard Taft, and the Republican convention dutifully nominated Taft. Most of the Progressive Republicans believed, as did Theodore Roosevelt, that Taft was a Progressive and would continue the work begun by his predecessor. The Democratic convention, after

W. A. Rogers, 1907; from The Bettmann Archive

"Do you think you could fly, Bill?"

Theodore Roosevelt prepares the way for William Howard Taft to receive the Republican nomination in 1908

its lapse in 1904, once again renominated Bryan. By 1908 the difference between the two parties was negligible. Roosevelt and the Progressive wing had forced the Republican party to adopt most of the demands that the Populists and Bryan had advocated in the previous decade. Not only were the Republicans successful in electing Taft in 1908, but they gained control of both houses of Congress. But Bryan still had tremendous drawing power and received 43 per cent of the popular vote.

Taft, before assuming the Presidency, had served as a circuit-court judge, governor of the Philippines, and Secretary of War. He had been a good subordinate in the Roosevelt cabinet, and Roosevelt felt that he was dedicated to continuing the Roosevelt policies. Taft apparently wished to do so, but in his own way. Taft, a constitutional lawyer, could not accept Roosevelt's view that the President had all the power not expressly forbidden him. Instead, as has been said, he felt that the President had only the powers expressly granted him. In this different conception of the Presidential power lies a great share of the reason for Taft's failure to win public favor for carrying on the Roosevelt reforms. Under Taft, initiative, to a degree, passed to Congress, where leaders like Cannon in the House and Aldrich in the Senate felt that reform had gone far enough. Taft, too, was inclined to be inert, whereas Roosevelt was a man of action. Taft would deliberate and procrastinate where Roosevelt would have dashed ahead. Although Taft agreed in theory with much of the Progressive platform, he was more unwilling than his predecessor to antagonize the Old Guard. Increasingly, during his administration, as the Progressives became skeptical of him, he listened to the advice of the conservatives.

The Republican platform of 1908 contained a pledge to revise the tariff. During the campaign Taft had gone on record as pledging himself to "a substantial revision downward." As a result, a special session of Congress was called by Taft to carry out the platform pledge. The House prepared a downward revision, but the Senate emasculated this bill. Special interests saw to it that their particular desires were incorporated. Even Senator Henry Cabot Lodge admitted, after watching the special interests work on the Senators, "The amount of ruthless selfishness that is exhibited on both sides surpasses anything I have ever seen." The Progressives launched a series of brilliant debates against the Payne-Aldrich Bill, but it passed Congress. The new bill made eight hundred and forty-seven changes, but six hundred were upward, and the free list was a joke. Mr. Dooley was quick to satirize the new tariff:

Th' Republican Party has been thru to its promises. Look at th' free list if ye don't believe it. Practically ivrything necessary to existence comes in free. Here it is. Curling stones, teeth, sea moss, newspapers, mix vomica, Pulu, canary bird seed, divvy-divvy, spunk, hog bristles, marshmallows, silk worm eggs, stilts, skeletons, an' leeches. Th' new tariff bill puts these familyar commodyties within th' reach iv all.[1]

The Progressives, led by La Follette and aided by Beveridge of Indiana and Cummins and Dolliver of Iowa, attacked the tariff schedules and showed the nation the connection between the rates and the special

[1]Reprinted from *Mr. Dooley Says.* Charles Scribner's Sons, New York, 1910.

interests. After Congress passed the bill, they called on Taft to veto it. After much vacillation Taft signed the bill. In the eyes of the Progressives he added insult to injury by calling it "the best tariff bill that the Republican party ever passed." From this time to the end of the administration, the Progressives increasingly grew more antagonistic to Taft. The interparty strife of these four years was of vital importance to the formation of the Bull Moose party in 1912. When Roosevelt returned from a hunting trip in Africa in the summer of 1910, he found the Republican party badly divided and the Progressive program checked, and before long he too became alienated from Taft.

The hotbed of Progressive or insurgent opposition to Taft was in the agrarian states of Kansas, Nebraska, Minnesota, Wisconsin, and Iowa. The movement also had some strength in the Dakotas and Indiana and on the east and west coasts, but its main strength was in the agrarian region of the Middle West. These were the states where the Populists had been popular and where Bryan had a strong following. The leaders of the insurgents were agrarians. They had Jefferson's faith in the common man, his social idealism, his distrust of urbanism, and his deep confidence in agriculture as the backbone of the nation. They felt that their agrarian society was fundamentally more democratic than an industrial society, since equality of opportunity was more of a reality in farming life. Also, caste lines were not so hard and so fast as in the urban world. Their people, they thought, had a better working philosophy of life as a result of really knowing their neighbors and sharing with them their joys and sorrows. The insurgents who fought Taft in Congress were, of course, only part of the larger Progressive movement of these years. Louis Post, in *The Public* magazine, captured the spirit of the insurgents when he remarked, "The Insurgents were Progressives who meant it."

The insurgent movement in the House of Representatives centered in an attack on the powers of the Speaker of the House, "Uncle Joe" Cannon of Illinois. Cannon used his office as Speaker to secure the greatest concentration of power ever enjoyed by an American legislator. He was chairman of the powerful Committee on Rules, he appointed all committees, and he ignored any member asking for recognition on the floor unless the member had consulted him in advance. "Uncle Joe" blocked those bills which he and his associates did not favor by letting them die in the committees. Cannon's economic and social philosophy was downright reactionary, and he used his power to kill Progressive bills. Toward reform he adopted the attitude indicated by his words "The Speaker stands pat on his declaration that 'this country is a hell of a success.'" Among the leading figures in the fight against Cannon were George Norris of Nebraska, John M. Nelson of Wisconsin, E. H. Madison and Victor Murdock of Kansas, and Charles A. Lindbergh of Minnesota. During 1910 and 1911 the insurgents were able to deprive Cannon of his membership on the Rules Committee and of his power to appoint the various House committees. President Taft lost prestige in this struggle because he failed to aid the insurgents.

At this time there raged also the unhappy Ballinger-Pinchot controversy. Richard Ballinger, Taft's Secretary of the Interior, felt that James R. Garfield, Roosevelt's appointee to that office, had taken some steps that were an unwarranted assumption of power. Therefore Ballinger restored to private sale vast sections of land that Garfield had set aside. Pinchot, head of the Forest Service and a favorite of Theodore Roosevelt, at once protested that this was undoing Roosevelt's work. Then an employee of the Department of the Interior charged that Ballinger was leasing valuable coal reserves in Alaska to the Guggenheim interests. Pinchot wrote an open letter to Senator Dolliver, which backed up the charges. Taft referred the affair to a Congressional investigation, which whitewashed Ballinger, and Taft dismissed Pinchot for insubordination. The significance of this episode was that it increased the suspicions which the Progressives had of Taft, and it helped to bring Theodore Roosevelt into sympathy with the insurgents. The impression that the country gained from the affair was that Taft was hostile to conservation. Actually, this was not correct. He established the Bureau of Mines, and considerable areas of oil, coal, and timberland were withdrawn from public sale.

Although the Progressives were incensed at Taft's administration, a number of Progressive laws were enacted. The Mann-Elkins Act of 1910 extended the power of the Interstate Commerce Commission by allowing it to suspend proposed rate increases until an investigation could reveal that such increases were justified. The Departments of Commerce and Labor were divided, and the secretary of each was given cabinet rank. A postal savings bank and a parcel-post system were established, and an act requiring publicity for campaign expenditures was passed. A Federal Children's Bureau was created and placed in the hands of Julia Lathrop of Hull House. Twice as many prosecutions for violation of the antitrust law were undertaken in Taft's four years as in Roosevelt's seven. In addition, two amendments were added to the Constitution. Congress passed the Sixteenth. or income-tax, Amendment in 1909, and the Seventeenth Amendment, granting the people the direct election of United States Senators, in 1912. Both amendments were ratified by the necessary number of states in 1913. The Sixteenth Amendment rivals the Fourteenth Amendment in importance, since it was a step toward achieving economic democracy through taxation based on the ability to pay. Little of this legislation, however, could be classed as administration-sponsored. The attitude of the public toward Taft's seemingly anti-Progressive policy was revealed in the mid-term election of 1910. Progressive Republicans generally were re-elected to Congress, but the Democrats made heavy inroads on the conservatives to gain a majority in the House and to cut down the Republican majority in the Senate. Furthermore, important Eastern states, such as New Jersey, Massachusetts, Connecticut, and New York, elected Democratic governors.

SELECTED BIBLIOGRAPHY

HENRY F. PRINGLE, *Theodore Roosevelt*, the best biography; *Theodore Roosevelt, an Autobiography*, throws a great deal of light on the man's views and actions; CHARLES E. MERRIAM, *Four American Party Leaders*, Chap. 2, an able study of Roosevelt as a political leader; MARK SULLIVAN, *Our Times*, Vols. I, II, enlightening material on the society of the day; C. R. VAN HISE, *Conservation of National Resources in the United States*, the best study on this subject; HENRY F. PRINGLE, *The Life and Times of William Howard Taft*, a good, critical biography of Taft. KENNETH W. HECKLER, *Insurgency Personalities and Politics of the Taft Era*, a good survey of the insurgent revolt; WALTER JOHNSON, *William Allen White's America*, material on the insurgents; L. WHITE BUSBEY, *Uncle Joe Cannon*, and N. W. STEPHENSON, *Nelson W. Aldrich*, valuable material on the conservative political figures.
H. S. COMMAGER (Ed.), *Documents of American History*, pp. 201–203, 228–230, 233–235, contains source material.

XXV

The New Nationalism
and the New Freedom

URING the insurgent struggle against "Uncle Joe" Cannon and the fight in the Senate against the Payne-Aldrich tariff, the Progressives had formed a fluid organization with a secretary and regular meetings. They remained, however, within the Republican party, hoping to capture control of the party machinery. William Allen White, in a letter to conservative Congressman Charles Scott, expressed the Progressive attitude toward the Republican party in this way:

> The difference between the insurgents and the Cannon Republicans is fundamental. They believe in the growing rights of men, you believe in the growing rights of property. The thing has got to be fought out in the Republican party and we will see who owns the party, the people or the corporations.

Theodore Roosevelt returned from Africa to this troubled political picture in the summer of 1910. He could not long remain from the scene of political activity. On August 31 he delivered an important speech, entitled "The New Nationalism," at Osawatomie, Kansas. Gradually this term was applied to Roosevelt's program in 1911 and 1912. The New Nationalism included the old Roosevelt policies of honesty in government, conservation, and the regulation of business in the interest of society, although now his emphasis was on government regulation of monopoly, not trust-busting. Roosevelt's belief in the reconstruction of society by political action was now much more developed than it was when he was President. He said at Osawatomie, among other things, that our democracy must guarantee equality of opportunity for all men; and he visualized the great issue of the day as a struggle of freemen to hold the government against special privilege. Special interests had to be driven out of politics, and to accomplish this he advocated the prohibition of the use of corporation money in politics. The positive state, he declared, clearly should reconstruct society by political action. One great factor preventing this, he added, was the conservative Supreme Court, which continually declared regulatory laws unconstitutional. He announced:

> The American people are right in demanding the New Nationalism, without which we cannot hope to deal with new problems.... This New Nationalism regards the executive power as the steward of the public welfare. It demands of the judiciary that it shall be interested primarily in human welfare, rather than in property, just as it demands that the representative body shall represent all the people rather than any one class or section.

Gradually Taft and Roosevelt grew apart. While this breach was widening, the insurgent Republicans in Congress formed the National Progressive Republican League, with Jonathan Bourne as president. The League included such Senators as La Follette, Moses Clapp, Albert Beveridge, Joseph Dixon, Joseph Bristow, Albert Cummins, and Miles Poindexter, and such Representatives as Victor Murdock, George Norris, Nils Haugen, and E. H. Madison. It was organized for the purpose of capturing the Republican party, and, with assurances from Roosevelt that he was not interested in 1912, began to unify sentiment in favor of La Follette for the Republican nomination to the Presidency. They refused to switch to the Democratic party for two principal reasons. Their constituency was "too Republican" to make this advisable, and they could see very little liberalism in the Democratic party, which they felt was based on the "solid South" and on corrupt city machines.

On February 2, 1912, La Follette collapsed in the midst of a speech on the "money trust." Although he soon recovered, a number of the insurgents withdrew their support and went over to Roosevelt. La Follette became bitter against Roosevelt and charged that Roosevelt had used him as a stalking-horse to test public opinion and then, when it was clear that the mood of the people was Progressive, had entered the fray himself. Even before La Follette's collapse Roosevelt had had his eye on the nomination. Taft, on February 12, in a public speech, attacked the people who supported the New Nationalism as "political emotionalists or neurotics—who have lost their sense of proportion." Naturally, Theodore Roosevelt did not enjoy being called a neurotic, and any lingering doubts that he might have had about running for the nomination now disappeared. Nine days after Taft's speech he openly announced his candidacy. Taft, Roosevelt, and La Follette carried on a bitter contest for the Republican nomination. In the thirteen states that chose their delegates to the party convention through primaries, Roosevelt swept the field, gaining 278 delegates to 46 for Taft and 36 for La Follette. The rank-and-file membership of the party clearly wanted Roosevelt; the bosses, however, were for Taft. Since the majority of states selected their delegates by conventions, the bosses delivered these delegates almost entirely to Taft.

When the national convention met, there were two hundred delegates in dispute. The Old Guard, by electing Elihu Root temporary chairman, ensured the awarding of the contested seats to Taft men. Claiming that his majority thus had been stolen, Roosevelt and his delegates withdrew, and Taft was renominated. The Roosevelt followers returned home and founded local units for a new political party. These Progressives hurled the charge of theft at Taft, and pointed out that Roosevelt was clearly the choice of the people, whereas Taft had been selected by the bosses. The Progressives made the following type of appeal to voters to gain their support:

The theft of the National Convention carried with it the theft of a Presidency; the theft of a great party, having in custody the destiny and welfare of ninety millions of people; the theft carried with it the privilege of the great corporations that are financing the men who stole the party to legally plunder the people. The plundering of the people, of course, is done a penny at a time in unjust prices on commodities of everyday life, here a fraction of a cent a pound, there a fraction of a cent on a yard and so on down the line. These unjust prices are made possible by unjust tariffs, unjust trust prices, unfair discriminations of various kinds in express rates, and other rates. Back of the men who are making these iniquitous prices, stand the big politicians who legalize these iniquities. These big politicians stole the Republican Convention, which in turn stole the presidential nomination, and thus stole the special privilege to plunder ninety million people. It was the greatest crime in history. No ancient throne that was ever despoiled, carried so much booty with it, carried the right to rob so many people with it, carried so much human injustice with it. That theft marks the climax of all feeling.

On August 5 the new Progressive party held its first convention, at Chicago, in a spirit of religious enthusiasm and frenzy that was reminiscent of the Populist convention of 1892. "Onward, Christian Soldiers" was the theme song of the convention, and Albert Beveridge, the keynote speaker, delivered a talk replete with catchy phrases. "We stand for a nobler America; we are against the interests; we are for the workingman; and we are against the bosses," he asserted. Some weeks before, Theodore Roosevelt had delivered one of the greatest speeches of his career. He had told his enthusiastic supporters, "We fight in honorable fashion for the good of mankind; fearless of the future; unheeding of our individual fates; with unflinching hearts and undimmed eyes; we stand at Armageddon, and we battle for the Lord." It was a magnificent speech, particularly the assumption that the Lord had suddenly become an opponent of William H. Taft!

The convention adopted a detailed Progressive platform and nominated Roosevelt by acclamation. A Rooseveltian phrase, "I am feeling like a bull moose," gave the new party a nickname and a symbol to match the Democratic donkey and the Republican elephant. To us today, with our historical perspective, the formation of the new party seems to have been a mistake. It ended all hope of liberalizing the Republican party for a long time to come; and when most of the Progressives returned to the Republican fold in 1916, they did so with their tails between their legs. They were to have remarkably little influence on party policies in the period following the close of the First World War.

THE LIBERAL DEMOCRATS AND THE ELECTION OF 1912

William Jennings Bryan's contribution to the Progressive movement after 1896 was his efforts to keep the Democratic party in the hands of the liberal element. In 1900 this was accomplished by his own candidacy. The following year he launched *The Commoner*, a weekly paper that served as a liberal Democratic organ. He was bitter in his condemnation of the Eastern wing of the party, which wanted to support big business in the same manner as the Old-Guard Republicans. During the four years 1900–1904, the conservative, Eastern Democrats succeeded in regaining control of the party machinery and nominated the New York lawyer A. B. Parker for the Presidency in 1904. Although Bryan supported the ticket, he warned, in *The Commoner:*

> As soon as the election is over I shall, with the help of those who believe as I do, undertake to organize for the campaign of 1908, the object being to marshal the friends of popular government within the Democratic party to the support of a radical and progressive policy to make the Democratic party an efficient means in the hands of the people for securing relief from the plutocratic element that controls the Republican party and for the time being is in control of the Democratic party.

Bryan was in complete control of the party in 1908, and he ran for the Presidency on an avowedly Progressive platform, basing his fight on the issue of plutocracy against democracy. While Bryan was struggling to keep the Progressives in control of the party machinery, Progressive Democrats were having notable success in Cleveland and Toledo, Ohio, and in New Jersey, from 1910 to 1912, under Governor Woodrow Wilson. In 1910 the Democratic bosses of New Jersey, thirsting for power after many years of defeats, decided that they needed a candidate for office who would be good "window dressing." At the suggestion of George Harvey, editor of *Harper's Weekly*, they selected Woodrow Wilson, President of Princeton University, with the expectation that he would be an excellent vote-getter and, after being elected, would leave the political details to the Democratic machine.

Thomas Woodrow Wilson, who was so greatly to influence the course of America and the world, had grown up in Virginia during reconstruction days. He had in his background a long list of distinguished Presbyterian preachers. The influence of his early Calvinistic training on his later actions cannot be overlooked, particularly as evidenced by his unwillingness to change his mind, once he had reached a decision. Along with this inflexible streak went an inability generally to compromise issues. Wilson attended Princeton as an undergraduate, and then took a doctorate at Johns Hopkins University in history and political science. In 1890 he obtained a chair of political science at Princeton, and in 1902 he was chosen president of that institution. While the Progressive movement was forging ahead in politics and literature, Wilson, at Princeton, attempted to make his institution more democratic. He tried unsuccessfully to transform the aristocratic undergraduate clubs into more democratic groups. Also, he insisted that the graduate school be integrated with the undergraduate college. Wilson received nationwide publicity when he refused a gift of half a million dollars to which were attached certain "strings," which he considered injurious to the welfare of the graduate school. Wilson's general attitude was that higher education was failing to serve American democracy. "The American College," he asserted, "must become saturated in the same sympathies as the common people. The colleges of this country must be reconstructed from the top to bottom. The American people will tolerate nothing that savours of exclusiveness."

During his campaign for governor in 1910 Wilson pledged his support to the enactment of Progressive legislation. He denounced boss rule in the interests of the predatory rich, and the bosses in the Democratic party applauded every speech, assuming that he did not mean it. Wilson was quite aware of the manner by which the bosses in both parties worked with corporations to make New Jersey's incorporation laws so lax that the state had become a haven for those corporations that sought to avoid the kind of legislation to which they might be subject in the more Progressive states. The Progressive Irish in New Jersey rallied to Wilson's support, and they helped Wilson, immediately after his election, to check the power of Democratic boss ex-Senator Smith.

In the preference primary for United States Senator, the voters of the state had expressed the desire that James E. Martine be sent to the Senate by the state legislature. Boss Smith felt under no obligation to follow the will of the people, and he schemed to have the legislature elect him instead of Martine. Wilson went to the people and was so successful in arousing them that the legislature did not dare elect Smith. After this victory over the boss, which made Wilson a dramatic figure, he began to push Progressive legislation through the legislature. Under his guidance New Jersey passed such laws as the direct primary, a corrupt-practices act, a public-utilities act, and an employers'-liability law. This legislation attracted the attention of the nation to Wilson, and he became a leading candidate for the Presidential nomination in 1912.

At the Democratic convention in 1912, with the split in the Republican party, the Democrats had a good chance for victory, provided they could present a Progressive candidate on a truly Progressive platform. Bryan helped to achieve this by forcing the convention to adopt a resolution renouncing "any candidate who is the representative of or under obligation to J. Pierpont Morgan, Thomas F. Ryan, August Belmont, or any other member of the privilege-hunting and favor-seeking class." Champ Clark of Missouri had the backing of the party conservatives and led on the early balloting for the nomination. When Tammany Hall threw its vote to Clark on the tenth ballot, Bryan dramatically transferred his support from Clark to Wilson. Gradually delegate after delegate followed Bryan, and Wilson was nominated on the forty-sixth ballot.

In the Presidential election that ensued, Taft was clearly the only conservative candidate. There was little to choose between the Democratic platform and the Progressive-party platform. Both rejected the Payne-Aldrich tariff, and both called for laws to curb predatory wealth. Roosevelt's platform was more explicit in stating the needed reforms, calling for the initiative, the referendum, the recall, woman suffrage, and a more detailed program of economic reform. Philosophically, however, there was a difference between Roosevelt's New Nationalism and Wilson's New Freedom. Roosevelt emphasized the need of regulating monopoly, whereas Wilson talked in terms of returning the control of business to the small operator. Actually, however, when Wilson became President, he had to alter his position somewhat and accept the need of regulating monopoly. The difference between the two men was marked. As Samuel E. Morison and Henry S. Commager have noted in *The Growth of the American Republic:*

> Roosevelt's tone was that of a fighting parson; Wilson already showed some glint of the spiritual quality of Lincoln. Roosevelt, with Biblical imagery and voice like a shrilling fife, stirred men to wrath, to combat, and to antique virtue; Wilson, serene and confident, lifted men out of themselves by phrases that sang in their hearts, to a vision of a better world. It was the Old Testament against the New, and the New won.[1]

During the campaign the followers of Roosevelt adopted the strategy of stating that a party that had needed forty-six ballots to nominate Wilson could not be trusted to carry out Progressive principles. They also asserted that although Wilson was a sincere Progressive, he would not have the support of the reactionary Democrats of the South and of the city machines in pushing through Progressive laws. When Theodore Roosevelt orated excitedly about the issues of the campaign, Finley Peter Dunne, through his character Mr. Dooley, sagely observed:

> I had no idee it was so bad. I wint to bed last night thinkin' th' counthry was safe. . . . Whin I got up I had a feelin' that somethin' was burnin', th' same as I had th' mornin' iv th' big fire. But I cudden't find annything wrong till I opened up th' papers an', much to me relief, found it was not me pants but th' republic that was on fire. Yes, sir, th' republic is doomed to desthruction again.[2]

Although Wilson gained only 42 per cent of the popular vote, he won an overwhelming victory in the Electoral College. Roosevelt gained 27 per cent of the popular vote, and Taft 23 per cent. Technically speaking, Wilson was a minority President; but since Roosevelt, and Eugene Debs on the Socialist ticket, had advocated many of the same general principles as Wilson, these three candidates, by winning over 75 per cent of the popular vote, clearly demonstrated that the mood of the nation was Progressive. The Democrats also swept into control of Congress, thus affording Wilson a working majority in the legislative branch of the government.

[1] Vol. II, p. 423. Oxford University Press, New York, 1942.
[2] Quoted by Elmer Ellis, *Mr. Dooley's America*, p. 248. Alfred A. Knopf, New York, 1941.

Theodore Roosevelt

William Howard Taft

Woodrow Wilson

Robert M. La Follette

THE WILSON ADMINISTRATION

Wilson, as President, became the greatest leader of the common man since Lincoln. His thoroughgoing belief in democracy, his alert consciousness of the abuses of the day, and his ability to express the spiritual aspirations of the common man made him an outstanding President. Wilson did his best to adapt the ideals of Jeffersonian democracy to the conditions of urban-industrial America. Although he was a firm believer in the common man, such are the paradoxes of history that he lacked the common touch. He believed in the people in the abstract, but he was aloof and cold to people in the concrete. Only to a few close friends did he show his humor and warmth.

Wilson, during the 1912 campaign, saw the struggle between freedom and industrial tyranny in the following light:

Don't deceive yourselves for a moment as to the power of the great interests which now dominate our development. They are so great that it is almost an open question whether the government of the United States can dominate them or not. Go one step further, make their organized power permanent, and it may be too late to turn back. The roads diverge at the point where we stand. They stretch their vistas out to regions where they are very far separated from one another; at the end of one is the old tiresome scene of government tied up with special interests; and at the other shines the liberating light of individual initiative, of individual liberty, of individual freedom, the light of untrammeled enterprise. I believe that that light shines out of the heavens itself that God has created. I believe in human liberty as I believe in the wine of life. There is no salvation for men in the pitiful condescensions of industrial masters. Guardians have no place in a land of freemen. Prosperity guaranteed by trustees has no prospect of endurance. Monopoly means the atrophy of enterprise. If monopoly persists, monopoly will always sit at the helm of the government. I do not expect to see monopoly restrain itself. If there are men in this country big enough to own the government of the United States, they are going to own it; what we have to determine now is whether we are big enough, whether we are men enough, whether we are free enough, to take possession again of the government which is our own.

Wilson's inaugural address gave to his administration a high tone of righteousness and justice. It is one of the most notable statements of the democratic faith in our literature and ranks in importance with Jefferson's first inaugural and Lincoln's second inaugural. After praising the American system of government, Wilson observed:

We have been proud of our industrial achievements, but we have not hitherto stopped thoughtfully enough to count the human cost, the cost of lives snuffed out, of energies overtaxed and broken, the fearful physical and spiritual cost to the men and women and children upon whom the dead weight and burden of it all has fallen pitilessly the years through. The groans and agony of it all had not yet reached our ears, the solemn, moving undertone of our life, coming up out of the mines and factories and out of every home where the struggle had its intimate and familiar seat. With the great Government went many deep secret things which we too long delayed to look into and scrutinize with candid, fearless eyes. The great Government we loved has too often been made use of for private and selfish purposes, and those who used it had forgotten the people.

After this criticism of America's waste and wreckage and failure to be interested in social welfare, Wilson proposed:

Our duty is to cleanse, to reconsider, to restore, to correct the evil without impairing the good, to purify and humanize every process of our common life without weakening or sentimentalizing it. There has been something crude and heartless and unfeeling in our haste to succeed and be great. Our thought has been "Let every man look out for himself, let every generation look out for itself," while we reared giant machinery which made it impossible that any but those who stood at the levers of control should have a chance to look out for themselves. We had not forgotten our morals. We remembered well enough that we had set up a policy which was meant to serve the humblest as well as the most powerful, with an eye single to the standards of justice and fair play, and remembered it with pride. But we were very heedless and in a hurry to be great.

We have come now to the sober second thought. The scales of heedlessness have fallen from our eyes. We have made up our minds to square every process of our national life again with the standards we so proudly set up at the beginning and have always carried at our hearts. Our work is a work of restoration.

Among the chief things that should be altered, said Wilson, were the tariff, which "makes the Government a facile instrument in the hands of private interests"; an outmoded banking and currency system; an exploitive industrial system; an inefficient agricultural system; and the immense waste of our natural resources. Wilson visualized the fully developed positive state by declaring that the government must be put to the service of humanity in safeguarding the health of the men, women, and children of the nation, as well as their rights in the struggle for existence. This was no sentimental duty, in Wilson's mind, because the firm basis of government was justice, not pity. There could be no equality of opportunity, the first essential of justice in the body politic he believed, if men and women and children were "not shielded in their lives and in their very vitality from the consequences of great industrial and social processes which they could not alter, control, or singly cope with." Society must see to it that it did not itself crush or weaken or damage its own constituent parts. The first duty of law was to keep sound the society that it served, Wilson declared, and sanitary laws, pure-food laws, and laws determining conditions of labor—in fact, those problems which individuals were powerless to handle for themselves— were intimate parts of the very business of justice and legal efficiency.

President Wilson was able to transform a large part of his idealistic thinking into concrete measures during the next four years because his party was in control of Congress and eager to follow his leadership. During his second administration, however, domestic reform had to be subordinated to the foreign situation. Shortly after his inaugural address on March 4, 1913, Wilson summoned Congress to a special session to revise the tariff of 1909. He delivered his message to Congress in person, a practice that had been abandoned by Jefferson. The tariff was a dangerous issue. It had been an important factor in defeating Cleveland in 1888, and the Wilson-Gorman and Payne-Aldrich tariffs had been emasculated by special interests. Wilson, in a forthright fashion, demanded a downward revision of tariff schedules. In the House a new tariff bill was soon drawn up and passed under the skillful leadership of Underwood of Alabama, Kitchin of North Carolina, and Hull of Tennessee. On reaching the Senate the Underwood bill fell prey to the special interests. When this situation developed, Wilson dramatically went to the people and said:

I think that the public ought to know the extraordinary exertions being made by the lobby in Washington to gain recognition for certain alterations of the Tariff bill. Washington has seldom seen so numerous, so industrious or so insidious a lobby. The newspapers are being filled with paid advertisements calculated to mislead the judgment of public men not only, but also the public opinion of the country itself. There is every evidence that money without limit is being spent to sustain this lobby and to create an appearance of a pressure of opinion antagonistic to some of the chief items of the Tariff bill.

It is of serious interest to the country that the people at large should have no lobby and be voiceless in these matters, while great bodies of astute men seek to create an artificial opinion and to overcome the interests of the public for their private profit. It is thoroughly worth the while of the people of this country to take knowledge of this matter. Only public opinion can check and destroy it.

The people supported Wilson in his plea, and the bill that passed the Senate marked a reversal in our tariff policy, a policy which had been largely unchecked since the Civil War. The average duties were reduced from about 37 per cent to 27 per cent, and the free list was "no joke"— goods like wool, sugar, iron ore, steel rails, agricultural implements, hides, boots, coal, and wood were to enter duty free. In all, duties were lowered on 958 items, lifted on 86, and maintained on 307. To make up for a loss in revenue, the bill called for a graduated income tax on incomes of over three thousand dollars.

At the same time that Congress was struggling with this tariff bill, the President presented a proposed reorganization of the banking and currency system. The Populists' protests against an inelastic currency were still valid, and since 1900 the control of the money of the nation had been increasingly concentrated in the hands of a few bankers. The investigations of the money problem by the Pujo Committee of Congress, in 1911, had thrown ample light on the unhealthful concentration of power in the hands of the Morgan and Rockefeller interests. Faced with Wilson's demand for a reorganization, conservatives advocated a central bank like the old Bank of the United States, with control of credit in the hands of the bankers. Secretary of State Bryan and his followers, however, wanted the government to issue bank notes and wanted the control of the new system to be in the government's hands. Carter Glass prepared a bill which incorporated many of Bryan's demands, but which at the same time retained some participation by private bankers. The resulting Federal Reserve Act of December 13, 1913, divided the country into twelve districts, each with a Federal reserve bank owned by the member banks, the member banks supplying the capital for the regional bank. All national banks had to join the system, and the state banks were permitted to join. A Federal Reserve Board, made up of the Secretary of the Treasury, the Comptroller of the Treasury, and six people appointed by the President, supervised the activities of the regional Federal reserve banks. A new type of currency—Federal reserve bank notes—was authorized. These bank notes were issued at the discretion of the Federal Reserve Board and were based on the amount of gold and government securities held by the regional banks. To give still greater elasticity to the currency, a second type of money— the Federal reserve note—was issued. When, for instance, a local bank required more currency to meet the demand for extra money at a harvest time, the bank deposited with its regional Federal reserve bank commercial paper (promissory notes of farmers or businessmen) and

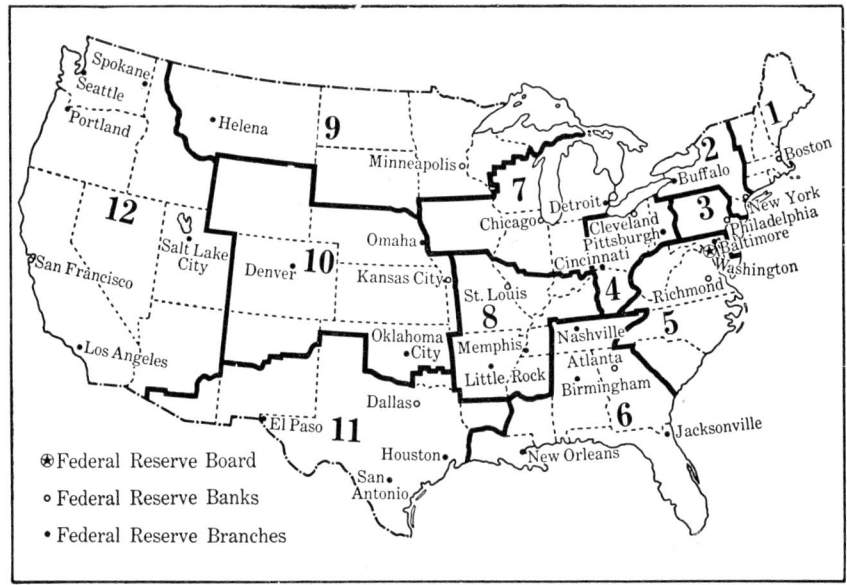

The Federal Reserve Districts

received at once a supply of Federal reserve notes. When the emergency passed, the local bank withdrew the notes from circulation, returned them to the regional bank, and received back its commercial paper.

The Federal Reserve Board could take the reserve of one regional bank and apply it in another region during a crisis, thus helping to increase elasticity. The Board also determined the rate of interest at which money was to be lent by local banks, and it determined the gold reserve that each bank had to maintain. Through these provisions the Board has tried to check speculation by raising the interest rate and gold-reserve requirements, and, by lowering the rate and requirements, has tried to force the local banks to lend money when they were being too cautious. Since 1913, the Federal Reserve System has worked well, and it has added to the financial stability of the country.

It was discovered, shortly after this act went into operation, that it did not sufficiently bring farm interest rates down, nor ease farm credit. To accomplish this, the Federal Farm Loan Act was passed in May, 1916. A Federal Farm Loan Board and twelve regional Farm Loan Banks were created after the Federal reserve pattern. These Farm Loan Banks were empowered to lend money for long periods at low interest rates to co-operative farm loan associations. Another step to aid the farmer was the Warehouse Act of 1916, which allowed licensed warehouses to issue warehouse receipts against farm produce, such receipts being usable as negotiable paper. This was scarcely different from the Populist demand for a Subtreasury system, which had been so severely denounced as too radical in the last decade of the nineteenth century.

Monopoly and the trust problem were the next issues to feel the cutting edge of the New Freedom. Theodore Roosevelt had recognized the need for additional antitrust legislation, but had failed to obtain any. Taft had dodged the issue. By 1913 the power of monopoly was greater than it had been in 1900, and the Sherman Antitrust Act was clearly ineffective in meeting the situation. Wilson called for "new laws" to meet "conditions that menace our civilization." Congress responded to Wilson's request by passing the Federal Trade Commission Act in September, 1914, and the Clayton Antitrust Act in October.

The Federal Trade Commission Act permitted the President to appoint a board of five to investigate corporations engaged in interstate commerce and to issue "cease and desist" orders against any corporation found guilty of violating the antitrust laws and of using unfair methods of competition. During the Wilson administration the board issued three hundred and seventy-nine "cease and desist" orders against such things as bribery, adulteration, misleading advertising, and unfair competition. In the decade following the First World War the board did not have sympathetic Presidents in power, and its work was hampered.

The passage of the Clayton Antitrust Act was a thoroughgoing strengthening of the Sherman Act. It forbade corporations to acquire stock in competing concerns and outlawed interlocking directorates (the same directors managing "competing" corporations) in corporations with a capitalization of more than a million dollars. It forbade such practices as price discrimination and "tying" agreements, which limited the right of purchasers to deal with competing manufacturers. Officers of corporations were made personally responsible for violations of the act. Labor unions and agricultural and horticultural organizations were exempted from the act, and the use of injunctions in labor disputes was forbidden "unless necessary to prevent irreparable injury to property." Actually, however, the courts interpreted this clause in such a way that injunctions were frequently granted until the Norris-La Guardia Anti-Injunction Act of 1932. The Clayton Act was suspended during the First World War, and in the postwar decade it was seldom used. When Franklin D. Roosevelt came into office, the regulating of trusts had to be attempted all over again.

Certain other Progressive laws deserve mention as constructive achievements of Wilson's administration. The La Follette Seamen's Act of 1915 improved the conditions of sailors in the American merchant marine, and the Merchant Marine Act of 1916 established a government Shipping Board empowered to acquire and to operate merchant ships. The Adamson Act of 1916 established the eight-hour day on all interstate railroads, the Smith-Lever Act of 1914 appropriated money for farm demonstration work, and the Smith-Hughes Act of 1917 made money available for vocational and agricultural education. The Democratic party, from 1913 to 1917, produced much worth-while, constructive legislation. It thus demonstrated that the Republican party was not the only party with a statesmanlike vision.

The future of Progressivism after the re-election of Wilson in 1916 was interwoven with events that were taking place elsewhere on the globe. The war brought a cessation of reform legislation, and in the postwar decade the conservative wing of the Republican party controlled the destinies of the nation. The Republicans turned away from Progressivism, and some writers during this period of Republican control began seriously to question the achievements of the prewar Progressivism. Lincoln Steffens, in his *Autobiography*, in 1931, and John Chamberlain, in *Farewell to Reform*, in 1932, adopted the attitude that it had all been in vain. When the New Deal came into power, however, it was recognized as a resurgence of Progressivism. Without doubt the work of the New Deal would have been severely handicapped had it not been for the groundwork done by the Populists, Bryan, Theodore Roosevelt, Woodrow Wilson, and other prewar Progressives.

SELECTED BIBLIOGRAPHY

Henry Pringle, *Roosevelt and Taft*; G. E. Mowry, *Theodore Roosevelt and the Progressive Movement;* Mark Sullivan, *Our Times*, Vol. III, present much of the color of the campaign of 1912.

F. L. Paxon, *The Pre-War Years, 1914-1917*, a general survey of the events of Wilson's administration; H. C. F. Bell, *Woodrow Wilson and the People*, the best one-volume biography; R. S. Baker, *Woodrow Wilson, Life and Letters* (8 vols.), the authorized biography.

W. E. Dodd and R. S. Baker (Eds.), *The Public Papers of Woodrow Wilson* (6 vols.); Woodrow Wilson, *The New Freedom*; Theodore Roosevelt, *The New Nationalism*, contain indispensable material.

Elmer Ellis, *Mr. Dooley's America*, contains many of Mr. Dooley's richest sayings.

H. S. Commager (Ed.), *Documents of American History*, pp. 262-264, 266-267, 278-282, 287-289, contains source material.

XXVI

The Emergence
of a New World Power

AMERICAN HISTORY is the fascinating story of the growth of a people from a solitary colony in 1607 to the greatest world power of the twentieth century. In a little more than three hundred years, a mere interlude in the long course of human history, the United States has developed from the Jamestown colony on the Virginia coast to the greatest industrial, financial, air, and naval power in the world. The nation grew so fast—John C. Calhoun once observed that we grew "fearfully"—that many people were confused by the changed situation of the country. Many Americans did not realize, after 1890, that the United States *was* a great world power and, as such, needed a positive foreign policy. Until the Japanese attack on Pearl Harbor in 1941, some even thought that the United States could isolate itself from the ebb and flow of world affairs. The thinking of a large segment of the American public lagged behind such technological developments as the radio and the airplane—developments which made the world a veritable neighborhood. It was thoroughly unconscious of the fact that what happened to peoples in other parts of the world was its business.

Broadly speaking, American foreign policy can be divided into three periods. From the time of independence to the days of Jacksonian democracy the nation had a constructive and understandable international policy. It consisted in establishing the United States as a nation among the nations of the world and in expanding into the West, where other nations still held claims. Such American statesmen as Thomas Jefferson, James Madison, James Monroe, and John Quincy Adams were able and well trained in diplomacy, and they had traveled widely in Europe and understood European ways and customs. During this period America's internal policies were directly affected by such developments in Europe as the French Revolution and the Napoleonic wars.

After the War of 1812, however, and particularly beginning with the days of Andrew Jackson, the United States turned its back on Europe and came to view the Old World as a remote place to be suspected. The American people literally turned their attention inward and faced the problem of developing a civilization in the West. No longer were relations with England and France to have an immense influence on American political parties or to alter the currents of American life. During the mid and late nineteenth century the American people devoted their activities to settling the West, crowding back the Mexicans, fighting a great civil war, and building an urban-industrial civilization. Only incidentally, in fixing our boundaries in Maine and the Northwest, did we come into touch with England. In this era, since foreign relations did not bulk large, the nation, as a relatively isolated power, developed no positive foreign policy. During this period, too, the United States was able to follow its own path without outside interference partly because its expanding population and growing industries made it secure, but also because the greatest maritime power, Great Britain, was no threat to American security. Furthermore, the fact that Great Britain was maintaining the balance of power, which prevented any great world conflict from breaking out between 1815 and 1914, helped to make it possible for the United States to develop in peace and to ignore the main currents of world politics.

In the decade of the 1890's, as a result of America's remarkable and quick development, it emerged on the world scene as a great power; as a nation it came out of a period of relative isolation to take its place as a significant force in world affairs. But its people now, unlike the Americans of the post-Revolutionary generation, lacked the background and understanding of world affairs necessary to a world power. As a result, America's international policy from the 1890's to the Second World War underwent a number of shifts from isolation to collective security and back from collective security to isolation. This lack of consistency was one of the many factors that helped to disturb world society in the opening decades of the twentieth century.

THE TRADITIONS OF THE GREAT POWERS

At the time that the United States emerged as a world power, the great powers were Great Britain, Russia, France, Germany, and Japan. All these powers, by 1900, except the United States, had definite policies and traditions built over many decades and, in some cases, over centuries. The United States, however, coming out of the negative and static period from 1828 to 1890, had no clear-cut diplomatic policy. Yet it had to carry on diplomacy in a world society where other powers had well-formulated attitudes. It is significant to note also that by 1900 two of the great powers were non-European. This meant, in the long run, that Europe would no longer be able to dictate to the rest of the world. It meant a change from European control of the world, which had existed since the sixteenth century, to a sharing of world control with the Western Hemisphere and the Far East.

Although space does not permit a lengthy discussion of the international policies of the great powers, a summary is necessary in order to comprehend properly the meaning of American history since the 1890's. Great Britain was the dominant world power from 1713 to 1914. Her outstanding tradition was her belief in the importance of sea power. As early as the Elizabethan period England had concentrated on sea power. By dominating the sea England controlled world trade and by blockade could starve an enemy into submission. During the nineteenth century England's superior sea power was particularly effective because Europe's rapid industrialization rendered that continent dependent on food supplies from overseas. The technology of the twentieth century, however, wreaked havoc on England's sea power. The airplane and submarine partially weakened the blockade, and mechanized warfare made it possible for Hitler's Germany to capture most of Europe so quickly in 1940 that the blockade could not be effective. Also, the rising sea power of the United States and of Japan complicated England's problem. In the 1890's England began to realize that she could not compete in the Western Hemisphere with the United States. As a result, the British fleet was withdrawn, and patrolling the Americas was left to the United States. Also, at the Washington Conference of 1922 Great Britain agreed to equality in sea power with the United States.

A second important British tradition was that of the balance of power on the European continent. England was able to maintain the balance of power during the nineteenth century because of her sea power. Essentially the policy meant never permitting one European country to become so strong that it was a threat to world peace. If any nation should threaten the balance of power, Great Britain would intervene. This she did when Philip II, Louis XIV, and Napoleon Bonaparte each attempted to control Europe. But, again, the development of technology in the twentieth century made it impossible for Britain alone to check the rising power of Germany. Tanks and airplanes made warfare too speedy for the balance of power maintained by sea power and the blockade to be effective. Since the 1890's Great Britain has added to these two traditions a definite belief in cultivating the friendship of the United States.

France, in the latter part of the nineteenth century and in the present century, was primarily concerned with checking the German threat to her security. Prussia had decisively defeated her in 1871, and from that time on she followed the policy of friendship with her neighbor's neighbors. This led her to ally herself with Russia and with Britain at the turn of the century.

Germany emerged on the world scene as a great power at about the same time as the United States and Japan. The German Empire had been created in 1871, but Prussia, the decisive force behind the empire, had been developing certain traditions for two centuries. The first outstanding German tradition was the belief in the importance of land power and of having the largest army in Europe. Foreign policy was usually controlled by the Prussian generals, who utilized diplomacy as part of a military policy designed to bring Germany into world domination. Closely allied to this tradition was the belief that the Germans were a superior race and needed *Lebensraum,* or living space. *Lebensraum,* to the Prussian ruling class, meant an area large enough to make Germany self-sufficient. This led Germany, by diplomacy and warfare, to seek control of the Balkans and Russia during the twentieth century. In the period leading up to the First World War this policy also led Germany to construct a large navy and to expand to an overseas empire.

Russia under the Czars had certain definite traditions, and Soviet Russia too has had these same traditions to a great degree. First was the Europeanization of Russia. Peter the Great, in the seventeenth century, began to introduce western-European techniques into a Russia that was strongly Asiatic in beliefs and customs. Until the Russian Revolution of 1917 and 1918, however, little progress was made in industrializing Russia. One of the outstanding accomplishments of Soviet Russia has been the remarkable industrialization of the country. A second tradition was the belief in Russia's need of access to the sea through a warm-water port, open the year round. In the Far East, Russia gained control of Port Arthur in Manchuria, only to lose it to the Japanese in the Russo-Japanese war of 1904–1905. During the nineteenth century Russia attempted to gain control of the Dardanelles and the Bosporus. After the First World War the Soviets established friendly relations with Turkey to ensure the free passage of goods from the Black Sea into the Mediterranean. The third major tradition of Russia has been Pan-Slavism. The small Slavic states in the Balkans received aid from Russia during the nineteenth century in their quest for liberation from Turkey, and during the Second World War Pan-Slavism was of particular importance in this region.

Japan was not part of world society until Commodore Perry of the United States navy opened the land to Western trade and intercourse in 1854. She was, however, an old nation in history, with well-developed beliefs in her superiority to other peoples. After 1854 she industrialized herself quickly, and she built a large army and navy. By the 1890's she was one of the great powers. After that time her policy consisted in having the dominant navy in the Far East and a great army. Her policy, for the fifty years before the Second World War, was based on the premise that she should dominate the Far East. She checked further acquisition of territory in that part of the world by non-Asiatic powers, and gradually, from the time of the Russo-Japanese War to the Japanese invasion of the Philippines, Burma, and the Dutch East Indies, she drove other powers out of the Far East. Referring to this policy as her Far-Eastern Monroe Doctrine, Japan interfered in the domestic affairs of China and acquired by conquest Manchuria, Formosa, Korea, and the areas mentioned above. The comparison with the American Monroe Doctrine was historically inaccurate. The United States, under the Monroe Doctrine, did not drive established powers out of the Americas, and under the "good neighbor" policy it did not intervene in a military fashion in Latin America.

Although oversimplified, the foregoing description of the traditions of the great powers suggests the scene in which the United States has worked as a great power. All the powers but the United States followed definite and concrete traditions. The United States, on the contrary, was inconsistent in its dealings with other nations, and during the twentieth century was struggling to achieve a constructive international policy. Two world wars in twenty-five years have been part of the price paid for the lack of a constructive diplomatic tradition.

THE UNITED STATES IN WORLD AFFAIRS, 1865–1898

Secretary of State W. H. Seward, in the Lincoln and Johnson cabinets, supplied the link between the American expansion of the "manifest destiny" years and the expansion overseas in the latter part of the nineteenth century. Seward dreamed of the United States controlling the Caribbean area, Central America, Hawaii, and Alaska. The United States Senate acquiesced in Seward's purchase of Alaska from Russia in 1867 for seven million two hundred thousand dollars and in the occupation of the uninhabited Midway islands in the same year, but refused to approve the Secretary's move to acquire Santo Domingo and the Danish West Indies. The Senate also, later, defeated attempts by President Grant to add Santo Domingo to the United States.

After the purchase of Alaska and the addition of Midway, the Senate and the people turned away from further expansion. Instead they concerned themselves with reconstructing the South, exploiting the Great Plains, and building American industry. The Grant administration, however, made one constructive contribution to world peace. Grievances that had arisen because of Britain's outfitting of ships for the Confederacy were settled by arbitration in 1872. Since that day the United States and England have settled their disputes by peaceful means. During Cleveland's second administration, for instance, a grave crisis developed between the two countries over the boundary between Venezuela and British Guiana. On July 20, 1895, Secretary of State Olney demanded of England whether she would arbitrate the dispute, which Olney stated involved the Monroe Doctrine. The English reply, which came three months later, denied that the Monroe Doctrine applied to this dispute and added that the United States had no right to enforce arbitration. President Cleveland notified Congress that, if necessary, he would determine the disputed boundary line himself. Cleveland's message stirred an outburst of warlike feeling here. But England had no desire to come into conflict with the United States, and the matter consequently was solved by arbitration.

By the time of the Venezuelan incident, 1895, the rising power of Germany was becoming a threat to Great Britain, and Britain needed friends. The growing German-British tension was nowhere better demonstrated than in South Africa. The British were about to extend their control over the Boer republics, but a British freebooting expedition—the Jameson Raid—was repulsed by the Boers on January 2, 1896. The German Kaiser immediately dispatched a telegram of congratulations to the Boers, and then he published the telegram. Under these circumstances, England could ill afford to antagonize the United States over the Venezuelan affair.

Although the years from 1867 to 1898 are generally considered to have been nonimperialistic years for the United States, actually the executive branch of the government took steps to acquire overseas possessions. This is best seen in the case of Hawaii and Samoa. President Grant secured the Senate's ratification, in 1875, of a trade treaty with Hawaii which actually placed the islands in the American sphere of influence. The treaty was renewed in 1884, and at that time the United States was given exclusive use of the naval base at Pearl Harbor. By 1890 Americans on the islands had secured control of Hawaii's parliamentary form of government. Three years later the last of the Hawaiian monarchs, Queen Liliuokalani, attempted to deprive the American group of control. This step precipitated a revolution, which resulted in the taking over of the islands by the American residents. The American minister abetted the revolution by landing marines and quickly drawing up a treaty of annexation to the United States. President Harrison was unable to rush the treaty through the Senate before President Cleveland took office; and when Cleveland postponed action, Hawaii's annexation had to wait until after the outbreak of the Spanish-American War. Similar steps on the part of the executive drew the United States into Samoa. In 1889 the United States, Great Britain, and Germany worked out a three-way protectorate of the islands. The American policy toward Hawaii and Samoa can best be described as a policy of "anticipated annexation." The executive took steps to acquire control, and eventually the enthusiasm of the Spanish-American War overcame the Senate's reluctance to expand.

THE SPANISH–AMERICAN WAR

Previous to the war with Spain in 1898, American expansion had been justified on the basis of the economic value of new areas, their geographical proximity to the United States, their strategic value to American security, and the opportunity that they offered for the extension of republican institutions. Before 1898 opposition to acquiring an overseas empire had long been vocal in the United States. It was argued by some that it was undesirable to add noncontiguous territory; that democracy required a homogeneous population, and therefore the addition of "backward" peoples would be a curse rather than a blessing. During the decade of the 1890's, however, new arguments, favoring expansion, gained wide acceptance and gradually overcame reluctance to acquiring an overseas empire.

Darwin's doctrine of evolution, for instance, was held to justify the absorption of "backward" people by "superior" people, since this was a method of contributing to the perfection of the species. Professor

John W. Burgess of Columbia University, under whom Theodore
Roosevelt had studied, observed that the Teutonic nations were called
upon "to carry the political civilization of the modern world into those
parts of the world inhabited by unpolitical and barbaric races; . . . If
a population was incompetent politically then Teutonic nations might
righteously assume sovereignty over, and undertake to create state order
for, such a politically incompetent population." Rudyard Kipling, the
poet of British imperialism, asserted that it was the "white man's burden" to manage "backward" peoples. This rationalization justifying
imperialism was part of a world-wide trend toward imperialism; by
no means was it indulged in solely by the citizens of the United States.

Another force stimulating imperialism was Captain Alfred T.
Mahan's prediction of a wider destiny for the United States. In his
writings on sea power he declared that "Americans must now begin
to look outward." He stated that sea power was essential to national
greatness, and he advocated that the United States acquire islands in
the Caribbean and in the Pacific as the basis for a world empire and
for a big navy. He noted in 1897:

Indications are not wanting of an approaching change in the thoughts and
policy of Americans as to their relations with the world outside their own
borders. . . . Within, the home market is secured; but outside, beyond the
broad seas, there are the markets of the world, that can be entered and controlled only by a vigorous contest. . . . Whether they will or not, Americans
must now begin to look outward. The growing production of the country
demands it. An increasing volume of public sentiment demands it.

To the ideological beliefs of the "white man's burden" and Mahan's
theory of sea power must be added economic factors to explain the
reasons why America became imperialistic. American investors in Cuba
and Hawaii, particularly, were a factor in leading the public to accept
a larger role for the United States. But anyway expansion in the 1890's
was as popular as it had been in the 1840's. Wall Street and business
interests generally did not have to finance imperialism; they were to
gain, of course, immense economic benefits from our overseas empire.

The Cuban revolution of 1895 was the event that precipitated the
United States onto the world scene as a major power. For decades
many Americans had been interested in adding this Spanish-controlled
island to the United States. The Cuban insurrection against Spain in
1895 coincided significantly with the passing of the American frontier
and with the emergence of the United States as a great industrial power.

By the 1890's American eyes were beginning to turn away from purely domestic activities and to seek adventure and markets overseas. The Cuban revolution, therefore, naturally attracted the public's attention and sympathy.

Amidst this awakening of American interest in activities beyond the United States was the coincidental situation that Joseph Pulitzer and William Randolph Hearst were engaged in a bitter battle for the control of circulation for their rival New York City newspapers. Through scare headlines and atrocity story after atrocity story, the *World* and the *Journal* inflamed American sympathies for the Cuban cause. At the same time, some younger political leaders, such as Henry Cabot Lodge, Dr. Albert Shaw, and Theodore Roosevelt, were interested in using the growing popular sympathy for Cuba to launch the United States toward overseas empire. Senator Lodge, for instance, wrote in a popular magazine:

> The tendency of modern times is toward consolidation. . . . Small states are of the past, and have no future. The great nations are rapidly absorbing for their future expansion and their present defence all the waste places of the earth. It is a movement which makes for civilization and the advancement of the race. As one of the great nations of the world the United States must not fall out of the line of march.

On February 9, 1898, Hearst's *New York Journal* printed a letter written by the Spanish minister at Washington, Dupuy de Lome, which had been stolen from the mails. In the letter the Spanish minister bluntly observed: "McKinley is weak and a bidder for the admiration of the crowd, besides being a would-be politician who tries to leave a door open behind himself while keeping on good terms with the jingoes of his party." This attack on the President only served to add fuel to the fire of hatred toward Spain. Six days after the publication of the De Lome letter, the United States battleship *Maine* was blown up in Havana harbor. The yellow journalists whipped up hysteria against Spain, and "Remember the Maine!" became the catchword of the day. Whether the *Maine* was destroyed by an accident, by a Spanish agent, or by a Cuban patriot trying to precipitate the United States into war is still unknown.

During February, 1898, the advocates of war echoed and re-echoed the slogan "Remember the Maine!" and aggressive young Republicans like Theodore Roosevelt saw this as the opportune moment to launch the United States on the path of empire. When McKinley tried to avert war by negotiations with Spain, Roosevelt remarked that "McKinley has no more backbone than a chocolate éclair." On April 9 the Spanish government acceded to American pressure by suspending hostilities in Cuba, and the American minister cabled from Spain that if the United States avoided humiliating Spain, the Cuban question would be settled according to American terms. McKinley's campaign-manager, Mark Hanna, and powerful Wall Street financial and business forces favored peace. McKinley, however, lacking the backbone necessary to oppose the frenzy stirred by the press and the pressure exerted by more militant groups of the public and Congress, sent his war message to Congress on April 11. The Congressional declaration of war on April 20 contained an amendment, suggested by Senator Teller, stating:

> The United States hereby disclaims any disposition or intention to exercise sovereignty, jurisdiction or control over said Island except for the pacification thereof, and asserts its determination, when that is accomplished, to leave the government and control of the Island to its people.

The other great powers of the world watched the developing crisis between Spain and the United States with mixed emotions. Germany (expanding overseas and about to buy many Pacific islands from Spain) and Austria-Hungary and France were inclined to be hostile to the United States. Although there were rumors of their intervention on Spain's behalf, no one nation wanted to take the lead in incurring American hostility. Great Britain, in contrast to these powers, was exceedingly friendly toward the United States and, after the war had broken out, urged the new world power to acquire the Philippines. The English attitude was reflected by a London newspaper on April 9, 1898: "If America were really attacked by a great Continental coalition, England would be at her side in twenty-four hours."

America embarked on the war in a gay, lighthearted fashion. The popular song of the day, "A Hot Time in the Old Town," expressed the general feeling toward the war. As Theodore Roosevelt once observed, "It wasn't much of a war, but it was all the war there was." The American people believed that they went to war to free the Cubans; the fact that the war was to create an empire for the nation was not forseen or expected by the mass of Americans.

Commodore Dewey's dramatic defeat of the Spanish fleet in Manila Bay on May 1, 1898, electrified the public. Assistant Secretary of the Navy Theodore Roosevelt, months before the outbreak of hostilities, had ordered Dewey to be ready for offensive action against Spain. During the troublesome times just before the coming of the war, Roosevelt's superior, Secretary Long, hardly dared leave Washington for fear of what Roosevelt would do with the navy. Long confided to his diary on February 25, 1898:

> These are trying times. In the evening Roosevelt, whom I left as Acting Secretary during the afternoon, came around. He is so enthusiastic and loyal that he is in certain respects invaluable; yet I lack confidence in his good judgment and discretion. He goes off very impulsively, and if I have a good night tonight, I shall feel that I ought to be back in the Department rather than take a day's vacation.

On February 26, 1898, the entry read:

> I had a splendid night last night and returned to the office both because I feel so much better and because I find that Roosevelt, in his precipitate way, has come very near causing more of an explosion than happened to the *Maine*.

The war was of short duration, and it revealed the significance of sea power for American security. Shortly after Dewey's victory in the Far East another American fleet, under Admiral Sampson and Commodore Schley, bottled up a Spanish fleet in Santiago Bay, Cuba. Late in June, American troops were landed in Cuba without opposition. When these troops threatened to capture Santiago, the Spanish fleet sailed out to destruction on July 3. Land battles were fought at Las Guasimas, El Caney, and San Juan. The battle of San Juan, participated in by Theodore Roosevelt, who had organized a picturesque volunteer cavalry of "Rough Riders," helped to lift him to the White House. After the war Roosevelt published a book about the Rough Riders, which inspired humorist Finley Peter Dunne with one of his shrewdest comments. Observed Mr. Dooley to Mr. Hennessy:

> "I haven't time f'r to tell ye the wurruk Tiddy did in ar-hmin' an' equippin' himself, how he fed himself, how he steadied himself in battles an' encouraged himself with a few well-chosen worruds whin th' sky was darkest. Ye'll have to take a squint into the book ye'erself to l'arn thim things."
>
> "I won't do it," said Mr. Hennessy. "I think Tiddy Rosenfelt is all r-right an' if he wants to blow his horn lave him do it."
>
> "True f'r ye," said Mr. Dooley. . . . "But if I was him I'd call th' book 'Alone in Cubia.'"[1]

[1] Quoted by Elmer Ellis, *Mr. Dooley's America*. Alfred A. Knopf, New York, 1941.

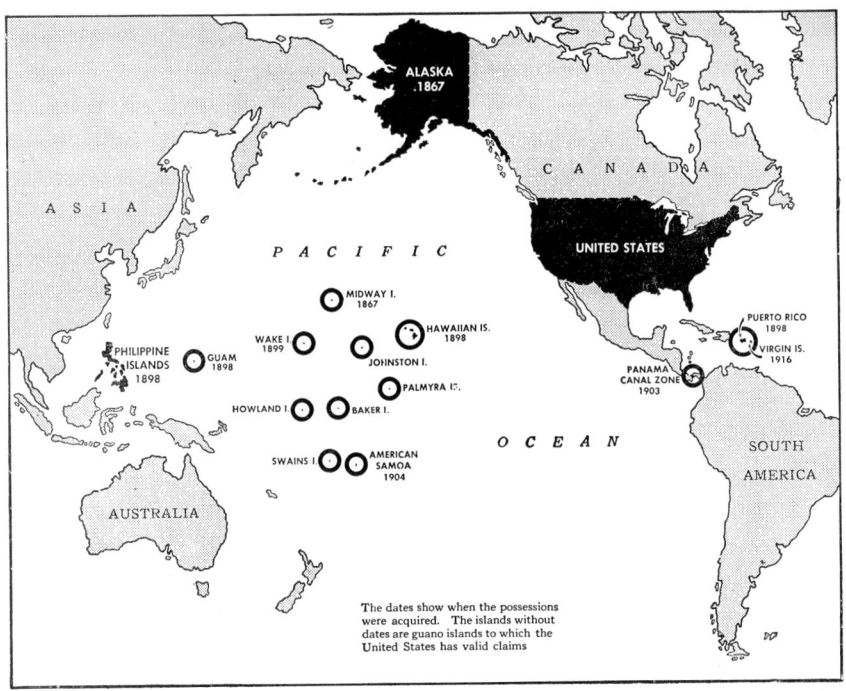

The Overseas Expansion of the United States between
1867 and 1916

Spain was forced to sue for peace and signed an armistice on August 12, 1898. The terms required Spain to evacuate Cuba, to turn Puerto Rico over to the United States, and to agree to American occupation of Manila until the peace treaty disposed of the Philippines. Spain sadly protested that these terms strip "us of the very last memory of a glorious past and . . . [expel] us from the Western Hemisphere, which became peopled and civilized through the proud deeds of our ancestors." The war actually did terminate Spanish control in a hemisphere which she had opened to Western civilization some four hundred years before, but by 1898 Spain was no longer a great world power.

By the treaty of peace, signed on December 10, Spain agreed to the independence of Cuba and to the cession of Puerto Rico and Guam to the United States. The disposition of the Philippines, however, was a troublesome question. McKinley, after much recourse to prayer and listening to public opinion, decided to acquire them for the United States. After Dewey's victory the press became fascinated with the idea of an American foothold in Asia. Business groups, which before the war had had no interest in the islands, saw a chance for business expansion and a base for trade with Asia. Followers of Captain Mahan advocated retention of the islands as a necessary step in the development of American sea power. Also, it seemed clear that, if the United States did not take the Philippines, Germany or Japan soon would. Japan had already suggested that she would be willing to share a protectorate with the United States, and Germany bought the last remaining Spanish islands during the months of peace negotiations. The United States paid Spain twenty million dollars for the Philippines, but in acquiring the islands it purchased also a first-class Filipino revolution. Filipino troops, under Emilio Aguinaldo, had been encouraged by Dewey to aid in the ending of Spanish rule, and now they took up arms against American domination. It was not until 1902 that the insurrection was stamped out.

When the peace treaty was submitted to the United States Senate, one of the greatest debates in American history was launched. Henry Cabot Lodge led the fight for ratification by observing:

> I cannot think calmly of the rejection of that Treaty by a little more than one-third of the Senate. It would be a repudiation of the President and humiliation of the whole country in the eyes of the world, and would show we are unfit as a nation to enter into great questions of foreign policy.

Senator George F. Hoar of Massachusetts opposed ratification because he felt that it violated the American belief in government by the consent of the governed. It was argued also that the annexation of the Philippines violated the Constitution; that the cost of administering and protecting the islands would be greater than they were worth; and that the acquisition would involve the nation in Far-Eastern politics. The treaty, however, was finally approved by a vote of fifty-seven to twenty-seven.

When the United States took the Philippines, it became a Pacific power, as well as a continental power. This also meant increased participation in European affairs, since the major European powers were active in the Far East. Like the other great powers, the United States had now embarked on the path of empire. Although many Americans were not fully aware of it until the Second World War, the United States in 1898 assumed responsibility for the development and protection of the Philippines. This was a responsibility that had to be implemented after December 7, 1941.

From 1898 to 1934 the United States gradually moved in the direction of independence for the Philippines. Congress passed the Organic Act of 1902, which permitted the Filipinos to elect the lower house of the legislature, and reorganized the islands as an unincorporated territory with the rest of the territorial government appointed by the United States. In 1916 the Jones Act was passed by Congress, which announced the American intention of withdrawing from the Philippines "as soon as a stable government can be established therein." Under American control a remarkable advance was made in education, health and sanitation, economic betterment, and self-government; but the Filipinos naturally continued their agitation for independence, and it was granted, to become effective in 1945, by the Tydings-McDuffie Act of 1934. American sugar interests disliked the competition of Filipino sugar with American-grown sugar, and American businessmen had failed to find the prosperous exploitation that they had once anticipated. But the grant of independence did not remove American responsibility for the islands. After the gallant manner in which the Filipinos had fought side by side with American forces against Japanese aggression after December 7, 1941, the American people realized their moral duty to guarantee the continued independence of the Philippines in the future.

THE UNITED STATES AND THE FAR EAST, 1898–1914

The Philippines were expected to be useful as a base for trade with the Chinese Empire. By 1899, however, the future of China was in doubt. Japan had defeated China in a war in 1894–1895 and had taken Formosa and other territories from China. During the next four years other great powers began to divide up China by leasing territory and establishing spheres of influence. This situation led the Chinese empress to remark, "The various powers cast upon us looks of tiger-like voracity, hustling each other in their endeavors to be the first to seize upon our innermost territories." In 1898 Germany took Kiaochow in the Shantung peninsula; Russia acquired Port Arthur; Great Britain added Weihaiwei, lying between the Russian and German leases, to her Chinese possessions; and France secured a lease of Kwangchow, adjoining Indo-China.

In their various spheres of influence the great powers established a monopoly of trade and investments for their own businessmen. Such a situation threatened to check any American business developments in China; Great Britain too was alarmed by this development, which threatened her commercial supremacy in China. In 1898, therefore, Britain suggested a joint statement by the two nations, calling for equality of commercial treatment for all nations, regardless of spheres of influence. This proposal was analogous to the Canning proposal to Rush in 1823 (p. 253), concerning a joint proclamation with regard to Latin America. As in 1823, however, the United States pursued an independent course.

On September 6, 1899, Secretary of State John Hay issued a note setting forth his famous "open door" policy, in which all the powers were asked to grant equality of opportunity in the Chinese areas that they controlled. Actually, only Great Britain specifically agreed to the policy, but all the other powers, except Russia, expressed approval. Developments in the next forty years, particularly in the Japanese-controlled areas, were to reveal that the open-door policy had not been maintained.

In 1900 another important American policy for China was announced. The ruthless foreign exploitation of China stirred a group of Chinese—the Boxers—to attempt to drive the "foreign devils" out of the country. The Boxers were quickly suppressed by an international expeditionary force, including some American troops. Fearing that this incident might lead to the further dismemberment of China, Secretary Hay announced that the United States would oppose any violation of the territorial sovereignty of China. It was clear from this stand that the American government would not be silent on Far Eastern questions. During the next few years, however, the great powers gave only verbal consent to the territorial sovereignty of China. In 1908 the Root-Takahira Agreement, signed by the United States and Japan, repeated the pledge of "the independence and integrity of China" and "equal opportunity for commerce and industry"; but Japan's real intentions were revealed in 1915, when she forced her "Twenty-one Demands" on China. These demands definitely infringed on China's sovereignty. Also, of course, Japan openly violated China's territorial integrity in 1931, when she seized Manchuria. Until 1941 the United States only protested with words these glaring violations of the territorial sovereignty of China.

One leading student of American diplomacy, S. F. Bemis, has stated that the open-door policy and the policy of the territorial sovereignty of China were great blunders on the part of the United States, since the United States had to retreat from them in the face of Japanese aggressions. On the other hand, these American policies delayed the partition

Foreign Concessions in the Far East in 1898

of China until China, under the Nationalist government, was able to fight back, and the American stand also helped to maintain China as a unit until the Allies came to her aid during the Second World War. Furthermore, in return for backing England in the Far East, the United States secured a free hand in the Western Hemisphere.

In addition to fostering the open-door and territorial-sovereignty policies for China, the United States played a significant role in another way in Far Eastern affairs. The Russo-Japanese War of 1904–1905 was brought to a close by the negotiations of President Theodore Roosevelt. He brought the belligerents together at Portsmouth, New Hampshire, and broke a deadlock in the peace negotiations. The victor, Japan, emerged from the conference with less than she had wanted, but with territorial gains, including the Russian lease of Port Arthur. She was bitter toward the United States, however, because she had not acquired all that she had desired. After 1905 relations between the two countries became increasingly difficult. Japan, seeking to dominate the Far East, resented America's increasing role in Oriental affairs and, particularly, America's interest in preserving the integrity of China.

THE UNITED STATES AND EUROPE, 1898–1914

During the sixteen years following the Spanish-American War, war clouds were gathering in Europe. The rising power of Germany, with her belief in the superiority of Germans and in her right to expand on the Continent and overseas, threatened the security of both England and France. Under this threat these powers drew together in an alliance in 1904. Three years later Russia, fearing German ambitions in the Russian Ukraine, joined this alliance. Germany, planning for world domination, countered with an alliance with Austria-Hungary and one with Italy. When the First World War broke out, however, Italy joined the Allied cause. In these grave years, when Germany was planning for war, the people of the United States had little comprehension of events outside their own borders. War seemed to be an inconceivable situation to the mass of Americans. But Presidents Theodore Roosevelt and Woodrow Wilson were aware of the effect that a European war might have on American security. As a result, both men interested themselves in helping to maintain the peace of Europe.

In the Moroccan crisis of 1905 and 1906 Theodore Roosevelt played a part in preserving peace. France claimed hegemony over Morocco, which was challenged by the German emperor, who personally visited Tangier and stressed his interest in the independence of the area. A severe diplomatic crisis quickly developed. Roosevelt, realizing that if war should break out, it would affect the United States, did his best to work out a peaceful solution. The United States was represented by Henry White at the international conference at Algeciras, which was called to solve the problem. As a result of the conference, war was postponed for a few years.

When the agreements of the Algeciras conference came before the United States Senate, the Senate ratified them, but stated that the ratification did not involve a departure "from the traditional American policy which forbids participation by the United States in the settlement of political questions which are entirely European in their scope."

The Senate, probably reflecting public opinion, had little realization that a conflict in Europe would involve the United States. Seemingly, only Theodore Roosevelt was aware that the development of technology had made it impossible for the United States to ignore world events. President Taft apparently lacked this vision. He refused, for instance, to participate in the second Moroccan crisis, in 1911, and observed that these were events "without direct political concern" to the United States.

Theodore Roosevelt also tried to maintain the peace of Europe by attempting to enlarge the activities and prestige of the international tribunal at the Hague. He referred a number of international disputes to the tribunal, such as the Venezuela controversy of 1902. Woodrow Wilson enlarged on these activities of Roosevelt. Before the outbreak of the First World War the Wilson administration, through Secretary Bryan, had signed twenty-six treaties with leading nations, in which it was agreed that disputes should be arbitrated before resort was had to war. Wilson also sent Colonel E. M. House on a trip to Europe in 1913 in an attempt to stabilize peace. In spite of such activities, however, the American people were ignorant of the gravity of the world situation, and as a result they were stunned and shocked when war broke out in 1914.

American international relations from 1898 to 1914 were marked by a growing cordiality between the United States and Great Britain. During the Spanish-American War, Britain alone of the European nations had been friendly to the United States, and from 1898 to 1914 Britain definitely cultivated amicable relations. She withdrew her fleet from the Western Hemisphere and supported American acquisition of the Philippines. In 1901, by the Hay-Pauncefote Treaty, England removed her objections, as expressed in the Clayton-Bulwer Treaty of 1850, to an American-owned and defended Panamanian canal. Also, British influence was behind the open-door policy in the Far East.

At the same time, German-American relations became extremely unfriendly. There gradually developed in the United States the idea that Germany was a menace to American security. Americans remembered that during the summer of 1898 a powerful German fleet, under Admiral von Diedrichs, had dropped anchor in Manila Bay. Diedrichs failed to observe some of Dewey's blockade regulations, and Dewey at once told Diedrichs, "If Germany wants war, all right, we are ready." On the other hand, the British fleet in Manila Bay, under Sir Edward Chichester, was extremely friendly to the United States. Americans also knew that Germany had had her eyes on the Philippines. Furthermore, the blockade of Venezuela in 1902 by German and British ships greatly disturbed the American public. The British were quick to realize American hostility to this action, whereas the Germans were slow to accept the Monroe Doctrine and arbitration in the affair. Out of this crisis came increasing suspicion of German designs on the Western Hemisphere. From 1902 to 1914 many Americans believed that Germany was trying to establish naval bases and colonies in the Caribbean. As a result, by the outbreak of the First World War there was, in the United States, a definite distrust of Germany, and a growing preference for Great Britain.

Developments in Europe and in the Orient in the years from 1898 to 1914 were to take the United States away from concentration on domestic affairs and require increasing attention to world affairs. The outbreak of war in 1914 and America's gradual involvement in the crisis dramatically symbolized the nation's new position in world affairs. Woodrow Wilson observed in 1919:

> The isolation of the United States is at an end, not because we chose to go into the politics of the world, but because by the sheer genius of this people and the growth of our power we have become a determining factor in the history of mankind, and after you have become a determining factor you cannot remain isolated, whether you want to or not. Isolation ended by the processes of history, not by the processes of our independent choice, and the processes of history merely fulfilled the prediction of the men who founded our republic.

SELECTED BIBLIOGRAPHY

S. F. Bemis, *Diplomatic History of the United States*, and T. A. Bailey, *Diplomatic History of the American People*, the two best general surveys; Dexter Perkins, *The Monroe Doctrine* and *America and Two Wars*, excellent.

J. W. Pratt, *Expansionists of 1898*, a good study of the psychological background of the Spanish-American War; P. T. Moon, *Imperialism and World Politics*, presents the world-wide situation; Walter Millis, *The Martial Spirit*, and Joseph Wisan, *The Cuban Crisis as Reflected in the New York Press*, are worth while.

Tyler Dennett, *Roosevelt and the Russo-Japanese War*, excellent for the Portsmouth Conference; Allan Nevins, *Henry White*, excellent for the Algeciras Conference; Tyler Dennett, *Americans in Eastern Asia* and *John Hay*, valuable.

H. S. Commager (Ed.), *Documents of American History*, pp. 152-154, 170-172, 181-198, 199-200, 232, 273, contains source material.

XXVII

The United States
and Latin America, 1898-1928

A MERICAN EXPANSION did not stop with the territorial acqui-
sitions resulting from the war with Spain. The United States
quickly expanded its domination over the Caribbean region
and over much of Central and South America and brought these areas
within the American sphere of influence. On the whole, the American
people seemed to be reluctant expansionists. The Senate vote on the
treaty closing the Spanish-American War was not a real indication of
the public's feeling toward expansion, since certain Senators voted for
the treaty out of fear that continued war would upset prosperity, and
also out of fear that the international situation was so dangerous that
the war with Spain, if it continued, might grow into a world war.
McKinley won the election of 1900, but not exactly on the imperialistic
issue; the prosperity of the country really determined the election.

The forces that overcame American reluctance to expand after 1898
were varied. Some of them had played a part in bringing on the
Spanish-American War. One very important force was the heavy investment of American capital abroad and the feeling that this had to
be protected by the government, particularly in Latin America. A
second force was the moral fervor created by the talk of the "white
man's burden." It was felt by many that the American people had
an obligation to expand their institutions and civilization to people
who were not as developed as they were. Enthusiasm for the Monroe
Doctrine was another factor. After 1895 the press was filled with discussion of it, and there was an intense emotional reaction to any threat
to the Doctrine. To forestall such threats, some Americans justified
expansion in Latin America. Furthermore, ardent expansionists were
in control of the nation's destinies during the first decade of the twentieth century. Theodore Roosevelt, John Hay, Henry C. Lodge, and
Elihu Root, particularly, urged the American people to expand their
control. The influence of these men should not be overlooked in eval-

uating the imperialistic forces of these years. Still another factor was the belief that Germany was a menace to the security of the United States. Germany began to be aggressive in world affairs when Bismarck's restraining hand was removed in the last decade of the nineteenth century, and she was looked upon as being ambitious for colonies and naval bases in the New World, in spite of the Monroe Doctrine. A recent study has disclosed that three fourths of the alleged threats to the Doctrine from 1871 to 1918 were attributed to Germany. As a result, some people justified American control of certain Latin-American countries as being necessary in order to forestall a German threat of occupation. Although the German menace may have been exaggerated, it was a motivating force behind American expansion.

During this same era, when Germany seemed to be a rival imperialistic power, Great Britain encouraged American expansion. She withdrew her fleet from the Caribbean area and recognized the prime interest of the United States in this region. She also encouraged this country to acquire the Philippines and to acquire a stake in China. She encouraged American domination of Latin America, realizing that American control meant more stable governments and therefore better opportunities for British trade and investment.

FROM ROOSEVELT TO COOLIDGE

American foreign relations from 1898 to 1928 were directly influenced by industrial, agricultural, and financial activities at home. Population pressure, however, was not part of America's expansionist drive; there was no surplus of people who were jostling one another. But American commodities and capital went out to the world; and especially to Latin America went financial experts, technologists, investors' agents, and adventurers. These people searched for sources of raw materials, they opened new markets for American goods, and they looked for investment opportunities. During these years the United States dominated the Caribbean region and also tried, in a number of instances, to make the governments of South America stable and democratic.

Theodore Roosevelt's policy toward Latin America was ruthless. He applied the Platt Amendment to Cuba in 1906, thus making Cuba a protectorate. He acquired the Canal Zone in 1903 and made Panama a protectorate. In 1905, by use of military force, he placed the customhouses of the Dominican Republic under United States supervision.

Using the Dominican Republic situation as a springboard, he proclaimed a new corollary to the Monroe Doctrine, which established the right of the United States to regulate Latin America in its relation to Europe. Up to this point, the Monroe Doctrine had regulated only European affairs in the Western Hemisphere, but under the Roosevelt corollary Latin America was to see its own activities regulated by the United States. Roosevelt also insisted upon peace in Central America. He forced the Central American countries to sign an agreement to arbitrate disputes, and, more important, he forced these states to renounce the right of revolution. This meant that the United States and the Central American republics would not recognize a government established by revolution in Central America. Since a revolution was the normal way for the Central American countries to change presidents, this policy of Theodore Roosevelt tended to perpetuate dictators in power. In practical application the policy generally meant that when a revolution broke out in one country, the United States and all the rest of the Central American nations would prevent arms and ammunition from reaching the revolutionists, while supplying the government in power with everything needed to suppress the revolt.

President Taft attempted to continue Roosevelt's policy. The three protectorates—Cuba, Panama, and the Dominican Republic—were retained, and the renunciation of the right of revolution and the Roosevelt corollary to the Monroe Doctrine were also maintained. In addition, Taft attempted to establish a protectorate over Nicaragua, but the Senate refused to ratify the treaty which would have accomplished this. Taft attempted also to establish control over the customhouses of Guatemala and Honduras, but he did not succeed.

Under Woodrow Wilson, America's empire reached its greatest extent. He retained the empire that had been achieved under Roosevelt and Taft and took further steps to expand America's sphere of influence in the Western Hemisphere. He added Nicaragua as a protectorate by the Bryan-Chamorro Treaty, which gave the United States a canal option in that country. He landed marines in Haiti in 1915 and placed that country under military government. In 1916, in the Dominican Republic, he extended the control of the United States from customs supervision to complete domination. Since his attitude toward Mexico, a country in the turmoil of revolution, was intertwined with the story of America and the First World War, it will be mentioned in Chapter XXVIII. Finally, he forced all of Latin America, not just Central America, to renounce the right of revolution.

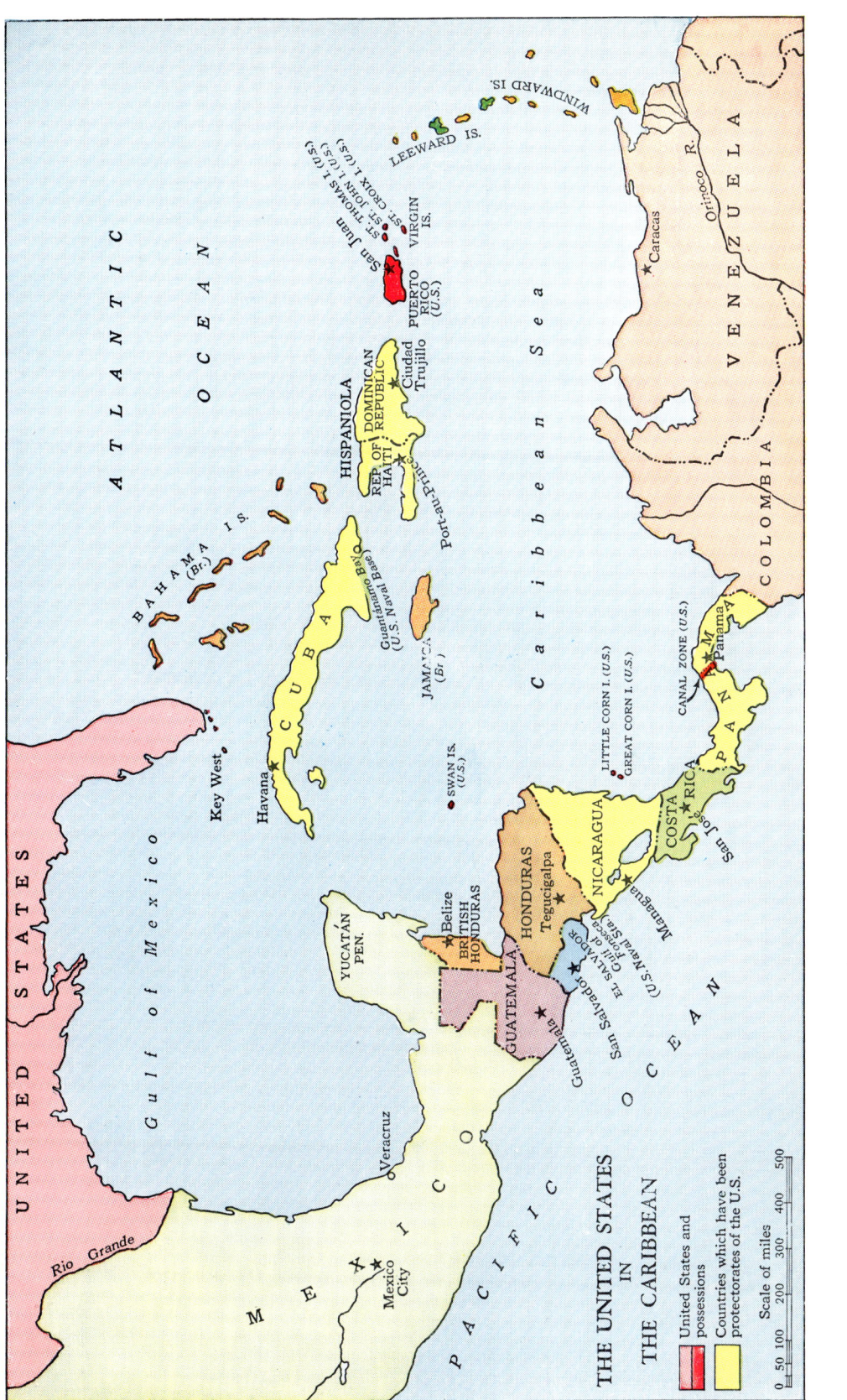

THE UNITED STATES
IN
THE CARIBBEAN

United States and possessions

Countries which have been protectorates of the U.S.

Scale of miles

0 50 100 200 300 400 500

Why did Woodrow Wilson, the great humanitarian and democrat, take the steps mentioned above? Wilson firmly believed that human rights were superior to property rights, and he openly denounced "dollar diplomacy." His opposition to the use of armed force on the part of the United States to protect the property and trade of American citizens in Latin America was so vigorous that the steps he took must have some explanation. The chief reason seems to be that he became irritated by Latin America's failure to achieve democracy and stable rule, and he decided, therefore, to teach it how to acquire these even if it required intervention. Furthermore, with a great war raging in Europe, Wilson was motivated by the strategic value of protectorates over Haiti and Nicaragua, as well as by the need of stability in the Western Hemisphere. Turmoil and strife in Latin America would endanger unity in the Americas. Upset conditions in Haiti, Nicaragua, the Dominican Republic, and Cuba might invite European occupation, and this would be a threat to the security of the Panama Canal.

The period of Republican control under Harding and Coolidge continued the empire acquired by Roosevelt, Taft, and Wilson. Both Warren G. Harding and Calvin Coolidge were more eager to collect the dividends of American investors in Latin America than their predecessors had been. Coolidge, for instance, said in 1927: "The person and property of a citizen are part of the general domain of the nation, even when abroad. . . . Wherever he goes the duties of our government must follow him." In Nicaragua, Coolidge exerted drastic control. Marines were landed to maintain the government desired by the Coolidge administration. Liberal opinion in the United States denounced this, and the marines were finally withdrawn. Relations with Mexico during the 1920's were unusually acute. The Mexican Constitution of 1917, Article 27, vested in the Mexican nation ownership of the subsoil mineral and oil deposits. American investments in mining and oil had reached, by this time, a value of about three hundred million dollars. If Article 27 were applied retroactively, this investment would be lost. Most of the American investment had been made during the dictatorial regime of Porfirio Díaz, from 1877 to 1911, when Díaz had practically given the country's resources away to foreign capitalists. He had abrogated an ancient Mexican and Spanish law which stated that the ownership of the subsoil deposits always resided in the nation. Article 27 was an attempt to return to this concept; but by 1917 foreigners had invested heavily in the exploitation of the subsoil deposits. The Harding administration refused recognition of President

Obregón's government because Obregón would not promise that Article 27 would not be retroactive, and American troops were placed along the Rio Grande. The situation was eased considerably in 1923, when the Mexican Supreme Court held that Article 27 was not retroactive.

Relations reached a crucial point again when the new Mexican President, Plutarco Calles, favored a retroactive interpretation of Article 27. Calles also made a start in carrying out the pledge of the Mexican Revolution that land would be given to the landless peons. This led to the confiscation of certain lands held by citizens of the United States. Calles furthermore placed curbs on the Catholic Church to reduce its economic and political power in Mexican life. Coolidge's Secretary of State, Kellogg, warned Calles: "The government of Mexico is now on trial before the world. . . . We have been patient and realize, of course, that it takes time to bring about a stable government, but we cannot countenance violation of . . . [Mexico's] obligations and failure to protect American citizens." But the Coolidge administration was unable to win any public support for military intervention in Mexico. On January 25, 1927, the Senate opposed any such proposal by voting unanimously for arbitration of the Mexican controversy. Coolidge now changed his tactics. Dwight W. Morrow, New York financier who had opposed "dollar diplomacy," was sent to Mexico as ambassador. By great tact and intelligence Morrow won the confidence of President Calles and ironed out many of the troublesome questions. Calles somewhat eased his restrictions on the Church and agreed not to make Article 27 retroactive. Dwight Morrow, in United States–Mexican relations, paved the way for the "good neighbor" policy.

CUBA, PANAMA, AND THE DOMINICAN REPUBLIC

In order to present a clearer and a somewhat more detailed picture of the Latin-American policy of the United States, it is necessary to trace specific action in the case of Cuba, Panama, and the Dominican Republic. Space does not permit a detailed description of relations with other Latin-American nations, but this can be obtained from the books mentioned in the bibliography at the close of this chapter.

The Teller Amendment, adopted in 1898 at the time that the United States declared war on Spain, pledged the restoration of Cuba to the Cubans. In 1901, however, the Platt Amendment was forced upon Cuba as the price of the evacuation of American troops. The amendment limited the sovereignty of Cuba in a number of ways. The government of Cuba could not conclude with any other power any treaty that would impair Cuban independence. She could not allow any foreign power to establish colonies or have naval bases on the island, nor could she borrow any money which her ordinary revenues could not repay. This really meant that the United States Department of State had the power to regulate Cuban loans. In addition, the United States was granted the right to intervene to protect Cuban independence and to maintain a government adequate for the protection of life, liberty, and property. Finally, in return for United States protection of the island, Cuba had to lease coaling stations and naval bases to the United States.

Trouble brewed in Cuba in 1906 over a fraudulent presidential election when the side that had been dishonestly defeated took up arms. Roosevelt sent W. H. Taft to investigate the situation. Taft reported that no man of conscience could assert that the man in power had been elected. On the other hand, he thought that it was dangerous to allow the insurgents to take command. As a result, Roosevelt appointed Taft as temporary executive, and then sent C. E. Magoon, as provisional governor, who ruled Cuba until 1909. In that year a reasonably fair election was held, and control of the island was turned over to the duly elected president. This government held power until 1917, when a revolt took place. Some charged that this revolt had been engineered by Germany to keep the United States occupied in the Western Hemisphere. Wilson landed troops and suppressed the revolution, and these troops were not withdrawn until after the First World War was over. In 1924 another revolution occurred on the island. Coolidge backed the government in power and prevented aid from reaching the rebels. By 1924 a billion dollars of American money was invested in Cuba. American bankers interested in Cuban affairs selected Gerardo Machado as their candidate for the presidency. A "slush fund" was collected in the United States to aid Machado's campaign, and he was duly elected. The next eight years were an unhappy period for the Cuban people. When the United States government had run the country, at least order was restored, schools were established, and sanitary projects were started. But under Machado, the American bankers' ally, the country suffered from "peculations, extravagances, and cruelties," which, as one historian has observed, places Machado "among the least pleasant of Latin-American dictators." The American bankers kept Machado in power by lending him money. In 1928 he called a constitutional convention and had himself re-elected for eighteen years. It was clear to the bankers and the Department of State that Machado was a dictator, but the Department did not oppose the bankers' loans that kept Machado in office.

In the United States, Machado was represented as a paragon of virtue. Journalists and lecturers in his pay fed American newspapers and the public with statements that made him appear to be a great president. All this time, however, he was securing the assassination of his opponents, suppressing freedom of speech and the press, and aiding in the exploitation of his people. Between 1927 and 1930, Cuban bonds to the value of many millions of dollars were floated on the American market. The bankers, as has been said, knew that Machado was a dictator, that Cuba was virtually bankrupt, and that the loans were unsound, but they sold the bonds to an unsuspecting American public. In none of the advertising of these bonds was there any hint of the true conditions in Cuba. When the New Deal came to power in 1933, the Securities and Exchange Commission was established to prevent such a thing from happening again. Under SEC regulations full information must be presented before any bonds may be sold to the public.

Machado stayed in power as long as American bankers financed him with money to pay the army and police, and as long as the State Department supported him. The depression following the stock-market crash of 1929 stopped further loans. By 1933 Cubans were starving, and a state of guerrilla warfare prevailed throughout the island. The army was more and more infrequently paid and became more and more restless. When Franklin D. Roosevelt became President, the Cuban army was told that the United States would not object to its removing Machado, and the dictator at once fled from the island. Subsequent dealings with Cuba, under the "good neighbor" policy, did much to counteract the earlier mistakes.

United States–Panamanian relations form another interesting and not too pleasant chapter in American diplomacy. A canal across Central America, desired for many decades, appeared vitally necessary after the United States had acquired possessions in the Caribbean and the Pacific. The voyage of the U.S.S. *Oregon* around Cape Horn during the Spanish-American War demonstrated the strategic need of a canal to make it possible to shuttle the fleet between the two oceans. The Clayton-Bulwer Treaty, however, stood in the way. Passed in 1850, this treaty stated that any canal in this region must be international in character and not exclusively either American or English. The treaty had been signed at the height of Anglo-American rivalry in Central

America, but by 1900 the British were willing to concede the United States a free hand in Latin America in return for support in the Far East. The Hay-Pauncefote Treaty of 1901 abrogated the Clayton-Bulwer Treaty and permitted the United States to fortify and otherwise protect a canal.

Congress now became the battleground of those who favored a route across Panama and those who favored one across Nicaragua. In 1876 a French company had purchased, from Colombia, the right to build a canal across Panama. By 1889 the company was bankrupt, after having spent $260,000,000 in a useless effort. A new company—the Panama Canal Company—was formed to sell the questionable assets of the old company to the United States. President McKinley appointed a commission to investigate the two routes, and the commission, finding that the Panama Canal Company wanted $109,000,000 for its assets, advocated the Nicaraguan route. The Panama Canal Company at once reduced its price to $40,000,000 and hired a New York lobbyist to influence Congress in its interest. At this point, nature worked to the advantage of the Panama route. A volcano erupted in Nicaragua, and the Panama lobbyists presented each Senator with a Nicaraguan stamp showing a volcano in eruption. Congress now passed the Spooner Act on June 28, 1902, authorizing the President to acquire the French concession for $40,000,000, provided that Colombia would cede a strip of land across the Isthmus of Panama; if not, the President was to negotiate with Nicaragua. Secretary of State John Hay persuaded the Colombian minister at Washington to sign a treaty on January 22, 1903, granting the United States a hundred-year lease of a ten-mile-wide canal zone for $10,000,000 down and $250,000 yearly rental.

The Colombian government rejected the treaty in August, 1903. Colombia apparently was holding out for more money, since the Panama Canal Company's concession would expire the following year and Colombia would then have the right to sell this concession herself. Theodore Roosevelt was outraged at "those contemptible little creatures in Bogotá," and in his headstrong way told John Hay, "I do not think the Bogotá lot of obstructionists should be allowed permanently to bar one of the future highways of civilization." The same thought was held by the Panama Canal Company and a group of Panamanian citizens led by Dr. Amador Guerrero. Dr. Amador Guerrero came to the United States, seeking support for the secession of Panama from Colombia, and he met with agents of the Company and some United States army officers to plan the next move. Philippe

Bunau-Varilla, agent of the Company, talked with Roosevelt and Hay. Bunau-Varilla said that from Roosevelt's face he could see that the United States would assist a revolt, and Dr. Amador Guerrero was sent back to Panama with plans for the revolt to take place on November 3. Roosevelt suggested his complicity when, sometime later, he wrote:

> I have no idea what Bunau-Varilla advised the revolutionists, or what was said in any telegrams to them as to Hay or myself: but . . . it was his business to find out what he thought our Government would do. I have no doubt that he was able to make a very accurate guess and to advise his people accordingly. In fact he would have been a very dull man had he not been able to make such a guess.

Back in Panama, Dr. Amador Guerrero was worried. He had one hundred thousand dollars to bribe the Colombian garrison, but he was afraid that United States aid would not arrive. Bunau-Varilla wired him that a United States warship would arrive on November 2. It did, and on the following day three more arrived. Their orders were to prevent the landing of any Colombian troops. Since an impassable jungle separated Colombia and Panama, such orders would prevent the suppression of the rebellion. On November 3 the acting Secretary of State cabled the United States consul at Panama: "Uprising on Isthmus reported. Keep Department promptly and fully informed." The consul replied: "No uprising yet. Reported will be in the night." That night he wired: "Uprising occurred tonight 6; no bloodshed. Government will be organized tonight."

Dr. Amador Guerrero, with the one hundred thousand dollars furnished by the Panama Canal Company, bribed the Colombian garrison of five hundred men, led by General Huertas, and these men, aided by the fire brigade of Panama City, constituted the revolutionary hordes! On November 4 General Huertas addressed his victorious soldiers in the following vein: "The world is astounded at our heroism. President Roosevelt has made good." On November 6 the United States recognized the Republic of Panama, and twelve days later signed a treaty obtaining the Canal Zone in perpetuity for ten million dollars and a yearly payment of two hundred and fifty thousand dollars. Roosevelt later boasted, "I took Panama," and the events seemed to bear him out. The basic issue at stake was the money to be paid the Panama Canal Company; and if Roosevelt had waited a few months, he probably could have bought the canal rights directly from Colombia. Instead he used the superior power of the United States, adopting what became known as the "big stick" policy, and made all Latin America tremble. Latin America's hatred of the United States increased by leaps and bounds after this affair. In 1921 the United States paid Colombia twenty-five million dollars, thereby admitting culpability. Roosevelt's unscrupulous and ruthless policy in this case was, in the long run, detrimental to America's best interests in Latin America.

The Panama Canal was opened to commercial traffic in August, 1914. Under the supervision of Colonel Goethals, it was a triumph of American engineering skill. The sanitary work done by Colonel Gorgas cleared up one of the world's greatest pestholes. The treaty that had been signed with Panama made Panama a dependency in that the United States was given the right to intervene to preserve order and to improve sanitation. The United States also had the right to take additional territory that might be thought necessary to the Canal, and had complete sovereignty over the Canal Zone. The treaty was abrogated in 1936. In the thirty-three years from 1903 to 1936 the United States permitted Panama the luxury of only one revolution. Since the opposition could not seize power through revolution, it had to rely on the ballot box. It found, however, that the group in power controlled the election machinery, voted "early and often," and failed to count the opposition's vote.

The third protectorate acquired by Roosevelt was that over the Dominican Republic. The Venezuelan affair of 1902 and 1903 formed an important background for the Dominican Republic situation. Venezuela was ruled by an unscrupulous dictator, Castro, who has been described as a mixture of Boss Tweed, P. T. Barnum, and Nero. Eleven foreign countries had debts against Venezuela, totaling over twelve million dollars. Germany and Great Britain blockaded the country in order to force Castro to come to terms. Gradually the people of the United States became aroused over this blockade. In England too public opinion opposed the government's action and particularly the tie-up with Germany. Under these circumstances, when Venezuela offered to arbitrate, the British government persuaded the Kaiser to accept the offer. England and Germany asked Roosevelt to arbitrate the dispute, but he referred it to the Hague Tribunal, which settled it satisfactorily. When, in 1905, the Dominican Republic fell into desperate financial straits, there was again the danger of European intervention, as there had been in the Venezuelan affair. To prevent intervention, Roosevelt announced his corollary to the Monroe Doctrine (page 584).

In addition to the danger of European intervention, there was that of American intervention, for which American investors clamored in order to protect their interests. Also, the expansionist impulses of army and navy officials were as strong as ever, and this pressure group worked on Roosevelt. The President himself believed in Captain Mahan's thesis that a nation, to be great, needed naval bases and colonies. It is difficult to say which pressure weighed most heavily in the case of the Dominican Republic, but all the above-mentioned pressures were present.

Roosevelt placed an American receiver in charge of the Dominican customs, and 55 per cent of the customs receipts were applied to the debts and 45 per cent to current governmental expenses. Within two years the Dominican Republic was transformed into a prosperous country, with revenues more than sufficient to meet expenses. Under Woodrow Wilson the United States took complete control of the country and from 1916 to 1922 ran it with the aid of marines. In 1922 Sumner Welles, as a special commissioner, established a provisional government, and in 1924 the United States withdrew from control of the Republic. Although American occupation had stabilized the country and its finances, the loss of sovereignty was resented by the Dominicans and by other Latin Americans.

No account of the territory acquired by the United States in the Western Hemisphere would be complete without a mention of the purchase of the Virgin Islands from Denmark. For strategic reasons American possession of the Virgin Islands was held to be indispensable. Denmark had been willing to sell this territory to the United States in 1867, but the United States Senate acted adversely on the proposal, urged by Secretary of State Seward. Again, in 1902, acquisition failed, but this time because the Danish senate refused to ratify the treaty. Finally, during the First World War, the United States bought the Virgin Islands for twenty-five million dollars. After the construction of the Panama Canal, the Virgin Islands were needed to form part of the defense of the Canal against foreign attack.

YANKEEPHOBIA

South of the Rio Grande, from 1901 to 1928, hatred of the United States was rampant. Latin America had a different civilization from that of the United States. Its heritage was that of Spain and Portugal, based on the broad foundation furnished by the numerous Indian groups. The cultural center of most of Latin America was in Spain and France, and the Latin American nations feared that the encroachments of the Anglo-Saxon United States were a threat to their civilization. The differences between the two Americas have been well described by Hubert Herring, in *Good Neighbors:*

There have always been two Americas . . . America North . . . the America of the Anglo-Saxon who settled Massachusetts and Virginia, established town meetings, and believed in the Word.

America South . . . from Mexico to Patagonia . . . the America of the Iberians, seekers after gold, builders of cities and cathedrals . . . peoples who lived by the sword and swore by the Cross.

The Americans North and the Americans South have gone their separate ways, four hundred years South, three hundred North . . . killing their Indians, importing their black slaves, breeding and intermingling . . . welcoming boatloads of Poles, Greeks, Italians, Germans, Swedes, Spaniards, Turks, Russians, to tend looms in Massachusetts, to dig tin in Bolivia, to raise wheat in Minnesota, to pick cotton in Alabama, to gather coffee in Brazil, to chop coal in Pennsylvania.

The Americans have found no common tongue, there has been little traffic in ideas between them . . . their peoples have not understood each other or cared whether they understood each other . . . Americans North have viewed Americans South as pleasant but impractical neighbors, always late for dinner, not to be trusted in business deals, knowing nothing of law or government . . . Americans South have viewed Americans North as ill-mannered fellows who do not shake hands, *mal-educados* intent upon closing a deal and without taste for the more leisurely gifts of the spirit.[1]

A leading Mexican lawyer has the following to say about Latin America:

In order to understand Latin America, you have to know not only our needs but also our ideals, because all our life and culture rest on what can be called "values." What we value most is a life which comes up to noble and spiritual levels. We are not pragmatic. We want the thing under certain conditions which satisfy our ideals. If you throw a penny to a beggar in Latin America, he would not take it. He wants not only your penny but your consideration. We have oil, but we want to exploit it according to certain standards. We have agricultural lands, but it is more important to distribute the land among the people and to delay production than to produce under a feudal regime. Our culture rests on the assumption that the most important part of life is the spirit. All our thinkers—José Enrique Rodó in Uruguay, Enrique José Varona in Cuba, Alejandro Korn and José Ingenieros

[1] *Good Neighbors*, p. 1. Yale University Press, New Haven, 1942.

in Argentina, Antonio Caso and José Vasconcelos in Mexico, and many others—have the same point of view: first, life, and, second, worthy, pure, noble life. In order to understand us, it is not enough to know about natural resources and our commerce and our finances. You have to know our thoughts, our ideals, our soul. This sounds romantic, but it is true.[1]

Every step taken to extend the control of the United States over Latin America increased Yankeephobia, and the United States came to be looked upon as the "Colossus of the North." Isaac Goldberg, in *Studies in Spanish-American Literature* (1920), in summing up the attitude of the writers of Spanish America, declared:

At best (always speaking generally) we are in their eyes as yet too engrossed in material ambitions to give attention to spiritual considerations; at worst we are the intriguing nation that despoiled Mexico of Texas and California, and who now, under the shield of the Monroe Doctrine and an alleged Pan-Americanism, cherish imperialistic designs upon the entire southern continent.

Roosevelt's activities in Panama, Cuba, and the Dominican Republic, Taft's "dollar diplomacy," and Woodrow Wilson's extension of the American sphere of interest stirred up an epidemic of Yankeephobia. Furthermore, the American attitude toward Mexico (1921–1927) and our intervention in Nicaragua (1926–1928) called forth great condemnation in Latin America. By the time of the administrations of Herbert Hoover and Franklin D. Roosevelt the United States had real need for a new diplomatic policy for the Western Hemisphere.

SELECTED BIBLIOGRAPHY

HENRY PRINGLE, *Theodore Roosevelt; A Biography*, and *Life and Times of William Howard Taft; A Biography*, valuable; S. F. BEMIS, *Diplomatic History of the United States*, Chaps. 28, 29, 30, 39, and T. A. BAILEY, *Diplomatic History of the American People*, Chaps. 32, 33, 35, 36, 42, surveys of the general field; J. F. RIPPY, *Historical Evolution of Hispanic America*, Chap. 15, a concise account of relations between the United States and Latin America.

HARLEY NOTTER, *Origins of the Foreign Policy of Woodrow Wilson*, the best study of Wilson's motives; J. F. RIPPY, *The United States and Mexico*, a thorough treatment; C. L. JONES, *Caribbean Interests of the United States* and *The Caribbean since 1900*, good surveys; MAX WINKLER, *Investments of United States Capital in Latin America*, an excellent, detailed account.

H. S. COMMAGER (Ed.), *Documents of American History*, pp. 200, 203–206, 209–214, 255–256, 265, 267–274, 292–293, 388–390, contains source material.

[1] "The Challenge of the Good Neighbor Policy," The University of Chicago Round Table, December 29, 1946.

XXVIII

The First World War

PRESIDENT WILSON, speaking from a deep knowledge of the American heritage, declared, on July 14, 1914:

My dream is that as the years go on and the world knows more and more of America it . . . will turn to America for those moral inspirations which lie at the basis of all freedom; that the world will never fear America unless it feels that it is engaged in some enterprise which is inconsistent with the rights of humanity; and that America will come into the full light of the day when all shall know that she puts human rights above all other rights and that her flag is the flag not only of America but of humanity.

Wilson's belief in America as the hope of the world required a peaceful world, but the assassination of the Austrian Archduke Ferdinand at Sarajevo on June 28, 1914, brought that peaceful world to an end.

In May, 1914, Colonel E. M. House had traveled to Europe as Wilson's representative to talk to the heads of the European governments. In England he had interviewed the leaders and had been told that he could count on England for peace. When he reached Berlin, the shock of reality appalled him. He wrote Wilson: "The situation is extraordinary. It is militarism run stark mad. Unless someone acting for you can bring about a different understanding, there is some day to be an awful cataclysm." The awful cataclysm broke in the week from July 28 to August 4. The First World War came as a complete surprise to America, since few Americans had any inkling that a great war was ready to break out. In this, of course, it was in marked contrast with the Second World War, which came only after a long series of incidents dating back as far as Japan's aggressions in Manchuria in 1931.

WHY AMERICA ENTERED THE WAR

When the war broke in 1914, the majority of the American people were at once sympathetic to the Allies. The United States eventually entered the war primarily because, from the outset, American sympathies were with the Allies. This fact is of basic importance, since Allied propaganda would have failed to have much influence without

American predisposition to it. Ties of language, literature, law, and custom bound the United States to England. London was the social, intellectual, and cultural capital of many American citizens, and it was the center from which most American newspapers received their European news. Few American newspapers maintained European staffs, and London bureaus supplied the European news printed in United States papers. The majority of American newspapers were pro-Ally from the start of the war. As early as August 2, 1914, the *New York Times* saw the war as a crusade for "the crushing out of the imperial idea, the end, once for all time, in those three empires [the Central Powers] of absolute rule and the substitution for all-powerful sovereigns and their titled advisors of an executive with power to carry out only the will of the people." In spite of Czarist Russia's participation on the Allied side, the issue was early seen, by the editors of the *Times* and many other editors, as democracy versus autocracy.

The political leaders of the nation—Woodrow Wilson, Theodore Roosevelt, William H. Taft, and others—were much closer to English traditions and ideas than to German. Furthermore, with France, American relations were, of course, sentimentally cordial. The work of Lafayette and other French aid to American independence were read about in every school textbook. Also, of course, the functioning French democracy was closer to our ideals than German and Austro-Hungarian autocracy and despotism.

In addition to all these ties, England and the United States had been growing closer and closer in world diplomacy. Ever since 1896 England had encouraged the expansion of American influence and empire, as can be seen, for example, in her friendliness toward American acquisition of the Philippines and in her encouragement of the doctrine of the "open door" in China. While this cordiality was increasing, the rising empire of Germany appeared to be more and more of a menace to the United States. As stated earlier, Germany was looked upon as having had covetous desires toward the Philippines, as having been largely responsible for the Venezuelan affair of 1902, and as seeking strategic posts in the Caribbean area.

The suspicion, held by Americans, that Germany was a militaristic nation made our entrance into the war on her side impossible. At the same time, it was felt to be inconceivable, in 1914, that the United States would join the Allies, although there can be little doubt of the American desire for an Allied victory. Such a leading Middle Western editor as William Allen White, of the *Emporia* (Kansas) *Gazette*, paid little attention to the war in his editorial columns until the sinking of the *Lusitania*, in May, 1915. Even after that event he probably expressed the temper of American opinion when he wrote: "Americans—South Americans and North Americans—hold the Ark of the Covenant of civilization. In a world war-mad, we have the peace that passeth understanding. By God's grace we should keep it."

On August 19, 1914, President Wilson issued a proclamation calling upon the people of the United States to be neutral in action, as well as in thought. Wilson personally was sympathetic to the Allies, but as President he seems to have worked to prevent this feeling from affecting national policy. In the eyes of one competent historian, Charles Seymour, Wilson was so successful in this "that he was attacked in turn by each belligerent group as being favorable to the other." President Wilson felt that his first duty was to maintain peace, and his second duty to preserve the neutral rights of the United States. If, however, one of the belligerents should attack the neutral rights of America, these two concepts would be contradictory. In a speech made at Milwaukee on January 31, 1916, he demonstrated his awareness of this dilemma:

> I know that you are depending upon me to keep this Nation out of war. So far I have done so and I pledge you my word that, God helping me, I will—if it is possible. But you have laid another duty upon me. You have bidden me to see to it that nothing stains or impairs the honor of the United States, and that is a matter not within my control; that depends upon what others do, not upon what the Government of the United States does. Therefore there may at any moment come a time when I cannot preserve both the honor and the peace of the United States. Do not exact of me an impossible and contradictory thing.

Wilson might have avoided a rupture with Germany by abandoning the rights of American ships and citizens on the high seas. Such a suggestion was made to him, but he felt that no nation should surrender its rights. If a country began to surrender its rights, there might be no end to the process. He told one Senator:

> If in this instance we allowed expediency to take the place of principle, the door would inevitably be opened to still further concessions. Once accept a single abatement of right, and many other humiliations would certainly follow. . . . What we are contending for in this matter is of the very essence of the things that have made America a sovereign nation. She cannot yield them without conceding her own impotency as a Nation and making virtual surrender of her independent position among the nations of the world.

Soon after Germany resumed her policy of unrestricted submarine warfare in 1917, President Wilson sent his war message to Congress. He was opposed to this type of warfare not merely because American property rights were endangered, but because principles of humanity were involved as well. Wilson viewed submarine warfare as war on humanity. In his note of June 9, 1915, after the sinking of the *Lusitania*, he had written Germany:

> The sinking of passenger ships involves principles of humanity which throw into the background any special circumstances of detail that may be thought to affect the cases. . . . The government of the United States is contending for something much greater than mere rights of property or privileges of commerce. It is contending for nothing less high and sacred than the rights of humanity, which every Government honors itself in respecting and no Government is justified in resigning on behalf of those under its care and authority.

Although President Wilson based American entrance into the war on Germany's resumption of unrestricted submarine warfare, there were others who saw the whole question in a larger perspective. They saw that the rising power of Germany threatened the European balance of power, and that a German victory would be a threat to the security of the United States. In 1913, for instance, Lewis Einstein, a minor American diplomat, wrote a remarkable article contending that the United States could no longer be indifferent to political events in Europe. He pointed out that Great Britain had contributed, for more than a century, to the security of the United States through her maintenance of the European balance of power; that the balance was now threatened by the rise of Germany; and that if Germany were able to defeat England and achieve dominance upon both land and sea, she would become a menace to the United States and to all other nations. He wrote:

> The European balance of power has been such a permanent factor since the birth of the Republic that Americans have never realized how its absence would have affected their political status. . . . At no time since the foundation of the Republic could a change materially altering the ancient European balance have been brought about without perceptibly affecting American interests and the position of the United States.[1]

This balance of power, which had worked so well for America's national interest, was now in danger because of the possibility of war

[1]"The United States and Anglo-German Rivalry," *Living Age*, Vol. 276 (1913), pp. 323–332.

between Germany and Britain. Einstein asserted that it would be a calamity to the United States if Germany subdued England and seized the British navy, because then Germany would be the supreme power on land and sea. His conclusion was:

Great Britain, by upholding the European balance of power, has contributed toward American development. If misfortune in arms awaits her it would be as politically unwise as it would be ungenerous to allow her to suffer unduly. A disastrous defeat inflicted by an opponent unwilling to use moderation should invite on the part of America a friendly mediation which in the last extremity might have to be converted into more effective measures.[1]

Colonel E. M. House, confidential adviser to Woodrow Wilson, and Secretary of State Lansing, who took office after Bryan's resignation in 1915, also realized that the United States should play a larger role in European politics. Lansing particularly believed that the future welfare of the United States depended upon an Allied victory. In his *Memoirs* he wrote that he had advocated American intervention in case such intervention became necessary to prevent a German victory. Lansing disliked Allied infringements on neutral rights, but nevertheless he was firmly convinced "that the German Government, cherishing the . . . ambition of world power which now possesses it . . . must not be permitted to win this war or to break even, though to prevent it this country is forced to take an active part." Although such was Lansing's attitude, he seems to have had little influence on Wilson. When Lansing argued that America had a stake in an Allied victory, the President was unmoved. When disputes between the United States and England over neutral rights were acute in the fall of 1916, Lansing observed:

On no account must we range ourselves even indirectly on the side of Germany, no matter how great the provocation may be. The amazing thing to me is that the President does not seem to grasp the full significance of this war or the principles at issue. . . . That German imperialistic ambitions threaten free institutions everywhere apparently has not sunk very deeply into his mind. For six months I have talked about the struggle between Autocracy and Democracy, and do not see that I have made any great impression.[2]

It was argued by some writers, during the 1930's, that Allied propaganda played an important role in bringing the United States into the

[1]Ibid.

[2]*War Memoirs of Robert Lansing*, p. 21. Used by special permission of The Bobbs-Merrill Company, Indianapolis, 1935.

war. American public opinion, however, was favorable to the Allied cause *before* Allied propaganda began to operate. Whatever success Allied propaganda had seems to have depended not so much on the skill and activity of the propaganda offices as on the fact that the climate of opinion in America was favorable to it. German propaganda had little success because, as the German ambassador, Von Bernstorff, said:

If in our propaganda in the United States, we had unqualifiedly found ourselves in agreement with the ideas which governed the American people, then of course we would have been much more successful with our propaganda. But since this was not the case . . . the natural result was that the propaganda fell to the ground.

Whenever German propaganda seemed to be progressing well, something like the sinking of the *Lusitania* or the deportation of Belgian citizens to Germany in 1916 would ruin it. Von Bernstorff, after the sinking of the *Lusitania*, frankly admitted, "Our propaganda in this country . . . has completely collapsed." In August, 1915, the New York *World* published evidence that the Germans were subsidizing writers and lecturers, as well as issuing pamphlet material. This aroused resentment in the public, though Americans knew that the Allies were doing the same thing; but there was little resentment against Allied propaganda. The fact that the Germans resorted to sabotage in munitions plants only served to emphasize that Germany's propaganda was unsuccessful.

During the 1930's, too, some people charged that America went into the war to protect the economic stake that some of its citizens had in the Allied cause. The economic stake of United States citizens in the Allied cause was large. At the beginning of the war the Allied powers applied restrictions on trade with the Central Powers and on any trade with European neutrals in goods that might be trans-shipped to the enemy. Trade with the Germans became negligible, while trade with the Allies mounted impressively. Allied trade, by the summer of 1915, had lifted the United States out of a depression. The English ambassador, Cecil Spring-Rice, wrote in November, 1915:

The brutal facts are that this country [the United States] has been saved by the war and our demands from a great commercial crisis. . . . We have therefore the claims of their best customers and at the present moment our orders here are absolutely essential to their commercial prosperity.

Any rupture with the Allies would have ruined our economic structure. Our trade with the Allies in munitions was particularly important. Allied command of the sea prevented the Central Powers from purchasing American munitions, while the Allies bought all they wanted.

A suggestion that the United States place an embargo on the munitions trade was rejected. In the first place, it was argued, the people wanted the Allies to win. Secondly, such an embargo would ruin American prosperity. "If it came to the last analysis," Colonel House wrote Wilson, "and we placed an embargo upon munitions of war and foodstuffs . . . our whole industrial and agricultural machinery would cry out against it." Furthermore, Wilson, a keen student of history, knew how Jefferson's embargo of 1808 had failed to achieve its objective of persuading the belligerents to respect American rights.

At first, the Allies paid for American goods by selling their American securities. By 1915, however, the Allies found it advisable to finance their purchases through loans floated in Wall Street. As a result of this process, the United States was transformed from a debtor nation to a creditor nation. While Bryan was in the cabinet, the government prevented such loans from being made, but after his resignation both Lansing and Secretary of the Treasury McAdoo persuaded the President to permit the loans. As Lansing wrote: "Popular sympathy has become crystallized in favor of one or another of the belligerents to such an extent that the purchase of bonds would in no way increase the bitterness of partisanship or cause a possibly serious situation." By April, 1917, about one and a half billion dollars had been lent by the public to the Allies and only twenty-seven million dollars to the Central Powers.

In 1934 the United States Senate appointed a committee, with Gerald Nye as its chairman, to investigate the activities of American bankers and munitions-makers. Senator Clark of Missouri, speaking before this committee, said that the American export of munitions to the Allies "ultimately led us into war. . . . There is no evidence whatever to show that we would ever have entered the war or ever fired a gun except for that course of action." The Nye Committee's final report declared that selfish industrial and financial interests had built up such a heavy stake in the Allied cause that "it prevented the maintenance of a truly neutral course." This whole thesis was overdone. Some people, perhaps, may have been influenced by our financial stake in the Allied cause. The financial group in America, however, generally favored neutrality rather than American participation. Neutrality produced adequate profits. War would mean increased taxation and governmental regulation of business. Furthermore, for all the sensationalism of the Nye investigations, no convincing data were revealed to show that the munitions-makers and bankers exercised any influence on the Congressional vote for war or on President Wilson, who asked Congress for war. Wilson himself answered the charge that munitions-makers were behind the American campaign for adequate American defense measures by saying, on February 1, 1916:

I have heard the preposterous statement made that the agitation for preparation for national defense has come chiefly from the men who make armor plate for the ships and munitions for the Army. Why, ladies and gentlemen, do you suppose that all the thoughtful men who are engaged upon this side of this great question are susceptible of being led by influences of that sort? . . . I have not found the impulse for national defense coming from those sources. . . . I found it coming from the men who have nothing to do with the making of profits, but who have everything to do with the making of the daily life of this country. And it is from them that I take my inspiration.

It was not loans or trade that led Woodrow Wilson to ask Congress for a declaration of war; it was rather Germany's unrestricted submarine campaign, which he considered to be an attack on humanity. As Charles Seymour has pointed out, "Whatever the emotional sympathy for the Allied cause in the United States and however close Allied and American commercial interests, the prevailing sentiment of the people was indelibly for peace until the submarine sank American ships."

THE PROBLEM OF NEUTRAL RIGHTS IN TIME OF WAR

Since the submarine precipitated the United States into war, some discussion of the problem of neutral rights in wartime is necessary. This had been a thorny problem for American statesmen during the great war that swept Europe from the French Revolution to the downfall of Napoleon in 1815. It was a grave problem for the United States, too, from 1914 to 1917. At the outbreak of the war England proclaimed a blockade of the Central Powers and drew up a list of trade restrictions. As the war continued, England increased these trade restrictions— cautiously, however, in order not to offend the United States. Sir Edward Grey, the British Foreign Secretary, explained England's problem in this way:

After Paris had been saved by the Battle of the Marne the Allies could no more than hold their own. . . . The Allies soon became dependent for an adequate supply [of their own war needs] on the United States. If we quarreled with the United States we could not get that supply. It was better, therefore, to carry on the war without blockade, if need be, than to incur a break with the United States about contraband. . . . The object of diplomacy, therefore, was to secure the maximum of blockade that could be enforced without a rupture with the United States. . . .

It was evident that the first step was to put on the list of absolute contraband all the articles that were essential for armies under modern conditions; and the second and more important step was to get the United States to accept that list. . . . These were articles that in old days had been of little or no use to armies but were now essential to them. Would the United States dispute our right to put some of these on the list? They might do so on the ground that they were articles of general use for general commercial as well as for military purposes. . . . It would be politic for us not to make the list too large at first.[1]

The United States protested England's restrictions, but to no avail. The basic trouble was, as Lloyd George pointed out, that nations at war cannot "always pause to observe punctilios. Their every action is an act of war, and their attitude to neutrals is governed, not by conventions of peace, but by the exigencies of a deadly strife." The Allies shut off direct trade with the Central Powers, and indirect trade through Holland or the Scandinavian countries was also largely checked. In addition, the Allies black-listed any American firms suspected of trading with their enemy. Wilson chose the policy of protesting these violations of neutral rights. War over them was unthinkable, since the nation wanted an Allied victory and the dispute involved only property rights. Wilson was too wise to permit a quarrel over neutral rights to place us on the side of autocracy and despotism, as in 1812. At times, however, he was furious at British trade restrictions. In the summer of 1916 he wrote Colonel House: "I am, I must admit, about at the end of my patience with Great Britain and the Allies. This blacklist business is the last straw."

The whole question of our economic dispute with the Allies was eliminated when Germany resumed unrestricted submarine warfare in

[1]From *Twenty-five Years, 1892–1916*, pp. 107–109. Frederick A. Stokes Company, New York, 1925. Quoted by permission of the executor of Viscount Grey of Fallodon, and by permission of Hodder & Stoughton, Ltd., London, and J. B. Lippincott Company, Philadelphia.

the beginning of 1917. According to Von Bernstorff, Wilson would not exert pressure on the Allies to remove restrictions as long as the submarine issue remained unsettled. For instance, on June 28, 1915, during the exchange of notes between the United States and Germany over the sinking of the *Lusitania*, Von Bernstorff wired his foreign office:

He [Wilson] wishes to come to some kind of settlement with us by means of this exchange of notes, in order that he may then turn his attention to England. . . . It should be clearly understood that Mr. Wilson does not want war with us, nor does he wish to side with England, despite all statements to the contrary in the Press of the Eastern States.

It is a safe generalization that every time Woodrow Wilson pressed the Allies on trade restrictions, Germany diverted the attention of the United States. For instance, American protest against Allied trade restrictions in December, 1914, was diverted by Germany's launching of unrestricted submarine warfare. Germany declared that the waters around the British Isles were a war zone and that all commerce with the Allies found there would be destroyed. Germany did not deny that the sinking of unarmed neutral ships was a violation of international law, but she justified her policy on the ground that it was necessary to counteract the equally lawless Allied blockade. Most Americans, however, saw a difference between Allied and German violations of neutral rights. Damages for property losses resulting from Allied violations could be collected after the war. German violations, on the other hand, entailed the loss of human lives. The submarine warfare took a toll of about two hundred American lives, twenty-eight of them being lost on American ships. The immediate result of the submarine warfare was what Winston Churchill foresaw:

We were sure that . . . [the submarine war] would offend and perhaps embroil the U. S.; and that in any case our position for enforcing the blockade would be greatly strengthened. We looked forward to a sensible abatement of the pressure which the American Government was putting upon us.

The United States was shocked by the policy of unrestricted U-boat warfare. President Wilson warned Germany, on February 10, 1915, "The United States . . . [will] be constrained to hold the Imperial German Government to a strict accountability for property endangered or lives lost." The American people, with their belief in neutral rights, probably would not have accepted any other stand on the part of the President than that of "strict accountability." A number of newspapers and leaders like Theodore Roosevelt actually criticized Wilson for being too weak in the steps that he took against Germany.

The torpedoing of the British liner *Lusitania*, on May 7, 1915, off the Irish coast, brought to a head the question of holding Germany to a "strict accountability." Over eleven hundred lives were lost, including those of one hundred and twenty-eight American citizens. The *Lusitania* carried munitions for the Allies, and the German embassy had published notices in American newspapers, warning against traveling on the ship; but the sinking was a stupid act. Theodore Roosevelt, the press, and many preachers clamored for war. Henry Watterson of the *Louisville Courier-Journal* editorialized that on "this Holy Sabbath every pulpit in America should send a prayer to God in protest; . . . and more than all—the Christian President of the United States . . . ceasing longer to protest, should act, leaving no doubt . . . that he is . . . a leader of men and nations, and that he holds aloft the Sword of the Lord and Gideon!"

Wilson knew that the country was not ready for war. He at once dispatched a note demanding that Germany disavow the sinking, make reparations, and take steps to prevent a recurrence. When no satisfactory answer was received, he dispatched a second note, on June 9, 1915. In it he stated that the United States was contending for the rights of humanity; that the United States would not admit that American citizens could not travel on merchant ships of belligerent powers; and that the United States would not admit the right of Germany to sink a ship without warning and without taking precautions for the safety of the passengers. Secretary of State Bryan thought that this note meant war with Germany, and he resigned rather than sign it. It was Bryan's feeling that the United States should renounce responsibility for Americans who traveled on belligerent ships. Wilson's position, already quoted, was "Once accept a single abatement of right, and many other humiliations would certainly follow."

In August, 1915, the British liner *Arabic* was torpedoed, with the loss of two American lives. A break with Germany now seemed inescapable. Von Bernstorff, however, explained to his government the dangerous tone of American opinion, and Germany agreed to stop sinking liners "without warning and without taking precautions for the safety of the lives of non-combatants." Then, in February, 1916, Germany once more resorted to unrestricted U-boat warfare. Wilson warned that unless Germany abandoned this warfare, the United States would break off diplomatic relations. Von Bernstorff and the Chancellor of Germany persuaded the Kaiser to accede, and on May 4, 1916, Germany agreed not to sink merchant vessels without warning, provided that the United States would make the Allies obey international law. In other words, if United States overtures to England proved unavailing, then Germany would again resort to unrestricted submarine warfare to counteract Allied trade restrictions. This note of May 4 was a victory for Wilson, but only so long as Germany was content to wait upon American action against the Allies. The moment that Germany decided that the U-boat campaign was worth more than American neutrality, Wilson would have to ask for a declaration of war.

AMERICAN PREPAREDNESS AND THE 1916 ELECTION

After the German note of May, 1916, the only way that Wilson could escape war for the United States was to bring peace to Europe. Throughout 1916 Wilson tried to achieve a peace based on mutual concessions. Colonel House had tried to persuade Germany, in January, 1916, that the time was ripe for a peace conference, but to no avail. In England, in the following month, House had made an agreement with Sir Edward Grey, who reported it as follows:

Colonel House told me that President Wilson was ready, on hearing from France and England that the moment was opportune, to propose that a conference should be summoned to put an end to the war. Should the Allies accept this proposal, and should Germany refuse it, the United States would *probably* enter the war against Germany. Colonel House expressed the opinion that, if such a conference met, it would secure peace on terms not unfavorable to the Allies; and, if it failed to secure peace, the United States would leave the conference as a belligerent on the side of the Allies, if Germany was unreasonable.[1]

When Wilson saw the agreement reached with Grey, he inserted the word *probably* before the words "the United States would leave the conference as a belligerent on the side of the Allies, if Germany was unreasonable." Wilson waited for Grey to say that the time was ripe for a peace bid on Wilson's part, but the British government did not act. The Allies were not victorious in 1916, and they were afraid that a peace treaty might leave their war aims unobtained. With no word from the Allies, Wilson's interest in the spring of 1916 centered in a campaign for American preparedness and in his own re-election. Ever

[1] Ibid. p. 27.

since the outbreak of war more belligerent individuals, like Theodore Roosevelt, had been trying to make political capital out of Wilson's desire for peace and neutrality. In order to check the Republicans and also to have an adequate force to protect the United States in case of war, Wilson pushed through Congress a series of acts to strengthen the defense of the country. The National Defense Act of June, 1916, enlarged the regular army to one hundred and seventy-five thousand, strengthened the National Guard, and provided for an officers' reserve corps. The Naval Appropriation Bill of August authorized the construction of a number of warships. The United States Shipping Board Act of September appropriated fifty million dollars to purchase or construct merchant ships. A Council of National Defense—consisting of six cabinet members and advisers drawn from industry and labor— was created to co-ordinate industry and other resources for defense.

It was during the preparedness campaign of 1916 that the relations between Mexico and the United States became extremely turbulent. In 1911 the Mexican people, led by Francisco Madero, ended the long dictatorship of Porfirio Díaz. Díaz, as dictator, had favored and helped foreign investors to exploit and to secure control of the resources of Mexico. The lands of the peons had been ruthlessly seized, and Díaz had modified historic Mexican law to permit foreign interests to secure control of subsoil resources. Madero, promising land to the people and the reclaiming of grants to foreigners, led a brief and unhappy existence. A group of army officers, led by Victoriano Huerta and backed by foreign interests, seized the government in February, 1913, and shot Madero. Wilson, although certain American interests clamored, refused to recognize Huerta as the ruler of Mexico. Wilson refused also to allow foreign nations to aid Huerta, and made sure that Huerta's opponents received arms. Veracruz was blockaded by United States ships to make sure that Huerta received no equipment. Then a boat crew of United States marines was arrested in Tampico. An apology was made by the Huerta government, but the American admiral in charge demanded also a salute to the American flag. When Huerta refused, United States troops were landed at Veracruz. At this point Wilson agreed to accept mediation by Argentina, Brazil, and Chile, and the result of the mediation was that Huerta resigned and left Mexico.

One of Huerta's opponents, General Carranza, was elected president and was officially recognized as such by Wilson. Carranza's government, however, was unable to maintain order. Pancho Villa, desiring to become president, decided that the best way to achieve this was to provoke the United States into sending troops into Mexico; then he could become the Mexican national hero by defeating the American army. On March 9, 1916, Villa attacked Columbus, New Mexico, and killed seventeen American citizens. After this raid Wilson ordered General John J. Pershing to invade Mexico and capture Villa. President Carranza protested against this invasion of Mexico, and relations reached a point of almost general hostilities between the two countries. Pershing did not capture Villa, and the American troops were withdrawn in January, 1917. The incident was important, however, since it stimulated enthusiasm in the United States for a real war, and it demonstrated how poorly prepared the United States was for a war. At the same time, it showed that Pershing was a capable general who could

C. K. Berryman in the *Washington Star*

Wilson as Preparedness Doctor

President Wilson instructs Secretary of War Garrison and Secretary of the Navy Daniels to improve the national defenses

carry out Presidential orders. When Wilson looked for a general to head the American Expeditionary Force to Europe, he chose Pershing rather than his superior, General Leonard Wood, who had been indulging in politics to aid the Republicans to defeat Wilson for re-election.

It was in this atmosphere of his attempts to bring peace in Europe, the Mexican affair, and the preparedness campaign that Wilson launched his 1916 campaign. The Democratic platform praised the progressive achievements of the New Freedom, and with reference to the European struggle the Democrats adopted the slogan "He kept us out of war." This, of course, was not a promise of future policy, and Wilson himself was aware of how close the United States had been to war and on what a slim basis peace was being maintained. The Progressive party, at its convention, nominated Theodore Roosevelt, but Roosevelt refused to run. He knew that a third-party campaign would ensure Wilson's re-election, and he persuaded most of his followers to return to the Republican fold. The Republicans refused to nominate Roosevelt partly because of his insurgency in 1912 and partly because his stand for war would have alienated votes. Instead they nominated Charles Evans Hughes, an associate justice of the Supreme Court.

During the campaign, since Wilson's defense steps had spiked the Republican desire to use preparedness as a campaign issue, Hughes talked vaguely of standing for "the firm and unflinching maintenance of all the rights of American citizens on land and sea." Hughes conducted a drab campaign—but not Theodore Roosevelt. Roosevelt stormed the country for Hughes because, as he wrote, "I felt that Wilson's re-election would be a damage to the moral fibre of the American people." Trembling with emotion, Roosevelt, in his last speech of the campaign, commenting on the fact that Wilson's summer White House was called Shadow Lawn, said:

> There should be shadows now at Shadow Lawn; the shadows of the men, women and children who have risen from the ooze of the ocean bottom and from graves in foreign lands; the shadows of the helpless whom Mr. Wilson did not dare protect lest he might have to face danger; the shadows of babies gasping pitifully as they sank under the waves; the shadows of women outraged and slain by bandits. . . . Those are the shadows proper for Shadow Lawn; the shadows of deeds that were never done; the shadows of lofty words that were followed by no action; the shadows of the tortured dead.

Roosevelt's bellicose utterances probably hurt Hughes more than they helped. The Republicans, however, were confident of victory. The Republican vote and the Bull Moose vote combined should have meant a comfortable margin of victory. Hughes, however, had revealed, during his campaign, that he was no Progressive, and many former supporters of the Bull Moose party cast their vote for Wilson, whose first term had been remarkably Progressive in spirit. The early returns pointed toward a Hughes victory, and Wilson went to bed on election night sure that he had been defeated. But as the returns from the Far West came in, it was seen that victory depended on California. Hughes, while campaigning in California, had snubbed Progressive Governor Hiram Johnson, and as a result lost the state by fewer than four thousand votes. California's electoral vote was just enough to give Wilson a majority in the Electoral College.

THE UNITED STATES ENTERS THE WAR

With the election over, Wilson turned once more to the problem of securing peace in Europe. On December 12, 1916, Germany issued an invitation to the Allies to open peace negotiations. This actually meant the end of all peace hopes, since the Allies interpreted it to signify that Germany was approaching exhaustion. Six days later Wilson called on the belligerents to state their war aims. To the Allies this move on Wilson's part seemed only an echo of the German invitation. The Allied terms, as expressed to Wilson, were "complete restitution, full reparation, and effectual guarantees" for the future. The German terms demanded part of France, economic control of Belgium, and a large amount of indemnities. It was obvious to Wilson that the belligerents would not be able to get together. On January 22, 1917, convinced that the United States must aid in securing and maintaining world peace, he formulated the conditions of such a peace. The terms were a forerunner of the Fourteen Points, containing such demands as government by the consent of the governed; freedom of the seas; limitation of armaments; and a league to enforce peace. The most important requirement, Wilson contended, was a "peace without victory" because a peace with victory "would mean peace forced upon the loser, a victor's terms imposed upon the vanquished. It would be accepted in humiliation, under duress, at an intolerable sacrifice, and would leave a sting, a resentment, a bitter memory upon which terms of peace would rest, not permanently, but only as upon quicksand. Only a peace between equals can last."

This speech was characterized by some in the United States as cowardly. Walter Hines Page, our ambassador to England, said that it gave "great offense in England, since it puts each side in the war on the same moral level." Page, for some time, had been attempting to arouse Wilson to the need of American aid to defeat Germany, but this only irritated Wilson. "It was not his [Page's] insistent demands in favor of the British," wrote Lansing, "but the gross misconduct of the Germans, which at last forced the President to break relations with the Imperial government." The Allies could not accept Wilson's proposal of a peace without victory, because they were bound by secret treaties which could be carried out only by a peace with victory. The real answer, however, to Wilson's speech had already been drafted by Germany. The war lords of Germany had decided to resume unrestricted submarine warfare on February 1, 1917. This resumption precipitated the United States into war in much the same manner as the Japanese attack on Pearl Harbor precipitated the United States into the Second World War.

Lord Grey, writing after the war, observed:

> It is clear that Germany missed a great opportunity of peace. If she had accepted the Wilson policy, and was ready to agree to a Conference, the Allies could not have refused. They were dependent on American supplies; they could not have risked the ill-will of the government of the United States, still less a *rapprochement* between the United States and Germany. Germans have only to reflect upon the peace that they might have had in 1916 compared with the peace of 1919.[1]

The German government was well aware that a resumption of unrestricted U-boat warfare would probably bring the United States into the war. Some writers, therefore, have looked upon Germany's decision as an act of great folly. Perhaps it was, but by no means as monumental as some have thought. The German navy carefully calculated how many ships it could sink, and it did not overestimate. In analyzing the military strength which the United States could give the Allies, the Germans did not underestimate, but they knew that it would take the relatively unprepared United States a long time to become effective. Actually, it was not until the summer of 1918 that United States troops entered the battle line in significant strength. The Germans expected that the U-boat would end the war before this occurred. The real mistake of the Germans possibly was not in overestimating the power of the submarine, but in underestimating their chances of victory without it. Germany did not foresee that Russia was about to collapse; nor did she appreciate the desperate financial straits of the Allies; nor did she foresee the mutinies in the French army during the winter of 1916–1917. When America entered the war, Allied finances were repaired, and French morale was revived.

On January 31, 1917, Ambassador von Bernstorff notified the American government that on the following day unrestricted submarine warfare would be resumed. Neutral and belligerent merchantmen alike would be sunk in a zone around the British Isles and in the Mediterranean. The United States would be permitted the privilege of sending one merchant ship a week to England. At once diplomatic relations with Germany were severed. On February 24 the English secret service handed the American State Department a copy of the famed "Zimmer-

[1] Ibid., p. 135.

The German Submarine Zone of January 31, 1917

mann note," in which Germany urged its ambassador in Mexico to try to interest Mexico in an offensive alliance with Germany and Japan if the United States entered the war. Mexico, as a reward, was to receive Texas and the Southwest. When the note was released to the press on March 1, the public's clamor for war increased. Several weeks later the news of the Russian Revolution and the destruction of the Czarist government reached the United States. Now the war could clearly be fought on the basis of democracy against autocracy. The sinking of five American merchant ships in March finally led Wilson to decide for war.

Wilson drafted his war message and the United States entered the war not to protect American investments in Allied securities, nor to enhance the profits of munitions-makers, but, as Wilson phrased it, "because we saw the supremacy and even the validity, of right everywhere put in jeopardy and free government likely to be everywhere imperilled by the intolerable aggression of a power which respected neither right nor obligation.... We entered the war as the disinterested champions of right." Wilson's desire for a peace without victory and his desire for a better world after the war were not achieved, but it was less his fault and more the fault of the European and American peoples, who could not reach his idealistic heights. On April 2, 1917, Wilson, in reading his war message to Congress, observed:

It is a fearful thing to lead this great peaceful people into war, into the most terrible and disastrous of all wars, civilization itself seeming to be in the balance. But the right is more precious than peace, and we shall fight for the things which we have always carried nearest our hearts,—for democracy, for the right of those who submit to authority to have a voice in their own Government, for the rights and liberties of small nations, for a universal dominion of right by such a concert of free peoples as shall bring peace and safety to all nations and make the world itself at last free. To such a task we can dedicate our lives and our fortunes, everything that we are and everything that we have, with the pride of those who know that the day has come when America is privileged to spend her blood and her might for the principles that gave her birth and happiness and the peace which she has treasured. God helping her, she can do no other.

Congress passed the war resolution on April 6. Six Senators and fifty Representatives opposed the war. President Wilson could have kept the United States out of war had he and the American public been willing to pay the price. The price involved a submission to German demands and a consequent surrender of national honor. And such submission probably would have meant that Germany would have won the war. England would shortly have been starved out by the U-boat; France was worn out; and the Russian Revolution soon took Russia out of the war. A triumphant Imperial Germany—not too dissimilar from Hitler's Germany—would have dictated the peace. The terms of the Treaty of Brest Litovsk, which Germany forced on Russia early in 1918, furnish evidence that a German peace would have been far more punitive than the peace that the Allies worked out at Versailles. With a German victory, the United States would have had to face alone the German military colossus. This was the price of peace in 1917. The alternative was to join in the war, defeat the German menace, and try to guide the peace into channels that would justify the sacrifice of human lives. The tragedy for the world was not that the United States entered the war and helped to defeat Germany, but that the United States failed to win a just and lasting peace. Wilson returned from Versailles in 1919 with a compromise peace, which might have worked, but the United States refused to join with its Allies in maintaining world peace through the League of Nations.

SELECTED BIBLIOGRAPHY

Charles Seymour, *American Neutrality*, and Charles C. Tansill, *America Goes to War*, the two best volumes; Bernadotte E. Schmitt, *The Coming of the War*, and S. B. Fay, *Origins of the World War*, excellent material on the European background of the war.

Robert Lansing, *War Memoirs*; Charles Seymour (Ed.), *The Intimate Papers of Colonel House*; Count von Bernstorff, *My Three Years in America*, afford a glimpse of the inside story of American entrance; Harold D. Lasswell, *Propaganda Technique in the World War*, adequately studies this phase; Harley Notter, *Origins of the Foreign Policy of Woodrow Wilson*, the best study of this subject; Sir Edward Grey, *Twenty-five Years, 1892–1916*; *War Memoirs of David Lloyd George*, valuable on the British attitude; A. M. Arnett, *Claude Kitchin and the Wilson War Policies*, critical of Wilson.

H. S. Commager (Ed.), *Documents of American History*, pp. 267–273, 276–277, 282–285, 290–292, 305–312, contains source material.

XXIX

The United States at War

THE ENTRY of the United States into the war touched off a gigantic contest: a race between American reinforcements to the Allies, and the U-boats, which were trying to bring the Allies to their knees before American aid became effective. The Allies were in a desperate condition in the months following April 6, 1917. During the first five months of unrestricted submarine warfare in 1917, Germany had sunk three and a quarter million tons of Allied shipping, and British Admiral Jellicoe warned American Admiral Sims that England could not remain in the war if such losses continued. By April England had only enough grain to last for six more weeks, and the government set November 1 as the limit of its endurance. Furthermore, the morale of the French army was low, and the Italians were in retreat before the Austrians. By this time, too, effective Russian resistance had collapsed.

THE HOME FRONT

America was inexperienced in the requirements of twentieth-century war. This was not a war in which the civilian could sit on the side lines and cheer a professional army. Factory and mine, farm and home, had to become parts of a complicated war machine. To produce war materials, thousands of workers had to be taken from peacetime tasks and transferred to war factories, and farmers had to alter their crops to fit the war needs. School children, housewives, and the men who remained as civilians had to change many of their accustomed habits of consumption and purchase. The United States, therefore, had to mobilize not just an army, but a nation. The Congress that voted the war by no means understood the demands of twentieth-century warfare. The Allies, however, knew what these demands were, and they sent missions to Washington to advise in the mobilization of total resources. These Allied missions revealed the desperate straits of the Allied nations, and urged that America immediately send money, ships, supplies, and men. The Allied needs made the American war effort doubly difficult. The United States not only had to equip its own army, but had to maintain supplies to the Allies. If it equipped only its own army and neglected supplies to the Allies, then victory would be in the grasp of Germany.

In spite of the individualistic tradition of America and the American's dislike of regulation, it was decided at the very beginning of the war to raise an army by the draft. The experience of England with the volunteer system was enough to convince American leaders of the unwisdom of that system in modern war. England had discovered that men vital to production had volunteered and left industry disorganized, and soon realized that it would have been better for the war effort to have left these men in the war plants. The real advantage of a conscription law was that an army could be raised in an orderly fashion, with relatively little shock to war production. On May 18, 1917, President Wilson signed the Selective Service Act. Men between the ages of twenty-one and thirty-one were subject to call for service. Exemptions were permitted for the physically unfit, the conscientious objectors, those with dependent families, and those necessary to war industries. The purchasing of exemption or the hiring of a substitute was not permitted, as it had been in Civil War days. An elaborate lottery system was devised to determine when each individual would be called to service.

The problem of volunteering was a difficult one to solve. It involved sentimental attachment to the older method of raising an army, even though this might not be efficient. The question was precipitated by the action of Theodore Roosevelt, who asked permission to enroll a volunteer force for service in France. Wilson rejected the offer on the advice of professional soldiers. The Civil War and the Spanish-American War had revealed the evil resulting from political commanders, and furthermore it was feared that Roosevelt's expedition would attract thousands of able, experienced men who were more needed in the training camps to make soldiers out of civilians. Although Roosevelt's offer was rejected, individual volunteering for service was still permitted. But by December, 1917, the army had shut most of its doors to volunteers. The navy and the Marine Corps did the same in August, 1918. By this time about 1,360,000 had volunteered, whereas 2,288,000 had been inducted under the Selective Service Act. A new man-power act was passed on August 31, 1918, changing the age limits of prospective draftees to eighteen and forty-five. Over thirteen million men registered under this new bill, bringing the total registered to 24,234,021. On November 11, 1918, there were 4,791,172 in the various military branches, whereas in April, 1917, there had been only 378,619 in all the branches of the service.

The training camps experienced a mushroom growth. Sixteen were constructed for the draft army and sixteen for the National Guard, which had been called into national service in May, 1917. The camps were constructed with great speed, although in many cases the soldiers arrived at still unfinished camps. The change from civilian to soldier was revolutionary to most of the men who entered the service. In the camps city men of recent immigrant extraction rubbed shoulders with the "native" American boys from the farms of Kansas and Iowa. Western ranch boys mingled with Southern mountain boys, and boys from the bayous of Louisiana came into contact with the Yankees from New England. Military life tended to bring standardization and conformity in thought and action, and provincial and sectional differences were modified. When the soldiers returned to civilian life after the war, they were much more like-minded than before their war experience. The army physical and mental examinations unearthed a vast amount of information about American life. One out of every four men was found to be illiterate and about one in every three physically unfit, and boys from the city were discovered to be not as fit as those from the prairies and Great Plains region.

Training in the camps generally lasted about six months. During this period the soldier learned obedience, drill, and care of equipment, and received physical training to enable him to withstand the rigors of active fighting. The Allies lent some eight hundred experienced officers, who aided in the basic training of the American army. Then the soldier went overseas for two months of specialized instruction, followed by a month in a quiet sector before actual fighting was allowed. This program was not always followed. The need of replacements sometimes resulted in the sending of inexperienced "rookies" to the battle zone a few weeks after they had been drafted. Trained officers for the growing army became an acute problem. Capable noncommissioned officers were raised in rank; civilians who had taken military drill in school or college were used; and the more able training-camp graduates were given officer training. By the end of the war approximately two thirds of the commissioned officers were graduates of the training camps.

To help to finance the war, Congress passed a loan act in April, 1917. Five great loans in all were floated, and a total of twenty-one billion dollars was raised from sixty-five million subscriptions. The first four loans were known as "Liberty Loans" and the fifth as a "Victory Loan," since it came after November 11, 1918. The Treasury Department launched a publicity campaign to sell Liberty and Victory Bonds to the people. Bonds were sold in low denominations, and war stamps could be purchased and accumulated until the price of a bond had been obtained. "Four-Minute Men" made speeches in theaters to spur the purchase of bonds, posters were designed to publicize the loans, and citizens' committees were organized to push sales. These committees sometimes treated anyone who did not buy bonds as unpatriotic, and occasionally yellow paint was applied to the door of the noninvestor's home. The money obtained from the loans was used to meet the costs of America's part in the war, as well as to make loans to our Allies. In addition to loans, taxation was used to help to pay the costs of the conflict. Income taxes and taxes on corporation profits were increased, although by no means as much as during the Second World War. Taxes on tobacco, liquor, amusement tickets, and other luxuries brought in some revenue. The money from taxes amounted to $11,280,000,000, just about one third of the cost of the war from April, 1917, to October, 1919. Of the roughly thirty-five-billion-dollar cost of the war, nine and a half billions consisted of the loan to the Allied governments.

Although the spectacular story of America's participation in the war can be told in terms of the exploits of the American army and navy, the more significant story is contained in the industrial mobilization at home. Without American food, munitions, and credit the Allies would have collapsed before American military aid was ready. The individualistic American economic system had to go through considerable change to reach a war footing. Government regulation of industry went far beyond the hopes of the most ardent Progressives. At a tremendous cost the American economic machine was geared to the task of winning the war. Congress conferred extraordinary powers on the President, allowing him to commandeer essential industries and mines, requisition supplies, control the distribution of goods, fix prices, and take over and operate the entire system of transportation and communication. These powers were delegated to boards organized under the guidance of the Council of National Defense, created in 1916. The Council became a civilian general staff, launching new boards to perform useful services and then tackling the next job to be done. All this work had to be done quickly and in an overcrowded capital city. As one writer has described the situation:

While Congress authorized loans and enacted the draft, and its committees deliberated upon next steps in war policy, the Council of National Defense presided as best it could over a patriotic madhouse. Honest devotion and hard work were the redeeming features in a job that had no precedents. . . . Every day brought the announcement of new war organizations and more committees. . . . When the new enthusiasts failed, no one had time to eliminate the wreckage. When they succeeded, batteries of desks crowded their gorged offices, overflowed into the corridors, shifted into apartment houses whose occupants were turned into the streets between dawn and bedtime, and migrated soon to mushroom buildings on vacant lots.[1]

One of the most important subordinate agencies of the Council was the War Industries Board, headed by Bernard Baruch. The War Industries Board, created on March 4, 1918, absorbed the work that had previously been done by a number of separate agencies. Baruch described the objectives of his Board in the following manner: "The Board set out to prevent competition among those buying for the war, and to regulate the use by the civil population of men, money, and materials in such a way that civilian *needs*, not merely *wants*, should be satisfied." Existing industries were co-ordinated to produce more efficiently, new industries were developed, waste was eliminated, and, with the President's permission, certain prices were fixed. The Board guided owners of nonessential plants into conversion for war production and helped war industries to secure capital for the construction of new plants. The Board discouraged unnecessary construction. Requests for permits for the building of churches and schools were rejected, and to save coal the number of stops that elevators could make, for example, was strictly regulated. Standardization in production was achieved by limiting the number of styles that could be manufactured. For instance, shoe-manufacturers were restricted to three colors in leather; the number of colors in typewriter ribbons was reduced from one hundred and fifty to five; automobile tires were reduced from two hundred and eighty-seven types to nine; buggy wheels, from two hundred and thirty-two to four. The value of this standardization was clearly seen, and after the war manufacturers continued the practice to some extent.

Many factories were turned from their normal peacetime production to war work. Women's-blouse factories made signal flags; radiator-manufacturers made big guns; automobile-builders made airplane parts;

[1]Frederic L. Paxson, *America at War: 1917–1918*, pp. 40–41. Houghton Mifflin Company, Boston, 1939.

and piano factories made airplane wings. This organization of a planned economy trained people and established precedents that were of great value when the United States had to meet the severe depression of the 1930's and the situation created by the Second World War. Among the men trained under the War Industries Board, who later were of significance in the New Deal, were Hugh S. Johnson, National Recovery Administration administrator, and George Peck of the Agricultural Adjustment Administration. Bernard Baruch himself was of inestimable help in an advisory capacity to President Franklin D. Roosevelt in converting America to wartime production, beginning in the summer of 1940. The conversion of industry to wartime production in the Second World War was, of course, a much bigger job than it was in the First.

David Lloyd George, English prime minister, said, shortly after American entrance into the war: "The road to victory, the guaranty of victory, the absolute assurance of victory, has to be found in one word, ships, in a second word, ships, and a third word, ships." In the second quarter of 1917 Great Britain lost 1,360,000 tons of shipping. The Allies could not launch new ships as rapidly as Germany was sinking them. One out of every four ships that left England never returned. To win the war, ships had to be built to transport supplies and men to the battle front. It was estimated that it required four tons of shipping in continuous operation to keep a single American soldier in France. The United States Shipping Board, which had been created in 1916, swung into action to deal with the problem of a government-owned and government-operated merchant marine. Edward Hurley was made chairman of the Shipping Board and worked with the Allied Shipping Board to create a "bridge to France."

Ten days after war was declared, Congress created the Emergency Fleet Corporation to help further in the problem. This Corporation took over German ships in American ports, bought neutral ships, leased private ships, and constructed new shipyards. Many shipyards in the Great Lakes region built ships in sections, and these sections were put together in east-coast yards. By the construction of steel ships, wooden ships, fabricated ships, and concrete ships the Emergency Fleet Corporation succeeded in increasing tonnage from one million to ten million tons. "Appalling prices," wrote Secretary of the Treasury McAdoo, "were paid for everything that had to do with a ship. Engines and other equipment were purchased at such a staggering cost that I fancied more than once that the machinery that we were buying must be made of silver instead of iron and steel." Four new shipyards were constructed, the largest of which was at Hog Island on the mud flats of the Delaware River below Philadelphia. One reporter wrote of the Hog Island shipyards:

> Here was an absolutely flat stretch of land circling back from a straight mile and a half of water front that last summer was nothing but a dismal, soggy, salt swamp inhabited only by muskrats and mosquitoes, now a beehive of industry, and one of the great manufacturing cities of the world. . . . Giant cranes were unloading huge pieces of steel and logs from the freight cars. Donkey engines were puffing. Sirens were blowing. Those titanic human woodpeckers, the compressed air riveters, were splitting the ears with their welding. A half dozen scows were dredging the river and a dozen pile drivers were descending with giant whacks upon the logs at the water's edge. . . . With begrimed faces and mud-encrusted shoes the men worked and walked along, laughing and shouting, singing and swearing. Hog Island was alive.[1]

On July 4, 1918, from the various new yards, a hundred ships were launched, but few of these actually carried cargoes to win the war. The Yanks and supplies went in other bottoms than those built in the new yards.

The construction of new shipyards and new factories made it necessary for the government to find housing for the workers. In many cases the government built houses, streets, sewers, water and lighting systems, schools, and places of amusement in areas that had been unoccupied before the war began. The Department of Labor took charge of this task in February, 1918. As a result, by the time peace came, another field for government planning had been opened. Under the New Deal the government, relying somewhat on this war experience, launched many governmental housing projects.

In the field of transportation within the United States, in order that war needs should have priority over civilian needs, the government took charge of the railroads in December, 1917. Private control of the various lines had not proved adequate. Frequently one line would have empty freight cars in its yards while another lacked cars to ship the freight in its yards. Freight cars tended to pile up at the Eastern ports of embarkation, and centralized control was necessary to route the cars back to the source of supply. McAdoo, Secretary of the Treasury, became Director-General of the United States Railroad Ad-

[1] Hamilton Holt, "Hog Island," *Independent*, Vol. XCIV, May 4, 1918, p. 196.

ministration and dictator of all traffic. The railroads were organized into regional units, competing companies were consolidated, and passenger service was cut to a minimum. McAdoo ran the railroads efficiently, but the rental paid by the government to the operators was too high, and the freight rates charged were too low. It cost the government $714,000,000 to operate the railroads; but it should be remembered that the primary purpose of Federal operation was to win the war, not to make a profit. In addition to the railroads, the government, before the war was over, took control of terminals, express companies, sleeping-car companies, grain elevators, warehouses, and telephone, telegraph, and cable services.

The branch of the war administration which reached the greatest number of citizens was the Food Administration. Herbert C. Hoover, who had gained valuable experience as chairman of the Commission for Relief in Belgium, was placed in charge of the task of carrying out the slogan "Food will win the war." The problem was to create a surplus of food in America for shipment to Europe to relieve an acute shortage among our Allies. This was accomplished mainly by persuasion; rationing was not used. Local citizen committees were organized to spread the message that foods must be conserved. The Bureau of Fisheries advocated that the people use the "meat of whales, porpoises, and dolphins . . . for food." Americans were called upon to deny themselves the luxury of meats, fine flour, fats, and sweets. "Wheatless" and "meatless" days were frequent. Restaurants added such delicacies as whale and horsemeat to the menu to make up for the omission of beefsteaks. Housewives particularly were urged not to waste food. That this campaign had a great deal of success was seen in Chicago, for instance, where in June, 1916, garbage to the amount of 12,862 tons had been collected, but in June, 1917, only 8386 tons was collected. During vacation time boys and women formed a "land army" to aid in farm work, and home vegetable gardens blossomed out in back yards and in vacant lots.

Mr. Hoover was given the power to fix the price of staples, license food-distributors, supervise exports, prohibit hoarding and profiteering, and stimulate production. The price of wheat was fixed high to increase production. Wheat-planting, as a result, greatly increased, particularly in submarginal land in the high plains of the West, later to be known as the "dust bowl." After the war this expansion had an unfortunate effect on the farmer when the falling off of European demand brought a great drop in price. Hoover also established a grain corporation to buy and to sell the staple grains, and he controlled the supply of sugar, as well as the supply and purchase of meat. The various activities designed to cut down American consumption were so successful that in 1918 the United States was able to export three times the normal amounts of grain, meat, and sugar.

These were the chief war agencies that regulated the American economy during the war years. There were other agencies, however, which deserve some mention. The Fuel Administration, to ensure sufficient coal for war factories and ships, closed down all nonessential manufacturing plants for five days and for a series of Mondays thereafter. This step really brought the war home to civilians, and Wilson observed that now "we are on a war footing." In order to make sure that there was gasoline for motor vehicles trucking vital war goods, car-owners were requested to forego pleasure driving, particularly on Sundays and holidays. All these various necessary restrictions on the use of gasoline, coal, and certain foodstuffs were carried out by persuasion and by voluntary co-operation on the part of citizens. Although the vast majority undoubtedly lived up to their obligations, it was possible for some to profiteer and to take advantage of the patriotism of their neighbors. When the United States entered the Second World War, to control hoarding and profiteering more effectively rationing was instituted, with coupons for each person.

The War Trade Board during the First World War licensed exports and imports in order to reduce drastically nonessential trade, and it also black-listed firms suspected of trading with the enemy. The property of enemy aliens in the United States was turned over to an Alien Property Custodian, A. Mitchell Palmer, who administered property worth close to a half-billion dollars. The problems arising from employer-employee relationships in wartime led to the creation of a labor administration. There were a number of strikes during the war, but few of them were purposely conducted to hamper the war effort. The workers were faced with rapidly rising prices and a growing number of nonunion people entering the ranks of industrial wage-earners. Strikes were conducted for higher wages and for union recognition in order to protect the union's position in a particular industry. Samuel Gompers, head of the American Federation of Labor and one of Wilson's advisers on labor problems, was insistent that the war must not be used to depress wage or labor standards. Strikes at times tied up vital war production. For three months a strike held up the production of the caterpillar tractors that were used in making tanks. The workers making the Browning machine gun went on strike at one time. To arbitrate industrial disputes a National War Labor Board was created, with William Howard Taft and Frank P. Walsh as co-chairmen. The Wilson administration preferred to solve industrial disputes through this agency rather than sponsor any law against war-time strikes. Injunctions were used, however, to prevent certain strikes when other methods had failed. Secretary of War Newton D. Baker, in commenting on the role of labor in the war, observed, "I have found labor more willing to keep step than capital."

The conflict between labor and capital was most acute in the Pacific Northwest, where the Industrial Workers of the World had some power. They sponsored strikes in the copper mines and in the lumber camps. Since they were a radical labor group, they were interested in striking a blow at the system of private capitalism. Violence was used by the I.W.W. and was countered with violence by their opponents. During and after the war, members of the I.W.W. were jailed as being guilty under either the Federal Sedition Act or similar state acts.

Seven days after the declaration of war Congress created the Committee on Public Information, headed by journalist George Creel, to tell the people what the war was about and to "sell" the war to the people. Some people were indifferent to the war, and others were definitely hostile to American participation. Socialist leader Morris Hillquit, for example, said, "The country has been violently, needlessly, and criminally involved in war." The Creel Committee launched a torrent of propaganda documents, posters, and films on the United States and the world. Over one hundred million pieces of "literature" were distributed by the Committee; pamphlets were printed in many languages; seventy-five thousand volunteer speakers—"Four-Minute Men"—invaded theaters, motion-picture houses, and civic meetings to urge the buying of bonds, a fuller support of the war effort, and the crushing of sedition. The Committee furnished the foreign-language press of the United States with news of the war, and every week dispatched an immense amount of "boiler plate" to twelve thousand country newspapers. Patriotic posters were made, and stereopticon slides and motion-picture films were widely distributed. Reading-rooms were fitted out where the Committee's Red, White, and Blue Books, War Information Series, and Loyalty Leaflets could be read. Furthermore, the Committee published daily an *Official Bulletin of the United States*, which contained the war news that had been released to correspondents for use in American papers. The Creel Committee's campaign tended to develop a conformity in point of view among the American people. Hatred of the enemy was cultivated, and gradually for many people tolerance and saneness were obliterated.

American public opinion was mobilized in part by George Creel and in part by volunteer committees sanctioned by state authorities. In Illinois, for instance, there were agencies covering the state, counties, and cities. These agencies took the form of women's committees, publicity committees, food committees, and various neighborhood committees, whose "primary function was the promotion of patriotic thought and action." For the suppression of real opposition to the war the Federal government had two far-reaching laws. The Espionage Act of June, 1917, fixed a fine of ten thousand dollars and twenty years' imprisonment for anyone guilty of inciting disloyalty or interfering with the Selective Service Act. The Sedition Act of May, 1918, extended that punishment to anyone who should "willfully utter, print, write or publish any disloyal, profane, scurrilous, or abusive language about the form of government of the United States, or the Constitution . . . or the flag . . . or the uniform of the Army or Navy . . . or bring the form of government . . . or the Constitution . . . into contempt . . . or advocate any curtailment of production in this country of anything necessary or essential to the prosecution of the war." These two acts were far more stringent than any of the steps taken by the North during the Civil War. At that time, whenever military courts went too far, Lincoln generally interfered and eased the decisions, but there was no such tempering in 1917 and 1918.

Under these two measures the government arrested over fifteen hundred people. Eugene V. Debs, who, as Socialist candidate for the Presidency in 1912, had received a million votes, was sent to jail. Victor L. Berger, Socialist Congressman, however, escaped a jail sentence when the Supreme Court reversed a lower court's decision. Those who opposed the war were not tolerated. As Justice Oliver Wendell Holmes observed, "When a nation is at war many things that might be said in time of peace are such a hindrance to its effort that their utterance will not be endured so long as men fight, and that no court could regard them as protected by any constitutional right." Among the magazines and newspapers that lost their second-class mailing privileges were the *Socialist Leader*, the *American Socialist*, and Max Eastman's *Masses*.

More repressive, however, of civil liberties than the work of the government was the action of certain "super"-patriots who took the law into their own hands. President Wilson, the night before he delivered his war message to Congress, had expressed a fear to Frank Cobb of the New York *World:*

> Once lead this people into war and they'll forget there ever was such a thing as tolerance. To fight you must be brutal and ruthless, and the spirit of ruthless brutality will enter into every fibre of our national life, infecting Congress, the courts, the policeman on the beat, the man in the street.

This prophecy was fulfilled. People who did not conform were treated as spies. The German-Americans, particularly, were victims of this over-zealous patriotism. The German language was just about eliminated from public-school teaching, German books were removed from public libraries, the playing of German music was frequently banned, and such distinguished musicians of German or Austrian background as Frederick Stock and Fritz Kreisler were publicly humiliated. Stock was deprived of his baton as conductor of the Chicago Symphony Orchestra, and Kreisler was refused a permit to appear in a New Jersey town. This orgy of intolerance was still mounting in intensity when the armistice ended the war. It was carried on after the war in such activities as those of the "Red scare" and the Ku Klux Klan.

PROPAGANDA ABROAD

During the war the United States carried on a propaganda campaign to destroy the will of the peoples of the Central Powers to continue fighting. Wilson, in his war message, had asserted that "we have no quarrel with the German people. We have no feeling toward them but one of sympathy and friendship." To the minority groups in the Austro-Hungarian empire he held out the hope of national independence. He also emphasized that the United States was in the war as the "disinterested champion of right," fighting for no material gains. In order to establish a high moral basis for peace, as well as to stir trouble among the peoples of the Central Powers, Wilson, on January 8, 1918, promulgated the Fourteen Points, necessary for the formulation of peace. These Fourteen Points, summarized, were

1. Open covenants openly arrived at.
2. Freedom of the seas alike in peace and in war.
3. The removal of all economic barriers and the establishment of an equality of trade conditions among all nations.
4. Reduction of national armaments.

5. A readjustment of all colonial claims in which the interests of the populations concerned must have equal weight with the interests of the governments whose titles are to be determined.

6. The evacuation of Russian territory and the independent determination by Russia of her own political development and national policy.

7. The evacuation and restoration of Belgium.

8. The evacuation and restoration of France and the return of Alsace-Lorraine.

9. A readjustment of the frontiers of Italy along national lines.

10. Self-determination for the peoples of Austria-Hungary.

11. A redrawing of the boundaries of the Balkan states along historically established lines of nationality.

12. Self-determination for the peoples under Turkish rule and freedom of the Dardanelles under international guarantees.

13. Independence of Poland, with free access to the sea guaranteed by international covenant.

14. The formation of a general association of nations under specific covenants for the purpose of affording mutual guarantees of political independence and territorial integrity to great and small states alike.

Wilson's Fourteen Points were in conflict with secret treaties that had been signed by the Allies with Italy, Japan, and Rumania to bring these nations into the war on the Allied side. Pledges of territory had been given these nations as the price of their participation in the war. Wilson knew in general that these treaties existed when he announced such points as open covenants and the self-determination of peoples. The new Soviet government of Russia, for instance, had published the terms of some of the treaties in November, 1917. Wilson's motive in announcing the Fourteen Points seems to have been to compel the Allies to revise their war aims; to secure the adhesion of Soviet Russia to the war; and to weaken the Central Powers by strengthening revolutionary forces within them. Some writers have felt that Wilson should have forced the repudiation of these agreements as the price of United States' aid. Wilson, however, told Colonel House, "If we stated that we would fight with the Allies but reserved the right later to dispute the application of the secret treaties, the only effect would be to cause irritation and to injure the chances of effective cooperative action against the enemy." If Wilson had insisted on the abrogation of the secret treaties, it is possible that this would have led to dissension among the Allies and a victory for Germany, since Germany, during 1917, was apparently well on the way to victory.

In the summer and autumn of 1918 millions of leaflets were dropped by Allied planes and balloons behind the German lines. These leaflets stressed the Fourteen Points and Wilson's distinction between the German people and the German government. According to the German general Ludendorff this propaganda was a major factor in bringing an end to the war. Actually, however, it was only when the German military leaders realized that they were facing defeat in the field that they insisted that their government make peace overtures. According to one authority:

> Propaganda would have been in vain without the Allies' victories and ... the latter distinctly preceded the former's effectiveness. I should even go as far as to say that, on the whole, the realization of German defeat came first to the soldiers in the field, from the generals down, and only then to the much surprised civilian population from the government down. What this propaganda had been offering, including the words of Wilson, on the one hand, and those of Lenin, on the other, was then—and only then—embraced by the Germans, since there was nothing else to grasp at.

THE MILITARY PHASE OF THE WAR

The Germans had expected that the U-boat would end the war before American aid could become effective. It was a year after the declaration of war before the American army became a telling force on the western front. Before that time, however, the American navy had played an important role in preventing the submarine from ending the war with a German victory. By May, 1917, the American navy had sent eighteen destroyers to Queenstown (Cobh), and by the end of the war eighty American destroyers were operating in the area from the British Isles to the Mediterranean. The British Grand Fleet was increased in striking power by the addition of five American battleships, and this in part persuaded the German command against sending their fleet out for another battle that might have been as disastrous as that of Jutland. All told, by the end of the war, the American navy had overseas about three hundred craft of various sizes, with a complement of seventy-five thousand officers and men.

Led by Admiral Sims, the American navy sowed the North Sea with mines, a barrier through which few submarines eventually were able to penetrate. By the date of the armistice this mine barrage extended two hundred and forty miles, and of the seventy thousand odd mines laid the American navy had laid fifty-six thousand. Various other techniques were used to curb the submarine. The sinking of

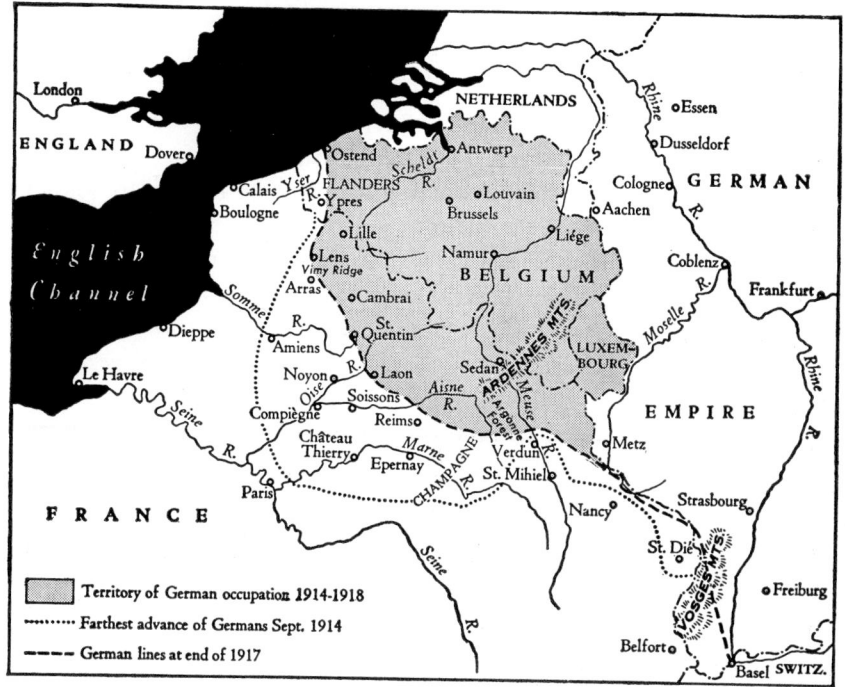

The Western Front, 1914–1917

Allied shipping just before American entrance had been exceedingly heavy. In February 532,000 tons of Allied and neutral shipping had been lost; in March 599,000 tons, and in April 869,000 tons. To counteract these losses the British developed the convoy system. American entrance into the war supplied the British with destroyers and smaller armed vessels needed to make the convoys safe. Freighters and troopships were given the protective custody of destroyers. By June and July, 1917, the convoy system was in full operation on the routes from America and Gibraltar, and in the North Sea. At a convenient port ships were organized into a convoy, and the convoy proceeded at the pace of the slowest ship. Soon the submarines discovered that an attack on a convoy was a hazardous operation. Surface attack became impossible, and a torpedo attack left the submarine exposed to depth bombs dropped by the protecting force. Separate destroyer detachments also operated in submarine-infested waters to cut down U-boat depredations. Under the convoy system, roughly two million American soldiers were landed in Europe. The majority of the ships carrying troops and supplies were of Allied registry, while the American navy supplied the bulk of the war vessels that did the protective work. Only one American troopship was torpedoed, with the loss of two hundred and ten lives, a remarkably small casualty list in view of the two million men who were carried across the Atlantic highway.

To bolster Allied morale, a small contingent of American soldiers, under the leadership of General John J. Pershing, landed in France in June, 1917. A few of these soldiers, marching in Paris on the Fourth of July, were greeted with tremendous enthusiasm by the French. One observer reported, "Our soldiers were covered by flowers—and always the steady roar of the crowd and now and then cries of *Vive l'Amérique!*" Pershing soon came to the conclusion that America must raise a large army and train it to take the offensive, rather than fight, and become exhausted by, the kind of trench warfare that had characterized the war ever since the first battle of the Marne, in September, 1914. Within three weeks of his arrival he notified Washington that he wanted a million men ready to take the field within a year and additional millions as they would be needed. He directed that "all instruction must contemplate the assumption of a vigorous offensive." Furthermore, he reached the conclusion that the American army should be kept intact in France as a separate unit and not be used solely as replacements in the existing Allied armies.

Training and transporting an army to France were not the entire task that faced the War Department. Clothing, arms, ammunition, gas masks, artillery, airplanes, and other important material had to be provided and shipped to Europe. At the European end, harbors had to be dredged, docks constructed, railroads built, telegraph wire strung, and hospitals, barracks, and warehouses assembled. A great deal of the material to do this gigantic job was shipped from America to France. Although American factories turned out two and a half million rifles, one hundred and eighty-one thousand machine guns, over five million gas masks, and quantities of other necessary equipment, at times French and English supplies had to be used, since American soldiers were shipped to France faster than had been anticipated.

Troops arrived in France, however, more slowly than Pershing desired. By the opening of 1918 there were only about two hundred thousand American troops in that country. After March, 1918, however, shipments increased rapidly, and by the armistice there was a total of 2,079,880. Late in 1917 the military situation in Europe underwent a drastic change. Germany threw some picked divisions into the Austrian campaign against Italy. On October 24 the German-Austrian armies pierced the Italian lines at Caporetto. Not until mid-November were the Italians able to stabilize their lines, and by this time Italy had lost six hundred thousand men and six thousand square miles of territory. French and English divisions were rushed to Italy to help to stop the rout. The prime minister of England and the premiers of France and Italy met and recommended a unified command against the enemy. Then, on November 7, the Soviets in Russia overthrew the Kerensky government, which had held power since the deposal of the Czar in the previous March. A month later the Soviets signed an armistice with the Germans. The year 1918 opened with the situation favorable for the Central Powers. With the Russian front ended, they could concentrate their forces on the western front to make a break-through and end the defensive trench warfare. Germany, however, had to strike quickly. Her allies—Austria-Hungary, Turkey, and Bulgaria— were war-weary and nearing exhaustion. General Ludendorff observed: "The state of our allies, of ourselves, and of the army all called for an attack that would bring about an early decision. This could only be accomplished on the Western front."

On March 21, 1918, Germany launched her great offensive on the western front with a terrific assault on the British lines from Arras to La Fère. At the end of two weeks Germany had gained fifteen hundred square miles of territory and inflicted one hundred and sixty thousand casualties on the British armies. On April 14 the French general Foch was placed in supreme command of the Allied armies in France. From this time on, the work of the French, British, and American armies was unified. During May and June, Ludendorff struck at the French armies along the front from Noyon to Reims. Within two weeks of this assault the Germans were threatening Paris from the right bank of the Marne. The heads of the French, English, and Italian governments warned the United States that "there is a great danger of the war being lost unless the numerical inferiority of the Allies can be remedied as rapidly as possible by the advent of American troops."

General Pershing temporarily suspended his demand for a separate American unit on the front, and American troops were added to the Allied armies where needed. During May and June the American army fought engagements at Cantigny, Château-Thierry, and Belleau Wood. On July 15 the last phase of the German offensive was launched along the Marne. American and French troops received the attack. Three days later Foch ordered a counteroffensive, led by the First and Second

American divisions and the First French Morocco Division. This was the turn of the tide. Later the German Chancellor stated: "I was convinced . . . that before the first of September our adversaries would send us peace proposals. . . . That was on the 15th. On the 18th, even the most optimistic among us knew that all was lost. The history of the world was played out in three days."

On August 8 the British army struck the Germans before Amiens. In the course of the first day's battle the British offensive, sparked by the use of tanks, captured sixteen thousand prisoners. The following day the French on the British right captured Montdidier. This offensive dealt a blow to the German army's morale. Large groups of soldiers surrendered, and Ludendorff referred to August 8 as "the black day of the German army." Pershing's desire for an independent American army, in charge of a sector of the front, was now carried out. The Americans were assigned to wipe out a salient at St. Mihiel, which the Germans maintained to protect the Mézières-Sedan-Metz railroad. Pershing's chief of staff, George C. Marshall, worked out the tactics of a remarkably well-planned campaign. On September 12 a force of half a million American soldiers attacked after a ferocious artillery barrage. In two days Pershing was able to report the capture of sixteen thousand prisoners and four hundred and fifty guns at the cost of seven thousand casualties. This success of the American army gave inspiration both to the men in uniform and to the public back home, and, as Pershing said, "No form of enemy propaganda could overcome the depressing effect on the morale of the enemy of this demonstration of our ability to organize a large American force and drive it successfully through his defenses."

Plans were now laid for a great Allied offensive all along the line from Ypres to Verdun. The American army was assigned to the sector between the river Meuse and the Argonne forest. Twenty-four miles of the active front between Verdun and the Channel coast were under Pershing's command. The Meuse-Argonne battle started on September 26. In spite of the difficult terrain, advances were quickly made. For the next month or more the Americans rolled the Germans back, as did the other Allied armies along the rest of the front. On September 30 General von Hindenburg notified his government that peace must be sought. The Germans had lost one million men since March, desertions were heavy, and fresh American troops were arriving every day. Bulgaria had been knocked out of the war by an Allied army in late September; Turkey and Austria-Hungary were exhausted.

On October 2 the Kaiser made Prince Max of Baden Chancellor of Germany, and on the following day the new Chancellor sent a note to President Wilson, requesting an armistice and peace negotiations based on the Fourteen Points. On October 4 the Austro-Hungarian government sent a similar request. At the end of October, Foch was empowered to negotiate an armistice. The German Armistice Commission met Foch on November 8, and on the morning of November 11 the terms were signed and fighting ceased. Meanwhile Austria-Hungary had signed an armistice with the Italians on November 3. Eight days later the Austrian emperor relinquished his throne, and the old Austro-Hungarian empire quickly dissolved. Germany, from October 2 to November 5, took steps which appeared to establish a responsible constitutional government, but actually the chief autocrats remained in power. On October 29 the crews of the German ships at Kiel mutinied rather than put to sea. Other mutinies quickly followed. The day before the armistice was signed, the Kaiser, deposed by action of the Chancellor, crossed the Dutch frontier. Under the pressure of growing military defeat the Germans hastened to sign the armistice because they realized that the best terms could be had while their army was still intact.

The ruling clique in Germany, however, did not lose power as a result of the end of the war. Though the Kaiser was deposed and the establishment of a republic accepted, the Prussian landlords, the military caste, and the industrial magnates continued to have tremendous strength. To head off the development of a real German democracy, these groups, in 1933, were to help to deliver Germany into the hands of Adolf Hitler and the Nazis. A real social revolution was needed in Germany in 1918 and 1919 to sweep these groups out of power, but the armistice helped to save their position.

American participation in the war, in addition to the campaigns mentioned, included some troops sent to aid the Italians and some to aid the French in Belgium. Five thousand American soldiers joined the Allies in the Archangel-Murmansk campaign, from September, 1918, to May, 1919, and ten thousand joined the Allied expedition to Vladivostok in eastern Siberia, which lasted until January, 1920. These two Allied activities on Russian soil were conducted in the hope of bringing a government to power in Russia that would resume the war against Germany and one also that would not repudiate the Russian debt, as the Soviets had done.

A judicial appraisal of America's contribution to victory, as well as

Pershing's role as commander of the A.E.F., would probably lead one to agree with this statement:

It is impossible to prove Pershing's rating as a general as it is to prove the degree to which the American reinforcement made it possible to defeat the enemy. Thrown by the strategy of his chief into a holding position not of his own choosing in the last engagement of the war, Pershing did more than hold. The human weight of the forces under his command was at least a vital factor in victory; the economic weight contributed by the American Government was another; the unity of direction, to which the United States had contributed greatly, was still a third. But the victory in the field which broke the Central Powers was the victory of a team in which the abstraction of co-operation was perhaps more significant than the weight of any single concrete factor.[1]

SELECTED BIBLIOGRAPHY

Frederic L. Paxson, *America at War: 1917–1918*, a good, solid survey; Benedict Crowell and Robert F. Wilson, *How America Went to War* (6 vols.), a thorough study of all phases of mobilization; W. F. Willoughby, *Government Organization in War Time and After*; W. G. McAdoo, *Crowded Years*; George Creel, *How We Advertised America*; Samuel Gompers, *American Labor and the War*; Bernard Baruch, *American Industry in the War*, contain valuable material on particular phases.

On the military phases of the war the following are valuable: John J. Pershing, *My Experiences in the World War*; T. G. Frothingham, *Naval History of the World War* and *American Re-enforcement in the World War*; Frederick Palmer, *America in France*; Shipley Thomas, *History of the A. E. F.*

H. S. Commager (Ed.), *Documents of American History*, pp. 324–326, contains source material.

[1]Frederic L. Paxson, *America at War: 1917–1918*, p. 387. Houghton Mifflin Company, Boston, 1939.

XXX

The Peace of Versailles

THE FIRST WORLD WAR lasted four years and three months. Thirty sovereign nations were involved; sixty-five million men were mobilized, of whom thirteen million were lost on the field of battle; valuable wealth was destroyed; and millions of civilians died from starvation and disease. The people of the world needed a real peace to recover from this destructive war. The victorious powers, however, were unprepared for a transition from war to peace. They had not sufficiently realized that the peace must be prepared for, even while the war was being fought. Woodrow Wilson's Fourteen Points occupied an important position in the peace considerations, but there was considerable opposition among some of the Allies to many of the points. Secret treaties, for instance, violated Wilson's belief in the self-determination of peoples. The one point that they were agreed upon, however, was the need of a League of Nations to maintain international peace.

The major decisions at the Peace Conference were made by the four chief powers—France, Great Britain, the United States, and Italy. The newspapermen were admitted to the General Sessions of the Conference, but they were not allowed at the meetings of the Big Four, where the major decisions were made. President Wilson justified these secret discussions in this way:

I am for all [the publicity] we can get, yet I must work with other men of other nations whose ideas of publicity are different from ours. We are at present merely comparing views, finding out where we stand. It is a kind of world cabinet meeting in which every member may express his views freely. If we announced partial results, or one decision at a time, it might easily result in bloodshed. We must do nothing that will invite more war, we must do everything to get a speedy peace. When we reach real decisions everything must be made known to the world.[1]

The enemy had no part in the negotiations and was called in only when the treaty was ready for signing. Russia also was not officially

[1] From *Woodrow Wilson and World Settlement,* by R. S. Baker. Copyright, 1922, by Doubleday & Company, Inc.

represented at the Conference. It took only four months to draft the treaty. Many of the delegates urged speed because of the unstable conditions in Europe. Small wars were either in progress or ready to start in central Europe, Poland, and Russia. It was feared that every day the final peace was delayed, there was more opportunity for communism to sweep through Europe. The hatreds engendered by the war and the desire for certain gains made it extremely difficult, of course, to achieve Wilson's ideal of peace. The Italians, led by Orlando, demanded land occupied by German-speaking people. The United States itself readily condemned secret and regional agreements, but disliked any criticism of the Monroe Doctrine. The Australian prime minister challenged Wilson to apply the principles of the Fourteen Points to the German islands occupied by the Australians. Lloyd George, the British prime minister, had been elected to office on the slogan "Make Germany pay," and he was charged with being statesmanlike at the expense of others, but not at the expense of the British Empire. Clemenceau of France was a narrow-minded, cynical old man who attacked Wilson's idealism by saying, "God was content with Ten Commandments, but Wilson must have fourteen!" Clemenceau seemed to be interested solely in the security of France. Larger world issues seemed not to concern him.

The leaders of the Big Four were responsible to public opinion in their homelands. Lloyd George, Orlando, and Clemenceau would probably have lost office had they yielded and displayed any signs of weakness at the Conference. Wilson too was faced with an American public aroused to hatred of Germany by the propaganda and events of the war years, and in his struggle for his type of peace could not rely upon a united American opinion. Just before the mid-term election of 1918 he had asked the electorate:

> If you have approved of my leadership and wish me to continue to be your unembarrassed spokesman in affairs at home and abroad, I earnestly beg that you will express yourselves unmistakably to that effect by returning a Democratic majority to both the Senate and House of Representatives.

The election, however, placed both houses of Congress in the hands of the Republicans. When Wilson left for France, Theodore Roosevelt announced:

> Mr. Wilson has no authority whatever to speak for the American people at this time. His leadership has just been emphatically repudiated by them. Mr. Wilson and his Fourteen Points and his four supplementary points and

all his utterances every which way have ceased to have any shadow of right to be accepted as expressive of the will of the American people.

To the Conference Wilson took Secretary of State Lansing, General Tasker H. Bliss, Colonel House, and Mr. Henry A. White. In addition, he took a number of experts in economic, geographical, and historical problems to help on the details of the Conference. No outstanding Republican, such as William H. Taft or Elihu Root, was included, nor any member of the United States Senate. Both these omissions proved to be strategic mistakes on Wilson's part.

At the Peace Conference, Wilson's primary purpose was to write the Covenant of the League of Nations into the treaty. Although the treaty, as finally drawn, had its faults, he felt that the League would compensate. Wilson, although agreeing to some compromises, forced a number of concessions on the Allies. For instance, he prevented Italy from taking Fiume, and he successfully protested against Japan's permanently occupying the Shantung peninsula in China. He also prevented the Allies from charging Germany with the entire cost of the war. A bitter fight ensued over the status of the German Rhineland, and the Conference almost broke up over France's demand for that area. Clemenceau argued that this was necessary for France's security and finally gave way only when Wilson and Lloyd George pledged American and British aid against Germany in the case of future aggression. This pledge never was submitted to the Senate and no action was taken when Hitler reoccupied the Rhineland in 1936.

THE TREATY OF VERSAILLES

On June 28, 1919, the Treaty of Versailles was signed in the palace of Versailles, where, forty-eight years before, the German Empire had been proclaimed. The essential part of the treaty was the Covenant of the League of Nations. The League was empowered to execute certain articles of the treaty, unsettled issues were to be referred to the League, and the new mandate system was answerable to it. Under the mandate system the conquered German colonies were handed over to Allied countries for administration, but not for outright annexation. In the collapse of collective security before 1939, as the League grew increasingly feeble and increasingly unable to control the mandate system, Japan, for instance, really annexed the former German colonies entrusted to her care and fortified them, in violation of the peace agreements.

Germany, under the treaty, had to disgorge many territorial conquests of the past. Alsace-Lorraine was returned to France; Belgium and Denmark received some border territory; and independent Poland received five sixths of Posen, Polish districts in West Prussia, and a corridor to the Baltic. The rich coal region of the Saar was turned over to the French for fifteen years. At the end of that time a plebiscite was to determine whether it should go to Germany or to France, or be run by an international commission. The amount of German reparations was left to a commission, which set the bill close to thirty-three billion dollars in 1921. Two years later the French, on the pretext that the Germans had defaulted, seized the Ruhr valley, not to relinquish it until 1925. Hitlerian Germany finally repudiated the debt obligations.

Under the treaty Germany agreed not to assemble an army or build fortifications on the left bank of the Rhine. The German army was reduced to one hundred thousand men, recruited by voluntary enlistment. The control of this army, unfortunately, was left in the hands of the Prussian militaristic group, which kept itself intact and later, under Hitler, built up a gigantic war machine. The manufacture of munitions was limited to the needs of this small army. Germany surrendered most of her naval strength and agreed not to make submarines, military aircraft, heavy artillery, tanks, and poison gas. Actually, however, Germany began to violate these provisions in the treaty soon after signing it. As a result, the settlement at Versailles was really never put into complete operation.

After the Treaty of Versailles was signed, treaties were made with Austria, Bulgaria, Hungary, and Turkey. The central structure of the peace agreements was the League of Nations. Postwar stability hinged upon an effective League. The purpose of the League was "to promote international co-operation and to achieve international peace and security." League membership was open to all nations, and every member had an equal vote in the Assembly. The executive body, the Council, consisted of the United States, Great Britain, France, Italy, and Japan as permanent members and four other nations as temporary members chosen by the Assembly. A permanent Secretariat at Geneva and the Permanent Court of International Justice, established at the Hague, completed the structure.

The members of the League agreed "to respect and preserve against external aggression the territorial integrity and existing political independence" of all the members. The Council could impose economic sanctions against any nation guilty of aggression, and in case military action was necessary it could recommend this to the League members. The Council was given power to organize plans for the reduction of armaments; to give publicity to treaties; and to establish an International Labor Organization with jurisdiction over labor conditions, traffic in women and children, health, and the drug trade. The humanitarian and social work done by the League up to the outbreak of war in 1939 was a remarkable achievement, accomplished in spite of the growing political weakness of the organization.

President Wilson felt that the Treaty of Versailles, in spite of certain flaws, was justified in view of the inclusion of the League. The peace treaty was by no means as drastic as Clemenceau had desired. Adolf Hitler was later to use the Treaty of Versailles as he used the Jews— as a scapegoat on which to heap blame for the troubles of Germany. The troubles that Hitler's Germany faced stemmed as much from defeat after four years of war as from the Treaty of Versailles. Those who have criticized the severity of the treaty have overlooked the fact that under it Germany was able to organize another military colossus and plunge the world again into war only twenty years after she had signed the treaty. The treaty, in other words, did not destroy Germany, as subsequent events amply revealed. Furthermore, the peace imposed on Germany was far less drastic than the one that she had forced on Russia at Brest Litovsk on March 3, 1918. Under this treaty Russia was required to give up Poland, Estonia, Finland, Livonia, Lithuania, Kurland, the Armenian provinces of Kars, Ardahan, and Batum, and the Ukraine. All in all, Russia had to relinquish about five hundred thousand square miles of territory and sixty-five million people. Germany took over control of the northern areas given up by Russia and established a pro-German government in the Ukraine. Russia was also required to pay an indemnity. The Treaty of Versailles set aside the Treaty of Brest Litovsk, but the drastic nature of the latter was an indication that the type of peace that would have been imposed on the Allies by a victorious Germany would have been far more rigorous than that which the Allies imposed on Germany.

The Treaty of Versailles was not nearly as severe as it became popular to say that it was in the United States before 1939 and, of course, valuable for Hitler to have the American public feel that it was. Had the League of Nations functioned according to Wilson's hopes, it is quite possible that the treaty might have endured for a long time.

THE FIGHT IN THE UNITED STATES

The Treaty of Versailles was a compromise peace that might have worked. The failure of the United States, however, to accept it and to enter the League of Nations helped to undermine hopes for a peaceful world at the very outset. Increasingly, more and more people have felt that if the United States had joined the League of Nations in 1919 or 1920, there would have been a strong possibility that the Second World War might have been prevented. In a blunt fashion Prime Minister Winston Churchill told the American Congress on December 26, 1941, that this war need not have happened had the peace-loving nations worked together during the past twenty years.

The failure of England and France to work together after 1919 also contributed to the collapse of collective security, but the United States, by withdrawing from the peace settlement, impaired its prestige, abdicated its leadership, and left the world in a state of confusion and despair. The rejection of the peace treaty, T. A. Bailey remarks, in *Woodrow Wilson and the Great Betrayal,* "was a betrayal of America's responsibility to assume that world leadership which had been thrust upon her. . . . Instead, we cravenly retreated, while our prestige sank to a new low in Europe, the Far East, and Latin America. Instead of trying to control events, we left ourselves at the mercy of events which inexorably drew us again into their vortex."[1]

Unfortunately the Treaty of Versailles, in which the Covenant of the League of Nations was incorporated, was not debated in the United States Senate purely on its merits. Instead of a reasonable atmosphere in which to discuss this proposed method of ending wars, the atmosphere of the Senate was one of bitterness, partisanship, and hostility. Some Senators, like Henry Cabot Lodge, had a deep personal hatred of Woodrow Wilson; some Senators were personally piqued that the President had not included any members of their body on the Peace Commission; some partisan Republicans did not want to pass a peace treaty drafted by a Democratic President, since this might ensure a Democratic victory in 1920. Then, of course, certain Senators were influenced by pressure groups among their constituents: many German-Americans were opposed to the treaty because, in their opinion, it was too severe on Germany; many Italian-Americans were against the treaty because Italy had not been given Fiume; many Irish-Americans looked upon the treaty as an English plot to control the world and were par-

[1]Page 359. The Macmillan Company, New York, 1945.

ticularly angry at England at that moment because of England's suppression of the Irish revolution; reactionaries were opposed to the treaty because it was not severe enough on Germany; and, on the other hand, a number of liberals, like O. G. Villard of the *Nation*, opposed the treaty because they felt that it was too hard on Germany.

When President Wilson presented the Treaty of Versailles to the Senate on July 10, 1919, that body did not divide into two groups, one for the treaty and the other against. Instead four groups were formed: (1) a protreaty group, composed of forty-three Democrats and one Republican, who were for ratification without any qualifications; (2) the "mild reservationists," consisting of about fifteen Republicans who were warmly for the treaty but desired reservations of a mild character; (3) the "strong reservationists," consisting of about twenty Republicans who favored ratification, but with "strong" reservations; and (4) the "irreconcilables," twelve Republicans and three Democrats, led by William E. Borah, who were opposed to ratification under any conditions.

The vast majority of the Senate, eighty out of ninety-six, were for the treaty, although groups 2 and 3 wanted certain reservations. The problem of strategy was to present the question in such a way that the three groups favorable to the treaty could unite. The tragedy was, as one writer has remarked, that the treaty "failed of ratification not because a constitutional majority desired to reject the treaty but because the different groups in favor of the treaty were unable to agree on the conditions of ratification." When the two votes on ratification occurred, on November 19, 1919, and on March 19, 1920, the treaty was defeated not by its enemies, the irreconcilables, but by its most ardent friends. On both occasions, when the treaty with reservations came to a vote, the reservationists voted for it and the irreconcilables, in combination with the administration Democrats (group 1), voted against it. The administration Democrats did not want to defeat the treaty; they wanted only to defeat the treaty with reservations in order that a vote could be had under more acceptable conditions. In so doing they were acting on the advice of President Wilson, who wrote to Senator Hitchcock just before the first vote was taken: "I sincerely hope that the friends and the supporters of the treaty will vote against the Lodge resolution of ratification. I understand that the door will then probably be open for a more genuine resolution of ratification."

A majority of the Senators, then, desired to accept the treaty, but they could not devise the strategy necessary to bring this majority together on the vote. This favorable majority was apparently backed up by a majority of the American public, who too wanted to accept the treaty and entrance into the League of Nations. The *Literary Digest* conducted a poll of newspapers in April, 1919, and found that 718 were for ratification, 478 were for ratification with conditions, and only 181 were against ratification. For a long time the idea of a League of Nations had been growing in the United States. Theodore Roosevelt, speaking before the Nobel Prize Committee in 1910, advocated a League of Peace to prevent war from breaking out. After the outbreak of the First World War he declared, "The great civilized nations of the world which do possess force, actual or immediately potential, should combine by solemn agreement in a great world league for the peace of righteousness." President Wilson was also thinking along the same lines in the fall of 1914. He told a friend that "all nations must be absorbed into some great association of nations whereby all shall guarantee the integrity of each so that any one nation violating the agreement between all of them shall bring punishment on itself automatically." Ex-President Taft expressed much the same opinion in October, 1914.

So many Americans were in agreement with these distinguished leaders that a League to Enforce Peace was formed on June 17, 1915. Within a year this League had branches in almost every Congressional district in the country, and in 1919 its members felt that the United States should join the League of Nations. Senator Lodge publicly gave his support to the proposal in 1916, as did Woodrow Wilson. On January 22, 1917, President Wilson told the Senate that one of the things necessary for permanent peace was a League of Nations. On January 8, 1918, in his message to Congress setting forth the Fourteen Points, on which he thought that the peace should be based, Wilson included, as the last point, a general association of nations to give "mutual guarantees of political independence and territorial integrity to great and small states alike."

But when Wilson sailed for Europe in December, 1918, to attend the Peace Conference, he did not have a united country behind his plan for a permanent peace. As has been said, he asked the country to elect a Democratic Congress. In the mid-term Congressional elections, however, the Republicans gained control of the Senate by a majority of two. Wilson made his request because he felt that a Republican Congress would divide the leadership of the nation. The Republicans in Congress had been prowar but antiadministration, and this was no time for divided leadership. Furthermore, Wilson believed that the election of a Republican majority in either house of Congress would be considered abroad to be a repudiation of his leadership.

Theodore Roosevelt denounced Wilson's appeal and repudiated the Fourteen Points. Other Republicans, such as Charles E. Hughes, William H. Taft, and Will Hays, chairman of the Republican National Committee, stated that they did not agree that Wilson's control of the government should be unhampered, nor was it necessary for the country's welfare. In the months that followed, when Taft fought shoulder to shoulder with Wilson, against the leadership of his own party in the Senate, for the Treaty of Versailles and the League of Nations, one writer has pointed out that Taft "must have wondered whether it might have been better to have given Wilson the continued control for which he asked. Wilson was destroyed in the conflict with a Republican Congress which followed the election of 1918."

Although Theodore Roosevelt said that the election results repudiated Wilson's leadership, this was not necessarily accurate. The election of Wilson in 1912 had been due largely to the splitting of the Republican party into two wings. In each of the elections from 1914 to 1918 the Republicans had regained seats in Congress. When it is remembered that there is usually a reaction against the party in power at a mid-term election when the Presidency is not at stake, the election of 1918 was not a great victory for the Republicans, nor a great defeat for the President. One observer has pointed out:

The forces which determined the several elections were sometimes local, sometimes general. They included support for or hostility to prohibition; the tendency of the business interests, large and small, to back the Republican party; pressure for a high tariff in industrial districts; objection on the part of food producers and distributors to the fixing of food prices, especially as the South had profited enormously from unregulated cotton prices; resentment in the states where General Leonard Wood was popular that the administration had not permitted him to go to France; the attitude of the Non-Partisan League or of its antiagrarian opponents, and the enthusiastic support by the women of those who had appealed for their new suffrage. There was virtually no issue contested and properly discussed which arose out of the policies that were the cause of our entering the war, of the degree of efficiency with which it was conducted, of the aims announced for the United States by its official spokesman, or of the effort which the United States was to put forth in the making of a durable peace.[1]

[1]Charles P. Howland, *American Foreign Relations*, pp. 239-240. Yale University Press, New Haven, 1918.

As soon as the armistice celebration had quieted down, Senators Knox, Poindexter, and Reed attacked the proposal of American entrance into a League of Nations. Former Senator Albert Beveridge of Indiana, in his correspondence, had been urging the defeat of a League of Nations for some time. He wrote Theodore Roosevelt and Will Hays that the Republican party would be injured if Wilson's plans were not opposed. He wrote Henry Cabot Lodge, Republican majority leader and chairman of the Senate Committee on Foreign Affairs, that the future of the party was in his hands and that its prospects would be "seriously, perhaps fatally, injured by the acceptance of Mr. Wilson's international plan, or any variation of it."

With the Democrats winning prestige for the successful prosecution of the war, some Republican politicians felt that they could not permit the Democratic party also to write a successful peace; if it did, victory for the Republicans in 1920 would be impossible. When Congress reassembled in December, 1918, partisan attacks were made on the way in which the war had been conducted and on Wilson's decision to attend the Peace Conference in person. Wilson's failure to include any Senator in his Peace Commission rankled in the breasts of some Senators. In the next three months the small group of irreconcilables, unalterably opposed to the League of Nations, seized the initiative in the Senate and assailed the idea of internationalism. The majority of Republicans, who favored the League in some form or other, remained quiet, and the country at large gained the impression that peace was becoming a partisan issue.

Just what role Henry Cabot Lodge was playing in these months and those to come is not entirely clear. His apologists maintain that he was honestly for a League of Nations, with reservations. There is evidence, however, to demonstrate that he was out to defeat American entrance into the League under any circumstance, and that he felt the best way to accomplish this was to attach reservations to the Covenant. Lodge was a partisan Republican, willing to sacrifice ideals to party loyalty. From 1893 to 1924, as a member of the Senate, he had never departed from strict party regularity. According to Nicholas Murray Butler: "The figure that made the least appeal throughout all these years was that of Henry Cabot Lodge. He was able, vain, intensely egotistical, narrow-minded, dogmatic, and provincial."

Lodge was a master of parliamentary technique. By 1919 no one knew better than he the devices to be used to kill a treaty in the Senate. That Lodge would oppose a treaty drawn up by a Democratic President, and one whom he personally hated, seems obvious. In his public statements on the treaty, however, he avoided furnishing any evidence of hostility toward the President. As Republican leader, it would have been unwise for him to attack the President. But in the book that Lodge wrote in 1925, justifying his conduct against the League, "his hatred for Wilson shines forth in its full intensity."

Some of Lodge's personal associates, including a grandson, believe that Lodge sincerely was for the entrance of the United States into the League, with reservations. Yet his daughter, who was close to him during the struggle, once said:

> My father hated and feared the Wilson league, and his heart was really with the irreconcilables. But it was uncertain whether this league could be beaten straight out in this way, and the object of his reservations was to so emasculate the Wilson pact that if it did pass it would be valueless. . . . My father never wanted the Wilson league, and when it was finally defeated, he was like a man from whom a great burden had been lifted.

Lodge, in his book *The Senate and the League of Nations*, admitted that he had told Senator Borah, the leader of the irreconcilables, that "any attempt to defeat the treaty of Versailles with the League by a straight vote in the Senate, if taken immediately, would be hopeless, even if it were desirable," and that the thing to do was "to proceed in the discussion of the treaty by way of amendment and reservation."

There is other information to indicate that Lodge used reservations as a method of preventing American entrance into the League. According to Senator James E. Watson of Indiana, Lodge planned to defeat the League through this technique. Watson said to Lodge, when the latter was planning the fight against the League:

> "I don't see how we are ever going to defeat this proposition. It appears to me that eighty per cent of the people are for it. Fully that percentage of the preachers are right now advocating it, churches are very largely favoring it, all the people who have been burdened and oppressed by this awful tragedy of war and who imagine this opens a way to world peace are for it, and I don't see how it is possible to defeat it." He turned to me and said, "Ah, my dear James, I do not propose to try to beat it by frontal attack, but by the indirect method of reservations." "What do you mean by that?" I asked. "Illustrate it to me." Then he went on to explain how, for instance, we would demand a reservation on the subject of submitting to our government the assumption of a mandate over Armenia, or any other foreign country. "We can debate that for days and hold up the dangers that it will involve and the responsibilities we will assume if we pursue that course, and we can thor-

oughly satisfy the country that it would be a most abhorrent policy for us to adopt. . . ." Senator Lodge then went on for two hours to explain other reservations, and went into the details of the situation that would be thus evolved, until I became thoroughly satisfied that the Treaty could be beaten in that way.[1]

As yet, evidence in the form of letters or memoirs has not come to light which would definitely indicate that the irreconcilables knew that Lodge was fighting for them from the camp of the reservationists. Lodge, however, was close to them during the fight and consulted with them on most major decisions. When ex-Senator Beveridge, for instance, urged on Lodge a more aggressive policy to defeat American entrance into the League, his reply indicated agreement with the end sought, but disagreement as to the method of obtaining it.

The initial plans to attack the League were made by Lodge and Theodore Roosevelt in December, 1918. Although no draft of the League Covenant had yet been published, these two men planned to attack whatever League proposal the President brought home. On the floor of the Senate, on December 21, Lodge made a speech, intended for the ears of the Allies, in which he warned that if certain "extraneous provisions [the Covenant of the League of Nations] were to be found in the treaty of peace, then they would be struck out or amended by the United States Senate."

The text of the Covenant of the League was first published in American papers on February 15, 1919. Immediately the small minority of irreconcilables rallied to the attack. There can be no question that the majority of Republican Senators wanted the United States to join the League. They saw some shortcomings in it, but they felt that it was bigger than the shortcomings. The most active Senators in debate, however, were the opponents of the League. Lodge, as Republican leader, had a difficult time in preserving party unity, but he struck upon a device to accomplish this. On March 3, in the Senate, he introduced a resolution, signed by thirty-seven Republican Senators and Senators-elect of the next Congress, to the effect that the peace treaty should be signed immediately and that the question of a "league of nations to insure the permanent peace of the world should then be taken up for careful and serious consideration." The real purpose of this round robin was to commit more than one third of the Republican Senators to a policy of united, partisan action on the treaty. This policy

---

[1] James E. Watson, *As I Knew Them*, pp. 190–191. The Bobbs-Merrill Company, Indianapolis, 1936. Used by special permission of the Publishers.

was a victory for the irreconcilables, since one of them, Senator Brandegee, had first suggested it to Lodge; but it was not a complete victory. In order to gain the signatures of many Republican Senators, a statement had to be inserted in the resolution that the signers could not accept the constitution of the League "in the form now proposed," the implication of which was that if changes were made, the signers would be free to accept the League.

When, shortly after this round robin, Lodge was discussing future plans with Borah, he had to admit that "the vocal classes of the community, most of the clergymen, the preachers of sermons, a large element in the teaching force of the universities, a large proportion of the newspaper editors, and

Greene in the *New York Evening Telegram*

Nailed!

The Senate, led by Senator Henry Cabot Lodge, defeats American entrance into the League of Nations

finally the men and women who were in the habit of writing and speaking for publication, although by no means thoroughly informed, were friendly to the League as it stood, and were advocating it." A month later Lodge admitted that a majority of the people favored the League.

Outstanding Republicans outside the Senate, such as ex-President Taft and A. Lawrence Lowell, were actively campaigning for the League. When the Covenant of the League was changed by the Peace Conference to meet the principal American objections, it became possible for the signers of the round robin to accept the League. Senator Hitchcock, the acting Democratic leader, had written Wilson in Paris: "A number of Republican Senators who signed Lodge's manifesto on the League of Nations will, in my opinion, vote for it nevertheless, if it is a part of the peace treaty. A still larger number will give it support if certain amendments are made." Taft and Lowell wired Wilson in the same vein, and the American delegation at Paris secured the consent of other nations to such changes as (1) the recognition of the

Monroe Doctrine by name; (2) the exclusion of domestic questions, such as immigration and tariff, from the League's jurisdiction; (3) the recognition of the right of a nation to withdraw from the League; and (4) the recognition of the right of a nation to refuse to accept a mandate over territory.

When the new Congress met in special session on May 19, 1919, the irreconcilable Republicans gained a great advantage. The Republicans controlled the Senate by a majority of two, and thus they had a majority on each committee. In control of the Committee on Foreign Relations, they could delay or hasten action on the treaty. Six of the ten Republican members of the Committee were openly irreconcilable. The other four were Lodge, the chairman, who was probably irreconcilable, McCumber, the most outspoken Republican for the League, and two party regulars, Harding and New, who would follow the party leaders.

Lodge seems to have deliberately packed the Republican membership of the Committee with men hostile to the League. Thus he gained the power to keep the treaty in the Committee's hands, while a campaign was launched to arouse public sentiment against the League. Millionaires H. C. Frick and Andrew W. Mellon contributed money, and a propaganda campaign, consisting of mailings and speaking tours, was started. The following advertisement is an example of the propaganda campaign:

AMERICANS, AWAKE!

Shall We Bind Ourselves to the War Breeding Covenant?
It Impairs American Sovereignty!
Surrenders the Monroe Doctrine!
Flouts Washington's Warning!
Entangles Us in European and Asiatic Intrigues!
Sends Our Boys to Fight throughout the World by Order
    of a League!
The Evil Thing with a Holy Name!

While this minority was working against the League, evidence continued to pile up of the great support that the League had among the people. Thirty-two state legislatures endorsed the League, two others made a conditional endorsement, and thirty-three governors of states endorsed it.

On July 10, 1919, the day after he returned from France, Wilson presented the Treaty of Versailles to the Senate. The Committee on Foreign Affairs kept the treaty in their hands for two months. They had to delay in this way, in order to defeat the treaty, because, as one of the irreconcilables, Senator Moses, later said, "If the rules of the Senate had permitted a quick vote, the Versailles Treaty would have been ratified without reservation." In order to delay action, the Committee read the treaty aloud line by line. This required two weeks. Then the next six weeks were devoted to permitting representatives of national groups which felt that the treaty was not fair to their homelands to vent their rage.

On September 10 the Committee on Foreign Relations presented its majority report to the Senate. The irreconcilables had realized by now that they could not persuade the majority of the Republicans in the Senate to reject the treaty. Not one of the irreconcilables signed a report calling for rejection. Instead they followed the advice of Lodge and proceeded "by way of amendment and reservation." With Lodge, Harding, and New, they recommended forty-five amendments and four reservations to the Covenant of the League. The minority report, filed by six of the seven Democratic members, urged acceptance of the treaty without change. Senator McCumber, one of the Republicans on the Committee, filed his own minority report, in which he rebuked the partisanship of the Republican majority:

> Not one word is said, not a single allusion made, concerning either the great purpose of the League of Nations or the methods by which those purposes are to be accomplished.
>
> Irony and sarcasm have been substituted for argument, and positions taken by the press or individuals outside the Senate seem to command more attention than the treaty itself. It is regrettable that the animosity which centers almost wholly against the League of Nations provisions should have been engendered against a subject so important to the world's welfare. It is regrettable that the consideration of a matter so foreign to any kind of partisanship should be influenced in the country, as well as on the floor of this Senate, by hostility toward or subserviency to the President of the United States. No matter how just may be any antagonism toward President Wilson, the aspirations and hopes of a wounded and bleeding world ought not to be denied because, under the Constitution, the treaty must first be formulated by him.

The majority report did not reflect the sentiment of the Senate. While the treaty was in the Committee, the debates on the floor of the Senate had demonstrated that the majority of the Republicans were going to vote for entrance into the League. Some wanted strong reservations, others mild; but both groups wanted acceptance of the treaty. Since the irreconcilables had failed to produce a majority against the League, their approach now was to hold all Republicans together by a program of amendments or reservations. The Wilson Democrats had two courses of action. They might reach an agreement with the mild reservationists and detach them from the other Republicans, or they could refuse any concessions and possibly win some Republican Senators who would be willing to give up all reservations rather than have the treaty rejected.

It was the latter course of action that the Wilson Democrats decided to follow. Wilson made no suggestion publicly that he might accept mild reservations. To his Senate leader, Hitchcock, he gave a list of reservations that he would accept if necessary, but he took no public step to win the support of the mild-reservationist Republicans. Apparently either he felt that it was not necessary to accept any reservations, or he was afraid that concessions made so early might lead to further demands.

In September the President started on a tour of the nation to arouse the people to vigorous support of the League. On this tour he collapsed and returned to Washington, broken and paralyzed. With his collapse, the most powerful protagonist of the League could fight no more. In a speech delivered just before he was stricken, the President prophetically said to his audience:

Stop for a moment to think about the next war. For I can predict with absolute certainty that within another generation there will be another world war if the nations of the world do not concert the method by which to prevent it. . . . I do not hesitate to say that the war we have just been through, though it was shot through with terror of every kind, is not to be compared with the war we would have to face next time.

The debate in the Senate, following the reports of the Committee on Foreign Relations, was one replete with demagoguery. The opponents of the League pandered to popular and emotional prejudices. They stated that the United States would become entangled in the broils of Europe; that the United States would lose its national sovereignty; that the League was a device to enable the British Empire to rule the world, since each Dominion, as well as Great Britain, had a vote; that the majority of countries in the League would be Catholic and thus the League would be under the Pope. They also tried to rally support by denouncing English activities in Ireland and the wrongs done to China in Shantung. In October, 1919, the voting began on the amendments. The mild reservationists joined with the almost solid Democratic membership, and all the amendments were defeated. On November 7 the voting began on the reservations, and then the mild reservationists joined with the rest of the Republicans to attach the reservations to the treaty. When the treaty, with fourteen reservations, came to a final vote on November 19, it was rejected by a vote of thirty-nine to fifty-five.

Space does not permit a discussion of the fourteen reservations, but a description of three of them will furnish an idea of their tone. Under the League a nation could withdraw on two years' notice, provided it had fulfilled its international obligations. The first reservation stated that Congress was the sole judge as to whether the United States had fulfilled its obligations. The second reservation declared that the United States would not furnish military force on the League's request without the consent of Congress. The fourteenth reservation was aimed at the separate votes given to the various Commonwealths of the British Empire. The reservation stated that the United States would not be bound by any decision in which it did not have equal voice with any other power.

Ratification was supported by the reservationist Senators and was opposed by the irreconcilables in combination with the Wilson Democrats, who voted for rejection in the hope of getting final acceptance of the Covenant, without reservations. McCumber, just before the vote was taken, pleaded with the administration Democrats to accept what could be obtained rather than lose everything; but Wilson sent a letter to them to vote against the treaty with reservations. Wilson did this in the expectation that a favorable vote could be obtained without any reservations, and also in the belief that if the United States placed conditions on its entrance into the League, other nations might do the same and the League would be greatly weakened.

The Senate's action came as a shock to the nation. As one authority has written: "It seemed absurd that the national policy adopted should be the one advocated by only seventeen Senators. Common sense revolted at seeing the votes of seventy-eight Senators to enter the League nullified because they could not agree among themselves on the terms of the entry." Immediately the Senate voted to reconsider the question in the next session. The confusion of the people over the action taken by the Senate can well be imagined from the observations of Ida Tarbell, who made a speaking tour of the West in the interests of the League in the summer of 1919:

As the days went by, I sensed a growing bewilderment at the fight against the League. These people had listened for years to people they honored urging some form of international union against war. They had heard Dr. Jordan and Jane Addams preaching a national council for the prevention of war, President Taft advocating a league to enforce peace. In many of these towns there had been chapters of these societies. . . . With such a background, was it strange that many people in the Northwest should have been puzzled that the Congress of the United States was seemingly more and more determined that we should not join this first attempt of the civilized world to find substitutes for war in international quarrels?[1]

When the demand swept the country for a compromise between the League Democrats and the reservationists, even Senator Lodge felt compelled to go into a conference on the question. He did so, however, from his own admission, with no idea of compromising. He refused to admit that the treaty had been defeated because of verbal differences between the pro-League groups. According to Lodge, the difference between those who supported the treaty and those who opposed it was "not verbal, but vital and essential." By this he could have meant only that the difference between the irreconcilables (of which he seemingly was one) and the administration Democrats was vital, because the difference between the reservationists (strong and mild) and the administration Democrats was one only of a verbal nature or at least of strategy.

A bipartisan conference met to discuss the method of common action of the reservationists and the Wilson Democrats. But this conference failed to work out a plan of action. The irreconcilables and the reservationists continued to vote together to add reservations to the Covenant of the League, which were not essentially different from those of November 19. In spite of the fact that the irreconcilables voted for adding reservations, there was no doubt that they would vote against ratification of the Covenant with these reservations. The question was whether enough Democrats would realize that there was no alternative but to vote for reservations, or the treaty would be defeated. Wilson wrote a letter from his sickbed urging his followers to oppose the treaty with the reservations. He still had faith that the public wanted the League, and he was willing to wait for the approaching Presidential election to serve as a popular referendum on the subject.

[1] *All in the Day's Work*, pp. 353–354. The Macmillan Company, New York, 1939.

The vote on March 19, 1920, on the question of ratification of the Treaty of Versailles with reservations, resulted in a majority for ratification, but nó the requisite two-thirds majority, since forty-nine votes were in favor and thirty-five were opposed. Some Democrats who had voted *against* in November voted *for* this second time, but the administration Democrats who again carried out Wilson's desire that they vote against were numerous enough to defeat the treaty. For the second time the responsibility for defeat lay not alone with the irreconcilables, but also with the League's warmest friends. If Wilson had not been quite so uncompromising in his position, the treaty with reservations could easily have passed.

When Senator James Watson mentioned to Lodge that Wilson might accept the reservations and then the country would be in the League, Lodge's reply was:

"You do not take into consideration the hatred that Woodrow Wilson has for me personally. Never under any set of circumstances in this world could he be induced to accept a treaty with Lodge reservations appended to it!" "But," I replied, "that seems to me to be rather a slender thread on which to hang so great a cause." "A slender thread!" he answered. "Why, it is as strong as any cable with its strands wired and twisted together."

That Lodge carefully estimated and studied Wilson at every step can be seen from Lodge's own book. After admitting that there was a possibility that the treaty might pass with the reservations, he observed: "I also felt convinced that President Wilson would prevent the acceptance of the treaty with the reservations if he possibly could. I based this opinion on the knowledge which I had acquired as to Mr. Wilson's temperament, intentions, and purposes."

Although Woodrow Wilson hoped that the Presidential election of 1920 might serve as a great national referendum on the question of the League, it did not do so. The majority of seven million for Harding cannot be translated into a majority of seven million against the League. The Republican platform, although ambiguous, did advocate the entrance of the United States into an international association of nations. In the platform committee there was a spectacular fight between the pro-League Republicans and the irreconcilables. There was a move to adopt a plank favoring the League with the Lodge reservations, but Lodge prevented this plank from being included. This action of Lodge's tended to demonstrate that he was an irreconcilable and had used reservations only as a technique to defeat the League.

During the campaign Warren G. Harding, on some occasions, inter-preted the plank on membership in an international association of nations as being pro-League and, on other occasions, as being anti-League. This equivocal stand was, of course, designed to confuse the voters and muddle the issue. Near the end of the campaign Harding seemed more and more to favor an international league. All this time the Democrats were campaigning for the League of Nations without reservations. Outstanding Republicans like ex-President Taft and Herbert Hoover campaigned for Harding and made it plain that they considered support of Harding equivalent to support of the League of Nations. On October 14, 1920, thirty-one leading Republicans, including Elihu Root, Charles E. Hughes, Henry L. Stimson, Herbert Hoover, and William Allen White, issued a public statement that the United States, under Harding's leadership, would enter a League of Nations with reservations.

Probably thousands of voters took these men at their word; undoubtedly many pro-League citizens voted for the Republican candidate on the strength of the statement of these men and the occasional pro-League stand of Harding. Calvin Coolidge observed:

I doubt if any particular mandate was given at the last election on the question of the League of Nations and if that was the preponderant issue. In the South, where there was decided opposition to the League, they voted the Democratic ticket. And as far as the League of Nations was concerned, in the North the vote was with equal and even greater preponderance in favor of the Republican ticket. Of course, many men voted thus who were in favor of the League. With them it became simply a question of supporting the Republican or Democratic party. So you can't say that there was a preponderance of votes against the League of Nations.

The fight in the Senate and the events of the campaign of 1920 demonstrated that the American people never had the opportunity to vote squarely on the question of the League of Nations. After Harding took office, he forgot any pledge that he and his party might have made. On August 25, 1921, Congress, by joint resolution, officially ended the war with Germany, and a separate treaty was made between the United States and Germany, which gave the United States all the advantages of the Treaty of Versailles without any of the responsibilities. Only a simple majority in each house is necessary to pass a treaty by a joint resolution of both houses. Had the Treaty of Versailles been accorded a vote by joint resolution, it would have passed the Senate in the March, 1920, voting.

A year before his death, on the eve of Armistice Day in 1923, Woodrow Wilson made his only speech as an ex-President. It was his farewell to the world, and he spoke in the spirit of tragic prophecy:

The anniversary of Armistice Day should stir us to great exaltation of spirit . . . although the stimulating memories of that happy time of triumph are forever marred and embittered for us by the shameful fact that when the victory was won—won, be it remembered, chiefly by the indomitable spirit and ungrudging sacrifices of our own incomparable soldiers—we turned our backs upon our associates and refused to bear any responsible part in the administration of peace or the firm and permanent establishment of the results of the war—won at so terrible a cost of life and treasure—and withdrew into a sullen and selfish isolation which is deeply ignoble because manifestly cowardly and dishonorable.

This must always be a source of deep mortification to us and we shall inevitably be forced by the moral obligations of freedom and honor to retrieve that fatal error and assume once more the role of courage, self-respect and helpfulness which every true American must wish to regard as our natural part in the affairs of the world.

That we should have thus done a great wrong to civilization at one of the most critical turning points in the history of the world is the more to be deplored because every anxious year that has followed has made the exceeding need for such services as we might have rendered more and more evident and more and more pressing, as demoralizing circumstances which we might have controlled have gone from bad to worse.

SELECTED BIBLIOGRAPHY

The standard work on the Peace Conference is H. W. V. Temperley and others, *History of the Peace Conference.*

R. S. Baker, *Woodrow Wilson and the World Settlement* and *What Wilson Did at Paris*; E. M. House and Charles Seymour (Eds.), *What Really Happened at Paris*; T. A. Bailey, *Woodrow Wilson and the Lost Peace*, all valuable; David H. Miller, *My Diary at the Conference of Paris*, very useful; Allan Nevins, *Henry White*, a well-written biography of a member of the American peace delegation.

D. F. Fleming, *The United States and the League of Nations, 1918–1920*, a detailed study of importance; Clarence A. Berdahl, "Myths about the Peace Treaties of 1919–1920," *American Scholar* (summer, 1942), Vol. 2, a valuable analysis of the Senate vote; W. S. Holt, *Treaties Defeated by the Senate*, and T. A. Bailey, *Woodrow Wilson and the Great Betrayal*, valuable.

H. S. Commager (Ed.), *Documents of American History*, pp. 331, 338–340, 352–353, contains source material.

XXXI

The "Roaring Twenties"

ARMISTICE DAY, November 11, 1918, was welcomed in the United States with great enthusiasm. In New York City eight hundred Barnard College girls snake-danced on Morningside Heights, and pretty girls kissed every soldier they saw. Offices and stores were closed, and the people gathered in the streets, blowing horns and creating a terrific din. The mood of the crowds was that of mingled exuberance and hate. The Kaiser was burned in effigy, and on Broadway a boy drew pictures of the Kaiser on the sidewalk so that people could step on them. The postwar era was launched in an environment supercharged with emotion and intolerance, and Socialist and other radical meetings were broken up by mobs which contained many ex-servicemen.

In the 1920's many Americans were excessively nationalistic and intolerantly patriotic. For instance, the door was virtually closed to immigrants by the adoption of the quota system. Immigrants from southern Europe were criticized as poor additions to the country, while the virtues of the Nordic stocks were highly praised. Furthermore, all unconventional political doctrines were attacked, and there was an extraordinary glorification of the "100 per cent American." In many other parts of the world, however,—in the Balkans and in Fascist Italy for example,— intense nationalism went much farther than in the United States.

What amounted to a high degree of fear swept through the nation for several years after the war. Many people seriously believed that a Red revolution was about to break out in the country, and rumors of marching Bolshevist armies filled the air. The newspapers, day after day, headlined the news of strikes and antiradical riots, and a jury in Indiana acquitted a man for killing an alien because he had cried, "To hell with the United States." The Vice-President of the United States stated that a dangerous example of radicalism was furnished when girl debaters of Radcliffe College upheld the affirmative in a debate on the topic "*Resolved*, That the recognition of labor unions by employers is essential to successful collective bargaining." A liberal English writer observed:

No one who was in the United States, as I chanced to be in the autumn of 1919, will forget the feverish condition of the public mind at that time. It was hagridden by the spectre of Bolshevism. . . . "Radical" covered the most innocent departure from conventional thought with a suspicion of desperate purpose.

During 1919 there were a number of serious strikes. In the inflation that developed in 1919, prices rose steadily while wages lagged behind, but many businessmen were in no mood to listen to the workers' demands. Bombarded during the war with spy stories, they were ready to believe that labor's struggle for better wages was the beginning of a planned, Bolshevist, proletarian revolution. Strikes swept through the steel, coal, textile, and railroad industries. Four million workers were on strike at various times in the year 1919. The attempt to organize the steel industry and the resulting strike attracted wide attention. The press ignored the strikers' side, but the Interchurch World Movement investigated conditions and found that the workers' grievances were extremely real. The church group revealed that the average work week was 68.7 hours and that wages were low. This group also showed that the employers used spies in the union and stirred up ethnic hatreds among the workers to prevent unified action by playing one group against another—the Italians, for instance, against the Serbs. The Bolshevist label was pinned on the strikers by the steel magnates, and the public uncritically accepted this characterization. As a result, the report of the Interchurch World Movement fell by the wayside, and the strike collapsed.

There can be no doubt that there were radicals in the twenties who wanted to change the system of private capitalism. The remnants of the I.W.W., the Socialists, the Communists, and the followers of Townley's Nonpartisan League constituted this radical horde. These groups, however, were an absurdly small minority of the American people, hardly more than two tenths of 1 per cent of the adult population—too few to make up a revolutionary mass movement; but the employer did not consider that in his fears. Frederick Lewis Allen has written, in *Only Yesterday:*

He, too, had come out of the war with his fighting blood up, ready to lick the next thing that stood in his way. He wanted to get back to business and enjoy his profits. Labor stood in his way and threatened his profits . . . he developed a fervent belief that 100-per-cent Americanism and the welfare of God's Own Country and Loyalty to the Teachings of the Founding Fathers implied the right of the business man to kick the union organizer out of his workshop . . . he was quite ready to believe that a struggle of American laboring-men for better wages was the beginning of an armed rebellion directed by Lenin and Trotsky, and that behind every innocent professor who taught that there were arguments for as well as against socialism there was a bearded rascal from eastern Europe with a money bag in one hand and a smoking bomb in the other.[1]

A series of bomb explosions in 1919 heightened the fear of radicalism. Thirty-six bombs were discovered in the mail addressed to prominent people such as Attorney-General Palmer, Justice Holmes, Judge Landis, J. P. Morgan, and John D. Rockefeller. One bomb damaged the house of Attorney-General Palmer in Washington. And at noon on September 16, 1920, a bomb exploded in front of the building occupied by J. P. Morgan and Company, on Wall Street, causing frightful damage. Thirty people were killed, hundreds injured, and windows smashed for blocks around. Mr. Morgan and his partners escaped injury; the victims of the explosion were clerks, stenographers, and messengers. The bomb went off in a horse-drawn wagon that had been left in front of the Morgan building. For years detectives followed up the clues, but were never able to discover the perpetrators of this dastardly deed. By this time the "Great Red Scare" was abating somewhat, and the people realized that such a deed was the work of a small group of fanatics rather than of a large segment of the left-wing movement.

The fear of radicalism was increased in September, 1919, when the Boston police went on strike. The police, who received a salary of $1100, which brought very little at the high prices of 1919, formed a union and joined the American Federation of Labor. Police Commissioner Curtis, of old Boston stock and a "stiff-necked martinet," had forbidden the police to join any outside organization. When they disobeyed his order, he suspended nineteen leaders of the union, most of them being police officers. A committee appointed by Mayor Peters of Boston proposed a compromise, but Curtis refused to budge. The police, many of them "fighting Irish," walked out on strike on September 9, 1919. One writer has observed:

[Commissioner Curtis] lived on another planet, in another era. As an industrialist he had an early Victorian habit of hiring and firing when and where and how he chose. But Curtis forgot that policemen and certainly higher police officials are embryonic statesmen, not operatives. They are not to be fired with impunity. Mayor Peters informed the Governor that when the nineteen officers were discharged the force would follow them out of office. The Commissioner felt sure the force would stand by him; probably

---

[1] Harper & Brothers, New York, 1931.

reasoning from a bread-and-butter angle, not knowing politics, certainly un-mindful of the Irish . . . the Governor, feeling profoundly his duty to maintain law and order, stood by the Commissioner in all of the preliminary maneuvers leading to the strike.[1]

With the city left without police, hoodlums smashed windows and looted some stores. On the following day Governor Calvin Coolidge called out the National Guard. Public opinion was overwhelmingly against the police. Mr. Curtis then proceeded to organize a new police force. Samuel Gompers wired Governor Coolidge, protesting the autocratic action of Curtis in suspending the union leaders; but Coolidge replied that there was "no right to strike against the public safety by anybody, anywhere, any time." Overnight this made Coolidge a national figure. Governor Coolidge could have prevented any violence by calling out the National Guard as soon as the police had left their posts, but the violence dramatized to the public what Calvin Coolidge felt was the heart of the problem, that a policeman cannot strike; he can only desert. In his *Autobiography* Coolidge remarked, "This was the important contribution I made to the tactics of the situation which has never been fully realized." With the national spotlight on him as a result of his actions in the strike, Coolidge's career took a turn which landed him in the White House.

Many ordinary citizens resorted to direct action in dealing with "dangerous radicals." Socialist clubs and newspapers were raided and destroyed, parades were broken up, and riots occurred when Socialists attempted to speak. Some states passed laws so drastic that any member of a left-wing party could be put in jail, and the American Civil Liberties Union was extremely busy defending case after case under these laws. A. Mitchell Palmer, Attorney-General of the United States, stepped into the fray. To head off a great coal strike, he secured an injunction restraining the leaders of the union from furthering a strike. Then Palmer sponsored a series of raids in which "Communist" leaders were rounded up and deported to Russia. A number of alleged "Communists" actually were anarchists, who did not find the climate of Soviet Russia at all favorable to their position. On New Year's Day, 1920, Mr. Palmer's aides raided Communist meetings all over the country and put the people arrested in jail. Over six thousand men were arrested in all and were left in jail for weeks, frequently without their

[1]W. A. White, *A Puritan in Babylon*, pp. 154–155. The Macmillan Company, New York, 1938.

knowing the charge made against them. Eventually a large number of them were released for want of any evidence to prove that they were Communists. The fear of radicalism went so far even that the New York legislature refused to admit five duly elected Socialists to their seats, and the House of Representatives in Washington barred a Wisconsin Socialist who also had been legally elected to office.

In April, 1920, during the height of the Red scare, a paymaster of a shoe factory in South Braintree, Massachusetts, was murdered. Two Italians with anarchistic leanings, Nicola Sacco and Bartolomeo Vanzetti, were convicted on extremely weak evidence. Since these men had radical ideas, the judge, the jury, and the community were prejudiced against them from the start. Liberals and radicals all over the world protested and made the case a *cause célèbre*. For seven years the men languished in jail, while attempts were made to have a new trial. In 1927 public opinion forced Governor Fuller to appoint a committee made up of President Lowell of Harvard, President Stratton of the Massachusetts Institute of Technology, and Judge Robert Grant to investigate the case. This committee reported, on even thinner evidence, that the verdict was just. On August 22, 1927, amidst a world-wide cry of protest, these two men went to the electric chair.

Far more destructive of civil liberties and democratic principles than the work of certain branches of the government was the activity of professional "super"-patriotic societies. The Allied Patriotic Societies, the American Defense Society, and the National Civic Federation, among others, were professional "Red-baiting" societies that even charged the liberal *Nation* and *New Republic* magazines with being "revolutionary." The National League of Women Voters, the Federal Council of Churches, and the Foreign Policy Association were placed under suspicion of being dangerously radical; Rabbi Stephen S. Wise, Oswald G. Villard, and Jane Addams were viewed as tainted with radicalism; movie stars like Will Rogers were charged with having their names in "Communistic" files; and a group of California "super"-patriots reported that they disliked Sinclair Lewis's novel *Main Street* because it "created a distaste for the conventional good life of the American." The effect of such statements was to frighten people from independent thought and action. In order to get on in business or professional activities one had to conform and could not afford to be looked upon as radical or even liberal. A writer in *Harper's Magazine*, in 1922, observed that, as a result of this antiliberal movement,

America is no longer a free country in the old sense; and liberty is, increasingly, a mere rhetorical figure. . . . No thinking citizen, I venture to say, can express in freedom more than a part of his honest convictions . . . free speech is choked off in one direction or another.

Old ladies of both sexes discovered, during the Red scare, that they could defeat whatever they wanted to defeat by charging it with radicalism. The hysteria that was created was not unlike the hysteria that Hitler was able to whip up in Germany against the pacifists and the liberals by the same technique of smearing them with the taint of "Communism." The American people, however, recovered from the Red scare early in the twenties and turned to other things. When, in the decade of the New Deal, Elizabeth Dilling published a book called the *Red Network*, and listed such a middle-class Republican liberal as William Allen White as a dangerous "Red," the public was seemingly not interested.

THE REVIVAL OF NATIVISM

Part and parcel of the Red scare and growing out of the same psychological background was the glorification of the "100 per cent American." Outbreaks against the Jews, the Roman Catholics, and the Negroes were frequent. Not only radicals, but any group that seemed alien or "un-American" to many of the dominant white Protestants was viewed with suspicion. Hundreds of thousands of Negroes had left the South to work in Northern factories during the war. They were compelled to live in the poorest slum areas and were excluded from many theaters and restaurants. Negro boys who had fought in the American army "to make the world safe for democracy" found that after the war they were expected to accept prewar restrictions and segregation. Naturally, after the war, some Negroes resented being placed in the category of "second-class" citizens and deprived of many of their rights.

One summer day in 1919 a Negro boy was swimming at a Chicago beach. Mutual understanding had set part of this beach off for whites and another part for colored people. The boy drifted across the invisible line, and he was stoned. He let go of the log with which he was swimming and drowned. A fight started on the beach over the stoning, and it set off a race riot throughout the city. For a week there were gang raids through the Negro area, with white mobs beating up and terrorizing Negro citizens. Negroes in defense fought back. When order returned, fifteen whites and twenty-three Negroes were dead, more than five hundred people had been injured, and a thousand had been left homeless by the destruction of property. In the following year another major race riot broke out in Tulsa, Oklahoma.

The Jews too found that they were regarded with great suspicion and hostility. Absurd charges that the Jews were plotting to subjugate the world to their rule appeared in Henry Ford's *Dearborn Independent*; some landlords refused to rent to Jewish tenants, and some schools refused to admit Jewish students. At the same time, the Catholics were charged with being under the control of the "foreign Pope."

It was in this atmosphere that the second Ku Klux Klan rose to power. The second Klan was the spiritual descendant of the Know-Nothing Movement of the 1850's. Its strength was that it was all things to all men. In its membership there were a few alarmed patriots, some fanatics, some political schemers; but the rank and file were just average Americans who would join any patriotic, secret society. The modern Klan was founded in 1915 by William J. Simmons of Atlanta, Georgia. In 1920 the organization assumed national proportions. Two figures—Edward Y. Clarke and Mrs. Elizabeth Tyler—saw the commercial possibilities in the Klan, and they sold it to the public. The ten-dollar membership fee was divided, four dollars going to the local Kleagle who sold the membership, one dollar and a half to the state headquarters, and the rest to Atlanta. But this commercial aspect alone cannot explain the stupendous growth of the Klan, which, by 1924, had between four and five million members. The official Klan literature reflected the average middle-class mind in its assertions of "100 per cent Americanism." The objects of the Klan, according to its constitution, were

> To unite white male persons, native-born Gentile citizens of the United States of America, who owe no allegiance of any nature to any foreign government, nation, institution, sect, ruler, person, or people; whose morals are good, whose reputations and vocations are exemplary . . . to cultivate and promote patriotism toward our Civil Government . . . to shield the sanctity of the home and the chastity of womanhood; to maintain forever white supremacy, to teach and faithfully inculcate a high spiritual philosophy through an exalted ritualism, and by a practical devotion to conserve, protect, and maintain the distinctive institutions, rights, privileges, principles, traditions and ideals of a pure Americanism.

The Jew, the Catholic, and the immigrant were excluded from membership. Although the Klan was a national organization, actually the local units were laws unto themselves, writing threatening letters to their opponents and whipping and tarring and feathering them. In one area the Klan might operate against Negroes, in another against Jews, in another against labor organizers, and in another against opponents of prohibition.

The Klan was essentially a village and small-town organization. It drew its membership from descendants of the old American stock residing in areas hardly disturbed by the immigration and industrialism of the post-Civil-War period. With its mysterious signs, its queer names like *Kleagle*, *Wizard*, and *Goblin*, its fantastic costumes, and its secret ritual, it offered relief from the deadly monotony of small-town life. The need of an escape from the drabness of much of rural life played no small part in the appeal of the Klan. Its cheap moral idealism filled a need not met by the business, social, or civic life of Main Street America. It tended to be the refuge of the mediocre man. Not very successful in business or in a profession, a man could join the Klan and become a Knight of the Invisible Empire for ten dollars. Surely knighthood had never been offered before at such a bargain! A man who had been "abused" all day by his customers, in the evening could adopt the disguise of the Klan and be revenged under the cloak of secrecy.

The Klan exerted a demoralizing influence upon the community and national life of the United States. It demanded like-mindedness, and its secret, terroristic methods nullified the democratic process. The non-Klan people in a community frequently feared to speak out in opposition because of the threatened reprisals. There were times when, in Oregon, Oklahoma, Texas, Arkansas, Indiana, Ohio, and California, the Klan had great political power. While the organization was at its height, Republican editor William Allen White characterized the menace of the movement in the following words:

To make a case against a birthplace, a religion, or a race is wickedly un-American and cowardly. The whole trouble with the Ku Klux Klan is that it is based upon such deep foolishness that it is bound to be a menace to good government in any community. Any man fool enough to be Imperial Wizard would have power without responsibility and both without any sense. That is social dynamite.

American institutions, our courts, our legislators, our executive officers are strong enough to keep the peace and promote justice and good will in the community. If they are not, then the thing to do is to change these institutions and do it quickly, but always legally. For a self-constituted body of moral idiots who would substitute the findings of the Ku Klux Klan for the processes of law, to try to better conditions would be a most un-American outrage which every good citizen should resent.

The Klan, conceived in the fear that the American way was in jeopardy, perpetuated fear by its cruelties and its crimes. After 1924, when middle-class America regained its balance, the movement rapidly declined. During the 1930's the Klan occasionally rode again, but never with the numbers or power that it had from 1920 to 1924.

THE BALLYHOO YEARS

When some two million soldiers returned from France, they found evidences everywhere that a new way of life was developing in America. Ahead of them were such things as radio broadcasting, bathing-beauty contests, racketeers, speak-easies where women drank publicly with men, the Sacco-Vanzetti case, the Teapot Dome scandal, the Florida real-estate boom, companionate marriage, broker's-loan statistics, and true-confession magazines and dull sex stories published by Bernarr MacFadden. Names like those of Al Capone, Daddy Browning and his "Peaches," Charles A. Lindbergh, Gene Tunney, and Bobby Jones were to be prominent in this decade. The decade began with women wearing skirts just six inches from the ground, with the beauty-parlor industry in its infancy, with the wearing of rouge still considered to be evidence of a scarlet career, and with women wearing long hair and a superabundance of petticoats. By the end of the decade women were wearing skirts above the knee and bobbed hair; automobiles had become not only a menace to pedestrians, but a place where lovers escaped the supervision of chaperons; and the beauty-parlor industry was a flourishing institution. It was a decade of tinsel, bright lights, flappers, bathing-beauty contests, and gang wars over bootlegging. It was an unreal world of nonsense that died in the stock-market crash of 1929.

By 1921 the Red scare had collapsed. It was believed that Communism was not a pressing threat. By this time, also, there was a great deal less enthusiasm for government surveillance because violators of prohibition felt that they also were being watched. In 1921 the country turned to fads. The mind of the average American was tired of the great intellectual effort of the Progressive era and of the war. Now the average American refused to concern himself with serious problems. Instead he sought escape in many trivial ways. Fads like mah-

Brown Brothers

Henry Ford

Keystone

Charles A. Lindbergh

Brown Brothers

Gene Tunney

Press Association

Babe Ruth

Wide World

Jack Dempsey

Brown Brothers

Bobby Jones

Some of the Leading Personalities of the Decade
Following the First World War

Rudolph Valentino

Underwood-Stratton

Mary Pickford

Brown Brothers

Douglas Fairbanks

Underwood-Stratton

jongg and the crossword puzzle swept the nation. Murder trials received an unhealthful amount of attention. Most Americans knew about the Hall-Mills murder case of 1922, but few cared or read about the basic problems of society. "The business of America" in this era, as Calvin Coolidge so succinctly put it, was "business." Next to business came sports. In typical American fashion sport was made a business and became highly competitive. The subjects of politics, religion, and education did not receive the same attention that was focused on sports. College football blossomed into a major industry. Great stadiums were built, and the greatest crowds that had watched athletic spectacles since the days of Rome filled them week after week. An amateur sport was transformed into a commercial amusement business run by coaches and alumni for the benefit of the sporting public. Hundreds of thousands of dollars were spent yearly on equipment, stadiums, coaching, and travel. Teams went touring for weeks at a time, the student-players acquiring, perhaps, what academic learning they could en route. In the fall of 1927 thirty million spectators paid fifty million dollars in gate receipts to watch this sport. Clever publicity offices built football-players like Red Grange of Illinois, Albie Booth of Yale, and the "Four Horsemen" of Notre Dame into dashing heroes for the public.

World-series baseball also attracted immense crowds. From spring to autumn millions of Americans followed their favorite teams and players in the American League or the National League. Then, for a week, came the struggle between the two top teams in the leagues. In 1923 the attendance at the world series totaled three hundred thousand people, and the receipts were over a million dollars. During the 1928 series one game alone attracted sixty thousand fans and netted two hundred and twenty-four thousand dollars. Stars like Babe Ruth of the New York Yankees, Walter Johnson of the Washington Senators, and Ty Cobb of the Detroit Tigers were valuable gate attractions and were much better known nationally than United States Senators and Representatives.

Prize fighting ranked next to football and baseball in popular appeal. Jack Dempsey was the crowned king of the fighting world, and he drew million-dollar gates. Weeks before the fights newspapers carried hundreds of stories about the gladiators. In 1926, when Gene Tunney defeated Dempsey, the public paid $1,895,000 for admission. The return engagement of these two men, in the following year, drew a gate of more than $2,650,000. The man who promoted prize fighting from an eclipse to a respectable affair was Tex Rickard, and with the attraction of the aggressive Dempsey, he made it another major American sport. During the twenties other sports also gained in popularity. Tennis and golf, for instance, ceased to be rich men's games. Basketball remained the favorite indoor sport, and ice hockey attracted more and more people. The sport of swimming received a great stimulus when Gertrude Ederle and Mrs. Corson swam the English Channel. The development of the one-piece bathing suit, growing more and more abbreviated as the decade continued, made it possible for women to become swimmers rather than just bathers.

The whole sports epic of the twenties suffered a decline in the depression years after 1929. When the economy of the United States received a boom after the outbreak of the Second World War, the sports world received another impetus. The ballyhoo included the touting of sport stars who were in the armed services. Gene Tunney, however, navy director of physical education, cautioned against a revival by the armed services of the gaudy sports exhibitions of the 1920's, since this would, he said, "turn the training of men as military warriors into a sideshow. If professional athleticism could win a war we would have won this by now. We led the world in such nonsense for 20 years. I am speaking from experience. I was a beneficiary of that foolishness—I made $1,000,000 in 30 minutes. But we weren't at war then. Our values were different. Now we're in a life and death struggle."

Another type of entertainment that attracted wide attention in the twenties was dancing. Dancing had long been an important phase of American life, but this decade witnessed rapid changes in dancing techniques. Instead of the waltz and the fox trot came all types of hops, wiggles, and squirms. One historian has written:

> This culminated in a climax of folly—the "dance-marathon" in which heroic imbeciles entered an endurance contest, keeping their feet in slow motion for several days and nights. Then the pace quickened; instead of the close hug and slow glide the dancers indulged in the violent acrobatics of the "Charleston" and the "black bottom" to the imminent peril of neighboring shins.[1]

Phonographs, radios, and jazz bands supplied music for the new dances. Ragtime music became the folk music of the decade, and Paul Whiteman, the "King of Jazz," best explained why this happened:

[1] P. W. Slosson, *The Great Crusade and After, 1914–1928*, p. 282. The Macmillan Company, New York, 1931.

Jazz is the folk music of the machine age. There was every reason why this music sprang into being about 1915. . . . In this country especially the rhythm of machinery, the over rapid expansion of a great country endowed with tremendous natural energies and wealth have brought about a pace and scale of living unparalleled in history. Is it any wonder that the popular music of this land should reflect these modes of living? Every other art reflects them.

THE REVOLT OF THE YOUNGER GENERATION

A revolt that had nothing to do with Communism was taking place in the postwar years. The sons and daughters of middle-class families, not alien agitators, were the proponents of the movement. It was not the Constitution, but the moral code that was endangered. Among the dicta of this old moral code were those that girls should not smoke and, of course, should not drink and certainly should not show the effects of alcohol; that girls were made of finer stuff than men and men should act accordingly; that "good" girls never succumbed to the lure of sex, but looked forward to a romantic love affair which would lead to the altar. The boys and girls, however, were wrecking this Victorian moral code. Dresses were going up rapidly, not to stop until they reached just above the knee; dresses were growing thinner; short-sleeved and sleeveless dresses were prominent; occasionally stockings were rolled below the knee; corsets were being abandoned. "Nice" girls were smoking cigarettes in public, and they were drinking. Tales were current of daughters of spotless parents getting drunk—"blotto," the younger generation called it—on the contents of hip-flasks, created by prohibition. Petting and necking in parked automobiles were upsetting dignified matrons. F. Scott Fitzgerald, in *This Side of Paradise* and *The Great Gatsby*, explained to the mothers and fathers just what his generation was doing.

The leaders of the old moral code rallied to its defense. The President of the University of Florida asserted, "The low-cut gowns, the rolled hose and short skirts are born of the Devil and his angels and are carrying the present and future generations to chaos and destruction." In 1921 the Utah legislature was considering a bill forbidding dresses that showed more than two inches of the neck or that accentuated the lines of the figure.

This revolt soon spread to men and women of all ages. There were many forces at work that accounted for the changing moral code. The war had shattered old values and social patterns and had created a spirit destructive of conventions. Two million American men in Europe had seen different moral codes, and willing *"mademoiselles"* had been plentiful in France. American girls who went across as nurses and war workers came under the influence of European standards, too. When these men and women returned, they were unwilling to settle back into the old routine. Their life of excitement and supercharged emotions, engendered by the ever present danger of death, left them skeptical of the standards of their elders. Another factor was the growing independence of women. In 1920 women won the right to vote, and the problem of housekeeping grew easier with the modern apartment, the can-opener, the spread of delicatessen stores, and the increase of electric appliances. Women were now free to do new things. Many went to work during the war and continued working afterward. They went not only into the old-time jobs open to women, such as teaching, but into new jobs in newspapers and writing; they ran tearooms, sold real estate, opened dress shops, and worked in department stores. With women acquiring economic independence, control of their activities by parents or husbands naturally declined; unmarried daughters left the family and went to live in apartments.

Still another factor in the revolt against the moral code was the popularity of psychoanalysis and the teachings of Sigmund Freud. The younger generation, interpreting Freud in their own way, talked about sex as the central and pervasive force which influenced human beings. To be mentally healthy, they argued, one must have an unrestrained and uninhibited sex life. One must obey one's libido. Freudian jargon —inferiority complex, sadism, masochism, etc.—was heard everywhere. Among the remaining forces that aided the revolt were prohibition, the automobile, movies, and sex magazines. Evasions of prohibition were widespread. The bootlegger and the speak-easy developed to serve the drinking public. The automobile too aided the newer freedom. The closed car was a room that could be moved to a secluded spot and thus afford escape from parental supervision. A judge of a juvenile court went so far as to charge that the automobile had become a "house of prostitution on wheels."

Lurid motion pictures and sex magazines with suggestive stories added to the flame of the revolt. One movie, for instance, was advertised as offering "brilliant men, beautiful jazz babies, champagne baths, midnight revels, petting parties in the purple dawn, all ending in one terrific smashing climax that makes you gasp." When the forces of morality objected to this trend in the movies, the producers appointed Will Hays, Harding's Postmaster-General, as arbiter of morals. According to Frederick Lewis Allen, in *Only Yesterday:*

> The result of Mr. Hays's labors was to make the moral ending as obligatory as in the confession magazines, to smear over sexy pictures with pious platitudes, and to blacklist for motion-picture production many a fine novel and play which, because of its very honesty, might be construed as seriously or intelligently questioning the traditional sex ethics of the small town. Mr. Hays, being something of a genius, managed to keep the churchmen at bay. Whenever the threats of censorship began to become ominous he would promulgate a new series of moral commandments for the producers to follow.[1]

The sex magazines meanwhile offered stories entitled "What I Told My Daughter the Night before Her Marriage" and "Watch Your Step-Ins." MacFadden's *True Story Magazine* had three hundred thousand readers in 1923 and almost two million in 1926.

A new frankness came into conversation and literature. Words like *damn* and *hell* were used in polite conversation, in the theater, and in literature, though they were generally taboo in such contexts in prewar days. Popular plays, like *What Price Glory* and *Strange Interlude*, were filled with epithets or stories of illicit love affairs which would not have been acceptable before the war. Novels like *An American Tragedy* and *The Sun Also Rises* treated sex openly and in defiance of the old Victorian code. Part of the revolution against morals and manners was the revolt of the high-brows. Sinclair Lewis, in *Babbitt* and *Main Street*, objected to the emotional and aesthetic starvation of American life, and portrayed the meanness, ugliness, and cultural bankruptcy of the small town. H. L. Mencken, in his *American Mercury* magazine, criticized Babbitts and reformers and denounced the low tastes of the mass of Americans. Realistic writers like Theodore Dreiser, Sherwood Anderson, and Sinclair Lewis found a champion in Mencken. John Dos Passos and Ernest Hemingway published novels like *The 42nd Parallel*, *The Big Money*, and *The Sun Also Rises*. These writers were of the generation that had emerged from the war and the collapse of Wilsonian idealism with their values shattered. They were repelled by the apparent meaninglessness of industrial America. Both men wrote, in these books, about love as though it were an obscene joke. Joseph Wood Krutch, in analyzing the spirit of the times, has observed:

[1]Harper & Brothers, New York, 1931.

Freedom has come, but with it a certain lessened sense of the importance of the passions that are thus freely indulged; and, if love has come to be less often a sin, it has come also to be less often a supreme privilege. If one turns to the smarter of these novelists who describe the doings of the more advanced set of those who are experimenting with life—to, for example, Mr. Aldous Huxley or Mr. Ernest Hemingway—one will discover in their tragic farces the picture of a society which is at bottom in despair because, though it is more completely absorbed in the pursuit of love than in anything else, it has lost the sense of any ultimate importance inherent in the experience which preoccupies it.[1]

This new moral code was born in disillusionment and bitterness. The generation was an unhappy one. The old values were shattered, and no new values appeared to replace them. Romantic love was cynically questioned. After 1928, however, a new code began to appear. The obsession with sex began to disappear, and the revolutionists began to adjust to the world. After that time the freer and franker life was continued, but in a more graceful and less blatant fashion.

PROHIBITION

The Eighteenth Amendment passed Congress easily in 1917 and was ratified by the necessary three fourths of the states by January, 1919. A year later national prohibition went into effect. A long period of agitation by the drys had preceded the adoption of the amendment. By 1914 prohibition by state law or by local-option legislation was in operation over one half the population of the country. Rural areas and small towns were the strength of the dry cause; cities were the stronghold of the wets. During the war the need to save grains for food led Congress to prohibit the manufacture of intoxicating beverages. Before this wartime restriction could be removed, the Eighteenth Amendment had blanketed the nation. A powerful pressure group, the Anti-Saloon League, had for years opposed any candidate for political office who was not a dry. Backed by the rural areas and the evangelical churches, the League demonstrated to Congress that public sentiment favored national action against the wets. Although the charge was later made that prohibition was slipped over while two million men were in France, actually the dry forces had enough areas already under their control to make the movement irresistible. Hardly had the amendment gone into effect, however, when the dry cause suffered an amazing

[1] *The Modern Temper*, p. 97. Harcourt, Brace and Company, New York, 1929.

relapse. The same type of emotional reaction that was affecting other phases of life struck the prohibition cause, and prohibition soon came to be violated in many ways.

Candidate Hoover Trying to Win the Votes of Both Wets and Drys in the 1928 Campaign

A long coast line and a long land border allowed smugglers to flourish; druggists, permitted to sell alcohol on doctors' orders, frequently misused prescriptions; alcohol manufactured for industrial purposes was redistilled and sold to bootleggers; and home manufacturing — "home-brewing" — and old-fashioned moonshining quickly developed. To grapple with this problem, the Federal government had too few prohibition agents. State and local governments gave little aid to Federal officials. Many times police and politicians were paid by bootleggers for protection against the enforcement of the law. Furthermore, public opinion gradually turned against the act, which made the problem of enforcement still more difficult.

The Canadian border provided bootleg liquor with an easy entrance into the United States. Fast trucks made it possible to convey great quantities of liquor across the border and then elude the prohibition agents. Bootlegging became so profitable an occupation that it quickly developed into a highly organized industry. In Chicago, Johnny Torrio, of the Four Deuces Club, saw the big money in organized bootlegging and set out to secure a monopoly of the business in the city. The spread of monopoly in other forms of business enterprise spurred the drive for monopoly in bootlegging. A gang of killers could drive out competition and force speak-easy proprietors to buy only Torrio liquor. A young hoodlum, Al Capone, was brought from New York to head Torrio's organization. Before long Torrio faded out, and Capone became the "big shot." He made millions. He took control of the suburb of Cicero and installed his mayor in office. Rival gangs threatened Capone's power, and this touched off a series of wholesale gang murders that made Chicago notorious. The murdering reached its climax on Saint Valentine's Day, 1929, when seven members of a rival gang were slaughtered in a garage on North Clark Street. All told, there were about five hundred gang murders in Chicago during the decade.

The Prohibition Enforcement Act, or Volstead Act, was the spark that stimulated the growth of gangsters. Automobiles also played a part, making it easy for gangsters to escape, and new deadly weapons increased their power. By 1929 Al Capone was an international

Talburt in *Cleveland Press*, 1933

Old Man River Keeps Rollin' Along

figure. Not only was he in charge of the Chicago liquor traffic, but he was supposed to have control of the sources of supply from Canada to Florida. He traveled around Chicago in an armored car; he had an estate in Miami; when he attended the theater, a bodyguard of eighteen men accompanied him; and it was charged that high politicians and judges took orders from him. The Federal government finally caught Capone, in the 1930's, on an income-tax-evasion charge and put him in jail.

Gang rule and violence, of course, were not restricted to Chicago. Many other cities witnessed the same developments. From the liquor traffic the gangs moved in and took control of gambling establishments, vice dens, and dance halls. Then came the rackets. Gangsters took over labor unions by force and exploited both the workers and the employers by threats of violence if their demands for money were not met. Gangsters organized cleaning-and-dyeing associations, garage associations, and window-washing associations. By 1929, in Chicago, for instance, there were ninety-one rackets in all. Businessmen were forced to join these associations, or their places of business would be bombed, their workingmen beaten up, and their delivery trucks destroyed. When prohibition was repealed, the bootleggers went bodily over to racketeering and posed a grave problem for Americans in the 1930's.

The price of liquor jumped considerably during the prohibition era, and the quality deteriorated. Unscrupulous bootleggers sometimes failed to remove all poison from their product, and the result was death from wood-alcohol poisoning. Bourke Cockran of New York, arguing against William Jennings Bryan's advocacy of prohibition in the 1920 Democratic convention, observed: "These ladies and gentlemen speak as if the use of liquor has been abolished by this amendment. It has not, but there is this difference: that formerly where the average drunkard was jolly, now he is paralyzed." Herbert Hoover, upon entering the White House, appointed a commission to study the problem of enforcing the Eighteenth Amendment. The commission's report revealed how widespread evasion of the law actually was. A majority of the commissioners, in individual reports, favored modification or repeal of the amendment, but the commission as a whole cast its vote for further trial. This was highly confusing, and Newman Levy, in the New York *World*, satirized it in the following manner:

> Prohibition is an awful flop.
> > We like it.
> It can't stop what it's meant to stop.
> > We like it.
> It's left a trail of graft and slime,
> > It's filled our land with vice and crime,
> It don't prohibit worth a dime,
> > Nevertheless we're for it.

During the 1932 campaign the Democrats favored outright repeal, while the Republicans favored a revision of the amendment which would have turned the problem over to the states. In February, 1933, Congress passed the Twenty-first Amendment, repealing Federal prohibition. The states ratified it within a year's time. So ended an amendment which had boomeranged completely on the dry group. Under it crime and corruption had flourished, and disrespect for law and order had been encouraged, since it was "the thing to do" to violate the Eighteenth Amendment. America breathed a sigh of relief when the act was repealed and once again began to drink pure liquor instead of the shoddy stuff of the prohibition era.

TECHNOLOGY CHANGES SOCIETY

Technological developments, such as rayon, refrigerators, telephones, and electric devices of all types, went far to alter life in the postwar decade. More important, however, than these developments were the improvements made in automobiles, airplanes, and movies, and the growth of the radio industry. The first "gasoline buggy" to operate successfully on a road had been constructed by Franklin and Charles Duryea in 1893 at Springfield, Massachusetts, but it was a long time before the automobile became popular. The first automobiles resembled carriages, and the motorists wore long linen dusters and goggles to protect themselves from the dust. There were no road maps and no filling stations, and gasoline had to be bought at general stores. Gradually, during the first decade of the twentieth century, the automobile caught on. By 1914 more than a half-million cars were sold each year, and by 1928 over twenty-four million cars were in use. The automobile industry, during the twenties, became America's largest industry, judged by the money value of the product. It had tremendous influence on allied industries in its consumption of large amounts of glass, iron, steel, leather, and rubber.

Henry Ford, who had been tinkering with a gasoline buggy at the same time as the Duryeas, built up a large industry on the basis of an inexpensive car, the "Model T." In 1927 the fifteen millionth automobile rolled off the Ford assembly line. By this time the leading producers in the automobile industry were Ford, General Motors, and Chrysler. They controlled about four fifths of the industry. The development of the automobile, the motorbus, and the truck had important effects on the steam railroads and on electric trolleys. Many electric lines were discontinued, and the railroads lost passengers and freight. By 1928 over three million trucks were in use either for short hauls or for cross-country trips. At the same time, the automobile led to significant changes in the farming communities. It ended isolation for the farmer and his family, his perishable goods could be speeded to market, and the tractor simplified his problems of plowing, cultivating, and reaping. For city folk it afforded an easy escape to the country on Sundays and holidays, and it also led many people to move to the suburbs, where they could live in semicountry conditions and yet drive to work in the city.

The increasing use of the automobile as the principal vehicle of American life required increasing expenditures of money by local governments for highway construction. Soon service stations, roadhouses, and "dog-carts" sprang up along the highways to serve traveling America. The automobile increased the migratory tendency already present in the people. Instead of using the car to drive to a vacation spot, people now spent their whole vacation driving. They carried tents and cooking utensils or put up in the new tourist camps. New England, which had suffered disastrous competition from Western farms and from the industrialization of other regions, now became a mecca of tourists. Its lovely scenery, combined with its historical lore, made an irresistible appeal. During the cold winters many people drove to southern California. Los Angeles had a great boom during the decade. It was the center of the tourist trade and the motion-picture industry, in addition to having important industrial and farming activities. It was during the twenties, too, that Florida became a popular winter resort. The automobile made it easy and inexpensive to drive to Florida for the winter. The year 1925 witnessed a mania of speculation in Florida real estate, and Miami, Palm Beach, Hollywood, and Coral Gables were among the cities that developed rapidly.

The automobile affected American life in infinite ways. It made it easier for the criminal to break the law and escape; it aided in the downfall of prohibition; it offered a new place for the younger generation to court; it broke the isolation of the farmer; it permitted people to leave the congested city for the suburbs; it helped to make Americans a migratory people; it stimulated related industries, such as glass and rubber; it helped to make Americans more mechanical; and it destroyed old-time provincialisms. Under the impact of this technological invention American life was drastically changed. The automobile was to the generation of the twenties what the airplane was to become to the generation following the Second World War.

The development of the radio industry was spectacular in the postwar decade. The first broadcasting station in America—KDKA of Pittsburgh—was opened on November 2, 1920. Within two years radio had become a craze. Although the radio industry did not occupy as important a place as the automobile industry, it had the distinction of being the new industry of the decade, and the sale of radio sets and parts increased rapidly. In 1922 total sales amounted to $66,000,000; in 1926, to $506,000,000; and in 1929, to $842,548,000. Radio reported the national conventions of the two parties in 1924 and the inauguration of Coolidge the following year. Jazz bands blared "It Ain't Gonna Rain No Mo'," and Rudy Vallee crooned over the air waves. Important sporting events, such as prize fights, world-series games, and college football contests, were broadcast, generally by Graham Mc-Namee, the best-known radio voice of the decade. Business firms began paying heavy sums to radio stations for the privilege of advertising their merchandise to the radio audience. By the end of the decade this industry, which had been launched in Pittsburgh in 1920, had developed into an industry of major proportions, creating new types of employment and, as in the case of the automobile, affecting the life of the average American. Every third home in the nation had a radio by 1929. People who could not afford or did not have the time to attend opera, symphony concerts, plays, and sporting contests could have the pleasure of hearing these in their own living-rooms while seated in their comfortable chairs, and all for the price of the radio set—and of having to listen, occasionally, to tiresome advertising.

In keeping with the trend to consolidation of American industry, the independent broadcasting stations gradually consolidated into chains. A chain would send out programs that were carried by the member stations in all parts of the country. The result was to increase the uniformity of what Americans heard. An indication of the tastes of the public was the division of time of programs broadcast from New York City stations in February, 1927: dance music, 26.42 per cent; other music, 48 per cent; education, 9.3 per cent; religion, 5.3 per cent; news, 2.8 per cent; drama, 2.6 per cent; sports, 1.8 per cent; children's programs, 1.1 per cent; miscellaneous, 2.6 per cent.

The motion-picture industry was still another industry that enjoyed a spectacular growth in the twenties and also had a powerful influence in molding American attitudes and life. It became the fourth largest industry, with an investment of over one and a half billion dollars. By 1927 there were twenty thousand five hundred theaters with an audience capacity of eighteen million. Each week, to these theaters, flocked close to a hundred million people. The postwar theaters and pictures displayed real technological improvement over those of prewar days. The favorite actors of the day were Charlie Chaplin, Douglas Fairbanks, Rudolph Valentino, Lillian Gish, and Mary Pickford. Among the most successful films of the decade were *The Covered Wagon, The Big Parade, The Iron Horse, The Pony Express, What Price Glory, The Ten Commandments, The King of Kings, Ben Hur, Beau Geste, The Sheik, The Three Musketeers,* and *Robin Hood.*

Hollywood, California, became the center of the industry. The brilliant sunshine, the mild winters, and the scenery appealed to motion-picture producers. Hollywood was the film center not only of the United States, but of the world as well. American films in Europe, Asia, and Latin America often accounted for 80 to 90 per cent of the pictures shown. Until 1927 all films were silent, so that actors who were skilled in the art of pantomime were the leaders in the profession. Then technology made it possible to synchronize sound with the film. One of the best of the early sound motion pictures was *The Jazz Singer,* in which Al Jolson sang his "Mammy" songs. During the next two years theaters were remodeled to carry sound, and many of the silent-film stars had to give way to new stars with better voices for the new medium.

In yet another field, the conquest of the air by flying machines, the twenties witnessed important steps, although the airplane's real utilization was to be left for the next decade. The First World War had given an impetus to airplane construction. During the war it was realized that the plane was not only a scouting machine, but an effective fighting machine as well. Vast amounts of money were spent in improving aircraft. After the war commercial aviation developed slowly. It was not until 1926 that it became profitable in the United States. Before this time, however, in 1924, the post office had inaugurated air-mail service between New York and San Francisco. One event in aviation history that attracted widespread public attention was Charles A. Lindbergh's successful flight from New York to Paris in May, 1927. Similar flights across the Atlantic soon followed. Richard E. Byrd explored the north pole by plane in 1926 and three years later used planes to explore the antarctic. By 1928 the aviation industry had developed to include forty-eight commercial airways, with a combined coverage of twenty thousand miles, and employed eleven thousand licensed aviators.

EDUCATION, LITERATURE, AND THE ARTS

In this period, also, certain changes that had been going on in American education reached their full expression. Since the Civil War the field of education had expanded rapidly. More and more children attended the public schools; instruction, once confined to the "three R's," now widened to include other subjects; new textbooks took the place of the Webster Spellers and the McGuffey Readers, which had done so much to acquaint an earlier generation with bits of poetry, good and bad; high moral values; and a sense of the fleeting character of life. High schools developed slowly until the turn of the century—there were only two hundred thousand pupils in the public high schools in 1890—and then grew rapidly as some persons began to speak of them as "the people's colleges" and asked that such schools prepare young people for their lifework. Normal schools, for teacher-training, expanded as rapidly as high schools, and American educators became familiar with the educational theories of Pestalozzi, Herbart, and Froebel. Soon John Dewey was talking of making the school a miniature of society itself. Between 1870 and 1920 enrollment in the public schools grew from 6,871,000 to 21,578,000.

Higher education also underwent change. In the early days most of the colleges had been under clerical control. The main object had been the training of young men for the ministry. Student bodies were small—five hundred constituted a large enrollment; courses of study were fixed, with Greek, Latin, and philosophy as their base; student life offered little enjoyment and was strictly regulated. After the Civil War, change began at once. A new group of college presidents, many with training at European universities, took charge—such men as White at Cornell, McCosh at Princeton, Eliot at Harvard, Porter at Yale, Angell at Michigan, and Gilman at Johns Hopkins. Under their leadership elective courses were added to the curricula, science was given wider attention, graduate schools were developed, standards were raised in law and medical schools, and, soon, schools of business were added to the professional group. The Morrill Act of 1862 provided funds, through land grants, for training in agriculture and "the mechanical arts," and opened the way for the establishment of state colleges in these fields either as separate institutions or as units of existing state universities. Higher education for women also made rapid advances. Vassar opened its doors in 1865, and Smith and Wellesley in the next decade. Western state universities pioneered in the admission of women on an equal basis with men, and by 1920 more than a hundred universities had followed their lead.

With these changes student bodies grew rapidly. Economic prosperity enabled parents to send their children to college in increasing numbers. Widened courses and increased facilities provided training according to the wishes and abilities of the students. Going to college enhanced social prestige. "Practical" courses ensured later financial returns. The growth of social clubs and of athletics made colleges attractive for other reasons than study. They became places where young people could have careers and achieve success which attracted local and even state and national attention. Luxurious dormitories and fraternity houses replaced the barren "college room" of earlier days; alumni searched "prep schools" for prize athletes who could bring victory over rival institutions, and went deep into their pockets to uphold the prestige of their alma maters. Universities counted their students by the thousands, which had once counted them by the hundreds, and the problems of mass education arose to plague faculties and administrators. Soon serious leaders, such as Woodrow Wilson at Princeton, began to ask whether the real ends of education were being served by such a system.

By the twenties, also, there had emerged something more solid in literature and the arts than the Gilded Age had produced. In the 1880's Samuel L. Clemens (Mark Twain), whose early works drew heavily on a Midwestern boyhood and therefore belonged, in a way, to that local-color literature which redeemed the Gilded Age, reached his peak as a humorist and interpreter of everyday American life. *Life on the Mississippi* and *Huckleberry Finn* reveal him at his best. After that a new and sharper note, one of bitterness, enters. Clemens had come to see the cheapness and the showiness of his age. He wrote to William Dean Howells in 1899:

> I have been reading the morning paper. I do it every morning well knowing that I shall find in it the usual depravities and baseness and hypocrisies and cruelties that make up civilization, and cause me to put in the rest of the day pleading for the damnation of the human race.

His was more than simple, personal bitterness; it was the cry of a philosopher whose contemporaries insisted on regarding him only as a "funmaker," the cry of "an artist cheapened by an overpowering demand for cheap wares." The brooding sense of futility in his later works definitely links him with a group of realists who set a new pattern in the early days of the twentieth century.

The great spokesman of this group was William Dean Howells. He too was a Midwesterner. His early novels dealt with the staid, unexciting life of New England, where he had gone to edit the *Atlantic Monthly*. There was realism of a sort in these works, but not the conscious effort to face the problems of a new day, and the bold acceptance of the task of "truthful presentation of materials," that mark his later novels. In these, new themes appear—woman's rights, marriage in the modern world, labor and class struggles, socialism, and spiritualism. He did not always come to grips with his problems, but the significant fact is that he was leading a movement away from "the moribund and tawdry romanticism" of the preceding period. Henry James, who left America to live in Europe, was a more capable craftsman. He was equally conscious of the shallowness of the day, but his influence was much less than that of Howells. The same is true of Hamlin Garland, who was more truly the pioneer realist of country life in Mid-America, and whose *Son of the Middle Border* and *Main-Traveled Roads* are works of enduring value. His later ventures into romanticism, however, were weak and robbed him of any important share in the ushering in of the new day.

It was, therefore, Howells who prepared the way for what has been called the period of naturalism. To this period belong such works as Stephen Crane's *Maggie: A Girl of the Streets* and his *Red Badge of Courage*; Theodore Dreiser's *Sister Carrie* and his *American Tragedy*; and Frank Norris's three novels *McTeague, Vandover and the Brute,* and *The Octopus*. There is a note of irony in most of these books and a refusal to pass moral judgment on characters or situations. There is something of the cold, scientific temper which observes and reports the world round about, as a scientist might report the results of his experiments. Crane had a rare gift for writing; Norris was more conscious of the sensational and of social wrongs; Dreiser, more plodding than either, had a firmer grip on his age and probably a more enduring influence. Together they represent a new era in American writing, and they blazed a trail which Sinclair Lewis, Sherwood Anderson, Willa Cather, O. E. Rölvaag, and many others were soon following. By the twenties America had, in things literary, come a long way from the Gilded Age.

In the field of architecture, as in the field of literature, a more solid group were at work even while the flamboyant extravagances of the Gilded Age predominated. Henry H. Richardson, Louisiana-born and French-trained, led the way. First in New York and then in Boston, he sought to check the influences which were erecting such hideous structures as the Smithsonian Institution in Washington and the old Grand Central Station in New York City, and to replace them with more dignified and simpler structures in the Romanesque style. His earlier buildings were mostly churches, but he was soon designing libraries, business houses, and homes. Some of his early churches were in a simplified Victorian Gothic, but in Trinity Church, Boston, he employed, for the first time, a modified French and Spanish Romanesque, which was soon termed "Richardsonian." The style was massive and heavy with solid walls and many arches, but there were great windows too, which added something of inspiration to the unity and strength conveyed by the rest of the building. Soon Chicago and Pittsburgh and Cincinnati, as well as many smaller communities, had Richardson buildings, a testimonial to the improved taste of a widening group of Americans.

Richard M. Hunt, born in Vermont and also trained in France, was another architect of great ability who labored in the seventies and eighties. In 1868 he opened an office in New York and soon was designing palatial town and country homes, in the French Renaissance style, for America's new millionaires. His work was thus more limited in scope than Richardson's, but he did design the Administration Building of the Chicago World's Fair and was responsible for the main portion of the Metropolitan Museum in New York, the Lenox Library at Yale, and the National Observatory in Washington.

The firm of McKim, Mead, and White, stressing a semiclassical type of public building, played an equally important part in discrediting the taste of the Gilded Age. These architects set the pattern for the World's Fair buildings in Chicago, in 1893, with their grand façades and their lesser structures in the rear. They borrowed heavily from the past and abroad, and added little to the creation of a native architecture; but they did help to span the gap between a "stuffy, artificial" past and a more native future.

To Louis Sullivan goes the credit for the final break which gave the United States its first structures in a truly native pattern. His Transportation Building at the World's Fair in Chicago stirred the admiration of foreign critics and opened the way for his greater work. This was in the field of the modern skyscraper, with its interior steel construction. His fundamental idea was that "form follows function," an idea that took into consideration the inflated values of real estate in American business centers and lifted buildings skyward, gave them abundance of light and air, and crowded into them a beauty all their own. Soon the sky lines of New York and Chicago testified to his foresight and the practical quality in all his dreams. His daring originality created a Chicago school of architects out of which came Frank Lloyd Wright, who, in the 1920's, more than any other, pushed America toward a truly native architecture, resting firmly on American soil.

American painters in the period after the Civil War have been divided into two groups, "the expatriates" and "those who stayed at home." Of the first group James McNeill Whistler was the most important. Trained in Europe and living most of the time in England, he followed the French realists for a time and then turned to a two-dimensional decorative style and a conscious effort at suppressing contrast in colors for the production of greater harmony in tone. His insistence on art for art's sake did not fit the temper of the Gilded Age, but such paintings as *Little White Girl* and *The Artist's Mother* have given him a permanent place in American art.

Of the "stay-at-homes" Winslow Homer stands out above all the rest. After an early period devoted to magazine illustration, he began painting scenes from American life with a straightforward objectiveness and a daring use of color that marked him as the greatest of American provincials. Later he turned to the sea for subjects, which he painted with grand yet simple power. His method of working directly from nature was particularly fitted to water colors, a field in which he soon excelled. No American has yet matched the breadth and mastery of color and mass and movement that Homer achieved in his pictures of the Maine woods and the Florida and West Indian shores.

In the decades from the seventies to the nineties three American landscape-painters, largely under European influences, broke sharply with the analytical realism of the Hudson River school, and achieved more freedom and more atmosphere in their work. George Inness, whose early works are classed with those of Cole and Doughty, now turned out light-filled, impressionistic canvases. Homer Dodge Martin and Alexander H. Wyant followed in his footsteps with authentic but poetic works that clearly showed the influence of both Constable and the Barbizon painters. Albert Ryder set a course all his own, in this period, with works that were both simple in design and mystical and dreamlike in quality. Thomas Eakins, who painted "with a sober, searching realism and a mastery of means," surpassed them all, except Homer, with his scenes of everyday American life and portraits of contemporaries. His works are solid and his figures soundly constructed. Only a weaker sense of design kept him from true greatness. Critics like to contrast him with the more gifted John Singer Sargent, whose brilliance as a portrait-painter has been unmatched by that of any other American, but who somehow lacked the depth and enduring strength of Eakins.

By their example and teachings these men opened the way for younger American artists of the next generation to secure sound training at home and to add something more native to their work. The Old World still held the upper hand and European study was still

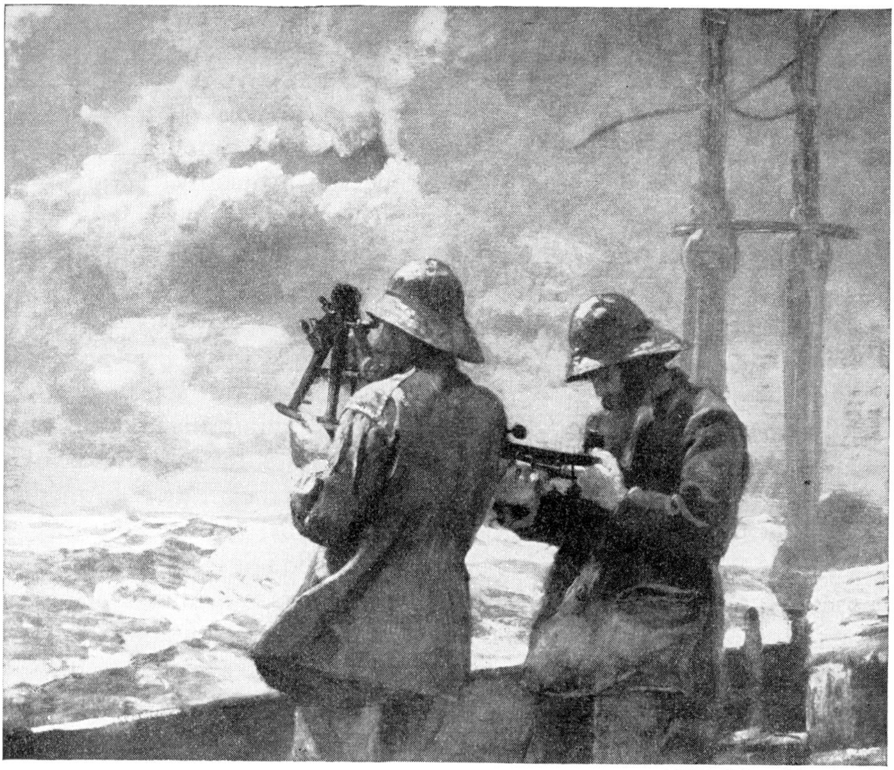

Addison Gallery of American Art

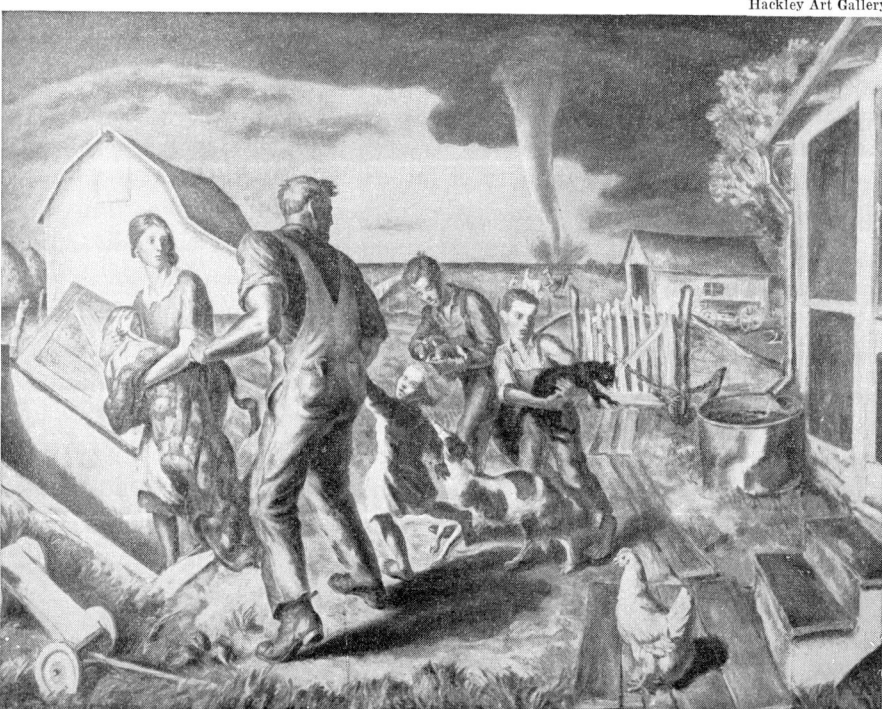

Eight Bells

PAINTING BY WINSLOW HOMER, 1886

The Tornado

PAINTING BY JOHN STEUART CURRY, 1929

Hackley Art Gallery

Stone City, Iowa

PAINTING BY GRANT WOOD, 1930

Significant American Paintings

Vermont Scene

PAINTING BY PAUL SAMPLE, 1936

essential, but artists such as John Twachtman, William Glackens, Mary Cassatt, Robert Henri, George Luks, John Sloan, and George Bellows found their way easier and the public more ready to grant them support because their predecessors had laid sound foundations.

In the field of sculpture only Augustus Saint-Gaudens and Daniel Chester French achieved first importance. Frederick MacMonnies, George Barnard, and Lorado Taft did acceptable, but not great, work. In the field of music the seventies and eighties saw American symphony societies organized in New York and Boston and, in the next decade, in Chicago, Cincinnati, and Pittsburgh. Of composers, however, only Edward MacDowell rose above the level of mediocrity. These accomplishments in the fields of architecture, art, and music must, of course, be viewed in the light of the youthfulness of the nation. They gave promise of greater cultural achievements in the years ahead.

Amidst the ballyhoo of the decade, it was difficult to see the progress that was being made in literature, education, art, architecture, and music. On the surface, life in the "roaring twenties" was dominated by an unbelievable, irrelevant potpourri of speak-easies, Teapot Dome scandals, bathing-beauty contests, and Bolshevist scares. It was a generation that was primarily interested in escaping from serious problems, domestic or international. It was an unreal world filled with raucous laughter, shoddy tinsel, and ballyhoo.

SELECTED BIBLIOGRAPHY

F. L. ALLEN, *Only Yesterday*, and P. W. SLOSSON, *The Great Crusade and After, 1914–1928*, delightful and valuable; JOHN M. MECKLIN, *The Ku Klux Klan, A Study of the American Mind*, a shrewd study of the psychological appeal of the Klan; JOSEPH WOOD KRUTCH, *The Modern Temper: A Study and a Confession*, an excellent survey of the mind of the decade; ROBERT G. and HELEN M. LYND, *Middletown*, a mine of valuable material; ZECHARIAH CHAFEE, *Free Speech in the United States*, facts on the illiberalism of the day; SILAS BENT, *Ballyhoo*, gives a real insight into the decade; WALTER LIPPMANN, *A Preface to Morals*, excellent in analyzing the disillusioned generation.

CHARLES MERZ, *The Dry Decade*, material on the prohibition experiment; S. F. DULLES, *America Learns to Play*, invaluable on sports; L. C. ROSTEN, *Hollywood*, an entertaining story; PAUL SCHUBERT, *The Electric World; the Rise of Radio*, worth while on radio.

Novels of the decade, like those of Ernest Hemingway, John Dos Passos, and F. Scott Fitzgerald, give insight into the times.

XXXII

Normalcy

PEACE brought to the American people the opportunity to escape from world problems and to immerse themselves in domestic bickerings. It was in this mood that the public approached the election of 1920. The Republicans, after a bitter convention fight between Governor Lowden of Illinois, General Leonard Wood, and Senator Hiram Johnson, nominated a dark horse—Warren Gamaliel Harding, Senator from Ohio—because, as one person observed, the weather was hot and the delegates wanted to get back home. Harding's outlook was in sharp contrast to Wilson's idealism. The convention, in the hands of Old Guard politicians, chose Harding because they wanted the party committed to policies reminiscent of the days of McKinley. Harding thoroughly expressed the attitude of the Old Guard when he stated, during the campaign: "America's present need is not heroics but healing; not nostrums but normalcy. We want a period in America with less government in business and more business in government." Calvin Coolidge of Massachusetts was nominated as Harding's running mate because of his work in the Boston police strike, including his statement that there was no right to strike against the public safety at any time.

The Democratic candidates, Governor James M. Cox of Ohio and Franklin D. Roosevelt of New York, represented what liberalism there was left in the party. It was fairly clear that Harding represented a return to conservatism, while Cox represented a continuation of Wilsonian Progressivism. War-tired America indicated, on election day, that it wanted Harding's pledge of a return to normalcy, a return to the benign days of William McKinley and Mark Hanna, when the government, run by business interests, failed to force that economic group to serve the public in the interest of a progressive democracy. During the entire decade of the 1920's the Republican party used the government as an instrument to advance business interests—one of the many similarities between the decade that followed the First World War and the decade after the Civil War. Other similarities were that both periods were conservative in social philosophy; both witnessed significant changes in industrial and business techniques; both were characterized by political and business corruption; and both were faced with the problem of liquidating the war. Industry, transportation, and agriculture had to be returned to a peacetime basis, and the problems of the national debt and veterans' aid were ever present.

THE LIQUIDATION OF THE WAR

The control of business by the government during the war led some to hope for the continuation of this control in peace as a means of achieving a more orderly society and one that distributed its benefits more equitably. This view, however, was repudiated during the years of Republican control. Actually, the last two years of Wilson's administration saw the beginning of the trend away from governmental regulation of the national economy. Congress repealed a great deal of the war legislation, war contracts were canceled, and the President was deprived of his special war powers. The trend away from governmental regulation was best seen in the field of the railroads. The government had taken over the railroads when private operation proved inadequate to meet the crisis created by the war. Since this was an abnormal period, no lesson could be learned as to whether governmental control was more efficient than private control. Therefore the Railroad Administration proposed the extension of its control for five years in order to give an "opportunity under proper conditions to test the value of unified control . . . the experience thus gained would of itself indicate the permanent solution of the difficulty." Congress, in the mood of the Red scare, was not in the least sympathetic to this proposal. The Transportation Act of 1920 returned the railroads to private ownership and operation. Instead of discouraging consolidation, the act encouraged it. Under the Interstate Commerce Commission's eyes, the railroads were allowed to make pooling agreements and consolidate themselves into a few large systems. The Commission was empowered to fix rates that would earn a "fair return" for the stockholders. Excess earnings by any road were to be taken by the government and used to aid weaker roads, and a Railway Labor Board was created to solve disputes over wages, hours, and working conditions.

It soon became clear that many railroads were happy to take advantage of the privileges of the act, but anxious to obstruct any governmental supervision. They defied the Railway Labor Board when it ordered them to cease antiunion practices, and they organized holding companies, which, being "noncarriers," were not subject to the I.C.C.'s supervision. The railroads and the Commission also disagreed on what basis to take for fixing a fair return. The Commission's valuation of railroad property was based on the actual cost of building the railroads, whereas the railroads wanted rates based on the cost of reproducing the railroads in the twenties. Since the twenties were a period of higher prices than those that had prevailed at the time when the roads had been constructed, this meant a wide variation between the two valuations. The Supreme Court, in 1929, took the side of the railroads. On the whole, the railroads did as they pleased under the act of 1920. But they did not prosper. By 1933 many were in bankruptcy, their credit was extremely low, and roadbeds and equipment were deteriorating.

Another grave problem of postwar liquidation was the merchant marine. War construction had greatly increased the number of government-owned ships. Under the Merchant Marine Act of 1920 the Shipping Board was allowed to sell these ships on extremely liberal terms; the government provided generous mail subsidies to private shipping lines; and trade with American colonies was restricted to American ships. These steps did not prevent the decline of the American merchant marine at a time when the merchant marines of other nations were improving. Finally, in 1929, the Jones-White Act was passed, which appropriated two hundred and fifty million dollars for construction loans to private companies; increased the mail subsidies; and provided for the sale of the remaining government-owned ships for as little as ten cents on the dollar. In spite of such lavish aid by the Republican administrations, the privately owned merchant marine by 1936 had liabilities greater than its assets; it owed the government sums which it could not pay; and it possessed ships which were old and slow compared with the ships of England, Germany, and Japan.

Veterans' compensation was another reconstruction problem. This problem had two parts: disability compensation and adjusted compensation for war service. Disability compensation was extremely liberal. For disabled veterans the government provided pensions, hospitalization, and vocational rehabilitation training. The second part of the problem involved the question of adjusted compensation for war service. A large number of soldiers, most of whom had been getting thirty dollars a month at the same time that civilians were receiving boomtime wages, thought that they should receive a bonus. In 1922 Harding vetoed a bill that would have paid a bonus of fifty dollars for each month of service. Two years later Congress succumbed to the pressure of the American Legion and passed a bonus bill over Coolidge's veto. This act gave every ex-serviceman a paid-up insurance policy based on a dollar and a quarter a day for service overseas and a dollar a day for each day's service in the United States. The average policy amounted to about one thousand dollars, and the total added to the national debt was three and a half billion dollars.

When the depression came and the rolls of the unemployed increased to dangerous proportions, a demand arose for immediate payment of these policies. In June, 1932, a "bonus army" marched on Washington to insist upon immediate payment. President Hoover was frightened by what he apparently considered to be the precursor of revolution, and he ordered out the army, which broke up the bonus army's camp. Public opinion was shocked at this use of force against ex-soldiers, and Hoover lost the support of many conservative people who disliked this show of militarism. During the next four years the bonus was a troublesome political issue. Over a Presidential veto Congress, in 1936, passed a bill permitting the cashing of these insurance policies.

CORRUPTION

During the Harding administration corruption flourished like a green bay tree. The public was apathetic toward politics and paid little attention to what was taking place in Washington. Warren G. Harding, whose political advancement had been the result of the work of local Ohio political bosses and machine politicians in control of the Republican National Committee, took these politicians into the national government with him. Harding was completely dependent on subordinates, and, unfortunately for the country, most of his subordinates were not of too high caliber. Will H. Hays, chairman of the Republican National Committee, was made Postmaster General; Albert B. Fall of New Mexico, who was openly friendly with big oil interests, was made Secretary of the Interior; and Harry M. Daugherty of the "Ohio gang" was made Attorney-General. The country, however, took some hope for a successful administration after the appointment of Charles Evans Hughes as Secretary of State and Herbert C. Hoover as Secretary of Commerce. The business groups were pleased, too, when aluminum monopolist Andrew W. Mellon was appointed as Secretary of the Treasury.

Harding had little notion of technical fitness for technical jobs. Instead he handed out offices as though they were plums. To his brother-in-law went the post of Superintendent of Prisons; to a Marion, Ohio, lawyer went the post of Comptroller of the Currency. Harding's loyalty was not to the best traditions of American democracy, but to his party and his friends, the Ohio politicians. It was natural for the "Ohio gang" to follow him to Washington, and Harding enjoyed nothing better than slipping away from the White House to where the group played poker and liquor flowed freely in spite of prohibition. Harding was basically the type of the rowdies of the "Ohio gang," although outwardly he had the appearance of a distinguished statesman.

Lobbyists poured into Washington to reap the harvest of a government which, after years of Progressive domination, would "do business." The major corruption developed in the field of oil. Secretary Albert Fall, with the acquiescence of Secretary of the Navy Denby, secretly leased, to the Doheny and Sinclair oil interests, control of valuable naval oil reserves, including the Teapot Dome reserve in Wyoming. Later it was discovered that Fall had received bribes of one hundred thousand dollars from Doheny and three hundred thousand dollars from Sinclair. After a long Congressional investigation, launched by Senator Tom Walsh of Montana, these leases were voided, and Fall was found guilty and sentenced to a term in jail. Secretary Denby was forced to resign. Doheny and Sinclair, the two bribegivers, escaped jail sentences, although Sinclair had to serve a term in prison in 1929 for refusing to answer questions put to him by a Senate Committee and for trying to bribe the jury during his trial.

There were other scandals, although oil was the aristocrat of them all. Charles R. Forbes, as head of the Veterans' Bureau, indulged in incredible corruption. It was charged that Forbes received a "cut" from contractors who built veterans' hospitals, and that hospital supplies were purchased in preposterous quantities—for example, seventy thousand dollars' worth of floor wax and cleaner was bought, enough to last a hundred years. In 1926 Forbes went to Leavenworth for fraud. Graft was rampant, too, in the Alien Property Custodian Office. German properties and patents were sold at ridiculously low prices. It was discovered that one purchaser had paid four hundred thousand dollars for an introduction to the custodian. The custodian, Thomas W. Miller, went to jail in 1927. Attorney-General Daugherty, leader of the "Ohio gang," was dismissed from office by President Coolidge after a Senate Committee had found him guilty of illegally selling liquor permits and pardons. On criminal trial, however, he escaped a sentence.

Harding personally seems to have been innocent of participating in this orgy of corruption. He was not unaware of it, however, nor of what it would mean to his reputation when the public learned of it. On a trip to Alaska his health broke under the strain, and he died on August 2, 1923. Years later, in dedicating a memorial to Harding at Marion, Ohio, President Herbert Hoover observed:

Warren Harding had a dim realization that he had been betrayed by a few men whom he trusted, by men whom he had believed were his devoted friends. It was later proved in the courts of the land that these men had betrayed not alone the friendship and trust of their staunch and loyal friend, but they had betrayed their country. That was the tragedy of the life of Warren Harding.

AID TO BUSINESS

Calvin Coolidge's laconic phrase "The business of America is business" and Harding's statement that the business of America was to take the government out of business expressed the attitude of the men in charge of the government in these years. There was a feeling that the nation was in danger from too much governmental activity. Calvin Coolidge observed that in the past, unfortunately, it had been necessary for the government to regulate industry, "but the present generation of businessmen has shown every disposition to correct its own abuses." The attitude of the group in power was that the government should not regulate business, but should aid business by high tariffs, by subsidies to the merchant marine and aviation, by the reduction of corporation and income taxes, and by searching for raw materials and markets for American businessmen. The philosophy of the administrations of Harding, Coolidge, and Hoover was a mixed one, however. There was much talk of "free enterprise" and "no government regulation." Yet the War had revealed certain values of central planning. War organization had brought standardization and efficiency. Businessmen wanted to return to private control of industry, but they wanted to retain all the advantages of integration, price-fixing, monopoly, and control of labor. Many businessmen, in the twenties, were willing to accept a planned economy, provided they did the planning. Regimentation was acceptable to many business firms, provided they ran the regiments.

The government obligingly responded during the years of Republican supremacy. It subsidized and aided business, it suspended the antitrust laws and facilitated the growth of monopoly, and it allowed business to run the show without regulation. The result was, according to an assistant Attorney-General, writing in 1943:

The industrial history of the United States from 1920 to Roosevelt is a well-documented mockery of the competitive system. Instead of building a free economy on the basis of exchange and fluidity, American industry continued to manacle itself to a policy of restrictions and agreements, all designed toward the common aim of advancing prices and limiting production. New waves of export quotas amounted to mere instruments of international cartels. Tariff barriers, culminating in the Hawley-Smoot act, built the final wall behind which American monopolies could dictate their own terms of competition. . . . The situation thus created helped to lay the groundwork for the disastrous economic depression of the early thirties.

Under Secretary of Commerce Hoover industry was encouraged to form trade associations which frequently limited competition and agreed upon monopoly prices. The Supreme Court extended its benediction to these monopolistic trade associations, and the antitrust laws were not invoked to control them. The courts frowned also upon action by the Federal Trade Commission aimed at curbing monopolistic practices. Hoover, the engineer, was outraged by competition and its inevitable waste. Under his sponsorship trade associations openly fixed prices and drew up codes of fair practice. A member of the Federal Trade Commission, in describing Hoover's policy, stated, "The Secretary of Commerce, far from appealing to Congress for legislation regulatory of business, allies himself with the great trade associations and the powerful corporations." Hoover explained his sponsoring of trade associations by saying, "We are passing from a period of extreme individualistic action into a period of associated activities."

Another way in which the government encouraged business in the twenties was the policy of tax reduction. Instead of keeping taxes up to pay off all the debt left by the war, Andrew Mellon obtained lower taxes. The excess-profits tax was repealed, and income taxes, the surtax, and estate taxes were lowered. But the government did not reduce one tax—the tariff. The low tariff passed by the Wilson administration never had a chance to function under normal conditions. A Republican-controlled Congress passed a high tariff bill in March, 1921, only to have it vetoed by Wilson, who pointed out, "If we wish to have Europe settle her debts, governmental or commercial, we must be prepared to buy from her." This bit of logic did not penetrate the minds of some, and in the following year the Fordney-McCumber tariff established the highest rates ever known in our history. A detailed study of the rates is not necessary, but the results are important. This tariff bill encouraged the growth of monopoly in the United States; it made it impossible for Europe to pay its debts to the United States in goods; and it brought reprisals by foreign countries in the form of retaliatory tariffs. As a result of the loss of foreign trade, many American manufacturers established plants overseas. Furthermore, under President Hoover the Hawley-Smoot tariff was passed, in 1930, increasing rates all along the line. Industries with foreign markets, the American Bankers Association, and 1028 economists protested, but Hoover signed the law. Foreign nations immediately retaliated, and our foreign trade dropped to an extremely low level. This type of economic isolation on the part of the United States stirred other countries to adopt similar policies. Gradually international trade became a mere trickle.

The Republican policy of high tariffs was carried out in a country whose financial status was different from what it had been before 1914. Until the war the United States had been a debtor nation, but during the war it had changed into a creditor nation. Its new creditor status required a willingness to accept goods as payments from debtor nations, but by raising tariffs it prevented foreign debtors from paying in goods. In order to enable foreign nations to buy from us, in spite of our refusal to take their goods, money had to be freely lent abroad. Private American loans abroad jumped from less than three billion in 1914 to about fourteen billion in 1930. These loans went all over the world, and American money was invested in government bonds, utilities, railroads, manufacturing establishments, mines, oil, and rubber. By 1930 the loans, by continents, were distributed in the following manner:

Europe	$6,707,000,000
North and Central America	4,391,036,000
South America	2,372,620,000
Australia	276,938,000
Far East	612,769,000

In the floating of many of these loans sometimes a good deal of corruption was present. Also, important information was kept from the purchasers of bonds which would have caused purchasers to question the soundness of some of the loans. This experience was to lead the New Deal to pass laws regulating the stock market to prevent such unethical practices from occurring again.

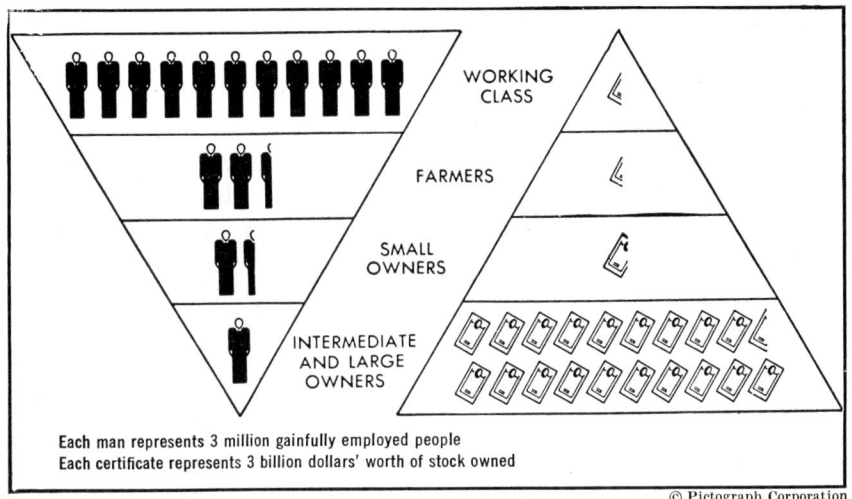

© Pictograph Corporation

Distribution of Corporate Ownership in 1928

All the various methods whereby the government officially encouraged business and finance in the twenties aided the development of monopoly and the concentration of control in the hands of the few. From 1919 to 1928 six thousand independent industrial and mining enterprises were absorbed by other companies, and four thousand public utilities were absorbed in mergers. By 1930 two hundred corporations controlled half the corporate assets in the country. Chain stores did one fifth of the retail-store business; 1.2 per cent of the utility corporations owned 84 per cent of the assets; Ford, Chrysler, and General Motors made nine tenths of all the automobiles; four tobacco companies produced nine tenths of all cigarettes; the Aluminum Corporation of America had a complete monopoly of aluminum production; the Du Ponts, the Allied Chemical and Dye Corporation, and the Union Carbide and Carbon Corporation controlled the chemical field; and twenty banks held 27.3 per cent of all the loans and investments of all banks in the country.

The holding-company device and interlocking directorates aided the concentration of power in the hands of the few. Through holding companies the Van Sweringen brothers, for instance, gained control of a railroad empire of thirty thousand miles. Their empire collapsed during the depression. Examples of interlocking directorates that flourished in those years, selected at random, are the Radio Corporation of

America directors, with 232 directorships in other companies; the New York Central directors, with 306; and the American Telephone and Telegraph directors, with 226. A Senate Committee on Banking and Currency estimated that J. P. Morgan's banking house controlled seventy-four billion dollars of corporate wealth, about one fourth of the total corporate assets of the country. Although the corporations of America, by 1929, were owned by between four and seven million stockholders, ownership and control were widely separated. The owner of a single share or of a few shares of American Telephone and Telegraph, for instance, had little influence on the policies of the company. Instead the directors controlled the corporation; and since they usually held directorships in many other corporations, their power was immense. It frequently was an irresponsible type of power, since the directors were far removed from any real responsibility to an electorate.

In the field of public utilities the Republican policy of encouraging the concentration of economic power is well illustrated. In 1930 three units—J. P. Morgan, the General Electric Company, and Insull—controlled half of the electric-power production. Samuel Insull expanded his empire by reckless and dishonest methods. When the depression came, innocent stockholders found their investments virtually wiped out by the collapse of the Insull empire. Insull had a labyrinth of holding companies, which controlled production companies in thirty states. Politically, Insull became a boss in Chicago politics, using his money to check decent government in that city. Any tendency toward the public ownership of electric-power plants was bitterly fought by the private companies, and they spent huge sums of money in financing campaigns against candidates who believed in public ownership.

During the twenties Senators Walsh of Montana, La Follette of Wisconsin, and Norris of Nebraska fought to have the Federal government operate power plants which would serve as yardsticks to test the fairness of rates charged by private companies. Their great struggle came over the dams at Muscle Shoals, on the Tennessee River, constructed during the war to furnish power for nitrate production. The Progressives in Congress prevented the reactionaries from turning Muscle Shoals over to Henry Ford on a hundred-year lease. In 1928 George W. Norris, a great fighter for a better life for the average man, guided a bill through Congress for government operation of Muscle Shoals, only to see it vetoed by Coolidge. In 1931 Norris persuaded Congress to pass the bill again, but Hoover vetoed it, saying:

I am firmly opposed to the Government entering into any business the major purpose of which is competition with our citizens. . . . The power problem is not to be solved by the project in this bill. The remedy for abuses in the conduct of that industry lies in regulation and not by the Federal Government entering upon the business itself. . . . I hesitate to contemplate the future of our institutions, of our country, if the preoccupation of its officials is to be no longer the promotion of justice and equal opportunity but is to be devoted to barter in the markets. That is not liberalism; it is degeneration.

In 1933 the New Deal embarked upon Senator Norris's plan of government operation of Muscle Shoals, with the creation of the Tennessee Valley Authority, a landmark in the planned use of one of America's most important resources.

The rapid consolidation of the control of industry and finance in the hands of the few, as well as the growing disparity in incomes during the twenties, explains the New Deal's desire to control and regulate industry and finance in the interests of the many, not the few. The New Deal's assault on the money power during the thirties was reminiscent of Jackson's attack on the money power during his Presidency. Many people seriously doubted that democracy could flourish with the great industrial and financial power of the country in the hands of a few people. Just as the Populists, Bryan, and Progressives like Theodore Roosevelt, "Fighting Bob" La Follette, and Woodrow Wilson had raised the question before 1917, so Franklin D. Roosevelt and his New Deal raised it after 1932. To make democracy work in an industrial world, Franklin D. Roosevelt proposed to regulate finance and industry in the interest of all the people. "If democracy is really to survive," the temporary National Economic Committee of Congress warned, in its final report, in 1941, "then all organizations through which man operates—industrial, social, and political—must also be democratic. Political freedom cannot survive if economic freedom is lost."

CALVIN COOLIDGE

Calvin Coolidge, who was once described as being "as crisp as a dill pickle and about as sour," assumed the Presidency in 1923. He was born in Plymouth, Vermont, and grew up in that state in the latter part of the nineteenth century. The turmoil that disturbed the rest of America in the years following the Civil War scarcely affected Coolidge's Vermont. There the old America lingered on, unspoiled by the devastation of industrial America. Vermont remained a social game preserve of the old rural order while the rest of America was embarking on new ways. The Vermont type of humor in Coolidge's time was the dry humor of rural areas. The story is still related in Vermont of a bragging Iowan who, returning to the Vermont that he had emigrated from, boasted of the nine-foot corn and the fat herds of cattle in Iowa. Then he said to his old friends, "How in the world do you people manage to get along here on these barren hillsides?" A lean Vermonter looked at him for a long time and then drawled, " 'Twould be hard if 't wa'nt for our Iowa six per cent mortgages, which help some."

Gluyas Williams in *Life*, 1928

President Coolidge Refuses Point-blank to Vacate the White House until His Other Rubber Is Found

Calvin Coolidge was descended from a hard-working, prosperous stock in a community whose government was the town meeting. There were few inequalities of wealth in his community. A man who worked hard at his calling was as good as any other man. Coolidge imbibed from his environment the Puritan belief in a morally guided universe. After attending college at Amherst he settled down at Northampton, Massachusetts, to practice law. A shrewd and calculating politician, he soon rose to power in Massachusetts politics, with the aid of conservative business people. To his belief in a morally guided universe, he added a belief in the benevolent feudalism of money. Coolidge was the average middle-class American of his generation. He believed that the rich were rich because they had worked hard and that the poor were poor only because they were lazy and slothful. He felt, as did many of his generation in the twenties, that the poor would be able to climb out of poverty if they became thrifty and persevering. Coolidge never understood the real problem facing the American working class. He was blind to such things as technological unemployment, the unequal distribution of wealth, and the exploitive features of twentieth-century America.

President Coolidge was a respectable mediocrity, and in the White House he became famous for his taciturnity. To illustrate this characteristic, the story is told of a clerk from the Treasury bringing Coolidge his first monthly salary check as President of the United States. The amount was impressive. It was one twelfth of seventy-five thousand dollars. Calvin Coolidge looked at the check intently. He said nothing. He drew the check toward him, folded it, and put it in his pocket, still saying nothing. He reached for the receipt and signed it and pushed it back to the clerk. Then, at that overpowering moment of his career, he looked up at the clerk and said, "Come again."

Yet this dour, dry Coolidge was a popular President in his day. "Silent Cal" was the symbol of what America wanted to be. His generation, which was so extravagant with its new automobiles, new clothes, installment-buying methods, and orgy of advertising and ballyhoo, seemed to gain vicarious satisfaction when they saw his frugality, his unpretentiousness, and his quiet nature. His frugality, as well as his lack of understanding of the fundamental forces in American society, is well illustrated by a question asked him, near the close of his administration, as to what had worried him most of all as President. These were the days of the greatest stock-market speculation in history and of acute agricultural distress in rural America. Coolidge replied:

"The White House hams; they would always bring a big one to the table. Mrs. Coolidge would always have a slice and I would have one. The butler would take it away and what happened to it afterward I never could find out." Almost wistfully he added: "I like ham that comes from near the bone."[1]

Coolidge, on assuming the Presidency, cleaned up the mess left by Harding. Attorney-General Daugherty was soon forced to resign, and the "Ohio gang" lost its dominant position. Coolidge, however, had no idealism, no desire to make the world a better place, and no fighting devotion to a cause except that of encouraging the benevolent feudalism of money. He regarded Progressivism with cynical disgust, and his administration witnessed more encouragement to business than had Harding's.

[1]W. A. White, *A Puritan in Babylon*, p. 416. The Macmillan Company, New York, 1938.

A year after death had placed him in the White House, Coolidge gained the Presidency in his own right. Coolidge's running mate in 1924 was conservative Charles G. Dawes of Illinois. The Democrats tried to defeat the Republican ticket by running equally conservative candidates. John W. Davis, Wall Street lawyer and Solicitor-General in Wilson's administration, was selected as the Presidential candidate, and, in the hope of placating the liberals, Charles W. Bryan, brother of the Great Commoner, was chosen as Davis's running mate. Many liberals, despairing of the two major parties, formed a Progressive party, and "Fighting Bob" La Follette ran on a platform calling for public ownership of water power, downward revision of tariff and railroad rates, farm relief, abolition of the injunction in labor disputes, and the election of all Federal judges. La Follette's five million votes that fall indicated that liberal sentiment was far from dead, but the country obviously preferred Coolidge's conservatism by giving him 15,725,000 votes; Davis received 8,386,500.

President Coolidge is best remembered for the years of the Coolidge bull market on Wall Street and the resulting years of Coolidge prosperity. Those were the halcyon days when the Republicans were promising a chicken in every pot and two cars in every garage. There were many reasons for the widespread prosperity of the Coolidge era. The war had impoverished Europe and had made the United States the economic master of the world; developments in mass production, standardization, and efficiency increased business prosperity; the Republican policy of aid to business furnished a stimulant to the boom; installment buying led to an overexpansion of purchasing, which, in turn, encouraged more production of goods; and the extensive stock-market speculation also spurred on the boom. An immense confidence that the Coolidge prosperity would last indefinitely led people to speculate in stocks as never before. The prices of common stocks shot up rapidly until by 1928 they reached what many hardheaded financiers considered to be alarming levels. The amount of money lent by bankers to brokers to carry accounts on margin increased during 1927, for instance, from $2,818,561,000 to $3,558,355,000, and more shares of stock changed hands in the week of December 3, 1927, than in any previous week in the history of the stock exchange. All sorts and conditions of people, who never before had played the market, now learned the meaning of such symbols as G.M. and A.T.&T.

The speculative market was encouraged by the actions and statements of President Coolidge and Secretary of the Treasury Mellon.

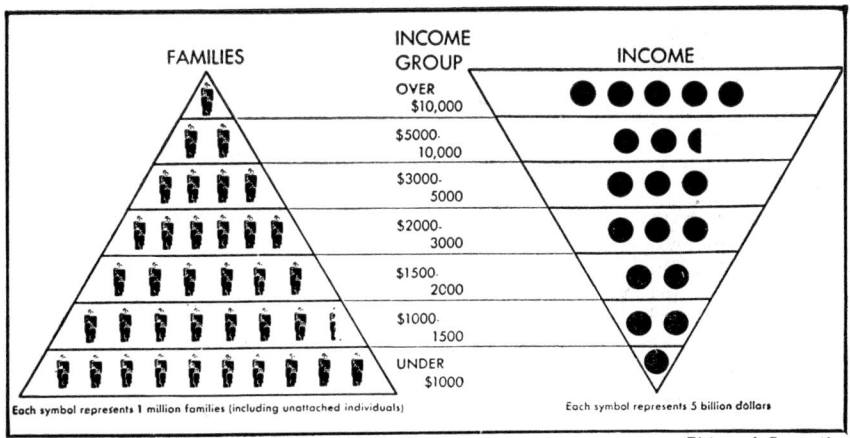

Pictograph Corporation

Distribution of Income

Whenever confidence in speculation seemed to be dropping, they issued statements that sent the prices up again. For example, on January 7, 1928, the President announced that he saw "nothing unfavorable" in the large amount of brokers' loans. According to the *New York Times,* "Stocks were turned over in huge volume on the New York Stock Exchange yesterday, largely as the result of enthusiasm aroused by President Coolidge's statement." Secretary Mellon, on December 31, 1928, stated: "In the industrial world conditions seem to be on an even keel. I look forward with confidence to continued progress in the years ahead." Such statements as these lulled the country into a false sense of security and helped the situation to get beyond control. During 1928 and 1929 the whole world was drawn into the maelstrom of Wall Street speculation. Banks in Cairo sent money to be lent on Wall Street, and speculative orders for stock were cabled from Algiers. On every side the rosiest type of optimism prevailed. "Prosperity due for a decline?" queried some, and then answered, "Why, man, we've scarcely started!" In Washington, with no comprehension of what the world was really doing, Calvin Coolidge, believing that "the business of America is business," gave his blessing to the witches' brew of speculation that was bubbling on Wall Street.

In the summer of 1927, while vacationing in the Black Hills, Coolidge, in a characteristic fashion, handed the newspapermen a ten-word message: "I do not choose to run for President in 1928." The Republicans then turned to Herbert C. Hoover as Coolidge's obvious successor. Hoover had the confidence of businessmen because of his policy of encouraging and aiding business as Secretary of Commerce, and he revealed, in a speech in August, 1928, that he was in tune with the widespread belief that the Coolidge prosperity was permanent when he said:

> We in America today are nearer to the final triumph over poverty than ever before in the history of any land. The poorhouse is vanishing from among us. We have not reached the goal, but, given a chance to go forward with the policies of the last eight years, we shall soon with the help of God be in sight of the day when poverty will be banished from this nation.

Herbert Hoover had a reputation as a great humanitarian as a result of his relief work during the war and his successful handling of relief problems arising from the Mississippi floods of 1927. He was a millionaire and a man of the world, but the fact that he had been born on an Iowa farm and had worked his way up the economic ladder appealed to the Horatio Alger instincts of Americans. His fame as an engineer did not handicap him with the people, since the America of the twenties worshiped machine technique and materialistic success. The Republican convention nominated Hoover on the first ballot and, as his running mate, selected conservative Senator Charles Curtis of Kansas. As a result, for the first time in American history, both candidates of a major party came from states west of the Mississippi River.

The Democratic convention met at Houston, Texas, and Franklin D. Roosevelt placed in nomination the governor of New York, Alfred E. Smith, the "happy warrior." Smith had been a strong contender for the nomination in 1920 and in 1924, and this time he was selected on the first ballot. Votes from the Southern delegates indicated that the South had not been entirely won over to Smith, and to placate this group Senator Joseph T. Robinson of Arkansas—a Southerner, a Protestant, and a dry—was made the Vice-Presidential candidate. Al Smith represented a different type of American democracy from that of Herbert Hoover. Having grown up on the "sidewalks of New York," he was the first lifetime urban dweller and the first Roman Catholic to receive the nomination of a major party. His record as governor of New York in regard to power regulation, labor affairs, and social reform had won him the respect of liberals and social workers. In regard to prohibition, then disturbing American politics, he was a wet. He had openly demanded the repeal of the Eighteenth Amendment and a return to state control of the liquor problem.

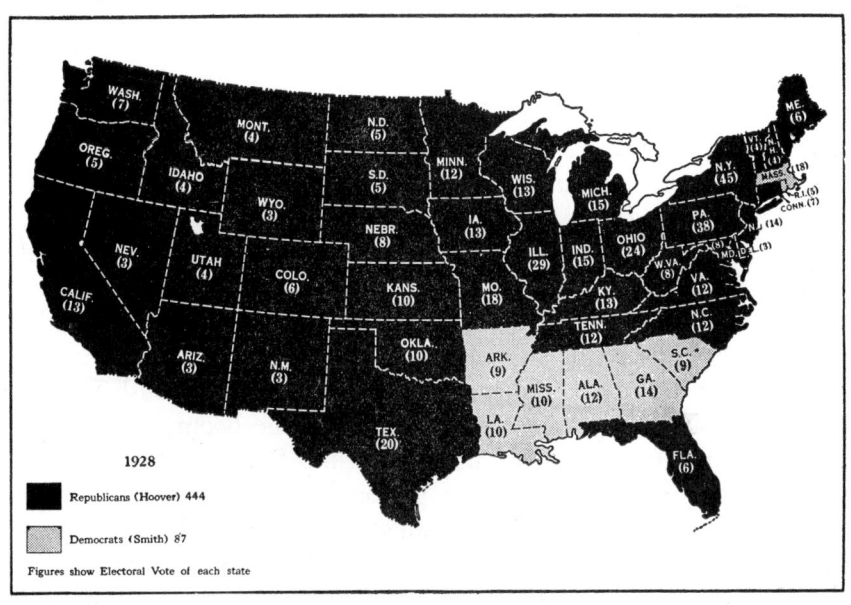

1928

■ Republicans (Hoover) 444

▨ Democrats (Smith) 87

Figures show Electoral Vote of each state

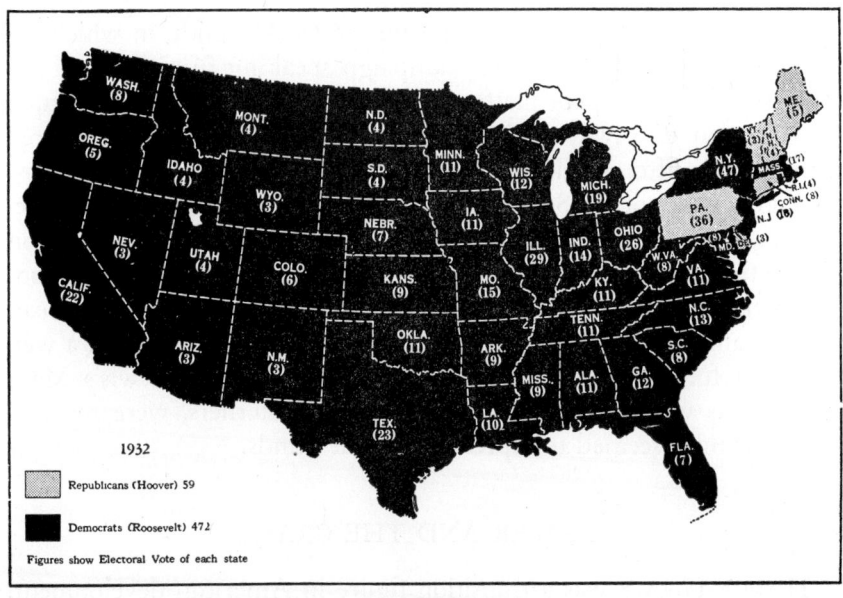

1932

▨ Republicans (Hoover) 59

■ Democrats (Roosevelt) 472

Figures show Electoral Vote of each state

The Presidential Elections of 1928 and 1932

Al Smith chose John J. Raskob, vice-president of General Motors, vice-president of Du Pont, and a director of a number of banks to head the Democratic National Committee. Raskob added three millionaires to the committee, thus indicating that a Democratic victory would not upset Coolidge prosperity. The amount of money spent by both parties was the largest in their history, the Republicans spending over ten millions and the Democrats over seven; and it was the first national election in which radio hookups carried the campaign directly to the people. Each party dodged such basic issues as the control of water power, the tariff, agricultural relief, and foreign affairs. The issues that exerted the greatest influence were those of prosperity, prohibition, and religion. On the issue of prosperity the Republicans obviously had the advantage, since they were in power during the boom; and Smith's wetness hurt him in the rural areas of the South and West. The issue of religion emphasized the personal aspects of the campaign. Probably, in the popular mind, Smith's Catholicism bulked large as an issue. The kind of Protestant who had supported the Klan believed that Smith's election would be the signal for the Pope to move to Washington.

In spite of the stirring campaign put on by Al Smith, in which his winning personality and expert campaign speaking furnished a sharp contrast to Hoover's poor platform appearance and his reserved nature, Hoover won decisively with twenty-one million votes, as compared with Smith's fifteen million. Smith carried only eight states and lost the border states of the South. This was the first time, since reconstruction days, that a Republican candidate had made a serious inroad on the South. Smith was defeated because the average American was content with the prevailing prosperity, which he attributed to Republican control; and since Al Smith was a Catholic, a New Yorker, and a wet, he was a foreigner to Middletown America. Sinclair Lewis's Main Streeters, as well as rural Southerners and Westerners, were repelled by what Smith seemed to represent in their minds.

HOOVER AND THE CRASH

Herbert Hoover was a transition figure in American development. Although he talked in terms of "rugged individualism," at the same time, as an engineer, he realized the value of social planning. The "American way" to him meant the attaining of social good through individual enterprise, the achieving of a planned society through the voluntary co-operation of businessmen. He believed that government should encourage business, not regulate or compete with it. His was the "seeping down" theory of prosperity, the belief that prosperity would trickle down from the rich at the top to the poor at the bottom.

With Hoover's victory over Smith, the bull market went into a frenzy. An unheard-of number of shares—seven million—were traded on November 23, 1928. The Federal Reserve Board, disturbed by the speculation, ordered its member banks to stop loans for speculative purposes, but this move of the Board was defeated in its effect because corporations lent their surplus for speculation. On September 3, 1929, stock-market prices reached their peak. In October came the crash. On October 24 twelve million shares changed hands. Five days later came a catastrophic drop in prices, and within a few weeks the value of stocks had fallen an average of 40 per cent. The following figures reveal the magnitude of the crash:

	Price:Mar. 3, 1928	*Price:Sept.* 3, 1929	*Price:Nov.*13,1929
American Can	77	$181\frac{7}{8}$	86
American Telephone and Telegraph .	$179\frac{1}{2}$	304	$197\frac{1}{4}$
Anaconda Copper	$54\frac{1}{2}$	$131\frac{1}{2}$	70
General Electric	$128\frac{3}{4}$	$396\frac{1}{4}$	$168\frac{1}{8}$
Montgomery Ward	$132\frac{3}{4}$	$137\frac{7}{8}$	$49\frac{1}{4}$
Electric Bond & Share	$89\frac{3}{4}$	$186\frac{3}{4}$	$50\frac{1}{4}$

The big bull market was dead. Billions of dollars' worth of profits disappeared. The grocer, the dressmaker, and the office clerk lost their investments. In every town families dropped from a showy display of wealth into debt. Day after day the newspapers printed reports of suicides. After the price collapse a whole series of ills hit American society. There had been an overproduction of capital goods at the given price level; there had been an unwise expansion by many concerns; installment buying and buying with stock-market profits had led to an overproduction of many commodities; an artificial price level had been maintained through monopoly conditions; and Europe too was in a depressed state. A major depression was soon under way. Prosperity had been more, of course, than just an economic thing. It had been a psychological experience as well. Rosy hopes of a povertyless world had been developed. When the blow came, it struck not only the pocketbooks but also the minds of America. Americans thus had to adjust their ideas, their manners, and their way of life to meet an altered world.

For the next three years the depression hit America harder than any other industrial nation. Stock prices continued to decline until, by July, 1932, they had fallen off 83 per cent; the wholesale-price index dropped from an average of 100 in 1929 to 63 by March, 1933; and industrial production was almost cut in half from 1929 to 1932. The depression struck various interests unequally. The farmers had been in a depression during the twenties, and after 1929 their difficulties were increased. Their debt load was unchanged, but the wholesale prices of farm goods fell 61 per cent from 1929 to the beginning of 1933. Since there were millions of farmers, mostly competing with one another, they were unable to join together and restrict production to keep prices up. On the other hand, in certain industrial fields production was restricted and prices were maintained. This, of course, meant that the workers bore the brunt of the depression. The rolls of the unemployed increased from one million in 1929 to about thirteen million in 1933.

Mortgage foreclosures were frequent in the farming communities, and farmers organized vigilance committees and used force to prevent the sheriff from selling their property. In the cities rents fell and vacancies increased as people moved in with relatives or friends. One third of the railroads went into bankruptcy. Some leading corporations, like Insull's utility empire, collapsed, and the banking structure began to totter. People became frightened, feeling that the banks were unsafe, and by 1931 over a billion dollars in currency had been withdrawn for hoarding, and during the first three months of 1933 a panic condition prevailed. Withdrawals increased so rapidly that the entire banking structure was threatened with collapse. To prevent this from occurring, governor after governor closed the banks and declared a bank holiday. On the morning that Franklin D. Roosevelt was inaugurated President, the governors of Illinois and New York closed the banks of their states, and before the day was over the banks of the remaining states were closed.

Before the stock-market crash President Hoover had called Congress into a special session "to redeem two pledges given in the last election—farm relief and limited changes in the tariff." The tariff act that resulted—the Hawley-Smoot Act—raised rates even higher than the Fordney-McCumber Act of 1922. The Hawley-Smoot Act raised consumer prices at home, aided monopolies, and brought American foreign trade to a standstill. As for farm relief, Hoover opposed price-fixing or the McNary-Haugen plan, which would have enlisted the government's support of agriculture by the creation of a government corporation to purchase selected agricultural products at a price that would yield a fair profit, sell the surplus abroad at whatever price it could command, and distribute among farmers, by an equalization fee, the loss on foreign sales. Hoover's solution of the farm problem was the Agricultural Marketing Act of June, 1929. Under the act a new Federal Farm Board was empowered to lend money to agricultural co-operatives and to purchase farm surpluses. In 1930 and 1931 the Board tried to peg the price of certain agricultural commodities by purchasing the surplus, but it found that the surplus was never-ending, and it reached the conclusion that the way to keep farm prices up was to restrict production. This step the Hoover Administration would not take.

Toward the ever growing depression the Hoover administration and the Republican party adopted the policy of minimizing its seriousness. The government had subsidized but not regulated business in the twenties, and the Republicans were not ready to admit that this policy was a failure. For a year or two the depression was treated as a transitory situation, and the nation was told that "prosperity is just around the corner." On the theory that the old formula of encouragement of business, without regulation, had not been used enough, the tariff was raised and the income tax was lowered. As more and more people were thrown out of work, President Hoover declared, "We *must* prevent hunger and cold to those of our people who are in honest difficulties." He was unwilling, however, to sanction direct work relief. Progressives urged the Federal government to finance large-scale work-relief programs, but the burden of relief was left to local governments and to private charity. Private agencies and local governments were unable to handle relief for the unemployed; still the President would not act. Hoover even vetoed a bill drawn up by Senator Wagner, which would have established a national system of employment agencies.

The continuing disintegration of economic activity finally forced the administration into action. In January, 1932, Hoover supported the Reconstruction Finance Corporation in its plan to lend money to railroads, banks, industry, and farmers. In July of that year an amendment permitted the R.F.C. to lend money for self-liquidating public works and to lend money to state and local governments "to be used in furnishing relief and work relief to needy and distressed people." Under the Roosevelt administration the R.F.C. became the banker for a variety of relief and recovery measures. Before 1933 R.F.C. aid saved many banks, railroads, and industries from complete collapse, and it did help local governments to meet their pay rolls. But it operated too slowly, and it did not materially aid the unemployed. It was hoped that the R.F.C. would bring prosperity to the banks, industries, and railroads and then that this prosperity would trickle down to the masses. The increasing number of unemployed showed that it was failing in this objective. More courageous steps were needed, but were not taken by the Hoover administration.

One other way in which Hoover hoped to check the depression was to inspire businessmen to enter into voluntary agreements to keep up wages, to expand their production, and to avoid industrial conflicts. Many conferences of businessmen were held, and agreements were entered into on these points. Then the agreements invariably broke down. Economic necessity and self-interest made it impossible to keep up wages and to expand production. President Hoover, believing in the co-operation of businessmen rather than the positive state, refused to take governmental action when the agreements broke down; instead the Hoover administration criticized the business forces. But the levels of production continued to decline, unemployment increased, and men drifted across the country, searching for work and living in little "shantytowns" constructed on the edges of industrial areas.

SELECTED BIBLIOGRAPHY

P. W. Slosson, *The Great Crusade and After, 1914–1928*; F. L. Allen, *Only Yesterday*; Samuel Hopkins Adams, *The Incredible Era*, offer valuable insight into the era; J. T. Adams, *Our Business Civilization*; A. A. Berle and G. C. Means, *The Modern Corporation and Private Property*; H. W. Laidler, *Concentration of Control in American Industry*; David Lynch, *The Concentration of Economic Power*, all valuable on the business developments; William Allen White, *A Puritan in Babylon*, and Herbert Hoover, *The Challenge to Liberty*, useful.

There is a great deal of valuable information in the reports of two committees appointed by President Hoover, *Recent Economic Changes in the United States*, and *Recent Social Trends in the United States*; Benedict Crowell and R. F. Wilson, *How America Went to War*, Vol. VI, the story of demobilization; Stuart Chase, *Prosperity, Fact or Myth?* a critical study of the prosperity of the twenties; W. Z. Ripley, *Main Street and Wall Street*; W. B. Donham, *Business Adrift*; Paul Douglas and Aaron Director, *Problems of Unemployment*, studies on the depression and the problems created by it.

H. S. Commager (Ed.), *Documents of American History*, pp. 353–358, 366–372, 374–377, 378–381, 384–388, 390–396, 402–405, 406–408, 412–417, contains source material.

XXXIII

The Resurgence of Progressivism

AT THE DEPTHS OF THE DEPRESSION a historian of the muckraking movement of the first decade of the century observed:

In some ways, it seems to the writer, conditions in this country are today very similar to those of thirty years ago. There is corruption in every type of government unit, from the small town or country up to the federal government. The buying and selling of votes is so common in certain sections that newspapers comment on it as a matter of course. And behind all this, today as thirty years ago, is business. The treatment that the laborers receive in some of the coal fields of Kentucky, West Virginia, and Pennsylvania is almost beyond belief. There is still the old problem of power, or the activities of the public utilities companies. Then there are new problems—the gangs, prohibition enforcement, corruption in unemployment relief, broadcasting, and the treatment of the so-called radicals. The list could be extended almost indefinitely. Are we not in need of exposures today?[1]

In 1932, amidst the suffering and increasing unemployment, the Republican party renominated Herbert Hoover on a platform that advocated, among other things, the extension of the protective tariff; the support of "any plan which will help to balance production against demand, and thereby raise agricultural prices, provided it is economically sound and administratively workable without burdensome bureaucracy"; and, in regard to prohibition, an amendment "retaining in the Federal Government power to preserve the gains already made in dealing with the evils inherent in the liquor traffic," but permitting "states to deal with the problem as their citizens may determine."

The Democrats, on the other hand, adopted a platform denouncing the Republican policy of economic isolation, the fostering of monopolies, and the encouragement of "the indefensible expansion and contraction of credit for private profit at the expense of the public." The platform charged that these policies had "ruined our foreign trade, destroyed the

[1]C. C. Regier, *The Era of the Muckrakers*, Preface. University of North Carolina Press, Chapel Hill, 1932. By permission of the University of North Carolina Press.

values of our commodities and products, crippled our banking system, robbed millions of our people of their life savings and thrown millions more out of work, produced widespread poverty and brought the government to a state of financial distress unprecedented in times of peace." Constructively the Democrats advocated reciprocal-trade agreements, aid for the farmers, Federal aid to the unemployed, the regulation of the stock exchange, the repeal of prohibition, reform of the banking structure, and independence of the Philippines.

Franklin D. Roosevelt, governor of New York, was nominated after a masterly preconvention campaign, managed by James A. Farley and Louis Howe. Roosevelt shattered precedent by flying to the Chicago convention and accepting the nomination from the convention itself. He then toured the country, talking farm relief, tariff reform, regulation of utilities, and economic reorganization. During the campaign he relied heavily on the advice of Raymond Moley, Rexford G. Tugwell, and Adolf A. Berle, all of the faculty of Columbia University. The group of advisers included, in addition, Judge Samuel I. Rosenman, Basil O'Connor, Hugh S. Johnson, Felix Frankfurter, and Bernard Baruch. This group became known as the "brain trust" and was violently denounced as the New Deal unfolded its program of relief, recovery, and reform in the next few years. In the campaign Roosevelt indicated the direction that his policies later followed. A speech delivered at the Commonwealth Club in San Francisco, for instance, was a clear and unambiguous statement of his program. In the course of the speech he said:

Our task now is not discovery or exploitation of natural resources, or necessarily producing more goods. It is the soberer, less dramatic business of administering resources and plants already in hand, of seeking to re-establish foreign markets for our surplus production, of meeting the problem of underconsumption, of adjusting production to consumption, of distributing wealth and products more equitably, of adapting existing economic organizations to the service of the people.

Although this was termed radicalism by some, it was in the tradition of Woodrow Wilson, Theodore Roosevelt, and William J. Bryan, who also had tried to adapt "existing economic organizations to the service of the people."

In the same speech Roosevelt said:

Every man has a right to life, and this means that he has also a right to make a comfortable living. . . . Every man has a right to his own property; which means a right to be assured, to the fullest extent attainable, in the

© Harris & Ewing

Franklin Delano Roosevelt

safety of his savings. By no other means can men carry the burdens of those parts of life which, in the nature of things, afford no chance of labor: childhood, sickness, old age. In all thought of property, this right is paramount; all other property rights must yield to it.

Here was a powerful declaration in support of private capitalism. In the years to follow, Roosevelt's reforms were aimed at preserving the system of private capitalism, not at substituting some other system for it. Reforms were necessary, however, to stave off some revolutionary movement from developing out of depression conditions. With regard to Roosevelt's desire to preserve capitalism by necessary reforms, one writer has said:

> Well-to-do people of Dutch ancestry and graduates of Groton and Harvard may not be promising material out of which to develop saints and martyrs, but they frequently exhibit a remarkable capacity to look after their own interests. It must never be forgotten that the world as it was suited Franklin D. Roosevelt admirably. His place in that world was pleasant and much more secure than that of most men. He must have been a fool of almost unexampled proportions to desire, much less to try to effect, the demolition of that world. On the contrary, such a man could be relied on to spare no effort to preserve it; and if he perceived that preserving it all was impracticable, he would do everything possible to preserve all of it that he could. If certain changes were necessary to shore up the toppling structure, it is precisely a man of Roosevelt's type who might be expected to be most energetic, resolute and emphatic in demanding that the changes be made, thoroughly and speedily.[1]

Socialists, Communists, and other extreme radicals were bitterly opposed to Roosevelt during the formative years of the New Deal. They were aware that instead of presiding at the demise of private capitalism and the profit system, he was expertly performing operations that might give capitalism a new hold on life.

The tidal wave that swept Franklin D. Roosevelt into office bears resemblance to the political "upsurges" that swept Thomas Jefferson, Andrew Jackson, and Abraham Lincoln into office in the nineteenth century. These movements were expressions of discontent with the *status quo*. The masses of the American people were profoundly stirred. At other times, however, American democracy has been sluggish, lazy, and careless, and has not aroused itself until there has been grave danger

[1] Gerald W. Johnson, *Roosevelt: Dictator or Democrat?* pp. 184–185. Harper & Brothers, New York, 1941.

to the democratic way of life. Then it has thrown aside its weak leaders and has turned to a leader devoted to fundamental democracy. But in 1932 there was more than discontent with the Republican rule. There was also a feeling of bitter despair, arising out of the collapse of the economic system. The discontent and the despair carried Roosevelt into office with the largest popular vote ever given a candidate in our history up to that time. The President-elect received almost twenty-three million votes to Hoover's fifteen and a half million. In the Electoral College the results were 472 to 59, with Hoover carrying only Maine, New Hampshire, Vermont, Connecticut, Delaware, and Pennsylvania.

F. D. R.

During the four Presidential campaigns that Franklin D. Roosevelt waged, a vocal minority attempted to create the impression that not only his program but his background was un-American. Franklin D. Roosevelt's early environment was aristocratic, but, as Gerald W. Johnson has written:

To say of an American President that he began life under highly advantageous circumstances proves nothing about him. It classifies him with John Tyler and William H. Taft, without doubt, but it also classifies him with Washington and Jefferson; so what can one reasonably infer from that? The log cabin-to-White House tradition is romantic, and delights the hearts of all sentimental Americans, but its value diminishes under realistic examination. It gave us Jackson and Lincoln, but it also gave us Fillmore and Garfield. Whether he be by origin proletarian or aristocrat, a President may be equally in line with American tradition—indeed, with either tradition, the great or the small.[1]

Franklin D. Roosevelt was born at Hyde Park, New York, in 1882. His father was a wealthy man, although of trifling wealth in comparison with that of the Rockefellers, the Vanderbilts, and the other richest families of the time. The first Roosevelt settled in New York when it was still a Dutch colony. Theodore Roosevelt sprang from the Republican wing of the family, while distant relative Franklin came from the Democratic wing. The Roosevelt family was a hard-working, prosperous one. To those who believe in the importance of hereditary traits, the following words of Gerald W. Johnson should be interesting:

In the whole Roosevelt record there is not a single great musician, painter, sculptor, or other artist, and not a single madman. No Roosevelt ever died

[1] Ibid. p. 37.

as a martyr to some great cause, and none was ever shot in a quarrel over a trollop. Up to the eighth generation there is no conspicuous instance in which a Roosevelt ever refused to do his duty, and none in which one ever did much more than his duty. In two hundred and fifty years the family was remarkably clear of both scandal and glory. Up to the last half-century they were simply worthy people, intelligent without genius, decent without saintliness, educated without erudition, not slothful in business, but not titans of industry—in short, admirable, but not inspiring.[1]

Franklin D. Roosevelt's early education was received from private tutors, with frequent trips abroad. He attended prep school at exclusive Groton and college at Harvard, in the class of 1904, and then received legal training at Columbia University's law school. Until 1910 he worked at the lawyer's trade. Then, in that year, he ran for the state senate from rock-ribbed Republican Duchess, Columbia, and Putnam counties. This district had not elected a Democrat since 1884, and therefore the regular party men were not interested in the candidacy. Franklin D. Roosevelt was asked to run, since his name would lend distinction to the ticket, and he could pay his own campaign expenses. Roosevelt toured his district in an automobile and met the people and talked to any who would listen. No candidate in the district had gone to the people in this way before. When the election returns came in, he carried the district by over a thousand votes. At Albany he distinguished himself by leading a courageous and successful fight against Tammany Hall, and he was one of the few New York delegates to the Democratic convention in 1912 to support Woodrow Wilson. After Wilson's election he was appointed Assistant Secretary of the Navy—a post once held by Theodore Roosevelt—as a reward for his efforts on Wilson's behalf and also because he long had had an ardent interest in things nautical. A political writer in Washington, during the Wilson administration, said of the Assistant Secretary of the Navy, "With his handsome face and his form of supple strength he could make a fortune on the stage and set the matinee girls' hearts throbbing with subtle and happy emotion." Secretary of the Navy Josephus Daniels called his assistant "a steam engine in breeches," and Daniels did little without Roosevelt's prior approval.

As Assistant Secretary, Roosevelt shook the navy out of its inertia and helped to prepare it for the war in 1917. During the war he was credited with originating the idea of the 110-foot submarine chaser,

[1] Gerald W. Johnson, *Roosevelt: Dictator or Democrat?* pp. 42–43. Harper & Brothers, New York, 1941.

which proved so effective. He was also credited with being one of the major figures behind the North Sea mine barrage against the U-boats. His experience in the Wilson administration during the First World War was, of course, to aid him considerably when he had to guide the destinies of the United States in the Second World War. The youthful Roosevelt was influenced in these years in Washington by President Wilson's philosophy of the New Freedom. Many of the ingredients of that philosophy later appeared in his own New Deal. In 1920, as a firm advocate of the New Freedom, he was nominated for the Vice-Presidency on the Democratic ticket. In the midst of the campaign he confronted Wilson, now paralyzed and confined to a wheel chair, and pledged his word to carry on the fight for the Wilsonian dream of collective security and international justice.

In the following year Mr. Roosevelt was stricken with infantile paralysis. His courageous fight for recovery in the next six years was of great significance. It gave him time for reading and reflection, and he emerged from these years with a deeper philosophy of life. It also gave him an opportunity to lay the groundwork for a progressive Democratic party. In this connection he carried on a wide correspondence with people all over the country. In 1928, upon the urgent request of Al Smith, Roosevelt ran for governor of New York. His victory in a year in which the Republican party swept the nation, and his re-election in 1930, made him a leading candidate for the Presidential nomination in 1932. As governor of New York, he showed that he really enjoyed the job, that he knew how to handle men, that he had a magnificent radio voice, and that he had the good will of the newspaper reporters.

THE PHILOSOPHY OF THE NEW DEAL

President Roosevelt's inaugural address on March 4, 1933, gave hope to a disillusioned and bitter America. Its confident tone seemed like the voice of a new messiah. The encouraging voice promised a "new deal" for the "forgotten man"—a promise which was carried out in the legislation of the next few years. Roosevelt asserted "that the only thing we have to fear is fear itself," although he did not minimize the dangers facing the country. He told the nation:

Values have shrunken to fantastic levels; taxes have risen; our ability to pay has fallen; government of all kinds is faced by serious curtailment of income; the means of exchange are frozen in the currents of trade; the withered leaves of industrial enterprise lie on every side; farmers find no markets for their produce; the savings of many years in thousands of families are gone.

More important, a host of unemployed citizens face the grim problem of existence, and an equally great number toil with little return. Only a foolish optimist can deny the dark realities of the moment.

Instead of exhortation, which Hoover had used, Roosevelt asserted, "We must act and act quickly." The number of steps that were taken in the next three months carried out this assertion. The new President was also vigorous in his denunciation of the "unscrupulous money-changers," who "stand indicted in the court of public opinion." The hope that he inspired in the people was contained in his closing remarks:

We face the arduous days that lie before us in the warm courage of national unity; with the clear consciousness of seeking old and precious moral values; with the clean satisfaction that comes from the stern performance of duty by old and young alike.

We aim at the assurance of a rounded and permanent national life.

We do not distrust the future of essential democracy. The people of the United States have not failed. In their need they have registered a mandate that they want direct, vigorous action.

They have asked for discipline and direction under leadership. They have made me the present instrument of their wishes. In the spirit of the gift I take it.

This speech was a typically Progressive speech that well might have been delivered by Theodore Roosevelt, "Fighting Bob" La Follette, or Woodrow Wilson. It did not advocate any overthrow of the American system of private enterprise, but it did propose to regulate private enterprise in the interests of the people. The problem, then, was to rearrange existing society. To carry out these objectives required planning: industrial planning to prevent the wasteful duplication of plants, obsolescence of machinery, and bankruptcies; planned use of the land in agriculture; and planning of the banking and utility structure. There was little difference between this planning and the older Progressive idea of regulation. There was a great difference, however, between this planning and that which had been carried on during the twenties. Under the New Deal the government played the dominant role in the planning. Washington and not Wall Street did the planning; business was no longer in control. The crash of 1929 and the resulting depression

George W. Norris   Felix Frankfurter   Cordell Hull

James A. Farley   Bernard Baruch   Harry Hopkins

Significant Leaders during the Days of the New Deal

John Nance Garner   Harold Ickes   Henry A. Wallace

Photographs by Harris & Ewing

demonstrated that business could not successfully plan the economic structure for the benefit of the many. Instead monopolists planned for only their own selfish class interest. Under New Deal planning, "the forgotten man" was to benefit, "the one third of the population which was ill-housed, ill-fed, and ill-clothed."

The New Deal's planning showed definite partiality for the average American. Every man must be protected in his "right to make a comfortable living" and be sure of "the safety of his savings." "The reward for a day's work will have to be greater on the average than it has been," Roosevelt observed, "and the reward to capital, especially the capital which is speculative, will have to be less." For such statements the New Deal was charged with stirring class consciousness. Actually, the Republican policies of the twenties, ending in the depression, had stirred class consciousness to a high degree. The New Deal, realizing this situation, sought to redress the class balance by improving the lot of the majority of Americans, and thus close the wide gap that had developed between the few and the many.

The New Deal carried on the Progressive philosophy of the pre-war years, but it did not have an immediate background of liberal movements upon which it could build. Before Theodore Roosevelt or Woodrow Wilson had developed Progressive principles in the national government, there had been a wide range of local and state movements, as well as the muckraking episode, Bryan, and the Populist era. The years just before the New Deal were lean years for liberal principles. The press of the nation was interested in protecting the *status quo* of exploitation, and there were no popular magazines carrying articles of exposure. The depression gave rise to some movements of an emotional type, like Huey Long's "Share-the-Wealth" program and the Townsend Plan, but these did not aid in the development of the New Deal. President Roosevelt, then, could not depend upon any well-developed movement when he took office. The New Deal had to be developed in a hurry in order to meet the grave crisis created by the depression. As a result of the speed which was required, mistakes were made in the implementation of the program.

The New Deal recognized, as the Old Deal had not, that the forces within the American economy were not in equilibrium, and it was aware of the fundamental defects in the capitalistic system. It saw that the danger of class hostilities was no longer remote, but was evident in many ways. The chief idea behind the remedy proposed by the New Deal was balance. Private ownership of the means of production was to continue, but private capitalism was to be checked from exploiting the raw materials and its labor supply. Roosevelt clearly stated this idea of a balance in the economic system in a speech on March 5, 1934:

What we seek is balance in our economic system—balance between agriculture and industry and balance between the wage earner, the employer, and the consumer. We seek also balance that our internal markets be kept rich and large, and that our trade with other nations be increased on both sides of the ledger.

AGRICULTURE AND THE PLANNED USE OF THE LAND

In the first place, President Roosevelt was faced with an appalling agricultural situation. The American farmer had, in most cases, been wasteful of the soil. Instead of conserving the land, he had used it to make a quick profit, and then had abandoned it and moved west to new land. But since the turn of the century, little desirable free land was to be had. Furthermore, now the American farmer was faced with competition from the newer lands of Canada, Argentina, and Australia. The Republican high-tariff policy since the Civil War and the official encouragement which that party had given to the growing industrial power had had definite adverse effects on the farmers' position, and ever since the First World War the farmer particularly had been in trouble. The depression and the resulting foreclosures of farm mortgages had only increased his desperation.

The New Deal moved quickly to alleviate the farm situation, which had been bringing the farmers of the West and the South closer and closer to the status of peasantry. The goals of its farm program were many. The government hoped to establish farm prices at the level at which they had been just before the First World War, in order to enable the farmer to secure "parity prices" for his products—that is, prices which would compare favorably with what he had to pay for goods and services. It hoped also to adjust farm production to meet the demands of the market. It proposed, too, to achieve soil conservation and the better use of the land. Finally, relief and rehabilitation were planned, as well as security against farm foreclosures and a reduction of the debt load of the farmer. Such competent farm advisers as Secretary of Agriculture Henry A. Wallace, George Peek, and Mordecai Ezekiel aided in the passage of the Agricultural Adjustment Act in May, 1933. Hoover's Farm Board had tried to raise farmers' prices by buying the surplus. Under the Agricultural Adjustment Act the same end was aimed at, but it was more effectively achieved by controlling production. The government paid farmers to reduce the acreage devoted to certain crops. The funds for this were raised by taxing the processors of these goods. The act was in operation from 1933 to 1935. Fifteen crops came under its supervision, although major attention was paid to wheat, cotton, tobacco, corn, hogs, beet and cane sugar, and cattle. Under the cotton program ten million acres of land were taken out of cotton production in 1933, and the price of cotton rose from five and a half to nine and a half cents a pound. The planters received about two hundred million dollars in payments for the shift in acreage. In the case of the wheat program, over eight million acres were removed from wheat production, over a hundred million dollars was paid in benefits, the price of wheat advanced, and the wheat farmer's income increased about 100 per cent.

An unprecedented drought also helped to destroy farm surpluses. The farm income, partly because of the drought, partly because of the program of crop reduction and benefit payments, and partly because of the devaluation of the dollar, increased from $5,562,000,000 in 1932 to $8,688,000,000 in 1935. On January 6, 1936, the Supreme Court declared the Agricultural Adjustment Act to be unconstitutional on two counts. The regulation of agriculture was "a purely local activity," and therefore it was a right reserved to the states, and secondly the processing tax was an improper use of the taxing power. Justice Stone, however, delivered a vigorous dissenting opinion, in which he warned the majority against a "tortured construction of the Constitution" and stated that the "courts are not the only agency of government that must be assumed to have capacity to govern."

Faced with this action on the part of the Supreme Court, the administration, without abandoning its desire to raise farm prices, shifted its emphasis to soil conservation. Shortly after the invalidation of the Agricultural Adjustment Act the Soil Conservation and Domestic Allotment Act was passed. This measure provided payments for farmers who put crop lands into pasture or into soil-conserving crops. The act, however, was only a stopgap. A more important act waited until the Supreme Court's attitude toward the legislation of the New Deal became more favorable. When this occurred, in 1938, another Agricultural Adjustment Act was passed, in February of that year. Under this act national quotas were established for certain crops; then the quotas were broken down to the individual farmer, and only those farmers who lived up to their quotas received soil-conservation payments.

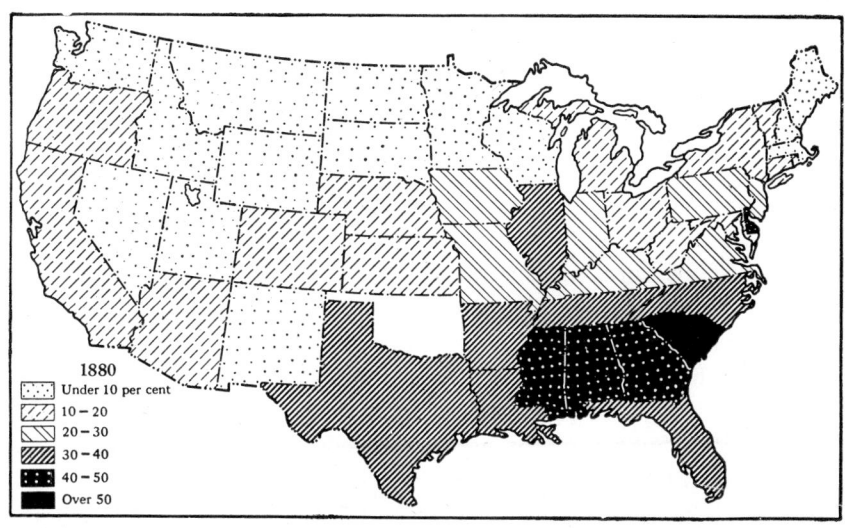

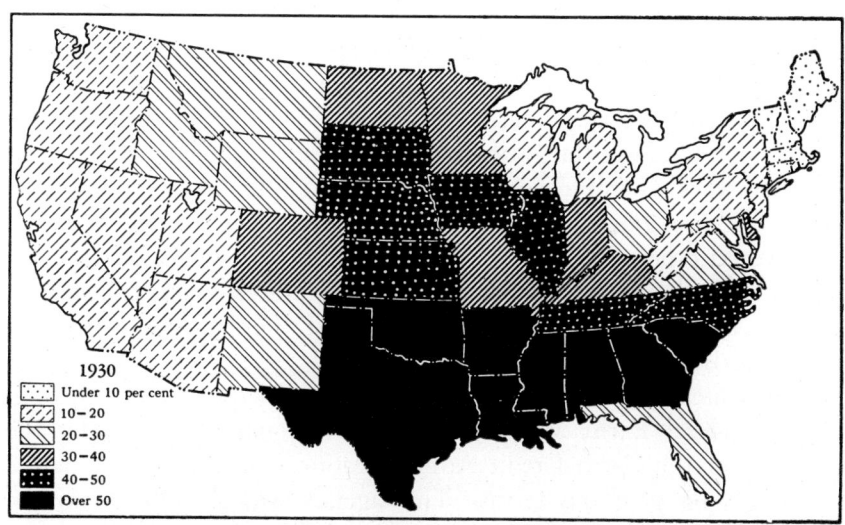

Farm Tenancy in 1880 and 1930

Penalty taxes were imposed on all production above the quotas. The act also provided for loans to the farmers, and crop insurance for wheat was tried. The insurance and loan features were expected to aid in the stabilization of production and the equalization of prices. This act did not receive the disapproval of the Supreme Court, since it controlled "commerce," which is national, and not "production." And it should be remembered that there were now two new justices on the Court.

Another phase of the New Deal's farm program was the removal of submarginal land from production and the resettlement of the depressed farmer on better land. The Division of Subsistence Homesteads (1933) and its successor, the Resettlement Administration (1935), bought up substandard land and set it aside as grazing areas, recreation places, and wild-life preserves. They also lent money to farmers for the purchase of seeds, tools, and livestock, and they resettled depressed farmers in new rural settlements. The Farm Security Administration, established in 1937, continued this work and added to it the establishment of co-operative farm communities, in which the land was operated in common. The first such community was opened at Lake Dick, Arkansas, in 1938. The FSA also took definite steps to aid migrant farm workers, whose plight was portrayed in John Steinbeck's novel *The Grapes of Wrath*. It constructed camps at which the migrants could reside in decent and hygienic surroundings, and it also worked to check the larger farm-owning groups from exploiting their labor. It experimented in the formation of health-insurance co-operatives to counteract the inadequate health facilities of many rural communities. After the United States entered the Second World War, the FSA was called upon to aid in the agricultural man-power problem. It arranged for farm workers employed only for a few months in one region to be transferred to regions where they were needed during the months when they would otherwise be idle. It set up minimum-wage and housing standards to be met before such migrant farmers were transferred. Also, it resettled on farming land some of the Japanese-Americans evacuated from the west coast.

The acute farm-mortgage situation was met by the creation, in 1934, of the Federal Farm Mortgage Corporation, which was under the direction of the Farm Credit Administration and which underwrote mortgages on generous terms. This agency was able to obtain the scaling down of both the interest rates and the principal of the mortgages. By 1935 Federal agencies owned about 38 per cent of the nation's farm indebtedness. The Reconstruction Finance Corporation meanwhile organized the Commodity Credit Corporation, which lent money to farmers. As a result of the policies pursued by these agencies, farm foreclosures largely ceased, and with the higher commodity prices created by the Agricultural Adjustment Administration many farmers were able to liquidate their debts.

At the same time, the State Department, under the leadership of Cordell Hull, was trying to recapture foreign markets for American goods through reciprocal-trade agreements. Treaties were signed with Canada, for instance, under which, in return for concessions on imported Canadian cattle and cheese, Canada granted concessions on American pork, potatoes, corn, poultry, food, and certain manufactured goods. The treaties signed with European and Latin-American nations greatly improved American trade beyond the state to which it had sunk as a result of the high Republican tariffs. Secretary Hull, of course, not only visualized the improvement of economic conditions at home and abroad from such treaties, but hoped that the treaties would break down excessive nationalism and be a force for world peace.

RELIEF AND SOCIAL SECURITY

The Roosevelt administration, in 1933, was confronted with the grave problem created by approximately fifteen million unemployed. The progressive nature of the New Deal was such that, even without an economic crisis, it would have sponsored laws to aid workers, but in 1933 it had the additional problem of the relief and re-employment of the millions who were idle. The Hoover administration had held that the relief of the needy was a local problem. The New Deal, however, looked upon it as a nationwide problem. By 1935 it had worked out the following program, whose point of departure was that the great mass of the unemployed were not lazy, but unfortunate: work should be given to the unemployed at once, preferably at their own skills and at wage rates that were the prevailing ones in their communities; thus the unemployed could maintain their self-respect, perform socially useful tasks, and at the same time receive a subsistence income until opportunities in private fields were opened. By this program the Federal government admitted its responsibility for the unfortunate. In spite of the work done by the New Deal to check unemployment, however, the number of people out of work in 1937 was still close to ten million.

Important steps had been taken before the above-mentioned policy was evolved. The Civilian Conservation Corps, created by Congress on March 31, 1933, gave work to young men in the rehabilitation of the nation's forests and soil. On May 22, 1933, Congress established the Federal Emergency Relief Administration. Under the FERA, grants of money were given to state and local governments, to be matched, or a percentage to be matched, by the recipients. Once the grants were made, the local authorities had charge of administering them. During the winter of 1933 and the spring of 1934, a special branch of the FERA, the Civil Works Administration, supplied emergency jobs for four million unemployed. By 1935 the FERA had developed a serious weakness. Many areas unloaded on the program persons who were not victims of the depression. Many chronic poor, who were the responsibility of local welfare agencies, were placed on FERA rolls. As a result, the Works Progress Administration, headed by Harry Hopkins, was launched in April, 1935, to replace the FERA. The WPA had, as its purpose, the creation of useful projects which would give employment to those on relief rolls and for which most of the money would go for wages. The Federal government retained a large measure of control over the expenditures of the funds so as to prevent unemployables from being placed on relief rolls by local communities.

In the carrying out of this huge program, there was some waste and confusion. A number of the projects were useless. On the other hand, *Fortune* magazine, in October, 1937, published an extensive report on the work of the WPA and observed: "This impartial and wholly unbiased survey gave strongest support to the feeling that the machinery (as opposed to the laborer cared for) of the damned and despised WPA functions with an efficiency of which any industrialist would be proud." A wide variety of projects were sponsored by the WPA. Roads, armories, sewers, school buildings, swimming pools, and bridges were constructed. Theater companies, music projects, artists, and writers were financed. For instance, unemployed writers were put to work in preparing state and regional guidebooks, and a number of significant historical and sociological investigations were made. WPA funds made adult-education projects possible all over the nation. A branch of the WPA, the National Youth Administration, paid small amounts to youths in school and college to help them to continue their education. It also employed young men and women beyond the school age in special projects. This youth program checked the demoralizing influence of idleness and enabled the leaders of the future to become better equipped for the tasks ahead of them.

The Federal government also attempted to cut unemployment and to improve the economic situation through the Public Works Administration, created in 1933. By the construction of public works, jobs would be provided and an impetus would be given to heavy industries, —steel, lumber, cement,—which were in a low state of operation. Harold Ickes, Secretary of the Interior, was made administrator and was empowered to make grants to states and local government units.

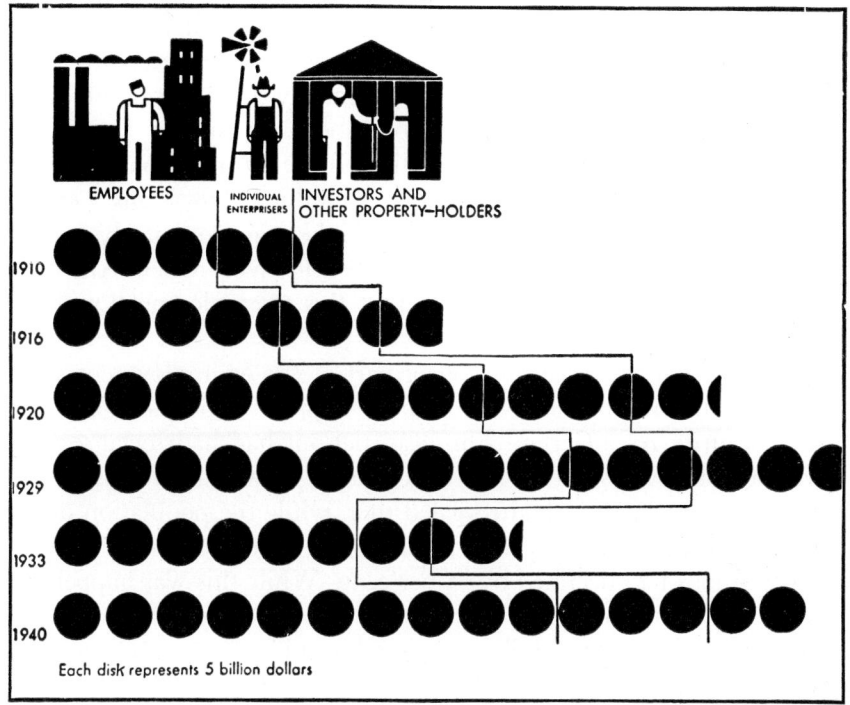

EMPLOYEES | INDIVIDUAL ENTERPRISERS | INVESTORS AND OTHER PROPERTY-HOLDERS

1910

1916

1920

1929

1933

1940

Each disk represents 5 billion dollars

Pictograph Corporation

Division of National Income

The recipients, in turn, had to supply a per cent of the funds needed for each project undertaken. The work was carried on by private firms, which were not required to hire relief labor. Harold Ickes's watchful eye prevented graft and politics from marring the PWA. By July 1, 1936, this agency had expended two and a half billion dollars on heavy-construction projects. These projects included waterworks, power plants, high-school and college buildings, municipal and state buildings, and naval construction. As Ickes said, these were "useful and enduring projects which will serve the people."

The number of people who were furnished jobs by the Federal government's various projects in February, 1936, is indicated by the following:

The WPA	3,035,852
The CCC	459,461
All other Federal agencies	340,774
Total	3,836,087

These figures, of course, represent only Federal relief projects. To these figures must be added the number who were receiving local, home relief. In February, 1936, approximately 2,130,000 family units were on local, home relief. Therefore about six million families or individuals were on some type of relief. If we estimate that there are three persons to a family, about eighteen million Americans were on relief. By 1938 the number was even higher, approximately twenty million. It was not until the Second World War, when American industry turned to war production, that this unemployment problem was temporarily solved.

A long-range, possible solution of part of the unemployment situation was launched by the New Deal in 1935 with the passage of the Social Security Act. Certain European nations had had social-security laws for many years before the United States government passed this measure. Investigations had revealed that, while the population of the United States had increased by about 20 per cent from 1920 to 1936, industrial jobs had declined by 25 per cent. While this was happening, the life expectancy of those over sixty-five years of age increased; but the number of industrial and professional openings for people over fifty decreased. Therefore it was felt necessary to frame legislation that would permanently help the unemployed and the aged. By 1934 twenty-eight states had old-age-pension plans, but only two—Ohio and Wisconsin—had unemployment-insurance legislation. It thus became necessary to have a national plan. The Social Security Act of 1935, in dealing with old age, provided that the Federal government should give grants to those states that passed old-age laws meeting certain specified standards. The Federal government matched the state grants, dollar for dollar, up to fifteen dollars a month. If a state appropriated fifteen dollars a month for those over sixty-five, the maximum payment would thus be thirty dollars a month. To meet the situation of those not yet sixty-five, a national system of compulsory old-age insurance was established. This plan applied to all workers except casual laborers, those engaged in agriculture, domestic work, and maritime work, and those working for Federal, state, and local governments. Money for this plan was obtained by taxes levied on both employers and employees.

No national plan was established for unemployment insurance. The Federal government levied upon employers of eight or more persons a 3 per cent tax on their payrolls. Ninety per cent of the Federal levy was returned to the social-security board of any state which passed insurance plans that met Federal specifications. By July, 1937, all the states, and Alaska, Hawaii, and the District of Columbia, had established systems that met these specifications. A Social Security Board of three members was set up to have supervision and management of these old-age-assistance and unemployment-insurance plans. The act also appropriated money to the states for aid to dependent children, and provided for yearly appropriations for maternal and child-health care, crippled children, the blind, and vocational-rehabilitation work. The act was immediately challenged on constitutional grounds. The Supreme Court on May 24, 1937, announced the constitutionality of the vital parts of the act, basing its decision on the "general welfare" clause of the Constitution. Justice Cardozo, in the decision on the unemployment-insurance plan, said, with reference to unemployment:

> The states were unable to give the requisite relief. The problem had become national in area and dimensions. There was need of help if the people were not to starve. It is too late today for the argument to be heard with tolerance that in a crisis so extreme the use of the moneys of the nation to relieve the unemployed and their dependents is a use for any purpose narrower than the promotion of the general welfare.

By this decision the Supreme Court helped to adapt the Constitution to the needs of twentieth-century, industrial America. The act, by most standards, was conservative. Needed health insurance was not included largely because of the pressure brought by insurance companies and the American Medical Association. The groups that were not included in the act suffered, and the payments under the act in many cases were not sufficient.

INDUSTRY AND LABOR

In order to increase employment opportunities and to rescue business from the chaos of the depression, the National Industrial Recovery Act was passed in June, 1933. This act was usually referred to as the NRA. The act was to achieve its purpose through the regulation and reform of industry. It was designed to speed up industrial production, to increase employment, to raise wages and shorten the hours of work, to protect the right of labor to organize and to strike, to eliminate child labor, and to check the waste of competition without aiding the growth of monopolies. The act permitted the industries of the nation to frame codes of self-government with the approval and super-

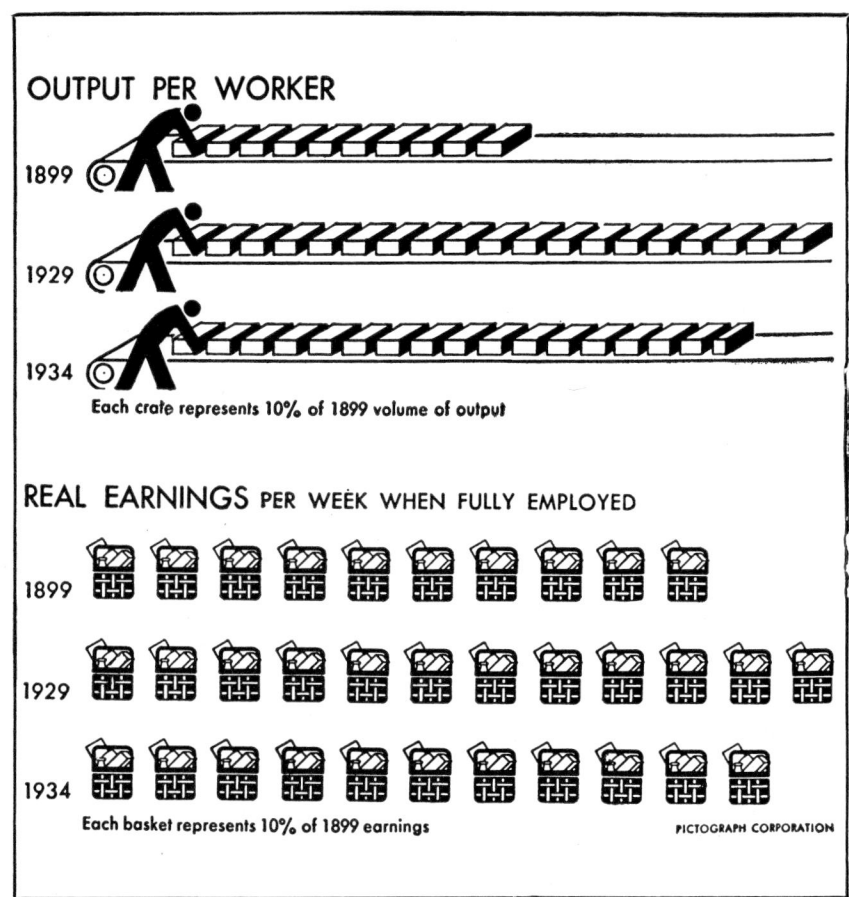

OUTPUT PER WORKER

1899

1929

1934

Each crate represents 10% of 1899 volume of output

REAL EARNINGS PER WEEK WHEN FULLY EMPLOYED

1899

1929

1934

Each basket represents 10% of 1899 earnings

PICTOGRAPH CORPORATION

Output and Earnings in Manufacturing Industries

vision of government administrators. The National Recovery Administration, with General Hugh S. Johnson as chief administrator, was to supervise the preparation of the codes and enforce their observance. By April, 1934, about five hundred codes had been drawn up, and over twenty million workers were under their provisions. The speed with which the codes had to be written allowed business a relatively free hand in formulating the provisions, and as a result big business was generally able to impose its desires on small business. Many of the old trade-association agreements of the twenties were taken over into the NRA codes. The New Deal required of business that it raise wages, lessen hours of work, and grant fair labor standards. In return, business was able to write its views into the codes. When an industry drew up a code, a code authority was established, under General Johnson's supervision, to administer it. Generally, the code authority was the old trade association. Although labor and the public were supposed to be represented on the code authority, these two groups actually played only a small part in the entire affair.

Except for the newspaper and retail-trade codes, child labor was successfully barred. Every code contained the following provisions affecting labor (Section 7A of the NRA):

(1) That employees shall have the right to organize and bargain collectively through representatives of their own choosing, and shall be free from interference, restraint, or coercion of employers of labor, or their agents, in the designation of such representatives or in self-organization or in other concerted activities for the purpose of collective bargaining or other mutual aid or protection; (2) that no employee and no one seeking employment shall be required as a condition of employment to join any company union or to refrain from joining, organizing or assisting a labor organization of his own choosing; and (3) that employers shall comply with the maximum hours of labor, minimum rates of pay, and other conditions of employment approved or prescribed by the President.

In order to protect the rights of labor and to settle industrial disputes by arbitration, the NRA created the National Labor Board. It was hoped that the provisions in the codes which limited the hours of labor would cause employers to hire more workers without reducing wages. Roughly 60 per cent of the workers under the codes gained a forty-hour week. Wage differentials were permitted. Higher wages were permitted for whites than for Negroes, for men than for women, for workers in the North than for those in the South. The minimum wages allowed, however, were higher than had prevailed before the act. In Northern cities about half the workers covered by the codes had a minimum wage of forty cents an hour.

A National Recovery Review Board, headed by Clarence S. Darrow, revealed, in May, 1934, that the NRA was fostering monopoly, that small industry was suffering, and that consumer prices were at the mercy of the monopolists. Doubts as to the constitutionality of the law led to noncompliance with the codes. During 1934 and 1935 the NRA was attacked on all sides. Small business criticized the encouragement of monopoly; big business now wanted the government to withdraw entirely, particularly because of the government's protection of labor; and liberals and consumers objected to the suspension of the anti-trust laws and to the rise in prices.

The NRA was tottering when the Supreme Court, on May 27, 1935, unanimously declared the National Industrial Recovery Act to be un-constitutional in the Schechter Poultry Corporation case. The NRA, the Court held, was an illegal delegation of Congress's power, since "Congress cannot delegate legislative power to the President to exercise an unfettered discretion to make whatever laws he thinks may be needed or advisable for the rehabilitation and expansion of trade or industry." Furthermore, the Federal government could not legislate for wages, prices, and industrial conditions in a business not clearly in interstate commerce. The Court also held that no "national emergency" justified these violations of the Constitution.

The administration, thus checked by the Court, proceeded, in the next few years, to achieve national regulation of labor in a more careful manner. Finally, in 1938, the Fair Labor Standards Act was passed. The purpose of the act was to establish "a ceiling over hours and a floor under wages." Certain Southern Congressmen tried to check the bill because wages and labor conditions in the South were far below those of the North. To this argument Representative Ellenbogen of Pennsylvania replied: "This nation cannot continue to exist half sweat-shop and half decent shop. Either the standard of living of the North must come down to the lower level of the South, or the wages in the South must come up to those of the North." Under the act all industries engaged in interstate commerce were to achieve the standard of a forty-hour work week and a forty-cent hourly wage. Industry was allowed seven years in which to make the adjustment; by 1945 the principle was to be reached. The act did not, however, force a maximum work week of forty hours. This was a minimum standard. Work could be done over that minimum at the rate of compensation of time and a half. After the Second World War broke out, antilabor forces tried to destroy the Fair Labor Standards Act by arguing that the forty-hour week was a maximum work week and thus impeded the war effort. This argu-ment was untrue, since workers were permitted to work more than forty hours. Farm laborers, retail employees, professional workers, and seamen did not come under the provisions of the act. Child labor was checked by excluding from interstate commerce goods produced by children under sixteen years of age and, in hazardous occupations, by those under eighteen. A Wage-Hour Administrator was to enforce the measure.

From the standpoint of organizing unions and conducting collective bargaining with employers, Section 7A of the NRA was of far more importance to labor than other provisions of that act. Organized labor had suffered a decline during the twenties, which was only accentuated by the widespread unemployment after 1929. Under Section 7A labor unions expanded their organizing efforts. Antilabor employers countered by firing union workers, hiring labor spies, and encouraging company unions. Company unions doubled in membership from 1932 to 1934, and independent unions launched many strikes. The employers, under Section 7A, were allowed to negotiate with all groups of workers rather than with the representatives of the majority. In this fashion, employers could divide their employees and still rule. The National Labor Relations Board, which replaced the National Labor Board in June, 1934, tried to curtail company unions; in order to ascertain the group that was representative of the majority of the employees in a plant, it held an election and then designated this group as the bargaining unit with the employer. Led by the National Association of Manufacturers, organized industry defied the Board and packed the courts with suits. When the NRA was invalidated, Congress quickly passed the Wagner Act in July, 1935. The purpose of the act was to encourage "the practice and procedure of collective bargaining." A new National Labor Relations Board was created to administer the act. The NLRB was authorized to conduct elections in the plants to determine what labor unit represented the majority of workers and thus should exclusively bargain with the employer. "Unfair practices"— discrimination against union members, domination of labor unions, and refusal to bargain collectively with employees—were forbidden.

In the course of the next two years the NLRB handled over five thousand cases involving "unfair practices," averted or settled close to two thousand strikes, conducted over fourteen hundred elections, and handled a total of more than sixteen hundred disputes. In many instances business refused to comply with the act. In April, 1937, however, the Supreme Court upheld the measure. Chief Justice Hughes observed that the "right of employees to self-organization and freedom in the choice of representatives for collective bargaining" was related to interstate commerce and was properly within the jurisdiction of Congress. He asked,

When industries organize themselves on a national scale, making their relation to interstate commerce the dominant factor in their activities, how can it be maintained that their industrial labor relations constitute a for-

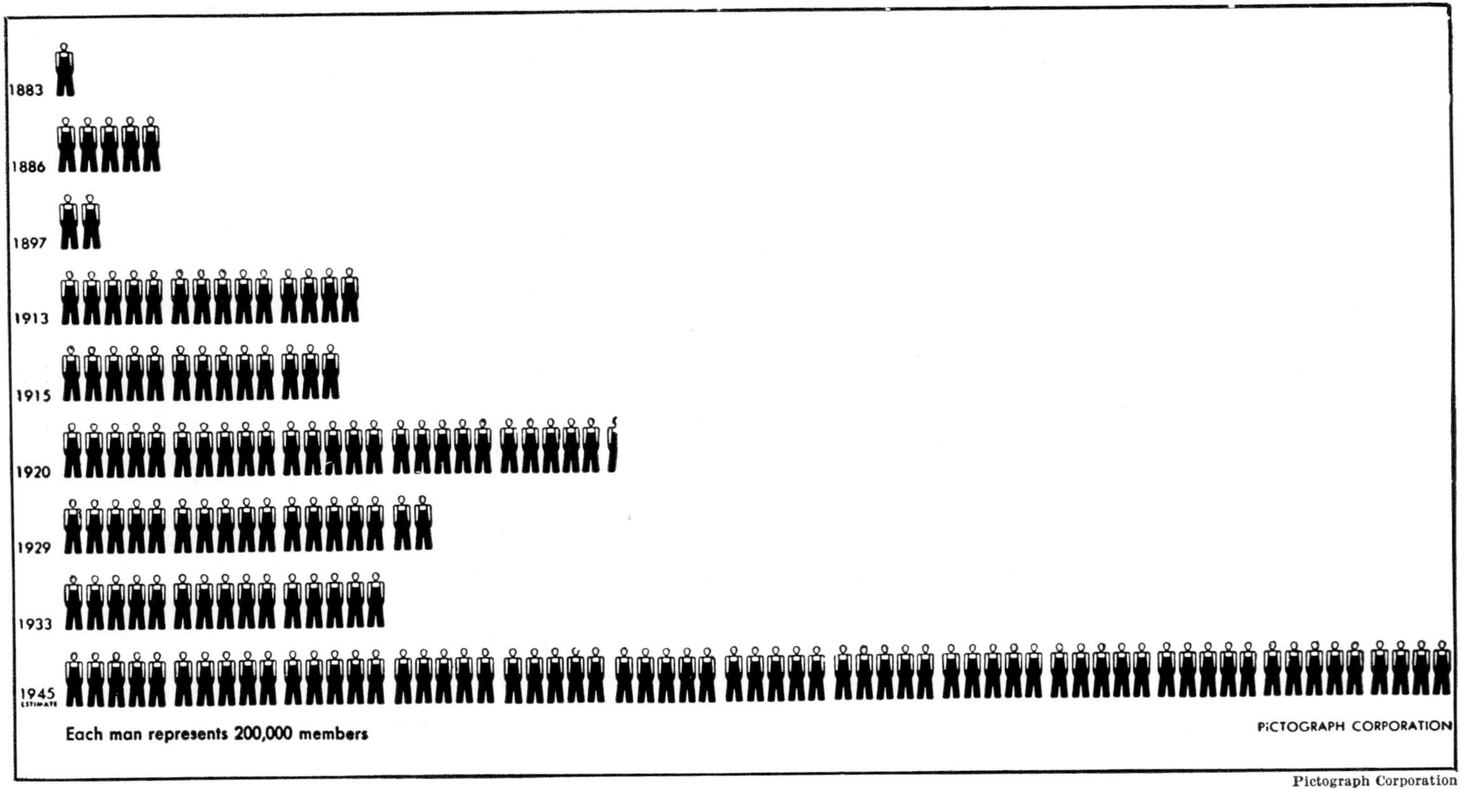

Trade-Union Membership

Each man represents 200,000 members

1883
1886
1897
1913
1915
1920
1929
1933
1945

PiCTOGRAPH CORPORATION

Pictograph Corporation

bidden field into which Congress may not enter when it is necessary to protect interstate commerce from paralyzing consequences of industrial war?

Organized labor received a great stimulus from New Deal legislation. The American Federation of Labor had had only two million members in 1933, a decline of two million since 1920. In the first three years of the New Deal the Federation gained a million and a half members. Within labor ranks the old problem of craft or industrial unionism came to the fore. The A. F. of L., essentially a craft movement, made no effort to organize the workers of such key industries as steel, automobiles, textiles, and rubber. In 1936 the Amalgamated Clothing Workers, the International Ladies' Garment Workers, and the United Mine Workers, three important industrial unions within the A. F. of L., led in the formation of the Committee for Industrial Organization. The C. I. O., headed by John L. Lewis of the United Mine Workers, planned to remain in the A. F. of L., but it was going "to encourage and promote organization of the workers in the mass production and unorganized industries of the nation." The temporizing and conservative leadership of the A. F. of L., typified by William Green, immediately looked upon this as a threat to its control of the Federation. Bitter words passed between the old-line Federation leaders and the C. I. O., which led to the expulsion of the C. I. O. from the Federation. In 1938 the C. I. O. adopted a constitution and changed its name to the Congress of Industrial Organizations.

The C. I. O. grew rapidly. By the fall of 1937 it claimed a membership of 3,700,000, while the A. F. of L. claimed 3,600,000 members. The C. I. O. organized the steel, automobile, rubber, electrical, and radio industries. Effective strikes in 1937 against the automobile industry led to union recognition by General Motors and Chrysler. The United States Steel Corporation signed a contract with the C. I. O. the same year, the first time that an independent union had been successful in this industrial field. "Little Steel," however,—Republic, Inland, Bethlehem, and Youngstown Sheet and Tube,—remained vigorously antiunion. In the spring of 1937 the C. I. O. launched a strike against this antiunion citadel. On Memorial Day the Chicago police fired into a union crowd picketing a Republic plant and killed ten strikers. The Inland Steel Company finally granted some of the union's demands, but the other companies refused to budge, and the men finally returned to work without any gains. The NLRB investigated the Republic Steel Corporation's labor policies and concluded:

Its spies shadowed union organizers; its police attacked and beat them; its superintendent and foremen threatened, laid off and discharged employees for union activities; its officers fostered and supported a whole series of puppet labor organizations which the company manipulated to oppose the union; and its president, Tom M. Girdler, publicly vilified the union's leaders, purposes and policies under circumstances intended to throw the weight of his influence against his employees' efforts at self-organization.

The NLRB found the company guilty of violating the Wagner Act, and ordered the reinstatement of about five thousand men who had been engaged in the strike.

During 1937 the workers used the technique of the sit-down strike. They stayed in the plants of the employer and refused to leave until their demands had been met. The United Automobile Workers of the C. I. O. used this device against General Motors. The corporation resorted to injunctions and appealed for the militia to remove the men from the plants. Governor Frank Murphy of Michigan refused to allow the militia to oust the strikers. He knew that this would lead to violence. Finally, through his negotiations, the workers achieved recognition of their union and secured improved conditions. Sit-down strikes spread until they involved about half a million workers, while the United States Senate adopted a resolution of denunciation, and some of the state and lower Federal courts held such strikes to be an unlawful seizure of property. The Supreme Court, in 1939, adopted the same attitude.

Organized labor made rapid strides in these years because the government no longer gave its support to the employers. The NLRB watched to see that employers bargained collectively with their employees and that they did not fire workers for union activities. Judges no longer granted injunctions so freely, and governors frequently refused to use the militia to break strikes. Labor made more gains under the New Deal than under any previous administration. But labor still had its problems, especially when the Second World War took the minds of the public off domestic matters. Powerful antiunion employers still fought unionization. A number of A. F. of L. unions were in the hands of racketeers, who used their power to exploit union members. The C. I. O. was shot through with a conflict between Communists and ordinary progressive union leaders. In 1939 and 1940 John L. Lewis broke with President Franklin D. Roosevelt and, during the 1940 campaign, endorsed Wendell Willkie. When labor voted for Roosevelt in spite of Lewis's action, the head of the C. I. O. resigned. Not long after he took his United Mine Workers out of the C. I. O.

THE FINANCIAL SITUATION

When President Roosevelt took office, a financial collapse of the nation seemed inevitable. The first step that the President took to check this was to order every bank in America closed, and to place an embargo on the export of gold and silver. Roosevelt had promised, during his campaign, a "strict supervision of all banking and credits and investment . . . and an end to speculation with other people's money," and Congress met in special session on March 9, 1933, to act upon measures that would implement this pledge. The Emergency Banking Act of March 9 provided for the speedy reopening of sound banks under adequate control, the Reconstruction Finance Corporation was permitted to buy the preferred stock of national banks, and a Bank Conservator was appointed to supervise the banks that were not ready to resume operation. On March 10 the President demanded salary cuts for government employees and the paring down of payments to war veterans. Ten days later Congress passed the necessary legislation to effect these economies. In the next year or two, however, Congress revoked these economies and restored salaries and pensions, and went on to vote a bonus to war veterans.

In order to raise commodity prices and ease the debt burden of the American public, vigorous steps were taken. The New Deal felt that the debts were too heavy to carry at the existing price level. Its idea, therefore, was "to make possible the payment of public and private debts more nearly at the price level at which they were incurred." On May 12 Congress granted the President the power to pursue a policy of inflation by reducing the gold content of the dollar, by issuing three billion dollars in new treasury notes to inflate the currency, and by providing for the unlimited coinage of silver and gold at a ratio to be set by him. A few weeks before this bill was passed, the United States had gone off the gold standard (April 19). European countries, particularly England, had already abandoned the gold standard and were on a basis of managed currencies. If the United States stayed on the gold standard, American goods would be expensive for foreign nations to buy; but, it was argued, if it went on a managed currency, exports would be stimulated.

Shortly after the United States had abandoned the gold standard and had forbidden the hoarding of gold and gold certificates (April 5), a world economic conference met at London. The American delegates were instructed not to accept the stabilization of the dollar, and, as a result, the conference broke up. Then the President experimented with a managed currency. He stated that he wanted a dollar "which a generation hence will have the same purchasing and debt-paying power as the dollar we hope to attain in the near future." All holders of gold were forced to turn their gold over to the Federal reserve bank. The export of gold was regulated by the government, and payment in legal-tender certificates, rather than in gold, was established for government obligations. The Supreme Court later upheld this, although the minority opinion was that "the impending legal and moral chaos is appalling." In January, 1934, since the government now possessed the gold supply of the nation, the President devalued the dollar by reducing its gold content from $25\frac{8}{10}$ grains to $15\frac{5}{21}$ grains. Out of the profit made from this step, a two-billion-dollar stabilization fund was created. Not long after this the government began to buy silver more heavily in order that one fourth the monetary stock of the country should be silver. Although prices did rise during the first years of the New Deal, critics of the above-mentioned steps charged that the rises were caused by other factors. There was no doubt that the policy of inflation had been carried out carefully, without resort to printing-press money with its attendant dangers.

As part of the policy of controlled inflation, the New Deal was interested in establishing better credit facilities and lower interest rates on loans. The Farm Credit Administration, already mentioned, provided money for new mortgages and for refunding old loans at much lower interest rates. The Home Owners' Loan Corporation, created in June, 1933, refinanced small mortgages on privately owned homes. All this activity to control the monetary supply of the nation was followed by reform of the national banking structure. Reform in this realm was so necessary that even conservative-minded people did not object. The collapse of so many banks, as well as the near-collapse of many others, and the unhealthy loans for speculation during the bull market pointed to the need of reform. The investigations of the Senate Committee on Banking and Currency, begun in April, 1932, revealed shocking practices. To clear up these evils, the Glass-Steagall Banking Act of June 16, 1933, called for the separation of commercial and investment banking; that is, banks were no longer allowed to underwrite stock issues and then sell them to their customers. The Federal Reserve Board was given positive power over credit for speculative purposes. The act also provided for a government-controlled corporation, the Federal Deposit Insurance Corporation, to insure bank deposits up to five thousand dollars.

The next step was the reform of stock-market practices. President Roosevelt, in his inaugural address, had denounced the "unscrupulous money-changers" who carried on their "speculation with other people's money." The period of the twenties, when many unsound bonds and stocks were floated, led the President to say:

> There is an obligation upon us to insist that every issue of new securities . . . shall be accompanied by full publicity and information, and that no essentially important element attending the issue shall be concealed from the buying public. . . . This . . . should be followed by legislation relating to the better supervision of the purchase and sale of all property dealt in on exchanges.

The Securities Act of May, 1933, and the Securities Exchange Act of June, 1934, were designed to secure these objectives. These laws required that all stock exchanges be licensed by the Securities and Exchange Commission; that all new securities issued be registered with the SEC; that every offering contain full information about the conditions of the corporation issuing the securities; and that the Federal Reserve Board be empowered to prescribe rules for the extension of credit for marginal loans.

POWER AND THE REGULATION OF UTILITIES

The New Deal launched a significant program for the future in the field of power. The great experiment was the Tennessee Valley Authority, created in May, 1933. It was soon popularly referred to as the TVA. It was to operate the Muscle Shoals dams "in the interest of the national defense and for agricultural and industrial development, and to improve navigation of the Tennessee River and to control the destructive flood waters in the Tennessee River and Mississippi River Basins." At last Senator George W. Norris's long fight for government operation in the field of power was won. The TVA was specifically permitted to construct and operate dams in the Tennessee Valley, a region cutting across seven states, to manufacture nitrate and fertilizer, to generate and sell electric power, to control floods, to improve navigation, and to advance "the economic and social well-being of the people living in the said basin."

The TVA launched a program of economic and social planning for this region to secure cheaper electric power, to use the water power that was being wasted, to conserve the natural resources, and to give

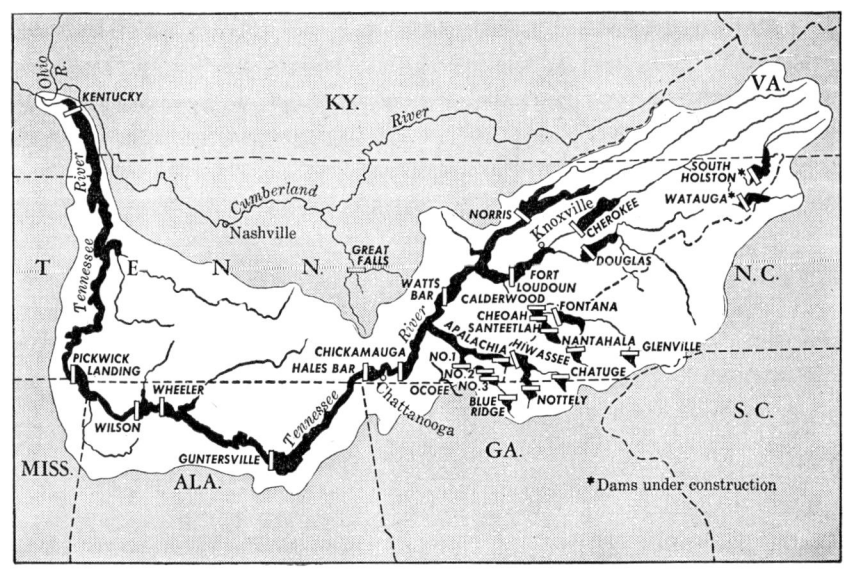

The TVA Region

the nation an indication of what could be achieved under planning. By 1938 four new dams had been completed and four more were under construction. The TVA built transmission lines, and in 1937 was supplying power to seventeen municipalities, to fifteen co-operative power associations, and to many industrial plants. Four years later over four hundred thousand customers were being served by the project. Farmers who never before had had electricity now had it to light their homes, to refrigerate their foods, and to perform many household chores. The rates for electricity charged by the TVA were lower than those of the private utilities in the area and in the rest of the country. Its rates became a yardstick to measure the fairness of private companies' rates. Although private utilities maintained that the TVA rates were not fair, many of them quickly scaled down their rates, and the resulting annual saving to consumers was estimated at close to fifty million dollars. Up to 1939 the average cost of the TVA current for home consumption was 2.14 cents per kilowatt-hour, whereas the country as a whole was paying 4.21 cents.

Conservatives objected to government competition with private industry. President Hoover had characterized this as "degenerate" when he vetoed a bill providing for government operation of Muscle Shoals. Wendell L. Willkie, president of the Commonwealth and Southern

Corporation, a holding company operating private utility concerns in the Tennessee region, launched a campaign to arouse private business by painting the TVA as "the entering wedge" for the "government ownership of all essential industries." Private utilities carried a case to the Supreme Court, challenging the constitutionality of the TVA. On February 17, 1936, the Supreme Court handed down an important decision, upholding the right of the TVA to generate electric power and to acquire transmission lines for electricity, as well as the right to improve navigation and to produce nitrates. C. Hermann Pritchett, in his scholarly volume *The Tennessee Valley Authority: A Study in Public Administration*, observes that the TVA has done a "clean and workmanlike job," and he concludes that "no other public instrumentality of our time has seemed to have more symbolic meaning, more usefulness as a tool, more promise for the future."

The Federal government had other projects for hydroelectric development under way. Hoover Dam, on the Colorado River, begun by the Hoover administration, was completed in 1936; Grand Coulee Dam, on the Columbia River, was begun in 1933, and Bonneville Dam, on the same river, in 1937. These last two dams were part of an immense project that was expected not only to provide a huge amount of power, but to make possible the irrigation and reclamation of over a million acres of land. The power generated by these dams, as well as by the TVA, was invaluable to American war production after 1940. The new industries that were quickly established in their area of service had an ample supply of electricity, which they could not have had without them. While all these dams were being constructed, the Rural Electrification Administration was building electric lines in rural areas, and the PWA was lending money to municipalities for publicly owned power stations.

The New Deal, in addition to these ventures in the public ownership of power, placed curbs on private utilities. During the twenties giant utility holding companies had been developed, which placed the control of the power of America in the hands of a few individuals or corporations. A group of English economists, after a study of the American power industry, wrote, in 1936:

The device of the holding company has been used more consistently and carried further towards its logical conclusion in the American electrical industry than in any other. There is some virtue in the device. It may serve to integrate a number of small companies and to secure for them operating and financial economies. But in the 1920's it was carried far beyond this and made to serve far wider purposes. Different utility magnates used holding companies to build up their rival utility "empires." They were ready to purchase any utility that was in the market, however remote it might be from their existing interests. Pyramiding was carried to fantastic lengths, and in many of these pyramids the operating companies were "milked" for the benefit of the holding companies.

Senator George W. Norris gave the following example of pyramiding: the Cumberland County Power and Light Company of Portland, Maine, was owned by the New England Finance and Investment Company, which was owned by the New England Public Service Company, which was owned by the Middle West Utilities Company, which was controlled by the Corporation Utilities Company, which was controlled by the Insull Utilities Company. Congress established control over this situation with the Wheeler-Rayburn Utilities Holding Company Act of August, 1935. The Federal Power Commission was given authority to control all utilities transmitting electricity across state lines, and all utility companies had to register with the Securities and Exchange Commission. No company could acquire additional property without the permission of the SEC. Rates were subject to control to prevent exorbitant profits. "As soon as practicable after January 1, 1938," the SEC was to limit the operations of holding companies "to a single integrated public-utility system." This meant that all members of every utility structure had to be geographically connected and capable of operating as a co-ordinated unit.

The private utilities denounced this part of the bill as a "death sentence." They exerted tremendous pressure on Congress to defeat the measure. After the bill was passed, they carried their case to the courts. In 1938 the Supreme Court upheld the act. The fourteen leading holding companies then pledged their co-operation to work out a solution with the SEC.

HOUSING

President Roosevelt announced to the nation that one third of the people were ill-housed. Housing conditions for the poor were wretched in both urban and rural areas, and a large number of dwellings fell far below minimum standards of safety and health. Private building had shrunk 95 per cent from 1928 to 1933. Some housing authorities estimated that the country needed eight million new urban housing units and three million new rural units. Construction costs were extremely high because of monopoly prices of materials and the monopoly price of labor maintained by some A. F. of L. building and trades unions in collaboration with the producers of housing materials. The New Deal was faced with the problem of reviving the housing industry, but more immediately it had to check the foreclosure of home-owners' mortgages. In March, 1933, mortgages on one thousand private homes a day were being foreclosed. The Home Owners' Loan Corporation, created by Congress in June, 1933, lent money over a long period at low rates of interest. By June, 1936, the HOLC had lent three billion dollars on one million mortgages, thus saving one million homes for their owners.

Low-cost housing for the poor lagged. The PWA, up to 1936, had constructed about thirty thousand new family units, but this was disappointing in view of the need. Local real-estate interests fought government housing, although they would not venture into the field of low-cost housing themselves. Finally, Congress, in 1937, took a significant step by creating the United States Housing Authority. The act (Wagner-Steagall Housing Act) which created the USHA empowered it to lend money to local public agencies for slum clearance and low-cost housing in order to remedy "a shortage of decent, safe, and sanitary dwellings for families of low income in rural or urban communities." The loans were for sixty years, at 3 per cent interest, and were to cover 90 per cent of the construction costs. The USHA also could grant annual subsidies to keep rents in any of the projects low enough for the pocketbooks of poor people. Under this program, during 1937 and 1938, many communities launched housing projects, such as the Ida B. Wells project in Chicago. By 1941 the USHA had been instrumental in the construction of housing units for approximately two hundred and forty thousand low-income families, but America still had a long way to go before adequate housing was provided for its people.

THE 1936 ELECTION

Three and a half years after the New Deal was launched, the electorate had the opportunity of expressing its opinion on the errors and achievements of the Roosevelt administration. Laws had been passed with bewildering speed. For instance, the list of measures called for or passed in the first ninety days read:

March 9: the Emergency Banking Act.
March 10: 25 per cent cut in the budget.
March 13: F.D.R. demanded repeal of the Volstead law.
March 16: F.D.R. demanded the AAA.
March 21: F.D.R. demanded the CCC.
March 29: F.D.R. demanded the SEC.
April 3: F.D.R. demanded the Farm Credit Act.
April 10: F.D.R. demanded the TVA.
April 13: F.D.R. demanded the Home Owners' Loan Act.
April 20: F.D.R. took the country off the gold standard.
May 4: F.D.R. demanded the Emergency Railroad Transportation Act.
May 12: F.D.R. signed the first Federal Emergency Relief Act.
May 17: F.D.R. demanded the NRA and $3,300,000,000 for work relief.

During the first ninety days the essential structure of the New Deal was laid before Congress. In the next three years the program was extended and modified in certain details, but only one aspect was reversed—the NRA. The results of the election of 1936 left no doubt as to how the country felt about the New Deal. It was an overwhelming endorsement. The Republican party in the years of the first New Deal administration lacked a constructive policy and able leadership. Old-time Progressive Republicans welcomed the New Deal and threw their support behind the program. One of them observed, in 1934: "On the whole and by and large, I am for the New Deal. It is neither Communist nor Fascist. Much of it is necessary. All of it is human. And most of it is long past due."

The New Deal's relief program had fed the hungry, had sustained the morale of millions of Americans, had restored in the minds of many confidence in democracy, and had preserved workers' skills that later were to be of extreme value when America had to "tool up" for war. The various reform and recovery measures had given business a shot in the arm, and a general revival of the business structure was in full bloom in 1936. This recovery was largely the result of governmental spending—"pump-priming." In spite of the revival, however, nine million were still unemployed and about three and a half million were on relief jobs. In the average voter's mind the New Deal's willingness to take unprecedented steps to meet the unemployment situation bulked very large. No previous President had supported such widespread humanitarian measures, and no other President had regulated business in the interest of the people on so broad a scale. As a good Progressive, Franklin D. Roosevelt had advocated and carried out Federal responsibility for the general welfare. He had increased the power of the central government to accomplish this, but this Hamiltonian move had been made to achieve Jeffersonian ends.

The bewilderment of Old-Guard Republicans, in the face of New Deal activity, was best expressed by ex-President Coolidge, who said: "When I read of the new-fangled things that are now so popular, I realize that my time in public affairs is past. I wouldn't know how to handle them if I were called upon to do so." When the Republicans opposed the New Deal, they did so in terms of championing states' rights against Federal centralization. The Congressional election of 1934, by adding to the Democratic majorities in Congress, had revealed the public's support of the Roosevelt administration. As the 1936 election approached, however, certain foes of the New Deal began to rally the opposition. Some men who had been important in the Democratic party during the days of the twenties, when it was as conservative as the Republican party, bolted the party in 1936. The group was a small one, of men who once had been distinguished leaders of the party. They were led by Alfred E. Smith and included Joseph B. Ely, ex-governor of Massachusetts, John W. Davis, 1924 Presidential candidate, John J. Raskob, 1928 chairman of the party, Bainbridge Colby, former Secretary of State under Wilson, and James A. Reed, former Senator from Missouri.

Before this action was taken, conservative elements had formed, in 1934, the American Liberty League. According to its own statement, the purpose of the Liberty League was to "combat radicalism, preserve property rights and uphold and preserve the Constitution." John W. Davis and Alfred E. Smith were on its board of directors, and wealthy industrialists like the Du Ponts contributed large sums of money. The real purpose of the League, of course, was to defeat the New Deal and return the country to the ways of the twenties. Charges were made that the New Deal was alien to the American way of life, that it was communistic, and that it was subversive of American liberties. The leaders of the League never demonstrated any realization that the work of Franklin D. Roosevelt might be saving their system of private capitalism from revolutionary changes such as were taking place in Germany.

The Liberty League spent about a million dollars on publicity in 1935 and 1936, and it organized a committee of corporation lawyers which charged the New Deal laws with being unconstitutional before the courts had tried the laws.

In spite of the bitterness displayed by the Liberty League, the Old Guard leaders of the Republican party realized that Franklin D. Roosevelt was unbeatable for re-election. They therefore allowed Western Republicans to select the Presidential candidate. A boom for Governor Alfred Landon of Kansas was launched by the Kansas City *Star* in co-operation with some Kansas editors, and Landon was nominated on the first ballot, as was his running mate, Colonel Frank Knox, publisher of the Chicago *Daily News*. Landon was supposed to appeal to the liberal vote. He was a leader of the progressive wing of the party in Kansas, which, however, was progressive only in terms of Kansas Republicanism, not in terms of the nation. Since he was an unknown in national politics, his views on vital problems were also unknown, and therefore it was felt that he could rally all anti-New-Deal sentiments to his cause.

The Republican platform charged:

America is in peril. The welfare of American men and women and the future of our youth are at stake. We dedicate ourselves to the preservation of their political liberty, their individual opportunity and their character as free citizens, which today for the first time are threatened by Government itself.

For three long years the New Deal Administration has dishonored American traditions and flagrantly betrayed the pledges upon which the Democratic Party sought and received public support.

The platform listed the "sins" of the Democrats; it charged that the powers of Congress had been usurped by the President, that the Supreme Court had been flouted, that the rights of states had been usurped, that the New Deal had prolonged the depression, and that the New Deal had appealed to passion and class prejudice. Then the Republicans pledged themselves to maintain constitutional government and to "preserve the American system of free enterprise, private competition, and equality of opportunity." The platform made it clear that the Republican party was for work relief, old-age security, aid to agriculture, the destruction of monopolies, the reduction of expenditures, and the balancing of the budget. Just how the Republicans intended to balance the budget and reduce expenditures while, at the same time, providing work relief and aid to the farmer was not clear in the platform or during the campaign. Former President Herbert Hoover, after the campaign, agreed that the platform was "a mixture of conflicting ideas and grab-bag offerings."

The Democrats, meeting at Philadelphia, joyously renominated

Franklin D. Roosevelt and John Nance Garner. The entire New Deal program was endorsed, and its extension was promised. The platform declared:

We hold this truth to be self-evident—that the test of a representative government is its ability to promote the safety and happiness of the people.

We hold this truth to be self-evident—that twelve years of Republican leadership left our nation sorely stricken in body, mind and spirit; and that three years of Democratic leadership have put it back on the road to restored health and prosperity.

We hold this truth to be self-evident—that twelve years of Republican surrender to the dictatorship of a privileged few have been supplanted by a Democratic leadership which has returned the people themselves to the place of authority, and has revived in them new faith and restored the hope which they had almost lost.

The platform praised the New Deal accomplishments, and asserted that the policies of government had been "humanized"; that the administration had thwarted and would continue to thwart the activities of malefactors of great wealth who defraud and exploit the people; and that Democratic rule had put the nation back on the road to restored health and prosperity. By inserting a plank to the effect that Congress did have the right to legislate nationally for such things as relief, child labor, minimum wages, hours of labor, and soil conservation, the platform took cognizance of the fact that the Supreme Court had invalidated many New Deal laws. Senator Barkley of Kentucky, in the keynote address to the Democratic convention, went farther than this and stated:

If in the future, further amendment [to the Constitution] should become necessary to enable the people to work out their destiny and protect their fundamental rights or to govern some archaic interpretation never intended by its framers, I doubt not that the people will face that duty with the same calm intelligence which has guided them in the past.

The ensuing campaign was bitter, but not exciting. Landon's speeches revealed a steady drift toward the conservatives in his party; his campaign-manager, John Hamilton, was clearly of that extraction. Landon showed himself to be an inept campaigner and a poor orator. Republicans thundered about the dangers of dictatorship and communism if the New Deal were retained. The vast majority of newspapers, reflecting their intimate tie with American business, opposed Roosevelt's re-election. The *Chicago Tribune* and the Hearst press reached new pinnacles of abuse and invective. The Hearst press, for instance, printed the following rhyme:

> The Red New Deal with a Soviet seal
> Endorsed by a Moscow hand,
> The strange result of an alien cult
> In a liberty-loving land.

Roosevelt, in return, with his exceptional radio voice, pointed out the contrast between the America of 1936 and the America of the tragic days of Hoover's Presidency. To his support there came not only the traditional Democrats, but independent citizens led by Senators Norris and La Follette, who established the National Progressive League. At the same time, union labor formed labor's Nonpartisan League, which worked for New Deal candidates; and the United Mine Workers contributed close to half a million dollars for Roosevelt's re-election. The Republican party spent nine million dollars to defeat the Democrats, and the Democrats spent about five and a half million in their campaign.

As election day approached, the *Literary Digest* and the Hearst press predicted Landon's election from the results of straw polls. James Farley, managing Roosevelt's campaign, confidently predicted that the Republicans would carry only two states. His prediction was fulfilled. Roosevelt was elected in the greatest landslide in American political history, and he carried every state but Maine and Vermont. The popular vote was 27,751,000 to 16,680,000. The third parties were swamped as well. Norman Thomas's Socialist party won only 194,000 votes, Earl Browder's Communist party 80,000 votes, and the new Union party 894,000 votes. Generally, in American history, third parties have polled strong votes only when the two major parties have refused to face the real issues and when there has been no fundamental difference between the two major parties. Then a third party has polled a heavy vote, as, for instance, in 1892 and 1924. In 1936, as in 1932, there was a clear difference between the two parties, and the voters ignored the third parties. The Union party was an odd assortment of elements, including some of the supporters of Fascist-minded Charles E. Coughlin, a Catholic priest, and some of the followers of Dr. Francis E. Townsend's plan for big Federal pensions for the aged. William Lemke, Republican representative from North Dakota, was the nominee of the new party, which quickly disappeared after the 1936 election.

Although some stunned conservatives charged that Roosevelt was re-elected by the relief vote, actually a poll taken by the American Institute of Public Opinion revealed that the President drew support from all classes of people and from all sections of the nation. The poll revealed that 47 per cent of the voters in the top-income bracket favored F.D.R. to 53 per cent for Landon, 67 per cent in the middle-income group to 33 per cent for Landon, and 75 per cent in the bottom-income bracket to 25 per cent for Landon. The Democrats also swept the Congressional elections, winning 334 of the 435 seats in the House and having 75 of the 96 Senatorial seats in their control.

THE SUPREME COURT

Franklin D. Roosevelt assumed that the vote was a mandate to continue his policies. In his inaugural address on January 20, 1937, he posed the question "Shall we . . . turn our back upon the road that lies ahead?" When Congress convened, he answered this question by asking for widespread legislation—hours of labor, housing, taxation, regional water-power development, and the reorganization of the government's administrative setup. Before he could really carry out this program, however, he felt that something had to be done about the Supreme Court. Just as in the days of Thomas Jefferson, the opposition party, repudiated at the polls, had found refuge in the Supreme Court. The Supreme Court had played havoc with New Deal legislation. In 1935 it had thrown out the NRA, the Farm Mortgage Act, and the Railroad Retirement Act. The next year it had invalidated the AAA, the Bituminous Coal Act, the Municipal Bankruptcy Act, and the New York State Minimum Wage Law. Roosevelt charged that the judges were "miners and sappers" of the Constitution, and he felt that "what was worse" was that "the language and temper of the decisions indicated little hope for the future. Apparently Marshall's conception of our Constitution as a flexible instrument—adequate for all times and therefore able to adjust itself as the new needs of new generations arose—had been repudiated."

The Supreme Court seemingly was nullifying the electorate's desires as expressed in 1932, 1934, and 1936. On January 6, 1937, the President explained to Congress that "means must be found to adapt our legal forms and our judicial interpretation to the actual present national needs of the largest progressive democracy in the modern world." The question of the Supreme Court's power long had been debated in American politics. At various times proposals had been made to deprive the Court of its power to kill a law by a mere majority vote or to empower Congress to override Court decisions. Instead of advocating such steps, however, President Roosevelt held "that the Constitution was not to blame, and that the Supreme Court as an institution was not to blame. The only trouble was with some of the human beings on the Court." Roosevelt had not made a single appointment to the Court. Seven of the nine had been appointed by Republicans, and six of the "nine old men" were over seventy years old. Four justices— McReynolds, Van Devanter, Sutherland, and Butler—could be counted upon to oppose any liberal measure. Generally, Justices Stone, Cardozo, and Brandeis had supported New Deal laws; Chief Justice Hughes and Justice Roberts wavered between the two points of view.

On February 5, 1937, President Roosevelt submitted a proposal to Congress for the reform of the Federal judiciary. The President asked to be empowered to appoint "additional judges in all Federal courts without exception where there are incumbent judges of retirement age who do not choose to resign." In the case of the Supreme Court, the voluntary retirement age was to be seventy years, and the President was to be allowed to appoint a new judge, up to a maximum of six, for every justice who did not retire at seventy. The President asserted, in a message accompanying this bill:

Modern complexities call for a constant infusion of new blood in the courts, just as it is needed in executive functions of the Government. . . . A lowered mental or physical vigor leads men to avoid an examination of complicated and changed conditions. Little by little, new facts become blurred through old glasses fitted, as it were, for the needs of another generation; older men, assuming that the scene is the same as it was in the past, cease to explore or to inquire into the present or the future. . . . A constant and systematic addition of younger blood will vitalize the courts and better equip them to recognize and apply the essential concepts of justice in the light of the needs and facts of an ever-changing world.

Outcries of alarm, consternation, and dismay met this proposal. Congress, the newspapers, radio, and public gatherings debated the measure. Some opponents held that it was part of Roosevelt's desire for power, others that it would wreck constitutional government and the theory of the separation of powers. Some conservatives organized societies to protect constitutional government. Many Southern Democrats, who never had been in sympathy with New Deal laws, but of necessity had had to vote for them, now bolted the President's leadership. Erstwhile liberals like Senators Wheeler and Borah opposed the proposed bill. Wheeler argued that changes in the Court's status should come through constitutional amendment. Newspapers, legal associations, college presidents, deans of law schools, a number of state legislatures, and columnists like Walter Lippmann and Dorothy Thompson militantly expressed their opposition to the President's plan. Those versed in the law, however, were divided over the bill. Professors E. S. Corwin and Charles Grove Haines, for instance, both distinguished students of the Constitution, supported the bill.

For months the debate raged. President Roosevelt, in two speeches, went to the public for support. In destroying social legislation, the Court, he pointed out, "has been acting not as a judicial body, but as a policy-making body. . . . We have, therefore, reached the point as a Nation where we must take action to save the Constitution from the Court and the Court from itself." The President asserted that his plan would "bring to the decision of social and economic problems younger men who have had personal experience and contact with modern facts and circumstances under which average men have to live and work. This plan will save our National Constitution from hardening of the judicial arteries." The Senate Judiciary Committee, in June, by a vote of ten to eight, declared against the bill. They denounced the proposed measure as a "needless, futile, and utterly dangerous abandonment of constitutional principle . . . without justification." The bill would "subjugate the courts to the will of Congress and the President and thereby destroy the independence of the judiciary."

While the debate was raging over the plan, the Supreme Court itself really decided the issue. On March 29, 1937, by a five-to-four decision, the Court upheld a minimum-wage law of the state of Washington. Nine months before, the Court had thrown out a similar measure from New York State. The Court now stated that the earlier decision "is overruled." Thus, in the opinion of the judges, the Constitution had changed its meaning since the President's bill had been proposed. The same day the Court upheld a new Railway Labor Act and a revised Farm Mortgage Act. Several weeks later the Court, in another five-to-four decision, upheld the Wagner-Connery Labor Relations Act. On May 24, by still another five-to-four vote, the Court gave judicial blessing to the Social Security Act. Justice Roberts switched his vote from the conservative to the liberal side and thus made the Court's about-face possible. As one observer put it, "A switch in time saved nine."

Conservatives now became worried anew. How could a Court rendering such decisions continue to serve as the defender of free contract, property rights, and free enterprise? While they were trembling at this thought, on June 1 Justice Van Devanter, a firm New Deal foe, announced his retirement from the Court. Now President Roosevelt could make a judicial appointment, and the majority in the Court would be liberal. Why, then, add more justices?

Although President Roosevelt's bill was defeated in the summer of 1937, he did secure a more liberal Court. Senator Hugo Black of Alabama was elevated to Van Devanter's position. Black had made a brilliant record as the head of Senate investigations of the merchant marine, aviation, and utility lobbies, and he had been an ardent supporter of New Deal laws. After he had taken the oath of office, it was revealed that he once had been a member of the Ku Klux Klan. His liberal Court record since his appointment, however, seemed to justify the President's faith in him. Within the next two or three years, other members of the Supreme Court followed Van Devanter into retirement. To fill the vacancies, President Roosevelt appointed Stanley Reed of Kentucky, former Solicitor-General; Felix Frankfurter, distinguished teacher of the Harvard Law School; William Douglas of the Yale Law School and the Securities and Exchange Commission; Robert Jackson of New York, former Attorney-General; Frank Murphy of Michigan, former governor of that state as well as governor-general of the Philippine Islands; and James Byrnes, Senator from South Carolina. Associate Justice Harlan Stone was elevated to the chief justiceship. The new Court retreated from the attitude of its predecessor, and interpreted the Constitution—as Marshall, Story, and Holmes had done—to fit the needs of a changing America. The number of broad, liberal decisions handed down by the Court led one writer to observe, "Never before in history has the Court so extensively altered so many basic principles in so short a time as in the three years since February, 1937." As a result, President Roosevelt could truthfully say, as he did in a fireside chat, that while he had lost a battle he had won the war.

THE BUSINESS RECESSION, 1937-1938

While public attention was focused on the Court fight, on the rise of the C. I. O. labor movement, and on the militaristic activities of Hitler and Mussolini in Europe and of the Japanese in China, a new depression struck America in August, 1937. The business slump continued until it hit bottom in June, 1938. But the bottom was not as low as in 1932. Close to fifteen million had been out of work in the summer of

1932, eleven million were unemployed in 1937. During 1936 and 1937, under pressure from big business, Congress had slashed relief and recovery appropriations. From 1934 to 1936 the government had added annually between three and four billion dollars to the national income, but in 1937 it added less than a billion. Meanwhile, however, private business had failed to expand enough to replace the Federal government's retrenchment.

Administration supporters charged that private business was on a "strike" to stop the New Deal, and the London *Economist* observed that the business community of America had worked itself into such "a lather of hatred" of Roosevelt that its violent temper was "choking the whole industrial and financial machine." Businessmen, on the other hand, charged that the mounting deficits, the unbalanced budget, and the tax structure made business uneasy and reluctant to expand. The new depression was met by a renewal of government pump-priming. The PWA, the RFC, and the WPA received increased appropriations to expand their activities. Other agencies, such as the CCC, the NYA, and the Rural Electrification Administration, launched new projects. The WPA purchased fifteen million dollars' worth of clothing from factories and gave it to the needy. In 1938 the Federal Surplus Commodities Corporation began to buy up surplus farm products and give them also to the needy. When middlemen complained of this practice, the FSCC started a stamp plan whereby private grocery stores distributed the surplus goods for the government free to the needy, in return for red and blue stamps which the latter received from their local relief agencies.

At the middle of the recession the public's attention was attracted to the failure of Richard Whitney, president of the New York Stock Exchange. He had been engaged in irresponsible speculation and had misappropriated his customers' securities. He had been a bitter enemy of the New Deal's regulation of the Stock Exchange, but his own manipulations only demonstrated further the need of such regulation. Whitney was sentenced to jail for embezzlement, and the Stock Exchange had to put in a management that now co-operated with the Securities and Exchange Commission.

The summer of 1938 witnessed an improvement in the economic situation Government pump-priming was partly responsible, but business too helped, by hiring more workers and increasing production schedules. A million people went back to work between June and November, 1938. Foreign trade also improved, largely because of **war** preparations abroad. Throughout 1939 progress toward better times continued, although government spending and war orders were heavily responsible for this.

POLITICAL AND GOVERNMENTAL REFORM

The New Deal had brought a heavy increase in government activities, new agencies, and new employees. Just before the First World War three hundred and seventy thousand civil servants were in the government's employ. By the end of the Hoover administration this figure had risen to five hundred and eighty-three thousand. By 1938 it had jumped to eight hundred and fifty-one thousand. Many people realized that increased government activity in such fields as agricultural relief, work relief, regulation of industry, and conservation might be more than temporary. People in increasing numbers were coming to expect the government, as the servant of the people, to regulate society in the interest of the people. The government was now playing, and would continue to play, a vital role in the citizen's life, but the government's administrative growth had been haphazard. Students of public administration pointed out the waste, overlapping, and inefficiency in the government's structure. From the time of Theodore Roosevelt every President had tried to achieve some reforms, but nothing more than piecemeal changes had been secured.

Franklin D. Roosevelt, after hearing the recommendations of a committee which he had appointed, laid before Congress, in 1937, plans for the reorganization of the civil service, the extension of the merit system, the addition of two new cabinet posts, the establishment of a planning agency to co-ordinate executive functions, and the development of an independent auditing system for the executive departments. The *Chicago Tribune* made the charge, which was quickly picked up by others, that this was a "dictatorship bill." Congress subsequently rejected the President's proposals. When Congress met in 1939, the President persisted, and finally in March a reorganization bill was passed, giving the President power to transfer, consolidate, or abolish some sixty of the more than one hundred executive agencies. Roosevelt regrouped twenty-three bureaus into three units—the Federal Works Agency, the Federal Loan Agency, and the Federal Security Agency.

Congress, in July, 1939, moved to deal with the divorcing of governmental administration from politics. To stop any political coercion of government employees or relief workers, Senator Hatch of New Mexico secured the passage of a measure forbidding Federal employees or state employees paid with Federal funds from engaging in "pernicious political activities." Under the Hatch Act no officeholder (below the policy-making level) was allowed to take an active part in campaigns. Congress also passed a law limiting the annual expenditure of any party to three million dollars, and restricted single contributions to not more than five thousand dollars. Later developments have seemed to reveal that these restrictions have been evaded.

As the Congressional campaign of 1938 approached, President Roosevelt took steps to cleanse his party of nonliberal influences. Many of the Southern Democrats were conservatives who really should have been in the Republican party, but who were not for reasons that went back to the Civil War and reconstruction. In Congress these Southern Democrats were inclined to vote against Presidential measures, and in the years after 1938 they did so to an increasing degree. Anxious that the label "Democrat" should mean a liberal-minded person, Roosevelt tried to secure the defeat of men like George of Georgia and Tydings of Maryland—tried to "purge" such men, his critics called it. Opponents of Roosevelt quickly denounced this step as dictatorial. George and Tydings were returned to the Senate, and the Republicans gained seven Senatorial seats and eighty seats in the House. Yet, in spite of this increased Republican membership, the Democrats still held a majority of 262 to 170 in the House and 69 to 23 in the Senate.

THE END OF A DECADE

The outbreak of war in Europe, in September, 1939, closed one chapter in American history and turned the page to a new one. After 1939 the legislation adopted and the issues debated were directly influenced by war conditions. The outbreak of the Second World War, therefore, forms a demarcation line in American history and offers a convenient opportunity to look back over the New Deal, from 1933 to 1939, and to examine its achievements or its failures.

The New Deal marked a reassertion and an extension of the ideals of the earlier Progressive movement, which had been wrecked by the First World War and its aftermath. President Roosevelt took the helm of the government at the depth of the depression, when the people were filled with despair. Financial chaos, industrial collapse, and widespread unemployment gripped the country. Twelve years of political conservatism, under Republican rule, had ended in economic disaster. Franklin

MONTPELIER,
VERMONT

Gall

ALBANY,
NEW YORK

RICHMOND,
VIRGINIA

Ewing Galloway

BATON ROUGE, LOUISIANA

State Capitols

D. Roosevelt's words of encouragement and idealism stirred the nation out of its apathy; and when these words were followed by action, the country "thrust forward to remake its national life after a fashion which, whether the old prosperity returned or not, would yield a larger social justice and meet the demands of a truer democracy." The President's willingness to extend governmental authority to meet the crisis and his ardent sympathy for the common man furnished a shot in the arm to American democracy.

The future course of world development was to be affected by Roosevelt's contribution to the revitalizing of American democracy. Democracy did not disappear in this country, as it did in many lands; and when Fascism threatened to dominate the world, the American people were ready to defend and fight for the democratic way of life. Without the intervening years from 1933 to 1939, many people might not have been so confident that theirs was a government worth shedding their blood to preserve. At noon, March 4, 1933, Franklin D. Roosevelt was inaugurated President. The following day the German Reichstag put absolute power in the hands of Adolf Hitler. Eight years afterward these two men were the champions of two ways of life so different that the world could not exist peaceably until one or the other had triumphed.

President Roosevelt and his followers were disturbed by the great gap between ideals and practices in American life. The nation boasted to the world of its democracy, yet at least one third of its people were ill-fed and ill-clothed. A report of the National Resources Committee revealed that in 1935–1936 the average family income of one third of the nation was only $471, whereas 1 per cent of the population, at the top, received 13 per cent of the national income. The New Deal set out to redistribute the American income. The Wages and Hours Act, the Social Security Act, and the increased income taxes on higher incomes were attempts to accomplish this redistribution. By such steps the New Deal was not aiming at destroying the private capitalist system, but only at reordering it. Franklin D. Roosevelt believed that the trouble with capitalism was the capitalists, not the system itself. Acting in accordance with the admonition "Reform in order to preserve," Roosevelt, by extending governmental regulation, hoped to prevent further abuses of power by the financial and industrial interests; to improve the condition of labor; and to secure for the common people a fuller, freer, and more secure existence. The system of private enterprise was on the verge of collapse in 1933. Franklin D. Roosevelt saved the system from the more revolutionary changes that might have come if he had not acted as he did. In view of this, history's final verdict on Roosevelt may well be that he was an outstanding conservative.

Roosevelt essentially wanted to make sure that the mass of the people ran the country, rather than the few who controlled the money. Some of the things that he did were failures, and some were only temporary palliatives leaving problems for the future to solve. Reform, relief, and recovery were the objectives of the New Deal. A great deal of reforming remained to be done after 1939. Relief and recovery ceased to be problems in the boom times created by the Second World War, but the postwar decade would have to meet the situation. Roosevelt, in the main, followed a middle-of-the-road policy. Those to his left assailed him for not moving faster, and those to his right charged that he was plunging the country into communism and chaos.

On November 10, 1938, the *New York Times* reached the following conclusion about the New Deal:

> The Roosevelt Administration can claim . . . that it has accomplished a fundamental change in the American point of view. This change is the process by which the Republican party, or all of the Republican party except a comparatively small die-hard faction of it, has now come around to the support of the basic purposes of such far-reaching measures as the Social Security Act, the Labor Relations Act, the various housing laws, the Government's regulation of the Stock Exchanges and its control of the issuance of securities. The unmistakable fact is that an increasing number of Americans, irrespective of party line, have come to regard, as both necessary and desirable, a larger share of responsibility on the Government's part in the policing of financial markets, in the achievement of essential social reforms and in the attainment of a generally higher standard of living for underprivileged people. For that quickening of the American conscience which has brought about this change in point of view, credit must be given to Franklin D. Roosevelt. It has been said of him that he may not have known the right answers to the questions he asked, but that at least he has asked the right questions. American opinion has moved forward to a new point of view primarily because of the unremitting pressure he has brought to bear and his ability to dramatize the issue.

SELECTED BIBLIOGRAPHY

The Public Papers and Addresses of Franklin D. Roosevelt, invaluable; GERALD JOHNSON, *Roosevelt: Dictator or Democrat?* provocative; C. A. and MARY BEARD, *America in Midpassage*, a good deal of material, but poorly assembled; RAYMOND MOLEY, *After Seven Years*, critical of F. D. R.; JAMES A. FARLEY, *Behind the*

Ballots; FRANCES PERKINS, *The Roosevelt I Knew*; HENRY A. WALLACE, *America Must Choose* and *New Frontiers*; HAROLD L. ICKES, *Back to Work*; R. T. McIN-TIRE, *White House Physician*; HUGH JOHNSON, *Blue Eagle from Egg to Earth*, personal accounts by people close to the President.

E. G. NOURSE, J. S. DAVIS, and J. D. BLACK, *Three Years of the AAA*; CAREY MCWILLIAMS, *Factories in the Field*; A. A. BERLE and others, *America's Recovery Program*; CARROLL DOUGHERTY, *Labor under the NRA*; EDWARD LEVIN-SON, *Labor on the March*; HORACE R. CAYTON, *Black Workers and the New Unions*; PAUL H. DOUGLAS, *Social Security in the United States*; M. D. LANE and F. STEEGMULLER, *America on Relief*; CAROL ARONOVICI, *Housing the Masses*; H. S. RAUSHENBUSH, *The Power Fight*; C. HERMAN PRITCHETT, *The Tennessee Valley Authority*; STUART CHASE, *Rich Land, Poor Land*; R. L. WEISSMAN, *The New Wall Street*; SIDNEY RATNER, *The Social History of Taxation*; FERDINAND PECORA, *Wall Street under Oath*, all dealing with phases of the New Deal.

The best book on the Supreme Court fight is ROBERT JACKSON, *Struggle for Judicial Supremacy*. Others worth reading are E. S. CORWIN, *The Twilight of the Supreme Court*; R. K. CARR, *The Supreme Court and Judicial Review*; MAX LERNER, *Ideas Are Weapons* and *Ideas for the Ice Age*.

Material on other phases of life during the 1930's can be found in F. L. ALLEN, *Since Yesterday*; R. S. and H. M. LYND, *Middletown in Transition*; W. G. OG-BURN (Ed.), *Social Change and the New Deal*; OSCAR CARGILL, *Intellectual America*; PERCY H. BOYNTON, *America in Contemporary Fiction*; GRANVILLE HICKS, *The Great Tradition*.

H. S. COMMAGER (Ed.), *Documents of American History*, pp. 417–466, 474–520, 521–558, 562–590, 604–613, contains source material.

XXXIV

America's Role
in World Affairs, 1920-1939

ALTHOUGH America had emerged as a great world power during the last decade of the nineteenth century, it was not until the country entered the First World War that the public at large realized America's changed status. The First World War brought a great revolution in American thinking. Instead of being concerned almost exclusively with domestic affairs, the American public suddenly became aware that great forces were altering the course of world events and that these forces were shaping American history far more than world affairs had shaped the history of this country in the nineteenth century. After the war, however, a reaction set in. American opinion swung back to isolationism in an exaggerated fashion. Attention was focused on "100 per cent Americanism" and on closing the doors to immigrants, and there was a general attitude of irresponsibility with regard to the more pressing social, economic, and international problems facing American life.

Isolationism in the United States had varied sources. There were those who felt that the oceans that separated the country from Europe and Asia permitted the United States to ignore events happening in those areas. Economically, the isolationist or nationalist argued that the United States had immense natural resources and therefore was nearly independent of other regions. The suspicion that the Founding Fathers had had of Europe led some to believe that Europe still was not to be trusted. Furthermore, it was held that America, being a mixture of Old World stocks, had to cut itself off from Europe until these peoples had developed a truly American character. Inertia and shortsightedness also helped to explain the prevalence of isolationist sentiment after 1920. It seemed cheaper to stay at home and not bother with the details of organizing the world and helping to suppress aggression.

The United States, in view of its great economic and naval strength, might well have been expected to play a powerful and statesmanlike role in international affairs in the post-Versailles world. The desire of the American people to return to "normalcy," which meant, actually, ignoring responsibilities, largely accounted for America's failure to do so. Having helped to win the war, America tried to ignore the equally serious problems of reconstruction. Twenty-four years after the United States entered the First World War, it was plunged into a second great conflict. The Japanese attack on Pearl Harbor stirred thinking Americans to a realization of the tragedy of their country's having ignored the responsibilities of a great power.

FOREIGN POLICY UNDER THE REPUBLICANS

Although Vice-President-elect Calvin Coolidge declared that the votes given Warren G. Harding could not be counted as votes against the League of Nations, nevertheless Harding promptly avoided the taking of any steps toward achieving American membership in the League. Perhaps the most adequate analysis of the Harding vote was made just after the election by the New York *World*: "The American people wanted a change and they have voted for a change. They did not know what kind of change they wanted, and they do not know today what kind of change they have voted for." Before long the public became aware that a decided change had taken place from the days of the domestic and foreign policies of Woodrow Wilson. Harding's Secretary of State, Charles E. Hughes, shunned any relation with the League, even refusing to answer communications from the League for months. Finally, in 1922, the United States began to send unofficial observers to participate in the League's handling of the opium traffic, white slavery, and many cultural and social activities, and in 1934 the United States officially joined the International Labor Organization. Although Harding and his successors were opposed to entrance into the League, they did urge membership in the World Court. This matter of the World Court dragged on for years, and entrance into the Court was finally defeated in the Senate, in 1935, partly as the result of an intensive isolationist propaganda campaign carried on by Father Coughlin and the Hearst press.

A bothersome question following the war was that of war debts. In 1914 the United States was a debtor nation, but the war changed it to a creditor nation. During 1917 and 1918 the United States government lent the Allies over seven billion dollars, and after the armistice lent them three billion dollars more for reconstruction purposes. Not long after the cessation of war the debtor nations began a campaign for the cancellation of their debts. They argued, with some justification, that this money was America's contribution to victory. They had expended lives to protect the United States while it was raising an army to fight the common enemy. Furthermore, the money lent had been spent in the United States for goods, and had given the American people prosperity. The debtor nations had only goods to send the United States to repay the obligations, but they said that the American high-tariff wall made it impossible for them to pay their debts in this way. This war-debt question embittered feelings on both sides of the Atlantic. The Euro-

Fitzpatrick in the *St. Louis Post-Dispatch*

"In Our Foreign Relations All Is Well"

PRESIDENT HARDING

peans looked upon the United States as a greedy "Uncle Shylock," and isolationists in the United States were convinced that the Europeans were deceitful wretches and that the United States would be wise to ignore Europe.

The United States insisted on payment. A factor that complicated the picture was the coupling of German reparations with the war-debt payments. Reparations to be paid by Germany were more than enough to cover Allied payments to the United States. Germany, however, defaulted on reparations in 1922, and the Allies then stopped payments to the United States. Secretary of State Hughes suggested the appointment of a committee of experts to study the reparations problem. The committee, headed by Charles G. Dawes, famous for his pipes and colorful profanity, provided, in 1924, for reparations more closely tied to Germany's ability to pay. Germany met these payments until 1928, but only by heavy borrowing in America. In 1929, when Germany faced defaulting again, a committee headed by Owen D. Young reduced the reparation payments. Two years later Germany, unable to borrow any more money in the United States, defaulted once again.

The spring of 1931 witnessed a desperate financial crisis in Austria and Germany. Financial chaos threatened to wipe out the heavy American investments that had been made in this area since the war. To prevent a widespread collapse, President Hoover recommended and Congress passed a moratorium for one year on war-debt payments. But Congress and the President made it clear that none of the foreign indebtedness to the United States was to be canceled or reduced. On June 16, 1932, the representatives of Great Britain, France, Belgium, Italy, Japan, and Germany met at Lausanne to discuss the debt problem. Chancellor Brüning of Germany had announced, a few months earlier, "The situation in Germany makes the contribution of political payments impossible, and any attempt to uphold the political debt system would lead Germany and the world to disaster." The Lausanne Conference lowered German reparations to seven hundred and fourteen million dollars, which really meant cancellation. This reduction, however, was made contingent on a satisfactory settlement of Allied war debts with the United States. President Hoover quickly replied that German reparations "are a solely European question in which the United States is not concerned," and repudiated any idea that the United States would scale down the Allied debt. When war-debt payments came due in June, 1933, Britain, Italy, Czechoslovakia, Rumania, Lithuania, and Latvia made "token payments"; Finland paid in full; and France and the remaining states defaulted. Congress, to demonstrate its irritation, in April, 1934, passed the Johnson Act, forbidding American loans to defaulting foreign governments. In the following June all debtor states except Finland defaulted.

One of the grave problems which faced the victors after the Peace Conference was the reduction of armaments. The burden of continued armaments was a heavy strain on the weakened economies of Europe. The Washington Conference of 1921–1922 set limits on the tonnage of capital ships and aircraft-carriers to be owned by any one power. President Coolidge and Secretary of State Frank B. Kellogg were anxious to limit the tonnage of smaller craft as well. In 1927 they called a naval conference, which met at Geneva. France and Italy, bitter rivals, refused to attend, and American shipping interests sent a lobbyist to prevent a disarmament program. The United States, Great Britain, and Japan were unable to reach any agreement, and the conference broke up without any action.

An outcome of the failure of the Geneva Conference was the belief in the United States that the way to have peace was not to limit armaments, but to abolish war completely. Professor James T. Shotwell of Columbia University presented this idea to Briand, the French foreign minister. Briand then sent a message to the American people, proposing a Franco-American agreement to "outlaw war." The State Department was at first unresponsive, but public opinion was aroused to support the proposal. President Nicholas Murray Butler of Columbia University and other publicists who believed strongly in collective action stirred the public's mind, and petitions bearing two million signatures forced the State Department into action. Secretary Kellogg persuaded Briand to include other nations in the pact which was signed in Paris on August 27, 1928.

The Kellogg-Briand Pact, or Pact of Paris, stated that the contracting parties "condemn recourse to war for the solution of international controversies, and renounce it as an instrument of national policy." Sixty-three nations eventually signed the pact, and it was ratified by the United States Senate on January 15, 1929. The Senate made it clear, however, that the pact did not commit the United States to punitive measures against violators. The Pact of Paris was absolutely lacking in sanctions. It was nothing but wishful thinking for peace. To have peace, it was necessary that provision be made for taking military action against an aggressor. This lack of coercive machinery rendered the pact meaningless when Japan attacked China in 1931. The interest of the United States in the Pact of Paris indicated a trend away from "ostrich isolationism," but American public opinion did not demonstrate any understanding that merely wishing for peace was insufficient.

A few months after the signing of the Kellogg-Briand Pact, President Hoover, in his inaugural address, revealed his attitude by saying, "I covet for this administration a record of having further contributed to advance the cause of peace." Increased naval building, however, seemed to be a threat to this hope. In 1930 President Hoover and English Prime Minister J. Ramsay MacDonald called a naval conference to meet in London. The results were disappointing. France and Italy refused to sign the main agreements; and although an upper limit for the construction of new ships was established, an "escalator clause" permitted construction above the maximum if any signatory considered itself to be endangered by the construction of a nonsignatory power. The Japanese were accorded a more favorable ratio than that of the Washington Conference, and Anglo-American parity in all ships was recognized. In 1934 Japan gave notice that she would not be bound by the agreement after 1936. Beginning in 1936 the powers resumed the race in naval armaments.

THE UNITED STATES AND LATIN AMERICA, 1928-1939: THE "GOOD NEIGHBOR"

Hatred of the United States was rife south of the Rio Grande until the introduction of the "good neighbor" policy. Calvin Coolidge, near the close of his administration, took steps to improve inter-American relations by sending Dwight Morrow to Mexico as ambassador in September, 1927. Morrow's intelligence and tact soon won the friendship of the Mexican government. The next move toward improved relations with our southern neighbors came in the administration of Herbert Hoover. Just before his inauguration Hoover toured Latin America. This tour made him realize the need of improving inter-American friendship. He therefore modified certain aspects of previous Republican policy. The denial of the right of revolution was applied only to Central America instead of to the whole hemisphere, as under his predecessors. The dividends and property of United States investors were protected with less vigor. The State Department quietly denounced the Roosevelt corollary to the Monroe Doctrine, and the marines were withdrawn from Nicaragua and steps were taken to withdraw them from Haiti as well.

These actions of the Hoover administration were harbingers of the "good neighbor" policy, to be developed by Franklin D. Roosevelt. They were taken, however, in a disconnected and almost secret fashion. President Roosevelt's Latin-American policy, continuing and building upon steps taken by Hoover, was well-planned and announced from the treetops. In 1928 Roosevelt had written an article for *Foreign Affairs* in which he had said that the United States should renounce territorial conquest and arbitrary intervention in the domestic affairs of its neighbors in behalf of vested interests. After 1933 he implemented these statements. In his inaugural address he asserted:

In the field of world policy I would dedicate this Nation to the policy of the good neighbor—the neighbor who resolutely respects himself and, because he does so, respects the rights of others—the neighbor who respects his obligations and respects the sanctity of his agreements in and with a world of neighbors.

With the aid of Secretary of State Cordell Hull and Undersecretary Sumner Welles, these words were translated into action. The situation in Latin America on March 4, 1933, was this: (1) Cuba was a protectorate under the Platt Amendment and was ruled by Dictator Machado;

(2) Panama was a protectorate under the 1903 treaty; (3) United States marines were in Haiti; (4) fiscal agents of the United States were in Haiti; (5) the right of revolution was denied Central America; (6) 80 per cent of the government bonds of Latin America were in default.

The convincing actions taken by President Roosevelt that made the United States a "good neighbor" were these: (1) revolutionists were allowed to overthrow Machado, and the Platt Amendment was abrogated, ending the protectorate over Cuba; (2) a new treaty was signed with Panama, restoring full sovereignty to that nation; (3) the marines and fiscal agents were withdrawn from Haiti; (4) the right of revolution was permitted to all Latin America; (5) pledges of nonintervention in the internal affairs of the Latin-American republics were made by the United States government.

At the Pan-American Conference of December, 1933, at Montevideo, Secretary Hull supported the pledge "No State has the right to intervene in the internal or external affairs of another." For years the Latin Americans had been attempting to procure such an agreement from the United States. Hull's pledge, which was repeated by President Roosevelt, proved to be more than mere words. It was carried out when, in March, 1938, the Mexican government confiscated all foreign oil holdings. American investors clamored for intervention, but President Roosevelt and Secretary Hull insisted only upon reasonable payment to the former owners of the oil wells.

Under the "good neighbor" policy the Monroe Doctrine was transformed from a policy exclusively of the United States to a Pan-American policy of security. President Roosevelt observed, shortly after his inauguration:

The maintenance of constitutional government in other nations is not a sacred obligation devolving upon the United States alone. The maintenance of law and orderly processes of government in this hemisphere is the concern of each individual nation within its own borders first of all. It is only if and when the failure of orderly processes affects the other nations of the continent that it becomes their concern; and the point to stress is that in such an event it becomes the joint concern of a whole continent in which we are all neighbors.

At a special Inter-American Conference for Peace, held at Buenos Aires in 1936, President Roosevelt implemented his idea of the Pan-Americanization of the Monroe Doctrine by telling the Conference that non-American states seeking "to commit acts of aggression against us will find a Hemisphere wholly prepared to consult together for our mutual safety and our mutual good." The delegates at the Conference signed a treaty, agreeing to consult with one another in order to maintain peace. Two years later the eighth Pan-American Conference met at Lima. By this time the world was horrified at the racial and religious persecutions being carried on by Nazi Germany. The delegates reiterated their pledge to consult with one another to maintain peace, and then they passed a series of resolutions condemning racial and religious persecution in the American republics, and denounced political activities by alien minorities in the interest of their native lands.

The increased cordiality between the United States and Latin America came none too soon. The totalitarian nations Germany, Italy, and Japan began to loom as threats to the peace of the world, and they openly denounced and ridiculed democracy. Germany, particularly, did its best in the years from 1933 to 1939 to stir Latin America against the United States. All the old anti-Yankee symbols were waved by German agents. If the United States had not become a "good neighbor," Germany might have found fertile ground for its anti-American seeds. As it was, when war finally broke out in 1939, the Latin-American nations worked, on the whole, closely with the United States. By 1939 the former "Colossus of the North" had been replaced by the "good neighbor." From an economic, as well as from a diplomatic, standpoint the United States and Latin America had strong ties by 1938. Latin-America's trade figures reveal that the United States had twice as much export and import business in Latin America as its nearest competitor, Germany. The *New Republic*, in 1940, looking over the years since 1933, observed that "the outstanding success of Mr. Roosevelt's foreign policy has undoubtedly been in this hemisphere."

ISOLATION VERSUS INTERNATIONALISM—
THE DECADE OF THE THIRTIES

From 1933 to 1939 the United States government followed a policy of attempting to improve international relations and thus prevent the collapse of world peace. This policy, however, was carried on in a world in which ruthless aggression was rampant. Japan seized Manchuria in 1931. Two years later Germany began to rearm under the dictatorship of Hitler. In 1935 Italy invaded Ethiopia. The following year Hitler tore up the Treaty of Locarno and fortified the demilitarized Rhineland. In 1937 Japan again attacked China, and the next year Hitler occupied Austria and dismembered Czechoslovakia. During the first six months of 1939 Hitler deprived Czechoslovakia of her independence and seized Memel, while Mussolini invaded Albania. On September 1, 1939, Hitler struck at Poland, and the world soon was at war.

President Franklin D. Roosevelt and Secretary Cordell Hull were avowed internationalists. They attempted to arouse America to the dangers that Hitler, Mussolini, and the Japanese signified to the democratic way of life. Both the Japanese and Nazi Germany, with their false theories of the superiority of their own peoples over other peoples of the world, were planning world domination. In the highly technological world of the twentieth century, President Roosevelt realized that no nation could escape this threat. No nation could isolate itself, because inventions in the field of transportation and communication had reduced the world to a veritable neighborhood. After the United States entered the Second World War, the State Department published a volume entitled *Peace and War: United States Foreign Policy, 1931–1941*, in which the following statement appears:

During a large part of the period with which this volume deals, much of public opinion in this country did not accept the thesis that a European war could vitally affect the security of the United States or that an attack on the United States by any of the Axis powers was possible. In this respect it differed from the President and the Secretary of State, who early became convinced that the aggressive policies of the Axis powers were directed toward an ultimate attack on the United States and that, therefore, our foreign relations should be so conducted as to give all possible support to the nations endeavoring to check the march of Axis aggression.

Our foreign policy during the decade under consideration necessarily had to move within the framework of a gradual evolution of public opinion in the United States away from the idea of isolation expressed in "neutrality" legislation and toward realization that the Axis design was a plan of world conquest in which the United States was intended to be a certain, though perhaps ultimate, victim, and that our primary policy therefore must be defense against actual and mounting danger. This was an important factor influencing the conduct of our foreign relations.

President Roosevelt and Secretary Hull worked to improve the mechanisms of collective security as a method of checking the ambitions of the aggressors. One way to accomplish this was to improve world-trade conditions. Congress, in June, 1934, passed the Reciprocal Trade Agreements Act, permitting the President to raise or lower tariffs by as much as 50 per cent in order to gain concessions from other governments. Secretary Hull, who was to make the agreements under this act, felt that world peace was impossible without freer world-trade conditions. By 1939 some twenty-one agreements had been made. These agreements were reached with Canada, France, Belgium, the Netherlands, Sweden, Switzerland, Czechoslovakia, Great Britain, Turkey, and twelve Latin-American nations. The reciprocal-trade agreements did stimulate world trade. In 1936–1937, for instance, American exports to countries with agreements increased 42 per cent over those of the year 1934–1935, whereas exports to nonagreement countries increased only 26 per cent. Although certain vested interests opposed the treaties, Congress, in 1937, 1940, and 1943, extended the life of the act.

The trade agreements, however, were only one step that the President and the Secretary of State had in mind to help to preserve world peace. The State Department had reports from its representatives in Germany which clearly set forth Germany's aim of world domination. One such report, in 1934, stated that the fundamental purpose of the Nazis "is to secure a greater share of the world's future for the Germans, the expansion of German territory and growth of the German race until it constitutes the largest and most powerful nation in the world, and ultimately, according to some Nazi leaders, until it dominates the entire globe." Such a situation led Roosevelt and Hull to urge United States' collaboration with peace-loving nations in order to maintain peace and order. One step was to enlarge American co-operation with the nonpolitical activities of the League of Nations, and on January 16, 1935, President Roosevelt urged the Senate to consent to membership in the World Court. He pointed out that such an act was of importance to the future of world peace, and that the United States now had an opportunity "once more to throw its weight into the scale of peace." The Senate, however, refused to permit the United States to take this step.

Both the President and the Secretary of State urged still another step for the maintenance of peace. This was to place an embargo upon the trade of an aggressor nation. Secretary Hull, in a letter to Congress on April 5, 1933, urged that Congress enact such legislation, and stated that such an embargo would be exercised by any President "to the sole end of maintaining the peace of the world and with a due and prudent regard for our national policies and national interests." Furthermore, Hull pointed out that the United States should not be left in the position of being unable to co-operate with other governments in the prevention of the shipment of arms to aggressors. Most important of all, the enactment of such a law "would strengthen the position of this Government in its international relations and would enable us to cooperate more efficiently in efforts to maintain the peace of the world."

Although this proposal was based on the sound premise that nations must work together if they desire peace, it failed to take into account the strength of isolationist sentiment in the United States. The belligerent attitudes of Hitler, Mussolini, and the Japanese threatened to plunge the world into war, and the American public's reaction was that we should keep out of it. It was commonly believed in those days that the United States actually could ignore a world war. The fear of a new war came just at the time when the country had grown skeptical of the wisdom of having entered the first war. In 1934 many books and articles were written about how munitions-makers and international bankers had profited from the first conflict, and the United States Senate appointed a committee in 1934, headed by Gerald Nye, to investigate such activities. The investigations revealed that excessive profits had been made by munitions-makers and by bankers who had floated Allied loans. Then the committee went too far in drawing conclusions. Senator Clark of Missouri asserted that the profits to be gained from the American export of munitions to the Allies were the only reason why the United States entered the first war. The Nye Committee, in its final report, declared that selfish industrial and financial interests had built up such a heavy stake in the Allied cause that it prevented a truly neutral policy. Then, in 1935, the reading public's attention was captured by Walter Millis's book *Road to War*, which dramatized and popularized the Nye contention. This attitude toward the First World War overlooked the basic forces which really accounted for the entrance of the United States into that war.

The public, however, readily accepted the Nye theory and became bitter and cynical about America's entrance into the first war. When the public was asked in a poll in April, 1937, "Do you think it was a mistake for the United States to enter the World War?" 71 per cent replied, "Yes." The public was so confused and so forgetful that it showed no realization that probably the alternative to American entrance would have been a German victory, a victory which, more than likely, would have been far more severe on the defeated Allies, and therefore, in the long run, on the United States, than the Treaty of Versailles was on Germany.

As a result of the Nye Committee's investigation and the books and articles attacking America's entrance into the first war, Congress moved to pass legislation designed to keep America neutral in the case of another conflict. President Roosevelt wanted a law which would place an embargo on trade with an aggressor. Such a law would make it possible for the United States to deter aggression or cripple it and at the same time aid the victim. The President's request was based on the frank assumption that it was vital to American security to aid the democracies if they were attacked by the dictators. This power to apply an embargo against an aggressor would have given the President a powerful weapon in world diplomacy. Any warning of his to the dictators against steps of aggression would have had behind it the threat that the world's most powerful industrial nation would throw its support to the victim. The President's bill also would have given him the power to forbid American ships to enter the war zone; prohibit loans to the belligerents; and warn Americans that they traveled on belligerent vessels at their own risk.

Congress, however, would not accept the President's suggestion. Its measure, signed by Roosevelt on August 31, 1935, prohibited the export of arms, ammunition, or implements of war to *any* belligerent nation; made it unlawful for an American vessel to carry arms for or to any belligerent; and empowered the President to warn Americans that they traveled on belligerent ships at their own risk. This measure did not permit the President to discriminate between aggressors and victims. As a result, it deprived the United States of the chance to play a powerful role in maintaining peace from 1935 to September, 1939, and definitely handicapped the President in his efforts to maintain peace.

From this law the dictators got the impression that if they plunged the world into war, the United States would refuse to aid their victims. This shortsighted policy on the part of Congress probably did aid the dictators in plotting their aggressions. An underlying assumption of the Congressional bill was that the people of the United States would be willing to close their eyes if the democracies of the world were threatened with extinction by the dictators. A few farsighted people, in 1935, realized that this was a false assumption. They knew that the people of the United States, when they saw the democracies being crushed, would demand aid for those victims. After September, 1939, as the mechanized columns of Hitler crushed democracy after democracy, the American people did rise up and demand aid to the remaining democracies opposing Hitler. It was not, however, until after war had broken out that the American people realized how foolish the Neutrality Act was. Then, and only then, did they support steps to revise it.

President Roosevelt signed the Neutrality Act, protesting that it "might drag us into war instead of keeping us out." Secretary Hull, a short time later, warned the country that to assume that by placing an embargo on arms we were making ourselves secure from war was "to close our eyes to manifold dangers in other directions." The outbreak of the war between Italy and Ethiopia, in October, 1935, led the President to apply the Neutrality Act. Since oil, copper, scrap iron, trucks, and tractors were not considered implements of war under the Neutrality Act, private American interests sold large amounts of these goods to Italy, which aided that country greatly in the prosecution of the war. This trade, denounced by the President and Secretary Hull, had some influence in weakening the halfhearted sanctions applied to Italy by the League powers. The Neutrality Act, in the case of this conflict, probably operated to make British diplomacy cautious in its opposition to Italy. If Britain went to war with Italy, it could not buy equipment from the United States, and Mussolini too was aware of this. Since there was no real co-operation among the democratic powers against the aggressor, Italy was able to conquer Ethiopia by the summer of 1936.

As a peaceful world further disintegrated with the Italo-Ethiopian war, President Roosevelt warned, on Armistice Day, 1935, that if the United States wanted peace, we could not "build walls around ourselves and hide our heads in the sand," but that we must strive to work with other nations to obtain peace. By this time the League was negligible as a force for peace. The aggressors knew that they could defy it with impunity. In July, 1936, came the next incident in the collapse of collective security: civil war broke out in Spain. General Franco and his Fascist following launched a revolt against republican Spain, but before long it was much more than an internal conflict. Germany and Italy sent men and equipment to aid Franco to destroy the democratically elected government, and Russia sent a little material to the government.

The American Neutrality Act did not specifically apply to civil conflict; so Congress amended it on January 8, 1937, extending its provisions to Spain. While this was taking place, England and France persuaded other governments to sign a pledge not to interfere in the Spanish conflict. Germany and Italy openly broke the agreement and continued to send aid to Franco; but the Loyalists, as those who supported the republican government were called, were deprived of any material aid from the United States and the other democracies. Germany and Italy used the Spanish war as a dress rehearsal for the great conflict to come. The military lessons learned were valuable to Germany in the early years of the Second World War. By their shortsighted policy the world's democracies allowed republican Spain to be destroyed by Franco, Germany, and Italy. Liberals in the United States protested the actions of the State Department, but the public was largely indifferent to the struggle, failing to see that the defeat of Spain's republic was another step toward attempted Fascist domination of the world.

The Neutrality Act expired on May 1, 1937, and Congress quickly passed a new bill. The new law retained the embargo on arms, munitions, and implements of war to all belligerents. Travel by Americans on belligerent ships was at their own risk, and it was illegal to buy or sell belligerent securities. A new feature was incorporated,—a "cash-and-carry provision,"—which stated that materials like scrap iron, cotton, and oil could not be exported to belligerents in American ships, and that the belligerents had to pay cash for such goods. Isolationists were extremely happy over this bill. They honestly believed that the way had now been discovered to keep the United States out of war, that this law would "insulate" the United States. The course of the Second World War from 1939 to Pearl Harbor, however, demonstrated that the Neutrality Act was working against the best interests of the United States. It began to be apparent that the United States might be left alone to fight a triumphant Germany in the West and a triumphant Japan in the East. Then the American people demanded the modification of the law and, just before Pearl Harbor, its repeal in order to aid those Allies who were still fighting against Fascism.

RELATIONS WITH JAPAN

In July, 1937, Japan invented an excuse to attack China. The Roosevelt administration followed a strong line of action against Japan. Ambassador Grew had warned the United States government, as early as 1934, that the Japanese were talking in terms of Japan's destiny to subjugate and rule the world. Grew, particularly, pointed out that the Japanese imperialists aimed at obtaining "trade control and eventually predominant political influence in China, the Philippines, the Straits Settlements, Siam, and the Dutch East Indies, the Maritime Provinces and Vladivostok, one step at a time, as in Korea and Manchuria, pausing intermittently to consolidate and then continuing as soon as the intervening obstacles can be overcome by diplomacy or force." The ambassador added that it would be "criminally short-sighted" to disregard the possibility of eventual war with Japan. His advice as to the best way of avoiding it was adequate military preparation. The Roosevelt administration expanded the size of the army and navy in the years just before 1939 over the protests of American pacifists, but that expansion was not comparable to the enormous expansions taking place in Germany, Italy, and Japan.

Toward China and Japan the United States had had a clear-cut policy since the turn of the century. The United States stood for the "open door" in China and the territorial sovereignty of that country. Having this stand, the United States obviously would be opposed to Japan's desire to dominate and run China. During the First World War the United States had objected to the "Twenty-one Demands," which Japan had served on China—demands which would have made China a protectorate of Japan. President Wilson also opposed Japanese control of the old German lease of the Shantung peninsula, and eventually helped to force the withdrawal of Japanese troops from that region. President Harding called a conference of the powers at Washington in 1921 and 1922, at which Great Britain, the United States, France, Japan, and five other nations signed a pledge (the Nine-Power Pact) to uphold the "sovereignty, the independence, and the territorial and administrative integrity of China."

The conference also made an agreement on capital naval ships. It was agreed that the ratio of capital ships should be five for England, to five for the United States, to three for Japan. In return, the United States promised Japan that it would not strengthen the fortifications of any of its Pacific islands except Hawaii. In 1934 Japan denounced the limitation that had been placed on capital ships; and long before this, competition in the construction of smaller craft had been taking place.

The sovereignty and the territorial integrity of China were shattered in 1931 when Japan ruthlessly invaded Manchuria as a step toward ultimate domination of the Far East. This action was an "utter and cynical disregard" of Japan's obligations under the Nine-Power Pact and the Kellogg-Briand Pact. President Hoover denounced the aggression as "immoral," and agreed that the United States had an obligation to China under the Nine-Power Pact and ought to co-operate with the League of Nations in the matter. Hoover felt, however, that if peaceful efforts failed to check Japanese aggression, the United States should not go to war with the League nations against Japan. His opinion was that Japan's "acts do not imperil the freedom of the American people, the economic or moral future of the people. I do not propose ever to sacrifice American life for anything short of this. . . . We will not go along on war or any of the sanctions either economic or military, for these are the roads to war." This stand on the part of President Hoover hampered action against Japan, a military power that respected only superior military power. As long as the President of the United States was willing to use only words against their aggression, the Japanese ignored the protests of America.

Another factor checking effective action by the United States was Secretary of State Henry L. Stimson's belief that if the liberals of Japan were not interfered with by outside threats, they would be able to check the militarists and end the Manchurian affair. The British Foreign Office, headed by Tory Sir John Simon, was unwilling to work completely with Stimson, which proved to be another circumstance impeding joint action against the aggressor. The League of Nations' first reaction to the aggression was to send an investigating commission to Manchuria. Stimson discouraged this move, not wanting to weaken the Japanese liberals. His attitude discouraged the League supporters, and one reporter stated that the favorable moment for checking Japan "had gone forever." Shortly after this, however, Stimson authorized the American consul at Geneva to attend the meetings of the League dealing with the aggression.

By the time the League finally sent a commission to Manchuria, Japan had crushed the last Chinese resistance there. President Hoover and Secretary Stimson, in order to express their disapproval, notified the Chinese and Japanese governments on January 7, 1932, that the United States would not recognize any "situation, treaty, or covenant" brought about by means contrary to the Kellogg-Briand Pact. The British Foreign Office failed to co-operate in this move, and the London *Times* justified Japan's actions and observed that foreign business interests would not suffer under Japanese control of Manchuria.

On January 28, 1932, the Japanese attacked Shanghai. A number of United States newspapers denounced Japan as "running amuck." There was some feeling for an economic boycott against Japan, but President Hoover and probably a majority of Americans opposed this for fear that it might be a step to war. Secretary Stimson was not unfavorable to co-operating with a League boycott. Close collaboration between England and the United States now seemed possible. Shanghai, unlike Manchuria, was the center of vast British financial and business interests. Secretary Stimson and Sir John Simon talked via the transatlantic telephone. Stimson, according to his own account, *The Far Eastern Crisis*, wanted economic sanctions applied to Japan. He asked England to join the United States in such a step, but Sir John Simon evaded any action. He apparently was not willing to apply economic pressure on Japan until he had a real assurance that Hoover and Congress would back up Stimson. Simon had good reason for this caution. President Hoover was unwilling to support sanctions, and Congress was isolationist.

As a result, nothing adequate was done about Japan. The League adopted the Stimson policy of the nonrecognition of any situation brought about by force. The League's investigating commission, late in 1932, censured Japan in its report, and Secretary Stimson stated that the United States was in agreement with the report. Japan then withdrew from the League of Nations, but retained Manchuria, and thus dealt a heavy blow to collective security. Allan Nevins has analyzed the significance of this entire incident in the following manner:

If the western powers, acting through a really strong League in which the United States was a loyal member, could have taken prompt and united action, they could easily have brought Japan to a halt. Their failure to act together advertised the weakness of the covenant and showed that the Kellogg Pact was yet little better than an empty formula. Hitler and Mussolini took careful note of the lessons taught by Japan. Within a few years Hull could truthfully declare that the attempt to disintegrate modern civilization had taken its beginnings in Manchuria in 1931–32.[1]

During the Manchurian crisis the American people failed to see the significance of the affair to American life. President Hoover's attitude that it did not imperil American freedom was echoed by the *Philadelphia Record*, which stated that "the American people don't give a hoot in a rain barrel who controls North China." Few Americans realized at this time that this really was the beginning of the Second World War, and that it would be cheaper in lives and wealth to cooperate militarily to check the outbreak of aggression at that point than to wait until a time (1939) when the aggressors should be far more powerful and better prepared for war against the democracies.

The Japanese attack on North China in July, 1937, came at a time when the diplomatic situation was extremely unfavorable for the United States. The rise of Hitler in Germany and Mussolini's belligerent attitude toward England and France left these two democracies too worried to pay much attention to the Far East. The League of

[1]*America in World Affairs*, p. 106. Oxford University Press, New York, 1942.

Nations, having failed to check Japan in Manchuria and Italy in Ethiopia, was too feeble to be of assistance. The United States was thus left alone to face this present act of aggression. Both President Roosevelt and Secretary Hull were anxious to aid China and hamper Japan. In this they were backed by the American people, who revealed, in a poll conducted in October, 1937, that 59 per cent were in sympathy with China, 1 per cent with Japan, and 40 per cent with neither. The President and the Secretary of State, however, were not willing to aid China to the extent of using force.

Under the pretext that neither side had declared war, President Roosevelt did not apply the Neutrality Act in this case. An arms embargo would have struck a great blow at China without hurting Japan too much. Industrialized Japan was able to produce her own guns, tanks, and airplanes, whereas China had to rely on outside areas. If the Neutrality Act had been applied, Japan would still have been able to buy raw materials like scrap iron. Therefore, if the President had invoked the Neutrality Act, the United States really would have taken the side of Japan against China. Such a step the American people would not have countenanced; but beyond not applying the Neutrality Act, they were reluctant to take steps to aid China.

On October 5, 1937, Mr. Roosevelt delivered a significant speech in Chicago, declaring that world peace was being threatened by international lawlessness, and that the countries that were contributing to gangsterism and disorder should be quarantined. Furthermore, he observed:

The peace, the freedom, and the security of 90 per cent of the population of the world is being jeopardized by the remaining 10 per cent, who are threatening a breakdown of all international order and law. Surely the 90 per cent who want to live in peace under law and in accordance with moral standards that have received almost universal acceptance through the centuries, can and must find some way to make their will prevail. . . . There must be positive endeavors to preserve peace.

The wisdom of this speech failed to attract the American public, which, at this moment, thought that the United States need not pay any attention to what was taking place in the Far East. The President was denounced by the isolationists for being a warmonger, although his idea of positive efforts to achieve peace appealed to the advocates of collective security as the only way for the United States to remain at peace. A conference of powers called by the League to discuss the

Chinese situation resulted in a total failure. Only military action would stop aggression, and the peoples in the democratic countries shrank from such a step.

THE EVE OF WAR

The year 1938 opened upon a dangerous world situation. Japan was continuing her aggressions against China. The Spanish civil war was slowly being won by the followers of Franco. In November, 1937, Italy had joined Japan and Germany in an alliance—the Anti-Comintern Pact. Germany was rearming at a feverish rate. Hitler and his National Socialist party had ridden into power with the backing of German militarists, Junker landlords, and industrialists, who supported him as a means of checking a democratic Germany. Hitler also drew support from the vast number of unemployed and from many in the middle class, whose security was threatened by the economic crisis in Germany. After 1933 he turned Germany into an armed camp. Differences of opinion were ruthlessly suppressed, and a free press and the right of free assembly disappeared. Hitler commanded, and the German people followed, except those who were murdered or thrown into concentration camps, or who fled the country. Schools and universities were forced to accept Nazi domination. Textbooks were rewritten to fit the Nazi philosophy, and German youth was regimented into Hitler Youth organizations. A Ministry of Propaganda controlled literature, journalism, radio, the films, theater, music, and painting. Independent trade unions were destroyed. The control of industry was placed in the hands of Nazi supervisors, and the unemployed were put to work on road-building projects and on a huge rearmament program.

Hitler was a master of mass rule. In *Mein Kampf* he explained how propaganda should be conducted:

The perception of the great masses is only very limited, their understanding is small, but their forgetfulness is great. Effective propaganda, for that reason, must keep to a very few points, and be used like slogans till the very last man comprehends its import.

Hitler whipped the Germans into a lather of fury over the supposed iniquities of the Treaty of Versailles. The Germans, suffering from an acute inferiority complex, were told by Hitler and Alfred Rosenberg, the philosopher of Nazism, that they were a superior people designed to rule first Europe and then the world. Before accomplishing this, however, the German race had to be purged of all Jews, Communists, internationalists, and democrats, who had corrupted the German race.

Low in *The New York Times*

The Difficulty Will Arise

when Someone Wants to Go Somewhere

The birth of the Axis in 1937. Germany, Italy, and Japan, aggressors all, united in the Anti-Comintern Pact ostensibly to fight Bolshevism

The race theory of the Nazis stated that the Nordic was born to rule, as the Latin, the Slav, the Jew, and the Negro were born to be ruled. The Jewish race, particularly, had to be disfranchised and destroyed. Corrupting forms of internationalism, like the Catholic Church, the Masons, and the Communists, had to be destroyed for the Nordic German race to reach its destiny. A pure race, of course, never existed, and anthropologists have demonstrated that there is no superior race; but the Nazis, nevertheless, were able to "sell" their doctrine to the German people. Anti-Semitism grew in other parts of the world, too, particularly in the United States, under the stimulus given it by Hitler.

The Nazis controlled a great industrial nation, a nation that, long before the Nazis, had talked of the imperial destiny of Germany. Hitler simply gave dynamic meaning to this old tradition. Nazi Germany built up armaments and tried to make itself self-sufficient. Unemployment soon gave way to a labor shortage. By 1938–1939 Germany had the most powerful military machine in the world, and the German people were ideologically conditioned for the business of waging war.

Americans viewed the militarization of Germany and the persecution of the Jews, the suppression of freedom, and the growth of the dictatorship of Hitler with horror. Most Americans, however, were unable to believe that Hitler was out to dominate the world. They considered his statements to be the ravings of a madman. But President Roosevelt urged on Congress, early in 1938, increased appropriations for military and naval rearmament. He pointed out that, in view of the increasing armaments of other nations, the American army and navy were inadequate for the purposes of national security. Although some quarters doubted that increased expenditures were necessary for national defense, Congress adopted most of the President's proposals. The President and Secretary Hull acted on the theory, in these days, that Germany was "bent on becoming the dominating colossus of Continental Europe."

On March 11, 1938, Hitler sent his army into Austria and two days later proclaimed the union of the two countries. Secretary Hull warned the United States, on March 17, that force would dominate world affairs unless the United States and other peace-loving nations worked together. Isolation, he observed, "is not a means to security; it is a fruitful source of insecurity." Only by helping to establish a world based on law "can we keep the problem of our own security in true perspective, and thus discharge our responsibility to ourselves." Hitler next cast covetous eyes on the Sudetenland in Czechoslovakia, and a "war of nerves" was launched against Czechoslovakia. War threatened to engulf Europe. President Roosevelt cabled Hitler, urging a peaceful settlement of the dispute. In a last-minute attempt to avoid war, the heads of the governments of Great Britain, France, Germany, and Italy met at Munich, on September 29, 1938. Russia was conspicuously ignored by the Chamberlain government in England and the Daladier government in France during this crisis, since these two governments were bent on appeasing Hitler rather than on collaborating with Russia to check Hitler.

The Munich Conference gave Hitler the Sudetenland. This conference was a great defeat for the democracies and a significant victory for an aggressor who was better prepared for war. Secretary Hull warned against the assumption that the Munich Pact meant peace, and he emphasized the need that the nations redouble their efforts for peace. A poll of the American people revealed that 77 per cent did not think that the German claim to the Sudetenland was justified. When they were asked which side they would favor if England and France had to go to war with Germany and Italy, 65 per cent replied, "England and France."

Toward Japan's continued aggression in China, the American State Department announced, in December, 1938, that it would not recognize Japan's "New Order," whereby Japan claimed complete domination of the Far East. Businessmen were asked to place a "moral" embargo on the shipment of airplanes to Japan, and credits were extended to the Chinese for purchases in the United States. Speaking to Congress on January 4, 1939, President Roosevelt pointed out: "There are methods short of war, but stronger and more effective than mere words, of bringing home to aggressor governments the aggregate sentiment of our people."

As war approached, farsighted internationalists were distressed at the implication of the Neutrality Act that the United States would stand aside in a conflict between the democracies and the totalitarian powers. If the democracies should win a quick victory, such a policy would be easy to follow. If, however, the course of the war should threaten the destruction of France and England, and if Germany, Italy, and Japan should achieve domination of Europe, Africa, and Asia, the United States would be in a dangerous position. If this situation should develop, the internationalists were sure that American intervention would be inevitable. Therefore their position, during 1938 and 1939, was that the United States, in order to avoid possible participation in a war to prevent a totalitarian victory, should join at once in steps to prevent that war from starting.

During 1939 President Roosevelt and Secretary Hull demonstrated their belief that collective efforts were necessary to avert war by urging Congress to revise the Neutrality Act. On January 4, 1939, President Roosevelt told Congress:

At the very least we can and should avoid any action, or lack of action, which will encourage or assist an aggressor. We have learned that when we deliberately try to legislate neutrality, our neutrality laws may operate unevenly and unfairly—may actually give aid to the aggressor and deny it to the victim. The instinct of self-preservation should warn us that we ought not to let that happen any more.

While debate was raging in the United States over the President's suggestion, Germany invaded and occupied Bohemia, in Czechoslovakia (March 14), and two days later declared that Czechoslovakia no longer existed as a nation. In emulation of his partner, Mussolini conquered Albania in April. The following month Secretary Hull urged Congress to revise the Neutrality Act to permit belligerents to buy munitions in the United States. The arms embargo worked against the democracies, the Secretary asserted, since they were behind the dictators in their rearmament programs. The dictators might be all the more willing to go to war if their less well-prepared enemies were shut off from American supplies by the arms embargo. On the other hand, they might be deterred from war if they realized that the democracies would be able to purchase war goods in the United States.

The Senate Foreign Relations Committee, by a vote of twelve to eleven on July 11, decided not to report the bill to repeal the arms embargo to the Senate. On July 18 President Roosevelt and Secretary Hull warned that failure to take action "would weaken the leadership of the United States in exercising its potent influence in the cause of preserving peace among other nations in the event of a new crisis in Europe between now and next January." The majority of the Senate Committee were not willing to free the President's hands so that he could threaten the dictators and thus, as he hoped, prevent war from breaking out. In a final attempt to persuade the Senate leaders that war in Europe was imminent, President Roosevelt and Secretary Hull called a group of them to the White House. Both the President and the Secretary were eloquent in their warnings that the arms embargo might encourage the dictators to start a war. Isolationist Senator Borah, however, disagreed with their contention that war was about to break out. Hull replied by saying, "I wish the Senator would come down to my office and read the cables. I'm sure he would come to the conclusion that there's far more danger of war than he thinks." To this Senator Borah petulantly replied, "So far as the reports in your Department are concerned, I wouldn't be bound by them. I have my own sources of information . . . and on several occasions I've found them more reliable than the State Department."[1] Shortly after this remark the meeting broke up without any action being agreed upon. Six weeks later Germany invaded Poland.

[1] Joseph Alsop and Robert Kintner, *American White Paper*, pp. 44–46. Simon and Schuster, Inc., New York, 1940.

SELECTED BIBLIOGRAPHY

Allan Nevins, *America in World Affairs,* an excellent, concise description of American diplomacy during the prewar decade; *Peace and War: United States Foreign Policy, 1931–1941,* the State Department's review of the decade; Joseph Alsop and Robert Kintner, *American White Paper,* interesting reading.

F. L. Schuman, *International Politics* and *Night over Europe* and *Design for Power*; G. A. Borgese, *Goliath: The March of Fascism*; Gaetano Salvemini, *Under the Axe of Fascism*; Otto Tolischus, *They Wanted War*; R. A. Brady, *The Spirit and Structure of German Fascism*; W. C. Johnstone, *The United States and Japan's New Order*; Willard Price, *Children of the Rising Sun*; A. W. Griswold, *The Far Eastern Policy of the United States*; Henry L. Stimson, *The Far Eastern Crisis*; Harley F. McNair, *The Real Conflict between China and Japan*; T. A. Bisson, *American Policy in the Far East, 1931–1940*; Frank P. Chambers, C. P. Grant, and C. C. Bayley, *This Age of Conflict, 1914–1943,* some of the worth-while books covering world changes and world diplomacy.

Among the valuable books on America's role in diplomacy are R. L. Buell, *Isolated America*; A. W. Dulles and H. F. Armstrong, *Can We Be Neutral?*; Norman Angell, *America's Dilemma: Alone or Allied*; C. A. Beard, *A Foreign Policy for America*; H. F. Armstrong, *We or They* and *When There Is No Peace*; Jerome Frank, *Save America First*; Philip C. Jessup, *International Security: The American Role in Collective Action for Peace.*

Important books dealing with inter-American relations are J. Fred Rippy, *Caribbean Danger Zone*; Hubert Herring, *Good Neighbors*; Charles Wertenbaker, *A New Doctrine for the Americas*; John MacCormac, *Canada: America's Problem.*

H. S. Commager (Ed.), *Documents of American History,* pp. 466–474, 558–562, 590–598, contains source material.

XXXV

From Poland to Pearl Harbor

IN THE EARLY DAWN of September 1, 1939, without a declaration of war, German troops marched into Poland and German planes rained death on Polish cities. Two days later England and France entered the war. Months before, the two Western democracies had warned Hitler that they would come to the aid of Poland in case of German aggression. After years of attempted appeasement, England and France had at last learned that Hitlerian Germany was seeking world domination and that their own security and independence were therefore in jeopardy.

Germany crushed Poland in one month. Co-ordinating air attacks with tank and mechanized-infantry assaults, the Germans cut the Polish armies to shreds. Germany's industrial plant had been keyed to war production for six years, and this gave her great military superiority over the Allies in the opening years of the war. England and France were not geared to war when it came in 1939, and, as a result, they had little with which to assist the Polish armies. Instead, during 1939 and early 1940, England and France waited behind the Maginot line, fighting a defensive war. On the high seas Great Britain hoped that her blockade of Germany would, in the long run, bring that nation to reason.

During this period of inaction on the western front, Soviet Russia built up her defenses against a German attack. Although late in August, 1939, Russia and Germany had signed a nonaggression pact, Russia seemed aware that Germany, in due time, would try to destroy her. Russia, therefore, used her interval of peace, until June 22, 1941, to build up her defenses. In the midst of the German war on Poland, Russia moved in from the east and established a boundary of her own. She also demanded and received from Latvia, Estonia, and Lithuania permission to establish military, naval, and air bases in their territories. Finland, however, refused the Russian request for bases, and a four-month war ensued. Although Finland fought with great courage, the outcome was a Russian victory. By the peace terms Russia gained the port of Viipuri, the Karelian Isthmus, and the strategic island of Hangö.

Low in the *New York Times*

"You May Have Begun Man—
but I, Adolf Hitler, Will Finish Him"

From his beginning Hitler had defied the precepts of humanity and God.
In 1939 he was ready for his supreme challenge—war

THE IMPACT OF THE WAR ON THE UNITED STATES

The outbreak of the Second World War made most Americans widen their horizons. They had tried to close their eyes to the realities of the international situation by such misguided legislation as the Neutrality Act of 1935. Isolationists had assumed that this bill would insulate the United States from war. The basic assumption behind the Neutrality Act was that the United States could stand aside in a conflict between the democracies and the totalitarian powers. This was a false assumption, as the events from 1939 to Pearl Harbor were to prove. As Hitler destroyed democracy after democracy, the American people awakened and realized that unless they aided the remaining Allies, the United States might be left alone to face a triumphant Germany. When this realization came, the American people supported the revision and finally the repeal of the Neutrality Act.

President Roosevelt vigorously asserted, in the period from September, 1939, to December, 1941, that the triumph of German militarism would be a threat to the security of the United States. The war began with a widespread American sympathy for the Allies and a definite belief that the democratic nations would win. It was felt that all that was necessary was to permit the Allies to acquire war materials in the United States. On September 21, 1939, President Roosevelt sent a message to Congress, urging the repeal of the embargo against selling arms and ammunition to nations at war and the substitution of a cash-and-carry plan instead. The embargo, Roosevelt pointed out, aided the aggressor and hurt the victim, since Germany was prepared for war and the Allies were not.

A vigorous debate ensued in Congress. Isolationist members like Hamilton Fish and Gerald Nye denied that the United States was threatened in any way by Germany. To rally support for the President's measure, William Allen White, liberal Republican and Middle Western newspaper editor, organized a committee which mobilized public opinion to influence Congress. White, reflecting the attitude of the majority of Americans, observed:

These European democracies are carrying our banner, fighting the American battle. These democracies . . . are digging our first-line trenches. We need not shed our blood for them now or ever. But we should not deny them access to our shores when they come with cash to pay for weapons of defense and with their own ships to carry arms and materials which are to protect their citizens and their soldiers fighting our common cause.

The prevailing attitude revealed that, though the American people wanted the defeat of Hitler, they wanted the United States to remain at peace. It was, of course, assumed by America that the Allies would win an easy and quick victory.

On November 3, 1939, the revision of the Neutrality Act passed Congress. The Republican members cast the vast bulk of the vote against the revision. The revised act retained the provisions banning American ships from war zones, forbidding the lending of money to belligerents, and warning Americans against traveling on belligerent ships. Under the revision, however, if the Allies had the money and the ships, they could buy war materials in the United States. Immediately England and France placed huge orders with American manufacturers. These orders led to an expansion of American war production, which, in turn, benefited the United States greatly after the Japanese attack on Pearl Harbor.

THE GERMAN BLITZKRIEG

President Roosevelt sent Undersecretary of State Sumner Welles on a mission to Europe in January, 1940, to investigate the possibilities of concluding a permanent peace. After visiting Italy, Germany, France, and England, Welles came to the conclusion that his mission had been a forlorn hope. He later wrote:

> Looking back now, with a fuller knowledge of the overwhelming confidence of the Nazi leaders, it is obvious that no verbal interposition by the United States in the winter of 1940 would have been effective. Only one thing could have deflected Hitler from his purpose: the sure knowledge that the power of the United States would be directed against him if he attempted to carry out his intention of conquering the world by force.[1]

Of course no such warning could be given Hitler, since the American people, although they wanted Hitler defeated, also wanted peace. That these were mutually contradictory desires was not realized by the American public.

On April 9, 1940, Germany slashed into Norway and Denmark. The invasion of Norway was carefully planned and co-ordinated with organized treachery within that country. The British landed forces to aid the Norwegians, but in less than two months Germany's supremacy was unchallenged. The defeat of England's army in Norway led to the appointment of Winston Churchill as prime minister of England on May 10, 1940. The day that he took office, Germany invaded Holland, Belgium, and Luxembourg. Churchill realistically told the British people:

> I have nothing to offer but blood, toil, tears, and sweat. . . . You ask what is our policy? I will say: It is to wage war by sea, by land and air with all our might and with all the strength that God can give us; to wage war against a monstrous tyranny never surpassed in the dark, lamentable catalogue of human crime.

In five days the Netherlands were conquered. On May 15 German panzer divisions cut through the French line near Sedan, and in a cataclysmic week German forces reached the English Channel. They cut off British and French forces in Flanders from France. On May 28 King Leopold of Belgium surrendered. In the next few days three hundred and thirty-five thousand English and French troops were

---

[1] *The Time for Decision*, p. 77. Harper & Brothers, New York, 1944.

evacuated from the port of Dunkirk. The British pressed into service every warship, sloop, launch, fishing boat, ferry, and tugboat that could be found. The Germans now turned from Dunkirk and launched the Battle of France. On June 10 Italy, under Mussolini, wanting to be in on the spoils of victory, entered the war on Germany's side. On June 10, too, the Germans crossed the Seine, and four days later Paris surrendered. In desperation, Premier Reynaud appealed to President Roosevelt for "clouds of planes" and warned that the only way to save France was to throw into the balance "this very day the weight of American power." But the American people were not ready for war. Reynaud resigned, and reactionary Marshal Pétain formed a government which signed an armistice with Germany on June 22.

At this point Germany committed a great blunder. In seventy days the blitzkrieg had placed the entire coast of Europe, from the arctic to Spain, in German hands. Germany dominated the industrial and agricultural resources of most of Europe. By July England was left in a position of precarious isolation. If Hitler had invaded England at that point, Germany might well have been successful in her attempt to dominate the world. Instead Hitler completed the conquest of France and consolidated his war gains.

During the summer and fall of 1940 Hitler threw his vaunted *Luftwaffe*—the German air force—at England. Great cities, such as London, Dover, Manchester, and Birmingham, were subjected to furious bombing assaults. The material damage to docks, factories, and homes was immense. Civilian casualties ran into the thousands. Through it all the British people were inspired by the intrepid leadership of Churchill. On June 18, 1940, he warned:

> The whole fury and might of the enemy must very soon be turned on us. Hitler knows that he will have to break us in this Island or lose the war. If we can stand up to him all Europe may be free, and the life of the world may move forward into broad, sunlit uplands. But if we fail, then the whole world, including the United States, and all that we have known and cared for, will sink into the abyss of a new Dark Age made more sinister, and perhaps more prolonged, by the lights of a perverted science. Let us therefore brace ourselves to our duty and so bear ourselves that, if the British Commonwealth and Empire lasts for a thousand years, men will say, "This was their finest hour."

The British Royal Air Force outfought the *Luftwaffe* in the air over Britain. By October the German air force had to admit that it had been unable to bring Britain's surrender by bombing. The R.A.F., plus the indomitable spirit of the average Englishman, saved the day for the democratic world. Referring to the magnificent courage of the outnumbered, but not outfought, R.A.F., Churchill trenchantly said, "Never in the field of human conflict was so much owed by so many to so few."

AMERICAN AID TO THE DEMOCRACIES

The epoch-making events in Europe definitely shaped America's attitude toward the war. The American people began to realize that the Western Hemisphere was in deadly peril because of the German successes in France and the Low Countries. Although isolationists insisted frantically that "this is not our war," the American people sensed that the future of America was being determined on the fields of France and in the air over England. Winston Churchill, with a keen knowledge of the American past, told Parliament, on June 4, 1940, that America would eventually come to the rescue of the Old World— and by this rescue save itself. He prophesied:

We shall not flag or fail. We shall go on to the end. We shall fight in France, we shall fight on the seas and oceans; we shall fight with growing confidence and growing strength in the air, we shall defend our Island whatever the cost may be. We shall fight on the beaches, we shall fight on the landing grounds, we shall fight in the fields and in the streets, we shall fight in the hills; we shall never surrender, and even if, which I do not for a moment believe, this Island or a large part of it were subjugated and starving, then our Empire beyond the seas, armed and guarded by the British fleet, would carry on the struggle, until, in God's good time, the New World with all its power and might, steps forth to the liberation and rescue of the old.

Would America meet the challenge? Would it rise to the rescue of the European democracies?

After Dunkirk it seemed possible that England might be defeated and the British fleet captured and sunk. This would leave the United States with a one-ocean navy facing probable attacks from the Japanese in the Pacific and from the Germans in the Atlantic. At the President's request, therefore, Congress appropriated two billion dollars for the army and a billion and a half for the navy. Before the close of 1940 the President's requests for defense, which Congress granted, had exceeded ten billion dollars. Furthermore, within a year after the German invasion of the Low Countries, Congress had appropriated thirty-seven billions for armaments and for aid to the Allies. This program envisaged a two-ocean navy, clouds of planes, and a large army. All this would take time to accomplish, and Hitler would not wait. The defense of the United States, from the summer of 1940 until American production became decisive, depended upon the ability of the British to hold out against Germany.

The bulk of the American people realized that it was good common sense to keep Britain in the fight while America armed for an inevitable attack. On June 10, 1940, the day that Italy entered the war, President Roosevelt expressed the prevailing American attitude when he said:

> Some indeed still hold to the now somewhat obvious delusion that we of the United States can safely permit the United States to become a lone island, a lone island in a world dominated by the philosophy of force. Such an island may be the dream of those who still talk and vote as isolationists. Such an island represents to me and to the overwhelming majority of Americans today a helpless nightmare, the helpless nightmare of a people without freedom; yes, the nightmare of a people lodged in prison, handcuffed, hungry, and fed through the bars from day to day by the contemptuous, unpitying masters of other continents.

Positively, Roosevelt asserted:

> Let us not hesitate—all of us—to proclaim certain truths. Overwhelmingly we, as a nation,—and this applies to all the other American nations—are convinced that military and naval victory for the gods of force and hate would endanger the institutions of democracy in the Western world. . . . In our American unity, we will pursue two obvious and simultaneous courses; we will extend to the opponents of force the material resources of this nation and, at the same time, we will harness and speed up the use of those resources in order that we ourselves in the Americas may have equipment and training equal to the task of any emergency and every defense.

Following this speech, the government of the United States took rapid steps to increase American security. Meeting with the other American nations on July 29, it told Germany that the Americas would not acquiesce in the transfer of French or Dutch colonies in the Western Hemisphere to Germany. In order to secure more unity at home, President Roosevelt, in late June, appointed two Republicans to his cabinet. Henry L. Stimson, Hoover's Secretary of State and Taft's Secretary of War, was made Secretary of War, and Colonel Frank Knox, publisher of the *Chicago Daily News* and Republican Vice-Presidential nominee in 1936, became Secretary of the Navy. On September 16 the first peacetime conscription bill in American history was passed by Congress and signed by the President. In view of the imminence of a German victory, America's small peacetime army was far too small for even the adequate

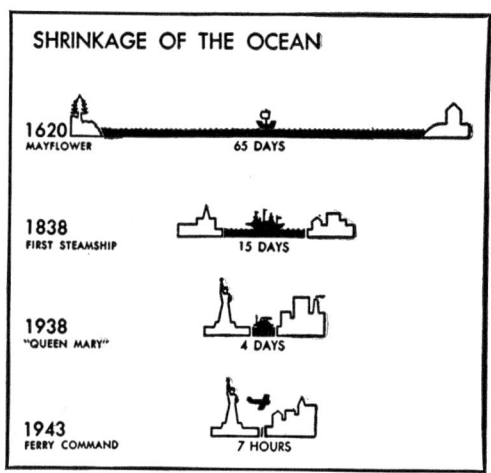

SHRINKAGE OF THE OCEAN

1620
MAYFLOWER   65 DAYS

1838
FIRST STEAMSHIP   15 DAYS

1938
"QUEEN MARY"   4 DAYS

1943
FERRY COMMAND   7 HOURS

Pictograph Corporation for McClure Newspaper Syndicate

The Facts of Technology
Destroy Isolationism

defense of the United States proper. Under the Burke-Wadsworth Selective Service Act, all men between twenty-one and thirty-five registered, and gradually the numbers necessary to build an adequate army were conscripted from these lists.

The second part of the President's policy, as set forth in his June 10 speech, was to keep the Allies fighting while the United States rearmed. To mobilize public opinion behind the President, William Allen White launched another organization, known as the Committee to Defend America by Aiding the Allies. This committee spread to all parts of the nation and by July 1 had three hundred local chapters. It sponsored gigantic rallies, ran newspaper advertisements, distributed leaflets, and focused a letter-writing campaign on Congress as part of its work in arousing support for aid to the Allies. A poll conducted by *Fortune* magazine in July, 1940, revealed that the public was overwhelmingly—67.5 per cent—in favor of aid to the Allies. Shorty after Dunkirk the United States government aided the Allies by turning over to private manufacturers, for sale to England, small arms, machine guns, and some planes and motor torpedo boats.

Secretary of State Cordell Hull warned the American people, on August 6, that great forces of lawlessness, conquest, and destruction were moving across the earth "like a savage and dangerous animal at large." Furthermore, observed Mr. Hull, "We cannot pursue complacently the course of our customary normal life." Yet a number of people still insisted that the United States could isolate itself from the effects of the German domination of Europe and the menace of Japan in the Far East. Charles A. Lindbergh, Gerald Nye, Hamilton Fish, Burton K. Wheeler, the *Chicago Tribune*, and the Communist and Socialist parties clamored that this was not America's war. The debate raged, but the course of events in Europe led the majority of Americans to realize their responsibility to the Allies.

A significant step in aiding the Allies was taken on September 3, 1940, when President Roosevelt announced the release of fifty American overage destroyers to Great Britain in return for a series of bases stretching from Newfoundland to British Guiana. The release of the destroyers was one of the decisive moves of the war. It enabled England to remain in the battle, and, at the same time, it gave America needed bases which, in the critical year after Pearl Harbor, were ready for operations against German submarines. Prominent men like General John J. Pershing had urged the release of the destroyers during the summer of 1940. Pershing stated:

> More than half the world is ruled by men who despise the American idea and have sworn to destroy it. . . . By sending help to the British we can still hope with confidence to keep the war on the other side of the Atlantic. . . . America will safeguard her freedom and security by making available to the British or Canadian governments at least fifty of the over-age destroyers, which are left from the days of the World War.

THE ELECTION OF 1940

The Presidential campaign of 1940 was waged at a time when the public's mind was concentrated on the air battle over Britain and on the threatening gestures of the Japanese in the Far East. On September 27 Japan, Germany, and Italy signed the Triple Alliance. According to the published version of the alliance, Japan bound herself to enter the war on Germany's side in the event that the United States entered the European conflict. The United States was now menaced by a war in two oceans. Before signing this pact, Japan had taken a number of important steps designed to increase her domination of the Far East. In June, 1940, she forced defeated France to allow Japanese "inspectors" in French Indo-China. Under duress, on September 22, Vichy France permitted the Japanese to have air bases in Indo-China and granted them the right to send troops into the area.

Hitler gave his approval to these Japanese steps, and, in return, a secret section of the Triple Alliance committed Japan to a war against the United States and the British Empire when the circumstances seemed appropriate. President Roosevelt answered the Triple Alliance threat on Columbus Day by saying:

No combination of dictator countries of Europe and Asia will halt us in the path we see ahead. . . . No combination of dictator countries of Europe and Asia will stop the help we are giving to almost the last free people fighting to hold them at bay.

Meanwhile the United States sent reinforcements to Hawaii and the Philippines, and on October 16 placed an embargo on the export of scrap iron and steel to Japan. Finished steel products, as well as gasoline, except aviation gasoline, could still be shipped to Japan. Of course the threat in the Triple Alliance did not stop American aid to the British.

With such world-shattering events taking place, the American people turned to a Presidential election. The Republican party faced decided handicaps. Its isolationist record since 1919 had been a major factor in aiding the unleashing of the forces of the Second World War. In domestic affairs the Old Guard Republicans were unwilling to recognize that the vast majority of the New Deal reforms were long overdue and were aimed at preserving capitalism rather than destroying it. As the time for the Republican convention approached, the three leading contenders for the Presidential nomination were Senator Robert Taft of Ohio, Senator Arthur Vandenberg of Michigan, and District Attorney Thomas E. Dewey of New York. All of them were isolationists or close to it, and they had not shown an acute awareness of the domestic crisis that had made the New Deal necessary and inevitable. The Presidential nomination, however, was not to be had by one of these regulars, approved by the organization Republicans.

A clever publicity build-up of Wendell L. Willkie had been taking place for about a year. Willkie was a Wall Street lawyer who had been president of the Commonwealth and Southern Corporation, which had fought a losing battle against the TVA. Although this record should have meant political death, Willkie overcame it by vigor, charm, and his forthright beliefs. He was no isolationist and said so unequivocally. Also, he was no reactionary when it came to social and individual rights. He was critical not of the ideas of the New Deal, but of the waste and inefficiency that accompanied the administering of the New Deal principles. No other Republican since Teddy Roosevelt had had such magnetism and glamour, and had inspired so many followers with fervent devotion, as Wendell L. Willkie. Telegrams from Willkie-supporters deluged the Republican convention, and Willkie-supporters packed the galleries and helped to stampede the delegates for their candidate. Dewey led on the first ballot, but gradually Willkie forged ahead and was nominated on the sixth ballot.

The Democratic convention renominated Franklin D. Roosevelt on the first ballot. Roosevelt's leadership in international affairs made his Presidency more popular and seemingly more essential than ever before. At Roosevelt's insistence, Secretary of Agriculture Henry A. Wallace was nominated for the Vice-Presidency. In the ensuing months Wendell Willkie conducted a vigorous and constructive campaign. He refused to play politics and pander to prejudice by attacking Roosevelt's international policy. He was enthusiastically for aid to the Allies. Since he also accepted the basic tenets of the New Deal, he centered his attempt to unseat the President on the issue of the third term. The third-term issue, however, failed to

"But why don't you become a Democrat and enjoy *politics?"*

Franklin D. Roosevelt's third- and forth-term elections prompted this *New Yorker* cartoon

be as important in the public's eyes as President Roosevelt's analysis of world affairs during the past eight years and the belief that his trained leadership was necessary in the great crisis facing American society.

Willkie's campaign suffered from the malcontents who flocked to his banner: Old Guard Republican reactionaries, who looked on Roosevelt as more dangerous than Hitler; John L. Lewis, in the ranks of labor; Fascist-minded Father Coughlin; and avowed isolationists and isolationist papers, such as Charles A. Lindbergh, Hamilton Fish, the *Chicago Tribune,* and the Hearst press. Although Willkie's sympathies were not with these forces, they helped to wreck his candidacy with the independents, whose votes determined the outcome. Roosevelt was overwhelmingly re-elected. He received 27,243,466 popular votes and won an electoral vote of thirty-eight states, totaling 449 votes. Willkie, however, received the largest popular vote ever given a Republican candidate—22,304,755.

LEND-LEASE

In the fall and winter of 1940 the war shifted its principal locale to the Balkans and the Mediterranean area. German troops entered Rumania in October; in January, 1941, German "tourists" infiltrated into Bulgaria, and that country formally joined the Germans on March 1. The Italians meanwhile had launched an invasion of Greece and were also fighting the British in North Africa and in East Africa. On April 6, 1941, German forces invaded Yugoslavia and Greece and quickly overcame those nations. At the end of March, German and Italian forces in North Africa drove the British, under General Wavell, back across the Egyptian frontier.

By December, 1940, the United States was faced with the hard fact that the British, the Chinese, and other nations fighting the Axis did not have enough money to continue to purchase arms and necessary equipment from the United States. If the United States held to its cash-and-carry policy, the Axis would win the war. In his weekly press conference on December 17, President Roosevelt told a homely story as a hint of his solution of the dilemma. Said the President:

Suppose my neighbor's house catches fire, and I have a length of garden hose four or five hundred feet away. If he can take my garden hose and connect it up with his hydrant, I may help him to put out the fire.

Now what do I do? I don't say to him before that operation, "Neighbor, my garden hose cost me $15; you have to pay me $15 for it."

What is the transaction that goes on? I don't want $15—I want my garden hose back after the fire is over. . . .

The President then advocated that the nation should act toward the war in the same fashion as an individual American would act if a fire were raging in a near-by house. The United States should send all the equipment that it could spare from its own defenses to aid its neighbors who were fighting the conflagration of war. In January, 1941, this proposal was submitted to Congress and called the Lend-Lease Bill. The bill authorized the President to "sell, transfer title to, exchange, lease, lend or otherwise dispose of . . . any defense article" to any nation whose defense he found vital to the security of the United States. The debate that resulted from the introduction of this bill was carried on in Congress, over the radio, in the press, at labor-union meetings, at the Rotary clubs, and in the colleges and churches. Some leading Republicans, such as William Allen White, Wendell L. Willkie, and Governor H. E. Stassen, supported the Lend-Lease Bill, and others, such as Alfred M. Landon, Herbert Hoover, and Senator Robert Taft, opposed the bill.

Isolationist committees reached the height of their fervor during the lend-lease debate. The America First Committee, headed by Robert E. Wood, was the most powerful of the isolationist forces. It preached a curious mixture of isolationism, Roosevelt hatred, and Anglophobia. Three other isolationist committees—the War Debts Defense Committee, the Make Europe Pay War Debts Committee, and the Islands for War Debts Committee—were founded under the sponsorship of certain isolationist Senators and Representatives (for example, Senators Lundeen and Reynolds and Representative Martin L. Sweeney); but the main inspiration for these committees came from George Sylvester Viereck, Nazi agent. Congressional franking privileges were used by all these isolationist groups to mail heavy amounts of isolationist propaganda to the American people. Nazi agents, such as Viereck and Laura Ingalls, and the Japanese agent Ralph Townsend made particular use of the America First Committee. This committee of American citizens was following a policy that was superbly adapted to furthering the plan that Germany and Japan had for the United States—namely, that it should embrace isolationism. By preaching isolationism, these committees did America a great disservice. They tried to keep America unprepared for a war that was inevitable, and they tried to persuade America to let its natural Allies be defeated by the Axis. If the United States had followed their advice, it probably would have had to fight the Axis alone after Pearl Harbor.

The Lend-Lease Bill passed Congress in March after weeks of debate had revealed the attitude of the country. The majorities for the legislation were impressive. The Senate voted in favor by a margin of 60 to 31 and the House by 317 to 171. From the standpoint of party politics, however, the voting revealed that the vast majority of Republicans were still isolationist. The bill made America "the arsenal of democracy." Under it American industrial might would squarely oppose the Axis. The United States was now pledged to keep Britain from being defeated and to enable Britain to take the offensive. It was obvious that the American people wanted the defeat of Hitler, but they still thought that this could be had without the military participation of the United States.

TOWARD MILITARY INTERVENTION

The events of the changing war, a war which was growing more and more inevitable for the United States every week, moved with amazing rapidity from March to December, 1941. Germany, on March 25, 1941, announced that it was extending the zone of war operations to Greenland. To forestall a German attack in that region, the United States occupied Greenland in April. During these months, too, German submarine and air warfare against British shipping was taking a very heavy toll. During March the Allies lost 437,730 tons of shipping. Unless such losses ceased, England would be forced out of the war. On April 9 ten American Coast Guard cutters were transferred to England, and in the following month fifty oil tankers were turned over to England. In June the United States froze all Axis assets in the country and closed all Axis consulates.

Then, on June 22, 1941, without warning, Germany attacked Russia. Hitler was confident that his undefeated armies would quickly destroy Russia, and he would then have the wheat of the Ukraine, the oil of the Caucasus, and the mighty industrial resources of the Volga and Donets basins. With the resources of Russia, Germany might well be able to defeat the rest of the world. Never did a conqueror miscalculate more than Hitler. The German army was bled white on the Russian countryside. Hitler expected that by posing as the destroyer of Communism, he could confuse the democracies sufficiently so that they would not render any assistance to Russia. Here, again, he made a serious blunder.

Winston Churchill announced to the world, immediately after the German attack on Russia: "We have but one aim and one single, irrevocable purpose. We are resolved to destroy Hitler and every vestige of the Nazi regime. . . . Any man or State who fights on against Nazidom will have our aid." Sumner Welles, acting Secretary of State, announced, on the following day:

Hitler's armies are today the chief dangers of the Americas . . . any defense against Hitlerism, any rallying of the forces opposing Hitlerism, from whatever source these forces may spring, will hasten the eventual downfall of the present German leaders, and will therefore redound to the benefit of our defense and security.

Some American isolationists tried to prevent any aid to Russia. Senator Taft, for instance, held that "a victory for Communism would

Low in the *New York Times*

"In the future," der Führer *said, "the army will be guided by my intuition."*

On June 22, 1941, against the advice of his generals, Hitler began the invasion of Soviet Russia, only to suffer his first major defeat

be far more dangerous to the United States than a victory for Fascism." Such isolationists, however, completely misjudged the mood of America. As Walter Lippmann observed, America and Russia were "separated by an ideological gulf and joined by the bridge of national interest." Although the American people disliked Communism, they nevertheless realized that a German defeat of Russia would increase the Nazi threat to American security. When isolationist Congressmen tried to exclude Russia from lend-lease aid, they were able to muster few votes.

In the months just preceding Pearl Harbor, the United States moved closer and closer to military intervention. German sinkings of Allied shipping in the Battle of the Atlantic were reaching appalling totals. American goods that were sunk on the high seas were not aiding the Allies, nor defending the security of the United States. Unless the Atlantic lane remained open, Great Britain would have to surrender. Therefore the United States occupied Iceland in July. By this move the United States assumed responsibility for keeping the Atlantic lane clear as far as Ireland.

The events which were making war more and more inevitable for the United States every week led to closer and closer collaboration with Great Britain. On August 14, 1941, it was announced to the world that President Roosevelt and Prime Minister Churchill had just met aboard ship in the Atlantic Ocean. The two men signed a joint declaration—the Atlantic Charter—which was not a plan to defeat Hitler, but the announcement of a peace program to be adopted "after the final destruction of the Nazi tyranny." The Charter recognized that future world peace depended upon international collaboration; the right of all peoples to choose the form of government under which they would live; access on equal terms, for all nations, to the trade and raw materials of the world; the freedom of the seas; freedom from war, from fear, from want; and the principle of no territorial aggrandizement.

During the fall of 1941 the American navy was finally forced into a shooting war. Units of the fleet patrolling the sea lane to Iceland had orders to defend themselves if attacked. On September 4 it was revealed that the American destroyer *Greer* had been fired on by a German submarine. Over the air, on September 11, President Roosevelt advised the country that the American navy had now been given instructions to shoot at the enemy on sight. By this time a number of American merchant ships had been sunk outside of what the United States viewed as the war zone. The *Robin Moor* had been sunk in the South Atlantic on May 21; the American-owned *Sessa* had been torpedoed on August 17; the *Steel Seafarer* had been sunk in the Red Sea on September 7; and the *Montana* was sunk on September 11.

On September 23 President Roosevelt announced that the sinking of American ships required the revision of the Neutrality Act to permit our ships to be armed for their own defense. Furthermore, to defeat Hitler, it was becoming necessary for the United States to deliver lend-lease material to the Allied ports. The Neutrality Act, however, prohibited this. At the time of the passage of the Lend-Lease Act, it had been hoped that the Allies could transport American equipment safely to their shores. By September, events had demonstrated that they were unable to do this. In a message to Congress on October 9, President Roosevelt recommended the repeal of those sections of the Neutrality Act which prohibited the arming of merchant ships and which forbade American ships to enter belligerent ports. The President pointed out:

In the Neutrality Act there are various crippling provisions. The repeal or modification of these provisions will not leave the United States any less neutral than we are today, but it will make it possible for us to defend the Americas far more successfully and to give aid far more effectively against the tremendous forces now marching towards the conquest of the world.

The revision of the Neutrality Act was speeded up by the announcement, on October 17, that the destroyer *Kearny* had been struck by a torpedo and eleven sailors killed. On October 27 the President acknowledged that the United States, as far as the navy was concerned, was in a shooting war. On October 30 the sinking of the destroyer *Reuben James* gave increased weight to the arguments in favor of revision of the Neutrality Act. The act, passed in 1935, had been designed to prevent the sinking of American ships, since it was held that this might lead the United States into war. But it had failed even to prevent the sinking of ships (the *Robin Moor*, for example) which were traveling waters far away from combat zones. Events of the *Robin Moor* type made it plain that the United States had no opportunity to choose between peace and war. And in spite of the propaganda efforts of the isolationist Congressmen and the America First Committee, the majority of the people were realizing, in the fall of 1941, that the only choice for the United States was between war and submission to the Axis powers.

On November 7 the United States Senate repealed those sections of the Neutrality Act which prevented the arming of merchant ships and which forbade American ships to enter combat zones and belligerent ports. Six days later the House concurred by a vote of 212 to 194. The close vote in the House revealed that many Congressmen had not adjusted their thinking to meet the situation of an inevitable war. The two major parties in the House voted as follows: Democrats, 187 for, 53 against; Republicans, 22 for, 137 against. Many men could not believe that the danger was as grave as the President depicted it. The decisive event that aroused these people was the Japanese attack on Pearl Harbor.

PEARL HARBOR

By the fall of 1941 the United States and Japan had arrived at a diplomatic impasse. America's traditional policies of the "open door" and the territorial sovereignty of China were in danger of being completely nullified by Japanese aggression. The United States, however, was in a difficult position after the summer of 1940. The defeat of France and the precarious position of Great Britain made it mandatory to direct all American aid to Europe. Protracted negotiations would be used in an attempt to immobilize and restrain Japan. Had a Japanese attack on the United States immediately followed the Triple Alliance of September 1940, the democratic world would have been in graver danger than it was after Pearl Harbor. The year and two months that elapsed between the signing of the pact and the Japanese attack made it possible for the United States to increase its own preparations for war.

Ray in the *Kansas City Star*

Giving Him Six Months to Think It Over

The United States warns Japan that trade relations will be severed unless Japan stops her aggression in the Far East

In March of 1941 the Japanese ambassador at Washington, Admiral Nomura, and the United States State Department began a series of diplomatic conversations, which lasted until December 7. When the Japanese marched troops into Indo-China in July, 1941, the United States countered by freezing all Japanese assets and suspending trade with the island empire. Measures were quickly taken also to reinforce American garrisons in the Philippines and Pacific island outposts. With Russia engaged in war against Germany, Japan was now, apparently, not greatly worried about the Russian threat in Siberia.

The Japanese devoted themselves to feverish preparations for war during the fall of 1941. General Tojo, who became head of the Japanese cabinet in October, dispatched Saburo Kurusu to Washington with the minimum demands of the Japanese Empire. This was nothing more than a ruse to divert attention from Japan's true intentions. Kurusu's demands were that Japan be given full access to the resources of the Netherlands Indies, that trade relations with the United States be restored, and that the United States stop all aid to China. Meanwhile Japanese troops poured into Indo-China for the coming assault on southeastern Asia, and the Japanese navy made ready for the attack on Hawaii, Midway, Guam, and the Philippines.

On December 6, in a final attempt to avert war, President Roosevelt sent an appeal direct to Emperor Hirohito. On the following day the Japanese replied by bombing Pearl Harbor. Early on Sunday morning, December 7, Japanese planes, operating from aircraft-carriers, devastatingly attacked Pearl Harbor, Midway, Wake, and Guam. Just as millions of Americans were about to eat their Sunday dinners, their radios brought news that seemed at first both fantastic and incredible. At the President's request, the next day

Battenfield in the *Chicago Times*, 1946

Maybe He Was a Little Distracted

Isolationists' votes in Congress slowed American preparedness

Congress voted a declaration of war. Three days later Germany and Italy declared war on the United States.

The attack on Pearl Harbor went far toward unifying the American people. Although, as President Roosevelt said, it was "a date which will live in infamy," the attack opened the eyes of many of those who had imagined that the United States could live at peace in a world dominated by the Axis dictators. The Japanese ended the dilemma that had faced the American people—the dilemma of wanting peace, but also wanting the defeat of the Axis. Japan proved that these were mutually contradictory desires, and after December 7, 1941, the United States joined with the Allies to remove the Axis menace. Those Americans who held to the isolationist position from 1939 to Pearl Harbor did a great disservice to the United States by morally disarming that segment of the people which accepted their leadership. Their statement that "it is not our war" and that the United States had nothing to fear from an Axis-dominated Europe and Asia completely overlooked the Axis desire to dominate the world.

Between 1939 and December 7, 1941, American foreign policy had undergone significant changes. Strict neutrality had been abandoned in order to give aid short of war to those countries whose resistance to aggression was helping to defend the security of the United States. When the *Reuben James* was sunk, the idea that America could be the arsenal while others did the fighting had to be abandoned; after this America became a limited belligerent by conducting operations along the Atlantic life line. All-out war came only with direct all-out attack on the United States by Japan.

It seems clear that the policy that America followed from September, 1939, to Pearl Harbor, of placing itself on the side of the Allies, had very little to do with actual involvement in the war. America was in the very same position as it was from 1914 to 1917. What course the United States should follow depended on what Germany and her allies might do, not on what the United States might do. Once war had broken out, it was inevitable that in time that war should engulf the United States. The only hope for peace for the United States lay in international co-operation *before 1939*, but the victors of the First World War had failed to work together from 1919 to 1939. The period of the war before American entrance was of great value in affording the United States an opportunity of training an army, of launching a larger navy, and of increasing the size of industrial plants devoted to war production. During that period, too, through the policy of aid to the Allies, the United States materially aided the nations opposing the Axis, and thus ensured allies for herself when she was plunged into the war.

SELECTED BIBLIOGRAPHY

Peace and War: United States Foreign Policy, 1931–1941, the State Department's view of the forces that brought war; FORREST DAVIS and ERNEST K. LINDLEY, *How War Came: An American White Paper*, American foreign policy from the fall of France to Pearl Harbor; HAROLD S. QUIGLEY, *Far Eastern War, 1937–1941*, helpful on this phase.

WALTER JOHNSON, *The Battle against Isolation*; JOHN R. CARLSON, *Undercover*; MICHAEL SAYERS and ALBERT E. KAHN, *Sabotage: The Secret War against America*; JOSEPH GREW, *Ten Years in Japan*; E. R. STETTINIUS, JR., *Lend-Lease: Weapon for Victory*; ROBERT BENDINER, *The Riddle of the State Department*, valuable books.

H. S. COMMAGER (Ed.), *Documents of American History*, pp. 599–608, 614–633, contains source material.

XXXVI

From Pearl Harbor to Hiroshima

I
N A SECRET SPEECH, on April 23, 1942, Winston Churchill told
Parliament:

Since Japan became our enemy and the United States our ally after December 7, the weight of the war upon us has become far more severe and we
have sustained a painful series of misfortunes in the Far East. . . . From the
beginning of our struggle with Hitler, I have always hoped for the entry of
the United States; and although the ideal was to have America in while
Japan remained out, I did not think that the injuries that Japan would certainly inflict upon us in our ill-guarded and even denuded Eastern theater
would be too heavy a price to pay for having the immense resources and
power of the United States bound indissolubly to our side and to our cause.
That is still my feeling. But I frankly admit that the violence, fury, skill and
might of Japan has far exceeded anything that we had been led to expect.[1]

American sea power in the Pacific, as Churchill implied in this
speech, suffered a temporary eclipse as a result of the disaster at Pearl
Harbor. Many of the battered ships were withdrawn from Pearl
Harbor to west-coast bases, and no Allied fleet capable of fighting a
general action with the Japanese navy existed in the fourteen-thousand-
mile stretch from San Francisco to Capetown. In this situation Japan's
failure to invade Hawaii and, later, to seize bases in Australia contributed greatly to a final Allied victory in the Pacific.

In the months after Pearl Harbor the United States and the United
Nations, which had been formally launched on January 2, 1942, had to
assume a defensive role in the war while they mobilized their resources
for an all-out fight in every part of the globe. Early in 1942 the Axis
nations won success after success, since, as dictatorships, they had long
been mobilizing their resources. The United States, however, as a
democracy, had, until Pearl Harbor, devoted most of its industrial power
to the production of consumer goods. As a result, it would not be until
August, 1942, that American resources would be sufficient for the nation
to take even limited offensive action in the Pacific. During the interval

[1]*Life*, January 28, 1946, p. 27.

from Pearl Harbor until American production, in co-operation with Allied production, could take the offensive, the United States was fortunate in having allies who could bear the brunt of the Axis attack. "Although we were woefully unprepared as a nation, we still had the time so essential to build a military force," General H. H. Arnold declared in 1945, "time given us by our Allies fighting with their backs to the wall, and by the distance of oceans."

THE WAR IN THE PACIFIC

After December 7, 1941, Japan was the undisputed master of the Pacific Ocean. Three days after Pearl Harbor the Japanese sank the British battleships *Repulse* and *Prince of Wales*, which had left Singapore, without air support, in search of an enemy convoy. Now the way was clear for assaults on the Philippines, the Netherlands Indies, and Singapore. Guam, Wake, and Hong Kong fell before the end of December, and, in addition, Japanese attacks were launched at British Malaya, Thailand (Siam), the Philippines, and Midway.

With insufficient troops and inadequate equipment for global war, the United States had to devote its first efforts to defending the Western Hemisphere and to protecting the Panama Canal Zone, Hawaii, and Alaska from hostile landings. As quickly as possible, the defenses of Hawaii and Midway were strengthened in order to protect lines of communication to Australia and New Zealand. Meanwhile the Japanese captured Manila on January 2, 1942, and invaded the Netherlands colonies of Celebes and Borneo on January 11. Faced with these rapid enemy advances, the United States and Great Britain created a unified command in the Pacific area, with General Sir Archibald Wavell as supreme commander and General George H. Brett as deputy supreme commander of American, British, Dutch, and Australian forces.

Military operations in the Pacific and Far Eastern areas presented a tremendous problem of logistics. It was seven thousand miles from San Francisco to Manila, and it required more than twice the ship tonnage to supply American troops in Australia than was necessary for the same number of American forces in Europe or North Africa. The supply line from the west coast to the Pacific war was later referred to by Admiral Chester W. Nimitz as "one of the Navy's greatest secret weapons," and Admiral Ernest J. King declared that the way it worked was "nothing short of colossal." The magnitude of the task of supply for offensive action against the Japanese can be illustrated by the case

*Wreckage of the
U. S. S.* Arizona
at Pearl Harbor

U. S. Navy official photo, from Press Association

A Convoy of Cargo Ships Heading toward Europe

Wide World

of Saipan, where, to maintain one hundred thousand men and to build a base, two million tons of freight, exclusive of supplies for warships, were shipped within a two-month period.

The British naval base at Singapore fell to the Japanese on February 15, 1942, and by the end of March they had captured the Netherlands Indies, had taken Rangoon, and were driving the British, Indian, and Chinese forces out of Burma. Meanwhile Philippine and American forces, under General Douglas MacArthur, were waging a losing fight in the Philippines. Overwhelmed by superior numbers, MacArthur made a defensive stand on the Bataan peninsula with an army that now numbered only slightly more than fifty thousand. Early in March, MacArthur, under orders from the War Department, flew to Australia to assume command of the Southwest Pacific Area and left General Jonathan M. Wainwright to continue the struggle on Bataan. Bataan fell on April 9, but the island fortification of Corregidor continued the struggle until May 6. On that day the exhausted forces were overwhelmed, and General Wainwright wrote in a letter:

As I write this we are subjected to terrific air and artillery bombardment and it is unreasonable to expect that we can hold out for long. We have done our best, both here and on Bataan, and although beaten we are still unashamed.

Unable to supply the Philippines, the United States, during the grim opening months of 1942, adopted the strategy of concentrating forces along the route to Australia and building up a base force on that continent. The desperate resistance on Bataan slowed the Japanese southward movement and gave the United Nations time to dispatch men, materials, and airplanes to Australia and to New Caledonia, Samoa, and other Pacific islands. On May 4, 1942, the Japanese, as part of their offensive against the supply line to Australia, seized Tulagi in the central Solomons. Three days later a large column of Japanese ships, moving southward in the Coral Sea, was attacked by United States carrier-based aircraft, and nineteen Japanese warships were sunk or damaged. The battles of the Coral Sea, the first major engagement in naval history in which surface ships did not exchange a single shot, were the high-water mark of the Japanese naval advance in the Southwest Pacific. One month after this engagement American planes inflicted a decisive defeat on a Japanese fleet off Midway. Thereafter Hawaii was never again in danger of attack, and the United Nations themselves were able to launch a series of offensive actions.

On August 7, 1942, United States marine and navy forces started a combined air-and-sea attack on Guadalcanal in the Solomons. Marines under General Vandegrift secured control of the airfield on Guadalcanal and held it against repeated enemy assaults. Japan, realizing that the Solomons were necessary as bases for her attacks on American supply lines to Australia, made repeated attempts to assist her forces there. A decisive battle between the Japanese fleet and the American fleet, under Admiral William F. Halsey, took place on November 13, 14, and 15, and the Japanese reinforcements were turned back.

Combined marine and army detachments, in co-operation with an air offensive, finally destroyed all organized enemy resistance on Guadalcanal by February 9, 1943. While the Japanese were hotly contesting the American action on Guadalcanal, other Japanese troops launched an offensive in the jungle of New Guinea for the Allied base at Port Moresby. The Japanese threat was turned back by ground troops in conjunction with effective air support. Not until early in 1943, however, did Australian and American troops, under General Robert L. Eichelberger, clear the northeast coast of New Guinea as far as Buna.

The United Nations' strategy in 1943 was for Admiral Nimitz to advance toward Japan across the great reaches of the Central Pacific; for General MacArthur's forces to proceed up the New Guinea coast; and for Admiral Halsey to move north in the Solomons. MacArthur's forces, with air and sea superiority, by a series of envelopment movements isolated hundreds of thousands of Japanese troops in pockets in New Guinea, from which they could not escape. In 1944 MacArthur reported: "The enemy garrisons which have been bypassed in the Solomons and New Guinea represent no menace to current or future operations. Their capacity for organized offensive effort has passed."

During the summer and fall of 1943 Australian forces moved along the New Guinea coast to capture Salamaua, Lae, and Finschhafen. Meanwhile New Zealand and American forces captured New Georgia, the Treasury Islands, and western Bougainville in the Solomons. In the Central Pacific, Admiral Nimitz's forces landed on Tarawa and Makin in the Gilbert Islands on November 21, 1943. At the same time that these gains were being made, the United Nations' air arm maintained a steady pounding against Japanese bases all along a three-thousand-mile arc from the Solomons to Timor, and, in addition, Allied planes and submarines destroyed many Japanese ships. In spite of the gains of 1943, however, the Allies were still only on a limited offensive and had not yet captured the key positions of Japanese strength.

Early in 1944, as a result of remarkable construction in American shipyards, the American fleet outweighed the Japanese fleet in both battleships and aircraft, and American task forces were striking into Japanese waters without serious opposition. On January 31, 1944, after two days of air and naval bombardment, the marines landed on Kwajalein in the Marshall Islands, the first Japanese territory to be taken by the Allies. On February 19, after severe bombing, another marine unit landed on Eniwetok. Control of the Marshalls soon was to furnish a base for B-24 attacks on the enemy naval base at Truk in the Carolines, which was the main point in the whole Japanese defense in the Central and Southwest Pacific.

After the capture of bases in the Marshalls, American task forces launched frequent air attacks on the Japanese in the Marianas, and in late March a task force began a two-day attack on a Japanese base twelve hundred miles west of Truk and only five hundred and thirty miles from the Philippines. For months American planes pounded the shipping and installations in the Marianas, and then, on June 15, 1944, Nimitz's forces landed on Saipan. A savage struggle took place with the defenders, well-entrenched in rugged terrain. By July 8 American forces were in complete control of the island at the price of 16,463 American casualties, including 3049 dead. The Japanese had over 20,000 dead. On July 21, after seventeen days of bombing, the marines landed on Guam. Two weeks later, resistance ceased, and the United Nations now had bases from which to hurl bomber attacks at Japan. On November 24, 1944, Superfortresses struck Japan from these bases in their first major attack. The capture of the Marianas neutralized the by-passed Japanese base at Truk, and the enemy defenses in the Central Pacific were now deteriorating at a rapid rate.

While Nimitz's forces were sweeping on to victory in the Central Pacific, MacArthur's Australian and American forces occupied the Admiralty Islands and, after a series of amphibious thrusts along the New Guinea coast, captured Hollandia, where General Krueger's Sixth Army Headquarters were established on July 6, 1944. From Hollandia's air bases Allied planes soon destroyed the remaining Japanese air power in that region, and, in spite of pockets of enemy troops scattered through the island, the Allies had effective control of New Guinea by the end of summer.

Early in September, 1944, Admiral Halsey's carrier-based planes struck at Yap and Palau in the Carolines, and on September 12 they hit at the central Philippines. During the month's activities Halsey's forces destroyed two thousand enemy planes and prepared the way for the invasion of the Philippines. On October 20 two assault forces, under Admirals Wilkinson and Barbey, approached the east coast of Leyte in the Philippines, and the first troops, under General Krueger, stormed ashore. At this point the Japanese fleet made a desperate attempt to stop the American attack, but Admiral Halsey's task force routed it and broke the backbone of the Japanese navy. The Allied air force and fleet destroyed repeated Japanese convoys attempting to reinforce Leyte, and by Christmas Day Allied forces were in complete command of the island. Meanwhile MacArthur's forces had landed on Mindoro on December 15, and the attack on Luzon was in preparation. On January 9, 1945, the United States Sixth Army landed at Lingayen Gulf north of Manila and by the end of the day had sixty-eight thousand troops ashore along a fifteen-mile beachhead. General Kenney's aircraft and the work of Philippine guerrillas made it extremely difficult for the Japanese to rush troops to check the invasion. Manila fell to the United Nations on February 23 and Corregidor and Bataan soon after that date.

While General Krueger's troops were completing the conquest of the Philippines, Admiral Spruance's Fifth Fleet landed marines on Iwo Jima on February 19, 1945. American possession of Iwo Jima was vital for the air assault on Japan. It soon became a base for escort fighter planes, and its airfields saved many damaged B-29's en route back to the Marianas after their nightly visits to Japanese cities. The effective B-29 raids from the Marianas and the work of American submarines in destroying enemy shipping were, more than any other factors, to account for the eventual Japanese defeat.

At the same time that the marines were fighting for Iwo Jima, Philippine-based planes secured air supremacy over Formosa and the China coast. Then, on March 26, the first Americans landed in the Ryukyu Islands, and five days later beachheads were established on the key island of Okinawa, only three hundred and thirty miles from Kyushu, Japan. Japanese resistance was fanatical, and not until June 21 did organized fighting cease. Suicide-plane attacks did heavy damage to the American fleet; and of the thirty-nine thousand American casualties up to the end of June, over ten thousand were among the personnel of the supporting fleet.

By May, 1945, with the close of the European war, the United States and England were ready to intensify their efforts in the Pacific. Chief of Staff General George Marshall noted, in his official report:

From California to the coast of China the vast Pacific abounded with American power. In the Philippines, the Marianas and the Ryukyus, our forces under steadily increasing reinforcements from the European continent massed for the final phase of the Pacific war. The enemy's shipping had been largely sunk or driven from the seas. The few remaining fragments of his once powerful naval force were virtually harbor bound and the industries and communications of Japan were crumbling under the mounting tempo of our aerial bombardment. Lord Mountbatten's forces in southeastern Asia were closing in on Malaysia and the Netherlands East Indies. Chinese armies, newly equipped, trained, and determinedly led, were gradually assuming the offensive.

Although the war in the Pacific area was secondary to the struggle in Europe, nevertheless it was necessary for the Allies, after 1941, to maintain such pressure on Japan that she should not be able to build an impregnable position. Continued Chinese resistance was fundamental to this. The Japanese conquest of Burma, however, isolated China except for the five-hundred-mile flight over the Himalayan "Hump" between Assam (India) and the Yünnan Plateau; furthermore, the Allies had little equipment to devote to the Chinese theater. Not until 1944 did Chinese, British, Indian, and American troops, under General Joseph Stilwell, have any real success in dislodging the enemy from northern Burma. Warfare in this area was dependent on the air force for the supply of both men and equipment. In spite of the handicaps, Stilwell continued to advance and to build a new overland route to China. China, before 1945, had already made a real contribution to the eventual defeat of Japan by its opposition to Japanese expansion as early as the decade of the 1930's. From 1941 to 1945 the Chinese phase of the war had to be subordinated to other theaters of action.

On January 28, 1945, the first American trucks reached China over the Stilwell Road. In the meantime, British forces closed in on Mandalay in March and captured Rangoon on May 3, 1945. By this time, the Burma campaign was virtually over, and more supplies could pour into China. Forty-six thousand tons of cargo a month was being flown into China by January, 1945. These supplies made it possible for General Chennault's American air force to aid the Chinese army against the enemy. Under General A. C. Wedemeyer, American-army officers aided in the retraining and re-equipping of the Chinese forces. The war was to end, however, before China should gain enough equipment to commence offensive operations.

Official U. S. Coast Guard photo

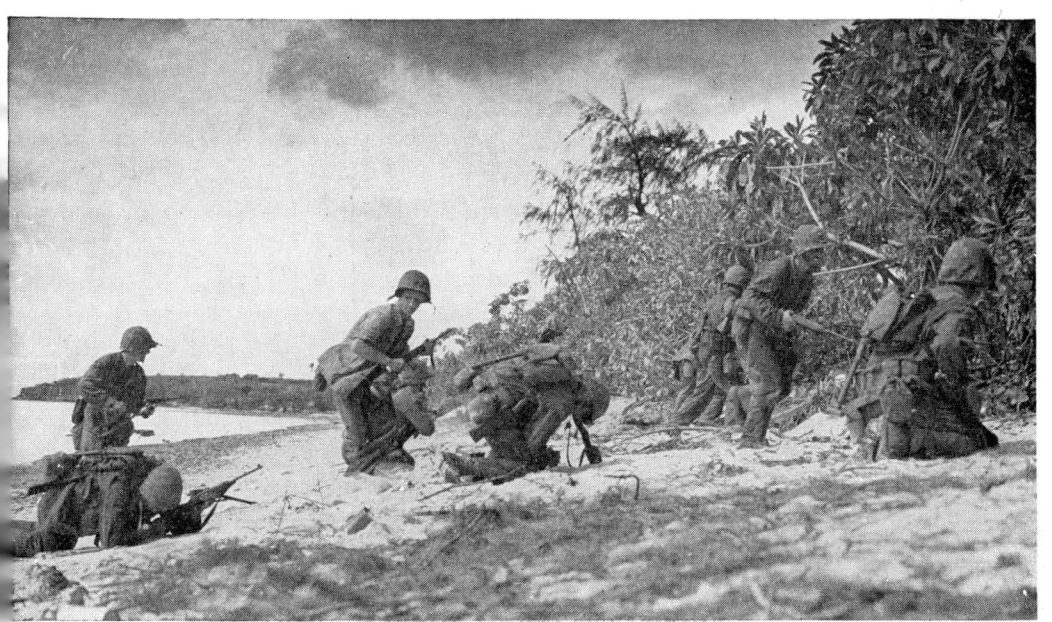

Marines Storming the Beach at Saipan

Allied Air Assault on the Shipyards at Kiel, Germany

U. S. Army A. A. F. photo

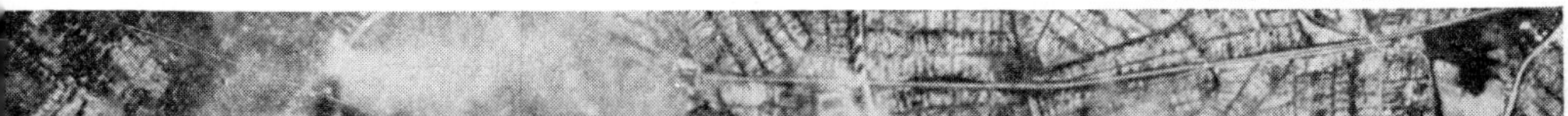

THE WAR IN THE WEST

By the time that the United States joined in the struggle against Germany, Hitler had had three years of phenomenal success. He had conquered more than one million square miles of territory and had brought approximately one hundred and sixty-eight million people under his control. Nazi Germany, however, had committed two major blunders by December 7, 1941. One was her underestimation of the British Royal Air Force and her failure to invade England after Dunkirk. The other was her invasion of the Soviet Union, where Hitler's armies suffered a series of disastrous defeats. When Hitler declared war on the United States, on December 11, 1941, it was the German belief that America was so torn with inner strife that all-out production could not be achieved in time to save Russia and Britain. This was the third major blunder made by Hitler.

In the months immediately after Pearl Harbor the initiative in the west continued to be in the hands of the Axis. America's first actions were to train the armed forces, convert its civilian industry, and, through lend-lease, dispatch as many supplies to Britain and Russia as could be spared. German U-boats, however, carried on a vigorous campaign to prevent American supplies from reaching Europe. During 1942 the Nazi raiders sank an average of one million gross tons a month, and Winston Churchill, in a secret speech delivered to Parliament on April 23, 1942, declared:

I will begin with the gravest matter, namely, the enormous losses and destruction of shipping by German U-boats off the east coast of the United States. In a period of less than 60 days, more tonnage was sunk in this one stretch than we had lost all over the world during the last five months of the Battle of the Atlantic before America entered the war. . . . We have done our best to aid the Americans in establishing a convoy system. . . . At their request, to assist the Americans we have sent over a number of our officers most experienced in anti-U-boat warfare, and upward of 30 corvettes and anti-submarine craft from our own hardpressed store. The figures for the last two months on the American coast, plus those in the Indian and Pacific Oceans from the Japanese attacks, constitute totals of monthly losses which are most alarming and formidable and comparable to the worst I have witnessed either in the last war or in this.[1]

During 1943, however, the convoy system and the use of the airplane, radar, and other antisubmarine devices overcame the U-boat menace,

[1]*Life*, January 28, 1946, p. 43.

and in December of that year President Roosevelt announced that the Allies were sinking submarines at a faster rate than that at which Allied merchant ships were being sunk.

By June, 1942, the United States had sufficient forces in the United Kingdom to organize the European Theater of Operations under the command of General Dwight D. Eisenhower, and on July 4, 1942, the first American fliers participated in a Royal Air Force assault against targets on the Continent. From that date to the end of the war the combined British-American bomber offensive increased its tempo every day and had as its objectives the destruction of German air strength; the disruption of German lines of communication; the crippling of the enemy's industrial and economic system; and the undermining of the morale of the German people. During 1943, for instance, the American air force was most interested in destroying Germany's airplane industry, and factories at Essen, Düsseldorf, and Mannheim received a regular pounding in day and night attacks.

During the summer of 1942, as German forces resumed their offensive in Russia and assaulted Stalingrad and captured oil fields in the Caucasus, the Soviets clamored for a second front to relieve the German pressure. At the same time, there were vocal demands from the American and British publics for a second front. Although the Anglo-American forces were not ready yet for a second front in Europe, General Sir Bernard L. Montgomery took the offensive in North Africa and attacked General Rommel's *Afrika Korps* at El Alamien on October 23, 1942, and soon drove the Germans out of Egypt. As Montgomery's forces pursued Rommel across the desert, American and British troops, under Eisenhower, landed in the western part of North Africa on November 8. Two days after the landing Winston Churchill remarked: "This is not the end. It is not even the beginning of the end. But it is, perhaps, the end of the beginning."

Before the landing American agents from the Office of Strategic Services had met with French officials in an attempt to secure cooperation, and General Charles de Gaulle and General Henri Giraud had broadcast pleas to the French not to resist. Resistance ceased, however, only on November 11, when Admiral Darlan, Pétain's designated successor as head of the Vichy government and the commander in chief of all French forces, took charge in North Africa and stopped hostilities. The Allied willingness to accept Darlan as head of the French North African government, in view of his previous subservience to the Nazis, was widely protested in some quarters, but the Allied governments justified the step on the ground that it had saved soldiers' lives and would speed the elimination of the Germans from North Africa.

Early in February, 1943, General Eisenhower was placed in command of the entire North Africa theater. While Montgomery pounded the Germans from the east, Eisenhower attacked from the west. On March 30 the British Eighth Army broke through the German Mareth line in Tunisia, and on April 8 the British and American forces joined for the final attack. During early May the last German and Italian resistance was smashed, and two hundred and fifty-two thousand enemy troops surrendered. While the land forces had sped across North Africa, the Allied navy and air force had aided materially in the victory by wrecking the enemy air force and by making it impossible for Rommel to be supplied from Sicily and, at the point of collapse, for the German-Italian army to be evacuated.

Soon the Allies were ready for the assault on Sicily. The experienced British and Dominion armies were now aided by an experienced American army. On June 12, 1943, the island of Pantelleria, off the Sicily coast, surrendered after two weeks of aerial attacks, and on July 10 American, British, and Canadian troops landed along a hundred-mile front in Sicily. The Allied success in Sicily resulted in the collapse of Mussolini's dictatorship and his replacement by Marshal Badoglio on July 26. Just before dawn on September 3, after four years of war for England, the British Eighth Army landed on the mainland of Italy. Five days later the Italian government surrendered, and the next day the Allies stormed ashore at Salerno, a few miles from Naples. The Germans struck back at Salerno, and for four critical days naval gunfire supported the troops on the beachhead while the air force flew 3000 sorties and dropped 2150 tons of bombs. In the first eighteen days at Salerno 189,000 troops, 30,000 motor vehicles, and 108,000 tons of supplies were landed. On October 2 the American army, under General Clark, captured Naples. Bad weather and rugged terrain made further progress in Italy difficult. From this time until the end of the war, progress in the Italian campaign was exasperatingly slow. The difficulties of fighting on this front are best to be seen in Bill Mauldin's cartoons of the front-line soldier and in Ernie Pyle's outstanding reporting of the details of the life led by the G.I. at the front. The United Nations' war in Italy was fought by a wide variety of forces, including Americans, British, Canadians, French, New Zealanders, South Africans, Poles, Indians, Brazilians, Italians, Greeks, Moroccans, Algerians, Arabs, Senegalese, and a Jewish brigade.

In order to speed up the Italian campaign, thirty-five thousand American combat air men had been sent to Italy by the end of 1943, and medium and heavy bomber missions pounded northern Italy, Austria, and southern Germany. Then, on January 22, 1944, Allied troops landed on the Anzio beachhead, twenty-five miles south of Rome, in an effort to outflank the Germans. The Germans stood off repeated assaults and pinned the Allies to a narrow area. South of the beachhead the American Fifth Army had already been stopped, in its northern advance, at Cassino, and some of the most difficult fighting of the war took place here. Finally, on May 11, the army of Field Marshal Alexander launched an offensive, which was co-ordinated with an attack from the American forces at Anzio, and by June 4, 1944, two days before the Allied invasion of France, Rome had fallen to the United Nations.

The German failure to invade England in 1940 has been mentioned as one significant step in the eventual defeat of Hitler, and the Russian campaign as a second. According to General George Marshall's final report on the war, the actual turning point of the war came when Germany invaded the Soviet Union. The German failure to capture Moscow before snow fell in 1941 proved to be disastrous, and the German offensive in 1942 failed, too, before the gallant defense of Stalingrad, where the Germans suffered an immense disaster. The British defense of North Africa during 1942 also played a role in paving the way for the eventual defeat of the Axis. According to General Marshall, the Russian and British stand in 1942 had the following significance for the United States:

> There can be no doubt that the greed and the mistakes of the war-making nations as well as the heroic stands of the British and Soviet peoples saved the United States a war on her own soil.
>
> Had the U.S.R.R. and the British Army of the Nile been defeated in 1942, as they well might if the Germans, Japanese and Italians had better co-ordinated their plans and resources and successive operations, we should have stood today [1945] in the Western Hemisphere confronted by a greater part of the world.

In November and December, 1943, the combined chiefs of staff met with President Roosevelt and Prime Minister Churchill in Cairo and shortly after with Roosevelt, Churchill, and Marshal Stalin at Tehran to plan the final defeat of Germany. By this time Anglo-American forces were pushing north in Italy from Naples, and the Russian army was on the offensive. During the winter of 1942–1943 the Russian winter offensive had reconquered one hundred and eighty-five thousand square miles of territory, and in July, 1943, the Russians launched an offensive that lasted ten months. From Leningrad to the Black Sea the Germans were sent reeling back, and the Russians reconquered most of their pre-1939 territory. "The success of the Russians," Secretary of War Stimson declared, in a public statement on October 28, 1943, "was primarily due to the superb fighting qualities of the Russian soldiers and the skill and resourcefulness of their leaders."

As the Russians were advancing westward late in 1943 and early in 1944, Allied bombers, day and night, softened up the fortress of Europe. From August 17, 1942, to V–E Day, United States fliers alone dropped over one million five hundred and fifty thousand tons of bombs on western Europe. In the year before the Allied landing in France, American bombers focused their attacks on plants manufacturing aircraft and ball bearings, on airfields, and on lines of communication, while British bombers concentrated on the destruction of the industries in the Ruhr and Rhineland regions. In the spring of 1944 synthetic-fuel plants and oil refineries became the targets, and between May and October, 1944, production was reduced to 5 per cent of the former monthly output. In May, 1944, too, over nine hundred locomotives and sixteen thousand freight cars were destroyed on the Continent. During the three months before D-Day, Allied air forces hammered the bridges and rail centers in the invasion areas so effectively that after the Allied landing, the enemy's ability to shift reserves to critical points was severely hampered. "This air preparation was a decisive factor in the success of Overlord [the code name of the operation]," General Marshall has observed.

General Dwight D. Eisenhower was selected as Supreme Commander of the Allied invasion forces in the operation designated as Overlord. Under his command were such generals as Bernard L. Montgomery, Omar N. Bradley, Jacob Devers, George Patton, Courtney H. Hodges, W. H. Simpson, Alexander Patch, Miles Dempsey, Carl Spaatz, Leigh-Mallory, Henry Crerar, and Jean de Lattre de Tassigny. On June 6, 1944, General Eisenhower launched the greatest amphibious operation in all world history. By this time 1,533,000 American soldiers had been transported to the British Isles, and American shipyards had broken all records in producing landing craft. On D-Day some four thousand ships, protected by eleven thousand airplanes, landed American, British, and Canadian armies along fifty miles of beaches on the coast of Normandy. Just before these troops landed, American and

British air-borne troops were dropped in vital areas in the rear of German coastal defenses. General Eisenhower has written,

That everything went according to plan is a remarkable tribute to the hard work, coordinated effort, and foresight of the thousands engaged in the initial planning and training, and, as Admiral Ramsay stated in his report, to the "courage of the tens of thousands in the Allied navies and merchant fleets who carried out their orders in accordance with the very highest traditions of the sea."

There was no effective German air resistance to the landing on June 6, although enemy ground resistance was stubborn. During the first hours of the assault the German communication and radar systems had been so thoroughly battered by Allied air forces that the German high command was completely ignorant of the magnitude of the Allied landing. By the second day the beachhead was secure, and the German coastal-defense system had been broken. On June 27 the vital port of Cherbourg fell to the American army, and supplies could now be landed on an increasing scale. The next step in Eisenhower's strategy was to break through the German lines and slice the German armies into segments. On July 26, while Montgomery's British and Canadian armies engaged the bulk of the German forces at Caen, General Patton's Third Army pierced the German line at St. Lô, and his armored columns raced through the gap.

American tanks roared through Brittany and over the roads of the area around Tours and Blois, destroying German communications and disrupting the Nazi army. At the same time, Canadian troops in the British Second Army drove south from Caen to Falaise, capturing one hundred thousand German troops and killing and wounding thousands. The disintegration of the German armies now was comparable to the disintegration of the French armies four years before, and by August 15 the Germans were reeling back to the west bank of the Seine.

On August 15 the United States Seventh Army, under General Alexander M. Patch, landed on the southern coast of France and, aided by the French underground, quickly sped up the Rhone valley. Ten days after the landing in southern France, Paris fell to General Leclerc and the Second French Armored Division of the First United States Army. By this time, in the French operation, the Nazis had suffered four hundred thousand casualties, of whom over two hundred thousand were prisoners of war; and at least 2378 German aircraft had been shot down, and 1167 had been destroyed on the ground.

While the Allied armies had speeded on to Paris, the Allied navy and merchant ships had brought constant reinforcements and supplies across the Channel and from the United States. By July 4 the millionth man had been landed, and by July 14 a million tons of stores and about three hundred thousand vehicles had gone ashore; and at the time of the fall of Paris, Eisenhower had two million men in France and over four hundred thousand vehicles.

© 1945, United Feature Syndicate, Inc.

"Radio the old man we'll be late on account of a thousand-mile detour." Sergeant Bill Mauldin Expresses the Reaction of Front-Line Soldiers to "Brass Hat" Requirements as to "Proper" Uniforms

After the fall of Paris, on August 25, Eisenhower's forces rolled over the battlefields of the First World War, and they were soon joined by the Franco-American forces from southern France. Under the over-all command of Eisenhower, Canadian and British forces moved northeastward in a sweeping drive through Belgium. Logistic difficulties, however, now began to slow the advance. Additional ports had to be opened, and railroads had to be repaired. The difficulties of supply finally halted the Allied armies at the German border, but General Eisenhower remarked that "only a miracle of hard work and brilliant improvisation by the supply services had carried our armored spearheads so far."

In mid-November Eisenhower launched an attack on the Siegfried defenses, with only small success. Then, on December 16, the Germans made a desperate gamble. Von Rundstedt attacked the weakly held Allied line between Monschau and Trier with twenty-four divisions. Panzer divisions broke through along a forty-mile front and, at the point of farthest penetration, drove more than fifty miles into the

American lines. Bad weather crippled the effectiveness of Allied air superiority until December 23, when severe blows were delivered to the German supply columns. The American Third and First armies finally eliminated the bulge in the Allied lines by the end of January, 1945. The Germans had delayed the invasion of their country by six weeks, but at a heavy price. They lost two hundred and twenty thousand men and more than fourteen hundred tanks and assault guns. "More serious in the final analysis," reported General Eisenhower, "was the wide-spread disillusionment within the German Army and Germany itself."

While the forces under Eisenhower were liberating France and threatening Germany, the Russians, in the east, were enjoying spectacular success. On June 23, 1944, they launched a massive offensive, which knocked Finland, Rumania, and Bulgaria out of the war and conquered White Russia, Bessarabia, Bucovina, and most of the Baltic states. By the end of 1944 the Red army had driven the Germans out of eastern Poland, eastern Czechoslovakia, Hungary, and Yugoslavia, and on October 19 the Russians stood on German soil in East Prussia. Then, on January 12, 1945, the Red army launched its great push to end the war and soon had conquered all of Poland, East Prussia, and most of Silesia, and by March 30 was only thirty miles from Berlin.

As the Russians were moving into Germany, Eisenhower, on February 23, 1945, hurled his armies at the line of the river Roer, protecting the Cologne plain. City after city fell. On March 23 the British Second Army crossed the Rhine, and on the following day the American Ninth Army secured a bridgehead six miles deep along a twenty-five-mile stretch of the Rhine. In the week just before the bridging of the Rhine, American aircraft had delivered 14,430 heavy-bomber attacks, 7262 medium-bomber attacks, and 29,981 fighter sorties against German targets. With the bridging of the Rhine and Allied armor piercing the German line, the complete rout of the *Wehrmacht* was under way. Allied armor raced for the heart of Germany, and on April 26 Russian and American forces met at Torgau on the Elbe.

Ten days before the Russian-American meeting the Russians had launched their attack on Berlin. On May 2 the German capital fell, and on that same day nearly one million German troops in Italy and Austria surrendered to the Allies. On April 28 Mussolini was killed by Italian partisans, and on May 1 Hitler, it is generally believed, took his life. Four days after Hitler's death the Germans in Holland, Denmark, and northern Germany stopped fighting, and two days later all land, sea,

Mein Kampf, Vol. II

In 1945 the Nazi Götterdämmerung was at hand. From the west and the east mighty Allied armies poured into the disintegrated Third Reich. Low interprets the Nazis' newest lie, that Hitler planned it that way

and air forces of the German government surrendered, at Reims, to General Eisenhower's chief of staff and to a representative of the Russian army.

General Eisenhower observed, in his official report:

It is difficult even for a professional soldier to appreciate the tremendous power which was achieved on the battlefields and in the skies of western Europe by the concerted efforts of the Allied nations. . . . More important even than the weapons, however, was the indomitable fighting spirit of the men of the Allied nations who wielded them. The courage and devotion to duty which they exhibited throughout the campaign, in the grim days of the Ardennes counter-offensive as well as in the excitement of the dash across France and later the advances into the midst of Germany, were unsurpassable. It was the spirit that had enabled them to withstand the shocks of Dunkirk and Pearl Harbor which brought us at the last to Lübeck, to Torgau, and to Berchtesgaden.

TOWARD UNITY

In 1809 Thomas Smith Grimké of Charleston, South Carolina, remarked,

He, who casts his eye over our happy land, must perceive that we form a little political world in ourselves: that our country seems, as was said of Laconia, to be but the patrimony of a band of brothers: that we appear to be another favored race, sent out by Heaven, from the storms and miseries of Europe, to dwell in this land of promise.

The trend of events from the First World War to Pearl Harbor convinced the bulk of Americans that the United States no longer could ignore "the storms and miseries of Europe," and Prime Minister Churchill bluntly told Congress, on December 26, 1941, that the war need not have happened had the peace-loving nations worked together during the previous twenty years. Shortly after the United States entered the war, Wendell Willkie flew around the world, covering thirty thousand miles in less than fifty days, and declared upon his return:

There are no distant points in the world any longer. I learned by this trip that the myriad millions of human beings of the Far East are as close to us as Los Angeles is to New York by the fastest trains. I cannot escape the conviction that in the future what concerns them must concern us, almost as much as the problems of the people of California concern the people of New York.

Our thinking in the future must be worldwide.[1]

On January 2, 1942, twenty-six of the nations fighting the Axis formed the United Nations and pledged their full resources against the enemy powers. Unity in commands and operations of the armed forces was quickly achieved between England and the United States and the smaller powers engaged in the conflict. Churchill had visited the United States just after Pearl Harbor to plan joint action; President Roosevelt traveled to Casablanca in January, 1943, to confer with Churchill on plans for the 1943 military offensive; and the two leaders met again at Quebec in August, 1943.

Meanwhile the necessities of war steadily brought about closer and closer collaboration between the United States and Russia. In June, 1942, President Roosevelt and V. M. Molotov, People's Commissar of Foreign Affairs, discussed not only co-operation in the war, but also

[1]*One World*, p. 3. Simon and Schuster, Inc., New York, 1943.

the problem of maintaining peace, freedom, and security after the war. The foreign ministers of the United States, Great Britain, and Russia, as well as the Chinese ambassador to Russia, met in Moscow in October, 1943, and agreed upon "the necessity of establishing at the earliest practicable date a general international organization, based on the principle of the sovereign equality of all peace-loving States." A few days later the United States Senate pledged that the nation, acting through its constitutional processes, would join in establishing an "international authority with power to prevent aggression and to preserve the peace of the world."

Two months after the Moscow agreement Churchill, Roosevelt, and Stalin met in a significant conference at Tehran. Before leaving for the conference Roosevelt had confided to Sumner Welles, his former Undersecretary of State: "We won't get any strong international organization unless we can find the way by which the Soviet Union and the United States can work together to build it up as the years go by." At Tehran the leaders of the Big Three planned the destruction of the armed forces of Germany and then stated:

And as to peace—we are sure that our concord will win an enduring peace. We recognize fully the supreme responsibility resting upon us and all the United Nations to make a peace which will command the good will of the overwhelming mass of the peoples of the world and banish the scourge and terror of war for many generations.

Just before Churchill and Roosevelt met with Stalin they had conferred with Generalissimo Chiang Kai-shek in Cairo and had agreed that Japan should be stripped of all the islands that she had acquired since 1914 and of all the territories that she had taken on the mainland of China.

Under Roosevelt's leadership a world food-and-agriculture conference met early in 1944, and the United Nations Relief and Rehabilitation Administration was established to deal with the relief problems that would arise after the collapse of Germany. During July, 1944, forty-five nations had representatives at the Bretton Woods Conference in New Hampshire, where the International Bank for Reconstruction and the International Monetary Fund were created. Then, in the autumn of 1944, representatives of the United States, England, and the Soviet Union, and later China, met at Dumbarton Oaks in Washington and drafted proposals for a world organization. "Franklin Roosevelt saw no need to fear Communism if an international organization existed,"

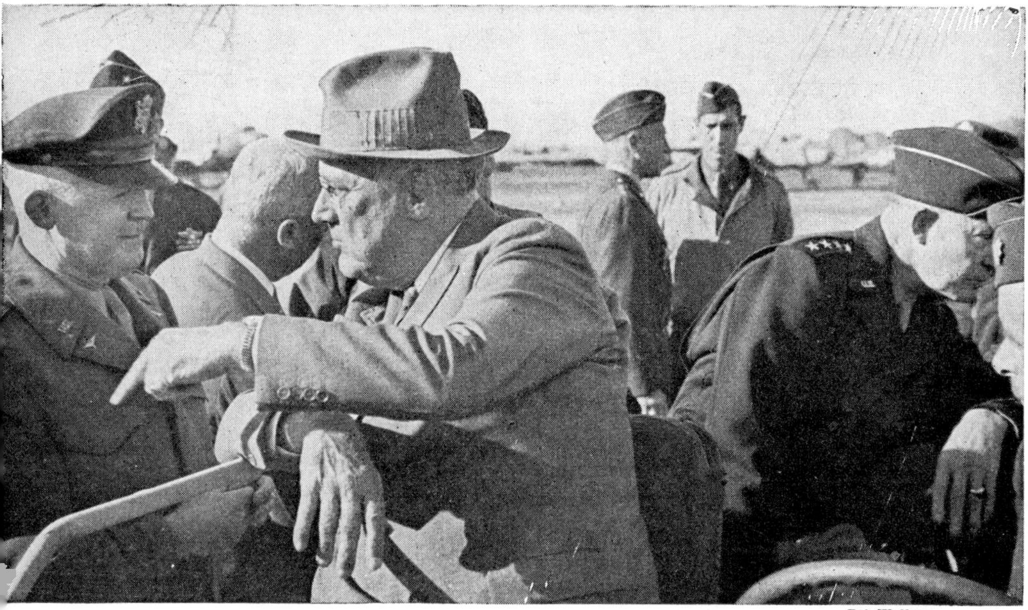

Bob Wallace

President Roosevelt Meets with American Generals during the War in Sicily

The Leaders of the Big Three and Their Advisers Meet at Yalta, February, 1945

Press Association

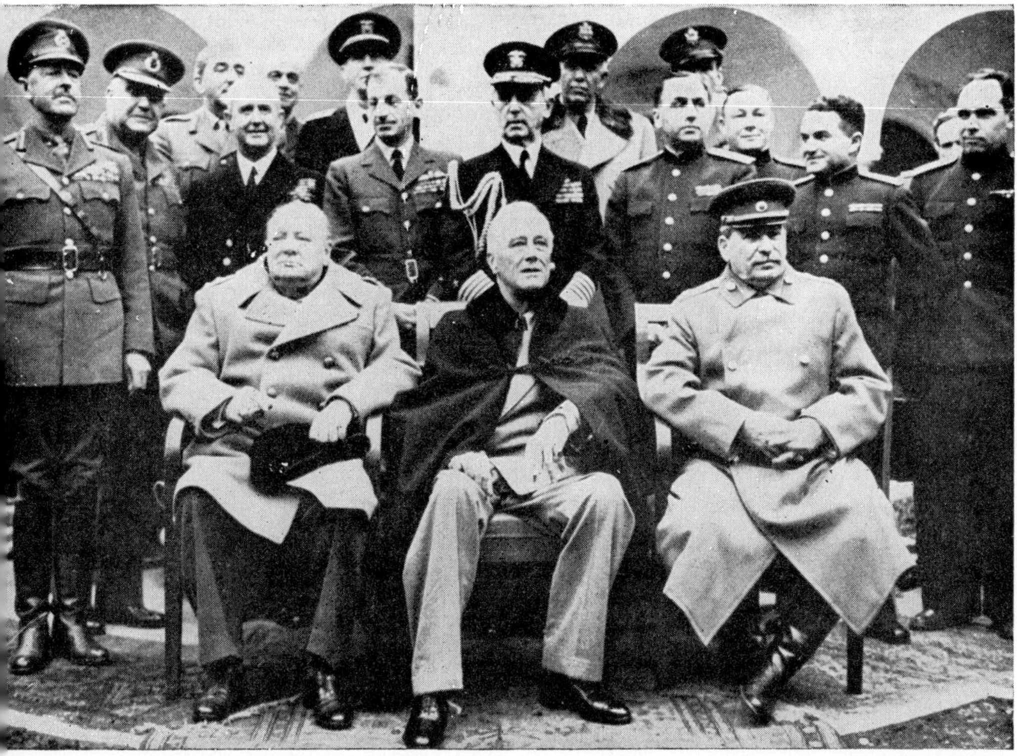

Sumner Welles has declared. "To him it need be feared as a disruptive force only if the world were divided into two armed camps, one headed by the Soviet Union and the other by the English-speaking powers."[1]

In February, 1945, Roosevelt met with Churchill and Stalin at Yalta to make plans for the final blows against Germany and Japan and also to solve differences of opinion that had arisen among the Big Three as to the structure of the proposed world organization. After solving the question of voting procedure in the world organization, the leaders of the Big Three agreed to call a conference of the United Nations to meet at San Francisco on April 25, 1945, to prepare a charter along the lines of the Dumbarton Oaks proposals.

The San Francisco Conference met in a spirit of gloom and uncertainty as a result of the death of President Roosevelt, just a few days before. It was agreed at the Conference to organize the United Nations:

1. To maintain international peace and security, and to that end: to take effective collective measures for the prevention and removal of threats to the peace, and for the suppression of acts of aggression or other breaches of the peace, and to bring about by peaceful means, and in conformity with the principles of justice and international law, adjustment or settlement of international disputes or situations which might lead to a breach of the peace;

2. To develop friendly relations among nations based on respect for the principle of equal rights and self-determination of peoples, and to take other appropriate measures to strengthen universal peace;

3. To achieve international cooperation in solving international problems of an economic, social, cultural, or humanitarian character, and in promoting and encouraging respect for human rights and for fundamental freedoms for all without distinction as to race, sex, language, or religion; and

4. To be a center for harmonizing the actions of nations in the attainment of these common ends.

All nations are equal in the UN, and membership is open to all peace-loving nations which accept the principles and obligations of the Charter. The principal organs of the UN are the General Assembly, the Security Council, the Economic and Social Council, the Trusteeship Council, the International Court of Justice, and the Secretariat. The General Assembly, which consists of all members of the UN, is primarily a "town meeting" for the airing of views and problems. It is to consider the question of the maintenance of international peace and disarmament; it is to promote co-operation in economic, social, cultural, and health fields; and it is permitted to call to the attention of the

[1] *Where Are We Heading?* p. 37. Harper & Brothers, New York, 1946.

toasted American war production, "without which our victory would have been impossible." In the days after Pearl Harbor the United States not only forged a magnificent fighting force, but also converted its economic system to meet the needs of total war. A British expert commented:

> For the first time in the history of war, battles were as much tussles between competing factories as between contending armies. The production of weapons, more so than the conscription of men, was the deciding factor in battle. God now marched with the biggest industries rather than with the biggest battalions.

Between July 1, 1940, and July 31, 1945, the United States spent $44,442,000,000 on aircraft; $40,694,000,000 on naval and merchant ships; $10,801,000,000 on guns and fire control; $19,734,000,000 on ammunition; $21,529,000,000 on combat and motor vehicles; $10,659,000,000 on communication and electronic equipment; $2,000,000,000 on the atomic bomb; and $38,148,000,000 on other equipment and supplies. These expenditures resulted in the remarkable production of 297,000 military airplanes, including 97,000 bombers; 71,060 naval vessels, aggregating 8,250,000 tons; 45,000,000 tons of merchant ships; 17,400,000 rifles, carbines, and side arms; 2,700,000 machine guns and over 315,000 pieces of field artillery and mortars; 165,528 naval-gun assemblies; 86,388 tanks; 16,438 armored cars; 88,077 scout cars and carriers; and 2,434,553 trucks, 991,299 light vehicles, of which most were jeeps, and 123,707 tractors.

In order to accomplish this miracle of production, the workers in the factories put in 45 per cent more man-days of effort in 1943, for instance, than they had in 1939, and labor increased its output by 89.6 per cent in 1943 over that of 1939. General George Marshall, commenting on one phase of this immense production, declared:

> The greatest advantage in equipment the United States has enjoyed on the ground in the fighting so far has been in our multiple-drive motor equipment, principally the jeep and the $2\frac{1}{2}$ ton truck. These are the instruments which have moved and supplied United States troops in battle while the German army, despite the fearful reputation of its 'panzer armies' early in the war still depended heavily on animal transport for its regular infantry divisions. The United States, profiting from the mass production achievements of its automotive industry, made all its forces truck-drawn and had enough trucks left over to supply the British armies with large numbers of motor vehicles and send tremendous quantities to the Red army.

During the Second World War, American armies, unlike our armies in 1917–1918, were equipped almost entirely with American-made products. Before Pearl Harbor, American industry had converted only slightly to war production under the supervision of the National Defense Advisory Commission, established in May, 1940, and headed by William S. Knudsen. In January, 1942, Donald M. Nelson took control of the new War Production Board, which guided the conversion of factories to war production. The automobile industry, for instance, moved its automobile machinery out into the snow and installed machinery designed to make tanks, planes, and trucks. By 1943 nearly 60 per cent of American industry had been converted, and both private and government funds were poured into the construction of new war plants. By the end of 1943 the government, through the Defense Plant Corporations, a subsidiary of the Reconstruction Finance Corporation, owned $14,500,000,000 in war plants.

Under the guidance of the WPB, a soft-drink company went into the business of loading shells, a citrus-fruit-canning company began to make parts for merchant ships, a maker of mechanical pencils produced bomb parts and precision instruments, and a grower and shipper of ferns made bomb chutes. Many civilian goods disappeared, and the production of others was curtailed, but the American consumer really did not suffer. "American industry," Donald M. Nelson has written, "turned out more goods for war than we ever produced for our peacetime needs—yet had enough power left over to keep civilian standards of living at an astonishingly high level." The biggest economic undertaking in our history was this wartime mobilization of the nation's resources. The value of goods and services produced in the United States in 1940 had been $97,000,000,000; this was increased to $150,000,000,000 in 1942, to $180,000,000,000 in 1943, and to nearly $200,000,000,000 in 1944. By the close of 1943, too, there were over ten million men in the armed services (over twice as many as in 1918), twenty-eight million people were engaged in civilian war work, and the country was spending money on the war at five times the rate of 1918.

Another miracle of the war effort was the work done by the transportation system. During the first six months of 1944 the loads on the railroads totaled 833,000,000,000 gross ton-miles, which was 106 per cent higher than in 1939, and freight carried by air reached 58,000,000 tons in 1943. Nor should the backbreaking job done by the individual worker and farmer be forgotten. The staggering production figures for industrial workers has already been mentioned. The farmer too met the challenge. Mountains of food poured from the farm after Pearl Harbor, giving the nation a greater food supply than any nation at war ever had. In 1944, for instance, the biggest wheat crop in American history—1,115,402,000 bushels—supplied all war, civilian, and export requirements. The corn crop of 3,100,000,000 bushels was second only to that of 1942. Meat production in 1944 included 19.4 billion pounds of beef and 13.3 billion pounds of pork, bacon, and ham. For the harvest of 1944 the farmers received more than $10,270,000,000 during the first seven months of the year—their greatest cash return in history.

After a nationwide tour in 1943 and 1944, John Dos Passos commented, in *The State of the Nation:*

> If you had had the chance that I've had during the last year to travel around among the various types of people in this country, I think you would agree with me that it is neither the farmers nor the factory workers who have been the worst offenders in putting their own interests before those of the country as a whole.[1]

Faced with mobilizing for total war, the government created many Federal agencies. The total Federal employees reached over three million, not including, of course, the men and women in the armed services. By 1944 war agencies were employing 2,168,366 individuals, and non-war agencies 1,037,755. Many of the war agencies overlapped and conflicted with one another, and the Federal government grew to an incomprehensible size.

In order to keep the public informed about the war and to carry on psychological warfare against the enemy, the Office of Facts and Figures was established and later merged with the Office of War Information. The OWI's most important work was done abroad, where it co-operated closely with the army and tried to undermine enemy morale.

The War Manpower Commission, headed by Paul McNutt, was a Federal agency that vitally affected the life of every American. It operated the Selective Service System for the armed forces, and it tried to regulate the employment of men and women in industry. Higher wages attracted workers to war industries, and the WMC discouraged workers from seeking employment in industries producing just civilian goods. As a result of the magnitude of the war effort, critical labor shortages occurred, and late in 1944 President Roosevelt urged Congress, but to no avail, to pass a National Service Bill, registering all men of

---

[1]Houghton Mifflin Company, Boston, 1944.

the ages eighteen through sixty-four under Selective Service, and making all women of eighteen through forty-nine liable to draft into war industries.

Another Federal agency directly affecting the American worker was the War Labor Board, headed by William H. Davis. The WLB averted many strikes and aided employers and employees in solving their differences over wages, hours, and grievances. Although newspapers frequently emphasized strikes in war industries, actually the man-hours lost as a result of strikes, in proportion to the total man-hours worked, were infinitesimal. President Roosevelt remarked, on October 27, 1944:

> The production necessary to equip and maintain our vast forces of fighting men on global battlefronts is without parallel. . . . The production which has flowed from this country to all the battlefronts of the world has been due to the efforts of American business, American labor, and American farmers, working together as a patriotic team.

The war agency which affected the daily lives of more people than either the War Manpower Commission or the War Labor Board was the Office of Price Administration. By the summer of 1943 gasoline, coffee, sugar, meat, and some canned goods had been rationed. Ration stamps and tokens were issued to assure an equitable distribution of the goods. The OPA had sixty thousand paid workers in branches all over the nation and hundreds of thousands of volunteers who sat on price and rationing boards. In spite of the efforts of these workers, however, black markets developed for gasoline, nylon stockings, and meats and other foods. But the OPA and other agencies did hold the line fairly well against rising prices until the end of the war. Chester Bowles, the head of the agency after 1943, wrote,

> OPA was created to control rents and the cost of living, to spread the supply of scarce products in the fairest possible way among all our citizens, and to maintain a stable economy on which to build a post war world which will provide economic security and true freedom for every American citizen.[1]

Working with the OPA to check runaway inflation was the Office of Economic Stabilization, directed by James F. Byrnes, later the head of the Office of War Mobilization and Reconversion, created in October, 1944, as the agency above all the other war agencies.

During the war, although taxes were the highest in American history, Congress lacked the courage to pay the bulk of the costs of the

[1]*Life*, December 13, 1943.

war by taxation. Roughly 40 per cent of the cost of the war was paid from taxes. The rest was borrowed from the people through War Bonds. Between May, 1941, and June, 1945, "E" Bonds (smaller-denomination bonds) in the amount of $36,000,000,000 were sold to the public. Only $7,000,000,000 of these were turned in for redemption during these same four years. The war brought widespread prosperity and made some Americans forget the difficult depression years of the previous decade. Some Americans bought $15,000 sapphire bracelets, $3500 mink coats, $200 cigarette-lighters, and $49.50 black chiffon nightgowns. The majority of Americans, however, saved their money

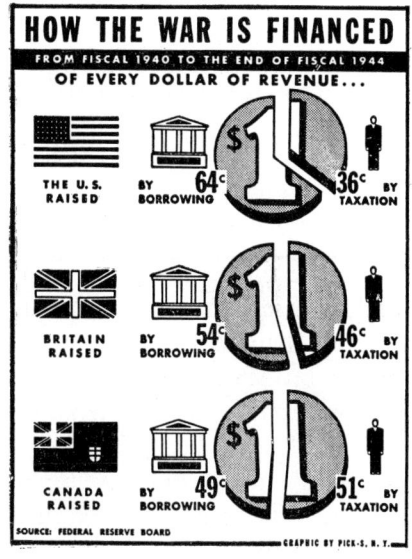

until radios, automobiles, and refrigerators should be again available. From May, 1941, to April, 1945, the savings of individuals reached $129,000,000,000. Perhaps the best analysis of a prosperous America at war was written by D. W. Brogan, English writer and teacher, in *Harper's Magazine* for May, 1944:

A country has the kind of army its total ethos, its institutions, resources, habits of peaceful life, make possible to it. The American army is the army of a country which is law-respecting without being law-abiding. It is the army of a country which, having lavish natural wealth provided for it and lavish artificial wealth created by its own efforts, is extravagant and wasteful. It is the army of a country in which melodramatic pessimism is often on the surface but below it is the permanent optimism of a people that has licked a more formidable enemy than Germany or Japan, primitive North America. It is the army of a country whose national motto was "Root, hog, or die." When convinced that death *is* the alternative, the hog roots. It is the army of an untidy country which has neither the time, the temperament, nor the need for economy. It is the army of a country in which great economic power is often piled up for sudden use; a final decisive military blow is merely a special variety of corner. It is the army of a country of gamblers who are more or less phlegmatic in taking and calculating their losses, but who feel with all their instincts that they can never go wrong over a reasonable period of time in refusing to sell America short.

So the American way of war is bound to be like the American way of life. It is bound to be mechanized like the American farm and kitchen (the farms and kitchens of a lazy people who want washing machines and bull-dozers to do the job for them). It is the army of a nation of colossal business enterprises, often wastefully run in detail, but winning by their mere scale and by their ability to wait until that scale tells. It is the army of a country where less attention is paid to formal dignity, of persons or occupations, than in any other society, where results count, where being a good loser is not thought nearly as important as being a winner, good or bad. It is the country where you try anything once, *especially* if it has not been tried before.

Before the American army and air force became effective fighting units overseas, American equipment was pouring onto the battle front through lend-lease agreements. Before the Lend-Lease Act had been passed on March 11, 1941, permitting the President to "sell, transfer title to, exchange, lease, lend, or otherwise dispose of . . . any defense article," England and France, as early as 1938, had begun to expand America's plant capacity for war production by placing munition orders. The orders placed under lend-lease from March, 1941, to Pearl Harbor, too, expanded American war production, and, as E. R. Stettinius, lend-lease administrator, has written, "The Lend-Lease orders placed in 1941 assured a much greater flow of arms and other essential supplies from our factories in 1942 and 1943, and by then this flow was needed not only for our allies but for our own forces as well."[1]

After Pearl Harbor, before any Allied nation could obtain lend-lease aid the United States had to be sure that the desired supplies were for the war effort; there had to be a sufficient supply of the articles in the United States; and, above all, the United States had to be convinced that the supplies would be more valuable in the hands of the requesting nation than in the hands of some other nation, including the United States. By the end of the war $43,950,000,000 of lend-lease aid had been furnished, of which 69 per cent went to the British Empire and 25 per cent to the Soviet Union. There is no doubt, as Stettinius has remarked, that American weapons in Allied hands speeded the end of the war and saved untold American lives.

Lend-lease was by no means a one-way street. The United States, by July 1, 1945, had received in reverse lend-lease $6,256,871,000. Belgium, for instance, furnished vegetables to the American army and

[1] *Lend-Lease, Weapon for Victory*, p. 99. The Macmillan Company, New York, 1944.

gave, in reverse lend-lease, twice as much as she had received. The largest amount of reverse lend-lease was supplied by Great Britain. The American air force used British-made bombs, auxiliary gas tanks, and other supplies, and England built over one hundred airfields for the use of American planes. Although some returning servicemen circulated the rumor that England charged heavy sums for the use of the airports, no money was paid for this service, but England received credits against her lend-lease from the United States.

The public's satisfaction with the American war effort was tested in 1944 by the first wartime Presidential election since 1864. As in 1940 and 1864, war aided the incumbent, and the people once again revealed that they did not, even at the price of a fourth term, favor changing horses in midstream. Long before election day President Roosevelt urged Congress to create a single Federal ballot in order to make it easy for the five million soldiers overseas to vote. Congress rejected the President's proposal and instead permitted a Federal ballot only if the soldiers applied for and failed to receive a state ballot or if a state certified that the Federal ballot was acceptable to it. Twenty states accepted the Federal ballot, but many soldiers failed to vote in the other states, since the securing of an absentee ballot from a state was a too cumbersome and a too discouraging process.

During the year before the Republican convention the leaders in control of the party machinery worked to prevent Wendell Willkie from again being their standard-bearer. Willkie was forthright and independent, and was too advanced on social issues and too much of a believer in world co-operation for the Old Guard. He conducted a dramatic campaign, but when he lost out in the Wisconsin primaries in April, 1944, he withdrew his candidacy. When the convention was held in Chicago, Willkie was conspicuously not invited to speak. Although Governor Bricker of Ohio waged a strenuous campaign for the nomination, by the time of the convention it was clear that Governor Thomas E. Dewey of New York was the man who had the best chance of defeating President Roosevelt. Dewey had grown up in Owosso, Michigan, had studied law at Columbia University, and had served as chief assistant to the United States District Attorney and convicted Waxy Gordon, the New York beer baron. After this success Governor Herbert Lehman appointed him special rackets prosecutor from 1935 to 1937. The prestige that came to him from these prosecutions won him the governorship of New York in 1942. He revealed that he was a competent administrator, although not a man greatly interested in theories. Though his supporters conducted an efficient campaign for the nomination, he spoke with great caution so as not to alienate the Old Guard, and he did not openly admit his candidacy.

Werner in the *Chicago Sun*

"I Don't Forget So Easy, Either"

The record of the Republican party on both domestic and international issues weakens their 1944 campaign

Dewey was nominated on the first ballot, and Bricker was awarded the second place. In his acceptance speech Dewey attacked "one-man government," pledged his suport to an all-out war effort, charged that the Roosevelt administration was inefficient and that "it has grown old in office. It has become tired and quarrelsome." The Republican platform pledged the party to the encouragement of private enterprise and criticized New Deal measures although in the field of agriculture and labor it was careful not to alienate votes. In regard to foreign policy the party favored "responsible participation by the United States in a post-war cooperative organization."

During the campaign the Republicans asserted that they could do a better job of winning the war and handle the reconversion situation more efficiently. They also denounced "New Deal bureaucracy," maintained that the Communists were really running the country, and warned of the dangers of a fourth term. Although the party stated that it believed in world co-operation, Dewey's opposition to aid to the Allies in 1940 and the Republican Congressmen's opposition to defense bills from 1939 to Pearl Harbor worked against its chances in 1944. The strategy of the Republican campaign was to repeat constantly that there was no indispensable man; that the New Deal was setting group against group and class against class; and that the New Deal was responsible for the depression of the 1930's.

A week before the Democratic convention President Roosevelt made it clear that, although he did not want to run, "if the convention should . . . nominate me for the Presidency, I shall accept. . . . I will accept and serve in this office, if I am so ordered by the Commander in Chief of us all—the sovereign people of the United States." Apparently persuaded by machine Democrats like National Chairman Robert Hannegan and Chicago Mayor Edward J. Kelly that liberal Henry Wallace, as the Vice-Presidential candidate, would cost the ticket votes, Roosevelt sanctioned the rejection of Wallace for Senator Harry S. Truman of Missouri. The Democratic platform boasted of the social reforms of the New Deal, of the world leadership of President Roosevelt, and of the successful administration of the war effort. The platform stated:

He [Roosevelt] stands before the nation and the world, the champion of human liberty and dignity. He has rescued our people from the ravages of economic disaster. His rare foresight and magnificent courage have saved our nation from the assault of international brigands and dictators.

Roosevelt delivered only a few campaign speeches, but in these he was at his best. Before the teamsters' union, on September 24, 1944, he burlesqued the Republicans in one of the ablest political speeches that he ever delivered. He said:

The whole purpose of Republican oratory these days seems to be to switch labels. The object is to persuade the American people that the Democratic party was responsible for the 1929 crash and depression, and the Republican party was responsible for all social progress under the New Deal. Imitation may be the sincerest form of flattery—but I am afraid that in this case it is the most obvious common or garden variety of fraud.

Near the close of the speech the President remarked:

These Republican leaders have not been content with attacks upon me, or my wife—they now include my dog, Fala. Unlike the members of my family, he resents this. . . . I am accustomed to hearing malicious falsehoods about myself—such as that old, worm-eaten chestnut that I have represented myself as indispensable. But I think I have a right to object to libelous statements about my dog.

On election day 25,602,505 votes were cast for Roosevelt and 22,006,278 for Dewey. Dewey carried Maine, Vermont, Ohio, Indiana, Wisconsin, Iowa, North Dakota, South Dakota, Nebraska, Kansas, Wyoming, and Colorado. Dewey lost the support of such independent forces as the *New York Times*, columnist Walter Lippmann, and many

Willkie adherents. As Lippmann wrote, "It is between Roosevelt with all his faults and Dewey with all his faults, and thus, reluctantly—because I dislike four terms and would have preferred a change—I cannot feel that Gov. Dewey can be trusted now with responsibility in foreign affairs." Organized labor, through such agencies as the C. I. O. Political Action Committee, rallied to Roosevelt's banner, as did many Americans who approved of the social reforms of the New Deal and of Roosevelt's international policies. Above all, Roosevelt still had an amazing hold on the average American. As Edwin A. Lahey, *Chicago Daily News* columnist, wrote on November 7, 1944: "Mr. Roosevelt's greatness, his indisputable psychological link with the little people of this country, is itself an objective fact. . . . The man has it. Dewey hasn't."

Roosevelt was destined to serve only a few weeks of his fourth term. On April 12, at 3.35 P.M., he died at Warm Springs, Georgia, in the "Little White House," as the result of a cerebral hemorrhage. Death came to the sixty-three-year-old President on the eve of his greatest victory—the defeat of the Axis and the establishment of an international organization to keep the peace of the world. The news of the President's death stunned Washington, the United States, and the world. Crowds in tears watched the funeral train roll north to Hyde Park. April 14, the day of the funeral, was proclaimed a day of mourning and prayer by President Harry S. Truman, who said: "His fellow countrymen will sorely miss his fortitude and faith and courage in the time to come. The peoples of the earth who love the ways of freedom and hope will mourn for him." For three days American radio canceled scheduled programs and devoted the time to the memory of Franklin D. Roosevelt, and newspapers all over the world were filled with praises of his contribution to world society. The House of Commons adjourned in the President's memory, and Winston Churchill declared, "It is also the loss of the British nation and the cause of freedom in every land." Joseph Stalin wired from Russia, "The American people and the United Nations have lost in Franklin Roosevelt a great politician of world significance and a pioneer in the organization of peace and security after the war."

Republican Senator George Aiken of Vermont observed, "The world can ill afford to lose him at this time." Senator Robert A. Taft remarked, "He dies a hero of the war, for he literally worked himself to death in the service of the American people." And a private in the army declared, "America will seem a strange, empty place without his

Press Association

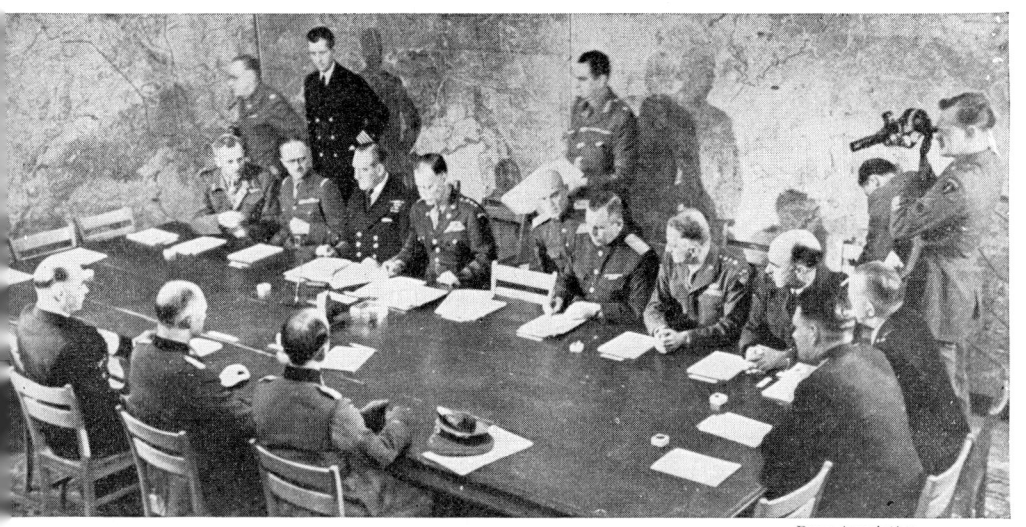

The Germans Complete the Surrender to the Allies at Reims, France, May 7, 1945

The Surrender of the Japanese

General Sir Arthur Percival, commander of Singapore, and General Jonathan Wainwright, hero of Corregidor, salute General Douglas MacArthur just before the latter signed the Japanese surrender document aboard the battleship *Missouri* in Tokyo Bay, September 2, 1945

Press Association

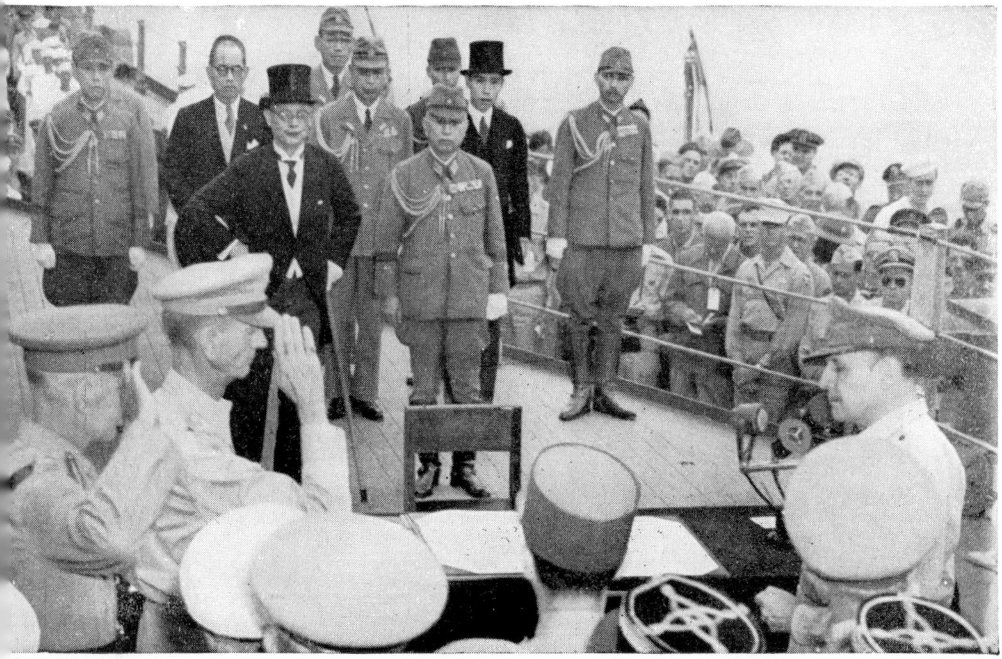

voice talking to the people whenever great events occur." From the standpoint of history, Henry Steele Commager wrote:

It should be possible to fix, if not with finality, at least with some degree of accuracy, the place occupied by Roosevelt in American history.

That this place still seems clouded by controversy cannot be denied. Yet this, too, is part of the picture and has its own significance. The Washington, the Jefferson, the Jackson, the Lincoln, the Wilson administrations, too, were characterized by controversy and bitterness; it is only the administrations of mediocre men like Monroe, Arthur, Harrison, that are memorable for placidity. The explanation of the controversy and especially of the bitterness is, however, less rational. It is a two-fold one: contemporaries tended to see in both the domestic and foreign policies of Roosevelt an abrupt and even revolutionary break with the past; they tended to personalize those policies, to regard them as largely an expression of Roosevelt's character, to focus all their attention—both their devotion and their hatred—on the man in the White House rather than on the ground-swell of opinion to which he gave expression.

We can see now that the "Roosevelt revolution" was no revolution, but rather the culmination of half a century of historical development, and that Roosevelt himself, though indubitably a leader, was an instrument of the popular will rather than a creator of, or a dictator to, that will. Indeed, the two major issues of the Roosevelt administration—the domestic issue of the extension of government control for democratic purposes, and the international issue of the rôle of America as a world power—emerged in the 1890's, and a longer perspective will see the half-century from the 1890's to the present as an historical unit. The roots of the New Deal, the origins of our participation in this war, go deep down into our past, and neither development is comprehensible except in terms of that past.[1]

THE OPENING OF A NEW AGE

At eight-fifteen in the morning of August 6, 1945, a B-29 roared over the Japanese city of Hiroshima and with one bomb destroyed many square miles of that city. One plane with one bomb created more devastation than a raid of two thousand B-29's could have produced. The new bomb, the atomic bomb, had a destructive power equivalent to that of twenty thousand tons of TNT. Of the estimated two hundred and forty-five thousand people in that Japanese city on August 6, one hundred thousand were killed outright or died soon from the effects of radioactivity or fire, and one hundred thousand more were injured. A

[1] *Franklin Delano Roosevelt: A Memorial*, pp. 214–215. Pocket Books, Inc., New York, 1945. Reprinted from an article in the *American Mercury*.

few days after the bombing, Philip Morrison, one of the atomic scientists, visited Hiroshima and later told the Senate Committee on
Atomic Energy:

I remember vividly the lunch
we had at the prefectural building in Hiroshima. The Japanese
officials came there to talk to
us and to describe their experiences. I spoke to the chief
medical officer of the district. He
had been pinned in the wreckage of his house for several days
after the explosion—he lived a
little more than a mile from the
point of impact—and was still
wearing splints. His assistant
had been killed, and his assist-

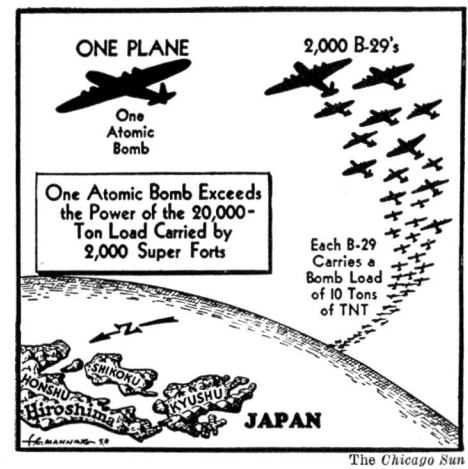

The *Chicago Sun*

ant's assistant. Of the three hundred registered physicians, more than two
hundred and sixty were unable to aid the injured. Of twenty-four hundred
nurses, orderlies, and first aid workers, more than eighteen hundred were
made casualties in a single instant. It was the same everywhere. There were
about thirty-three modern fire stations in Hiroshima. Twenty-six were useless
after the blast, and three-quarters of the firemen killed or missing. The military organization was destroyed; the commanding general and all his staff
were killed, with some five thousand of the garrison of eight thousand. Not
one hospital in the city was left in condition to shelter patients from the rain.
The power and telephone were both out over the whole central region of the
city. Debris filled the streets, and hundreds, even thousands of fires burned
unchecked among the injured and the dead. No one was able to fight them.

There is a word for this kind of attack; it is described as an attack of
saturation. If you strike at a man or a city, your adversary protects himself.
If you attack a man, he runs or strikes back at you; if you attack a city, it
throws up flak, it musters its firemen, it treats the wounded. But if you strike
all at once with overwhelming force, your enemy cannot protect himself. He
is stunned. The flak batteries are all shooting as fast as they can; the firemen
are all busy throwing water at the flames. Then your strike may grow larger
without increased resistance. The defenses are saturated. The atomic bomb
is a weapon of saturation. It destroys so quickly and so completely such a
large area that defense is hopeless. Leadership and organization are gone.
Key personnel are killed. With the fire stations wrecked and the firemen
burned, how control a thousand fires? With the doctors dead and the hospitals smashed, how treat a quarter of a million injured?

There is one more novelty. A Japanese official stood in the rubble and said to us: "All this from one bomb; it is unendurable." We learned what he meant. The cities of all Japan had been put to flame by the great flights of B-29s from the Marianas. But at least there was warning, and a sense of temporary safety. If the people of Kobe went through a night of inferno, you in Nagoya were going to be all right. The thousand-bomber raids were not concealed; they even formed a pattern of action which the war-wise Japanese could count on. But every hour of every day above any Japanese city there might be one American plane. And one bomber could now destroy a city. The alert would be sounded day and night. Even if the raiders were over Fukuoka, you in Sendai, a thousand miles north, must still fear death from a single plane. This is unendurable.

For approximately four years American scientists, with government subsidies, had raced with enemy scientists to see which could split the atom first and unleash a destructive force unparalleled in world history. American scientists won that race and brought a quick end to the war. On August 9 a second atomic bomb fell, on Nagasaki, and two days later Tokyo appealed for peace. On August 11 Secretary of State James F. Byrnes, on behalf of the United States, Great Britain, the Soviet Union, and China, accepted the surrender on this basis: "From the moment of surrender the authority of the Emperor and the Japanese government to rule the State shall be subject to the Supreme Commander of the Allied Powers, who will take such steps as he deems proper to effectuate the surrender terms."

The end of the war was, of course, welcomed by the United Nations with great hilarity and joy, mixed with an uneasiness and concern over the implications of atomic energy for the future of civilization. The Atomic Scientists of Chicago stated:

It is anticipated that in a relatively short time, perhaps five to ten years, many nations will have large stocks of atomic bombs, unless they are prevented from amassing them by an international agency for atomic energy. Even though our population and our industry are dispersed to a large number of small towns, enough bombs probably can be made, sooner or later, to destroy a large fraction of even such small towns. Enough bombs may, in fact, be accumulated to lay waste a significant fraction of the land area of this country.

It was clear that the casualties of an atomic war would be far greater than those of the Second World War, which had been the most devastating war in all history. According to General Marshall's final report,

201,367 Americans had been killed, by the end of June, 1945, approximately 600,000 had been wounded, and 57,000 were missing. Army battle deaths alone were greater than the losses of the Union and Confederate armies in the Civil War. The ground forces suffered 81 per cent of all American casualties; the army air force suffered 120,000 casualties; and the navy and the marines had over 66,000. American losses, however, were low compared with those of the British Empire, Russia, Germany, and Japan. The tentative figures for battle deaths alone (not including civilian deaths, which were many) were 3,250,000 Germans, 3,000,000 Russians, 375,000 men of the British Empire, and 1,500,000 Japanese.

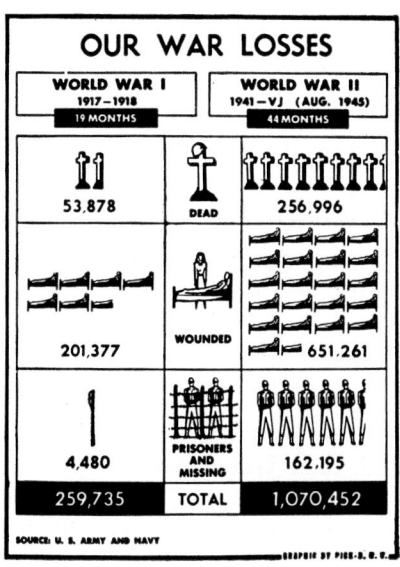

OUR WAR LOSSES

WORLD WAR I 1917–1918 19 MONTHS		WORLD WAR II 1941–VJ (AUG. 1945) 44 MONTHS
53,878	DEAD	256,996
201,377	WOUNDED	651,261
4,480	PRISONERS AND MISSING	162,195
259,735	TOTAL	1,070,452

SOURCE: U. S. ARMY AND NAVY

SELECTED BIBLIOGRAPHY

The official published reports of Chief of Staff George C. Marshall, of General Dwight D. Eisenhower, of Admiral Ernest King, and of General H. H. Arnold are invaluable; Edgar McInnis, *The War* (5 vols.); *Prelude to Invasion: An Account Based upon Official Reports by Henry L. Stimson, Secretary of War*, useful. Among the best accounts of phases of the fighting are Ralph Ingersoll, *The Battle Is the Pay-Off*; R. E. Merriam, *Dark December*; W. L. White, *They Were Expendable* and *Queens Die Proudly*; Richard Tregaskis, *Guadalcanal Diary* and *Invasion Diary*; Robert Corse, *Lifeline*; C. C. Wertenbaker, *Invasion*; Gilbert Cant, *The Great Pacific Victory—From the Solomons to Tokyo*; Stewart Alsop and Thomas Braden, *Sub Rosa: The O.S.S. and American Espionage*; John Mason Brown, *To All Hands: An Amphibious Adventure*. The diplomatic problems are covered in Sumner Welles, *Where Are We Heading?* Wendell Willkie, *One World*; V. M. Dean, *The Four Cornerstones of Peace*. Developments on the home front are described in John Dos Passos, *The State of the Nation*; Donald Nelson, *Arsenal of Democracy*; Jack Goodman (Ed.), *While You Were Gone*; Frances Perkins, *The Roosevelt I Knew*. Among the best books on the atomic bomb are John Hersey, *Hiroshima*; Dexter Masters and Katherine Way (Eds.), *One World or None*; Henry DeWolf Smyth, *Atomic Energy for Military Purposes*; Selig Hecht, *Explaining the Atom*.

XXXVII

The New Age

THE atomic bomb that dropped on Hiroshima opened a new era for mankind. The ability of men to destroy life and property in warfare had reached new levels; the necessity of ending war and insuring peace had become more urgent. For the United States it meant new responsibility. Great Britain, long the dominant power in the western world, had spent her strength in the two world wars. Germany lay in ruined defeat; France had long since become a secondary power. Only Russia and the United States had emerged from the struggle stronger than when it began. The future for weal or woe lay with these young giants.

Near the close of the Second World War, the feeling that war must never occur again led the Allied and Associated Nations to meet at San Francisco to write the charter of the United Nations. The holding of the meeting in the United States was in itself an indication of America's new world position. Whereas after the First World War the United States had withdrawn from the peace settlement and the League of Nations, now this country was in the vanguard in forming the world organization. In fact, it is doubtful that the United Nations would ever have been launched without the impetus supplied by President Roosevelt. More than any other figure on the world stage, he seemed to express the longing for peace and an efficient organization for its maintenance.

Although difficulties had developed between the United States and the Soviet Union before the San Francisco Conference met in late April, 1945, it seemed at the Conference itself that the two powers might be able to work together for a peaceful world. Former Secretary of State Edward R. Stettinius Jr. has written that President Roosevelt believed that "If the Soviet Union, through patience and understanding, could be brought into a functioning world organization, it might become a constructive force in world affairs. If, on the other hand, the world were divided into two armed camps, then the Soviet Union would become a disruptive force in world affairs."[1]

[1]*Roosevelt and the Russians: The Yalta Conference*, Walter Johnson, ed., p. 25. Doubleday & Co., New York, 1949.

In spite of the great expectations to flow from the San Francisco Conference, it soon developed that the Soviet Union and the West were not in accord. The meetings of the United Nations Assembly and Security Council during the next few years revealed the deep split between the East and the West. Shortly after the Yalta Conference (February, 1945), the Soviet Union began to violate the pledges it had made that the countries of Eastern Europe would be permitted to choose governments representative of the people through free elections. Instead, the Soviet authorities forced puppet governments on Bulgaria, Rumania, Hungary, and Poland. Soon Soviet pressure was applied to Greece and Turkey. To the United States this was not only a violation of sacred agreements but a threat to peace as well. Consequently in what seemed a direct reversal of traditional policy, the United States threw its power behind these nations threatened by Soviet expansion. The time had come, as August Belmont had predicted in 1850, "when self-preservation will dictate to the United States the necessity of throwing her moral and physical force into the scales of European republicanism."

On March 12, 1947, President Truman announced to Congress that the United States should enter upon a policy which would "support free peoples who are resisting attempted subjugation by armed minorities or by outside pressures." He then added, "I believe we must assist free peoples to work out their own destinies in their own way."

Congress quickly appropriated money to send military equipment and economic aid to Greece and Turkey. The Truman Doctrine proved to be, however, only a stop-gap program. Western Europe needed help to recover from the war. Unless the United States appropriated money to aid in the rebuilding of the shattered economies of Europe, unrest in these nations might encourage Communist *coup d'etats* supported by the Soviet Union. It was essential to the security of the United States that Western Europe not be absorbed by the Soviet Union. Economic stability had therefore to be restored to Europe.

In keeping with this purpose, Secretary of State George C. Marshall announced in June, 1947, that the United States stood ready to aid those free nations of Europe which would also take steps to aid themselves. President Truman justified such a program when, on March 17, 1948, he pointed out that "Rapid changes are taking place in Europe which affect our foreign policy and our national security. There is an increasing threat to nations which are striving to maintain a form of government which grants freedom to its citizens. The United States is deeply concerned with the survival of freedom in those nations."

This was an open recognition of the fact that a "cold war" had developed between Russia and the United States. It was a bold acceptance of American leadership against Russian aggression and a call for popular support and sacrifice in carrying it forward. The willingness of the American people and of Congress to underwrite the Marshall Plan or the European Recovery Program was apparent from the beginning and it was greatly increased by the Communist seizure of power in democratic Czechoslovakia in February, 1948. Although Congress agreed to appropriate a total of close to eighteen billions for European recovery by 1952, the intensification of the "cold war" soon made it clear that further steps were necessary to bulwark the security of Western Europe.

The immediate occasion was Soviet suspension of rail, motor, and canal connections between the Western zones of Germany, which had been placed under American, English, and French control, and the city of Berlin. Such a move weakened Western economic support and threatened its political influence. Only by the development of what came to be known as "the air lift" could Berlin be reached. For nearly a year this continued. Not until the spring of 1949 did the Soviet Union admit its failure and lift its blockade. The Soviet Union, too, suffered a critical setback in its plans for expanding its domination when Marshal Tito of Yugoslavia in 1948 broke with the Russians. Although Tito remained a firm Communist, he believed in the independence of each Communist nation. Such a theory was unacceptable to the Soviet leaders, who wanted all nations in their sphere of influence to be mere puppets of Russian policy. Gradually, the United States began to extend limited help to Tito as part of the policy of the containment of the Soviet Union.

In spite of the stimulus given European recovery by the Marshall Plan, the growing intensity of the "cold war" only increased European insecurity. Consequently Great Britain, France, Belgium, Luxembourg, and the Netherlands signed the Brussels Pact on March 17, 1948, pledging collaboration "in economic, social and cultural matters and for collective self-defense." It was a promising step but lacked the force to become effective. The United States alone had the armaments and resources that seemingly could make a European defense pact feasible. As a result discussions looking toward a more effective North Atlantic defense pact were launched in Washington in July, 1948. President Truman had already indicated his support of such a step when he, in referring to the Brussels Pact, had stated on March 17, "I am sure that the determination of the free countries of Europe to protect themselves will be matched by an equal determination on our part to help them do so."

The United States Senate, meanwhile, at the suggestion of Arthur Vandenberg, on June 11 had adopted a resolution which prepared the way for a formal treaty of alliance of the Atlantic powers. The adoption of the Vandenberg Resolution by the impressive vote of 64 to 4 was a dramatic indication of the fact that the United States had at last accepted its responsibility as the leader in world affairs.

Late in January, 1949, Secretary of State Dean Acheson, who had succeeded General Marshall, in commenting on the negotiations for the Atlantic Treaty, declared: "Our national security is vitally affected by the security of the North Atlantic area. The peoples of the North Atlantic area have a common heritage and civilization. We North Atlantic peoples share a common faith in fundamental human rights, in the dignity and worth of the human person, in the principles of democracy, personal freedom, and political liberty . . . We believe that these privileges and this common heritage can best be fortified and preserved and the general welfare of the people of the North Atlantic area advanced by an arrangement for coöperation in matters affecting their peace and security and common interest. . . ."

On April 4, 1949, the representatives of Belgium, Canada, Denmark, France, Great Britain, Iceland, Italy, Luxembourg, the Netherlands, Norway, Portugal, and the United States signed the North Atlantic Pact in Washington. Article 5 of the Pact stated: "The Parties agree that an armed attack against one or more of them in Europe or North America shall be considered an attack against them all; and consequently they agree that, if such an armed attack occurs, each of them, in exercise of the right of individual or collective self-defense recognized by Article 51 of the Charter of the United Nations, will assist the Party or Parties so attacked by taking forthwith, individually and in concert with the other Parties, such action as it deems necessary including the use of armed force, to restore and maintain the security of the North Atlantic area."

American signature of the North Atlantic Pact again demonstrated the distance that the nation had traveled in world affairs since the Neutrality Act of 1935. By 1949, the United States clearly faced the fact that the security of Western Europe was essential to American security. The lesson of two great conflicts in a generation had been learned. No longer would the United States retreat into isolation. It was now, a bit unwillingly, the keystone in the security structure of the non-Soviet world.

By 1950, although the United States and Western Europe had seemingly checked Soviet expansion in the West, significant developments were now focusing world attention on Asia. Immediately following the war, Great Britain had granted Dominion status to India, Pakistan, and Ceylon, and Burma had left the Empire entirely. Stirrings of nationalism all over the Far East left not only Britain but the other European nations as well the alternatives of withdrawing gracefully from the area or of facing dangerous civil conflicts. The Netherlands in late 1949 finally relinquished its imperial control over Indonesia. The French, however, retained their hold on Indo-China despite a bitter internal conflict.

China meanwhile was undergoing a major transformation. The Chinese Communists by late 1949 had driven the Nationalist government of Chiang Kai-Shek from the mainland. Although the Chiang government had had superior resources and a larger army than the Communists at the close of the war, and the United States had poured into Chiang's government considerable economic and military aid after 1945, his armies by 1950 had melted away and he had to take his stand on the island of Formosa. Incompetence, corruption, and the loss of respect of the Chinese for the Nationalist government led to the disintegration of the Chiang forces. Into this disintegrating situation moved the well-disciplined Communist armies until they had control of the entire mainland.

Demands arose from some sources in the United States that we should send a military expedition to defend Formosa from the Communist forces. The American government, however, refused. The doctrine of anti-Communism alone as a basis of policy had demonstrated its insufficiency in China. The people of China had needed a Government that would attempt to solve problems of poverty and disease, and the Nationalists had failed to supply the social reforms necessary. In setting forth American policy toward Asia after the Communist success in China, Secretary of State Acheson declared on January 12, 1950:

... I hear almost everyday someone say that the real interest of the United States is to stop the spread of communism. Nothing seems to me to put the cart before the horse more completely than that. Of course we are interested in stopping the spread of communism. But we are interested for a far deeper reason than any conflict between the Soviet Union and the United States. We are interested in stopping the spread of communism because communism is a doctrine that we don't happen to like. Communism is the most subtle instrument of Soviet foreign policy that has ever been devised and it is really the spearhead of Russian imperialism which would, if it could, take from these people what they have won, what we want them to keep and develop which is their own national independence, their own individual independence, their own development of their own resources for their own good and not as mere tributary states to this great Soviet Union.

. . . So after this survey, what we conclude, I believe, is that there is a new day which has dawned in Asia. It is a day in which the Asian peoples are on their own and know it and intend to continue on their own. It is a day in which the old relationships between east and west are gone, relationships which at their worst were exploitation and which at their best were paternalism. That relationship is over and the relationship of east and west must now be in the Far East one of mutual respect and mutual helpfulness. We are their friends. Others are their friends. We and those others are willing to help but we can help only where we are wanted and only where the conditions of help are really sensible and possible. So what we can see is that this new day in Asia, this new day which is dawning, may go on to a glorious noon or it may darken and it may drizzle out. But that decision lies within the countries of Asia and within the power of the Asian people. It is not a decision which a friend or even an enemy from the outside can decide for them.

Thus the United States, by 1950, was ready in Asia as well as in Europe to extend economic and technical aid to free nations that desired such assistance. Whether such aid would enable these nations to maintain internal stability and promote security from outside attack was an unanswered question as the world reached the midpoint in the twentieth century.

DIFFICULTIES OF ADJUSTING TO THE NEW AGE

In the months following the dropping of the atomic bombs on Hiroshima and Nagasaki, a feeling of uneasiness and concern for the future of civilization spread among the people of the United States. If one atomic bomb could devastate the heart of a great city and kill nearly one hundred thousand people, many asked themselves what would improved atomic bombs do in another war?

For the first year of the atomic age, there was a vigorous discussion over whether a military or civilian agency should control the research and production in the atomic field. The atomic scientists and many citizens focused pressure on Congress in favor of civilian control and Congress in 1946 established the Atomic Energy Commission as a civilian agency. The work of the Commission, however, was closely co-ordinated with that of the military and tight secrecy regulations were thrown about the entire operation.

Meanwhile in March, 1946, a group of citizens led by David E. Lilienthal and Undersecretary of State Dean Acheson presented a report for international control of atomic-bomb production. Mr. Acheson said of the report on April 23:

> In plain words, the report sets up a plan under which no nation would make atomic bombs or the materials for them. All dangerous activities would be carried on—not merely inspected—by a live functioning international authority with a real purpose in the world. . . .

To further such ends President Truman now appointed Bernard M. Baruch to head the American delegation to a United Nations Atomic Energy Commission. In presenting the report for an International Atomic Development Authority with managerial control or ownership of all atomic-energy activities potentially dangerous to world security and with power to control, inspect, and license all other atomic activities, Mr. Baruch began with the solemn warning:

"We are here to make a choice between the quick and the dead."

The Baruch proposals also stated that when an adequate system of control and inspection had been established, the United States would then stop making any more bombs and would dispose of its existing supply. These proposals were unacceptable to the Soviet Union. Not only was that nation working on atomic-bomb production itself but its delegate to the United Nations, Andrei Gromyko, said that the American plan proposed that "a system of inspection be established in such a way that it should be given unlimited power and the possibility of interfering with the internal economic life of nations." This was, of course, exactly what the American people wanted. This alone seemed to afford world security.

Russian refusal to co-operate, however, left matters as they were and both nations went ahead with their own plans and efforts—the United States confident that its atomic program was well ahead of that of the Russians. Late in 1949, however, this confidence was sadly shattered when President Truman suddenly announced that the Soviet Union had just set off a successful atomic explosion. That announcement altered the whole picture and launched a new drive for additional national defense. Russia and the United States had begun a new kind of "armament race." Early in 1950 the President told the American people that the Government was proceeding with the production of a new type of bomb—the hydrogen bomb. Some scientists warned that when this bomb was made it would have a destructive power of 1000 times that of the atomic bomb and would devastate at least a 50-square-mile area. Some even talked of the possibility of wiping out the entire human race.

In spite of the seriousness of this threat to civilization, no agreement with the Soviet Union for a workable plan of international security seemed possible. Although the United Nations had performed valuable service in mediating war in Palestine and Indonesia, and in disposing of the former Italian colonies in Africa, the Security Council had failed to bring the two super powers together on critical issues. Veto after veto by the Soviets demonstrated the split between the East and the West. With the United Nations rendered ineffective by Soviet vetos, an increasing number of Americans and Europeans began to advocate a federal organization of the Atlantic nations.

Not only did the United States proceed with the manufacture of new and more deadly bombs in the immediate post-war years, but the nation supported a military establishment far larger than ever before in peacetime. In 1949, for instance, approximately 15 billions out of the total yearly budget of about 43 billions went to the Department of Defense. It was estimated that the costs of past wars, veterans' expenses, defense preparations, and aid to Europe accounted for nearly three fourths of the national budget.

The need for greater central efficiency to deal with the new situation soon called for certain administrative changes. To co-ordinate military policy with the activities of the Department of State, Congress created the National Security Council. By law, in 1949, the President, the Vice President, the Secretary of State, the Secretary of Defense, and the Secretary of the Treasury were made regular members while others could be invited to the meetings. The meetings were conducted in the utmost secrecy and served as a clearing house to formulate policy. In another critical area, too, Congress tried to make the Government more efficient for its new role in the new day. The Central Intelligence Agency was created to improve American intelligence information and to co-ordinate the work of various military and civilian agencies in this general field.

The American government thus became increasingly complex in the postwar years. The creation of new agencies plus the expansion of certain older branches meant more and more government employees and additional expenses. Many citizens became restless under the heavy taxation necessary to support the governmental structure. Demands for reforms were frequently heard in Congress and ex-President Hoover headed an important citizen's committee that in 1949 submitted reports calling for widespread reform of the executive branch of government.

DOMESTIC TURBULENCE

The difficulties of living peacefully and optimistically in the new age were not alone restricted to the world sphere. At home the vigor of debate and conflict over the role of the government in the economy was more critical than in New Deal days. President Truman in various messages to Congress and in his 1948 campaign proclaimed among other things the need for increased Federal aid to housing, for Federal aid to education, for a Federal health program including a Federal insurance plan, for Federal laws to outlaw the poll tax as a deterrent to voting, for a fair-employment-practice law to prohibit discrimination in employment based on race, color, religion, or national origin, and for the strengthening of the antitrust laws against monopoly.

The Truman "Fair Deal" program, as the President called it, was bitterly denounced by most Republicans as "statism," "the welfare state," and "socialism." A sharp reaction seemed to be in the making. Even before the Truman policies had entirely taken form in 1946, the Republican party had secured control of both houses of Congress for the first time since 1928. Although on foreign issues most Republicans supported the Truman policies, there was little agreement on domestic issues. President Truman's request to the Eightieth Congress for strengthening controls over inflation, for new antitrust measures, for civil-rights legislation, for increased social-security benefits, and for new housing legislation were rejected by the Republican-controlled Congress. Its leaders felt that the traditional American way of life was being threatened. They talked much of "free enterprise" and "individual initiative."

The President and his Congress were, therefore, often at odds. In 1947, this Eightieth Congress passed a tax program over the President's veto which he denounced as "a rich-man's tax bill that gives a tremendous reduction in taxes to the wealthy, and leaves a heavy tax burden on the people with low incomes." In the field of labor legislation came the sharpest conflict. Republican leaders felt the need for new labor laws to replace the Wagner Act (1935), which had been drafted when labor was in a far weaker position than it was after 1945. By 1947 organized labor claimed over 15 million members. Continuing strikes, particularly on the part of John L. Lewis's United Mine Workers, made many citizens feel that some segments at least of organized labor were not accepting responsibility commensurate with their power. The Republican-controlled Congress, with votes from some Democrats, passed the Taft-Hartley labor law over the President's veto in the late spring of 1947. Among other things, this new labor legislation banned the closed shop, required labor leaders to sign anti-Communist affidavits before their unions could use the National Labor Relations Board's procedures, and provided for the right of the President to ask for an injunction against a threatened strike or a strike already underway whenever the situation reached the state of a "national emergency."

The merits and demerits of the Taft-Hartley Law were widely debated. One thing that could be said for sure was that the law mobilized labor leaders in the Railroad Brotherhoods, the Congress of Industrial Organizations, and the American Federation of Labor against the Republican party. Although the CIO had organized its Political Action Committee in 1943 and had supported Franklin D. Roosevelt's re-election in 1944, the American Federation of Labor had not before taken such direct political action. The national executive committee of the Federation had not endorsed Mr. Roosevelt and some members had supported the Republican ticket. The Taft-Hartley Law, however, particularly with its ban against the closed shop, led the American Federation of Labor to organize Labor's League for Political Education and support President Truman in 1948 and Congressional candidates opposed to the law.

The President was quick to take advantage of labor's reaction to the Taft-Hartley Law, and he made it an important aspect of his campaign in 1948. "Do you," he asked, "want to carry the Taft-Hartley Law to its full implication and enslave totally the workingman, white collar and union man alike, or do you want to go forward with an administration whose interest is the welfare of the common man?"

The President's quest for election in 1948 was beset by many difficulties. During the first year or two of his presidency, he had seemed to lack sureness and the ability to lead the nation through its difficulties in the new age. Many former New Deal figures left the Truman Administration, outraged by what they considered to be an increasingly conservative group of advisers close to the President. Former Vice-President Henry A. Wallace resigned from the Truman cabinet in a dispute over foreign policy and early in 1948 launched the Progressive party. Secretary of State Byrnes resigned in 1947 and a coolness was apparent between him and the President. Furthermore, a number of Southern

Democrats objected to the President's request for civil-rights laws from Congress and threatened trouble unless the party forgot the issue. Refusal brought open revolt with Thurmond as the Dixiecrat candidate.

Meanwhile the Republican party looked forward to victory for the first time since 1928. Governor Thomas E. Dewey was nominated for the second time but only after a struggle with the forces supporting Senator Robert A. Taft and Harold E. Stassen. The foreword to the party platform stated: "To establish and maintain peace, to build a country in which every citizen can earn a good living with the promise of real progress for himself and his family, and to uphold as a beacon light for mankind everywhere, the inspiring American tradition of liberty, opportunity and justice for all—that is the Republican platform."

In the text of the platform the Republicans pledged an attack on inflation, on governmental waste, on monopoly; they pledged support of Federal aid to housing, of farm prices, of laws to establish fair employment practices, outlaw the poll tax, and increase social-security benefits. In the field of foreign affairs, the party pledged itself to continue aid to Europe, but it promised the country, "We shall protect the future against the errors of the Democratic administration, which has too often lacked clarity, competence or consistency in our vital international relationships and has too often abandoned justice."

The Democratic party at its convention adopted a platform that pledged a continuation of the policies of the Roosevelt and Truman administrations. "We chart our future course," the platform declared, "as we charted our course under the leadership of Franklin D. Roosevelt and Harry S. Truman in the abiding belief that democracy—when dedicated to the service of all and not to a privileged few—proves its superiority over all other forms of government." The platform denounced the actions of the Eightieth Congress and reasserted its support of the President's request for civil-rights legislation, antimonopoly laws, curbs on inflation, housing legislation, the repeal of the Taft-Hartley law, Federal aid to education, extension of social security, and adequate supports for farm prices.

President Truman, in accepting the nomination, set forth the issue between the two parties in the following way:

The situation in 1932 was due to the policies of the Republican party control of the Government of the United States. The Republican party . . . favors the privileged few and not the common every-day man. Ever since its inception, that party has been under the control of special privilege; and they have completely proved it in the 80th Congress. They proved it by the things they did *to* the people and not *for* them.

. . . In 1932 we were attacking the citadel of special privilege and greed. We were fighting to drive the money changers from the temple. Today, in 1948, we are now the defenders of the stronghold of democracy and equal opportunity, the haven of the ordinary people of this land and not of the favored clases or the powerful few. . . .

Although the President also told the Democratic Convention that "Senator Barkley and I will win this election," few people thought that the Democrats had any chance of victory. George Gallup and other public-opinion pollsters predicted an overwhelming victory for Governor Dewey and his running mate, Governor Earl Warren of California. *Life* magazine featured a cover picture of Governor Dewey the week before election and called him the next President. *United States News* devoted fifteen pages of its issue for election week to the policies of the "newly elected" President Dewey.

In the closing speech of his campaign, Governor Dewey, on what was supposed to be the "eve of victory," observed:

. . . Love of freedom has blessed our land and made it great. We shall now go forward to keep our freedom in a world where intolerance and strife and godless materialism are on the march. As a nation we shall again make human liberty our intense, devoted active concern. Here at home we will carry on this fight against injustice and discrimination, the fight for the civil liberties of all our people in all our land.

These things we can do. With our faith in ourselves renewed, with competence and devotion restored to our Government, with unity and strength of purpose among us there is nothing as a people we cannot do. There is nothing we cannot do, provided only that we have peace.

The results on election evening stunned many people but not President Truman and Senator Alben Barkley. They had carried a fighting campaign to the nation, constantly attacking the record of the 80th Congress and comparing that record with the promises in the Republican platform. "The record of the 80th Congress," charged Mr. Truman in Chicago on October 25, "is a sad tale of the sell-out of the people's interest to put more and more power in the hands of fewer and fewer men.

. . .The Republican 80th Congress repeatedly flouted the will of the people. And yet the Republican candidate has the gall to say: 'The 80th Congress delivered as no other Congress ever did for the future of our country.'

I'll say it delivered.

It delivered for the private power lobby. It delivered for the big oil company lobby. It delivered for the railroad lobby. It delivered for the real estate lobby.

That's what the Republican candidate calls delivering for the future. Is that the kind of future you want?

When the votes were counted Truman had received 24,104,836; Dewey, 21,969,500; Wallace, 1,157,100; and Thurmond, 1,169,312. In the electoral college the results were Truman, 303; Dewey, 189; and Thurmond, 39.

The Truman victory led to widespread questioning of the methods and value of public-opinon polls. The Social Science Research Council commented: ". . . the recent polling difficulties apparently stemmed in part from insufficient knowledge of several aspects of political behavior. The forecasts relied heavily upon past voting behavior as reflected in election statistics. Statistical data alone cannot give effective recognition to factors which are the product of special local political situations, or influences which may range from the dynamics of personal leadership to the apathy of voters or from indecision on the part of individuals to organized action by pressure groups."

An analysis of the 1948 elections reveals that the Republican party was apathetic in its campaign and too smug over its "certain victory." The Democratic party, which seemed to be torn to pieces by the Wallace wing on the left and Governor Strom Thurmond's States Rights Democrats or Dixiecrats in violent opposition to Truman's stand on civil liberties on the right, displayed remarkable vigor. Columnist Walter Lippmann wrote after the election: "The Democratic victories attest the enormous vitality of the party as Roosevelt led it and developed it from 1932 to 1944. Mr. Truman is very nearly the only man who can say that he really believed that the party still had such strength and could exert it without Roosevelt's personal leadership."

Extremely important to the Truman victory had been the work of the CIO and the AFL, but by no means could these labor forces claim more than a share of the credit. The Negro vote in the northern cities, too, was a significant factor in the Democratic victory. In Chicago, for instance, Truman received 71 per cent of the Negro vote, and he could not have carried the state without his smashing victory in the Negro area. He also had the great advantage of patronage which goes with the party in power—an advantage now doubly great in a period of government aids and expanded government activity.

Above all it was important to note that New Dealish candidates for Governor and Senator frequently received more votes in their state than Mr. Truman. The election demonstrated that a growing dependence on government and a faith in welfare policies was not dead in the post-war era. Senator-elect Estes Kefauver of Tennessee commented on the Democratic victory: "The people want to move on. They want progress, not just a negative, stand-pat program. They are looking for better opportunity, for security and a chance for a better life for themselves and their children; and they want the resources of our nation, the rivers and the soil, developed. They felt that Truman and the Democrats offered the best chance of getting these things and other things which they want."[1]

FREEDOM AT HOME

The uneasiness and distress over living in a new age were clearly revealed in the area of civil liberties. During the war, there had been an extension of civil liberties and a remarkable lack of hysteria and intolerance. The disintegration of American-Soviet relations in the atomic age, however, created a feeling of great unrest. "Excitement, bordering on hysteria," commented the American Civil Liberties Union in 1947, "characterized the public approach to any issue related to Communism, accentuated by the declaration of a foreign policy aimed at blocking the advance of Soviet influence." Former Assistant Secretary of State Archibald MacLeish, writing in the *Atlantic Monthly* for July, 1949, stated that the fear of Soviet Russia and Communism was dictating our foreign policy and much of our domestic activities.

The Attorney General issued a long list of organizations charged with being under Communist influence and any member of these organizations was held to be at the least pro-Communist by the act of association. A loyalty check was made on the two million Federal employees and a Loyalty Review Board was established to hear any cases of alleged subversives. After two years of work, the Loyalty Review Board had discovered only a few cases of doubtful loyalty on the part of governmental employees.

Charges of "Red" and "disloyal" were levied against some people without substantial evidence. Some legislative investigations violated common-law traditions of the right of the accused to see the evidence and to present information on his own behalf. "Under the pressure of the

[1]University of Chicago Round Table, Nov. 7, 1948.

cold war hysteria," noted the American Civil Liberties Union in 1949, "against everything conceived to be Communist, the efforts to distinguish the loyal from the disloyal in all public positions were expanded beyond anything ever known before in American life."

Three court trials occupied the public spotlight in 1949–50. Eleven Communist leaders were tried under the Smith Act making criminal a conspiracy to advocate the overthrow of the government by force and violence. Judith Coplon, an employee in the Attorney General's office, was charged with passing secret information to the Russians. Alger Hiss, former State Department figure and Secretary-General of the San Francisco Conference, was indicted for perjury when he denied meeting with and giving material to Whitaker Chambers, confessed ex-Communist spy courier. Appeals from convictions in the Communist leaders case and the Hiss case failed and those involved went to jail. The Coplon case was still in the courts at the beginning of 1952.

THE KOREAN CONFLICT

The "cold war" between the east and the west exploded into a "hot war" on June 25, 1950, when the Russian-sponsored North Korean Government attacked the Republic of South Korea. Within a few hours President Truman authorized General MacArthur in Japan to release equipment to the Republic of Korea (R. O. K.). That same afternoon of June 25, the Security Council branded the North Korean attack as aggression and called for peace.

Events now moved rapidly. On June 27 President Truman ordered General MacArthur to use American air and sea forces to support the Korean Republic. The same day the Security Council called on all UN members to give assistance to the Korean Republic, and by July 8 fifty-three of its fifty-nine members had signified their support of the resolution. Although a number of the United Nations, including Great Britain, Canada, Australia, New Zealand, and Turkey, put armed forces into Korea, the United States and the Republic of Korea furnished the great bulk of the UN forces.

American action in Korea was a gamble. We had few troops in the Far East, and the problem of supplying these troops across the Pacific was immense. President Truman's attitude was, however, that if the United States allowed the South Koreans to be destroyed then other nations friendly to the United States would assume that we would do nothing to aid them if and when they were victims of aggression.

During the last half of 1950, the Korean conflict went through three phases. The first phase was marked by North Korean victories which by August left UN forces with little more than a beachhead. American ground troops had been committed to action on June 30, and General MacArthur had been made Commander of all UN forces on July 7. The second phase consisted of a series of UN counterattacks begun in September, which entrapped many North Koreans, and carried the Allies across the 38th parallel. As the UN forces pushed toward the Manchurian border, late in October, a third phase developed. In this the North Koreans were led by Chinese Communist troops which were supposedly made up of volunteers but which were, in reality, part of China's regular army. The next few months were filled with bitter and bloody fighting.

In the spring of 1951, a stalemate developed. Although the fighting was still bitter, neither side could bring a decision without committing larger forces. Under such conditions conflicting opinion quickly developed as to the best policy to be pursued. General MacArthur felt that "limited war" in Korea would mean endless slaughter of American troops. He favored bombing Manchuria and argued that this would bring victory. The Administration, on the other hand, favored punishing the enemy in Korea, but feared that extending the war to Manchuria might bring Russia into the conflict and touch off a general war. Because of this difference of opinion, President Truman, on April 11, relieved General MacArthur of his command.

The new UN Commander, General Matthew Ridgway, sent his troops grinding ahead to the 38th parallel and just beyond. On June 23 Russia's delegate to the UN, Jacob Malik, proposed a cease fire. Truce talks were soon started but faced long interruptions and much disagreement. On November 27, however, the belligerents did reach an agreement that the respective battle lines would be a provisional cease-fire line. This did not end the fighting, for air and naval attacks continued even though ground action eased up somewhat after this. By early 1952, the truce teams of the two sides were deadlocked. The whole business had been costly. By January 23, 1952, American casualties alone totalled 104,644, with 18,049 of this figure being deaths.

In addition to the Korean conflict, the United States in 1951 increased its military aid to the French fighting in Indo-China. We also drafted a peace treaty with Japan which fifty nations, over strong Russian protests, signed in September, 1951. Mutual defense pacts were signed, at the time of the treaty, with Australia, New Zealand, and the Philippines, pledging American co-operation with them to repel aggression.

CHANGES IN EUROPE AND AMERICA

At the outbreak of the Korean conflict, Western Europe was divided and disarmed. The emphasis during the last six months of 1950 and all of 1951 was, therefore, to increase the tempo of European rearmament. To aid this, the nations of the North Atlantic Treaty Organization agreed on December 18, 1950, to the appointment of General Dwight Eisenhower as Supreme Commander of the Atlantic Pact forces. During 1951, also, Congress appropriated six billion dollars in military and economic aid to Western Europe under the Mutual Security Agency which replaced the Marshall Plan administration. The Western European nations, although undertaking rearmament, expressed fears that their economies could not stand the strain. In an attempt to integrate Europe better, the Schuman Plan was developed to pool the steel and coal resources of Western Germany with those of France, Italy, Belgium, the Netherlands, and Luxembourg. Steps were also taken to raise a Western German army, but one that was integrated in a European army composed of troops from the above-mentioned countries. This European army was to serve under General Eisenhower's command. It was hoped through the Schuman Plan and the European army to integrate Western Germany in such a way that Germany would not again become a threat to the peace of Western Europe.

The Moslem world, stretching from Morocco to the Middle East, added to the tense world situation in 1951. The declining power of Great Britain and France led to a nationalistic upsurge against them in Morocco, Tunisia, Egypt, and Iran.

At home in the United States, the armed forces were quickly expanded from about 1,450,000 in June, 1950, to 3,500,000 by early 1952. The production of weapons, planes, and tanks was greatly increased. Approximately forty billion dollars were spent on military preparations in the one budget year of July 1, 1951, to June 30, 1952. In December, 1950, Charles E. Wilson, president of General Electric, was made head of the new Office of Defense Mobilization. Strategic materials were allocated to defense industries and price and wage controls were applied. Taxes, too, were increased considerably.

The opening of the Korean conflict touched off a vigorous debate on foreign policy. Many Republicans in Congress accused the Truman Administration of being responsible for the defeat of the Nationalist Chinese. The most dramatic episode in the debate on Far Eastern policy came with the recall of General MacArthur in 1951 and his testimony before Congress. In spite of the debate, the Administration continued to favor a "limited war" in Korea.

The Administration's policy of increasing the number of American troops in Europe also came under attack. Ex-President Hoover, one of the critics, urged in December, 1950, that we avoid committing troops on the European continent and concentrate instead on building the air force and the navy and the defenses of the Western Hemisphere. "We can, without any measure of doubt," Mr. Hoover stated, "with our own air and naval forces, hold the Atlantic and Pacific Oceans with one frontier on Britain (if she wishes to co-operate); the other, on Japan, Formosa and the Philippines." This position received considerable support in old isolationist areas.

The Administration, however, in 1951 increased the number of American troops in Europe and poured supplies into the Atlantic Pact armies under General Eisenhower. Secretary of State Acheson set forth the Administration's point of view on December 30, 1950:

This country must remain true to its tradition of standing by its friends. To abandon our allies would gratify the Kremlin. To do so would be appeasement on a gigantic scale. The Soviet Union, holding in unhappy bondage the peoples of Eastern Europe, wields enough power without making the Soviet imperialists a gift of the productive capacity and technical skills of Western Europe, plus the strategic resources and the manpower of the Middle East and Asia.

Dean Acheson, himself, came under bitter attack with most Senate and House Republicans demanding his resignation on December 15, 1950. President Truman replied: "I refuse to dismiss Acheson."

Senator Joseph McCarthy of Wisconsin, beginning early in 1950, accused the Department of State of being "infested with Communists" who had "handed over" China to the Communists. Although the majority on a Senate subcommittee on July 17, 1950, cleared the Department on these charges, the attack continued. On June 14, 1951, the Senator vigorously attacked General George C. Marshall, former Secretary of Defense and Secretary of State, and accused him of making common cause with Stalin. A number of prominent leaders, in turn, accused Senator McCarthy of "smearing" the reputations of many American public servants. The attacks of the Senator nevertheless met with some approval from suspicious and war-weary peoples and became part of the atmosphere of the Presidential campaign of 1952.

A Senate Committee, led by Democrat Estes Kefauver of Tennessee, conducted a series of investigations into crime in 1950 and 1951, and revealed the tie-up of criminals with local political and police officials. Many of the hearings were put on television and the Kefauver investigations attracted wide attention.

At the tense Republican convention in Chicago in July, 1952, General Dwight Eisenhower, who had resigned as Supreme Commander of the NATO forces, defeated Senator Robert A. Taft's last bid for the nomination. Two weeks later the Democratic convention drafted Governor Adlai E. Stevenson of Illinois to be its standard-bearer. The resulting campaign was bitter, intense, and hectic. Governor Stevenson set the tone for his campaign in his acceptance speech:

I hope and pray that we Democrats, win or lose, can campaign not as a crusade to exterminate the opposing party, as our opponents seem to prefer, but as a great opportunity to educate and elevate a people whose destiny is leadership, not alone of a rich and prosperous country as in the past, but of a world in ferment.

. . . Let's face it. Let's talk sense to the American people. Let's tell them the truth, that there are no gains without pains, that we are now on the eve of great decisions, not easy decisions . . .

General Eisenhower characterized his campaign as a crusade to "clean up the mess in Washington," criticized the Truman Administration for being "soft on communists," and pledged that he personally would visit Korea. In one speech he stated:

The Administration in its fear, in its exhaustion, has tried to label our party as the party of reaction, the party that looks backward. But the plain truth is that the Fair Deal's economic treadmill is a philosophy of those who "look backward."

. . . We are looking forward to an equal justice and an equal fairness for all our citizens . . .

In the election, the popular vote was approximately 33 million for Eisenhower and 27 million for Stevenson, with Eisenhower carrying the electoral vote by 442 to 89. Eisenhower's large margin of victory, however, did not carry over very strongly in the Congressional elections, where the Republicans captured control of the Senate by the margin of one and of the House of Representatives by seven votes.

The Eisenhower victory brought to a close twenty years of Democratic administration. It reflected Eisenhower's commanding prestige and a belief that it was time for a change.

INDEX